THE

WAR OF THE REBELLION:

A COMPILATION OF THE

OFFICIAL RECORDS

OF THE

UNION AND CONFEDERATE ARMIES.

PUBLISHED UNDER THE DIRECTION OF

The Hon. RUSSELL A. ALGER, Secretary of War,

BY

COL. FRED C. AINSWORTH, U. S. ARMY,
MR. LESLIE J. PERRY, CIVILIAN EXPERT,
MR. JOSEPH W. KIRKLEY, CIVILIAN EXPERT,
Board of Publication.

SERIES II—VOLUME V.

WASHINGTON:
GOVERNMENT PRINTING OFFICE.
1899.

PREFACE.

The work of preparing the records of the war for public use was begun under the resolution of Congress of May 19, 1864, by Adjt. Gen. E. D. Townsend, U. S. Army, who caused copies to be made of reports of battles on file in his office and steps to be taken to collect missing records.

Under the provisions of joint resolution No. 91, of 1866, Hon. Peter H. Watson was appointed to supervise the preparation and formulate a plan for the publication of the records, but he did no work and drew no pay under this appointment, which expired July 27, 1868, by limitation of the resolution. This resolution also repealed the former one and work ceased.

The first decisive step taken in this work was the act of June 23, 1874, providing the necessary means "to enable the Secretary of War to begin the publication of the Official Records of the War of the Rebellion, both of the Union and Confederate Armies," and directing him "to have copied for the Public Printer all reports, letters, telegrams, and general orders, not heretofore copied or printed, and properly arranged in chronological order." Appropriations have been made from time to time for continuing such preparation. Under this act the preliminary work was resumed by General Townsend, who first outlined the plan on which the records are printed, though it appears that originally he contemplated publishing to the world only the more important military reports.

Subsequently, under meager appropriations, it was prosecuted in a somewhat desultory manner by various subordinates of the War Department until December 14, 1877, when the Secretary of War, perceiving that the undertaking needed the undivided attention of a single head, detailed Lieut. Col. Robert N. Scott, U. S. Army, to take charge of the bureau and devote himself exclusively to the work.

The act of June 23, 1874, greatly enlarged upon the first crude scheme of publication. On this more comprehensive basis it was determined that the volumes should include not only the battle reports, but also "all official documents that can be obtained by the compiler, and that appear to be of any historical value." Colonel Scott systematized the work and the plan and presented the records in the following order of arrangement, which has been adhered to by his successors:

The first series will embrace the formal reports, both Union and Confederate, of the first seizures of United States property in the Southern States, and of all military operations in the field, with the correspondence, orders, and returns relating specially thereto, and, as proposed, is to be accompanied by an Atlas.

In this series the reports will be arranged according to the campaigns and several theaters of operations (in the chronological order of events), and the Union reports of any event will, as a rule, be immediately followed by the Confederate accounts. The correspondence, etc., not embraced in the "reports" proper will follow (first Union and next Confederate) in chronological order.

The second series will contain the correspondence, orders, reports, and returns, Union and Confederate, relating to prisoners of war, and (so far as the military authorities were concerned) to state or political prisoners.

The third series will contain the correspondence, orders, reports, and returns of the Union authorities (embracing their correspondence with the Confederate officials) not relating specially to the subjects of the first and second series. It will set forth the annual and special reports of the Secretary of War, of the General-in-Chief, and of the chiefs of the several staff corps and departments; the calls for troops, and the correspondence between the National and the several State authorities.

The fourth series will exhibit the correspondence, orders, reports, and returns of the Confederate authorities, similar to that indicated for the Union officials, as of the third series, but excluding the correspondence between the Union and Confederate authorities given in that series.

The first volume of the records was issued in the early fall of 1880. The act approved June 16, 1880, provided "for the printing and binding, under direction of the Secretary of War, of 10,000 copies of a compilation of the Official Records (Union and Confederate) of the War of the Rebellion, so far as the same may be ready for publication, during the fiscal year;" and that " of said number 7,000 copies shall be for the use of the House of Representatives, 2,000 copies for the use of the Senate, and 1,000 copies for the use of the Executive Departments." Under this act Colonel Scott proceeded to publish the first five volumes of the records.*

---

*All subsequent volumes have been distributed under the act approved August 7, 1882, which provides that:

"The volumes of the Official Records of the War of the Rebellion shall be distributed as follows: One thousand copies to the Executive Departments, as now provided by law. One thousand copies for distribution by the Secretary of War among officers of the Army and contributors to the work. Eight thousand three hundred copies shall be sent by the Secretary of War to such libraries, organizations, and individuals as may be designated by the Senators, Representatives, and Delegates of the Forty-seventh Congress. Each Senator shall designate not exceeding twenty-six, and each Representative and Delegate not exceeding twenty-one, of such addresses, and the volumes shall be sent thereto from time to time as they are published, until the publication is completed. Senators, Representatives, and Delegates shall inform the Secretary of War in each case how many volumes of those heretofore published they have forwarded to such addresses. The remaining copies of the eleven thousand to be published, and all sets that may not be ordered to be distributed as provided herein, shall be sold by the Secretary of War for cost of publication with ten per cent. added thereto, and the proceeds of such sale shall be covered into the Treasury. If two or more sets of said volumes are ordered to the same address, the Secretary of War shall inform the Senators, Representatives, or Delegates who have designated the same, who thereupon may designate other libraries, organizations, or individuals. The Secretary of War shall report to the first session of the Forty-eighth Congress what volumes of the series heretofore published have not been furnished to such libraries, organizations, and individuals. He shall also inform distributees at whose instance the volumes are sent."

Col. Robert N. Scott died March 5, 1887, before the completion of the work, which, during a ten years' service, he had come to love so dearly. At his death some twenty-six books only had been issued, but he had compiled a large amount of matter for forthcoming volumes; consequently his name as compiler was retained in all the books up to and including Vol. XXXVI, although his successors had added largely to his compilations from new material found after his demise.

The Secretary of War, May 7, 1887, assigned Lieut. Col. H. M. Lazelle, U. S. Army, to duty as the successor of Colonel Scott. He had continued in charge about two years, when, in the act approved March 2, 1889, it was provided—

That hereafter the preparation and publication of said records shall be conducted, under the Secretary of War, by a board of three persons, one of whom shall be an officer of the Army, and two civilian experts, to be appointed by the Secretary of War, the compensation of said civilian experts to be fixed by the Secretary of War.

The Secretary of War appointed Maj. George B. Davis, judge-advocate, U. S. Army, as the military member, and Leslie J. Perry, of Kansas, and Joseph W. Kirkley, of Maryland, as the civilian expert members of said board. The board assumed direction of the publication at the commencement of the fiscal year 1889, its first work beginning with Serial No. 36 of Vol. XXIV.

July 1, 1895, by direction of the Secretary of War, Maj. George W. Davis, Eleventh Infantry, U. S. Army, relieved Maj. George B. Davis, U. S. Army, as the military member and president of the Board of Publication. Subsequently Col. Fred C. Ainsworth, U. S. Army, was appointed the military member and president of the board, relieving Maj. George W. Davis June 1, 1898.

Each volume includes a copious and accurate index, and for the further convenience of investigators there will be, in addition, a general index to the entire set when complete, in a volume by itself.

Nothing is printed in these volumes except duly authenticated contemporaneous records of the war. The scope of the board's work is to decide upon and arrange the matter to be published; to correct and verify the orthography of the papers used, and occasionally to add a foot-note of explanation.

FRED C. AINSWORTH, *Colonel, U. S. Army,*
LESLIE J. PERRY, *Civilian Expert,*
JOSEPH W. KIRKLEY, *Civilian Expert,*
Board of Publication.

Approved:

RUSSELL A. ALGER,
Secretary of War.

WAR DEPARTMENT, *Washington, D. C., June 23, 1898.*

CONTENTS.

VII

1862.

	Sunday.	Monday.	Tuesday.	Wednesday.	Thursday.	Friday.	Saturday.
Jan				1	2	3	4
	5	6	7	8	9	10	11
	12	13	14	15	16	17	18
	19	20	21	22	23	24	25
	26	27	28	29	30	31	
Feb							1
	2	3	4	5	6	7	8
	9	10	11	12	13	14	15
	16	17	18	19	20	21	22
	23	24	25	26	27	28	
March							1
	2	3	4	5	6	7	8
	9	10	11	12	13	14	15
	16	17	18	19	20	21	22
	23	24	25	26	27	28	29
	30	31					
April			1	2	3	4	5
	6	7	8	9	10	11	12
	13	14	15	16	17	18	19
	20	21	22	23	24	25	26
	27	28	29	30			
May					1	2	3
	4	5	6	7	8	9	10
	11	12	13	14	15	16	17
	18	19	20	21	22	23	24
	25	26	27	28	29	30	31
June	1	2	3	4	5	6	7
	8	9	10	11	12	13	14
	15	16	17	18	19	20	21
	22	23	24	25	26	27	28
	29	30					
July			1	2	3	4	5
	6	7	8	9	10	11	12
	13	14	15	16	17	18	19
	20	21	22	23	24	25	26
	27	28	29	30	31		
August						1	2
	3	4	5	6	7	8	9
	10	11	12	13	14	15	16
	17	18	19	20	21	22	23
	24	25	26	27	28	29	30
	31						
Sept		1	2	3	4	5	6
	7	8	9	10	11	12	13
	14	15	16	17	18	19	20
	21	22	23	24	25	26	27
	28	29	30				
October				1	2	3	4
	5	6	7	8	9	10	11
	12	13	14	15	16	17	18
	19	20	21	22	23	24	25
	26	27	28	29	30	31	
Nov							1
	2	3	4	5	6	7	8
	9	10	11	12	13	14	15
	16	17	18	19	20	21	22
	23	24	25	26	27	28	29
	30						
Dec		1	2	3	4	5	6
	7	8	9	10	11	12	13
	14	15	16	17	18	19	20
	21	22	23	24	25	26	27
	28	29	30	31			

1863.

	Sunday.	Monday.	Tuesday.	Wednesday.	Thursday.	Friday.	Saturday.
Jan					1	2	3
	4	5	6	7	8	9	10
	11	12	13	14	15	16	17
	18	19	20	21	22	23	24
	25	26	27	28	29	30	31
Feb	1	2	3	4	5	6	7
	8	9	10	11	12	13	14
	15	16	17	18	19	20	21
	22	23	24	25	26	27	28
March	1	2	3	4	5	6	7
	8	9	10	11	12	13	14
	15	16	17	18	19	20	21
	22	23	24	25	26	27	28
	29	30	31				
April				1	2	3	4
	5	6	7	8	9	10	11
	12	13	14	15	16	17	18
	19	20	21	22	23	24	25
	26	27	28	29	30		
May						1	2
	3	4	5	6	7	8	9
	10	11	12	13	14	15	16
	17	18	19	20	21	22	23
	24	25	26	27	28	29	30
	31						
June		1	2	3	4	5	6
	7	8	9	10	11	12	13
	14	15	16	17	18	19	20
	21	22	23	24	25	26	27
	28	29	30				
July				1	2	3	4
	5	6	7	8	9	10	11
	12	13	14	15	16	17	18
	19	20	21	22	23	24	25
	26	27	28	29	30	31	
August							1
	2	3	4	5	6	7	8
	9	10	11	12	13	14	15
	16	17	18	19	20	21	22
	23	24	25	26	27	28	29
	30	31					
Sept			1	2	3	4	5
	6	7	8	9	10	11	12
	13	14	15	16	17	18	19
	20	21	22	23	24	25	26
	27	28	29	30			
October					1	2	3
	4	5	6	7	8	9	10
	11	12	13	14	15	16	17
	18	19	20	21	22	23	24
	25	26	27	28	29	30	31
Nov	1	2	3	4	5	6	7
	8	9	10	11	12	13	14
	15	16	17	18	19	20	21
	22	23	24	25	26	27	28
	29	30					
Dec			1	2	3	4	5
	6	7	8	9	10	11	12
	13	14	15	16	17	18	19
	20	21	22	23	24	25	26
	27	28	29	30	31		

SERIES II.–VOL. V.

CORRESPONDENCE, ORDERS, ETC., RELATING TO PRISONERS OF WAR AND STATE FROM DECEMBER 1, 1862, TO JUNE 10, 1863.

UNION CORRESPONDENCE, ETC.

Extract from Annual Report of the Secretary of War, December 1, 1862.

*　　　*　　　*　　　*　　　*　　　*　　　*

The Adjutant-General's Office has also had charge of the exchange of prisoners. In the month of July a cartel of exchange was arranged by General John A. Dix, on the part of the United States, and General [D. H.] Hill, of the rebel army, under which large numbers of prisoners of war have been exchanged. There still remain some paroled prisoners belonging to the U. S. Army whose exchange will be effected at the earliest opportunity.

*　　　*　　　*　　　*　　　*　　　*　　　*

EDWIN M. STANTON,
Secretary of War.

HEADQUARTERS ARMY OF TENNESSEE,
Murfreesborough, Tenn., December 1, 1862.

Maj. Gen. W. S. ROSECRANS,
Commanding U. S. Forces, Nashville, Tenn.

GENERAL: I am in receipt of your communication of the 29th* [ultimo] in reply to mine in reference to the case of Adjutant Hawkins. The circumstances which formed the basis of complaint occurred in a distant part of my department and I have no information in regard to the matter other than that transmitted you in my last. I concur fully with you in your suggestions in regard to the uses of the flag as a means of communication between the opposing armies. Official courtesy no less than a precaution against the improper use of the flag requires that it should come from the commanding general and follow the most direct route. Entertaining these views I was surprised to receive a communication of equal date with yours from one of your subordinates, Major-General McCook, addressed to me directly and sent by a circuitous route. The selection of the Franklin pike for a flag was certainly singular, as no one desiring to reach this place in ordinary times would make choice of that road. On the same day I also received a communication from another of your subordinate officers, General Negley, who sought by flag to effect an object highly unpleasant to me, and which he afterwards accomplished contrary to my expressed and imperative regulations. I can only account for these discrepancies by presuming

---

* See Series I, Vol. XX, Part II, p. 109.

(1)

that these violations of courtesy were without your knowledge or approval. I cordially reciprocate your views in making known your intention to conform in this as in all other things to the laws and usages of war. It shall be my aim strictly to conform to such a line of policy, and should any deviations inadvertently occur the errors shall be promptly corrected when brought to my attention.

I am, general, very respectfully, your obedient servant,

BRAXTON BRAGG,
General, Commanding.

HEADQUARTERS ARMY OF TENNESSEE,
Murfreesborough, Tenn., December 1, 1862.

Maj. Gen. W. S. ROSECRANS,
Commanding U. S. Forces, Nashville, Tenn.

GENERAL: Inclosed I send you a communication for Major-General Wright in reply to one from him received under cover from Major-General McCook.

Hereafter I must insist that all communications from your lines intended for me shall come from the commander of the forces and not as in this instance from a subordinate officer.

Respectfully, your obedient servant,

BRAXTON BRAGG,
General, Commanding.

[Inclosure.]

HEADQUARTERS ARMY OF TENNESSEE,
Murfreesborough, Tenn., December 1, 1862.

Maj. Gen. H. G. WRIGHT.

SIR: I have the honor to acknowledge the receipt of your communication of the 23d ultimo* proposing an exchange of a citizen of Kentucky, now a prisoner in your hands, for another represented to be held by our forces as a hostage. As the party is not within my control and I am without any information as to the circumstances or cause of his arrest the matter will be referred to my Government.

I cannot refrain in this connection from calling your attention to the action of your Government in its treatment of citizens of Kentucky and other States who are simply suspected or who express sympathy with the Confederate cause. Numbers of individuals, non-combatants, are daily arrested and sent to Ohio prisons for acts which the Confederate forces commit and for which they alone should be held responsible. Though strongly urged when in Kentucky to retaliate upon Union men by similar treatment in order to procure the release of the true and loyal Kentuckians in Federal prisons I resolutely declined to recognize or countenance such a principle as that practiced by your authorities. If any arrests were made they were unauthorized, and the isolated instances in which they occurred were but exceptions to a positive rule to the contrary. The Confederate authorities, military and civil, have uniformly observed the principle of the exemption of non-combatants from molestation for the acts of the organized forces of the United States. It would be a gratifying feature in a war full enough of horrors without such unnecessary adjuncts if the Federal Government would observe a similar action. Instead, however, of such being now the practice private property is destroyed or confiscated and citizens are mulcted and retaliated upon even unto death. It is

---

* Omitted.

not to be denied that the patience of the Confederate Government is becoming threadbare. It has in vain resorted to every resource recognized by civilized warfare in retaliation of such outrages, but with no avail except in individual cases. It has failed to elicit any disavowal of the principle on which the Federal Government acts, and it is to be apprehended that as a natural result a system of retaliation in kind will be resorted to. It will rest chiefly with the Federal Government to decide hereafter the character which the contest shall assume.

These acts of retaliation upon individuals, together with the indignities to our clergy at different periods and more recently in a Southern city, are steeling the hearts and nerving the arms of our people to the last degree of desperation. Union—social association with a people guilty of such acts—is henceforth an impossibility. Destitution, the prison—death itself—is preferable.

Respectfully, your obedient servant,

BRAXTON BRAGG,
General, Commanding.

[Indorsement.]

HEADQUARTERS DEPARTMENT OF THE OHIO,
Cincinnati, December 9, 1862.

Respectfully referred to the assistant adjutant-general, Headquarters of the Army, for the information of the General-in-Chief. The within is in reply to my letter of the 23d ultimo* to General Bragg relative to the exchange of A. H. Townly, a citizen of Campbell County, Ky., captured by a party of General Kirby Smith's command in September last, and reported to be held as a hostage for one L. C. Norman, of Boone County, Ky., and now a prisoner of the United States.

The matter of their exchange was referred to me to negotiate by the commissary-general of prisoners, Colonel Hoffman.

H. G. WRIGHT,
Major-General, Commanding.

———

JUDGE-ADVOCATE-GENERAL'S OFFICE, *December 1, 1862.*

On the application of Capt. Benjamin P. Walker, late assistant commissary of subsistence, to be restored to the service from which he was recently dismissed by order of the President:

The grounds on which this officer was dismissed are in the order stated to be "habitual absence from his post and gross and willful neglect of duty." These charges rest upon a report made to Colonel Hoffman, Third Infantry, U. S. Army, commissary-general of prisoners, by Capt. H. M. Lazelle, Eighth Infantry, U. S. Army, under date of 7th of August, 1862, and on a letter addressed to the latter on the 27th of July, 1862, by Col. C. W. B. Allison, temporarily commanding at Camp Chase. The report goes very much in detail and professes to be the result of an examination made into the administration of Captain Walker at Camp Chase. Captain Lazelle seems to have found nothing to commend but very much to condemn. The points which he presents against Captain Walker are principally:

1. Continued absence without leave from his post.
2. Inefficiency or unfaithfulness in receiving from the contractors and issuing to the troops inferior provisions.

———

* Omitted.

3. In charging to the department the expense of issuing the rations and the wastage which occurred and in unnecessarily keeping on hand large quantities of provisions at the risk of the Government.

As Captain Lazelle was at Camp Chase but a short time his own testimony in support of the charge of habitual absence without leave cannot be regarded as entitled to much more weight than belongs to the expression of an opinion formed from rumor or from the statements of others. The same remark may be made in reference to the letter of Colonel Allison, who in speaking of Captain Walker says, "He is absent three-fourths of the time. He has never asked or obtained my authority for his absence." It is ascertained that Colonel Allison who certifies so emphatically was in command at Camp Chase but for three or four weeks. Against these statements, based upon such limited opportunities for acquiring correct information on the point, we have the positive averment of W. J. Holmes that for eight months preceding the 19th of November, 1862, he had acted as military secretary of the post and had as such written leaves for Captain Walker by order as well of Colonel Moody as of Colonel Allison during their administrations. He adds: "I have no recollection of the captain ever being absent without leave or overstaying his leave of absence." John W. Sayre, Captain Walker's clerk through the entire time of his service, swears that to his knowledge the captain was never absent except on leave and that he never neglected his duties. This charge of absence without leave is fully refuted by various other persons of unquestionable credibility. The proof on the point is entirely satisfactory and removes all doubt as to the groundlessness of the imputation. Captain Lazelle seems to have based his report on a very cursory and superficial examination. Several of the witnesses state that he came "with kid gloves" and did not cut or handle anything but condemned everything on sight alone. It is but charitable to infer from the mistakes he made that he accepted as true complaints and hearsay which reached him without giving himself the trouble of scrutinizing them and ascertaining whether they were true or false. For example he states that "rock salt" alone was furnished by Captain Walker to the troops, whereas the proof is ample that not a pound of rock salt was ever issued to them. Again he says he was told that the "necks" of the beef had been habitually issued before his arrival at the post, and that he learned from one of the contractors that the shanks "to just below the knee" were also issued, whereas it is shown and by witnesses speaking under oath that neither shanks nor necks had ever been issued. His allegations as to the inferiority of the provisions and the complaints made of them are completely swept away by a mass of testimony, the greater part of it given under oath, which establishes that the beef was first quality and the flour extra superfine and the provisions such as were used by the citizens of Columbus at their own tables; that they were of good quality and that the rations were as good as are generally served and better than those frequently accepted by the Government.

Little or no complaint at all was heard. On these points the testimony comes from men of high character and occupying high official positions, many of whom from their immediate connection with the service had abundant opportunities of knowing personally the truth of the statements they have made. Brigadier-General Garfield passed three months at the post with his regiment, and he says: "My own regiment was well served, nor did I hear of any complaints from others."

I regard the evidence offered as showing beyond any reasonable ground for question that Captain Walker is a man of integrity and good business habits; that as an officer he was faithful and efficient and that his duties were discharged in a manner entirely satisfactory to the troops and to the Government. The report of Captain Lazelle was the first impeachment of his official conduct that had been made. Among the persons who have borne testimony to the effect which I have stated may be mentioned the quartermaster-general and the adjutant-general of Ohio; Captain Burr, assistant quartermaster, U. S. Army; John H. Wheeler, deputy U. S. marshal of Ohio; Samuel Galloway, special U. S. commissioner; Captain McClung, assistant quartermaster; Major Kilburn; Capt. Franklin Ernst, assistant quartermaster; N. B. Maple, post sutler; Capt. S. F. Allen; John E. Darby, assistant surgeon; Thomas J. Kerr; Thomas Jones, who supplied a large part of the flour; Alexander McBride, late post surgeon; Charles H. Goss, postmaster at Camp Chase; Louis Zettler, one of the contractors; John M. White and James R. Rusk, who supplied the beef, together with many others. It is not possible to suppose that all the witnesses—most of whom had personal knowledge of Captain Walker's administration from its beginning to its close—were deceived and that Captain Lazelle and Colonel Allison, who observed it for a few weeks, were alone acquainted with its true character.

The wastage which is made so conspicuous a feature in the complaint lodged against this officer does not appear to have exceeded what the Army Regulations allow. That this as well as the expense of issuing the rations should have been borne by the Government was in accordance with previous usage at the post and with the interpretation given to the contract by the parties to it and seems to have been acquiesced in without objection by the Commissary-General. The proof is conclusive that instead of keeping large amounts of provisions on hand only so much was received each day from the contractors as was required to be issued. Captain Lazelle no doubt mistook the warehouse of the contractor for that of the commissary. It is another evidence how superficial and unreliable was his examination. Without further going into particulars I will state in general terms that could the testimony now on file be submitted to the consideration of a court-martial I believe that Captain Walker would be unhesitatingly acquitted of all the charges made against him, and so believing I cannot but recommend his restoration to the service.

J. HOLT,
Judge-Advocate-General.

[First indorsement.]

DECEMBER 2, 1862.

On authority of this report I direct that Capt. Benjamin P. Walker be restored if practicable without detriment by the dismissal.

A. LINCOLN.

[Second indorsement.]

DECEMBER 2, 1862.

Report of Judge-Advocate-General approved and restoration ordered.

EDWIN M. STANTON,
Secretary of War.

OFFICE COMMISSARY-GENERAL OF PRISONERS,
Washington, D. C., December 1, 1862.

Hon. EDWARD SALOMON,
Governor of Wisconsin, Madison, Wis.

GOVERNOR: I have the honor to acknowledge the receipt of your letter of the 24th ultimo,* together with the accompanying papers from paroled troops of Wisconsin at Camp Parole, near Annapolis, complaining of their treatment, and I beg to offer the following reply: Two or three weeks since I made a personal inspection of the condition of that camp and I found the men there as well provided for as it was possible for them to be under the circumstances, and wherever there were deficiencies, of which there were very few, measures were taken for their immediate supply. I went into a great many tents and made many inquiries as to their condition, but there were few or no complaints. Some few men wanted a jacket or some other article of clothing and these were being supplied as fast as possible. Provisions were in a superabundance. The police of the camp within the company grounds was very good, but just outside it was in places very filthy, because these very men probably who complain, with others, would not obey the orders in relation to such matters. I endeavored to provide a remedy for this evil by ordering a guard-house to be built in which to confine and punish such offenders. Men in camps away from their homes make many groundless complaints in the hope to obtain through the interference of their friends a transfer to their own States, and they do all they can by disobedience of orders and neglect of police to give themselves good cause to say that they are badly treated. An order announcing the recent exchanges will be published as soon as it is received from the printers, and it covers nearly all our paroled troops, except a part of those taken at Harper's Ferry and subsequently. Since the exchange the paroled troops from Iowa at Annapolis have been ordered to Benton Barracks, and any from Wisconsin who may be in this section will be immediately ordered to the same point. Ohio troops go to Camp Wallace, in that State.

Trusting that the above explanations will be satisfactory, I am, Governor, very respectfully, your obedient servant,

W. HOFFMAN,
Colonel Third Infantry, Commissary-General of Prisoners.

OFFICE COMMISSARY-GENERAL OF PRISONERS,
Washington, D. C., December 1, 1862.

Col. G. DE KORPONAY,
Commanding Camp Banks, near Alexandria, Va.

COLONEL: All paroled men in your camp delivered at Aiken's Landing September 13, 1862, have been exchanged (see General Orders, No. 134, of September 19, 1862). The date (13th) is omitted in the order. Private I. J. Barry, Company A, One hundred and second Pennsylvania, is one of these men, and he and all exchanged at the same time should be mustered for their pay as soon as practicable. Some days since I gave to your adjutant a scale of rations to be issued to the fragments of companies under your command, the savings to be converted into a fund for the benefit of the whole command. With this fund purchase all articles that will in any way promote the health and comfort of the sick. If

---

you have not already comfortable hospitals, kitchens and outhouses have them made immediately and defray the expenses out of this fund. As the fund accrues disburse any not required for the sick in providing all necessary conveniences for your camp and anything necessary for the general good. Farmer's boilers for cooking are much more convenient than camp-kettles and cause a greater saving of fuel. Introduce them as soon as you can. One of forty gallons will cook for 100 men. Two or three camp-kettles may be required in addition to small articles. A horse-power saw-mill for sawing wood for the stoves will be very useful and economical, and I wish you to purchase one when you have funds to spare for the purpose. The horse will be furnished by the Quartermaster's Department. Out of the fund pay extra pay to the clerks in your office, not to exceed 40 cents per day.

Very respectfully, your obedient servant,

W. HOFFMAN,
Colonel Third Infantry, Commissary-General of Prisoners.

PROVOST-MARSHAL'S OFFICE,
New Berne, N. C., December 1, 1862.

Major HOFFMAN, *Assistant Adjutant-General:*

I have caused a sanitary inspection to be made of Craven Street Jail and have the honor to transmit Doctor Galloupe's report, to which I would respectfully ask your attention. I would also respectfully represent that the rooms and cells under this building are in the most deplorable condition—cold, damp, foul and utterly unsuitable for the confinement of human beings—and for the sake of humanity I would recommend that the following change be made, viz: That timber and materials be furnished to build a guard-house in the garden adjoining and that the rooms in this building with the exception of this office be fitted up for prisoners. You will notice that the surgeon advises the appointment of a new jailer and in a few days I shall recommend a suitable person; and remain,

Very respectfully, yours,

JONES FRANKLE,
Major, Provost-Marshal.

[Inclosure.]

NEW BERNE, *November 27, 1862.*

Maj. JONES FRANKLE, *Provost-Marshal.*

SIR: I have this day made the sanitary inspection of the Craven Street Jail and have the honor to submit the following report:

1. The cells and rooms occupied by the prisoners are in the most disgusting and filthy state, seriously endangering the health and lives of the prisoners; there is apparently no attempt to make the apartments either decent or healthy; no efficient means are provided for heating or ventilation; the prisoners urinate in tubs kept in the rooms; these tubs are saturated with urine and at the time of the inspection were nearly full, giving out an intolerable stench.

2. The clothing, blankets, &c., are damp, filthy and lousy; no pains are taken to sun and air these articles; the men are unwashed and untidy and many of them diseased.

3. Rations provided for the prisoners are of good quality but not properly cooked or served.

4. The rooms least suitable for occupation are overcrowded by prisoners while the best rooms are nearly empty.

Upon the whole the sanitary condition of this prison is most unfavorable and dangerous to the health and lives of its inmates. In view of this I would respectfully make the following suggestions:

1. That a man of experience, energy and discretion be selected for jailer.

2. All the rooms occupied by the prisoners should be thoroughly cleansed and suitable means for warming and ventilating them be provided.

3. Every man should be thoroughly bathed and provided with new and clean clothing; blankets, &c., should be sunned and aired daily; every man should be allowed at least two hours' exercise in the jail yard daily and should bathe at least once a week.

4. One room should be set apart for the sick, as a hospital, and an entire change made in the arrangement of the prisoners' quarters. The cells are totally unfit for occupancy; no one can be confined there twenty-four hours without danger to health.

Respectfully submitted.

ISAAC F. GALLOUPE,
Surgeon in Charge of Jails.

FORT MONROE, December 1, 1862.

Hon. E. M. STANTON:

Two hundred and seventy-seven released prisoners of war, 58 released Government laborers and 40 released political prisoners are sent to Annapolis to-day. Among the former are Major Jordan, Seventh [Ninth] Pennsylvania Cavalry, and 151 men and officers of Fifty-fourth Pennsylvania Regiment, captured at Paw Paw, who are exchanged and can be at once sent to their regiment.

WM. H. LUDLOW,
Lieutenant-Colonel and Agent for Exchange of Prisoners.

(Copy to Colonel Hoffman, commissary-general of prisoners.)

FORT MONROE, December 1, 1862.

Col. W. HOFFMAN, Commissary-General of Prisoners:

Where are the rolls of prisoners captured by General Rosecrans, reported as being 2,500? Can you send them to me?

WM. H. LUDLOW,
Lieutenant-Colonel and Agent for Exchange of Prisoners.

YORKTOWN, December 1, 1862.

Captain BARSTOW, Acting Assistant Adjutant-General:

Retain lists of prisoners and any papers and communications from Mr. Ould, and send Captain Mulford with the steamer New York and all the released prisoners to Annapolis to be turned over to the commanding officer of that post. Order Captain Mulford to bring back the steamer.

WM. H. LUDLOW,
Lieutenant-Colonel.

GENERAL ORDERS, ⎱ HDQRS. DEPARTMENT OF THE MISSOURI,
　　No. 23. ⎰　　　　　*Saint Louis, Mo., December 1, 1862.*

*　　　*　　　*　　　*　　　*　　　*　　　*

VII. Officers of the provost-marshal's department during the existence of civil war are especially intrusted with the peace and quiet of
their respective districts, counties and sections, and to this end may
cause the arrest and confinement of disloyal persons, subject to the
instructions and orders of the department. They will have charge of
all prisoners taken from the enemy; the keeping of the records as far
as possible of the prisoners taken by the enemy, that the proper data
for an exchange may be at any time obtained; the arrest and return or
imprisonment of deserters, and in general all duties relating to prisoners
of war or state.

VIII. Before any assistant provost marshal or the commander of any
troops or post shall send any prisoners to the provost-marshal-general
at these headquarters or to district provost-marshals he shall make a
list of such prisoners, stating when and where and by whom captured
(and if prisoners of war the rank, regiment and company to which
they belong), and also the charge against each prisoner, with the substance of the evidence against each, which statement and evidence
must be sent with the prisoners. And where persons arrested by
assistant provost-marshals are sent to the provost-marshal-general or
to district provost-marshals the witnesses against them must be first
examined, their residence stated and their testimony written down and
sworn to and sent along with the prisoners. Assistant provost-marshals and commanders should dispose of prisoners not charged with
serious offenses without sending them to Saint Louis, and they must be
careful not to send prisoners unless there is some evidence to warrant
imprisonment.

IX. Prisoners of war are entitled to be exchanged as soon as practicable, and all officers holding or capturing such prisoners will send
them forward at once to these headquarters to the provost-marshal-
general, to be exchanged or to be sent to the commissary-general of
prisoners as may be ordered.

X. All orders or parts of orders heretofore issued conflicting herewith are rescinded.

By command of Major-General Curtis:

　　　　　　　　H. Z. CURTIS,
　　　　　　　　　Assistant Adjutant-General.

　　　　　ADJUTANT-GENERAL'S OFFICE,
　　　　　　　Washington, December 2, 1862.
COMMANDING OFFICER, *Fort Delaware, Del.:*

The Secretary of War directs that you discharge Judge Carmichael
from custody. Report receipt of this.

　　　　　　　　E. D. TOWNSEND,
　　　　　　　　　Assistant Adjutant-General.

Resolution adopted by the United States Senate December 3, 1862.

Resolved, That the Secretary of War be requested to furnish to the
Senate any information he may possess with reference to the sale into
slavery of colored freemen captured or seized by the rebel forces, and
to state what steps have been taken to redress this outrage upon
human rights.

HEADQUARTERS PAROLED PRISONERS,
Near Annapolis, Md., December 3, 1862.
Col. W. HOFFMAN, *Commissary-General of Prisoners.*

SIR: In compliance with your instructions I have the honor to report the number of men from the different Western States as follows: Ohio, 2 officers, 238 enlisted men; Tennessee, 1 officer, 122 enlisted men; Michigan, 2 officers, 122 enlisted men; Indiana, 51 enlisted men; Wisconsin, 2 officers, 64 enlisted men; Virginia, 20 enlisted men; Missouri, 7 enlisted men; Minnesota, 2 officers, 18 enlisted men; Kentucky, 1 officer, 3 enlisted men; Illinois, 6 enlisted men. Total, 10 officers, 651 enlisted men.

Very respectfully, your obedient servant,
GEO. SANGSTER,
Lieutenant-Colonel, Commanding Paroled Prisoners.

OFFICE FOR EXCHANGE OF PRISONERS,
Vicksburg, Miss., December 3, 1862.
Captain BICKFORD, U. S. Army,
Agent for Exchange of Prisoners, near Vicksburg, Miss.

CAPTAIN: I have the honor to hand inclosed copy of a letter received from Maj. Gen. M. L. Smith, C. S. Army. I am sorry that his complaints are true and frequently complained of by our returning prisoners of war, and hope you will disavow any participation in the matter on the part of your Government.

I have the honor to be, very respectfully, your obedient servant,
N. G. WATTS,
Major, C. S. Army, and Agent for Exchange of Prisoners.

[Inclosure.]

VICKSBURG, *December 3, 1862.*
Major WATTS, *Agent for Exchange of Prisoners.*

MAJOR: You are to call the attention of the Federal agent for exchange of prisoners to the fact that our men state on returning that all their money is invariably taken from them and not returned. Every blanket resembling a Federal blanket is claimed. The watches and money of officers are taken from their possession and kept and trunks emptied of clothing. No such treatment that I am aware of has been experienced by their prisoners, and it is hoped the above is not done by any authority of their officers and that it may not recur in future.

Very respectfully,

M. L. SMITH,
Major-General, Commanding.

HEADQUARTERS DEPARTMENT OF THE MISSOURI,
Saint Louis, December 3, 1862.
Brig. Gen. C. P. BUCKINGHAM, *Assistant Adjutant-General.*

GENERAL: Yours of the 26th ultimo* in relation to the return to duty of the Iowa officers and soldiers exchanged is duly received. The trouble is to know who are exchanged. No lists or descriptions have been sent and I am constantly importuned on this subject. Occasional newspaper notices inform us of some officers being exchanged

---

* Not found.

and I have acted on these, but I respectfully submit that immediate notice should be brought home to department and district commanders of exchanges, so we may know who to detail for duty. Exchanged or not exchanged should they not return to their rendezvous?

I have the honor to be, general, your obedient servant,

S. R. CURTIS,
Major-General.

HEADQUARTERS ARMY OF TENNESSEE,
Murfreesborough, Tenn., December 3, 1862.

Maj. Gen. W. S. ROSECRANS,
Commanding U. S. Forces, Nashville, Tenn.

GENERAL: I inclose for your information the following papers, viz:

1. General Orders, No. 84, from the Adjutant and Inspector General's Office, Richmond, in reference to Federal military violations of the laws and usages of war, with retaliatory provisions, special and general.

2. An extract of a communication from Clarksville, Tenn., giving a statement of the outrages committed upon private citizens and their deplorable condition under the military authority as administered there.

3. A copy of a report from the commanding officer of my picket forces in your front detailing the depredations which marked the route of one of your reconnoitering parties a few days since, under the orders and sanction of its officers.

4. Extract from the report of another picket officer on the Lebanon road, in which he gives the statement of a reliable citizen as to the system of rapine indulged in by another one of your reconnoitering parties.

I deem it unnecessary to enlarge upon the subject as presented in the papers submitted to you. I could multiply almost indefinitely authentic complaints from widely separated parts of my department setting forth a similar condition of affairs, as consequent upon a visit or occupation by your troops. Inasmuch, however, as in your highly esteemed favor of the 29th ultimo* you foreshadowed a correction of the previous existing causes of complaint by declaring your intention to observe the usages and laws of war I shall place a generous construction upon the late occurrences and hope that they were without your knowledge and will meet with a prompt correction and punishment.

Awaiting your reply I shall abstain from the disagreeable duty of considering the steps which a suffering people and an outraged civilization will demand in order to put a stop to such an extended and uniform system of unparalleled and savage warfare.

I am, general, very respectfully, your obedient servant,

BRAXTON BRAGG,
General, Commanding.

[Inclosure No. 1.]

GENERAL ORDERS, }   ADJT. AND INSP. GENERAL'S OFFICE,
      No. 84.   }   *Richmond, November 10, 1862.*

I. The following orders are published for the information and guidance of the Army:

II. Whereas, reliable information has been received that Colonel Lowe and Col. A. C. Harding, Eighth Illinois Regiment, U. S. Army, have been engaged in a series of wanton cruelties and depredations in Clarksville,

---

* See Series I, Vol. XX, Part II, p. 109.

Tenn., and the surrounding counties, which in many instances have resulted in the arrest, incarceration and maltreatment of non-combatants and peaceful citizens of the Confederate States, and in others in the unjustifiable destruction of private property without compensation and contrary to the rules and practice of civilized warfare: Therefore, it is ordered that the aforesaid Colonel Lowe and Col. A. C. Harding, Eighth Illinois Volunteers, U. S. Army, be and they are hereby declared no longer entitled to be regarded as soldiers, and that they have forfeited all claim to the benefits of the cartel existing between the Governments of the Confederate States and the United States for the exchange of prisoners of war, and further that in the event of their capture they shall be kept in close confinement and treated as felons until otherwise ordered by the President of the Confederate States.

III. And whereas, other officers of the U. S. Army yet unknown to the Confederate Government are represented and believed to have participated in the wrongs and outrages before referred to: Therefore, it is also ordered that the provisions of the first paragraph of this order shall be applicable to any other officers of the Federal Army in the State of Tennessee, upon proof of their guilt deemed satisfactory by the commanding officer of the department in which they may be captured and held.

*   *   *   *   *   *   *

By order: S. COOPER,
                              Adjutant and Inspector General.

[Inclosure No. 2.]

Extract from a communication from Clarksville, Tenn.

The commander above named and others have been and still are engaged in arresting many of the citizens of this portion of country and placing them in a loathsome dungeon and keeping them there unless they take the oath of allegiance, these citizens being in no way connected with the Confederate Army.

They have gone to the premises of many citizens seizing them and destroying or carrying away all their property of every description. In some cases they burn everything before them. They have taken away hundreds of negroes; they have visited houses insulting ladies and threatening to shoot, stab, bayonet and even burn them. They have robbed them of their wardrobes—not only of men, but those of women and children.

They are also in the habit of taking all the negroes. We in this city have been visited by these men and treated in a savage and brutal manner, and they daily threaten to return and utterly destroy the city and imprison all the citizens who do not take the oath of allegiance to the Federal Government.

The aforesaid Harding visited a church in the country and arrested two ministers of the gospel and placed them in prison, where they still are. He also took the horses and carriages from the congregation and required the persons present, both male and female, to take the oath or go to prison, and he proclaims that every man in the country shall be arrested and either take the oath or go to the dungeon. This is our present condition.

Now we are wholly unprepared to repel these insults and oppressions. It is true there are still many men here who are willing to meet them, but we are wholly destitute of both arms and ammunition, nor is there any military force in this vicinity that is able to repel them.

[Inclosure No. 3.]

HEADQUARTERS CAVALRY BRIGADE,
La Vergne, Tenn., December 1, 1862.

[GEORGE WM. BRENT.]

COLONEL: I have the honor to state that the enemy have been for the last month burning all unoccupied houses between La Vergne and Nashville. Up to this time they have to my knowledge burned more than twenty houses. At and near La Vergne last Thursday they burned several under the immediate direction of their officers. They stated that they did not intend to leave any shelter for rebels.

They take special care to burn houses near which our pickets have been stationed, but by no means confine themselves to these.

Respectfully, colonel, your obedient servant,

JOS. WHEELER,
Brigadier-General and Chief of Cavalry.

[Inclosure No. 4.]

Extract from report of officer commanding pickets on the Lebanon road, December 1.

* * * * * * *

He says they are destroying and burning everything in their route, taking even the shoes from the feet of the women. They have a large number of wagons and are evidently on a marauding expedition.

HEADQUARTERS ARMY OF TENNESSEE,
Murfreesborough, Tenn., December 3, 1862.

Maj. Gen. W. S. ROSECRANS,
Commanding U. S. Forces, Nashville, Tenn.

GENERAL: I inclose you a copy marked A of reports made by medical officers of my command in regard to the indignities to which they were subjected while they were in the hands of your predecessor. As the officer from whom they received such severe and unjustifiable treatment is probably not within your jurisdiction I beg that you will forward the papers with a copy of this communication as far as pertains to the case to his proper commander. The rumor which was made the pretext for the confinement of these officers in violation of the cartel existing between the two Governments was wholly unfounded. It would be most painful to me to be compelled to resort to retaliation for such acts of cruelty or bad faith, but if their committal is encouraged in subordinate officers by allowing them to go unpunished or unremarked there will be but one course left me.

I desire also to call your attention to the case of Surgeon Horton, Tenth Regiment Tennessee Volunteers, who is reported to me as confined on parole within the limits of the city of Nashville and prohibited from communicating with his Government. You will oblige me by informing me of the reasons of this exceptional course toward this officer.

The case of Private R. K. Kerchival, Fourth Tennessee Volunteers, imprisoned in Nashville by General Negley and refused an exchange, as set forth in the inclosed statement marked B, is submitted also to your special attention.

It will afford me unalloyed pleasure to learn that in these cases of great apparent hardship and abuse "the laws and usages of war" have been enforced and the parties guilty of violating them brought to just and merited punishment.

I am, general, very respectfully, your obedient servant,
BRAXTON BRAGG,
General, Commanding.

[Inclosure A.]

NICKAJACK, *November* 10, 1862.

General BRAXTON BRAGG.

SIR: In company with K. C. Divine, brigade surgeon, Fourth Brigade, Second Division, Left Wing, Army of the Mississippi, I left our hospitals near Perryville, Ky., October 20, and proceeded to Harrodsburg to confer with Surgeon Moore, left in charge. On the 21st we left Harrodsburg for Danville, at which place we arrived in the evening and found General Buell and a large part of his forces just arrived from Crab Orchard en route for Lebanon, Ky. Having been refused permission to pass out of Kentucky by any other route than via Somerset, I obtained through the instrumentality of my personal friend, Dr. Robert Murray, General Buell's medical director, passes for myself and Doctor Divine to rejoin our command by that route, but on starting that way was deterred from continuing by the information that the Knob counties of Kentucky and Tennessee were infested by gangs of Union bushwhackers and thieves and the report that several persons on that route had been shot and plundered, a Confederate surgeon among the number. We therefore went to Lebanon, Ky., disposed of our horses and took the cars for Louisville, to which place General Buell had gone. We were insulted by Yankee officers in the cars and threatened with arrest.

On our arrival at Louisville on Saturday night, October 25 (in a violent snow-storm), we put up at the Galt House, registering our names as surgeons, C. S. Army. On examining the register after supper we discovered the letters C. S. A. had been erased. In the morning after breakfast I saw Lieutenant Bush, aide to General Buell, and asked him to procure us permits to pass down the river to Vicksburg on a boat that was to leave that night with paroled Confederate prisoners. He promised to see General Buell and procure passes for us and leave a note for me at the hotel office. We left the hotel in the morning for the house of a friend. In the evening we were informed by a friend in the Federal service that the boat would leave that night and that he understood we were to be sent to the military prison. At my request he went to the office of the Galt House and brought me a note from Lieutenant Bush (herewith annexed) referring us to General Boyle. Upon repairing at once to General Boyle we were referred to Colonel Dent, provost-marshal, who informed us we were under arrest and must go to the prison hospital "as hostages for a Federal surgeon who was reported to be confined in a dungeon at Knoxville, Tenn., on bread and water." We were courteously allowed by Colonel Dent to return to our friend's house to supper and report at the prison at 8 p. m., which we did, protesting, however, against our imprisonment. We were assigned beds in the hospital wards and ate at the surgeons' table. We found in the hospital as hostages like ourselves Surgeons Alexander and Leak and Assistant Surgeon Meux, C. S. Army, who had been confined to the prison but transferred to the hospital. We found many of our wounded soldiers in the hospital, whom we took charge of and attended to their wounds. On the following [day] after our imprisonment we addressed a joint note to General Boyle (copy annexed), to which we received no reply.

On Wednesday evening, the 29th instant, we were ordered by Surgeon Head, U. S. post surgeon at Louisville, to be transferred from the military hospital to the military prison, in which were confined some 500 Confederate soldiers (paroled), political prisoners and others, among whom we found three more Confederate surgeons who had that day been imprisoned, viz, Assistant Surgeons Phillips, Fenner and Clark. I addressed a note to Doctor Murray, General Buell's medical director, and through his interference we were released and ordered to report on the evening of the 30th to Doctor Cowan, C. S. Army, at the Louisville Hotel, where we found he had been furnished with transportation for us to Cairo, via railroad through Indiana and Illinois. At Cairo we reported to the general in command (General Tuttle), who telegraphed to General Grant for permission to send us through the Federal lines at Memphis. General Grant replied, ordering General Sherman at Memphis to "pass through the lines rebel surgeons."

We left Cairo on the Belle Memphis on the evening of Saturday, November 1, transportation given us, and arrived at Memphis on Monday morning, the 3d instant, where we procured a pass from General Sherman and conveyance to Hernando. Thence next day to Coldwater, where we took the cars, and I proceeded via Grenada, Jackson, Mobile and Atlanta hither. Please find notes, &c., annexed. Surgeon Jones, C. S. Army, who was also imprisoned at Louisville, was sent down on the boat to Vicksburg with our paroled men, on his parole to return in forty days. Surgeons Leak, Fenner and Clark were robbed by the Federals of their knives, pocket instruments and some clothing.

Deeming it proper to communicate the above facts to the general commanding, I remain, very respectfully,

H. HINKLEY,
Brigade Surgeon.

[Sub-inclosure No. 1.]

HEADQUARTERS 121ST REGIMENT OHIO VOLUNTEERS,
Perryville, Ky., October 19, 1862.

The guard will pass the bearer, H. Hinkley, brigade surgeon, First Brigade, Second Division, Army Mississippi, Left Wing, through our lines.

W. P. REID,
Colonel, Commanding Post

[Sub-inclosure No. 2.]

HEADQUARTERS ARMY OF OHIO,
In Camp, October 21, 1862.

Pass Surgeon Hinkley, C. S. Army, through our lines south via Somerset, he having given his parole not to divulge anything to the prejudice of the U. S. service.

By order of Major-General Buell:

T. J. BUSH,
First Lieutenant.

[Sub-inclosure No. 3.]

OCTOBER 24, 1862.

Doctor HINKLEY.

SIR: The general has given directions to General Boyle about your getting South. You will find him at his headquarters on Seventh street near Broadway.

Very respectfully, your obedient servant,

T. J. BUSH.

[Sub-inclosure No. 4.]

MILITARY PRISON HOSPITAL, *October 29, 1862.*
[General J. T. BOYLE.]

SIR: We take the liberty of addressing you to-day to call your attention to a change in our situation, ordered yesterday by Doctor Head, medical director. Confederate surgeons, we were on our arrival here (on our way South from attending to our wounded in Perryville) arrested and sent to the prison hospital to be held (so we were informed) as hostages for a Federal surgeon said to be confined in Knoxville, Tenn. We are now to be sent to the military prison by order of Doctor Head. While we ask leave to doubt the truth of any Federal surgeon being confined merely for being a Federal surgeon, we would respectfully request of you if we are held as prisoners to be confined to some other quarters more comfortable to us as non-combatants and more suited to our condition. We will cheerfully give our parole of honor not to leave any premises or house you may confine us to, or give you bond here in the city if released on parole to return here in a specified time if the Federal surgeon should prove to be confined. We respectfully request that if we are to be held as prisoners we be assigned quarters better suited to our condition than the military prison, provided we have to leave the hospital.

Respectfully,

K. C. DIVINE,
[J. M.] ALEXANDER,
H. HINKLEY,
Brigade Surgeons.

T. W. LEAK,
Surgeon.

[T. R.] MEUX,
[N. D.] PHILLIPS,
[J. S.] FENNER,
[A. T.] CLARK,
Assistant Surgeons.

[Sub-inclosure No. 5.]

HEADQUARTERS DISTRICT OF MEMPHIS,
Memphis, November 3, 1862.

Dr. J. B. Cowan, C. S. Army; Doctor Hinkley, C. S. Army; Doctor Phillips, C. S. Army; Doctor Clark, C. S. Army; Doctor Leak, C. S. Army; Doctor Divine, C. S. Army; Doctor Fenner, C. S. Army, and Doctor Meux, C. S. Army, are hereby permitted to proceed southward to the Confederate lines pursuant to instructions from Maj. Gen. U. S. Grant. They will proceed by the Hernando road to-day.

By order of Major-General Sherman:

J. H. HAMMOND,
Assistant Adjutant-General.

[Inclosure B.]

TULLAHOMA, TENN., *November 22, 1862.*
Dr. A. J. FOARD, *Surgeon and Medical Director.*

SIR: In company with Dr. H. Hinkley, brigade surgeon, First Brigade, Second Division, Army of the Mississippi, I left McDowell Hospital, near Perryville, Ky., October 20 and proceeded to Harrodsburg to report to and confer with Doctor Moore, left in charge. On 21st at 2 p. m. we left for Danville, at which place we arrived in the evening. Found General Buell and the major part of his forces just returning from Crab Orchard (General L. Wallace having been left at Big Hill) en route for Lebanon, Ky.

Having been refused permission to pass out of Kentucky by way of the Gap (reason assigned, the general did not want us to pass through his army) we were granted permission to pass via Somerset, but on starting that way we were assured that General Bragg's army was making for Nashville or Murfreesborough, and receiving information that the Knob counties of Tennessee and Kentucky were infested by gangs of bushwhackers and thieves, and the report that several persons on that route had been shot and plundered, a Confederate surgeon among the number, we concluded to go to Lebanon, Ky., and if possible to get in advance of the Federal Army and make our way to Murfreesborough. Failing in our intentions we were advised by Dr. R. Murray, General Buell's medical director, to sell our horses and go by way of Louisville, to which place General Buell had preceded us.

Whilst on the cars we were insulted by a couple of drunken Federal officers and threatened with arrest. On our arrival at Louisville at 9 p. m. Saturday, 25th, in a violent snow-storm, we put up at the Galt House, registering our names as surgeons, C. S. Army. On examining the register after supper we found the letters C. S. A. had been erased, whereupon I demanded to know the perpetrator of so low and base an act. The clerk denied knowing. After we had left the house I was told that it was done by the proprietor, Silas Miller, former captain of steam-boat Robert J. Ward, a man who had made all of his money from the patronage of Southern people.

Sunday morning, October 25, after breakfast I requested to see General Buell, but was told by his aide-de-camp, Lieutenant Bush, that he was yet in bed, but that he would see him and have a note at the office bar, with passes, &c., so that we might go down the river on the boat to leave that evening with paroled prisoners. Finding it unpleasant to remain longer at the hotel, we repaired to the house of a friend, Lighter Huffman. In the afternoon we were informed by a friend, Captain Sherley, in the Federal service, that the boat would leave that night, and that there was an order for our arrest from Brigadier-General Boyle. He (Captain Sherley) advised us to remain quiet indoors until near the time of the boat's starting. Supposing that General Boyle merely wished to pay his respects to us until the time for the boat to leave, we did as advised. At our request Captain S. went to the Galt House and returned with a note from Lieutenant Bush, in which Lieutenant B. stated that General Boyle had instructions as to our getting South. This confirmed us in our former opinion.

At 6.30 p. m. we reported to General Boyle's adjutant-general (General B. refusing to see us). We were directed by him to Colonel Dent, provost-marshal, who informed us that we were to go to the prison hospital, there to remain as hostages for one Doctor Goins, a surgeon of theirs, whom a citizen (Doctor Hall) reported was in a dungeon at Knoxville on bread and water. We were further told he was immured because of his being a Tennesseean, and was therefore held as a traitor. We were kindly allowed by Colonel Dent to return to the house of our friend obtain our articles and report at the prison at 8 p. m., which we did, protesting, however, against our imprisonment in the strongest terms. Finding that of no avail I told him that should our Government so far forget its principles and its dignity as to commit so infamous an act that I would not serve it another day. Colonel Dent replied that it was bad treatment and not acting in good faith, but that he had his orders and must obey them. We were assigned beds in the hospital wards and ate at the surgeons' table.

We found in the prison hospital J. M. Alexander, surgeon Second Brigade, First Division, Army of the Mississippi; Surgeon Leak, Fourth Tennessee Regiment; N. D. Phillips, assistant surgeon Smith's battery, General Maney's brigade; J. S. Fenner, assistant surgeon Sixth Tennessee Regiment; T. R. Meux, assistant surgeon Thirty-Fourth Tennessee Regiment, and A. T. Clark, assistant surgeon Sixth Tennessee Regiment, who had been transferred from the prison to the prison hospital, which is in the same general inclosure and closely guarded. We found many of our wounded whom we took charge of.

On the day after our imprisonment we addressed a joint note to General Boyle, a copy of which was furnished by Doctor Hinkley, to which we received no reply. On Wednesday, October 29, we were ordered by General Boyle, approved by Doctor Head, post surgeon, to the prison proper, in which were 500 of our soldiers who had been paroled at and near Perryville, their money and pocket knives having been taken from them. The money they returned to all except Morgan's men, refusing, however, to return the knives.

Whilst in the prison they gave us prison fare, and that was given from the hands of filthy and disgusting Dutchmen. On the evening of the 29th Dr. J. B. Cowan, surgeon-general Forrest's brigade, reached Louisville. Hearing of our confinement he sought an interview and complained to General Buell, who ordered our release stating that he did not know of our imprisonment. His adjutant-general, General Fry, did, but stated that he thought that we had been released long ago. General Boyle gave to Doctor Cowan as the reason for our arrest and imprisonment "that we had cut up" and used seditious language, therefore required punishment, admitting, however, that the officers who complained of Doctor Hinkley and myself were drunk. There was no complaint lodged against the other surgeons, consequently giving the lie to his first assertion. The reason assigned for imprisoning our paroled soldiers was to prevent their receiving the sympathy of the "Secesh;" that they would furnish them clothing which would enable them to stand the winter campaign. G. D. Prentice said it was to prevent their sharing the sympathies of the she-devils.

General Boyle sent a written order for us to report to Doctor Cowan at the Louisville Hotel without delay. This order we promptly obeyed, glad enough to get out of such a place. We were ordered to leave immediately and were furnished transportation through Indiana and Illinois on the cars to Cairo, where we were treated kindly by General Tuttle, who telegraphed to General Grant asking [permission] for us to pass via Memphis. He replied telling General Tuttle to pass us through his lines in ambulances. On reaching Memphis finding that we would be detained a day or more if we waited for the ambulances some citizens of Memphis kindly procured a couple of hacks for which they paid $50, and sent us to Hernando, Miss.; there our money being good, we procured wagons and went to Coldwater station, on Mississippi and Tennessee Railroad, from which place we took cars, &c., to this place.

Respectfully,

K. C. DIVINE,
Surgeon, C. S. Army.

OFFICE COMMISSARY-GENERAL OF PRISONERS,
Washington, D. C., December 3, 1862.

Lieut. Col. W. H. LUDLOW,
Agent for the Exchange of Prisoners, Fort Monroe, Va.

COLONEL: I inclose herewith a letter* from Judge Goodloe, of Lexington, Ky., inclosed by Major-General Wright, commanding Department of the Ohio, in relation to the capture and parole of home guards in Kentucky.

Under the cartel there can be certainly no propriety in the rebel authorities imposing any other than the usual restrictions on those whom they may capture. Have you the views of Mr. Ould in this matter or can you make any suggestions as to the best course to be pursued?

I inclose a list† of Federal officers and men captured at different places, which I have picked up at different times. No rolls are furnished.

Rolls of General Rosecrans' captures have been forwarded to this city but they have not yet arrived. I will forward to you as fast as I receive them all rolls of Federal or rebel prisoners.

Very respectfully, your obedient servant,

W. HOFFMAN,
Colonel Third Infantry, Commissary-General of Prisoners.

OFFICE COMMISSARY-GENERAL OF PRISONERS,
Washington, D. C., December 3, 1862.

Capt. S. E. JONES,
Headquarters Western District, Louisville, Ky.

CAPTAIN: Your letter of the 22d ultimo‡ is received and I have to reply that deserters from the rebel army cannot be considered prisoners of war but to insure their loyalty they should be required to take the oath of allegiance with the penalty of death for its violation.

If professed deserters come within our lines they may be spies and every commander should judge of each case after careful inquiries according to the circumstances. All soldiers taken in arms, whether recruits or conscripts, are prisoners of war, and if they desire not to be exchanged but to be released on bond a special report should be made in each case with a recommendation for or against. All civilians who took part with the rebels during their recent inroad into Kentucky should be sent to the depot at Johnson's Island, Sandusky, with a clear statement of the charges in each case. Doubtful cases may be sent to Camp Chase.

Very respectfully, your obedient servant,

W. HOFFMAN,
Colonel Third Infantry, Commissary-General of Prisoners.

HEADQUARTERS DEPARTMENT OF VIRGINIA,
Fort Monroe, December 3, 1862.

ROBERT OULD, Esq., *Agent for Exchange of Prisoners.*

SIR: Your communication of the 29th§ of November has been received and forwarded to the Secretary of War. In my letter to you of the

---

* See Vol. IV, this Series, p. 706. ‡ See Vol. IV, this Series, p. 745.
† Omitted. § See Vol. IV, this Series, p. 770.

20th* November I informed you that orders had been issued and were being executed to send all the prisoners at the West belonging to irregular organizations to Vicksburg for exchange. The same orders are intended to apply to those in the department of General Butler. The political prisoners at Forts Warren and Lafayette and the Old Capitol Prison at Washington have with a few exceptions been unconditionally released. These orders will show you the policy of the United States Government and will probably cover points 2 and 3 in your official communication of the 29th November. In view of these releases I hope you will no longer hesitate to reciprocate by ordering the release of the Robinsons, father, son and son-in-law, and all others similarly confined. I send you to-day in addition to prisoners of war Mr. S. H. Lyon, who goes to Richmond in exchange for Alfred Schleg, released on condition to procure this exchange. I intend to meet you in a few days. Please send me by Captain Mulford a list of persons wishing to come via flag of truce through our lines. Within a few days a number of persons, mostly women and children, will apply to be sent to City Point. Will they be permitted to land at that place? They belong at the South.

I am, very respectfully, your obedient servant,
WM. H. LUDLOW,
Lieutenant-Colonel and Agent for Exchange of Prisoners.

HEADQUARTERS, *Fort Monroe, Va., December 3, 1862.*
Hon. ROBERT OULD, *Agent for Exchange of Prisoners.*

SIR: Since I wrote you this morning information has been given me that some thirty or forty citizens of Pennsylvania, non-combatants, were seized by order of General Stuart in his late incursion into Pennsylvania and Maryland and were conveyed to Richmond. This is so clearly in contravention of the positions you have laid down that I need only mention the fact to you to insure their immediate delivery to Captain Mulford, in charge of the flag of truce.

Your obedient servant,
WM. H. LUDLOW,
Lieutenant-Colonel and Agent for Exchange of Prisoners.

OFFICE PROVOST-MARSHAL-GENERAL,
Saint Louis, Mo., December 3, 1862.
Brig. Gen. LEWIS MERRILL,
Headquarters District of Northeast Missouri, Warrenton, Mo.

GENERAL: A considerable number of citizens from the interior of the State—and amongst them are several undoubted Union men who have suffered in the cause—have made urgent application to me to give a hearing to the prisoners who have been captured and sent down by you as sentenced to imprisonment for the war. It is urged upon me that amongst those prisoners will be found a considerable number of young men whose fathers and connections are true Union men who never before took up arms and who went off most indiscreetly under the excitement produced by the enrolling orders, and that they are now willing to give their adhesion to the side of the Government

---

* See Vol. IV, this Series, p. 738.

and give bond for the performance of their promise; also to enroll in the Enrolled Missouri Militia. Amongst those pressing this matter is Judge A. Leonard, of Fayette, whom I personally know and esteem. He requests the release of the sincerely penitent who have never before been in arms and who will enroll and give bond. I understand from General Curtis that he is in favor of so dealing with them. Will it not be better to select out from the mass those who will probably conduct themselves in a loyal manner in the future if their first offense be passed over? My wish is to take that course with them, but I consider it due to you that I present the matter to you before taking any steps. My aim will be not to release any one unless I believe that he will honestly keep his engagements, which I will secure by a good bond. May I ask, general, that you will give this your early consideration and reply to this as soon as practicable.

I have the honor to remain, your obedient servant,

F. A. DICK,
Lieutenant-Colonel and Provost-Marshal-General.

WAR DEPARTMENT, *Washington, December 3, 1862.*
Lieut. Col. WM. H. LUDLOW, *Commanding at Fort Monroe.*

COLONEL: You will please communicate with Mr. Ould the intention of the War Department to escort to the lines all ladies and their children who desire to join their husbands and relatives who make proper application previous to the 16th instant. It is proposed to send them from this city about the 25th instant. Please make such arrangements as will obviate detention.

By order of the Secretary of War:

L. C. TURNER,
Judge-Advocate.

OFFICE PROVOST-MARSHAL-GENERAL,
Saint Louis, Mo., December 3, 1862.
Col. W. HOFFMAN, *Commissary-General of Prisoners.*

COLONEL: J. J. Clarkson, of Dade County, Mo., is now a prisoner in the jail of this county. He is held upon an indictment found against him in the U. S. circuit court. As a rebel officer he was engaged in the battle at Lexington, Mo., in September, 1861. His indictment is based upon his service in the rebel army, under the late act of Congress, for conspiracy. He claims to be a colonel in the C. S. Army. He was commissioned July, 1861, by C. F. Jackson as Governor of Missouri, as colonel Fifth Infantry Missouri State Guard. He states that he was transferred from the infantry Missouri State Guard to cavalry C. S. Army and carried his rank with him. He was never formally commissioned by any one in the Confederate service but was constantly recognized as a colonel in the Confederate Army by Generals Van Dorn and Hindman under both of whom he served. The evidence he produces shows that he acted in the C. S. Army as a colonel, and after his transfer from the Missouri State Guard received no orders from General Price. In March, 1862, he was authorized by General Van Dorn to raise a battalion of six companies of cavalry for the war, and a majority of the regiment which he commanded when captured were from Arkansas. He was captured in July, 1862, with about fifty of his men in the Cherokee

Nation. Two of his lieutenants captured with him he states have been exchanged. He was held a prisoner of war from July to October, 1862, when under the indictment he was delivered to the U. S. marshal and put in jail. Under the cartel he claims the right to be exchanged. Not being in my custody upon his application I have had him examined, and he now remains in jail until the questions involved in his case shall be decided. I am anxious to receive specific directions as a guide to determine such questions as they arise, and I ask:

1. Do the facts stated place Clarkson upon the footing of a colonel in the Confederate service so that it is safe to send him forward for exchange as an officer of that rank, or should he be detained until it is ascertained that one of our colonels will be returned in exchange for him?

2. Supposing him entitled to be treated as a colonel in the Confederate service is the pending indictment to interfere with his being exchanged? If recognized as a Confederate officer must he not at once be granted an exchange? The indictment is based upon the ground that he is a citizen; the cartel treats him as a belligerent.

3. He was captured in arms and is a prisoner of war, and if not considered an officer what shall be his status?

4. Colonel Clarkson being now in the custody of the U. S. marshal by order of the circuit court of the United States it is the duty of the marshal to produce his body in court at its next sitting. The marshal insists upon holding the prisoner. The court does not sit until April, 1863, so that the matter cannot be brought before it that it may make an order to deliver the prisoner to the military authorities. If it is decided that I am to take the prisoner from the marshal by superior force I ask specific instructions in relation to the matter. Should there not be either an order from the Secretary of War directing me to take this man from the marshal and send him forward to be exchanged as a prisoner of war, or else an order in terms embracing all such cases? And in view of other cases now being examined by me I also need instructions upon other points.

5. There are prisoners of war under my control against whom indictments have been found in the U. S. circuit court based upon the said law for conspiring through this rebellion to overthrow the Government. The U. S. marshal asks me to surrender these prisoners to him that they may be arraigned in court upon the indictments. Will you direct what course I shall pursue? And under this head arise two questions: First, what answer should I give the marshal if such prisoners desire to be exchanged according to the terms of the cartel? And second, in your letter to Colonel Gantt of 20th September, 1862, the last paragraph states: "All prisoners belonging to the Confederate Army who desire it will be released upon taking the oath of allegiance." If Confederate prisoners held by me avail themselves of this means of obtaining a discharge and the marshal demands their delivery to him what should be my action? The prisoners have no means of learning that such indictment has been found against them.

6. There is a large number of prisoners in my custody, probably over 200, who have been captured in the central and northern part of Missouri within the last three months who state that they have been sworn into the Confederate service. It appears that persons claiming to be authorized to recruit for the Confederate army entered the State, passing up from Arkansas into the northern part of the State. They went amongst the guerrilla bands of Porter, Poindexter and others and claiming to be duly authorized swore these men into the rebel service, and when most of these men were captured they were working their

way toward Arkansas with the intention of serving in the rebel army. Many of these men now claim to be exchanged as prisoners of war. I ask to be instructed as to what I shall do with them. And at this point I desire to call your attention to that clause in your letter of the 20th of September above quoted. I have acted upon that, as making it obligatory upon me to release any prisoner of war who offers to take the oath. Would it not be safer to leave it to my discretion to refuse a release where I entertain serious suspicions as to the good faith of the prisoner? And another question has arisen in my mind under that clause. It is whether deserters from the rebel army who deliver themselves up as prisoners are to be entitled to a release upon taking the oath. A few days ago a man came to my office professing to be a deserter, having safely passed the lines and reached Saint Louis without being questioned. He asked to take the oath and be released. From his manner and appearance I thought it not unlikely that he was a spy, and yet it was but suspicion that I felt. In such a case if the rule you have established leaves it to my discretion I would hold the man in custody until satisfied of his honesty.

In your letter to Colonel Gantt of the 13th* of October you direct that prisoners sent to Alton must be accompanied by a full list, giving all the details required by the printed rolls, and that they must be sent to arrive in the daytime. A large number of irregular prisoners are sent to Saint Louis picked up by detached companies in this State. They sometimes pass through two or three hands before they reach me. They are guerrillas or bushwhackers and marauders of various kinds. All that I can learn about them is from the evidence taken to prove their acts, and it contains generally no particular beyond the county, and not always that. It is impossible to give all the particulars in such cases. When bands of men are captured they are often sent forward with only their names and the general proof against the entire body. The officers who capture them send them here for imprisonment without delay, and all that they can know is that they were captured as a marauding band in arms but without permanent officers or organization. When prisoners sent from here reach Alton after dark it is in consequence of the necessity of sending them by the daily packet which starts in the afternoon and is sometimes detained.

I have the honor to be, very respectfully, your obedient servant,

F. A. DICK,
Lieutenant-Colonel and Provost-Marshal-General.

HEADQUARTERS DEPOT PRISONERS OF WAR,
Near Sandusky, Ohio, December 3, 1862.

Col. W. HOFFMAN, *Commissary-General of Prisoners:*

Inclosed you will find return† of prisoners for November. I have designed to make it comply with your directions of the 29th November by putting on the back all changes. I have, however, excepted the rolls of prisoners sent during the month and also this day. I have heretofore been in the practice of notifying you by letter of every discharge and so supposed the dead were the only prisoners necessary to name on the returns. You will observe that our list of dead is very large. I think I can get along without hiring a clerk as you permit me, and if I can think it my duty so to do.

Very respectfully, your obedient servant,

WM. S. PIERSON,
Major Hoffman's Battalion, Commanding.

---

* See Vol. IV, this Series, p. 618.   † Omitted.

MADISON, WIS., *December 4, 1862.*

Hon. E. M. STANTON:

It is almost four weeks since I advised you of the arrest of men who forcibly resisted draft in Ozaukee County. They were arrested under President's proclamation, to be tried by court-martial. They are in General Pope's custody but should be tried at once. To release on parole or keep them without trial would be unjust and very injurious. Has no conclusion been arrived at yet? Please answer.

E. SALOMON,
Governor of Wisconsin.

HDQRS. 14TH ARMY CORPS, DEPT. OF THE CUMBERLAND,
Nashville, December 4, 1862.

His Excellency ANDREW JOHNSON,
Military Governor of Tennessee, Nashville, Tenn.

GOVERNOR: Applications for permission to take the parole not to take up arms, &c., are being made to officers commanding detached portions of this army. This induces me to request that you will appoint commissioners in the various counties of the State where it is practicable or politic to do so for the purpose of administering the oath of allegiance or non-combatant parole and taking the necessary bonds. I would also be pleased if you could appoint a commissioner to accompany this army in order to release on oath or parole all persons falling into our hands who are desirous of taking either.

I have the honor to be, with much respect, your obedient servant,

W. S. ROSECRANS,
Major-General, Commanding Department.

OFFICE COMMISSARY-GENERAL OF PRISONERS,
Washington, D. C, December 4, 1862.

Col. E. D. TOWNSEND, *Assistant Adjutant-General.*

COLONEL: Only the Indiana troops taken at Munfordville, Ky., have been exchanged (see paragraph 10, General Orders, No. 191*). There are no rolls in this office of the Kentucky troops taken at Munfordville. I presume Colonel Ludlow has them.

Very respectfully, your obedient se——

W. HOFFMAN,
Colonel Third Infantry, C——— ary-General of Prisoners.

OFFICE CO——— GENERAL OF PRISONERS,
———ington, D. C., *December 4, 1862.*

Lieut. Col. W. H. LUDLOW,
Agent for Exchange of P——oners; Fort Monroe, Va.

COLONEL: I send by this mail rolls received to-day of rebel prisoners recently delivered at Vicksburg. Other rolls must be received in a few days of prisoners sent from Sandusky (Ohio), Alton and Louisville, and there should be more from General Grant's army.

Yesterday six political prisoners arrived here under a parole for thirty days for the purpose of effecting the release and exchange for themselves of six named persons, as follows: (1) Jesse B. Kimes for C. F. Ward,

---

* See Vol. IV, this Series, p. 736.

Confederate; (2) Joseph Winger for George Carter, Confederate; (3) George G. Rupley for Doctor Jackson, Confederate; (4) J. M. McCowan for John C. Spiggs, Confederate; (5) Sanford Schroeder for Henry A. Ball, Confederate; (6) Andrew Hartman for John Dowell, Confederate. Of the rebel prisoners I can find records of but three, viz, C. F. Ward, escaped from prison in this city November 17, 1862; J. C. Spiggs, released on oath November 25, 1862, and H. A. Ball, still held in the Old Capitol. George Carter, Doctor Jackson and John Dowell cannot be found on the rolls.

Under these circumstances what can be done for the men whose equivalents cannot be found?

Very respectfully, your obedient servant,

W. HOFFMAN,
Colonel Third Infantry, Commissary-General of Prisoners.

OFFICE COMMISSARY-GENERAL OF PRISONERS,
Washington, D. C., December 4, 1862.

Lieut. Col. F. A. DICK,
Provost-Marshal-General, Saint Louis, Mo.

COLONEL: I desire to call your attention to certain matters connected with the Alton Prison which occasion much confusion and detriment to the service. It is reported to me that recently 273 prisoners arrived at the prison about 10 o'clock of a dark and bitter cold night. No rolls or papers of any kind were sent with these prisoners and as a consequence it was only with much labor, if not impossible, to make a correct report of them. Orders from the War Department and instructions from this office require that when prisoners are sent to any station full rolls shall accompany them, and I request that hereafter rolls may be sent with all prisoners ordered from Saint Louis to Alton, and I request also if it is practicable that transportation may be provided in such a way that they may arrive before night.

By the orders from the War Department prisoners can only be released from the Alton Prison by its authority, but as you will perceive by my correspondence with your predecessor, Colonel Gantt, I directed the commanding officer to release on the order of the provost-marshal-general such prisoners as he might have sent up on charges which proved to be without foundation, but at the same time I requested him to reserve as far as practicable the Gratiot Street Prison for all cases under investigation.

Except in these cases all releases not ordered by the Secretary of War or the commander of the department are unauthorized, and the commander of the prison disobeys his instructions in consenting to them.

It is reported to me that great inconvenience is experienced by the daily calls for the release of prisoners made from your office, and I must request that hereafter you will order the release of no prisoner except under the circumstances mentioned in the instructions which I have heretofore given.

I have sent you copies of my printed circulars and I beg to call your attention to my written instructions to Colonel Gantt.

The management of the prison is under my exclusive control, and only such regulations as I approve will be carried out there.

Very respectfully, your obedient servant,

W. HOFFMAN,
Colonel Third Infantry, Commissary-General of Prisoners.

OFFICE COMMISSARY-GENERAL OF PRISONERS,
Washington, D. C., December 4, 1862.

Maj. PETER ZINN,
Commanding Camp Chase, Columbus, Ohio.

MAJOR: Your letter of the 28th has been received. Deserters from the rebel army cannot be considered as prisoners of war; but as spies may come in under that garb or it may be assumed as a ground for release, great caution must be observed that no imposition is practiced. You will refer to this office all cases where this claim is set up, with all the circumstances which are given to sustain them, in order that a decision may be made. All soldiers taken in arms whether recruits or conscripts are prisoners of war, and if they desire not to be exchanged but to be released on bond a special report should be made in each case with a recommendation for or against. Make a special report in all cases where prisoners have entered the rebel service in violation of their oath. Parole bonds do not seem to come within the meaning of the law requiring stamps and I presume no such stamp will be necessary.

Very respectfully, your obedient servant,

W. HOFFMAN,
Colonel Third Infantry, Commissary-General of Prisoners.

HEADQUARTERS DEPARTMENT OF VIRGINIA,
Fort Monroe, December 4, 1862.

Col. W. HOFFMAN, Commissary-General of Prisoners.

COLONEL: I inclose to you to-day various papers with indorsements. Some of them are old references to me by General Thomas, but they can now be acted on by you. I must have the list of General Rosecrans' paroled prisoners before meeting with Mr. Ould. It will be worth the while if not otherwise speedily obtained to send a special agent for them. Have the Confederate prisoners, members of irregular organizations, been released and sent to Vicksburg?

Yours, very respectfully,

WM. H. LUDLOW,
Lieutenant-Colonel and Agent for Exchange of Prisoners.

ON BOARD TRANSPORT METROPOLITAN,
Off Vicksburg, Miss., December 4, 1862.

Maj. N. G. WATTS, C. S. Army,
Agent for Exchange of Prisoners:

In reply to your communication of the 3d instant I beg leave to state that I have no personal knowledge of or participation in the detention from prisoners of war of any money or other property on the part of my Government except such as is authorized by the usages of war, but that the statement of any specific cases of a different nature which you may be pleased to make together with your note will be by me laid before the proper authorities for examination.

With great respect, I remain, your obedient servant,

W. W. BICKFORD,
Captain, U. S. Army, and Agent for Exchange of Prisoners.

[DECEMBER 4, 1862.—For General Orders, No. 31, Department of the Cumberland, relating to the return to their homes of those Kentuckians who had abandoned the rebel armies. see Series I, Vol. XX, Part II. p. 122.]

Resolution adopted by the United States Senate December 5, 1862.

Resolved, That the President be requested to inform the Senate if not incompatible with the public service the number and the names of citizens of Kentucky who have been and who are now confined in the military prisons and camps of the United States outside the limits of said State, and what are the charges against them, by whom made and by whose order the arrest was made.

HDQRS. 13TH ARMY CORPS, DEPT. OF THE TENNESSEE,
Oxford, Miss., December 5, 1862.
Lieutenant-General PEMBERTON,
Commanding Confederate Forces.

GENERAL: I have now several hundred Confederate prisoners who by the Dix-Hill cartel will have to be sent to Vicksburg for exchange unless by agreement they will be received elsewhere.

I propose to deliver them at such point on the Mississippi Central road as you may suggest and where an officer of your command may be to receive and receipt for them. Or I will parole and release them here, sending rolls certified to for an officer of your army to receipt if you prefer it.

Please inform me of your pleasure in this matter and I will conform to it.

I am, very respectfully, your obedient servant,
U. S. GRANT,
Major-General.

HEADQUARTERS DEPARTMENT OF THE OHIO,
Cincinnati, Ohio, December 5, 1862.
Brig. Gen. L. THOMAS,
Adjutant-General U. S. Army, Washington, D. C.

GENERAL: I have the honor to inclose a communication from Brig. Gen. J. T. Boyle, commanding District of Western Kentucky, in reference to the course to be pursued toward rebel deserters who have delivered themselves up to the military authorities in Kentucky. The views presented by General Boyle upon this subject are so entirely in accordance with my own that I would ask that his letter be presented to the Secretary of War for his information and such action as he may deem proper. I do not clearly understand why General Boyle desires or has looked for further instructions. Those he has are ample to meet all the various requirements so far as they can be foreseen, and I have therefore instructed him in replying to his letter to carry out the orders already given him from these headquarters.

Very respectfully, your obedient servant,
H. G. WRIGHT,
Major-General, Commanding.

[Inclosure.]

HEADQUARTERS DISTRICT OF WESTERN KENTUCKY,
Louisville, November 30, 1862.

Maj. Gen. H. G. WRIGHT,
Commanding Department of the Ohio, Cincinnati, Ohio.

GENERAL: I have received no orders or instructions for execution of General Orders, No. 49, modified by you, since I reported to you the action under the existing orders. Colonel Hoffman telegraphs, "Send rebel deserters to Camp Chase." Now, general, the execution of Orders, No. 49, and its modifications with all errors that may be committed were infinitely better than to send all rebel deserters to Camp Chase. The expense to the Government will be very great, and the evils resulting from such a policy will be incalculable, to say nothing of the great injustice to individuals. Many of these new recruits deserting are small boys from under fourteen to eighteen years of age—foolish, deluded youths, who should not be confined with a pack of scoundrels. Many of them are ignorant men, made to believe they were conscripted— some forced into the service and some inveigled into the rebel army. Nearly the whole of them are deserters, some being paroled at their request supposing it released them from rebel obligations. If extreme measures are taken forcing these men to Vicksburg we convert our State into a recruiting field to fill the thinned and decimated ranks of the rebels. If they are forced to prison they will never surrender themselves but make their way South, or form bands in our State rather than be immured in prisons. I feel sure I would prefer anything rather than be sent to prison, and I doubt not these men will; whereas a lenient policy compared to this will recover these men from their fallen condition and win them to allegiance to the Government and restore them to good citizenship. There are a good many of these men who ought to be sent North and some who should be confined in prison. But the great body of them are better men, better citizens and deserving more leniency than hundreds in the city and thousands in the State who enjoy the protection of the Government in their lives and property and business. The Secretary of War has repeatedly complained as I understand his communications against arrest of this class of citizens who are tenfold more guilty than these deserters. I have a very large acquaintance throughout this State and I think I can form a pretty correct judgment in regard to these men and can separate pretty justly between the classes who should be released and those who should be sent to Vicksburg or to prison. Besides these rebel recruits deserting there are a good many deserters of Northern birth and foreigners belonging to Northern States. Surely these men should not be sent to prison or to Vicksburg. There are yet in the rebel army hundreds of them who will desert if opportunity offers. Shall all inducement to desert be withdrawn? Shall we punish for desertion from the rebel army? Shall we announce to them that they shall have a felon's cell in our prisons or be sent to Vicksburg to a rebel gallows? What then shall be done with discharged rebels—with those who served their time out, who wish to remain at home or go North? I beg, general, that you will submit this subject with this letter to the Government if you do not feel authorized to give orders for execution of the modified orders on this subject. I cannot doubt that these views will meet your approval as they are in perfect harmony with the modifications made by you.

I regret very much to be placed continually in a position to subject me to censure at one time for extreme rigor and severity and at another for inactive leniency. I can be relieved of this if full instructions are given on these subjects. I believe I understand this subject and our people and the true interests of the Government, and I could administer the matter to the real interest of the whole country.

I am, general, very respectfully, your obedient servant,

J. T. BOYLE,
Brigadier-General.

WASHINGTON, D. C., *December 5, 1862.*

Col. E. D. TOWNSEND, *Assistant Adjutant-General.*

COLONEL: General Orders, No. 191, directing the assembling of paroled U. S. prisoners at the general camps at Benton Barracks and Indianapolis does not finally dispose of them by ordering them to their respective commands.

The General-in-Chief directs that special orders be sent to the commanding officers of the general camps through department commanders to forward the exchanged prisoners there assembled to the armies to which they belong with the least delay. They will be distributed to their respective regiments by army commanders. They will be sent in all cases under charge of commissioned officers, who before leaving the camp will have rolls of the detachment of each regiment, battery, &c., made out.

Prisoners belonging to regiments in the Department of the Missouri will be forwarded by orders from the department commander, Saint Louis. Those belonging to the Department of the Tennessee will be sent to Memphis, touching at Columbus, Ky., for orders. Those belonging to the Departments of the Ohio and the Cumberland will be sent to Louisville, Ky., reporting to the commanding officer at Louisville, who will forward to Nashville the men whose regiments are serving in the Department of the Cumberland. Commanders of camps can ascertain where regiments are serving by applying to the Adjutant-General's Office at Washington, D. C.

Very respectfully, your obedient servant,

J. C. KELTON,
Assistant Adjutant-General.

OFFICE COMMISSARY-GENERAL OF PRISONERS,
Washington, D. C., December 5, 1862.

Maj. W. S. PIERSON,
Commanding Depot of Prisoners, Sandusky, Ohio.

MAJOR: S. B. Greenfield and G. C. Bronaugh, political prisoners from Kentucky, so far as the books show come under paragraph II of General Orders, No. 193, of November 22, from the War Department, and if there are no other charges against them they and all others similarly situated in your charge are entitled to release on parole under the above order. Those who go to Kentucky should be required to report to the provost-marshal at Louisville; those to Tennessee to the provost-marshal at Nashville; those to Missouri to the provost-marshal at Saint Louis, and those to Virginia to the provost-marshal at Wheeling. In other Western States they should report to the nearest military authority to their homes.

Very respectfully, your obedient servant,

W. HOFFMAN,
Colonel Third Infantry, Commissary-General of Prisoners.

FORT MONROE, *December 5, 1862.*

Col. W. HOFFMAN, *Commissary-General of Prisoners:*

All of the Shiloh prisoners, officers and men, wherever found are exchanged. The rolls of exchanges were left by me in the Adjutant-General's Office. Many Shiloh prisoners were delivered on the Commodore.

WM. H. LUDLOW,
Lieutenant-Colonel and Agent for Exchange of Prisoners.

HEADQUARTERS DEPARTMENT OF VIRGINIA,
Fort Monroe, December 5, 1862.

Col. W. HOFFMAN, *Commissary-General of Prisoners.*

COLONEL: In addition to the lists of paroled men it will be necessary for me to have the original paroles or a receipt or something to show that they have been delivered within the Confederate lines. All the Indiana troops captured at Munfordville, Ky., are exchanged. The order covers all. I return the lists* sent to me and I will arrange the difference in the sum total with Mr. Ould, whom I cannot meet until I have the rolls of General Rosecrans' captures.

I am, very respectfully, your obedient servant,

WM. H. LUDLOW,
Lieutenant-Colonel and Agent for Exchange of Prisoners.

HEADQUARTERS PAROLED PRISONERS,
Near Annapolis, Md., December 5, 1862.

Col. W. HOFFMAN, *Commissary-General of Prisoners.*

SIR: Yours of yesterday in relation to officers visiting Washington without proper authority is received, and in reply I would say that in all cases where officers have applied to me for permission I have informed them that the authority rested entirely with the War Department. I know that officers are in the habit of going to Washington and to other cities without any authority, and I have been very anxious that some measures be adopted to prevent it. Frequently when officers have been absent without authority and I attempt to reprove them for it they inform me that they were at the Adjutant-General's Office; that he did not say anything to them about it and that they thought the Adjutant-General was my superior officer. There is not an officer at this camp that has not been informed that they are disobeying orders by going to Washington, but some having gone and transacted their business with the Department it has encouraged others to go, and I do not think there is a day that there are not some of them at the capital. All officers upon their reporting here are assigned to duty with companies. We have quarters now in camp for all the officers, and if the provost-marshal at Annapolis had instructions to arrest all officers in that city without proper authority it would be a great assistance in conducting the business of this camp. Their presence with the men would have a salutary effect upon their discipline. There are a number of officers who are attentive to their duties and are good officers. There are also a large number who are scarcely ever in camp and who seldom do any duty. These officers we have reported to you.

---

* Omitted.

I shall do everything in my power to meet your views in the conducting of this camp, and you may rest assured that no officer goes to Washington with my consent unless he is sent there on business of these headquarters with yourself.

I am, colonel, very respectfully, your obedient servant,

GEO. SANGSTER,
Lieutenant-Colonel Commanding Paroled Prisoners.

HEADQUARTERS DEPOT PRISONERS OF WAR,
Near Sandusky, Ohio, December 5, 1862.

Col. W. HOFFMAN, *Commissary-General of Prisoners:*

I am just in receipt of General Orders, No. 193, with regard to which I wrote you some days ago. I am embarrassed with the order because I think it probable that many of the prisoners should not be discharged from exceptions in paragraph III, and I have no information in this office as to the cases. I have charges against very few, and in many instances do not know by what authority they were arrested. I have directed a list of the citizens to be copied from the roll books. I shall then examine each case, and where I find no charge or evidence against the prisoner within the meaning of paragraph III from the States of Kentucky, Missouri, Tennessee and Virginia I shall offer him his parole. To-day is Friday, and as I think great care should be taken in this matter I shall not probably get the list and be able to commence action under it before Monday. I shall then proceed as fast as I can offer the prisoners their parole as above, and prepare them (the paroles) and execute them and let them go. Please telegraph me at once if this course is not correct. I suppose Missouri and Kentucky are rebel States within the meaning of this order.

Very respectfully, your obedient servant,

WM. S. PIERSON,
Major Hoffman's Battalion, Commanding.

P. S.—Forty prisoners arrived last evening from Henderson, Ky.; among them are citizens [who] I think will have to be discharged under Orders, No. 193. The lieutenant of the guard says they are very bad men. I will send roll to-morrow.

WAR DEPARTMENT, *Washington, December 6, 1862.*

The COMMANDANT OF FORT DELAWARE:

You will immediately release I. C. W. Powell, a prisoner, who is said to have been arrested at the same time with Judge Carmichael, and who is said to be now in Fort Delaware.

EDWIN M. STANTON.

ATTORNEY-GENERAL'S OFFICE,
Washington, December 6, 1862.

Hon. WILLIAM A. HALL, *Member of Congress.*

DEAR SIR: Your letter of yesterday in behalf of Henry Foot, of Randolph County, Mo., states that he stands indicted of both conspiracy and treason, and after stating some mitigating circumstances asks "that these prosecutions be discontinued." Pardon me for suggesting (for your further consideration) that the discontinuance or *nolle prosequi* of these indictments would leave the party still open to accusation upon the same grounds; whereas a pardon if the case be proper for one would leave him safe from future prosecution.

Very respectfully, your obedient servant,

EDWARD BATES.

HEADQUARTERS DEPARTMENT OF THE OHIO,
Cincinnati, Ohio, December 6, 1862.

Maj. Gen. W. S. ROSECRANS,
Commanding Department of the Ohio.

GENERAL: I have the honor to acknowledge receipt of your letter of the 27th ultimo in regard to persons professing to be deserters from the rebel army returning to Kentucky. The instructions issued from these headquarters for the guidance of district commanders are to the effect that those persons who are for good reasons believed to be *bona fide* deserters from the rebels may be allowed to return to the State and there remain at liberty upon their taking the oath of allegiance and giving bond with reliable surety of its proper observance. Professed deserters or others to whom suspicion attaches to be arrested and sent to some place of security provided for the safe-keeping of political prisoners, Camp Chase being a convenient and proper place for such purpose.

I am, general, respectfully, your obedient servant,

H. G. WRIGHT,
Major-General, Commanding Department.

HDQRS. DEPT. OF MISSISSIPPI AND EAST LOUISIANA,
Grenada, Miss., December 6, 1862.

Maj. Gen. U. S. GRANT, *Commanding U. S. Forces, &c.*

GENERAL: Your communication of 5th instant just received. The prisoners referred to I presume to be the sick who were necessarily left and stragglers from this army. The former if agreeable to you I would prefer should be kept in hospital until they can be sent for and proper receipts given. The latter as the roads are in bad condition and railroad bridges destroyed I would ask to be sent to Vicksburg, Miss., as is required by terms of the cartel.

I have some forty prisoners taken in action who will be sent to Vicksburg for exchange.

I am, general, very respectfully, &c., your obedient servant,

J. C. PEMBERTON,
Lieutenant-General, Commanding.

OXFORD, MISS., *December 6, 1862.*

Brig. Gen. GRENVILLE M. DODGE, *Corinth, Miss.:*

The general commanding has communicated with the general commanding Confederate forces on the subject of army surgeons who are captured having the right to retain their horses and other private property, indicating his willingness to let them take with them when released everything that is necessary to enable them to perform their vocations in the field, but has not yet received a reply, and until he does their horses and surgical instruments will be held, they having set the example in depriving our surgeons when captured of such property.

By order of Maj. Gen. U. S. Grant:

JNO. A. RAWLINS,
Assistant Adjutant-General.

HEADQUARTERS DEPARTMENT OF THE OHIO,
Cincinnati, Ohio, December 6, 1862.

Col. WILLIAM HOFFMAN,
Commissary-General of Prisoners, Washington, D. C.

COLONEL: Inclosed* is a letter from General John W. Finnell, adjutant-general of the State of Kentucky, in regard to exchange of prisoners, which letter is referred to you with request for advice at these headquarters upon the points in question, viz, can home guards or recruits for incomplete regiments, in service when captured though not mustered in, be duly exchanged as and for prisoners of war, and must they report in person at Camp Lew. Wallace before being entitled to exchange?

There are a great many paroled prisoners, stragglers, about the country who have never reported as required at Camp Lew. Wallace, some of them belonging to detachments of prisoners which have so reported and been exchanged.

Have such men been included in the recent exchange? If so they will readily come in and join their regiments. While their dislike to going to Camp Wallace is so great that they will manage to keep out of the way and avoid the authorities if reporting there is presented as the only alternative.

Asking early consideration and reply, respectfully, by command of Major-General Wright, commanding department,

J. M. RICE,
Captain and Aide-de-Camp.

OFFICE COMMISSARY-GENERAL OF PRISONERS,
Washington, D. C., December 6, 1862.

Maj. PETER ZINN,
Commanding Camp Chase, Columbus, Ohio.

MAJOR: Your letter of the 1st instant is received and your action in the matter of the release from parole of W. H. H. Plummer by the military commander of Covington is approved. If the prisoner was to be discharged under the orders from the War Department it was your duty and not Colonel Sipes' to carry out the order and his interference was unauthorized. Orders, No. 193, of November 22, from the War Department, require that two classes of prisoners shall be released and it is for you as the commander of the prison at Camp Chase to execute the order. The first paragraph refers to those who have discouraged enlistments or interfered with the draft in any State where the drafting has been completed (see paragraph I). If there are cases of this kind at Camp Chase you must ascertain from the Governor of the State where the offense was committed whether the draft has been completed before the prisoner can be released. The

---

* Not found.

second paragraph refers to prisoners who have been sent from Virginia, Kentucky, Tennessee and Missouri by the Governors or other military authorities charged with disloyal practices. The records in your office must decide the character of the offense, and when prisoners are released you will require them to report to the provost-marshal at Wheeling, Louisville, Nashville or Saint Louis according to the State in which they reside, or to the military commander nearest to their homes.

The third paragraph points out the exceptions to be observed. In cases where you have any doubt it will be proper that you should consult with Judge S. Galloway.

Very respectfully, your obedient servant,

W. HOFFMAN,
Colonel Third Infantry, Commissary-General of Prisoners.

HEADQUARTERS DEPARTMENT OF VIRGINIA,
Fort Monroe, December 6, 1862.

Col. W. HOFFMAN, *Commissary-General of Prisoners.*

COLONEL: The various applications for exchanges referred to me are reserved for my next interview with Mr. Ould, which will be as I have before mentioned as soon as I receive the rolls and papers relating to the captures of General Rosecrans. I will endeavor to arrange the release of three men whose equivalents cannot be found before the expiration of their parole and will inform you of the result. If I cannot they must of course return. Thomas McKay, William D. Bartlett and Benjamin Hicks were arrested by some of General Pope's officers under circumstances detailed in a letter* a copy of which was furnished to me by Mr. Ould and which is inclosed. Will you please have these cases investigated and the men released if the facts are as stated in the letter of Mr. Jacobs? The Confederate authorities have frequently called my attention to these cases and I wish to give them a decided answer now.

I am, very respectfully, your obedient servant,

WM. H. LUDLOW,
Lieutenant-Colonel and Agent for Exchange of Prisoners.

OFFICE COMMISSARY-GENERAL OF PRISONERS,
Washington, D. C., December 6, 1862.

Col. WILLIAM HOFFMAN,
Commissary-General of Prisoners, Washington, D. C.

COLONEL: In compliance with your instructions dated Washington, November 11, 1862, I on the 28th ultimo, having completed my duties at Alton, repaired immediately to Louisville, arriving thereon Saturday, the 29th. I immediately conferred with Col. Henry Dent, Thirty-fourth Kentucky Volunteers, provost-marshal-general of Kentucky, and from him ascertained that all prisoners, both political and military, as soon as arrested within the State were forwarded to him at Louisville with such charges or explanations of their offenses as the nature of their arrests would require. Acting under instructions from the commanding officer of the department all minor cases were adjudicated by him and in every case his action had been submitted to the commanding officer for approval. All political prisoners against whom serious charges

---

* Not found; but see Jacobs to Davis, Vol. IV, this Series, p. 873.

were preferred were sent to Camp Chase, Ohio. All prisoners of war were forwarded via Cairo to Vicksburg for exchange.

On Sunday, the 30th, I inspected the prison, the main entrance to which is on Broadway, near Tenth street. The prison is a temporary one, erected on the inside of a square, three sides of which are formed by the quarters of the Thirty-fourth Regiment Kentucky Volunteers, which constitutes the guard of the prison. The prison quarters are temporary frame buildings, conveniently arranged, entirely separated from the quarters of the troops and inclosed by a high fence, which includes sufficient grounds for exercise. The guards were suitably posted and the prison was as secure as possible for a temporary one. It was under the command of Lieut. Col. L. H. Ferrell, Thirty-fourth Kentucky Volunteers. The capacity of the prison accommodations is about 300, but can be readily extended to 1,000 with but little expense. The food furnished the prisoners was ample for their subsistence and of the first quality. The cooking arrangements were excellent. The cooks were contrabands. The prison was crowded, containing over 300, but their general health was quite good. The police of the prison is good. The hospital is separate from the prison but is within the main inclosure. It is used by the guard and prisoners. It is under the charge of Asst. Surg. George W. Ronald, Thirty-fourth Kentucky Volunteers, and is superior in neatness and comfort to any I have yet visited. There is no reason why the regulations as contained in your circular of July 7 should not be enforced here, but the changes that daily occur will cause it to be difficult to maintain the division or company organization as directed in paragraph I of that circular. Paragraph XI will also require alteration. All other paragraphs may be strictly enforced. A prisoners' fund may be accumulated here to great advantage to the Government. Although your regulations have not been enforced here everything in relation to the prison has been conducted with due regard to economy to carry out the intentions of the Government and to secure to the prisoners kind but firm treatment. The following releases and transfers have occurred since November 1 to November 24, inclusive, viz: 2,417 prisoners of war sent to Cairo, Ill.; 74 recent recruits from General Bragg's army sent to Cairo, Ill.; 190 deserters from the rebel army, natives of England, Ireland and Scotland and claiming to belong to Northern States, discharged upon oath of allegiance; 186 deserters, recent recruits, who joined Bragg while in Kentucky, discharged on oath and bond; 30 political prisoners sent to Camp Chase; 50 political prisoners discharged on oath and bond; 2 political prisoners sent to Vicksburg for exchange. I inclose herewith a roll* of the prisoners confined at Louisville, which will explain their character. I also inclose herewith a letter from the provost-marshal-general.

Respectfully submitted.

H. W. FREEDLEY,
Captain, Third U. S. Infty., Assistant to Com. Gen. of Prisoners.

[Inclosure.]

HDQRS. PROVOST-MARSHAL-GENERAL OF KENTUCKY,
Louisville, Ky., December 1, 1862.

Captain FREEDLEY.

SIR: In the short interview with you on yesterday you requested me to state in writing the various suggestions made on that occasion.

First. The duties of provost-marshal at this point are very onerous, as you will perceive by examination of prison report. Wherefore the

---

* Omitted.

department of provost-marshal of this State is one of great labor, and every facility should be given to enable that officer to furnish the commissary-general with accurate information.

Second. If the department should wish me to continue those duties I would ask to be detached from my regiment, as the labor is so great I cannot perform it.

Third. There should be at least three clerks in this department to keep up the work. For the last sixteen months I have performed the labor myself with the assistance of one man, and he an ordinary clerk. I am broken down and I can perform it no longer without the above-named assistance.

Fourth. The provost-marshal's department should be separate from that of the military and be required to report direct to the department at Washington in relation to everything connected with prisoners.

Fifth. Giving general supervision to the commanding officer of the district over said department.

Sixth. An order should be made giving the provost-marshal the power to permit such prisoners as are bare of clothing to be furnished with same by their friends or to be furnished by Government.

Seventh. All articles of contraband of war found with prisoners should be sold for the benefit of prison.

Eighth. Several slaves have been brought to the prison with their masters who were captured, said slaves having acted as cooks, &c. I should like to know what shall be done with them. If we turn them loose in Kentucky they are liable to be arrested by the civil authorities, placed in the county jail and sold for jail fees, and if individuals or corporations put them across the Ohio River they are liable for their value by civil proceeding. Our people protest against their being let loose in our midst.

Ninth. There is a divided sentiment in this State as to what disposition shall be made of deserters and what we term political prisoners. There are but few men arrested but what have friends among the Union people, who make strong appeals for their release. Some general rule on this subject would save us much trouble.

Respectfully,

HENRY DENT,
Colonel and Provost-Marshal-General.

HDQRS. MILITARY DISTRICT OF WASHINGTON, D. C.,
December 6, 1862.

WILLIAM P. WOOD, *Superintendent Old Capitol Prison.*

SIR: You will please forward as soon as possible a list of Union men released from the Salisbury Prison, N. C., by your intercession while you were there in your capacity as commissioner from the Military District of Columbia.

This list is necessary for the information of Colonel Hoffman, commissary-general of prisoners, in order that he may see the situation of the prisoners recently sent from Richmond, who instead of being treated as exchanged prisoners have been released on parole.

I wish the information to be such as to show Colonel Hoffman that the Southern Confederacy, so-called, repudiated a proper, legal and honorable exchange.

I am, sir, very respectfully, your obedient servant,

JOHN P. SHERBURNE,
Assistant Adjutant-General.

OFFICE COMMISSARY-GENERAL OF PRISONERS,
Washington, D. C., December 7, 1862.

Col. E. D. TOWNSEND,
   Assistant Adjutant-General, Washington, D. C.

COLONEL: Much embarrassment and injury to the service is experienced from the practice which generally prevails of sending paroled Federal troops from the lines to interior camps without rolls of any kind or with very imperfect ones, and also of paroling rebel prisoners without making any report of the circumstances or furnishing any rolls. Recently a detachment of 200 or 300 paroled troops arrived at Camp Parole unaccompanied by rolls, and officers and men paroled by the enemy have straggled in from the Army of the Potomac and reported to me having nothing in writing to show their position. But partial rolls have yet reached this office of the rebels captured at Corinth and Iuka, and these are far from satisfactory. To remedy this evil I respectfully suggest that an order be issued immediately and widely circulated to all commanders requiring that in all cases where our troops are captured by the enemy and paroled the senior officer present shall cause to be prepared and forwarded to this office with as little delay as practicable a full list by regiments and companies of all so paroled, giving the rank, regiment and company of each person, the time and place of capture and the disposition made of them; also that like rolls shall be prepared and furnished to this office of all rebel prisoners captured by our forces.

When the circumstances are such that a roll cannot be immediately prepared a written report giving the number of officers and men, the time and place of capture and the disposition made of them shall be made, to be followed by the necessary rolls at the earliest practicable moment. I would suggest also that when rebel prisoners are sent to Vicksburg for exchange commanders be required to send duplicate rolls with them, one to remain with the agent who receives them and the other with his receipt upon it to be forwarded to the Adjutant-General marked for the commissary-general of prisoners.

Very respectfully, your obedient servant,

W. HOFFMAN,
Colonel Third Infantry, Commissary-General of Prisoners.

[Indorsement.]

ADJUTANT-GENERAL'S OFFICE, *January 7, 1863.*

Attention is respectfully invited to the subject of this letter and of the inclosed General Orders, No. 163.

By order of the Secretary of War:

E. D. TOWNSEND,
Assistant Adjutant-General.

[Inclosure.]

GENERAL ORDERS, } WAR DEPT., ADJT. GENERAL'S OFFICE,
   No. 163.   }   *Washington, October 22, 1862.*

Whenever prisoners of war are released on parole and sent through the lines the officers who release them will immediately send rolls to the Adjutant General of the Army containing an exact list of the prisoners' names, rank, regiment, date and place of capture and date of release on parole. These rolls are indispensable in effecting exchanges of prisoners.

By order of the Secretary of War:

L. THOMAS,
Adjutant-General.

WAR DEPARTMENT, *Washington, December 7, 1862.*
Lieut. Col. WM. H. LUDLOW, *Fort Monroe, Agent, &c.:*

I am directed by the Secretary of War to say in answer to the interrogatory in your letter of the 4th instant that the reception by the Confederates of the women and children we sent cannot be reciprocated by the reception of those they send. If the Confederates refuse to receive them we can bring them back. If they advise you in time that they will not be received none will be forwarded. I have now a large number (150) of applications.

L. C. TURNER,
Judge-Advocate.

HEADQUARTERS PAROLED PRISONERS,
Near Annapolis, Md., December 7, 1862.

Col. W. HOFFMAN, *Commissary-General of Prisoners.*

SIR: In obedience to your instructions of the 29th instant [ultimo] I have the honor to submit the following report:

After a thorough investigation of all the points spoken of in your letter I would respectfully refer you to the orders issued from these headquarters from time to time showing that the practices of which you spoke have been suppressed as far as I have had the power to do so.

So far as murder is concerned no official report has ever reached me; neither had I heard of any previous to the date of your letter, and am satisfied none ever occurred as shown by the accompanying report of the commandant of cavalry.

The whole trouble arises in my opinion from not having a sufficient guard—175 is the whole number of men and officers on guard duty. I have not only issued orders to the commandant of the guard but made the proper requisition on Col. John F. Staunton, Sixty-seventh Pennsylvania Volunteers, for a proper guard according to instructions from Major-General Wool, a copy of which is inclosed, together with the letters sent to Colonel Staunton and to which I received no reply.

The instructions to the guard which I inclose will show what steps have been taken to suppress drunkenness and the concomitant evils.

In relation to the murders reported to the Secretary of War I have found one of the men who made it, and his examination now pending has delayed this paper.

So far he has proved nothing and the testimony will be forwarded to you in a few days.

The condition of the camp is all I could desire and in accordance with your orders, except the deficiency in a guard to enforce them.

I have the honor to be, very respectfully, your obedient servant,

GEO. SANGSTER,
Lieutenant-Colonel, Commanding Paroled Prisoners.

[Inclosure No. 1.]

CAMP PAROLED PRISONERS,
Near Annapolis, Md., December 7, 1862.

Lieut. Col. GEORGE SANGSTER,
Commanding Paroled Prisoners, near Annapolis, Md.

COLONEL: I have the honor to report that in accordance with Special Orders, No. 122, from your headquarters, dated December 7, 1862, I have personally superintended a thorough search of the woods and fields adjacent to the camp and have discovered nothing which would warrant a suspicion of death by violence of any soldier or citizen. I respectfully beg leave to state further that since our arrival in your camp our men have daily scoured the whole country within a circuit of six miles from camp in search of straggling soldiers, and had any dead bodies been concealed within the extent of their search they could not have failed to discover them. No such discovery has been made.

My company has been on duty in this camp since October 6, 1862.

I am, very respectfully, your obedient servant,

HENRY L. CLAYTON,
Lieut., Commanding Company B, Purnell [Legion] Cavalry.

[Inclosure No. 2.]

GENERAL ORDERS, } HEADQUARTERS PAROLED PRISONERS,
    No. 14.   }   *Annapolis, Md., September 18, 1862.*

I. The following order has been submitted to Major-General Wool. He approves and directs its enforcement. Refusal to obey by commissioned officers will result in arrest and be reported to headquarters of the Eighth Army Corps:

II. The general order of the day will be until further orders as follows: Reveille, 5 a. m.; breakfast, 6 a. m.; police, 7 a. m.; recall, 8.30 a. m.; surgeon's call, 9 a. m.; dinner, 12 m.; police, 1 p. m.; recall, 2.30 p. m.; inspection of camp, 4.30 p. m.; battalion assembly for reading orders, 5 p. m.; surgeon's call, 6 p. m.; supper, 6.30 p. m.; tattoo, 8.45 p. m.; taps, 9 p. m.

III. At all calls except breakfast, dinner and supper the commissioned officers will be present with their commands.

IV. The calls will be intimated by the bugle at headquarters when the bugles of the different battalions will take up the call.

V. Sunday morning inspection at 8 a. m., when a report of the condition of each command will be made to these headquarters.

By order of—

GEO. SANGSTER,
Lieutenant-Colonel, Commanding Paroled Prisoners.

[Inclosure No. 3.]

GENERAL ORDERS, } HEADQUARTERS PAROLED PRISONERS,
    No. 24.   }   *Near Annapolis, Md., December 4, 1862.*

I. General passes will be given only to employés at headquarters, quartermaster's, commissary and hospital departments, each of which will bear the same on its face. All other passes will be issued daily from headquarters bearing a stamp to be changed daily, and only one name shall be placed upon the same pass.

II. No wagon, cart or other vehicle will be permitted to pass within the lines without written permission from headquarters stating the purpose of the driver, whose name must appear on the same and which is not transferable.

III. No spirituous or malt liquors, wine or cider will be permitted in camp. If any such be found it will be confiscated and with the party or parties brought to these headquarters.

IV. The guards will permit neither teams nor individuals to pass in or out except at Post No. 1.

V. The health of the men and common cleanliness demand that no soldiers shall defecate on any part of the camp grounds other than the proper sinks for that purpose. If any soldier disobeys this order he shall be immediately arrested, confined to the guard-house and his name sent to these headquarters.

VI. Any gambling, drunkenness or disorder noticed by the guard will be reported to the officer of the guard who will at once have the party or parties arrested and confined.

VII. The countersign will be given out at 6 p. m., after which no officer or soldier will be permitted to pass in or out of camp unless by proper authority from headquarters.

VIII. The officer commanding the troops guarding the camp will be held strictly responsible for the enforcement of the above orders.

By order of Lieut. Col. George Sangster:

A. P. SCHURTZ,
Acting Adjutant.

[Inclosure No. 4.]

SPECIAL ORDERS, }   HEADQUARTERS PAROLED PRISONERS,
No. 40.   }   *Annapolis, Md., September 18, 1862.*

*   *   *   *   *   *   *

II. Pursuant to instructions received from headquarters Eighth Army Corps, dated September 16, 1862, the following order is promulgated:

The officers paroled are not exempt from taking care of the non-commissioned officers and privates, and are bound to perform all police duties and anything that may be necessary to the welfare and comfort of the paroled troops. Their duties would violate no obligations required by their paroles.

If any officer disobeys any order requiring the duties here mentioned he will be reported to these headquarters for dismissal from the service.

By order of—   GEO. SANGSTER,
Lieutenant-Colonel, Commanding Paroled Prisoners.

[Inclosure No. 5.]

GENERAL ORDERS, }   HEADQUARTERS PAROLED PRISONERS,
No. 16.   }   *Annapolis, Md., September 20, 1862.*

I. Agreeable to the direction of Adjt. Gen. L. Thomas the following order is promulgated:

II. On and after September 21, 1862, commissioned officers and men will remain in camp and no passes will be given out to go to the city.

By order of Lieut. Col. George Sangster:

D. E. GREGORY,
First Lieutenant and Adjutant.

[Inclosure No. 6.]

SPECIAL ORDERS, }   HEADQUARTERS EIGHTH ARMY CORPS,
No. 127.   }   *Baltimore, Md., October 7, 1862.*

*   *   *   *   *   *   *

V. Col. J. F. Staunton, commanding Sixty-seventh Pennsylvania Volunteers, at Annapolis, Md., will upon the proper requisition of Lieutenant-Colonel Sangster, Forty-seventh New York State Militia, furnish such guard as may be deemed necessary to enforce the paroled prisoners to keep their camp in such a state of thorough police as the regulations of the service require. The chief quartermaster of this army corps will fill promptly all requisitions for tools called [for] by the commanding officer of the paroled prisoners necessary to facilitate the carrying out of this order.

Lieutenant-Colonel Sangster will be held to strict accountability that hereafter no cause be found to complain of the condition of the camp at Annapolis.

By command of Major-General Wool:

SEPT. CARNCROSS,
Acting Assistant Adjutant-General.

[Inclosure No. 7.]

HEADQUARTERS PAROLED PRISONERS,
Near Annapolis, Md., October 21, 1862.

Col. J. F. STAUNTON,
Comdg. Sixty-seventh Pennsylvania Vols., Annapolis, Md.

SIR: In accordance with instructions from Major-General Wool and Special Orders, No. 127, paragraph V, you will furnish such guards as is deemed necessary to guard and enforce the proper policing of my camp at all times.

I therefore make a requisition on you for 600 men to be here at all times, subject to my orders.

I am, sir, very respectfully,

GEO. SANGSTER,
Lieutenant-Colonel, Commanding Paroled Prisoners.

[Inclosure No. 8.]

SPECIAL ORDERS, }   HEADQUARTERS PAROLED PRISONERS,
No. 79.   }   *Near Annapolis, Md., October 25, 1862.*

*   *   *   *   *   *   *

II. Major Day, commanding detachment of One hundred and thirty-first New York Volunteers, will at once take means to dislodge the men who occupy shanties along the line of tents who are known to be drinking and gambling against the rules and discipline of this camp.

If moral persuasion will not do the military force must be used.

By order of Lieut. Col. George Sangster:

A. P. SCHURTZ,
[Acting] Adjutant.

[Inclosure No. 9.]

HEADQUARTERS PAROLED PRISONERS,
Near Annapolis, Md., October 27, 1862.

Col. JOHN F. STAUNTON,
Commanding Sixty-seventh Pennsylvania Volunteers.

SIR: The requisition for 600 men which I made on the 21st instant in accordance with instructions from headquarters Eighth Army Corps has not been complied with. Please explain why this has not been done.

Very respectfully, yours, &c.,

GEO. SANGSTER,
Lieutenant-Colonel, Commanding Paroled Prisoners.

[Inclosure No. 10.]

HEADQUARTERS PAROLED PRISONERS,
Near Annapolis, Md., October 28, 1862.

Col. JOHN F. STAUNTON,
Commanding Sixty-seventh Pennsylvania Volunteers.

SIR: I would again respectfully call your attention to my requisition of October 21, 1862, and the letter of the 27th instant and solicit of you a reply in writing whether you can furnish me the guard called for and needed.

I am, colonel, very respectfully, your obedient servant,

GEO. SANGSTER,
Lieutenant-Colonel, Commanding Paroled Prisoners.

[Inclosure No. 11.]

SPECIAL ORDERS, }   HEADQUARTERS PAROLED PRISONERS,
No. 84.   }   *Near Annapolis, Md., October 30, 1862.*

*   *   *   *   *   *   *

VI. The commanding officer is compelled to call the attention of battalion commanders to General Orders, No. 14, paragraph II, and direct that until further orders that portion ordering a battalion assembly each day at 5 p. m. is revoked, and hereafter there will be two roll-calls daily; one at 7 a. m., the other at 5.30 p. m., which will be superintended by a commissioned officer or reliable non-commissioned officer. There will be a battalion formation at 4 o'clock every p. m. for the purpose of reading orders.

The rolls of each company will be called in their respective streets, superintended by a commissioned officer, if any; if not then by the senior non-commissioned officer. The absentees will be noted and will be reported on the morning report of the next day as absent without authority and no rations shall be drawn or issued to them.

Commanders of companies will be held strictly responsible for the execution of this order, and if any soldier who has absented himself from the said roll-calls without the proper authority shall by neglect or otherwise receive his rations for the day immediately succeeding his absence the company commander shall be subjected to a court-martial if a commissioned officer, and if a non-commissioned officer have the money value of the rations deducted from his pay.

Commissioned officers absent from these formations without sufficient cause will be reported to headquarters Eighth Army Corps for disobedience of orders.

This order will be read at each battalion assembly for one week.

By order of George Sangster, lieutenant-colonel:

A. P. SCHURTZ,
[Acting] Adjutant.

WAR DEPARTMENT, *Washington, December 8, 1862.*
Hon. H. HAMLIN, *President of the Senate.*

SIR: In answer to the resolution of the Senate of the 3d instant requesting to be furnished with any information which may be in the possession of this Department "with reference to the sale into slavery of colored freemen captured or seized by the rebel forces," and asking "what steps have been taken to redress this outrage upon human rights," I have the honor to state that no information, official or otherwise, pertaining to the matter mentioned in the first branch of the resolution has been received by this Department, and that no action has therefore been taken by it upon the subject.

I have the honor to be, very respectfully, your obedient servant,

EDWIN M. STANTON,
Secretary of War.

WAR DEPARTMENT, *Washington, December 8, 1862.*

Maj. Gen. HORATIO G. WRIGHT,
  Commanding Department of the Ohio, Cincinnati, Ohio.

GENERAL: The Secretary of War directs me to transmit to you the inclosed copy* of a resolution adopted by the Senate on the 5th instant, and to instruct you to procure from General Boyle and from any officer in your command who has had or who has exercised the authority to make arrests within the State of Kentucky a list of the citizens of that State "who have been and who are now confined in the military prisons and camps of the United States outside of the limits of the said State, together with a statement of the charges against them, by whom made and by whose order the arrests were made." You will also procure the like information from the commandants of military prisons within the limits of your department. It is important that the information should be transmitted to this Department at the earliest practicable moment.

Very respectfully, your obedient servant,

C. P. WOLCOTT,
Assistant Secretary of War.

[Indorsement.]

HEADQUARTERS DEPARTMENT OF THE OHIO,
  Cincinnati, December 12, 1862.

Respectfully referred to Colonel Burbank, Second Infantry, and military commander, Cincinnati, Ohio, who will furnish to these headquarters at the earliest practicable moment a list and accompanying statement furnishing the information called for in the within letter from the War Department and the accompanying resolution of the Senate adopted on the 5th instant.

By command of Major-General Wright:

W. P. ANDERSON,
Assistant Adjutant-General.

HEADQUARTERS DEPARTMENT OF THE OHIO,
  Cincinnati, Ohio, December 8, 1862.

Brig. Gen. G. GRANGER,
  Commanding Army of Kentucky, Lexington, Ky.

GENERAL: I return herewith the letter† of Lieutenant-Colonel Sipes, military commander of Covington and Newport, dated the 1st instant, presenting the case of Capt. T. M. Coombs, Fifth Regiment Kentucky Cavalry, in the Confederate Army, a paroled prisoner, bound to report himself as such within a specified time at Louisville to be sent to Vicksburg for exchange, and who was arrested before reporting on the charge of treason and confined in the Williamstown jail. Colonel Sipes deems this to be a case demanding the interposition of military authority for the release of the prisoner from jail and the restoration of his rights as a prisoner of war.

The Federal Government has so far recognized the belligerent rights of the so-called Confederate States as to enter into an agreement with the military authority of those States acknowledging the right of prisoners captured from them as prisoners of war and as entitled to exchange. So far then as the acts of an individual engaged in a military capacity in the enemy's service are concerned he is not individually

---

* Omitted here; see p. 27.   † Not found.

responsible for them so long as they are not in violation of the laws of war, and no person not in the military service of the Federal Government has been held guilty of treason for taking service in the Confederate Army. Captain Coombs is not therefore liable to that charge unless he has committed some act other than that of entering the rebel ranks and performing the duties of a soldier, and you will make a demand upon the civil authorities for his delivery up to your custody as a prisoner of war. It appears that General Burbridge or some other officer gave permission to Captain Coombs to visit his family in Kentucky, granting him certain time within which he was to report at Louisville. This was wrong and no such indulgence should hereafter be granted.

Very respectfully, your obedient servant,
H. G. WRIGHT,
Major-General, Commanding.

HEADQUARTERS ARMY OF TENNESSEE,
Murfreesborough, December 8, 1862.
Maj. Gen. W. S. ROSECRANS,
Commanding U. S. Forces, Nashville, Tenn.

GENERAL: As an act of humanity I send to your lines under a flag a large number of prisoners captured by the forces under my command and paroled. It would be a great hardship to send them at this inclement season by the route to either place designated by our cartel for exchange. My inspector-general, Lieutenant-Colonel Beard, is charged to deliver them to you and accept your receipt.

I am, general, very respectfully, your obedient servant,
BRAXTON BRAGG,
General, Commanding.

HEADQUARTERS ARMY OF TENNESSEE,
Murfreesborough, December 8, 1862.
Maj. Gen. WILLIAM S. ROSECRANS,
Commanding U. S. Forces, Nashville.

GENERAL: I am in receipt of your communication of the 4th instant* in reply to one from me calling your attention to the treatment of certain medical officers of my command and to the case of Private Kerchival. I am gratified to find that the officers who were concerned in the arrest of Doctors Hinkley and Divine were not of your command and that they were ultimately indebted to your advice for their release. The charge upon which they were imprisoned still seems to me inadequate to have warranted such severity. If they were guilty of misconduct the testimony of intoxicated men was insufficient to establish the fact, while the charge seems to have fallen to the ground upon investigation. Any abuse of the privileges of a parole if called to the attention of my Government will receive prompt attention. In reference to Private Kerchival I must respectfully insist that the statement of General Negley does not alter the aspects of the same. He admits the use of gross language to the prisoner, and when a general officer so far forgets himself as to bandy abusive epithets with a private while performing the duties of a subordinate he should not make his prisoner

---

* Not found.

because possessing spirit to resent an insult suffer for an offense to which his own conduct invited him. I shall look for the release of Private Kerchival at an early day with confident interest. With respect to matters of complaint indirectly communicated through General Negley's letter they shall have prompt attention and correction as far as lie within my power.

I am, general, very respectfully, your obedient servant,

BRAXTON BRAGG,
General, Commanding.

HEADQUARTERS TRANS-MISSISSIPPI DEPARTMENT,
Little Rock, December 8, 1862.

Brig. Gen. FREDERICK STEELE,
Commanding U. S. Forces at Helena.

GENERAL: Please find tabular statement marked A* containing the list of U. S. prisoners of war whom I have exchanged for Lieutenant-Colonel Giddings, Lieut. C. W. Carnes, 1 sergeant and 12 privates of the Twenty-first Texas Cavalry. Tabular statement marked B* which I also send you, carefully prepared from papers on file, will explain the error of Colonel Ritter, U. S. Army, and also show the balance of prisoners due to the Confederate States in this department. From this balance must, however, be deducted any Confederate prisoners received by Lieutenant Stevenson. Robert Craig, a private of the Fifth Missouri Cavalry, having been taken a prisoner and paroled has been again taken prisoner by the forces under my command without any evidence of his having been exchanged. Will you please inform me if you have any record of his having been exchanged?

I am, very respectfully, your obedient servant,

TH. H. HOLMES,
Major-General, Commanding Trans-Mississippi Department.

[First indorsement.]

HEADQUARTERS DEPARTMENT OF THE MISSOURI,
Saint Louis, December 19, 1862.

Respectfully referred to the provost-marshal-general, who will state briefly the action of this department [in] sending prisoners immediately under the national cartel arrangement.

By order of Major-General Curtis:

H. Z. CURTIS,
Assistant Adjutant-General.

[Second indorsement.]

OFFICE PROVOST-MARSHAL-GENERAL,
December 30, 1862.

Respectfully returned to Major Curtis, assistant adjutant-general, with the information that: 1st. When prisoners come here from the armies of the department in the field and reported as prisoners of war they are forwarded to Cairo for shipment to Vicksburg as soon as rolls can be prepared and other arrangements made. 2d. The entire lists of prisoners are being examined, and whenever prisoners appear to be entitled to the rights of prisoners of war they are noted for shipment to Cairo as soon as any considerable number have accumulated. 3d. There are scores of prisoners who claim the rights of exchange who

---

*Not found.

are not entitled to them nor receive them, such as sly recruiting officers, C. S. Army, bushwhackers and guerrillas, men who have violated oath, &c.

N. B.—I have written to the commanding officer of the Fifth Missouri Cavalry inquiring concerning R. Craig.

F. A. DICK,
Lieutenant-Colonel and Provost-Marshal-General.

[Third indorsement.]

HEADQUARTERS DEPARTMENT OF THE MISSOURI,
Saint Louis, January 27, 1863.

Respectfully referred to Col. C. Bussey, commanding post, Helena, Ark., who will please ascertain concerning the private mentioned and reply by first flag of truce.

By order of Major-General Curtis:

H. Z. CURTIS,
Assistant Adjutant-General.

[Fourth indorsement.]

HEADQUARTERS DISTRICT OF EASTERN ARKANSAS,
Helena, January 31, 1863.

I have sent a communication explaining this to General Holmes, commanding the Confederate forces at Little Rock. Respectfully returned to the Department of the Missouri.

W. A. GORMAN,
Brigadier-General, Commanding.

OFFICE COMMISSARY-GENERAL OF PRISONERS,
Washington, D. C., December 8, 1862.

Col. W. W. DUFFIELD,
Ninth Michigan Volunteers, Detroit, Mich.

COLONEL: I have the honor to acknowledge the receipt of your letter of the 29th ultimo in relation to Lieutenant-Colonel Parkhurst, of your regiment, and in reply thereto to inform you that this officer was exchanged on the 10th ultimo for Lieut. Col. Emory F. Best, Twenty-third Georgia Regiment. Please communicate this fact to Lieutenant-Colonel Parkhurst in order that he may join his regiment without delay.

I am, colonel, very respectfully, your obedient servant,

W. HOFFMAN,
Colonel Third Infantry, Commissary-General of Prisoners.

OFFICE COMMISSARY-GENERAL OF PRISONERS,
Washington, D. C., December 8, 1862.

Col. G. DE KORPONAY,
Commanding Camp Banks, Alexandria, Va.

COLONEL: Send all exchanged [troops] at your camp to join their regiments with as little delay as practicable. Prepare as full rolls as possible, each regiment by itself, and furnish cooked rations for the journey. The men who belong to regiments serving in the West will be sent under an officer to join a command belonging to the same regiments from Camp Parole at the Annapolis Junction on Thursday next, the 11th instant, by the 3 p. m. train. The officer will return from Baltimore unless he belongs to one of the regiments. The Quartermaster's Department will furnish the necessary transportation.

By order of the General-in-Chief:

Very respectfully, your obedient servant,

W. HOFFMAN,
Colonel Third Infantry, Commissary-General of Prisoners.

OFFICE COMMISSARY-GENERAL OF PRISONERS,
Washington, D. C., December 8, 1862.

Lieut. Col. GEORGE SANGSTER,
Commanding Camp Parole, Annapolis, Md.

COLONEL: The exchanged troops at your camp belonging to regiments serving in and west of Virginia will leave to join their regiments by the evening train on Thursday next, the 11th instant. Send as full rolls with the detachment as possible, each regiment by itself, and furnish cooked rations for the journey. The exchanged men of these regiments at Camp Banks will be ordered to join this command at the Annapolis Junction and the commanding officer must be prepared to take charge of them. Direct him to distribute his command as follows, viz: At Wheeling, for General Wright's department, First, Second, Fourth, Tenth Infantry, Eighth Cavalry and Second Artillery Regiments [West] Virginia Volunteers; and for General Cox's command, Thirty-fourth, Thirty-seventh, Forty-second and Forty-seventh Ohio Infantry. At Camp Wallace, for General Wright's department, the Twenty-third, Thirtieth and Eighty-third Regiments Ohio Infantry. At Nashville, for General Rosecrans' army, Twenty-first and Twenty-fourth Regiments Ohio Infantry and Third and Fourth Regiments Ohio Cavalry; Tenth, Sixteenth, Twenty-second, Twenty-fourth, Twenty-seventh and Fifty-first Illinois Infantry; First, Second, Third, Fourth, Fifth and Sixth Regiments Tennessee Infantry and Second Regiment Tennessee Cavalry; Thirty-seventh Regiment Indiana Infantry, Eleventh Kentucky Infantry and First and Fourth Regiments Kentucky Cavalry. At Benton Barracks, for General Grant's army, First Regiment Ohio Cavalry; Eleventh, Twelfth, Fifteenth, Twenty-eighth, Twenty-ninth, Thirtieth, Thirty-first and Fifty-eighth Illinois Infantry and Twelfth Illinois Cavalry; Seventh Regiment Tennessee Infantry; Third, Sixth, Seventh, Eighth, Twelfth, Fourteenth, Fifteenth, Sixteenth Regiments Iowa Infantry and Second Iowa Cavalry, and Eighteenth Regiment Missouri Infantry.

The Quartermaster's Department will furnish the necessary transportation. Notify the quartermaster at Baltimore in season so that there may be no delay there.

Report immediately the regiments and the number of officers and enlisted men in each that will move under this order. The sick in hospital will not go.

By order of the General-in-Chief:

Very respectfully, your obedient servant,

W. HOFFMAN,
Colonel Third Infantry, Commissary-General of Prisoners.

OFFICE PROVOST-MARSHAL-GENERAL,
Saint Louis, Mo., December 8, 1862.

Col. W. HOFFMAN, *Commissary-General of Prisoners.*

COLONEL: I have received your letter of the 4th. I was very much disappointed that the shipment of prisoners from Saint Louis to Alton spoken of by you was attended by untoward circumstances, and I am 'not surprised at the dissatisfaction expressed by you. I wish to explain the matter. I took charge of the provost-marshal's office on the 5th of November. At that time the Gratiot Street Prison held about 800 prisoners. Its maximum number should not have exceeded 500. I found that the Myrtle Street Prison, capable of containing comfortably 100 prisoners, had been taken possession of by my predecessor but for want of some necessary repairs was not occupied. I had it made ready and removed 150 prisoners there from Gratiot Street, which by that time had over 1,000 prisoners. In a few days thereafter the number in Gratiot Street again ran up to about 1,100. About the middle of November sickness in Gratiot Street Prison began increasing at an alarming rate. The number sick about that time was over 100, and within a week it ran up to 235 so that a large number of sick and dying men were lying on the floors. Every morning men would be found dead on the floor in the common rooms who had received no attention because from the crowded condition of the rooms it was impossible with the ordinary hospital attendance. With this condition of things it was impossible to observe the ordinary police and sanitary regulations. The men could not be even taken out of doors, for the prison has no yard. Of the 150 well men removed to Myrtle Street 35 were taken sick within four days, the consequences of the infection at Gratiot Street—and with all this prisoners were coming in daily from the country at the rate of from 30 to 100 a day. Fearing that the worst consequences would result from keeping these men longer in Gratiot Street and ascertaining that there was abundant room in Alton for a large number I decided to remove several hundred of those whose cases would not probably be disposed of at an early day. Upon looking over the lists in this office it was reported to me that there were about 400 of that class and I notified Colonel Hoffman to expect about that number. But the actual number sent was 276, and the difference between that and the estimated number arose thus: Upon the lists were a large number who were found too sick to go. Some had died, some been discharged and two pages of names were duplicated. Had the books of this office been in proper condition such inaccuracy would not have existed, but for that I am not in fault for half my time has been occupied in overhauling the confused state of things found by me in this office. The day before the prisoners were to go the guard was provided and transportation engaged. It was found impossible to get a special boat and it was necessary to use the Alton packet. But the crowded and confused state of things at the prison, the unavoidable result of its overcrowded condition and the intermingling of the sick and the well created great delay in getting the prisoners out, and as a corrected list had to be made out to send with them the boat did not get off until nearly dark. This list ready to go with the prisoners unfortunately was left behind in the prison. Notwithstanding the hour was so late, the prisoners being out and ready, it would have been worse to turn them back than to go forward. Since then, last Saturday I sent 237 additional prisoners from Gratiot Street Prison to Alton and the number now at Gratiot Street is about 570,

On to-day the quartermaster has begun making most important and necessary repairs and improvements in the Gratiot Street Prison, and when completed it will be comfortable and can be kept clean. To send off the last body of prisoners arrangements were made to start the boat by 11 a. m. It did not start until 1, and was so impeded by the ice that it did not arrive at Alton until dark. But for the ice the boat could have arrived before 4 o'clock. In no case will any effort be wanting to have things so arranged that prisoners sent from here to Alton will hereafter arrive in the day, and invariably will full rolls be sent. But the prisoners that were sent by me were men who had been captured as guerrillas in Missouri and the only rolls of them ever sent to this office contain merely their names and by whom captured, with the remark that they were to be imprisoned. Having at an early day made myself familiar with your instructions I have carefully followed them and not deviated from them in a single instance that I know of. You said that prisoners might be sent to Alton; if impracticable to keep them here until their cases were disposed of. The foregoing facts show that the case provided for by you existed, and I wrote to Colonel Hildebrand that these prisoners' cases had not been disposed of by me so that he might keep them distinct from others. I have confined my releases from the Alton Prison strictly to those authorized to be released by me in your letter of 29th of October. Beyond that I have not given an order relating to a prisoner at Alton. I was told to-day that General Grant had lately ordered prisoners there to be released, and perhaps you may have supposed that releases made if any were upon orders from this office. I have not given a solitary pass or permit to visit the Alton Prison, it being forbidden in your letter of October 29. You state:

It is reported to me that great inconvenience is experienced by the daily calls for the release of prisoners made from your office.

The releases which I have ordered have been strictly within your instructions. I nowhere find in them directions as to the time when I shall make the orders. The releases that I have ordered were of prisoners who were there when I became provost-marshal. As I have reached their cases and ascertained that the charges against them were unfounded I have sent up the orders for the release, for I have considered that after it is determined that a man should be discharged he ought at once to be released; and as it is an expense to the Government to subsist him the sooner that stops the better. I think there must be some misapprehension as to the inconvenience from this cause, for it will less interfere with the prison routine to release the men gradually than in large bodies. Upon the closing sentence of your letter I remark I regret that you have the impression that I have not confined myself within the orders of the War Department and your instructions relating to the Alton Prison. At all times it will give me great satisfaction to have you point out any misconstruction of mine of the orders and regulations made, and I assure you that any mistake that I may make will not be intentional and when pointed out will not occur again. In a late letter I stated that "a large number of my prisoners are men captured in Missouri in bands, and a part of them sworn into the Confederate service by recruiting officers from the rebels who had reached the northern part of the State," and I asked if these men are to be sent forward to be exchanged. My impression is that a large number of irregular prisoners, such as men captured in small bodies without organization, and also disloyal citizens who would have joined the Confederate Army if they could have reached it, have been sent forward from Johnson's Island and Alton to Cairo to be exchanged. If such prisoners are to be sent forward I believe that amongst those in my custody will be found a large number who will gladly go South. I ask an early reply to this inquiry that I may send such men off at once and in that way relieve our overcrowded prisons.

Inclosed are copies of two letters* sent to Colonel Hildebrand.

I have the honor to be, most respectfully, your obedient servant,

F. A. DICK,
Lieut. Col. and Provost-Marshal-General, Dept. of the Missouri.

[Inclosure.]

OFFICE PROVOST-MARSHAL-GENERAL,
Saint Louis, Mo., November 29, 1862.

Col. J. HILDEBRAND, *Commanding Alton Military Prison.*

COLONEL: The necessity for removing a considerable number of the prisoners from Gratiot Street Prison was pressing for the reason stated in my letter of the 27th. A large list of prisoners was made out in this office by the clerk who has always had charge of that kind of work from the rolls sent to this office by General Merrill. In the pressure of business time was not taken to call off the prisoners by the list to ascertain if they agreed with it. In making up the list from different rolls done by different clerks it happened that two pages of it were duplicated. Upon calling upon the prisoners to go it was found that a few of them had been released, a considerable number were dead and a large number too sick to be moved. For these reasons the number actually sent, 276, fell short of the number I expected to send. Had the records of my office been in proper condition those discharged would have been so entered and could due time have been taken beforehand to ascertain the state of health of the men the sick would not have been entered upon the list. All such irregularities are being corrected as rapidly as possible but order cannot be brought out of confusion instantaneously. What made the matter appear worse the officer in command of the guard left at the prison the rolls of the prisoners actually sent. This will be sent to you at once.

I am, colonel, very respectfully, your obedient servant,

F. A. DICK,
Lieut. Col. and Provost-Marshal-General, Dept. of the Missouri.

FORT DELAWARE, *December 8, 1862.*

Col. WILLIAM D. WHIPPLE,
Assistant Adjutant-General, Eighth Army Corps.

SIR: Will you please instruct me as soon as convenient whether the paroled prisoners, numbering about 550 enlisted men of the U. S. service now at this post, are to be forwarded by me without further orders in the case than is embraced in General Orders, No. 191, from Adjutant-General's Office, Washington, to any other post or camp for return to their regiments. Provision first of general order referred to covers the case of all the paroled prisoners at this post; that is they are captured and paroled in Virginia and Maryland previous to November 1, 1862, and were delivered at Aiken's Landing prior to November 11, 1862, but in the after enumeration no mention is made of this post or

---

* For Dick to Hildebrand, November 27, see Vol. IV, this Series, p. 762.

the department to which it belongs. If they are to be sent away at once will you please indicate to what point I shall forward them.

I am, very respectfully, your obedient servant,

D. D. PERKINS,
Lieutenant-Colonel, Commanding Post.

OFFICE COMMISSARY-GENERAL OF PRISONERS,
Washington, D. C., December 8, 1862.

Col. WILLIAM HOFFMAN,
Commissary-General of Prisoners, Washington, D. C.

COLONEL: In addition to my report of the 6th instant I have the honor to submit the following statement in relation to the disposal of rebel prisoners captured in Kentucky so as to fully inform you of their character and so that you may be enabled to give proper directions for their treatment and disposal. By reference to my former report you will find the prisoners are classed as follows, viz: First, prisoners of war; second, political prisoners; third, rebel deserters; fourth, rebel recruits. It is regarding that class of prisoners termed rebel recruits and deserters that I wish to call your particular attention. These prisoners are men who have joined the rebel army while in Kentucky; many of them are persons of extreme youth almost incapable of bearing arms who have by means of false inducements been led to join the army. Residing in that portion of Kentucky recently occupied by Bragg's army they have been made to believe that its occupancy by that army would be permanent. These men have served in the rebel army from a few days to six weeks, and after finding it impossible for the rebels to hold that portion of the State and that they were woefully disappointed in their expectations of the service some have deserted and gone to their homes; others have voluntarily surrendered themselves to the Federal authorities; others have permitted themselves to be captured, while all are tired and disgusted with the rebel service and desirous of returning to their homes, taking the oath of allegiance and becoming loyal citizens. Some of these prisoners are young men of wealth and position. Some are the sons of gentlemen of undoubted loyalty, and there are but few among them who have not friends or relatives among gentlemen of the highest respectability and occupying influential positions in the State. These gentlemen who have the interest of the country at heart are desirous that these prisoners should be leniently treated, and hope that the bitter lesson they have already received has taught them the duties of loyal citizens. They also represent that the effect of this lenient treatment in the present condition of Kentucky will be most beneficial. If on the contrary they are sent to the rebel army and exchanged it will only add so many more desperate men to fight against the country; will make Kentucky a recruiting field for the rebels, and will so much contribute to increase the domestic distress already existing in that State. Again it is represented that the Kentucky regiments in the rebel army when they were forced to leave the State were much disaffected and demoralized. This is so represented by deserters and others, who state if Kentuckians in that army were at all assured that they could return to their homes, take the oath of allegiance, become loyal citizens and be permitted to remain unmolested by the Federal authorities nearly the whole number not obligated by oath to remain would return to their homes and allegiance. The Union people of Louisville are intensely Union in all their sentiments, uncompromisingly hostile and excessively bitter against all who are opposed to them in opinion. While they can look with some degree of leniency upon deluded Kentuckians they view with suspicion every act of kindness shown to rebel prisoners, even when this act is demanded by humanity.

These representations have been made to me by the provost-marshal-general of Kentucky, who requested that they be informally presented to you so that he might receive the proper instructions to guide him in his official duties. The commanding officer at Louisville has also requested definite instructions on all matters relative to the care, treatment and disposal of the different classes of prisoners.

Very respectfully, your obedient servant,

H. W. FREEDLEY,
Capt., Third Infty., Assistant to Commissary-General of Prisoners.

ALTON MILITARY PRISON, *December 8, 1862.*

Col. F. A. DICK, *Provost-Marshal-General.*

SIR: In answer to the note of your clerk of the 5th instant inquiring for prison regulations I have the honor to submit the following as our system of management: The business of the prison is done by the following officers under the direction of the commanding officer: 1 prison adjutant, 1 prison provost and 5 clerks and sergeants. The duty of the adjutant is to keep a correct record of all prisoners received, transferred, died, and make the monthly return; receive all money and valuables belonging to the prisoners. The adjutant is allowed three clerks; one who assists in keeping the records of the office, one who examines all mail matter passing to and from the prisoners and one who makes out the morning reports. The prison provost has charge of the prisoners, yard, cells, superintends the calling of the prison-roll, the policing, and is directly responsible for the correctness of the morning ward reports. He draws the rations, receives all packages passing through to the prisoners, &c. He has two clerks, one who examines all packages received by the provost and has charge of the police force, and one who calls the ward rolls and reports all changes to the adjutant. The prison provost draws and issues all clothing to the prisoners. There is connected with the prison a sutler who furnishes the prisoners with various articles, taking orders on the adjutant. We have the prisoners divided in wards, calling the roll twice a day, and all changes immediately reported. The hospital steward is required to report all changes daily.

I am, colonel, respectfully, your obedient servant,

I. B. KINKEAD,
Captain and Prison Adjutant.

HEADQUARTERS ARMY OF SOUTHEAST MISSOURI,
Patterson, Mo., December 9, 1862.

Brig. Gen. M. JEFF. THOMPSON, *Holcomb's Island.*

GENERAL: Your communication of November 29 was received at my camp during my absence. I take the earliest opportunity on my return to reply.

I do not agree with you that the enrolled militia of the State are subject to capture and exchange unless embodied and in active service, which the men whom you send me were not.

Order No. 21, enrolling the militia of the State, provides that those who enroll themselves as Southern sympathizers shall not be molested if engaged at home in the peaceful pursuit of their domestic duties. I think the same should be held by you of our militiamen.

Colonel Pheelan before leaving my camp released, I learn by his order, some of the men whose names appear on your list.

Reciprocating the hope that the war on this side of the Mississippi may be carried on hereafter more in accordance with the rules of civilized warfare,

I remain, sir, your most obedient servant,

J. W. DAVIDSON,
Brigadier-General.

P. S.—Your communication will be referred to my department commander for further decision.

———

INSTRUCTIONS.] HEADQUARTERS DEPARTMENT OF VIRGINIA,
Fort Monroe, Va., December 9, 1862.

Capt. JOHN E. MULFORD, *Charge of Flag-of-Truce Boat:*

No communication or intercourse whatever with the enemy will be allowed to any persons on flag-of-truce boats other than such as is necessary to accomplish the objects of the flag. The officer in command of the flag of truce will see that these instructions are rigidly enforced.

By command of Major-General Dix:

D. T. VAN BUREN,
Assistant Adjutant-General.

———

OFFICE COMMISSARY-GENERAL OF PRISONERS,
Washington, D. C., December 9, 1862.

Hon. E. M. STANTON, *Secretary of War, Washington.*

SIR: I desire very respectfully to lay the following case reported to me by Lieut. Col. F. A. Dick, provost-marshal-general at Saint Louis, before the Secretary of War for his decision:

J. J. Clarkson, of Dade County, Mo., is held a prisoner in jail of said county upon an indictment found against him in the U. S. court under the late act of Congress for serving in the rebel army. He served at the battle of Lexington under a State commission, and subsequently served in the Confederate Army as a colonel, where he was constantly recognized as such by Generals Van Dorn and Hindman under whom he served, though he was never formally commissioned. In March, 1862, he raised six companies of cavalry for the war, and a majority of the regiment he commanded when captured were from Arkansas. He was held as a prisoner of war from July till October, when under the indictment he was delivered to the U. S. marshal and put in jail. The provost marshal-general asks:

First. Do the facts presented entitle Clarkson to be considered as a colonel of the Confederate Army and to be exchanged as provided for in the cartel?

Second. If recognized as a colonel of the C. S. Army how is he to be taken out of the hands of the U. S. marshal that he may be exchanged?

The court does not sit till April, 1863.

I would respectfully suggest that as the case is presented by Colonel Dick there can be little doubt that he should be recognized as a colonel in the rebel army, and there is no room for question that the rebels should receive him in exchange for a colonel of our army.

The second question is a legal one and it is not proper that I should suggest a reply if I could.

Colonel Dick has in his possession prisoners of war against whom indictments have been found in the U. S. court. They have been demanded of him by the U. S. marshal and he desires to be instructed as to the course which he should pursue. By the cartel these men can claim to be sent to Vicksburg and paroled or exchanged.

Very respectfully, your obedient servant,

W. HOFFMAN,
Colonel Third Infantry, Commissary-General of Prisoners.

OFFICE COMMISSARY-GENERAL OF PRISONERS,
Washington, D. C., December 9, 1862.

Lieutenant-Colonel DOSTER,
Provost-Marshal, Washington City.

COLONEL: At the instance of Lieutenant-Colonel Ludlow, agent for exchange of prisoners, I have the honor to request that Henry A. Ball, reported to be held as a spy in this city, may be released upon parole to report to Lieutenant-Colonel Ludlow, at Fort Monroe, Va. It is demanded under the cartel.

I am, colonel, very respectfully, your obedient servant,

W. HOFFMAN,
Colonel Third Infantry, Commissary-General of Prisoners.

WASHINGTON, *December 9, 1862.*

Lieut. Col. F. A. DICK, *Provost-Marshal-General:*

Release no more prisoners of war on their taking the oath of allegiance. Will answer your letter of 3d instant by mail.

W. HOFFMAN,
Commissary-General of Prisoners.

OFFICE COMMISSARY-GENERAL OF PRISONERS,
Washington, D. C., December 9, 1862.

Lieut. Col. W. H. LUDLOW,
Agent for Exchange of Prisoners, Fort Monroe, Va.

COLONEL: I inclose herewith a number of applications for exchange together with some original rolls.

Many Union men from border States are held in a most shameful condition in the rebel prisons, and I am sure you will spare no efforts to secure their speedy parole and exchange. The names I send to you have come to me from various sources, and I shall perhaps be able to send you a more complete roll in a few days from Major Wood, superintendent of the Old Capitol Prison.

I have again telegraphed to General Grant for rolls of captures made by Rosecrans and have asked that a duplicate set be sent. It is probable they have gone to Vicksburg and will be forwarded from thence with the receipt of the Confederate agent. Three thousand eight hundred and sixty-five prisoners of war have been sent from Alton, Sandusky, Camp Chase and Louisville to Vicksburg, and for these receipts will be returned from Vicksburg.

Very respectfully, your obedient servant,

W. HOFFMAN,
Colonel Third Infantry, Commissary-General of Prisoners.

HEADQUARTERS ARMY OF SOUTHEAST MISSOURI,
Patterson, Mo., December 9, 1862.

Colonel HARDING, *Commanding Post, Patterson, Mo.*

COLONEL: Accompanying please find letter to General Thompson and safeguard for officers bearing the flag of truce. The prisoners brought in by them should be restored to their custody until further action by the authorities at headquarters Department of the Missouri.

Very respectfully, your obedient servant,

HENRY C. FILLEBROWN,
Assistant Adjutant-General.

[Indorsement.]

HEADQUARTERS POST, *December 9, 1862.*

Capt. W. T. THOMPSON.

SIR: Please read the within and send me word whether you wish to take your prisoners back or to parole them. We must get them off our hands until the questions arising shall be determined. I will either deliver them to you or send them for parole, as you think best.

Very respectfully, &c.,

CHESTER HARDING, JR.,
Colonel, Commanding Post, Patterson, Mo.

JUDGE MAXWELL'S, *December 9, 1862.*

Col. CHESTER HARDING, U. S. Army,
Commanding Post, Patterson, Mo.

COLONEL: The prisoners were put upon parole before leaving our headquarters and were only brought along by me to expedite and facilitate the exchange in case it could be effected. They can be released upon your reminding them of the fact. Have you a desire that we should return upon any particular route? If you have not we would prefer going through Greenville and Bloomfield, as it saves us a long stretch of swamp.

Yours, most respectfully,

W. T. THOMPSON,
Aide-de-Camp to Brigadier-General Thompson, C. S. Army.

[Indorsement.]

HEADQUARTERS POST, *December 9, 1862.*

Capt. W. T. THOMPSON, C. S. Army,
Judge Maxwell's House.

CAPTAIN: You are at liberty to take the Greenville and Bloomfield route on the condition that you do not reveal anything in regard to the position, numbers, &c., of the U. S. troops that you may meet or pass on the road.

I am, sir, very respectfully, your obedient servant,

CHESTER HARDING, JR.,
Colonel, Commanding Post, Patterson, Mo.

———

HEADQUARTERS MILITARY DISTRICT OF WASHINGTON,
December 9, 1862.

Brigadier-General MARTINDALE,
Military Governor of Washington.

GENERAL: I have the honor to state that in the course of investigation of prisoners at the Old Capitol Prison for the past two months I have found a great many prisoners of State whose only objection to taking the oath of allegiance to the United States being apparently that their property and families were beyond the lines of the U. S. forces, and such a course on their part would only subject them to arrest and incarceration by the Confederate authority and their property by the existing laws of the Confederate Government to confiscation.

As the policy of the United States Government is and has been to allow persons freedom of opinion and speech and not to make arrests on account of proclivities or sympathies with the Southern Confederacy, I would earnestly suggest that the next commission on the part of the United States for the exchange of civilian prisoners be instructed to confer with the Confederate authorities with the view of preventing the arrest by either Government of any person or persons for their sympathies or loyalty to either section, and that such arrests shall not be made unless some overt act has been committed.

By such a course we would soon have a large number of loyal and avowed Unionists in the seceding States, the number increasing as their confidence increased, and this confidence extending through the several Southern States now partially occupied by the U. S. forces. Such a course could not fail to be of incalculable value to the Government and its interests.

I have the honor to be, general, very respectfully, your obedient servant,

JOHN P. SHERBURNE,
Assistant Adjutant-General.

———

DEPARTMENT OF STATE, *Washington, December 10, 1862.*

Hon. EDWIN M. STANTON, *Secretary of War.*

SIR: Mr. Mercier, the minister from France, has submitted to me a correspondence which has taken place between Major-General Butler and Admiral Reynaud* in regard to the case of Mr. Le More, said to be a French subject, whom the general has caused to be confined in Fort Pickens at hard labor with a ball and chain attached to his leg. Mr. Le More is charged by Major-General Butler with having been engaged in supplying the insurgents with stores and with contumacy in refusing to submit to an examination and to produce papers. But Major-General Butler has promised the admiral that the accused shall have a military trial.

———

* See Butler to Seward, November 29, Vol. IV, this Series, p. 767.

Having taken the instructions of the President I have to request that instructions may be given to Major-General Butler or to whomsoever may be in command at New Orleans that those additions to the confinement be removed, that he be released from labor and from the ball and chain.

I have the honor to be, sir, your obedient servant,

WILLIAM H. SEWARD.

HDQRS. DEPT. OF MISSISSIPPI AND EAST LOUISIANA,
Jackson, Miss., December 10, 1862.

Maj. Gen. U. S. GRANT, *Comdg U. S. Forces, West Tennessee, &c.*

GENERAL: I am credibly informed that Lieutenant-Colonel Hedgpeth, Sixth Missouri Infantry, C. S. Army, who was severely wounded in the engagement near Corinth, is now at the Overton Hospital, Memphis, subjected to unusually hard treatment—his parole, watch, and money taken from him. If this statement is correct I respectfully request that you will inform me of the reasons why the privileges assured by the cartel for the exchange of prisoners are denied in Colonel Hedgpeth's case, and further request that he be either paroled at once or sent to Vicksburg for exchange by the first opportunity.

I am, general, very respectfully, your obedient servant,

J. C. PEMBERTON,
Lieutenant-General, Commanding.

MURFREESBOROUGH, *December 10, 1862.*

General BRAGG.

SIR: Some months since Hon. A. J. Marchbanks, of Warren County, was arrested by the Federals and sent to Camp Chase, where he has been confined up to this time as a political prisoner. At the time of his arrest he was one of the circuit judges of the State, but his official term has expired since that time. He is a quiet and most excellent citizen, firm and unwavering in his devotion to the Confederate cause, but modest, quiet, and unobtrusive. About a month since Doctor Charlton (of the neighborhood of La Vergne), a Union man, was arrested by General Forrest and sent to this place. At my instance the commandant of the post, Captain O'Harra, and Doctor Charlton each wrote to the Federal authorities at Nashville proposing to exchange Charlton for Judge Marchbanks, but I have not been able to hear anything in answer to this proposition up to this time, and address you for the purpose of asking that you correspond with General Rosecrans upon the subject and, if possible, secure the release of Judge Marchbanks.

Respectfully, ISHAM G. HARRIS.

[First indorsement.]

HEADQUARTERS DEPARTMENT No. 2,
Murfreesborough, Tenn., December 14, 1862.

Referred to Maj. Gen. W. S. Rosecrans, who will no doubt promptly secure the release of this citizen under our recent agreement.

BRAXTON BRAGG,
General, Commanding.

[Second indorsement.]

HDQRS. DEPARTMENT OF THE CUMBERLAND,
Nashville, December 16, 1862.

Respectfully referred to His Excellency Governor Johnson, who may know something about this case.

By command of General Rosecrans:

J. P. GARESCHÉ,
Assistant Adjutant-General, Chief of Staff.

[Third indorsement.]

EXECUTIVE OFFICE,
Nashville, Tenn., December 16, 1862.

Respectfully returned.

There has been no correspondence with this office on the subject of an exchange of Judge Marchbanks for Doctor Charlton. On the 5th instant Rev. C. D. Elliott, a political prisoner, was paroled for twenty days from that date to effect an exchange for Dr. James Charlton, of La Vergne, a political prisoner held by the Confederates, as set forth in the pass beyond our lines furnished Mr. E. by the provost-marshal-general. I have not as yet been advised as to the result of Mr. Elliott's efforts to effect said exchange.

Judge Marchbanks is held as a political prisoner at Camp Chase, as stated within.

ANDREW JOHNSON, *Military Governor.*

[Fourth indorsement.]

HDQRS. DEPARTMENT OF THE CUMBERLAND,
Nashville, December 17, 1862.

Respectfully forwarded to the Adjutant-General.

W. S. ROSECRANS,
Major-General, Commanding Department.

SAINT LOUIS, *December 10, 1862.*

Col. J. HILDEBRAND, *Commanding Alton Military Prison.*

COLONEL: Will you find out the facts of the arrest of W. H. Hawkins, Twenty-second Tennessee Volunteers, and report at once to this office all the facts in the case? This man has been the subject of a demand by General Bragg through a letter forwarded to General Curtis by General Wright, from Cincinnati. It is important to know of him at once. He is said to have gone in with flag of truce and been improperly retained and to be now at Alton.

I am, colonel, very respectfully,

F. A. DICK,
Lieutenant-Colonel and Provost-Marshal-General.

HEADQUARTERS PAROLED PRISONERS,
Near Annapolis, Md., December 10, 1862.

Col. W. HOFFMAN, *Commissary-General of Prisoners.*

SIR: I have the honor to report the result of the examination of the men in camp who complained to the Secretary of War of murders being committed in camp which I spoke of in my letter to you of 7th instant. The men ordered away will leave here at 3 p. m. to-morrow and I will send you the rolls complete by the next mail. There are about 300 men going.

I am, colonel, very respectfully, your obedient servant,

GEO. SANGSTER,
Lieut. Col. 47th N. Y. S. M., Commanding Paroled Prisoners.

[Inclosure.]

Statement of Private M. Shaw, Company D, Forty-fourth New York Volunteers, December 7, 1862.

Question. Do you know of any murder being committed in or about this camp?

Answer. No.

Question. Have you any reliable information of any murder being committed in or about this camp?

Answer. I think I have.

Question. Of what does your information consist?

Answer. Of reports.

Question. Give a report of one murder.

Answer. The report of Prentiss S. Frink, of Company D, Forty-fourth New York Volunteers, that he was informed at the hospital of the burial of a man who died from the effects of injuries received in camp.

Question. Do you know the name of the person murdered?

Answer. No.

Question. Was it a man or a boy?

Answer. I don't know. I suppose it was a man.

Question. What reason have you [to suppose] that it was a man?

Answer. I have no reason only that there are very few boys that stay in camp nights.

Question. Do you know who the parties were who committed the offense?

Answer. No.

Question. Was the act committed inside the chain of sentinels or outside?

Answer. Reported to have been inside.

Question. Who reported it to be within the chain of sentinels?

Answer. Corpl. A. J. Hurd, Company A, Forty-fourth New York Volunteers, and W. E. Chineworth, First Maryland Cavalry.

Question. At what particular part of the camp was the offense committed?

Answer. In front of the tent of A. J. Hurd.

Question. Did Hurd or Chineworth say that they saw the murder committed?

Answer. No.

Question. Did they say they saw the body of the person murdered?

Answer. Yes; Chineworth said so.

Question. Did either Hurd or Chineworth say they saw the persons that committed the deed?

Answer. They did not.

Question. How did Hurd know that a murder had been committed in front of his tent?

Answer. I don't know.

Question. When did they tell you this murder had been committed?

Answer. Some time the latter part of October or the first part of November, perhaps.

Question. Why do you think it was about that time?

Answer. Because I think it was about that time.

Question. Did you ever attempt to ferret out the murderers?

Answer. I did not.

Question. Do you know or have you heard of any other murder having been committed in or about this camp?

Answer. I have heard it remarked that there have been several murders committed.

Question. Who have you heard make these remarks?

Answer. Sergt. James O'Neil, Company B, Ninth Massachusetts Volunteers; Josiah M. Darrel, Company E, Twentieth Massachusetts Volunteers; James N. Lynch, Company F, Fortieth New York Volunteers, and Harry Wilson, Company E, Fortieth New York Volunteers.

Question. What information did you receive from these men?

Answer. I got no information except the talk.

Question. Have you ever heard anything in reference to the several murders of which you speak except vague and indefinite reports?

Answer. No.

Question. Do you know of any gambling being carried on in this camp?

Answer. Yes.

Question. Can you give me the names of the party or parties engaged in gambling?

Answer. Yes. W. E. Chineworth.

Question. Was Chineworth engaged as the dealer or bettor?

Answer. I supposed he was the one that owned the bank.

Question. Did you ever gamble yourself?

Answer. No.

Question. What kind of a game was Chineworth playing?

Answer. I don't know the name of the game but it was with dice.

Question. How often did you see Chineworth playing?

Answer. I saw him several times.

Question. When you say several times, do you mean several times in one day or several times in several days?

Answer. Several times in several days.

Question. Do you know of any one else engaged in gambling?

Answer. I do not know the name of any one else.

Question. Did you ever see Prentiss S. Frink gambling?

Answer. No. I have seen Frink standing by Chineworth but did not know whether there was gambling going on or not.

Question. What were the actions of Chineworth when you saw him gambling?

Answer. He was rattling dice.

Question. Did you see any money on the table?

Answer. I saw money and checks.

Question. Do you know how much capital Chineworth had invested in this business?

Answer. No; I do not.

Question. Did you ever report Chineworth as having gambled to any officer?

Answer. No.

Question. Did you report Chineworth's gambling to anybody?

Answer. I have spoken of it to his chum, A. J. Hurd.

Question. When you knew that the offense of gambling—violating the regulations of the U. S. Army—was being committed why did you not as a good soldier report the same to these headquarters?

Answer. Because I supposed the fact of their gambling was known at these head-quarters and that they had the power to break it up if they felt so disposed.

Question. Why did you suppose the fact was known at these head-headquarters?

Answer. Because it is so open, so universal and so near these headquarters I sup-posed all must know it who wished to.

Question. How near these headquarters was the nearest gambling you know of?

Answer. As near as I can estimate, 100 yards.

Question. Who kept the table you estimate as 100 yards from here?

Answer. I do not know.

Question. Was the table in the front or in the rear of this camp?

Answer. In the rear.

Question. In the rear of what battalion was this table?

Answer. In the rear of the Third Battalion.

Question. What kind of a game was played at this table?

Answer. I do not know the name of the game. I saw cards and dice.

Question. Did you see any money bet?

Answer. I have seen money on the table.

Question. Was this carried on in the open air or in a booth or tent?

Answer. In the open air.

Question. Did you ever see the guard of this camp attempt to sup-press this gambling?

Answer. I saw the guard endeavoring to do so last Sunday, the second time they came around.

Question. Did you ever see any officer or officers of the guard endeav-oring to break this gambling up?

Answer. Only this time that I have mentioned that I recollect.

Question. Can you stand in front of these headquarters and see the place where the table stood that you estimate as being 100 yards from headquarters?

Answer. I think not.

Question. Have you seen any liquor sold in this camp?

Answer. I have, to the best of my knowledge.

Question. Why did you think it was liquor?

Answer. It looked like it; its being dealt out of a canteen and their taking pay for it led me to suppose it was liquor.

Question. Who did you see selling liquor?

Answer. I tried to ascertain his name but could not.

Question. How many men did you see selling liquor?

Answer. I have seen two.

Question. What was their *modus operandi?*

Answer. They carried canteens and glasses with them.

Question. Had they a fixed position or were they moving?

Answer. Moving.

Question. Can you give me any information upon which I can arrest some of these individuals?

Answer. I can.

Question. Will you do it?

Answer. I will.

Statement of Prentiss S. Frink, Company D, Forty-fourth New York Volunteers, December 7, 1862.

Question. Do you know of any murders being committed in or about this camp?

Answer. No.

Question. Have you any reliable information of any murder being committed in or about this camp?

Answer. Nothing only what I have heard.

Question. Did you ever tell M. Shaw that there had been murder committed in this camp?

Answer. I told Shaw I had been told so by others.

Question. Who told you there had been a murder committed?

Answer. There were two men came into our booth last Sunday to buy some stationery and they said that there had been two men murdered in this camp. One had his throat cut and the other had his head mashed in with a club.

Question. Have you heard of any other murder?

Answer. While I was in the hospital a man who said he was a steward told me that one man had died from the effects of his wounds received by being kicked and knocked about the camp.

Question. In either of the cases of which you spoke have you any personal knowledge?

Answer. No.

Question. Do I understand you to say that all the knowledge you have of this affair is from mere camp rumors?

Answer. All I know is what others told me.

Question. At what particular part of the camp did your informants tell you the murder had been committed?

Answer. They did not say.

Question. Did ever Chineworth tell you that any murders had been committed here?

Answer. No.

Question. Did you ever make any efforts to find out whether these statements were true or not?

Answer. No.

Question. Why did you not try to find out?

Answer. I did not consider it any of my business.

Question. Did you believe these reports when you heard them?

Answer. There was so much said about it that I did not know but what there might be some truth in it.

Question. Do you know of any gambling being carried on in this camp?

Answer. I do.

Question. Can you give me the names of the party or parties engaged in gambling?

Answer. Yes; Sergeant Walker, Forty-fourth New York Volunteers, since discharged from the service.

Question. Did you ever see Chineworth gambling?

Answer. I saw Chineworth standing by a table, not playing, but looking as though he would play if he could find some one to play with.

Question. Had Chineworth the implements of gambling before him?

Answer. He had a dice-box and dice.

Question. Did you ever see Shaw gambling?

Answer. No.

Question. Did you ever see any effort on the part of the guard to suppress gambling?

Answer. Yes; last Sabbath.

Question. Did you ever see any effort on the part of the guard to suppress gambling at any other time than last Sabbath?

Answer. I think not.

Question. Do you know of any liquor being sold in this camp?

Answer. I do.

Question. To the best of your judgment what kind of liquor was it?

Answer. Whisky.

Question. Why do you think it was whisky?

Answer. I drank some.

Question. Who has sold liquor in this camp?

Answer. I do not know their names.

Question. How many have you seen selling liquor in this camp?

Answer. Seven or eight.

Question. What was their mode of operations?

Answer. They carried it in jugs, canteens and bottles.

Question. Had they fixed positions or were they moving?

Answer. They were moving.

Question. Can you give any information that would lead to the apprehension of these individuals?

Answer. I think I can.

Question. Will you do it?

Answer. I will try.

Statement of W. E. Chineworth, First Maryland Cavalry, December 7, 1862.

Question. Do you know of any murders being committed in or about this camp?

Answer. I do not.

Question. Do you know of any one being badly beaten or killed in front of your booth?

Answer. Nothing more than I heard.

Question. Did you ever tell Shaw that you saw the body of a person murdered?

Answer. No.

Question. Do you know of any man being killed or badly beaten in this camp?

Answer. To the best of my knowledge there were four men passed my booth and they met a man and asked him if he had any money. The man said no. They asked him if he had not been paid off. The man said no. They then asked him if he belonged to Pennsylvania and he said no. They said he lied, and to the best of my judgment knocked him down. I heard some men coming along afterwards. I heard them stop and say, "Halloo, here is a man stretched out. What is the matter with you, old fellow?" That is the last I heard of it.

Question. When you got up in the morning were there any dead men lying around your shanty?

Answer. No.

Question. Were there any marks of a scuffle or blood around your shanty?

Answer. No.

Question. Did you learn anything subsequent to that relating to this affair?

Answer. No.

Question. Who was in the shanty with you when you heard this?

Answer. A. J. Hurd, Hank Tompkins, Forty-fourth New York Volunteers; Nichols, Forty-fourth New York Volunteers.

Question. Did you ever hear of any men having their throats cut in this camp?

Answer. I heard that there was a man found with his throat cut in this camp.

Question. Who told you this?

Answer. I could not say who told me. I only heard it. The rumor was that Colonel Sangster and Colonel Staunton were riding out and found the body.

Question. Do you know of any one being engaged in gambling in this camp?

Answer. I do.

Question. Who were they?

Answer. I do not know.

Question. Did you ever gamble yourself?

Answer. I bet on the board two different days.

Question. Did you ever keep a table yourself?

Answer. I did not.

Question. Do you know of anybody in this camp engaged in selling liquor?

Answer. I know of two places where I think they sell liquor.

Question. Did you ever buy any yourself there or did you ever see anybody else buy any?

Answer. I did not.

Question. Why do you think they sold liquor there?

Answer. Because I heard others say it was a whisky shanty.

Question. Who did you hear say it was a whisky shanty?

Answer. John Brewer.

Question. Can you give me any information that would lead to the apprehension of the perpetrators of the murders, gamblers and liquor dealers?

Answer. I can point out some men who have been engaged in gambling; I think I can point out some liquor dealers but I know nothing about the murders.

Statement of E. B. Richardson, Company K, Twenty-first Massachusetts, December 8, 1862.

Question. Do you know of any murder or murders that have been committed in or about this camp?

Answer. Only what I have heard.

Question. Give me a statement of what you have heard.

Answer. I have heard rumors that there have been murders committed in and about this camp but can give nothing definite.

Question. Who did you get these rumors from?

Answer. I could not tell the names.

Question. Do you know anything of any gambling in this camp?

Answer. I have seen considerable of what they call gambling.

Question. What kind of gambling have you seen?

Answer. I have seen considerable of what they call the sweat-board.

Question. Who have you seen gambling at these boards?

Answer. I could not give the names but could recognize them.

Question. Will you assist me all you can in the apprehension of the gamblers?

Answer. I will.

Question. Do you know any one who has sold liquor in this camp?

Answer. I have seen men with canteens and glasses and asking who wanted the next drink but did not see them sell any so I could not give any direct information.

Question. Who have you seen with canteens and glasses?

Answer. I can't give the names but could recognize them.

Question. Will you give the name of the person or persons who you suppose have sold liquors?

Answer. A man by the name of Robbins. I will find his company and regiment. Also a man by the name of Keyser and a man by the name of Babcock, who assisted Robbins.

Statement of A. H. Reed, Company G, Sixty-seventh Pennsylvania Volunteers, December 8, 1862.

Question. Do you know of any one in your company or in any other company or any one connected with this camp in any way that has been murdered?

Answer. I do not but I have heard that there have been six murders committed from one Friday till the next Friday.

Question. Did you ever gamble?

Answer. No.

Question. Did you ever see any attempt on the part of the guard to suppress gambling?

Answer. I have. Yesterday week we arrested sixty gamblers.

Question. Do you know any of the men that have been arrested?

Answer. I do not know them personally.

Question. Have you ever seen any liquor sold in this camp?

Answer. No. I have seen them have liquor but did not see them sell any.

Question. Can you give any information that would lead to the apprehension of these individuals?

Answer. I have been told that they sold liquor on the left of the camp in the shanties.

Question. Can you point out the shanties?

Answer. I could not.

Question. Can you point out the places where there was gambling?

Answer. I can.

Statement of John H. Fisher, hospital steward, Fourteenth New York State Militia, December 8, 1862.

Question. How long have you been in this camp?

Answer. Since the 12th of September.

Question. What has been your business since you have been in this camp?

Answer. Hospital steward.

Question. Do you know of any one having died in the hospital from the effects of wounds and bruises received in this camp?

Answer. Yes.

Question. What was the name of the party?

Answer. Andrew Drewlock, Second New York Artillery.

Question. How did he receive his injuries?

Answer. Shot by the guard.

Question. Do you know of any one else?

Answer. No.

Question. Could any one in the hospital die and be buried without your knowing it?

Answer. No. I give the orders for all the coffins and no one can get a coffin without an order.

Statement of Josiah M. Darrel, Company E, Twentieth Massachusetts, December 8, 1862.

Question. How long have you been in this camp?

Answer. Since the 3d of November.

Question. Do you know of any murders having been committed in or about this camp?

Answer. I have heard that there have been murders committed but have no personal knowledge of them. The night before I heard of the rumor I was reading in my tent. I heard the cry of murder distinctly and the next morning a man came in my tent and said that a murder had been committed during the night. I do not know the man that told me.

Question. Do you know of any person or persons who have been engaged in gambling in this camp?

Answer. I do not.

Question. Did you ever see any attempt on the part of the guard to suppress gambling?

Answer. No.

Question. Have you ever seen liquor sold in this camp?

Answer. I have.

Question. Do you know of any spot where liquor has been sold?

Answer. I know where there is a shanty kept by a man by the name of Wright who I suppose sells liquor.

Question. Can you give any information that would lead to the apprehension of these parties engaged in selling liquor?

Answer. I have given all the information that I know of.

Statement of Sergt. James O'Neil, Company B, Ninth Massachusetts December 8, 1862.

Question. Do you know of any murder having been committed in or about this camp?

Answer. Nothing; only rumors.

Question. Who told you that there had been a murder committed?

Answer. I could not tell. I have heard several talk about it.

Question. Do you know of any one that has been engaged in gambling in this camp?

Answer. I have seen gambling going on but could not tell who were engaged in it.

Question. Did you ever gamble yourself?

Answer. I did once. I played at a sweat-board.

Question. Do you know the man who owned the board?

Answer. I do not know his name but can point him out.

Question. Have you ever seen any attempts of the guard to suppress gambling.

Answer. I have not.

Question. Have you ever seen any liquor sold in this camp?

Answer. Yes.

Question. Can you point any one out who has sold liquor?

Answer. I can.

Statement of James N. Lynch, Company F, Fortieth New York Volunteers, December 8, 1862.

Question. Do you know of any murders having been committed in or about this camp?

Answer. I have heard rumors of murders being committed but nothing definite.

Question. Do you know of any person or persons being engaged in gambling in this camp?

Answer. I have seen gambling in this camp but do not know who were engaged in it.

Question. Have you seen the guard attempt to suppress this gambling?

Answer. I have not but heard that they did.

Question. Have you seen any liquor sold in this camp?

Answer. I have seen men giving liquor out of canteens but did not see them take money for it and so could not say that they sold it.

Question. Can you point out any place where liquor has been sold or is sold?

Answer. I cannot.

Statement of William Eckerson, Jr., Forty-fourth New York Volunteers, December 8, 1862.

Question. Do you know of any murders having been committed in or about this camp?

Answer. I do not; only what I have heard others talk. A week ago yesterday I was talking with one of the guard at the post-office just as I returned from church. The guard said he was a Methodist preacher, and in the course of our conversation we talked about murders that had been committed during the past week. He said that there had been six murders committed from one Friday until the next Friday night, and from the conversation I heard I inferred that he had seen some of the dead bodies in the woods. The guard's name was Reed. I have heard others speak of the same subject but could not remember any names.

Question. Do you know of other occurrences of this character?

Answer. I have heard of several murders being committed but can give no correct account of them.

Question. Do you know of any persons that have been engaged in gambling in this camp?

Answer. I have seen a great deal of gambling in this camp but could not mention any names as I do not know the persons.

Question. Did you ever gamble yourself?

Answer. No.

Question. Did you ever see any attempt on the part of the guard to suppress gambling?

Answer. No.

Question. Have you ever seen liquor sold in this camp?

Answer. Yes.

Question. By whom?

Answer. I do not know any names.

Question. Where have you seen liquor sold in this camp?

Answer. In two of the wooden shanties.

Question. Can you give any information that would lead to the apprehension of any of these individuals?

Answer. I can point out the places where liquor has been sold.

Question. Will you give me all the information and assistance in your power?

Answer. I will endeavor to do so.

Statement of Peter Bowman, Company G, Nineteenth Indiana, December 8, 1862.

Question. Do you know of any murders having been committed in or about this camp?

Answer. I do not.

Question. Do you know of any gambling being carried on in this camp?

Answer. I have seen gambling in some wooden shanties but I do not know who were engaged in it.

Question. Have you seen the guard attempt to suppress this gambling?

Answer. I have not seen the guard arrest any.

Question. Have you seen liquor sold in this camp?

Answer. I sold five gallons myself last month.

Question. Do you know of any one else who has sold liquor in this camp?

[No answer found.]

Statement of Harry Wilson, Company E, Fortieth New York Volunteers, December 8, 1862.

Question. Do you know of any murders being committed in or about this camp?

Answer. I have heard of murders being committed but could not tell who told me.

Question. Do you know of any gambling being carried on in this camp?

Answer. I have seen gambling carried on here but do not know who were engaged in it. I do not know of any gambling being carried on at the present time.

Question. Have you seen the guard attempt to suppress this gambling?

Answer. I have once.

Question. Have you seen any liquor sold in this camp?

Answer. I have but do not know who sold it. I do not know of any liquor being sold now.

Statement of George Wright, Company C, Fortieth New York Volunteers, December 8, 1862.

Question. Do you know of any murders having been committed in or about this camp?

Answer. No.

Question. Do you know of any gambling being carried on in this camp?

Answer. No.

Question. Did you ever gamble yourself in this camp?

Answer. No.

Question. Have you ever seen liquor sold in this camp?

Answer. I sold it myself about two months ago but have sold none since I heard it was against the regulations of the camp. I know of no one else that has sold liquor.

HEADQUARTERS DEPARTMENT OF THE CUMBERLAND,
Nashville, December 11, 1862.

General BRAXTON BRAGG.

GENERAL: Your letter inclosing list of prisoners captured at Hartsville and paroled by you has been received. It is reported to me that the flag of truce presented itself about dark and during a skirmish.

The officer who conducted them to our lines insisted upon our receiving them as I am informed upon the ground of humanity. We take care of your prisoners, feed them, make them as comfortable as we can and conduct them to the proper place of exchange. That is our idea of humanity. Our prisoners were sufficiently clad when taken and I think ought to have been similarly treated. Whether your idea of humanity consists in robbing them of their blankets and overcoats I know not, but such they assure me was the treatment they received from your troops.

Without entering further into that question, however, I must be permitted to observe that to send these prisoners to my lines without any previous agreement with me to receive them is a violation both of the letter and spirit of the cartel.

I regret to notice this act of injustice and discourtesy, which is aggravated by the fact of their not being sent to us at a proper hour of the day when all the business could have been transacted without inconvenience to either party.

Paroled prisoners will hereafter only be received by me in accordance with the terms of the cartel. Herewith you will please receive receipts for the prisoners taken at Hartsville conformed to the lists of them forwarded by you. Although purporting apparently to be originals these lists are evidently mere copies, not attested by the signature of any officer of either army. As regards the third list sent by you inasmuch as it contains the names of persons of whom I know nothing it is impossible for me to say or do anything.

Very respectfully, your obedient servant,

W. S. ROSECRANS,
Major-General, Commanding.

HEADQUARTERS ARMY OF TENNESSEE,
Murfreesborough, December 11, 1862.

Maj. Gen. W. S. ROSECRANS,
Commanding U. S. Forces, Nashville, Tenn.

GENERAL: In your letter of the 4th instant you express your abhorrence of the system of harassing and arresting non-combatants. In a previous letter I have intimated my entire concurrence in these views and nothing shall swerve me from the faithful observance of a policy which is dictated by every proper sentiment. I am credibly informed, however, that on the very day on which your communication was written a number of citizens of Tennessee charged only with political offenses or proclivities were arrested and imprisoned in the penitentiary at Nashville. It is of little moment to me whether this was done by your immediate order or by your subordinates for whose conduct you are responsible, and I hereby notify you that I shall enforce rigid and unyielding retaliation against the commissioned officers who fall into my hands until this violation of good faith be corrected in deeds as well as words.

Very respectfully, your obedient servant,

BRAXTON BRAGG,
General, Commanding.

CINCINNATI, *December 11, 1862.*

Hon. EDWIN M. STANTON, *Secretary of War:*

A battle at Nashville seems imminent. I am not yet exchanged. I trust my command will not go into action without me. Can I not be exchanged at once and put under orders?

WM. H. LYTLE,
Colonel Tenth Ohio.

OFFICE COMMISSARY-GENERAL OF PRISONERS,
Washington, D. C., December 11, 1862.

Lieut. Col. GEORGE SANGSTER,
Commanding Camp Parole, Annapolis, Md.

COLONEL: The exchanged troops at your camp will be ordered to join their respective regiments with as little delay as practicable. Place all belonging to the same army under the senior officer who will conduct them to headquarters and report to the general commanding. Send as complete rolls with them as practicable, each regiment by itself, and furnish cooked rations for the route. The Quartermaster's Department will furnish the necessary transportation.

By order of the General-in-Chief:

Very respectfully, your obedient servant,
W. HOFFMAN,
Colonel Third Infantry, Commissary-General of Prisoners.

OFFICE COMMISSARY-GENERAL OF PRISONERS,
Washington, D. C., December 11, 1862.

Maj. JOSEPH DARR, Jr.,
Provost-Marshal-General, Wheeling, Va.

MAJOR: Your several letters of the 3d and 4th instant communicating the recommendation of Governor Peirpoint for the release of certain named prisoners are received, and I have to reply that General Orders, No. 193, of November 22, will probably cover all these cases, and it is therefore not necessary at present to present them to the War Department.

Very respectfully, your obedient servant,
W. HOFFMAN,
Colonel Third Infantry, Commissary-General of Prisoners.

RICHMOND, VA., *December 11, 1862.*

Lieut. Col. WILLIAM H. LUDLOW, *Agent of Exchange.*

SIR: With reference to the Pennsylvania non-combatants captured by General Stuart and whose release you ask in your letter of the 3d instant* I beg respectfully to state that they were captured and are now held only in retaliation for captures of non-combatant citizens of the Confederate States. As soon as your Government releases the non-combatants of the Confederate States now held by you and agrees to abandon the policy of making such captures in the future; or in other words as soon as your Government agrees substantially to the

* See p. 20.

proposition relating to such captures which I made to you at our last interview, these citizens of Pennsylvania will be unconditionally released. You have in your military prisons at this time a far larger number of persons who were arrested on Confederate soil while engaged in no acts of hostility to your Government than we have in ours. How can you claim the release of your non-combatants when you retain ours? How can you ask us to release your non-combatants when you refuse to agree that ours shall not be captured? In retaining these Pennsylvanians the Confederate Government does not abandon its position so often reiterated that the capture of non-combatants is illegal and contrary to the usages of civilized warfare. The Government of the Confederate States is anxious to put an end to any such practice. It has protested earnestly and persistently against it. When those protests failed to accomplish the desired end a sense of duty to its own citizens demanded that the Confederate Government should resort to other means. May I not hope that the United States Government will promptly settle this whole matter by a release of such Confederate citizens as are now in prison who when captured were connected with no military organization and by a disavowal of any purpose to make such arrests in future?

Respectfully, your obedient servant,

ROBT. OULD,
Agent of Exchange.

RICHMOND, *December 11, 1862.*

Lieut. Col. W. H. LUDLOW, *Agent of Exchange.*

SIR: I have directed that all the military prisoners now in Richmond shall be sent to you. Mrs. Anderson will also go down in the same train. There are quite a number of persons, mostly ladies, whose friends, connections and means are in the North who are extremely anxious to go to the United States by flag-of-truce boat. Some of them have already the permission of the Confederate Government and others are applying for permission. Others again whose families are in Norfolk are very desirous of going to them. I cannot at this time give you a list of these applicants. They, however, all come within the above description. You would probably not recognize their names if they were given. I am very much harassed and pressed by these applications and hardly know what to do or say in the premises. What rule have you adopted about them? If I send them to the flag-of truce boat will you receive them and forward them to their destination? I can assure you that I will only send such as come within the categories I have mentioned.

We on the other hand will receive such as have their friends, connections and means in the South. You can send such to City Point where they will be received.

Respectfully, your obedient servant,

RO. OULD,
Agent of Exchange.

WAR DEPARTMENT, *Washington, December 12, 1862.*

Hon WILLIAM H. SEWARD, *Secretary of State.*

SIR: The Secretary of War has had the honor to receive your communication of the 10th instant covering a copy of correspondence between Major-General Butler and the French Admiral, Mr. Reynaud, relative to the imprisonment of the Messrs. Le More, alleged French subjects residing at New Orleans.

Replying thereto I am directed to inform you that a copy of your letter has been transmitted to General Butler with instructions to remit the punishment of the ball and chain and hard labor.

I have the honor to be, very respectfully, your obedient servant,
C. P. WOLCOTT,
Assistant Secretary of War.

WAR DEPARTMENT, *Washington, December 12, 1862.*

Maj. Gen. B. F. BUTLER, *Commanding, &c., New Orleans, La.*

SIR: The Secretary of War instructs me to transmit a copy of a letter from the State Department relative to your order for the imprisonment of the Messrs. Le More, and especially in reference to the case of Alfred Le More, confined at Fort Pickens, and additionally punished with the attachment of a ball and chain to his leg. The Secretary also directs me to say that under the instructions of the President mentioned in the communication of the Secretary of State the prisoner must be released from the ball and chain and from hard labor.

Very respectfully, your obedient servant,
C. P. WOLCOTT,
Assistant Secretary of War.

[Indorsement.]

HEADQUARTERS DEPARTMENT OF THE GULF,
New Orleans, January 26, 1863.

The commanding officer of the District of Pensacola will carry out the within orders of the War Department and communicate his action to these headquarters, returning these papers.

By command of Major-General Banks:
RICHARD B. IRWIN,
Lieutenant-Colonel and Assistant Adjutant-General.

Received back February 13, 1863, and respectfully referred to the Board of Prison Inspectors to ascertain and report where Mr. Le More now is.

By command:
RICHARD B. IRWIN,
Assistant Adjutant-General.

OFFICE COMMISSARY-GENERAL OF PRISONERS,
Washington, D. C., December 12, 1862.

Lieut. Col. F. A. DICK,
Provost-Marshal-General, Saint Louis, Mo.

COLONEL: Your letter of the 6th instant is received and in reply I can give you only general instructions in relation to the discipline of the prisons. To insure good order, good police and healthy condition of the prison regularity and system must be introduced into the management of every department, and the manner of accomplishing this I must leave to your own judgment. A thorough policing of every part of the prison should take place every morning, and a thorough and frequent airing of clothing should be required when practicable.

Prompt obedience to orders and regulations must be exacted, and for any violation of orders you will fix a punishment at your own discretion.

General Orders, No. 193, herewith inclosed,* directs the release of two classes of prisoners, and it is left to your discretion to decide who are to be released under it. If there are any who would be released under the first paragraph you must ascertain from the Governor of the State they come from if the draft or quota has been furnished. The second paragraph covers all cases of persons sent from the border States by the Governor or military commander—Virginia, Kentucky, Tennessee and Missouri.

Very respectfully, your obedient servant,

W. HOFFMAN,
Colonel Third Infantry, Commissary-General of Prisoners.

OFFICE COMMISSARY-GENERAL OF PRISONERS,
Washington, D. C., December 12, 1862.

Lieut. Col. F. A. DICK,
Provost-Marshal-General, Saint Louis, Mo.

COLONEL: In the case of J. J. Clarkson, who claims to be a colonel in the Confederate Army, I have to reply to the inquiries contained in your letter of the 3d instant that inasmuch as he has no commission from the rebel Government a decision of the question will not be made until he is claimed as an officer of that Government. Prisoners of war held by you will not hereafter be turned over to any civil authority except by order of the War Department. The prisoners you refer to as having been taken with or without arms in the central and northern parts of Missouri while on their way to join the rebel army will be held as political prisoners not entitled to the privileges of prisoners of war, and you will as often as may be necessary furnish to this office rolls of all captures of this character, giving on the rolls all necessary particulars of time, place, &c. Prisoners of war will not be released on taking the oath of allegiance except by authority of the War Department. Deserters from the enemy will not be held as prisoners of war, but it must be clearly established that they are deserters, and to insure their loyalty the oath of allegiance should be administered to them. When prisoners are sent to you without rolls if possible detain them until rolls are prepared before they are sent to Alton. When you have none of the particulars of the capture let that be stated on the rolls.

Very respectfully, your obedient servant,

W. HOFFMAN,
Colonel Third Infantry, Commissary-General of Prisoners.

HDQRS. 2D BRIG., 1ST DIV., ARMY OF THE FRONTIER,
Camp near Cane Hill, December 12, 1862.

The PRINCIPAL SURGEON, C. S. Army,
Cane Hill or Boonsborough.

SIR: I am instructed by the general commanding the U. S. forces in this vicinity to require the following: That you furnish me with a complete list of your wounded and attendants; that they be kept close about the hospitals and not allowed to straggle about town or our camps. Under no pretext will any of them attempt to pass the lines.

Those able to move about must wear a badge and be furnished with a certificate signed by me, which they must hold in readiness to produce when called upon. The propriety of these regulations will at once occur to you. Should you desire anything more explicit I should be pleased to see you at my quarters.

Your obedient servant,

WM. WEER,
Colonel, Commanding.

Proceedings of a board which met at Saint Louis, Mo., December 12, 1862, pursuant to Special Orders, No. 16, paragraph III, dated at Headquarters District of Missouri, Saint Louis, December 10, 1862, of which the following is a true copy:

SPECIAL ORDERS, } HEADQUARTERS DISTRICT OF MISSOURI,
No. 16.   } *Saint Louis, Mo., December 10, 1862.*

*   *   *   *   *   *   *

III. A board of officers is hereby appointed for the following purposes:
1. To inquire into the necessity of having additional prison accommodations for the prisoners now at the Gratiot and Myrtle Street Prisons, and whether provision should be made for others who may be sent to this city for confinement.
2. In case additional accommodations are found to be necessary to select a suitable building for the purpose, fix the compensation which should be made for such building and state what will be the probable amount of other expenses connected with its occupation.
Detail for the board.—Col. S. A. Rice, Thirty-third Iowa Infantry Volunteers; Maj. L. D. Hubbard, Third Illinois Cavalry; Surg. A. Parks, Thirty-third Iowa Infantry Volunteers.
The board will confer with the honorable Sanitary Commission, who are respectfully requested to express their opinions on the above points.
The board will make a full and complete report and express a decided opinion on the points submitted as soon as possible.
The board will assemble to-morrow, December 11, at 10.30 a. m., at the headquarters of Colonel Rice.
By order of Brigadier-General Carr:

C. H. DYER,
Assistant Adjutant-General.

The board having carefully examined the Gratiot and Myrtle Street Prisons has the honor to report: That there are but 471 prisoners in the Gratiot Street Prison, and that 750 prisoners can be therein accommodated without risk of detriment to their comfort and health. New hospital arrangements are being perfected by Surgeon Hood, in charge, which are very useful and beneficial, and your board deems it unnecessary that more space be provided to meet any present necessities. The sick average about 20 per cent. of the prisoners on account of the prevalence of the mumps and measles. The Myrtle Street Prison is in good order and can contain with compliance to every necessity of health 150 prisoners throughout the winter. It now contains 145. The board is of opinion that no necessity exists for more prison room, as the honorable Sanitary Commission lately report that the Alton Prison will receive 550 additional prisoners and have sufficient capacity for their accommodation without detriment to their health and comfort.

The board deems that unless a large number of prisoners are to be transferred to this point it would be an unnecessary expense to the Government to fit up another building for a prison unless rendered absolutely necessary by a great increase of prisoners, and submit the following report of two buildings which have been examined:
1. The Lytle Factory would require an expense of at least $5,000 to remove and replace its heavy machinery and $5,000 additional to place

it in suitable condition for a prison.   It would accommodate 750 prisoners.   Your board estimate its rent at $7,000 per annum.

2. The Milo Factory would accommodate 1,200 prisoners and is a preferable building in many respects; but being situated on the rock it would be necessary to blast or hew a place for the purpose of a privy and the deposits would have to be pumped away. The rent is estimated at $10,000 per annum and expenses incurred to fit it for a prison would be at least $7,000. This report has been submitted to the honorable Sanitary Commission, whose opinion is indorsed hereon.

[Indorsement.]

The Western Sanitary Commission, to whom the report of the commissioners appointed by Brigadier-General Carr to examine and report on prison accommodation was submitted, would suggest that after careful measurements of the rooms in the Gratiot and Myrtle Street Prisons they found that not over 625 should be admitted into the Gratiot Street Prison and 100 in the Myrtle Street Prison. The numbers named are the largest admissible. * * *

The Myrtle Street Prison.—There are 155 bunks. The space allotted to them will not average over 150 feet, which is entirely too little. By reducing the number of bunks to 100 the average then would only be 211 cubic feet, which is scarcely enough. Eighty men would be a better number. The Alton Prison will accommodate from 600 to 800 more. Having the use of this prison, [we] would agree with the commissioners that additional buildings would not be necessary, especially as prisoners taken in battle are to be at once exchanged. The arrests in the State are not likely to increase more than discharges will take place; but of this the military authorities can alone judge.

Very respectfully,

JAMES E. YEATMAN.

Respectfully submitted.

SAMUEL A. RICE,
Colonel Thirty-third Iowa Infantry Volunteers.
LOUIS D. HUBBARD,
Major, Third Illinois Cavalry.

Capt. C. H. DYER,
Assistant Adjutant-General, Hdqrs. District of Saint Louis.

[Indorsement.]

HDQRS. DIST. OF SAINT LOUIS, DEPT. OF THE MISSOURI,
Saint Louis, December 18, 1862.

The inclosed report of a board which was convened for the purpose of investigating into the necessity of additional prison room in this city is respectfully forwarded to department headquarters. The board reports that at present there is no need of additional prison room, in which I fully concur.

E. A. CARR,
Brigadier-General, Commanding District.

HEADQUARTERS DEPARTMENT OF THE MISSOURI,
Saint Louis, December 12, 1862.

Col. WILLIAM HOFFMAN,
Commissary-General of Prisoners, Washington, D. C.

COLONEL: I have the honor to request information as to whether the officers and men of the Twenty-fifth Missouri Infantry and others paroled at Lexington, Mo., in 1861, and all prisoners taken and paroled at the battle of Wilson's Creek, Mo., in 1861, have ever been exchanged. Also as to prisoners taken at the battle of Pittsburg Landing or

Shiloh. The exchange of none of those above mentioned appears to be announced in General Orders, No. 191.

I have the honor to be, colonel, very respectfully, your obedient servant,

H. Z. CURTIS,
Assistant Adjutant-General.

HDQRS. DEPT. OF MISSISSIPPI AND EAST LOUISIANA,
Grenada, December 13, 1862.

Maj. Gen. U. S. GRANT, *Commanding U. S. Forces.*

GENERAL: I am credibly informed that Capt. W. W. Faulkner, Captain Meriwether, Lieut. L. N. Johnson, Lieutenant Blakemore and sixteen privates belonging to Partisan Ranger Corps, C. S. Army, have been refused the benefits of the late cartel for the exchange of prisoners of war. These officers and men are as much a part of the C. S. Army as are any other composing it, and as much entitled to the benefits of the cartel as any of your prisoners whom I now hold. I request therefore to be informed of your intentions in reference to the prisoners above referred to, and have to state that I shall cause an equal number of your prisoners to be held in close confinement if the information conveyed to me be correct.

I am, general, very respectfully, &c., your obedient servant,

J. C. PEMBERTON,
Lieutenant-General, Commanding.

HEADQUARTERS DISTRICT OF EASTERN ARKANSAS,
Helena, December 13, 1862.

Major CURTIS, *Assistant Adjutant-General.*

MAJOR: I have the honor to forward papers and abstracts relating to the exchange of prisoners. They were received to-day under a flag of truce. I have simply replied to General Holmes saying that I had forwarded them to department headquarters.

I am, major, your obedient servant,

W. A. GORMAN,
Brigadier-General, Commanding.

[Inclosure.]

HEADQUARTERS TRANS-MISSISSIPPI DEPARTMENT,
Little Rock, Ark., December 7, 1862.

COMMANDING OFFICER U. S. FORCES, *Helena, Ark.*

SIR: I inclose under cover to you several communications* marked 1 and 2, addressed to Major-General Curtis or other officer commanding Department of Missouri, Saint Louis, Mo. I beg that these communications be forwarded immediately and the answer returned to me as soon as received.

I am, sir very respectfully, your obedient servant,

TH. H. HOLMES,
Major-General, Commanding.

---

* Not found.

HDQRS. SECOND CAVALRY MISSOURI STATE MILITIA,
Palmyra, December 13, 1862.

Brigadier-General MERRILL,
Commanding Northeastern District of Missouri.

GENERAL: I have the honor to acknowledge receipt of your order of the 12th ordering full statement of causes of arrest of Misses Lizzie Powell and Maggie Creath and a report of the manner of their confinement. Having had no official connection with these young ladies or control over their detention I called upon Colonel Strachan, late provost-marshal-general of this district, whose reply I have the honor to inclose. The active disloyalty of these two women is notorious, and their beauty, talents and superior education have made many a man a bushwhacker who except for that influence would have been an honest man. They are even openly and persistently disloyal. I regard them each of sufficient importance to either justify a strict surveillance or banishment from the State.

I have the honor to be, your obedient servant,

JOHN McNEIL,
Brigadier-General, Missouri State Militia.

[Inclosure.]

[PALMYRA, MO., *December 13, 1862.*]

General McNEIL:

SIR: In answer to your inquiries about Misses Powell and Creath, the evidence sent to the office from Doctor Hueston, near Santa Fé, I think, and several others, established that these young ladies had taken a carriage of Armstead Botts, of Monroe County, driven to Hannibal, and brought out under the protection of the petticoat flag a quantity of gun caps, some 50,000, and other essentials to the guerrillas. Miss Creath made quite a sensation in Monroe County traveling with one Clay Price, a noted captain of guerrillas, dressed in rebel colors and a brace of rebel pistols ornamenting her taper waist. Their influence, being young ladies of large talking propensities, was particularly pernicious, they openly declaring that they acknowledge the authority of no Government but that of "Jeff Davis, the noblest and wisest man that ever graced a presidential chair." Their cases were submitted by me to Colonel Gantt, provost-marshal-general, and he advised their banishment from the State, but gave me no written order to that effect. The manner of their detention has been on their personal parole that they would abstain from writing and talking treason. They remained at the house of Elder Creath without guard, and Miss Powell has since been allowed the liberty of Hannibal, her native town, at your order.

I am, very respectfully,

WM. R. STRACHAN,
Provost-Marshal, Palmyra.

OFFICE COMMISSARY-GENERAL OF PRISONERS,
Washington, D. C., December 13, 1862.

Maj. Gen. JOHN E. WOOL,
Commanding Eighth Army Corps, Baltimore, Md.

GENERAL: The conflict of authority between the military commanders at Annapolis is of frequent occurrence and leads to inconvenience and to the detriment of the service. I therefore beg to request that specific instructions placing the camp of paroled prisoners at

Annapolis under the exclusive command of Lieutenant-Colonel Sangster, Forty-seventh New York Volunteers, may be issued from your headquarters, and that the guards furnished for duty at the camp from the Sixty-seventh Regiment Pennsylvania Volunteers may be recognized while thus employed as subject to the orders of Lieutenant-Colonel Sangster and not to those of Colonel Staunton.

Very respectfully, your obedient servant,

W. HOFFMAN,
Colonel Third Infantry, Commissary-General of Prisoners.

OFFICE COMMISSARY-GENERAL OF PRISONERS,
Washington, D. C., December 13, 1862.

Maj. Gen. H. G. WRIGHT,
Commanding Department of the Ohio, Cincinnati, Ohio.

GENERAL: I have the honor to acknowledge the receipt of your letter of the 6th instant* with the inclosed letter from General John W. Finnell, adjutant-general of Kentucky volunteers, and in reply I am directed by the Secretary of War to say that all military organizations engaged in service if captured before being mustered in are entitled to the same consideration as if the muster had been perfected, and the home guards and recruits to whom you refer in order that they may receive pay and be exchanged should at once repair to Camp Wallace as required by General Orders, No. 72, of 28th of June. It is presumed that when these troops entered the service they were enrolled, so that there can be no doubt where they belong. Rolls will be prepared at Camp Wallace of these men which will be forwarded through this office to the agent for exchange of prisoners, and on these rolls he will negotiate their exchange. The exchanges thus far of prisoners taken at Munfordville cover only the Indiana regiments.

Very respectfully, your obedient servant,

W. HOFFMAN,
Colonel Third Infantry, Commissary-General of Prisoners.

OFFICE COMMISSARY-GENERAL OF PRISONERS,
Washington, D. C., December 13, 1862.

Lieut. Col. F. A. DICK,
Provost-Marshal-General, Saint Louis, Mo.

COLONEL: Your letter of the 8th is received and in reply I have to say that the explanations you give of the matters referred to in my letter of the 4th instant are quite satisfactory.

Hereafter when your prisons are likely to become too much crowded give me timely notice, that prisoners may be transferred from Alton to Sandusky to make room for those held in Saint Louis. Such a state of things as you represent should never occur again if it is possible to avoid it, and there should be always ample room to spare in at least one of your prisons. Endeavor to systematize your calls for the release of prisoners from Alton so that they may be prepared for as much as twice or three times a week. The matter of the latter part of your letter is covered by mine of the 12th instant.

Very respectfully, your obedient servant,

W. HOFFMAN,
Colonel Third Infantry, Commissary-General of Prisoners.

---

* See p. 33.

HDQRS. 2D BRIG., 1ST DIV., ARMY OF THE FRONTIER,
                    Cane Hill, Ark., December 13, 1862.
Lieutenant-Colonel MOONLIGHT, *Chief of Staff:*

A flag of truce has just reached here. I send the communication he brings, which I opened at his request. I have already taken steps to bring in the medicines for the rebel invalids. The ambulances I have detained at the lines. The bearer states that in his opinion the intention is to convey the rebel wounded southward. On this account I have refused them admittance and await the orders of the general. The bearer of the flag is with me.

Your obedient servant,
                                        WM. WEER,
                              Colonel, Commanding Brigade.

HDQRS. 2D BRIG., 1ST DIV., ARMY OF THE FRONTIER,
                    Camp, Cane Hill, December 13, 1862.
Captain McCOY, C. S. Army:

I am forbidden until further instructions to allow any of your party to enter the lines. However, for the sake of your wounded I send an ambulance to bring in your medicines. I instruct the person in charge to report them to Doctor Welch, in charge of your hospitals. When I receive a communication from General Blunt I will inform you as to what privileges you will be allowed.

Your obedient servant,
                                        WM. WEER,
                                   Colonel, Commanding.

WASHINGTON, *December 13, 1862.*
Col. MARTIN BURKE, *Fort Hamilton:*

You will discharge * * * and all other political prisoners whose discharges have been ordered, without any conditions, in case they refuse to take the oath of allegiance, &c.

By order of the Secretary of War:
                                        L. C. TURNER,
                                      Judge-Advocate.

SAINT LOUIS, *December 13, 1862.*
Colonel HILDEBRAND,
    Commanding Military Prison, Alton, Ill.

COLONEL: I have the honor to say that any prisoners from Missouri now held in Alton subject to the orders of this office except those hereinafter mentioned may if they desire be released on parole and bond to go to any locality in the free States east of the Illinois Central Railroad and north of line drawn due east from Springfield, Ill., and there remain for the war. No person who is under sentence of a military commission or who is charged with crime which should be tried by a military commission will be included in this permission. It is believed that many of the young men under your charge from this State will accept the offer. Quite a number have already done so. They will thus find themselves in a peaceful community where labor of all kinds is in great demand, wages are high and schools abundant. If you find any among your prisoners who wish to accept these terms of release from confinement please be kind enough to communicate their names to this office and their cases will be attended to at once.

I have the honor to remain, colonel, your obedient servant,

F. A. DICK,
Lieut. Col., Provost-Marshal-General, Department of the Missouri.

OFFICE PROVOST-MARSHAL-GENERAL,
Wheeling, December 13, 1862.

Col. W. HOFFMAN, *Commissary-General of Prisoners.*

SIR: I have the honor to acknowledge receipt of your communication of 11th instant. Please send me the Orders, No. 193, of November 22; also any orders that may have been issued relating to exchange of prisoners. May I trouble you to remember me and send me the orders of the War Department as they are issued?

Very respectfully,

JOS. DARR, JR.,
Major and Provost-Marshal-General.

HEADQUARTERS EIGHTH ARMY CORPS,
Baltimore, December 14, 1862.

Maj. L. C. TURNER,
Judge-Advocate, Washington, D. C.:

I. C. W. Powell and William Nabb were arrested with Judge Carmichael. Powell was discharged on the 6th instant, but Nabb is still at Fort Delaware. Can he not be discharged? If so on what terms?

[JOHN E WOOL,]
Major-General.

BALTIMORE, *December 14, 1862.*

COMMANDING OFFICER, *Fort Delaware:*

The commanding officer at Fort Delaware will have all the rebel prisoners of war at Fort Delaware prepared to embark for Fortress Monroe to report to Lieut. Col. William H. Ludlow for exchange, he being the agent. Duplicate rolls will be made of the prisoners. They will be placed under a guard of twelve men, an officer and two non-commissioned officers, with the rolls, which will be delivered to Colonel Ludlow. Colonel Belger will furnish transportation.

JOHN E. WOOL,
Major-General.

HEADQUARTERS DEPARTMENT OF THE TENNESSEE,
Oxford, Miss., December 14, 1862.

Lieutenant-General PEMBERTON,
Commanding Confederate Forces, Jackson, Tenn.

GENERAL: Your communication in the case of Colonel Hedgpeth is just received. I did not even know that Colonel Hedgpeth was in the hospital at Memphis and cannot answer as to the misfortune that may possibly have befallen him in the way of losses sustained. Where there are large armies and particularly in large cities there are always persons ready to steal where an opportunity occurs, and especially have many of our Federal troops who have been so unfortunate as to fall into the hands of the Southern Army found this true.

As to the other or any other bad treatment toward Colonel Hedgpeth you will find when the facts are before you he has received none.

All prisoners of war are humanely treated by the Federal authorities, and many a wounded or sick soldier has remonstrated against being sent back for exchange on the ground that the treatment received at the hands of the Union authorities was so much better than they could get among what they denominated their friends.

All prisoners who desire it are sent by the first opportunity that occurs to Vicksburg for exchange. Sick and wounded are paroled in hospitals, and as soon as able to travel are furnished passes out of our lines or are sent with other prisoners to the depot agreed upon for exchange.

Unless there is some good reason for it Colonel Hedgpeth has not nor will not be made an exception to the rule.

I am, sir, very respectfully. your obedient servant,
U. S. GRANT,
Major-General.

OFFICE COMMISSARY-GENERAL OF PRISONERS,
Washington, D. C., December 14, 1862.

Maj. Gen. H. G. WRIGHT,
Commanding Department of the Ohio, Cincinnati, Ohio.

GENERAL: I respectfully beg leave to call your attention to the utter inattention to General Orders, No. 163, by officers in your department who have charge of prisoners of war. I have to-day received four sets of rolls all without signatures or verification of any kind. They were addressed to the Adjutant-General in one package and accompanied by two letters, one addressed to Lieut. T. G. Beaham, acting assistant adjutant-general, December 6, by Capt. Ed. M. Hulburd, provost-marshal at Lexington, and the other addressed to the Adjutant-General at Washington, December 8, by Maj. Gen. G. Granger, commanding at Lexington. Three of these rolls have the dates when the prisoners were sent to Louisville and no other date; the fourth roll has no date at all. The time and place of capture are not given, nor anything by which they may be identified with any particular command. Generally the names are entered in a promiscuous way without giving the rank of the person named. For the convenience of reference the names should be entered on the rolls by regiments and companies and in alphabetical order. It is difficult to say which rolls the two letters referred to and one of them is not referred to at all. The same character of rolls is required for our own troops when captured and paroled by the enemy and for rebel prisoners when paroled by us. May I beg your early attention to this matter, as much embarrassment and delay in effecting exchanges is occasioned by the careless manner in which rolls have heretofore been prepared. New rolls should be forwarded to replace those just received containing all necessary details as required in General Orders, No. 32, of April 2; General Orders, No. 54, of May 17, and General Orders, No. 163, of October 22, 1862.

Very respectfully, your obedient servant,
W. HOFFMAN,
Colonel Third Infantry, Commissary-General of Prisoners.

GENERAL ORDERS, ╲ HDQRS. DEPARTMENT OF THE OHIO,
      No. 31.   ╱   *Cincinnati, Ohio, December 14, 1862.*

I. In pursuance of instructions from the Headquarters of the Army, Adjutant-General's Office, of the 19th instant, it is ordered that commanders of camps of paroled prisoners of war within the Department of the Ohio immediately forward the exchanged prisoners under their command to the armies to which they belong by detachments under charge of commissioned officers, the detachments to be sent to their respective regiments, batteries, &c., by commanders of armies in which they are serving. Correct rolls of detachments, according to regiments, batteries, &c., will be furnished the several commanding officers before starting. The quartermaster's department will provide the necessary transportation on requisitions of the commanders of the respective camps.

II. All exchanged officers and soldiers now absent from the several camps of rendezvous for paroled prisoners, whether with or without leave, except in cases of sick leave granted by the proper authority, who fail to promptly report in person to the respective commanders of those camps will be reported as deserters and dealt with accordingly.

By command of Major-General Wright:

N. H. McLEAN,
Assistant Adjutant-General and Chief of Staff.

Resolution adopted by the House of Representatives December 15, 1862.

Resolved, That the Secretary of War be directed to inform the House what steps, if any, have been taken for the relief of sutlers and other non-combatants attached to our Army, now held as prisoners at Richmond and elsewhere.

HEADQUARTERS DEPARTMENT OF THE TENNESSEE,
      Oxford, Miss., December 15, 1862.
Lieutenant-General PEMBERTON,
      Commanding Confederate Forces.

GENERAL: Your communication of the 13th instant in relation to the detention of Captain Faulkner and other guerrillas is just received.

These moving bands have been a pest to the communities through which they passed but no detriment to the cause of the Union. They have not observed the rules of civilized warfare, and I did not suppose were authorized or under any control except such as they agreed upon among themselves. As you acknowledge them, however, and as most of their belligerency is directed against sympathizers and abettors of this rebellion I will send them to Vicksburg for exchange or set them loose.

I will state here that this is the third communication from you to General Sherman and myself since the present advance commenced that has been threatening in tone. One of your communications also implied a doubt of my veracity in the statement made by me as to prisoners taken as well as casting reflections upon the character of those prisoners.

I will now state to you that the number of prisoners taken by my forces on this advance has been exclusive of sick and stragglers over 1,000. Most of this latter class have been persons who have become tired of the war and have been permitted to take the oath of allegiance and return to their homes.

All communications heretofore received from officers of the Southern Army have been courteous and kind in spirit and have been replied to in the same tone. I regret the necessity for any other class of correspondence.

On my part I shall carry on this war humanely, and do what I conceive to be my duty regardless of threats and most certainly without making any.

I am, very respectfully, your obedient servant,
U. S. GRANT,
Major-General.

HEADQUARTERS ARMY OF TENNESSEE,
Murfreesborough, Tenn., December 15, 1862.

Maj. Gen. W. S. ROSECRANS,
Commanding U. S. Forces, Nashville, Tenn.

GENERAL: Your communication in reference to an alleged error in the number of prisoners as compared with the lists furnished has been received.

I have the honor to inclose you copy* of a receipt given by your officer who conducted the transfer. By it you will perceive that he attested the correctness of the number and certified accordingly. If any were permitted to escape after being turned over to him I am certainly not responsible for the loss.

I am, general, very respectfully, your obedient servant,
BRAXTON BRAGG,
General, Commanding.

SAINT PAUL, *December 15, 1862.*

The PRESIDENT OF THE UNITED STATES:

Your order of the 6th instant for the execution of thirty-nine Indians just received by special messenger. They are imprisoned at Mankato, ninety miles distant, and the time fixed (19th) is too short for preparations for concentrating the troops necessary to protect the other Indians and preserve the peace. The excitement prevails in all sections of the State, and secret combinations exist embracing thousands of citizens pledged to execute all the Indians. Matters must be managed with great discretion and as much secrecy as possible to prevent a fearful collision between the U. S. forces and the citizens. I respectfully ask for authority to postpone the execution one week from the 19th instant if I deem [it] necessary. Please reply at once. Your directions of 9th relative to Chakaydon received to-day by mail and will be obeyed.

Respectfully,   H. H. SIBLEY,
Brigadier-General, Commanding.

OFFICE COMMISSARY-GENERAL OF PRISONERS,
Washington, D. C., December 15, 1862.

Surg. L. A. EDWARDS,
U. S. Army General Hospital, Portsmouth Grove, R. I.

SIR: The paroled troops received at the general hospital, Portsmouth Grove, have been exchanged, and those fit for duty will be immediately ordered to join their respective regiments.

---

* Not found.

Send as complete rolls with them by regiments and companies and accounts of pay and clothing as practicable, and furnish cooked rations for the route. The accompanying memorandum will show the points to which they should be sent. Three officers will be ordered to report to you to conduct the command. The Quartermaster's Department will furnish the necessary transportation.

By order of the General-in-Chief:

Very respectfully, your obedient servant,

W. HOFFMAN,
Colonel Third Infantry, Commissary-General of Prisoners.

[Inclosure.]

OFFICE COMMISSARY-GENERAL OF PRISONERS,
December 15, 1862.

Memorandum.—Men belonging to the Army of the Potomac will join at Fredericksburg via Washington. Men belonging to General Grant's army or General Curtis' department will be sent to Benton Barracks thence to join their regiments; those of General Wright's department to Camp Wallace, near Columbus, Ohio, and those of General Rosecrans' army to Nashville, Tenn. Men belonging to Mitchel's corps will be sent to Port Royal via New York. Two officers will conduct the detachment going west and one the detachment for New York and this city.

W. HOFFMAN,
Colonel Third Infantry, Commissary-General of Prisoners.

OFFICE COMMISSARY-GENERAL OF PRISONERS,
Washington, D. C., December 15, 1862.

Hon. RICHARD YATES,
Governor of Illinois, Springfield, Ill.

GOVERNOR: Your letter of the 6th instant addressed to the Secretary of War has been referred to me and in reply I have the honor to inform you that the prisoners taken at Lexington, Mo., have not been exchanged.

Lieutenant-Colonel Ludlow, agent for the exchange of prisoners, will endeavor in his next interview with the agent of the rebel Government to effect an exchange of all prisoners captured in Missouri in mass, as very little is known by either party of captures made there. Some irregular exchanges have been made of which there is no official information.

I am, Governor, very respectfully, your obedient servant,

W. HOFFMAN,
Colonel Third Infantry, Commissary-General of Prisoners.

HDQRS. PROVOST-MARSHAL-GENERAL OF KENTUCKY,
Louisville, Ky., December 15, 1862.

Brigadier-General BOYLE,
Commanding District of Western Kentucky.

GENERAL: A few days ago you instructed me to forward to Camp Chase all discharged rebel soldiers, also all deserters from the rebel army that had been in said army any length of time, and in pursuance of said order I have prepared a descriptive list of such persons confined in the military prison of this city and intended forwarding them as directed, but I find in this morning's Journal General Orders, No. 31, which issued from headquarters of General Rosecrans (said order please find inclosed*) on the subject of desertions from Confederate Army to which I beg leave to call your attention, and will hold the prisoners subject to your further orders. It seems to me that General Rosecrans invites these men to desert, and says to them on their entering into bond for future good conduct they shall have protection as long as they faithfully observe the laws of the Government and deport themselves as peaceable citizens. Now, general, if this class of men are confined at Camp Chase it will place the Government in the attitude of holding out false reports—hopes to her people—and in lieu of making friends we embitter them against their country. Hoping that you will approve my action I await further instructions.

I am, sir, very respectfully, your obedient servant,

HENRY DENT,
Colonel and Provost-Marshal-General of Kentucky.

SPECIAL ORDERS, }   HEADQUARTERS EIGHTH ARMY CORPS,
No. 186.   }   *Baltimore, Md., December 15, 1862.*

*   *   *   *   *   *   *

The camp of paroled prisoners at Annapolis, Md., is hereby announced as under the exclusive command of Lieutenant-Colonel Sangster, Forty-seventh New York State Militia, and the guards furnished for duty at the camp from the Sixty-seventh Regiment Pennsylvania Volunteers will be recognized while thus employed as subject only to the orders of that officer.

*   *   *   *   *   *   *

By command of Major-General Wool:

SEPT. CARNCROSS,
Acting Assistant Adjutant-General.

EXECUTIVE MANSION, *Washington, December 16, 1862.*
Brig. Gen. H. H. SIBLEY, *Saint Paul, Minn.:*

As you suggest let the executions fixed for Friday, the 19th instant, be postponed to and be done on Friday, the 26th instant.

A. LINCOLN.

Private.—Operator please send this very carefully and accurately.

A. L.

INDIANAPOLIS, *December 16, 1862.*
Hon. EDWIN M. STANTON, *Secretary of War:*

Will you please order the paroled Indiana prisoners taken at Hartsville, Tenn., sent here? It is conceded on all hands that they behaved most gallantly. We have comfortable barracks for 8,000 men, and telegraphed you a few days ago asking that all the paroled Indianians at Columbus, Chicago and elsewhere be sent here. If this is done I will

---

* Omitted here; see Series I, Vol. XX, Part II, p. 122.

have them reorganized and in good condition for service by the time they are exchanged. Answer by telegraph.

O. P. MORTON,
Governor.

HEADQUARTERS CENTRAL DISTRICT OF MISSOURI,
Jefferson City, December 16, 1862.

Col. C. S CHARLOT,
Asst. Adjt. Gen., Missouri State Militia, Saint Louis, Mo.

COLONEL: Herewith I have the honor to transmit a request of certain officers and soldiers formerly belonging to the Thirteenth [afterwards Twenty-fifth] Infantry Missouri Volunteers (Colonel Peabody), and who are now in Benton Barracks as paroled prisoners, they having been captured at the surrender of Lexington, and under the belief that they had been exchanged who have since their capture entered the U. S. service as members of the Fifth Regiment Cavalry Missouri State Militia. I am aware that good faith would prohibit the return of these men to their regiment without being exchanged, but my object in forwarding their request is to have some arrangement made at once which will result in their exchange as they are good soldiers and we require their services.

Very respectfully, your obedient servant,

BEN. LOAN,
Brigadier-General, Missouri State Militia.

[Indorsement.]

HEADQUARTERS DEPARTMENT OF THE MISSOURI,
Saint Louis, Mo., December 18, 1862.

Respectfully forwarded to the commissary-general of prisoners, with the request that these and all Lexington prisoners may be exchanged as soon as possible.

S. R. CURTIS,
Major-General.

[Inclosure No. 1.]

BENTON BARRACKS, *December 16, 1862.*

[Brig. Gen. BEN. LOAN.]

GENERAL: I have received from Col. B. L. E. Bonneville, U. S. Army, commanding post at Benton Barracks, a communication addressed to you by Jeremiah Murray, William Baker and other members of Company K, Twenty-third Regiment Missouri Volunteer Infantry, asking that they be discharged from the service of the United States on account of having been taken prisoners at the surrender of Lexington and paroled as prisoners of war on or about the 10th of September, 1861. I would most respectfully state that the above-mentioned parties were formerly members of Company D, Fourteenth Regiment Missouri Volunteer Infantry [Home Guards], commanded by Lieutenant-Colonel White at the battle of Lexington, and that they were discharged from and mustered out of the U. S. service in the month of September, 1861, on account of having been paroled as prisoners of war at Lexington, Mo. The above-mentioned parties soon after voluntarily enlisted in Company K, Twenty-third Regiment Missouri Volunteer Infantry, in which company they served until the 6th of April, 1862, when they were taken prisoners at the battle of Shiloh. They returned to Benton Barracks with the balance of the Shiloh prisoners July 10, 1862, since which time they have been under the command of the officer in charge of the paroled prisoners. Being exchanged they were ordered to report for duty on Saturday last by W. P. Robinson, colonel commanding Twenty-third Regiment Missouri Volunteer Infantry, but have not as yet obeyed the order, and state that they are not willing to rejoin their company until they are exchanged as Lexington prisoners. Also, I find on the communication above alluded to an indorsement by H. Z. Curtis, assistant adjutant-general, ordering these men to report to the commander of the paroled men at Benton Barracks to wait an exchange, as no official notice of the exchange of Lexington prisoners has been received at the headquarters of this department. General, I would most respectfully ask if these men are entitled to an exchange or a second discharge from the U. S. service on account of their being paroled at Lexington, after voluntarily enlisting in another regiment knowing that they had been paroled. I am the more anxious to get an explicit answer to this question as, although but four names are attached to the communication above alluded to, there are twelve men in my company and upward of 300 in the various regiments awaiting a decision on this question.

I am, general, very respectfully, your obedient servant,

R. H. BROWN,
Capt. Company K, Twenty-third Regt. Missouri Vol. Infantry.

[Inclosure No. 2.]

Brig. Gen. BEN. LOAN, *Commanding Central District of Missouri.*

SIR: I respectfully herewith tender you a request of several members of the Fifth Regiment Missouri State Militia, now paroled prisoners of war in Benton Barracks, formerly belonging to the Thirteenth Regiment Missouri Volunteers, Col. E. Peabody, taken prisoners at the battle of Lexington on the 21st of September, 1861, to have us ordered to our regiment for duty, we taking all the consequences of not being exchanged. The reasons for asking the above favor are that we—George Meyer, formerly second lieutenant of Company B, Maj. M. P. Berry's battalion of cavalry, attached to Thirteenth Regiment Missouri Volunteers, now sergeant-major Fifth Regiment Missouri State Militia; Sergt. John Engesser, formerly corporal of same company, now sergeant Company E, Fifth Regiment Missouri State Militia; Corpl. Fred. Wiedman, formerly private of same company, now corporal Fifth Regiment Missouri State Militia; Charles Ackermann, formerly private of Company B, Thirteenth Regiment Missouri State Militia, now Company C, Fifth Regiment Missouri State Militia; Edward Schaltenbranch, formerly private of Company B, Thirteenth Regiment Missouri State Militia, now corporal Company E, Fifth Regiment Missouri State Militia— after having been notified by Col. E. Peabody that we had been exchanged and mustered out of service, joined the Fifth Regiment Missouri State Militia, and after serving for eight months in said regiment were ordered to Saint Louis as prisoners of war. Prisoners of war that were taken by the C. S. Army in 1862 have almost all been exchanged or will be in a short time, and the prisoners of 1861 were never mentioned. Therefore the above-mentioned prisoners of war now at Benton Barracks prefer to join their regiment for duty instead of staying at Benton Barracks or being mustered out of service, believing they would do more good with their regiment in the field than in garrison at Saint Louis.

Respectfully referring the above to your consideration, I am, your obedient servant,

GEORGE MEYER,
Acting Adjutant Fourth Battalion Paroled Men, Benton Barracks.

WASHINGTON, D. C., *December 16, 1862.*

Maj. Gen. S. R. CURTIS:

The prisoners taken at Lexington, Mo., have not been exchanged.

W. HOFFMAN.

FORT MONROE, *December 16, 1862.*

Col. W. HOFFMAN, *Commissary-General of Prisoners:*

Have you yet received the lists of paroles of Rosecrans' captures?

WM. H. LUDLOW,

Lieutenant-Colonel and Agent for Exchange.

HEADQUARTERS PAROLED PRISONERS,

Near Annapolis, Md., December 16, 1862.

Col. W. HOFFMAN, *Commissary-General of Prisoners.*

SIR: I have the honor to report that I have completed the shipment of men to the Army of the Potomac by water and to all other corps by railroad with the exception of men in hospital and such stragglers as may come in, which I am confining in the guard-house as a reward. In a day or two I will be able to say how many are sick in hospital here and at Annapolis. I send complete rolls of all the men I have sent away. To-morrow I will be able to again complete my new organization of camp and will report to you a complete list of last arrivals from Richmond.

Hoping you will excuse my delay, having worked all my force night and day to forward the transportation of exchanged men,

I remain, very respectfully, your obedient servant,

GEO. SANGSTER,

Lieutenant-Colonel, Commanding Paroled Prisoners.

HEADQUARTERS, *Camp Chase, December 16, 1862.*

Col. W. HOFFMAN,

Commissary-General of Prisoners, Washington, D. C.

COLONEL: Having been absent from camp for a few days on account of illness I returned yesterday and found yours of the 6th instant in regard to Order 193. Upon consultation with Commissioner Galloway we had come to the conclusion before writing you on the 1st instant that the order did not apply to prisoners confined at this post, because excepted in the third paragraph as amenable for trial before Mr. Galloway, the military commissioner appointed for that purpose. Without containing any specific instructions on this point the tenor of your letter appears to contemplate separate action on my part without regard to the commissioner at all. If I have been mistaken in my construction of the order please telegraph me and I will proceed to execute the order as fully as circumstances will permit. I have thought my construction of this order correct, particularly as the examinations of Commissioner Galloway have been sent from time to time to the War Department, and the discharges continued on his recommendations as formerly. Had the order contemplated a different disposition of these prisoners it appears to me they would have so directed. There is but one prisoner from this State and his discharge is ordered on executing loyalty bond. There are only about 300 still remaining in prison, of which say 200 are from Virginia and perhaps 50 from Kentucky. Of this number about 100 have been examined and their discharge recommended on different terms.

I am, very respectfully, your obedient servant,

PETER ZINN,
Commanding Post.

SPECIAL ORDERS, ⎱   HEADQUARTERS PAROLED PRISONERS,
No. 131.   ⎰   *Near Annapolis, Md., December 16, 1862.*

*   *   *   *   *   *   *

XIV. The officer commanding detachment Sixty-seventh Pennsylvania Volunteers doing guard duty at Camp Parole will make his morning report at these headquarters every day at 9 a. m., bringing the guard book for examination and to receive instructions.

XV. Guard mounting will hereafter be conducted strictly in accordance with Army Regulations and at 8 a. m.

XVI. There will be an officer of the day and an officer of the guard who will be held to a strict accountability for the carrying out of General Orders, No. 24, and Special Orders, No. 126, paragraph XVI, from these headquarters.

XVII. No officer of the detachment will be at any time absent from his command without authority from these headquarters, and then only if approved by the officer commanding the detachment.

XVIII. All passes to men to Annapolis must be approved at these headquarters.

XIX. The officer commanding detachment doing guard duty at this camp in accordance with Special Orders, No. 186, paragraph IV, from headquarters Eighth Army Corps, being subject by it to the orders only from these headquarters will make no change in his officers or men without authority from these headquarters.

By order of George Sangster, lieutenant-colonel, commanding paroled prisoners:

JAMES E. DOUGHTY,
Adjutant.

WAR DEPARTMENT, *Washington, December 17, 1862.*

Hon. GALUSHA A. GROW,
Speaker of the House of Representatives.

SIR: In reply to a resolution of the House of Representatives directing the Secretary of War "to inform the House what steps if any have been taken for the release of sutlers and other non-combatants attached to our army now held as prisoners at Richmond and elsewhere" I have the honor to transmit the inclosed report of the commissioner for exchange of prisoners, stating what steps have been taken in reference to the subject of inquiry.

EDWIN M. STANTON,
Secretary of War.

[Inclosure.]

WASHINGTON, *December 17, 1862.*

Hon. EDWIN M. STANTON, *Secretary of War.*

SIR: In reference to the resolutions in the House of Representatives of the 15th instant calling for information in regard to the exchange of sutlers who are or have been held as prisoners at Richmond and elsewhere I have the honor to report that the cartel of September 25, current year, requires that "captured sutlers, teamsters and all civilians in the actual service of either party shall be exchanged for prisoners in similiar positions."

In conformity with this requirement a number of exchanges have already been made, and lists or rolls are now in course of preparation in the office of the commissary-general of prisoners embracing the names of sutlers and sutlers' clerks, with a view to their exchange, which will be perfected as soon as possible, and no time will be lost in effecting the exchange. The rolls now in preparation will embrace all classes of citizens referred to in the cartel.

I have the honor to be, very respectfully, your obedient servant,
E. A. HITCHCOCK,
Major-General of Vols., Commissioner for Exchange of Prisoners.

FORT MONROE, *December 17, 1862.*
Hon. EDWIN M. STANTON:

There is no reason here why the women and children to go to City Point should not go now. They should, however, be sent in a transport which can proceed there without trans-shipment here. There are some women and children at Norfolk desirous of going not to return, and I ask your authority to send them. I send 550 prisoners of war to-day. I think it important that Colonel Ludlow should see you and I will send him by the Baltimore boat this evening.

JOHN A. DIX,
Major-General.

HEADQUARTERS DEPARTMENT OF THE CUMBERLAND,
Nashville, December 17, 1862.
General BRAXTON BRAGG.

GENERAL: I have the honor to acknowledge the receipt of your communication of the 15th instant.

On reference to article 7, the first of the supplementary articles of the cartel, you will find that a mutual agreement between the commanders of either army is necessary to authorize the exchange of prisoners at any other than the two points designated in the article. By the course pursued by you I was compelled to receive the Hartsville prisoners. However, I merely state this in explanation of my letter without intending further to dwell on the point. But I cannot accept your statement that we have inaugurated the practice of stripping prisoners of their overcoats and blankets. I cannot even admit that it is a practice with us; on the contrary I know that we have furnished blankets and overcoats to your soldiers and we shall continue to do so.

I have the honor to be, general, your obedient servant,
W. S. ROSECRANS,
Major-General, Commanding.

HEADQUARTERS DEPARTMENT OF THE CUMBERLAND,
Nashville, December 17, 1862.
General BRAXTON BRAGG.

GENERAL: I have the pleasure to acknowledge the receipt of your communication announcing the release of three of my men unlawfully captured behind a flag of truce.

I am gratified to say that I expected it of you. I trust the more recent outrage behind your own flag under Lieutenant Colonel Hawkins, complained of in my letter of yesterday, will be as promptly and honorably redressed.

Your communication of the 15th as to the difficulty of having uniforms for your men is also received. The reasons you give have weight, but are not in my judgment sufficient since a designation badge however slight is all that I ask.

    With great respect, your obedient servant,

W. S. ROSECRANS,
Major-General, Commanding Department.

HEADQUARTERS DEPARTMENT OF THE CUMBERLAND,
Nashville, December 17, 1862.

General BRAXTON BRAGG.

GENERAL: I have the honor to acknowledge receipt of your communication in reference to Judge Marchbanks, a political prisoner confined at Camp Chase, whose release as a non-combatant you therein ask. And in reply I am constrained to inform you that I have no power to act in this case, Judge Marchbanks being under the exclusive control of the Secretary of War, to whom your letter has accordingly been referred.

    I have the honor to be, general, very respectfully, your obedient servant,

W. S. ROSECRANS,
Major-General, Commanding Department.

OFFICE COMMISSARY-GENERAL OF PRISONERS,
Washington, D. C., December 17, 1862.

Capt. H. W. FREEDLEY, *Washington, D. C.*

CAPTAIN: After completing the duty assigned to you at Indianapolis you will proceed to Alton and Saint Louis and obtain from the commander of the prison at the former place and the provost-marshal-general at the latter the orders announcing the trial and sentence of political prisoners now held at either of the two places named or at the depot at Sandusky. You will then return to this city.

    Very respectfully, your obedient servant,

W. HOFFMAN,
Colonel Third Infantry, Commissary-General of Prisoners.

HEADQUARTERS PAROLED PRISONERS,
Near Annapolis, Md., December 17, 1862.

Col. W. HOFFMAN, *Commissary-General of Prisoners.*

SIR: I have the honor to report that General Wool yesterday placed under my command the guard which was at my camp, amounting to 175 men, and to-day Colonel Staunton, commanding at Annapolis, has taken them and officers away, which are the best I have had here from his regiment, and left me 110 men. I issued the order I received to the commandant of the detachment of guard in accordance with your orders, and also the orders to obey promptly all orders from these head-quarters. I hope you will take this matter in hand so that I can have a guard that I can depend upon at all times and that understand the duties of my camp.

I am, colonel, very respectfully, your obedient servant,

GEO. SANGSTER,
Lieutenant-Colonel, Commanding Paroled Prisoners.

DEPOT PRISONERS OF WAR,
Near Sandusky, Ohio, December 17, 1862.

Maj. Gen. H. G. WRIGHT,
Commanding Department of the Ohio:

I have the honor to acknowledge the receipt on the 16th instant of the resolutions of the Senate* of the United States calling for the number and names, charges and by whom [made] against citizens of Kentucky in the military prisons outside of the limits of said State, and by whose order arrested, together with your order for me to forward the information therein called for at the earliest practicable moment; in reply to which I forward herewith a roll of the citizens from Kentucky from the roll books of these headquarters. This roll will give the names, when and where captured, the date of receipt at this post; from whence received and when discharged, and so far as information has been forwarded to these headquarters the charges. I have, however, no information on the subject of the charges except as they are marked on the rolls, no charges having been forwarded with the prisoners, most of the prisoners having come from other camps. I have no knowl-edge when or by whose order they were arrested. Indeed I do not see as I can give any information beyond what is disclosed on the roll forwarded herewith.

I have the honor to be, very respectfully, your obedient servant,

WM. S. PIERSON,
Major Hoffman's Battalion, Commanding Post.

[Inclosure.]

Kentucky citizen prisoners.

T. W. Allen, George Anderson, G. C. Bronaugh, E. H. Burnett, J. Chadwell, B. F. Chrissman, A. P. Davis, J. M. Dishman, J. H. Davis, T. F. Fisher, W. F. Gentry, S. B. Greenfield, J. R. Gentry, James Howell, J. C. Johnson, Elijah Jones, Patten Jones, T. B. Jones, W. Jones, J. H. Jones, J. D. Lillard, Jake A. Lowey, T. Murphy, John McCarney, John Mealer, G. W. Norris, Newton M. Osment, M. N. Powell, B. F. Reed, W. D. Ryan, C. C. Skillman, Harvey Tanner, Mathew Thompson, Robert Vowells, William Wallace, R. J. Warsham, George Whitsell.

[DECEMBER 17, 1862.—For General Orders, No. 11, Department of the Tennessee, expelling Jew traders, see Series I, Vol. XVII, Part II, p. 424.]

---

* Reference is to resolution of December 5, p. 27.

HEADQUARTERS C. S. FORCES,
Murfreesborough, December 18, 1862.

General W. S. ROSECRANS,
Commanding U. S. Forces, Nashville, Tenn.

GENERAL: As you express your determination in your letter of the 11th instant to receive no more prisoners through your lines I am at a loss to know whether or not this will embrace Lieutenant-Colonel Moore and Lieutenant Dewald, his aide-de-camp. These officers were among the captured at Hartsville and included in the list furnished you and have been receipted and left behind by accident.

They await here your decision before being sent by the long and tedious route to Vicksburg or Aiken's Landing.

I am, general, respectfully, your obedient servant,
BRAXTON BRAGG,
General, Commanding.

HEADQUARTERS FIRST CORPS, TRANS-MISSISSIPPI ARMY,
December 18, 1862.

Brig. Gen. J. G. BLUNT, *Comdg. U. S. Forces, Cane Hill.*

GENERAL: I have received by the hands of Colonel Orme, bearer of flag of truce, your letter of the 17th instant in relation to the exchange of prisoners. It was agreed upon between us that flags for this purpose should be at Cane Hill every Wednesday. According to this agreement I sent on last Monday in time to reach Cane Hill by Wednesday 1 lieutenant and 259 enlisted men, prisoners in my hands, the officer being instructed to exchange for any of my command in your hands and to parole the balance until exchanged. Previously I sent within your lines nine officers and three enlisted men under the same instructions to my bearer of flag.

You therefore depart from the agreement in sending a flag elsewhere and I would be justified in detaining the bearer. I do not care to do so. The officer bearing this is directed to receive what prisoners he actually brings as in exchange for the proper number of those before paroled by me. Such as you claim exchanged for as paroled by you must first be known to be of the C. S. Army and properly captured. This requires more time than it would be agreeable on either side to keep your flag party at my outpost, and the matter can be better arranged at Cane Hill on next Wednesday.

Respectfully,

T. C. HINDMAN,
Major-General, Commanding.

HEADQUARTERS, *Goldsborough, December 18, 1862.*

COMMANDING OFFICER, U. S. Army, *Kinston, N. C.*

SIR: I send under flag of truce a train to Kinston with Surgeons Willey and Taylor and a few men to act as nurses for the wounded Confederate soldiers at that place. I would thank you to give them any assistance in your power consistent with duty.

I am, very respectfully, your obedient servant,
J. G. MARTIN,
Brigadier-General.

OFFICE COMMISSARY-GENERAL OF PRISONERS,
Washington, D. C., December 18, 1862.

Hon. GIDEON WELLES,
Secretary of the Navy, Washington, D. C.

SIR: I have the honor to acknowledge the receipt of your letter of the 16th instant, addressed to General E. A. Hitchcock, agent for exchange of prisoners of war, and to inform you that it will be forwarded to Lieutenant-Colonel Ludlow, at Fort Monroe, who is attending to the exchanges in the absence of General Hitchcock, in order that the prisoners therein named may be exchanged as early as practicable. I have the honor to inform you also that your letter of the 26th of November addressed to the Adjutant-General, giving the names of the six paroled seamen, was forwarded to Colonel Ludlow for his early attention.

I have the honor to be, very respectfully, your obedient servant,
W. HOFFMAN,
Colonel Third Infantry, Commissary-General of Prisoners.

OFFICE COMMISSARY-GENERAL OF PRISONERS,
Washington, D. C., December 18, 1862.

General S. R. CURTIS,
Commanding Department of the Missouri, Saint Louis, Mo.

GENERAL: In reply to your letter of the 12th instant I have the honor to state that the prisoners taken and paroled in Missouri have not yet been exchanged owing to the entire absence of rolls. The officers taken at Shiloh were declared exchanged in General Orders, No. 191; the exchange of enlisted men taken at the same place was announced in General Orders, No. 147, of September 30. At the next negotiations for exchanges it is hoped all the Missouri prisoners will be exchanged *en masse.*

I am, general, very respectfully, your obedient servant,
W. HOFFMAN,
Colonel Third Infantry, Commissary-General of Prisoners.

WASHINGTON, D. C., *December 18, 1862.*

Maj. Gen. S. R. CURTIS:

All Shiloh prisoners are exchanged. Enlisted men by Orders, No. 147; officers by Orders, No. 191, first clause.

W. HOFFMAN,
Commissary-General of Prisoners.

HEADQUARTERS MILITARY COMMANDANT,
Covington and Newport, Ky., December 18, 1862.

Major-General WRIGHT,
Commanding Department of the Ohio.

GENERAL: In obedience to your order of the 12th instant inclosing a copy of a letter from the War Department in which was embraced a resolution adopted by the Senate of the United States on the 5th day of December requiring a list of the citizens of the State of Kentucky who have been and who are now confined in the military prisons and camps of the United States outside of the limits of said State, together with a statement of the charges against them, by whom made and by whose order the arrests were made, I have the honor to submit the following report:

I was appointed to the command of this post on the 10th day of September last by order of Major-General Wallace, commanding U. S. forces in Northern Kentucky, and on the 15th day of the same month was ordered by General Wallace to examine all citizens now held as prisoners in the two cities under your (my) command and see that they have an impartial hearing. Also that the witnesses for the prosecution are present when such examination takes place, and make written report to these headquarters of cases, advising as to the disposition of each with a synopsis of the evidence. Under this order I without delay proceeded to investigate the cases of citizens held in military custody in the cities of Covington and Newport, Ky.

Before any of these investigations were concluded Major-General Wallace was relieved and Brig. Gen. A. J. Smith appointed to the command of the U. S. forces here, and a number of cases were submitted to the last-named officer for his final approval or disapproval. Major-General Granger was next placed in command of the Army of Kentucky and he instructed me to decide finally on all cases coming before me without referring the testimony or sentences to any higher authority. I have continued to do so up to the present time, and find on reference to the records of my office that I have examined and decided 241 cases, exclusive of the prisoners of war who have come before me. Of this number I have sent out of the State, to be confined at Camp Chase, Columbus, Ohio, ten prisoners. Copies of the evidence in these cases both for and against the prisoners are appended* to this report.

It is but proper that I should here remark that several prisoners have been ordered to Camp Chase by officers exercising the authority in the interior of the State and have received transportation to that post from me. But I did not examine their cases and consequently can furnish no report in reference to them. Having thus briefly complied with the requirements of the Senate's resolution as contained in your order I beg your indulgence while I submit a few remarks bearing upon the subject of the arrest and imprisonment of the citizens of Kentucky charged with disloyalty to the Government of the United States or with giving aid and comfort to its enemies. That the power to make such arrests and imprisonments has been too indiscriminately exercised cannot be doubted by any one who has investigated the subject, but justice compels me to say that the abuse of this power can rarely be traced to regular military officers acting under the authority of the United States. By far the larger number of arrests and imprisonments for alleged offenses against the Government have been made by acting provost-marshals who although appointed by a military commander were themselves citizens. The will of these gentlemen was the law, and in many instances they appear to have exercised their official functions with but little regard for any rule of action either civil or military. Many of them kept no records, and instances are not rare where prisoners were confined by their order for months without the shadow of a written charge of any kind against them.

This exercise of power on the part of citizen provost-marshals applied to property as well as persons. Cases are known where the effects of individuals were seized and appropriated without any military or legal sanction and in violation of all principles of justice and right.

I am firmly convinced that much of the bad feeling which has existed and still exists in Kentucky is to be attributed to the causes which I have enumerated. Had a different course of policy been pursued—a policy which would have kept distinct and well defined the military from the civil power—a policy which would have made property and liberty both secure except in clearly proven cases of disloyalty, and would have prevented the incarceration or banishment of citizens through feelings of personal enmity and prejudice—much of the bloodshed and devastation which has marked the State for a year past would have been avoided.

It may be asked, how was this to be done? I answer by placing military power in the hands of military men only, who could be held amenable to military law for the abuse of that power, and by leaving the civil authorities unobstructed whenever their loyalty was known. If instead of appointing a hundred or more civilians as provost-marshals with no guide for their action but their individual judgment and prejudice those positions had been filled by officers of the Army only and a regular system established by competent authority for their government, complaints would not now be so generally nor so justly made about despotic arrests and seizures. The system that has been in operation was no system at all, for under it in one county citizens would be arrested and imprisoned by scores while in the adjoining county parties equally guilty would go unmolested.

I refer to these matters only for the purpose of doing what I can to remedy an evil and prevent its continuance. I consider Kentucky a loyal State. Her civil government and courts of justice are known to be loyal to the Constitution and laws of the United States. Her soil is now free from the dominion of rebel soldiery and it is difficult to imagine a case of disloyalty arising among her citizens which cannot be met and punished under the operation of civil power. The mistake in my judgment has been all along in considering this Commonwealth as a treasonable Commonwealth and in endeavoring to crush her by the exercise of power instead of appealing to her in the language of reason.

In the disposition of some cases brought before me and in many tried by other military commanders and provost-marshals throughout the State bonds were taken for the good and loyal conduct of the accused. These bonds vary in amount from $20,000 to $500 and are I believe generally drawn in proper form and well secured. It is questionable whether these obligations if forfeited by the traitorous conduct of the parties bound by them could be collected by due process of law, because there is so far as my knowledge extends no statute authorizing or empowering the military authorities to take them. I would therefore respectfully suggest that the omission be remedied by having these bonds legalized and that they be ordered to be filed with the clerks of the U. S. courts in Kentucky to be enforced under the direction of those tribunals.

I have the honor to be, general, with great respect, your obedient servant,

WM. B. SIPES,
Lieutenant-Colonel, Commanding Post.

[Indorsement.]

HEADQUARTERS DEPARTMENT OF THE OHIO,
Cincinnati, Ohio, December 23, 1862.

Respectfully returned to Colonel Sipes, Seventh Pennsylvania Cavalry, military commander, Covington, Ky., who will prepare a tabular statement furnishing the information called for by the resolution of the Senate. This report will be returned to these headquarters with the statement called for.

By order of Major-General Wright: C. W. FOSTER,
Assistant Adjutant-General.

———

HEADQUARTERS ARMY OF NORTHERN VIRGINIA,
December 19, 1862.

Maj. Gen. A. E. BURNSIDE,
Commanding U. S. Forces opposite Fredericksburg, Va.

GENERAL: I have been informed that Private John W. Irwin, of Company A, Ninth Virginia Cavalry, has been captured by some of the troops under your command and is being tried* as a spy. Presuming if this information be correct that the object of the investigation is to ascertain the truth I have thought proper to make known to you the facts connected with the absence of Private John W. Irwin from his regiment as reported to me by Colonel Beale, commanding Ninth Virginia Cavalry, and Brig. Gen. W. H. F. Lee, commanding the brigade to which the regiment belongs. While the brigade was at Brandy Station, in Culpeper County, Private Irwin received permission from his brigade commander about the 14th of November to visit his home in Stafford County to procure a fresh horse. This is a permission commonly given in similar cases and at the time it was not known that the place to which Private Irwin wished to proceed was within the lines of your army.

The person in question is described to me as follows: Small figure, about 5 feet 9 inches high, complexion dark, hair mahogany and eyes blue. Age about eighteen years and manner rather sprightly.

Very respectfully, your obedient servant,

R. E. LEE,
General.

———

OFFICE COMMISSARY-GENERAL OF PRISONERS,
Washington, D. C., December 19. 1862.

Maj. Gen. W. S. ROSECRANS, *Commanding, Nashville, Tenn.:*

Duplicate rolls should accompany prisoners sent to Vicksburg for exchange, one with a receipt to be returned by a messenger to the Adjutant-General for this office.

By order of the Secretary of War:

W. HOFFMAN,
Commissary-General of Prisoners.

———

WASHINGTON, D. C., *December 19, 1862.*

Maj. Gen. S. R. CURTIS:

All prisoners delivered at Aiken's Landing up to 11th of November are exchanged. See Orders, No. 191, first clause.

W. HOFFMAN,
Commissary-General of Prisoners.

———

* See p. 103 for case of Irwin.

ALTON MILITARY PRISON, *December 19, 1862.*

Maj. Gen. U. S. GRANT,
Commanding Department of the Tennessee.

SIR: In answer to yours of the 15th instant I have to inform you that in transferring a lot of prisoners from this prison to Johnson's Island on the 15th of last month Colonel Faulkner made his escape and has not been heard from since. Captain Meriwether has been sent to Cairo for exchange.

I am, sir, very respectfully, your obedient servant,
J. HILDEBRAND,
Colonel, Commanding Post, Alton, Ill.

ALTON MILITARY PRISON, *December 19, 1862.*

Lieut. Col. F. A. DICK,
Provost-Marshal-General, Department of the Missouri.

COLONEL: Am I to understand from the last clause of your letter that I am to find out the names of those who are willing to accept your terms of release and report their names to you, or am I to release them and report their release to you?

I am, sir, your obedient servant,
J. HILDEBRAND,
Colonel, Commanding Post.

P. S.—There will be from 100 to 200 who are willing to accept your terms of release.

I. B. KINKEAD,
Prison Adjutant.

SAINT LOUIS, *December 19, 1862.*

To the PRESIDENT:

I submit most respectfully to the consideration of Your Excellency the following remarks: I was informed to-day by Major-General Curtis that the President had telegraphed him to inquire if it would be advisable to suspend martial law in Missouri. Officially I have most complete and reliable information as to the condition of this State. I have been in Missouri nearly all the time during the rebellion and I say positively that at no previous time have the efforts and evil purposes of the rebels in this State and city been more active and hopeful than now. All through the portions of the State occupied by our troops traitors are indefatigable in their efforts to aid their Southern friends. The successful military efforts of such brave men as General Merrill, who has captured thousands of these traitors, have made them somewhat cautious for a time but their hopes never die and their purposes and efforts remain the same. Appeals and representations to the contrary may be made by Major Rollins and Judge Hall and other gentlemen who live in the worst part of the State but those gentlemen are not regarded in Missouri as fair representatives of the Union men who uphold the Government. It is not unfair to say that those gentlemen were elected by the votes of disloyal men. I make these statements not from a desire to injure them, for I esteem them both as gentlemen, but that their dependence upon disloyal men may be known. I have daily evidence that in the interior and in Saint Louis secretly information and material aid is being furnished by many of our most respectable citizens to the enemy. The most bitter hostility exists between them and the Union people. I have daily appeals from the interior for the adoption of a more stringent policy that Union men may have security from their rebellious neighbors. I have instructed provost-marshals in the interior to select out the leading dangerous men and banish them from the State during the war. General Merrill and the other generals in the interior are pursuing the same system.

I came into this office on the 1st of November. I then found General Curtis in consequence of the persistent appeals of pretended Union men at times really in doubt as to what course to pursue, but the powerful evidence of this active disloyalty daily furnished him through my office and other sources has completely satisfied him of the necessity of a vigorous policy with so malignant an enemy. No one who has contended with these people as we in Missouri have done and who is a true friend of the Government is in doubt as to this. But pretended Union men who never work for the cause and encounter no hardships nor risks can well cry out in behalf of the rebels. I therefore most respectfully ask of the President that he will not require that we relax in our efforts to fight this enemy in the most effective manner. It is no light matter to stand here in conflict with these people and if we are in a fair way to get the upper hand it should be remembered that upon the least opportunity they will spring at our throats again.

I trust that the President will not consider me officious in offering these suggestions, but placed as I have been by the order of General Curtis at the head of a most responsible and powerful office I am convinced of the necessity of maintaining the ascendency of the Federal Government in Missouri by force. To remove military supremacy will be to let loose these evil-doers again upon true Union men. There is one other point that I beg leave to present to the President. I find that a considerable number of the Southern sympathizers desire to go South. General Curtis has evinced decided willingness to allow them to go but he is of the impression that to do so is not favored by the Government. If permission can be given to allow such persons to go we will be rid of many unchangeable enemies who will do us less injury there than here.

I applied to General Curtis to-day to allow me to permit a wife, daughter and four small boys of a rebel preacher in the South to go and I understood from him that he doubted if it would meet with favor at Washington. There are several prominent rebels in Saint Louis who ought to be sent South. There are many female spies in good society who ought to be sent. They are efficient aiders of the rebellion. I urgently ask that such persons of both sexes I may be permitted with the approval of General Curtis to send to their Southern friends. If the lines were opened and Southern sympathizers with their slaves were permitted to go it would work a most wonderfully good effect upon Missouri, and in a short time its result would be permanent peace and tranquillity to the State.

I have the honor to be, Your Excellency's most obedient servant,

F. A. DICK,
Lieut. Col., Provost-Marshal-General, Dept. of the Missouri.

HEADQUARTERS PAROLED PRISONERS,
Near Annapolis, Md., December 19, 1862.

Col. W. HOFFMAN, *Commissary-General of Prisoners.*

SIR: I have the honor to report that on the receipt of the orders from General Wool I took command of the guard, being 6 officers and 175 men, and soon after Colonel Staunton, commanding at Annapolis, removed the guard leaving me 110 men and to-day he has taken them away and sent me 90 men and 1 officer. I inclose a copy of letter to General Wool and I think I will have relief immediately. I send this inclosed that you may know my acts in the premises.

I am, colonel, very respectfully, your obedient servant,

GEO. SANGSTER,
Lieutenant-Colonel, Commanding Paroled Prisoners.

[Inclosure.]

HEADQUARTERS PAROLED PRISONERS,
Near Annapolis, Md., December 19, 1862.

Col. W. D. WHIPPLE,
Assistant Adjutant-General, Eighth Army Corps.

SIR: The guard which you placed under my command by Special Orders, No. 186, numbered 175 men and 6 officers. On receipt of that order the inclosed order,* with a copy of Special Orders, No. 186, was sent to Captain Arndt, then in command. On the receipt of your order Col. J. F. Staunton ordered the detachment that was present off. I protested against such a movement. He then sent me 4 officers and 110 men. To day he takes away this detachment and gives me only 1 officer and 90 men. So small a number of guard is totally inadequate to protect the Government property and preserve the good order and discipline of this camp. I have camp equipage standing sufficient to accommodate 12,000 troops and am ordered by the General-in-Chief to keep them standing for the accommodation of new arrivals.

By Special Orders, No. 127, October 17, I am held to a strict accountability that hereafter no cause be found to complain of the condition of the camp at Annapolis. To assume this responsibility it is absolutely necessary that I shall have a much larger guard than 90 men. With the guard under command of Captain Arndt (6 officers and 175 men) the discipline was much better than it had previously been although the number was so small. Captain Arndt being an active and efficient officer did all I could have desired or expected with the number of men. In view of these facts I respectfully ask that Colonel Staunton be ordered to return the officers and men under Captain Arndt at once.

I am, colonel, very respectfully, your obedient servant,

GEO. SANGSTER,
Lieutenant-Colonel, Commanding Paroled Prisoners.

GENERAL ORDERS, }　HEADQUARTERS ARMY OF KENTUCKY,
　　No. 36.　　 }　　　　*Lexington, Ky., December 19, 1862.*

Deserters from the rebel service and persons who are returning to their homes in this State, having been followers of the rebel army but not in the service, will upon coming within the limits of the Military District of Central Kentucky report in person to these headquarters to the major-general commanding the Army of Kentucky and submit their respective cases to be properly adjudged upon and disposed of.

Persons included within the terms of this order who shall fail to observe the same will be arrested and treated as spies or prisoners of war according to the circumstances of each particular case.

Civil officers and loyal citizens are requested to aid in the enforcement of this order.

By order of Maj. Gen. G. Granger:

THOS. G. BEAHAM,
First Lieut., First [Second] Iowa Cavalry, Actg. Asst. Adjt. Gen.

---

* Not found.

HEADQUARTERS ARMY OF TENNESSEE,
Murfreesborough, Tenn., December 20, 1862.

Maj. Gen. W. S. ROSECRANS,
Commanding U. S. Forces, Nashville.

GENERAL: In your letter of the 11th instant you complain that there was in several respects a want of regularity and humanity in the delivery of the Hartsville prisoners.

You charge, first, that the flag presented itself about dark and during a skirmish; second, that the officer who conducted them to your lines insisted upon your receiving them upon grounds of humanity; third, that the lists accompanying them were not original nor attested copies; and fourth, that a third list was sent of which you knew nothing. These charges are so fully met by the communication of my inspector-general which is herewith inclosed as to convince me that you were misinformed as to the facts and that your complaints are groundless.

Your assertions as to the uniform kindness and humanity with which our prisoners are treated by Federal commanders are strangely at variance with facts well known to me. Men now in my camp were recently transported from Cairo to Vicksburg in such a state of destitution from official robbery and so exposed to the cold and inclement weather that forty died on one boat during the passage. You are pleased to compare your " idea" of humanity with ours; I confess to a striking difference. From Butler to Boyle a system is practiced the milder features of which as in this case we practice only in retaliation and with repugnance. The alacrity of your own men to fall into our hands and the humiliating expedients you have seen proper to enforce in order to put a stop to it are convincing evidences of the falsity of the charge of inhumanity as practiced by us.

On the other hand the uniform testimony of our returned prisoners and their unyielding aversion to capture indicate their repugnance to your kind of hospitality.

Disagreeable as is this subject it is proper that we should understand each other. The course which has been pursued by Federal commanders and their subordinates in the treatment of Confederate prisoners both of war and of state must cease, and until it does I shall retaliate in kind for every violation of humanity and justice. Our soldiers are either traitors to be hung or prisoners of war to be treated as such. It is not enough for you to say you condemn such actions as form the subject of my complaint. Your condemnation must show its fruits. Your department is small and the stay of prisoners within your jurisdiction limited. They are then turned over to the mercies of others who entertain different views of humanity perhaps from yourself. My surgeons are imprisoned and treated with indignity and to my protest I am referred to some distant commander on whom I have no means of operating directly. My soldiers are returned from Northern captivity stripped of all but enough to hide their nakedness and with constitutions undermined from exposure to the weather. It is in vain to appeal for proper redress and I shall hereafter enforce a policy strictly corresponding to that practiced by your commanders, never, however, losing sight of the higher duties of humanity which will prohibit my imitation of your " idea" except in its least objectionable features.

I have attentively noted your remarks in regard to the future delivery of prisoners. When you received instead of rejecting those last sent I considered you as estopped from further complaint and regard your remarks as wholly irrelevant. Under your decision such of your prisoners as fall into my hands shall hereafter be sent to the regular points of exchange subject to the exposures of so long a journey which my "idea" of humanity would spare them. They may thereby, however, escape the degradation of the nightcap parade, which it seems under your system all, brave and cowardly alike, must endure as the penalty of falling into your hands.

I regret the evident annoyance of which your letter too plainly gives proof, but as it may be traced to your own lines it is not in my power to remove the causes except as I have attempted.

I am, general, very respectfully, your obedient servant,

BRAXTON BRAGG,
General, Commanding.

[Inclosure.]

HEADQUARTERS INSPECTOR-GENERAL'S OFFICE,
Murfreesborough, December 18, 1862.

General B. BRAGG,
Commanding Army of Tennessee, Murfreesborough, Tenn.

GENERAL: In reply to the letter of General W. S. Rosecrans of December 11, 1862, referred to me, I have the honor to state:

The flag of truce did "present itself" about dark by reason of a delay caused by skirmishing in front. This delay could not be anticipated or avoided, and but for this the prisoners would have been turned over in time to reach Nashville by dark.

The skirmishing had entirely ceased and the enemy fallen back when the flag passed our lines.

The officer who conducted them (the prisoners) did not insist on grounds of humanity or any other ground that they should be received.

The officer who received the flag (Lieutenant-Colonel Wood) did not make nor intimate the least objection to receiving the prisoners, for in less than ten minutes after I met him I had received his receipt for them and all official dispatches I had for General Rosecrans.

The prisoners were sufficiently fed, for I had caused two days' rations to be issued to them the evening before, and Colonel Wood remarked that they had enough to eat as he saw them cooking. The lists furnished were certified by me to be "copies of original paroles on file in my office" and did not purport to be original. The third list if I understand correctly what is referred to was a list of prisoners headed by Lieutenant-Colonel Kerr, numbering sixty-nine, captured at various times and places, and the prisoners accompanied the list.

I am, general, very respectfully, your obedient servant,

W. K. BEARD,
Inspector-General.

SPECIAL ORDERS,
No. 358.

HDQRS. ARMY OF THE POTOMAC,
Camp near Falmouth, Va., December 21, 1862.

I. Before a general court-martial convened at the office of the provost-marshal-general Army of the Potomac, pursuant to Special Orders, No. 347, of December 9, 1862, from these headquarters, and of which Col. J. S. Crocker, Ninety-third Regiment New York Volunteers, is president, was arraigned and tried Private John W. Irwin, Company A, Ninth Virginia Cavalry (so-called), Confederate Army, on the following charge and specification:

CHARGE: Being found and arrested within the lines of the Army of the Potomac as a spy.

Specification.—In this that the said Private John W. Irwin, Company A, Ninth Virginia Regiment, being a rebel soldier in arms against the Government of the United States, on or about the 27th day of November, A. D. 1862, did come within the lines of the Army of the Potomac at or near Hartwood, Va., disguised in citizen's clothing, having previously lurked about in that locality during a time when important movements of that army were being made, concealing himself so as to gain information of the said movements with hostile intent.

Plea.—Not guilty.

Finding and Sentence.—After mature deliberation on the testimony adduced the court finds the accused, Private John W. Irwin, Company A, Ninth Virginia Cavalry, as follows :

Of the specification of the charge, Guilty.

Of the charge, Guilty.

And does therefore sentence him, Private John W. Irwin, Company A, Ninth Virginia Cavalry, to be hung by the neck until he be dead; two-thirds of the members of the court concurring in the sentence.

II. The proceedings, finding and sentence of the court are confirmed. The commanding general on reviewing the evidence finds abundant grounds for the finding and sentence of the court, but having since its adjournment received from General R. E. Lee, commanding the so-called Army of Northern Virginia, a communication representing that the accused had obtained a furlough to visit his home and procure a fresh horse—a permission commonly given in the said army in similar cases— and that at the time it was not known that the place to which Private Irwin wished to proceed was within our lines, he has and does remit the sentence.

Private John W. Irwin will be treated as a simple prisoner of war, to be paroled and returned in ordinary and usual course.

By command of Major-General Burnside :

LEWIS RICHMOND,
Assistant Adjutant-General.

HEADQUARTERS DISTRICT OF SOUTHWEST MISSOURI,
Springfield, December 21, 1862.

Maj. Gen. S. R. CURTIS,
Commanding Department of the Missouri, Saint Louis.

GENERAL: The military commission that has been in session in this district since June has sentenced a number of guerrillas to be shot. The evidence was clear and fully sustains the charges of violation of the laws of war. The proceedings were in form and properly referred to department headquarters. Months have elapsed without their being again heard from; and in the meantime our Union citizens and soldiers are being murdered by the companions of the condemned men. It is true that numbers of the guerrillas have been killed, but the moral effect of the execution in a formal manner after a full, fair trial of one guerrilla would far exceed that of shooting them in open warfare or from the brush. I respectfully urge that the quiet of this country demands a sterner measure of justice upon the part of the Government than has heretofore been practiced. Mercy to these outlaws is cruelty and death to the Union men of the southwest.

I am, very truly, your obedient servant,

E. B. BROWN,
Brigadier-General, Commanding.

[First indorsement.]

HEADQUARTERS DEPARTMENT OF THE MISSOURI,
Saint Louis, December 26, 1862.

Respectfully returned for General Brown to please state when the proceedings therein referred to were forwarded. No record of them whatever can be found here.

By order of Major-General Curtis: H. Z. CURTIS,
Assistant Adjutant-General.

[Second indorsement.]

HEADQUARTERS DISTRICT OF SOUTHWEST MISSOURI,
Springfield, January 2, 1863.

Judge-advocate will send me a statement of all cases tried by military commission between the 5th of July and 29th of August, 1862. These are the class referred to in my letter to General Curtis.

E. B. BROWN,
Brigadier-General, Commanding.

[Third indorsement.]

SPRINGFIELD, MO., *January 3, 1863.*

Charles H. Clifford was tried by military commission. Trial commenced October 29 and ended November 1, 1862. Sentence: "To be hung by the neck until he is dead at such time and place as the commanding officer of the department may designate." There is no date showing when the record was sent up for review. The original is in my possession. The prisoner is now in military prison at Springfield, Mo.

Smith Crim was tried by military commission. Trial commenced September 25 and ended September 26, 1862. Sentence: "To be shot to death by musketry at such time and place as the commanding officer of the district may designate." The original record is now in my possession. Smith Crim was sent to Saint Louis, Mo., as shown by the books of the acting provost-marshal-general, December 30, 1862. There is [no] date showing when the record was sent up for review.

James A. Stoker was tried by military commission. Trial commenced September 4 and ended September 6, 1862. Sentence: "To be hung by the neck until he is dead, at Springfield, Mo., on the first Friday in October, 1862." Proceedings sent to commanding general Southwest District September 9, 1862. The original record is now in my possession. James A. Stoker was sent to Saint Louis December 30, 1862, as shown by the books of the acting provost-marshal-general, District of Southwest Missouri.

William T. Cox was tried by military commission. Trial commenced and concluded November 18, 1862. William T. Cox was sentenced to be shot. He has escaped from prison, as shown by the books of the district provost-marshal.

WM. RAGAN,
Lieutenant, Eighteenth Iowa Infantry, Judge-Advocate.

HOUSE OF REPRESENTATIVES,
Washington, December 22, 1862.

Hon. E. B. WASHBURNE.

MY DEAR SIR: I return you the papers in the matter of the Sixty-fifth Regiment with the suggestion that you send them with a note to Colonel Hoffman. I have seen him on the subject and he promises action.

Yours, truly,

I. N. ARNOLD.

[Inclosure.]

ADJUTANT-GENERAL'S OFFICE,
Springfield, December 16, 1862.

Hon. E. B. WASHBURNE, *Washington.*

DEAR SIR: I inclose letter just received from Colonel Cameron, of the Sixty-fifth Illinois Volunteers, now stationed at Chicago; also the report therein referred to. The Sixty-fifth and Phillips' battery are Illinois troops captured and paroled at Harper's Ferry. Although they all behaved most gallantly they were disgracefully surrendered and they feel mad at the shadow resting upon them. They are impatient for a fight. The troops of other States have been exchanged and why in the name of all that is fair and just are Illinoisians to be kept shut up on their parole when others are exchanged? Several thousand have gone out of Camp Douglas exchanged and our own troops detained paroled prisoners. Do take hold of this thing at once and let these men loose. I have a brother who is a captain in the regiment and he says this discrimination against our men has demoralized them and they are breaking out of camp and running away every day. Let me hear from you by telegraph as soon as possible.

Yours, truly,

ALLEN C. FULLER,
Adjutant-General.

[Sub-inclosure.]

HEADQUARTERS, *Camp Douglas, Chicago, December 13, 1862.*
Hon. ALLEN C. FULLER, *Adjutant-General, Springfield, Ill.*

HONORED SIR: I send you herewith a copy* of the consolidated morning report of paroled troops remaining in this camp. While I am anxious to see them all exchanged I feel a special interest in the Sixty-fifth Illinois and Phillips' battery. What I ask is that the regiment and battery be at once exchanged, armed and allowed a reasonable time to call in furloughed men and prepare for the field. By the decision of the War Department dated November 16, 1862, in my possession, we cannot drill, do guard duty or discharge any duty usually performed by soldiers. The men have recently received six months' pay, and tired of inaction and disgrace, surrounded by sympathizing friends, offered large bounties in cavalry regiments and mortified at not being placed on an equality with troops they feel to be inferior to themselves, I need not say that it is almost impossible under these circumstances to keep a regiment together. Do what you will men get tired and dissatisfied when they have nothing to do. I hope the Department at Washington will be induced to act speedily on our case and send us off to the Southwest.

I have the honor to be, general, truly, yours,

DANIEL CAMERON,
Colonel Sixty-fifth Illinois, Commanding.

[Indorsement.]

HOUSE OF REPRESENTATIVES, *January 7, 1863.*
Will Colonel Hoffman please inform the bearer in this regard.

E. B. WASHBURNE.

HEADQUARTERS DEPARTMENT OF THE CUMBERLAND,
Nashville, December 22, 1862.
General BRAXTON BRAGG.

GENERAL: I have the honor to acknowledge the receipt by flag of truce to-day of four letters from yourself.

I regret, however, to say that I have not yet the pleasure to acknowledge the return of that picket of some forty cavalrymen which was captured by some of your cavalry in the presence of your flag of truce and under the eyes of its bearer, Lieutenant-Colonel Hawkins.

---

* Omitted.

After your non-condemnation of the behavior of your men on the preceding day under similar circumstances and the return of the three men thus captured—albeit minus overcoats and holsters—I will only most respectfully quote your own phrase: "Words will not suffice, we must have deeds." In short, my dear general, the *sine qua non* to our further correspondence or official intercourse is the prompt return of these men with all their clothes, arms and equipments When you speak by such deeds of simple justice I shall be able to understand you.

Very respectfully, your obedient servant,

W. S. ROSECRANS,
Major-General, Commanding.

HEADQUARTERS ARMY OF TENNESSEE,
Murfreesborough, Tenn., December 22, 1862.

Maj. Gen. W. S. ROSECRANS,
Commanding U. S. Forces, Nashville, Tenn.

GENERAL: A. J. Marchbanks, a citizen of Warren County, Tenn., fifty-six years of age, was arrested in Van Buren County, of this State, by order of General Dumont on the 14th day of June. He is now confined at Camp Chase, Ohio. The charge preferred against him was his loyalty to the Confederate Government. I desire to call your attention to this case and respectfully claim the return of Mr. Marchbanks to my lines according to the agreement existing between us.

I have the honor to be, general, very respectfully,

BRAXTON BRAGG,
General, Commanding.

HEADQUARTERS, *Cincinnati, December 22, 1862.*

Brig. Gen. J. T. BOYLE,
Comdg. District of Western Kentucky, Louisville, Ky.

GENERAL: I have to acknowledge the receipt of the letter of Colonel Dent, provost-marshal, &c, dated the 15th instant, presenting the cases of discharged rebel soldiers and deserters confined in the military prison at Louisville who under your orders were to be sent to Camp Chase, but whom he was retaining in consequence of the orders of Major General Rosecrans in regard to the same classes of persons in which he authorizes a more lenient policy. This letter you refer to me for instructions in the matter.

If any of the prisoners referred to have been liberated by General Rosecrans under the orders alluded to they should be discharged unless they have by their subsequent acts laid themselves liable to arrest; but I see no reason for departing [in] the cases of those first arrested by your authority from the policy we have been pursuing, as expressed in my letters to you of November 1 and 24 and December 5, 1862, and by the modified orders of General Buell, No. 49. The oath of allegiance and not the non-combatant oath of General Rosecrans should in all cases be administered.

It is to be regretted that orders from Washington do not indicate some general policy to prevail in all departments and thus avoid the differences which must otherwise exist in respect to the treatment of persons of these classes found within the jurisdiction of the various commanders, but until this is done these differences must continue.

The policy we have followed has received the sanction of the General-in-Chief and has not been disapproved by the War Department.

Very respectfully, your obedient servant,

H. G. WRIGHT,
Major-General, Commanding.

INDIANAPOLIS, *December 22, 1862.*

Hon. E. M. STANTON, *Secretary of War:*

I mail an important letter* for the consideration of the President, Cabinet and General-in-Chief. A secret order exists in this vicinity to incite desertion of soldiers with their arms, to resist arrest of deserters, to stop enlistments, to disorganize the army, to prevent further drafting—in short, a distinct avowal to stop this war. There are oaths and signs and watchwords, all to forward the foregoing designs. I shall try and prepare a case for the court in session, of which Brevet Brigadier-General Van Rensselaer is president; but how shall we reach citizens who are the originators? The affidavits of soldiers arrested and examined separately prove conclusively all above alleged and implicate citizens as well as soldiers. It affords a clue to the alarming desertions now so prevalent in this State and very serious.

H. B. CARRINGTON,
Colonel, U. S. Infantry.

OFFICE COMMISSARY-GENERAL OF PRISONERS,
Washington, D. C., December 22, 1862.

Hon. E. M. STANTON, *Secretary of War, Washington, D. C.*

SIR: In compliance with your instructions I have the honor to report that it has been stated that an exchange of the Twenty-third Regiment Illinois Volunteers and other troops captured in Missouri for rebels captured by the Union forces was arranged between General Frémont and General Price, but no official report of this exchange has ever been made nor can any record of it be found on the files in the office of the commanding general at Saint Louis, and the exchange is no longer recognized.

It is expected that at his next interview with the agent from Richmond Colonel Ludlow will be able to arrange an exchange of all prisoners captured on either side in Missouri up to a recent date, covering all those about which there is so much doubt.

I have the honor to be, very respectfully, your obedient servant,

W. HOFFMAN,
Colonel Third Infantry, Commissary-General of Prisoners.

OFFICE COMMISSARY-GENERAL OF PRISONERS,
Washington, D. C., December 22, 1862.

Maj. Gen. S. R. CURTIS,
Comdg. Department of the Missouri, Saint Louis, Mo.

GENERAL: In reply to the letter of Col. W. W. Lowe, commanding Fort Henry, of the 30th ultimo, referred by the Adjutant-General, I have the honor to state that by the cartel for the exchange of prisoners it is provided that agents shall be appointed by each party whose duty

---

* Not found; but see "Memorandum," etc., p. 363.

it shall be to arrange all exchanges, and such agents must be appointed by the War Department. It is therefore not proper that a subordinate should assume such duties for himself or assign them to another, and Colonel Lowe can scarcely be warranted in exercising the duties of an agent for the exchange of prisoners.

I am, general, very respectfully, your obedient servant,
W. HOFFMAN,
Colonel Third Infantry, Commissary-General of Prisoners.

OFFICE COMMISSARY-GENERAL OF PRISONERS,
Washington, D. C., December 22, 1862.
General CHARLES W. HILL,
Adjutant-General of Ohio, Columbus, Ohio.

GENERAL: In reply to your letter of the 6th instant addressed to the Adjutant-General I have the honor to state that Lieutenant-Colonel Ludlow, agent for the exchange of prisoners, will have an interview with the agent from Richmond in the early part of next month when an exchange of all prisoners on parole on either side will be arranged as far as numbers will warrant it. It is hoped that all of our paroled men will be exchanged whether still in the service or not, but if there are not enough rebels in our hands it is probable those of our troops in service will have the preference. I will forward your list to Colonel Ludlow.

I have the honor to be, very respectfully, your obedient servant,
W. HOFFMAN,
Colonel Third Infantry, Commissary-General of Prisoners.

OFFICE COMMISSARY-GENERAL OF PRISONERS,
Washington, D. C., December 22, 1862.
General W. W. MORRIS,
Commanding Fort McHenry, Baltimore, Md.

GENERAL: A boat will leave this city in eight or ten days for Fort Monroe with prisoners for exchange, and if there are any prisoners at Fort McHenry belonging to the rebel army I respectfully request you will send them to the provost-marshal in this city that they may be sent South.

I am, very respectfully, your obedient servant,
W. HOFFMAN,
Colonel Third Infantry, Commissary-General of Prisoners.

OFFICE COMMISSARY-GENERAL OF PRISONERS,
Washington, D. C., December 22, 1862.
Col. JESSE HILDEBRAND,
Commanding Military Prison, Alton, Ill.

COLONEL: Orders, No. 193, of the 22d November from the War Department, a copy of which is herewith inclosed,* require that two classes of prisoners shall be released, and it is for you as commander of the prison at Alton to execute the order. The first paragraph refers to those who

---

* See Vol. IV, this Series, p. 746.

have discouraged enlistments or interfered with the draft in any State where the drafting has been completed. (See paragraph I.) If there are cases of this kind at the Alton Military Prison you must ascertain from the Governor of the State where the offense was committed whether the draft has been completed before the prisoner can be released.

The second paragraph refers to prisoners who have been sent from Virginia, Kentucky, Tennessee and Missouri by the Governor or other military authorities charged with disloyal practices.

The records in your office must decide the character of the offense, and when prisoners are released you will require them to report to the provost-marshal at Wheeling, Louisville, Nashville or Saint Louis according to the State in which they reside, or to the military commander nearest to their homes.

The third paragraph points out the exceptions to be observed.

Very respectfully, your obedient servant,

W. HOFFMAN,
Colonel Third Infantry, Commissary-General of Prisoners.

OFFICE COMMISSARY-GENERAL OF PRISONERS,
Washington, D. C., December 22, 1862.

Col. DANIEL CAMERON,
Sixty-fifth Illinois Vols., Comdg. Camp Douglas, Chicago, Ill.

COLONEL: Please report at as early a day as practicable the cost of the property destroyed at Camp Douglas by the paroled troops stationed there. Let this report be as much in detail as possible, showing the cost of the buildings, fencing, lumber and tools. Designate the regiments or parts of regiments engaged in these outrages and note as far as practicable the part taken by each in order that they may be held to a proper accountability. If you can establish the principal facts by affidavits.

Very respectfully, your obedient servant,

W. HOFFMAN,
Colonel Third Infantry, Commissary-General of Prisoners.

OFFICE PROVOST-MARSHAL-GENERAL,
Saint Louis, December 22, 1862.

REGULATIONS:

Lists of prisoners of war for exchange will be made up by Capt. J. F. Dwight, who will forward them to Cairo in pursuance to the instructions of Col. William Hoffman, commissary-general of prisoners.

Captain Dwight will also as far as practicable see persons calling upon matters of general business and will require where it can be done that communications shall be made in writing, so that time may not be wasted by listening to needless details.

Prisoners who are to be held for the war should be sent to Alton and the facts at once made known to the commissary-general of prisoners, that he may remove them to another prison and leave room at Alton for others.

There are many prisoners who have been sentenced to be imprisoned at Alton for the war, but that having been done when the present regulations about prisoners did not exist they should be reported to Colonel Hoffman.

It is advisable to inform General Merrill and perhaps other generals that these prisoners for the war will be removed to Johnson's Island, Sandusky, whereupon they become subject only to the orders of the War Department.

In determining the punishment of prisoners great weight will be given to the opinion of the officers who examine the cases, and especially where they personally examine the prisoner. In every such case the appearance and manner of the prisoner should be noted, and in my own examinations that not unfrequently determines my judgment.

Prisoners will be held for the war when having taken up arms they have returned home, taken the oath and again taken up arms. When these facts appear the officer examining the case will make a memorandum on the papers with the sentence. Let it be at once noted on the prisoners' book and a list of such without delay sent to Colonel Hoffman.

The most difficult class is where men have taken the oath and afterwards taken up arms. The circumstances and motives which have induced men to take the oath are so various, its influence so various, and then the circumstances of violating it so various and difficult to appreciate that each case will have its peculiarities. If practicable this class should have a personal examination and be attended to by the same officer, whose decision will be final.

The class who during the last year have taken up arms for the first time is distinct. My impression of them is unfavorable, and as a general rule they should be imprisoned for the war. Men who have withstood the effect of the early heat and zeal of the rebels and who have seen the evil effects of the war upon this State, and who at last went off when by the effect of enrolling orders they considered themselves forced to take one side, have proven themselves rebels. Many such pretend that they acted under sudden influences; but that is not so, for the influences have been operating daily since the war began. Yet there are some of this class who were so weak as to blindly follow others. Theirs, however, is a permanent blindness. My opinion therefore is that this class should be either imprisoned for the war or be banished to the free States.

There is a troublesome class, being those who are traitors at heart, but who not having committed any palpable acts yet have so encouraged the rebellion that they have been put under bonds, and after that have after an interval recommenced their first conduct. The difficulty with these is in getting at the proof. If such conduct is proven they should be imprisoned for the war and they should be noticed as proper subjects to be sent South.

Those concerned in marauding and going to Union men's houses and taking their arms, pressing horses, &c., expelling Union men, supplying provisions to rebel bands, especially those concerned in small bands who have infested neighborhoods, and such other crimes as make them triable by a military commission, should be sentenced to imprisonment for the war and sent to Alton. But they should be noted on the rolls as triable, to be tried by a military commission. And all such cases should be entered on a list to be reported to headquarters for trial by a military commission.

It is important to know as soon as practicable if the evidence has been sent against each prisoner. And in every such case it should be called for at once. But to avoid unnecessary labor a number of cases could be reported to the same provost-marshal at the same time.

It is necessary to keep in sight the execution of each order given. Prepare regulation with Mr. Speak and he will secure this.

It is absolutely necessary that the prisoners' book be made complete every day. It must be written up each night.

Proper rules and discipline for the prisoners is a subject of great importance. Brigadier-General Carr has in use certain good rules, but as the prison keepers and prisoners are under charge of this office it is necessary to give daily attention to the indexes of the prisons.

As at Alton they are prisoners of war it is necessary constantly to keep them in irons. I cannot parole my prisoners there. It is necessary to keep in view the strict rules of Colonel Hoffman as to the Alton Prison.

A subject of importance is the money and property affairs of the provost marshals in the interior. Several of them have been reported as having collected money which they have not accounted for, and as yet other things have so engrossed the time of this office that this subject has not been properly looked after.

George Partridge, chief clerk, will continue in the exclusive charge of all evidence against prisoners. It will be kept in his custody. He will arrange and make proper indexes to it. Evidence will be obtained from and returned to him. It will be his duty to ascertain and note the cases that are ready for investigation and see that evidence is written for. He will especially keep in view those cases where the evidence cannot be procured so that no prisoner shall remain confined from oversight or neglect. All cases decided will pass through his hands, the decision noted by him and turned over to the order clerk to be carried out. It is his duty to keep a special docket or list, noting the cases for trial, the nature, sentence, &c. He will also as far as practicable examine the cases of prisoners. Orders for prisoners to be brought up for examination will be made up and executed by him. It is his duty to select out the cases that ought to be tried so as always to have ready in advance a sufficient number.

It is found to be necessary for the dispatch of business to fix hours when persons calling to inquire for prisoners can receive attention. From 9 to 10 and from 12 to 1 such persons will be referred to Mr. Partridge; and from 12 to 1 persons upon business can have access to any one in the office. As far as practicable during other hours persons calling will be required to state their object in writing and send it in by the messenger.

The examination of the cases of prisoners will be made by Captain Heath, Captain Allen, Lieutenant Howe and Mr. Partridge.

Where a case comes clearly within certain rules the officer having it will note the decision with the date and his name. Where the decision is a release it shall be at once executed. Cases of doubt or difficulty will be referred to me with a memorandum of the facts and recommendation.

Prisoners who have been longest confined should be first disposed of.

There are some cases where there is neither charge nor evidence against the prisoner. It is important to hunt up such cases that their release may be ordered. Prisoners are being released every day because the evidence does not prove any act of disloyalty; but if it shows the prisoner to be in active sympathy with the rebellion it is proper to release such men in case they consent to leave the State for the war.

Persons released to remain in Missouri will be required to enroll in the Enrolled Missouri Militia, take the oath and give bond of $1,000 or more. Most releases are accompanied by oath or bond.

F. A. DICK,
Lieutenant-Colonel and Provost-Marshal-General.

OFFICE GRATIOT STREET MILITARY PRISON,
Saint Louis, Mo., December 22, 1862.

Lieut. Col. F. A. DICK,
Provost-Marshal-General, Department of the Missouri.

COLONEL: It becomes my duty to report to you the shooting by one of the guard on duty of a prisoner in the hospital at this post. It seems from what I can learn of the affair that William Lohmann (the prisoner killed) put his head out of the window and being ordered by the guard to take it in refused or at least did not do so, whereupon the guard fired his rifle at him, the bullet striking him between the eyes and killing him instantly. The instructions of the guard in such cases as given by Colonel Almstedt, commanding post of Saint Louis, are as follows:

Prisoners are positively forbidden to project their heads, arms or legs outside of the windows or to spit out of the windows, the sentinels being instructed to (after warning the prisoner offending) shoot at any prisoner violating this rule.

This order was immediately upon its receipt copied and copies posted on the walls in the halls and rooms of the prison so that no prisoner should through ignorance of the rules be in any danger of receiving a bullet from the guard unawares. This order was received at this prison November 21, 1862.

I am, colonel, very respectfully, your obedient servant,
W. J. MASTERSON,
Commandant of Prison.

———

HEADQUARTERS U. S. PAROLED FORCES,
Columbus, Ohio, December 23, 1862.

Col. W. HOFFMAN,
Commissary-General of Prisoners, Washington, D. C.

COLONEL: I have the honor to inform you that your order to send the paroled prisoners to their respective regiments and commands was duly received and has been executed except in the case of stragglers and absentees who we continue to send off as they come in. The prisoners formerly in camp here with the exception of some 300 or 400 captured at Perryville on the 8th of October and subsequently at Harrodsburg and vicinity are all now on duty with their respective commands or on their way to join them. There is nothing insuperable or greatly inconvenient in removing from Camp Wallace to Camp Chase according to the order of the Secretary of War transmitted through you.* The principal loss in removing will consist in the buildings, hospitals, storehouses, &c., which General Wallace caused to be erected and which will be rendered useless for the present by the removal to Camp Chase. These buildings, however, can be generally taken down without great injury and removed to some other point where they are needed and put up again. The only other loss accruing from the removal is in the wood which has been purchased for the winter, and which in anticipation of hard roads and having been cut green might have a little time to dry before being used was provided in advance. There is about 1,200 cords on hand and the distance from Camp Wallace to Camp Chase (eight miles) is too great to justify its removal to the latter place. It can, however, probably be sold with but a small loss (what the deliv-

---

*Camp Wallace was established by General Lew Wallace as a camp for paroled soldiers organizing for service against Indians in the Northwest. General James Cooper was assigned to command on October 3, 1862.

ery will cost) to a railroad which passes within half a mile of the camp. Two regiments are removing from Camp Wallace to Camp Chase to-day and they will be followed by the others as soon as their quarters are cleaned and ventilated for their reception.

Very respectfully, yours,

JAMES COOPER,
Brigadier-General.

OFFICE COMMISSARY-GENERAL OF PRISONERS,
Washington, D. C., December 23, 1862.

J. B. KIMES, Esq., *Philadelphia.*

DEAR SIR: Your letter of yesterday is just received, and I regret to say in reply that there is no alternative but for you to return to Richmond. The matter is entirely in the hands of the rebel Government, and it is for them to say on what terms you can be released. By the conditions of your parole you were to be exchanged for a certain-named person, and that person having made his escape from our custody it is for the party who paroled you to say on what further terms you can be released and no act of our Government can put the case in any other shape.

I have referred the matter to Colonel Ludlow and possibly when you see him he may be able to suggest some way of relieving you from a very painful position. It would give me great pleasure to announce to you your exchange or to do anything to bring it about speedily but it is not in my power to do anything.

Very respectfully, your obedient servant,

W. HOFFMAN,
Colonel Third Infantry, Commissary-General of Prisoners.

HEADQUARTERS CAMP OF INSTRUCTION,
Benton Barracks, Mo., December 23, 1862.

Maj. H. Z. CURTIS,
Assistant Adjutant-General, Saint Louis, Mo.

SIR: I inclose you two lists of paroled officers and enlisted men officially announced in General Orders, No. 191,* War Department, Adjutant-General's Office, Washington, November 19, 1862, as exchanged. In accordance with my instructions Colonels Cromwell and Woods have furnished lists arranged to correspond with the various paragraphs of the general order. As paragraph 8 appears to be particular in its dates of 1st, 5th, 7th, 12th and 26th of September and 18th of October I have not included in these lists a number of men delivered to Captains Lazelle and Swan between the 12th and 26th of September, awaiting your further instructions.

Colonel Cromwell's list which should have been signed by himself is signed by his adjutant, but to prevent delay in his absence I allowed it to be thus signed, but have directed the colonel to come to your office and give his own signature.

I am, major, very respectfully, your obedient servant,

B. L. E. BONNEVILLE,
Colonel, U. S. Army, Commanding.

---

* See Vol. IV, this Series, p. 735.

HOLLY SPRINGS, *December 23, 1862.*
COMMANDING OFFICER, *Grand Junction, Tenn.:*

Arrest and return to this place all officers and men who may find their way to your post claiming to be paroled, and permit no one connected with the Army under any pretext to pass North without written authority from these headquarters, sending back under guard all who do not properly belong to your post.

By order of Maj. Gen. U. S. Grant:

JNO. A. RAWLINS,
Assistant Adjutant-General.

HEADQUARTERS ARMY OF THE POTOMAC,
Office of the Provost-Marshal-General, December 23, 1862.
Brig. Gen. L. THOMAS, *Adjutant-General U. S. Army.*

GENERAL: By direction of the provost marshal-general I have the honor to inclose descriptive lists* and paroles* of 463 prisoners of war captured in the recent battles at Fredericksburg and paroled for exchange at this office, who were sent into the enemy's lines upon condition of a transfer arranged between Major-General Parke, on the part of the United States, and Lieutenant-General Longstreet, in behalf of the enemy. Two hundred and seventy-one U. S. prisoners of war paroled for exchange were delivered by the enemy into our possession. These have been forwarded through Lieutenant Colonel Doster, provost-marshal at Washington, for entrance into the camp at Annapolis for paroled prisoners. Previous to this arrangement we as well as the enemy had sent a large number of prisoners of war to the rear—we to Fortress Monroe, they to Richmond. Paroles of prisoners to be exchanged are sent in duplicate, one copy being intended for the Adjutant-General's Office, the other for such disposition as may be decided upon with reference to this anomalous transfer. Duplicates for the Adjutant-General's Office of the parole papers of officers recently paroled at this office for exchange and of men paroled to remain within the loyal States are sent here, together with paroles taken by officers of the army apart from this office. A copy of the correspondence relating to the transfer of prisoners of war at Fredericksburg is also inclosed.

Very respectfully, your obedient servant,

J. P. KIMBALL,
Assistant Adjutant-General.

[Inclosure No. 1.]

HEADQUARTERS, *Near Fredericksburg, December 16, 1862.*
GENERAL COMMANDING U. S. FORCES,
Opposite Fredericksburg.

SIR: I am authorized by General R. E. Lee, commanding Confederate forces, to express his desire that you send over to the late battle-grounds and collect the bodies of such officers and soldiers as may be left there. He also desires me to express his willingness to parole and return to you the prisoners taken since your passage of the Rappahannock.

I am, sir, very respectfully, your most obedient servant,

JAMES LONGSTREET,
Lieutenant-General, Commanding.

---

* Omitted.

[Inclosure No. 2.]

HEADQUARTERS ARMY OF THE POTOMAC,
Before Fredericksburg, December 16, 1862.

Lieut. Gen. JAMES LONGSTREET,
Commanding Confederate Forces near Fredericksburg.

SIR: I am directed by the general commanding this army to acknowledge the receipt of your note of this morning delivered under flag of truce by Major Sorrel and to say that he will in accordance with the first proposition send over a party of a field officer and 100 officers and soldiers on our right at the position of the upper pontoon bridge to remove the dead and wounded of our troops who may remain on the field above the town. He proposes also to send a party of a field officer and 100 men on our left at the position of the lower bridges to remove those of our dead and wounded who may be there. The parties as it is now late in the day may be compelled to remain on the field possibly all night and perhaps for a short time in the morning in order to fully accomplish their mission. The parties will be detailed and sent on as soon as possible after the delivery of this reply to the officer of your staff who receives it. The general commanding further desires me to say that he will be glad to receive at any hour General Lee may designate at some place in front of the town the prisoners belonging to our troops now in your possession. The prisoners of your troops now in our hands have been sent to the rear. Communication will be had with the rear at once, and if practicable the prisoners sent there will be returned without delay within your lines at the point most convenient for their delivery.

I am, very respectfully, your obedient servant,

JOHN G. PARKE,
Major-General and Chief of Staff.

[Inclosure No. 3.]

HEADQUARTERS, *Near Fredericksburg, December 16, 1862.*

GENERAL COMMANDING U. S. FORCES,
Opposite Fredericksburg.

SIR: By direction of Lieut. Gen. James Longstreet I have the honor to acknowledge receipt of your communication of this date. I am directed to inform you that such prisoners of your army as remain in our possession since your passage of the Rappahannock will be delivered to you to-morrow across the river at some convenient point near the city about the hour of noon.

I have the honor to be, sir, very respectfully, your most obedient servant,

G. M. SORREL,
Major and Assistant Adjutant-General, C. S. Army.

[Inclosure No. 4.]

HEADQUARTERS ARMY OF THE POTOMAC,
December 17, 1862.

GENERAL COMMANDING CONFEDERATE FORCES,
Near Fredericksburg.

SIR: Your note by Major Sorrel, assistant-adjutant general, of yesterday has been received. Preparations will be made to receive the prisoners to be delivered at noon near Fredericksburg. The prisoners of your troops who remain in our possession since the passage of the Rappahannock will be delivered to you at the same place at or before the same hour. The foregoing is communicated by direction of the general commanding. (A portion of the prisoners have been sent to Fortress Monroe.)

I am, very respectfully, your obedient servant,

JOHN G. PARKE,
Major-General and Chief of Staff.

WAR DEPARTMENT, *Washington, December 23, 1862.*

Hon. H. HAMLIN, *President of the Senate.*

SIR: In answer to the resolution of the Senate of yesterday's date requiring me to inform the Senate "if citizens arrested by his authority, or by those acting under his authority, have been required before they could obtain their release from imprisonment to take an oath or give an obligation that they would not sue or bring an action for damages against those who arrested or caused them to be arrested," I have the honor to state that no citizen has with my knowledge or by my authority been required to take an oath or give an obligation that they would not sue or bring an action for damages against those who arrested or caused them to be arrested. By order of this Department arrests and releases are committed to the supervision and direction of Major Turner, judge-advocate, and the resolution of the Senate having been referred to him his report upon the subject is herewith subjoined. When information of the cases mentioned in his report reached me directions were immediately given to make no such requirement in any case or under any circumstances.

With the exceptions mentioned by the judge-advocate I have no knowledge, information or belief that any persons arrested by order or authority of this Department have been released upon any terms or conditions but of taking the oath of allegiance to the Government of the United States, or upon parole or unconditionally.

I have the honor to be, your obedient servant,

EDWIN M. STANTON,
Secretary of War.

[Inclosure.]

WAR DEPARTMENT, JUDGE-ADVOCATE'S OFFICE,
Washington, December 23, 1862.

Hon. EDWIN M. STANTON, *Secretary of War.*

SIR: I have the honor to acknowledge the receipt from you of a resolution of the Senate of the United States of which the following is a copy:

IN THE SENATE OF THE UNITED STATES,
December 22, 1862.

Resolved, That the Secretary of War be directed to inform the Senate if any citizens arrested by his authority or by those acting under his authority have been required before they could obtain their release from imprisonment to take an oath or give an obligation that they would not sue or bring an action for damages against those who had arrested or caused them to be arrested.

Attest:

J. W. FORNEY, *Secretary.*

And as judge-advocate acting under your authority I respectfully report that no citizen or citizens have been required by me to take an oath or give an obligation before they could obtain their release from imprisonment "that they would not sue or bring an action for damages against those who had arrested or caused them to be arrested."

There were four citizens imprisoned in the Old Capitol Prison, but not by any order or warrant from this office, charged with uttering and publishing treasonable and disloyal sentiments and discouraging enlistments, who before their discharge and at their own request and solicitation without any suggestion from me severally made oath among other things that he would not at any future time commence or cause any action or suit against the officers of any loyal State or of the United States for causing his arrest and imprisonment.

The facts and circumstances are as follows:

The four persons above alluded to are Messrs. D. A. Mahony, John H. Mulkey, D. Sheward and Andrew D. Duff, and the oath was sworn to November 11, 1862. Previous thereto they had been before me at my office for personal examination and the investigation of the charges against them, and on these occasions they had refused to take the oath of allegiance unconditionally and to support the Government in its efforts to crush the rebellion. By reason thereof they were not discharged, while others were discharged who took the oath of allegiance unconditionally.

About the 9th or 10th of November last I was informed by the friends of the said prisoners that they were willing to take the oath of allegiance unconditionally, and I immediately requested the superintendent of the Old Capitol Prison to bring them to my office. This I think was the evening of the 9th of November, and they were to be brought to my office the next day.

The next morning I received a letter from the U. S. marshal of Illinois advising me that certain persons who had been discharged and upon heavy bonds conditioned for loyalty and good citizenship were commencing criminal and civil proceedings against the persons who were in anywise connected officially in that State in making the charges and arrests, thereby hindering and deterring public officers from executing the laws and orders of the Government. Upon the receipt of this letter I informed the superintendent of the Old Capitol Prison and Judge Mason (the counsel or friend of the prisoners) that inasmuch as the said four persons were from the same section of country as those who were instituting suits to harass and intimidate public officers and were also their associates in the Old Capitol Prison I must postpone their discharge till further consideration.

This determination to defer the release temporarily was communicated to the four prisoners as I infer by Judge Mason or the superintendent, because the afternoon of the same day the said prisoners sent word to me by the superintendent that they were not only willing to take the oath of allegiance unconditionally but also desired to make oath that they would not annoy and harass public officers by vexatious suits, as Mehaffy and O'Dell had done.

I accordingly drafted the form of an oath as suggested by them and sent it by the superintendent for their consideration. The next day (November 11) the four persons came to my office and said the oath was according to their suggestion and met their approbation, and they severally subscribed and swore to it before me.

I report therefore that the oath of allegiance with the clause not to commence suits was inserted at their express request and solicitation to have it inserted and without any request or suggestion from me.

This is the only oath with such a clause inserted that I ever administered, and this was done at the request of those making the oath.

I have the honor to be, very respectfully, your obedient servant,

L. C. TURNER,
Judge-Advocate.

Inclosed copy of oath as administered.

I, —— ——, of ——, do solemnly swear that I will support, protect and defend the Constitution and Government of the United States against all enemies whether domestic or foreign, and that I will bear true faith, allegiance and loyalty to the same any ordinance, resolution or law of any State convention or legislature to the contrary notwithstanding; and further that I do this with a full determination, pledge and purpose without any mental reservation or evasion whatsoever; and further that I will neither enter any of the States now in insurrection against the authority of the Federal Government nor hold any correspondence whatever with them or with any person in them during the present rebellion without permission of the Secretary of War; and that I will in all things deport myself as a good and loyal citizen of the United States; and that I will not at any future time commence or cause any action or suit against the officers of any loyal State or of the United States for causing my arrest or imprisonment: So help me God.

Sworn to and subscribed before me this 11th day of November, 1862.

L. C. TURNER,
Judge-Advocate.

OFFICE COMMISSARY-GENERAL OF PRISONERS,
Washington, D. C., December 23, 1862.

Lieut. Col. W. H. LUDLOW,
Agent for Exchange of Prisoners, Fort Monroe, Va.

COLONEL: I inclose herewith a number of letters* urging individual exchanges, military and civil, together with some small rolls.* You will find the names of those mentioned in the letters on the rolls prepared in this office, except where there is a roll with the letter. Please notice the indorsement on the letter of Major Turner with names of prisoners at Camp Chase who refuse to be released on parole. I send by the mail the rolls received from Corinth. I have telegraphed to Generals Grant, Rosecrans and Tuttle, commanding in the Southwest, to forward receipted rolls of prisoners delivered at Vicksburg or elsewhere as soon as possible.

Very respectfully, your obedient servant,

W. HOFFMAN,
Colonel Third Infantry, Commissary-General of Prisoners.

GENERAL ORDERS, ⎱   HDQRS. DEPARTMENT OF THE GULF,
    No. 115.   ⎰   *New Orleans, December 23, 1862.*

Upon consultation with Maj. Gen. B. F. Butler and with his concurrence and advice the commanding general directs as follows:

First. The following-named persons will be released from arrest immediately upon the receipt of this order at the posts at which they are confined and upon their giving parole not to commit any act of hostility to the United States or render any aid or comfort to the enemies of the United States during the existing war:

At Ship Island.—James C. Batchelder, William H. Sheppard, Fred. Losberg, Aaron H. Dale, Eugene Morris, H. M. Wright, P. E. Wiltz, jr., B. F. Perry, L. J. Dodge, Joseph Bloom.

Fort Saint Philip.—Martin Fallor.

---

*Not found.

Fort Jackson.—Peter Keveny, W. J. Delano, G. H. Stewart, Michael Bowen, L. Delpit, J. M. West, Charles Hobdy, John Hickey.

Fort Pike.—Dr. Theodore Clapp.

Fort Pickens.—J. Dacres, E. N. Rossey, Doctor Booth, C. Morse, D. C. Lowber, C. B. Metcalf, R. Crosby, A. N. Baker, J. Creen, G. T. Grinnell, R. W. Porter, J. Corbitt, J. H. Huckins, C. Bacon, W. Kelly, A. Forsyth, N. Bauber, W. Cush, E. A. Hamilton, J. D. Kermey.

Parish prison of Parish of Orleans.—Hermogene Perry, Leonard Marins, L. Collis, girl of Mrs. Cornes, John Louistella, N. Bonaparte, G. Morngenstine, James Cunningham, Thomas Riley, Andrew of Reed, John Short, K. S. Derrickson, J. J. Mitchell, M. Coudon, Didui, f. m. c., George of Williamson, Jim, Captain Maurin, A. Catching, T. Hargis, John Williams, William Miller, D. Scully, W. Hamilton, A. Bulger, James Gariltaldy, Nelson (slave), S. Roberts, Alfar of Cosby, Joseph Raffle, Levy Keys, A. Lucotte, Robert Phillips, W. Hunter, J. Donahue, C. Horran, R. Allen, Sam. Peters, J. Fremaux, V. Forin, W. E. Niles, John Newille, Peter Finn, James Haherty, James Doherty, J. Sheriden, J. J. Foley, J. Capdeville, D. Graig, S. Boydet, William Buckley, John Denis, A. Reider, John G. King, W. Pulton, M. Eagan, William Jones, P. Swett, Tim. Haley, John Mooney, Pelise Boyle, C. Wilcox, N. Doyle, J. Herod. Ed. Green, Joseph Levy, Tim. Knight.

Second. The following-named persons will be released from arrest upon taking the oath of allegiance to the United States:

At Ship Island.—James Beggs, Michael Murphy, Frederick A. Taylor, P. E. Wiltz.

At Fort Pickens.—John T. Monroe.

By command of Major-General Banks:

RICHARD B. IRWIN,
Lieutenant-Colonel and Assistant Adjutant-General.

HEADQUARTERS DISTRICT OF WESTERN VIRGINIA,
Marietta, Ohio, December 24, 1862.

Maj. N. H. MCLEAN,
Assistant Adjutant-General, Department of the Ohio.

SIR: I have the honor herewith to transmit report of Maj. J. Darr, jr., provost-marshal-general for the District of Western Virginia, upon the order* from War Department, inclosed.

Very respectfully, your obedient servant,

J. D. COX,
Major-General, Commanding.

[Inclosure.]

OFFICE PROVOST-MARSHAL-GENERAL, STATE OF VIRGINIA,
Wheeling, December 19, 1862.

Maj. G. M. BASCOM, *Assistant Adjutant-General.*

SIR: I have the honor to state in reply to demand for information concerning the arrest and detention of citizens of the State of Kentucky not taken in arms that I have at no time arrested or caused to be arrested or held in custody any such citizens of Kentucky. Information on that subject can be obtained of Maj. R. M. Corwine, aide-de-camp, Cincinnati, Ohio, and the commanding officer at Camp Chase, Ohio.

Very respectfully, your obedient servant,

JOS. DARR, JR.,
Major and Provost-Marshal-General.

---

* See Wolcott to Wright, December 8, 1862, p. 43.

OFFICE COMMISSARY-GENERAL OF PRISONERS,
Washington, D. C., December 24, 1862.

Maj. Gen. S. R. CURTIS,
Commanding Department of the Missouri, Saint Louis, Mo.

GENERAL: I have the honor to acknowledge the receipt of letters from Brigadier-General Loan and others in relation to the exchange of Lexington, Mo., prisoners, referred by you to this office. My letter of the 18th instant will have advised you of the steps already taken to secure the exchange of these prisoners. In the meantime it of course will not be proper for officers or soldiers who were paroled at that time to enter upon active service, nor would it be advisable to discharge any of these men while waiting for this exchange, which there is little doubt will be effected within two or three weeks.

Very respectfully, your obedient servant,
W. HOFFMAN,
Colonel Third Infantry, Commissary-General of Prisoners.

OFFICE PROVOST-MARSHAL-GENERAL,
Wheeling, December 24, 1862.

Col. W. HOFFMAN, *Commissary-General of Prisoners.*

SIR: I have the honor specially to report the receipt of a prisoner of war sent here by Brigadier-General Crook in the shape of a female wearing male apparel charged as a spy for the rebels, arrested in the streets of Charleston, Va. Her statements are contradictory, at one time asserting she was in the rebel army, at another time affirming she served with the Twenty-third Kentucky Volunteer Infantry, U. S. Army. She is a coarse-looking creature, scarcely answering the description of *la fille du regiment.* I have placed her in the Ohio County jail for the present, ordered clothes for her suitable to her sex, and await your order regarding her.

Very respectfully,

JOS. DARR, JR.,
Major and Provost-Marshal-General.

[Indorsement.]

Respectfully referred to Colonel Doster, provost-marshal, to know if he can provide for the within-named woman in the Old Capitol Prison if she is ordered to this city. Please return this letter.

W. HOFFMAN,
Colonel Third Infantry, Commissary-General of Prisoners.

[Inclosure.]

A FEMALE SOLDIER IN CUSTODY—AN EVENTFUL CAREER.

Among the prisoners brought up yesterday on the steamer Bostona, No. 2, was the somewhat famous female soldier, Harry Fitzallen, of whom our readers have doubtless heard something through the Cincinnati papers. Harry, who was dressed in a tightly-fitting cavalry uniform, was taken to jail yesterday soon after his arrival, when the provost-marshal, Major Darr, with a view of ascertaining if possible the truth in relation to the charge that has been made against Harry of being a rebel spy, held an interview with her. During the conversation she said her name was Marian McKenzie. She was born in Glasgow, Scotland. Her mother died when she was an infant and her father removed with her to this country when she was only four years old.   Her father dying a short time after reaching New York Marian was left alone upon the world and managed to make her living in various ways, as she expressed it.   She educated herself and studied for the stage but finding the profession of an actress not exactly suited to her taste she traveled about from place to place engaging in divers employments. Shortly after the breaking out of the war she enlisted in a Kentucky regiment at Newport and served two months.   Upon her sex being discovered she had to quit.   She enlisted several times after this in as many different regiments and was several times arrested.   The last time she was arrested in Charleston, Kanawha County, in men's apparel by the provost-marshal.   She says that she has brothers and sisters residing in Canada.   Upon being asked what part of Canada her relations inhabited she declined to answer, saying: "This sensation will have publicity enough if it has not already and I do not wish the innocent to suffer for the guilty."   When told that she would be detained until her statements could be corroborated she said: "Very well, I cannot help it.   The only way in which I have violated the law is in assuming men's apparel.   The injury that I have done is principally to myself." She speaks fluently and uses the best of language, and is evidently an educated woman, well skilled in the iniquities of the world.   She visited this city about three years ago under the name of Miss Fitzallen and in the character of a prostitute.   She says she went into the army for the love of excitement and from no motive in connection with the war, one way or another.   She is about twenty-five years of age, very short and very thick.   She has heretofore acknowledged that she has been engaged in the rebel service but now denies the soft impeachment. As there are several suspicious circumstances connected with the case Harry will be furnished with appropriate clothing and detained until all doubts are removed.

HEADQUARTERS, *Camp Chase, December 24, 1862.*
Col. WILLIAM HOFFMAN,
   Commissary General of Prisoners, Washington, D. C.

COLONEL: By order of Brigadier-General Cooper I will be relieved of the command of this post to-morrow.   I am notified that the guard and prison will remain under my control but at the same time constitute a part of General Cooper's command.   I have respectfully to ask specific instructions as to how far this control will extend as to the reception and discharge of prisoners, the control of their funds and generally such information as will enable the commandant of the post and myself to draw the line between our several duties.

   I am, very respectfully, your obedient servant,

PETER ZINN,
Major First Battalion of Governor's Guards, Comdg. Post.

OFFICE COMMISSARY-GENERAL OF PRISONERS,
   Washington, D. C., December 25, 1862.
Capt. H. M. LAZELLE,
   Asst. to Commissary-General of Prisoners, Washington, D. C.

CAPTAIN: You will proceed immediately to Camp Chase and make an inspection into the condition of the prison at that camp.   Examine into everything that relates to the condition of the prisoners, their clothing, their provisions, personal cleanliness, the supply of bedding, the general police of the prison, and into all matters that have a bearing upon the measures taken to provide for their welfare and safe keeping. Make a detailed report upon these points and also upon the number of prisoners held there, the character of the charges against them, and whether it would be advisable to send any or how many to the depot on Johnson's Island, Sandusky Bay. Having performed this service you will report in person at this office.

Very respectfully, your obedient servant,

W. HOFFMAN,
Colonel Third Infantry, Commissary-General of Prisoners.

OFFICE COMMISSARY-GENERAL OF PRISONERS,
Washington, D. C., December 26, 1862.

Lieut. Col. GEORGE SANGSTER,
Commanding Camp Parole, Annapolis, Md.

COLONEL: If there are any exchanged prisoners at Camp Parole belonging to regiments serving in the West you will send them to their regiments without delay under the instructions heretofore given you, as you will also any that may arrive at your camp hereafter. Governor Kirkwood, of Iowa, will visit your camp to consult you about the men from his State. In all cases when you forward men under a non-commissioned officer or a private you will report by mail to the commander of the camp to which they are ordered the number of the party and the day of their departure.

Very respectfully, your obedient servant,

W. HOFFMAN,
Colonel Third Infantry, Commissary-General of Prisoners.

FORT HAMILTON, *N. Y. Harbor, December 26, 1862.*

Brig. Gen. L. THOMAS,
Adjutant-General U. S. Army, Washington, D. C.

SIR: Inclosed please find a package of papers which were received with eleven prisoners who were sent from Key West, Fla., to Fort Lafayette. I would respectfully request that the attention of the judge-advocate be called to the documents, as they give the history of the prisoners.

I am, very respectfully, your obedient servant,

MARTIN BURKE,
Lieutenant-Colonel Third Artillery.

[Inclosure No. 1.]

HEADQUARTERS,
Island of Key West, Fla., December 10, 1862.

COMMANDING OFFICER, *Fort Lafayette, New York Harbor:*

The inclosed information respecting the within-named twelve prisoners is taken from the records and evidence at this office. I therefore beg respectfully to forward it.

I have the honor to be, sir, most respectfully, your obedient servant,

JOS. S. MORGAN,
Colonel Ninetieth New York Regiment, Commanding Post.

[Inclosure No. 2.]

SPECIAL ORDERS, }   HEADQUARTERS U. S. FORCES,
                         FORT PULASKI, KEY WEST, &C.,
No. 11.   }   *August 12, 1862.*

Whenever any vessel shall be brought into the port of Key West, charged with breaking or attempting to break the existing blockade of the rebel coasts, upon the condemnation of such vessel as a prize and the discharge of its officers and crew by the civil authority all persons captured on such vessel who cannot show satisfactorily that they are not citizens of the United States shall be immediately arrested by the commandant of the post of Key West and kept in close custody, their arrest being reported at once to the brigadier-general commanding. Should any such person pending adjudication in the case of the vessel be permitted to go at large the commandant of the post will arrest him if he consider it necessary to prevent his escape and keep him in custody until the discharge or condemnation of the prize, when they will be dealt with according to the directions of this order.

By order of Brig. Gen. A. H. Terry:

THEODORE BACON,
Captain, Seventh Connecticut Volunteers, Actg. Asst. Adjt. Gen.

[Inclosure No. 3.]

HDQRS. U. S. FORCES, FORT PULASKI, KEY WEST, &C.,
Hilton Head, October 3, 1862.

Col. JOSEPH S. MORGAN,
Ninetieth New York State Volunteers, Comdg. Post at Key West.

COLONEL: I have the honor to acknowledge the receipt of your communications of August 30 and September 10 and 13, reporting the arrest of certain citizens of the United States who were captured on board prize vessels attempting to violate the blockade. The major-general commanding the department has directed that all the persons whose arrests are reported shall be sent to Fort Lafayette, N. Y. You will send with the prisoners a copy of Special Orders, No. 11, from these headquarters, a statement of the facts in regard to each of them and a copy of this letter. I am instructed that a report in regard to the whole matter will be made to the honorable Secretary of War from the headquarters of the department.

I am, colonel, very respectfully, your obedient servant,

ALFRED H. TERRY,
Brigadier-General, Commanding.

EXECUTIVE MANSION, *Washington, December 26, 1862.*
Honorable SECRETARY OF WAR.

SIR: Two Ohio regiments and one Illinois regiment [which] were captured at Hartsville have been paroled and are now at Columbus, Ohio. This brings the Ohio regiments substantially to their homes. I am strongly impressed with the belief that the Illinois regiment better be sent to Illinois where it will be recruited and put in good condition by the time they are exchanged so as to re-enter the service. They did not misbehave as I am satisfied, so that they should receive no treatment nor have anything withheld from them by way of punishment.

Yours, truly,   A. LINCOLN.

[Indorsement.]

COLONEL: Please add the accompanying letter to the papers I left with you a few moments ago.

Yours,   W. HOFFMAN,
            Colonel Third Infantry, Commissary General of Prisoners.

This letter has not been laid before the Secretary.

                                                                W. H.

———

HEADQUARTERS DEPARTMENT OF THE GULF,
                    New Orleans, December 26, 1862.
Col. JOHN S. CLARK,
    Provost-Marshal-General, Department of the Gulf.

COLONEL: In answer to your letter of the 25th instant the commanding general directs me to say that your suggestions are approved. The orders heretofore given to you to send certain paroled prisoners to the enemy's lines will therefore include all such prisoners now in the Department of the Gulf excepting such as wish to remain and take the oath of allegiance and also such as cannot safely on account of wounds or ill-health be removed.

    Very respectfully, your obedient servant,
                                    [RICHARD B. IRWIN,]
            Lieutenant-Colonel and Assistant Adjutant-General.

———

                        SAINT PAUL, *December 27, 1862.*
The PRESIDENT OF THE UNITED STATES:

I have the honor to inform you that the thirty-eight Indians and half-breeds ordered by you for execution were hung yesterday at Mankato at 10 a. m. Everything went off quietly and the other prisoners are well secured.

    Respectfully,
                                    H. H. SIBLEY,
                                        Brigadier-General.

———

            ATTORNEY-GENERAL'S OFFICE, *December 27, 1862.*
Hon. E. M. STANTON, *Secretary of War.*

SIR: On the 8th instant I received certain papers relative to the application of a certain negro slave to Major-General Rosecrans, commanding the Army of the Cumberland, for " free papers." Major-General Rosecrans having referred this application to the Adjutant-General for " the decision of the Secretary of War" it is inclosed to me with the following indorsement:

Respectfully referred to the Attorney-General of the United States for his opinion. By order of the Secretary of War:

                                    CHAUNCEY McKEEVER,
                                        Assistant Adjutant-General.

The law makes it my duty to give my advice and opinion to the heads of Departments when requested by them upon questions of law touching any matters that may concern their Departments. Although it has been the invariable practice of the heads of Departments to ask the advice of the Attorney-General by direct communication from themselves, stating the facts upon which the question arises and the question itself, I am yet bound to suppose that the reference of these papers to me by Mr. McKeever "for my opinion" was by your order. I therefore waive the question of the propriety of this method of asking my opinion.

But as no question is stated "by your order" for my opinion, and as I have no means of ascertaining the point upon which you desire my advice and as moreover I am unable to perceive from the papers that any question which might be extracted from them "concerns the Department" over which you preside, I do not think that I have any legal authority to search the papers for a point on which to give an opinion. I therefore have the honor to return them to you.

I am, sir, very respectfully, your obedient servant,
EDWARD BATES,
Attorney-General.

OFFICE COMMISSARY-GENERAL OF PRISONERS,
Washington, D. C., December 27, 1862.

Maj. Gen. H. G. WRIGHT,
Commanding Department of the Ohio, Cincinnati, Ohio.

GENERAL: In reply to the letter of Surg. C. McDermont, medical director, Right Wing, Fourteenth Army Corps, referred to this office, I have the honor to state that the circumstances under which the sick and wounded referred to by Doctor McDermont were delivered are such as to make it right and proper that all should be considered as on parole though a part of the number did not through an oversight give their individual paroles. Their names will be sent to Colonel Ludlow, agent for the exchange of prisoners, to be included in the next exchanges.

I have the honor to be, very respectfully, your obedient servant,
W. HOFFMAN,
Colonel Third Infantry, Commissary-General of Prisoners.

OFFICE COMMISSARY-GENERAL OF PRISONERS,
Washington, D. C., December 27, 1862.

Lieut. Col. W. H. LUDLOW,
Agent for Exchange of Prisoners, Fort Monroe, Va.

COLONEL: I inclose herewith further rolls* of prisoners for exchange. In relation to the twenty-seven prisoners referred to in Doctor McDermont's letter* herewith inclosed I have written to General Wright that they should be considered as on parole and that I would refer the names to you for exchange. I have recently learned that Capt. John W. Alley, of the Third U. S. Infantry, who was taken at Brownsville. Tex., in April, 1861, has not been exchanged. Will you be kind enough to put his name on your rolls and effect his exchange as early as possible.

Very respectfully, your obedient servant,
W. HOFFMAN,
Colonel Third Infantry, Commissary-General of Prisoners.

---

* Not found.

FORT MONROE, *December 27, 1862.*

Col. W. HOFFMAN, *Commissary-General of Prisoners:*

No Confederate prisoners who have taken the oath of allegiance should be sent South against their will. They would be immediately impressed into the Confederate military service. It is best to set them at liberty.

WM. H. LUDLOW,
Lieutenant-Colonel and Agent for Exchange of Prisoners.

OFFICE U. S. MILITARY COMMANDER,
Detroit, December 27, 1862.

Col. W. HOFFMAN, *Commissary-General of Prisoners.*

COLONEL: Nineteen men of the Fifteenth Michigan Infantry, captured at Corinth 2d and 3d of October, and some of the Third Cavalry and Twelfth Infantry same days; some fifty-odd men captured by Morgan's men on the Lexington turnpike and three or four other squads of two or three captured at different places—I cannot determine whether they are exchanged or not. On reading your letter to Colonel Duffield I made up my mind that all Michigan troops were exchanged, for you said in that letter: "An order will be published to-morrow or next day announcing all the recent exchanges according to the place of capture, and it is intended to cover all our paroled troops up to 11th of November, exclusive of a few at Harper's Ferry." You further state: "The exchanges are fully perfected and the announcement is in the order relieving every officer and soldier from responsibilities of his parole, * * * and covers all classes." On reading the above I was convinced that all our Michigan troops were exchanged who had been captured prior to the 11th of November. But yesterday Capt. James E. Mackey, of Fourteenth Michigan Infantry, showed me a letter from your office declaring that he was not exchanged. He was left sick with one or two men down toward Tuscumbia somewhere and picked up. I had announced in orders that all Michigan troops were paroled and had given other orders for their movement, but Captain Mackey's letter throws me all back. What can I depend upon as regards those I have mentioned above? Please give an early answer.

Very truly, yours,

J. R. SMITH,
Lieutenant-Colonel and Military Commander.

FORT MONROE, *December 28, 1862.*

Hon. E. M. STANTON, *Secretary of War:*

In view of the recent proclamation of Jeff. Davis directing that no commissioned officer of the United States taken prisoner shall be released on parole before exchange until General Butler is punished shall not all Confederate commissioned officers taken prisoners be detained instead of being forwarded as usual for exchange? I shall go to City Point to meet Mr. Ould immediately after the 1st of January. Do you wish to see me at Washington before I go?

WM. H. LUDLOW,
Lieutenant-Colonel and Agent for Exchange of Prisoners.

WASHINGTON, *December 28, 1862.*

Colonel LUDLOW:

You will not make any exchange of commissioned officers until further instructions and come to Washington previous to going to City Point.

EDWIN M. STANTON,
Secretary of War.

HEADQUARTERS CAMP OF INSTRUCTION,
Benton Barracks, Mo., December 28, 1862.

Col. W. HOFFMAN,
Commissary-General of Prisoners, Washington, D. C.:

In answer to your telegram asking for the number of paroled men at this camp not now exchanged I have the honor to inform you that there are 501 reported present and 410 absent without leave. Many of these have been captured in small squads by guerrillas. I will forward you in a few days complete lists of those men giving information of when and where captured and where paroled, &c.

I am, colonel, very respectfully, your obedient servant,

B. L. E. BONNEVILLE,
Colonel, U. S. Army, Commanding Post.

HEADQUARTERS ARMY OF THE POTOMAC,
Office Provost-Marshal-General, December 28, 1862.

Col. W. HOFFMAN, *Commissary-General of Prisoners.*

COLONEL: I have the honor to send you by direction of the provost-marshal-general the parole papers* received from the enemy in the recent transfer of prisoners of war captured by both forces and paroled for exchange, the enemy returning into our lines 271 of our men whom they captured, we into theirs 463 captured by us, the rest on both sides having been sent to the rear previous to this arrangement. The number paroled for exchange sent from this office to Fort Monroe was 107. The officers and men paroled by the enemy have been already forwarded to you for disposal through Captain Forsyth, provost-marshal, Aquia Creek, and Lieutenant-Colonel Doster, provost-marshal, Washington, successively. In pursuance of General Orders, No. 163, War Department, descriptive rolls of the prisoners paroled for exchange at this office sent beyond the lines and paroles of all prisoners have been duly forwarded to the Adjutant-General's Office, together with a copy of the correspondence between Major-General Parke in behalf of the U. S. Army and Lieutenant-General Longstreet in behalf of the enemy, relating to the above-mentioned transfer.

Very respectfully, your obedient servant,

J. P. KIMBALL,
Assistant Adjutant-General.

PHILADELPHIA, *December 28, 1862.*

Hon. WILLIAM H. SEWARD, *Secretary of State.*

DEAR SIR: I inclose a petition drawn up by myself while incarcerated in the military prison at Tupelo, Miss., and signed by thirty-seven others, my fellow-prisoners. In the good providence of God I

---

* Not found.

escaped. My fellow-prisoners were not so fortunate and I since learn that the majority of them were executed. Would you be so kind as to reply to our petition that I may publish it for the benefit of others who are suffering in the dungeons of the South for their Union sentiments? By so doing you will much oblige,

Your friend and fellow-citizen,

JOHN H. AUGHEY.

[Inclosure.]

CENTRAL MILITARY PRISON,
Tupelo, Itawamba County, Miss., July 11, 1862.

Hon. WILLIAM H. SEWARD.

DEAR SIR: A large number of citizens of Mississippi holding Union sentiments and who recognize no such military usurpation as the so-called Confederate States of America are confined in a filthy prison swarming with vermin and are famishing from hunger, sufficient quantity of food not being furnished us. We are separated from our families and suffered to hold no communication with them. We are compelled under a strong guard to perform the most menial services and are insulted on every occasion by the officers and guards of the prison. The nights are very cool and we are furnished with no bedding and are compelled to lie down on the floor of our dungeon, where sleep seldom visits us till exhausted nature can hold out no longer. Then our slumbers are broken, restless and of short duration. Our property is confiscated and our families are destitute of the necessaries of life, all that we have, yea, all their living, being seized upon by the Confederates and converted to their own use. Heavy fetters are placed upon our limbs and daily some of us are led to the scaffold or to death by shooting. Many of us are forced into the Army, instant death being the penalty in case of refusal, "thus constraining us to bear arms against our country, to become the executioners of our friends and brethren or to fall ourselves by their hands." These evils are intolerable and we ask protection through you from the United States Government. The Federal Government may not be able to release us, but we ask protection which the Federal prisoner receives. Were his life taken swift retribution would be visited upon the rebels by a just retaliation; a rebel prisoner would suffer death for every Federal prisoner whom they destroyed. Let this rule hold good in the case of Union men who are citizens of the South. The loyal Mississippian deserves protection as much as the loyal native of Massachusetts. We ask also that our confiscated property be restored to us or in case of our death to our families. If it be destroyed let reparation be demanded from the rebels or the property of known and avowed secessionists sequestered to that use. Before this letter reaches its destination the majority of us will have ceased to be. The writer has been informed by the officers that "his chances for living long are very slender;" that he has confessed enough to cause him to lose his life, and the judge-advocate has specified Tuesday, the 15th instant, as the day of his execution. We have therefore little hope that we individually can receive any benefit from this petition, though you regard it favorably and consent to its suggestions, but our families who have been so cruelly robbed of all their substance may in after time receive remuneration for their great losses. And if citizens of avowed secession proclivities who are within the Federal lines are arrested and held as hostages for the safety of Union men who are and may hereafter be incarcerated in prison in Tupelo and elsewhere the rebels will not dare to put another Union man to death.

Hoping that you will deem it proper to take the matters presented in our petition under advisement, we remain, with high considerations of respect and esteem, your impressed and imprisoned fellow-citizens,

JOHN H. AUGHEY.
BENJAMIN CLARKE.
JOHN ROBINSON.
[And 37 others.]

BENTON BARRACKS, *Saint Louis, December 29, 1862.*
Col. W. HOFFMAN, *Commissary-General of Prisoners:*

Are deliveries of prisoners made at Vicksburg from the 1st of September to the 18th of October exchanged?

B. L. E. BONNEVILLE.

WAR DEPARTMENT, *Washington, December 30, 1862.*
Major-General CURTIS, *Saint Louis:*

No officers, prisoners of war, will be released on parole till further orders.

H. W. HALLECK,
General-in-Chief.

(Same to General Wright, Cincinnati; General Rosecrans, Nashville; General Grant, Mississippi; General Dix, Fort Monroe; General Foster, New Berne, via Fort Monroe; General Schenck and General Banks.)

OFFICE COMMISSARY-GENERAL OF PRISONERS,
Washington, D. C., December 30, 1862.
Maj. Gen. H. G. WRIGHT,
Commanding Department of the Ohio, Cincinnati, Ohio.

GENERAL: I am directed by the General-in-Chief to say that he does not think it proper that an officer on parole should command at Camp Douglas, Chicago, Ill., and he desires that you select an available and suitable officer to relieve Col. Daniel Cameron, Sixty-fifth Illinois Volunteers, who is now in command.

I am, general, very respectfully, your obedient servant,

W. HOFFMAN,
Colonel Third Infantry, Commissary-General of Prisoners.

OFFICE COMMISSARY-GENERAL OF PRISONERS,
Washington, D. C., December 30, 1862.
Maj. JOSEPH DARR, Jr.,
Provost-Marshal-General, Wheeling, Va.

MAJOR: In reply to your letters of the 24th and 25th instant asking for instructions in relation to a female prisoner I have to say that the only offense charged against her of which the Government should take

notice is that of being a spy; and to hold her for this offense it is necessary that some definite act which can be established by reliable testimony should have been committed by her. If such charge can be
made with any reasonable probability of being established prepare it
in due form, giving time and place, and with the names of the witnesses
and what they know and any other testimony you may have submit it
to this office. If no such charges can be made release her.

Very respectfully, your obedient servant,

W. HOFFMAN,
Colonel Third Infantry, Commissary-General of Prisoners.

SAINT LOUIS, *December 30, 1862.*
COMMANDING OFFICER FIFTH MISSOURI CAVALRY,
Helena, Ark.

SIR: General Holmes, commanding the rebel forces of the Trans-
Mississippi Department, in an official communication from Little Rock
December 8, 1862, states that " Robert Craig, a private of the Fifth
Missouri Cavalry, having been taken prisoner and paroled has been
again taken prisoner by the forces under my command without any
evidence of his having been exchanged." This if correct places Craig
in a most unfortunate position and demands attention. I will thank
you to look into the matter and report to me at your earliest convenience all the facts in the case of which you are apprised. I would
suggest also that you bring the case to the attention of the general
commanding at Helena, that it may be the subject of explanation
between the opposing forces if opportunity arises.

Very respectfully, your obedient servant,

F. A. DICK,
Lieutenant-Colonel and Provost-Marshal-General.

OFFICE COMMISSARY-GENERAL OF PRISONERS,
Washington, D. C., December 31, 1862.
Brig. Gen. J. H. MARTINDALE, *Commanding, Washington.*

GENERAL: Lieutenant-Colonel Ludlow, agent for exchange of prisoners, informs me that there is some doubt whether there will be any
further exchanges of officers and he desires that no more rebel officers
be sent to Fort Monroe for exchange until this question is decided.

I am, general, very respectfully, your obedient servant,

W. HOFFMAN,
Colonel Third Infantry, Commissary-General of Prisoners.

OFFICE COMMISSARY-GENERAL OF PRISONERS,
Washington, D. C., December 31, 1862.
Col. J. R. SMITH, *Military Commandant, Detroit, Mich.*

COLONEL: Your letter of the 27th instant is just received and I beg
to say in reply that in my letter to Colonel Duffield I spoke of the
exchanges which I expected the order to cover, " according to the
place of capture," and it was not intended that the letter should be
understood as announcing any exchanges except so far as it was specified. Captures had been made at many places which I know nothing

about which were not covered by the order. I explained that the exchanges had been fully perfected in order that all might know that the order relieved them from all responsibilities and that a certificate of exchange was not necessary. Of course none can serve whose exchange is not announced in the order (191), a copy of which I forwarded to you as soon as it was issued.

I am, colonel, very respectfully, your obedient servant,

W. HOFFMAN,
Colonel Third Infantry, Commissary-General of Prisoners.

OFFICE COMMISSARY-GENERAL OF PRISONERS,
Washington, D. C., December 31, 1862.

Maj. PETER ZINN,
Commanding Camp Chase Prison, Columbus, Ohio.

MAJOR: In reply to your letter of the 22d instant reporting the cases of prisoners charged with violating their oaths and one case reported as a spy, I have to say that as the first step for such and all similar cases you should ascertain by a careful examination of the witnesses or such written testimony as you may have whether a clear and distinct charge as to the facts (alleged), with time and place, can be presented with a probability of being sustained, and when it appears that a charge can be established it should be drawn up in due form with specifications and submitted with the names of the witnesses and what they know and any written testimony you may have to the proper authorities through this office. If there is not sufficient testimony to warrant a trial make a report in each case giving all the information you have. It may be necessary in some cases to obtain the details of the case from the officer making the arrest. In reporting cases of rebel deserters give all the details of their desertion as far as they are known to you, that there may be no doubt of the position they occupy.

Very respectfully, your obedient servant,

W. HOFFMAN,
Colonel Third Infantry, Commissary-General of Prisoners.

COLUMBUS, OHIO, *December 31, 1862.*

Col. WILLIAM HOFFMAN,
Commissary-General of Prisoners, Washington, D. C.

COLONEL: In obedience to instructions received at the office of the commissary-general of prisoners dated December 25, 1862, I have the honor to inform you that I proceeded immediately to Camp Chase, near this point, and made an inspection of the prison at that place with a view of ascertaining its condition and as a result of that examination I respectfully submit the following report:

Upon my arrival I found in immediate command of the prison Maj. Peter Zinn, of the First Battalion, Governor's Guards, Ohio volunteers. On the 29th instant this officer, resigning his commission in the Army, relinquished his command to the senior officer next to him of that battalion, Capt. E. L. Webber, who now has control of the prison under the general orders of the commanding officer of Camp Chase, Colonel Kautz, of the Ohio volunteer service, who is under the orders of Brigadier-General Cooper, of the U. S. volunteer service, headquarters at Columbus. The prisoners at Camp Chase, 266 in number, political and military, are all confined in the prison known as Prison No. 2. It is inclosed by a firm, high, double-board fence, in excellent repair. Near the top of this and overlooking completely all of the inside of the prison balconies are arranged upon which are constantly posted eight sentinels, whose beats afford a complete survey of the whole interior. At night two additional sentinels are placed on each of the four sides of the walls on the outside of the prison and at a distance of about thirty feet from it. In the four corners of the prison on the inside and at the four corners on the outside at the end of the beats of the sentinels are placed lights at night of the same character as the ordinary street lights, thus placing the whole prison at all times under the surveillance of the guard and in my opinion insuring the complete security of the prisoners at all times. The guard from the prison is daily detailed from the First Battalion of Governor's Guards, to which is assigned the special duty of the security of the prisoners. It is at present commanded by Capt. E. L. Webber, and its organization and strength are fully detailed in a consolidated morning report marked A* inclosed. I desire especially in this connection to call your attention to an indorsement placed upon this report by Major Zinn.

The prison will readily and comfortably accommodate 350 prisoners and as will be seen from the present number of inmates it is not at all crowded. The barrack and hospital accommodations are in excellent condition both as regards police and repair, with two or three slight exceptions in the roofs of these buildings which I directed to be remedied. The frequent whitewashing of the quarters, fence and sinks has been neglected. It is desirable that it should be done at once. The prison is generally speaking quite well drained, though material changes are needed to make it complete in arranging and grading the drains. Raised walks and roadways have been made in the prison which if the ground was firm and made of gravel or clay mixture would retain their shape and answer the purpose for which they were designed, viz, to promote drainage and present so far as possible a hard surface to the foot or the passage of wagons; but the site of the prison is on low ground not easily drained and the soil is of a soft, loamy character which in wet weather absorbs and retains the moisture, rendering at such times the interior of the prison exceedingly disagreeable from the accumulation of mud. For this reason too the proper police and cleanliness of the floors of the quarters in wet weather is next to impossible. From causes already referred to it is obvious that the ground would except in long continued dry weather be damp and that the floors of the buildings placed very near it would also be so and for that reason unhealthy. The floors of both the barracks and hospital have been laid close to the ground, but a few inches separating their surfaces from it, and the vertical walls of these buildings extending below the floors generally to the ground prevents the circulation of air under the floors and as a consequence they are almost always damp. To insure dry barracks and hospital accommodations and a dry interior of the prison the floors should be raised at least one foot from the earth, the portion of the walls projecting vertically below them sawed off and the walks and the roads of the prison covered with a layer of gravel to a proper depth. As all this could be readily done at an expense not exceeding $300 and as this sum is much less than the present amount of the prison fund I have in obedience to your order directed it to be immediately done and that the roads and walks should be properly graded as well as the drains and sewers.

* Not found.

I have also directed the constant and free use of lime which has been seldom if ever distributed as it should be. The prison is infested with rats which make their hiding-places under the floors, so that if those were raised as described the number would undoubtedly greatly diminish. No objection has ever been made by the authorities against the destruction of these vermin by the prisoners. On one occasion, however, a large number of the prisoners armed themselves with clubs with the intention they stated of killing rats, but the officer in charge of the guard very properly suspecting other designs, since the rats could readily retreat under the buildings, caused the clubs to be taken from the prisoners. Camp Chase has been infested in all parts by immense numbers of rats, and from inquiries among officers I am satisfied that the prison is quite as free from them as other parts of the occupied quarters and camp ground.

The prison is well policed daily under the direction of the provost-marshal by the prisoners, and in this as in all matters when required to perform the duties of the prison they are tractable and obedient. The provost-marshal is an officer permanently detailed for the police and general care of the prisoners. He has under him two trusty subordinates, non-commissioned officers, who assist him in the issue of the provisions and clothing, police and other daily duties of the prison. He attends the daily roll-calls and makes his report to the commanding officer daily. The prisoners generally are well supplied with tubs for washing and bathing and washing basins, so that no complaint is made. Brooms, however, are much needed, and I have directed their purchase and that they be constantly supplied to the inmates of the prison when needed unless they are uselessly destroyed.

From a personal inspection of all the prisoners and from statements made to me by the officer and non-commissioned officers having the immediate charge of them I am convinced that the cause of vermin upon the persons of the prisoners is in but few and rare instances their personal habits while in prison, and that it can never be attributed to the want of means to prevent such nuisance, but that such accumulation is very frequently and disgustingly discernible upon their persons and clothing when brought to the prison from their own homes or when captured and brought to Camp Chase from the camps of the enemy. It is obvious that without great care, which has not been properly exercised generally speaking, the quarters occupied by these prisoners would be quickly infested. So far as is possible I have directed that in such cases in future the prisoners should be separated from those free from vermin, and to remove it and prevent further accumulations I have directed the frequent and thorough scrubbing of the infested quarters with salt brine and their fumigation with sulphur

I respectfully submit for your examination the paper marked B, a copy of instructions given by me to the present commanding officer of the prison for improvement in its condition. The prisoners are divided into messes varying in number from seven to fifteen, each mess occupying the accommodations of a single division of the barracks, or rooms. Each mess cooks its own provisions, for which purpose it has a convenient stove, a great sufficiency of cooking implements and the proper amount of table furniture for the prisoners' use in almost all cases. I have directed that where a deficiency exists it should be supplied. The ration is that prescribed by the Board of Council of last year and which has governed the issues to the prisoners at Camp Chase, with the exception of the modification introduced at that place last summer by your approval relating to the issue of beans, rice or hominy in the same ration and the substitution frequently of fresh vegetables for certain vegetable portions of the ordinary issue. From personal inspection and conversations with the prisoners I am satisfied their food is wholesome and abundant, and in not a single instance in much questioning did I learn of a complaint either as to the quantity or quality of the food. The provisions are drawn from the commissary department in the usual manner and received by the two non-commissioned officers called stewards having under the provost-marshal the immediate care of the prisoners, who issue the provisions directly to the stewards of the different messes. I call your attention to the paper inclosed marked C from the assistant commissary of subsistence at Camp Chase, which gives in detail statements relating to the ration and the issue of vegetables.

The quarters of the prisoners are comfortably warmed and no restriction has been placed upon the quantity of fuel which each mess consumed, yet notwithstanding this there has been a considerable saving of fuel without an effort having been made so to do. The issue or allowance has invariably been the same as that permitted to the private soldier. I desire in relation to this matter to call your attention to the facts embraced in the paper inclosed marked D. Upon a personal examination of all the prisoners I found but exceedingly few of them, not exceeding four or five in number, who were not sufficiently clothed, and invariably with these the fault had been their own, as they had not made application in any manner for clothing nor did they appear to care for it. The same substantially may be said of bedding, and upon inspection of all the blankets in the possession of the prisoners it was found to average two and two-sevenths blankets per man. I could learn of no complaints of cold. For confirmation of this please examine the report* marked E of the issues of clothing to prisoners. I will add that the officer having charge of the clothing informed me that in all cases upon the application of a prisoner for clothing it was given him if after a personal examination it was found that the articles called for were needed and that the clothing previously given the applicant had not been improperly disposed of.

As an index to the general health of the prison I inclose a copy of the hospital record of the prison from the 1st of November, and if the sickness and mortality be compared with that of the exterior camp I believe it will be found that proportionally its general health has been much better. From the accompanying paper* marked F it will be seen that the average number of sick was about eighteen, and this is the proportion of sick in a camp prison of nearly 300 inmates. The hospital is well supplied with wholesome food, cooking utensils, fuel, medicine and bedding. Of the latter there was in the hospital on the 17th ultimo the following amount: Fifty-nine calico comforts, 16 Government blankets, 23 straw ticks, 43 cotton sheets, 31 pillows, 38 pillow covers, and requisitions had been made on the 17th ultimo for an additional quantity of more than one-half this amount. The hospital at present contains but sixteen patients. The prisoners are supplied by the sutler with articles to the extent of the amount of their money deposited with the commanding officer. The supplies of the sutler seem to be proper and suitable, both in their variety and quality.

I desire to call your particular attention to the inclosure marked G relative to the disposition by Major Zinn of the sutler's tax amounting to $149.20. He has permitted the post council first to tax the sutler, which should have been done by himself, and then has permitted this

---

* Not found.

amount of tax to be diverted from its proper destination and it is now in the hands of the post treasurer at Camp Chase, instead of in the possession of the officer in charge of the prison, as by article 6 of the general regulations from your office. I deemed it better to leave this matter to your action, as a partial disposition had been made of the money by the post council which was in no manner under its control and appropriated to a purpose entirely without its jurisdiction.

The prisoners so far as I have been able to ascertain are never inter fered with by the sentinels either in the night or daytime unless they go beyond the prescribed limits of the prison, which is within about three yards of the high fence which surrounds it. On one occasion a disturbance took place at night between some of the prisoners, who were repeatedly ordered by a sentinel to disperse, and upon their indifference to and disobedience of his order he fired and killed one of them. The paper marked H is a copy of a letter from Major Zinn to Major Darr upon the subject and has been given me as explanatory of the affair by the commanding officer at Camp Chase.

With regard to the general treatment of the prisoners, their receipt of moneys and packages by express and other matters relating in detail to their comfort, I desire especially to call your attention to the series of papers marked K in which many statements occur over the signatures of the prisoners themselves of satisfaction and contentment.

The paper* marked M contains a list of the prisoners now confined at Camp Chase, with their homes, date of confinement, place of arrest and the nature of the charges against them stated in general terms. Judge Galloway is now engaged in the examination of the prisoners. The charges and statements made are recorded, and every opportunity is afforded to the prisoner to furnish evidence of his innocence as in his favor. If there is not proper evidence to sustain the accusation against the prisoner he is by the authority delegated to the judge discharged. If his offense warrants it as in many cases the prisoner is discharged under bonds, the amount of the bonds depending upon the degree of the offense, and the prisoner is made upon his release to report in person to the Federal constituted authorities in those sections of the country to which he belongs. Judge Galloway has informed me that he will probably complete his duties by the middle of February or the 1st of March of this year.

I submit for your information the inclosure* marked O, of the number of prisoners who have arrived at Camp Chase and who have been discharged or transferred from there during the month of December, 1862, by detachments or singly. This gives the date, number of prisoners, authority directing their movements and the place of their arrest and when discharged of their destination. From this it will be seen that Governor Tod has made many releases. He has granted over 400 permits from the 1st of March to the 26th of December, 1862, for parties to visit the prison and have interviews with their friends.

The amount of the prisoners' fund is $1,843.63 to the 1st of December, 1862, and the hospital fund is $56.31. I respectfully recommend an increase of the sutler's tax on his sales to prisoners and that this amount or a portion of it be devoted to the prison hospital fund and that more delicacies be provided for the sick. At present its small amount will permit but little useful expenditure. To the general prisoners' fund above stated there should be added the sum of $149.20 stated in paper marked G and which has been by the recent commanding officer improperly diverted. In general the prison is much more

------

* Not found.

favorable in every respect than on the date of my last report to you of it, and with the improvements already authorized by you will certainly if properly controlled be above any reasonable grounds for complaint. With the exception of articles 6 and 9 of the general regulations from your office the rules for the government of prisoners are well observed, considering the want of experience of the officers who have had the control of the prison, their short term of continuance in that position and the interference with the prisoners from many other sources than from this office, as well as the multiplied orders and requests received there from other quarters than the authority constituted for the control of prisoners by the War Department.

With much respect, I am, colonel, your obedient servant,

H. M. LAZELLE,
Captain, Assistant to Commissary-General of Prisoners.

[Inclosure B.]

HEADQUARTERS, *Camp Chase, December 29, 1862.*

Capt. E. L. WEBBER,
In Charge of Prisoners, Camp Chase, near Columbus, Ohio.

CAPTAIN: By the direction of the commissary-general of prisoners I have the honor to submit the following instructions for your guidance: You will immediately have raised all the buildings in Prison No. 2 so that the floors will be one foot from the ground and so secure them upon firm and permanent foundations by means of string pieces supported upon wooden blocks, and cause that portion of the vertical walls of the buildings to be removed when extending below their floors. The walks and roads in the prison and all low portions of the prison ground will be covered with gravel to such depth (not to exceed nine inches) as will make the ground firm and hard and insure rapid drainage. You will cause the drains at all times to be kept free and clean and so graded as will cause all surface water to be carried well without the walls of the prison and the prison limits. Cause lime to be freely used in the sewers and sinks, and particularly in the hospital vicinity. Cause all the buildings of the prison and the inside surface of the fence to be whitewashed at least once a month, and let all precautions within your power be used to prevent and destroy vermin, whether existing in the quarters or the prison grounds, and to this end you will enforce so far as is practicable habits of personal cleanliness among the prisoners where their disposition is opposed to this condition. You will cause the prisoners to be properly supplied with tubs for washing and bathing, with brooms and with all other facilities necessary for their cleanliness. The labor of grading, whitewashing, &c., will so far as is possible be performed by the prisoners, as well as all that is necessary for their own comfort or improved condition.

Very respectfully, your obedient servant,

H. M. LAZELLE,
Assistant to Commissary-General of Prisoners.

[Inclosure C.]

OFFICE OF THE COMMISSARY OF SUBSISTENCE,
Camp Chase, Ohio, December 29, 1862.

STATEMENTS.

The ration issued by me to prisoners of war (in obedience to instructions from the commander of this post) consists of the following articles, viz: Three-fourths of a pound of pork or bacon or 1 pound of fresh beef, 18 ounces of bread or 1¼ pounds of corn-meal, and at the rate of every 100 rations 8 quarts of beans or 10 pounds of rice or hominy, 5 pounds of roasted coffee, 14 pounds of sugar, ⅚ of a pound of adamantine candles, 4 pounds of soap, 2 quarts of salt, and thrice per week potatoes at the rate of 1 pound per man, and molasses at the rate of 4 quarts for every 100 rations twice per week. Also in addition to the foregoing ration vegetables, &c., consisting of cabbage, beets, parsnips, carrots, onions and apples (green) have been issued twice per week at the rate of 227 pounds for every 100 rations. This proportion of the amount of vegetables is derived from my bill of purchases from December 1st to the present date, showing the whole amount purchased to have been 7,070 pounds and the average number of men drawn for the time specified above is 388, and the issues having been made twice per week regularly shows the amount issued in the proportion above stated. The stores issued from the commissary are of the same quality as those issued to the U. S. troops, all of which I deem to be of the best quality. The vegetables purchased by me and issued to the prisoners have always been of a good and wholesome quality and of such kind as the market affords. The ration has been issued ordinarily for two days at a time, the actual weight of each and every article composing the ration being given. Fresh beef is being issued four times per week and pork and bacon the remainder of the time by a special order received from Maj. Peter Zinn, commandant of post. The stewards of the prison receive the rations at the commissary department from me after they are weighed and are always present to see that the weight is given correctly.

I have the honor to be, very respectfully, sir, your obedient servant,

JOHN McMURRAY,
Captain and Commissary of Subsistence.

[Inclosure D.]

HEADQUARTERS CAMP CHASE,
Provost-Marshal's Office, December 28, 1862.

Capt. H. M. LAZELLE:

First, the allowance of wood to each prisoner is one-sixth of a cord; second, issued in the same manner as to regular soldiers; third, requisition made upon the quartermaster; fourth, during the present month 58 cords have been issued; fifth, the aggregate number this month is 386; sixth, 6 cords. November 1, 1862, an order was issued for 105 cords. The aggregate during the month of November was 600. December 1, 1862, an order was issued for 89 cords, and the aggregate is 386, making the aggregate for November and December 493, the amount of wood the prisoners were entitled to being 158 cords, and upon measurement we find 34 cords on hand, making a saving of 6 cords. It may be stated that the prison hospital has been furnished out of the above requisitions during the last two months and the prisoners had an abundance to keep them comfortable.

Very respectfully, your obedient servant,

JAMES C. HENLEY,
Lieutenant and Provost-Marshal of Prisons.

[Indorsement.]

There has been no restriction of wood to prisoners, as their wood racks are never empty.

ALEXANDER SANKEY,
Steward.

[Inclosure G.]

Statement of taxes levied on the post sutler by the post council of administration for the following months:

August, 1862, 1,579 prisoners, at 4 per cent........................ .... $63. 16
September, 1862, 815 prisoners, at 4 per cent.................................. 32. 60
October, 1862, 739 prisoners, at 4 per cent..................................... 29. 56
November, 1862, 597 prisoners, at 4 per cent 23. 88

Sum total... 149. 20

ROBERT LAMB,
First Lieutenant and Post Treasurer.

DECEMBER 29, 1862.

NOTE.—I have permitted the tax from the prisoners to remain in the post fund because at my request the post council ordered to be paid from the fund to the prison clerks and stewards a compensation of 17 cents per day above their usual compensation. If Colonel Hoffman or other competent authority may think proper to order the above amounts to be paid over to the prison savings fund I have no doubt it will be done.

PETER ZINN,
Major, Governor's Guards.

[Inclosure H.]

HEADQUARTERS, *Camp Chase, Ohio, November 21, 1862.*
Maj. JOSEPH DARR, Jr.,
Provost-Marshal-General of Virginia, Wheeling.

MAJOR: Yours of the 19th instant is at hand. I shall endeavor to have you informed of the death of prisoners from Virginia that may take place hereafter at this post, but in the multiplicity of business here it may be omitted. William Jones, of Ritchie County, was shot by a sentinel Saturday night, November 1. On learning of the fact Sunday morning I ordered an investigation to be made and it appeared after the hour of extinguishing lights had passed the officer of the guard had difficulty in having them put out in messes 4 and 5, in one of which Jones lodged. Shortly after a furious uproar broke out in these messes and the men rushed in the open space in front thereof. The sentinel ordered the men into quarters in a loud and determined voice some half dozen times, which was entirely disregarded. After snapping his gun the sentinel recocked and fired into the crowd, shooting Jones, who died suddenly. It appears he thought the prisoners were trying or preparing to break out, and after giving so much warning he thought it his duty to shoot as he did. I was fully satisfied of the honesty and sobriety of the sentinel, and though greatly regretting the circumstance could not attach blame to him in the matter. It turned out that a fight was going on between two prisoners belonging to two different messes and as frequently happens Jones, a mere looker on, suffered because of his undue curiosity and not obeying the order to go in.

I am, very respectfully, your obedient servant,
PETER ZINN,
Major, Commanding Post.

[Inclosure K.]

CAMP CHASE, *December 27, 1862.*

The following are only a few of the many extracts that I might have copied from prisoners' letters during the past three days ending

December 26, 1862, speaking of the treatment that they receive at Camp Chase Prison, and I would here add that the following extracts are only a counterpart of thousands of others of similar character that I have read during the past few months.

D. B. TIFFANY,
Prison Provost-Marshal and Examiner of Letters.

[Extracts.]

We have plenty to eat and are doing well.

JOSEPH McGILL (*Virginia*).

I want nothing; I have everything that heart could wish except my freedom. I am doing well and living fine and fat.

JONATHAN MUSGRAVE (*Virginia*).

We get plenty to eat and are treated very well by the officers.

W. A. WOMACK (*Kentucky*).

Bill of fare at the Virginia House December 25, 1862: Bean soup, hog and corn, pork and hominy, roast beef, turkey, duck, Shanghai chicken, oysters, apple dumplings, pound cakes, sweet cakes, green peaches, peach pie, &c.

ED. (*Virginia*).

DECEMBER 28, 1862.

We have nothing to do but eat and sleep. We have plenty to eat and to drink and a very good bed to sleep on. We have no reason to complain. We have very nice officers here; as nice as any need have.

JOHN A. CARSON (*Virginia*).

I received a letter from you dated the 18th of this month in which you express a great deal of uneasiness about my suffering here. I have a good husk mattress and a parcel of cotton comforts and a couple of pillows, so that I can sleep quite comfortably. I have no need of clothing. The good Being has blessed me in the midst of my afflictions.

D. D. DAVIDSON (*Virginia*).

I expect to be exchanged in two or three weeks. This is the best prison I ever saw. We live as well here as in our hotels in Dixie.

J. W. HAYWOOD (*Virginia*).

Judge, this is a good place to stay. The officers here are the nicest men; we have plenty to eat and to wear here.

JOHN H. PAINE (*Virginia*).

My, what a dinner—turkey, chicken, roast beef, oysters, green peaches, pound cake, honey, apple-dumplings, pies and in fact a thousand little things too tedious to mention. My health is fine and I am getting fleshy and too big for my clothes.

M. E. RUSSELL (*Virginia*).

We are doing very well. The officers are very pleasant and agreeable gentlemen about the prison.

F. P. M. ESTIS (*Missouri*).

We have plenty to eat here and to wear and the officers that command this place are nice men.

JOHN H. HENSON (*Virginia*).

From March to July I received, by letter and express, $4,991, all of which I have delivered to the prisoners and have their receipts for the same. Since August the prisoners have not been allowed money inside the prison, but have had receipts for their money, which receipts were good with the sutler, as they, the prisoners, could buy anything not contraband through the sutler they wanted.

D. B. TIFFANY,
Provost-Marshal of Prison.

From September to December I have received and delivered to the prisoners 140 express packages containing eatables and mostly clothing, and nothing has been considered contraband but whisky and fire arms.

D. B. TIFFANY,
In Charge of Express Goods.

[Newspaper Article.]

CAMP CHASE PRISON.

There have been some very heartless and reckless strictures made of late by the editor of the Crisis on the management of the military prison at Camp Chase. We were yesterday enlightened on the subject by an interview with one of the prisoners who has been confined there for five months past and who has been released on taking the oath of allegiance and giving an appropriate bond. He is a man worth $40,000 in land and slaves and has five sons in John Morgan's army. But he assured us that the stuff that was published in the article alluded to about the management of the prison department of the camp was, in his own expressive prose, all a d—d pack of lies. He said that he was an old man and not used to hardships, but that now at the end of five months in the prison he never had better health and finds that he has gained fifteen pounds of flesh during the time. He says the rations are good and abundant. Some of the prisoners he declares willfully and wantonly waste their food, and this he says is done by some of them who never were half as well fed at home as they are there. And he expressed himself as being quite willing to let such fellows go hungry a little while. As to cleanliness, &c., he assures us that anything disorderly in this particular is all blamable upon certain prisoners themselves. He says if they grew dirty and lousy it is their own fault and the result of their own negligence and laziness. It is true he says that some are filthy and covered with vermin, but they are such as he says "who never did anything but stink all their lives." They refuse to wash properly and to observe any special care of themselves or of their quarters, and our informant said that he told them that he "didn't care a d—n if they were eaten up with lice, they deserved it for their laziness." He said he had been careful and cleanly and washed himself frequently and he never had a louse on him. Others could do the same if they would.

He was asked by some of the prisoners who remain, preferring lice to their allegiance, to take home with him some copies of the Crisis to show how badly they were treated in the prison. He told them, "No, I won't carry that much filth and falsehood around my person." This kind of prison experience is quite enough to stamp the statements made concerning the barbarities of Camp Chase with the character they deserve.

Reuben Sebree, the man spoken of in this article, was a citizen prisoner from Kentucky and was released on giving $1,500 bond. The same statements were made to me (only a little stronger) that appear in this article.

D. B. TIFFANY,
Prison Provost-Marshal.

(Sebree was released on the 19th of December.)

[Inclosure—From the Columbus, Ohio, Crisis.]

HORRIBLE DISCLOSURES IN RELATION TO A POLITICAL PRISON.

We speak wholly of the political prison, the prison of the State, as we know nothing whatever of what occurs in the prison where "rebels taken in arms" are kept; that is, the prisoners of war. It must not be forgotten that there have been from 600 to 700 political prisoners at Camp Chase at a time, and although 700 have been lately discharged without trial there are yet there some 400. One hundred or 200 of these have arrived there within a few days past from Kentucky and Western Virginia. These men are taken from their homes, some from their beds at night, some from their houses in daytime, and a great many of them are picked up in their fields at work and never suffered to see their families before being spirited off to Ohio and incarcerated in this cele brated Bastile, which will soon be as famous as Olmutz itself. Our Ohioans are put in the same prison with these men from other States and from them we have learned some facts which the people of Ohio ought to know. Many of these men have been kept in this prison for over one year, a great many for five, six, seven and eight months, without even seeing outside or being allowed to communicate personally with any one, not even wife, child, father, mother or stranger. They are furnished with nothing but a single blanket even these cold nights unless they are able to purchase additional comforts with money they may be able to command. Many are poor men and unable to purchase. They were not permitted to bring along a change of clothing and many had on when seized nothing but summer wear, and that has become filthy, worn out and scarcely hangs upon their backs. They have no bedding and are therefore compelled to sleep on the bare boards. They have not enough wood furnished to keep fires up all night, hence the suffering is intensified by the cold weather. If they attempt after night to walk out in the yard to take off the chills of the dreary night they are instantly threatened to be shot by the guards as ordered by those in command.

Doctor Allen, of Columbiana County, Ohio, said he lay on a bare board until his hips were black and blue. The wood furnished them is four feet long and they are compelled, each mess, to chop it up for themselves, and the provisions being furnished raw they have to cook for themselves. Recollect always that these are political prisoners against whom no one appears as accuser and no trial is permitted. The prison has become filthy, awfully so, and the rats are in droves. If the prisoners attempt to kill one of these rats they are forbidden and threatened with being shot instantly. Recollect always as we said above these are political prisoners against whom some malicious negro worshiper has created a suspicion of disloyalty but whose name is kept a secret and hence there can be no trial. The prison is perfectly alive with lice and no chance is given to escape the living vermin. A dead man, one of the prisoners, was carried out to the dead yard and laid there over night and when visited in the morning by other prisoners who heard there was a dead man there they found the hair on his head stiff with lice and nits, the lice creeping into his eyes in great numbers, and as he lay with his mouth open the lice were thick crawling in and out of his open mouth. Not long since two of the prisoners got into a scuffle in trying their strength and finally into a fight as was supposed, and several other prisoners rushed to part them when the guards from the lookouts above fired on them killing an old man by the name of Jones from Western Virginia, and the ball grazing the skull of another he fell and it was supposed at first he was killed also. Another of the balls passed through a board at the head of a sick man in the hospital and only escaped him by a few inches. The two men in the scuffle were not hurt. We might go further, but God knows this is enough for once. It is enough to make one's blood run cold to think of it. Now if any one doubts this—if the authorities at camp or at the State-House doubt it—if the Legislature when it meets will raise a committee we promise to name the witnesses who if sent for will under oath prove all this and as much more, some of which is too indecent to print in a newspaper for the public ear. We do not bring these things to light for any other purpose than an act of humanity, of respect for the fair fame of Ohio and to direct public attention to them that the brutal authorities of that camp may have justice done them. The commandant of the camp is himself a member of the Ohio House of Representatives. He will no doubt appear on the first Monday of January to take his seat. Let him answer to his peers on that floor; let him answer to his constituents who elected him; let him answer to the whole people of Ohio if he dare whether these things are so or not. Heaven be blessed if any modification can be put upon these transactions, any excuse of the most trivial nature by which the fame of Ohio may be vindicated from the crime and stigma which otherwise must go down to all time upon the pages of our history. We copied a paragraph from the Herald on Tuesday to the effect that—

The colonel and every field officer of the Ninth New York State Militia were in this city on Friday last when they should have been with their command at Fredericksburg. Colonel Stiles, of the regiment referred to, explains his absence as follows: On the 3d of December N. Isham, acting surgeon, pronounced Colonel Stiles unfit for duty on account of pleurisy, and recommended an absence of twenty days in order to prevent permanent disability or death.

THE CRISIS' SYMPATHY WITH REBELS—IT THINKS THEIR PRISONERS BETTER THAN OUR SOLDIERS.

CAMP CHASE, *December 17, 1862.*

Mr. EDITOR:

It sometimes occurs that honest men require a defense against the vituperations of sympathetic traitors. The present case is doubtless one. An article appeared in the Crisis of December 10 entitled "The Prisoners at Camp Chase." The article is nothing more nor nothing less than a tissue of falsehoods by a well-known falsifier. The evidence is founded on the statements of citizens of Ohio who have been confined in prison at Camp Chase, and a promise is given to name the witnesses that they can be sent for to substantiate the charges, and much more too indecent to appear in a newspaper. The first charge of any significance is that "the inmates of the prison are not allowed to communicate with any one outside." This is not true. No one has been forbidden to hold interviews with persons outside when application has been made to the proper authority. Interviews and personal communications are of daily occurrence and regular transmission of letters through the U. S. mails is allowed to the prisoners; and remittances of money, clothing and in fact every and all things necessary for the comfort and enjoyment of the inmates are allowed to be sent and given them by their friends outside. "They are furnished with nothing but a single blanket even these cold nights," exclaims the Crisis with as much gusto as the boldest calumniator could command. Indeed this seems horrible to this hoary-headed old sinner who manufactures slanders on honest men and patriots. No Union soldier is furnished any more than one blanket and it is considered ample for field service, and they must provide any surplus out of their hard earned funds.

The Crisis says, "They are not allowed to bring along a change of clothing." Of all the lies in the category of the *denito texto* this is the most barefaced. I have seen large trunks filled to their largest capacity taken into the prison and the transportation paid by the Government. Among the cruelties so elaborately enumerated by the Crisis are the facts of the prisoners having "to chop their own wood and cook their rations." The soldiers of all armies and the prisoners taken by all the armies of the civilized world are required to do the same, and no one but the editor of the Crisis ever pretended to call it cruel, and in doing so he but shows his ignorance and folly, not to say ignorance and malignity. The "Old Wheel Horse" thinks that the prisoners ought to be allowed to kill the rats that infest the prison! They are allowed to kill as many as their taste dictates, and frequently when I have been on guard I have seen numbers of the prisoners engaged in killing them. The shooting of Jones seems to be the fainting point when the editor looks for a good place and falls into a swoon, occasioned by so much barbarity. A court of inquiry justified the sentinel in shooting Jones, and I personally know that the men who composed that court of inquiry are honest men; as far above the editor in point of patriotism and love of truth and justice as our Savior was above the false-hearted Jews. The provost-marshal who has charge of the prison is a man loved and respected by all who know him, and although a stern, unyielding patriot, will not permit the meanest rebel to suffer. When the prisoners have not sufficient funds to purchase clothing they are furnished at the expense of the Government. No longer ago than December 16 nearly $200 worth of clothing was dispensed to inmates of the prison. They are allowed the same rations as soldiers and in addition are allowed beef five times a week—soldiers only four. They are furnished with a greater variety of vegetables than soldiers, and from two to four barrels of first-rate apples are given them above the usual rations per week. Nowhere in the history of prisons is such generosity known. Yet despite all this the editor belies and slanders those who are using their best endeavors to render comfortable and tolerable the necessary confinement of our country's designing enemies. The summary character of martial law so necessary in times of public danger may for a time visit unnecessary punishment upon the innocent. Even civil courts are not always free from cruelty to guiltless persons. But the love of truth and fairness seems entirely foreign to the Crisis and its notorious editor in characterizing Major Zinn as a person who will pollute his seat in the Legislature. The major is doubtless heir to the common frailties of human nature, but no man can truthfully say that his administration at Camp Chase has not been as commendable as any of his predecessors. I am satisfied that he will not fear to allow any investigation the Legislature or the law may set on foot. It is unnecessary to prolong this article. All I have said I can prove beyond the cavil of a doubt by dozens of men at Camp Chase who are uninterested and unbiased.

A. S. HEMPSTEAD,
Private, Company A, Zinn's Battalion.

[Indorsement.]

The writer of this communication is a graduate of Central College, Ohio, and a young man of good character.

E. L. WEBBER,
Captain, Commanding Battalion, Governor's Guards.

HDQRS. DEPT. OF MISSISSIPPI AND EAST LOUISIANA,
Vicksburg, January 1, 1863.

Maj. Gen. N. P. BANKS,
Commanding U. S. Forces, New Orleans, La.

SIR: By an official communication from Major-General Butler received some time since I was informed that it was his intention to retain fourteen of the "chiefest" Confederate prisoners of war then in his hands, including Brig. Gen. Charles Clark, until he should receive instructions from his Government as to what disposition should be made of them. I request to be informed whether it is your purpose to carry out the provisions of the cartel for the exchange of prisoners of war. If so I will be pleased to receive all those now held by you at such points on the Mississippi River below our lines as you may choose to designate. I also include in this communication the following extract from a letter lately received from Robert Ould, esq., agent of the Confederate States for the exchange of prisoners of war, for your information:

On the 21st of September last Captain Murphy was exchanged for Maj. Charles E. Livingston, Seventy-sixth New York Volunteers; General Butler has therefore no claim for any further equivalent for Captain Murphy. The exchange was a special one and was made by me in consequence of an urgent letter from Governor Moore, of Louisiana, in whose service Captain Murphy had been acting. I informed Governor Moore of the consummation of the exchange nearly three months ago. If General Butler will refer to General Orders, No. 147, issued by the United States Government September 30, 1862, he will see the above exchange therein published.

The same communication refers to Partisan Rangers. The following agreement has been made between the respective commissioners of exchange, to wit:

The body of Confederate troops known by the designation of Partisan Rangers and whose officers are commissioned by the Confederate Government and who are regularly in the service of the Confederate Government are to be exchanged when captured.

The Federal Government has recently professed to carry out the above agreement to its full extent. I believe it has done so in the East. Perhaps General Butler has not as yet been notified of the action of his Government. The agreement above quoted comes from the War Department at Washington and is signed by their agent for exchange.

I am, very respectfully, your obedient servant,

J. C. PEMBERTON,
Lieutenant-General, Commanding.

HEADQUARTERS EIGHTEENTH ARMY CORPS,
                    New Berne, N. C., January 1, 1863.
General EVANS, *Commanding C. S. Forces, Kinston, N. C.*

GENERAL: I send by this flag of truce eleven prisoners of war paroled and released according to the terms of the cartel. The remaining twenty-nine prisoners, announced verbally by the last flag of truce, preferred to take the oath of allegiance and remain in this town. Inclosed please find list* of the eleven referred to. I would also again request that an officer and private who accompany this flag be permitted to go to White Hall for the purpose of disinterring the bodies of two relatives killed in the engagement at that place, and two more bodies at Kinston.

I have the honor to remain, general, very respectfully, your obedient servant,

                                   J. G. FOSTER,
                                   Major-General, Commanding.

HEADQUARTERS DEPARTMENT OF THE MISSOURI,
                    Saint Louis, January 1, 1863.
Col. J. C. KELTON,
        Assistant Adjutant-General, Washington, D. C.

COLONEL: I have the honor to send herewith copy of my reply to Major-General Holmes' letter of the 7th ultimo in which by direction of his commander-in-chief he asks full information in regard to the execution of ten men by order of Brigadier-General McNeil, Missouri State Militia, some time since in Northeast Missouri.

The question is one of some delicacy and I hope my solution of it will meet the approval of the General-in-Chief.

I am, colonel, very respectfully, your obedient servant,
                                   S. R. CURTIS,
                                   Major-General.

[Inclosure.]

HEADQUARTERS DEPARTMENT OF THE MISSOURI,
                    Saint Louis, December 27, 1862.
Maj. Gen. T. H. HOLMES,
        Commanding Trans-Mississippi Department.

GENERAL: Yours of the 7th instant containing a slip from the Memphis Daily Appeal of the 3d of November concerning what you denominate an account "of the murder of ten Confederate citizens of Missouri by order of General McNeil of the U. S. Army," and asking full information in regard to the circumstances related is duly received.

The matters of correspondence between us must be confined to the operations of belligerents and the exchange of prisoners. The idea of "Confederate citizens of Missouri" in Missouri is inconsistent with a state of war between opposing sections and utterly repugnant to the attitude heretofore allowed you as a belligerent, which I have cordially approved for the sake of preserving the immunities recognized by civilized warfare. You have no military power in Missouri and have had none in North Missouri for a year past, much less a civil organization which would induce any man to call himself a "Confederate citizen."

There is but one class of "citizens of Missouri;" they are Federal citizens, not Confederate. They universally acknowledge allegiance to Federal and State authority.

---

* Omitted.

The rights of such citizens cannot be adjudicated by appeal through the military authorities of the so-called Confederate States. I have no disposition to overlook the conduct of any officer in my command or shift any responsibility which it may attach to me, but while the State of Missouri can guard her own citizens through the regularly constituted authorities I cannot even by implication justify any interference by you with what by your own showing relates to her "citizens in Missouri."

I have the honor to be, general, very respectfully, your obedient servant,

S. R. CURTIS,
Major-General.

EXECUTIVE DEPARTMENT, *Richmond, Va., January 2, 1863.*
His Excellency ABRAHAM LINCOLN,
President of the United States.

SIR: * * * In addition to this flagrant case* of unusual and severe treatment of a prisoner of war another and equally glaring instance has been brought to my notice—a case appealing equally to my sense of justice and calling loudly for redress.

Under a proclamation from the Executive of this State calling upon the citizens of Northwestern Virginia to organize themselves into companies to repel the invasion of this State by her enemies Capt. Daniel Dusky and Lieut. Jacob Varner, two patriotic officers, one a citizen of Calhoun County and the other a citizen of Jackson County, in this State, organized a small force and took military possession of the town of Ripley, in the county of Jackson, and held it in opposition to the Federal authority and to the usurped government in Virginia. While so in possession of this town they took military possession of the mails for the purpose of ascertaining the military purposes of the enemy as they had a right to do by all the rules of warfare over the world. Some time afterwards they were overpowered by a much larger force and required to surrender which they refused to do until their captors who were soldiers of the United States agreed that they should be treated as prisoners of war. After this agreement was made they and the force under them surrendered, and immediately thereafter in violation of the express stipulation to the contrary they were taken to the city of Wheeling, confined in jail there, indicted, tried and convicted and sentenced to the penitentiary upon a charge of robbing the mail for a term of four years, and they are now and have been ever since confined in the penitentiary at the city of Washington, treated as common felons. Both he and his companion, Jacob Varner, are citizens of high character and patriotism, honorable and heretofore honored by public positions in their counties. For such violations of the plainest dictates of justice and propriety and against all the usages of war some remedy must be found. I have determined therefore to put in execution the principle of retaliation and I have ordered two of the prisoners captured by General Floyd, to wit, Capt. William Gramm, of Philadelphia, and Lieut. Isaac A. Wade, of Putnam County, Eighth Regiment of troops under the usurped government of Virginia belonging to the Army of the United States, to be also imprisoned in the penitentiary of this State and to be safely kept there at hard labor until Captain

---

*The omitted portion of this letter relates to Richard Thomas Zarvona, whose case will be found in Vol. II, this Series, p. 379 *et seq.*

Dusky and Lieutenant Varner are either exchanged under some suitable agreement to be entered into between the Government of the United States and the State of Virginia or until they are unconditionally discharged. And I deem it a duty I owe to the cause of humanity and civilization to hold the residue of the prisoners I have now in custody as well as all who may hereafter come into the possession of this State as hostages for the good treatment of unoffending citizens of Virginia who have been incarcerated for no other cause than being loyal to their own State and the government of their choice—a government which has in a thousand instances been recognized and acknowledged by the Government of the United States as one of the sovereign and independent States of the former Union and which they are now waging a hopeless war to restore to its position. Believing, however, that it would be better for the Government of the United States, better for the Confederate States, better for the individual States, better for the citizens, better for the cause of humanity and of civilization that these departures from the rules of modern warfare should no longer be permitted to exist I respectfully ask that some arrangement should be made for the proper exchange of the prisoners named and some agreement be entered into for the exchange of all state prisoners hereafter. If no such agreement be made and the course hitherto pursued be continued I shall without hesitation, so long as the honor of Virginia and the safety and welfare of her citizens are intrusted to me as her Chief Magistrate, unflinchingly retaliate to the utmost of my ability and power for any improper, unusual or harsh treatment practiced upon officers, soldiers or citizens of Virginia. The sin of its commencement shall rest upon the Government of the United States; the virtue of its continuance shall be proudly upheld by the authorities of this Commonwealth.

Respectfully,

JOHN LETCHER,
Governor of Virginia.

WAR DEPARTMENT, ADJUTANT-GENERAL'S OFFICE,
Washington, January 2, 1863.

Maj. Gen. A. E. BURNSIDE,
Commanding Army of the Potomac, Falmouth, Va.

SIR: The record of proceedings of the general court-martial before which John W. Irwin, a rebel soldier, was tried and convicted of being a spy together with your Special Orders, No. 358, of December 21, 1862, remitting the sentence of death in his case has been received. The following indorsement on the record has been made by the Judge-Advocate-General of the Army:

The remission of the sentence in this case by General Burnside is inoperative. Having confirmed the proceedings the pardoning power can be exercised by the President of the United States alone. The question is whether a simple letter from a rebel general shall be held sufficient to overthrow the sworn testimony given before the court-martial and thus protect a spy from the gallows to which he has been condemned.

I am directed in accordance with the above opinion to say that the prisoner, Irwin, will be held in custody until the President's pleasure is made known.

I have the honor to be, sir, &c.,

E. D. TOWNSEND,
Assistant Adjutant-General.

HEADQUARTERS U. S. FORCES,
Columbus, Ohio, January 3, 1863.

Col. N. H. McLEAN, *Cincinnati, Ohio.*

COLONEL: I am frequently subject to embarrassment from the irregular manner in which orders respecting paroled prisoners are transmitted to me from Washington. Instead of such orders reaching me through Major-General Wright, commanding the department, as I presume they ought to do, they are sent directly to me. The result of the neglect to send such orders through the major-general commanding the department has been in several instances a conflict in the commands which I have received. A conflict of this kind at present exists. On the 10th instant I received through Colonel Hoffman an order from Washington to have the paroled prisoners immediately mustered for payment in order that they might be paid before being sent forward to their regiments. This I could scarcely construe otherwise than as an order to muster the prisoners and retain them here until they should be paid. Notwithstanding I had at the same time a general order from the commander of this department to forward the paroled prisoners to their respective commands as soon as I was informed of their exchange. A day or two ago I received from General Boyle an order* to send the Kentucky prisoners who have been exchanged to their regiments in the field. This I cannot do without violating the order of the Secretary of War received through Colonel Hoffman, commissary-general of prisoners. I presume I am not wrong in supposing that the major-general commanding the department has the command of all troops, paroled and non-paroled, within the limits of his department. If this be so to prevent embarrassment all orders to officers subordinate to him should be transmitted through his headquarters. I cannot with propriety suggest this to the authorities at Washington, but I am sure it would promote regularity and order as well as prevent such embarrassments as those I have referred to.

I have the honor to be, with great respect, your obedient servant,

JAMES COOPER,
Brigadier-General.

[Indorsement.]

HEADQUARTERS DEPARTMENT OF THE OHIO,
Cincinnati, Ohio, February 6, 1863.

Respectfully referred to the Adjutant-General of the Army with the request that instructions to the commanding officers of camps of prisoners within this department may be transmitted through these headquarters, and as far as practicable all orders or instructions for commanding officers serving in this department may be so transmitted to them.

By order of Major-General Wright:

C. W. FOSTER,
Assistant Adjutant-General.

OFFICE COMMISSARY-GENERAL OF PRISONERS,
Washington, D. C., January 3, 1863.

Lieut. Col. W. H. LUDLOW,
Agent for Exchange of Prisoners, Fort Monroe, Va.

COLONEL: I have the honor to inclose herewith receipts† for 1,131 prisoners of war delivered at Vicksburg, and also rolls of Federal pris-

---

* Refers to General Order No. 31, December 14, p. 83.   † Omitted.

oners taken in Kentucky now at Camp Chase. I am expecting to-day by express rolls of 1,643 prisoners delivered at Vicksburg from Sandusky and other Western camps. Some individual cases are inclosed.
Very respectfully, your obedient servant,
W. HOFFMAN,
Colonel Third Infantry, Commissary-General of Prisoners.

OFFICE COMMISSARY-GENERAL OF PRISONERS,
Washington, January 3, 1863.

In all cases where money is taken from prisoners the commanding officer is required to keep an accurate account of it and to pay it out only to the order of the prisoner, any balance being returned to him on his release. (See accompanying regulations.*) Personal baggage of prisoners not contraband is not to be taken from them; on the contrary it has been transported for them at considerable expense to the Government. Charges of this character I believe can be sustained against the Confederate officials.

Respectfully referred to Lieut. Col. W. H. Ludlow, agent for the exchange of prisoners.
W. HOFFMAN,
Colonel Third Infantry, Commissary-General of Prisoners.

INDIANAPOLIS, IND., *January 3, 1863.*
Col. WILLIAM HOFFMAN,
Commissary-General of Prisoners, Washington, D. C.

COLONEL: I have the honor to report that I have verbally authorized the temporary employment of an additional physician at the military prison at Alton. The smallpox is raging terribly there, having increased within the past week from 6 to about 100 cases. All the prisoners have been vaccinated.
I am, colonel, very respectfully, your obedient servant,
H. W. FREEDLEY,
Captain, Third Infantry.

WASHINGTON, D. C., *January 4, 1863.*
Major-General CURTIS:

It is understood that the rebel Government has refused to parole and exchange our officers. We shall neither parole nor send forward for exchange any more officers till this question is settled. The most important move now is to open the Mississippi and you will give all possible aid to that object. It is hoped that General Grant will now be able to assist Sherman without any more troops from Columbus. Arm the transports the best you can.
H. W. HALLECK,
Major-General, General-in-Chief.

HEADQUARTERS, *Cincinnati, Ohio, January 5, 1863.*
Hon. EDWIN M. STANTON, *Secretary of War:*

On 31st ultimo I ordered Major McDowell to arrest by military force certain gamblers in Louisville, Cincinnati, Columbus and Cleveland

---

* See Vol. IV, this Series, p. 152.

who had won large sums of Government money at play from Paymaster Cooke and take them to Cairo where other parties were already in arrest on same charges. Most of the persons have been arrested as ordered and arrangements entered into by them to refund the sums they had won, but the process is resisted in the cases of Philo O. Jones and August Olmstead, of Columbus, Ohio, George Gilbert, Cleveland, Ohio, and Samuel Smithers, of Cincinnati. Writs of *habeas corpus* have been issued in two of the cases. It was believed that nothing could be effected by civil suit, hence the action of the military authorities which has been perfectly successful in all but the cases referred to. Can the writ of *habeas corpus* be suspended in these cases? It is very important that it should be in order to secure to the United States a large amount of money and also by this example to show such men that they can be reached for defrauding the Government in gaming with disbursing officers. Action to-day is necessary as the writ in the case of the Columbus gamblers comes before the judge to-day.

H. G. WRIGHT,
Major-General.

WAR DEPARTMENT, *Washington, January 5, 1863.*
Major-General WRIGHT, *Cincinnati, Ohio:*

The President directs that the writ of *habeas corpus* be suspended in the cases mentioned in your telegram and that you hold Jones, Olmstead, Gilbert and Smithers and the other gamblers arrested by you in secure military custody for trial and punishment before a military commission, and that in the meantime they be imprisoned at Cairo or such other military camp, fort or post as may keep them securely. A written order will be forwarded by mail.

EDWIN M. STANTON,
Secretary of War.

HEADQUARTERS, *Cincinnati, January 5, 1863.*
Hon. E. M. STANTON, *Secretary of War:*

All the gamblers connected with Major Cooke so far as known, excepting those named in my dispatch of this morning, have been arrested and have paid over the amounts which they are charged to have won on the promise of Major McDowell, approved by Majors Larned and Coon, paymasters, and Major Rowley, provost-marshal at Cairo, that they should be released from further liability so far as Major McDowell could do it, and they were discharged accordingly. The proof against those parties rested solely on the statements of Major Cooke and their own admission and perhaps could not be legally proved against them. Shall they be again arrested? The amount thus recovered is over $121,000. The parties still to be arrested are asserted to have won $73,500. I think in view of the pledge given by Major McDowell, at which he believed he was doing the best and perhaps the only thing that could be done, that no further action against them should be taken. The rest will be arrested and held unless you direct a similar arrangement with them. Please answer to-night.

H. G. WRIGHT,
Major-General.

HEADQUARTERS DEPARTMENT OF VIRGINIA,
Fort Monroe, Va., January 5, 1863.

Maj. Gen. H. W. HALLECK, General-in-Chief.

GENERAL: I have the honor to inclose a letter* from Lieut. T. G. Baylor, of the Ordnance Department, protesting against the trial and sentence of one of his employés, a citizen, under an order of which I also inclose a copy,* appointing a provost judge for the trial of certain cases arising within the limits of this command. The letter is addressed to my assistant adjutant-general and asks that it may be referred to the Judge-Advocate-General of the Army. I forward it to you for such action as you may think proper. When I took command of the troops at this post and its vicinity at the beginning of the month of June last I found Fort Wool filled with prisoners charged with a great variety of offenses and misdemeanors not of a military character. I undertook to examine these cases myself, but finding it impossible consistently with my other duties I appointed a provost judge on the 27th of the same month with a view to the speedy punishment of the guilty and the release of the innocent and he has until now discharged his duties unquestioned as far as I know, either in regard to his authority or the equity of his decisions. I have usually designated specially the cases he was to try and decide, and the highest penalty he has imposed in any instance is imprisonment at hard labor for ninety days. All cases of a highly criminal character have been brought before a military commission. I infer from the tenor of Mr. Baylor's letter that he does not deny my right to bring such cases before a military commission, his "protest" being aimed at the trial of his employé by a court "consisting of one individual alone." It is proper to add that there is not a civil magistrate in this district or any existing authority to appoint one and that the entire department under my command was declared to be out of the Union by the Legislature of Virginia, and all except a limited territory around this fort has been acquired from the enemy by conquest. Under these circumstances I consider myself warranted by the laws of war to appoint special tribunals for the administration of justice. (See Halleck's International Law, chapter 32, sections 1 to 7.) I request an early decision on Mr. Baylor's "protest" that the party under sentence if he has been tried coram non judice be brought before a military commission.

I have the honor to be, very respectfully, your obedient servant,
JOHN A. DIX,
Major-General.

———

HDQRS. U. S. FORCES, FORTS HENRY, HEIMAN AND DONELSON,
January 5, 1863.

Col. WILLIAM HOFFMAN,
Commissary-General of Prisoners, Washington, D. C.

SIR: I am directed by the colonel commanding to say to you that he was authorized by General U. S. Grant to make exchanges.

I have the honor to be, colonel, your obedient servant,
CHAS. A. B. LANGDON,
Acting Assistant Adjutant-General.

———

* Not found.

[First indorsement.]

OFFICE COMMISSARY-GENERAL OF PRISONERS,
January 15, 1863.

Respectfully referred to the General-in-Chief.

W. HOFFMAN,
Colonel Third Infantry, Commissary-General of Prisoners.

[Second indorsement.]

HEADQUARTERS OF THE ARMY, *January 15, 1863.*

Respectfully returned to Colonel Hoffman, inquiring what unauthorized exchanges have been made by the commanding officer of U. S. forces at Forts Henry, &c.

By order of Major-General Halleck:

J. C. KELTON,
Assistant Adjutant-General.

[Third indorsement.]

OFFICE COMMISSARY-GENERAL OF PRISONERS,
January 15, 1863.

Respectfully returned, with the letters which gave rise to the question.

W. HOFFMAN,
Colonel Third Infantry, Commissary-General of Prisoners.

[Fourth indorsement.]

General Grant could not confer upon Colonel Lowe the authority he attempts to exercise.

H. W. HALLECK,
General-in-Chief.

[Inclosure No. 1 to third indorsement.]

HDQRS. U. S. FORCES, FORTS HENRY, HEIMAN AND DONELSON,
November 30, 1862.

Brigadier-General CURTIS, *Saint Louis, Mo.*

GENERAL: As I now have a considerable excess of rebel prisoners and have received authority to make exchanges I have the honor to request that the following men of my regiment, paroled and now on duty at Benton Barracks, be returned here as soon as possible to be exchanged: Sergts. James H. Wing, George McLeane; Corpl. George Loppin; Privates C. S. Franklin, O. H. Bowman, R. Braschinsky, P. A. Bevington, P. McGeary, George R. Travor, Company B, Iowa paroled prisoners, Barracks No. 61, Benton Barracks.

I am, sir, your obedient servant,

W. W. LOWE,
Colonel, Commanding.

[Inclosure No. 2 to third indorsement.]

OFFICE COMMISSARY-GENERAL OF PRISONERS,
Washington, D. C., December 22, 1862.

Maj. Gen. S. R. CURTIS,
Commanding Department of the Missouri, Saint Louis, Mo.

GENERAL: In reply to the letter of Col. W. W. Lowe, commanding Fort Henry, of the 30th ultimo, referred by you to the Adjutant-General, I have the honor to state that by the cartel for the exchange of prisoners it is provided that agents shall be appointed by each party whose duty it shall be to arrange all exchanges, and such agent must be appointed by the War Department. It is therefore not proper that a subordinate should assume such duty for himself or assign them to another, and Colonel Lowe can scarcely be warranted in exercising the duties of an agent for the exchange of prisoners.

I am, general, very respectfully, your obedient servant,

W. HOFFMAN,
Colonel Third Infantry, Commissary-General of Prisoners.

WASHINGTON, *January 5, 1863.*

Col. W. H. LUDLOW, *Agent for Exchange of Prisoners:*

Shall rebel officers captured in the West be sent to Vicksburg for exchange as heretofore?

W. HOFFMAN,
Commissary-General of Prisoners.

CINCINNATI, *January 5, 1863.*

Col. WILLIAM HOFFMAN,
Commissary-General of Prisoners, Washington, D. C.

COLONEL: At the battle of Perryville, Ky., while engaged in rallying one of my regiments momentarily thrown into some disorder by an attack of the enemy in great force I was disabled by a wound and taken prisoner. On the day following I was paroled at Harrodsburg. On the night of my arrival in this city I received a telegram from Washington of which the following is a copy:

WASHINGTON, *October 14, 1862.*

Col. W. H. LYTLE:

Your telegram respecting exchange has been received and the Adjutant-General instructed to negotiate your exchange as speedily as possible. Allow me to express my high estimation of your gallantry and hope for your speedy recovery and restoration to your command with appropriate rank.

E. M. STANTON,
Secretary of War.

Notwithstanding this order to the Adjutant-General I have not yet after the lapse of more than two months received any notification of my exchange, and recently at Murfreesborough to my intense regret my old command has been in action without me. May I not ask, colonel, your earliest attention to my case and that if practicable my exchange may be effected without further delay?

I have the honor to be, colonel, your obedient servant,

WM. H. LYTLE,
Colonel Tenth Ohio Volunteer Infantry,
Lately Commanding Seventeenth Brigade, Rousseau's Division.

P. S.—I will add that my address is to Cincinnati, under orders from Major-General Wallace, commanding camp paroled prisoners at Columbus, dated October 25, 1862, to remain here until I was "recovered, exchanged and received orders."

W. H. L.

OFFICE PROVOST-MARSHAL-GENERAL,
Wheeling, January 5, 1863.

Col. W. HOFFMAN, *Commissary-General of Prisoners.*

SIR: I have the honor to reply to yours of the 3d instant asking for the charges, &c., against Mary Jane Green. In the month of August, 1861, when on the staff of General Rosecrans and acting as provost-marshal in the field I had this girl in custody in the jail of the town of Sutton, Va., charged as a spy for the guerrillas. She did not deny the same and cursed terribly, vowing what she would do if ever released. I directed that she should be sent to Wheeling, where she was confined until December, 1861, when General Rosecrans made his headquarters in this city. I called upon her to see if any change had taken place in her disposition but found her as bitter as ever. General Rosecrans had her brought before him when she abused him well with her tongue and he ordered her back to jail. Shortly before General Frémont assumed command of the Mountain Department General Rosecrans directed me to send Mary Jane Green to her home in Braxton County with the hope and expectation that the Union troops would shoot her. I released her, gave her transportation and in a very short time she was returned to me having been caught in the act of destroying the telegraph line near Weston, Lewis County, Va. This was in May, 1862. On her arrival here she took sick, refused to take medicine and came near dying. This seemed to cool her somewhat and since August last she has professed penitence. She is an ignorant creature, but at times has the ferocity of a perfect she-devil about her. I cannot advise her release and respectfully suggest, as in the case of Marian McKenzie *alias* Harry Fitzallen, reported to you December 24 and 25 (to which I have no reply*), that she be sent if possible to some house of refuge or detention and be held there until the end of the rebellion. I omitted to say that in April last before I sent her home I let Mary Jane Green out of jail on parole and got her a place to work with a family here, but owing to her bad temper and conduct I was obliged to place her again in custody. Her three brothers are now guerrillas.

Very respectfully, your obedient servant,

JOS. DARR, JR.,
Major and Provost-Marshal-General.

HEADQUARTERS FIRST TENNESSEE PARTISAN RANGERS,
January 5, 1863.

COMMANDER OF THE POST, *Bolivar, Tenn.*

SIR: About ten days ago the U. S. forces stationed at Bolivar captured John B. Scarborough, assistant surgeon, and Thomas W. Bass, forage master, of my regiment of Partisan Rangers. They have not yet been paroled, in violation of the cartel. In the case of the assistant surgeon, in retaliation I have captured two surgeons of the U. S. Army, one of whom, Ezekiel P. Buell, surgeon of the Eightieth Ohio Regiment of Volunteers, I propose to exchange for John B. Scarborough, assistant surgeon. I also propose to exchange Second Lieut. Thomas L. Patton, of Company A, Eightieth Ohio Regiment Volunteers, for Thomas W. Bass, forage master. In this exchange I give you advantages in giving officers of superior rank for others of inferior rank, and in the instance of the forage master a commissioned officer for a private detailed to act as forage master, but I can afford to be generous to an enemy who

---

* See Hoffman to Darr, p. 130.

violates the usages of civilized war and a solemn compact between belligerents.

I have now in my possession Second Lieut. Robert Hill, Company D, and Adjt. James E. Philpott, of Eightieth Ohio Regiment Volunteers, also Surg. Joseph S. Martin, of Seventh Kansas Regiment U. S. Volunteers, whom I intend to hold as hostages for the violations of civilized usages of war and the cartel already committed and threatened against my command. If my surgeon and forage master are exchanged I will parole the other officers named. Capt. A. W. Cushman and Privates John A. Hill, Henry B. Bullard, Thomas Bates, William Johnson, Henry S. Dancey, Spencer B. Shelton, John M. Lewis, Marcus Lott and Cullin McCray, as an escort, are bearers of flag of truce and this dispatch.

Very respectfully,

R. V. RICHARDSON,
Colonel, Comdg. Regiment of Partisan Rangers, C. S. Army.

HOUSE OF REPRESENTATIVES, Washington, January 6, 1863.
Hon. E. M. STANTON, Secretary of War.

SIR: Inclosed you will find the application* of certain officers of the Second Regiment of New Mexico Militia for exchange. The application is submitted by the Acting Governor of New Mexico to the commandant of the Department of New Mexico and has the favorable indorsement of Brig. Gen. James H. Carleton upon it, and I hope it may be convenient and agreeable to have the exchange made.

Yours, respectfully,

JOHN S. WATTS,
New Mexico.

[Indorsement.]

FORT MONROE, May 12, 1863.

Respectfully returned to Col. W. Hoffman, commissary-general of prisoners. All captures in New Mexico up to January 1, 1863, have been declared exchanged.

WM. H. LUDLOW,
Lieutenant-Colonel and Agent for Exchange of Prisoners.

HEADQUARTERS DEPARTMENT OF THE GULF,
New Orleans, January 6, 1863.
Lieut. Gen. J. C. PEMBERTON,
Comdg. Dept. of Mississippi and East Louisiana, Vicksburg:

Your communication of the 1st instant was received this day at 12 meridian. It is my desire to conform to and carry out the provisions of the cartel for the exchange of prisoners of war. I have not the requisite information to enable me to state exactly what proposition of exchange I can make, but at the earliest possible moment I will communicate with you as requested in your letter.

I do not know that it is necessary for me to carry out the intention attributed by you to General Butler to retain fourteen of the chiefest Confederate prisoners of war then in his hands, including Brig. Gen. Charles Clark, until he should receive instructions from his Government as to the disposition to be made of them. As soon as I can ascertain the facts in the case I will communicate with you, and also in

---

* Not found.

relation to Captain Murphy, named in the extract from the letter of Robert Ould, esq., agent of the Confederate States for the exchange of prisoners of war. General Orders, No. 147, of 1862, from the War Department, Adjutant-General's Office, recognize the exchange of Captain Murphy.

I have the honor to be, very respectfully, your obedient servant,

N. P. BANKS,
Major-General, Commanding.

NEW ORLEANS, *January 6, 1863.*

Maj. N. G. WATTS,
Agent for the Exchange of Prisoners, Lakeport:

Partisan Rangers will be exchanged in accordance with the terms specified in the cartel in relation to them. I will communicate an answer on the subject of exchanges as soon as I can examine the subject and will transmit it to some point such as General Pemberton requests in his letter.

N. P. BANKS,
Major-General, Commanding.

HEADQUARTERS DEPARTMENT OF THE OHIO,
Cincinnati, Ohio, January 6, 1863.

Col. W. HOFFMAN, *Commissary-General of Prisoners.*

COLONEL: I have the honor to acknowledge the receipt of your letter of the 30th ultimo in regard to selecting a suitable and available officer to relieve Col. Daniel Cameron, Sixty-fifth Illinois Volunteers, a paroled officer, from the command at Camp Douglas, Chicago, Ill. Brig. Gen. J. Ammen, U. S. Volunteers, has been ordered to the command of Camp Douglas, he being the only suitable officer available for the duty, which seems to require that rank in order to enable the officer to command any colonels who may be at the camp, and General Ammen has only now become available by the removal of most of the troops from Camp Dennison, where he has been for some time stationed.

Very respectfully, your obedient servant,

H. G. WRIGHT,
Major-General, Commanding.

WELDON, N. C., *January 6, 1863.*

Maj. Gen. J. G. FOSTER, U. S. Army,
Commanding Eighteenth Army Corps, New Berne, N. C.

GENERAL: I have the honor to acknowledge the receipt of your communication of the 31st ultimo and a copy of a letter addressed to you by Edward Stanly, who signs himself military governor of North Carolina. In relation to prisoners of war when they have been paroled I can say never to my knowledge have they been nor have I ever heard of their having been employed in the performance of any duty for the Government. As my Government has so faithfully respected the parole of prisoners I am the more astonished that you should have brought a merely hearsay rumor that came to the ears of the editor of the Raleigh Standard to my notice when an order was issued from the War Department of the United States requiring as I remember paroled prisoners to instruct recruits, garrison fortresses in the rear of the army, guard prisoners, &c. While our press as the extract you sent me shows would denounce such violation of a parole of

honor I have seen yours teeming with the demand that the prisoner,
we had captured and paroled should be sent to Minnesota to repel the
Indians then at war with your people.

*   *   *   *   *   *   *

I am, general, very respectfully, your obedient servant,

S. G. FRENCH,
Major-General, Commanding.

HEADQUARTERS DEPARTMENT OF THE MISSOURI,
Saint Louis, January 6, 1863.

Brig. Gen. LEWIS MERRILL,
Commanding District of Northeast Missouri, Warrenton, Mo.

GENERAL: It is understood that the rebel Government has refused
to parole and exchange our officers, in consequence whereof the general
commanding is directed to exchange no more officers until this question
is settled. I am directed to say that until further orders you will
please cause all rebel officers taken prisoners within your command to
be forwarded under guard to the provost-marshal-general at these
headquarters.

I have the honor to be, general, very respectfully, your obedient
servant,

H. Z. CURTIS,
Assistant Adjutant-General.

(Same to Brig. Gen. Ben. Loan, commanding District of Central Mis-
souri, Jefferson City; Brig. Gen. E. B. Brown, commanding District of
Southwest Missouri, Springfield; Brig. Gen. E. A. Carr, commanding
District of Saint Louis, Saint Louis.)

HEADQUARTERS DEPARTMENT OF THE CUMBERLAND,
Murfreesborough, January 6, 1863.

General R. B. MITCHELL.

GENERAL: The general commanding directs that the Confederate
prisoners be forwarded to Alton. Officers will not be paroled on
account of Jeff. Davis' proclamation and order. Official letters will
be written which you will cause to be read to them.

Our own paroled prisoners who have no written evidence of their
parole will be ordered to their regiments their parole being unlawful.

Continue your vigilance in arresting every officer who is in the city
without permission from division approved by corps commanders or
from these headquarters.

Confine them and send lists of names promptly.

Very respectfully, your obedient servant,

C. GODDARD,
Major and Acting Assistant Adjutant-General.

HEADQUARTERS FIRST TENNESSEE PARTISAN RANGERS,
January 6, 1863.

COMMANDER OF THE POST, *Bolivar, Tenn.*

SIR: I am informed that Forage Master Thomas W. Bass and Asst.
Surg. John B. Scarborough, of my regiment, First Tennessee Partisan Rangers, C. S. Army, who have been captured as prisoners of war

by the U. S. forces at Bolivar, are now on trial before a military commission upon charges of murder, arson, robbing and I suppose all the black crimes that are customarily committed by your Government. This proceeding is most savage and brutal and a gross violation of every usage and law of civilized war.

I wish to state simply that these men are duly mustered into the military service of the Confederate States by myself acting under the authority and commission duly issued by the Secretary of War under special order of the President of the Confederate States. Thomas W. Bass has been appointed by me forage master and Dr. J. B. Scarborough has been appointed assistant surgeon of the First Tennessee Regiment of Partisan Rangers, C. S. Army. The Partisan Ranger service is a legally organized branch of the C. S. Army under an act of the Congress of the Confederate States. In my operations I have not violated the laws of war; your army has done it time and again. This pretended trial of Bass and Scarborough is one of the many gross and wanton violations of the military law of nations. If this proceeding is not immediately stopped and these men treated as prisoners of war or if they are punished capitally or cruelly treated as prisoners of war I will retaliate tenfold, and that you may know I have the means to execute my threat of retaliation I refer you to my note of the 5th instant sent to you under flag of truce.

U. S. officers and soldiers have been stealing negroes, horses, mules, money, &c.; they have plundered houses, broken open bureau drawers, searched the person of ladies and insulted women; they have burnt houses and assassinated unoffending men, women and children all over the land, and yet when they have been captured although we had every reason to avenge these injuries they have been promptly paroled except when necessary to retaliate. No unusual trials have been resorted to to scare prisoners and extort from them the oath of allegiance to a belligerent government. Your command has pillaged my own premises and grossly insulted my wife and very nearly shot one of my children and have threatened to burn my houses. I wish to notify you and your command that if I can get hold of the demons who have perpetrated these acts or who shall perpetrate them again, or who shall order or excute these threats, I will not treat them as prisoners of war but as outlaws and enemies of mankind. Further if any non-combatant citizen of the Confederate States and of West Tennessee shall be captured or their houses burned or other property destroyed I will retaliate by capturing two Union citizens for each Confederate citizen and will take or destroy from Union men and U. S. soldiers and Government twice the amount of property taken or destroyed. My family resides near your army and those also of my relations and friends; for every depredation and insult committed against them I will retaliate upon Union men, Union soldiers and property.

Capt. Albert W. Cushman and escort will bear this note and flag of truce.

Yours, &c.,

R. V. RICHARDSON,
Col., Comdg. First Tennessee Regt. Partisan Rangers, C. S. Army.

P. S.—Capt. J. Slaughter Caruthers with escort composed of John Ford, Henry McCain, T. T. Bennet and F. W. Hughes will bear this dispatch under flag of truce.

Yours, &c.,

R. V. R.

SAINT LOUIS, *January 7, 1863.*

Brig. Gen. E. B. BROWN, *Springfield:*

If men come from enemy's lines they must be taken and held as prisoners of war or as spies unless they swear and give bond to abjure all connection with the so-called Confederate rebellion and swear allegiance to the United States.

S. R. CURTIS,
Major-General.

HEADQUARTERS CAMP OF INSTRUCTION,
Benton Barracks, Mo., January 7, 1863.

Col. WILLIAM HOFFMAN,
Commissary-General of Prisoners, Washington, D. C.

SIR: Having been directed by the major-general commanding the department to correspond with you directly in matters pertaining to paroled prisoners I have the honor to represent that cases are constantly occurring of the capture of civilians in the employ of the Government in the capacity of mechanics and otherwise. Upon being paroled they come here destitute of the means of subsistence or of returning to their homes sometimes as distant as New Orleans. They are referred for instructions from one headquarters to another, till at last they are sent to this post with no definite orders. They are generally anxious to be exchanged and to resume their employment. Until that is effected ought they [not] to be borne upon our list and subsisted like paroled soldiers? I would not trouble you with these questions, but these instances are occurring so frequently that I deem it well that the wishes of the Government on this subject should be distinctly understood.

All of which is respectfully submitted.

I am, colonel, very respectfully, your obedient servant,

B. L. E. BONNEVILLE,
Colonel, U. S. Army, Commanding.

[Indorsement.]

OFFICE COMMISSARY-GENERAL OF PRISONERS,
January 14, 1863.

Respectfully referred to the Quartermaster-General. Probably most of these men referred to have been exchanged under the recent declaration and they may be again employed by the Government.

W. HOFFMAN,
Colonel Third Infantry, Commissary-General of Prisoners.

HEADQUARTERS ARMY OF THE POTOMAC,
Office Provost-Marshal-General, January 7. 1863.

Col. W. HOFFMAN, *Commissary-General of Prisoners, &c.*

COLONEL: I beg leave to invite your attention to the loose and irregular manner in which exchanged U. S. prisoners from the Parole Camp at Annapolis are returned to the Army of the Potomac. Three large detachments have been recently landed at Aquia Creek under mere nominal control without orders or instructions of any kind. They come under the cognizance of this office only as stragglers, for through no fault of their own they are nothing else from the moment of their landing. No descriptive papers concerning them have been received by me excepting in one instance a list of upward of 1,000 men, while but few, upward of 100, reported at this office for distribution to their regiments. Through existing regulations commanders look to me for the proper return of their men dismissed from such camps; but my own part in the transmission of men from Annapolis is simply accidental as above indicated. On the 5th instant there arrived at Aquia Creek 380 men from the Parole Camp at Annapolis under charge of First Lieutenant Barker and two more lieutenants. They were sent off by the commandant of the camp the day previous with some 480 men via Washington, without a guard, without rolls and apparently without orders. On reaching the Soldier's Rest at Washington some 50 men were missing—lost along the way. The remainder, 430, were forwarded from Washington on the 6th instant, but on arriving at Aquia Creek only 380 could be accounted for. Of this number 211 it was found did not belong to this army and were sent accordingly back to Alexandria under a suitable guard for delivery to Maj. W. H. Wood, Seventeenth U. S. Infantry, assistant provost-marshal-general, Army of the Potomac, who will return them in due course to their respective regiments. Even the number thus accounted for were disposed of with great difficulty and embarrassment, for the confused condition of this transfer and indeed the transfer itself came to my knowledge only by accident.

I have the honor to inclose a copy of General Orders, No. 192, and to suggest that its provisions be made to cover the transfer of exchanged U. S. soldiers dismissed from the several camps for paroled prisoners. By this arrangement soldiers will be returned *de facto* when dismissed from parole camps, and moreover they will be properly equipped for service when they are received. At least I must earnestly request that I be duly apprised by telegraph when such a transfer is to be made in order that I may either arrange for the transmission of all large detachments under a guard of my own or for their reception here by my own guard to relieve an efficient guard accompanying them from the start.

Very respectfully, your obedient servant,

M. R. PATRICK,
Provost-Marshal-General.

[Inclosure.]

GENERAL ORDERS, } HDQRS. ARMY OF THE POTOMAC,
No. 192. } *Camp near Falmouth, Va., December 24, 1862.*

I. In order to facilitate the return to duty of officers and men detained at the camp of convalescents, stragglers, &c., near Alexandria, Maj. W. H. Wood, Seventeenth Infantry, assistant provost-marshal-general, Army of the Potomac, will repair to Alexandria and take charge of all such officers and men in the various camps of that vicinity as are reported for duty in the field, superintending their muster and embarkation by corps under the direction of the corps officers designated for that purpose and providing the proper escort for the detachment on board the steam-boat to Aquia Creek.

II. As the men in those camps are without arms, frequently without proper clothing and therefore useless with their regiments until supplied each corps commander will appoint subject to the approval of the commander of his grand division a suitable officer to take charge of the arming, equipping, clothing and conducting to corps headquarters for the distribution to their respective regiments and commands all officers and men of the corps who may be turned over to him by Major Wood.

11 R R—SERIES II, VOL V

III. The corps officer charged with this duty must keep himself thoroughly posted as to the caliber and description of all arms, kinds of equipments, clothing, &c., used by the various regiments and commands of his corps, and on being notified from the office of the provost-marshal-general that a detachment of convalescents, &c., is in readiness for him at Alexandria will repair to that place with a copy of this order and of the order detailing him for the duty, report to Major Wood and make requisitions for such arms, clothing, &c., as may be necessary to fit out every man of the detachment for immediate service with forty rounds of ammunition.

IV. As soon as possible after the requisitions are filled the corps officer will make the necessary issues to the men (taking such receipts from and making such charges against them as will enable him to transfer the accountability for the property issued to the commanders of regiments and companies to which the men belong and furnish the necessary data for the settlement of their account) and conduct them to the headquarters of his corps for distribution to their respective regiments and commands.

V. Capt. H. S. Welton, Nineteenth Infantry, now at Alexandria, will report with his company to Major Wood and assist him in the execution of this order.

By command of Major-General Burnside:

LEWIS RICHMOND,
Assistant Adjutant-General.

HDQRS. RIGHT WING, FOURTEENTH ARMY CORPS,
In Camp near Murfreesborough, January 7, 1863.

Brigadier-General DAVIS, *Commanding First Division.*

GENERAL: By authority of the general commanding General McCook directs that all of your command claiming to have been paroled by the enemy but who have no written evidence of it or whose paroles are signed by any other than a commissioned officer of the Confederate Army be returned to duty with their regiments, all such paroles being illegal. He directs that all paroled men in your command be collected together and the evidence of their parole examined and the men disposed of as herein indicated.

Lists of those properly paroled will be furnished by division provost-marshal to the provost-marshal-general at headquarters Department of the Cumberland, who will give directions concerning them.

Very respectfully, your obedient servant,

J. A. CAMPBELL,
Major and Assistant Adjutant-General.

GENERAL ORDERS, }   HDQRS. DEPT. OF THE CUMBERLAND,
No. 1.   }   *Murfreesborough, Tenn., January 7, 1863.*

The general commanding is pained to inform the commissioned officers of the Confederate Army taken prisoners by the forces under his command that owing to the barbarous measures announced by President Davis in his recent proclamation denying paroles to our officers he will be obliged to treat them in like manner. It is a matter of regret to him that this rigor appears to be necessary, and he trusts that such remonstrances as may well be made in the name of justice, humanity and civilization will reach the Confederate authorities and induce them to pursue a different course thereby enabling him to accord to their officers those privileges which he is always pleased to extend to brave men even though fighting for a cause which he considers hostile to our nation and disastrous to human freedom.

By command of Major-General Rosecrans:

C. GODDARD,
Assistant Adjutant-General and Chief of Staff.

MURFREESBOROUGH, *January 8, 1863.*

Colonel HOFFMAN:

We desire to send our prisoners to the most convenient point for prompt exchange. Where shall it be?

W. S. ROSECRANS,
Major-General.

WASHINGTON, D. C., *January 8, 1863.*

Brig. Gen. L. THOMAS, *Adjutant-General U. S. Army.*

GENERAL: I have the honor to submit the following for the consideration of the honorable the Secretary of War:

Eleven months ago I was arrested in this city, conveyed to Fort Lafayette and placed in close confinement.

At the time my division headquarters were at Poolesville, Md., where were kept all my papers, public and private, which had accumulated during a continuous field service of many months and where I had the private property belonging to the usual equipment of a general officer in the field.

All this property and papers was as I am informed taken possession of by the Government and conveyed to the office of the War Department.

Subsequently a portion of my clothing and equipment was sent to the residence of my family in this city.

A considerable portion of my clothing, &c., has never been returned, nor have any of my papers, public or private, been restored.

The papers and articles retained (including the letters of my wife and family) embrace many which have great value to me and can have little to any one else—none whatever to the Government.

These articles are my property and mine only and the only effect of their retention will be inconvenience and annoyance to me.

I therefore request that orders may be given directing the restoration of my property and papers, which have now been eleven months out of my possession without a receipt or catalogue furnished to me.

Very respectfully, I am, general, your most obedient servant,

CHAS. P. STONE,
Brigadier-General.

[Indorsement.]

WAR DEPARTMENT, *January 9, 1863.*

Return to the Adjutant-General with the information that the property and papers were brought to this Department by one of General Stone's aides; that the property was delivered to Mr. Parker, General Stone's brother-in-law; that the papers were at the time sealed up and remain so still, and that the Judge-Advocate was instructed nearly two months ago to examine the papers and such as were of a private nature returned to General Stone, retaining only such as were of a public character or important as evidence.

P. H. WATSON,
Assistant Secretary of War.

OFFICE COMMISSARY-GENERAL OF PRISONERS,
Washington, D. C., January 8, 1863.

Col. W. H. LYTLE, *Tenth Ohio Infantry, Cincinnati, Ohio.*

COLONEL: Your letter of the 5th instant is just received, and in reply I would state that to guard against the possibility of your name not being on the rolls for exchange I have written to Colonel Ludlow, agent for exchange of prisoners, to call his particular attention to your case which I hope will result in your speedy exchange.

Very respectfully, your obedient servant,

W. HOFFMAN,
Colonel Third Infantry, Commissary-General of Prisoners.

OFFICE COMMISSARY-GENERAL OF PRISONERS,
Washington, D. C., January 8, 1863.

Lieut. Col. W. H. LUDLOW,
Agent for Exchange of Prisoners, Fort Monroe, Va.

COLONEL: I have just received a note from Col. W. H. Lytle, Tenth Ohio Infantry, expressing great anxiety to be exchanged, and fearing that his name may not be on the rolls I call your attention to his case and I beg that you will not lose sight of it should the exchange of any officers [be] acted upon. He was captured at Perryville.

Very respectfully, your obedient servant,

W. HOFFMAN,
Colonel Third Infantry, Commissary-General of Prisoners.

OFFICE COMMISSARY-GENERAL OF PRISONERS,
Washington, D. C., January 8, 1863.

Asst. Surg. N. A. HURSAM,
Twentieth Maine Volunteers, Washington, D. C.

SIR: I am informed by Lieutenant-Colonel Ludlow, agent for exchange of prisoners, that it is understood between him and R. Ould, esq., agent for exchange on the part of the Confederate service, that all paroles exacted of medical officers in either army by subordinate commanders are null and void; the parole exacted of you by Major Fairfax, of the Confederate Army is therefore not binding and you will proceed to join your regiment without delay.

By order of the General-in-Chief:

Very respectfully, your obedient servant,

W. HOFFMAN,
Colonel Third Infantry, Commissary-General of Prisoners.

MADISON, WIS., *January 9, 1863.*

Hon. E. M. STANTON:

In the matter of *habeas corpus* of the Ozaukee County prisoners arrested and held in custody for resisting the draft the supreme court will make a decision on the 12th instant. Should they decide that the President has not the power to suspend the writ of *habeas corpus* or to punish by court-martial persons forcibly resisting the draft and should issue an attachment in order to enforce their decision shall I release the prisoners? If not released in such a case there may be collision between State and U. S. authorities. I have information of a confidential nature which warrants this dispatch and renders an early reply necessary.

W. L. ELLIOTT,
Brigadier-General, Commanding.

HEADQUARTERS EIGHTH ARMY CORPS,
Baltimore, Md., January 9, 1863.

Col. WILLIAM HOFFMAN,
Commissary-General of Prisoners, Washington, D. C.

COLONEL: A large number of persons are found bearing paroles similar to the inclosed. The persons who hold these paroles claim the privilege of going at large without restriction as long as they keep within the loyal States. This it will readily be seen might lead to great abuse and serve as a protection to spies and all kinds of disloyal persons and this too without the parties being detected in any misconduct or overt act which would authorize a revoking of the parole. The major-general commanding this department desires to know whether such paroles as these shall be regarded or shall the persons bearing them be arrested or sent beyond the Union lines? Please return the parole inclosed, which is an original taken from a person who has been arrested and is now in confinement until your decision is known.

I am, sir, very respectfully, your obedient servant,

WM. D. WHIPPLE,
Assistant Adjutant-General.

[Inclosure.]

OFFICE PROVOST-MARSHAL-GENERAL,
Camp near Sharpsburg, Md., September 27, 1862.

I, Victor Brand, private, Seventh Louisiana, prisoner of war, taken at battle of Antietam, do hereby request that I be not returned by exchange or upon parole, and I do give my parole of honor that I will not take up arms against the Government of the United States or in any manner give aid or information to its enemies or go within any of the States now in rebellion until released from this obligation by competent authority.

his
VICTOR x BRAND,
mark
Private, Seventh Louisiana.

Subscribed in presence of—
JAMES W. FORSYTH,
Captain and Acting Assistant Adjutant-General.

The above-named Victor Brand is permitted to proceed to and remain in any of the loyal States.

By command of the provost-marshal-general, Army of the Potomac:

JAMES W. FORSYTH,
Captain and Acting Assistant Adjutant-General.

OFFICE COMMISSARY-GENERAL OF PRISONERS,
Washington, D. C., January 9, 1863.

Maj. JOSEPH DARR, Jr.,
Provost-Marshal-General, Wheeling, Va.

MAJOR: Your letters of 24th and 25th ultimo in relation to Marian McKenzie were answered on the 30th ultimo but my letter was missent and I therefore rewrite it and inclose* it herewith, but do not release her until you have referred her case again with such charges as may be presented against her. I approve of your suggestion that Mary Jane Green should be placed in a house of refuge, and if there is one within reach where she will be received the Government paying for her board you are authorized to send her there, and you may make the same disposition of Marian McKenzie if she cannot be brought to trial as a spy and her character is like that of Mary Jane Green. Should you be unable to have them received at a house of refuge what are your means for holding them at Wheeling? I approve of your action in paroling Kate Brown.

Very respectfully, your obedient servant,

W. HOFFMAN,
Colonel Third Infantry, Commissary-General of Prisoners.

HEADQUARTERS DEPARTMENT OF VIRGINIA,
January 9, 1863.

Col. W. HOFFMAN, *Commissary-General of Prisoners.*

COLONEL: I have the honor to inclose to you the within declarations† of exchanges agreed upon by Robert Ould, esq., Confederate agent for exchange of prisoners, and myself at City Point, Va., on the 8th instant.

I am, very respectfully, your obedient servant,

WM. H. LUDLOW,
Lieutenant-Colonel and Agent for Exchange of Prisoners.

OFFICE PROVOST-MARSHAL-GENERAL,
Saint Louis, Mo., January 9, 1863.

Col. WILLIAM HOFFMAN,
Commissary-General of Prisoners, Washington, D. C.

COLONEL: I have the honor of transmitting for your consideration the following extract from a letter received from J. B. Douglass, colonel commanding Sixty-first Regiment Enrolled Missouri Militia, Columbus, Mo., under date of December 29, 1862:

I wish to know whether John T. Singleton has been released as he was in my county a few days since. He was an officer in Price's army and a very bad and dangerous man. He once made his escape from Alton and was rearrested at Liberty, in this State. I know him well. He is a bad man and should not be set at liberty. Let me hear from you at your earliest opportunity in this case. For God's sake do not let out the worst men and keep the poor ignorant boys in prison.

I will say that I am personally acquainted with Colonel Douglass and can vouch for his integrity and patriotism. His statements are worthy of credence. Colonel Hildebrand, commanding post at Alton, writes me January 5 that Singleton was released upon your order on the 6th of September or 1st of November and that some ninety others were discharged about the same time. It is important for me to know if prisoners at Alton who have been sent from this office before I came into it are liable to be released by order from Washington without first notifying me. If so it will be necessary for me at once to send you the charges or evidence against such prisoners, for pretended Union men from Missouri are constantly applying for the release of bad rebels. I

---

* See p. 130.   † See General Orders, No. 10, January 10, p. 169.

would respectfully suggest that applications for such release should be referred to this office before being acted upon, otherwise such men as Singleton may be released upon the belief that they are worthy of it. I ask that you will instruct Colonel Hildebrand to report immediately to this office all released from the Alton Prison, and that also all released from Sandusky of Missouri prisoners be reported here. I am often embarrassed for the want of such information.

I am, colonel, very respectfully, your obedient servant,

F. A. DICK,
Lieut. Col. and Provost-Marshal-General, Dept. of the Missouri.

SPECIAL FIELD ORDERS, ⎰ HDQRS. DEPT. OF THE CUMBERLAND,
    No. 6.   ⎱ *Murfreesborough, Tenn., January 9, 1863.*

*   *   *   *   *   *   *

XIII. To insure proper care of the Confederate sick and wounded within our lines Surgeon Avent, C. S. Army, is appointed medical director for them. All Confederate and other surgeons employed in care of their sick in hospitals and private houses and all citizens having Confederate sick or wounded in either case will promptly report their location, names, number and condition to Surgeon Avent, and will be held responsible for their care and conformity to his orders or the orders of our military authorities. No medical men, nurses or invalids will leave their hospitals or places without his permission, and none will be removed without written application sanctioned by him and approved by the medical director of our army. All nurses or patients leaving without such permission will be treated as deserters and medical officers violating these orders will be severely punished. Needful supplies will be issued on requisitions sanctioned or submitted by Surgeon Avent and approved by authority of the medical director of this army. Surgeon Avent will furnish with the least possible delay lists of the Confederate sick and wounded within our lines, and morning reports of the nurses and sick certified to on honor as the basis on which he makes his requisitions. He will promptly report for negligence or disobedience of orders all delinquent medical officers and others under his control. These regulations being for the good of those whom it concerns the general commanding trusts they will be fully and cheerfully complied with.

*   *   *   *   *   *   *

By command of Major-General Rosecrans:

HENRY STONE,
Lieutenant and Acting Assistant Adjutant-General.

GENERAL ORDERS, ⎰ HEADQUARTERS EIGHTH ARMY CORPS,
    No. 3.   ⎱ *Baltimore, Md., January 9, 1863.*

In all cases when the troops of this army corps are captured by the enemy and paroled the senior officer present shall cause to be prepared and forwarded to the office of the commissary-general of prisoners at Washington with as little delay as practicable a full list by regiments and companies of all so paroled, giving the name, rank, regiment and company of each person, the time and place of capture and the disposition made of them. Like rolls shall be prepared and furnished to the same office of all rebel prisoners captured by our forces. When the circumstances are such that a roll cannot be immediately prepared a written report giving the number of officers and men, the time and place of capture and the disposition made of them shall be forwarded followed by the necessary rolls at the earliest practicable moment.

By command of Major-General Schenck:

WM. D. WHIPPLE,
Assistant Adjutant-General.

WAR DEPARTMENT, *Washington, January 10, 1863.*
Major-General WRIGHT, *Cincinnati:*

*   *   *   *   *   *   *

All our paroled prisoners taken prior to December 10 are declared exchanged. Get them back to their regiments in the field as rapidly as possible.

H. W HALLECK,
General-in-Chief.

HEADQUARTERS U. S. PAROLED FORCES,
Columbus, Ohio, January 10, 1863.
Col. W. HOFFMAN, *Commissary-General of Prisoners.*

SIR: In reply to your communication of the 29th ultimo I beg leave to state that rolls of Kentucky Home Guards are being made out and will be forwarded to you as soon as completed. The reason that a reply to your communication has been deferred is that parties reporting here as paroled prisoners are without descriptive lists or any evidence whatever of their being in the service. The consequence is that an examination, often difficult, is required to ascertain from whence they came and where they belong. This has been the case with prisoners belonging to the Kentucky Home Guards referred to in your late communication. Your suggestions relative to furnishing you with lists of the paroled prisoners will be complied with. I would respectfully call your attention to what cannot be regarded otherwise than an abuse. I refer to the fact that exchanged prisoners from Camp Parole (Annapolis) belonging to regiments in West Virginia frequently arrive here after having gone to Louisville or other places on the Ohio from whence they have been sent here. They arrive here without descriptive lists or any evidence of their connection with the service, demanding transportation to their regiments after having taken the roundabout trip above stated. The want of care in giving this class of prisoners a proper direction in the first instance is not only productive of a useless expense to the Government but often of great hardship and inconvenience to the prisoners themselves, who are often without means to supply themselves with subsistence. If this evil could be corrected it would subserve the interests of the Government and the convenience of the prisoners exchanged.

I have the honor to be, very respectfully, your obedient servant,

WM. VON DOEHN,
Assistant Adjutant-General to General Cooper.

WHEELING, VA., *January 10, 1863.*
DIRECTORS HOUSE OF REFUGE, *Cincinnati.*

GENTLEMEN: The Government desires to place in an institution similar to your own two female prisoners over the age of twenty, one charged with destroying the telegraph line in Western Virginia, the other with frequenting our camps in male attire—it is supposed in the character of a spy. The object is to hold them until the rebellion is crushed and in the meantime place them at work. Please advise me whether you can receive them and hold them at the expense of the Government. It is desired if possible to reform these creatures.

Very respectfully,

JOS. DARR, JR.,
Major and Provost-Marshal-General.

HEADQUARTERS ARMY OF THE POTOMAC,
Office Provost-Marshal-General, January 10, 1863.

Col. W. HOFFMAN, *Commissary-General of Prisoners.*

COLONEL: Concerning the subject-matter of your letter of the 7th ultimo to Col. E. D. Townsend, assistant adjutant-general, a copy of which has been referred to this office, General Patrick wishes me to say that all paroled U. S. soldiers who have been returned to the Federal lines since the army has been upon the Rappahannock have been forwarded to you under proper conduct, together with all the rolls and records pertaining to them made out in accordance with existing regulations excepting men perhaps who eluded the restraints necessarily put upon them, such probably having made their way to Washington individually without orders. In the event of your having failed to receive any of the requisite documents relating to paroled soldiers sent from this office you are requested to state what is missing. General Patrick wishes me to call your attention to the fact that it has become a common form of desertion in this army to forge parole certificates. By means of these men straggle off or rather desert to parole camps where too frequently their claims are recognized. So far as this office is informed no U. S. soldiers of this army have been liberated by the enemy on parole without individual certificates of parole excepting those paroled at Fredericksburg, whose original parole papers were passed over to this office and upon the 28th ultimo forwarded to you. At this office the word of no man claiming to be paroled is taken unless he produce a certificate of parole and usually his statement is referred to his officers for an official report in his case. Several cases of desertion under false parole claims have recently come to the notice of this office and the men have been punished accordingly, while it is known that many deserters of this description have succeeded in making their way by land to Alexandria and Washington.

Very respectfully, your obedient servant,

J. P. KIMBALL,
Assistant Adjutant-General.

GENERAL ORDERS, ⎰ WAR DEPT., ADJT. GENERAL'S OFFICE,
No. 10. ⎱ *Washington, January 10, 1863.*

I. The following officers and men have been declared duly exchanged as prisoners of war since the announcement in General Orders, No. 191, of November 19, 1862:

1. All the officers and enlisted men who were delivered at City Point, Va., from the 11th of November, 1862, to the 1st of January, 1863.

2. All officers and enlisted men captured at Harper's Ferry.

3. All officers and enlisted men paroled at Winchester November 15 and 26, 1862, and December 1, 1862.

4. All officers and enlisted men paroled by Colonel Imboden November 9, 1862.

5. All officers and enlisted men paroled at Goldsborough, N. C., May 22, 1862, and delivered at Washington, N. C.

6. All captures of officers, enlisted men and camp followers in Missouri, Kansas, Arkansas, New Mexico, Texas, Arizona and Louisiana up to January 1, 1863.

7. All captures of officers, enlisted men and camp followers in Kentucky, Tennessee, Mississippi, Alabama, South Carolina and Florida up to December 10, 1862.

8. All captures on the sea, the sea and Gulf coasts and the waters flowing into the same up to December 10, 1862.

II. The paroled troops herein declared to be exchanged will be without delay equipped for the field and forwarded to the armies to which they belong from posts or camps wherever they may be collected. All officers and enlisted men absent in virtue of being on parole will now that they are exchanged immediately return to duty with their proper commands.

By order of the Secretary of War:

E. D. TOWNSEND,
Assistant Adjutant-General.

MURFREESBOROUGH, *January 11, 1863.*

Hon. EDWIN M. STANTON, *Secretary of War:*

The crimes of spying, murder, arson, rape and others as well as desertion are increasing, and the power to check them by inflicting the penalty of death is a nullity, for by the delays necessary to get them a regular trial by general court-martial and then holding them until the matter is reviewed and approved by the President such a time elapses that the troops are relieved and the culprit escapes. This ought to be remedied.

W. S. ROSECRANS,
Major-General.

HEADQUARTERS DEPARTMENT OF THE CUMBERLAND,
Murfreesborough, January 11, 1863.

Lieut. FRANCIS BRADY.

LIEUTENANT: You appeared at our picket-lines on a side road bearing a white flag and conducting two ladies who you say wished to enter our lines.

You produce an order or what purports to be an order from John W. Green, acting assistant adjutant general of Morgan's division, to Captain Quirk, commanding a company of scouts at Liberty, to send the ladies under a flag of truce to Murfreesborough.

Under the laws of war you and your party are arrested as spies and will be held for trial.

A feeling of humanity and your appearance and statements, however, induce the general commanding the department to permit you to return to General Morgan and procure such testimony as you can to relieve you from the position in which you are placed.

General Rosecrans desires me to state to you: First, a flag of truce is a solemn public embassy sent for important purposes of war or humanity by the superior commanders of opposing forces and duly accredited by the sender. No subordinate can send a flag of truce nor can it pursue any by or side road. Second, any one using a flag of truce otherwise is liable to be denied the privileges of civilized soldiers in battle and those who carry the flag to be treated as spies.

General Morgan ought to know this. It has been the subject of correspondence between General Rosecrans and General Bragg. General Bragg informed General Rosecrans before General Morgan was married that he had already given orders in reference to this matter. General Rosecrans therefore desires me to say to you that if under these circumstances by going to General Morgan's headquarters you can produce any evidence that will relieve you from the charge and save you from the fate of a spy you may go on your parole to return in three days and bring with you such sworn and other testimony as you may be able to procure.

I am, lieutenant, very respectfully, your obedient servant,

G. P. THRUSTON,
Captain and Acting Aide-de-Camp.

OFFICE COMMISSARY-GENERAL OF PRISONERS,
Washington, January 12, 1863.

Brig. Gen. M. R. PATRICK,
Provost-Marshal-General, Army of the Potomac, Falmouth, Va.

GENERAL: I have the honor to acknowledge the receipt of your letter of the 7th instant, and I must express my regret that there has been so much neglect in forwarding exchanged troops from the camp at Annapolis to your headquarters. It shall be remedied. I required that they should be sent under the command of the senior officer by water and that as complete rolls as possible by regiments should be sent with them. After consulting with the Adjutant-General at Army Headquarters it was deemed not advisable to furnish the detachments with arms and equipments because regiments in the field are generally encumbered with surplus arms, and as the number of men to a regiment rarely exceeds fifty, generally much less, it was thought there would be no difficulty in equipping them after joining. To carry out your wishes in this particular it will be necessary to put in force at Annapolis the order issued for Camp Banks, and I respectfully urge that officers be sent from the Army of the Potomac for this service. Guards were not ordered to accompany the detachment because I assumed that not being prisoners they would be conducted by their officers as all other troops are, but if a guard had been necessary there were no troops at Annapolis to furnish it. I inclose herewith a copy* of a letter just received from the commanding officer at Camp Parole, Annapolis, reporting the condition of paroled prisoners just arrived from Richmond, Va., and this is only a repetition of what has been done before more than once. It is a matter of great difficulty to force officers in charge of such commands to perform their duty properly. Instructions however specific are of little avail.

I am, very respectfully, your obedient servant,

W. HOFFMAN,
Colonel Third Infantry, Commissary-General of Prisoners.

---

* Not found.

OFFICE COMMISSARY-GENERAL OF PRISONERS,
Washington, D. C., January 12, 1863.

Brig. Gen. W. L. ELLIOTT,
Commanding Department of the Northwest, Madison, Wis.

GENERAL: In reply to your letter of the 5th instant addressed to General Hitchcock I have the honor to inform you that the exchange of all prisoners taken in Arkansas up to January, 1863, will be announced in orders in a few days.

I am, general, very respectfully, your obedient servant,

W. HOFFMAN,
Colonel Third Infantry, Commissary-General of Prisoners.

OFFICE COMMISSARY-GENERAL OF PRISONERS,
Washington, D. C., January 12, 1863.

Lieut. Col. GEORGE SANGSTER,
Commanding Camp Parole, Annapolis, Md.

COLONEL: I inclose herewith a letter* just received from General Patrick, provost-marshal-general of the Army of the Potomac, from which you will see that there has been great neglect somewhere in forwarding exchanged troops from your camp to the Army of the Potomac, and I desire immediately a report from you showing the manner in which the detachments forwarded by you were organized and the instructions for their conduct given to the officer in charge. My letter of the 11th December gave sufficiently definite instructions to you. Parties of the same army were to be placed under the command of the senior officer and as complete rolls as possible by regiments were to be furnished. By telegram I directed they should be sent by water. If these instructions were not carried out please explain why. A statement of all payments and issues of clothing made at your camp should accompany each detachment. About this there can be no difficulty as it is all on your own records, and any other information should be given which the records received with the men contain. Instructions will be sent to you in relation to furnishing arms and equipments for exchanged troops. Your weekly report does not show the number of troops present exchanged nor the number on parole. Let these numbers be given in each report. Send by mail the numbers for last week. Learn from the men themselves to what corps they belong.

Very respectfully, your obedient servant,

W. HOFFMAN,
Colonel Third Infantry, Commissary-General of Prisoners.

FORT MONROE, *January 12, 1863.*

Colonel HOFFMAN:

The declarations of exchange include all prisoners of war and camp followers but not political prisoners.

WM. H. LUDLOW,
Lieutenant-Colonel and Agent for Exchange of Prisoners.

GENERAL ORDERS, }   HEADQUARTERS ARMY OF KENTUCKY,
No. 5.   }   *Lexington, Ky., January 12, 1863.*

The general commanding is reminded by the number of inquiries addressed to him on the subject that a variety of opinions exist in the

---

* Omitted here; see Patrick to Hoffman, January 7, p. 160.

minds of provost-marshals and others within this command as to the proper treatment of soldiers discharged from the rebel service and of those whose term of enlistment has expired. Inquiries have also been made as to the treatment of captured soldiers and officers of the rebel army and as to the effect in certain causes of administering the oath of allegiance. To set at rest such inquiries and to secure uniformity of action in these particulars for the future the following instructions are issued. They will be hereafter strictly observed within the limits of the Military District of Central Kentucky:

I. When the oath of allegiance has been taken and sufficient bonds entered into the loyalty of the party may under ordinary circumstances be regarded as sufficiently well assured. But taking the oath and giving bond will not be regarded as furnishing an indemnity for past offenses, and overt acts such as taking up arms against the Government or engaging in military service of the enemy although previously committed may nevertheless be inquired into and punished, except where upon fair investigation the party has once been discharged by the major-general commanding this army or by superior authority.

II. Captured soldiers of the rebel army and persons other than officers in the military service of the so-called Government of the Confederate States will if they are not deserters from our own service and do not from their conduct or the circumstances of their capture deserve the treatment of spies be treated as prisoners of war and forwarded to Vicksburg, Miss., for exchange. To such persons it will not be proper to administer the oath of allegiance. They will be treated as prisoners of war and when they have taken such oath will if in custody of a proper officer be released from its obligations provided the case has not been passed upon by authority superior to that of the major-general commanding this army. Captured officers of the rebel army will, however, be kept in confinement and neither paroled nor forwarded for exchange until further orders.

III. Officers and soldiers discharged from the rebel service and those whose term of enlistment has expired will be arrested unless they have once been set at liberty upon the charge by authority of the general commanding this army or some superior officer, and will be kept in custody until a report in each case has been made to these headquarters and action taken thereon. In these cases the oath of allegiance will not be administered unless orders to that effect are received, but if such oath has already been taken the fact will be stated in the report.

IV. As to deserters from the rebel service and others named in General Orders, No. 36, from these headquarters, a plain rule of action has been furnished. They will report here. That order, however, applies only to such as had not been when it was issued already passed upon and disposed of.

V. Where the bond for the observance of an oath of allegiance is not a sufficient security the oath will be readministered and a new bond taken in a sufficient amount and with sufficient sureties.

VI. Provost-marshals and officers acting in that capacity within the limits of this command will report at once to these headquarters the names of all persons now in their custody with the charge against them. This report will also include a list of the cases disposed of since November 17, 1862, with a statement of the disposition made in each case.

VII. Semi-monthly reports will be hereafter sent from provost-marshals and those acting as such upon the first and fifteenth days of every month. Such reports will be arranged in tabular form, containing, first, the names of prisoners; second, their rank, company and regiment if in military service; third, the time and place of their capture, and fourth, the disposition made in the second cases, with the date of such disposition.

In all cases where prisoners are forwarded for exchange or sent under custody beyond the limits of the State reports similarly arranged will be at once forwarded to these headquarters.

By order of Maj. Gen. Gordon Granger:

WM. C. RUSSELL,
Captain and Assistant Adjutant-General.

GENERAL ORDERS, }   HDQRS. DEPARTMENT OF THE GULF,
No. 9.   *New Orleans, January 12, 1863.*

I. Any person registered as a public enemy of the United States within this department will be permitted to withdraw such designation and description upon taking the oath of allegiance, and any person who may have been unable to take the oath within the time prescribed by previous orders will upon satisfactory proof of the facts be admitted to that privilege upon application to the provost-marshal general.

II. All commanding officers of this department who have captured or who shall capture prisoners of war are directed to make duplicate lists thereof, giving whenever possible the name, rank, company, regiment and brigade of each prisoner, the place and time of capture and the name of the officer by whom captured. One copy of the list will be sent to the provost-marshal-general and the other will be sent to these headquarters through the proper channels.

III. It is provided by the general cartel of exchange adopted July 22, 1862, "that all prisoners of whatever arm of service are to be exchanged or paroled in ten days from the time of the capture if it be practicable to transfer them within their own lines in that time; if not as soon after as practicable."

IV. Commanding officers will give attention to the comfort and health of prisoners of war while they remain in their charge.

By command of Major-General Banks:

RICHARD B. IRWIN,
Lieutenant-Colonel and Assistant Adjutant-General.

MADISON, WIS., *January 13, 1863.*

Hon. EDWIN M. STANTON, *Secretary of War:*

In the *habeas corpus* cases of the Ozaukee County prisoners the supreme court, consisting of loyal and patriotic judges, has just decided that the President has not the power to suspend the writ of *habeas corpus* in Wisconsin nor to declare martial law therein to subject persons resisting the draft to trial by court-martial. I recommend therefore that the prisoners be discharged to avoid a conflict between the civil and military authorities. Please order General Elliott immediately to discharge them. Answer immediately.

EDWD. SALOMON,
Governor of Wisconsin.

OFFICE COMMISSARY-GENERAL OF PRISONERS,
Washington, D. C., January 13, 1863.

Hon. GIDEON WELLES,
Secretary of the Navy, Washington, D. C.

SIR: I have the honor to inform you that at the recent meeting of the agents for the exchange of prisoners of war it was declared that all captures on the sea, the sea and gulf coasts and waters flowing to the same up to December 10, 1862, are duly exchanged.

I have the honor to be, very respectfully, your obedient servant,

W. HOFFMAN,
Colonel Third Infantry, Commissary-General of Prisoners.

OFFICE COMMISSARY-GENERAL OF PRISONERS,
Washington, D. C., January 13, 1863.

Brig. Gen. M. R. PATRICK,
Provost-Marshal-General, Army of the Potomac, Falmouth, Va.

GENERAL: I have the honor to inclose herewith copies of the orders* under which exchanged troops were sent from the camp near Annapolis to the Army of the Potomac. You will see that they were all sent by water to Aquia Creek and that proper rolls were sent with them. The colonel commanding the camp informs me that he sent all the descriptive rolls he had with the dates of payments to the commanders of the regiments. The orders should have required the commander of the detachment to conduct it to the headquarters of the Army of the Potomac as I directed, but the omission was certainly not a sufficient excuse for the negligent manner in which the duty was performed. If there was a commander at Aquia Creek he should have seen that they were properly forwarded from there. Colonel Sangster should have detailed officers of higher rank to command the 430 men under Lieutenant Barker. That no guard was furnished was not a neglect for there was no guard at the camp available; and if there had been as I have before said I would not have deemed it necessary to send a guard with soldiers who were not prisoners. They should have furnished their own guard, and with officers of any energy this would have been sufficient. The great neglect it would appear was in the commander of the detachments and if such is the case you will know what steps to take.

I am, general, very respectfully, your obedient servant,

W. HOFFMAN,
Colonel Third Infantry, Commissary-General of Prisoners.

OFFICE COMMISSARY-GENERAL OF PRISONERS,
Washington, D. C., January 13, 1863.

Brig. Gen. JAMES COOPER,
Commanding Camp Chase, Columbus, Ohio.

GENERAL: I have the honor to give below a copy of a telegram this day addressed to you:

All troops captured and paroled in Kentucky, Tennessee, Mississippi, Alabama, South Carolina and Florida up to 10th December are exchanged. Those at Camp Chase will be prepared for the field without delay; then they will be mustered and paid before marching. Call in all absentees.

By order of the General-in-Chief.

A general order will be published in a few days announcing the exchanges recently made which will direct that all exchanged troops will be prepared for the field and forwarded to their several commands without delay. Where troops were mustered for pay on the 31st ultimo no other muster is necessary, but the payment will not be made till

---

* Not found; but see Patrick to Hoffman, with inclosure, pp. 160, 161.

they are ready to march. Fragments of companies not heretofore mustered will be mustered for pay to 31st December.

I am, general, very respectfully, your obedient servant,

W. HOFFMAN,
Colonel Third Infantry, Commissary-General of Prisoners.

(Copies to Col. B. L. E. Bonneville, commanding Benton Barracks, Saint Louis, Mo.; Brig. Gen. J. Ammen, commanding Camp Douglas, Chicago, Ill.)

OFFICE COMMISSARY-GENERAL OF PRISONERS,
Washington, D. C., January 13, 1863.

General J. H. MARTINDALE,
Military Governor of Washington.

GENERAL: In reply to the matter of transportation for the deserters from the rebel army referred by you to the Secretary of War I have the honor to say that as these men have been recognized as deserters and have been set at liberty they are placed on the same footing with other citizens and must provide for their own necessities by their labor.

By order of the Secretary of War:

Very respectfully, your obedient servant,

W. HOFFMAN,
Colonel Third Infantry, Commissary-General of Prisoners.

OFFICE COMMISSARY-GENERAL OF PRISONERS,
Washington, D. C., January 13, 1863.

Col. E. D. TOWNSEND, *Assistant Adjutant-General.*

COLONEL: All the paroled troops in the West captured previous to the 10th December are embraced in the recent exchanges, and I respectfully request that they be assembled and prepared for the field at Camp Chase, Camp Douglas and Benton Barracks and that they be there mustered and paid before marching.

Very respectfully, your obedient servant,

W. HOFFMAN,
Colonel Third Infantry, Commissary-General of Prisoners.

HEADQUARTERS ARMY OF THE MISSISSIPPI,
Post Arkansas, January 14, 1863.

Maj. Gen. U. S. GRANT,
Commanding Department of the Tennessee.

GENERAL: I have all the prisoners embarked for Saint Louis, Mo. My reasons for sending them are these: First, I have received no orders to exchange them; second, the headquarters of the commissioner for the exchange of prisoners is there; third, it would seem to me criminal to send the prisoners to Vicksburg if they may be properly sent elsewhere. To send them there would be to re-enforce a place with several thousand prisoners at the moment we are trying to reduce it. I would sail from here to Little Rock and reduce that place but for want of sufficient water in the channel of the Arkansas River. This being the case I will proceed as soon as I have completed the demolition of the enemy's works here to Napoleon, by which time I hope to hear from you.

Your obedient servant,   JOHN A. McCLERNAND,
Major-General, Commanding.

HEADQUARTERS DEPARTMENT OF THE OHIO,
Cincinnati, January 14, 1863.

Hon. E. M. STANTON, *Secretary of War, Washington, D. C.*

SIR: In compliance with the instructions contained in your letter of the 8th ultimo I have the honor to forward herewith a list* prepared from the records at these headquarters of the citizens of Kentucky who have been and are now confined in the military prisons and camps of the United States outside of the limits of said State, with a statement of the charge against them, by whom made and by whose order the arrests were made. I also forward herewith official copies of General Boyle's letter of the 8th instant and letter of Col. Henry Dent, provost-marshal-general of Kentucky, as report made in regard to prisoners sent from said State and now held in prison.

I am, sir, very respectfully, your obedient servant,

H. G. WRIGHT,
Major-General, Commanding.

[Inclosure No. 1.]

HEADQUARTERS DISTRICT OF WESTERN KENTUCKY,
Louisville, January 8, 1863.

Maj. Gen. H. G. WRIGHT,
Commanding Department of the Ohio, Cincinnati, Ohio.

GENERAL: I inclose letter of Col. Henry Dent, provost-marshal-general of Kentucky, as report made in regard to prisoners, &c., sent from Kentucky and now held in prison. Colonel Dent has been provost-marshal-general in this place since the beginning of the war. It is impossible to make any detailed report. Some of the prisoners were sent by order of military commanders at Lexington, Covington, Cynthiana, Henderson, &c., and by U. S. commissioners and U. S. marshals, of which no report ever reached these headquarters or the provost-marshal-general. I believe there are but few citizens if any held as civil or political prisoners. There are a number held as prisoners of war. The whole subject as connected with prisoners of all classes has been intrusted to the provost-marshal-general and under orders received and issued by me he has administered this department of duty with prudence and wisdom. The information desired can much more readily be obtained at the several prisons in the different States to which they have been sent.

I am, very respectfully, your obedient servant,

J. T. BOYLE,
Brigadier-General.

[Inclosure No. 2.]

HDQRS. PROVOST-MARSHAL-GENERAL OF KENTUCKY,
Louisville, Ky., January 5, 1863.

Brigadier-General BOYLE,
Commanding District of Western Kentucky.

GENERAL: In compliance with your directions please find response to inquiry made by the Senate of the United States, under resolution of the 5th of December, 1862, calling on the President of the United States, if not incompatible with the public service, to report the number and names of citizens of Kentucky who have been and who are now confined in the military prisons and camps of the United States

---

* Omitted.

outside of the State of Kentucky. I find on examination of the records in my office that all prisoners forwarded to camps outside of this State from this city and vicinity and all papers and charges were sent with said prisoners. Consequently it will not be in my power to give the desired information. Most of the prisoners forwarded were sent here by commanding generals, post commanders, U. S. commissioners and provost-marshals together with the charges, and forwarded as directed by the commanding general of this department. The records of Camp Chase, Camp Morton and Camp Douglas will give the names and charges of all citizens sent from this post. Not expecting to be called on for such a statement no complete record was kept in this office.

I am, general, very respectfully, your obedient servant,

HENRY DENT,
Colonel and Provost-Marshal-General of Kentucky.

CITY POINT, VA., *January 14, 1863.*

Hon. ROBERT OULD, *Agent for Exchange of Prisoners.*

SIR: May I have the pleasure of an early as possible interview with you? I desire to know whether in compliance with the terms of the cartel the commissioned U. S. officers now in your hands are to be released, and also what disposition has been made of the case of Mrs. Piggott who was taken from her home at Williamsburg, Va., with forty of her slaves and who is now detained at Richmond or some other place within the Confederate lines.

Major General Dix some time since communicated with you on this case. He has received pressing applications to retaliate by the arrest and imprisonment of ladies within our lines whose avowed sentiments and conduct have been persistently disloyal to the United States Government: Can you not have this matter arranged by the prompt return of Mrs. Piggott and all her property to her home?

I am, very respectfully, your obedient servant,

WM. H. LUDLOW,
Lieutenant-Colonel and Agent for Exchange of Prisoners.

OFFICE COMMISSARY-GENERAL OF PRISONERS,
Washington, D. C., January 14, 1863.

Col. E. D. TOWNSEND,
Assistant Adjutant-General, U. S. Army, Washington, D. C.

COLONEL: I am directed by the commissary-general of prisoners to inform you that there never have been received in this office the rolls of Federal prisoners of war delivered at Washington and Tarborough, N. C., and who were sent from those points to New Berne. They are designated in paragraph IV, of General Orders, No. 118, War Department, August 27, 1862, as the deliveries to General Burnside at Hatteras and Fort Macon. The commissary-general of prisoners respectfully requests that if these lists are in the office of the Adjutant-General they may as soon as convenient be sent to this office.

Very respectfully, your obedient servant,

H. M. LAZELLE,
Captain, U. S. Army, Asst. to Com. Gen. of Prisoners.

WAR DEPARTMENT, *Washington, January 15, 1863.*
Brigadier-General ELLIOTT, *Madison, Wis.*:

The questions presented on the *habeas corpus* have been referred by the President to the law officer of the Government with a view to procuring the judgment of the Supreme Court of the United States. As soon as this opinion can be had you will receive instructions, but in the meantime the President directs that you retain the prisoners until you receive further instructions from him.

EDWIN M. STANTON,
Secretary of War.

OFFICE COMMISSARY-GENERAL OF PRISONERS,
Washington, D. C., January 15, 1863.
Lieut. Col. F. A. DICK,
Provost-Marshal-General, Saint Louis, Mo.

COLONEL: Your letter of the 9th instant with the accompanying letter* of Mr. Bradley has been received. The latter has been referred to the President according to your indorsement thereon. In reply to your letter of the 9th instant† I have to say that the prisoner (Singleton) referred to by you was released under a general order from the War Department which directed the release of all military prisoners who were willing to take the oath of allegiance under the instructions which I have heretofore given. All prisoners sent to Alton whose cases are under investigation are entirely beyond your control, and in order that their cases may be well understood at the prisons where they are held it is important that a full history of each individual case should be sent with them when they are transferred from Saint Louis. Nothing of the kind has heretofore been done and to supply this deficiency which has been much felt in determining on applications for release I some time since ordered Captain Freedley to Alton and Saint Louis to obtain the charges, trial and sentence of all prisoners now held at any of the prisons above named. When a prisoner is transferred from Saint Louis to another prison this fact noted on your books closes his history with you.

Very respectfully, your obedient servant,
W. HOFFMAN,
Colonel Third Infantry, Commissary-General of Prisoners.

WASHINGTON, *January 15, 1863.*
Lieut. Col. W. H. LUDLOW, *Agent for Exchange of Prisoners.*

Is the declaration of exchanges published in the Herald of 13th, signed R. Ould, correct? Are sutlers and their employés now on parole considered exchanged?

W. HOFFMAN,
Commissary-General of Prisoners.

ALTON MILITARY PRISON, *Alton, Ill., January 15, 1863.*
Col. W. HOFFMAN, *Commissary-General of Prisoners.*

COLONEL: Nearly 800 prisoners who were sent to Vicksburg for exchange but could not be landed there owing to the recent fight at

---

*Not found.   † See p. 166.

that point were returned to this prison and many of them (nearly or quite fifty) do not wish to be exchanged but would prefer being sent home and enroll themselves in the militia of the State of Missouri, in which State they formerly lived. Others would prefer taking the oath of allegiance and give bonds in any amount reasonable not to aid or abet by word or act the rebellion. We therefore refer the matter to you for instruction.

Your obedient servant,

J. HILDEBRAND,
Colonel, Commanding Post.

MEMPHIS, TENN., *January 16, 1863.*

Maj. Gen. SAMUEL R. CURTIS,
Commanding Department of the Missouri, Saint Louis, Mo.

I was just starting down the river to join the Mississippi expedition when I met some steamers loaded with prisoners ordered by Major-General Sherman to Saint Louis. I find no dispatches to myself and do not know what there may be directed to you. As I am leaving Memphis and can make no orders for the disposal of these prisoners I hope you will have the kindness to take charge of them and communicate with the General-in-Chief as to their final disposition. You can state that the last prisoners sent to Vicksburg were refused by the Southern commander there. I have received instructions from Washington that no more commissioned officers are to be paroled. This I presume is in retaliation for the course pursued by Southern authorities toward our prisoners.

U. S. GRANT,
Major-General.

P. S.—The probable reason the last prisoners were not received at Vicksburg was in consequence of the attack having commenced before their arrival. I am opposed to sending any more prisoners to Vicksburg just at this time, however, if I knew they would be received because they would go at once to re-enforce the very point we wish to reduce.

OFFICE COMMISSARY-GENERAL OF PRISONERS,
Washington, January 16, 1863.

Lieut. Col. GEORGE SANGSTER,
Commanding Camp Parole, Annapolis, Md.

COLONEL: The following paroled troops have been exchanged, viz: All officers and enlisted men delivered at City Point, Va., from November 11, 1862, to January 1, 1863; all officers and men captured at Harper's Ferry; all officers and men paroled at Winchester, Va., November 15 and 26 and December 1, 1862; all officers and men paroled by Colonel Imboden November 9, 1862, and all officers and men paroled at Goldsborough, N. C., May 22, 1862, and delivered at Washington, N. C.

These and other exchanges will be announced in orders in a few days, and in the meantime you will equip for the field without delay all of the paroled troops at your camp covered by the above exchanges. They may now be ordered to any duty.

Make requisitions immediately for arms and equipments and for clothing if necessary.

Very respectfully, your obedient servant,

W. HOFFMAN,
Colonel Third Infantry, Commissary-General of Prisoners.

HEADQUARTERS DEPARTMENT OF VIRGINIA,
Fort Monroe, Va., January 16, 1863.

Major-General HITCHCOCK,
Commissioner for the Exchange of Prisoners.

GENERAL: I have the honor to inclose to you a copy of the Richmond Enquirer* containing Jeff. Davis' message. His determination avowed in most insolent terms to deliver to the several State authorities all commissioned officers of the United States that may hereafter be captured will I think be persevered in. You will recollect that after the proclamation of Jeff. Davis of the 23d of December, 1862, I urgently advised another interview (the last one I had with Mr. Ould and in which very important exchanges were declared). I then did so anticipating that the cartel might be broken and wishing to make sure of the discharge from their parole of 10,000 of our men. This was effected, and in a manner so advantageous to our Government that we gained in the count of 20,000 exchanged about 7,000 men. I had almost equal good success in the exchange declared on November 11, 1862. If an open rupture should now occur in the execution of the cartel we are all well prepared for it. I am endeavoring to get away from Confederate prisons all our officers captured previously to the date of the message of Jeff. Davis (the 12th instant), with what success I shall know early next week.

As you may receive this copy of the message in advance of any other may I ask that it be transmitted to the Secretary of War or the General-in-Chief with the additional information conveyed in this communication to you.

I am, very respectfully, your obedient servant,

WM. H. LUDLOW,
Lieutenant-Colonel and Agent for Exchange of Prisoners.

FORT MONROE, *January 16, 1863.*

Col. W. HOFFMAN, *Commissary-General of Prisoners.*

The declaration of exchanges published by Robert Ould is on his side, not ours, and does not apply to our officers and men. The declarations I gave you are correct. All sutlers and their employés are exchanged.

WM. H. LUDLOW,
Lieutenant-Colonel and Agent for Exchange of Prisoners.

FORT MONROE, VA., *January 16, 1863.*

Col. J. C. KELTON, *Assistant Adjutant-General:*

About 1,000 Murfreesborough prisoners are at Richmond. Shall they be received without the officers? The flag-of-truce boat is awaiting your direction.

WM. H. LUDLOW,
Colonel, &c.

WAR DEPARTMENT, *Washington, January 16, 1863.*

Lieut. Col. WILLIAM H. LUDLOW,
Agent for Exchange of Prisoners, Fort Monroe:

Receive the Murfreesborough prisoners with or without the officers. By order of Major-General Halleck:

J. C. KELTON,
Assistant Adjutant-General.

---

* Of January 15, 1863. See p. 193, for extract from the message, in Hitchcock to Stanton.

ON BOARD STEAM-BOAT HASTINGS, *January 16, 1863.*

Major-General ROSECRANS,
        Commanding Department of the Cumberland.

SIR: Agreeably to instructions received from Major Sidell by telegraph dated Nashville, January 13, 1863, a copy of which is hereto attached, I beg to state that I was one of the passengers aboard the steamer Hastings (in Government employ transporting wounded men from Nashville to Louisville) on the 13th instant, the day she was fired into by a party of rebel guerrillas of General Wheeler's cavalry brigade, under command of Colonel Wade. The Hastings had on board 212 wounded soldiers under charge of Surgeon Waterman, with instructions to report the same at Louisville. The Hastings left Nashville without any convoy. On nearing Harpeth Shoals we saw the burning hull of the steamer Charter, opposite a group of some half dozen or more small houses that had also been burned. A short distance below a fleet of six steamers were engaged in loading and unloading Government stores under the protection of the gun-boat Sidell, commanded by Lieutenant Van Dorn. Suspicious of some danger below I hailed Van Dorn and inquired as to who burned the boat and houses. He replied that the guerrillas had burned the steamer and that he had retaliated by burning the houses. "Is there any danger below?" "No;" said he, "you can pass on safely. I have cleaned them out." The steamer Trio also ladened with wounded was in advance of us some four or five miles. Believing all safe below we passed on. On reaching the head of Harpeth Shoals we saw the Trio lying to in a cove on the south bank of the Cumberland River, thirty-five miles from Nashville and thirty miles from Clarksville. Having heard the captain of the Trio say that he was nearly out of fuel I presumed that he was taking on wood. On a nearer approach to her I discovered a company of cavalry drawn up in line on the bank just above the Trio. Two of the company took off their hats, waved them at us and ordered us to come to. I inquired, "Why, and what do you want? We are loaded with wounded and have no time to stop." "Come to, or we will fire into you." And at that instant the whole line came to a ready. Being the only commissioned officer on board (not wounded) with the exception of Surgeon Waterman I immediately assumed command and ordered the captain of the Hastings to land. The boat in the meantime had moved past the designated landing point, and the guerrilla commander gave the order to fire and three volleys of musketry were fired all taking effect upon the upper and forward portion of the steamer. The volleys were followed by one discharge of cannon, the ball passing through the clerk's office on the starboard side and out on the opposite side of the cabin. I told them to cease firing as we were landing as rapidly as possible. On landing they boarded the steamer and ordered the men all to leave the boat as they must burn her. In connection with Doctor Waterman I urged the claims of humanity upon them, and finally through a personal acquaintance with Captain Burford, General Wheeler's assistant adjutant-general, we extracted from them a promise to spare the boat on condition of the captain entering into bonds that she should carry no more supplies for the Army of the United States. I pass by a description of the horrible scenes enacted by Wade's men. They plundered the boat, even to the knives, forks, spoons, &c.; rifled passengers' baggage; robbed wounded soldiers of their rations, and money from their pockets; took the officers' side arms, overcoats, hats, &c. I reasoned with their officers to no purpose, save Captain Burford, who was utterly unable to control the men. I then took on board the wounded of the Trio and her crew and asked permission to leave. This was granted and the colonel ordered his men off. On his leaving he noticed several bales of cotton on which our wounded men were lying; he instantly became furious and ordered us to remove the same ashore and burn it, a task almost impossible. Many of the men were badly wounded; night was coming on; no rations nor medicines and thirty miles distant from any military post. Seeing all this I asked for other terms. He then agreed if I would burn the cotton on my arrival at Louisville he would spare the boat and allow us to go on unmolested, and in the event of my failing to comply with the order I must return to the line of the Confederate States as a prisoner of war. These terms were harsh, but in view of the suffering men I instantly complied. During the interim the steamer Parthenia hove in sight; was also brought to, her crew and passengers transferred to us, and preparation was then made to burn the Trio and Parthenia. In order to save the Hastings from coming in contact with the steamers when fired I again asked to leave. This they would not grant, but through the entreaties of Captain Burford we were allowed to cross to the other side of the river under range of their cannon. We hardly landed when the gun-boat Sidell hove in sight. On her appearance the enemy mounted their horses and awaited her action. She came on under a full head of steam, carrying her when the engine had ceased within 150 yards of our boat, on the same side of the river. I hailed Van Dorn; told him to take the middle of the stream and not endanger the lives of the wounded during the engagement, for we had no other idea but that he would fight. To our utter astonishment he ignominiously surrendered without firing a single shot. He then crossed her over to the enemy, who boarded her, threw over her cannon, then fired the three steamers and ordered us across the river again. I took on what was left of the crew and soldiers and after waiting one hour and a half according to their orders I started with the Hastings for Clarksville, reaching there at 8 p. m. and reporting to Colonel Bruce. He acted promptly and soon furnished us with supplies. I telegraphed the facts to General Rosecrans at Nashville and received the answer under which I am ordered to make a statement* of the whole affair for your consideration. The commissioned officers and privates were all paroled, they taking complete lists of the same, but furnishing no evidence of parole in return. I await at Louisville your decision in regard to myself. I do not desire to burn the cotton; neither to return as a prisoner of war. I shall reach Louisville on the 18th. Too much praise cannot be awarded to Surgeon Waterman, Thirty-ninth Indiana Volunteers, in charge as medical director for his efficiency and energy during the trying hour. He will turn the wounded men over to medical director at Louisville. I might add that large hospital flags were flying at the head of the jack-staff and that Colonel Wade admitted that he knew we had wounded on board. General Wheeler's orders to him were to burn all boats irrespective of what they carried.

Respectfully submitted from your most obedient servant,

M. P. GADDIS,
Chaplain Second Regiment Ohio Volunteer Infantry.

---

* See Series I, Vol. XX, Part I, p. 980.

[Inclosure.]

NASHVILLE, *January 13, 1863.*

Chaplain GADDIS:

The wounded must be got to Louisville without delay. Report at Cincinnati to General Wright on arrival at Louisville. Send him a written statement. Will report before your arrival.

W. H. SIDELL,
Assistant Adjutant General.

I certify the above to be a correct copy of telegram.

M. P. GADDIS,
Chaplain.

HEADQUARTERS ARMY OF TENNESSEE,
Tullahoma, Tenn., January 17, 1863.

Maj. Gen. W. S. ROSECRANS,
Commanding U. S. Forces, Murfreesborough, Tenn.

GENERAL: I inclose a copy of a letter* from Brig. Gen. John H. Morgan in reference to the letter of Captain Thruston which has been forwarded for my consideration and reply.

It is only necessary for me to protest with all solemnity against your action in the matter as unsustained by any article of war or usage of civilization and as not comprehended in the letter or spirit of my communication with you on the subject. A flag of truce is always entitled to respect, and whenever its bearers are treated as spies it can only be done by the abnegation of all intercourse. In coming to an outpost it may be received or refused, but the bearer cannot be charged with being a spy as until voluntarily within your lines he is not within the limits which define him as such, the definition of a spy being one who is found lurking in or about the camps or fortifications of an enemy. The accused were not in your lines until forcibly carried there by you nor did they propose to enter them.

The proposition by which I limited myself to a particular road while you were in Nashville if strictly construed now that you are in Murfreesborough would render the bearer of the flag which covers this equally liable to the treatment and charge preferred against the parties whom you hold. The omission to notify General Morgan of the arrangement is explained by the fact that his is of the nature of an independent command, constantly detached and necessarily requiring to be exempted from the operation of such a regulation. Since the communication between us referred to both he and General Forrest have sent and received flags to which no objection has been raised. He respected your "white flag" at Hartsville and spared the lives of your prisoners. More recently in his Kentucky expedition on several occasions he sent flags which were respected although not covering communications from me and against which I have received no remonstrance.

To these expressions of my views upon the injustice and inhumanity of the position you have assumed in the premises I must add that I deem your action unworthy of one occupying your high official position. These unfortunate men are in your power and it is left entirely to your decision whether they shall be the victims of your threats if it will gratify your vindictiveness to sacrifice them without the shadow of cause or if you regard it necessary in order to protect the flag from

---

* Omitted here; Morgan to Brent, January 15, p. 813, Confederate Correspondence.

abuse. Be your own judge, but I shall regret the unpleasant duty which such a course will necessitate on my part.

I am, sir, very respectfully, your obedient servant,

BRAXTON BRAGG,
General, Commanding.

HEADQUARTERS, *Corinth, Miss., January 17, 1863.*

Colonel RODDEY,
Commanding Confederate Forces at Tuscumbia:

I herewith send by hands of one of your men a list of prisoners in my hands whom I desire to exchange for any men of this command in your hands. If it meets your approbation please return the men whom you exchange under flag of truce to Glendale, with the exchange papers signed, and I will deliver the prisoners in my hands to the flag at that place.

It is represented to me that your command has been burning the houses of and turning out the families of Alabamians who have enlisted in the U. S. service. I desire to know if this is done by your order or by your sanction. They also report the hanging of one Union man whose sons are in this army and the shooting of others for no other reason than their sentiments.

Southern families are fleeing to these lines for protection from these cruelties and depredations, some of whom I find do not even sympathize with our cause, but are driven out merely upon suspicion or because some relative has joined this army. If you purpose to drive out of your lines all Union men and their families I desire to know that fact.

I am, very respectfully, your obedient servant,

G. M. DODGE,
Brigadier-General, Commanding District of Corinth.

HEADQUARTERS CAMP OF INSTRUCTION,
Benton Barracks, Mo., January 17, 1863.

Maj. H. Z. CURTIS,
Assistant Adjutant-General, Saint Louis, Mo.

SIR: I have the honor herewith to transmit a copy of a communication* this day received from Col. W. Hoffman, commissary-general of prisoners, and a return of the officers and men at this post affected by it. Immediately on the reception of the telegram indicated I placed the exchanged men present in a separate battalion and directed all absentees to report at once in person, so that on the arrival of the orders mentioned you can dispose of these troops without delay. As so few of these men belong to any single regiment it seems certain that to arm them here would be nothing but an injury to the service. Since these troops were mustered on the 31st of December, 1862, on the same rolls with men not yet exchanged a new and separate muster before payment appears a necessity.

I am, major, very respectfully, your obedient servant,

B. L. E. BONNEVILLE,
Colonel, U. S. Army, Commanding.

---

* See Hoffman to Cooper, p, 175.

HEADQUARTERS DEPARTMENT OF VIRGINIA,
Fort Monroe, January 17, 1863.

Col. W. HOFFMAN, *Commissary-General of Prisoners.*

COLONEL: The rolls of North Carolina captures were used by me in my last interview with Mr. Ould and are already counted. I have just returned from City Point but have not yet received a decisive answer on the subject of the release or parole of our officers. I shall receive it early next week. I am endeavoring to get all captured before the 12th of January out of Confederate prisons for I have every reason to believe that all captured after that date will be disposed of as directed in the message of Jefferson Davis, viz, be handed over to the different State authorities. But upon all these points I shall be better advised in a few days. I would recommend you to retain all the political or citizen prisoners until I can communicate with you again. I expect from Confederate sources further information relating to them. Your four letters for the South received and forwarded. A large number of the Murfreesborough prisoners are at Richmond. I have sent a boat up for them to-day.

Yours, very respectfully,

WM. H. LUDLOW,
Lieutenant-Colonel and Agent for Exchange of Prisoners.

P. S.—The release of W. J. Peters was promised to me by Mr. Ould without any equivalent. I had long pressed for his release. The substitution of Voegler for White will doubtless be satisfactory.

W. H. L.

RICHMOND, VA., *January 17, 1863.*

Lieutenant-Colonel LUDLOW, *Agent of Exchange.*

SIR: I regretted very much on reaching City Point meridian on the 16th instant to find you had left. I did not receive any notice that you would be obliged to leave at 11 o'clock on that day. If I had, however, I do not see how I could have been at City Point any sooner.

In your communication of the 14th instant you desire to know whether the Federal commissioned officers now prisoners will be released. I have already furnished you with an official copy of the proclamation of President Davis dated December 23, 1862. In conformity therewith officers will not be released on parole but will be exchanged for those of corresponding rank. If you have any Confederate officer in your possession and will deliver him an officer of like grade will be delivered to you and they will be mutually declared to be exchanged. So if you have released any officer on parole we will deliver to you an officer of corresponding rank and declare them exchanged. The Federal officers, however, now in our possession will not be surrendered to you on parole. This rule will apply only to commissioned officers. We are ready at any time to release on parole and deliver to you your non-commissioned officers and privates.

This course has been forced upon the Confederate Government not only by the refusal of the authorities of the United States to respond to the repeated applications of this Government in relation to the execution of Mumford but by their persistence in retaining Confederate officers who were entitled to parole and exchange. You have now of captures that are by no means recent many officers of the Confederate service who are retained in your military prisons East and West.

Applications have been made for the release of some without success, and others have been kept in confinement so long as to justify the conclusion that you refuse both parole and exchange.

One prominent instance I will bring to your notice. General B. F. Butler has retained Brigadier-General Clark and thirteen others for several months. At the latest advices received by us they were still in custody. During the whole of the time that they have been thus detained we had a large excess of Federal prisoners all of whom were either promptly exchanged or delivered to you on parole.

This is by no means a solitary case. I have now and have had for a long time authentic evidence in [my] possession of the retention of a large number of Confederate officers by your military authorities. Several prominent cases have also very recently been presented to me. You are very well aware that this has been a subject of complaint ever since the adoption of the cartel. In view of all these facts the Confederate Government has determined to refuse any parole to your officers until the grievances of which it has complained are redressed. Of course this applies to such commissioned officers as were captured before the date of President Davis' message. He himself has indicated what disposition will be made of such as may be captured after that date.

In your communication of the 14th instant you also refer to the case of Mrs. Piggott who you say "was taken from her home at Williamsburg, Va., with forty of her slaves and who is now detained at Richmond or some other place within the Confederate lines."

Without any comment upon the singularity of the request that slaves made free by President Lincoln's proclamation should be promptly returned as the property of Mrs. Piggott I inform you that Mrs. Piggott was released from custody on *habeas corpus* a long time ago. She is a citizen of Virginia, responsible to the laws of that State and the Confederacy. The Confederate and State authorities will not allow any interference by the United States with the course of justice in any one of the Confederate States. They will not entertain even a protest. No fears of retaliation upon "ladies" or any one else will ever make them relinquish their rightful and exclusive control.

I perceive by your published notice of exchanges that you have made a mistake in declaring exchanged the Federal prisoners paroled at Goldsborough and delivered at Washington, N. C. These are the 1,300 that I have so constantly pressed upon you and for whom you have given no equivalent or credit. You have the list in your possession. I delivered it to you that you might examine more fully into the matter. Those men have not been exchanged. I hope you will make the proper correction.

When shall I see you at City Point again?

Respectfully, your obedient servant,

RO. OULD,
Agent of Exchange.

OFFICE PROVOST-MARSHAL-GENERAL,
Wheeling, January 17, 1863.

Col. WM. HOFFMAN, *Commissary-General of Prisoners.*

SIR: I have the honor to inclose* copy of letter from the president of the board of directors of the House of Refuge at Cincinnati stating

---

* Omitted; substance herein stated.

the impracticability of receiving the female prisoners already reported to you.

Very respectfully, your obedient servant,

JOS. DARR, Jr.,
Major and Provost-Marshal-General.

HEADQUARTERS DEPARTMENT OF THE CUMBERLAND,
Murfreesborough, January 18, 1863.

General JOSEPH E. JOHNSTON, C. S. Army.

GENERAL: It is with regret that I find myself compelled by a sense of duty to humanity to decline communicating with General Bragg by flag of truce until redress has been made for a violation of the rights of a flag of truce committed by a party of Confederate cavalry on the Murfreesborough pike between La Vergne and Nashville.

The nature of this outrage is explained and the facts set forth in a copy of my letter to General Bragg herewith inclosed* marked A, to which I will add that the mother of Lieutenant-Colonel Hawkins, who applied to me on the morning of my arrival at Murfreesborough for permission to go home assured me that her son persistently stated the facts as they are represented, the same trick of going behind a flag of truce and capturing three pickets having been practiced upon us a day or two before, General Bragg having acknowledged it to be wrong and promised to repair it. I confidently expected such apology and reparation of the second outrage, instead of which General Bragg wrote a letter justifying it on the ground of the ignorance of the scouting party of the post that the flag was there and also on the ground that his flag was unlawfully detained, both of which allegations were false, the truth being as will appear in the papers herewith inclosed† marked B, C, D and E. And as I must officially regard General Bragg as the responsible author of the statement which he indorses it is obviously inconsistent with military safety as well as with self-respect to continue an official intercourse with him.

I regret also to state it has been the habit of subordinate officers under your command to degrade flags of truce by sending them on side roads and to remote points on our lines accredited in no proper manner and obviously for the purpose of spying. This is the common practice of General Morgan. This abuse I appeal to you to stop, as I shall treat every flag that comes in such a way as unlawful and its bearers as spies or as prisoners of war, as the evidence against them may indicate.

I am, general, very respectfully, your obedient servant,

W. S. ROSECRANS,
Major-General, Commanding.

HEADQUARTERS DEPARTMENT OF THE CUMBERLAND,
Murfreesborough, January 18, 1863.

General BRAXTON BRAGG, *Commanding, &c.*

GENERAL: Major-General Rosecrans directs me to return your communication directed to him from Tullahoma, dated the 17th instant, in

---

* Not found, but see Stone to Bragg of this date, *post.*
† Not found.

reference to the detention of the bearer of a white flag accredited by Mr. John W. Green, acting assistant adjutant-general, &c., for the following reasons:

When you were officially informed and acknowledged an outrage committed on the rights of a flag of truce on the Murfreesborough pike you returned the three pickets captured without their overcoats and robbed of part of their equipments. When on the very next day you coolly came behind your own flag, borne by Lieutenant-Colonel Hawkins, and halted at our lines and captured some forty of our cavalrymen in his presence and against his protestations, you neglected promptly to repair the outrage although in principle the same as the former one, but under circumstances far more aggravating, and when your attention was subsequently called to this neglect and you were informed that such reparation would be regarded as a *sine qua non* to further official intercourse you replied by a communication justifying the outrage and moreover accusing the general's authorities of twenty-four hours' detention of your flag of truce, the justification being a manifest contradiction of acknowledged principles and facts, and the statement concerning the detention false, for which you made yourself responsible by saying that you had fully examined the case.

The general will forward herewith the communication directed to your official superior, trusting that more enlightened and just views will be taken by him and that there may yet be preserved that respect for the sacred character of a flag of truce which the interests of humanity require. All the general asks is that a flag of truce shall not be used to cover tricks and spying but confined to its legitimate objects—needful and honorable intercourse on great public matters between opposing armies. To prevent individual hardships he directs me to suggest that due notice ought to be given that persons presenting themselves at our line with white flags but without due authority from the superior officer of your forces on any of these lines will be liable to be treated as spies for lurking about our lines and for disgracing the sacred character of a flag of truce.

I am, general, very respectfully, your obedient servant,

HENRY STONE,
Lieutenant and Acting Assistant Adjutant-General.

HEADQUARTERS DEPARTMENT OF VIRGINIA,
Fort Monroe, Va., January 18, 1863.

Hon. ROBERT OULD, *Agent for Exchange of Prisoners.*

SIR: Will you please send me by Captain Mulford a reply to my communication to you of the 14th instant in reference to your retention of U. S. officers in violation of the cartel and also to the case of Mrs. Piggott? Will you also inform me whether you will release the citizen prisoners now held by you and especially those captured by General Stuart in his raid into Maryland and Pennsylvania?

William J. Peters whose release you promised me some time ago has reported to me with a copy of parole to procure the release of one White, a citizen, or return in thirty days. I should have been glad if his release had been unconditional as agreed on, but having given his parole he has diligently but unsuccessfully sought out White. Only three Whites have been found on the rolls, two at Fort McHenry and one at Fort Monroe, but all were released some time since. It being impossible to furnish the equivalent named will you accept for him one Henry Voegler, now held at Baltimore? If so please notify me through Captain Mulford.

I am, very respectfully, your obedient servant,

WM. H. LUDLOW,
Lieutenant-Colonel and Agent for Exchange of Prisoners.

MADISON, WIS., *January 19, 1863.*

Hon. EDWIN M. STANTON, *Secretary of War:*

I think the record in the *habeas corpus* cases will answer. We have agreed to argue the motion for writ for error on Friday, the 30th, provided you will authorize General Elliott to parole the prisoners. I recommend you to do so. Please answer at once.

T. O. HOWE.

WAR DEPARTMENT, *Washington, January 19, 1863.*

Hon. T. O. HOWE, *Madison, Wis.:*

General Elliott is authorized to parole the prisoners if you so advise, and to do whatsoever you as counsel of the United States may deem proper to be done upon the subject. Please show him this telegram.

EDWIN M. STANTON,
Secretary of War.

WAR DEPARTMENT, *Washington, January 19, 1863.*

Brigadier-General ELLIOTT, *Madison, Wis.:*

You will please follow the instructions of the Hon. T. O. Howe, special counsel of the United States, in respect to the prisoners in your custody.

EDWIN M. STANTON,
Secretary of War.

ATTORNEY-GENERAL'S OFFICE, *January 19, 1863.*

R. J. LACKEY, Esq.,
U. S. Attorney, Western District of Missouri.

SIR: In answer to your letter of the 9th I have no directions to give as to the propriety of prosecuting indictments pending in your court. The Government here have not any settled purposes on the matter of prosecution so as to interfere with my views of prudence and policy in the matter of prosecutions. And I, trusting to the good judgment of the district attorneys, am willing to leave the matter very much to their discretion. They know (what I cannot know) the tone of feeling in their localities, the character and amount of testimony, the sort of juries likely to be had and the likelihood of fair trial and conviction. Still I wish to make to you a few suggestions which perhaps may aid to conclusions of your own judgment. It is not desirable to try many cases of treason. It is a crime hard to prove, being guarded by a variety of legal technics. And even conviction makes the convict all the more a martyr in the eyes of his partisans. In a clear case against a person of eminence, of notoriety, I would be glad to see a conviction for the public effect rather than the punishment of the individual. But it would be unfortunate to be defeated in many such cases. It is far better policy I think when you have the option to prosecute offenders for vulgar felonies and misdemeanors than for romantic and genteel treason. The penitentiaries will be far more effectual than the gallows. Prosecute your best cases—not the weak and doubtful. It will not do for us to be habitually beaten. With these few hints I trust the matter to your own good judgment.

Very respectfully, your obedient servant,

EDWARD BATES.

HEADQUARTERS DEPARTMENT OF THE CUMBERLAND,
Murfreesborough, January 19, 1863.

General JOSEPH E. JOHNSTON, C. S. Army.

GENERAL: I addressed you a letter yesterday in reference to abuses and outrages of flags of truce and the consequent suspension of official intercourse with General Bragg until reparation should be made for a very great outrage by the return of troops captured.

Sincerely desirous of conducting war according to the laws of humanity and civilization and not doubting that my feelings are responded to by yourself, who I have known through mutual friends and admirers in your earlier days, I am induced to address you at some length on two or three other matters of interest to humanity, premising that I have never practiced abuses nor allowed them to be practiced under my command.

1. The cartel requires that the prisoners captured by either party shall be delivered at Aiken's Landing or Vicksburg, or at such other points as may be agreed upon by the commanding generals of opposing armies. General Bragg in violation of this and without any previous notice to me on the subject marched the Hartsville prisoners, robbed of their overcoats and without rations, from Murfreesborough to our lines, they arriving at night in order to force the acceptance of them, thereby cheating us of what is justly due by the provisions of the cartel.

2. The Confederate cavalry are in the constant habit of disembarrassing themselves of the prisoners which they capture by paroling and releasing them wherever they find them, thereby forcing us to accept a delivery at any point which suits their convenience and after a delivery made in violation of the cartel to avoid recapture, in this way attempting to gain credit for prisoners which they probably might not be able to hold and certainly have not properly delivered. By thus violating the agreement they forfeit their rights to the benefit of the capture; were it otherwise they would be permitted to claim the benefit of their own improper action.

3. No lists of these prisoners are ever furnished us. As I shall conform to the provisions of the cartel and confidently expect conformity thereto from the Confederate authorities no such persons can be regarded as prisoners of war, nor will credit be claimed or given for them in exchange, but when prisoners are lawfully taken, assembled, listed and paroled I shall be ready to select a convenient point at which to receive those you capture and deliver to you those whom we capture.

I have also to call your attention to the fact that at the recent battle at Murfreesborough our surgeons who fell temporarily into your hands were in several or all instances robbed of their horses and other private property and that some of them were carried off.

I also regret to state that the bodies of our wounded officers and soldiers were found stripped of their clothing—even the body of General Sill was robbed of its uniform.

The acts of injustice to our surgeons and inhumanity to the dead I am sure you must condemn and in future will be able to prevent. I regret to inform you also that the officers of the regular brigade report that some regiment of your troops approached them on the field wearing our uniforms and bearing our flag.

This has been continually practiced by General Morgan's men. Such conduct is unworthy of a civilized people and I trust that you will promptly put a stop to it as I shall give orders that Confederate troops meeting [us] in battle or lurking about our lines wearing our uniform or bearing our colors shall not receive quarters nor shall they be treated as prisoners of war.

I am, general, very respectfully, your obedient servant,

W. S. ROSECRANS,
Major-General, Commanding.

MURFREESBOROUGH, *January 19, 1863.*

Colonel HOFFMAN, *Commissary-General of Prisoners:*

I see by the papers that all prisoners taken in Kentucky have been exchanged. Does this include General William H. Lytle, of Cincinnati ?

W. S. ROSECRANS,
Major-General.

WASHINGTON, D. C., *January 19, 1863.*

Hon. EDWIN M. STANTON, *Secretary of War.*

SIR: I have the honor to attach hereto a slip taken from the Richmond Enquirer of the 15th instant, being a passage from what purports to be a message from Jefferson Davis as President of the Confederate States to the Senate and House of Representatives of those States, indicating the course proposed to be pursued in the South toward officers of the U. S. Army who may be taken prisoners within such portion of the Southern States as are designated in the proclamation of His Excellency the President of the United States, dated the 1st instant, on the subject of slaves within such designated portions of the Southern States.

In view of this threat to deliver captured officers into the hands of civil officers of Southern State governments to be dealt with as criminals under State laws I beg to call your attention to a proclamation issued by the same functionary, Jefferson Davis, about a month since, directed chiefly against Major-General Butler, in which in violation of an existing cartel for the exchange of prisoners Mr. Davis declares his purpose of holding a certain class of prisoners in duress, putting their lives in jeopardy contrary to the laws of war. In consequence of this proclamation you were constrained to give the necessary orders for holding in close custody certain officers of the rebel army taken in arms with the simple design of awaiting the further action of the rebel authorities in the premises. This precautionary measure on your part is believed to be all that can be done in the present case until it can be seen whether the rebel authorities in the South shall attempt to outrage the public sentiment of the civilized world by putting into practice the savage threat indicated in slip hereto annexed.

It would be proper, however, that the officers of the Union armies should be informed of the existence of the threat in question which I respectfully request may be done through the General-in-Chief.

I have the honor to be, very respectfully, your obedient servant,

E. A. HITCHCOCK,
Major-General of Vols., Commissioner for Exchange of Prisoners.

Extract from the Richmond Enquirer, January 15, 1863.

*　　*　　*　　*　　*　　*　　*

So far as regards the action of this Government on such criminals as may attempt its execution I confine myself to informing you that I shall unless in your wisdom you deem some other course more expedient deliver to the several State authorities all commissioned officers of the United States that may hereafter be captured by our forces in any of the States embraced in the proclamation that they may be dealt with in accordance with the laws of those States providing for the punishment of criminals engaged in exciting servile insurrection. The enlisted soldiers I shall continue to treat as unwilling instruments in the commission of these crimes and shall direct their discharge and return to their homes on the proper and usual parole.

OFFICE COMMISSARY-GENERAL OF PRISONERS,
Washington, D. C., January 19, 1863.

Hon. OLIVER KEYSER,
House of Representatives, Columbus, Ohio.

SIR: I have the honor to acknowledge the receipt of your letter of the 14th instant informing me that a committee has been appointed by the Legislature of Ohio of which you are the chairman to examine into the condition of the prisoners at Camp Chase, and requesting a copy of the report of the inspection recently made under my order by Captain Lazelle, U. S. Army, and in reply I beg to say that I will direct the commander of the prison to afford every facility to the committee to investigate the management of the prison, but as the report of Captain Lazelle was only intended for this office and can have no influence on the opinion of the committee it is not deemed advisable to furnish the copy desired. All orders and regulations for the government of the prison will be submitted for the consideration of the committee.

Very respectfully, your obedient servant,

W. HOFFMAN,
Colonel Third Infantry, Commissary-General of Prisoners.

OFFICE COMMISSARY-GENERAL OF PRISONERS,
Washington, D. C., January 19, 1863.

Lieut. Col. GEORGE SANGSTER,
Commanding Camp Parole, Annapolis, Md.

COLONEL: Your letter of January 15 is received and the arrangements you made for transferring troops West are generally satisfactory. In order to insure hereafter if possible that there shall be no delay when you send troops West, if you have no officer to take them through and the party is small you will send an officer with them to Baltimore to see them well started from that point and on the most direct route. If the party is over twenty-five men and there is no officer belonging to it you will detail an officer from the guard to conduct it to its destination. Always give the officer in charge special instructions and request an acknowledgment of the men and all papers from the officers to whom they are delivered. Lieut. W. Einstein, Seventh Pennsylvania Cavalry, will report to you this afternoon and you will send under his charge to the West all men at the camp whether exchanged or on parole whose regiments are serving in the West. Those on parole will be left at Camp Chase, and he will leave there all exchanged men whose regiments are farther west to be forwarded by the commanding officer. He will himself conduct to the Army of the Cumberland at or near Nashville all exchanged men who may be placed under his command. Virginia troops will be left at Wheeling and the Kentucky Home Guards at Camp Chase. You will muster for pay up to the 31st ultimo all exchanged troops at your camp and a payment will be made before they march. This does not include the troops ordered West.

Very respectfully, your obedient servant,

W. HOFFMAN,
Colonel Third Infantry, Commissary-General of Prisoners.

HEADQUARTERS PAROLED PRISONERS,
Camp near Annapolis, January 19, 1863.

Col. W. HOFFMAN, *Commissary-General of Prisoners.*

SIR: I have the honor to inclose my report* for the week ending January 17, 1863, all of which I hope is in accordance with your orders except the army corps column. I find by inquiry that there are not 500 men here that know what army corps they belong to, and those even who pretend to know I find upon examination that the half of them are wrong and rather than make you a wrong report I have omitted it entirely. If the men of my camp were a sample of our Army we would have nothing but a mob of stragglers and cowards. I am convinced more and more every day that three-fourths of paroled men are stragglers and cowards. It would be well to have an order bearing strictly on stragglers so that the officers commanding companies or regiments could report those men whom they know to be stragglers, and as they arrive from Richmond or elsewhere we could deal with them accordingly.

I am, colonel, most respectfully, your obedient servant,

GEO. SANGSTER,
Lieutenant-Colonel Commanding Paroled Prisoners.

ORDERS.]   HDQRS. DISTRICT OF WESTERN KENTUCKY;
Louisville, January 19, 1863.

Chaplain M. P. Gaddis, Second Ohio Volunteer Infantry, having reported to these headquarters that he was taken prisoner on the 13th day of December on the Cumberland River by the rebel General Wheeler and released on the following conditions: That upon the arrival of the steamer Hastings with wounded men at the city of Louisville, Ky., the 111 bales of cotton on the boat said to belong to private parties should be burned on the wharf of the said city and in the event of this not being done he was to report himself to the Confederate authorities within twenty days from date of parole—

Mr. Gaddis, being a non-combatant and not being a prisoner of war according to the terms of the cartel agreed upon by the representatives

----

* Not found.

of the United States and the so-called Confederate States, he is hereby positively forbid burning the aforesaid cotton and will not deliver himself up to the Confederate authorities.

Mr. Gaddis will proceed to Cincinnati at once and will report to Maj. Gen. H. G. Wright, commanding the Department of the Ohio.

By command of Major-General Boyle:

A. C. SEMPLE,
Assistant Adjutant-General.

MACHIAS, [ME.,] *January 20, 1863.*
Hon. E. M. STANTON, *Secretary of War, Washington.*

SIR: About eighteen months ago the Confederate steamer Sumter made prizes of several merchant vessels off the coast of Cuba and carried them to a port in that island. The officers and crews of these vessels were liberated by Captain Semmes on parole. Will you be good enough to inform me whether under the recent arrangement for exchanges made by Colonel Ludlow, particularly under the eighth section of this arrangement, the officers and men referred to are or not included? I write for the benefit of certain persons residing here who are interested in the decision.

I have the honor to be, your very obedient servant,

WM. B. SMITH.

OFFICE COMMISSARY-GENERAL OF PRISONERS,
Washington, D. C., January 20, 1863.
Col. B. L. E. BONNEVILLE,
Commanding Benton Barracks, Saint Louis, Mo.

SIR: In reply to your letter of the 7th instant presenting the cases of paroled Government employés who report to you I have the honor to communicate the following instructions just received from the Quartermaster-General: Civilians employed by Quartermaster's Department captured by the enemy are considered as entitled to pay until released. They should if on parole be discharged from the service on reaching the first convenient place and are entitled to receive a certificate of the material facts to enable them to establish their claim for pay until released. Those who have been exchanged can generally obtain employment from the quartermaster upon making their cases known. If they do not choose to enter the service or if not being exchanged their paroles prevent them from serving the United States there is no other course left but to discharge them. The United States cannot support them in idleness. It is not considered proper to allow them transportation to return to their homes or distant places of employment.

Very respectfully, your obedient servant,

W. HOFFMAN,
Colonel Third Infantry, Commissary-General of Prisoners.

OFFICE PROVOST-MARSHAL-GENERAL,
Saint Louis, Mo., January 20, 1863.
Col. W. HOFFMAN, *Commissary-General of Prisoners.*

COLONEL: I have the honor to acknowledge receipt of your letter of the 15th instant. You state that Singleton was released from Alton [Prison] under a general order which directed the release of all military prisoners who were willing to take the oath. While I am aware of the fact that I have no control over prisoners at Alton merely because they are there, yet it is important that I make known to you the fact that there are many prisoners at Alton sent there by my predecessors against whom there are serious charges and whose cases have never been fully investigated by this office. You will recollect that Colonel Gantt was at one time under the impression that the Alton prisoners were under the control of this office and consequently he considered I suppose that prisoners there would not be released until acted upon by this office. I have as yet never been able to dispose of the cases of those prisoners who were sent to Alton by Colonel Gantt and Colonel Farrar. The whole force in this office has been kept engaged upon the cases in the prisons at Saint Louis. My object has been to dispose of the Saint Louis cases first and then send the prisoners who are to be permanently confined to Alton, and have the Alton prisoners whose cases have not been acted upon taken up and disposed of. In view of these facts I suggested that inquiry be made at this office before ordering the release of prisoners at Alton. If, however, that course should not be adopted it will be necessary for me to have the Alton cases first disposed of. In your letter of October 29, 1862, to Colonel Gantt you state that prisoners at Alton may be released by this office who have been sent there upon charges which upon investigation prove to be unfounded. I have been incessantly engaged in having these cases investigated; but there has been great difficulty in procuring the evidence, and nearly every case requires a personal examination of the prisoner. It takes much time to dispose of so many cases. I desire to be informed whether prisoners at Alton sent from here whose cases have not been disposed of are liable to be released by orders from Washington for the reasons above stated.

I have the honor to be, your obedient servant,

F. A. DICK,
Lieutenant-Colonel and Provost-Marshal-General.

FORT MONROE, *January 20, 1863.*

Hon. G. V. FOX, *Assistant Secretary of the Navy:*

Not only the cartel but also the declaration of exchange of all captures on the sea up to the 10th instant requires the release of Captain Vincent and others now confined in Fort Lafayette and other prisons. When will they be sent here for exchange?

WM. H. LUDLOW,
Lieutenant-Colonel and Agent for Exchange of Prisoners.

WAR DEPARTMENT, *Washington, January 20, 1863.*

Hon. WILLIAM H. SEWARD, *Secretary of State.*

SIR: I have the honor to report in answer to your communications of the 5th and 12th instant relative to Captain Wynne that the facts and circumstances within my knowledge relative to the arrest, imprisonment, &c., of Edward Wynne, representing himself to be a captain of the Grenadier Guards, Canada, are briefly as follows:

Captain Wynne when brought before me respectfully declined making any disclosures touching the object of his visit to Richmond or the ways and means whereby he effected his passage through the Federal lines, but during our conversation he stated in answer to interrogatories that he left Canada the last of October and came to this city where he remained a day or two; that he passed the Federal lines on his way to Richmond from Washington near Leonardtown, having no pass or permission from the Federal authorities. In answer to the question, "From whom did you obtain information as to the best plan to pass through the Federal lines?" he answered, "I picked up the information about town" (Washington). That after getting into the rebel lines he proceeded to Richmond and remained at and in the vicinity of that city until about the 24th ultimo and then left with a pass from the rebel authorities for the North. He came to the Point of Rocks and crossed over and was there arrested, sent to this city and committed to the Old Capitol Prison. He informed me that he carried but one letter South and that to a lady whose name he declined giving, but in a letter found on his person written by C. Q. Tompkins, a rebel officer, to Col. Robert H. Chilton, adjutant-general in the rebel army, Captain Wynne and Captain Phillips, a British officer, are represented as gentlemen highly accredited by friends in Baltimore. Captain Wynne informed me that he was at Fredericksburg before and after the battle, and he had in his possession a map of the battle drawn by Hotchkiss, of the rebel topographical engineers, on which the position of the rebel forces and the topography of the battle-ground are correctly and artistically delineated. Among the papers and letters found in his possession was one from Col. G. W. C. Lee, the rebel secretary of Jeff. Davis, inviting him and Captain Phillips to dine; another from the said rebel Colonel Lee stating that he (Colonel Lee) "will speak to General Fitz. Lee in reference to your wishes," &c., and "to serve you in any respect;" another from the said rebel Colonel Lee addressed to his uncle, the rebel Capt. S. S. Lee, at Drewry's Bluff, introducing Captains Wynne and Phillips, saying among other things, "I believe they are acquaintances of Miss Ellen Magruder whom they met in Canada;" another from C. Q. Tompkins, a rebel officer, to Col. Robert H. Chilton, a rebel adjutant-general, introducing Captains Wynne and Phillips as officers of the British army, who will visit "your headquarters with the sanction of this Government;" a pass from the rebel Major-General Stuart directing guards and pickets to pass to Richmond from headquarters cavalry division Hon. F. Lawley, F. Vizetelli (London Illustrated News artists), Captains Wynne and Phillips; a pass from War Department of the Confederate States of America giving permission to Captain Wynne to visit at will thirty days, upon his honor not to communicate in writing or verbally any fact that might be injurious to the Confederate States, &c.; a lithographic map of the battle-grounds of the Chickahominy; the Virginia ordinance of secession largely displayed, with *fac similes* of the signatures of the members of the convention of secessionists; photographs of the rebel President and cabinet ministers of the rebel Confederacy; a book of lithographic figures displaying the uniforms of the C. S. Navy and another displaying the uniforms and dress of the Army of the Confederate States; a book of 215 pages of the war songs of the South and a book of 490 pages, being the pro-slavery argument as maintained by the most distinguished writers of the Southern States. Captain Wynne in answer to an interrogatory frankly and earnestly declared that his sympathies were with the rebels. The communication* of Lord Lyons is returned as requested.

I have the honor to be, very respectfully, your obedient servant,
L. C. TURNER,
Judge-Advocate.

---

* Not found.

GENERAL ORDERS, {   HDQRS. DEPT. OF THE CUMBERLAND,
    No. 3.   }   *Murfreesborough, Tenn., January 20, 1863.*

The following extracts from the cartel under which prisoners are exchanged in the existing war with the Southern States are published for the information of this army:

*   *   *   *   *   *

ARTICLE 4. All prisoners of war to be discharged on parole in ten days after their capture, and the prisoners now held and those hereafter taken to be transported to the points mutually agreed upon at the expense of the capturing party. The surplus prisoners not exchanged shall not be permitted to take up arms again, nor to serve as military police or constabulary force in any fort, garrison or field-work held by either of the respective parties, nor as guards of prisons, depots or stores, nor to discharge any duty usually performed by soldiers until exchanged under the provisions of this cartel.   *   *   *

*   *   *   *   *

ARTICLE 7. All prisoners of war now held on either side and all prisoners hereafter taken shall be sent with all reasonable dispatch to A. M Aiken's, below Dutch Gap, on the James River, Va., or to Vicksburg, on the Mississippi River, in the State of Mississippi, and there exchanged or paroled until such exchange can be effected, notice being previously given by each party of the number of prisoners it will send and the time when they will be delivered at those points respectively; and in case the vicissitudes of war shall change the military relations of the places designated in this article to the contending parties so as to render the same inconvenient for the delivery and exchange of prisoners other places bearing as nearly as may be the present local relations of said places to the line of said parties shall be by mutual agreement substituted. But nothing in this article contained shall prevent the commanders of two opposing armies from exchanging prisoners or releasing them on parole from other points mutually agreed on by said commanders.

In pursuance of the terms of the cartel it is ordered that all officers and soldiers captured by this army be immediately paroled and sent to the nearest military post, duplicate descriptive rolls being sent to the provost-marshal-general at these headquarters, whose duty it will be to see that such prisoners are promptly forwarded for exchange. No Confederate officers or soldiers captured by this army that may be paroled and set at liberty without proper delivery as provided in the cartel will be claimed as prisoners of war and proper subjects of exchange. No U. S. officers or soldiers so captured, paroled, and set at liberty without proper delivery, as provided in the cartel, will be considered as prisoners of war and proper subjects for exchange, but will be immediately ordered back to duty, such paroles being a violation of the terms of the cartel. An attempt on the part of the capturing party thus to force delivery to their own advantage forfeits their right to hold the prisoners.

By command of Major-General Rosecrans:

C. GODDARD,
Assistant Adjutant-General and Chief of Staff.

WASHINGTON, D. C., *January 21, 1863.*

Maj. Gen. E. A. HITCHCOCK.

GENERAL: A party of soldiers dressed as citizens were sent out by the late General Mitchel to destroy railroads in that vicinity. They were captured by the enemy and held as spies and a number of them were executed. Two of them recently escaped and have reported to me under orders to join their regiment which is serving with General Rosecrans. If they should be captured again would they not be liable again to be held for trial as spies? I think they would but I would prefer to be governed by your better judgment.

Respectfully, your obedient servant,   W. HOFFMAN,
Colonel Third Infantry, Commissary-General of Prisoners.

[Indorsement.]

I concur in the opinion expressed within and think the men referred to ought not to be exposed to the danger of falling into the hands of the enemy under the circumstances.

E. A. HITCHCOCK,
Maj. Gen. of Vols. and Commissioner for Exchange of Prisoners.

FORT MONROE, *January 21, 1863.*

Hon. EDWIN M. STANTON, *Secretary of War:*

A dispatch from Mr. Ould, Confederate agent for exchange of prisoners, informs me that all officers now in the hands of the Confederates and captured before the 12th of January, the date of Jeff. Davis' message, will not be released on parole but will be exchanged for those of corresponding rank. All officers captured after the 12th instant will be handed over to the Governors of the States where captured, as indicated in Jeff. Davis' message. "All non-commissioned officers and men will be released on parole as heretofore." I am now receiving the Murfreesborough prisoners and sending them to Annapolis.

WM. H. LUDLOW,
Lieutenant-Colonel, &c.

HEADQUARTERS DEPARTMENT OF VIRGINIA,
Fort Monroe, January 21, 1863.

Major General HITCHCOCK,
Commissioner for Exchange of Prisoners.

GENERAL: I have the honor to inclose to you communications* just received from Mr. Robert Ould, Confederate agent for exchange of prisoners; also a copy of communication of December 11. These show the condition of matters as connected with citizen prisoners. I would recommend that no civilians be released from any of our prisons to go South unless to procure exchanges. Such exchanges can be made. Before resorting to reprisals would it not be better to use up all the material for exchanges now on hand? The mail is just closing and I am obliged to write in haste.

I am, very respectfully, your obedient servant,

WM. H. LUDLOW,
Lieutenant-Colonel and Agent for Exchange of Prisoners.

HEADQUARTERS DEPARTMENT OF VIRGINIA,
Fort Monroe, January 21, 1863.

Col. W. HOFFMAN, *Commissary-General of Prisoners.*

COLONEL: William J. Peters is released from his parole and goes up to Annapolis this afternoon with 700 Murfreesborough prisoners just received from City Point. I would recommend that no civilians be released from any of our prisons to go South unless to procure exchanges there. Such exchanges can be made. I do not think any general plan can be agreed on unless after long delay, and before resorting to reprisals we had better use up all the material for exchanges now on hand.

*Not found; but see Ould to Ludlow, January 17, p. 186, and for letter of December 11, see p. 71.

If you are at a loss to find equivalents you can send the parties released on parole to report to me.

I am, very respectfully, your obedient servant,

WM. H. LUDLOW,
Lieutenant-Colonel and Agent for the Exchange of Prisoners.

WAR DEPARTMENT, *Washington, January 21, 1863.*

Hon. WILLIAM H. SEWARD, *Secretary of State.*

SIR: In answer to your note of this date I have the honor to say that Captain Wynne declined answering any and all questions touching the object of his mission to the rebel capital or who he saw, or where he lodged while in this city. I have directed him to be again brought before me and will report the result of the examination. When brought before me as stated in my report he declined making disclosures, but after a brief familiar conversation he answered a few questions and declined answering many. His confinement since the 5th instant may have impressed him with the importance of disclosing the truth and the whole truth.

I have the honor to be, very respectfully, your obedient servant,

L. C. TURNER,
Judge-Advocate.

HEADQUARTERS DEPARTMENT OF THE OHIO,
Cincinnati, Ohio, January 21, 1863.

Chaplain M. P. GADDIS, *Second Ohio Volunteer Infantry.*

SIR: I am directed by the commanding general to acknowledge the receipt of your report of the 16th instant in relation to the burning of Government steamer on the Cumberland River, and to state that as seen in General Orders, No. 90, War Department, 1862, you as a chaplain if captured by the enemy cannot be held as a prisoner of war; that you had no authority to enter into any obligation to destroy the cotton on your arrival at Louisville.

The decision of General Boyle in relation thereto is approved.

Very respectfully, your obedient servant,

W. P. ANDERSON,
Assistant Adjutant-General.

[Indorsement.]

CINCINNATI, *January 23, 1863.*

I desire to state in connection with the above indorsement of Briga-dier-General Boyle's order that on reaching Louisville I took steps to carry out my plighted faith with the so-called Confederate States, viz, the burning of the cotton; but having first deemed it my duty to report to General Boyle was by him forbidden to do the same or to return as a prisoner of war. Believing that under the circumstances I was fully justifiable in entering into such an obligation I hereby enter my solemn protest against said orders and demand permission to carry out the intentions of the obligation.

Very respectfully,

M. P. GADDIS,
Chaplain Second Ohio Volunteer Infantry.

War Department, Adjutant-General's Office,
Washington, January 22, 1863.

Brig. Gen. C. P. Stone, *Washington, D. C.*

Sir : Your letter of the 8th instant has been submitted to the Secretary of War. I have respectfully to inform you in reply that the property and papers were brought to this Department by one of your aides; that the property was delivered to Mr. Parker, your brother-in-law; that the papers were at the time sealed up and remain so still. Maj. L. C. Turner, judge-advocate, has been instructed to examine the papers and in a few days will return to you such as are of a private nature, retaining only such as are of a public character or important as evidence.

I am, sir, &c.,   L. THOMAS,
                                        Adjutant-General.

WASHINGTON, *January 22, 1863.*

Maj. Gen. S. R. Curtis :

All rebel enlisted prisoners of war should be sent to Vicksburg for exchange. If this cannot be done distribute them at Camps Morton, Douglas and Washburn, near Milwaukee. I will telegraph to the commander to notify you how many they accommodate.

By order of the General in Chief :

                              W. HOFFMAN,
                    Commissary-General of Prisoners.

Office Commissary-General of Prisoners,
Washington, D. C., January 22, 1863.

Col. W. E. Doster, *Provost-Marshal, Washington.*

Colonel : Please inform me if Assistant Surgeon Green, of the Fifth Virginia Cavalry, has yet been sent to Fort Monroe. It is not desired that any more political prisoners be sent South until I hear further from Colonel Ludlow.

Very respectfully, your obedient servant,

                              W. HOFFMAN,
        Colonel Third Infantry, Commissary-General of Prisoners.

War Department, *Washington, January 22, 1863.*

Hon. William H. Seward, *Secretary of State.*

Sir : I have the honor to inclose to you a copy of statement verified by oath made by Captain Wynne last evening before me at my office. He did not disclose frankly and fully but reluctantly and partially, refusing positively to disclose facts, names and circumstances of vital importance to characterize the object of his visit to Richmond. This refusal on his part is significant and stamps this surreptitious messenger to the rebel capital as a spy. It seems that Captain Phillips, of the same corps, was his companion from Canada and while in Richmond and passed our lines without being arrested. The letter found on Captain Wynne written by a rebel officer stated that Captains Phillips and Wynne came highly accredited to the rebels from Baltimore, and although Wynne took no letters himself he reluctantly swore that Captain Phillips did take letters from Baltimore. These grenadier captains belong to the same corps as Colonels Fletcher and Neville, who were with General McClellan on the Peninsula. Neville returned to England, but Fletcher went to Baltimore and then returned to Richmond and other parts South, returning to Canada I am told about five weeks since through this city.

I have the honor to be, very respectfully, your obedient servant,

L. C. TURNER,
Judge-Advocate.

[Inclosure.]

WASHINGTON CITY, *District of Columbia, ss:*

Edward Wynne upon oath makes the following statement: I am lieutenant and captain of the Grenadier Guards, in Canada, and a British subject. I left Montreal about the 27th of October last for New York. I stopped in New York at the Brevoort House and staid there five days. From New York I went to Baltimore and staid there till the 17th of November and stopped at Guy's Hotel. I saw in Baltimore General Morris, commandant of the fort, Mr. William Brune, Mr. Weld, two Messrs. Gilmore and Captain Balfour, an English officer. I had a letter of introduction to Mr. William Brune from his brother, John C. Brune, in Canada. I had also a letter of introduction to Mr. W. Wilkins Glenn, of Baltimore, from an English officer in Canada, and I had letters to no other persons in Baltimore. I had a letter to Colonel Browner in New York, an English officer, which I did not deliver, and letters to no other persons in New York. From Baltimore I went to Washington City and stopped at Willard's Hotel for dinner but did not sleep in Washington. I had letters to no one in Washington and I saw no one in Washington to converse with save Mr. Weld, of Baltimore, or rather near Cumberland. I went back to Baltimore the evening of the same day I came to Washington. I left Baltimore the second time on the 17th of November last in company with Capt. Guy Phillips, an English officer in the Grenadier Guards. Captain Phillips left Canada with me and traveled with me. We left Baltimore on the 17th on a steamer and went to Kent Island, where we staid till evening and then went on board a smack, which we hired to take us into the mouth of Patuxent River. We landed at the mouth of the Patuxent River after about four days' sailing. At Patuxent River we hired a two-horse wagon and driver to take us to the Potomac River near Piney Point and the night after leaving Patuxent River we crossed over the Potomac near Piney Point. After crossing the river we hired another conveyance that took us to Farnham. We slept there and then hired another conveyance to take us to the Rappahannock River. We slept that night about a mile on the other side at a place called Center Cross. The next day we went to the White House and the next day to Richmond by the cars, which was the 26th of November. I decline to answer whom we consulted as to the best way of getting from Baltimore to Richmond, and I decline telling who advised us how to go or the best way of going or aided or assisted us in going, but several persons were consulted and several persons advised us but the names I decline giving. I took no letters from Baltimore to Richmond, but Captain Phillips did, but how many I know not. The day I spent in Washington I did not visit any of the camps or fortifications. I only went about town and to the Capitol. Captain Phillips did not accompany me to Washington but he came over to Washington the afternoon of the day that I came over and returned to Baltimore the next. When I left Canada with Captain Phillips we had an idea of going to Richmond and we matured our plans for going while in Baltimore, although we made up our minds to go when in New York. We stopped first in Richmond at the Spotswood and then at the Exchange Hotel. I saw and conversed with General Stuart, Col. [G. W.] Custis Lee, the officers of General Stuart's staff, Colonel Brown, Major-General Lee, Colonel Baldwin and other rebel officers. We went to Drewry's Bluff and to Fredericksburg while staying at Richmond, having passes from the rebel authorities. We dined with Col. [G. W.] Custis Lee and with General Stuart, but no rebel officers dined with us. Captain Phillips and myself left Richmond together and went to the Point of Rocks, having passes from the rebel authorities. Captain Phillips crossed over first alone and was not arrested. I followed him about 7 p. m. and was arrested. This was on Sunday, the 27th of December last. I took no letters from Richmond to any person North and I have no knowledge that Captain Phillips did. We avoided that as we knew it was a dangerous thing to do.

ED. WYNNE,
Lieutenant and Captain Grenadier Guards.

Subscribed and sworn to before me this 21st day of January, 1863.

L. C. TURNER,
Judge-Advocate.

HEADQUARTERS DEPARTMENT OF THE MISSOURI,
Saint Louis, January 23, 1863.

Maj. Gen. U. S. GRANT,
    Commanding Department of the Tennessee, Memphis, Tenn.

GENERAL: The prisoners are arriving here and what to do with them is a difficult question. I have them on Arsenal Island without shelter. I am obliged to put them where a small guard will do for I have sent everything down to help you in the down-river matters.

*   *   *   *   *   *   *

With my best wishes for your success, I remain, general, very truly, yours,

SAML. R. CURTIS,
Major-General.

SAINT LOUIS, January 23, 1863.

Colonel HOFFMAN,
    Commissary-General of Prisoners, Washington:

Adjutant-general of Indiana reports room for 2,000 prisoners but no guard. We have barracks here but no guard for 6,000 prisoners. I have them at Arsenal Island still on their boats. Shall I have sheds built on island? Will you take charge of them? It is not in my power to make them safe and comfortable.

S. R. CURTIS,
Major-General.

WASHINGTON, January 23, 1863.

Major-General CURTIS,
    Commanding Department of the Missouri:

Send your prisoners to Camps Douglas and Morton; the former can receive 4,000 and the latter 2,000. General Wright will furnish guard.

Notify him of the number sent to each place. If General Rosecrans has not sent wounded prisoners to Camp Butler substitute it for Camp Morton.

By order of the General-in-Chief:

W. HOFFMAN,
Commissary-General of Prisoners.

QUARTERMASTER-GENERAL'S OFFICE,
Washington, January 23, 1863.

Col. WILLIAM HOFFMAN,
    Commissary-General of Prisoners, Washington City.

COLONEL: The letter of Col. B. L. E. Bonneville, commanding Benton Barracks, Mo., relating to civilians employed by the Government captured and paroled by the enemy referred by you to this office on the 14th instant is herewith returned. Civilians employed by the Quartermaster's Department captured by the enemy are considered as entitled to pay until released. They should if on parole be discharged from the service on reaching the first convenient place and are entitled to receive certificates of the material facts to enable them to establish their claim for pay until released. Those who have been exchanged can generally obtain employment from the quartermaster upon making their cases known. If they do not choose to re-enter the service or if not being exchanged their paroles prevent them serving the United States there is no other course left but to discharge them. The United States cannot support them in idleness. It is not considered proper to allow them transportation to return to their homes or distant places of employment.

Very respectfully, your obedient servant,

M. C. MEIGS,
Quartermaster-General.

COLUMBUS, *January 23, 1863.*

Col. W. HOFFMAN, *Commissary-General of Prisoners:*

We can accommodate from 300 to 400 wounded prisoners. Prison No. 3 requires repairing, which has been ordered.

JAMES COOPER,
Brigadier-General, Commanding.

WASHINGTON, *January 23, 1863.*

Lieutenant-Colonel LUDLOW, *Agent for Exchange of Prisoners:*

Does the phrase "all captures on the sea" in the declaration of exchanges cover citizens running the blockade?

W. HOFFMAN,
Commissary-General of Prisoners.

FORT MONROE, *January 23, 1863.*

Col. J. C. KELTON,
    Headquarters of the Army, Washington, D. C.:

We have three Confederate officers confined at Fort Norfolk. Shall they be paroled and sent to Richmond to be exchanged for specific equivalents of our officers confined there or return in ten days?

WM. H. LUDLOW,
Lieutenant-Colonel and Agent for Exchange of Prisoners.

HEADQUARTERS DEPARTMENT OF VIRGINIA,
Fort Monroe, January 23, 1863.

Col. WM. HOFFMAN,
Commissary-General of Prisoners, Washington, D. C.:

The phrase "all captures on the sea" in the declaration of exchange does not cover citizens running the blockade but applies to persons captured in arms or hostile array against the United States.

Please so inform Mr. Fox, Assistant Secretary of the Navy.

WM. H. LUDLOW,
Lieutenant-Colonel and Agent for the Exchange of Prisoners.

HEADQUARTERS DEPARTMENT OF VIRGINIA,
Fort Monroe, January 23, 1863.

Hon. ROBERT OULD:

Permit me to call your attention to a point in our exchanges which is operating (though probably unnoticed by you) with great unfairness.

At our last interview, and not anticipating such decisions as you have arrived at in reference to exchanges of U. S. officers, in order to facilitate our business I assented to the plan of exchanging by captures and reducing to equivalents in privates. The result now is that while I reduce to such equivalent all your officers captured at Fredericksburg who had been paroled and sent through the lines you retain all of our officers captured at the same place. Whatever action may be taken in violation of the cartel in reference to officers captured at Fredericksburg, they should be released on their parole. Will you please send me your decision on this point? The declaration of exchange of our officers and men paroled at Goldsborough, N. C., May 22, 1862, and delivered at Washington, N. C., was only intended to apply to seven and not to the large capture referred to by you.

I am, very respectfully, your obedient servant,

WM. H. LUDLOW,
Lieutenant-Colonel and Agent for Exchange of Prisoners.

INDIANAPOLIS, IND., *January 23, 1863.*

Col. WILLIAM HOFFMAN,
Commissary-General of Prisoners, Washington, D. C.

COLONEL: In reply to your telegram of the 20th instant I have to reply that I have no means of obtaining accurately the number of patients in the rebel hospitals at La Fayette. I wrote to Doctor Chesnut to furnish me with the required information but he cannot state accurately. I inclose his reply just received.

I am, colonel, very respectfully, your obedient servant,

H. W. FREEDLEY,
Captain, Third Infantry.

[Inclosure.]

LA FAYETTE, IND., *January 22, 1863.*

Captain FREEDLEY:

In answer to your communication of the 20th instant I have to state that the two regiments of rebel prisoners quartered at this place had been stationed at Bowling Green; were marched from there to Fort Donelson and were kept in the rifle-pits four days and nights before they were captured. They were then placed in open boats and without overcoats and very poorly dressed were brought here, half famished with cold, exposure and hunger. For the first two days they were furnished with food by the citizens, consisting of meats, poultry, vegetables, fruits and pastries of great varieties. The result of this imprudence was in addition to the large sick list which they brought with them the great majority of both regiments were attacked within a few days with camp diarrhea. Immediately after their arrival typhoid pneumonia, under which the rebels had suffered so severely at Bowling Green, broke out among them in its most malignant form. Tippecanoe Hospital and the hospital at Welsh's Hall were opened on February 25, 1862, and both were filled immediately with patients, and by the 10th of March 140 patients had been received into the hospitals and at least 50 more were under treatment in the barracks, as hospital room could not be procured for them. I kept a list of all the patients returned cured and also of the deceased, but it was lost during my visit to Corinth and consequently I cannot give you quite so accurate an account of the second month. The first month would average 150 patients per day, while perhaps the second month would not average more than 50 or 60 per day, and the last ten or twelve days would not average more than 20. I had during the entire time not only to prescribe for the patients in both hospitals (which were located one mile apart) and in the barracks but put up the prescriptions myself, which consumed my entire time and was exceedingly laborious. I trust that my claim will not suffer any further reduction, as the whole amount would scarcely compensate me for the labor and toil of the first month. Although I applied for an assistant surgeon and had the promise of one I had neither assistant surgeon nor apothecary at any time.

Yours, respectfully,   THO. CHESNUT,
                                              Surgeon.

LOUISVILLE, *January 23, 1863.*
Capt. A. C. SEMPLE, *Assistant Adjutant-General.*

SIR: On the recent passage of the steamer Hastings down the Cumberland on the 13th instant she was attacked and captured by a squadron of rebel cavalry under command of Colonel Wade. It was the intention of the captors to regularly parole all on board; but as much time would be required to accomplish this work they finally determined to take the lists of the sick and wounded in possession of the surgeon in charge and report them to the Confederate authorities as regularly paroled prisoners on condition that the surgeon would so consider them and so report them to the Federal authorities. As it seemed evident that nothing could be gained by a refusal to enter into this arrangement it was readily agreed to. There being no list of the commissioned officers one was made out and they were required to stand in line and with uplifted hand to take the parole. After its administration they were informed that the surgeon in charge would furnish them with such papers as would show that they had been made prisoners of war and regularly paroled. This, however, the surgeon subsequently refused to do on the ground that he was in charge only of the wounded from certain hospitals; that having furnished the lists of these he had fulfilled his part of the agreement, and as the names of the officers did not appear on these lists they were not under his care and he had nothing to do with them.

Thus the matter stands. A dozen or more Federal officers have been reported to the Confederate authorities as paroled prisoners of war and they are without the papers needful to establish the fact. The case as presented then involves a question of military law of which I cannot pretend to be a judge. I report the facts as briefly as I can and in behalf of all concerned respectfully ask the attention of the proper authority to a consideration of them.

Very respectfully,

L. H. RALSTON,
Captain Company C, Third Kentucky Volunteers.

CHICAGO, *January 23, 1863.*
Col. W. HOFFMAN, *Commissary-General of Prisoners:*

Camp Douglas will accommodate 300 wounded and 3,000 to 4,000 well prisoners. The troops there are without arms but requisition has been made for a supply. Camp Washburn, at Milwaukee, and Camp Randall, at Madison, Wis., both full. One thousand prisoners could be taken care of at Prairie du Chien and 1,000 at Oshkosh, Wis. Notify me if any are sent to either place.

J. A. POTTER,
Captain and Assistant Quartermaster.

CHICAGO, *January 23, 1863.*
Col. W. HOFFMAN, *Commissary-General of Prisoners:*

Colonel Cameron is still at Camp Douglas though under orders. Plenty of troops in Wisconsin to guard prisoners there.

J. A. POTTER,
Captain and Assistant Quartermaster.

WAR DEPARTMENT, *Washington, January 24, 1863.*
Colonel LOOMIS,
Commanding at Fort Columbus, New York Harbor:

You will produce before Judge Sutherland the man Peter Miller, in respect to whom a writ of *habeas corpus* is pending, whenever you are notified to do so by any judicial authority. It is the desire of the Department to have no dispute in his case. I have also directed the provost-marshal-general to inform you when he should be produced.

EDWIN M. STANTON,
Secretary of War.

SAINT LOUIS, *January 24, 1863.*
Major-General HALLECK:

I have formerly discharged prisoners of war who seem worthy and willing to renounce rebel service, no United States order conflicting. I ask the discretionary power. Some 200 of the Murfreesborough prisoners desire to take the oath.

S. R. CURTIS,
Major-General.

CAMP BUTLER, *Illinois, January 24, 1863.*

Col. W. HOFFMAN:

Have the prisoners captured at Lexington under Colonel Mulligan been exchanged?

W. F. LYNCH,
Colonel Fifty-eighth Illinois.

HEADQUARTERS DEPARTMENT OF VIRGINIA,
Fort Monroe, January 24, 1863.

Col. W. HOFFMAN, *Commissary-General of Prisoners.*

COLONEL: I perceive an announcement of the arrival at Cairo of nearly 5,000 prisoners captured at Arkansas Post. Will you please inform me how many commissioned officers there are among them and send me a list of their names, rank, &c.? You are aware that the Confederate authorities have refused to release our captured officers on parole and intend to hand over to the Governors of the States where captured all taken after the 12th instant. This latter intention indicated by Jeff. Davis in his message is now under debate in the Confederate Congress, but I have no doubt that it will be carried out. An officer captured before the 12th instant will not be paroled but exchanged so that if our military authorities consent to the arrangement we can only get such officers released by releasing Confederate officers to procure the exchange of a special equivalent. What are you doing toward releasing citizen prisoners to procure special equivalents?

I am, very respectfully, your obedient servant,

WM. H. LUDLOW,
Lieutenant-Colonel and Agent for the Exchange of Prisoners.

P. S.—I inclose to you a copy of a communication from Mr. Ould. Have we not citizen prisoners captured by our officers who can be at once sent here for exchange for those taken by General Stuart? Please inform me.

W. H. L.

[Inclosure.]

RICHMOND, *January 19, 1863.*

Lieut. Col. WILLIAM H. LUDLOW, *Agent of Exchange.*

SIR: I have nothing new to add to my former communication to you in relation to the release of citizen prisoners. The Confederate Government is willing to adopt any fair and reciprocal rule. If you will release citizen prisoners captured by your generals in their raids into Confederate territory we will most cheerfully release such as have been captured by us including those taken by General Stuart. Is there anything unreasonable in this position? I know nothing about Henry Voegler whom you propose for William J. Peters. Peters need not return. I will inquire if we can receive Voegler for Peters. If not, I will hereafter suggest some name to you.

Respectfully, your obedient servant,

ROBERT OULD,
Agent of Exchange.

CINCINNATI, *January 24, 1863.*

Col. W. HOFFMAN, *Commissary-General of Prisoners:*

Three hundred and fifty of Confederate wounded can be accommodated at Camp Dennison and the medical director has been directed to provide accommodations for others elsewhere in the department. Will arms for the regiments at Camp Douglas be sent from Washington? Please answer immediately.

By order of Major-General Wright:

N. H. McLEAN,
Assistant Adjutant-General and Chief of Staff.

CINCINNATI, *January 24, 1863.*

Maj. N. H. McLEAN,
Assistant Adjutant-General, Department of the Ohio.

SIR: Please have my case settled as soon as possible. I am of the opinion that nothing short of an understanding between Secretary Stanton or General Halleck with the rebel Secretary will insure my safety either in the Army or out of it. I know them too well.

Respectfully, yours,

M. P. GADDIS,
Chaplain Second Regiment Ohio Volunteers.

[Indorsement.]

HEADQUARTERS DEPARTMENT OF THE OHIO,
Cincinnati, Ohio, January 27, 1863.

Respectfully referred to Col. W. Hoffman, commissary-general of prisoners, for reference if necessary to the Secretary of War.

On the first statement presented by Chaplain Gaddis I was confident the decision of Brigadier-General Boyle was the proper one and therefore approved it. The papers subsequently submitted by the chaplain cast some doubt on the correctness of that decision, particularly the statement that the rebels refused to parole him as a chaplain, such proceeding being in violation of the cartel, and required as the condition of letting the cotton remain on board for the use and comfort of the sick and wounded that he should pledge himself not as chaplain but as an individual in care of the wounded to destroy the cotton or deliver himself up. While I remain of the opinion still that the rebels cannot under any understanding had between the parties hold Chaplain Gaddis, I am not conversant enough with the understanding existing with the so-called Confederate authorities to be positive and therefore refer the case for decision.

Instructions have been given to hold the cotton till the matter shall be finally decided.

H. G. WRIGHT,
Major-General, Commanding.

CINCINNATI, *January 24, 1863.*

Maj. N. H. McLEAN,
Assistant Adjutant-General, Department of the Ohio.

SIR: After more mature reflection in regard to my present position toward the so-called Confederate States I am convinced that the "orders" issued to me by Brigadier-General Boyle and subsequently indorsed by Major-General Wright are wrong and do me unintentional injustice, and place me in a position not at all desirable to one who values his veracity and honor at any time, much less in a case like the present. I must either burn the cotton, return to the Confederate lines, or my Government must through the proper channels assume the responsibility of my actions and thus publicly relieve me. I being the only commissioned officer on either steamer able to treat with our captors certainly did my duty in making the best terms possible. In doing this you in the indorsement of General Boyle's order condemn me. My position as chaplain does not relieve me. General Wheeler did not parole me; he said it would be a violation of the cartel. The cotton was a lawful capture by them and under the circumstances they would have been justified in burning the same. Placed as both parties then were the cotton could not be burned without endangering the lives of many of the sufferers on the Hastings. Hence General Wheeler ordered me to be held personally responsible for the burning of the cotton on my reaching Louisville. I accepted the terms not dreaming that commanding generals would condemn instead of indorsing my course.

So long as there were other lives at stake I cared not for my own, but as it is now reduced to one and that my own it is just as valuable to me as yours and far more valuable than the paltry price of 111 bales of cotton, in order to save which it is now proposed to consign me to a doom not desirable to any man. I am fully aware of what that doom will be if I return without having tried to burn the cotton and I would rather submit to that doom than live and bear the disgrace necessarily involved in the violation of a faith plighted to a recognized "belligerent power" under such circumstances.

In conclusion allow me to say that I have been connected with the army ever since the commencement of the war and have tried to do my duty. I have been on detached service part of the time as recruiting officer, quartermaster, transporting supplies, &c., and have always had the commendation of my superiors and at this period of the war I can ill-afford to be thus cast off.

Hoping, my dear sir, that you now fully understand my position and will give it the attention that it deserves,

I remain, most respectfully, your obedient servant,

M. P. GADDIS,
Chaplain Second Regiment Ohio Volunteer Infantry.

HEADQUARTERS PRISONS,
Camp Chase, Ohio, January 24, 1863.

Captain LAZELLE,
Asst. to Commissary-General of Prisoners, Washington, D. C.

CAPTAIN: First, pursuant to your instructions I have contracted for the grading with gravel the walks and wells in the prisons at this post, *i. e.*, the east prisons, and herewith inclose the agreement* in duplicate for the approval of the commissary-general of prisoners and upon the return of the same if approved the work will be immediately begun. The price of $1 per cubic yard is the lowest responsible bid I had.

I have separated the prisoners of war from political [prisoners] and placed them and the officers recently received in prison No. 1 (east), No. 2 becoming too much crowded, and as it is equally as muddy as No. 2 the graveling will have to be done in it also. In that case the present contract could be extended.

2. I hold the commissioned officers, prisoners of war, from parole and exchange as directed by the commissary-general of prisoners.

---

* Omitted.

3. I have forwarded no prisoners of war to Cairo for exchange very recently, desiring first to learn from the commander at Cairo whether under late events on the Mississippi they could be received at present there.

4. The orders of Colonel Hoffman dated 19th instant are received and accordingly all facilities and information possible will be furnished the legislative investigating committee concerning prisons and prisoners.

I am, captain, very respectfully, your obedient servant,

EDWIN L. WEBBER,
Captain, Commanding Prisons.

PRIVATE AND CONFIDENTIAL.]

NEW YORK CITY, *January 24. 1863.*

Hon. W. H. SEWARD, *Secretary of State.*

SIR: The contents of this letter will explain briefly why I have presumed to trespass upon your time. For a year and a half I have been actively engaged in aiding the South in its attempt to overthrow the Government of the United States. For this I have suffered sufficiently and after mature reflection have returned to my ancient allegiance, having quietly renounced all connection with the rebels and sought repose from excitement by a residence in the North. Whilst I have thus lived in solitude the thought has often disturbed me when I reflected upon my present inactivity compared with my former life, and I have been led to ask myself if I were not wrong in not attempting some effort in behalf of the United States Government when I was capable of doing so much harm and injury to the Confederates from the knowledge which I possess of their movements in Europe and of their plans for securing the ultimate dismemberment of the Union. I know that I can better serve the Government in furnishing it with late reliable information than any man in the North. Whilst in Europe in 1861 and 1862 I was perfectly familiar with all secession movements and intrigues, having been one of the agents from the South.

I read regularly the dispatches of Messrs. Yancey, Mann and Rost, as well as those of Mr. Slidell after his arrival. I knew of the efforts of Bulloch and Semmes to fit out the Oreto and "290," or Alabama, and I could have frustrated them had I so desired. But I was then revolutionary in my opinions. I have since become conservative and peaceful. Since my change of opinion I will engage to place myself at the disposal of the President and repair to England and France and furnish the Department of State with regular abstracts of all dispatches and arrange with the Navy Department for the capture of the Alabama. I will be able to ascertain the depot where she will coal and steamers can be dispatched for her capture. In addition I can furnish a list of all vessels engaged in the contraband trade in order that they may be overhauled and properly dealt with.

I have thus furnished you with only an outline of that which I can do. In a personal interview I could explain myself more fully and at greater length than the mere limits of a letter will allow. I have made these propositions in earnest because I desire to see the war closed and the Union restored. If desired I can give the highest references as to my antecedents before the war and of operations since its commencement from among men of the North.

I desire that you shall show this letter only to the President in the event that you notice it at all, because if I place myself at his disposal and by any means the agents of Jefferson Davis should become apprised of the fact I would be powerless for good. As it is many would regard my proposals as dishonorable, but against treason and rebellion all means are honorable. At present I possess the unlimited confidence of all the rebel agents and commissioners.

Hoping soon to hear from you upon the subjects contained in this hurried and imperfect note,

I remain, honorable sir, with the highest consideration, your most obedient servant,

                                                B. WARD.

Address care of Astor House, New York.

                    HEADQUARTERS OF THE ARMY,
                        Washington, D. C., January 25, 1863.

Major-General CURTIS, *Saint Louis:*

Prisoners of war (not officers) who ask to take the oath of allegiance may in your discretion be released.

                                        H. W. HALLECK,
                                            General-in-Chief.

                HEADQUARTERS DEPARTMENT OF VIRGINIA,
                        Fort Monroe, January 25, 1863.

Maj. Gen. E. A. HITCHCOCK,
        Commissioner for Exchange of Prisoners.

GENERAL: I have the honor to acknowledge the receipt of your communication of the 23d instant* relating to the case of Doctor Rucker, with its [inclosure?]. I sincerely regret that his case has been so long neglected, as many opportunities have been presented since his arrest to procure his liberation or exchange. Governor Letcher, of Virginia, is assuming power and performing acts in gross violation of the cartels, so much so that Mr. Ould has spoken to me on the subject in tones of regret and at the same time hinted that he was powerless to remedy. There is a continual clashing and conflict of authority going on in Virginia between the State and Confederate authorities. The latter are afraid to quarrel openly with the former and would let Letcher have his own way with Doctor Rucker. I would earnestly recommend that some Confederate medical officer or prominent citizen of Virginia now in our hands (if we are so fortunate as to have one) be immediately set apart as hostage for Doctor Rucker. I will of course promptly make a demand for him and desire to have a hostage to present as an alternative. I am satisfied that nothing but most vigorous measures can be efficient in such a case. Colonel Hoffman may know of some suitable prisoner for a hostage and I would be glad to be furnished with his name, as I shall meet Mr. Ould in a few days.

I am, very respectfully, your obedient servant,

                                        WM. H. LUDLOW,
                        Lieutenant-Colonel and Agent for Exchange of Prisoners.

                            RICHMOND, *January 25, 1863.*

Lieutenant-Colonel LUDLOW, *Agent of Exchange.*

SIR: Your letters of the 23d have been received.

1. J. A. Flagg will be sent off by to-morrow's boat.
2. I prefer to retain the sutlers until I see you.

---

* Not found.

3. It is not true that many of your prisoners at Richmond and Salisbury are suffering from want of clothing. I will hereafter inform you whether any clothing for their use will be received.

4. I will make due inquiry into the alleged fact that parties belonging to the Fourth Regiment East Tennessee and other Tennessee and Ohio regiments have been detained in Atlanta and Castle Thunder for over eight months. I do not think that such is the fact. If it is so they shall be delivered to you.

5. You say "that all the men taken in arms against the United States who belonged to your (our) irregular organizations have been released and delivered at Vicksburg." The representations daily made to me are exactly to the contrary. If credible testimony can be believed you have now many hundreds of our officers and men in confinement. By the express terms of our last agreement all such are to be immediately released, to whatever organization they may have belonged. They heretofore have been refused a release because they were styled "bushwhackers." They were not so in any sense of the term. Will you release them?

6. Some few of the officers captured at Fredericksburg were paroled and sent to your lines. If any injustice has been done to you by our agreement about reducing officers to privates or in any other subject-matter I will promptly redress it. It will, however, be impossible to arrange that matter without an interview. There must be many officers in your and our possession who by our agreement made at the last interview were declared exchanged. Such certainly ought to be mutually delivered up. The excess is on our side but I will stand it because I have agreed to it. I must, however, insist upon the immediate delivery of such of our officers as are included in the agreement.

7. The letter to the widow of the late General D. R. Jones was sent to her in a few minutes after its receipt.

8. I have many subjects upon which I desire to have a conference with you. Inform me unless you yourself come when you will be at City Point.

9. Inform me by the next communication whether you have any of our non-commissioned officers and privates on hand and when you will send them; also whether you intend to keep in confinement the citizen prisoners whom you have arrested.

Respectfully, your obedient servant,

RO. OULD,
Agent of Exchange.

WAR DEPARTMENT, *Washington, January 26, 1863.*
Major-General SCHENCK, *Baltimore:*

Please make official report of all the circumstances of the arrest of Captain Wynne, calling himself of the British army, and also any testimony or facts leading to the suspicion of his being a spy.

H.W. HALLECK,
General-in-Chief.

HEADQUARTERS EIGHTEENTH ARMY CORPS,
New Berne, N. C., January 26, 1863.
Brig. Gen. N. G. EVANS, *Commanding, Kinston, N. C.*

GENERAL: I herewith have the honor to send prisoners of war taken by my forces at and near Trenton, N. C.

These men are released on their parole of honor. The list* of names please find inclosed.

I am, with great respect, your obedient servant,

J. G. FOSTER,
Major-General, Commanding.

SAINT LOUIS, *January 26, 1863.*

Colonel HAWKINS,
Commanding Escort of Confederate Prisoners at Alton:

You will ascertain what privates among the prisoners under your control desire to take the oath of allegiance and renounce the rebel service. And those who do so desire you will leave under proper guard upon the boats at Alton. The rest you will immediately send on to Chicago. Show this to Colonel Hildebrand.

S. R. CURTIS,
Major-General.

OFFICE COMMISSARY-GENERAL OF PRISONERS,
Washington, January 26, 1863.

Brig. Gen. M. C. MEIGS,
Quartermaster-General U. S. Army, Washington, D. C.

GENERAL: I have the honor to inclose herewith the papers which were referred to me from your office in relation to the destruction of public property at Chicago, Ill., by paroled troops, together with a report on the same matter made to me by Col. D. Cameron, commanding the camp, as required by my order† of the 22d ultimo, a copy of which is herewith inclosed.

By the report of the Board of Survey which inquired into the value of the property destroyed at Camp Douglas it is shown that the loss amounts to $7,652.70. Of this amount it is stated in the report of Colonel Cameron that the troops as a body are responsible for $2,169.65. For the balance no known person is responsible. The proceedings of the court of inquiry which investigated the circumstances of the destruction of this property are not furnished.

I would respectfully recommend that the troops who were at the camp when the property was destroyed be required to reimburse the loss to the Government. The following troops were at the camp at the time, viz: One hundred and eleventh New York, Colonel Segoine, aggregate 829; One hundred and twenty-fifth New York, Colonel Willard, aggregate 803; One hundred and twenty-sixth New York, Lieutenant-Colonel Bull, aggregate 787; Company A, Fifth New York Artillery, Captain Graham, aggregate 94; Company F, Fifth New York Artillery, Captain McGrath, aggregate 121; Thirty-second Ohio, Lieutenant-Colonel Swinney, aggregate 576; Sixtieth Ohio, Lieutenant-Colonel Hixon, aggregate 861, since mustered out of service; First Indiana Battery, Captain Rigby, aggregate 50; Fifteenth Indiana Battery, Captain Von Sehlen, aggregate 94; Company M, Second Illinois Artillery, Captain Phillips, aggregate 83; detachment Eighth New York Cavalry, aggregate 79; detachment Twelfth Illinois Cavalry, aggregate 97, and detachment First Maryland Cavalry, aggregate 31. Of these Colonel Cameron states that the Thirty-second and Sixtieth

---

* Omitted.   † See Hoffman to Cameron, p. 110.

Ohio, First Indiana Battery and Eighth New York Cavalry took the most active part. I have given the numbers present.

By the report of the Board of Survey which inquired into the leaving of the property at Camp Tyler it appears that the value of the property destroyed cost the Government $7,937.84. For this it appears by the report of Colonel Cameron that the One hundred and fifteenth New York, Colonel Sammon, aggregate 849, is mainly responsible, and I respectfully recommend that they should be required to refund this amount.

No report is made by Colonel Cameron of the tools and quartermaster's stores destroyed.

I am, very respectfully, your obedient servant,

W. HOFFMAN,
Colonel Third Infantry, Commissary-General of Prisoners.

OFFICE COMMISSARY-GENERAL OF PRISONERS,
Washington, January 26, 1863.

Lieut. Col. W. H. LUDLOW,
Agent for Exchange of Prisoners, Fort Monroe, Va.

COLONEL: I inclose herewith a letter* addressed to General Hitchcock requesting that inquiries may be made for Maj. E. F. Blake, Fifth Connecticut Volunteers, and the general wishes me to ask of you the favor to learn if possible through Mr. Ould whether he has ever been in their hands and what has been his fate. The general desires that you will return this letter to him with an indorsement which will show to the friends of Major Blake what has been done to get trace of him. I have frequent applications of this kind and have intended asking you to furnish me with a list of such officers or soldiers as may now be in their hospitals. Among the many sick and wounded who have fallen into their hands there may be still a number living who have not been well enough to be delivered for exchange. When paroled prisoners are delivered at Annapolis it will be only necessary for their commander to notify Colonel Sangster, the commander at Camp Parole, of their arrival, and he will send an officer and guard to receive them. I am preparing rolls of citizens held by us who may be offered for exchange and hope to send them down to-morrow. You can select from the rolls or you may permit Mr. Ould to select such persons as are acceptable and they will be immediately forwarded to you, or if Mr. Ould prefers it those in the West can be delivered there.

Very respectfully, your obedient servant,

W. HOFFMAN,
Colonel Third Infantry, Commissary-General of Prisoners.

WASHINGTON, *January 26, 1863.*

Lieut. Col. W. H. LUDLOW, *Agent for Exchange of Prisoners:*

Can medicine be sent to our citizen prisoners at Richmond? When will sutlers and their employés be released? Rebel prisoners of war are ordered from Tennessee to City Point for exchange.

W. HOFFMAN,
Commissary-General of Prisoners.

---

* Not found.

FORT MONROE, *January 26, 1863.*

Col. J. C. KELTON, *Assistant Adjutant-General, Washington.*

Shall I not retain here for the present Asst. Surg. J. C. Green, Confederate prisoner, as hostage for Surgeon Rucker, threatened with death by the authorities of Virginia? Rucker's case is the one referred to the General-in-Chief by the President on the 20th instant.

W. H. LUDLOW,
Lieutenant-Colonel, &c.

GENERAL ORDERS, }　　HDQRS. DEPT. OF THE TENNESSEE,
　　No. 10.　　　}　　　　*Memphis, Tenn., January 26, 1863.*

I. It being a violation of the provisions of the Dix-Hill cartel to parole prisoners at any other points than those designated in said cartel except by agreement between the generals commanding the opposing forces no paroles hereafter given to Federal soldiers in violation of such provisions of said cartel will be respected.

II. Officers or soldiers who by straggling from their commands are captured and paroled will at once be arrested and brought to trial before a court-martial.

III. Guerrillas or Southern soldiers caught in the uniforms of Federal soldiers will not be treated as organized bodies of the enemy but will be closely confined and held for the action of the War Department. Those caught within the lines of the Federal Army in such uniforms or in citizen's dress will be treated as spies.

IV. Officers, soldiers and citizens are prohibited from purchasing horses, mules or military clothing from any one connected with the Army without special authority. In order that improper and dishonest appropriation of captured property may be prevented commanding officers will exercise vigilance in enforcing this order and report every violation of it, to the end that offenders may be summarily punished.

V. Steam-boats are prohibited from carrying stock of any description North without permits granted by division or army corps commanders or the provost-marshal general, and violations of this restriction will be punished at the discretion of a military commission.

By order of Maj. Gen. U. S. Grant:

JOHN A. RAWLINS,
Assistant Adjutant-General.

DEPARTMENT OF STATE, *Washington, January 27, 1863.*

Hon. E. M. STANTON, *Secretary of War.*

SIR: The attention of this Department has unofficially been invited by the British pro-consul at Philadelphia to the condition of the cells in which prisoners are confined in Fort Delaware. The occasion of his communication to which I have had access was a visit to the fort which he made in connection with two of his countrymen who are there confined as deserters or enlisted men.

The granite walls of the dungeons are represented to be wet with moisture, the stone floor damp and cold, the air impure and deathly, no bed or couches to lie upon and offensive vermin crawling in every direction. It is also represented that the prisoners are allowed no water with which to wash themselves or change of clothing and are on every side surrounded by filth and vermin.

Although I have no doubt that these representations are exaggerated I have taken the liberty to make them known to you.

I have the honor to be, sir, your obedient servant,

WILLIAM H. SEWARD.

———

HEADQUARTERS OF THE ARMY,
Washington, D. C., January 27, 1863.

Lieutenant-Colonel LUDLOW, *Fort Monroe:*

The Secretary of War directs that you retain Surg. J. C. Green as a hostage for Surgeon Rucker.

Confederate officers will not for the present be exchanged for specific equivalents.

H. W. HALLECK,
General-in-Chief.

———

OFFICE COMMISSARY-GENERAL OF PRISONERS,
Washington, D. C., January 27, 1863.

Hon. E. M. STANTON,
Secretary of War, Washington, D. C.

SIR: I have the honor to submit herewith a report* made pursuant to your instructions of the 8th ultimo by General H. G. Wright, commanding Department of the Ohio, accompanied by a list of citizens of the State of Kentucky who have been and are now confined in the military prisons and camps of the United States outside of the line of said State, with a statement of the charges against them, by whom made and by whose order the arrests were made. This report was made to furnish the information called for by a resolution of the Senate adopted on the 5th of December, 1862. To simplify the list I have caused the names of all not noted as released to be entered in separate lists for the two prisons. Some of them have been released since the date of General Wright's letter, and they are so noted. I have also had prepared and submit herewith lists of citizens of Kentucky held at Camp Chase, Sandusky and Alton whose names do not appear on the list of General Wright, he having no control over the Alton Prison and the arrests at the other prisons having been made since the date of his report. I have the honor to inclose herewith a copy† of the Senate's resolution calling for the report.

Very respectfully, your obedient servant,

W. HOFFMAN,
Colonel Third Infantry, Commissary-General of Prisoners.

———

ADJUTANT-GENERAL'S OFFICE,
Washington, D. C., January 27, 1863.

Col. WILLIAM HOFFMAN, U. S. Army,
Commissary-General of Prisoners, Washington, D. C.

SIR: Please inform this office if within your knowledge whether charges have been preferred against Capt. R. W. Baylor, Twelfth Vir-

———

* See p. 177 for Wright to Stanton inclosing reports of General Boyle and Colonel Dent.
† Omitted here; see p. 27.

ginia Cavalry, for violation of a flag of truce near Harper's Ferry, Va., about the 6th of February, 1862, and if this officer is in confinement at Fort Delaware.

I am, sir, very respectfully, your obedient servant,
E. D. TOWNSEND,
Assistant Adjutant-General.

OFFICE COMMISSARY-GENERAL OF PRISONERS,
Washington, D. C., January 27, 1863.
Col. E. D. TOWNSEND,
Assistant Adjutant-General, Washington.

COLONEL: There is nothing on the records of this office in relation to Capt. R. W. Baylor, of the Twelfth Virginia Cavalry. My impression is that I received an application a short time since for the exchange of a rebel officer of that name who was a prisoner at Fort Delaware, but I have no roll on which the name appears. I will telegraph there and inquire for him.

Very respectfully, your obedient servant,
W. HOFFMAN,
Colonel Third Infantry, Commissary-General of Prisoners.

WASHINGTON, *January 27, 1863.*
Major-General CURTIS:

Please have a list of captured rebel officers furnished to this office giving rank, regiment and company and where captured.
W. HOFFMAN,
Commissary-General of Prisoners.

OFFICE COMMISSARY-GENERAL OF PRISONERS,
Washington, January 27, 1863.
Lieut. Col. W. E. DOSTER, *Provost-Marshal, Washington.*

COLONEL: Efforts are being made to effect the exchange of as many civilians now held as prisoners at Richmond as possible, and to further this object I have to request you will furnish me with the names of all citizens from the Southern States who are held in this city as prisoners and who are subjects for exchange.

Very respectfully, your obedient servant,
W. HOFFMAN,
Colonel Third Infantry, Commissary-General of Prisoners.

OFFICE COMMISSARY-GENERAL OF PRISONERS,
Washington, January 27, 1863.
Lieut. Col. W. H. LUDLOW,
Agent for Exchange of Prisoners, Fort Monroe, Va.

COLONEL: Please find inclosed herewith four lists* of rebel prisoners captured and paroled in Kentucky, Tennessee and Mississippi; also a number of applications* for the exchange of loyal citizens held as prisoners in Richmond; application* for the exchange of disloyal prisoners held by us and the recommendation of Judge Galloway for the exchange of eight political prisoners held at Camp Chase. There is a Mr. William

---

* Omitted.

H. Child, of Alabama, who wishes to be exchanged that he may go home, and being a very gentlemanly man I think you may make a good exchange for him. He is in this city, recently released from Fort Lafayette. The Mr. Price now on parole in Baltimore who applies for an exchange might be exchanged for a Doctor Thatcher, of Greenbrier, Va., who I am told is held at Richmond. I inclose two lists* of prisoners in confinement in Richmond given to me by persons recently released. They may be of service to you in making up the exchanges. We hold at Fort Lafayette I believe Zarvona *alias* Mr. Thomas, who attempted to capture a steamboat at Baltimore, who I understand is a man of note with the rebels, and that they hold seven officers in close confinement as hostages for him. I don't know whether this man is for exchange but I will inquire and let you know. Is it true that they are in our debt over 150 prisoners who should have been released from Salisbury? I hear that Mr. Wood said so, and he I believe represents that they would give the seven officers and the prisoners at Salisbury for Zarvona. I have no faith in this story. I mention it to get at the truth. I send you some rolls* of Kentucky prisoners at Sandusky and Camp Chase that you may ascertain if they can be exchanged for our people who are held at Richmond; those marked under sentence could not be exchanged. We have other prisoners of the same class from all the border States, and if you can negotiate an exchange it will be a great blessing to those who are suffering in their horrible prisons. I will send you full rolls if you think exchanges can be made and the prisoners selected can be sent down immediately. I have called on the provost-marshal in this city for a list of the prisoners at the Old Capitol and will forward it to you as soon as it is received.

Very respectfully, your obedient servant,

W. HOFFMAN,
Colonel Third Infantry, Commissary-General of Prisoners.

FORT MONROE, VA., *January 27, 1863.*
Maj. Gen. H. W. HALLECK, *General-in-Chief:*

A Richmond paper of this morning gives the information that Jeff. Davis' retaliatory proclamation is strongly opposed in the Confederate Congress. W. L. Yancey has made a speech against it.

WM. H. LUDLOW,
Lieutenant-Colonel and Agent for Exchange of Prisoners.

(Copy to Hon. Edwin M. Stanton, Secretary of War.)

GENERAL HOSPITAL NO. 17,
Nashville, Tenn., January 27, 1863.
Maj. Gen. W. S. ROSECRANS,
Commanding Department of the Cumberland.

SIR: I have the honor to report that on January 13, 1863, as surgeon in charge, I started with 212 wounded and sick soldiers of the U. S. Army on the steamer Hastings on the Cumberland River bound for Louisville, Ky. At Harpeth Shoals on that same day the boat was captured by the Confederate forces after being fired upon by artillery and musketry, the hospital flag flying. The lists of about 212 soldiers and officers from General Hospitals No. 8, No. 15 and No. 6, Nashville, Tenn., were taken and the boat and men permitted to proceed only on

---

* Omitted.

condition that I certified to the lists as captured and paroled. They dictated and I appended the following certificate to each of the hospital lists, no copy of which was left me:

ON CUMBERLAND RIVER, *Near Ashland, January 13, 1863.*

I certify that the above lists of sick and wounded U. S. soldiers on board the steamer Hastings were captured by the Confederate forces (or forces of the Confederate States) on January 13, 1863, on the Cumberland River, and duly paroled by E. S. Burford, assistant adjutant-general of General Wheeler's Cavalry Corps.

L. D. WATERMAN,
Surgeon Thirty-ninth Indiana Volunteers, in Charge of Sick and Wounded.

There were also eight or nine wounded officers of the U. S. Army on board whose names were taken and who were sworn not to take up arms, &c., but who being passengers and not under my charge and immediately mingled with 500 others from other steam-boats I am unable to name. The Confederate officers being intoxicated and getting rapidly more so took the lists names and plunder and hurried off in spite of my protest and demands for copies, only giving me in return the following statement the original of which I have:

HEADQUARTERS CAVALRY,
On Board the Hastings, on the Cumberland River, Tenn., January 13, 1863.

The steamer Hastings having been captured by the Confederate forces on the 13th of January, 1863, and having 212 U. S. soldiers, wounded in the late battles before Murfreesborough, do swear that they will not aid or abet or in anywise do anything prejudicial to the interests of the Confederate States until they are duly exchanged according to the cartel.

Witness:

E. S. BURFORD,
Assistant Adjutant-General, General Wheeler's Cavalry Corps.

These wounded officers and soldiers were mingled with others unavoidably and scattered to different hospitals, with no evidence, some of them without an understanding of the transaction. Such are very briefly the essential facts concerning this capture and attempt at parole the report of which has been somewhat delayed by sickness.

I have the honor to be, very respectfully and obediently, yours,

L. D. WATERMAN,
Surgeon Thirty-ninth Indiana Volunteers,
In Charge General Hospital No. 17, Nashville, Tenn.

WAR DEPARTMENT, *Washington, January 28, 1863.*
Hon. WILLIAM H. SEWARD, *Secretary of State.*

SIR: I have the honor to acknowledge the receipt of your letter of the 27th instant and to inform you in reply that orders have been issued for an immediate and thorough inspection into the condition of the prisoners confined at Fort Delaware.

Very respectfully, your obedient servant,

EDWIN M. STANTON,
Secretary of War.

WAR DEPARTMENT, *Washington, January 28, 1863.*
Maj. Gen. R. C. SCHENCK, *Commanding at Baltimore, Md.*

GENERAL: I inclose herewith a copy of a letter* of the 27th instant from the Department of State calling attention to certain representations made by the British pro-consul at Philadelphia in regard to the condition of the prisoners at Fort Delaware and of the cells in which

---

* See Seward to Stanton, January 27, p. 216.

they are confined. Please detail a competent officer to make an immediate and thorough inspection of the quarters assigned to the prisoners, and also to inquire as to the alleged neglect of their health and comfort. When his report is received be good enough to transmit it to this Department for such action as the case may seem to require.

Very respectfully, your obedient servant,

EDWIN M. STANTON,
Secretary of War.

SPRINGFIELD, ILL., *January 28, 1863.*

Honorable SECRETARY OF WAR:

The following dispatch was just received:

PARIS, EDGAR COUNTY, *January 28, 1863.*

Adjutant-General FULLER:

By proper authority I arrested a deserter from my company and mob rescued him. What shall I do? Answer immediately.

SIMPKINS,
Lieutenant Company E, Sixty-sixth Illinois Volunteers.

One or two similar instances have occurred in other counties. What shall I do? I learn that 2,500 prisoners are being sent here. If so, you will have to send force to guard them. We cannot.

RICHARD YATES,
Governor.

OFFICE COMMISSARY-GENERAL OF PRISONERS,
Washington, D. C., January 28, 1863.

CLERK OF THE SENATE OF THE UNITED STATES, *Washington.*

SIR: I have the honor to request that you will furnish me with a copy of the resolution adopted by the Senate on the 5th of December, 1862, calling on the President for information in relation to citizens of Kentucky who have been arrested and confined outside the limits of said State. The copy is required to accompany a report which is to be submitted to the Secretary of War.

I am, very respectfully, your obedient servant,

W. HOFFMAN,
Colonel Third Infantry, Commissary-General of Prisoners.

FORT MONROE, *January 28, 1863.*

Col. W. HOFFMAN, *Commissary-General of Prisoners:*

What orders if any have been given for the delivery to Confederate authorities of the non-commissioned officers and privates captured at Arkansas Post?

WM. H. LUDLOW,
Lieutenant-Colonel and Agent for Exchange of Prisoners.

FORT MONROE, *January 28, 1863.*

Major General HITCHCOCK,
Commissioner for Exchange of Prisoners:

I intend to go to City Point to-morrow to meet Mr. Ould and would much like to have the list of our citizen prisoners which W. P. Wood made. Can they be sent by mail this afternoon?

WM. H. LUDLOW,
Lieutenant-Colonel and Agent.

FORT MONROE, *January 28, 1863.*

Col. W. HOFFMAN, *Commissary-General of Prisoners:*

Our prisoners can receive medical and other supplies. Send them to me. I expect all the sutlers and employés to be deliverd next week. Where are the Arkansas Post prisoners? Jefferson Davis' retaliatory proposition is strongly opposed in Confederate Congress and I now think will not be carried out.

WM. H. LUDLOW,
Lieutenant-Colonel and Agent for Exchange of Prisoners.

WASHINGTON, *January 28, 1863.*

Lieut. Col. W. H. LUDLOW:

I will mail the rolls to-day. Post of Arkansas prisoners are held at Western camps till they can be sent to Vicksburg. Please exchange Brig. Gen. August Willich, captured at Murfreesborough December 31.

W. HOFFMAN,
Commissary-General of Prisoners.

HEADQUARTERS, *Fort Monroe, January 28, 1863.*

Col. W. HOFFMAN, *Commissary-General of Prisoners.*

COLONEL: I have just received the inclosed communications from Capt. William Gramm and others. They are addressed to the Secretary of War and if it be necessary you can hand them to him. The subject-matter has been brought to the attention of the President by Governor Letcher, and I understand that he has directed his private secretary to examine into and report the facts. Will you please furnish me with the facts? I must have them to act understandingly upon and would be glad to receive them as soon as possible. If the Confederate officers are at hard labor as alleged what is the offense?

I am, very respectfully, your obedient servant,

WM. H. LUDLOW,
Lieutenant-Colonel and Agent for Exchange of Prisoners.

[Inclosure No. 1.]

PENITENTIARY, *Richmond, Va., January 4, 1863.*

Hon. EDWIN M. STANTON,
Secretary of War, Washington, D. C.

SIR: I have the honor of addressing this communication from out of the penitentiary to you for the purpose of giving you information that myself and Lieut. Isaac A. Wade, both of the Eighth Regiment West Virginia Volunteer Infantry, U. S. Army, are held here in close confinement at hard labor by order of Governor Letcher, of Virginia, as hostages for Capt. Daniel Dusky and Lieut. Jacob Varner, both commissioned by him and reported to be held in close confinement at hard labor in the penitentiary at Washington, D. C. We were taken prisoners of war by Major-General Floyd's command on the 25th day of November while on a reconnoitering expedition into Logan County, W. Va., ordered by Major-General Cox, commanding the District of Kanawha. My command consisted of 70 men and 3 commissioned officers, of which 11 enlisted men, Lieut. Wade and myself were captured.

The regiment at the time was stationed at Coalsmouth, Kanawha River, a distance of over fifty miles from the place of our capture. Permit me, Mr. Secretary, to beg of you to order our exchange if possible as soon as practicable, so that we may be released at an early day and enjoy the liberties of freedom once more and have our innocent sufferings ended.

Hoping that you may grant our most earnest request as soon as possible. I remain, Mr. Secretary,

Very respectfully, your most obedient servant,

WM. GRAMM,
Capt. Co. B Eighth Regt. W. Va. Volunteer Infantry, U. S. Army.

[Inclosure No 2.]

PENITENTIARY, *Richmond, Va., January 5, 1863.*
Mr. STANTON, *Secretary of War.*

SIR: We are prisoners of war held by the State of Virginia and we are confined in the State Penitentiary as a means of retaliation for the confinement of one Colonel Zarvona* and others held by the Government of the United States. Said Zarvona bears a commission from the State of Virginia and is said to be in confinement in some of our Northern prisons. We were taken prisoners in Floyd County, Ky., by Maj. Gen. John B. Floyd, commanding State troops. We were handed over to Governor Letcher, who issued an order confining us to solitary confinement in the State Penitentiary until we were exchanged for Colonel Zarvona and others. We therefore beseech you to effect an exchange for us as soon as possible. A copy of the Governor's order has been forwarded to you already.

Very sincerely, yours,

DAVID V. AUXIER.
ISAAC GOBLE.
JOHN W. HOWE.

The first two of the above-named are soldiers of the Thirty-ninth Regiment Kentucky Volunteers. The last is a citizen of Johnson County, Ky.

[Inclosure No. 3.]

IN THE CELLS OF THE PENITENTIARY,
Richmond, Va., January 6, 1863.
Secretary STANTON:

We, the undersigned prisoners, and a number of others who are held here for delivery of Col. Thomas Zarvona, have no other redress only through you and our Government for release of that officer. Once he is released they will release us prisoners, all which is most desirable. Nothing more at present.

We remain, your obedient servants,

WILLIAM S. DILS.
SAMUEL PACK.

SAINT LOUIS, *January 28, 1863.*
Major-General CURTIS, *Commanding Department of the Missouri.*

GENERAL: There are among those confined at the Gratiot Street Military Prison 200 prisoners sent up from below under charge of Colonel Hawkins. These are part of the captured at Murfreesborough;

* See Vol. II, this Series, for case of Zarvona, p. 379 *et seq.*

some of them conscripts, and all have expressed their wish on being questioned thereto to take the oath of allegiance and be discharged. In view of your memorandum instructions of January 26 I desire your orders in regard to the disposition I shall make of them. These prisoners expressed their desire to Colonel Hawkins while under his charge to be released on oath and therefore he landed them here and delivered them into my charge. Afterwards being each questioned by my orders all stated that they did not wish to be exchanged, but preferred to take the oath. I recommend that they be released on the terms they request. The Gratiot Street Prison is very much crowded and I desire to ease it as soon as possible in this way. There are also prisoners of war for exchange to the number of about 130—sent from Springfield and elsewhere—in Gratiot Street Prison. What disposition shall I make of them; forward them to Camp Douglas? What disposition is to be made of the Arkansas Post prisoners remaining on the J. J. Roe? The Nebraska and Gaty have gone to Alton.

Very respectfully, your obedient servant,

F. A. DICK,
Lieutenant-Colonel and Provost-Marshal-General.

PROVOST-MARSHAL'S OFFICE,
New Orleans, La., January 28, 1863.

COMMANDING OFFICER OF CONFEDERATE FORCES,
Port Hudson, La.

SIR: I am directed by the commanding general to inform you that there are in this department 376 Confederate prisoners of war enrolled for exchange. All the requisite arrangements upon the part of the United States having been complied with it remains for you to designate the time when you will deliver the like number of Federal prisoners of war in exchange at the place agreed upon in the cartel between the United States and the Confederate Government.

If possible please give this your immediate attention and return answer by the bearer.

I am, sir, very respectfully, your obedient servant,

C. W. KILLBORN,
Captain and Provost-Marshal of New Orleans, La.

[Indorsement.]

HEADQUARTERS DEPARTMENT OF THE GULF,
New Orleans, January 30, 1863.

Respectfully referred to Maj. Gen. C. C. Augur, commanding, &c., who will please send a communication of the same purport as the within to the commanding officer of the Confederate forces at Port Hudson over his own signature.

By command of Major-General Banks:

RICHARD B. IRWIN,
Lieutenant-Colonel and Assistant Adjutant-General.

HEADQUARTERS DEPARTMENT OF NORTH CAROLINA,
New Berne, January 29, 1863.

Col. W. HOFFMAN, *Commissary-General of Prisoners.*

COLONEL: In reply to your communication of the 15th instant to General Foster I beg to state that I am informed that the circumstances were as follows, viz: At the time of the capture of the prisoners mentioned no blank rolls for prisoners had ever been received in this department and consequently the exact form in which these rolls were to be made out was not known here; and further that these prisoners were paroled on the battle-field and the paroles are in consequence probably not as perfect as they should be. It was impossible to carry the prisoners with the army on the forced marches, not only on account of the guard required but also on account of the limited supply of commissary stores with which the army was furnished. Inclosed I have the honor to forward the paroles* taken from the prisoners. Most of the prisoners you will observe were captured at or near Kinston, N. C., during the fight there December 14. These men agreed, in addition to the parole signed by them, not to leave the town of Kinston for forty-eight hours after the departure of the U. S. forces from that place. All the others with the exception of those whose parole is dated at New Berne were captured between New Berne and Kinston and sent to New Berne under guard and thence sent by flag of truce December 25, 1862, to the enemy's line. This statement will account for our not having a receipt from a Confederate officer for the prisoners. As it may aid in effecting an exchange I would also state that an exact copy of the list sent to General Hitchcock was forwarded by flag of truce to Maj. Gen. S. G. French, C. S. Army, commanding Department of North Carolina. I also inclose* a list of three Confederate officers now confined at this post.

Hoping that these paroles and this explanation will do away with the difficulties in the way of an exchange,

I am, very respectfully, your obedient servant,

H. W. WESSELLS,
Brigadier-General of Volunteers, Commanding.

OFFICE COMMISSARY-GENERAL OF PRISONERS,
Washington, D. C., January 29, 1863.

Hon. J. K. MOORHEAD, *Member of Congress, Washington.*

SIR: In reply to your letter of the 25th instant inclosing complaints from paroled soldiers at Camp Parole I have the honor to inform you that those complaints are without any real foundation. The rations have been reduced by my order with the approval of the Secretary of War because the allowance was much greater than was at all necessary, and the surplus is converted into a fund through the Subsistence Department which is disbursed under my orders for the benefit of the camp. As one step toward preserving discipline two roll-calls are required a day, and to punish those who neglect to attend the commanding officer stops their rations almost the only means of punishment in his power. Arrangements are being made for their payment. It may already have been done. There is no interference with their correspondence.

Very respectfully, your obedient servant,

W. HOFFMAN,
Colonel Third Infantry, Commissary-General of Prisoners.

---

* Not found.

OFFICE COMMISSARY-GENERAL OF PRISONERS,
Washington, D. C., January 29, 1863.

Lieut. Col. F. A. DICK, Provost-Marshal-General, Saint Louis, Mo.

COLONEL: I have the honor to acknowledge the receipt of your letters of 20th and 21st instant.* I was not aware that there was necessarily so much delay in investigating the cases of prisoners sent to Alton, and to guard against the possibility of the release of those whose cases have not been acted on I will give instructions to the commanding officer of the prison to release none such without first calling my attention to their position. But that he may act advisedly in such cases it will be necessary that you should furnish him with full rolls with charges for his guidance. On the application of Colonel Lowe, commanding Fort Henry, you will send him Alexander Holsapple, of Calloway County, Ky., a prisoner in your charge, to be by him discharged. Orders have been issued for the release of John H. Dameron. I cannot authorize the release of Thomas Maxwell (or Maxfield) without a report in his case. I have the case of Enoch Harding, a prisoner at Johnson's Island, under consideration.

Very respectfully, your obedient servant,
W. HOFFMAN,
Colonel Third Infantry, Commissary-General of Prisoners.

SAINT LOUIS, January 29, 1863.

Col. R. J. EBERMAN,
Assistant Provost-Marshal, Macon County, Mo.

COLONEL: In answer to your letter of inquiry of January 22 I have to reply that all persons returning from the rebel service are at once to be arrested and placed in custody. If they desire to be released on oath and bond you may investigate their cases and upon being satisfied that their return is honest and that they (really tired of the rebel service) desire to become loyal citizens you are authorized to release them on oath of allegiance and approved bond with two sureties in a sum not less than $1,000. None are to be released who have previously taken and broken the oath, but are to be forwarded to Saint Louis with all the evidence against them. You will have to exercise much care and discretion in preventing the return of recruiting officers, spies and those who may desire to make trouble in future raids.

Very respectfully, your obedient servant,
F. A. DICK,
Lieutenant-Colonel and Provost-Marshal-General.

Resolution adopted by the House of Representatives January 30, 1863.

Resolved, That the General-in-Chief of the Army be directed to inform the House of Representatives whether any rebel officers captured by the Army of the United States have been granted parole since the proclamation of Jefferson Davis refusing to parole or exchange captured officers of Union regiments.

---

* Letter of the 21st not found.

ADJUTANT-GENERAL'S OFFICE,
Washington, January 30, 1863.

Brig. Gen. M. R. PATRICK,
Provost-Marshal-General, Army of the Potomac:

A dispatch is just received from commanding officer Fort Delaware reporting Capt. Robert W. Baylor confined there charged with murder of one of our men while bearing a flag of truce.

L. THOMAS,
Adjutant-General.

OFFICE COMMISSARY-GENERAL OF PRISONERS,
Washington, D. C., January 30, 1863.

Maj. Gen. H. G. WRIGHT,
Commanding Department of the Ohio, Cincinnati, Ohio.

GENERAL: In reply to your reference of the letter of Lieut. Col. D. B. Wright, of the Confederate Army, to this office I have the honor to say that the order directing that rebel officers shall not be paroled does not apply to cases where the officers have already been exchanged as appears to be the position of Colonel Wright. The battle of Perryville took place on the 7th of October and all officers captured then or previous to the 10th December, 1862, are declared by General Orders, No. 10, to be exchanged, and all such should be sent through our lines by the nearest suitable route. The cartel does not require that prisoners shall be paroled within ten days but that they "shall be sent with all reasonable dispatch" to the two points designated for exchange or parole.

I have the honor to be, very respectfully, your obedient servant,

W. HOFFMAN,
Colonel Third Infantry, Commissary-General of Prisoners.

OFFICE COMMISSARY-GENERAL OF PRISONERS,
Washington, D. C., January 30, 1863.

Lieut. Col. W. E. DOSTER,
Provost-Marshal, Washington, D. C.

COLONEL: Can you give me any information in relation to Capt. Daniel Dusky and Lieut. Jacob Varner, commissioned officers belonging to the rebel army of Virginia, said to be held in confinement at hard labor in the penitentiary of this city? Officers of our army are held in the penitentiary at Richmond in retaliation for the confinement of the above-named men and I desire the information asked for that such steps may be taken as the case demands. Please reply at your earliest convenience.

Very respectfully, your obedient servant,

W. HOFFMAN,
Colonel Third Infantry, Commissary-General of Prisoners.

INDIANAPOLIS, IND., *January 30, 1863.*

Col. WILLIAM HOFFMAN,
Commissary-General of Prisoners, Washington, D. C.

COLONEL: I have made a thorough inspection of Camp Morton to-day. I find it much dilapidated and sadly in need of repairs. The buildings already there can be made to accommodate about 2,000 wounded prisoners but the accommodations will be poor. A fatigue party is now at work policing the camp. I would respectfully recommend a more judicious arrangement of the barracks and that some of the temporary barracks at Camp Carrington be removed to within the inclosure. The camp may then be made to accommodate 4,000 prisoners. What disposition shall be made of the rebel surgeons who accompany the prisoners? Of the force stationed here there are only 224 men for guard duty. There is a regiment stationed here, the Seventy-first Indiana Volunteers (Colonel Biddle), which has 738 men. Of these 504 are paroled, having been recently captured in Kentucky. The number of secession sympathizers and anti-war and anti-administration politicians here renders it injudicious to keep many rebel prisoners at Camp Morton without an officer of firmness and experience in command. I leave for Cincinnati this evening.

Very respectfully, your obedient servant,
H. W. FREEDLEY,
Captain, Third Infantry.

WAR DEPARTMENT, *Washington, January 31, 1863.*
Major-General GRANT, *Memphis:*

The commissary-general of prisoners has referred to me a list of exchanges effected by General Dodge on the 19th of December. General Dodge was not authorized by the cartel to make exchanges and such assumption of authority necessarily leads to difficulty and trouble.

H. W. HALLECK,
General-in-Chief.

WASHINGTON CITY, D. C., *January 31, 1863.*
Hon. EDWIN M. STANTON, *Secretary of War.*

SIR: In the case of the Rev. M. P. Gaddis, chaplain of the Second Ohio Regiment, I have the honor to report that the circumstances appear to be these as gathered from the papers submitted:

The steamer Hastings on the 13th instant was passing down the Cumberland River from Nashville bound to Louisville having on board 212 wounded soldiers of the U. S. Army, and at a point some thirty-five miles from Nashville fell into the hands of an armed force acting under Confederate authority, whose commander observing that she was a sanitary vessel gave her permission to pass "without molestation," but on discovering soon after some cotton bales on board of the vessel on which some of the wounded men were lying he gave orders to remove and burn it. Chaplain Gaddis, who was on board, appears to have assumed command of the vessel, and by his interposition representing the danger to the wounded if disturbed he obtained permission to proceed with the vessel and with the cotton upon a promise made by him, not as chaplain but in his individual capacity, to burn the cotton "on the wharf" at Louisville or return within twenty days and deliver himself up to the Confederate authorities as a prisoner of war.

On arriving at Louisville and reporting the circumstances General Boyle ordered, January 19, that the cotton should not be burned and that Chaplain Gaddis should not return to the Confederate authorities. This order was approved by General Wright, commanding Department of the Ohio, by an order dated at Cincinnati, January 21, but subsequently, January 24, on an appeal from Chaplain Gaddis General Wright expresses some doubt as to the propriety of the order given by General Boyle and refers the subject for the disposal of the War Department.

Being required to report in this case I have the honor to observe that there can be no doubt as to the humane purpose of Chaplain Gaddis, but there is as little doubt that he had no authority to pledge himself to burn the cotton "on the wharf" at Louisville; a pledge the invalidity of which must have been known to the Confederate commander who might with as much propriety have required from Chaplain Gaddis a pledge to fire the city of Louisville as a condition for allowing the Hastings to pass. Under such circumstances it might be assumed that the Confederate commander had no expectation of a compliance with such a pledge and only accepted it as a matter of form under cover of which to allow the wounded men to proceed undisturbed. I suppose the pledge is a nullity on the face of it. The alternative condition by which Chaplain Gaddis promised to return as a prisoner of war presents a case for himself to decide upon, and his determination in view of it ought not to be interfered with by external authority. In the event of his deciding to return with the evidence clearly in his power to furnish of his own personal good faith in the matter the Confederate authorities would be answerable to humanity and to civilized history that his treatment should not disgrace the usages of modern warfare.

The further action of the War Department it would seem must depend upon the decision of Chaplain Gaddis.

I have the honor to be, very respectfully, your obedient servant,

E. A. HITCHCOCK,
Major-General of Vols., Commissioner for Exchange of Prisoners.

WASHINGTON, D. C., *January 31, 1863.*
WM. P. WOOD, *Superintendent Old Capitol Prison.*

SIR: Inclosed you will find a copy of the memorandum for Colonel Ludlow from Mr. Ould, dated City Point, Va., January 8, 1863.

If you desire to make any answer to this statement from Mr. Ould I will forward it through Colonel Ludlow if it is such as he can present with propriety.

I desire you to furnish me a report of your proceedings in your communications with Mr. Baxter or other Confederate authorities, especially any pledge you may have from any one assuming to act by that authority tending to the release or exchange of any citizen of the United States held as prisoner by that authority.

Respectfully, your obedient servant,

E. A. HITCHCOCK,
Major-General of Vols., Commissioner for Exchange of Prisoners.

[Inclosure.]

CITY POINT, VA., *January 8, 1863.*

MEMORANDUM FOR COLONEL LUDLOW.

When Mr. Wood reached Varina with the prisoners under his charge I informed him distinctly and repeatedly that no equivalent of any kind would be given for non-combatants arrested on Confederate soil. I did not offer to exchange any person of whatever condition or nationality for such. I did say that if any citizen of the

Confederate States was arrested outside the limits of those States in such a case it might be a fair subject of negotiation. Mr. Wood did not say to me that he would not negotiate at any other place than Richmond. So far from it he tried repeatedly to negotiate with me at Varina. He only asked as a preliminary for their delivery that I would agree to consider his prisoners as subjects of exchange. If Mr. Wood had made any such declaration as he avers he did make he never would have gone to Richmond, and he having now made such a declaration he never will be allowed to go there.

Mr. Wood entreated me again and again for permission to go to Richmond. At first I refused and remarked to him jestingly that he would not be safe there. I did not, however, even in jest put it on the score of his "violent Unionism." I knew many of the gentlemen on Mr. Wood's boat, some of them very intimately. They besought me to permit them to be delivered and expressed their horror of being retained. At this stage after I had repeatedly refused to allow Mr. Wood to go to Richmond he came to me and said he was willing to go to Richmond under arrest. I reluctantly consented and accordingly during the following night he was put under a guard and sent to the provost-marshal of Richmond. It is utterly untrue that the issue between Mr. Wood and myself was that he should proceed to Richmond or return with the prisoners. The matter of going to Richmond was an afterthought with Mr. Wood. Mr. Wood's first application was to have the prisoners recognized as subjects of exchange. If I had agreed to that there would have been no proposition to go to Richmond. Mr. Baxter was not appointed to treat with Mr. Wood. Mr. Baxter for more than a year before that time had been engaged in reporting upon the cases of parties confined in prison. Mr. Baxter was not a commissioner for determining the exchange of any kind of prisoners and our Government did not in any way so consider Mr. Wood. Mr. Baxter simply reported cases to the War Department and so far as I have ever heard was never authorized to make stipulations and regulations concerning such or any other matters.

RO. OULD.

HEADQUARTERS,
Camp Douglas, Chicago, Ill., January 31, 1863.
Col. W. HOFFMAN, Commissary-General of Prisoners.

SIR: A number of prisoners now in this camp have called upon me, others have written to me, for information as to the probability of their being permitted to take the oath of allegiance. Some have even proposed to enter our service, as they were forced into the rebel. These are generally from Kentucky, Tennessee or Arkansas. Those from Arkansas especially being generally poor men make strong Union professions. Those from Texas and Mississippi are very hostile and do not wish any terms except to fight it out.

Very respectfully, your most obedient servant,
J. AMMEN,
Brigadier-General of Volunteers, Commanding.

OFFICE COMMISSARY-GENERAL OF PRISONERS,
Washington, D. C., January 31, 1863.
W. B. SMITH, Machias, Me.

SIR: In reply to your letter of the 20th instant addressed to the Secretary of War I have to inform you that the eighth section of General

Orders, No. 10, issued from the War Department on the 10th January, 1863, applies only to persons taken in arms. Sailors captured on merchant vessels and paroled must be exchanged for persons of a similar class taken from the enemy's vessels or for other civilians.

Very respectfully, your obedient servant,

W. HOFFMAN,
Colonel Third Infantry, Commissary-General of Prisoners.

HEADQUARTERS DEPARTMENT OF THE CUMBERLAND,
Murfreesborough, January 31, 1863.
Surg. L. D. WATERMAN,
39th Indiana Vols., Hospital No. 17, Nashville, Tenn.

SIR: The general commanding directs me to acknowledge the receipt of your report of the capture of the steamer Hastings by the Confederates while conveying sick and wounded under your charge to Louisville. He directs me to say that no prisoner can be considered as properly paroled except those delivered in accordance with the terms of the cartel published in General Orders, No. 142, War Department, series 1862. The men under your charge will not therefore be considered as paroled.

Very respectfully, your obedient servant,

C. GODDARD,
Assistant Adjutant-General and Chief of Staff.

HEADQUARTERS DISTRICT OF CORINTH,
Corinth, Miss., February 1, 1863.
Col. W. HOFFMAN,
Commissary-General of Prisoners, Washington, D. C.:

I herewith forward roll* of prisoners taken from this command in accordance with the instructions of your communication of January 22, 1863. I give all particulars so far as I have them. The enemy are in the habit of paroling men and sending them North without living up to the Dix-Hill cartel, and we have no mode of preventing it. The men accept the parole and make for home.

I am, very respectfully, your obedient servant,

G. M. DODGE,
Brigadier-General.

HEADQUARTERS CAMP OF INSTRUCTION,
Benton Barracks, Mo., February 1, 1863.
Col. WILLIAM HOFFMAN,
Commissary-General of Prisoners, Washington, D. C.

SIR: Herewith I have the honor to transmit you a roll* of the paroled men at this post for the month of January, 1863, as required by your instructions, containing 75 commissioned officers present, 16 commissioned officers absent, 818 enlisted men present, 971 enlisted men absent, 1,880 aggregate.

I am, colonel, very respectfully, your obedient servant,

B. L. E. BONNEVILLE,
Colonel, U. S. Army, Commanding.

---

* Omitted.

HEADQUARTERS, *Annapolis, Md., February 1, 1863.*

Col. W. HOFFMAN, *Commissary-General of Prisoners.*

SIR: I have the honor to report that I have completed my arrangements at Annapolis for the receiving of paroled men from Richmond. The new Government barracks built at Annapolis able to accommodate 2,000 men has been put to the use of paroled men arriving from Richmond and every arrangement will be made for their comfort. Cooking stoves will be put up to-morrow when we can give them food at once and that properly cooked. This will satisfy the men better than anything else on their arrival. I can keep them there until I get every comfort for them provided and then remove them to camp. These barracks will be the finest feature in my command, and hereafter I will have things so arranged that there can be no complaint on the arrival of men. We never had a complaint after we got the men made comfortable. All our trouble has been on their arrival. Some of the poor fellows would drop down from want of food as well as from the effects of prison life long before they could reach my camp, but this will never occur again. The Government barracks have just been put up and they are boarded on the sides and have pitched roofs, good floors, with kitchens, officers' quarters and all that is needed for comfort. Three or four of the buildings are not yet completed inside. These I will complete with an eye to the comfort and convenience of my paroled men. I hope, colonel, that these arrangements will be satisfactory to you, as I know it is to General Schenck by his granting my request thus to use the new barracks. I inclose you a copy of my order* to Col. Charles Gilpin, who will command the guard in Annapolis, as well as the guard at Camp Parole and along the line of railroad. Capt. F. J. Keffer, Seventy-first Pennsylvania Volunteers, and Lieut. J. E. Doughty, Second U. S. Sharpshooters, have been detailed in accordance with your request. A copy of the order I inclose. I have also received an order from the commander-in-chief ordering Captain Ames, brigade commissary, as commissary at my camp. A copy of the order I inclose. Major Given is still with me but I have received no order for his being detailed here. The major as well as myself is very anxious to know what is to be done with him.

I am, colonel, most respectfully, your obedient servant,

GEO. SANGSTER,
Lieutenant-Colonel, Commanding Paroled Prisoners.

[Inclosure No. 1.]

SPECIAL ORDERS, }   HEADQUARTERS EIGHTH ARMY CORPS,
No. 29.   }   *Baltimore, Md., January 29, 1863.*

*   *   *   *   *   *   *

7. By authority of the War Department Capt. F. J. Keffer, Seventy-first Regiment Pennsylvania Volunteers, and Second Lieut. James E. Doughty, Second Regiment U. S. Sharpshooters, exchanged prisoners of war, now at Parole Camp, near Annapolis, are hereby detailed for duty with the paroled prisoners, and will report in person to Lieut. Col. George Sangster, commanding Camp Parole, Annapolis, Md.

By command of Major-General Schenck:

WM. H. CHESEBROUGH,
Assistant Adjutant-General.

---

* Not found.

[Inclosure No. 2.]

SPECIAL ORDERS, } HEADQUARTERS OF THE ARMY,
   No. 46. }   *Washington, January 28, 1863.*

*   *   *   *   *   *   *

2. Capt. George L. Ames, brigade commissary of subsistence of volunteers, will proceed to Annapolis, Md., and report for duty to the commanding officer of Camp Parole at that place.

*   *   *   *   *   *   *

By command of Major-General Halleck:

L. THOMAS,
Adjutant-General.

HEADQUARTERS, *Annapolis, Md., February 1, 1863.*
Col. W. HOFFMAN, *Commissary-General of Prisoners.*

SIR: I have the honor to inclose you complete rolls* of 981 men which arrived here from Richmond on the 29th and 30th of January in charge of Captain Mulford, Third Regiment New York Volunteers. I had the pleasure of an interview with him on the 30th at which time he reported to me, I then being in command of Annapolis as well as Camp Parole. I found him to be a gentleman and ready to do anything for the comfort of our paroled men and the forwarding of business of this office. I gave him a blank to make out his rolls on so as to conform with your orders and save the loss of time in making the proper rolls for you, which will be done hereafter. He will be here again on Wednesday with more men. I do hope I will have clothing by that time to clothe the men which I have got and those who will be here on Wednesday. These men are the best I have ever received from Richmond and I attribute it to the fact that they are soldiers and not stragglers. They are satisfied to wait the will of the Government, believing we are doing the best we can for their comfort. But, oh! what a sad condition they are in. It would have made one's heart sick to have seen them when they arrived here, but all they said was give us a loaf of bread; we will wait for anything else. I also had to provision the men on the transports to enable them to return. They being in the storm for three days used up all their rations.

I am, colonel, most respectfully, your obedient servant,

GEO. SANGSTER,
Lieutenant-Colonel, Commanding Paroled Prisoners.

INDIANAPOLIS, *February 1, 1863.*
Col. W. HOFFMAN, *Commissary-General of Prisoners:*

Have returned from Cincinnati. It is advisable to send wounded rebel prisoners to Camp Morton. Have telegraphed General Rosecrans to this effect.

H. W. FREEDLEY.

HEADQUARTERS, *Hilton Head, S. C., February 2, 1863.*
Maj. Gen. H. W. HALLECK, *General-in-Chief, Washington.*

GENERAL: I have the honor to transmit herewith for your consideration certified copies of a correspondence had with General Mercer,

---

* Omitted.

commanding rebel forces at Savannah, relative to the treatment of prisoners of war. The correspondence so fully explains itself that I feel comment to be unnecessary in submitting the matter to your judgment and awaiting your further orders.

I have much pleasure in reporting the safe arrival in this harbor of 10,000 re-enforcements under command of Major-General Foster. The troops are in excellent condition and spirits, having experienced pleasant weather and not having been overcrowded in the transports.

I have the honor to be, general, with the highest esteem, your most obedient servant,

> D. HUNTER,
> *Major-General, Commanding.*

[Inclosure No. 1.]

HEADQUARTERS DISTRICT OF GEORGIA,
Savannah, January 21, 1863.

Maj. Gen. DAVID HUNTER,
Commanding, &c., Hilton Head, S. C.

GENERAL: I beg leave respectfully to call your attention to the case of Mr. D. McDonald, of McIntosh County, in this State.

Mr. McDonald is a non-combatant and has never been in military service. He was taken from his own residence and made no resistance of any kind whatever. He was conveyed it is now understood to Hilton Head and is retained as a prisoner by you. I must request that you will take the case into consideration and trust that you will at once conclude to release Mr. McDonald so that he may return to his family, who are much in need of his attention.

I am, general, very respectfully, &c.,

> H. W. MERCER,
> *Brigadier-General, Commanding.*

[Inclosure No. 2.]

HEADQUARTERS DEPARTMENT OF THE SOUTH,
January 30, 1863.

General MERCER, *Commanding, &c., District of Georgia.*

GENERAL: I have the honor to acknowledge the receipt of your communication dated January 21, 1863, calling attention to the case of Mr. D. McDonald, of McIntosh County, Ga., claimed by you to be a non-combatant who has never been in military service, now held as a prisoner at this post, and asking that I take Mr. McDonald's case into consideration and that he be released and returned to his family.

Without pausing to enter upon the merits of this particular case I would most respectfully inform you that by the same flag of truce which conveyed your letter I received notification that First Lieut. Virgil H. Cate, Company C, Seventh Regiment New Hampshire Volunteers, recently captured in the vicinity of Saint Augustine, Fla., is held as a prisoner in Charleston jail, General Beauregard having notified him that "being a commissioned officer he is not subject to exchange," but that he will "probably be turned over to the local authorities of the State of Florida for trial under the statutes made and provided in that State for the punishment of persons engaged in inciting negro slaves to insurrection." This action is doubtless based on the declaration made in the recent message of Mr. Jefferson Davis that "hereafter unless Congress (meaning the Confederate Congress) think some other course more expedient" he will cause all commissioned officers of the

United States taken prisoners of war to be turned over for punishment as before recited to the authorities of the several States in which they may have been taken.

Under these circumstances and until this policy in violation of all the rules of war amongst civilized nations be distinctly and practically repudiated I announce to you that all commissioned officers of your service now prisoners, or hereafter to become so, in my hands will be kept in close confinement and held answerable with their lives for the safety of my officers who are prisoners, and that I will not discharge or entertain applications for discharging upon any pretext whatever any citizens or residents of Georgia, South Carolina or Florida now in my hands or who may hereafter be captured by coastwise expeditions and incursions. Regretting that a previous departure from the recognized rules of civilized warfare on the side of your authorities should compel this retaliatory declaration and the acts to follow it on my part,

I have the honor to be, general, very respectfully, your obedient servant,

D. HUNTER,
Major-General, Commanding.

———

HEADQUARTERS,
Camp Douglas, Chicago, Ill., February 2, 1863.

Col. W. HOFFMAN, *Commissary-General of Prisoners.*

SIR: There are now about 3,900 prisoners in this camp. Many of them are sick and nearly all poorly clothed and without blankets. As the weather is cold there must be a good deal of suffering. A number profess to be conscripts forced into the service and request to be allowed to take the oath of allegiance. They say they do not wish to be exchanged as they are determined not to go into the rebel service again. I have no instructions and can find none in this office on these points.

Very respectfully, your most obedient servant,

J. AMMEN,
Brigadier-General of Volunteers, Commanding.

———

INDIANAPOLIS, IND., *February 2, 1863.*

A. LINCOLN, *President:*

Armed resistance to arrest of deserters was made yesterday. This is a practical issue where the military authority is clearly paramount. There must be more ample authority by law or otherwise while this Congress is in session. I shall send all but the soldiers arrested to the grand jury, U. S. court, this day. Prompt and decided action is required.

HENRY B. CARRINGTON,
Colonel Eighteenth Infantry, Commandant.

———

HEADQUARTERS, *Annapolis, Md., February 2, 1863.*

Col. W. HOFFMAN, *Commissary-General of Prisoners.*

SIR: I have the honor to report that there are now at the general hospital at Annapolis, Md., some 350 men who came in with the men from Richmond on the 29th and 30th of January. They are afflicted with a variety of diseases, but a great number with broken legs and arms, others bruised badly internally and externally, caused by an accident on leaving Richmond. While crossing a bridge the bridge gave way and some thirty were drowned; the others in the condition as stated above. As soon as I get the facts gathered I will report the same to you.

I am, colonel, very respectfully, and obediently, yours,

GEO. SANGSTER,
Lieutenant-Colonel, Commanding Paroled Prisoners.

RICHMOND, *February 2, 1863.*

Lieutenant-Colonel LUDLOW, *Agent of Exchange.*

SIR: Your communications of the 31st have been received.

1. I will meet you at 1 p. m. on Tuesday, the 10th of February.

2. At the present hurried moment I cannot lay my hands on what you term my " proposition of the 19th instant for the release of citizen prisoners." If it was that all citizen prisoners on both sides are to be released it meets my most hearty approbation. I will immediately take means to have all in our custody ready for delivery.

3. Sutlers, sutlers' clerks and employés will be treated as heretofore.

4. When we meet we will talk over the case of the Robinsons.

5. As to the Fredericksburg officers I have already written you.

6. I will inquire into the case of Captain Harris and conform to the rules we have established.

7. There is much difficulty in the case of Doctor Rucker. He is charged with such crimes as you could never say were ordered to be perpetrated by your Government. He has not been tried at all. Do you mean to assert that if an officer or private commits an outrage not warranted by the usages of war or by his orders that he is not amenable to our laws if he is captured? Suppose he has committed a crime in direct violation of the orders of his Government. Is he then also to have our immunity? You have stated your proposition too broadly. With qualifications I have no disposition to contest it.

8. All the officers and men who have been declared exchanged will be delivered to you as speedily as possible.

9. I will make inquiries about Major Blake and George W. Bryant and let you know.

10. We have heard nothing as to the whereabouts of the officers and men captured on the Harriet Lane. I have not sufficient time to send the parties for whom you have asked in the train that leaves to-morrow morning but will hasten matters as much as possible. I hope you will be urgent in furthering the delivery of all officers and men whom we have declared exchanged. You have many hundreds in your prisons. Your agreement as to them and citizen prisoners will release all.

Respectfully, your obedient servant,

RO. OULD,
Agent of Exchange.

HEADQUARTERS, *Annapolis, Md., February 2, 1863.*

Col. W. HOFFMAN, *Commissary-General of Prisoners.*

SIR: I have the honor to inclose a complete roll of 306 men from Richmond, which arrived here on the 30th of January in charge of Captain Mulford, Third Infantry New York Volunteers, who are now at the barracks in Annapolis and not accounted for in my monthly return nor in my seven-day report. Their condition is such that I could not take them to camp and this accounts for their not being entered on the seven-day and monthly returns; and I hope the clothing will arrive soon for they will need a complete outfit. I have some of them wrapped in blankets instead of pants. There are now 200,000 suits at Philadelphia and I do not see why they delay a shipment, and especially for such men as these. The blankets they had when they reached Richmond they had to make shirts of for the enemy's soldiers, and the tailors found among our men by them were forced to make the shirts out of our soldiers' clothing.

With this I am, colonel, very respectfully, your obedient servant,
GEO. SANGSTER,
Lieutenant-Colonel, Commanding Paroled Prisoners.

BALTIMORE, *February 3, 1863.*
Major-General HALLECK, *General-in-Chief:*

Not remembering the extent of your verbal instructions I repeat the question, Shall rebel surgeons be refused parole under the order of December 30?

ROBT. C. SCHENCK,
Major-General.

HEADQUARTERS OF THE ARMY,
Washington, D. C., February 3, 1863.
Major-General SCHENCK, *Baltimore:*

Rebel surgeons, prisoners of war, are to be treated as provided in the cartel so long as the enemy observes the cartel in respect to medical officers.

H. W. HALLECK,
General-in-Chief.

MURFREESBOROUGH, TENN., *February 3, 1863.*
Hon. E. M. STANTON:

The rebels have been in the habit in utter violation of the terms of the cartel of paroling and releasing our prisoners without delivering either at Aiken's Landing, Vicksburg or any other place agreed upon between myself and the commanding general of the opposing army, and without any evidence or notice of such parole and delivery. I have published an order announcing that persons thus turned loose are lawfully released from their parole by the wrongful act of the rebels and that all such within my department shall be returned to duty by special orders, naming them. I respectfully request authority to order back those who have strayed into other departments.

W. S. ROSECRANS.

HEADQUARTERS FIFTEENTH ARMY CORPS,
Camp before Vicksburg, February 4, 1863.
Col. E. D. TOWNSEND,
Assistant Adjutant-General, Washington, D. C.

SIR: The letter of Col. William Hoffman of December 7, 1862, referred to me by your indorsement of January 7, 1863, is received, and

General Orders, No. 163, of the series 1862, sent therewith also is at hand. The letter shall be published to my troops and enforced as far as possible. A wide difference of opinion exists among officers in the matter of paroling prisoners of war. The enemy has a very loose practice of picking up our men, stragglers and others, by their properly organized troops as well as irregular guerrillas, of paroling them and turning them loose to find their way back to our lines as best they may. Hundreds of such men are now to be found in every army corps and at every post. In like manner our scouting parties and detachments pick up stragglers who invariably represent themselves, sometimes truthfully but more frequently falsely, as having abandoned their cause and on their way home. These invariably get off somehow or other and compose the gangs of robbers and guerrillas that infest the whole Southern country. Since the Dix-Hill cartel for the exchange of prisoners of war, published to the army in General Orders, No. 142, of September 25, 1862, I contend that neither party can claim a credit for prisoners delivered or exchanged in any manner other than that therein set forth, and that commanders of detachments, guerrillas or regulars, who take prisoners and set them free on parole cannot claim exchange for such prisoners; that the parole is void and of no effect, and the soldiers thus returned may be made to rejoin and do duty with their companies. If we insist upon the enemy taking our men prisoners, holding them and exchanging them at the place and in the manner set forth in the cartel it will break up a system that is operating against us.

I have the honor to be, your obedient servant,
W. T. SHERMAN,
Major-General, Commanding.

QUARTERMASTER-GENERAL'S OFFICE,
Washington, February 4, 1863.

Col. ROBERT ALLEN, *Saint Louis, Mo. :*

It is stated that the paroled prisoners taken [in] Arkansas may be sent this way for delivery at Richmond. I see no reason for incurring such an expenditure when they can be sent directly to Vicksburg; but if it should be ordered you will of course send them by the cheapest route, which if they are on the river will probably be by the Ohio to Parkersburg or Pittsburg. As the Baltimore and Ohio Railroad has been excepted from the railroad contracts and has charged higher rates per man per mile than others, do not let them come by that road unless their agents agree to put their charges down to the convention rates as to fare and baggage and distances. Their ticket agent (L. M. Cole) now offers this.

M. C. MEIGS,
Quartermaster-General.

QUARTERMASTER-GENERAL'S OFFICE,
Washington City, February 4, 1863.

Col. W. HOFFMAN, *Commissary-General of Prisoners.*

COLONEL: Application has been made to me by the agents of the Baltimore and Ohio Railroad for the transportation of the Arkansas prisoners on the road if sent to Richmond. They say that the cheapest transportation will be by the Ohio River to Parkersburg and by their road to Baltimore, thence by water to City Point, and they offer to reduce their fare to the regular rates of other roads—2 cents per mile, shortest route—if they do the work. But why go to the great expense of transporting 5,000 rebels by railroad and steam-boat to the Atlantic for exchange when the cartel makes Vicksburg a point of delivery? If operations prevent their being delivered there just now can they not be kept awhile; and in any case can they not be delivered on any day under flag of truce when battle is not actually formed? They should be delivered with the least possible baggage and clothing. While we had no cartel and retained prisoners it was right and humane to supply them with absolutely necessary clothing, but I think that none of this should be allowed to go within the rebel lines and relieve their great want of such supplies.

I am, very respectfully, your obedient servant,

M. C. MEIGS,
Quartermaster-General.

HEADQUARTERS EIGHTEENTH ARMY CORPS,
New Berne, N. C., February 4, 1863.

Maj. Gen. G. W. SMITH,
Commanding Department of North Carolina, Raleigh, N. C.

GENERAL: I have the honor to call your attention to the following statements of facts: Two prisoners, Oliver Warren and Henry Welsh, were taken by the Confederate forces near Washington, N. C., last November. These men are both in the First Regiment North Carolina (Union) Volunteers and regularly mustered into the service of the United States and are therefore clearly entitled to the benefit of the cartel agreed upon by our respective Governments providing for the release of prisoners on their parole within ten days of their capture. I regret to say that these men have not been released but were thrown into the Libby Prison, Richmond. I trust that calling your attention to these facts will be sufficient to procure the release of these men without any further action on my part.

I am, general, with great respect, your obedient servant,

I. N. PALMER,
Brigadier-General, Commanding.

CINCINNATI, OHIO, *February 4, 1863.*

Hon. EDWIN M. STANTON:

General Rosecrans telegraphs me if exchanged to report to him in person immediately. I have received no official notification of my exchange.

WM. H. LYTLE,
Colonel Tenth Ohio Infantry.

OFFICE COMMISSARY-GENERAL OF PRISONERS,
Washington, D. C., February 4, 1863.

Capt. H. W. FREEDLEY,
Third Infantry, U. S. Army, Indianapolis, Ind.

CAPTAIN: Your letter of the 30th ultimo has been received. You will direct such improvements made at Camp Morton as may be necessary to put the barracks in a condition to accommodate comfortably the wounded who have been sent there or who may be sent there so far as its capacity will admit. The sheds along the fence are scarcely suitable for this purpose. You recommend that some of the temporary barracks at Camp Carrington be removed to Camp Morton; but as you give me no information as to the character of that camp, its extent or the purpose for which it was established I have no grounds on which to approve of such an arrangement. In all reports which you make I desire that you will go into full details so that it will not be necessary for me to ask for further information. Report fully about the condition of Camp Morton. How many buildings can be appropriated to the wounded and how many can they accommodate? Can the sheds be made available? What are you doing in the way of improvements? I have an order in my possession from the War Department for you to join your company but it is suspended for the present.

Very respectfully, your obedient servant,

W. HOFFMAN,
Colonel Third Infantry, Commissary-General of Prisoners.

HEADQUARTERS, *Camp Butler, Ill., February 4, 1863.*

[N. H. McLEAN.]

MAJOR: This will introduce Quartermaster George Sawin, Fifty-eighth Illinois Volunteers, who comes upon business the nature of which you will see by the papers he brings. In addition I would say that nearly one-half the prisoners confined here were pressed into the Confederate service and are anxious to take the oath of allegiance and then join loyal regiments. They are foreigners, Germans, Polanders, &c. Please give instructions in regard to them.

Respectfully, your obedient servant,

W. F. LYNCH,
Colonel Fifty-eighth Illinois Volunteers, Commanding Post.

[Inclosure.]

HEADQUARTERS DEPARTMENT OF THE OHIO,
February 4, 1863.

ADJUTANT-GENERAL, *Department of the Ohio.*

(Through Col. W. F. Lynch, Fifty-eighth Regiment Illinois Volunteers, commanding Camp Butler.)

SIR: Is it consistent with the policy of the Government to allow such of the prisoners of war now confined at Camp Butler, Ill., and who are believed to be worthy of confidence to take the oath of allegiance to the United States and then enlist in such regiments now in said camp as they may select?

GEORGE SAWIN,
Lieutenant and Quartermaster, Fifty-eighth Illinois Regiment.

MEMORANDUM.—The prisoners of war now confined at Camp Butler are principally from regiments raised in and about Texas. A large number are of Irish, German and Polish nationality. They state they were conscripted and forced into the rebel army against their will; that the battle of Arkansas Post was the first in which they were engaged. Some are known to have gone from Illinois to the South for employment and some have near relatives and friend, in Illinois. They are willing to take the oath of allegiance and fight for the Union, and but for the misfortune of locality would ere this be found in the ranks of loyal regiments.

GEORGE SAWIN,
Lieutenant and Quartermaster, Fifty-eighth Illinois Infantry.

[Indorsement.]

HEADQUARTERS DEPARTMENT OF THE OHIO,
Cincinnati, Ohio, February 7, 1863.

Respectfully referred to the commissary-general of prisoners for instructions.

As a general rule prisoners of war cannot be discharged on taking oath of allegiance, but the case has been presented as a peculiar one, it having been alleged that many of the prisoners are not only of foreign birth, have their residences in Northern States and had gone South only for the sake of employment, but that they had been conscripted and forced against their will to serve in the rebel army. Under these circumstances I would advise that those of the men who are undoubted conscripts should be discharged on their application on taking the oath of allegiance, unless such course is considered to be in contravention of the cartel concerning prisoners of war.

H. G. WRIGHT,
Major-General, Commanding.

NEW YORK, *February 4, 1863.*

Col. W. HOFFMAN:

There are at present at Fort Lafayette about twenty-four blockade-running prisoners. I do not know whether they are considered citizen prisoners or not.

M. BURKE,
Lieutenant-Colonel.

SAINT LOUIS, MO., *February 5, 1863.*

General MEIGS:

Barracks for prisoners should be on islands to save guards. I concur with Colonel Allen in recommending Arsenal Island instead of Cairo for prison barracks.

S. R. CURTIS,
Major-General.

[Indorsement.]

QUARTERMASTER-GENERAL'S OFFICE,
February 9, 1863.

Respectfully referred to Colonel Hoffman, commissary-general of prisoners, for his advice. Barracks for prisoners were ordered to be built at Cairo.

By order:

E. S. SIBLEY,
Brevet Colonel, U. S. Army, and Deputy Quartermaster-General.

SAINT LOUIS, *February 5, 1863.*

General M. C. MEIGS, *Quartermaster-General:*

All the Arkansas prisoners have been sent to Chicago and Springfield, Ill. The 4,000 sent to Chicago cost $9,000 less than the conventional price, being carried for 1⅓ cents per mile.

ROBERT ALLEN,
Chief Quartermaster.

OFFICE COMMISSARY-GENERAL OF PRISONERS,
Washington, D. C., February 5, 1863.

Capt. ISAAC B. KINKEAD,
Seventy-seventh Ohio Volunteers, Alton Military Prison.

CAPTAIN: In reply to your letter of the 30th ultimo asking permission to enlist men from the different military prisons I have to inform you that the War Department has not and probably will not authorize any enlistments of the character you mention.

Very respectfully, your obedient servant,

W. HOFFMAN,
Colonel Third Infantry, Commissary-General of Prisoners.

HEADQUARTERS DISTRICT OF PENSACOLA,
February 5, 1863.

Lieut. Col. RICHARD B. IRWIN, *Assistant Adjutant-General.*

SIR: I have the honor to report that on yesterday, 4th instant, a flag of truce from the enemy arrived at our lines conveying a communication from General Buckner, Confederate Army, of which inclosed is a copy (marked A), to which I made a reply of which I likewise inclose a copy (marked B).

I am, sir, very respectfully, your obedient servant,

ISAAC DYER,
Colonel, Commanding.

[Inclosure A.]

HEADQUARTERS DISTRICT OF THE GULF,
Mobile, January 31, 1863.

OFFICER COMMANDING U. S. FORCES, *Pensacola, Fla.*

SIR: I am directed by General Braxton Bragg, commanding this department, to inform you that the following-named officers of the Federal Army captured at Murfreesborough, Tenn., will be held in close confinement at Atlanta, Ga., as hostages for Judge Wright, Mr. George W. Wright and Mr. Merritt, citizens of Pensacola, who he understands are now inhumanly and contrary to the rules of civilized warfare confined in Fort Pickens for refusing to take the oath of allegiance to the Abolition Government, viz, Capt. B. W. Canfield, Company E, One hundred and fifth Ohio Regiment; First Lieut. A. W. Tourgee, Company G, One hundred and fifth Ohio Regiment; Second Lieut. Alonzo Chubb, Company D, One hundred and fifth Ohio Regiment. Should the general commanding have been incorrectly informed with reference to the circumstances attending the incarceration of the citizens of the Confederate States named above it will give me pleasure to advise him of any facts with which you may furnish me which may tend to alleviate the condition of the U. S. officers now held as hostages.

Respectfully, your obedient servant,

S. B. BUCKNER,
Major-General, C. S. Army, Commanding District.

[Inclosure B.]

HEADQUARTERS DISTRICT OF PENSACOLA,
February 4, 1863.

Maj. Gen. S. B. BUCKNER, *Confederate Army.*

SIR: I beg leave to acknowledge the receipt of your communication of 31st ultimo in regard to the intention of General Bragg to keep in close confinement certain Federal officers in retaliation for the confinement at Fort Pickens of Judge Wright, Mr. George W. Wright and Mr. Merritt, citizens of Pensacola. I inclose herewith copy of Orders, No. 14, from these headquarters, in conformity with which and letters those gentlemen have been liberated. Judge Wright is at present in Pensacola, Mr. George W. Wright has passed out of our lines and Mr. Merritt has left this place for New Orleans.

I am, sir, very respectfully, your obedient servant,

ISAAC DYER,
Colonel, Commanding District of Pensacola.

[Sub-inclosure.]

SPECIAL ORDERS, } HEADQUARTERS DISTRICT OF PENSACOLA,
No. 14. } *January 19, 1863.*

The commanding officer at Fort Pickens will release from confinement G. W. Wright on condition of his giving his parole of honor.

By command of Brigadier-General Dow:

OLIVER MATHEWS,
Acting Assistant Adjutant-General and Aide-de-Camp.

CAMP BUTLER, ILL., *February 5, 1863.*
Col. W. HOFFMAN:

About one-half the rebel prisoners confined here are foreigners, conscripts. They are anxious to take the oath of allegiance. I am satisfied of their truthfulness. Shall I administer it to them and discharge? Rolls will be sent you to-morrow.

W. F. LYNCH,
Colonel Fifty-eighth Illinois Volunteers.

HEADQUARTERS DEPARTMENT OF VIRGINIA,
Fort Monroe, February 5, 1863.
Col. W. HOFFMAN, *Commissary-General of Prisoners.*

COLONEL: I inclose to you a copy of letter sent a few days since to Major-General Hitchcock. This morning I received from him a telegram stating that orders will be issued as desired by me. I have just received a communication from Mr. Ould in which in reply to me he expresses a willingness to exchange all citizen prisoners. I wish therefore that the orders asked for in my letter to General Hitchcock may be immediately executed and that all citizen prisoners be forwarded from their various places of detention to Washington as speedily as possible. Please inform me on what day they will be ready and I will send a steamer from here under charge of a discreet officer to bring them down. Mr. Ould states that he will have our prisoners ready. I urge prompt action on this subject as all such exchange arrangements are liable to be interrupted and it would be a source of general regret if such interruption should now occur. How many citizen prisoners are now in the Old Capitol Prison? Will you please show this letter to the Secretary of War and to Major-General Hitchcock?

I am, very respectfully, your obedient servant,

WM. H. LUDLOW,
Lieutenant-Colonel and Agent for Exchange of Prisoners.

[Inclosure.]

HEADQUARTERS DEPARTMENT OF VIRGINIA,
Fort Monroe, February 2, 1863.

Major-General HITCHCOCK,
    Commissioner for Exchange of Prisoners.

GENERAL: I have the honor to inform you that I have concluded arrangements with Mr. Ould for the release of all citizen prisoners who have been captured by the Confederates in their raids. This will include of course those taken by General Stuart in Maryland and Pennsylvania. I think I can make the agreement to cover all our citizen prisoners, and I suggest that orders be immediately given to have all the citizen prisoners who have been captured by our military officers forwarded to Washington from their various places of detention. I will send a steamer from here to take them up to City Point for exchange. I consider it very desirable that the number sent should be as large as possible, the Confederates having more than 250 of our Union men. Would not this be a favorable opportunity to send all not under sentence? The information asked for and referred to me in relation to some of our officers and men will be communicated as soon as obtained. The demand has been made for Doctor Rucker and Assistant Surgeon Green is held a hostage for him. I have entered my earnest protest against any of our officers and men being retained in gross violation of the cartel and placed under the operation of State laws. I do not think the threat of Jeff. Davis will be permitted to be carried out by the Confederate Congress. The fact that we have more of their officers than they have of ours is a troublesome one to them. I shall be in Washington in a few days. May I ask the favor that you will show this letter to the Secretary of War and to Colonel Hoffman and inform me what orders are issued in relation to its subject-matter?

I am, very respectfully, your obedient servant,

WM. H. LUDLOW,
Lieutenant-Colonel and Agent for Exchange of Prisoners.

FORT HAMILTON, N. Y., February 5, 1863.

Hon. EDWIN M. STANTON.

SIR: A person calling himself Mr. Ray came to this post to-day and asked to see me. Upon the officer of the day inquiring his business he stated that he was a civil officer and had papers to serve on me. Upon my refusing to see him or allow the papers to be served he said that he had an interview with the Governor and was acting under instructions; and he further said that the civil authorities were determined and that my refusing to allow the papers to be served would certainly lead to a conflict. Please answer.

MARTIN BURKE,
Lieutenant-Colonel Third Artillery.

FORT HAMILTON, N. Y., February 5, 1863.

Hon. EDWIN M. STANTON:

In connection with my dispatch to you of this date I have understood that the papers desired to be served on me was a habeas corpus, for whom I know not.

MARTIN BURKE,
Lieutenant-Colonel Third Artillery.

OFFICE PROVOST-MARSHAL-GENERAL,
Saint Louis, Mo., February 5, 1863.

Col. W. HOFFMAN, *Commissary-General of Prisoners.*

COLONEL: Your dispatch of the 4th asking the number of citizen prisoners arrested by military authority, including guerrillas, received. The answer is being made up and will be sent in an hour by telegraph. It will be impossible to have the precise number stated, as I do not receive constant reports from Alton and especially not as to the deaths there. I request that Colonel Hildebrand be instructed to report to this office once a week the deaths and releases of prisoners at Alton under charge of this office. I wish to make known to you what work I am now having done in this office. Finding no reliable records of prisoners excepting one single book, which was a mere list stating the time of capture, county and place where imprisoned, and that book considerably behind I have for weeks been engaged in calling the roll of every prisoner under my control. I ascertain if there is evidence in the office against the prisoners. I have the prisoners personally examined and in a large number of cases I have to send to other points for evidence. When all the evidence can be obtained then the case is made up and passed upon. I have already ascertained by this process that a large number of prisoners about whom I could get no reliable impression are criminals of the worst character, and having now procured the evidence against them I have asked Major-General Curtis to appoint a military commission or a court-martial that these men may be tried. This tribunal will be sitting in a short time and its decisions will be reported to you without delay. I am having made a roll of every prisoner in my charge which states briefly his case and the disposition made of him. To-day I send to Alton a clerk to procure an accurate list of the prisoners there, and as soon as the cases in Saint Louis have been disposed of I will take up the Alton list and go through with it as rapidly as possible. When these lists are completed I will send to you a copy of them. It may appear to you that it takes a long time to have these back cases examined, but the work has been kept constantly going forward. The greatest obstacle that I have to contend with is the insufficient evidence sent forward by the officers who capture the prisoners. They deliver them over to the nearest post and from there they are sent forward, with an imperfect list and a few remarks; the officers are off again in the field and do or can furnish but little evidence, so that the most of the evidence I act upon is the statements made by the prisoners.

I have the honor, colonel, to be your obedient servant,

F. A. DICK,
Lieutenant-Colonel and Provost-Marshal-General.

HEADQUARTERS, *Annapolis, Md., February 5, 1863.*

Col. W. HOFFMAN, *Commissary-General of Prisoners.*

SIR: I have the honor to inclose you a report* which I procured from Captain Mulford to-day as to the accident at Richmond which I reported to you. I am happy to see that the report after his investigation has much reduced the loss of life and limb. To-day I received 750 men from Richmond and a complete set of rolls, in care of Captain Mulford, Third Regiment New York Volunteers. Three of the men had individual paroles, which I sent to you to-day. Captain Mulford sent

---

* See inclosure to letter from Sangster to Hoffman, same date, p. 246.

a letter about one, the others have the papers with them. In eight hours after their arrival I had them comfortably quartered and clothed. The rolls I will send to-morrow.

I am, colonel, very respectfully, your obedient servant,
GEO. SANGSTER,
Lieutenant-Colonel, Commanding Paroled Prisoners.

HEADQUARTERS, *Annapolis, Md., February 5, 1863.*
Col. W. HOFFMAN, *Commissary-General of Prisoners.*

SIR: Through the carelessness of one of the clerks this report was left out of the letter I wrote this morning. Please find it inclosed and excuse the oversight.

I am, colonel, very respectfully, your obedient servant,
GEO. SANGSTER,
Lieutenant-Colonel, Commanding Paroled Prisoners.

[Inclosure.]

STEAMER NEW YORK,
Annapolis, Md., February 5, 1863.
Lieutenant-Colonel SANGSTER,
Commanding Post, Annapolis, Md.

SIR: In compliance with your request I have the honor to report the following in regard to an accident which occurred to paroled (Federal) prisoners while on their way from their prison to the railroad for City Point to meet flag-of-truce steamer New York, January 27, 1863. The detachment of 800 paroled (Federal) prisoners left the prison at about 4.30 a. m. and on their way to depot while crossing the canal a bridge, an iron structure over which 1,000 of our men had passed the day before, gave way and precipitated about 100 men into the canal. Private George Epart, Company H, Thirtieth Indiana Volunteers, and Private David Lampa, Company K, Thirtieth Indiana Volunteers, were drowned. Sergt. J. M. Arnold, Company K, Twenty-fourth Wisconsin Volunteers; Private W. Morgan, Company E, Eleventh Pennsylvania Volunteers, and Private F. Cramer, Company A, Twenty-fourth Wisconsin Volunteers, were injured and left in Richmond. There were also several others bruised and one or two limbs broken, whom I brought down and left at this post on my last trip. The supposed cause of the falling of the bridge was in consequence of the head of line having halted and the men breaking from their ranks filled the bridge full thereby overloading it.

I am, colonel, very respectfully, yours,
JNO. E. MULFORD,
Capt., 3d Inf. N. Y. Vols., Comdg. Flag of Truce, James River.

SANDUSKY, OHIO, *February 5, 1863.*
Col. W. HOFFMAN:

One hundred and eighty citizens and guerrillas, excluding those under sentence. Suppose all arrested by military authority, but as many come from other camps cannot tell. Heavy snow-storm. Ice safe for prisoners on foot. Have written.

WM. S. PIERSON,
Major, Commanding.

COLUMBUS, OHIO, *February 5, 1863.*

Col. W. HOFFMAN:

We have 156 citizen prisoners arrested by military authority, about half of whom are recommended by War Department for release by Commissioner Galloway. No guerrillas.

EDWIN L. WEBBER,
Captain, Commanding.

HEADQUARTERS COMMANDANT OF PRISONS,
Camp Chase, Ohio, February 5, 1863.

Col. W. HOFFMAN,
Commissary-General of Prisoners, Washington, D. C.

COLONEL: I have the honor to this day forward the monthly returns* of prisoners at this post and the prisoners' savings fund and prison hospital fund, with abstracts* and vouchers* for the month of January, 1863. The sutler tax on account of prisoners has not been collected for the months of December, 1862, and January, 1863. The average number of prisoners for each month is about the same, say 383, which at 10 cents per head per month will add to the savings fund some $76.40, and should have been included in the present return. I will see that this is attended to. The recent large receipts of prisoners of war at this post, commissioned officers, rendered it necessary to open the west prison, No. 3, the east prisons being greatly crowded and insufficient hospital room for the numbers of sick and wounded. I therefore with the approval of the colonel commanding post had the quartermaster build a partition across Prison No. 3, excluding the first four company quarters now occupied by the battalion of guards but which could be ready on short notice for prisoners should they be needed, and into the larger part I have moved all the prisoners of war except the sick and wounded, who with the citizens remain in the hospital prison. Prison No. 1 is now vacated, except three female prisoners, whom for the present I have placed in there having no other accommodations for them. These last, a mother and two daughters, also a son, were sent here for confinement from Nashville by order of Major-General Rosecrans, charged as spies and smuggling contraband articles. I am informed that a number more are to come. If so some separate confinement should be arranged for them. Prisoner Thomas L. Jones is still on parole. I am in receipt of orders from the War Department January 31, 1863, to release him on his oath of allegiance as recommended by Special Commissioner Galloway, and have notified him to report here.

I am, colonel, very respectfully, your obedient servant,

EDWIN L. WEBBER,
Captain, Commanding Prisons.

WAR DEPARTMENT, *Washington, February 6, 1863.*

Hon. G. A. GROW, *Speaker of the House of Representatives.*

SIR: I have the honor to transmit herewith a report from the General-in-Chief in reply to the resolution of the House of Representatives of the 30th ultimo calling for information as to "whether any rebel officers

---

* Omitted.

captured by the Army of the United States have been granted paroles since the proclamation of Jefferson Davis refusing paroles or exchange to the captured officers of Union regiments."

I am, sir, very respectfully, your obedient servant,

EDWIN M. STANTON,
Secretary of War.

[Inclosure.]

HEADQUARTERS OF THE ARMY,
Washington, D. C., February 2, 1863.

Hon. E. M. STANTON, *Secretary of War.*

SIR: I inclose herewith a resolution of the House of Representatives dated January 30, probably through inadvertence directed to me.

In answer to this resolution I have the honor to report to the War Department that immediately on receiving official information that the enemy had retained our officers who were taken prisoners of war, in violation of the cartel, the following order was telegraphed to all commanders of military departments and of armies in the field:

WASHINGTON, D. C., *December 30, 1862.*

No officers, prisoners of war, will be released on parole till further orders.

H. W. HALLECK,
General-in-Chief.

I have no information that any rebel officer captured by the Union forces has been released on parole since that time. Medical officers are made an exception to the order, it being understood that in respect to them the enemy continues to observe the stipulations of the cartel.

Very respectfully, your obedient servant,

H. W. HALLECK,
General-in-Chief.

WASHINGTON, D. C., *February 6, 1863.*

Maj. Gen. S. R. CURTIS, *Saint Louis, Mo.*

GENERAL: I beg leave to call your attention to the inclosed slip* of newspaper which purports to give the substance of a recent order of General Loan. Such an order if it be genuine is in violation of the laws of war and may lead to serious difficulties. It was to prevent such excesses that the law of July last was passed requiring sentences of death to first receive the approval of the President before execution.

Very respectfully, your obedient servant,

H. W. HALLECK,
General-in-Chief.

OFFICE COMMISSARY-GENERAL OF PRISONERS,
Washington, D. C., February 6, 1863.

Brig. Gen. M. C. MEIGS,
Quartermaster-General U. S. Army, Washington, D. C.

GENERAL: I have the honor to acknowledge the receipt of your letter of the 4th instant and beg leave to offer the following reply: It would doubtless be the shortest and possibly the cheapest route for prisoners of war from Louisville to Baltimore to take the steam-boat to Parkersburg and thence by the Baltimore and Ohio Railroad to Baltimore, but it would be hazardous to take them through the disaffected

---

* Not found.

country through which that road passes, where there would be so many temptations for them to try to make their escape or to overcome the guard. The movement was ordered only on condition that the prisoners could not be sent to Vicksburg for exchange and it applies only to the Murfreesborough prisoners. Those captured in Arkansas and elsewhere will be held at the camp in the West. Eight hundred prisoners were recently sent to Vicksburg for exchange but were returned in consequence of the operations against that city. If these prisoners are held at all it seems to be unavoidable that some clothing must be issued to them, but it will be confined to that which is absolutely necessary to cover their nakedness. Whether we hold them or send them to City Point for delivery the expense must be very heavy and I will urge that some other point than Vicksburg be agreed upon for the delivery of prisoners so that we may be relieved at once of the care of them.

I have the honor to be, very respectfully, your obedient servant,

W. HOFFMAN,
Colonel Third Infantry, Commissary-General of Prisoners.

NEW ORLEANS, *February 6, 1863.*
Maj. Gen. N. P. BANKS,
Commanding Department of the Gulf, New Orleans.

GENERAL: As agent for the exchange of prisoners under the cartel between the two Governments I ask the pleasure of a personal interview in reference to Brig. Gen. Charles Clark's release and other prisoners. As regards the murderers mentioned in Lieutenant-General Pemberton's letter I have nothing to say, but will take them if delivered to me. I am very anxious to see General Clark as I was on his staff for months.

Very respectfully, your obedient servant,

N. G. WATTS,
Major, C. S. Army, and Agent.

HEADQUARTERS COMMANDANT OF PRISONS,
Camp Chase, Ohio, February 6, 1863.
Col. W. HOFFMAN,
Commissary-General of Prisoners, Washington, D. C.

COLONEL: Your communication of the 31st ultimo called my attention to General Orders, No. 193, and your letter of instructions of December 6, 1862. Those orders were received before I had any official connection with the prisons. Since the receipt of your last I have carefully investigated the case and I cannot see why all the citizen prisoners confined here should not be released. General Orders, No. 193, and your instructions seem clear enough to me in the light I view them, but I am puzzled to know why a special commissioner under authority of the War Department as I understand it is kept here to examine and pass upon such cases. In a majority of the cases examined and reported upon by the special commissioner, Galloway, up to this time, and in the cases of nearly all the citizen prisoners now in my custody, the charge is "disloyalty," or "rebel sympathizer," or "aiding and abetting the rebels:" rarely anything else and seldom do any papers come fully substantiating these charges, and it looks to me that all such prisoners come under the provisions of paragraph 2 of General Orders, No. 193, and should be released without regard to trial by commissioner. This same class of prisoners is being sent here continually from Wheeling, Va., Louisville and Lexington, Ky., and other places, and that I may act advisedly and without doubt I would respectfully ask specific instructions in the following cases:

1. Are all citizen prisoners in custody at Camp Chase from the States of Virginia, Kentucky, Tennessee and Missouri against whom the only charge is "disloyalty" or "aiding and abetting the rebels" to be released by me under General Orders, No. 193, and your instructions of December 6, 1862, without reference to the special commissioner here and without requiring them to take the oath of allegiance, only requiring them to report to the provost-marshals of their districts? And as the same class of prisoners continue to arrive shall I treat them in the same way?

2. The commissioner has examined a large number of the cases of citizens now here and recommended them to the Secretary of War for release on different conditions, and they await the orders for their release.

3. What class of cases comes under the jurisdiction of the commissioner?

The case of Thomas L. Jones, of Kentucky, was taken up by Commissioner Galloway and he was recommended to be released on taking the oath of allegiance, which he refused to do. He was paroled by Governor Tod to his home in Kentucky. His time expired and he asked a renewal of parole. The Governor recommended him to return and have his case disposed of. He was not ordered to return by me and has not reported himself.

I am, colonel, very respectfully, your obedient servant,

EDWIN L. WEBBER,
Captain, Commanding Prisons.

HEADQUARTERS, *Cincinnati, February 7, 1863.*

Col. WILLIAM HOFFMAN,
Commissary-General of Prisoners, Washington, D. C.

COLONEL: I have the honor to inclose a copy of letter addressed to Col. W. F. Lynch, commanding at Camp Butler, instructing him to procure and furnish certain supplies represented to be necessary to the comfort of the rebel prisoners confined at that post. From the representations made to me I am satisfied that the sufferings of these prisoners during the present inclement weather have been intense and that common humanity required that some alleviation should be promptly provided. I have therefore taken the responsibility of giving the inclosed instructions without awaiting for a reference of the matter to your office.

Very respectfully, your obedient servant,

H. G. WRIGHT,
Major-General, Commanding.

[Inclosure.]

HEADQUARTERS, *Cincinnati, February 7, 1863.*

Col. W. F. LYNCH,
Fifty-eighth Regt. Ill. Vols., Camp Butler, near Springfield, Ill.

COLONEL: It has been represented at these headquarters that the rebel prisoners of war confined at Camp Butler have suffered severely rom the severity of the weather owing to the want of straw, blankets, stoves for heating the barracks in which they are confined and possibly for the want of adequate clothing. General Orders, No. 67, series of 1862, from the War Department, Adjutant-General's Office, provides hat clothing and other necessaries shall be supplied to prisoners of war under regulations to be prescribed by the commissary-general of prisoners. The needful regulations in this respect are presumed to have been furnished you and the supplies in accordance therewith should be obtained of the proper staff departments on requisitions approved and ordered by you. In case no such regulations have been supplied for your government you will cause to be furnished the stoves necessary to heating the prison barracks, the proper allowance of straw or bedding and a blanket apiece for such of the prisoners as are not already provided with one. You will please report your action under these instructions to these headquarters.

Very respectfully, your obedient servant,

H. G. WRIGHT,
Major-General, Commanding.

WASHINGTON, *February 7, 1863.*

Mr. WILLIAM P. WOOD, *Superintendent Old Capitol Prison.*

SIR: I have received your letter of the 5th instant, together with the list accompanying it, a copy of Mr. Baxter's receipt to you of the 29th October last and a copy of your letter prepared for Mr. Baxter.

I inclose herewith a certified copy of Mr. Baxter's receipt,* which I offered you in conversation.

As you refer to my letter calling for that receipt as if my use of the term "official" in connection with it had changed its character from that of a private to that of a public document I must explain that you had no authority to hold any private intercourse with people in arms against the Government of the United States. When your authority to act under the orders of General Wadsworth (approved by the Secretary of War) ceased your acts, unauthorized in fact, might be said to be extra official, but your proceedings did not the less belong to the United States Government and ought to have been submitted to the Government.

I presume I understand now the reason of your recall. By the copy of the memorandum of agreement between yourself and Mr. Baxter you appear to have exercised functions not committed to you. By the order of General Wadsworth September 28, 1862, you were directed "to proceed to Richmond via Fortress Monroe for the purpose of delivering exchanged State prisoners, marked A, and for tendering exchange of State prisoners, marked B, for Union State prisoners now held in confinement by the authorities in Richmond." This paragraph covers your authority and it does not empower you to enter into general negotiations with Confederate authorities, yet the copy you furnish shows that you assumed that power and formally signed your name to an agreement the effect of which if sanctioned would have committed the United States Government to a policy which would virtually have paralyzed its power to act upon rebels under the law of reason. It appears to me that you could not yourself have been aware of the grave character of the act you committed. But I do not question your motives.

---

* Not found.

I regret to see the tone and temper in which you write to Mr. Baxte about other public functionaries as anxious to discharge their duty t the public as you can be. I consider that you have written the lette under a misapprehension of the powers committed to you and of th circumstances under which those powers were annulled.

Respectfully, your obedient servant,

E. A. HITCHCOCK,
Major-General of Vols., Commissioner for Exchange of Prisoners.

OFFICE COMMISSARY-GENERAL OF PRISONERS,
Washington, D. C., February 7, 1863.

Col. W. H. LUDLOW,
Agent for Exchange of Prisoners, Fort Monroe, Va.

COLONEL: I inclose herewith a list* of rebel officers captured by General Rosecrans' army. I have not yet received a list of those cap tured in Arkansas. I inclose also rolls* of rebel prisoners of war captured at different places in the West. I have not yet been able to obtain al the information requested in your letter of the 28th ultimo. We have in the West 1,200 or 1,500 citizen prisoners and it is proposed to selec from those as many as may be necessary to balance all held by the rebels at Richmond. You will probably be called to this city before the exchange is consummated in order that the announcement may be clearly understood.

Very respectfully, your obedient servant,

W. HOFFMAN,
Colonel Third Infantry, Commissary-General of Prisoners.

P. S.—I gave to-day to Mr. Child, the gentleman about whom I wrote to you a few days since, a pass to Fort Monroe where he is to report to you for exchange.

W. H.

WASHINGTON, *February 7, 1863.*

Lieut. Col. W. H. LUDLOW, *Agent for Exchange of Prisoners:*

Your letter of 5th is received. I am making arrangements to collect citizen prisoners here and will let you know when they arrive.

W. HOFFMAN.

HEADQUARTERS DEPARTMENT OF THE GULF,
New Orleans, February 7, 1863.

Maj. Gen. N. P. BANKS, *Commanding Department of the Gulf.*

GENERAL: I have the honor to report that in obedience to your instructions I yesterday proceeded to Lake End to receive the flag of truce under which the letter of Lieut. Gen. J. C. Pemberton was sent to you. I found Major Watts, of C. S. Army, and delivered to him your answer to General Pemberton's note. Major Watts' especial busi ness, however, was to confer in relation to exchange of prisoners, he being the accredited agent of the Confederate Government and charged with that duty. I found him to be intelligent, affable and courteous

---

* Omitted.

After explaining in detail the object of his visit he made two propositions in writing (see copy annexed), to both of which I acceded.

He called my attention especially to his correspondence with General Butler in October last relative to prisoners of the Eighth Vermont Regiment captured by General Taylor and assured me he had endeavored to carry out the provisions of the cartel and also the particular request of General Butler as to delivery of prisoners, as the correspondence will show.

He regretted that any misunderstanding had arisen regarding Brigadier-General Clark and his fellow-prisoners and assured me the prisoners detained by the Confederate Government in consequence of such misunderstanding should be immediately delivered to General Grant on the fulfillment of the arrangement entered into between us.

I called his attention to the matter of shooting a number of Federal prisoners of war some months since and for which General Butler revoked the parole of the prisoners taken by General Weitzel in La Fourche.

He explained by declaring it the act of the State authorities and not of the Confederate Government, but denounced it as an outrage and unjustifiable and assured me that President Davis looked upon it in like manner. He also said that although the act was one of war and committed by State officers it must be assumed by the Government as its own act, and he had no doubt if the matter was properly presented as a grievance explanation and prompt disavowal would be rendered. He had discussed the matter personally with the President and did not hesitate from opinions advanced by him at that time to express the opinion above mentioned.

I also called his attention to the fact that Federal prisoners were still held in Texas and had been since the commencement of the war. He answered promptly that he would correct that matter immediately, and thereupon proposed to proceed to Galveston for the purpose of having a conference with General Magruder, and pledged his honor to do everything in his power to have all the prisoners in Texas delivered at the earliest possible moment to the Federal authorities; said that many taken in the early part of the war were not at present in custody of the Confederate authorities, some having been paroled, others escaped; he would, however, do his best to gather them together and forward them to Galveston.

Copies of the correspondence annexed. All of which is respectfully submitted.

JOHN S. CLARK,
Colonel and Aide-de-Camp.

[Inclosure No. 1.]

NEW ORLEANS, *February 6, 1863.*

Col. JOHN S. CLARK, U. S. Army, *New Orleans.*

COLONEL: I will meet you on the 21st instant for the purpose of receiving Brigadier-General Clark and any other prisoners your Government may choose to deliver to me. At which time if it meets the sanction of your Government I will either in person or by an authorized agent proceed to Texas to carry out the cartel to its fullest extent as regards all prisoners taken before the 23d of January, 1863, and will n accordance with the President's proclamation carry out the cartel.

Respectfully, your obedient servant,

N. G. WATTS,
Major and Agent for Exchange of Prisoners at Vicksburg.

[Inclosure No. 2.]

HEADQUARTERS DEPARTMENT OF THE GULF,
New Orleans, February 6, 1863.

Major WATTS, C. S. Army, *Agent for Exchange of Prisoners.*

MAJOR: Your communication of to-day received in which you propose to meet me as agent to deliver prisoners at Baton Rouge on the 21st instant and to receive such prisoners of war as the Federal authorities may be ready to turn over at that time, mentioning especially Brigadier-General Clark.

Also that you will at that time if it meet the sanction of my Government, either in person or by authorized agent, proceed to Texas to carry out the provisions of the cartel to its fullest extent as regards all prisoners taken previous to January 23, 1863.

In answer I am directed to say that Brigadier-General Clark together with some 350 prisoners of war now on parole have been awaiting the action of the Confederate authorities for some days, a letter having been forwarded by the general commanding to Lieutenant-General Pemberton under flag of truce some days since advising him of the above fact.

I will meet you at the place proposed with the prisoners, say in the river above Baton Rouge, at 9 a. m. on the 21st instant.

In answer to your second proposition I will immediately lay the matter before the general commanding and have no doubt it will meet with his approbation. It may be necessary, however, before giving a definite answer to confer with the naval authorities.

Nothing will give the general greater pleasure I assure you than to see the provisions of the cartel carried out to the letter.

I have the honor to be, very respectfully, your obedient servant,

JOHN S. CLARK,
Colonel and Aide-de-Camp.

[Inclosure No. 3.]

NEW ORLEANS, *February 7, 1863.*

Col. J. S. CLARK, *Aide-de-Camp, &c.*

COLONEL: On referring to my letter addressed to you on yesterday I find that I stated that the cartel would be carried out to its fullest extent as regards all prisoners taken before the "23d January, 1863." I should have stated the 23d December, 1862. Please note the correction.

I inclose copy of request* made to General Banks on the 6th January, 1863, through an officer who only took a memorandum of it. Please give it consideration, especially as regards Deputy Surveyor P. E. Walden, who I learn is at Fort Pickens.

Your obedient servant,

N. G. WATTS,
Major and Agent.

SPECIAL ORDERS, }   HDQRS. DEPARTMENT OF THE OHIO,
No. 60.   }   *Cincinnati, Ohio, February 7, 1863.*

*   *   *   *   *   *   *

4. Col. H. Van Rensselaer, Inspector-General of the U. S. Army, will proceed without delay to Camp Butler, near Springfield, Ill., and make

*Not found.

a thorough inspection of that post, including all that relates to the prisoners of war confined thereat. Special care will be taken in the examination into the management of the commissary and quartermaster's
department at the post, and the officers of those departments stationed
in Springfield will furnish on the call of the inspector-general such information as he may require in making the investigation ordered. On
the completion of this duty he will return and report at these headquarters.

By order of Major-General Wright:

W. P. ANDERSON,
Assistant Adjutant-General.

HEADQUARTERS, *Port Hudson, February 8, 1863.*
Brig. Gen. C. GROVER, *Commanding Post, Baton Rouge, La.*

SIR: Your note of the 5th instant has just been received. In reply
I have to state that as the U. S. prisoners of war are at Jackson, Miss.,
it will be necessary to send your communication to Lieutenant-General
Pemberton, commanding the Department of Mississippi and East
Louisiana.

I am, sir, very respectfully, your obedient servant,

FRANK GARDNER,
Major-General, Commanding.

HEADQUARTERS, *Annapolis, Md., February 8, 1863.*
Col. W. HOFFMAN, *Commissary-General of Prisoners.*

SIR: I have the honor to inclose you complete rolls* of 740 men
who arrived here on the 5th instant from Richmond. I am happy to
say that my new arrangements for the comfort of paroled men arriving
from Richmond has far exceeded my expectations, although the sleet
and snow was driving everything before it. On their arrival here I
had them in barracks in half an hour after reaching the dock, and in
eight hours after their arrival every man had clean clothes on, with a
good overcoat and blanket and plenty of good food with comfortable
quarters. Every man's name was taken down and his clothing charged
to him. Had I not had these new barracks to put them in I feel satisfied we should have lost several lives from the severeness of the weather
and the naked condition of the men as it would have been impossible
to have given them any comfort at camp. The recent frosts and snow
and rain storms have torn my canvas very much, but I hope in a
month to complete my work of building huts at camp. I am working
120 men building these huts. I have got several streets completed and
the men in them. They are of a very perfect and comfortable nature.
I will require some 100,000 feet of lumber to complete my work, but we
have plenty of funds for that and all other purposes. I will send for
30,000 feet of lumber to-morrow and will urge the work on with the
greatest of speed.

I am, colonel, very respectfully, your obedient servant,

GEO. SANGSTER,
Lieutenant-Colonel, Commanding Paroled Prisoners.

---

*Not found.

GENERAL ORDERS, }   HDQRS. DEPT. OF THE CUMBERLAND,
No. 14.   }   *Murfreesborough, Tenn., February 8, 1863.*

I. Whereas, by the cartel for the exchange of prisoners agreed upon by commissioners, Maj. Gen. John A. Dix, on the part of the United States, and Maj. Gen. D. H. Hill, on the part of the Confederate authorities, dated Haxall's Landing, on James River, July 22, 1862, and published by the War Department in General Orders, No. 142, September 25, 1862, the provisions of which are to be binding during the war, it is provided among other things that all prisoners captured by either party shall be delivered at the expense of the capturing party at either Aiken's Landing or Vicksburg, or at such other point as may be mutually agreed upon between the commanding generals of opposing armies; and

Whereas, in violation of these provisions the Confederate authorities opposed to this army have without due notice or agreement and often without furnishing any lists or evidence of their capture and parole released and set free certain officers and men belonging to this army at such time and place as best suited their own convenience, thus avoiding the expense and trouble of delivering them according to the cartel and the danger of their recapture, thereby forfeiting their right to claim an exchange and releasing by their own act the persons so captured and set free—

It is ordered, That all officers and men so released subsequent to the 10th day of December, 1862, will be returned to duty, and that hereafter the names of any so captured and released will be forwarded to these headquarters that special orders may be issued in each case for their return to duty.

II. General Orders, No. 10, War Department, January 10, 1863, announces the exchange of all prisoners captured by the Confederate forces in the States of Kentucky, Tennessee, Mississippi, Alabama, South Carolina and Florida previous to the 10th of December, 1862. All officers and soldiers captured from this command previous to that date will therefore at once return to their regiments or commands.

By command of Major-General Rosecrans:

C. GODDARD,
Assistant Adjutant-General and Chief of Staff.

WAR DEPARTMENT, *Washington, February 9, 1863.*
Brigadier-General LYTLE, *Cincinnati, Ohio:*

The inquiry as to your exchange could not be answered until a specific report by the commissioner of exchanges, who has just reached here. He reports that all captures prior to the 10th of December are exchanged and so declared. You are included in the declaration and are exchanged and can report to General Rosecrans.

EDWIN M. STANTON,
Secretary of War.

Indorsement on case of William J. Livingston.

JUDGE-ADVOCATE-GENERAL'S OFFICE,
February 9, 1863.
The PRESIDENT OF THE UNITED STATES:

Usage and the course of decision have enforced in regard to military commissions the same principles which prevail in the organization of courts-martial. These principles require that it shall appear from the record not only that the court and judge-advocate were sworn, but also that the oath was administered in the presence of the accused.

This does not appear in the present case. The accused no doubt deserved severe punishment for the crimes proved against him, but an insuperable obstacle to the execution of the death sentence pronounced against him is found in the fact that he was captured as a prisoner of war and this is distinctly admitted by the prosecution on the record. Under the cartel which exists for the exchange of prisoners he can claim as he does that he is entitled to be exchanged and the Government should do nothing that would disable it from complying with its obligations in this regard.

J. HOLT,
Judge-Advocate-General.

HEADQUARTERS,
Camp Douglas, Chicago, Ill., February 9, 1863.
Col. W. HOFFMAN, *Commissary-General of Prisoners.*

SIR: Inclosed please find roll* of prisoners of war captured at Arkansas Post and forwarded to this camp under charge of Col. George W. Clark, Thirty-fourth Regiment Iowa Volunteer Infantry. Colonel Clark was not able to make a list during the trip. We have prepared this roll with great care and feel assured that it is correct or as nearly so as practicable.

Very respectfully, your most obedient servant,
J. AMMEN,
Brigadier-General of Volunteers, Commanding.

RICHMOND, VA., *February 9, 1863.*
Lieut. Col. W. H. LUDLOW, *Agent of Exchange.*

SIR: 1. Inasmuch as you have established a regulation that no citizens shall be allowed to depart on your flag-of-truce boats without the special permission of your Secretary of War hereafter no citizens, male or female, will be allowed to land at City Point without having received the previous permission of the Confederate authorities. Moreover no permission of Secretary Stanton will be respected the application for which is not made through me.

2. I see from your own papers that some dozen of our men captured at Arkansas Post were allowed to freeze to death in one night at Camp Douglas. I appeal to our common instincts against such atrocious inhumanity.

3. I send two official reports* in the case of Doctor Rucker. They emanate from such high authority that the most implicit reliance can be placed on them.

Respectfully, your obedient servant,
RO. OULD,
Agent of Exchange.

RICHMOND, VA., *February 9, 1863.*
Lieut. Col. WILLIAM H. LUDLOW, *Agent of Exchange.*

SIR: I send by the steamer to-day all the non-commissioned officers and men whom we have. I have also directed that all the officers now

---
* Not found.

here who were captured before December 10, 1862, should be sent. Such of them as are not here will be forwarded to this place as speedily as possible and sent to you.

How is it that you send only one officer by this boat? I know you have several others who have been exchanged under our agreement. I send all the sutlers' clerks, employés, agents, &c., whom we have in Richmond.

Many of the persons named in your list of citizen prisoners were sent off long ago. It will be necessary for me to see you before all citizen prisoners are released or delivered. I will carry out the agreement fully.

George W. Bryant, Twelfth Massachusetts, died of his wounds on the 26th of December last. Major Blake has never been in Richmond. Not one of the Tennessee and Ohio men to whom you referred in one of your letters is in Richmond. If they are elsewhere they will be delivered to you.

The clothing, &c., have been received and your directions will be complied with.

I will meet you at 1 o'clock on the 17th instant. I have taken steps to have all the citizen prisoners brought to Richmond.

Respectfully, your obedient servant,

RO. OULD,
Agent of Exchange.

INDIANAPOLIS, IND., *February 9, 1863.*

Col. WILLIAM HOFFMAN,
    Commissary-General of Prisoners, Washington, D. C.

COLONEL: Your letters of the 4th and 5th instant were received yesterday. I have directed no improvements at Camp Morton excepting such as could be made without additional expense to the Government. The camp has been carefully policed by fatigue parties detailed from the troops for that purpose. Captain Ekin has furnished a carpenter and had some bunks constructed, additional windows, glazing and window sash supplied and other general repairs made. No further prisoners have arrived. The four buildings in the center of the camp are occupied by the prisoners, one of which—the old hospital—is supplied with cots and is occupied by the wounded who are unable to walk and require constant medical treatment and nursing. The worst cases of the wounded are at the center hospital under the care of Doctor Kitchen. The sheds on the north side of the camp are not occupied. They, however, can be made suitable for such wounded prisoners as are capable of visiting the hospital for medical treatment. There are only 224 troops here for guard. Should more prisoners arrive and it be necessary to occupy these sheds a greater guard will be required. I have explained this to General Wright and he has promised to send another regiment if necessary. You may rest assured that everything possible will be done that can be compatible with the regulations you have established for the comfort and security of the prisoners and with the least possible expense to the Government. I have not considered it necessary to trouble you with a report of all the little details of the rules I have established for their government as they are all included in your circular of regulations. I will report to-morrow the dimensions of the barracks now occupied by the prisoners and the numbers confined in each. The barracks I have recommended to be removed from Camp Carrington are barracks that have been erected for the temporary accommodation of troops organizing here and can be removed at but little expense. They are temporary frame barracks, 16 by 100 feet, divided into four rooms and capable of accommodating 100 troops each. Should no more prisoners arrive their removal will not be necessary. The accounts against the prisoners' fund which I have forwarded have not been received. The creditors are clamorous for their payment. Should I be permitted to draw on the prisoners' fund at Alton these accounts, materially diminished, can readily be paid.

Very respectfully, your obedient servant,

H. W. FREEDLEY,
Captain, Third Infantry.

GENERAL ORDERS, }   HDQRS. DEPARTMENT OF THE OHIO,
No. 9.   }   *Cincinnati, Ohio, February 9, 1863.*

I. It is reported that much embarrassment and injury to the service is experienced from the practice of sending paroled Federal troops from the lines to interior camps without rolls of any kind or very imperfect ones, and also of paroling rebel prisoners without making any report of the circumstances or furnishing any rolls. To remedy this evil hereafter in all cases where our troops are captured by the enemy and paroled the senior officer present will cause to be prepared and forwarded to the office of the commissary-general of prisoners at Washington, D. C., with as little delay as practicable a full list by regiments and companies of all so paroled, giving the rank, regiment and company of each person, the time and place of capture and the disposition made of them. Like rolls of all rebel prisoners captured by our forces will be furnished by the officer in command of the troops by whom such captures are made.

When the circumstances are such that a roll cannot be immediately prepared a written report giving the number of officers and men, the time and place of capture and the disposition made of them will be made, to be followed by the necessary rolls at the earliest practicable moment.

When rebel prisoners are sent to Vicksburg for exchange commanders will also send duplicate rolls with them, one to remain with the agent who receives them, the other with his receipt upon it to be forwarded to the commissary-general of prisoners.

II. The following general orders and extracts from general orders, Adjutant General's Office, Washington, D. C., are published for the information and government of all concerned, and it is enjoined that the requirements thereof be strictly complied with:

No. 44, 1861:

In compliance with a resolution of the House of Representatives the Secretary of War directs that officers report to this office the names and residences of all prisoners that may be hereafter taken and released upon their oath of allegiance to the United States.

In like manner officers will report the names and residences of all prisoners who have been taken and released upon their oath of allegiance to the United States previous to this date, July 13, 1861.

No. 9, 1862:

The Secretary of War directs that officers and soldiers of the United States who are or may be prisoners of war shall during their imprisonment be considered entitled to and receive the same pay as if they were doing active duty.

No. 14, 1862:

The Secretary of War directs that the rations of prisoners held in the rebel States shall be commuted for and during the period of their imprisonment; the commutation to be rated at cost price.

No. 52, 1862:

The names of officers and men taken prisoners by the enemy must not be dropped from the muster-rolls, but will be placed at the foot of the list of names in their respective companies until they are exchanged or discharged.

No. 54, 1862:

The commissary-general of prisoners and commanding officers having charge of prisoners of war will as soon as practicable forward to this office lists of the prisoners, showing their rank, regiment, where captured, date of confinement and where confined. Similar lists will be furnished of new detachments as often as they may arrive at their several places of confinement.

No. 67, 1862:

The supervision of prisoners of war sent by generals commanding in the field to posts or camps prepared for their reception is placed entirely under Col. William Hoffman, Third Infantry, commissary-general of prisoners, who is subject only to the orders of the War Department. All matters in relation to prisoners will pass through him.

He will also establish regulations for issuing clothing to prisoners, and will direct the manner in which all funds arising from the saving of rations at prison hospitals or otherwise shall be accounted for and disbursed by the regular disbursing officers of the departments in providing under existing regulations such articles as may be absolutely necessary for the welfare of the prisoners.

Loyal citizens who may be found among the prisoners of war, confined on false accusations or through mistake, may lay their cases before the commissary-general of prisoners, who will submit them to the Adjutant-General.

The commissary-general is authorized to grant paroles to prisoners on the recommendation of the medical officer attending the prison in case of extreme illness, but under no other circumstances.

No. 71, 1862:

In every case of prisoners taken in arms against the United States who may be tried and sentenced to death the record of the tribunal before which the trial was had will be forwarded for the action of the President of the United States, without whose orders no such sentence in such cases will be executed.

No. 72, 1862:

I. Whenever sick men, paroled prisoners or others, under circumstances entitling them to their descriptive lists and accounts of pay and clothing, &c., are sent away from their regiments, or being already separated from their regiments are discharged from any hospital or moved from point to point in a body, they will be put under charge of a trusty officer or non-commissioned officer (to be selected if possible from their own number) who will exercise command over the party and conduct it to its destination. And to this officer or non-commissioned officer will be confided the descriptive lists of all for the safe-keeping of which until properly turned over with each soldier he will be held strictly accountable. Detailed instructions in writing for his guidance and government during the journey will in every case if possible be furnished to such officer by his last commander, and should he himself be compelled to make any detachments from his party he will in each case observe the same rules.

II. That paragraph of General Orders, No. 65, of June 12, 1862, which authorizes the discharge when requested by them of paroled prisoners is hereby rescinded.

III. No more furloughs will be granted to paroled prisoners. All furloughs heretofore given to them are hereby revoked and all prisoners now at large on their parole or who may hereafter be paroled by the rebel authorities will immediately repair if belonging to regiments raised in the New England and Middle States to the Camp of Instruction established near Annapolis, Md.; if belonging to regiments raised in the States of Virginia, Tennessee, Kentucky, Ohio, Indiana and Michigan to Camp Chase, near Columbus, Ohio; if belonging to regiments raised in the States of Illinois, Wisconsin, Minnesota, Iowa and Missouri to the camp near Jefferson Barracks, Mo. (Camp Wallace, near Columbus, Ohio, since substituted for Camp Chase, and Benton Barracks, near Saint Louis, Mo., for Jefferson Barracks), and report for such duty compatible with their parole as may be assigned to them by the officers in command of said camps. And all whether officers or soldiers who fail to comply with this order within the space of time necessary for them to do so will be accounted deserters and dealt with accordingly.

The attention of all commanding, mustering and recruiting officers is particularly directed to this order, and they are required to use their utmost exertions not only to give it the widest circulation in their neighborhoods but to see that it is faithfully carried out. And their Excellencies the Governors of the several States are respectfully solicited to lend their efforts to the same end.

IV. The transportation necessary to a compliance with this order can on application be procured from the Governors of the several States or from the U. S. mustering or commanding officers in the various cities within them.

V. The commanders of the different camps of instruction to which paroled men are sent will have them organized into companies and battalions, keeping those of the same regiment and of the same State as much together as possible, and will have correct muster-rolls of them made out and forwarded to this office; and on the 15th day of every muster month will furnish a list of them to the company commanders, from whom in return they will procure full and exact descriptive lists of each man and accounts of the pay, clothing, &c., due to or from him to the Government.

No. 163, 1862:

Whenever prisoners of war are released on parole and sent through the lines the officers who release them will immediately send rolls to the Adjutant-General of the Army containing an exact list of the prisoners' names, rank, regiment, date and place of capture and date of release on parole. These rolls are indispensable in effecting exchanges of prisoners.

No. 176, 1862:

The commissary-general of prisoners has charge of the U. S. officers and men on parole, and correspondence relating to them as well as all details concerning them will pass through him.

III. The foregoing instructions relative to prisoners of war are thus compiled and published that every officer serving in the Department of the Ohio and on whom the duties prescribed may be devolved may be fully informed in relation thereto, and future negligence on the part of any one will be punished as willful disobedience of orders.

The reports and rolls called for, except those directed to be sent with prisoners to Vicksburg, will by officers serving in this department be neatly and carefully prepared, properly folded and indorsed and forwarded through these headquarters.

By command of Major-General Wright:

N. H. McLEAN,
Assistant Adjutant-General and Chief of Staff.

SPECIAL ORDERS, } HDQRS. DEPARTMENT OF THE GULF,
No. 16.   }   *New Orleans, February 9, 1863.*

I. All prisoners of war in this department taken from the enemy and now on parole and who have not taken the oath of allegiance will report on Friday, the 20th instant, at 1 p. m., at the foot of Canal street, in this city, for passage via Baton Rouge through the lines under flag of truce. Such as have not already been registered will report at the provost-marshal's office, 177 Canal street, in time to be registered. Officers of the United States having Confederate prisoners of war in custody will forward them to this city under guard in time for registration and passage on transport as above provided.

II. By General Orders, No. 10, January 10, 1863, from the War Department, Adjutant-General's Office, the following officers and men are declared duly exchanged as prisoners of war: All captures of officers, enlisted men and camp followers in the States of Texas and Louisiana up to January 1, 1863; all captures of officers, enlisted men and camp followers in the States of Florida, Alabama and Mississippi up to December 10, 1862; all captures on the sea, the sea and Gulf coasts and the waters flowing into the same up to December 10, 1862. All officers and enlisted men of the United States in this department herein declared exchanged will immediately report for duty to their proper companies and regiments.

By command of Major-General Banks:

RICHARD B. IRWIN,
Lieutenant-Colonel and Assistant Adjutant-General.

WAR DEPARTMENT, *Washington, February 10, 1863.*

Major-General SCHENCK, *Baltimore:*

The commanding general of a department has authority to try or to release prisoners whom he arrests. It is not necessary to refer such cases to these headquarters.

H. W. HALLECK,
General-in-Chief.

BRIGADE HEADQUARTERS,
Columbia, Tenn., February 10, 1863.

General J. C. DAVIS, *Commanding U. S. Forces.*

GENERAL: I have recently captured forty-eight non-commissioned officers and privates belonging to the Federal Army which were paroled and sent into Fort Donelson. We have here six of your men captured a few days since which have not been paroled, also Captain Von Minden, of the Fifth Iowa Cavalry, and First Lieut. Samuel Mitchell, the latter captured at Fort Donelson on the 3d instant. At the earnest solicitation of Captain Von Minden I send a flag of truce in charge of Lieut. J. G. Clouston, of Major-General Wheeler's staff, for the purpose of exchanging him for Captain Rambaut, my commissary, who I am informed was captured by your forces a few days since. I am willing to exchange the six men here for an equal number of men of mine [now in your] possession, or any of my command you may have paroled and sent out of your lines. Lieutenant Clouston also has in his charge a list of the forty-eight prisoners sent into Fort Donelson, which list has not yet been forwarded to the War Department of the Confederate States, any of whom I will release from their paroles in exchange for any of my men who may have fallen into your hands. Lieutenant Clouston is fully authorized and empowered to receive any prisoners of my command you may have and erase from the list the names of an equal number of those captured by us and to give you official notification in writing of the release from parole of the men whose names are thus erased. He is also authorized, should it meet your approbation, to arrange time and place for the exchange of Captains Von Minden and Rambaut and the six men now here in our possession. Any arrangements made by Lieutenant Clouston will be ratified by me and carried out in good faith.

I am, general, very respectfully, yours,

N. B. FORREST,
Brigadier-General.

OFFICE COMMISSARY-GENERAL OF PRISONERS,
Washington, D. C., February 10, 1863.

Brig. Gen. J. AMMEN, *Comdg. Camp Douglas, Chicago, Ill.*

GENERAL: In reply to your letter of the 6th instant I have the honor to inform you that by General Orders, No. 60, of January 6, 1862, from the War Department, all medical officers taken prisoners are to be unconditionally released, but of course it is expected that their position will be well established. It is very possible that the two prisoners who apply to be recognized as surgeons are entitled to the position, but it is necessary that there should be some official evidence of the fact, and I have therefore to request that you will telegraph to General Curtis or General McClernand for information. When it is established that they are medical officers of the rebel army they should be sent on parole to the nearest convenient point of our lines to be released. In the absence of these medical officers should you find it necessary you will employ private physicians to attend the sick and wounded prisoners.

I am, general, very respectfully, your obedient servant,

W. HOFFMAN,
Colonel Third Infantry, Commissary-General of Prisoners.

OFFICE COMMISSARY-GENERAL OF PRISONERS,
Washington, D. C., February 10, 1863.

Col. HENRY DENT, *Provost-Marshal-General, Louisville, Ky.*

COLONEL: By your telegram of the 11th instant it appears that you have sixty deserters from the rebel army. On the 3d of December last I communicated to Captain Jones, aide-de-camp to General Boyle, instructions as to the disposition to be made of such prisoners. Lest they may not have reached you I will give you the substance of them: Deserters from the rebel army who are really such cannot be held as prisoners of war and they should be released; but to insure their future loyalty they should be required to take the oath of allegiance with the penalty of death for its violation. If you have any such cases in charge please make a report for each case with your recommendation for or against discharge. There may be those who will represent themselves as deserters who are in fact spies. To guard against cases of this kind commanders must make a careful examination of each case presented.

Very respectfully, your obedient servant,

W. HOFFMAN,
Colonel Third Infantry, Commissary-General of Prisoners.

OFFICE COMMISSARY-GENERAL OF PRISONERS,
Washington, D. C., February 10, 1863.

Lieut. Col. GEORGE SANGSTER,
Commanding Camp Parole, Annapolis, Md.

COLONEL: Your letter of the 8th instant is received. The second paragraph of General Orders, No. 10, current series, required that "all exchanged troops will be forwarded to the armies to which they belong as soon as properly equipped." This order,* a copy of which is inclosed, covers all the exchanged troops at Annapolis, and you will accordingly forward them without delay. You will assign an officer to command the detachments ordered to different armies, and these officers will receipt to you for all arms and other public property in the hands of the men, which property will be turned over on receipt to the officers commanding the companies to which the men belong. Send with each detachment full accounts of clothing, pay, &c. If a payment has not been made it should be made at once. You will not send any more paroled troops West till I give you further orders. Colonel Waite, of the First Infantry, has been ordered to take command at Annapolis, and you will command Camp Parole as heretofore. I have no doubt the colonel will carry out your arrangements, which seem to me very judicious, and his presence will relieve you of much labor. Maj.

---

*Omitted here; see p. 169.

James Given, Seventh Pennsylvania Cavalry, having been exchanged and the General-in-Chief having declined to permit him to remain on duty at the camp you will order him to his regiment, availing yourself of his services if necessary in conducting troops to their regiments.

Very respectfully, your obedient servant,

W. HOFFMAN,
Colonel Third Infantry, Commissary-General of Prisoners.

[FEBRUARY 10, 1863.—For General Orders, No. 16, Department of the Cumberland, relating to the capture of rebel soldiers dressed in Union uniforms, see Series I, Volume XXIII, Part II, p. 53.]

[FEBRUARY 10, 1863.—For Reynolds to Flynt concerning treatment of the inhabitants of Middle Tennessee, see Series I, Volume XXIII, Part II, p. 54; and for Halleck to Rosecrans, March 5, in answer to Reynolds' suggestions, see p. 107, same volume.]

HEADQUARTERS U. S. FORCES,
Franklin, Tenn., February 11, 1863.

Brig. Gen. N. B. FORREST,
Commanding Confederate Forces.

GENERAL: Your communication in regard to the exchange of prisoners was received by Lieutenant Wilson and party, who met your messenger under flag of truce a few miles in advance of my lines and by whom they were promptly delivered.

All Confederate prisoners captured by my command since leaving Murfreesborough the 31st ultimo (except a few sick) have been sent to that place and Nashville to be disposed of according to Department orders regulating exchanges. Colonel Carroll and Major Rambaut have both been sent to Nashville.

I have no authority to negotiate an exchange of prisoners, general, and cannot therefore entertain your proposition however much I might desire to do so. Captain Von Minden's communication will be forwarded and an early exchange recommended.

Very respectfully, yours,

JEFF. C. DAVIS,
Brigadier-General, Commanding.

FORT MONROE, *February 11, 1863.*

Hon. EDWIN M. STANTON, *Secretary of War:*

In reply to my demand Mr. Ould, Confederate agent for exchange of prisoners, has just informed me that all U. S. officers captured before December 10, 1862, the date of Jeff. Davis' proclamation, would be immediately released. All the sutlers' clerks and Government employés confined in Richmond have been released and have arrived here on flag-of-truce boat New York. I shall meet Mr. Ould on the 17th at City Point.

WM. H. LUDLOW,
Lieutenant-Colonel and Agent for Exchange of Prisoners.

(Copy to Colonel Hoffman, commissary-general of prisoners, and Major-General Hitchcock, commissioner for exchange of prisoners.)

ASSISTANT QUARTERMASTER'S OFFICE,
Camp Douglas, Chicago, Ill., February 11, 1863.

Col. W. HOFFMAN,
Commissary-General of Prisoners, Washington.

SIR: I have the honor to inclose you an estimate* of clothing necessary for the comfort of the rebel prisoners in Camp Douglas, Ill. This estimate was made by Lieutenant George, of the Sixty-fifth Regiment Illinois Volunteers, appointed for that purpose by General Ammen. Some of the prisoners are very much in need of clothing as they suffer severely with the cold. If this is satisfactory please approve the same and return it to me. Clothing that is not fit to issue to our own men can be procured from Captain Potter, assistant quartermaster in Chicago, Ill.

Very respectfully, your obedient servant,
J. P. RUTHERFORD,
Captain and Assistant Quartermaster, U. S. Army.

CAMP CHASE, OHIO, *February 11, 1863.*

[Maj. Gen. W. S. ROSECRANS.]

GENERAL: Your order relative to the general treatment of Confederate officers captured by your forces and here incarcerated is continually being violated. Not only (as I have understood by a commissary clerk) by filling out such requisitions as are forbidden by your order, but they are permitted to buy any edibles they wish of the prison sutler. This comes under my observation whenever on guard. I wish to know if you tolerate such violation. You certainly will not when once aware of the fact. For any further information please reply and you will be furnished with a letter of exposition in full containing other matters worthy of notice.

G. W. CAMPBELL,
Private Co. A, First Batt., Eighty-eighth Regt. Ohio Vol. Infty.

[First indorsement.]

DEPARTMENT OF THE CUMBERLAND,
February 19, 1863.

Respectfully forwarded to Major-General Wright, commanding, Cincinnati, Ohio.

W. S. ROSECRANS,
Major-General, Commanding.

---

* Omitted.

[Second indorsement.]

HEADQUARTERS DEPARTMENT OF THE OHIO,
Cincinnati, Ohio, February 23, 1863.

Respectfully referred to the commanding officer at Camp Chase, through whom this communication should have been forwarded.

By order of Major-General Wright:

C. W. FOSTER,
Assistant Adjutant-General.

[Third indorsement.]

HEADQUARTERS U. S. FORCES,
Columbus, Ohio, February 24, 1863.

Respectfully referred to the provost-marshal at Camp Chase who will report on the within subject to these headquarters.

By order of Brigadier-General Cooper:

WM. VON DOEHN,
Assistant Adjutant-General.

TULLAHOMA, TENN., *February 12, 1863.*
Major-General ROSECRANS, U. S. Army.

GENERAL: I have had the honor to receive your letters of the 18th and 19th ultimo addressed to me as I understand because you "find yourself compelled by a sense of duty to humanity to decline communicating with General Bragg by flag of truce," &c.

Being unable to perceive how the interests of humanity are to be promoted by suspension of correspondence between the commanders of opposite armies I very much regret your determination, the more so because it is not in my power to re establish that correspondence.

General Bragg is the commander of the Army of Tennessee not I. One of his functions as such is of course the conducting of such correspondence as you propose to hold with me. I can assume none of the duties or privileges of the position in which our common superior, the President of the Confederacy, placed him.

I gladly avail myself of this opportunity to express to you my appreciation of your humanity exhibited in the case of our wounded who fell into your hands at Murfreesborough.

Most respectfully, your obedient servant,

J. E. JOHNSTON,
General.

HOUSE OF REPRESENTATIVES, *February 12, 1863.*
Hon. E. M. STANTON, *Secretary of War.*

SIR: About a month since I cut from the Chronicle of this city the following, purporting to [be] the latest news from Richmond:

One hundred and eighteen men, captured by the Virginia Line at Petersburg and at Pikeville, Ky., are confined at Richmond, and the Governor has announced to* President Lincoln the terms upon which such exchange can alone be made.

He has placed at hard labor in the penitentiary Captain Gramm and Lieutenant Wade as hostages for Captain Dusky and Lieutenant Varner, now confined in the District of Columbia penitentiary. * * *

---

* For Letcher to Lincoln, January 2, 1863, see case of Richard Thomas Zarvona, Vol. II., this Series, p. 401. For the omitted portion of this letter, see this Volume, p. 147.

Dusky and Varner were convicted at Wheeling, Va., for robbing the mail, having been captured after the commission of the act. They were received in the penitentiary in this District January 10, 1862, and are now in the Albany, N. Y., penitentiary. They were sentenced for four years.

I believe an examination of the facts will show that Dusky and Varner were commissioned officers in the so-called Southern Confederacy. If this is the true state of the case ought not Captain Gramm and Lieutenant Wade be relieved by making the exchange and by treating Dusky and Varner as prisoners of war?

Very respectfully,

JAMES R. MORRIS.

. [Indorsement.]

ADJUTANT-GENERAL'S OFFICE, *March 13, 1863.*

Respectfully submitted with report* of commissary-general of prisoners.

E. D. TOWNSEND,
Assistant Adjutant-General.

———

HEADQUARTERS, *Annapolis, Md., February 12, 1863.*
Col. W. HOFFMAN, *Commissary-General of Prisoners.*

SIR: I have the honor to inclose you complete rolls† of soldiers and citizens who arrived here yesterday from Richmond on board of steam transport New York, Capt. A. A. Mann, Third New York Volunteers, being in charge of the men and flag-of-truce boat, Captain Mulford being sick of fever at Fort Monroe. I also received Col. A. B. Moore, of the One hundred and fourth Regiment Illinois Volunteers, and First Lieut. J. Dewald, One hundred and eighth Ohio Volunteers. These officers were receipted for by General Rosecrans, and on that receipt General Dix sent them through to report to Major-General Rosecrans. A statement of the facts of the case I inclose which I got from the colonel. You will find that the rolls show ninety-five citizens. Eighty-nine were present as I telegraphed to you yesterday. Six of them were sent to Baltimore by the order of Major-General Dix thus accounting for the difference.

I am, colonel, with great respect, your obedient servant,

GEO. SANGSTER,
Lieutenant-Colonel, Commanding Paroled Prisoners.

[Inclosure.]

ANNAPOLIS, MD., *February 11, 1863.*
Col. GEORGE SANGSTER, *Commanding Post.*

SIR: I arrived at this city this morning by flag-of-truce boat, having been a prisoner in the hands of the rebels since December 7, 1862. I was paroled on the 11th of December, 1862, at Murfreesborough, Tenn., with some thirteen other officers. Instead of being allowed to depart as a paroled prisoner I with the other officers was held. All excepting myself and Lieut. J. Dewald were sent to prison at Atlanta, Ga., and have been and still are there in close confinement. After keeping me some three weeks in Murfreesborough after being paroled I was sent to Atlanta prison and kept closely guarded and confined. After keep-

---

* See Hoffman to Thomas, March 12, p. 350. † Omitted. ·

ing me there a short time they took me from Atlanta prison to Richmond and confined me in the Libby Prison for three weeks. During the whole of this time myself and other officers taken at the same time had our paroles in our pockets which were totally disregarded, as they said it was no evidence that an officer was entitled to release notwithstanding his parole. The non-commissioned officers and privates captured with us were paroled and sent home and the officers' names were included in the list and was receipted for by General Rosecrans, but none of us were allowed to go. These facts were told me by Colonel Beard, inspector-general for General Bragg.

The treatment we have received by the commandants at the two prisons named has been shameful and entirely destitute of humanity. We have lived on corn-meal, bad meat and cold water, these being the only things furnished us to subsist upon. We think that such treatment exhibited toward paroled prisoners is an outrage and I sincerely hope that rebel officers in our hands will be compelled to live on similar short allowances. I desire you to have me forwarded to my regiment at Camp Douglas, Ill., which is now on duty guarding the rebel prisoners at that place. I also wish to go to Washington to get my pay. By rendering me this assistance you will greatly oblige,

Yours, forever in favor of my country and the old flag,
ABSALOM B. MOORE,
Colonel 104th Regiment Illinois Infantry and
Comdg. 39th Brigade, 12th Division, Dept. of the Cumberland.

WASHINGTON, D. C., *February 13, 1863.*
Lieut. Col. WILLIAM H. LUDLOW.

SIR: I inclose a note* referring to the case of Sergt. M. Mullen (from one of his daughters I understand) to which I would ask particular attention. He is a Union Virginian and for this reason doubtless has been made a special sufferer.

Fairfax Minor has been ordered to be held here as a hostage for him, whose treatment when you can be heard from in the case of Mullen will depend upon your report.

Very respectfully, your obedient servant,
E. A. HITCHCOCK,
Major-General of Vols., Commissioner for Exchange of Prisoners.

OFFICE COMMISSARY-GENERAL OF PRISONERS,
Washington, D. C., February 13, 1863.
Brig. Gen. J. H. MARTINDALE,
Commanding District of Washington, Washington.

GENERAL: It is proposed to send to City Point for exchange with as little delay as practicable all citizen prisoners arrested by [the] military in this city and now on parole or held in confinement who wish to be exchanged, and I have respectfully to request that you will cause notice to be given requiring all on parole to report without delay to the provost-marshal that it may be determined who are to be exchanged.

Very respectfully, your obedient servant,
W. HOFFMAN,
Colonel Third Infantry, Commissary-General of Prisoners.

---

* Not found.

WASHINGTON, *February 13, 1863.*

Lieut. Col. W. H. LUDLOW, *Agent for Exchange of Prisoners.*

How many citizen prisoners do you want for exchange?

W. HOFFMAN,
Commissary-General of Prisoners.

OFFICE COMMISSARY-GENERAL OF PRISONERS,
Washington, D. C., February 13, 1863.

Lieut. Col. W. H. LUDLOW,
Agent for Exchange of Prisoners, Fort Monroe, Va.

COLONEL: I have the honor to inclose herewith all the information*
I have been able to obtain in relation to the two prisoners in the penitentiary at Albany. From their own statements it is plain that they
belong to no proper military organization and that neither of them was
an officer. It was not till recently that the rebel authorities would
recognize guerrillas, bushwhackers and other irregular bands as fit
subjects for exchange, and within a few weeks past they have rejected
some of this class. They cannot now therefore go back to 1861 and
claim to exempt a band of marauders who break into a post-office and
steal the mail from proper punishment on the ground that they
belonged to the Army and were acting under the authority of their
Government. You will fully understand how to bring this matter
before Mr. Ould so as to insure the release of our officers who are held
in their penitentiaries as hostages for these robbers, and I need only
put the papers in your hands. Nothing has yet been decided in
Zarvona's case. General Hitchcock has been confined to his room for
several days, and probably nothing will be done till he can attend to it.

Mr. W. L. McDonald, sutler of the Twenty-sixth New Jersey Volunteers, called on me this morning with a parole in which he was pledged
to effect the exchange of S. J. Anderson, on parole in New York, for
himself within thirty-five days or to return to Richmond. His parole is
January 19 [1863]. As you have already made provision for the exchange
of sutlers and their employés I told Mr. McDonald it was unnecessary
that he should make a special exchange, and that he might consider
himself exchanged unless he hears further from me. Mr. Anderson was
arrested in August, 1861, by order of the Secretary of State and sent
to Fort Lafayette from whence he was paroled. I presume there will
be no objection to his being exchanged and I will apply to have him
sent to report to you to be given as an equivalent for Mr. McDonald if
that should be necessary, or to be exchanged for some person of standing held by them. I inclose the papers† in this case. I have to-day
telegraphed to persons in the West to send citizen prisoners here for
exchange. I doubt if I can get as many as 300 unless I send unwilling
persons. I will notify you by telegraph of their arrival and their
number. You are aware that all captured rebel officers are held by us.
Did you have any understanding with Mr. Ould about them when he
announced that all our officers captured before the 10th of December
would be released? I have been two days confined to my bed by illness
which has delayed the necessary arrangements for the delivery of citizen prisoners.

Very respectfully, your obedient servant,

W. HOFFMAN,
Colonel Third Infantry, Commissary-General of Prisoners.

---

* See Morris to Stanton, p. 266.

† Not found; but see case of Samuel J. Anderson, Vol. II, this Series, p. 602 *et seq.*

OFFICE COMMISSARY-GENERAL OF PRISONERS,
Washington, D. C., February 13, 1863.

Lieut. Col. W. E. DOSTER, *Provost-Marshal, Washington, D. C.*

COLONEL: I beg leave to notify you that I have ordered from the West about 150 citizen prisoners to this city for exchange. They have been directed to report to you. The number may be increased to 300.

Very respectfully, your obedient servant,

W. HOFFMAN,
Colonel Third Infantry, Commissary-General of Prisoners.

OFFICE COMMISSARY-GENERAL OF PRISONERS,
Washington, D. C., February 13, 1863.

Capt. E. L. WEBBER,
Commanding Camp Chase Prison, Columbus, Ohio:

Send under a guard of an officer and ten men to report to the provost-marshal of this city all citizen prisoners who wish to be exchanged, including those recommended by Judge Galloway, excluding spies. Send to me rolls with charges and sentences in full. Notify me when they leave. Among those to be exchanged include all who are unwilling to take the oath of allegiance if permitted to do so, though they may not desire to be exchanged. Judge Galloway recommends that Lewis W. Luther, of Cabell County, Va., be released on taking the oath of allegiance. Governor Peirpoint recommends that he be sent South and you will therefore include him among those to be exchanged. Order 193 applies only to prisoners in confinement at its date. I will write you further in relation to it.

Very respectfully, your obedient servant,

W. HOFFMAN,
Colonel Third Infantry, Commissary-General of Prisoners.

OFFICE COMMISSARY-GENERAL OF PRISONERS,
Washington, D. C., February 13, 1863.

W. L. McDONALD,
Sutler of Twenty-sixth New Jersey Vols., Washington, D. C.

SIR: In reply to your application to me to effect an exchange between yourself and Mr. S. J. Anderson, now on parole in New York, I have to inform you that by an arrangement recently entered into between Lieut. Col. W. H. Ludlow, agent for the exchange of prisoners, and Robert Ould, esq., the agent from Richmond, all sutlers and their employés have been exchanged and it is therefore not necessary that a special exchange should be made in your case. But that there may be no doubt on the subject I will refer the matter to Colonel Ludlow, that your release from your parole may be fully acknowledged. Unless you hear further from me you may consider yourself exchanged.

Very respectfully, your obedient servant,

W. HOFFMAN,
Colonel Third Infantry, Commissary-General of Prisoners.

FORT MONROE, VA., *February 13, 1863.*

Col. W. HOFFMAN, *Commissary-General of Prisoners:*

I want 500 citizen prisoners for exchange.

WM. H. LUDLOW,
Lieutenant-Colonel and Agent for Exchange of Prisoners.

HEADQUARTERS DEPARTMENT OF VIRGINIA,
Fort Monroe, February 13, 1863.

Colonel HOFFMAN, *Commissary-General of Prisoners.*

COLONEL: I am informed that the men of the Eighth U. S. Infantry captured in Texas and so long detained there are now at Carrollton, La. These men have all been declared exchanged and can be immediately ordered into service.

I am, very respectfully, your obedient servant,

WM. H. LUDLOW,
Agent for Exchange of Prisoners.

WHEELING, VA., *February 13, 1863.*

Col. W. HOFFMAN, *Commissary-General of Prisoners:*

Had shipped all prisoners to Camp Chase. Only hold here now the nine hostages reported to you January 31.

JOS. DARR, JR.,
Major and Provost-Marshal-General.

GENERAL ORDERS, }   HDQRS. SIXTEENTH ARMY CORPS,
No. 9.   }   *Memphis, Tenn., February 13, 1863.*

The attention of the general commanding is called to irregularities in sending paroled prisoners to interior camps. The following General Orders, No. 163, of the War Department, Adjutant-General's Office, Washington, October 22, 1862, is therefore republished for the information of all concerned:

Whenever prisoners of war are released on parole and sent through the lines the officers who release them will immediately send rolls to the Adjutant-General of the Army containing an exact list of the prisoners' names, rank, regiment, date and place of capture and date of release on parole. These rolls are indispensable in effecting exchanges of prisoners.

By order of Maj. Gen. S. A. Hurlbut:

HENRY BINMORE,
Assistant Adjutant-General.

OFFICE COMMISSARY-GENERAL OF PRISONERS,
Washington, D. C., February 14, 1863.

Maj. Gen. R. C. SCHENCK,
Commanding Eighth Army Corps, Baltimore, Md.:

Please have furnished to this office immediately a list of prisoners held in Baltimore with the date of arrest, the charges and by whose order arrested, also a list of those paroled with the same particulars and by whose authority and to what limits paroled, with date. Make the two lists separate.

By order of the Secretary of War:

W. HOFFMAN,
Commissary-General of Prisoners.

(Same to Brig. Gen. W. W. Morris, Fort McHenry, Baltimore, and Col. M. Burke, Fort Hamilton, N. Y.)

OFFICE COMMISSARY-GENERAL OF PRISONERS,
Washington, February 14, 1863.
Maj. Gen. H. G. WRIGHT,
Commanding Department of the Ohio, Cincinnati, Ohio.

GENERAL: I have the honor to acknowledge the receipt of your letter of the 7th instant informing me of your action in the matter of furnishing necessary supplies for the prisoners of war at Camp Butler and I am much indebted to you for your considerate attention.

Captain Freedley is quite conversant with the manner in which prisoners of war have heretofore been provided for and it was for this reason that I directed him to confer with you in relation to them, expecting that he would then visit the different camps and see that the regulations heretofore issued were properly enforced. Finding that he was delayed at Indianapolis I ordered him to visit Camp Butler and Camp Douglas to inspect and report on the condition of the prisoners.

The prisoners' fund if well managed would cover a large part of the expenses necessary to provide for their indispensable wants.

We must furnish them blankets for the time we have them and more or less clothing, but of course this should be limited to what is absolutely requisite.

Please find inclosed a copy of the regulations providing for the control of prisoners.

I am, general, very respectfully, your obedient servant,
W. HOFFMAN,
Colonel Third Infantry, Commissary-General of Prisoners.

WASHINGTON, February 14, 1863.
Lieut. Col. F. A. DICK, Provost Marshal-General:

Select at Saint Louis and Alton Prisons and send under a suitable guard to report to the provost-marshal in this city for exchange 350 citizen prisoners. Include guerrillas and those under charges or sentenced to confinement for the war or a less period, not spies. Send them by Pittsburg and report by telegram when they will leave.
W. HOFFMAN,
Commissary-General of Prisoners.

OFFICE COMMISSARY-GENERAL OF PRISONERS,
Washington, D. C., February 14, 1863.
Lieut. Col. W. E. DOSTER, Provost-Marshal, Washington.

COLONEL: Can you provide for 500 citizen prisoners for a few days? They may be expected from the West in ten days.
Very respectfully, your obedient servant,
W. HOFFMAN,
Colonel Third Infantry, Commissary-General of Prisoners.

HEADQUARTERS PROVOST-MARSHAL'S OFFICE,
Washington, D. C., February 14, 1863.
Col. W. HOFFMAN,
Third Infantry, Commissary-General of Prisoners.

COLONEL: In reply to your inquiry as to whether provision could be made for 500 citizen prisoners for a few days I have the honor to state that I do not apprehend any difficulty but that the accommodations could be furnished.

I have the honor to be, colonel, very respectfully, your obedient servant,

W. E. DOSTER,
Lieutenant-Colonel and Provost-Marshal.

HEADQUARTERS DISTRICT OF ARIZONA,
Mesilla, February 15, 1863.

Capt. BENJAMIN C. CUTLER,
Assistant Adjutant-General, Santa Fé.

CAPTAIN: I learn from two parties who have recently arrived here from San Antonio, Tex., that there are in that vicinity 300 prisoners, enlisted men of the U. S. service, treated like felons and miserably fed and clothed. My informants say that they are a part of the old regular force who were taken prisoners when General Twiggs turned over to the Texas commissioners. Cannot something be done from here for their exchange?

I am, captain, very respectfully, your obedient servant,

J. R. WEST,
Brigadier-General, Commanding.

HDQRS. C. S. FORCES N. E. ARKANSAS AND S. E. MISSOURI,
Near Batesville, Ark., February 15, 1863.

Brigadier-General DAVIDSON, U. S. Army,
Commanding U. S. Forces, West Plains, Mo.

GENERAL: After the action at Hartville, Mo., I left my wounded in charge of several surgeons, some of whom have returned to my camp paroled stating that surgeons, attendants and wounded had been paroled by U. S. officers.

There was an agreement made between General Hindman, C. S. Army, and General Blunt, U. S. Army, commanding Army of the Frontier, forbidding this act, which has been honestly and faithfully carried out by the C. S. authorities. The conduct of the U. S. officers at Hartville is in direct violation of it.

Again: It has not been the usage of either the United States or Confederate States Government in this war to parole the surgeons.

I hope and believe that when this letter reaches you justice will be done my Government with regard to the surgeons, attendants and wounded left at Hartville.

I must also call your attention to the fact that in the little dash made by a detachment of your cavalry into Batesville the officer in command carried off some twenty-five miles the only attendant of a wounded soldier and paroled him.

This act was unofficerlike, cruel and inhuman, for the poor soldier was unable to move and as far as that officer was concerned was left to die.

I cannot, do not, believe that you will countenance such an act.

Very respectfully,

J. S. MARMADUKE,
Brigadier-General, C. S. Army.

[Inclosure.]

HEADQUARTERS SHELBY'S CAVALRY BRIGADE,
Camp Kirtley, February 15, 1863.

Brigadier-General MARMADUKE,
Commanding Cavalry Division.

GENERAL: One of the surgeons attached to my brigade and left in attendance upon our wounded at Hartville, Mo., has recently returned, reporting to me that he with the other surgeons detailed there had been arrested by the Federals, somewhat badly treated and finally paroled, though not without first having the gloomy prospects of going to Saint Louis as prisoners offered to them.

What sudden change has come over Federal rule and usage in Missouri? Are agreements made to be broken and the tender offices of surgeons rendered nugatory by insults, arrests, separations and confinements? General Blunt could have no such ideas, General Hindman certainly had none such, or the treaty at Prairie Grove would have remained unmade.

Our action toward Federal surgeons has always been one of uniform kindness, tempered with a desire to aid rather than detract from their works of mercy, but I seek in vain for their reciprocation of multiplied kindnesses and look only to find them abusing the chief attributes and virtues of humanity.

To arrest and imprison a surgeon causes him to neglect his patients; wounds neglected produce irritation, mortification, death, and death too caused by those who have received countless favors at our hands.

General, some understanding must be reached that will cover this matter, and if needs be retaliation however repugnant to every human feeling will be adopted as a matter of stern and urgent self-defense.

Very respectfully, yours, &c.,

JO. O. SHELBY,
Colonel, Commanding Cavalry Brigade.

[Indorsement.]

HDQRS. C. S. FORCES, N. E. ARKANSAS AND S. E. MISSOURI,
Camp near Batesville, Ark., February 16, 1863.

Brigadier-General DAVIDSON,
Commanding U. S. Forces near West Plains, Mo.

GENERAL: I beg to call your attention to the within letter.

Very respectfully,

J. S. MARMADUKE,
Brigadier-General, Commanding.

OFFICE PROVOST-MARSHAL-GENERAL,
Saint Louis, Mo., February 15, 1863.

Col. W. HOFFMAN, *Commissary-General of Prisoners.*

COLONEL: I have received your telegram of the 14th directing me to select at Saint Louis and Alton Prisons and send under guard to report to the provost-marshal in Washington for exchange 350 citizen prisoners, including guerrillas and those under charges or sentenced to confinement for the war or a less period (not spies), to report by telegram when they will leave. I will proceed at once to execute this order and will report by telegram when they will leave. My first impression is that it will take about a week to get them ready to start.

I have the honor, colonel, to be, your obedient servant,

F. A. DICK,
Lieutenant-Colonel and Provost-Marshal-General.

HDQRS. C. S. FORCES N. E. ARKANSAS AND S. E. MISSOURI,
Batesville, Ark., February 16, 1863.

BRIGADIER-GENERAL COMMANDING U. S. FORCES,
West Plains and Springfield, Mo.

GENERAL: I have the honor to send under flag of truce in charge of Capt. A. D. Brown, C. S. Army, dispatches for yourself.

Very respectfully,

J. S. MARMADUKE,
Brigadier-General, C. S. Army.

[Inclosure No. 1.]

HDQRS. C. S. FORCES N. E. ARKANSAS AND S. E. MISSOURI,
Camp near Batesville, February 15, 1863.

Brigadier-General BROWN, U. S. Army,
Commanding at Springfield, Mo.

GENERAL: I have learned from reliable sources that my surgeons left with my wounded at Springfield, Mo., have been arrested, taken from the care of the wounded and sent as prisoners to Saint Louis or elsewhere. It is difficult to believe that conduct so contrary to the usages of war—so cruel to the unfortunate wounded—indeed inhuman, can be countenanced by the U. S. authorities. I write to demand the release of these officers and their return to the duty assigned them by me. I beg also to call your attention to the fact that many of my wounded at Springfield, Mo., have been paroled contrary to the express understanding and agreement between General Hindman, C. S. Army, and General Blunt, U. S. Army, commanding Army of the Frontier. This agreement has been faithfully and fully carried out by General Hindman and all officers serving under him. A like faithful execution of the agreement is expected of all U. S. officers. Again, I learn that Captain Frazier, of MacDonald's Missouri Cavalry Regiment, left wounded and in charge of my surgeons at Springfield, Mo., has been confined in a miserable dungeon and is to be tried for his life. Can this be possible? I do assure you that I hope this is false, but if true I do most solemnly pledge you that I will retaliate tenfold, seeing it is the only remedy for the wrongs done my men. I regret the necessity made by you of writing this letter but the rights and lives of those under my command demand it.

Very respectfully,

J. S. MARMADUKE,
Brigadier-General, Commanding.

[Inclosure No. 2.]

HEADQUARTERS SHELBY'S CAVALRY BRIGADE,
Camp Kirtley, February 15, 1863.

Brigadier-General MARMADUKE,
Commanding Cavalry Division.

GENERAL: From direct information recently received by me and from such sources as to leave no doubt of its entire correctness I have to inform you that contrary to laws and usages of civilized warfare the surgeons left in care of our wounded at Springfield, Mo., have been unconditionally arrested, taken away from their charges of mercy and sent as prisoners of war to Saint Louis. Why is this? The terms of the agreement between General Hindman and General Blunt on the field of Prairie Grove were such as to secure all surgeons, wounded and nurses from molestation or parole. In good faith I have invariably kept this contract, and I demand that the Federals be held to the performance of theirs. I am unwilling to believe that this action on their part is a willful intention to thwart the merciful object held in view by the officers who formed the treaty; but if our wounded are to be deprived of the benefit of their surgeons and that too in direct violation of a solemn agreement the sooner it is known the better, for the sooner will we learn that we are fighting an enemy who has snatched the soothing chalice from the lips of their own wounded and suffering and embittered a war already rapidly tending to extermination. I would suggest that you send a flag of truce to inquire into the matter.

Very respectfully, yours, &c.,

JO. O. SHELBY,
Colonel, Commanding Cavalry Brigade.

[Indorsement.]

HEADQUARTERS FOURTH DIVISION,
Camp near Batesville, Ark., February 15, 1863.

Brigadier-General BROWN,
Commanding U. S. Forces, Springfield, Mo.

GENERAL: I beg to submit for your consideration the within letter.

J. S. MARMADUKE,
Brigadier-General, Commanding.

OFFICE COMMISSARY-GENERAL OF PRISONERS,
Washington, D. C., February 16, 1863.

General J. H. MARTINDALE,
Commanding District of Washington.

GENERAL: By direction of the Secretary of War I have the honor to request that you will cause a list to be furnished me of all citizen prisoners held at the Old Capitol Prison, giving the dates of arrest, the charges and by whose order arrested; also a list of all on parole, giving the same particulars, with the authority for and date of parole and the limit. May I ask your immediate attention to this matter?

Very respectfully, your obedient servant,

W. HOFFMAN,
Colonel Third Infantry, Commissary-General of Prisoners.

OFFICE COMMISSARY-GENERAL OF PRISONERS,
Washington, D. C., February 16, 1863.

Lieut. Col. W. H. LUDLOW,
Agent for Exchange of Prisoners, Fort Monroe, Va.

COLONEL: I have the honor to inclose herewith a list* of military and civil prisoners now held at Richmond, Va., and also a list* of Federal

---

* Not found.

prisoners at Atlanta, Ga., which was furnished to me by Col. A. B. Moore, One hundred and fourth Illinois, recently released from Richmond. Many or all of these names may already have been presented to you, but I am anxious that no person should by any chance be overlooked. There are some conspicuous cases and for these I am sure you will make every effort to secure their exchange. General Hitchcock has given me the name of Doctor Rucker whom I believe he has spoken to you himself about as one whose release should be insisted on in the most positive manner. Governor Peirpoint has given me the name of Mr. Trahern, sheriff of Barbour County, W. Va., who is a prisoner at Richmond, and the Governor desires that his exchange be effected. John Owens, of Wolfe County, Ky., was released at Richmond on parole for thirty days from February 3 to procure an exchange. Please name some person as his equivalent among those who will be sent to you. I am making up the number of citizens you require (500), but it will require some little time to accomplish it. The Secretary has asked for rolls of all held before he decides who may be exchanged. It may be three or four days before all will be assembled here. Are you expecting to make exchanges of military prisoners and to what extent? Some 300 Murfreesborough prisoners went down to-day from Baltimore unexpectedly to me. Please bear in mind my request to obtain a list of all military prisoners who have died in the Richmond prisons and also the names of all who are still confined in the hospitals too unwell to be delivered. I have many inquiries about missing officers and soldiers, and it would be a great relief to their friends to know something positive about them. Some special applications for exchanges are herewith inclosed.

Very respectfully, your obedient servant,

W. HOFFMAN,
Colonel Third Infantry, Commissary-General of Prisoners.

WASHINGTON, *February 16, 1863.*
Lieut. Col. F. A. DICK:

Citizen prisoners will not leave Alton till a report is made to me by the surgeon there in relation to the smallpox. Wait till you hear from me.

W. HOFFMAN,
Commissary-General of Prisoners.

ALTON MILITARY PRISON, *Alton, Ill., February 16, 1863.*
Col. W. HOFFMAN, *Commissary-General of Prisoners.*

COLONEL: On the night of the 23d of January last a Mrs. Clara Judd, a female prisoner, was brought to this prison in company with several male prisoners, all of whom were easily provided for except the female. I did not know what to do with her as there were no rooms about the building where cooking could be done without a great expense, as I myself with several other officers am boarding at these headquarter buildings and have her boarded at $2 per week. But I do not feel justified to continue such board without advising you of the fact and ask you to approve or disapprove of said board of Mrs. Judd. Mrs. Judd was arrested and sent to this prison as a spy by order of

General Rosecrans. She has never had any trial but is held in this prison as a spy. Please let me know what I shall do in regard to her board. She resides near Winchester, Tenn.

I ask what can be done for prisoners of war who do not want to be exchanged and return to the rebel army and rebel service but say they would positively rather be hung than return to such army and service and continue in such a war? These prisoners are nearly all Union men in feeling and some are anxious to join our ranks. Please instruct me in regard to this class of prisoners.

Col. F. A. Dick, provost-marshal general at Saint Louis, Mo., has in some instances released prisoners of war other than those he sent to this prison, which by a letter of instructions previously [sent] to him and myself from you allowed him to release those only that he may have sent here. I call your attention to this but feel confident that Colonel Dick does not intend to assume power and improperly exercise it. A word from you on that subject is sufficient. All such prisoners as come under General Orders, No. 193, with your instructions added, are released by me as fast as we can satisfy ourselves as to the fact of their or they being entitled to such release. Please answer my three inquiries for instructions and oblige.

Very respectfully submitted.

J. HILDEBRAND,
Colonel, Commanding Post.

HEADQUARTERS DEPARTMENT OF VIRGINIA,
Fort Monroe, February 16, 1863.

Col. W. HOFFMAN, *Commissary-General of Prisoners.*

COLONEL: I shall go to City Point to-morrow to meet Mr. Ould and will write to you more in full on my return in relation to the cases of the two men confined in the penitentiary at Albany. The Secretary of War desired me to ascertain the best exchange for Zarvona. W. L. McDonald, sutler of the Twenty-sixth New Jersey Volunteers, need not return. Please send S. J. Anderson with the other civilians when they arrive at Washington. The arrangement made with Mr. Ould for the release of our officers captured before the 10th of December does not call for the release of any rebel officers. Will you please give the necessary orders for the release of rebel officers who have been declared exchanged? The Confederates are delivering to us our officers who have been declared exchanged. Also please retain all civilians intended for exchange until they can be sent all together on the steamer intended for them. I would recommend that you send all civilians for exchange now in your custody and who are not unwilling to go South. The guerrillas and other members of irregular organizations can be reserved and sent to Vicksburg for delivery. Although the most of them have been declared exchanged according to the published declarations in general orders yet by a special agreement with Mr. Ould I am to be credited with all deliveries at Vicksburg which had not been previously counted, and these had not been. When is it proposed to send them and also the Fort Hindman [Arkansas Post] captures to Vicksburg?

I regret to learn of your illness and hope that ere this both General Hitchcock and yourself have recovered.

I am, very respectfully, your obedient servant,

WM. H. LUDLOW,
Lieutenant-Colonel and Agent for Exchange of Prisoners.

DEPOT PRISONERS OF WAR,
Near Sandusky, Ohio, February 16, 1863.

Col. WILLIAM HOFFMAN,
Commissary-General of Prisoners, Washington, D. C.

COLONEL: Before the dispatch of the 10th was sent a paper had been thoroughly circulated for all to sign who wish to go South for exchange. On sending in the roll of those and also to ascertain about the twenty-nine who had since then arrived many more expressed the wish to go. Your dispatch on the 13th reads "send all," and I therefore advised you that our roll had increased to 212. I am in receipt of your dispatch of to-day in which you direct to hold till I hear from you again and shall wait. I wrote you this afternoon about ice. It appears to be growing colder; and if so it will be safe crossing in a day or two by the time this reaches you. This is written in the evening.

Very respectfully, your obedient servant,

WM. S. PIERSON,
Major, Commanding.

CIRCULAR.] HEADQUARTERS DEPARTMENT OF THE GULF,
New Orleans, February 16, 1863.

The accompanying order and circulars relating to the immediate employment of negroes will explain a system of labor that has been suggested and adopted for the present year. The provost-marshals are authorized and directed to receive and record the assent of planters or other persons thereto, and when such written consent is given officers and soldiers and especially the chaplains of the Army and all other persons acting under the authority of the United States are requested to assist as far as practicable without violence in inducing the return of negroes and their families to the plantations where they have been accustomed to labor.

Without regular employment many thousands of negroes must perish during the year. More than $60,000 were applied to the support of dependent and destitute persons in the month of January. The support of many thousands of unemployed negroes will increase the burden to such extent as to make it impracticable to continue the charity. The immediate cultivation of corn, sugar, cotton and other products is imperatively demanded upon every consideration of public interest and for this no other labor is now available. On the plantations they will have secured to them by the officers of the Government sufficient and wholesome food, clothing, kind treatment and a share of the crop they produce.

The compensation may seem small but in view of the pecuniary advances that must be made and the risks that attend industry in a period of war it is not unreasonable. Those who are not thus engaged will be employed on the public works or in the quartermaster's department without pay except their food and clothing, medical attendance and such instruction and care as may be furnished to them and their women and children.

In view of all the facts and after most anxious consideration the commanding general believes it to be the best system of labor that can now be adopted, and assuming the entire responsibility of the act he calls upon the commanding generals and all officers of the Government to assist in its immediate execution.

N. P. BANKS,
Major-General, Commanding.

HEADQUARTERS ARMY OF THE POTOMAC,
February 17, 1863.

Major-General HALLECK:

After my experience in exchanging the Pennsylvania Reserves by which I gave 270 more officers and men than I received no further exchange will be made with my consent.

HOOKER,
Major-General.

CINCINNATI, OHIO, *February 17, 1863.*

Maj. Gen. H. W. HALLECK, *General-in-Chief:*

Colonel Lynch, commanding at Camp Butler, telegraphs that General Curtis has instructed him to release rebel prisoners upon their taking the oath of allegiance, Camp Butler being in this department. Colonel Lynch refers the matter here for instructions. What shall be done?

H. G. WRIGHT,
Major-General.

HEADQUARTERS OF THE ARMY,
Washington, D. C., February 17, 1863.

Colonel HOFFMAN, *Commissary-General of Prisoners.*

COLONEL: Copy of the following telegram is respectfully furnished for your information:

WASHINGTON, D. C., *February 17, 1863.*

Major-General WRIGHT, *Cincinnati:*

Rebel prisoners who do not wish to be exchanged and offer to take the oath of allegiance are released when upon proper examination and evidence it is believed that they are sincere in this course. If there is good reason to doubt their sincerity they will not be released.

H. W. HALLECK,
General-in-Chief.

H. W. HALLECK,
General-in-Chief.

SPECIAL ORDERS, }   WAR DEPT., ADJT. GENERAL'S OFFICE,
No. 79.   }   *Washington, February 17, 1863.*

*   *   *   *   *   *   *

9. Capt. W. T. Hartz, assistant adjutant-general of volunteers, will report in person without delay to Col. W. Hoffman, Third U. S. Infantry, commissary-general of prisoners, in this city.

*   *   *   *   *   *   *

By order of the Secretary of War:

L. THOMAS,
Adjutant-General.

OFFICE COMMISSARY-GENERAL OF PRISONERS,
Washington, D. C., February 17, 1863.

Maj. L. C. TURNER, *Judge-Advocate, Washington.*

MAJOR: Can you furnish me a list of political prisoners paroled from Fort Lafayette giving the date, the authority for and the limits of the paroles? I would like also if possible the authority for the arrest and the time.

Very respectfully, your obedient servant,

W. HOFFMAN,
Colonel Third Infantry, Commissary-General of Prisoners.

OFFICE COMMISSARY-GENERAL OF PRISONERS,
Washington, D. C., February 17, 1863.

Capt. E. L. WEBBER,
Commanding Camp Chase Prison, Columbus, Ohio.

CAPTAIN: Your letter of the 11th instant is received.

General Orders, Nos. 60 and 90, of 1862, are still in force and all medical officers and chaplains received among the prisoners of war should be discharged and sent beyond our lines.

Send them on their parole to report to General Wright at Cincinnati and write a letter to the general requesting him to forward them by such points in our lines as he may deem proper.

None can be recognized as holding the place of a medical officer or chaplain but those who are so designated on the rolls.

I am not yet prepared to say that "contract surgeons" can be classed with medical officers.

It will be determined in a few days whether rebel officers can be permitted to take the oath of allegiance.

You are not at liberty to grant paroles to rebel officers under any circumstances without the authority of the Secretary of War except in case of illness which is provided for by the circular of regulations.

Very respectfully, your obedient servant,

W. HOFFMAN,
Colonel Third Infantry, Commissary-General of Prisoners.

OFFICE COMMISSARY-GENERAL OF PRISONERS,
Washington, D. C., February 18, 1863.

Brig. Gen. JACOB AMMEN,
Commanding Camp Douglas, Chicago, Ill.

GENERAL: Pursuant to instructions from the General-in-Chief you are authorized to release all prisoners of war belonging to the Confederate Army not officers on their taking the oath of allegiance in good faith. A careful examination will be made in each case to ascertain the sincerity of the applicant, and it will be explained that by taking the oath of allegiance he becomes liable to be called on for military service as any other loyal citizen. Whenever there is a doubt the application must be rejected. The oath will be taken in duplicate, one copy for the person to whom it is administered and one with roll of all so discharged to be sent to this office. This permission does not extend to guerrillas or other irregular organizations. None of these will be released except on special report in each case, approved at this office. The above instructions will cover the several applications made by individuals to be released on taking the oath of allegiance.

Very respectfully, your obedient servant,

W. HOFFMAN,
Colonel Third Infantry, Commissary-General of Prisoners.

(Same to commandants of all other important prison posts.)

HEADQUARTERS DEPARTMENT OF THE POTOMAC,
Fort Monroe, February 18, 1863.

Col. W. HOFFMAN, *Commissary-General of Prisoners.*

COLONEL: I have the honor to inclose to you a list* of paroles of prisoners of war by Capt. Joseph P. Black, provost-marshal at Harrodsburg, Ky., from December 28, 1862, to January 9, 1863; also a list* of thirty-one prisoners captured by officers under command of General Weitzel and paroled by him; also list* of prisoners taken by Colonel Thomas at Bayou Teche, La.; also a descriptive list* of wounded prisoners paroled. I cannot use these papers in effecting exchanges until it is shown or known what has become of the paroled men, or whether after being paroled they were sent through the lines. Will you please give orders that all parole papers shall show these points? It will be a very simple matter for the officer sending you the paroles to do it.

I am, very respectfully,

WM. H. LUDLOW,
Lieutenant-Colonel and Agent for Exchange of Prisoners.

ALTON, ILL., *February 18, 1863.*

Col. W. HOFFMAN, *Commissary-General of Prisoners:*

Your question † is difficult to answer. One-half the prisoners have had smallpox and varioloid. I think it would be unsafe to send even those not diseased without complete change of clothing.

A. WALL,
Surgeon, Military Prison Hospital.

QUARTERMASTER-GENERAL'S OFFICE,
Washington, February 18, 1863.

Col. WILLIAM HOFFMAN,
Commissary-General of Prisoners, Washington, D. C.

COLONEL: You are respectfully informed that Captain Potter, assistant quartermaster at Chicago, has this day been directed to issue for the comfort of rebel prisoners at Camp Douglas from the stock of inferior gray clothing on hand at Chicago the 300 pairs trousers specified in Captain Rutherford's requisition of the 11th instant. The balance of the articles called for have been ordered from the inferior stock on hand at New York.

By order of the Quartermaster-General:

Very respectfully, your obedient servant,

ALEX. J. PERRY,
Assistant Quartermaster.

HEADQUARTERS DEPARTMENT OF THE CUMBERLAND,
Murfreesborough, February 19, 1863.

General JOSEPH E. JOHNSTON, C. S. Army.

GENERAL: Inclosed I transmit a letter sent you yesterday by flag of truce, which was returned to my lines to-day, indorsed as you will see and signed "Jos. Wheeler, Major-General and Chief of Cavalry."

----

* Omitted.   † Reference is to Hoffman to Dick, February 16, p. 277.

I also inclose copies of the list* of medical officers robbed during the battle of Stone's River, and Chaplain Gaddis' statement† of the treatment of some wounded men on a hospital boat.

I presume your customs do not warrant subordinates in stopping communications addressed to their superior commanders, nor is it necessary to call attention to the discourtesy of an officer of high rank who had the meanness to stop such a communication and to abstract therefrom the inclosure, which he presumed to return because he was unwilling to forward it, the papers referring to his own conduct.

Very respectfully, your obedient servant,
W. S. ROSECRANS,
Major-General, Commanding.

[NOTE.—See indorsements on the letter following. It is probable that the foregoing letter with its inclosures did not reach its destination, having been found with the files of the Department of the Cumberland.]

[Inclosure No. 1.]

HEADQUARTERS DEPARTMENT OF THE CUMBERLAND,
Murfreesborough, Tenn., February 17, 1863.

General JOSEPH E. JOHNSTON, C. S. Army.

GENERAL: Yours of the 12th instant dated at Tullahoma by flag of truce is just received. I very much regret that you have not the power to redress the outrage and punish the perfidy which compels me to avoid communicating with General Bragg by flag of truce.

I was in hopes that by our joint efforts we should have been able to put the sacred claims of justice and humanity high above passion and revenge in the estimation of the troops of our respective armies and thus reduce the terrible amount of human suffering to the necessities of a state of war and those resulting from individual acts of crime and outlawry.

I know that no success would compensate for the degradation and shame that I should feel in allowing my troops to sneak in behind a flag of truce to make a capture or allowing them to go into battle dressed in your uniforms and carrying your colors or in robbing your surgeons of their private property, all of which was done by General Bragg's troops before and at the battle of Stone's River.

Inclosed is a copy of a list* of thirty-eight medical officers robbed.

Inclosed also is the statement† of the Reverend Chaplain Gaddis, showing that under the tacit if not active sanction of General Wheeler a hospital boat loaded with desperately wounded and sick soldiers was fired into by musketry and artillery.

Now, general, my difficulty is that while these outrages actually occur it seems from the official statements of your officers that different reports come to them.

Thus General Bragg in one of his voluminous epistles to me complains that your prisoners were robbed of their clothing. I did not think it proper to say it to him but I do to you that in all my experience I have neither seen nor heard of anything of the kind. They have seldom if ever had blankets or clothing enough and have been provided with such things by my order when possible.

I only ask what I feel bound and resolved to observe—that which is right and humane according to the usages of civilized war.

_____
* Omitted.   † Omitted here; Gaddis to Rosecrans, p. 284.

I appeal to you and through you if you have not the power to your superiors to know if my efforts and wishes in this matter cannot be met in a spirit of frankness and cordiality.

Hoping that in all official intercourse we may pursue mutual respect and feelings of personal kindness,

I remain, general, your obedient servant,

W. S. ROSECRANS,
Major-General.

[First indorsement.]

HEADQUARTERS CAVALRY, *February 19, 1863.*

Respectfully returned.

Being an officer of General Bragg's army I do not feel authorized to forward a communication the language of which, when referring to the commanding general of the army, indicates so little regard for the courtesies that are presumed to govern gentlemen in their intercourse.

JOS. WHEELER,
Major-General and Chief of Cavalry.

[Second indorsement.]

HEADQUARTERS DEPARTMENT OF THE CUMBERLAND,
Murfreesborough, February 19, 1863.

Respectfully reforwarded to General Joseph E. Johnston to whom the letter is addressed.

The inclosures mentioned within have been abstracted. Duplicates are reinclosed.

W. S. ROSECRANS,
Major-General, Commanding.

[Inclosure No. 2.]

CAMP AT MURFREESBOROUGH, TENN., *February 4, 1863.*

Major-General ROSECRANS,
Commanding Department of the Cumberland.

SIR: In accordance with your request I herewith transmit a condensed account of the capture and subsequent destruction of a portion of your transportation by fire on the Cumberland River on the 13th day of January, 1863, at the head of Harpeth Shoals, thirty miles from Nashville and thirty-five miles from Clarksville.

I was on the steamer Hastings at the time of her being ordered by the guerrillas to land and at the request of the captain of the Hastings and the officers and men on board (near 260 wounded) assumed command. I answered their hail and order by saying "that we were loaded with wounded and could not stop;" they again ordered us to come to and backed their order by three volleys of musketry, after which I ordered the pilot of the Hastings, "Round the steamer to the shore." This he immediately endeavored to do; the current being swift the boat yielded slowly and the enemy again fired two rounds of artillery, one of the balls taking effect on the steamer, seriously wounding one of the men. As soon as the boat struck the steamer that had been captured some two hours previously "a gang of drunken rebels under command of Colonel Wade took possession of the Hastings." Then followed a scene of plunder and theft never before witnessed. They robbed soldiers and passengers indiscriminately, took from your wounded soldiers their blankets, rations, medicines and in many cases their clothing; robbed the officers of their side-arms, overcoats, hats, &c., the boat of all her freight, stores and money and her officers of their personal property.

I demanded of Colonel Wade some explanation of this inhuman course; he being so drunk only made me an idiotic reply. I then looked round for some other officer and discovered Captain Burford, General Wheeler's assistant adjutant-general, in whom I recognized an old acquaintance. I appealed to him; he was powerless from the fact that the whole gang was drunk. He, however, reported the facts to General Wheeler, who authorized him to parole the Hastings on condition that she carry no more supplies for the Federal Government. I accepted the parole. I then took on board the wounded off the steamer Trio, also from the steamer Parthenia, and had succeeded in obtaining permission to pass on, when they for the first time discovered that the deck of the Hastings was covered with bales of cotton on which our wounded were lying. Wade instantly ordered me to put ashore all the wounded (over 400) that he might burn the cotton, it being theirs by capture and with them a contraband of war. To move the men again was almost impossible. They had been virtually stripped of everything, medicines, rations, clothing; were thirty-five miles from any military post; night coming on, no place of shelter; no place to put our wounded and dying men save a muddy corn-field; a heavy snow had begun to fall and in view of all this and my sympathy for men who for eighteen months had done their duty as true soldiers and who for days had fought under you and only ceased when borne from the field I demanded other terms. I told them I would not move a soul from the boat, &c. All this was reported to Wheeler (at least they said so) and he ordered that I should be held personally responsible for the burning of their cotton on reaching Louisville under penalty of my return to their lines as a prisoner of war. I deemed the terms mild under the circumstances and I immediately accepted them, in which I claim I did my duty. The passengers and soldiers of the Trio and Parthenia were robbed in like manner. After they had done us all the harm they could, barely escaping with our lives, they allowed us to cross the river during the burning of the steamers. While they were preparing to burn the gun-boat Sidell hove in sight and to all appearance made preparations to drive the enemy away but from some cause or other Van Dorn made no fight and surrendered the boat without firing a single shot. They then took possession of her, threw over her guns and arms, fired the three boats and in a short time nothing remained but the charred hulls. On reaching Clarksville I reported by telegraph to Major Sidell, who ordered me to proceed on as rapidly as possible to Louisville and report to Generals Boyle or Wright. This I did, and the inclosed papers* will explain the final result of the unfortunate affair.

Thus hoping that in all this you will not condemn me,

I remain, most respectfully, your obedient servant,

M. P. GADDIS,
Chaplain Second Regiment Ohio Volunteer Infantry.

WASHINGTON, *February 19, 1863.*

Lieut. Col. F. A. DICK:

In consequence of the prevalence of smallpox at Alton you will send no prisoners to this city till further orders. How many could you send from Saint Louis?

W. HOFFMAN,
Commissary-General of Prisoners.

---

* See preceding correspondence.

FORT MONROE, *February 19, 1863.*

His Excellency the PRESIDENT,
Hon. EDWIN M. STANTON, *Secretary of War,*
Major-General HALLECK,
Major-General HITCHCOCK:

I have just returned from City Point from a conference with Mr. Ould. The Legislature of Virginia will overrule Governor Letcher in his late attempt at retaliation in imprisoning U. S. officers and will transfer to the Confederate authorities where it properly belongs under the cartel all matters connected with exchange of prisoners. It is now quite certain that the Confederate Congress will overrule Mr. Jefferson Davis in his retaliatory proclamation and message and exchanges will go on as heretofore under the cartel. I have perfected arrangements for exchange of civilians.

WM. H. LUDLOW,
Lieutenant-Colonel and Agent for Exchange of Prisoners.

HEADQUARTERS, *Fort Monroe, February 19, 1863.*
Col. W. HOFFMAN, *Commissary-General of Prisoners.*

COLONEL: Wholesale desertions are going on to the enemy from the First Regiment [New York] Mounted Rifles stationed at Suffolk. Twenty-five since the 1st of January. The motive I think is to dispose of equipments and get paroled. Some of these men are now at Camp Parole at Annapolis. Solomon Fowler, Thomas Ransom, Charles French, William Cresswell are represented to have been captured. All other cases are desertions. Will you please order the commanding officer at Camp Parole to send back on the steamer which will probably be at Annapolis on Saturday or Sunday all men including the above named belonging to the First Regiment New York Mounted Rifles. The captured I will declare exchanged and they will be returned to their regiment. The others will be treated as deserters.

I am, very respectfully, your obedient servant,

WM. H. LUDLOW,
Lieutenant-Colonel and Agent for Exchange of Prisoners.

RICHMOND, VA., *February 19, 1863.*
Lieut. Col. WILLIAM H. LUDLOW, *Agent of Exchange.*

SIR: I send to you all the officers captured at Fredericksburg. Major Zentmeyer and Captains Marchand and Schaffle have died.

In the list of Fredericksburg captures given by you to me you have the names of Lieut. John A. Billingsley, F. H. B. Randolph and James Carey. These officers have never been delivered to us. Of course you will send them in your next delivery.

I send you about 250 military prisoners, some sutlers and one political prisoner. This embraces all the military prisoners and sutlers whom we have at the Libby. Lieut. Col. Douglas Hapeman and Maj. John Widmer are at Atlanta.

I have not had time to inquire into your other memoranda. I will, however, send any that have been declared exchanged if there be any in Richmond on the next flag-boat.

Respectfully, your obedient servant,

RO. OULD,
Agent of Exchange.

WHEELING. VA.. *February 19, 1863.*

SECRETARY OF WAR:

Writ of *habeas corpus* to take deserters out of possession of officers sent by me to arrest them issued at Steubenville, which is in this district, commanded by General Cox, was not respected by me, and have instructed officers not to notice the writ. Am I right? It is a "butternut" proceeding and I think intended to be carried further.

JOS. DARR, JR.,
Major and Provost-Marshal.

CHICAGO, *February 19, 1863.*

Col. WILLIAM HOFFMAN,
Commissary-General of Prisoners, Washington, D. C.

DEAR SIR: A number of C. S. prisoners now in Camp Butler, Springfield and Camp Douglas, Chicago, Ill., all of them Germans who have been pressed into the rebel army, desire to take the oath of allegiance and join my regiment (German), the Sixteenth Illinois Cavalry, part of it now in the field, known as Thielemann's Cavalry. On an application to the post commanding officers to grant permission to take those men out of camp and into U. S. service I was advised to write to you by them to that effect. You will do me as well as Governor Yates, with whom I had conversation in regard to the matter, a great favor by complying with my wishes. An early answer would oblige, colonel,

Your obedient servant,

CHR. THIELEMANN,
Major of Thielemann's Cav., appointed Col. Sixteenth Illinois Cav.

[Indorsement.]

I respectfully ask favorable attention to this and a reply.

I. N. ARNOLD.

HEADQUARTERS DEPARTMENT OF VIRGINIA,
Fort Monroe, Va., February 20, 1863.

Acting Rear-Admiral S. P. LEE,
Commanding North Atlantic Blockading Squadron.

ADMIRAL: I have just received your communication of yesterday. The list of steamers sent you by Colonel Van Buren yesterday shows the additions made to the list furnished you in October. These steamers should have been reported to you at the time they were respectively taken into the service of the Quartermaster's Department, but through a misapprehension in the assistant adjutant-general's office explained in Colonel Van Buren's letter they were not reported to me. I will see that no such mistake occurs hereafter and that all changes are reported on the day they are made. I think no inconvenience has resulted from it as all these steamers have a flag number and none others are passed without special permits.

All steamers in the service of the army communicate with the guard vessel now both by night and day and when it is possible. If they are in the quartermaster's service they exhibit a flag with a number corresponding with that on the list which has been furnished. If not in his service they are passed under special permits.

There is a difficulty at night in distinguishing the guard vessel from others and I respectfully suggest that the one here as well as the one at Norfolk may hoist a red light at night so that our steamers may know and be able to communicate with them.

In regard to flag-of-truce boats their purpose always is to reach here before night. But Colonel Ludlow is sometimes unavoidably detained and it may happen too that our prisoners cannot be put on board the transports at City Point in time to reach your picket boat until after dark. The prisoners are generally miserably provided for and a delay of a single night at Newport News would be inconvenient. I therefore propose that you suggest some signal by whistle or lights by which the flag-of-truce boats may advise you of their approach. It is not likely that it will be often necessary to use it.

I have the honor to be, very respectfully, your obedient servant,
JOHN A. DIX,
Major-General.

GENERAL ORDERS, } WAR DEPT. ADJT. GENERAL'S OFFICE,
     No. 46.   }   *Washington, February 20, 1863.*

With a view to the more prompt and effective execution of so much of General Orders, No. 191, of November 19, 1862, as relates to the collecting of paroled troops at the camps designated the attention of mustering and disbursing officers and recruiting officers of the Regular Army is again specially called to the provisions of General Orders, No. 72, of June 28, 1862; and that it may be known what is done under these orders the officers referred to will make to the superintendent of the volunteer recruiting service in each State tri-monthly reports of men collected and forwarded and the superintendents will make like reports to the commissary-general of prisoners in this city, Col. W. Hoffman, Third Infantry. These reports will not only give the numbers but will also state the steps taken to carry out the order, with such suggestions as they may have to make to promote the object in view.

All stragglers from the army whether paroled, exchanged or otherwise come within the reach of this order; and that none may be ignorant of it officers charged with its execution will give it circulation in the local newspapers, announcing at the same time that all absentees who fail to report within five days will thereafter be considered deserters for whom the usual reward will be paid on delivery. At stations where it would be more convenient to do so detachments will be sent directly to Camp Parole, at Annapolis, rather than to Elmira, N. Y.

By order of the Secretary of War:
L. THOMAS,
Adjutant-General.

WAR DEPARTMENT, *Washington, February 21, 1863.*
SIMEON DRAPER, *Provost-Marshal-General, New York:*

You are not authorized to parole any person who has held a rebel commission or been in the rebel service. Such action cannot be approved by this Department. The person referred to in your dispatch if he has held a rebel commission should be immediately arrested and brought to Washington.

EDWIN M. STANTON,
Secretary of War.

INDIANAPOLIS, *February 21, 1863.*

Hon. EDWIN M. STANTON, *Secretary of War:*

I am informed that it is the intention of the War Department to send the paroled prisoners of Western regiments to some Western camp. I would respectfully suggest that those belonging to Indiana regiments be sent here if no others, and beg leave to call your attention to the satisfactory manner in which the camps have been conducted here.

O. P. MORTON,
Governor.

OFFICE COMMISSARY-GENERAL OF PRISONERS,
Washington, D. C., February 21, 1863.

Hon. L. W. POWELL, *U. S. Senate, Washington.*

DEAR SIR: The Secretary of War directs that no guerrillas or citizens charged with aiding them be released except on the recommendation of the Governor of the State in which they reside. Such recommendation will insure their immediate release. This order covers all the cases which you have presented to me and their release awaits the recommendation of the Governor of Kentucky.

I am, very truly, your obedient servant,

W. HOFFMAN,
Colonel Third Infantry, Commissary-General of Prisoners.

(Same to Hon. George H. Yeaman, Hon. Robert Mallory, Hon. C. A. Wickliffe, members of Congress, Washington, D. C.)

OFFICE COMMISSARY-GENERAL OF PRISONERS,
Washington, D. C., February 21, 1863.

Col. T. P. ANDREWS,
Paymaster-General U. S. Army, Washington, D. C.

COLONEL: I have this moment learned from General Cooper, commander, that the exchanged troops at Camp Chase have been under orders for the field for a month. They are detained there waiting payment. Will you please give orders for their immediate payment?

Very respectfully, your obedient servant,

W. HOFFMAN,
Colonel Third Infantry, Commissary-General of Prisoners.

QUARTERMASTER-GENERAL'S OFFICE,
Washington, February 21, 1863.

Col. ROBERT ALLEN,
Quartermaster, U. S. Army, Saint Louis, Mo.

COLONEL: Your telegram of the 5th instant and that of General Curtis of the same date relating to the erection of barracks for prisoners was referred to Colonel Hoffman, commissary-general of prisoners, who reports that "barracks for prisoners are required at Cairo to receive those sent there on the way to Vicksburg for exchange. They are at times assembled there in small parties till enough are collected to load a boat or more. They are not to be held there permanently and the barracks are intended only for transient prisoners passing up or down."

M. C. MEIGS,
Quartermaster-General.

DEPOT QUARTERMASTER'S OFFICE,
Baltimore, Md., February 21, 1863.

Col. WILLIAM HOFFMAN,
Commissary-General of Prisoners, Washington, D. C.

COLONEL: Some 700 rebel prisoners are confined in the city jail here, there being no room for them at Fort McHenry or Fort Delaware. I have made a contract with the warden of the jail to feed and lodge them at 20 cents a day each and they are very well taken care of, but they are in a miserable, destitute situation for clothing, and Colonel Bliss, chief quartermaster Eighth Army Corps, has applied to me to know whether I can issue old clothing to about 100 desiring to take the oath of allegiance but for whose release there is no authority. I have the honor to refer the matter to you under General Orders, No. 67, War Department, 1862.

Very respectfully,

J. L. DONALDSON,
Quartermaster.

OFFICE COMMISSARY-GENERAL OF PRISONERS,
Washington, D. C., February 23, 1863.

Maj. Gen. H. G. WRIGHT,
Commanding Department of the Ohio, Cincinnati.

GENERAL: The accompanying papers have been referred to Lieutenant-Colonel Ludlow, agent for exchange of prisoners, who has returned them* with the following comment:

I cannot use these papers in effecting exchanges until it is shown or known what has become of the paroled men, or whether after being paroled they were sent through the lines. Will you please give orders that all parole papers shall show these points?

I have the honor to refer the matter to you that the attention of commanders may be called to what is required in such cases.

I am, general, very respectfully, your obedient servant,

W. HOFFMAN,
Colonel Third Infantry, Commissary-General of Prisoners.

(Same to Maj. Gen. N. P. Banks, Nineteenth Army Corps, commanding Department of the Gulf.)

[First indorsement.]

HEADQUARTERS DEPARTMENT OF THE OHIO,
Cincinnati, Ohio, February 26, 1863.

Respectfully referred through Major-General Rosecrans, commanding Department of the Cumberland, to Brigadier-General Baird, who is requested to return these papers to these headquarters with a statement as to the disposition made of these prisoners when paroled. What became of them?

By order of Major-General Wright:

C. W. FOSTER,
Assistant Adjutant-General.

[Second indorsement.]

HDQRS. THIRD DIVISION, ARMY OF KENTUCKY,
Franklin, Tenn., March 15, 1863.

It having been reported to me that a portion of the rebel sick left about Harrodsburg after the battle of Perryville had by some oversight

---

* See Ludlow to Hoffman, February 18, p. 282.

not been paroled and that as they recovered they were in the habit of trying to escape to their homes without any obligation upon them I reported the fact to the headquarters of the Army of Kentucky and received instructions to have them paroled. This was done by the provost-marshal at Harrodsburg, after which the men remained as the other sick and were forwarded as they became able to travel to the headquarters at Lexington. What afterwards became of them I do not know. Some may still be at Harrodsburg. Respectfully forwarded through headquarters of Major-General Granger.

A. BAIRD,
Brigadier-General, Commanding.

[Third indorsement.]

HEADQUARTERS ARMY OF KENTUCKY, March 17, 1863.

The prisoners referred to within were duly forwarded to Vicksburg for exchange.

G. GRANGER,
Major-General, Commanding.

[Inclosure.]

CAMP NEAR FRANKLIN, TENN., March 13, 1863.

Brig. Gen. A. BAIRD,
Commanding Third Division, Army of Kentucky.

GENERAL: In answer to the question of Col. W. Hoffman, commissary-general of prisoners, wishing to know what had been done with the prisoners paroled at Harrodsburg, Ky., by me while acting provost-marshal I have the honor to make the following statement: Ten of the officers were sent to General Granger's headquarters, Lexington. There were thirty in the hospitals at Harrodsburg unable to move when I left. The balance were forwarded to your headquarters at Danville at two different times under escort.

I am, general, your most obedient servant,

JOSEPH P. BLACK,
Captain Company E, Ninety-sixth Illinois Volunteer Infantry.

WAR DEPARTMENT, Washington, February 23, 1863.

Hon. EDWIN M. STANTON, <i>Secretary of War.</i>

SIR: I have the honor to report in the case of T. T. Tunstall,* late consul at Cadiz and now in Old Capitol Prison, that said Tunstall applied in writing to the Secretary of State December 15, 1862, for a permit or pass to return to "my home and family in the State of Alabama;" and in his said application among other things is the following:

Ill-health, sir, the distance that divides me from my means and friends, my long absence from my home (now nearly seven years) and the interval of twenty months having elapsed with no tidings of my family or intercourse with them, inspire me with the hope that you will give a prompt and favorable consideration to the subject of this communication.

That on the 9th of December, 1862, the Secretary of State addressed me a note inclosing the application of said Tunstall recommending that a permit be given in the words following:

Under the circumstances of the case should there be no special reason to the contrary I have to suggest that Mr. Tunstall be permitted whenever a suitable occasion is presented to pass our lines under a flag of truce.

---

* For the arrest and detention of Tunstall, see Vol. III, this Series, p. 284 <i>et seq.</i>

It is proper here to remark that Mr. Tunstall had been confined at Fort Warren and been discharged by the Secretary of State on his parole not to give aid and comfort to the enemies of the United States. After the receipt of the note from the Secretary of State Mr. Tunstall called at my office repeatedly to obtain a permit but I gave no encouragement until some time after it was publicly announced that women and children could avail themselves of going South. I then presented his case with the recommendation of the Secretary of State to the Secretary of War, and he directed me to give Mr. Tunstall permission to go to his home and family on the flag-of-truce steamer of the 7th of January last and the permit was accordingly given. That Mr. Tunstall did return by said flag-of-truce steamer New York the 7th ultimo and was delivered over to the rebel agent, Mr. Ould, at City Point; that on the passage from this city to City Point the detectives on board the steamer found among his luggage quinine and other prohibited articles, and they reported language used by him on the steamer that was offensive and objectionable—so much so that I took from him some money which had been intrusted to him to take to the prisoners in Libby Prison. In his communication to the Secretary of War Mr. Tunstall says that—

I frequently in conversation with Maj. L. C. Turner on my way down on the flag-of-truce boat expressed my wish and determination to return as soon as I could see my people, &c., and asked him if he thought the Government would molest me in the event of my return here. To which he replied: "Oh, I suppose not, I guess not," or some such phrase of similar assurance that it would not was to the best of my memory the language he used.

As to Mr. Tunstall's wish and determination to return to Washington or to the loyal States his statement in said letter to the Secretary of War and one to myself is the first knowledge or intimation I ever had of said wish and determination. Had he expressed such wish or determination to me I am quite sure I should have distinctly remembered it, for the reason that all persons who went South at that time and under my superintendence were distinctly and repeatedly informed (when they asked) that their going South was without any assurance whatever that they could obtain permission to return during the war. I recollect that Mr. Tunstall said to me some time during the passage that he claimed to be a Spanish citizen and intended eventually to return to Spain (Cadiz) and spend his days, but that he intimated that it was his wish and determination to return here or anywhere in the loyal States, and that I responded that "I guessed" or "supposed" or intimated by any other phrase that the Government would not molest him if he did return is not true. He had no such assurance direct or indirect from me, and I had no intimation that he entertained a wish or determination to return here, either during his application for a permit or during his passage to City Point.

I have the honor to be, very respectfully, your obedient servant,
L. C. TURNER,
Judge-Advocate.

ADJUTANT-GENERAL'S OFFICE,
Springfield, Ill., February 23, 1863.

Col. WILLIAM HOFFMAN,
Commissary-General of Prisoners, Washington, D. C.

SIR: I am directed by His Excellency Governor Yates to call attention to the condition of paroled prisoners of war belonging to regiments of this State who have been exchanged at Richmond and sent to Annapo lis, Md. Letters from enlisted men of the Twenty-first Regiment Illinois Volunteers, whose truth and sincerity are personally known to His Excellency, state that some thirty members of this regiment were reported at the paroled camp at Annapolis on or before the 12th instant who on passage from Richmond and since arrival at Annapolis have received harsh treatment from officers in charge; allowed to go without rations for thirty-six to forty hours, and for two days after landing at Annapolis not provided with quarters, subsistence or blankets. These men have been in service since June, 1861, have fought at Donelson and Shiloh and passed months in Southern prisons without necessaries of life, and upon their return to Annapolis where they should be bountifully supplied by Government officials they receive attentions which are under the circumstances more disheartening than while in rebel hands. Believing that these abuses grow out of carelessness of subordinate officers immediately in charge of paroled men at different camps and that neglect could only be chargeable for a very short time the State authorities have passed without attention many letters of complaint received direct and others sent by friends to the Governor, but the number and nature of complaints now made leads to the request that you will so far as may be consistent cause proper attention to be paid our volunteers at Annapolis whenever any may be reported, and in case of those now there that they may be sent to Camp Butler, Ill., or to Benton Barracks, Saint Louis, where they can receive attentions of friends and fitted at an early day to resume active duty.

Very respectfully, your obedient servant,

ALLEN C. FULLER,
Adjutant-General.

HEADQUARTERS SECOND DISTRICT,
Vicksburg, February 24, 1863.

Maj. Gen. U. S. GRANT,
Commanding U. S. Forces in front of Vicksburg.

GENERAL: I am instructed by the lieutenant-general commanding this department to transmit to you the inclosed copy of a notice purporting to have been issued by Admiral David D. Porter, U. S. Navy.

I request that you will inform me whether this document is authentic and if it be whether the operations of any part of the forces under you are to be conducted in accordance with the principles announced by Admiral Porter or with those of a civilized warfare.

While the troops of this Confederacy whom I have the honor to command will actively repel the invasion of our territory by the forces of the United States it is my desire that their operations shall be in accordance with the usages of war, of humanity and of civilization. I shall deplore the necessity for any departure from them.

Therefore I hope this notice of Admiral Porter is not authentic or that it will be reconsidered, and that in no case will its threats be executed because I am instructed to say if they are the fullest retaliation will be inflicted upon the Federal prisoners now in our hands or whom we may capture; and no quarter will be given to any officer, soldier or citizen of the United States taken in the act of burning houses, laying waste the plantations or otherwise wantonly destroying the property of the citizens of this Confederacy; and that all such persons suspected of having been guilty of such acts will not if taken be treated as prisoners of war but will be kept in close confinement.

Relying upon your disposition to co-operate with me in averting the necessity for a resort to such measures,

I am, general, respectfully, your obedient servant,

C. L. STEVENSON,
Major-General, Commanding.

[Inclosure.]

NOTICE.

Persons taken in the act of firing on unarmed vessels from the bank will be treated as highwaymen and assassins and no quarter will be shown them.

Persons strongly suspected of firing on unarmed vessels will not receive the usual treatment of prisoners of war but will be kept in close confinement.

If this savage and barbarous Confederate custom cannot be put a stop to we will try what virtue there is in hanging.

All persons no matter who they are who are caught in the act of pillaging the houses of the inhabitants along the river, levying contributions or burning cotton will receive no quarters if caught in the act, or if it is proved upon them

By order of—

DAVID D. PORTER,
Acting Rear-Admiral, Commanding Mississippi Squadron.

OFFICE COMMISSARY-GENERAL OF PRISONERS,
Washington, D. C., February 24, 1863.

Maj. Gen. S. R. CURTIS,
Comdg. Department of the Missouri, Saint Louis, Mo.

GENERAL: I have the honor to return herewith the descriptive list of rebel prisoners paroled at Des Arc, Ark., for further information. Colonel Ludlow, agent for exchange of prisoners, returns similar papers* to me with the following comment:

I cannot use these papers in effecting exchanges until it is shown or known what has become of the paroled men, or whether after being paroled they were sent through the lines.

May I request that you will order this information to be furnished in all cases? Orders heretofore issued by the War Department require that rolls of prisoners captured shall give the rank, regiment and company and the time and place of capture. To effect exchanges it is necessary to be known in addition the time and place of delivery to the rebel authorities.

I am, general, very respectfully, your obedient servant,

W. HOFFMAN,
Colonel Third Infantry, Commissary-General of Prisoners.

[Indorsement.]

OFFICE PROVOST-MARSHAL-GENERAL,
Saint Louis, March 4, 1863.

Repectfully forwarded to the commanding officer at Helena, Ark., with a request that these papers be returned with the information needed by Colonel Hoffman. This as expeditiously as possible.

F. A. DICK,
Lieut. Col. and Provost-Marshal-General, Dept. of the Missouri.

---

* See Ludlow to Hoffman, February 18, p. 282.

OFFICE COMMISSARY-GENERAL OF PRISONERS,
Washington, D. C., February 24, 1863.

Brig. Gen. W. A. HAMMOND,
Surgeon-General U. S. Army, Washington, D. C.

SIR: At the request of Lieut. Col. W. H. Ludlow, agent for exchange of prisoners, I inclose to you a list* of U. S. officers and soldiers together with a few citizens who have died while held as prisoners within the lines and in the hospitals of the rebel army. On examination of the list some repetitions of names are found to occur probably to the number of ten or twelve.

Very respectfully, your obedient servant,
W. HOFFMAN,
Colonel Third Infantry, Commissary-General of Prisoners.

OFFICE COMMISSARY-GENERAL OF PRISONERS,
Washington, D. C., February 24, 1863.

Col. G. DE KORPONAY,
Commanding Camp Banks, Alexandria, Va.

COLONEL: The paroled and exchanged troops belonging to regiments serving in the West will be sent out to Western camps from Camp Parole, Annapolis, in a few days, and you will please send to that camp any men at Camp Banks belonging to such regiments to be joined to those going West. Let this be done at once and send full rolls with them. Your weekly report of the 20th instant shows upwards of 400 exchanged troops still at the camp. Please explain what it is that detains them.

Very respectfully, your obedient servant,
W. HOFFMAN,
Colonel Third Infantry, Commissary-General of Prisoners.

OFFICE COMMISSARY-GENERAL OF PRISONERS,
Washington, D. C., February 24, 1863.

Capt. E. L. WEBBER,
Commanding Camp Chase Prison, Columbus, Ohio.

CAPTAIN: Yours of the 5th instant with the accompanying papers has been received. Your arrangements for the accommodation of prisoners of war are satisfactory. It will scarcely be possible to provide for the female prisoners sent to you by General Rosecrans at the camp and if you find it necessary and can do so you will place them in the jail in Columbus making the best terms for their keeping you can. You can issue them rations at the jail if it is advisable.

In reply to your letter of the 6th instant I have to say that all instructions given to your predecessor are still in force and are for your guidance. I am not informed of the particular instructions given to Judge Galloway but until other orders are given by the Secretary of War you will of course recognize his position. Order 193 applies only to prisoners held at its date and so far as they are concerned its execution was left in the hands of the commanding officer. Those arrested since that date can only be released by authority of the Secretary of War. No recommendations from Judge Galloway have come to me

---

* Omitted.

except for the exchange of prisoners and they I presume are among those recently arrived in this city from Camp Chase. The foregoing will answer the three inquiries contained in your letter. Should T. L. Jones decline to take the oath of allegiance his parole should not be extended.

Very respectfully, your obedient servant,

W. HOFFMAN,
Colonel Third Infantry, Commissary-General of Prisoners.

U. S. QUARTERMASTER'S DEPARTMENT,
Springfield, Ill., February 24, 1863.

Col. WILLIAM HOFFMAN,
Commissary-General of Prisoners, Washington, D. C.

COLONEL: I have received no instructions from you concerning issues to the Arkansas prisoners now confined at Camp Butler, near this city. I have a quantity of gray clothing on hand unfit for issue to volunteers which might answer for the prisoners if desirable. Please forward copies of any general regulations concerning prisoners which may have been recently adopted and oblige,

Very respectfully, your obedient servant,

W. H. BAILHACHE,
Captain and Assistant Quartermaster.

OFFICE COMMISSARY-GENERAL OF PRISONERS,
Washington, D. C., February 25, 1863.

Hon. L. W. POWELL, *U. S. Senate, Washington, D. C.*

SIR: Your letter of yesterday is received and I have the honor to reply that after seeing you and before I had given directions for the release of prisoners from Kentucky in whose behalf you have presented petitions under general instructions for the release of prisoners of war on their taking the oath of allegiance I received further instructions verbally that petitions for the release of guerrillas and those charged with aiding them would not be acted on until they had received the approval of the Governor of the State. When I stated in my note that his approval would insure the immediate release of the prisoner I gave only my own impression and should have stated it would finally depend on the decision of the Secretary of War.

I inclose herewith in accordance with your request the petitions* presented by you.

Very respectfully, your obedient servant,

W. HOFFMAN,
Colonel Third Infantry, Commissary-General of Prisoners.

OFFICE COMMISSARY-GENERAL OF PRISONERS,
Washington, D. C., February 25, 1863.

GUSTAVUS V. FOX, Esq.,
Assistant Secretary of the Navy, Washington, D. C.

SIR: I have the honor to request you will furnish me with the names of citizen prisoners confined at Fort Lafayette by order of the Secre-

---

*Not found.

tary of the Navy with the charges against them.   This information is
desired with a view to effect their exchange.

Very respectfully, your obedient servant,

W. HOFFMAN,
Colonel Third Infantry, Commissary-General of Prisoners.

OFFICE COMMISSARY-GENERAL OF PRISONERS,
Washington, D. C., February 25, 1863.

Col. CHRISTIAN THIELEMANN,
Sixteenth Regiment Illinois Cavalry.

COLONEL: In reply to your letter of the 19th instant asking that
certain rebel prisoners of war at Camp Douglas and other camps be
permitted to take the oath of allegiance and join your regiment I have
to say that the Secretary of War forbids the enlistment into our ranks
of prisoners of war who have been released on taking the oath of
allegiance.

Very respectfully, your obedient servant,

W. HOFFMAN,
Colonel Third Infantry, Commissary-General of Prisoners.

OFFICE COMMISSARY-GENERAL OF PRISONERS,
Washington, D. C., February 25, 1863.

Maj. Gen. JOHN E. WOOL,
Commanding Department of the East, New York.

GENERAL: I am directed by the Secretary of War to request that
you will cause to be furnished to this office the names of all citizen
prisoners on parole in your department, giving the authority for and
the time of the arrest, the date and limits of parole and by whose
order. This information is desired with a view to effect an exchange
for prisoners held by the rebels at Richmond.

I have the honor to be, very respectfully, your obedient servant,

W. HOFFMAN,
Colonel Third Infantry, Commissary-General of Prisoners.

NEW YORK, *February 25, 1863.*

Col. W. HOFFMAN, *Commissary-General of Prisoners.*

COLONEL: I have sent to Mr. Fox, Assistant Secretary of the Navy,
a declaration of exchange of the men of the gun-boat Isaac Smith,
detained at City Point on the 21st instant and who were sent hence to
Annapolis.   Will you please have him give the necessary order transferring to your order all the prisoners at Fort Lafayette held under the
order of the Navy Department who were captured previously to
December, 1862, that date covering all captures on the sea?   Zarvona
is also to be exchanged so I understood the Secretary of War.   If I
am correct in this he can be sent with the other prisoners.   It would
be well to parole all of them (before they leave their various places of
detention) not to make any attempt at escape or hold any outside communication until delivered within the Confederate lines.   I hear that
there are a large number of prisoners of war at Fort Delaware.

Would it not be best to order at once the sending to Fort Monroe for delivery at City Point all the enlisted men confined there?

I am, very respectfully, your obedient servant,

WM. H. LUDLOW,
Lieutenant-Colonel and Agent for Exchange of Prisoners.

HEADQUARTERS EIGHTH ARMY CORPS,
Baltimore, Md., February 25, 1863.

Col. WILLIAM HOFFMAN,
Commissary-General of Prisoners, Washington, D. C.

COLONEL: In compliance with your request of the 15th instant I have the honor herewith to forward you the accompanying list* of prisoners, political and otherwise, that have been received at Fort McHenry during the months of October, November, December, January and February, how disposed of, and also those now on hand. I also hand you a list showing the paroles taken at the provost-marshal's office and the circumstances under which they were granted. I regret much the delay attending the preparation of these papers. It has, however, been unavoidable and they have been forwarded as soon as the information could be obtained.

I am, colonel, very respectfully, your most obedient servant,

W. H. CHESEBROUGH,
Lieutenant-Colonel and Assistant Adjutant-General.

NAVY DEPARTMENT, *February 26, 1863.*

Col. WILLIAM HOFFMAN,
Commissary-General of Prisoners, Washington.

SIR: Your note of the 25th instant requesting the names of citizen prisoners confined in Fort Lafayette by order of the Secretary of the Navy with the charges against them with a view to effect their exchange has been received, and in reply I transmit herewith a copy of a letter of this date addressed to the Secretary of War by the Secretary of the Navy requesting that the naval captures turned over to the military authorities may be detained for future action.

Very respectfully,

G. V. FOX,
Assistant Secretary of the Navy.

[Inclosure.]

NAVY DEPARTMENT, *February 26, 1863.*

Hon. E. M. STANTON, *Secretary of War.*

SIR: I have the honor to inform you that this Department desires the detention of all those persons captured by the naval forces and now chiefly confined in Fort Lafayette. Most of them are pilots whose places cannot be supplied by the rebels. The cartel of September 25, 1862, published in general orders of the War Department, No. 142, has been annulled by Jefferson Davis by public proclamation and officers and sailors of the U. S. naval force are retained in prison on bread and water. Under these circumstances it is proper that the naval captures turned over to the military authority should be held for

---

* Omitted.

future action.   In any new arrangement for a cartel I request that this Department may be allowed to associate an officer or officers to arrange the terms.

Very respectfully,

GIDEON WELLES,
Secretary of the Navy.

[Indorsement.]

WAR DEPARTMENT, *March 6, 1863.*

Respectfully referred to Major-General Hitchcock, commissioner for the exchange of prisoners of war.

By order of the Secretary of War:

P. H. WATSON,
Assistant Secretary of War.

HEADQUARTERS DEPARTMENT OF THE GULF,
New Orleans, February 26, 1863.

ADJUTANT-GENERAL OF THE ARMY, *Washington, D. C.*

SIR: I have the honor to transmit herewith duplicate lists* of prisoners of war taken from the enemy and delivered on the 23d instant to Major Watts, Confederate agent for the exchange of prisoners, by Col. John S. Clark, aide-de-camp, of my staff.

Very respectfully, your obedient servant,

N. P. BANKS,
Major-General, Commanding.

HEADQUARTERS, *Cincinnati, Ohio, February 26, 1863.*

Brigadier-General WHITE,
Commanding Eastern District, Louisa, Ky.

GENERAL: Yours of the 22d was received this morning on my return to Cincinnati from a visit to Kentucky. I am not aware that any instructions were given to Colonel Cranor in regard to the disposition to be made of persons who having served in the rebel ranks have subsequently returned to their homes, as no such cases seem to have been referred to by him in his report to these headquarters. The rule established in other portions of the State where the question of the proper disposition to be made of such persons is constantly arising is this:

1. Deserters from the rebel ranks, recognized as being such, are to be treated according to the laws of war with all the leniency compatible with our own safety, it being an established principle to weaken the enemy as much as possible by encouraging desertion from his ranks. Under this rule the practice has been to permit the deserter to remain at home on his taking the oath of allegiance and giving proper bonds for its observance, the amount of the bond being at the discretion of the district commander and depending upon the condition of the party as regards property, &c. Should any doubt exist, however, of the reliability of the individual then such other steps should be taken, such as sending him to Camp Chase as a political prisoner, as will give reasonable security against his doing harm.

2. Persons returning home after serving their term in the rebel service but who are believed to be truly penitent may if deemed reliable be permitted to remain on similar terms. They are not entitled to

---

* Omitted.

the same consideration as deserters, but as they might if prevented by dread of imprisonment from returning remain in the rebel ranks it is good policy to encourage their return home, always provided they are to be trusted. If any doubt exists as to their reliability they should be sent with proper written charges and proofs to Camp Chase as political prisoners. They cannot be considered as prisoners of war and are not entitled to the immunities granted that class by the cartel agreed upon by the United States with the rebel authorities.

3. Still another class is to be found in Kentucky who while never having left their homes or taken up arms in the rebel cause have by their acts proved themselves enemies to the United States. These on proper proof should be arrested and sent always with written charges and proofs to Camp Chase as political prisoners. Many such give no chance for obtaining evidence of their disloyalty, while they are notoriously disloyal. Such persons are arrested whenever a sound judgment indicated a necessity for it as they are often more dangerous than open enemies. Often they are discharged when the necessity for their confinement passes. In applying the preceding principles you will observe that much is left to your own judgment necessarily.

I would, however, state that great prudence should be exercised in the matter of arrests. Old feuds, more recent dislikes, have an influence in controlling the judgments of the most loyal, and experience has shown that individuals entirely innocent of any disloyal design may be arrested and imprisoned upon the evidence of the over-zealous patriot or of the designing enemy. The numerous discharges of prisoners from Camp Chase illustrates this. I refer to this experience to put you on your guard against hearsay evidence. While every real enemy of the Union should be put where he could do no harm it is all important for the good of the cause that the innocent should not suffer even for a time through false representations.

I would further state that any permission such as seems to be granted by Colonel Cranor does not protect a person from another arrest. To be entitled to this immunity the individual must have so conducted himself as to have proved his loyalty. He must be beyond suspicion.

Very respectfully, your obedient servant,
H. G. WRIGHT,
Major-General, Commanding.

HEADQUARTERS EXCHANGED AND PAROLED PRISONERS,
Near Alexandria, Va., February 26, 1863.

Col. W. HOFFMAN, U. S. Army,
Commissary-General of Prisoners, Washington, D. C.

COLONEL: I received your letter of 24th instant yesterday afternoon directing me to forward all paroled and exchanged prisoners in this camp belonging to regiments serving in the West to Camp Parole, Annapolis, Md., at once. I will be unable to comply with your directions immediately as I do not know the regiments that are serving in the West. I therefore respectfully request to be furnished with a list of such regiments and on receipt of it I will promptly comply with your orders.

With regard to the 400 exchanged troops here reported on my weekly report of the 20th instant and calling for an explanation as to their detention here I beg to refer you to the column " for duty " on that report the figures of which only show 147. Out of that number there is a camp guard as you will perceive of eighty-eight, and the guard has been formed in compliance with orders from the Military Governor of Alexandria. These men, however, have been selected for that duty on account of being pronounced unfit for duty in the field by the medical officer of this command, and when medical authority pronounces any members of this command unfit for field duty I cannot forward them to their regiment.

I am, colonel, very respectfully, your obedient servant,

GABRIEL DE KORPONAY,
Colonel Twenty-eighth Pennsylvania Volunteers, Comdg. Camp.

SURGEON-GENERAL'S OFFICE,
Washington, February 26, 1863.

Col. WILLIAM HOFFMAN,
Commissary General of Prisoners, Washington, D. C.

COLONEL: To enable me to complete by careful comparison of all data a list of such Confederate prisoners of war as have died within our lines I respectfully request that you will furnish me with a list of such prisoners as are so reported to your office, this list including the following information:

Name.	Rank.	Company.	Regiment.	Cause of death.	Date of death.	Place of death.

By order of the Surgeon-General U. S. Army:

Very respectfully, your obedient servant,

JOS. R. SMITH,
Surgeon, U. S. Army.

WHEELING, *February 26, 1863.*

Col. W. HOFFMAN, *Commissary-General of Prisoners:*

Has any order been issued about exchange of prisoners since that of January 10, 1863, No. 10? I consider those not exchanged who were captured near Romney and paroled there December 8, 1862, and send them to Camp Chase.

JOS. DARR, JR.,
Major and Provost-Marshal-General.

MURFREESBOROUGH, *February 26, 1863.*

Col. W. HOFFMAN, *Commissary-General of Prisoners:*

I forwarded this day complete lists of Federal prisoners belonging to this department captured at the battle of Stone's River, and to this date 1 brigadier general, 1 colonel, 3 lieutenant-colonels, 1 major, 14 captains, 30 subordinates, 2,502 enlisted.

WM. M. WILES,
Captain and Provost-Marshal-General.

WASHINGTON, D. C., *February 27, 1863.*

Major-General ROSECRANS, *Murfreesborough, Tenn.*

GENERAL: It is deemed best that you should not enforce your General Orders, No. 14, by placing the men improperly paroled into the ranks. The principle established by your order is correct but it is deemed best that both the enemy and our own men should be notified before it is enforced. A general order will be prepared and issued on this subject.

Very respectfully, your obedient servant,

H. W. HALLECK,
General-in-Chief.

HEADQUARTERS DEPARTMENT OF VIRGINIA,
Fort Monroe, Va., February 27, 1863.

Hon. E. M. STANTON, *Secretary of War.*

SIR: I learn from Colonel Ludlow that citizen prisoners are to be mutually released. I have a letter from Hon. Washington Barrow, who is on parole at Saint Louis and who is desirous of going to Washington. I do not know the grounds of his arrest but if as I suppose it is for disloyalty in Tennessee he will no doubt fall within the general arrangement for the exchange of citizen prisoners. If I am mistaken in supposing that such an exchange is definitely arranged I would suggest that he be discharged upon the release of some one of our own prisoners at Richmond.

I am, very respectfully, your obedient servant,

JOHN A. DIX,
Major-General.

HEADQUARTERS DEPARTMENT OF THE GULF,
New Orleans, February 27, 1863.

Brig. Gen. JAMES BOWEN,
Provost-Marshal-General, Department of the Gulf.

GENERAL: The general commanding directs that you immediately provide suitable quarters and keep in close custody all prisoners of war taken from the enemy, both officers and enlisted men, whose names appeared on the late register and who refused or neglected to comply with the special order requiring them to report on the 20th instant at the foot of Canal street for passage through the lines, &c.; and that hereafter neither officers nor enlisted men be allowed their liberty within our lines without first taking the oath of allegiance, but will be kept in custody until a favorable opportunity offers to forward them through the lines under orders from these headquarters.

JOHN S. CLARK,
Colonel and Aide-de-Camp.

OFFICE COMMISSARY-GENERAL OF PRISONERS,
Washington, D. C., February 27, 1863.

Brig. Gen. L. THOMAS,
Adjutant-General U. S. Army, Washington, D. C.

GENERAL: To enable me to distribute exchanged troops to their respective regiments and batteries it is necessary that I should know the army corps to which they belong and the department in which they are serving, and I have therefore the honor to request that I may be furnished with all requisite information for the above purpose.

I am, general, very respectfully, your obedient servant,

W. HOFFMAN,
Colonel Third Infantry, Commissary-General of Prisoners.

OFFICE COMMISSARY-GENERAL OF PRISONERS,
Washington, D. C., February 27, 1863.

Capt. H. M. LAZELLE,
  Assistant to Commissary-General of Prisoners.

CAPTAIN: You will proceed immediately to Camp Parole, near Annapolis, and make a minute inspection into its condition in every branch of the service—discipline, supplies, quarters, records, &c. Ascertain what provision is made at Annapolis for the reception of paroled troops arriving there by water under orders to repair to Camp Parole. You will particularly inquire into the matter referred to in the accompanying papers.* Having performed this service you will return to your duties in this office.

Very respectfully, your obedient servant,
W. HOFFMAN,
  Colonel Third Infantry, Commissary-General of Prisoners.

———

OFFICE COMMISSARY-GENERAL OF PRISONERS,
Washington, D. C., February 27, 1863.

Capt. H. M. LAZELLE,
  Asst. to Commissary-General of Prisoners, Washington, D. C.

CAPTAIN: I intended to make some verbal suggestions to you in relation to the inspection you are to make at Camp Parole which as I will not see you again before you leave I will put in writing. It is frequently said that soldiers are encouraged by the officers to leave the camp and go to their homes without authority. Make particular inquiries into this matter of officers and non-commissioned officers. Send for sergeants of Illinois regiments and ascertain what statements they make as to the manner of their treatment on arriving at Annapolis. Of course you will see what preparations are made for their reception, and from Colonel Sangster's report will know if there is any foundation for their complaints. Examine into the manner in which guard duty is done and find if my instructions on this subject are observed. Look into the condition of the camp fund and see what purchases are made from it. Inspect the hospital and see that the sick are comfortably provided for. Your orders cover all these points and I suggest them only that none may be lost sight of.

Yours, very truly,

W. HOFFMAN,
  Colonel Third Infantry, Commissary General of Prisoners.

———

OFFICE COMMISSARY-GENERAL OF PRISONERS,
Washington, D. C., February 27, 1863.

WILLIAM B. SMITH, Esq., *Machias, Me.*

SIR: In reply to your letter of the 16th instant requesting the exchange of the captain and crew of the brig Machias, of Machias, Me., who were captured near the Island of Cuba by the rebel steamer Sumter July last and released on parole I have to inform you that since my letter to you of the 31st ultimo I have learned from Lieutenant-Colonel Ludlow, agent for the exchange of prisoners, that the eighth section of General Orders, No. 10, is intended to cover on our side

———

* Not found.

all seamen captured by rebel vessels on the waters referred to, and under this construction the captain and crew of the brig Machias are exchanged.

Very respectfully, your obedient servant,

W. HOFFMAN,
Colonel Third Infantry, Commissary-General of Prisoners.

WAR DEPARTMENT, *Washington, February 28, 1863.*

Brigadier-General PATRICK,
Provost-Marshal-General, Army of the Potomac:

Send to this Department under guard Arnold Harris,* recently arrested in Maryland, with his papers, horse and all his property.

By order of the Secretary of War:

P. H. WATSON,
Assistant Secretary of War.

HEADQUARTERS DEPARTMENT OF VIRGINIA,
Fort Monroe, Va., February 28, 1863.

Hon. E. M. STANTON, *Secretary of War.*

SIR: I have the honor to transmit a report of the examination of political prisoners by Judge Pierrepont and myself under your order of the 27th February, 1862, and of the disposition made of the cases acted upon by us. The minutes of the proceedings and the testimony having been forwarded to you by the judge, there are a few details in regard to the cases disposed of at Fort McHenry which I am unable to furnish and for which I respectfully refer to the papers in your possession.

I am, very respectfully, your obedient servant,

JOHN A. DIX,
Major-General.

OFFICE COMMISSARY-GENERAL OF PRISONERS,
Washington, D. C., February 28, 1863.

Lieut. Col. W. H. LUDLOW,
Agent for Exchange of Prisoners, New York City.

COLONEL: Your letter of the 25th instant is received and in accordance with your request I have asked that the prisoners of war held at Fort Lafayette by order of the Secretary of the Navy may be placed at my disposal for exchange. In reply I am furnished by Mr. Fox, Assistant Secretary of the Navy, with a copy of a letter addressed by the Secretary of the Navy to the Secretary of War, a copy† of which I inclose herewith, from which you will perceive that the Secretary of the Navy for reasons which he gives declines to consent to the exchange of the prisoners referred to. Mr. Fox stated to me in conversation that pilots are rated as officers and inasmuch as the rebels have retained our naval officers they feel at liberty to detain others of like class. I am at a loss to know how to consider rebel officers who were captured in Virginia and Maryland previous to the date of your last interview with Mr. Ould and who are now in our hospitals. There is nothing in Order No. 10 to meet such cases nor is there anything

---

*For case of Arnold Harris, see Vol. II, this Series, p. 1515 *et seq.*
†See p. 298.

in Mr. Ould's declaration as published in the Herald to meet the case. I understand from what you said to me that all such prisoners have been exchanged but to make sure I wish you would write me on the subject at your earliest convenience. I will consult the Secretary of War in relation to the exchange of Zarvona and if approved will have him accompany the other prisoners. I will also have it decided whether the two men in [the] penitentiary at Albany can be exchanged. My last report from Fort Delaware gives only some fifteen or twenty enlisted rebel prisoners. I will send down from this city, Fort McHenry and Fort Delaware all enlisted persons for exchange as soon as the number is large enough to make it advisable.

Very respectfully, your obedient servant,

W. HOFFMAN,
Colonel Third Infantry, Commissary-General of Prisoners.

OFFICE COMMISSARY-GENERAL OF PRISONERS,
Washington, D. C., February 28, 1863.

Capt. E. L. WEBBER,
Commanding Camp Chase Prison, Columbus, Ohio.

CAPTAIN: If there are officers or enlisted men belonging to the rebel Army held as prisoners of war at Camp Chase who are embraced in any of the classes declared exchanged in General Orders, No. 10, they will be sent beyond our lines by the earliest opportunity. Report to General Wright how many there are and ask when and by what route they can be forwarded. Say to Lieut. J. H. Jones, Twenty-fourth Alabama Regiment, that you have received these instructions.

Very respectfully, your obedient servant,

W. HOFFMAN,
Colonel Third Infantry, Commissary-General of Prisoners.

HEADQUARTERS COMMANDANT OF PRISONS,
Camp Chase, Ohio, February 28, 1863.

Capt. H. M. LAZELLE,
Assistant to Commissary-General of Prisoners, Washington.

CAPTAIN: I have the honor of addressing you for the purpose of asking information on several subjects:

1. The rebel commissioned officers confined here are receiving large remittances of money from their friends and as the money costs nothing but the asking for it they are very lavish in expending it. There are many of them who wish to purchase uniforms; expensive cloth that could be readily turned into uniforms when they get back to the South, and large supplies of extra clothing that they cannot obtain in the South; also the best quality of boots. I am at a loss to know where to draw the line in this respect. My judgment is that they should be permitted to buy sufficient to keep them comfortable and nothing to carry away with them. Should a man who has a comfortable suit and a change of underclothing be permitted to buy other clothing? Shall I permit friends to furnish unnecessary articles of clothing to prisoners? Also should the prisoners be permitted to purchase any articles of food or should any delicacies be given them by their friends? There is much talk upon this subject and I should be thankful for your opinion and instructions.

20 R R—SERIES II, VOL V

2. There are three female prisoners here, sent from Nashville by order of General Rosecrans. They are charged with aiding the rebels and carrying contraband articles across our line. The evidence against them is here. We have poor facilities for female prisoners. What shall be done with them? Shall their cases be turned over to Special Commissioner Galloway for investigation?

Very respectfully, captain, your obedient servant,   .

EDWIN L. WEBBER,
Captain, Commanding Prisons.

CAMP CHASE, *February 28, 1863.*

Col. WILLIAM HOFFMAN,
Commissary-General of Prisoners, Washington City.

SIR: I have the honor respectfully to call your attention to the following statement: On the 23d of October, 1862, I was appointed by the direction of Captain Freedley, assistant commissary-general of prisoners, provost-marshal of prisons in this camp. In such capacity I have acted as such, without any specific instructions being given to me that would guide me in the performance of any duty that might arise of an extraordinary nature incident to the confinement of such a large number of prisoners as are now here. In view of the above fact I would respectfully ask you to give me instructions on the following points, viz:

1. Would it be my duty as provost-marshal to permit friends or prisoners themselves to purchase such articles of clothes that would on their return to the South answer for a uniform in the rebel army?

2. Would it be inconsistent with the dignity of the United States to require every person who has interviews with prisoners to take an oath of allegiance previous to the interview?

To my first question I would state that the numerous friends of the rebels in the North send here daily large boxes, trunks and packages of clothing and other articles that cannot be purchased in the South except at a large sum. To my second question I would state that of the numerous interviews held with the prisoners but few who desire the interview are in speech and actions any more loyal than the prisoners.

In view of the above facts and as a loyal officer striving to aid his Government be kind enough to give me the necessary information that I may be guided hereafter.

I have the honor to be, very respectfully, your obedient servant,

JAMES C. HENLEY,
Lieutenant, Company A, Battalion Governor's Guards.

GENERAL ORDERS, {   WAR DEPT., ADJT. GENERAL'S OFFICE,
No. 49.   }   *Washington, February 28, 1863.*

I. The following rules in regard to paroles established by the common law and usages of war are published for the information of all concerned:

1. Paroling must always take place by the exchange of signed duplicates of a written document in which the name and rank of the parties paroled are correctly stated. Any one who intentionally misstates his rank forfeits the benefit of his parole and is liable to punishment.

2. None but commissioned officers can give the parole for themselves or their commands, and no inferior officer can give a parole without the authority of his superior if within reach.

3. No paroling on the battle-field. No paroling of entire bodies of troops after a battle and no dismissal of large numbers of prisoners with a general declaration that they are paroled is permitted or of any value.

4. An officer who gives a parole for himself or his command on the battle-field is deemed a deserter and will be punished accordingly.

5. For the officer the pledging of his parole is an individual act, and no wholesale paroling by an officer for a number of inferiors in rank is permitted or valid.

6. No non-commissioned officer or private can give his parole except through an officer. Individual paroles not given through an officer are not only void but subject the individuals giving them to the punishment of death as deserters. The only admissible exception is where individuals properly separated from their commands have suffered long confinement without the possibility of being paroled through an officer.

7. No prisoner of war can be forced by the hostile Government to pledge his parole, and any threat or ill-treatment to force the giving of the parole is contrary to the law of war.

8. No prisoner of war can enter into engagements inconsistent with his character and duties as a citizen and a subject of his State. He can only bind himself not to bear arms against his captor for a limited period, or until he is exchanged, and this only with the stipulated or implied consent of his Government. If the engagement which he makes is not approved by his Government he is bound to return and surrender himself as a prisoner of war. His own Government cannot at the same time disown his engagement and refuse his return as a prisoner.

9. No one can pledge his parole that he will never bear arms against the Government of his captors, nor that he will not bear arms against any other enemy of his Government not at the time the ally of his captors. Such agreements have reference only to the existing enemy and his existing allies and to the existing war and not to future belligerents.

10. While the pledging of the military parole is a voluntary act of the individual the capturing power is not obliged to grant it, nor is the Government of the individual paroled bound to approve or ratify it.

11. Paroles not authorized by the common law of war are not valid until approved by the Government of the individual so pledging his parole.

12. The pledging of any unauthorized military parole is a military offense punishable under the common law of war.

II. This order will be published at the head of every regiment in the service of the United States and will be officially communicated by every general commanding an army in the field to the commanding general of the opposing forces and will be hereafter strictly observed and enforced in the armies of the United States. *

By order of Maj. Gen. H. W. Halleck:

L. THOMAS,
Adjutant-General.

---

* This order was printed in circular form by General J. E. Johnston, through his assistant adjutant-general, Benjamin S. Ewell, and "published for the information of General Johnston's command."

AQUIA CREEK, *March 1, 1863.*

P. H. WATSON, *Assistant Secretary of War:*

By direction of Brigadier-General Patrick, provost-marshal-general, Army of the Potomac, I forward in charge of guard Arnold Harris, citizen, to report to you. The guard and prisoner left this place on the steamer John Brooks at 1.30 p. m. and will arrive at Washington at 4.30 p. m. to-day.

J. W. FORSYTH,
Captain and Provost-Marshal.

SPRINGFIELD, ILL., *March 1, 1863.*

COMMISSARY-GENERAL OF PRISONERS:

Camp Butler well conducted. Leave for Chicago to-morrow unless otherwise instructed.

H. W. FREEDLEY.

BEFORE VICKSBURG, *March 2, 1863.*

Lieut. Gen. J. C. PEMBERTON,
Commanding Department of Mississippi and East Louisiana:

Maj. Gen. C. L. Stevenson's letter of the 24th ultimo written at your dictation was received last evening. This letter inclosed what purports to be a copy of an order issued by Admiral D. D. Porter to his squadron and makes inquiry if it is authentic.

I will state that Admiral Porter's command over the Mississippi squadron is as complete as mine over the army in this department and that he alone is responsible for any orders he may issue. One thing, however, I can guarantee: Admiral Porter has never departed from the rules of civilized warfare and never will until driven to do so in retaliation for offenses committed by persons who by their acts cease to be entitled to the treatment due soldiers captured in legitimate warfare.

There has been much done by the citizens of the Southern States that is not in accordance with any known rules of civilized warfare and for which they individually are responsible and can call for protection in their acts upon no people or Government. These are persons who are always in the guise of citizens, and on the approach of an armed force remain at their homes professing to be in no way connected with the army but entitled to all the indulgences allowed non-combatants in a country visited by an opposing army. These same persons, many of them, are ever ready to fire upon unarmed vessels and to capture and sometimes murder small parties of Federal soldiers who may be passing. I do not here instance an isolated case but a rule that seems to have been adopted, particularly in Mississippi and Arkansas. In the absence of any standard authority on this subject I believe all persons engaged in war must have about them some insignia by which they may be known at all times as an enemy to entitle them to the treatment of prisoners of war. Then their hostilities must be carried on in accordance with the rules of civilized warfare.

In the absence of these two conditions being fulfilled they who violate them become responsible for their own acts.

I have never threatened retaliation upon those recognized as engaged in warfare against the Government for these illegal acts, and until the

Southern authorities formally recognize them as their own do not propose to do so. It is not my intention nor do I believe it to be the intention of Admiral Porter to hold the innocent responsible for the acts of the guilty.

I regret that General Stevenson's letter whilst making inquiries should contain a threat. I have yet to hear for the first time of such a course securing any alleviation from the hardships necessarily produced by a state of war.

All prisoners that have fallen into my hands have been kindly and humanely treated.

Unprincipled and over-zealous persons many times may exaggerate unavoidable suffering but a sensible commander will always know how to receive such reports.

I will refer General Stevenson's letter to Admiral Porter who alone can answer the queries.

U. S. GRANT,
Major-General.

U. S. MISSISSIPPI SQUADRON,
Near Vicksburg, March 2, 1863.

Maj. Gen. U. S. GRANT, &c.

GENERAL: On consideration I thought it best to write the inclosed letter (a copy of which I send you) in answer to General Pemberton.

I don't think he will gain any great consolation from it and it may enlighten him on the subject of civilized warfare.

Very respectfully, &c.,

DAVID D. PORTER,
Acting Rear-Admiral, Commanding Mississippi Squadron.

[Inclosure.]

U. S. MISSISSIPPI SQUADRON,
Near Vicksburg, March 2, 1863.

Maj. Gen. C. L. STEVENSON, *Vicksburg, Miss.*

SIR: Major-General Grant, commanding this department, has handed me a communication from you written by authority of General Pemberton, commanding Department of Mississippi and East Louisiana. I might very properly object to notice it, as all communications relating to the Mississippi Squadron should be addressed to me as commander-in-chief of the naval department on the Mississippi River. I decline, however, to stand on a point of etiquette.

I inclose* you a communication I wrote to one of my officers in relation to the notice your general has taken exceptions to; it will fully explain my views on this subject.

No one is more desirous than myself that operations within the limits of my command should be conducted in accordance with the usages of war, of humanity and of civilization, which sentiment I am pleased to see is expressed by yourself. I can see no easier way to arrive at the desired end than by putting a stop to the inhuman practice of firing on unarmed vessels and peaceful citizens.

I am quite satisfied that it is not civilized for parties who are over-seer civilians one day (trading with our people) and soldiers the next

* Not found.

to be traveling around the country firing upon hospital vessels and river steamers. The hospital vessel of this squadron was attacked in sight of me and a volley of musketry fired into the windows while she had on board and being attended with all care some of the wounded prisoners taken at the Post of Arkansas.

A few days since a band of armed desperadoes jumped on the deck of the tug Hercules and killed in cold blood some of the unoffending crew. Men lurk in the woods without a flag or distinguishing mark and fire at any human being they may see on the deck of a steamer without caring or knowing whether it is friend or foe they are about to murder, and this we are called upon to recognize as civilized warfare. If, sir, you call this carrying on war in a civilized manner we differ very widely in our opinions.

If those who profess to be your followers make war on us after the manner of highwaymen I see no·reason why they should be treated with that courtesy and kindness which I believe I have the reputation of extending to all prisoners captured in honorable warfare.

I think on due consideration that you will find I have announced no principle not strictly in accordance with the usages of civilized warfare. In this respect I endeavor to set an example of moderation that it would be well to follow. I have enjoined upon every person under my command to exact the strictest obedience to my order against pillaging or injuring the property of persons on the rivers, and while doing all I can to avert the calamities of war I intend to exact a strict compliance with the usages of war, of humanity and of civilization. If persons claiming to be soldiers deviate from them they can scarcely expect to be treated to any of the amenities of war and their leaders should not claim for them more than they expect themselves.

In this matter of firing on unarmed vessels no good results have arisen. On the contrary it has led to a system of retaliation where unfortunately the guilty parties did not always suffer. It has led to perfect demoralization and brought to the river-banks a set of desperadoes who plunder alike both friend and foe.

This system can do no good toward ending this war and is only destructive to those who had no hand in making it. If General Pemberton is desirous that the war should be conducted on the principle of humanity and civilization all he has to do is to issue an order to stop guerrilla warfare. He can exercise his judgment with regard to any retaliatory measures he may think proper to institute. I presume our soldiers and sailors could easily prepare themselves for any ordeal they might be subjected to and we might hope to see our country aroused at last to a sense of the injuries inflicted upon it.

Very respectfully,

DAVID D. PORTER,
Acting Rear-Admiral, Commanding Mississippi Squadron.

WASHINGTON, *March 2, 1863.*

Lieut. Col. F. A. DICK:

Send here for exchange 150 [citizen] prisoners. See my telegram of 14th ultimo. Send to me rolls with charges and sentences. Reply.

W. HOFFMAN,
Commissary-General of Prisoners.

HEADQUARTERS DEPARTMENT OF THE GULF,
New Orleans, March 2, 1863.
Brig. Gen. T. W. SHERMAN,
Commanding Defenses of New Orleans.

SIR: To avoid the possibility of a misunderstanding on so important a point the commanding general directs me to state that the prisoners of war belonging to the Forty-second Massachusetts who came down on the Iberville are, with the exception of the chaplain, paroled but not exchanged. The chaplain is unconditionally released. The conditions of the parole are thus stated in the fourth article of the cartel between the United States and the enemy promulgated in General Orders, No. 146, of 1862, from the War Department, Adjutant-General's Office:

The surplus prisoners not exchanged shall not be permitted to take up arms again nor to serve as military police or constabulary force in any fort, garrison or field-work held by either of the respective parties, nor as guards of prisons, depots or stores, nor to discharge any duty usually performed by soldiers until exchanged under the provisions of the cartel.

Very respectfully, your most obedient servant,
[RICHARD B. IRWIN,]
Lieutenant-Colonel and Assistant Adjutant-General.

OFFICE PROVOST-MARSHAL-GENERAL,
Saint Louis, Mo., March 2, 1863.
Col. W. HOFFMAN,
Commissary-General of Prisoners, Washington, D. C.

COLONEL: I desire to submit to your consideration the matter of rebel prisoners of war now within the department and that have recently passed through here. On the 12th of December I forwarded from here toward Cairo 82 prisoners of war for exchange at Vicksburg and on the 5th January 63 others. These were never exchanged, as when the boat containing about 1,100 prisoners (the 82 of December 12 among the others) which had been sent from Cairo reached Vicksburg Admiral D. D. Porter would not permit the prisoners to land on account of the battle then going on and they were ordered up to Helena. From Helena they were sent up to Memphis, thence to Cairo, thence hither, and I having no accommodation for them here by orders from General Curtis sent them to Alton. Since that time all the Arkansas Post prisoners have passed through Saint Louis, the sick only being left here, and have gone to Camp Butler, Springfield, Ill., and Camp Douglas, Chicago. There were about 4,000 of them I think. I was never furnished with complete rolls. I have here 200 other prisoners of war for exchange and last week sent up to Alton about 200 more, not having room for them here. I am constantly written to by the prisoners inquiring concerning their exchange and can only answer by saying that they will go by the first exchange. By the terms of the cartel all prisoners of war if not exchanged are to be paroled within ten days and yet here are those I have mentioned now confined many weeks beyond the stipulated time. I do not feel authorized in paroling these men and respectfully request that some means be taken to rid our prisons and camps of those who under the cartel are entitled to their liberty so far as we are concerned. May I request your early attention to this subject, colonel, and that I may be informed concerning the prospect of an exchange?

Very respectfully, your obedient servant,
F. A. DICK,
Lieutenant-Colonel and Provost-Marshal-General.

HEADQUARTERS PROVOST-MARSHAL'S OFFICE,
Washington, D. C., March 2, 1863.

Col. W. HOFFMAN, Commissary-General of Prisoners:

I have the honor to inform you that there are at present confined in the Old Capitol Prison 160 prisoners of war for exchange excluding officers and those held for other purposes.

I am, sir, very respectfully, your obedient servant,

HENRY B. TODD,
Captain and Provost-Marshal.

———

An act of the U. S. Congress approved March 3, 1863, relating to habeas corpus, &c.

Be it enacted by the Senate and House of Representatives of the United States of America in Congress assembled, That during the present rebellion the President of the United States whenever in his judgment the public safety may require it is authorized to suspend the privilege of the writ of habeas corpus in any case throughout the United States or any part thereof. And whenever and wherever the said privilege shall be suspended as aforesaid no military or other officer shall be compelled in answer to any writ of habeas corpus to return the body of any person or persons detained by him by authority of the President; but upon a certificate under oath of the officer having charge of any one so detained that such person is detained by him as a prisoner under authority of the President further proceedings under the writ of habeas corpus shall be suspended by the judge or court having issued the said writ so long as said suspension by the President shall remain in force and said rebellion continue.

SEC. 2. And be it further enacted, That the Secretary of State and the Secretary of War be and they are hereby directed as soon as may be practicable to furnish to the judges of the circuit and district courts of the United States and of the District of Columbia a list of the names of all persons, citizens of States in which the administration of the laws has continued unimpaired in the said Federal courts, who are now or may hereafter be held as prisoners of the United States by order or authority of the President of the United States or either of said Secretaries in any fort, arsenal or other place as State or political prisoners or otherwise than as prisoners of war; the said list to contain the names of all those who reside in the respective jurisdictions of said judges or who may be deemed by the said Secretaries or either of them to have violated any law of the United States in any of said jurisdictions, and also the date of each arrest—the Secretary of State to furnish a list of such persons as are imprisoned by the order or authority of the President acting through the State Department and the Secretary of War a list of such as are imprisoned by the order or authority of the President acting through the Department of War. And in all cases where a grand jury having attended any of said courts having jurisdiction in the premises after the passage of this act and after the furnishing of said list as aforesaid has terminated its session without finding an indictment or presentment or other proceeding against any such person, it shall be the duty of the judge of said court forthwith to make an order that any such prisoner desiring a discharge from said imprisonment be brought before him to be discharged; and every officer of the United States having custody of such prisoner is hereby directed immediately to obey and execute said judge's order; and in case he shall delay or refuse to do so he shall be subject to indictment for a misdemeanor, and be punished by a fine of not less than $500 and imprisonment in the common jail for a period not less than six months, in the discretion of the court: *Provided, however,* That no person shall be discharged by virtue of the provisions of this act until after he or she shall have taken an oath of allegiance to the Government of the United States and to support the Constitution thereof, and that he or she will not hereafter in any way encourage or give aid and comfort to the present rebellion or the supporters thereof: *And provided, also,* That the judge or court before whom such person may be brought before discharging him or her from imprisonment shall have power on examination of the case and if the public safety shall require it shall be required to cause him or her to enter into recognizance with or without surety in a sum to be fixed by said judge or court to keep the peace and be of good behavior toward the United States and its citizens, and from time to time and at such times as such judge or court may direct appear before said judge or court to be further dealt with according to law as the circumstances may require. And it shall be the duty of the district attorney of the United States to attend such examination before the judge.

SEC. 3. *And be it further enacted,* That in case any such prisoners shall be under indictment or presentment for any offense against the laws of the United States and by existing laws bail or a recognizance be taken for the appearance for trial of such persons it shall be the duty of said judge at once to discharge such persons upon bail or recognizance for trial as aforesaid. And in case the said Secretaries of State and War shall for any reason refuse or omit to furnish the said list of persons held as prisoners as aforesaid at the time of the passage of this act within twenty days thereafter, and of such persons as hereafter may be arrested within twenty days from the time of the arrest, any citizen may after a grand jury shall have terminated its session without finding an indictment or presentment as provided in the second section of this act by a petition alleging the facts aforesaid touching any of the persons so as aforesaid imprisoned, supported by the oath of such petitioner or any other credible person, obtain and be entitled to have the said judge's order to discharge such prisoner on the same terms and conditions prescribed in the second section of this act: *Provided, however,* That the said judge shall be satisfied such allegations are true.

SEC. 4. *And be it further enacted,* That any order of the President or under his authority made at any time during the existence of the present rebellion shall be a defense in all courts to any action or prosecution, civil or criminal, pending or to be commenced for any search seizure, arrest or imprisonment made, done or committed or acts omitted to be done under or by virtue of such order, or under color of any law of Congress; and such defense may be made by special plea or under the general issue.

SEC. 5. *And be it further enacted,* That if any suit or prosecution, civil or criminal, has been or shall be commenced in any State court against any officer, civil or military, or against any other person for any arrest or imprisonment made or other trespasses or wrongs done or committed or any act omitted to be done at any time during the present rebellion by virtue or under color of any authority derived from or exercised by or under the President of the United States or any act of Congress; and the defendant shall at the time of entering his

appearance in such court or if such appearance shall have been entered
before the passage of this act, then at the next session of the court in
which such suit or prosecution is pending file a petition stating the
facts and verified by affidavit for the removal of the cause for trial at
the next circuit court of the United States to be holden in the district
where the suit is pending, and offer good and sufficient surety for his
filing in such court on the first day of its session copies of such process and other proceedings against him, and also for his appearing in
such court and entering special bail in the cause if special bail was
originally required thereon, and it shall then be the duty of the State
court to accept the surety and proceed no further in the cause or
prosecution and the bail that shall have been originally taken shall be
discharged. And such copies being filed as aforesaid in such court of
the United States the cause shall proceed therein in the same manner
as if it had been brought in said court by original process, whatever
may be the amount in dispute or the damages claimed or whatever the
citizenship of the parties, any former law to the contrary notwithstanding.

And any attachment of the goods or estate of the defendant by the
original process shall hold the goods or estate so attached to answer
the final judgment in the same manner as by the laws of such State
they would have been holden to answer final judgment had it been rendered in the court in which the suit or prosecution was commenced.
And it shall be lawful in any such action or prosecution which may be
now pending or hereafter commenced before any State court whatever
for any cause aforesaid after final judgment for either party to remove
and transfer by appeal such case during the session or term of said
court at which the same shall have taken place from such court to the
next circuit court of the United States to be held in the district in which
such appeal shall be taken in manner aforesaid. And it shall be the
duty of the person taking such appeal to produce and file in the said
circuit court attested copies of the process, proceedings and judgment
in such cause; and it shall also be competent for either party within six
months after the rendition of a judgment in any such cause by writ of
error or other process to remove the same to the circuit court of the
United States of that district in which such judgment shall have been
rendered; and the said circuit court shall thereupon proceed to try and
determine the facts and the law in such action in the same manner as
if the same had been there originally commenced, the judgment in such
case notwithstanding. And any bail which may have been taken or
property attached shall be holden on the final judgment of the said
court in such action in the same manner as if no such removal and
transfer had been made as aforesaid. And the State court from which
any such action, civil or criminal, may be removed and transferred as
aforesaid upon the parties giving good and sufficient security for the
prosecution thereof shall allow the same to be removed and transferred,
and proceed no further in the case: *Provided, however,* That if the party
aforesaid shall fail duly to enter the removal and transfer as aforesaid
in the circuit court of the United States agreeably to this act the State
court by which judgment shall have been rendered and from which the
transfer and removal shall have been made as aforesaid shall be authorized on motion for that purpose to issue execution and to carry into
effect any such judgment the same as if no such removal and transfer
had been made: *And provided also,* That no such appeal or writ of
error shall be allowed in any criminal action or prosecution where final
judgment shall have been rendered in favor of the defendant or respondent by the State court. And if in any suit hereafter commenced the

plaintiff is nonsuited or judgment passed against him the defendant shall recover double costs.

SEC. 6. *And be it further enacted*, That any suit or prosecution described in this act in which final judgment may be rendered in the circuit court may be carried by writ of error to the Supreme Court whatever may be the amount of said judgment.

SEC. 7. *And be it further enacted*, That no suit or prosecution, civil or criminal, shall be maintained for any arrest or imprisonment made or other trespasses or wrongs done or committed or act omitted to be done at any time during the present rebellion by virtue or under color of any authority derived from or exercised by or under the President of the United States or by or under any act of Congress unless the same shall have been commenced within two years next after such arrest, imprisonment, trespass or wrong may have been done or committed or act may have been omitted to be done: *Provided*, That in no case shall the limitation herein provided commence to run until the passage of this act, so that no party shall by virtue of this act be debarred of his remedy by suit or prosecution until two years from and after the passage of this act.

WAR DEPARTMENT, *Washington, March 3, 1863.*
Hon. GIDEON WELLES, *Secretary of the Navy.*

SIR: The Secretary of War directs me to inform you that in compliance with the request made in your letter of the 28th ultimo the Adjutant-General has been ordered to detail Brigadier-General Totten as an associate with Rear-Admiral Shubrick and Commodore Davis, of the Navy, for the consideration of the case of paroling of the officers and men of the U. S. steamer Mercedita off Charleston, S. C., during the late attack from the rebels.

Very respectfully, your obedient servant,
P. H. WATSON,
Assistant Secretary of War.

HEADQUARTERS CAMP OF INSTRUCTION,
Benton Barracks, Mo., March 3, 1863.
Col. W. HOFFMAN,
Commissary-General of Prisoners, Washington, D. C.

SIR: I have the honor to herewith transmit returns of the paroled men at this post for the month of February, 1863, as required by your instructions, containing 105 commissioned officers present; 2 commissioned officers, without leave, absent; 1,440 enlisted men present; 624 enlisted men, without leave, absent; 2,171 aggregate present and absent.

I am, colonel, very respectfully, your obedient servant,
B. L. E. BONNEVILLE,
Colonel, U. S. Army, Commanding.

HEADQUARTERS U. S. FORCES,
Columbus, Ohio, March 3, 1863.
Maj. N. H. McLEAN,
Assistant Adjutant-General and Chief of Staff, Cincinnati, Ohio.

SIR: I have the honor to inclose you the report of the provost-marshal at Camp Chase in respect to the too great indulgence allowed to Confederate prisoners. You will observe from this report that these prisoners are under the direct and immediate control of Colonel Hoffman, commissary-general of prisoners, and that we have no authority in the premises.

By order of Brigadier-General Cooper:

WM. VON DOEHN,
Assistant Adjutant-General.

[Inclosure.]

PROVOST-MARSHAL'S OFFICE,
Camp Chase, Ohio, February 25, 1863.

Brigadier-General COOPER,
    Commanding U. S. Forces, Columbus, Ohio.

SIR: In reply to the inclosed letter* I have the honor to report that prisoners of war in this camp have been and are allowed to purchase from the sutler such articles as the following—hams, flour, molasses, canned fruits, apples, pies, cakes, raisins, nuts, clothing, boots and shoes, tobacco, &c., besides the other minor articles which a sutler usually keeps. They are also allowed the few delicacies which sympathizing friends furnish. I cannot learn that a copy of General Rosecrans' order relating to this matter has ever been sent here, or that it applies in this camp. The provost-marshal of Camp Chase has nothing to do with the prison. It is under the control of Captain Webber and Provost-Marshal of Prisoners Lieutenant Henley, the whole being subject to Colonel Hoffman at Washington.

Very respectfully, your obedient servant,

C. W. STEWART,
First Lieutenant and Provost-Marshal. Camp Chase.

OFFICE COMMISSARY-GENERAL OF PRISONERS,
Washington, D. C.. March 3. 1863.

Lieut. Col. GEORGE SANGSTER,
    Commanding Camp Parole, Annapolis, Md.

COLONEL: I am directed by the commissary-general of prisoners to say in answer to communications received that furloughs cannot be granted to soldiers on parole except in extreme cases.

Very respectfully, your obedient servant,

W. T. HARTZ,
Captain and Assistant Adjutant-General.

(Same to Col. R. A. Constable, Seventy-fifth Ohio Volunteers, Washington, D. C.)

HEADQUARTERS DEPARTMENT OF VIRGINIA,
Fort Monroe, Va.. March 4, 1863.

General WINDER, *Richmond.*

GENERAL: I send by Captain Mulford, U. S. Volunteers, with the flag-of-truce boat which leaves for City Point to day a portrait of Washington and request that it may be restored to its owner. The inclosed correspondence† (copies of letters numbered 1, 2 and 3) will explain the circumstances under which the picture was taken and is now sent to you for restoration to the owner.

I am, general, very respectfully, yours,

JOHN A. DIX,
Major-General.

---

* See Campbell to Rosecrans, p. 265, *ante.*   † Not found.

SAINT LOUIS, *March 4, 1863.*

Colonel HOFFMAN:

I have this day sent 150 citizen prisoners in compliance with your last orders. They go to Washington via Pittsburg in charge of Captain Dean, additional aide-de-camp.

F. A. DICK,
Lieutenant-Colonel and Provost-Marshal-General.

OFFICE PROVOST-MARSHAL-GENERAL,
Saint Louis, Mo., March 4, 1863.

Col. W. HOFFMAN, *Commissary-General of Prisoners.*

COLONEL: I send forward to-day under guard in response to your telegraphic orders of the 2d instant and 14th ultimo 150 citizen prisoners. The charges against them are entered opposite their names in the column of remarks. In nearly every case these charges are based upon the voluntary statements of the prisoners made upon a personal examination in accordance with the form* herewith inclosed. In those cases in which the remark is made, "evidence on file," the evidence referred to is that of witnesses filed in this office. In no case is a prisoner sent forward upon this list who could with safety or propriety be enlarged in this department. Some of the worst cases are those who have been arrested for refusal to enroll in the Missouri militia. They are traitors at heart who wish to enjoy the protection of the Government here and yet will not take any part in defending this State from the rebel invasion.

I have the honor to remain, colonel, very respectfully, your obedient servant,

F. A. DICK,
Lieut. Col. and Provost-Marshal-General, Dept. of the Missouri.

OFFICE COMMISSARY-GENERAL OF PRISONERS,
Washington. D. C., March 4, 1863.

Capt. EDWIN L. WEBBER,
Commandant of Prison, Camp Chase, Ohio.

CAPTAIN: Your letter of February 28, 1863, addressed to Capt. H. M. Lazelle, assistant to commissary-general of prisoners, was received, and I am directed by the commissary-general of prisoners to say in answer to same that the indulgences therein mentioned should not be allowed. Rebel officers are not to have any more clothing than what they actually require for immediate and actual use and which must be of a quality such as to insure its not lasting for any length of time on their return to the South. As to their boots or shoes, they may be of the commonest quality or rather of a quality that will suffice but for immediate use. They are not to be allowed to purchase uniform clothing of any kind or have it or anything in that line furnished by their friends. They will be allowed to purchase a moderate or reasonable allowance of food or delicacies, and those who are too poor to purchase may have it furnished by their friends in reasonable quantities. Regulations made by the commissary-general of prisoners in June last show under what circumstances money may be received and expended. Orders

---

* Not found.

have been sent in relation to general prisoners. All communications to this office must be addressed to the commissary-general of prisoners.

Very respectfully, your obedient servant,

W. T. HARTZ,
Captain and Assistant Adjutant-General.

OFFICE COMMISSARY-GENERAL OF PRISONERS,
Washington, D. C., March 4, 1863.

J. N. CHESTER, Esq., *Box 2766, New York Post-Office.*

DEAR SIR: Your letter of the 25th was duly received and I am directed by the commissary-general of prisoners to inform you that all officers captured subsequent to December 13, 1862, are to be held until a further understanding or until arrangements can be made for exchange.

Very respectfully, your obedient servant,

W. T. HARTZ,
Captain and Assistant Adjutant-General.

SPECIAL ORDERS, ?   WAR DEPT., ADJT. GENERAL'S OFFICE,
No. 103.   }   *Washington, March 4, 1863.*

*   *   *   *   *   *   *

XXXII. Brig. Gen. Joseph G. Totten, U. S. Volunteers, is hereby detailed as an associate with Rear-Admiral Shubrick and Commodore Davis, of the Navy, for the consideration of the case of the paroling of the officers and men of the U. S. steamer Mercedita, off Charleston, S. C., during the late attack from the rebels.

*   *   *   *   *   *   *

By order of the Secretary of War:

L. THOMAS,
Adjutant-General.

[MARCH 5, 1863.—For records relating to the affair at Thompson's Station, Tenn., and the capture of the Union forces under Col. John Coburn, see Series I, Volume XXIII, Part I, p. 73 *et seq.* Also, see Part II, same volume, for correspondence relating to Coburn's operations.]

EXECUTIVE DEPARTMENT, *Wheeling, March 5, 1863.*

Col. W. HOFFMAN, *Washington, D. C.*

DEAR SIR: I am anxious to know if any progress has been made in the exchange of non-combatants now in custody on the Federal and Confederate side. I have frequent letters and requests from parties interested and have little information to give them, and am eager to arrest more hostages if I can [not?] get the exchanges made. I don't desire to make arrests. I see from information I received from Richmond that Doctor Hughes has got to Richmond. I don't understand how this was done without the release of Trout. Trout was a member of the loyal Legislature of Virginia and was captured last fall and taken to Richmond. I supposed I had done everything to have him placed against Hughes but all failed and Trout is still in a loathsome jail.

I am, yours, &c.,

F. H. PEIRPOINT.

MURFREESBOROUGH, TENN., *March* 5. *1863.*

Maj. Gen. H. W. HALLECK, *General-in-Chief:*

Your letter of February 27 in regard to General Orders, No. 14, of this Department, is just received. I desire to ask if the objection to that order rests on the ground that notice has not been given to the enemy or to our own army. I wrote to General Bragg December 11 that though his mode of paroling the Hartsville prisoners was irregular I would let it pass for that time, but that thereafter no parole would be recognized that was not made in accordance with the terms of the cartel. There has been great abuse in the mode of paroling and the most stringent measures are necessary to prevent our men from being paroled so as to escape duty. I respectfully suggest that sufficient notice has been given to the enemy, and that the discipline of this army will suffer if the men irregularly paroled since that notice are [not] returned to duty.

W. S. ROSECRANS,
Major-General, Commanding.

OFFICE COMMISSARY-GENERAL OF PRISONERS,
Washington, D. C., March 5, 1863.

Lieut. Col. GEORGE SANGSTER,
Commanding Camp Parole, Annapolis, Md.

COLONEL: You will without delay forward to Camp Chase, Columbus, Ohio, and Benton Barracks, Saint Louis, Mo., all the paroled troops at Camp Parole including those in the general hospital at Annapolis who are recommended for the transfer by the surgeon in charge belonging to regiments serving in the West in accordance with General Orders, No. 72, of June 28, 1862. Furnish the command with cooked rations for the route and send as full rolls by companies and regiments as possible with the officer in charge. Apply to Colonel Waite, commanding at Annapolis, for five officers and seven non commissioned officers to conduct the detachment, three officers and four non-commissioned officers to go to Camp Chase, and two of the former and three of the latter to Benton Barracks. These officers will return to their proper station after performing this duty. The Quartermaster's Department will furnish the necessary transportation.

By order of the General-in-Chief:

Very respectfully, your obedient servant,

W. HOFFMAN,
Colonel Third Infantry, Commissary-General of Prisoners.

OFFICE PROVOST-MARSHAL-GENERAL,
Saint Louis, Mo., March 5, 1863.

Col. W. HOFFMAN,
Third Infty., Commissary-General of Prisoners, Washington.

COLONEL: Yesterday as you have already been informed by telegram and letter I sent in obedience to your orders 150 citizen prisoners for exchange to Washington City.

There remain of the guerrilla and irregular prisoners, many of them captured last fall and others along with them in prison, a large number of similar cases.

For the release of many of these prisoners a great influence and pressure is brought to bear. Many of them fall into bad health, the circumstances of the families of others excite the sympathies of their neighbors and other circumstances combine to induce great efforts to release these prisoners.

I believe that some of them ought to be released, but a large proportion of them are as obstinate rebels as they ever were and it will not be safe to enlarge such characters while the war lasts. I respectfully suggest that such prisoners be passed through the lines to be exchanged.

A considerable number of such irregular prisoners who are being captured continuously are determined rebels whose purposes no length of imprisonment will change.

Would it not be advisable upon the capture of such men to exchange them at once? To detain them fills our prisons at heavy expense to the Government.

Several rebel mails have been taken in the last few weeks and I find that a large number of women have been actively concerned in both secret correspondence and in carrying on the business of collecting and distributing rebel letters. I have now the evidence upon which these women can be convicted. I have for some time past been thinking of arresting and trying them but the embarrassment is to know what to do with them. Many of them are the wives and daughters of officers in the rebel service; for example, Mrs. Frost, a wealthy, influential woman, wife of the rebel General D. M. Frost; Mrs. McPheeters, wife of a rebel surgeon at Richmond; Mrs. Cook, the wife of a rebel Senator [Representative] from Missouri; Mrs. Polk (and daughters), wife of Trusten Polk, lately of the U. S. Senate, and now in the rebel service as judge I believe; Mrs. Bredell, mother of Captain Bredell, on staff of rebel General Bowen, and very many others.

These women are wealthy and wield a great influence; they are avowed and abusive enemies of the Government; they incite our young men to join the rebellion; their letters are full of encouragement to their husbands and sons to continue the war; they convey information to them and by every possible contrivance they forward clothing and other support to the rebels. These disloyal women, too, seek every opportunity to keep disloyalty alive amongst rebel prisoners. I have been appealed to very many times by our loyal people to know why these disloyal women were not sent through the lines to join their husbands and sons. I respectfully suggest that such an order be issued by the Secretary of War.

Again there is a large number of active, intelligent, wealthy, disloyal men in Saint Louis who keep up a constant intercourse with the rebels in arms and by every means that they dare they urge them on in the rebellion. These men exercise a telling influence upon the rebels in arms and upon the disloyal masses in this State. Open, notorious disloyalty is preferred by these men to even a reputation for neutrality. They abstain from open acts, such as giving money, arms and other supplies, but their secret acts, words, associations and sympathies are unmistakably hostile to the Government and they openly rejoice at our reverses and lament at our victories. Forbearance toward this class of people was first adopted because it was thought that leniency would reform them, but that forbearance has settled into a usage which has produced evil consequences and has led these people to believe that it is their "constitutional" right to speak and conspire together as they may choose. The quiet, secret influence of this class is injurious and greatly so. I suggest that they be sent to join their Southern friends if such a course should be approved by the Secretary of War.

I have at last accomplished the work of examining all the old cases of prisoners excepting only those who were too sick to be brought out.

I have the honor, colonel, to be your obedient servant,

F. A. DICK,
Lieutenant-Colonel and Provost-Marshal-General.

EXECUTIVE DEPARTMENT, *Springfield, Ill., March 6, 1863,*
Col. W. HOFFMAN, *Commissary-General of Prisoners.*

COLONEL: I have the honor to inclose three communications* from paroled prisoners of war requesting their removal from Annapolis to a camp in this State. The frequency of appeals of this kind impels me to suggest the propriety of having a camp established in this State for the reception and keeping of all paroled prisoners belonging to Illinois regiments until they are exchanged. It is but fair to presume from the tone of the numerous letters received here asking for transfers to camps in Illinois that it is the general wish of these men to be nearer to their homes than they are now. In their opinion they will receive better attention and treatment when in their own State under the immediate supervision and control of their own officers than they do at the places where they are now kept. From section III of General Orders, No. 72, issued June 28, 1862, I infer that it was the intention of the War Department to have the prisoners sent to a camp as near to their respective homes as possible. Why this has not been carried out I cannot conceive. The fact is that more dissatisfaction exists among the paroled prisoners from the cause of their being kept at camps distant from their homes than from any other. After they have endured the hardships of imprisonment while in custody of the enemy they look with joy for the day when they may be allowed to return to the State which they left to fight for their common country and are bitterly disappointed when kept in camps so far from home. The complaints about this are so numerous that I would specially request you to give this matter your special attention. If the location of the camps is under your supervision I wish you to locate one in this State. If the War Department makes the selection I wish you to do all in your power to have the change made and to have the prisoners in the different camps transferred to the one selected.

I am, colonel, very respectfully, your obedient servant,

RICHD. YATES,
Governor.

HEADQUARTERS, *Camp Douglas, Ill., March 6, 1863.*
Col. W. HOFFMAN, *Commissary-General of Prisoners.*

SIR: I have the honor herewith to transmit the report* of deaths, releases and deserters of the prisoners of war at Camp Douglas, Chicago, Ill., for the month of February, 1863.

Very respectfully, your most obedient servant,

J. AMMEN,
Brigadier-General of Volunteers, Commanding.

---

* Omitted.

OFFICE COMMISSARY-GENERAL OF PRISONERS,
Washington, D. C., March 6, 1863.

Brig. Gen. W. W. MORRIS,
Commanding Fort McHenry, Baltimore, Md.

GENERAL: I am directed by the Secretary of War to assemble in this city all citizen prisoners whom it is desirable to exchange and I have therefore to request you will forward immediately to the provost-marshal, Eugene Williamson, of Baltimore, and C. J. Thompson, of Queen Anne County, Md. If the charge of being a spy against E. S. Edwards cannot be established by evidence before a court martial he too had better be forwarded for exchange. Knowing all the circumstances you can better judge of this than I can. If any have been paroled from Fort McHenry and are liable to exchange from having a residence, business or intimate relations with the South please forward them also, with charges, &c. All should arrive here on or before the 13th instant.

Respectfully, your obedient servant,   W. HOFFMAN,
Colonel Third Infantry, Commissary-General of Prisoners.

OFFICE COMMISSARY-GENERAL OF PRISONERS,
Washington, D. C., March 6, 1863.

Lieut. Col. D. D. PERKINS,
Commanding Fort Delaware, Del.

COLONEL: You will please forward to this city without delay to report to provost-marshal all citizen prisoners in your custody who from being residents of the South or having intimate relations of any kind there are subjects for exchange provided the charges against them are not such as to debar them from this favor. None will be exchanged except those charged with disloyalty in some shape. If there are any charged as spies unless the charge is very specific, with the testimony given on which it is to be established, you will forward them. Please send a roll giving the place, date and cause of arrest with the authority therefor and the place of residence.

Very respectfully, your obedient servant,
W. HOFFMAN,
Colonel Third Infantry, Commissary-General of Prisoners.

OFFICE COMMISSARY-GENERAL OF PRISONERS,
Washington, D. C., March 6, [1863.]

Lieut. Col. W. H. LUDLOW,
Agent for Exchange of Prisoners, Fort Monroe, Va.

COLONEL: Fearing that my letter of the 28th ultimo addressed to New York may not reach you I inclose a copy* herewith.

Since its date I have consulted the Secretary of War in relation to Zarvona and he declines to authorize his exchange. It is also decided not to release the two prisoners in the penitentiary at Albany. The papers already forwarded to you cover this case and justify their detention. If the rebel authorities persist in holding our officers as hostages for these two men such measures will be taken as may be necessary to meet such a state of things.

Very respectfully, your obedient servant,
W. HOFFMAN,
Colonel Third Infantry, Commissary-General of Prisoners.

---

* Omitted here. See p. 304.

CLARKDALE, SAYVILLE, L. I., *March 6, 1863*.
Col. W. HOFFMAN, *Commissary-General of Prisoners*.

COLONEL: I expect to leave here to-morrow and am going to West Point to visit my son, a cadet there. I shall start for Fort Monroe on Tuesday morning. I do not know of any necessity calling me to Washington. Orders have been given for the steamer to be at Washington on Thursday to convey the prisoners to be exchanged to City Point and the officer in charge is directed to report to you. Will you please send to me by him lists of the prisoners with statements opposite each name of all charges against them. Also please return me the list or memoranda I gave you and which was furnished by Mr. Ould with statements opposite each name, of charges, and whether included in the delivery, and if not, why not. I shall also be happy to receive any other information which in your judgment will facilitate the exchange.

I am, very respectfully, your obedient servant,
WM. H. LUDLOW,
Lieutenant-Colonel and Agent for Exchange of Prisoners.

RICHMOND, VA., *March 6, 1863*.
Lieut. Col. WILLIAM H. LUDLOW.

SIR: Your several communications and lists have been received.

First. You send a list of seven U. S. officers who you say are now in the Libby Hospital wounded. All of these officers were sent to you on the 20th ultimo.

Second. You send a list of eighteen U. S. officers headed by Major Withers who you say are now in the Libby Prison. Of these twelve, being captures at Fredericksburg, have already been sent off. The other six were captured in Virginia since December 1, 1862, and several of them since January 1, 1863.

Third. I think you have a right to complain of your informants in the above matters. Not one undelivered is entitled to exchange under our agreements.

Fourth. Surgeon Marvin I send to you; also Lieutenant Bruck (not Brooks) who has just sufficiently recovered. I also send you some 300 non-commissioned officers and privates, being all that we have on hand.

Fifth. You say we have a number of your men who were captured as stragglers from the Army of the Potomac last summer and that some of your officers just released from Richmond have seen and talked with these men. Your informants have again deceived you. I defy them or any human being to point out one name. I have made the most rigid personal scrutiny and have found out that the intimation is grossly unfounded.

Sixth. I must express my profound astonishment at your extraordinary declaration that we have a larger number of officers and men and civilians who have been declared exchanged than you have. 'Tis true we have some officers and you well know how that happened. Their number, however, is not a tithe of yours. I have offered to deliver every one of them and now only await the same act on your part. As to men who have been declared exchanged we have none. If we wished to retain your men why would we send them off when you had no equivalent to offer? The deliveries we have recently made on parole furnish a sufficient contradiction. On the other hand, you captured some 4,000 of our men at Arkansas Post and have made no sort of effort to deliver them. I send you now men that have been captured nearly two months after they were. Moreover at the very time that you dispatched the steamer that carries this letter from Fortress Monroe you had lying round about your headquarters hundreds of men, some of whom have been already exchanged and most of whom, if not all, were embraced in our agreements, and yet with this material around you you sent two prisoners of war and expected to get all we have; which you have done. I appeal to you whether I have not the right to complain of this. What in Heaven's name does it mean? I tell my people frankly what you have agreed to do and say to them I believe it will be accomplished. Upon such a return as you have made at this time I am met with the inquiry everywhere which I have just propounded to you. Will you do me the favor to answer it?

Seventh. You also referred in your communication to the case of an officer who was detained in Atlanta on the charge of passing counterfeit money. Is such an act authorized by the military orders of your Government? If so let us know and we may deliver the accused over to you. If it is not so authorized he has committed an offense against the known laws of the land and is not in the commission of the same shielded by the laws of war or the usages of belligerents. You talk of trying him for such an offense upon complaint by us. How can you? It is no offense against your laws. If it was it could only be tried in the district where the offense was committed. Moreover how could you obtain the attendance of the witnesses even if you proceeded to trial? You would not let them come within your borders. First and foremost, however, comes the question, Do you by virtue of your military orders or in pursuance of the same command your officers and soldiers to counterfeit our money? If so let us know and we will be illuminated. The officer shall have a fair trial. He will be entitled to compulsory process for his witnesses and if the guilty intent is not proved he will be discharged. If innocent of the fraud he is as safe as you are.

Eighth. I have not had time to have an examination made as to your lists of Hartsville, Murfreesborough and Atlanta prisoners. I have to say the same as to those from Western Virginia. As to the former and latter I stand by our agreement.

Ninth. I very much regret that you did not say one word in your several communications in regard to the officers whom you captured before the date of the President's message. Will you exchange them by personal delivery? If so, when and where? I hope it will be done at City Point.

Tenth. I send you herewith a list* of officers and men who are detained in your prisons. Most of them have been already declared exchanged. The information as to almost all of them is of a very reliable kind. Most of the cases have been presented to me since my last interview with you. If it is only half true it presents a case upon which from my respect for you I cannot venture to comment.

Respectfully, your obedient servant,

ROBT. OULD,
Agent of Exchange.

WAR DEPARTMENT, *Washington, March 7, 1863.*
Hon. GIDEON WELLES, *Secretary of the Navy.*

SIR: The Secretary of War directs me to acknowledge the receipt of your letter of the 26th ultimo requesting "the detention of all those

---
* Not found.

persons captured by the naval forces and now chiefly confined in Fort Lafayette," and also "that in any new arrangement for a cartel" the Navy Department "may be allowed to associate an officer or officers to arrange the terms."

In reply the Secretary instructs me to inform you that your communication has been referred to Major-General Hitchcock, commissioner for exchange of prisoners.

Very respectfully, your obedient servant,

P. H. WATSON,
Assistant Secretary of War.

[Indorsement.]

WASHINGTON, *March 13, 1863.*

The subject of the inclosed communication was by me submitted to the Secretary of War with a statement that notwithstanding the proclamation of Jeff. Davis exchanges have been made and are in progress of being made now under the cartel referred to, and I asked whether the cartel shall be considered valid. He answered that the prisoners captured by the Navy now at Fort Lafayette are not to be exchanged.

It is doubtful whether they came under the cartel, not having been captured on board of armed vessels but for the most part arrested in the act of running the blockade.

E. A. HITCHCOCK,
Major-General of Vols., Commissioner for Exchange of Prisoners.

WAR DEPARTMENT, *Washington, March 7, 1863.*
Hon. A. S. WHITE, *Stockwell, Ind.*

SIR: The Secretary of War instructs me to acknowledge the receipt of your letter of the 5th instant covering a communication from Mr. D. H. Cowan, of Louisville, Ky., asking your influence in obtaining the release of his two nephews now prisoners of war at Johnson's Island. In reply I am directed to inform you that the rule of this Department in such cases is that all persons taken in arms against the United States must be held to count according to rank in a general exchange of prisoners, but no person thus counted on arriving at neutral ground will be forced into the rebel lines contrary to his wish provided he is willing to take the oath of allegiance to the Government of the United States.

Very respectfully,

P. H. WATSON,
Assistant Secretary of War.

OFFICE COMMISSARY-GENERAL OF PRISONERS,
Washington, D. C., March 7, 1863.
His Excellency RICHARD YATES,
Governor of the State of Illinois, Springfield, Ill.

DEAR SIR: In reply to your communication of February 26 in relation to the granting of furloughs, transfers and discharges to the paroled prisoners of our Army I have the honor to refer you to General Orders, No. 72, from the War Department, a copy of which I herewith inclose,* and by reference to paragraph III, you will see that no more furloughs will be granted to paroled prisoners, and also that certain camps are specified as places of rendezvous for troops belonging to the several

---

*See Vol. IV, this Series, p. 94.

States. Any deviation from said order can only be granted by the Secretary of War. The rules for the discharge of paroled prisoners are the same as in all other cases, either by expiration of term of service on surgeon's certificate of disability or by order of the Secretary of War. As to prisoners of war belonging to the rebel army instructions have been sent to the commandants of military prisons authorizing them to release all prisoners of war (no officers) who were willing to take the oath of allegiance in good faith. This privilege does not extend to guerrillas or other irregular organizations, who can only be released on application or recommendation of the Governor of the State in which he resides.

Very respectfully, your obedient servant,

W. HOFFMAN,
Colonel Third Infantry, Commissary-General of Prisoners.

OFFICE COMMISSARY-GENERAL OF PRISONERS,
Washington, D. C., March 7, 1863.

Maj. Gen. JOHN E. WOOL,
Commanding Department of the East, New York City.

GENERAL: There are two political prisoners on parole in New York whom it is intended to send South for exchange and I have written letters to them directing them to report to the provost-marshal in this city without delay. Fearing that the letters may not be received I have the honor to ask for your assistance in securing their prompt arrival here. They are S. J. Anderson, paroled before June from Fort Lafayette, and John Innerarity, paroled January 20, 1862. The latter's address is care of O. G. Carter, esq., New York Mutual Insurance Company, 61 William street, New York. These men should come to this city under their parole to report as directed. There are also paroled from Fort Lafayette the following named, viz: F. W. Williams, in Connecticut; Samuel Hoffman, no place given; John Benson, no place; A. A. Jackson, no place; John Loony, no place; Samuel Pike, no place, and Adolphe Mazureau, Boston. I have no means of knowing with what understanding these men were paroled, nor in most cases the place where they may be found nor whether they are subject to exchange. May I request of you the favor to ascertain if it is in your power those particulars for me, and in the cases where an exchange seems to be advisable to send the parties to this city immediately under their parole to report to the provost-marshal. Where there is a doubt about the propriety of an exchange the person might be sent here to have the question decided. Those who belong South only are expected to be exchanged. A steamer will leave this city on the 14th probably for City Point and citizens to be exchanged will be sent in her. It is therefore desirable that those coming from New York should arrive before that day.

I have the honor to be, very respectfully, your obedient servant,

W. HOFFMAN,
Colonel Third Infantry, Commissary-General of Prisoners.

OFFICE COMMISSARY-GENERAL OF PRISONERS,
Washington, D. C., March 7, 1863.

Col. J. C. KELTON,
Asst. Adjt. Gen., Headquarters of the Army, Washington, D. C.

COLONEL: I have the honor to inclose herewith a report presented by Captain Lazelle, Eighth Infantry, of an inspection made by him pursuant to my orders of the condition of Camp Parole in all its details. From this report the General-in-Chief will see that there are many things in the management of the camp that might be changed for the better. This state of affairs has mostly grown out of the great want of proper officers at the camp to command and supervise the wants of so many men. The presence of paroled officers in too many cases is the foundation of much complaint and discontent among the men, for instead of attending to their necessities and encouraging them by their authority and advice to be patient with their condition and to strive by attention to the few duties exacted of them to make themselves as comfortable as possible, they do just the reverse of all these things, exaggerating in every way the unavoidable inconveniences which troops so situated must experience and inducing them to believe that their hardships are too much to bear. Lieutenant-Colonel Sangster, the commanding officer, has been indefatigable in his efforts to perform all the duties required of him, but they are more than one man can attend to. His instructions have been very full and explicit and his faithful efforts to carry them out have been attended with commendable success. On the 15th of December I urged that a guard of 350 men with a proper complement of officers should be permanently established at the camp and an order to that effect was given, but it was only partially carried out and recently it has been entirely set aside by the details of a guard of 90 men daily from a regiment at Annapolis. How useless such a guard is is abundantly shown by the report of Captain Lazelle.

The report also shows the great necessity for the presence permanently at the camp of good officers not on parole, enough to furnish one to each battalion of 500 men. Without these officers it is impossible that the wants of the men can be properly attended to or that anything like respectable discipline can be kept up. There are doubtless many invalid officers or those unfit for field service who could render good service at this camp without taking from the efficiency of the army in the field. I respectfully approve the recommendation of Captain Lazelle that the regiment now at Annapolis which is reduced in numbers be ordered to the camp for guard duty, or that it relieve a regiment of the Army of the Potomac small in numbers for this purpose. The charge made by Sergeant Ewing, the deserter, that he was induced or advised to desert by the commanding officer or any other officer I have no doubt is wholly false, and I have directed that he shall be apprehended and brought to trial for this and the offense of desertion. Colonel Sangster's report* on this matter is herewith inclosed. Whatever can be done to remedy the many defects in the condition of things at the camp will be attended to at once, but nothing like a respectable degree of discipline and good order can be hoped for until a fair complement of efficient and reliable officers are assigned to duty there.

Very respectfully, your obedient servant,

W. HOFFMAN,
Colonel Third Infantry, Commissary-General of Prisoners.

[Indorsement.]

HEADQUARTERS EIGHTH ARMY CORPS,
Baltimore, Md., March 11, 1863.

Respectfully referred to Col. C. A. Waite, U. S. Army, commanding at Annapolis, Md., who will carefully examine the report of the inspecting officer in relation to the condition of affairs at Camp Parole and report as soon as possible his views in regard to carrying out the suggestions

---

* Not found.

made in that report. Colonel Waite will in the meantime make such changes in the disposition of the troops under his command as will furnish the most effective guard he can for that camp and apply such other remedies as may be within his power to remove or remedy the evils complained of.

ROBERT C. SCHENCK,
Major-General, Commanding.

[Inclosure.]

OFFICE COMMISSARY-GENERAL OF PRISONERS,
Washington, D. C., March 3, 1863.

Col. WILLIAM HOFFMAN,
        Commissary-General of Prisoners, Washington.

COLONEL: I have the honor to inform you that in compliance with instructions received from this office on the 27th ultimo I proceeded to Annapolis, Md., to make an inspection of Camp Parole, to inquire into the measures taken for the reception of prisoners upon arrival at Annapolis and to examine into certain accusations against officers relating to their duties while in charge of prisoners, and upon these matters respectfully submit the following report:

Federal prisoners sent to Camp Parole from the South arrive there by water conveyance and in detachments ranging in number from a few hundred in some to several thousand in others. The commanding officer at Camp Parole has informed me that no intimation is received by him of the sending of these prisoners to Camp Parole until the boat touches the wharf at Annapolis with them on board. They generally arrive in a state of extreme destitution, with little or no clothing and that covered with filth and vermin. They are often physically emaci-. ated and suffering from hunger and disease. Of course not only a variety of necessaries are to be provided for them but in most cases the number of prisoners is so large that the arrangements for their immediate comfort must be of an extended character. Upon landing at the wharf they are conducted to what are termed the College Green Barracks. These consist of eight wooden frame buildings each 90 by 20 feet, one story in height, with sides and roof boarded and battened. They are partially provided with bunks and will temporarily accommodate during cold weather 150 men each. At present three of these buildings have been set aside for the reception of prisoners. In rear of them is a cook house well provided with cooking utensils necessary for cooking for 600 men at a time. This cook house, as well as the three buildings above referred to, is under the charge of a non-commissioned officer and a few men, whose duty it is to keep them in a state to receive prisoners. Upon arriving here the prisoners are formed and their number compared with the accompanying rolls. When this is done a list is immediately made of all who are in need of clothing from a personal inspection of each man by an officer, and in almost all cases a complete suit, including overcoat and blanket, is issued to each soldier upon the day of his arrival. Before he is allowed, however, to put on any article of the clothing the men are marched to the river, made to throw away their old clothing and cleanse themselves. They remain two or three days in these barracks until they are provided with clothing and until accommodations are set aside for them at Camp Parole, about two miles from these barracks, where they are then taken. The barracks referred to were built for the use of the Sixty-seventh Regiment Pennsylvania Volunteers, now at Harper's Ferry. They are at present partially occupied by 347 men of the Potomac Home Brigade, and the three buildings above mentioned as used by prisoners are thus occupied by permission of General Schenck, granted recently. While here the prisoners are provided with full rations regularly issued, the cooking of which is done by details from among them, with the exception of bread, which is sent from the Navy-Yard Hospital. They are also well provided with fuel. The arrangements above referred to have all been made within about three weeks, previous to which time the men were upon their arrival taken to Camp Parole as soon as possible and provided for there, and with but a single exception they have been made comparatively comfortable upon the day of arrival at Annapolis. This exception occurred about two weeks since when about 300 men of 700 arriving late in the day and during a storm were for the night placed in a large store-house near the wharf. They were, however, given an abundance of fuel, 1,700 pounds of straw and one blanket each for the night and were immediately provided with rations. It appears that before the arrangement above described was made there was delay (owing to the large number sent to Annapolis and without previous notice) in properly providing for the wants of the prisoners, and of course at an inclement season of the year considerable suffering must have attended such tardiness. But at present the quartermaster's stores, except a few kept for immediate use at the camp store-house, are all stored in convenient buildings near the wharf, and as all commissary stores required by prisoners are drawn from the post commissary the requisitions upon these officers made by the inspecting officer in charge of the prisoners while at the College Green Barracks are immediately filled, the post bakery supplying fresh bread, and consequently unless the number of prisoners arriving is very large there can be no just cause for complaint. It is evident, however, that the present facilities could be greatly extended if the commanding officer at Camp Parole was duly notified of the probable arrival of prisoners. Increased accommodations should also in my opinion be prepared at the College Green Barracks.

Guards.—At present the 347 men of the Potomac Home Brigade occupying them furnish daily to the Navy Yard Hospital a guard of six men and to Camp Parole a daily guard of ninety men, which is the entire and only infantry guard at Camp Parole. I would recommend that instead of marching these ninety men to the camp each day, a distance of two miles from the barracks, all the Potomac Home Brigade now at College Green Barracks be sent to Camp Parole, with the exception of about twenty-four men and non-commissioned officers. These could occupy one of the buildings above referred to and have the care of them all and furnish the daily guard at the general hospital, while it is evident that not only the inconvenience of sending the guard so long a distance to Camp Parole daily would be avoided, but the moral effect of the presence of a larger body of men as a guard at that point, permanently stationed there, would be beneficial both to the prisoners and the guard, for the latter now seem to consider it a special personal favor conferred by them daily upon the camp and its commanding officer by their going there, and they do not perhaps attend so faithfully to their duties as they should and could be better made to do were the guard and its officers immediately under the control of the officer in charge at Camp Parole instead of the officer commanding the post of Annapolis (see Paper A1*), to whom only do they seem to think themselves wholly accountable. Besides this the vacation of the barracks now occupied would leave seven large buildings readily accommodating 1,000 men in all for the reception of the

* Not found.

prisoners immediately upon their arrival. I omitted to mention that there is one company (B) of the Purnell Legion, numbering about eighty men in all. About thirty-five of this number are permanently stationed at Camp Parole, from whom five men as picket guards are daily detached to ride about the country in the vicinity of the camp and the roads leading to it, arresting marauders and stragglers. The remainder of this company (B) are stationed at the town of Annapolis as a provost guard and they occupy as quarters a portion of the College Green Barracks. Yet it is obvious that one of the buildings would readily accommodate not only this guard but that portion of the general hospital guard which might remain at the barracks in case of the removal to Camp Parole of the main body.

I now desire to call your attention to the guards at Camp Parole. Commanding the detail of ninety men above mentioned as daily furnished are two officers, one acting as officer of the day at the camp and the other as officer of the guard. There are thirty infantry posts about the camp at which are nominally thirty sentinels, but great carelessness prevails among them while on post and their duty is very indifferently performed and very often totally neglected. This is illustrated by the inmates of the camp constantly passing and repassing their posts in every direction for fuel to the forests and other purposes, and by the nuisances constantly committed everywhere outside the immediate camp limits by the prisoners in full view of the sentinels and without molestation by them. I invite your attention to accompanying papers* marked A, (2) (3) (4), from which it will be seen that if the orders given had been strictly enforced but little complaint could be justly made of the manner of performing the guard duty. But the guard is inefficient and not large enough to perform in a proper manner the duties required for even the present strength of the camp, which at times contains a far greater number of prisoners. An increase of the number of sentinels to at least fifty, with a permanent guard of at least 400 men stationed at the camp, properly officered and under efficient discipline, would be necessary for the carrying out of the camp regulations even in a tolerable manner. To establish this I will refer to some of the daily practices at the camp by the prisoners—the constant habit of defecating all about the immediate vicinity; the constant passing of sentinel's posts whenever convenient; the stopping of the fuel wagons by the soldiers of one part of the camp when the fuel is designed for another part; the interference by soldiers with the delivery of the particular quantity of fuel designed for any company, regardless of the teamster of the cavalry patrol accompanying the team, they not unfrequently tossing the black teamster in a blanket if he remonstrates; the destruction of wooden buildings by the soldiers for the purpose of using the boards whenever convenient; the seizing of the tents in camp which may be vacated by exchanged men leaving and doubling the canvas of their own by placing these tents over those occupied, and many other irregularities inconsistent with the first principles of order or discipline.

Discipline.—With regard to the general discipline of the camp I have to inform you that it is extremely slack as the above facts will illustrate. There are no parades, except for morning and evening roll-calls. These are company parades and for the purpose of reporting absentees. It will be seen from the paper* marked B (1) that the whole camp is divided into six battalions, each embracing certain State's troops. One

---

* Not found.

of these battalions, the Fourth, embracing the Western troops is composed of about 3,000 men, divided into thirty-three companies and the whole under the charge of Captain Miller, who is the only commissioned officer with the whole battalion; and the company organization is a merely temporary matter, with non-commissioned officers acting as such for the time they are at the camp, and under these circumstances it could not be expected that the same interest could be manifested in the company's welfare, with an organization composed of men of various States and only for a temporary purpose, as under other circumstances. Of the eleven paroled officers at Camp Parole but four are convalescents, so as to be reported for duty, and consequently two of the battalions are without any commissioned officer at all, and Colonel Sangster has but two permanent assistant officers, his major and adjutant, besides these four, in the whole camp of nearly 6,000 men, with the exception of the officer in command of the portion of the cavalry stationed at the camp. The disposition generally manifested by the paroled officers is to avoid duty if possible rather than attend to the wants of their men, and the spirit exhibited seems to be a prominent desire to complain and encourage discontent among the men rather than to remedy their discomforts. The commanding officer at Camp Parole represents that he has great difficulty in getting them to perform duty necessary for the simple care of the paroled men, and in this connection I respectfully call your attention to the inclosed paper* marked B (2), in which by an order it is attempted to enforce the performance of certain duties. It is evident that proper attention cannot be given to the wants of men by officers of this disposition and by non-commissioned officers who regard their appointment as only temporary and which they may consider as increasing their duty at a time when so much desire is manifested to avoid duty under the restrictions of their paroles. It is in consequence of this characteristic of the paroled officers and the heterogeneous and temporary character of the organization of the men from various States, battalions and companies that I respectfully recommend that at least one energetic and efficient officer be permanently detailed at Camp Parole to take constant charge of every 500 men of which each battalion may be composed, and that each battalion should be divided into companies of 100 men each, to be under the control of an intelligent and competent non-commissioned officer permanently stationed at Camp Parole. I shall again refer to what I believe to be the advantage of this latter provision under the matters of supplies and records. In this manner the duties of the officers in charge of the various battalions could be reduced to a system and the comfort of the men immediately attended to through non-commissioned officers interested in the requirements of their positions. At present one paroled officer having the Fourth Battalion in charge is alone in command of the 2,900 men of whom it is composed and of course cannot properly attend to all its duties, while some other battalions of a few hundred men have also one officer or none at all. The total number of men at the camp will be seen from the morning report* inclosed, marked B (3).

Records.—Upon the arrival of prisoners at Camp Parole the rolls of prisoners received are copied upon other sheets of the form commonly used for Confederate prisoners of war, giving the name, rank, regiment, company, where and when captured, where and when released and explanatory data. Upon the departure of detachments of prisoners quadruplicate rolls are made out. One copy is given to the officers

---

* Not found.

sent with them, one sent to the officer in command receiving the prisoners, one retained and one copy sent to this office. An order book is kept, a letter book and an index book, but no guard report book and no morning report book. A book of accounts of the savings and expenditures from the general camp fund is also kept. It would appear that as each battalion company is often composed of men from several States, and as no record of men is kept except on rolls, a complete history of the man so far as connected with his stay at camp would be seen better by arranging in the form of a book the necessary data. This has been in my opinion very well done by Colonel Sangster in the inclosed form,* marked C (1). He has had six of these books printed, one of which is designed for each battalion organization. From these if properly kept much labor will be systematized and much avoided in making up the various reports and returns sent from the adjutant's office at the camp. At present all that is known of the inmates of the camp is gotten from the rolls, and the names on returns of men sent away show those left on the original rolls, but the confusion and labor and liability to mistakes, losses of rolls, &c., which might result from this method are very obvious. At present or up to the time of the arrival of these books no company or battalion records have been kept of the men of the companies beyond the morning report gotten from the sergeant's roll and its regular morning roll-call, and it would seem from the limited assistance permanently at Camp Parole, from the large number of men arriving and departing and the dispatch often necessary to be used in sending them away, that much inaccuracy must have been at times from want of books unavoidable. I inclose a copy* of charges against deserters for expenses incurred in their apprehension, always sent by Colonel Sangster to the commanding officer to whom the exchanged prisoners are sent. It is marked C (2).

Supplies.—All commissary stores are drawn from the post commissary at Annapolis on a consolidated ten-days' return. They are issued in bulk, hauled to Camp Parole, where the acting assistant commissary issues every three days to the sergeants in charge of the various battalion companies, who in turn divide the stores received among the messes of the company, composed of numbers varying from eight to fifteen in each mess. The bread is all baked at the post and issued fresh, eighteen ounces to each ration. The provision returns are sent in the usual manner from the companies consolidated into battalion returns and the post commissary is held accountable for the amount of provisions which ought to be on hand at any time, as would appear from the number of men borne on the morning report. I inclose for your inspection copy* of an abstract of three days' issues to show the form, the quantity and the articles issued and to whom issued, marked D (1). D (2) is a schedule* showing the quantity of each article now issued in fifty rations and the amount in each article reserved and credited. D (3) is a statement* of the amount saved in seven days. After diligent inquiry among many men and non-commissioned officers I am unable to find any complaint either of the quality or quantity of the food, with the exception of the single article of bread. Some few men complain that the amount is not sufficient, but this deficiency is by no means generally felt. I personally weighed several average loaves of bread and found them to be fully eighteen ounces. I am satisfied that if care and economy were at all exercised in preparing the food the present ration would be found abundant. But after the sergeant

* Not found.

has subdivided the rations as above indicated each mess cooks the rations allotted in such manner as is thought best, and this embraces many methods. There are but four Farmer's boilers in use in the entire camp so far as I could learn by personal inspection, and no proper shelter is constructed for the use of these. There is much complaint among the men about a want of cooking utensils and such common furniture as a tin plate, cup, knife and fork, and this complaint is well founded in very many instances. As well illustrating this I refer you to paper* marked D (4) inclosed and the accompanying letter.* This is a list of the camp and garrison equipage and cooking utensils now in possession of the Fourth Battalion. I desire to call your attention to the manner in which these articles are absorbed by some of the companies while others have none at all of particular articles. The Fourth Battalion it will be observed numbers nearly 3,000 men, divided into thirty-three companies and but one officer with them all. One reason of the unequal distribution of the articles referred to is that on the departure of troops the articles of camp furniture left behind in their tents are immediately seized upon by the companies remaining instead of being turned in to the quartermaster's department and reissued proportionally to the wants of the troops remaining. The quartermaster has not assistance enough, nor are there permanently stationed officers enough in camp to attend to this matter. And it would appear that the paroled officers leaving with the troops under the present arrangements do not interest themselves sufficiently to see that it is done. As a consequence of this neglect the quartermaster at the camp has informed me that on the departure of any considerable number of troops he goes to the tents vacated by them with a wagon and picks up whatever he can. Generally this is such property as has not been appropriated by the soldiers remaining. The paper* marked D (4) will show some facts relating to this matter. It will be seen that much of this irregularity and present neglect of the paroled officers and non-commissioned officers placed temporarily in charge of the troops would be avoided by having at least one commissioned officer to each 500 men and one non-commissioned officer to each company of 100 men permanently stationed at the camp, not only to attend to the wants of the men and to see that the furniture is properly provided, distributed and cared for but to attend to the records of the various battalions, which have been greatly neglected from a want of proper officers. · I desire to call your attention to the inner page of the paper* marked D (4). These are several requisitions for camp and garrison equipage and clothing which have been recently submitted but the articles never have been issued. The men have been and are greatly complaining for want of these articles and the officer (Captain Miller) has informed me that his requisitions are not honored and that he cannot get the articles. The quartermaster at the camp (Captain Kiersted) informs me that the requisitions were returned to Captain Miller to be put in proper form and that Captain Miller did not do this and that consequently the articles were not issued. In the meantime the soldiers are without these necessaries, many of them, while others have an abundance as will be seen from the list* D (4). There seems to exist considerable unpleasant feeling in the matter and I do not think that in all cases the necessary care is taken by the officers at the headquarters of the camp to avoid this and to consult only the true interests of the service. The commanding officer, Colonel Sangster, does everything in his power but he lacks experience, and as he is not properly assisted there is but little method in the labor compared to what there should be.

---

* Not found.

Quartermaster's supplies.—The quartermaster at Camp Parole informed me that he had on hand about 1,500 suits of all articles of clothing except dress coats. He states that since November 1 the clothing has been received on requisitions through this office and that the delay has been seldom over ten days from the sending of the estimate until the arrival of the clothing, with the exception of the last estimate, sent about the 1st of February ultimo, for 2,000 overcoats and dress coats and 500 mess pans, [and] camp-kettles. These have not been received. He thinks that the supply kept on hand is larger than would be necessary if it were possible to be informed of the probable arrival of prisoners in advance. None of the prisoners at present so far as I could learn complain of the want of clothing except the article of dress coats, and my inquiries were much extended among them. I respectfully call your attention to the letter* marked E (1) from the quartermaster. The deficiency in camp and garrison equipage and cooking and table furniture arises partially as has been shown from the unequal distribution of these articles in the companies of the camp, many companies having far more than the regulation allowance while many men among the Illinois and other Western troops are entirely unprovided for, some of them stating to me that they were compelled to eat with their fingers, others to borrow cooking utensils and eight or ten to eat from a single mess pan with wooden spoons and forks of their own manufacture, and some others are without a cup to drink from. The allowance of wood regularly hauled into the camp and delivered is that authorized by the regulations. But as before mentioned the constant and forcible interference with the wagons delivering the fuel by the prisoners prevents any proper distribution of it and while many companies have a superabundance others are greatly deficient and are compelled to resort to the forest daily for a supply. This should be remedied by a strong mounted patrol to each wagon instead of seeking to remedy the matter by delivering all the fuel at the headquarters of each battalion (as is now sought to be done), since it is taken away by the men who are the most active—at least the greater share of it. The abstract* marked E (2) will show the amount of fuel delivered. The fuel used is all hauled from the wharf in Annapolis to the camp by the Government wagons and costs at the wharf $5.25 per cord. Ten wagons are now employed constantly for this purpose.

Ordnance stores are constantly kept on hand, together with such garrison equipage as is necessary to furnish the soldier with a complete outfit on leaving Camp Parole to return to duty. The rifle regularly issued is of the caliber .58. Abstracts are made in triplicate on the departure of troops, one for the officer in charge of the troops, one for the commanding officer to whom the troops are sent and one for the officer at Camp Parole. Duplicate invoices are also sent to the commanding officer of the companies to which the troops belong.

Quarters.—The inclosed statement,* marked F (1), will show the number and kind of tents now used in the camp, also the buildings and huts furnished and unfurnished, occupied and unoccupied, in the camp and the purpose for which the buildings are used. About two-thirds of the tents in the camp are floored and nearly all the huts are so. The Sibley tents, though ordinarily capable of accommodating eighteen men, do not generally contain over eight or ten at the camp, they are so cut down, many of them, at the bottom from the decay of the canvas, while others are much contracted by the manner of erecting them, and from these causes and from being banked up they are much contracted, and

---

* Not found.

the same remarks will generally apply to the other tents of the camp. The small huts are extremely low and very badly constructed and in the summer season would be of little use. Larger log buildings are in process of construction, but the labor on them has been delayed, partially from a want of lumber. The roofs of the log buildings are covered with boards battened at the joints. Some of them are yet unfinished though occupied. Generally speaking the soldiers seem comfortably provided with quarters for the present with the exception of the Fourth Battalion of 3,000 men, which is composed of Western troops. Among these men there is much complaint and in many instances from their own account and from what I could learn it is not without foundation. Upon arriving at Camp Parole some of them for a week or more occupied the log frames constructed for huts without roofs, others lived in crowded tents or others occupied huts, and as before stated there was not always fuel sufficient. This induced some few of them to go to the forest with their blankets and construct for themselves shelters, a few others constructed pits covered with boughs in which they lived. I sent a sergeant to inspect the latter and he reported nine men living inside them outside of camp limits. I saw one man that told me he was living with several others in the woods, and from all I was able to find out I should estimate that about twelve or fifteen were living in the woods, besides those living in pits with temporary shelters, returning to camp only when they required provisions. These facts were unknown to the commanding officer until communicated by me, when he sent a mounted patrol to bring them all in, but the officer did not succeed in finding them. His report is in paper* marked F (2). Six privies enumerated. I saw but one privy for the men in the whole camp and that badly constructed, with the vault filled to the top. I was told that the others had been pulled down by the soldiers, they desiring to use the lumber for their quarters. I respectfully recommend the immediate construction of suitable privies of logs with board coverings and that the soldiers be made to use them instead of creating what would in warm weather be an intolerable nuisance about camp in all directions. Also the immediate construction of kitchens for 100 men, each of logs, and to each kitchen, if a Farmer's boiler were supplied, great economy would appear both in fuel and rations. From the inclosed estimate,* marked F (3), it will be seen that the construction of barracks of logs of certain dimensions is cheaper than the construction of similar barracks of frame and boards, and I think that it would be found that the construction of log quarters for the whole camp would be cheaper if used for eighteen months than the use of tents for a similar period, for the reason that the destruction of tents by troops here is very great, and they sometimes upon the leaving of troops take the canvas of the vacated tents and double it over those used by themselves. Of course this is done without the consent of the quartermaster, who himself informed me of this practice, though I found no tents with the canvas thus doubled.

Police.—The police of the camp is far from being good nor is the rubbish sufficiently far removed from the camp vicinity. But with the limited guard and officers now at the camp it is impossible this should be efficiently done. Many of the company grounds are in extremely bad condition.

Sutler.—The sutler's store is more a refreshment saloon than sutler's store, though a tolerable assortment of necessary articles is kept.

---

* Not found.

Oysters in every style and a species of lager beer are sold without restriction. I cannot say whether the beer is intoxicating or not, but was told by the commanding officer that the use of it was recommended by the surgeon to aid in physically recruiting the system of the soldiers. The sutler does not credit soldiers so he informed me, nor is he taxed for the privilege of sutlering at the post. The commanding officer has informed me, however, that the sutler gives tobacco and beer and other small articles to the soldiers when they are destitute and that he has presented many delicacies and necessaries to soldiers in the hospital. The hospital of the camp is in excellent condition, being well supplied with every necessary for the sick, with medicine, bedding and material. The kitchen is in good condition and is well and abundantly provided with cooking utensils and table furniture. A wash house is in course of construction for the use at the hospital.

I inclose a schedule* of the number of patients and the general types of diseases and the number of deaths occurring within a specific period, marked G. There are three large hospital tents situated in the hospital camp, which are very badly located, being in a depression of ground between two slopes and of course receiving the absorbed moisture from the slopes (even if there is no surface water) in the vicinity of their floors. I recommended their removal to a more favorable locality, which can be readily done, as there is good ground in close proximity. The guard-house and prison room are sufficient under the present arrangement and in good order. The punishment of offenders is confinement at the guard-house and a bread and water diet. Sometimes the men are sent to the jail at Annapolis by the commanding officer for confinement temporarily. I respectfully recommend the discontinuance of this practice, since it does not seem proper that a soldier without a felon's guilt should share his quarters, and that the proper guard-house prisons be constructed at the camp. The water at the camp is abundant and good. It is supplied by wells of about fifteen or twenty feet in depth.

Camp fund.—For a complete statement of all matters of savings and expenditures at the camp from the fund I refer you to the general abstract* marked H (1); to the abstract* of purchases marked H (2); to the copies of drafts* marked H (3); to the abstract* of employés marked H (4), and to the explanatory letter* of Colonel Sangster marked H (5).

I received from you instructions to inquire into the case of Sergt. G. W. Ewing, of Company G, Third Pennsylvania Cavalry. I return the several letters* given me and the letter* of Colonel Sangster in relation to the matter, together with the names of the various officers of the Third Pennsylvania Cavalry to whom the sergeant refers. The letter* is marked K. In reference to soldiers ever having received any encouragement from their officers to desert after diligent inquiry among soldiers and non-commissioned officers I am prepared to say that I believe it to be entirely without foundation, as I was unable to learn that there had ever been such an expression of encouragement used toward any soldier.

With reference to the letter of the adjutant-general of the State of Illinois which reports in general terms complaints made by soldiers from that State at Camp Parole I believe that I have already given such facts in relation to the matter as will show how far they are based upon truth. I reinclose the letter* to you. I also submit for your consideration the application of J. E. Cassel, first lieutenant of the

---

* Not found.

Seventy-seventh Regiment Pennsylvania Volunteers, to be permanently detailed as the acting assistant commissary at Camp Parole. It is marked L. In general terms it would be very desirable in my opinion if the guards at Camp Parole were permanently stationed there and much increased, and a sufficient number of officers permanently detailed for duty at the camp to render all necessary assistance; if the quarters were all composed of large buildings of logs both for economy and comfort at all seasons; if privies and kitchens were built as already indicated; if the guard-house was enlarged; if mounted patrols attended and protected the proper distribution of supplies; if the quarters of the Western troops were more enlarged and rendered more comfortable; if a change was made in the location of a portion of the hospital quarters, and if drills when the weather should permit and stricter discipline were introduced into every branch of duty at the camp, and if more complete records were kept at the headquarters of each battalion of the men composing it. Camp Parole is located about two miles from the town of Annapolis and the road leading to it is extremely bad at this season of the year. At present with about 6,000 men in camp sixteen wagons are constantly employed in hauling supplies to it.

Generally all supplies come to Camp Parole by way of Baltimore by rail except the wood, which is hauled to the camp from the city. If the whole camp were moved to near the railroad, which could be readily done as it is but about three-quarters of a mile from it, all supplies could be delivered immediately at the camp, thus avoiding the labor and transportation which though at present large (resulting from the delivery of all stores first at the town) must be greatly increased when the number of troops at Camp Parole is greater. A favorable site could be readily found. I am satisfied and believe that the removal of the camp would be less expensive than the cost of transportation for one year under the present circumstances. The ground immediately outside the present camp is so covered with accumulations of rubbish and filth and the sites of old tents and huts as to have rendered it unfit for any considerable expansion of the camp in any direction. If, however, it should not be deemed expedient to remove the camp I respectfully recommend an entire change in the present location of the quarters of that portion of the camp occupying the low ground to the sandy slopes which in my opinion the direction of the quarters should follow for the purpose of securing immediate drainage, which at present is very imperfect though the nature of the soil is favorable to the rapid absorption of moisture. The compactness or symmetry of the camp would not by this measure materially differ from that which it now has, and if it is designed to continue the building of the log quarters or to make the camp bear anything of a permanent character this mode of location is in my opinion very essential.

In conclusion I have to add that if my report exhibits the spirit of constant criticism, without the excuses which unquestionably might be justly offered by the commanding officer and the officers permanently detailed at Camp Parole for many irregularities, I can only say that I have simply attempted to detail facts, without comments more than were explanatory.

With the highest respect, I am, colonel, your obedient servant,

H. M. LAZELLE,
Captain, Assistant to Commissary-General of Prisoners.

OFFICE COMMISSARY-GENERAL OF PRISONERS,
Washington, D. C., March 7, 1863.

Mrs. MARGARET A. RUCKER, *Marietta, Ohio.*

MADAM: Your letter of the 15th ultimo to His Excellency the President and that of the 1st instant to the Secretary of War desiring that measures may be taken for the release of your husband, W. P. Rucker, from the dungeons of Richmond have been referred to me and I hasten to inform you that everything that is possible is being done by the Government to secure his release. His case has been brought to the notice of the rebel authorities and his immediate release demanded. The agent for the exchange of prisoners will meet the agent from Richmond when an answer to this demand is expected. I will forward your letters to Lieutenant-Colonel Ludlow, agent for the exchange of prisoners, that he may be fully acquainted with all the circumstances of the case and I hope you will not be disappointed in soon having your husband sent to you.

Very respectfully, your obedient servant,

W. HOFFMAN,
Colonel Third Infantry, Commissary-General of Prisoners.

OFFICE COMMISSARY-GENERAL OF PRISONERS,
Washington, D. C., March 7, 1863.

Lieut. Col. F. A. DICK,
Provost-Marshal-General, Saint Louis, Mo.

COLONEL: In reply to your communication of March 2, 1862, I am directed by the commissary-general of prisoners to say that as you appear to misapprehend the provisions of the cartel for the exchange of prisoners you are referred to article 7 of the cartel, where you will see that certain points are specified where prisoners may be sent for exchange without regard to time. As soon as there is a way open they will probably be ordered to be sent to some point on the Mississippi for exchange or parole, or otherwise be held to be sent to City Point.

Very respectfully, your obedient servant,

W. T. HARTZ,
Captain and Assistant Adjutant-General.

HEADQUARTERS OF THE ARMY,
Washington, D. C., March 8, 1863.

Col. W. HOFFMAN, *Commissary-General of Prisoners.*

COLONEL: The report upon the camp of paroled prisoners at Annapolis submitted by you has been examined by the General-in-Chief and he wishes you to designate such officers as you can recommend and who are subject for detail on duty at that camp. The papers have been referred to General Schenck for such remedies as he may be able to apply. The necessary orders have been issued in regard to Captain Hendrickson at Alton Prison, Ill.

Respectfully, &c.,

J. C. KELTON,
Assistant Adjutant-General.

GENERAL ORDERS, }   HDQRS. DEPT. OF THE CUMBERLAND,
      No. 43.   }   *Murfreesborough, Tenn., March 8, 1863.*

I. The general commanding finds within his lines many helpless and suffering families whose natural protectors and supporters are in arms against us. These people need food, clothing and protection which it is neither our duty nor in our power adequately to provide. Many others whose sympathies and connections are such as to surmount all the obligations that arise from their permission to remain within our lines, forbidding them to communicate with the enemy or act as spies against us. The residence of these persons within our lines not only continually endangers us but their own integrity and personal safety. It is therefore ordered that:

1. All those whose natural supporters are in the rebel service, and
2. All whose sympathies and connections are such that they cannot give the assurance that they will conduct themselves as peaceable citizens shall hold themselves in readiness to go south of our lines within ten days from the date of notice.

II. They will be permitted to take with them all their personal effects not contraband of war. They will apply to the nearest provost-marshal or commanding officer for the requisite passes and will be required to give assurance that they have taken no contraband of war.

III. Persons thus going South who shall thereafter enter our lines without permission will be regarded and treated as spies.

IV. All who acknowledge their obligations as citizens of the United States; all who give by the non-combatant's oath and bond or in any other satisfactory manner the requisite assurance that they will behave themselves as peaceable citizens may remain at home, following their usual avocations, subject to military orders and regulations

By command of Major-General Rosecrans:

                          C. GODDARD,
                    Assistant Adjutant-General.

GENERAL ORDERS, }   HEADQUARTERS MIDDLE DEPARTMENT,
      No. 15.   }   *Baltimore, Md., March 8, 1863.*

Whereas, by the cartel for the exchange of prisoners agreed upon by Commissioners Maj. Gen. John A. Dix on the part of the United States and Maj. Gen. D. H. Hill on the part of the so called Confederate States, dated Haxall's Landing, on James River, July 22, 1862, and published by the War Department in General Orders, No. 142, September 25, 1862, the following terms and stipulations among other things were agreed upon and determined:

1. It is provided by Article 4 that all prisoners then held and all those thereafter taken will be transported to the points mutually agreed upon at the expense of the capturing party.
2. Article 6 provides that the stipulations and provisions of the cartel shall be of binding obligation during the continuance of the war.
3. Article 7 (supplementary articles) provides that all prisoners then held or thereafter captured by either party shall be sent to A. M. Aiken's, below Dutch Gap, on the James River, Va., or to Vicksburg, on the Mississippi River, in the State of Mississippi, and there exchanged or paroled until such exchange can be effected, or at such other place as may be hereafter mutually agreed upon by the commanding generals of opposing armies.

And whereas, in violation of these stipulations and provisions certain of the rebel forces and also bands of armed marauders and guerrilla parties, all professing to act under and by the authority of the so-called Confederate States, have without due notice or agreement and often without furnishing any list or evidence of their capture and parole released and set free certain officers and men belonging to this army corps, particularly in the Shenandoah Valley, at such time and place as best suited their own convenience, thus avoiding the expense and trouble of delivering them according to the provisions of the cartel and the danger of their recapture, thereby forfeiting their right to claim an exchange and releasing by their own act the persons so captured and set free:

It is ordered, That all officers and men so released or who may here-after in such manner be released and who have not been regularly exchanged will be returned to duty.

And it is further ordered, That all officers and men of this command who have in this manner been released and are now absent from their respective posts, regiments or companies shall return to duty with their respective commands on or before the 1st day of April next or be entered on the rolls and considered as deserters and treated accordingly.

By command of Major-General Schenck:

WM. H. CHESEBROUGH,
Lieutenant-Colonel and Assistant Adjutant-General.

FORT MONROE, *March 9, 1863.*

Hon. E. M. STANTON, *Secretary of War:*

Colonel Ludlow informed me that the political prisoners, about 500 in number, would be ready at Washington on the 12th. Shall I send up Captain Mulford with the State of Maine, the flag-of-truce boat, to-morrow? She is ready now. Will you direct Colonel Hoffman to have complete lists of the prisoners prepared? There are two or three at Fort Norfolk whom I wish to send.

JOHN A. DIX,
Major-General.

OFFICE PROVOST-MARSHAL-GENERAL,
Wheeling, March 9, 1863.

Col. W. HOFFMAN, *Commissary-General of Prisoners.*

SIR: I have to apologize for an unintentional error in my late report of the female prisoner Mary Jane Prater. I set her down as one, but it now appears she is two. The jailer informs me that she has been *enceinte* about five months. This complicates the matter somewhat. I presume I will soon receive final instructions from you concerning this one and Marian McKenzie, both arrested on same charge, wearing soldiers' apparel and frequenting our camps in that garb.

Very respectfully,

JOS. DARR, JR.,
Major and Provost-Marshal-General.

HDQRS. VOLUNTEER RECRUITING SERVICE FOR VIRGINIA,
Wheeling, Va., March 9, 1863.

Col. W. HOFFMAN,
Commissary-General of Prisoners, Washington, D. C.

SIR: General Orders, No. 46, War Department, Adjutant-General's Office, 20th February, 1863, require that reports be made to superintendents of volunteer recruiting service in regard to the collection of paroled prisoners and that superintendents make like reports to you,

&c. In relation to the above order I have the honor to report that there are no mustering or disbursing officers in Western Virginia except myself and only one recruiting officer, who is stationed in this city, and there will be no reports for me to consolidate. The duties prescribed in General Orders, Nos. 72 and 191, of series of 1862, have been executed by Maj. Joseph Darr, jr., major First [West] Virginia Cavalry and provost-marshal of Virginia. This officer is stationed in Wheeling and he devoted his whole time to this and similar subjects which he seems to have reduced to a system. He is in correspondence with all regimental and post commanders and in the collection of deserters and stragglers has been very active and energetic. I have had a conversation with him in relation to the subject and I recommend that the present system be continued. He informs me that he has made regular reports to you and if you so direct he will hereafter make these reports through me.

Please let me know what your wishes are.

Very respectfully, your obedient servant,

B. H. HILL,
Major Second Artillery, Supt. Volunteer Recruiting Service.

WASHINGTON, *March 10, 1863.*

Maj. Gen. J. A. DIX, *Commanding:*

The political prisoners will not be ready to leave before Saturday, the 14th. Please let the steamer arrive here on the 12th.

W. HOFFMAN,
Commissary-General of Prisoners.

BENTON BARRACKS, *March 10, 1863.*

Maj. H. Z. CURTIS, *Assistant Adjutant-General:*

The following telegram just received I have the honor to transmit for your information:

About 1,000 paroled prisoners are ordered from Annapolis to Benton Barracks.

W. HOFFMAN,
Commissary-General of Prisoners.

B. L. E. BONNEVILLE,
Colonel, U. S. Army, Commanding.

LOUISVILLE, KY., *March 10, 1863.*

Col. WILLIAM HOFFMAN:

We received some time since orders to send no prisoners of war to City Point till further orders. Have now on hand 300 privates. Colonel Carrington telegraphs they cannot be received at Camp Morton, Ind. What shall we do?

STEPHEN E. JONES,
Captain and Aide-de-Camp.

OFFICE COMMISSARY-GENERAL OF PRISONERS,
Washington, D. C., March 10, 1863.

Col. JESSE HILDEBRAND,
Commanding Military Prison, Alton, Ill.

COLONEL: I am directed by the commissary-general of prisoners to say in answer to communication from H. A. Galloway that instructions have been sent to the various commandants of the military prisons authorizing them to release all Confederate prisoners of war not officers who were willing to take the oath of allegiance in good faith. This privilege does not extend to guerrillas or other irregular organizations who can only be released upon the recommendation of the Governor of the State in which they reside. Application from George W. Stanfill has been returned with directions to furnish more satisfactory evidence that he has not been an officer in the rebel service. Also an application from Capt. W. H. Brown and which has been returned with the request to furnish more satisfactory evidence of the fact of his having resigned from the Confederate service previous to his capture. I also return application from Capt. J. K. P. Randolph. Rebel officers cannot be released upon taking the oath of allegiance.

Very respectfully, your obedient servant,

W. T. HARTZ,
Captain and Assistant Adjutant-General.

MURFREESBOROUGH, *March 11, 1863.*

Col. J. C. KELTON:

I telegraphed the General-in-Chief the date and character of the notification given to General Bragg—that I would receive no more paroled prisoners except in accordance with the terms of the cartel—and requested his decision whether or not after this full and fair notification I shall refrain from carrying into effect my General Orders, No. 3, current series, as to paroled prisoners delivered by turning them loose in defiance of notice and the provisions of the cartel. Please say to him that desertions consequent in the suspense of this question induces me to ask decision as early as practicable and that if possible it may not disturb the past policy which works well, as does also the order against those wearing our uniform.

W. S. ROSECRANS,
Major-General.

HEADQUARTERS DEPARTMENT OF THE OHIO,
Cincinnati, March 11, 1863.

Col. WILLIAM HOFFMAN,
Commissary-General of Prisoners, Washington, D. C.

COLONEL: I have the honor to inclose a letter from Captain Webber, commandant of prisons at Camp Chase, in which he states that he has some fifty officers and enlisted men prisoners of war who come under paragraphs 6 and 7 of General Orders, No. 10, current series, and calling upon me by your order to indicate the route by which they shall be forwarded through our lines. I presume the captain has misinterpreted your instructions as General Orders, No. 10, relate exclusively to our own men. I therefore refer the matter to you before proceeding further. I would remark that General Grant, having given orders that no more prisoners be sent to Vicksburg, and as General Rosecrans sends his prisoners in this direction instead of through his lines, I know of no point to which rebel prisoners can be sent for exchange except City Point.

Very respectfully, your obedient servant,

H. G. WRIGHT,
Major-General, Commanding.

[Inclosure.]

HEADQUARTERS COMMANDANT OF PRISONS,
Camp Chase, Ohio, March 7, 1863.

Major-General WRIGHT,
Commanding Department of the Ohio, Cincinnati.

GENERAL: I am directed by the commissary-general of prisoners to report to you for exchange all prisoners of war in my custody coming under General Orders, No. 10, War Department, current series, to be sent beyond our lines at the earliest opportunity, and to ask you when and by what route they can be forwarded. I respectfully report that I have some fifty prisoners, officers and enlisted men, who come under paragraphs 6 and 7 of General Orders, No. 10, and they can be forwarded at a day's notice to whatever point you may designate.

I am, general, very respectfully, your obedient servant,
E. L. WEBBER,
Captain, Commanding Prisons.

OFFICE COMMISSARY-GENERAL OF PRISONERS,
Washington, D. C., March 11, 1863.

Hon. F. H. PEIRPOINT,
Governor of Virginia, Wheeling, Va.

SIR: Your letter of the 5th instant is received, and in reply I have the honor to inform you that arrangements have been made for the departure from this city on Saturday next of a steamer with the political prisoners who are to be exchanged for citizens now held by the rebels at Richmond or elsewhere. The collecting together of those who are to be sent South has been attended with unavoidable delay, but I hope it will be but a few days now before all Union men who have suffered so much at the hands of the rebels will be restored to their friends. Doctor Hughes was paroled for thirty days by order of the Secretary of War to proceed to Richmond and effect the exchange of Samuel A. Pancoast for himself, but as yet I have not heard that he has either effected the exchange or returned himself.

I have the honor to be, very respectfully, your obedient servant,
W. HOFFMAN,
Colonel Third Infantry, Commissary-General of Prisoners.

OFFICE COMMISSARY-GENERAL OF PRISONERS,
Chicago, Ill., March 11, 1863.

Col. WILLIAM HOFFMAN,
Commissary-General of Prisoners, Washington, D. C.

COLONEL: I find the condition of the prisoners at Camp Douglas much improved. The barracks have all been repaired. The fence which was partly torn down by the paroled men has been reconstructed. The barracks are not crowded and are comfortably heated. Each one is provided with a comfortable bunk, and the prisoners are in every way as comfortably provided for as our own troops. The camp is under the command of Brig. Gen. Jacob Ammen, U. S. volunteers, who has given every care and attention to the troops and prisoners under his charge. He has confined himself strictly to your instructions and they are rigidly enforced. I find the camp in good police. The continuous rainy weather together with the low location of the camp have been quite uncomfortable. A system of drainage has been established which when completed promises the best results. The labor is performed by the prisoners themselves.

The guard of the prisoners is composed of the Sixty-third and One hundred and fourth Illinois and Ninth Vermont Infantry with a battery of the Illinois artillery, making a total of 1,737 enlisted men present for duty. The commissary department is under the charge of Capt. C. C. Pomeroy, acting assistant commissary of subsistence and mustering and disbursing officer at Chicago. This department is conducted with economy and to the entire satisfaction of all interested. The rations were found to be good, wholesome and of the first quality. The reduced ration is issued in accordance with your instructions. Captain Pomeroy resides in Chicago and his duties as mustering officer require a large share of his attention. He employs an agent who remains constantly at the camp. The number of troops and prisoners at Camp Douglas would warrant and require that an officer of the commissary department should be stationed there. The rations are furnished by contract at a cost of $14.43 per 100 rations; William F. Tucker, of Chicago, contractor. The quartermaster's department is under the charge of Capt. J. A. Potter, assistant quartermaster at Chicago, having for his assistants Capts. J. P. Rutherford and Charles Goodman, assistant quartermasters, U. S. volunteers, at the camp. The affairs of the quartermaster's department are properly and economically administered. There is no necessity for two quartermasters at this camp and I respectfully recommend that Capt. J. P. Rutherford be relieved. Captain Rutherford is senior to Captain Potter in date of commission, although acting in a subordinate capacity. Captain Potter concurs with me in this recommendation, which will prevent any conflict in regard to rank.

The medical department is under the charge of Dr. George H. Park, surgeon Sixty-fifth Illinois Infantry. I found the hospitals generally neat and clean and are well supplied with cots and bedding. The sick prisoners were well cared for. The medical supplies were sufficient. Doctor Park is kind in his treatment of the sick prisoners and endeavors to perform his duties satisfactorily. He is zealous, energetic and attentive and will endeavor faithfully to carry out your instructions. He has four physicians employed by contract as his assistants with the prisoners. There has been and still is a large amount of sickness here. This is to be attributed mainly to the fact that when these prisoners came up the river they were crowded upon transports without proper protection from the weather and without proper facilities for cooking their rations. They were delayed en route, many of them sick, with only the clothing they had on their backs. They had been subjected to much exposure for some days previous to their capture and were literally broken down in health and spirits. On their arrival 800 were under medical treatment. Among the prisoners are four persons who represent themselves to be medical officers of the C. S. Army. I have no reason to doubt their statement. No roll accompanied them by which to verify their statements. They represent themselves as follows, viz: D. F. Stewart, surgeon Tenth Texas Regiment; Thomas C. Foster, assistant surgeon Tenth Texas Regiment; John A. Schomblin, assistant surgeon Fifteenth Texas Regiment; James W. Motley, assistant surgeon Seventeenth Texas Regiment. These medical officers are employed at the prisoners' hospital and their services are quite valuable. They desire to remain and take care of their sick fellow-prisoners. The commanding officer has permitted them to remain until he receives contrary instructions from you. Besides the diseases usually found in camps smallpox is prevailing to some extent. There are now 125 cases under treatment. A smallpox hospital has been erected separate from the camp and outside of the inclosure. Every endeavor has been made to prevent the disease spreading and every precaution is adopted that is general under similar circumstances. The mortality of the prisoners is quite large, but this is to be attributed to their wretchedly broken-down condition. Their general health has greatly improved since their arrival at the camp. Three hundred and eighty-seven prisoners have died in the month of February; 262 are now sick in hospitals, while a number are being prescribed for and receiving medical treatment in their quarters. This is exclusive of the 125 cases of smallpox. Large contributions have been made to the hospitals of medicines, clothing and delicacies for the sick by charitable persons and friends of the prisoners residing in the loyal States.

Quite a number of prisoners express a desire to take the oath of allegiance and a number have been permitted to do so. Before a prisoner is permitted to take the oath he is carefully examined and if there is no reason to doubt his sincerity the oath is administered. On the contrary, if there is cause to doubt or to suppose that the oath will not be sacredly kept this privilege is not granted. The oath was administered to fifty-one prisoners during the month of February. This was but a small fraction of the number of applications. The guards are vigilant and attentive to their duties. They are well instructed and the discipline is more rigid than in any camp I have yet visited. But six prisoners have escaped since their arrival.

The prisoners' fund at this camp amounts to $1,473.38, of which $1,115.34 accrued during the month of February. I found that the prisoners upon their ration returns were drawing salt meat almost exclusively and I recommended that fresh beef be issued five days in the week. This will not only increase the fund and lessen the cost to Government of their maintenance, but will be conducive to the health of the camp. I have examined the money accounts of the prisoners and find them all correct and properly kept. All the books and records of the adjutant's office regarding prisoners are kept as directed in your circular of instructions. There has been but little clothing furnished by Government, only in extreme cases, but there have been large contributions by their friends. The following articles were contributed during the month of February: 620 pairs of shoes, 597 overshirts, 303 flannel shirts, 12 cotton shirts, 312 woolen blouses, 1,980 knit socks, 1,846 pairs cotton drawers, 60 flannel drawers, 148 hats, 101 pairs pants, 3 gray undercoats and a large number of articles of lesser value. These articles have been received, examined and distributed as required by your circular.

The total number of prisoners at present confined in this camp is 3,520. They are principally from the States of Texas and Arkansas. They appear cheerful and contented. Their treatment is much better than they had been led to expect and many say better than they received in the Southern Army. A number who have taken the oath have enlisted in the U. S. volunteers. The general condition of the camp is good but the quarters occupied by the prisoners are in need of some repairs. I do respectfully recommend that they all be raised so as to permit a current of air to pass under them. I recommend this as an important sanitary measure for the camp is quite low and damp. There is a bakehouse at the camp which has not been completed. I recommend its completion and that the prisoners bake their own bread. The saving which would result and which is now lost to the Government would constitute quite an important item of the prisoners' fund.

When I take into consideration the unfavorable state of the weather, the wretched condition of the prisoners when they arrived, the reported discipline of the command (paroled men) previous to their arrival I cannot but assure you that the utmost satisfaction has been given in the administration of affairs at this camp, and the general appearance of improvement in every department that the camp now presents leads me to expect the most satisfactory results. I inclose herewith a report of a board of physicians appointed by the city of Chicago to visit and report upon the smallpox hospital of Camp Douglas.

I am, colonel, very respectfully, your obedient servant,
H. W. FREEDLEY,
Captain, Third Infantry.

[Inclosure.]

The rapid increase of smallpox among the prisoners at Camp Douglas has occasioned considerable alarm among the people resident thereabouts and during last week they united in an earnest appeal to the Board of Health complaining of the hospital used for the smallpox patients and asking for some action in their behalf. General Ammen being appealed to said that he was perfectly willing to adopt any measure which would render the neighborhood safe and abate the fears of citizens. The Board of Health appointed Doctors Brainard, McVickar and Cheney to visit the camp and report. General Ammen also appointed a committee of surgeons to meet them and consult. The result is contained in the following report:

CHICAGO, *March 11, 1863.*

Hon. F. C. SHERMAN, Esq., *Mayor,* and
The BOARD OF HEALTH OF THE CITY OF CHICAGO:

The undersigned appointed by the Board of Health of the city to visit the smallpox hospitals at Camp Douglas and confer with the surgeons on service there have discharged that duty and respectfully beg leave to report: That they find the smallpox first occurred among the troops there about the 10th of November but did not appear to any extent until the arrival of the Confederate prisoners now there, about the 27th of January, since which time it has been gradually increasing until there are now 125 cases in the hospital. There have been 19 deaths. Among our own troops there have occurred 19 cases and 1 death. Under the judicious care of Doctor Park, surgeon of the Sixty-fifth Illinois Volunteers, post surgeon, and Doctor Carpenter, surgeon of the Ninth Vermont Volunteers, attending physician in the hospital, thorough vaccination has been introduced and the patients are well cared for and treated and everything in their power is being done to minister to their comfort and the arrest of the disease. As a result of their examination they have to assure their fellow-citizens that under the providential occurrence of this disease within their borders everything is being done which a due regard to their interests demand. The disease has occurred and the victims of it must be cared for somewhere and they do not see where they can be cared for better than they are now. The only suggestions they desire to make to discharge faithfully their duty and the responsibility devolved upon them in the premises are that a new structure be erected for hospital purposes midway between the present site of the hospital and the western border of the camp and that an efficient guard be thrown around the same to completely isolate the sick from all communication with the well; that perfect non-intercourse be established between the camp and the city until an entire subsidence of the disease; that all bodies of deceased patients be interred at least six feet beneath the surface of the ground; that thorough and perfect vaccination be introduced under direction of the authorities of the camp and that all clothing and other fruits of contagion be burned as soon as possible. With these precautions they feel that our citizens may yield all alarm, that no extension of the disease need be apprehended and that it will soon cease to exist among them.

B. McVICKAR, M. D.
DANIEL BRAINARD, M. D.
L. P. CHENEY, M. D.

SPECIAL ORDERS, ⟩   HDQRS. DEPARTMENT OF THE OHIO,
   No. 78.   ⟨   *Cincinnati, Ohio, March 11, 1863.*

*   *   *   *   *   *   *

III. Lieut. Col. S. Eastman, First U. S. Infantry, military commander, Cincinnati, Ohio, will send under charge of an officer the rebel surgeons now in his charge in Cincinnati, Ohio, to Columbus, Ohio, where they will be joined by the rebel surgeon Haldeman and the two nurses there held by the military commander, whence they will proceed to Baltimore, Md., where they will be turned over to the military commander to be sent to City Point. The officer in charge will see that these prisoners are not allowed to communicate with persons along the route to Baltimore, and will obtain from the military commander a receipt for their delivery. On the completion of this duty the officer will return and report to the military commander, Cincinnati, Ohio. The quartermaster's department will furnish the necessary transportation.

*   *   *   *   *   *   *

By order of Major-General Wright:

W. P. ANDERSON,
Assistant Adjutant-General.

WAR DEPARTMENT, *Washington, March 12, 1863.*
Major-General ROSECRANS, *Murfreesborough:*

The matter of paroled prisoners has once been decided by the Secretary of War. He has your telegrams and if he reverses his decision you will be duly notified.

H. W. HALLECK,
General-in-Chief.

U. S. MISSISSIPPI SQUADRON,
Yazoo River, March 12, 1863.
Acting Master GEORGE HENTIG, U. S. Navy,
Commanding Curlew.

SIR: Your communication in relation to the detention of two men claiming to be under a flag of truce has been received. It is desirable that flags of truce should be respected when properly sent, but the men should have gone off when told that Captain Sutherland was not on the station. Allow the men to return to Colonel Ferguson and inform him that Captain Sutherland has left the squadron and is in Saint Louis; that I have received a communication from General Stevenson on the part of General Pemberton which I have answered which will perhaps render it unnecessary to send any more flags of truce in relation to this matter.
Send Colonel Ferguson a copy of this letter.
Very respectfully,

DAVID D. PORTER,
Acting Rear-Admiral, Commanding Mississippi Squadron.

NAVY DEPARTMENT, *Washington, March 12, 1863.*
Hon. GIDEON WELLES, *Secretary of the Navy.*

SIR: The board convened by your order of March 3, 1863, for the purpose of considering the present status or condition under the laws

of war of the officers and others attached to the U. S. steamer Mercedita at the time of the surrender of that vessel off Charleston, S. C., on
the 31st of January last, and of reporting whether or not in its opinion
the paroles stated to have been given on that occasion are valid and
subsisting, have the honor to report that it has given the subject its
most careful study and reflection and is of the opinion that inasmuch
as Lieutenant-Commander Abbot assumed the responsibility of giving
the parole for the officers and others on board of the Mercedita, and
inasmuch as his act was immediately sanctioned by his commanding
officer, Commander Stellwagen, the validity of the parole should be
admitted and the corresponding status or condition of the officers and
men should be recognized.

Very respectfully, your obedient servant,

W. B. SHUBRICK,
Rear-Admiral and President.
C. H. DAVIS,
Rear-Admiral.
JOS. G. TOTTEN,
Brevet Brigadier-General, U. S. Army.

OFFICE COMMISSARY-GENERAL OF PRISONERS,
Washington, D. C., March 12, 1863.

Hon. E. M. STANTON, *Secretary of War, Washington, D. C.*

SIR: Pursuant to the instructions on the accompanying papers* I
have the honor to submit the following report in relation to the management and condition of the troops at Camp Parole, near Annapolis:

Previous to the receipt of these papers I had directed Captain
Lazelle, Eighth Infantry, who is on duty in my office, to make a minute
inspection of the condition of Camp Parole in all its departments, and
I have the honor to submit herewith his report,† which is very full and
satisfactory. From this report it appears that though much has been
done to secure good discipline in the camp, and that the troops should
be well provided for in every way, much remains yet to be done before
anything like perfection will be arrived at. The great obstacle in the
way of a favorable state of things there is the anxiety of the men to
go to their homes and their unwillingness to do anything to better their
condition, which would deprive them of any reasonable ground of complaint and the claims which they base upon it for furloughs. Few of
the paroled officers care to exert themselves to correct this state of feeling. On the contrary they prefer to encourage it in the hopes that it
will secure their being ordered away. Whenever there is any deficiency
in the supplies it is only temporary and unavoidable or else it is
mainly produced by the misconduct of the men themselves. By a comparison of the report of Captain Lazelle with the statements in the
accompanying papers it will be perceived that the complaints are,
except perhaps in some rare instances, wholly false or very much
exaggerated the little occasion for them which really exists.

I have made repeated applications for a permanent guard for the
camp but it has not been practicable to furnish it, nor has it been
practicable to retain for duty there a sufficient number of reliable and
efficient officers to insure a satisfactory state of discipline. The commanding officer, Lieutenant-Colonel Sangster, has very full instructions,
and he has been very faithful in his efforts to carry them out, but the

---

*Not found; but see preceding correspondence.   †See p. 328.

work was more than he with the few officers he had to assist him could accomplish, and his success though very commendable has come short of his wishes. I have made such recommendations to the General-in-Chief as I hope will insure in future a better state of the camp. The paroled troops at the camp belonging to regiments serving in the West have been ordered to Camp Chase and Benton Barracks, pursuant to General Orders, No. 72, of June 28, 1862, which was perhaps the chief object hoped to be gained by these complaints.

I have the honor to be, very respectfully, your obedient servant,

W. HOFFMAN,
Colonel Third Infantry, Commissary-General of Prisoners.

OFFICE COMMISSARY-GENERAL OF PRISONERS,
Washington, D. C., March 12, 1863.

Brig. Gen. J. H. MARTINDALE,
Commanding District of Washington, Washington, D. C.

GENERAL: I have the honor to inclose herewith rolls of citizen prisoners held in Old Capitol Prison who under the direction of the Secretary of War will be embarked on board the steamer State of Maine on Saturday, the 14th instant, under the charge of Capt. J. E. Mulford, Third New York Volunteers, for City Point via Fort Monroe, there to be exchanged for prisoners to be delivered from Richmond. It is possible that some of those on the Old Capitol Prison list may be charged with offenses which will debar them from the privilege of an exchange, and others may be added to the list. Please direct that all shall be prepared to embark on Saturday and have rations issued for the voyage. Three days will I presume be sufficient. Each prisoner will be permitted to take for himself such reasonable supply of clothing as he may have in use and a sum of money not to exceed $500; but this allowance will depend somewhat on the person and the circumstances. A guard will be ready to receive the prisoners on the steamer, and it will only be necessary to conduct them from the prison to her. Prisoners are expected from Sandusky to go in the steamer and I am therefore unable now to say at what hour she will be ready to leave, but by to-morrow evening I will be able to fix the time. Have the kindness to direct that the accompanying rolls be delivered to Captain Mulford with the prisoners. Charles K. Sherman, now a prisoner at the Old Capitol, is not to be exchanged at present; and though his name is not on the list I think it best to mention his case lest by accident he should be included among those sent to the steamer.

Very respectfully, your obedient servant,

W. HOFFMAN,
Colonel Third Infantry, Commissary-General of Prisoners.

P. S.—Since writing the foregoing I have learned that there are prisoners at the Old Capitol whose names have not been furnished to me. I expect a list this morning and will send it to you as soon as received.

W. H.

OFFICE COMMISSARY-GENERAL OF PRISONERS,
Washington, D. C., March 12, 1863.

Col. H. B. CARRINGTON,
Eigthteenth Infantry, U. S. Army, Indianapolis, Ind.

COLONEL: In reply to your telegram of the 5th instant to the Adjutant-General I have the honor to inform you that the General-in-Chief requires that officers who arrest men for political offenses should be able to present specific charges on which the accused can be brought to trial, and they should also know what disposition is to be made of the person arrested in the meantime. In the present case you are authorized to send the prisoner arrested by you to Camp Chase if the necessary charges can be sent with him.

Very respectfully, your obedient servant,

W. HOFFMAN,
Colonel Third Infantry, Commissary-General of Prisoners.

OFFICE COMMISSARY-GENERAL OF PRISONERS,
Washington, D. C., March 12, [*1863*].

Brig. Gen. L. THOMAS, *Adjutant-General, Washington, D. C.*

GENERAL: Pursuant to instructions in the accompanying letter* I have the honor to report that with a view to effecting the release of the officers held as hostages at Richmond for the two men Dusky and Varner, now in the penitentiary at Albany, I called on the provost-marshal at Wheeling and the officer in charge of the penitentiary for such information in relation to the charges against these men, their trial, &c., as they could give.

From the report of the trial and from their own statements it appeared that they were not officers and had but little claim to be considered anything else than as mail robbers and I referred the papers to Colonel Ludlow, agent for the exchange of prisoners, on the 13th ultimo with a letter from which the following is an extract:

I have the honor to inclose herewith all the information I have been able to obtain in relation to the two prisoners in the penitentiary at Albany. From their own statement it is plain that they belonged to no proper military organization and that neither of them was an officer.

It was not till recently that the rebel authorities would recognize guerrillas, bush-whackers and other irregular bands as fit subjects for exchange, and within a few weeks past they have rejected some of this class. They cannot now, therefore, go back to 1861 and claim to exempt a band of marauders who break into a post-office and steal the mail from proper punishment on the ground that they belonged to their army and were acting under the authority of their Government.

You will fully understand how to bring the matter before Mr. Ould so as to insure the release of our officers who are held in their penitentiaries as hostages for these robbers and I need only put the papers in your hands.

After an interview with Mr. Ould Colonel Ludlow suggested that notwithstanding the clear right to detain these men in the penitentiary it would be the best policy to consent to their release if it were practicable and I submitted the matter by direction of the Secretary of War to Major-General Hitchcock, commissioner for exchange of prisoners, who decided that an exchange could not be consented to. This decision I communicated to Colonel Ludlow on the 6th instant, the following being an extract of my letter to him:

It is also decided not to release the two prisoners in the penitentiary at Albany. The papers already forwarded to you cover this case and justify their detention. If the rebel authorities persist in holding our officers as hostages for these two men such measures will be taken as may be necessary to meet such a state of things.

Colonel Ludlow will have an interview with Mr. Ould on the 16th instant, the result of which in this matter will be reported without delay.

I have the honor to be, very respectfully, your obedient servant,

W. HOFFMAN,
Colonel Third Infantry, Commissary-General of Prisoners.

---

* Not found.

OFFICE COMMISSARY-GENERAL OF PRISONERS,
Washington, D. C., March 12. 1863.

Col. GEORGE SANGSTER,
Commanding Camp Parole, Annapolis, Md.

COLONEL: Your letters of the 7th and 10th instant have been received. I return herewith the order on Captain Sullivan for $1,000 approved. You have not yet furnished me an account of the camp fund as required by my instructions of the 11th of November last. As the savings are paid by the commissary in Baltimore instead of the commissary at your camp the account must be kept in your name unless you prefer to make your commissary your treasurer, in which case he can make the disbursements on your order and the accounts will be rendered through you as directed. You will immediately prepare and submit to me an account for February showing the receipts and expenditures with vouchers. This fund must be carefully expended for the relief of the troops at the camp, and to this end much may be used in making them comfortable in their quarters. Be careful that the funds are not lavished on employés or in the purchase of articles not for the benefit of the men. Tobacco may be purchased from time to time in reasonable quantities.

My instructions in relation to company kitchens and cooking boilers have not been carried out. These are things of the first importance and must be attended to without delay. If your engineer corps cannot accomplish better results they do not earn their extra pay. The little pens which have been put up for quarters are more than useless and the labor and money expended on them has been worse than thrown away. I shall probably direct a change in the location of the camp within its present ground or near the railroad, and until you get further instructions you need only make your arrangements for putting your camp in its best possible condition. Captain Lazelle will visit your camp early next week to advise with you on the subject.

The General-in-Chief has referred the matter of a suitable guard for the camp to General Schenck which I hope will relieve you from any further trouble on this account. As soon as I can find suitable officers not on parole available for the service several will be detailed to report to you to assist in conducting the affairs of the camp. Under all the circumstances your management of the camp is very satisfactory. When anything in discipline or good order is deficient I attribute it not to any want of attention or energy on your part but mainly to the peculiar character of the command and the want of the assistance of reliable officers which your numerous duties absolutely require.

Very respectfully, your obedient servant,

W. HOFFMAN,
Colonel Third Infantry, Commissary-General of Prisoners.

WASHINGTON, *March 13, 1863.*

Col. W. H. LUDLOW, U. S. Army.

SIR: The Secretary of the Navy has by letter requested that certain prisoners may be held in confinement at Fort Lafayette, captured by the navy. He refers in his letter to the proclamation of Jeff. Davis abrogating the terms of the cartel announced in orders of the 25th September, 1862 (agreed upon in July), but over and above this he seems to think that the Navy ought to have been represented in the making of the cartel.

At all events he requests that in case of any new cartel being made an officer of the Navy may be associated with the commission employed in making it.　The prisoners referred to (in Fort Lafayette) are not considered as coming under the existing cartel, so far as they were not captured in armed vessels but on board of merchant vessels engaged in attempting to run the blockade.

Upon referring this subject to the Secretary of War he has directed that the prisoners in question are not to be exchanged.

It is to be hoped that as far as possible exchanges may continue to be made and if difficulties arise that they may be the subject of friendly intercourse under the ninth article of the cartel.　We must do all we can in the name of humanity.

Very respectfully, your obedient servant,

E. A. HITCHCOCK,
Major-General of Vols., Commissioner for Exchange of Prisoners.

OFFICE COMMISSARY-GENERAL OF PRISONERS,
Washington, D. C., March 13, 1863.

Hon. RICHARD YATES,
Governor of Illinois, Springfield, Ill.

SIR: In reply to your communication, through General Fuller, of the 23d ultimo, I have the honor to inclose herewith an extract from a report made by Captain Lazelle, U. S. Army, under my instructions, of the condition of the paroled troops at Camp Parole, and particularly in regard to the matter referred to in your letter.　The report will assure you that nothing has been neglected in the arrangements for the comfortable reception in every way of troops arriving at Annapolis.　Captain Lazelle speaks of one case where men were for one night not as well provided for as they should have been, but this arose from unavoidable circumstances which at that time could not be guarded against. I regret to say that there is a spirit of discontent and fault-finding among officers and men under such circumstances which induces them to exaggerate the inconveniences they experience rather than by a little effort on their own part to remove them entirely.　All paroled troops at Annapolis belonging to regiments serving in the West have been ordered to the camps designated for their occupation in General Orders, No. 72 of June 28, 1862.

I am, Governor, very respectfully, your obedient servant,

W. HOFFMAN,
Colonel Third Infantry, Commissary-General of Prisoners.

FORT MONROE, VA., *March 13, 1863.*

Col. W. HOFFMAN, *Commissary-General of Prisoners:*

Please inform me when the Western prisoners will be delivered at Vicksburg.　I must give some information on this subject to Mr. Ould.

WM. H. LUDLOW,
Lieutenant-Colonel and Agent for Exchange of Prisoners.

WASHINGTON, *March 13, 1863.*

Lieutenant-Colonel LUDLOW, *Agent for Exchange of Prisoners.*

Western prisoners cannot be delivered at Vicksburg. Orders will be given immediately for their delivery at City Point. Have written to you about them.

W. HOFFMAN,
Commissary-General of Prisoners.

OFFICE COMMISSARY-GENERAL OF PRISONERS,
Washington, March 13, 1863.

Lieut. Col. W. H. LUDLOW,
Agent for Exchange of Prisoners, Fort Monroe, Va.

COLONEL: Your letter of the 11th instant is just received. I return herewith the list* of Confederate officers and men sent you by Mr. Ould, accompanied by explanations showing where they are and why they are still held. Those who have been exchanged have not been delivered at Vicksburg because of the impossibility of reaching that city whilst operations are being carried on against it. I have sent instructions to Camp Chase to forward all exchanged officers and men who may be held there by any route which the commanding general of the Department of the Ohio may point out as practicable. To-morrow or next day I will order all the enlisted prisoners at the Western stations and all officers already exchanged to be forwarded for delivery at City Point. Guerrillas will be included and I will cause separate rolls to be prepared for them as you requested. There are some rebel officers who have been exchanged still in our hospitals who will be sent South as soon as they are able to travel. Mr. Innerarity is here and will go down on the steamer for exchange. Washington Barrow of Tennessee, a gentleman of standing and influence in his State and formerly in Congress, is here on parole and will be sent forward for exchange. On January 12 Dr. Alfred Hughes left here on parole for thirty days to proceed to Richmond to effect the release and exchange for himself of Mr. Samuel A. Pancoast. Since then I hear nothing of him except that Mr. Pancoast remains in prison while he remains at Richmond in violation of his parole. Call Mr. Ould's attention to the case and insist that Mr. Pancoast be immediately released. Gideon S. Bolton was paroled by Mr. Ould for thirty days to effect an exchange for John McDowell, Hampshire County, Va., who was at the time on parole from Camp Chase. I ordered him to be sent here immediately, but he has not yet arrived. I learned to-day where he can be found and dispatched a messenger for him. Mr. Bolton will go down on the boat to consult you as to what he had better do. I have not been able to get a letter to Mr. S. J. Anderson as I have not his particular address in New York. I believe it is on his letter which I referred to you. I inclose herewith a number of individual applications* for the release of prisoners at Richmond. Some of them I know have already been brought to your attention. The rolls of the prisoners to be sent from here are not yet completed nor have the prisoners expected from Sandusky arrived. I shall write you further before the boat leaves. Remember to call Mr. Ould's attention to the fact that

---

* Not found.

prisoners of war were sent from Johnson's Island to Vicksburg for exchange who were rejected and sent back because they were crazy or imbecile.

Very respectfully, your obedient servant,
W. HOFFMAN,
Colonel Third Infantry, Commissary-General of Prisoners.

OFFICE COMMISSARY-GENERAL OF PRISONERS,
Washington, D. C., March 13, 1863.

W. P. WOOD, Esq., *Superintendent of Old Capitol Prison.*

SIR: If possible please send by the bearer the probable number of prisoners to be exchanged not including those just arrived under my orders and now at the Old Capitol, nor those on the list furnished by the provost-marshal, Captain Todd, and say when you can hand me the list called for by General Hitchcock.

Very respectfully, your obedient servant,
W. HOFFMAN,
Colonel Third Infantry, Commissary-General of Prisoners.

OFFICE COMMISSARY-GENERAL OF PRISONERS,
Washington, D. C., March 14, 1863.

Brig. Gen. J. H. MARTINDALE,
Commanding District of Washington, Washington, D. C.

GENERAL: I have the honor to request that you will have furnished to this office a list of all prisoners of war belonging to the rebel army now in confinement at the Old Capitol Prison, and I request you will oblige me by requiring hereafter that when any number of prisoners over twenty arrive or are transferred a list may be immediately furnished. At the end of the month a return is required showing the number present, the number received, transferred, died, &c., during the month, giving on the back of the return the names of all noted under the head of "alterations" except where they have been furnished during the month. Blanks for these rolls and returns will be furnished from this office.

I am, general, very respectfully, your obedient servant,
W. HOFFMAN,
Colonel Third Infantry, Commissary-General of Prisoners.

OFFICE COMMISSARY GENERAL OF PRISONERS,
Washington, March 14, 1863.

Lieut. Col. W. H. LUDLOW,
Agent for Exchange of Prisoners, Fort Monroe, Va.

COLONEL: I have turned over to Capt. J. E. Mulford, Third New York Infantry, 309 citizen prisoners to be delivered at City Point for exchange. Two hundred and eleven have been ordered from Sandusky, but by an unusual state of the ice in the bay they have not been able to cross from the island and they will consequently not be present for the trip of the steamer. When she returns with those delivered to you they will doubtless have arrived and will be sent down on her. Captain Mulford is furnished with full rolls of them and I inclose herewith the duplicate rolls.* I return herewith the lists* handed you by

---

* Not found.

Mr. Ould which you left with me, with duplicates of them prepared in my office showing what has become of the prisoners named in the lists so far as our records give the information. You will notice that a large majority of the persons named have been released or exchanged. A number cannot be found on our rolls. As I stated in my letter of yesterday all officers and men in our possession already exchanged will be delivered in a few days either in the West or at City Point. Among the prisoners of war there are several, Colonel Morehead and Doctor Dixon among them, who are charged with being spies and they will not be released till their cases are investigated. Colonel Morehead was arrested in Kentucky within our lines dressed in citizen's clothes. Doctor Dixon after having been released, being a medical officer, obtained passes for two different routes by misrepresentations. I cannot recall the other cases. Governor Peirpoint is anxious that J. H. Trout, a member of the loyal Legislature of Virginia now in confinement at Richmond, should be exchanged, as he hoped Doctor Hughes would be reserved for this purpose. Select some suitable person to make an equivalent for him and effect the exchange if possible. I hope you will be able to induce Mr. Ould to release any surplus he may have over the number I send down to be fully covered by those who will be on the way from Sandusky. I inclose three lists* of Federal and rebel troops paroled in Arkansas though I have doubts whether you can make any use of them. Though there is no evidence of the fact the rebels were doubtless sent beyond our lines. General Wright, commanding Department of the Ohio, strongly urges the exchange of Private H. C. Lilly, Fourteenth Kentucky Cavalry, that he may accept the place of colonel of the regiment. The agent of Adams Express Company has been called upon for information relating to the box of jewelry forwarded by Colonel Dent for Capt. R. R. Ross. His report has not yet been received. I will make inquiries into the case of John H. Boyle, held as a spy, and will inform you of the facts when they are ascertained. I am not certain whether it was intended I should retain the three papers* marked "Copy" and one marked "Memoranda" or not. I send them to you. If you do not require them please return them for future reference. I repeat my request to be furnished with the list of the sick and wounded of our officers and soldiers still confined in prisons and hospitals in Richmond and elsewhere.

Very respectfully, your obedient servant,

W. HOFFMAN,
Colonel Third Infantry, Commissary-General of Prisoners.

OFFICE COMMISSARY-GENERAL OF PRISONERS,
Washington, D. C., March 14, 1863.

Capt. H. B. TODD, *Provost-Marshal, Washington.*

CAPTAIN: I have not yet been furnished by Mr. Wood, superintendent of the Old Capitol Prison, with a list of the prisoners under his charge who may be exchanged and I have therefore [been] unable to say at what time they will be ready to leave. I would like to have all things prepared for their departure as far as is practicable so that there may be no delay after I hear from Mr. Wood.

Very respectfully, your obedient servant,

W. HOFFMAN,
Colonel Third Infantry, Commissary-General of Prisoners.

---

* Not found.

OFFICE COMMISSARY-GENERAL OF PRISONERS,
Washington, D. C., March 14, 1863.

Lieut. Col. W. H. LUDLOW,
Agent for Exchange of Prisoners, Fort Monroe, Va.

COLONEL: I inclose herewith a copy of the general orders* just issued in relation to paroles which is to govern officers on our side hereafter. Its provisions are all very proper and are consistent with the requirements of the cartel. Whether the Richmond Government will be satisfied with it remains to be seen. In many instances small squads of men and individuals have been paroled by only doubtful authority, and just turned loose with no report of them, or a very meager one. The parties, nevertheless, are under the obligation of their paroles, and can only be relieved by an exchange or by a mutual understanding of the authorities. Is it not possible for you to make an arrangement with Mr. Ould by which such paroles may be canceled and that hereafter in all matters of parole the usage of war as announced in General Orders, No. 49, shall govern all parties? I have no instructions in relation to this order, and offer the above only as my own suggestions.

Very respectfully, your obedient servant,

W. HOFFMAN,
Colonel Third Infantry, Commissary-General of Prisoners.

P. S.—Since writing the foregoing I have consulted the General-in-Chief, who approves the suggestions.

W. H.

MURFREESBOROUGH, TENN., *March 16, 1863.*

Brig. Gen. L. THOMAS, *Adjutant-General:*

About December 10 I notified General Bragg that no more prisoners would be received from the Confederates unless delivered in accordance with the terms of the cartel. Finding they continued to parole and release our men and that men went out to get paroled, and even rebel citizens paroled them, I published an order carrying out my notice to General Bragg. Under this order almost an entire stop has been put to paroling, but General Halleck says it was inexpedient to enforce it until further notice to the rebels as the Department was not advised that I had given official notice more than a month before this order was published. As it is of vital importance to the service that the order should be enforced here I respectfully ask a reconsideration of these instructions. The troops awaiting this decision are now a nuisance in our camp and many who have been paroled make their way across the country home and are lost. I hope the rigor of the order will cause its execution to be approved.

W. S. ROSECRANS,
Major-General.

WASHINGTON, *March 16, 1863.*

Col. WILLIAM HOFFMAN:

Doctor Rucker is said to be held a prisoner at Liberty, Bedford County, Va. Renew your demand for his release and say that if he is treated otherwise than as a prisoner of war I shall recommend retaliation and in the strongest terms. Place Doctor Green in close confinement.

E. A. HITCHCOCK,
Major-General of Volunteers, &c.

---

* See p. 306.

OFFICE COMMISSARY-GENERAL OF PRISONERS,
Washington, D. C., March 16, 1863.

Maj. Gen. S. R. CURTIS,
Commanding Department of the Missouri, Saint Louis, Mo.

GENERAL: The General-in-Chief directs that all enlisted prisoners of war of the rebel army be forwarded to City Point for delivery and I have the honor to request you will give the necessary orders for the movement of the prisoners in the two prisons at Saint Louis and the Alton Prison. At the latter prison the prevalence of smallpox for some time past may make it objectionable to send prisoners from there more or less infected with the disease so far through the interior of the country and it is left to you to decide how far the order in relation to these prisoners can be carried out. This order covers all guerrillas, rangers, &c. The Pittsburg and Baltimore route will I presume be most direct and convenient, and I would respectfully suggest that the quartermasters of these two places be notified of the movement in time so that there may be no delay for transportation. I will write to the provost-marshal-general at Saint Louis and the commanding officer at Alton Prison in relation to rolls, &c.

I am, general, very respectfully, your obedient servant,
W. HOFFMAN,
Colonel Third Infantry, Commissary-General of Prisoners.

OFFICE COMMISSARY-GENERAL OF PRISONERS,
Washington, D. C., March 16, 1863.

Maj. Gen. H. G. WRIGHT,
Commanding Department of the Ohio, Cincinnati, Ohio:

The General-in-Chief directs that all enlisted prisoners of war of the rebel army be forwarded to City Point for delivery and I have the honor to request you will give the necessary orders for the movement of the prisoners at Camp Chase, Camp Morton, Camp Douglas, Camp Butler and Louisville. The Pittsburg and Baltimore route I presume will be the most convenient, and I would respectfully suggest that the provost-marshals at these two places have timely notice to provide the necessary transportation, &c., and the movement should be so arranged as to time that parties from different camps would not interfere with each other on the Pittsburg and Baltimore road. I will write to the commanders of the camps in relation to rolls, &c.

In reply to your letter of March 11 I have the honor to say that the announcement of exchanges in General Orders, No. 10, paragraphs 6 and 7, apply to both parties, it being understood by the agents for exchange that all captures on both sides up to the time and in the States named have been exchanged. The rebel authorities in announcing the exchanges use the same language with some explanations. The two articles apply to all military organizations, guerrillas, rangers, &c. I refer Captain Webber to you because I was doubtful whether it was possible to send prisoners beyond our lines in the West, and since it is not I will direct that they be sent with other prisoners of war on separate rolls to City Point.

I am, general, very respectfully, your obedient servant,
W. HOFFMAN,
Colonel Third Infantry, Commissary-General of Prisoners.

OFFICE COMMISSARY-GENERAL OF PRISONERS,
Washington, D. C., March 16, 1863.

Brig. Gen. JACOB AMMEN,
   Commanding Camp Douglas, Chicago, Ill.

GENERAL: You will receive instructions from General Wright to forward to City Point, Va., all enlisted prisoners of war in your charge. In addition to the duplicate rolls required to go with them by General Orders, No. 9, Department of the Ohio, please send a roll also to this office. If you have any guerrillas or other irregular organizations among the prisoners not officers make rolls of them distinct from the regular organizations. Any money that you may have in charge belonging to prisoners should be placed in the hands of the officer commanding the guard, with the names of those to whom it is due and the amount, to be delivered to them at City Point. Please give particular instructions to the commander of the guard in writing that he will suffer the prisoners to have no intercourse with persons by the way and that at all changes of cars he will arrange his guard so as to insure that none may escape. If the strength of the guard is not designated by the general it should not exceed one to eight persons, with a proper complement of officers and non-commissioned officers. Cooked provisions for the guard and prisoners should be provided to serve them to Baltimore. Should there be any prisoners remaining at the camp on the 1st of April next please send me full rolls of them, giving under the head of remarks all necessary information not coming under the several headings, as time of arrival, where from, &c. These rolls are required for a new set of books and I hope they will be carefully prepared and forwarded to this office at the time named.

Very respectfully, your obedient servant,
W. HOFFMAN,
Colonel Third Infantry, Commissary-General of Prisoners.

(Same *mutatis mutandis* to commandants of other prison posts.)

FORT MONROE, *March 17, 1863.*

His Excellency A. LINCOLN:

The Virginia Legislature has transferred to the Confederate Government the whole subject of prisoners of war. Gold has risen at Richmond to $4.50, so the papers state. A private statement makes it $6.
JOHN A. DIX,
Major-General.

OFFICE COMMISSARY-GENERAL OF PRISONERS,
Washington, March 17, 1863.

Hon. E. M. STANTON, *Secretary of War, Washington, D. C.*

SIR: In reply to your order for a report on the matter presented by the Hon. S. Colfax I have the honor very respectfully to refer to my report of the 12th instant on the same subject.

I would state in addition that by authority of the Secretary of War I have ordered the surplus rations—that is what remains after giving an ample supply for the use of the men—to be converted through the commissary department into a fund to be expended exclusively for the benefit of the command, an account of which fund is presented to me monthly.

The troops at Camp Parole are paid from time to time as the interests of the service demand.

I have the honor to return herewith the letter presented by Mr. Colfax.

I have the honor to be, very respectfully, your obedient servant,

W. HOFFMAN,
Colonel Third Infantry, Commissary-General of Prisoners.

OFFICE COMMISSARY-GENERAL OF PRISONERS,
Washington, D. C., March 17, 1863.

Maj. Gen. H. G. WRIGHT,
Comdg. Department of the Ohio, Cincinnati, Ohio.

GENERAL: In reply to the matter submitted in your indorsement on the letter of General White accompanying a report of Major Davidson of the capture and parole of certain officers and men by guerrilla bands I have the honor to state that such paroles, though of doubtful force, have heretofore been recognized as binding by both parties, and Union troops so paroled will be considered as bound by their paroles until General Orders, No. 49, has been generally promulgated to the Army; after which time any officer or soldier violating any of its provisions by giving his parole improperly will be held as an offender and punished accordingly. I have consulted the General-in-Chief on this subject and the above are his views. Order No. 49 will be presented to the agent from Richmond for the exchange of prisoners and it is expected that the rebel authorities will be willing to adopt that order as their rule in relation to paroles, and an effort will be made by a mutual agreement of the agents for exchange to cancel paroles so irregularly given on either side.

I am, general, very respectfully, your obedient servant,

W. HOFFMAN,
Colonel Third Infantry, Commissary-General of Prisoners.

OFFICE COMMISSARY-GENERAL OF PRISONERS,
Washington, D. C., March 17, 1863.

Col. G. LOOMIS, *Commanding Fort Columbus, N. Y.:*

Please furnish to this office the names of any state or political prisoners in your charge other than prisoners of war, giving the authority for date and place of arrest, charges and place of residence.

By order of the Secretary of War:

W. HOFFMAN,
Commissary-General of Prisoners.

(Same to other prison commandants.)

HEADQUARTERS DEPARTMENT OF VIRGINIA,
Fort Monroe, Va., March 17, 1863.

Major-General FOSTER.

GENERAL: Mr. Ould, the Confederate agent for the exchange of prisoners, has often spoken to me in reference to the men referred to in the copy of affidavit inclosed. Will you please give me such information as you may possess concerning them. Mr. Ould claims that credit for these men has never been given the Confederate authorities in the settlement of exchange of prisoners.

I am, very respectfully, your obedient servant,

WM. H. LUDLOW,
Lieutenant-Colonel and Agent for the Exchange of Prisoners.

[Inclosure.]

CITY OF PETERSBURG, *State of Virginia:*

Personally appeared before the undersigned notary public W. H. Ker, major and assistant adjutant-general, who states on oath that in the month of May, 1862, A. D., he paroled at Salisbury, State of North Carolina, 1,383 Federal prisoners of war, and that the said prisoners were sent to Washington, State of North Carolina, in detachments of 200, each detachment under charge of a commissioned officer. Affiant further states that the paroles were signed in duplicate, one of which was left with Maj. A. C. Godwin, commanding the military prison at Salisbury, State of North Carolina, the other given to the officer in charge of the respective detachments.

WM. H. KER,
Major and Assistant Adjutant-General.

STATE OF VIRGINIA, *Corporation of Petersburg, to wit:*

I, Robert H. Mann, a notary public in and for the corporation aforesaid in the State of Virginia, do hereby certify that William H. Ker, major and assistant adjutant-general, whose name is signed to the foregoing affidavit, this day personally appeared before me in corporation aforesaid and made oath to the truth of the facts therein stated. Given under my hand this 2d of March, 1863.

ROBERT H. MANN,
Notary Public.

HEADQUARTERS, *Annapolis, Md., March 18, 1863.*

ASSISTANT ADJUTANT-GENERAL,
Headquarters Middle Department, Baltimore, Md.

SIR: In compliance with the indorsement on Colonel Hoffman's letter of the 7th instant, referred to me from your office with Captain Lazelle's report, I have carefully read the latter and find that nearly all the suggestions therein contained must be carried into effect by the commanding officer at Camp Parole or by instructions from Washington. That camp is placed under the immediate command of Lieut. Col. G. Sangster in all matters connected with its police or interior arrangement, who receives his instructions through Colonel Hoffman, the commissary-general of prisoners, directly from the General-in-Chief.

I shall order the Third Regiment Potomac Home Brigade to Camp Parole to strengthen the guard, except such portions as may be necessary for a guard at the general hospital and to protect the public property at the navy-yard, so soon as the snow shall disappear and the ground be sufficiently dry to render it safe to change the men from comfortable barracks to tents where they will be compelled to sleep on the ground.

The number of paroled prisoners has been recently so much reduced, being now only some 2,000, that the present guard is sufficient for a few days.

I think that the recommendations of Captain Lazelle if carried out will materially improve the condition of things at the camp and I respectfully recommend them to the favorable consideration of those in authority.

I have retained Captain Lazelle's report but will return it to department headquarters in a few days.

I am, sir, with much respect, your obedient servant,

C. A. WAITE,
Colonel First Infantry, Commanding Post.

OFFICE COMMISSARY-GENERAL OF PRISONERS,
Washington, D. C., March 18, 1863.

Hon. E. M. STANTON, *Secretary of War, Washington, D. C.*

SIR: I have the honor to report, in explanation of my orders to the provost-marshal in relation to rebel prisoners and deserters received from the Army of the Potomac, that at the request of the provost-marshal-general of the Army of the Potomac and with the approbation of the General-in-Chief I have directed that deserters from the rebel army should be forwarded to the commanding general in Philadelphia, there to be released on taking the oath of allegiance. In the case where an order for rebel prisoners of war to be sent North was issued in my name by Captain Hartz, assistant adjutant-general, he was led astray by the letter from the office of the provost-marshal-general of the Army of the Potomac which accompanied the prisoners and which stated that they were rebel prisoners paroled to go North. Hereafter I will guard against such mistakes.

Very respectfully, your obedient servant,

W. HOFFMAN,
Colonel Third Infantry, Commissary-General of Prisoners.

HAMMOND GENERAL HOSPITAL,
Beaufort, N. C., March 18, 1863.

Surg. F. G. SNELLING,
Medical Director, Eighteenth Army Corps, New Berne, N. C.

SIR: I have the honor of submitting to you a report of the condition of the prisoners' quarters at Fort Macon. I would, however, state that it is made by direction of Surg. F. S. Ainsworth, U. S. volunteers, by whose order I visited the sick there previous to receiving the special order from Lieutenant-Colonel Hoffman, whenever a boat could be had. Their quarters are in the northeast casemate of the inner parapet, so that sunshine never enters to such an extent as to make printed matter discernible in all parts of the room, consequently the place is constantly damp. The dimensions are as follows: Length 24 feet, breadth 17 feet, height at center of the arch 13 feet, height to commencement of the arch $7\frac{1}{3}$ feet, making the cubical contents about 3,180 feet, giving to each of the 24 occupants about 130 cubic feet, which I submit is too contracted a space for a human being. I have from my first visit at the fort repeatedly called the attention of the commander, Major Giles, Third New York Artillery, to this crowded room and have advised that they should be provided with more space, of which there is enough. To obtain some data in regard to the healthiness of this damp place I consulted the report of surgeon's call back to the 18th of February, being just one month, and find whole number of prescriptions 265—for prisoners 103, for garrison 162; number in fort, including the prisoners, 236—garrison 206, prisoners 30. You will see the proportion of sickness is almost five times greater among the prisoners than among the troops and I can give no other cause than miserable quarters, as all have the same food. Any instructions from you will be gladly received and all orders promptly obeyed.

I am, sir, very respectfully, your obedient servant,
                                    L. H. PEASE,
        Tenth Connecticut Vols., Asst. Surg. Hammond General Hospital.

[First indorsement]

MEDICAL DIRECTOR'S OFFICE,
        EIGHTEENTH ARMY CORPS.

Respectfully referred to Lieutenant-Colonel Hoffman, with a request that the prisoners of Fort Macon be provided with other and suitable quarters, to be approved of by the surgeon in charge.
                                    F. G. SNELLING,
                Medical Director Eighteenth Army Corps.

[Second indorsement.]

HEADQUARTERS EIGHTEENTH ARMY CORPS,
        New Berne, N. C., April 20, 1863.

Respectfully forwarded to the commanding officer of Fort Macon for his attention and action. The health of the prisoners should of course be attended to.

By order of General Foster:
                                    S. HOFFMAN,
                        Assistant Adjutant-General.

———

HEADQUARTERS COMMANDANT OF PRISONS,
        Camp Chase, Ohio, March 18, 1863.

Col. WILLIAM HOFFMAN,
        Commissary-General of Prisoners, Washington, D. C.

SIR: Owing to the large influx of rebel prisoners and paroled soldiers our camp is full. We have now here 1,008 rebel prisoners, 3,000 paroled soldiers, 8 companies of the Second Ohio Volunteer Cavalry, part of 2 batteries and some detachments of recruits, 30 deserters. I also understand that at Louisville are a number of rebel prisoners (700) that will be ordered here as soon as room can be had for them. In view of these facts I take the liberty of asking if the fence now around Prison No. 3 can be removed and inclose a piece of ground on the south end of Prison No. 2 large enough to hold 2,000 prisoners. This would place the prisons all together and give us quarters for 1,000 more paroled soldiers. Prison No. 3 being situated in the middle of the camp the sewerage from it has to pass through two regimental quarters on the east and the stench arising from the drains make it not only unhealthy but very unpleasant for those quarters below. Our prevailing winds in hot weather are from the west and southwest and if the prisons were all at the east end of camp where Prisons Nos. 1 and 2 are the drainage would all be from the camp and no smell from privies would annoy our soldiers. My plan would be to inclose with good substantial fence, same as Prisons 1 and 2, the ground necessary to hold what rebel prisoners will probably be sent here more than Prisons

1 and 2 will hold. Instead of building them houses I would put them
in tents, or at least I would build nothing more than kitchens for
them to cook in.

This fence could be made from the fence around Prison No. 3, in
part. There is also I understand at Camp Lew. Wallace a large
amount of lumber in vacant quarters that is liable every day to be
stolen, as there are no soldiers there to prevent it. That could be
hauled here and used for that purpose without purchasing any new
lumber to build either fence or kitchens. Another thing in favor of
this arrangement would be that it would take less men and officers for
guard than under the present arrangement and would be entirely separate from the soldiers' quarters. But the great benefit would be to
remove the prisons from the center of the camp and to get rid of the
nuisance arising from its sewerage.

Very respectfully, your obedient servant,

[THOMAS J. KERR.]

[Indorsement.]

COLONEL: The above was written by Captain Kerr, of the quartermaster's department, and he wishes my approval. It would seem from
the above that our prisons are full. This is not the case. We can
accommodate 800 more prisoners than we have now. Prisons Nos. 1
and 2 will not accommodate all that are here and as our guard force
is small that a less number of guards may be sufficient Prison 1 is
vacated and Prison 2 and a large portion of Prison 3 is occupied. I
heartily approve of the above in all respects except as regards the use
of tents. It seems to me that the style of barracks in Prisons 1 and 2
are preferable. That the prison might be removed from the center of
the camp is very desirable. Were the prisons all together the same
number of guards would be sufficient for double the number of prisoners now here.

Hoping that you will give this subject your consideration,

I am, colonel, very respectfully, your obedient servant,

EDWIN L. WEBBER,
Captain, Commanding Prisons.

INDIANAPOLIS, IND., *March 19, 1863.*

Memorandum of condition of public affairs in Indiana to be submitted
to the President* and honorable Secretary of War.

I submit facts that are within my personal knowledge indicative of
the sentiment and purposes that underlie domestic treason in Indiana.

I.—ORIGIN AND PROGRESS.

About the time of the draft the Knights of the Golden Circle organized to break up the army. I have abundant affidavits and adequate
proof. I advised the honorable Secretary of War as well as the President in personal communications. Their success was considerable
until the arrest and conviction of John O. Brown, now under sentence
of death suspended at my request, that he may be used as a witness
before the U. S. district court in May next. The oaths embodied:

1. To secure the desertion of soldiers with their arms and the protection of said deserters.

---

* See p. 108 for Carrington to Stanton, December 22, 1862.

2. Resistance to further drafts and interference with enlistments.

3. To stop this war.

Signs, grips and passwords were devised and sentinels were posted at each meeting to warn of the approach of any not members. In December the organization assumed new force and significance. The signs, grips and passwords were changed. The obligations became more directly treasonable and the organization assumed military form and purpose. To illustrate:

1. The signs included battle signals for infantry and cavalry; upon giving which a soldier would be treated as a friend by the rebel foe; also five-pointed copper stars, to be worn upon the left breast, to be disclosed upon opening the coat before an enemy if made a prisoner, or if this State should be visited by Confederates. Others of German silver are hung in small frames to protect houses in which they belong.

2. The oath included resistance to confiscation of the goods of the fraternity either North or South; provided night and day signals upon which the order should rally to the defense of a brother member and made the pledge of mutual support significant by extreme penalties in case of disclosure of the nature of the order. The following is the form of oath prescribed for the second degree (and is the same in a large number of counties) from which copies have been procured and is undoubtedly general in its use:

"Do you believe this to be the word of God?" (Hands in the Bible.)

"Do you believe the present war now being waged against us to be unconstitutional?"

"Then receive the obligation."

I, —— ——, do solemnly swear in the presence of Almighty God that I will support the Constitution of the United States and the State in which I reside, and keep it holy. I further promise and swear that I will go to the aid of all true and loyal Democrats and oppose the confiscation of their property either North or South; and I further promise and swear that I will suffer my body severed in four parts— one part east, out of the East gate; one part at the west gate; one part at the north gate; one part at the south gate—before I will suffer the privileges bequeathed to us by our forefathers blotted out or trampled under foot forever. I further promise and swear that I will go to the aid from the first to the fourth signal of all loyal Democrats either North or South. I further promise and swear that I will not reveal any of the secret signs, passwords or grips to any not legally authorized by this order, binding myself under no less penalty than having my bowels torn out and cast to the four winds of heaven: So help me God. I promise and swear that I will do all in my power to bring all loyal Democrats in this Circle of Hosts. I further promise and swear that I will do all in my power against the present Yankee abolition, disunion Administration: So help me God.

3. The order has enjoined upon its members thorough arming. The extent of this may be derived from the fact that in February and March alone nearly 30,000 arms, revolvers, &c., have entered Indiana as derived from invoices of sales, and undoubtedly thousands more have been brought from the East of which I have no knowledge. On the day the sale of arms was prohibited at Indianapolis nearly 1,000 revolvers were contracted for and the trade could not supply the demand. Two small establishments at La Fayette, Ind., had each sixty kegs of powder which at other times would last for years. Sixteen boxes came from Lexington, Ky., under disguise of household goods. One box from Cincinnati was marked pick-axes, another hardware, another nails. These are instances which daily occurred until decided action was adopted.

4. The country lodges drill in the steps and facings, and with such muskets and rifles as they have practice the manual.

5. The subjects of discussion are the despotism of the Government; the preponderating power of the North-East in proportion with size;

the restoration of the Democratic party and overthrow of the present Administration by force if it must be; the restoration of the South or a union with it would give them again control of the Senate and the power. Systematic falsification of the purposes and acts of the Government is made use of to prejudice and exasperate the people and portions of the press so thinly disguise their treason as to make whatever they do or say for appearance sake only more destructive to the morals of the public.

6. Their connection with Southern traitors is to be noted. It is claimed in their lodges that they have the co-operation of the fraternity in Kentucky, Tennessee, &c.; that at the next raid of Morgan he will leave the command and quietly appear to raise the standard of revolt in Indiana. Thousands believe this, and his photograph is hung in many houses. In some counties his name is daily praised. Besides this some of the prisoners of war now here have the same views as to the intent of these domestic traitors; have the same signs, grips, watchwords and the same battle signals.

II.—Present condition of the organization.

This has been incidentally adverted to. Additional facts are given to illustrate its practical workings and extent. Not long since over 200 mounted men, many of them armed, rode into Franklin, Johnson County, and openly declared for Jeff. Davis, denounced our Government and declared their desire for immediate peace under the supremacy of Davis as a substitute for Mr. Lincoln. On the 18th instant in Putnam County a procession openly resolved that they were ready to renounce the United States, cheered for Jeff. Davis and were cheered in turn. On Thursday last a sergeant and six men went to Raleigh, Rush County, to arrest deserters (whom a party of two could not secure and were driven away) and within two hours after an alarm signal about 200 mounted men gathered armed with rifles, shotguns and revolvers, and compelled the detail to return. I sent a special train with 100 men the same night and arrested the deserters, however, and shall turn the ringleaders over to the U. S. court.

In the Morgan County case the leaders of the party who attacked the cavalry detachment were proven to be Knights of the Golden Circle. At Brown County last week a committee of them drove out a Union Democrat, threatening the penalty of death upon him for having left the Knights. Two cases have happened in this city where the lives of men suspected of turning informers were in danger. One gave notice where he was and he was arrested by me (*pro forma*) and his assailant was confined for trial, being a soldier. Another was kept confined one night by nine men and escaped by cunning. Several companies have been nearly ruined by them. I am investigating a case where I do not believe there are twenty loyal men in the company. The foregoing are instances of the boldness of the order, which could be multiplied.

In the central lodge at this city the members of the order were reported at 92,000 between sixteen and seventy years of age four weeks ago. This was then extravagant, but there must be nearly or quite that number now as they are known to have lodges in nearly every county—I think all but seven—and daily assume greater boldness. That a large number of the common classes in some of the rural districts who are members of the order watch for some armed overthrow of the Administration is certain. The numbers of good and true citizens who report and the concurrent statements of deserters prove this.

The ostensible leaders here are not the leaders of the Democratic party; but I mention a few facts to show how confident the leading men are of the power of the order. At the suggestion of Governor Morton I invited the State officials and leading men of both parties to a conference as to public affairs. They agree to address the Democracy in a manner that shall check this discontent. It remains to be seen whether it will be done.

Hon. T. A. Hendricks, U. S. Senator, assured me "that the majority of the people of Indiana were desperate under the despotism of the Government and no one could tell how long it would be endured."

Doctor Athon, Secretary of State, says that "in visiting Southern Indiana every man in many counties is armed to the teeth and asking 'How long is this to endure?'"

The people have been grossly and wickedly deceived by this order until they believe the most infamous lies as to the Government and its designs. Plans have been carefully discussed in the lodges respecting seizure of the arsenal, the railroads and the telegraph; and especially have several lodges made it obligatory upon the members to protect deserters and resist the conscription. They are promised arms from Kentucky and really believe they are to have them, absurd as it may seem.

To meet these dangerous tendencies I have followed up every resistance to arrests by use of force and perfecting the arrest without delay. Seven of the Morgan County men were convicted. Lawyers of this city refused to testify before the grand jury on the plea that it would criminate themselves and subject them to indictment for treason. I shall use the accumulated evidence before the grand jury that meets to-day with the view to indict these lawyers and a considerable number of leaders from various counties, hoping for a good effect from the same.

The fact is that the order has grown faster than the party leaders wished and has assumed a shape and bitterness that may not be controlled if it breaks forth even by them; but I know that these leaders feel that they have a power at their backs which they hold as invincible. I am convinced that the tension cannot long last; reaction or violence is certain. While avoiding all needless collision my aim has been by firmness but discretion to aim at such a popular reaction without an outbreak and thus let the people down to their old quietude. The people will thus fall back soon or precipitate an issue in some locality. If it be not simultaneous and general it can and will be handled and handled severely. But if the difficulties here should be complicated by a successful inroad upon Kentucky as anticipated by Generals Rosecrans, Wright and Boyle there would be great danger. The only perfect assurance in such case would be in the support of a division from the East. The reaction in the New York Democratic politicians has not reached the West and the popular daring of Vallandigham makes him so mischievous that either he or Morgan could raise an army of 20,000 traitors in Indiana. If this Vallandigham counsels resistance or defiance to any U. S. statute in Indiana I wish authority to arrest him.

In furnishing the foregoing statement at the request of Governor Morton, whose good judgment has been my chief auxiliary in matters of a civil order, I will also refer to him for fuller information as to the condition of the State. I will respectfully add a word of my personal views. I believe that no city paper should use the mails or cars or circulate if it counsels resistance to the conscript act. I should like discretionary power in Indiana in this particular, if the Government contemplated any interference with the press, should conscription be resisted. I believe that no person should be allowed in sober and deliberate mood to support the archtraitor Davis by act or word of mouth. Union farmers in their innocence come to me and say that such a person "Hurrahs for Jeff. Davis; what shall we do?" This seems a small matter, but I say in all seriousness that the feelings of retired country-men are as much irritated by this as a citizen of the town would be by armed treason. This delicate sense of national honor in the rustic is not to be overlooked and we cannot spare the men whose feelings revolt at such cries. We are at the crisis. We shall pass it safely. But we must encourage the loyal Union men; they must feel that they are protected. Disloyal men if their name be legion must feel that they are in danger. When the detachment under my command passed through Livingston to arrest Judge Constable, of Marshall, Ill., a gray-headed old man knelt down in the mud, crying, as he prayed, "Thank the Almighty Father we have a Government again."

The Government must be felt as the protector of the people. Now is the time. Come what will, firmness is our safety and the result is certain. Victory in the field is valuable, but we must show the power and goodness of the Government at home or disaster in the field will have ten-fold damage here and victory in the field will lose half its force.

Respectfully submitted,

HENRY B. CARRINGTON,
Colonel Eighteenth U. S. Infantry, Comdg. at Indianapolis.

OFFICE COMMISSARY-GENERAL OF PRISONERS,
Washington, D. C., March 19, 1863.

Brig. Gen. JACOB AMMEN,
Commanding Camp Douglas, Chicago, Ill.

GENERAL: I desire to call your attention to the circular issued from this office July 7, 1862,* for the government and care of prisoners of war, and particularly to the disbursement of the prison fund. By reference to article 5 of the circular you will see how it is to be accumulated, how used and for what purposes. The principal object of the fund is to make the prisoners as comfortable as circumstances will admit and at the same time to relieve the Government as far as possible of the expense of their keeping. It is not desirable to accumulate any large fund on hand, nor is it intended to be wasted in the purchase of articles not necessary to the health and comfort of the prisoners or in the purchase of an undue quantity of luxuries. A reasonable quantity of tobacco may be purchased, vegetables, &c., and any surplus after the purchase of necessaries will be used to purchase clothing, fuel, straw and in the payment of such incidental expenses consequent upon the care of prisoners which are now paid by the Government.

Very respectfully, your obedient servant,

W. HOFFMAN,
Colonel Third Infantry, Commissary-General of Prisoners.

(Same to Col. William F. Lynch, commanding Camp Butler, Spring-field, Ill., and officer commanding military prison, Alton, Ill.)

---

* See Vol. IV, this Series, p. 152.

FORT MONROE, *March 19, 1863.*

Hon. EDWIN M. STANTON, *Secretary of War:*

A large number of released citizen prisoners, including those captured by General Stuart in his raid into Maryland and Pennsylvania, have arrived here and leave for Washington to-day. These were confined in Richmond. Those confined in Salisbury, N. C., will be delivered next week.

WM. H. LUDLOW,
Lieutenant-Colonel and Agent for Exchange of Prisoners.

———

FORT MONROE, *March 19, 1863.*

Col. WM. HOFFMAN, *Commissary-General of Prisoners:*

About 200 more citizen prisoners will be wanted.

WM. H. LUDLOW,
Lieutenant-Colonel, &c.

———

OFFICE PROVOST-MARSHAL GENERAL,
Saint Louis, Mo., March 19, 1863.

Col. W. HOFFMAN, *Commissary-General of Prisoners.*

COLONEL: I send forward to-day by express the list of prisoners other than prisoners of war called for by your telegraphic order of the 4th instant. The number of those who are strictly citizens is comparatively small. The larger share of the list is composed of those whom I have styled bushwhackers. The members of this latter class cannot claim to be prisoners of war, neither can they claim as citizens a trial by the slow and expensive methods of civil law. I would recommend that the most desperate among them be tried by military commissions on the charge of violation of laws and customs of war and that the rest be exchanged.

I have the honor to be, colonel, your obedient servant,

F. A. DICK,
Lieutenant-Colonel and Provost-Marshal-General.

———

OFFICE COMMISSARY-GENERAL OF PRISONERS,
Washington, D. C., March 19, 1863.

W. P. WOOD,
Superintendent Old Capitol Prison, Washington, D. C.

SIR: The roll of citizen prisoners which you are preparing should have been furnished some days since under the instructions of General Hitchcock and is required immediately. You will therefore please have it made up by this evening at least.

Very respectfully, your obedient servant,

W. HOFFMAN,
Colonel Third Infantry, Commissary-General of Prisoners.

———

OLD CAPITOL PRISON, *Washington, March 19, 1863.*

Col. W. HOFFMAN, *Commissary-General of Prisoners.*

SIR: I have received your note of this date and assure you I have received no communication from General Hitchcock or yourself since the state prisoners left here for exchange Saturday last. The only instructions in relation to state prisoners came from the military governor yesterday. In obedience to said instructions I am now preparing a roll of state prisoners and will forward the same to the military governor as soon as completed. Had I received any orders from General Hitchcock or yourself in relation to the subject alluded to in your note, viz, " the rolls of citizen prisoners which you are now preparing should have been furnished some days since," I should have complied with such instructions, but I cannot understand how I am to execute orders which I never receive and which are not anticipated by me. Endeavoring to be prompt and faithful to all requirements which may be expected from me,

I remain, your obedient servant,

WILLIAM P. WOOD,
Superintendent Old Capitol Prison.

MILITARY PRISON, *Alton, Ill., March 19, 1863.*
Col. W. HOFFMAN,
Commissary-General of Prisoners, Washington, D. C.

COLONEL: Having at length been placed in command of this prison a question has arisen between Colonel Hildebrand, the commandant of this post, and myself as to the nature of my duties and the extent of my authority and control over the prison and its inmates. This question is one of some consequence, and if not settled soon and the duties of the prison commander more clearly defined will I fear lead to trouble and may be an obstacle in the way of my performance of my duties in a satisfactory manner to myself at least. There is nothing on file here that I can find which defines the duties and extent of authority of the commandant of the prison separate and apart from that of the commandant of the post. Both these duties have heretofore been confided to the one officer, but as this command is now to be divided it appears to me that the duties of each commander should be properly determined in order that the one may not unnecessarily encroach upon the prerogatives of the other. Colonel Hildebrand has I believe laid his view of this subject before you. Mine is that being commander of the prison I ought to have the entire control of it and of the prisoners confined subject only to such orders as I may receive from time to time from you. This subject is submitted to you with the hope that you will give it your earliest attention so that I may be able to perform my share of the duties here such as they be understandingly and in a satisfactory manner. I find also that the provost-marshal-general of the Department of the Missouri, Lieutenant-Colonel Dick, of the Missouri State Militia, assumes authority over this prison so far as to send prisoners here and to take them away upon his own order. I would like to be informed how far I am subject to the orders of Lieutenant-Colonel Dick, and to what extent I am under the control of Colonel Hildebrand, the commander of the troops here, in the performance of my duties in the prison.

I have the honor to be, sir, with much respect, your most obedient servant,

T. HENDRICKSON,
Major Third Infantry, Commandant of Prison.

HEADQUARTERS MILITARY GOVERNOR,
Alexandria, Va., March 19, 1863.

Brig. Gen. JOHN P. SLOUGH,
Military Governor, Alexandria, Va.

GENERAL: Upon inspection of the paroled and exchanged prisoners' camp I find hundreds of tents lying in the open air water-soaked and fast becoming worthless in spite of your repeated orders to the contrary. There are but 342 men now in camp, all but 32 of whom have been exchanged; 70 men are detailed as camp guard; 29 are upon extra or daily duty. There are 8 commissioned officers, 7 teams for transportation and 3 ambulances.

In my opinion there is no good reason why this camp should not be broken up and the property on hand turned in to the depot quartermaster. It is in a very unhealthy situation; the ground being so level that proper drainage is impossible, the soil being of the worst for the site of a camp.

Taking away the guard and the detailed men who are fit to go to their regiments there will be but 243 men left, proper subjects for any camp but that of their regiments. Of these the 32 paroled men should be sent to Annapolis and the balance to the convalescent camp where they will faster recover their health than in tents.

It may be thought that this camp should be kept up in anticipation of its being needed in case of an advance of our army and the consequent chances of an influx of paroled and exchanged prisoners, but with the present facilities at this point a camp could be established upon three days' notice sufficient to accommodate all likely to be sent here.

If it is concluded to keep the camp in this vicinity it should be removed to a new and more healthy location.

Respectfully, your obedient servant,

D. J. RICH,
Captain and Aide-de-Camp.

[First indorsement.]

HEADQUARTERS MILITARY GOVERNOR,
Alexandria, Va., March 19, 1863.

Approved and respectfully forwarded.

For the reasons within named I respectfully recommend that this camp be broken up.

JNO. P. SLOUGH,
Brigadier-General of Volunteers, Military Governor.

[Second indorsement.]

HEADQUARTERS DEPARTMENT OF WASHINGTON,
March 20, 1863.

Respectfully referred to Colonel Hoffman.

By breaking up this camp and sending these thirty-two men to Annapolis these eight officers will be available and can be ordered to Annapolis where their services are much needed. The other men can be comfortably accommodated at the convalescent camp.

S. P. HEINTZELMAN,
Major-General, Commanding.

IUKA, MISS., *March 19, 1863.*

Colonel HANNON, C. S. Army,
  Commanding at Tuscumbia, Ala.

COLONEL: On the 15th instant in violation of the cartel by which the hospital was established at this point Capt. J. N. George, C. S. Army, with fifty men more or less burned two bridges or trestles between the villages of Iuka and Burnsville, thereby rendering the railroad impassable for cars between here and Corinth.

If the above-mentioned acts were committed under orders emanating from Confederate authorities or are sanctioned by the same I, as the Federal officer in charge of the Confederate hospital at Iuka, demand of you as the successor of Colonel Roddey, with whom the last agreement in regard to the neutrality was made, to be placed with my assistants, all U. S. property brought here for the use of the hospital and our personal baggage beyond the break in the railroad, say the village of Burnsville, under a flag of truce, where we can be reached by a train from Corinth under a similar flag, leaving the Confederate sick and wounded and attendants now in hospital upon your hands, without rations, taking back with me to Corinth the present amount on hand, medicines and hospital stores; or if you deny the authority and condemn the burning of the railroad bridges I ask for official permission for the citizens with any assistance that may be sent from our lines unmolested to rebuild the bridges and put the road in running order again. The citizens of Burnsville, Iuka and vicinities have expressed a willingness to rebuild the bridges with the consent of the Confederate commander at Tuscumbia, Ala., and a safeguard for the future protection of everything connected with this hospital until it is broken up, which in my judgment can be done within three weeks.

For any particulars regarding the cartel and how far the Federals have carried it out on their part I respectfully refer you to any C. S. Army surgeon who has been on duty at this hospital, especially Surgs. D. C. Roberts, J. C. Roberts and Felton.

Hoping that our official and personal relations may be as pleasant as that of your worthy predecessor, Colonel Roddey,

  I remain, your obedient servant,

  A. B. STEWART,
  U. S. Volunteers, Medical Director Confederate Hospital, Iuka.

WAR DEPARTMENT, *Washington, March 20, 1863.*

Maj. Gen. JOHN A. DIX, *Commanding at Fort Monroe, Va.*

GENERAL: I send herewith copies of a letter from the State Department dated the 11th instant and of the inclosure to which reference is therein made, and am directed by the Secretary of War to request that you will forward to its destination the inclosed sealed package addressed to Mr. E. William de Voss, Bremen consul at Richmond, Va., and that you will also issue the requisite orders to enable Mr. De Voss and family to come within our lines, together with their personal effects by means of any truce boat of which they may desire to avail themselves, provided Mr. De Voss shall before entering our lines give a written assurance—

1. That neither himself nor any member of his family has rendered any aid or support directly or indirectly to the rebel cause during the period of his residence in the rebel States.

2. That neither himself nor any member of his family has undertaken to execute any commission for any person beyond our lines; nor to bring any written or verbal message nor any other matter or thing for or from any person beyond our lines, nor will execute any such commission.

3. That neither himself nor any member of his family will bring or deliver any letter, message, matter or thing except what properly belongs to the official business of his consulate or his own Government or that of the United States, excepting also the personal effects of himself and family.

Very respectfully, your obedient servant,

P. H. WATSON,
Assistant Secretary of War.

[Inclosure No. 1.]

DEPARTMENT OF STATE, *Washington, March 11, 1863.*

Hon. E. M. STANTON, *Secretary of War.*

SIR: I have the honor to inclose a letter to Mr. E. W. de Voss, consul of Bremen at Richmond, Va., addressed to him by the minister of the Hanseatic Republics. I annex also a transcript of the minister's note which accompanied the letter to Mr. De Voss, and will thank you if there be no objections to such a course to comply with the wishes of Mr. Schleiden.

I am, sir, your obedient servant,

WM. H. SEWARD.

[Inclosure No. 2.]

HANSEATIC LEGATION,
Washington, D. C., March 10, 1863.

Hon. WILLIAM H. SEWARD,
Secretary of State of the United States, Washington, D. C.

SIR: The Bremen consul at Richmond, Va., Mr. Edward William de Voss, has requested me by letter, dated the 19th ultimo and just received under flag of truce, to grant him a leave of absence for the purpose of visiting Europe, accompanied by his wife, his three children, aged from three to ten years, and a nurse, and to cause the necessary orders to be given that he may embark with his said family on board one of the first steamers proceeding under a flag of truce to Fortress Monroe to continue his voyage by the way of New York to Bremen. Appreciating the motives of his request I have complied with the same, have issued a passport for Mr. Consul De Voss and family and appointed his partner and brother-in-law, Mr. Frederick William Hanewirickel, as acting consul and the necessary instructions to be forwarded under flag of truce to its destination. I entreat you at the same time to be pleased to cause the necessary orders to be given to the commanding general at Fortress Monroe that Mr. Consul De Voss and his family may be allowed to proceed under flag of truce through the military lines of the Federal Army for the purpose of proceeding to New York where he is to embark for Bremen. As you have under similar circumstances extended on the 5th of April last a similar favor to the Bremen consul at Savannah, Mr. H. Muller, I am confident that you will cheerfully comply with my present request, and beg beforehand to accept my thanks for doing so.

I am, sir, with high consideration, your obedient servant,

R. SCHLEIDEN.

HEADQUARTERS OF THE ARMY,
Washington, March 20, 1863.

Commodore W. D. PORTER, U. S. Navy, *Washington.*

COMMODORE: I have to acknowledge the receipt of your letter of the 19th. A demand will be immediately made upon the Confederate authorities for the exchange of Spencer Kellogg if living, or that he be accounted for if dead.

Very respectfully, your obedient servant,
H. W. HALLECK,
General-in-Chief.

OFFICE COMMISSARY-GENERAL OF PRISONERS,
Washington, D. C., March 20, 1863.

Hon. GIDEON WELLES,
Secretary of the Navy, Washington, D. C.

SIR: I have the honor to inform you that forty-three paroled seamen belonging to the U. S. Navy have just arrived in this city from Richmond and I have respectfully to request you will designate an officer to take charge of them. They are now on the State of Maine at the foot of Sixth street.

Very respectfully, your obedient servant,
W. HOFFMAN,
Colonel Third Infantry, Commissary-General of Prisoners.

OFFICE COMMISSARY-GENERAL OF PRISONERS,
Washington, D. C., March 20, 1863.

Brig. Gen. J. H. MARTINDALE,
Commanding Military District of Washington.

GENERAL: The steamer State of Maine has just arrived with about 325 prisoners, paroled Union soldiers and citizens from Richmond, and I have respectfully to request that you will order a guard to conduct them from the boat to the Soldiers' Rest where they will have to be provided for for the present. I have to request also that you will order a guard of an officer and twenty men to conduct the soldiers to Camp Parole, at Annapolis, as soon as arrangements can be made for their transportation.

Very respectfully, your obedient servant,
W. HOFFMAN,
Colonel Third Infantry, Commissary-General of Prisoners.

OFFICE COMMISSARY-GENERAL OF PRISONERS,
Washington, D. C., March 20, 1863.

Col. J. C. KELTON,
Assistant Adjutant-General, Washington, D. C.

COLONEL: I have the honor to submit herewith for the action of the General-in-Chief a communication* from His Excellency Governor Yates, of Illinois, recommending the establishment of a camp for paroled troops of that State somewhere within its limits. On this application I beg leave to suggest that on account of convenience of

*Omitted here; Yates to Hoffman, March 6, p. 321.

access and the necessary barracks provided at them Camps Morton, near Indianapolis, Ind., and Butler, near Springfield, Ill., offer good points for collecting together the paroled troops of these two States, and the chief objection to this arrangement is that other States more remote to which transportation would be very expensive would expect like camps to be established within their borders.   There are no troops more difficult to control, officers and men, than those on parole, and the greater the number assembled at any one camp the greater the difficulty, and for this reason it would be advisable to have additional camps in the West, provided reliable and efficient commanders could be found for them.   The two camps named and Camp Douglas, at Chicago, are now occupied by rebel prisoners of war who will in a few days be delivered at City Point when the camps may be occupied by our paroled troops.   Camp Douglas might be designated for the regiments from Michigan, Wisconsin, Iowa and Minnesota, which would bring the men much nearer to their homes than as at present located without great additional cost.

It is possible that conceding this much to State feelings might produce good effect in reconciling men to the irksome restraints and *ennui* of the parole camp thereby bringing about a better state of discipline than now prevails and which is so much to be desired.   At all events it would remove in great part the grounds for the many complaints now so often presented.   At each camp of paroled troops there should be a suitable guard with officers for the staff departments who are not on parole, and the duties which the paroled troops may properly be called on to perform should always be pointed out in general orders.

Very respectfully, your obedient servant,

W. HOFFMAN,
Colonel Third Infantry, Commissary General of Prisoners.

[Indorsement.]

MARCH 21, 1863.

If deemed necessary the number of parole camps may be increased. It, however, is not advisable to have particular camps for the troops of particular States.   If they know they are to be sent home to their own States when paroled it serves as an inducement to surrender to the enemy.

H. W. HALLECK,
General-in-Chief.

———

OFFICE COMMISSARY-GENERAL OF PRISONERS,
Washington, D. C., March 20, 1863.

Col. J. C. KELTON,
Assistant Adjutant-General, Washington, D. C.

COLONEL: After a conversation with Major-General Heintzelman in relation to the advantages of Camp Banks for paroled troops I agree with him that it would be to the interest of the service to break it up and transfer the exchanged men who are mostly invalids to the convalescent camp, and those still on parole to Camp Parole.   I am informed by the general that at the convalescent camps accommodations can be set aside, especially for such paroled troops as cannot be provided for at Camp Parole, and by this arrangement the officers now at Camp Banks can be assigned to duty at Camp Parole or so many of them as may be necessary.   Colonel De Korponay's services will not be required and he may be ordered to his regiment.   I would therefore respectfully recommend that instructions be given for the breaking up of Camp Banks and for carrying out the above suggestions. I am informed at the headquarters of General Heintzelman that Capt. S. W. Burbank, Fourteenth Infantry, and Lieut. H. Asbury, Third Infantry, are in the city and available for service at Camp Parole in consequence of impaired health, and I have to request that they may be ordered there for duty.

Very respectfully, your obedient servant,

W. HOFFMAN,
Colonel Third Infantry, Commissary-General of Prisoners.

HEADQUARTERS DEPARTMENT OF VIRGINIA,
Fort Monroe, March 20, 1863.

Col. W. HOFFMAN, *Commissary-General of Prisoners.*

COLONEL: There are a number of Confederate officers and men who have been declared exchanged and who are yet within our lines. It is very desirable that they should be delivered as soon as possible. Some of our own officers captured at Hartsville and declared exchanged are now in Richmond and can be delivered to us as soon as there is reciprocity. Can you not arrange to have the Confederate officers and men above referred to put on board of the State of Maine, now on her way to Washington with citizen and other released prisoners? The State of Maine can bring back here 800. If you send 200 citizen prisoners, 600 others can be also sent. Have you lists of all the Confederate officers in your custody? Shall be in Washington on Monday next and will call upon you. I have propositions for exchange of officers to submit to the Secretary of War, and if accepted by him the exchanges can be immediately thereafter made.

I am, very respectfully, your obedient servant,

WM. H. LUDLOW,
Lieutenant-Colonel and Agent for Exchange of Prisoners.

STEAMER STATE OF MAINE, *Washington, March 20, 1863.*

Col. W. HOFFMAN, *Commissary-General of Prisoners.*

SIR: I have the honor to call your attention to the complaints of a number of citizen prisoners sent in my charge from Washington on the 14th instant on board steamer State of Maine to City Point, Va., for delivery and exchange, in regard to certain private funds which they allege had been taken possession of by officials having them in charge and which were to have been returned to them. On my arrival at City Point, Va., a number of the prisoners demanded of me their money of which I had no knowledge and so informed them, whereupon they represented that upon application to Mr. Wood, keeper of the Old Capitol Prison, just previous to having been sent on board the steamer for the funds belonging to them respectively he had informed them that the amounts belonging to each individual would be placed in my hands for delivery to them on our arrival at City Point. This was not done nor was any reference whatever made to me about money until after I had left Washington and as above stated. Of this, however, I was unable to convince a portion of the claimants and was by some denounced as a Yankee robber, &c. Robert Ould, esq., Confederate agent for exchange of prisoners, officially called my attention to this matter and informed me that he was authorized to receive any funds belonging to prisoners whenever forwarded and claimed that those referred to in this communication should be.

I submit the foregoing statement for your consideration, and have the honor to be,

Your obedient servant,

JOHN E. MULFORD,
Captain, Commanding Flag of Truce, James River.

[Indorsement.]

MARCH 31, 1863.

Mr. Wood will report on this with the other papers delivered to him this morning.

HEADQUARTERS DEPARTMENT OF THE SOUTH,
Hilton Head, Port Royal, S. C., March 21, 1863.

General G. T. BEAUREGARD,
Commanding at Charleston, S. C.

SIR: I have the honor to communicate for your information a general order* issued by the War Department of the United States promulgating the rules and principles which will hereafter be observed and enforced in U. S. Armies in relation to paroles.

I have the honor to be, very respectfully, your obedient servant,

D. HUNTER,
Major-General, Commanding.

SAINT LOUIS, *March 21, 1863.*

Captain CRANDALL, *Washington, Mo.:*

It is charged that you resist the civil process in Washington relating to fugitive slaves of loyal masters. If true you exceed the laws and orders on this subject. You should not interfere with slaves of loyal owners either to restrain or deliver up, but as far you can avoid trouble with them.

S. R. CURTIS,
Major-General.

WAR DEPARTMENT, *Washington, March 21, 1863.*

The commissary-general of prisoners will issue the articles of clothing that may be necessary to the citizen prisoners who have just arrived from Richmond.

By order of the Secretary of War:

ED. R. S. CANBY,
Brigadier-General.

HEADQUARTERS DISTRICT OF NORTH ALABAMA,
Florence, March 21, 1863.

Surgeon STEWART.

SIR: Your communication of the 19th instant addressed to Colonel Hannon, commanding C. S. forces at Tuscumbia, has been laid before me.

The existence of any "cartel by which the hospital was established at Iuka" is a matter wholly unknown to me or any officer now in this

---

command. To know whether it has been violated we must first have a copy. It was natural, however, for us to suppose that some agreement of neutrality as to the particular place where the hospitals were established had been made. Before, however, you can ask us to carry out any agreement the terms of the agreement must be known. A copy then of any paper [in] writing concerning this matter is requested with the assurance that as far as practicable it will be cheerfully conformed to.

The "demand" to be placed with your assistants and property beyond the break of the railroad need not be considered until the matter can be settled as any violation of a cartel on our part.

So far as I am now informed the destruction of the railroad was a proper act of military defense and as at present advised is justified by me. Neither will any one be permitted to reconstruct it so far as I can prevent until sufficient testimony is shown that it was embraced in an agreement to do so.

All the property of yourself, assistants and of the United States at Iuka will be protected by our forces and delivered to you to be removed so far as the same relates to the hospitals there should you determine to leave. The rations, however, should be left with the sick and wounded and nothing could justify an act leaving them to starve.

It will not be expected that the recent outrages committed at and near Tuscumbia by a band of robbers from Corinth shall go unpunished; if so, those who think so will be disappointed.

Your expression of a desire for pleasant relations in conducting the hospitals at Iuka are heartily reciprocated and nothing will be done to bring about any different state of feeling.

For the delivery of the hospital furniture, &c., belonging to the ladies of Florence and Tuscumbia, we acknowledge an act of courtesy usual to your profession.

The parties referred to in your letter who can give particulars of cartel are not here to do so, and therefore I will await your reply to this.

I have the honor to be, surgeon, respectfully, your obedient servant,

S. A. M. WOOD,
Brigadier-General, C. S. Army, Commanding.

OFFICE COMMISSARY-GENERAL OF PRISONERS,
Washington, D. C., March 21, 1863.

Brigadier-General CANBY, War Department.

GENERAL: In order to account properly for the issue of clothing to citizen prisoners just received from Richmond it will be necessary that the order of the Secretary of War should accompany the vouchers. The Secretary directs me this morning to make the issue and I will be obliged to you if you will give me an order to that effect.

Very respectfully, your obedient servant,

W. HOFFMAN,
Colonel Third Infantry, Commissary-General of Prisoners.

OFFICE COMMISSARY-GENERAL OF PRISONERS,
Washington, D. C., March 21, 1863.

Brig. Gen. W. A. HAMMOND, Surgeon-General.

GENERAL: I cannot answer your note of this morning in a better way than by furnishing you with an extract from Captain Freedley's report of an inspection made by him under my instructions of the condition of the prisons at Camp Douglas.* This will assure you that there is no just foundation for the complaints contained in the accompanying note.

Very respectfully, your obedient servant,

W. HOFFMAN,
Colonel Third Infantry, Commissary-General of Prisoners.

OFFICE COMMISSARY-GENERAL OF PRISONERS,
Washington, D. C., March 21, 1863.

Brig. Gen. J. H. MARTINDALE,
Comdg. Military District of Washington, Washington, D. C.

GENERAL: The steamer State of Maine will leave this city early next week, possibly on Tuesday, for Fort Monroe, and I have respectfully to request that all enlisted prisoners of war belonging to the rebel army now at the Old Capitol Prison may be sent on her to report to Lieut. Col. W. H. Ludlow, agent for exchange of prisoners, at Fort Monroe, Va., under charge of Capt. John E. Mulford, Third New York Volunteers, who will be on the steamer with a guard prepared to receive them. The prisoners are to be delivered at City Point for exchange and I have to request that duplicate rolls may be sent with them. If there are any rebel officers in the prison whose exchanges have already been announced in orders I have respectfully to request that they may be delivered at City Point at the same time. By direction of the Secretary of War the Rev. J. P. B. Wilmer, now in the Old Capitol Prison, will be sent on the State of Maine under a guard to Fort Monroe and delivered to Major-General Dix to be forthwith placed beyond the U. S. lines at City Point. He is not to be permitted to have communication with any unauthorized person until he is beyond our lines. Please give the necessary orders to have the Secretary's instructions carried out.

Very respectfully, your obedient servant,

W. HOFFMAN,
Colonel Third Infantry, Commissary-General of Prisoners.

GENERAL DEPOT RECRUITING SERVICE MISSOURI VOLS.,
Benton Barracks, Mo., March 21, 1863.

Col. W. HOFFMAN,
Commissary-General of Prisoners, Washington, D. C.

COLONEL: In compliance with General Orders, No. 46,† current series, I respectfully submit the following report of stragglers from the Army, paroled, exchanged or otherwise, who have reported at this post for the period beginning March 10 and ending March 20, inclusive, to wit, two commissioned officers [and] twenty-eight enlisted men. Further I would report on my actions to carry out this order that I have caused 100 copies of it and an extract from General Orders, No. 72, December, 1862, to be printed. These I distributed to all regular officers on duty in this State with instructions to make reports and act in accordance thereto (see copy of order inclosed).‡ I also had the order published for six days in the daily paper of this city which has the largest circu-

---

*See p. 343.   † See p. 288.   ‡ Omitted.

lation. Therefore I have reason to believe the order has been widely circulated and generally read throughout the entire State.

I am, colonel, very respectfully, your obedient,

B. L. E. BONNEVILLE,
Col., U. S. Army, and Supt. Recruiting Service, Missouri Vols.

OFFICE COMMISSARY-GENERAL OF PRISONERS,
Washington, D. C., March 21, 1863.

Col. WILLIAM HOFFMAN,
Commissary General of Prisoners, Washington, D. C.

COLONEL: I have the honor to submit the following report of the condition of the prisoners of war confined at Camp Butler, near Springfield, Ill.:

This camp is situated on the Great Western Railroad, about six miles east of Springfield, and is commanded by Col. W. F. Lynch, Fifty-eighth Regiment Illinois Volunteers. There are at present confined in this camp 1,620 prisoners of war who were captured at Arkansas Post, and are principally from the States of Texas, Arkansas and Louisiana. These prisoners are quartered in twenty-one frame buildings, including hospitals, each one erected for the purpose of quartering 100 U. S. volunteers. These buildings are ample for their accommodation, are provided with comfortable bunks and in every way fitted up as quarters for our own troops.

The rations issued to the prisoners I find to be quite as large as they can consume. They are cheerful and contented, and all agree in saying that their provisions are now much better in quality and larger in amount than those issued to them when in the service of the Confederate States. The prisoners are divided into companies. The roll is called daily under the superintendence of the provost-marshal and all changes and alterations reported to the commanding officer. These reports are frequently verified by counting all the prisoners when on parade. Every precaution has been adopted to secure correctness and security. The guard is detailed from the Fifty-eighth Illinois Infantry and from a detachment of the Sixteenth Illinois Cavalry stationed at the post. The sentinels were quite sufficient in numbers and well posted. They appeared well instructed in their duties but perform them in a loose and indifferent manner. The prisoners are, however, held securely and but few escapes have been made. They appear to have become so indolent and so contented with their treatment that they do not desire to escape.

The discipline of the camp is not good. A loose manner of performing all the duties of a soldier seems to prevail. There is a decided want of force and of energy among the officers and there is not a sufficiently broad line of demarcation between them and the enlisted men under their command. Indolence and want of energy seem to prevail among the troops as well as among the prisoners. The police of the camp was very poor. No attention whatever had been paid to it. Large amounts of filth and offal had been permitted to accumulate in the vicinity of the prisoners' quarters until they were almost too filthy to visit. This was partly to be excused as it had rained almost daily for some weeks. The camp had never been dry since the prisoners arrived. This long-continued rainy weather had caused the roads to be almost impassable and it required all the transportation of the camp to supply it with wood. Such was the condition of the roads that wagons were unable to reach the camp from Springfield. The camp was indeed exceedingly muddy and it was almost impossible to enforce any police regulations, but had proper attention been paid to drainage there would have been no necessity of its being in such a wretched condition. I applied to Captain Bailhache, assistant quartermaster at Springfield, and he temporarily furnished three additional wagons for the use of the camp. As soon as these reached camp they were enabled to supply it with wood and some measures were taken to have it properly policed.

The prisoners' barracks, internally and without, were exceedingly filthy, the prisoners taking no means or trouble to insure their own cleanliness or comfort although every necessary means was within their reach. The officers in charge of the camp did not attempt to enforce cleanliness among the prisoners and appeared not to be aware of its importance. The prisoners on their part were content to remain in indolence amidst filth and vermin.

The duties of the adjutant's office have been properly performed. I have examined the books and records and find them correct. The money accounts have been properly kept and all remittances are recorded and receipts given. Proper economy is exercised in all the accounts of the prisoners. I found everything in this office satisfactorily performed. The quartermaster's department is under the charge of Captain Bailhache, assistant quartermaster, U. S. volunteers, having for his assistant at the camp Lieut. George Sawin, regimental quartermaster Fifty-eighth Illinois Volunteers. Affairs in this department have been administered with proper economy but there has been a disposition to do as little as possible to promote the comfort of the prisoners. No expense has been incurred in their behalf. On my arrival I found many destitute of proper clothing and succeeded in obtaining for their use a small quantity of gray clothing (somewhat damaged) which had been turned over by the State of Illinois to the quartermaster's department. This issue supplied all their immediate wants.

The barracks occupied by the prisoners are sadly in need of repairs. New bunks should be constructed, additional modes of ventilation provided while repairs in floor and roof are required. There have been no repairs to this camp for some time and it presents a general appearance of neglect. It appears that this camp was built by Capt. Charles B. Watson, Fourteenth U. S. Infantry, late mustering and disbursing officer at Springfield, out of the fund for collecting, organizing and recruiting U. S. volunteers. Upon being relieved Captain Watson did not turn over this camp to his successor and consequently it is not properly accounted for nor kept in that state of repair that the interests of the service demand. The repairs required by this camp do not require much expense to the Government and the labor could all be performed by the prisoners.

The commissary department is under the charge of Capt. Ninian W. Edwards, acting commissary of subsistence, U. S. volunteers, at Springfield, having for his assistant at the camp Lieut. John H. Barret, Tenth Illinois Cavalry, acting assistant commissary of subsistence. The rations furnished are good and wholesome. The reduced ration is issued. The affairs of this department are conducted with a due regard to economy and in every respect satisfactorily. The rations are furnished by contract at a cost of $14.97 per 100 rations; Fowler & Co., of Springfield, contractors.

The medical department is under the charge of Asst. Surg. E. A. Merrifield, Fifty-eighth Illinois Volunteers, and is plentifully supplied with medicines and other hospital supplies. I have inspected the hospitals and find [in] them but little improvement over the barracks as regards cleanliness. I was indeed surprised to find such a filthy place for sick men. These hospitals have a large number of nurses and attendants who have been detailed from the prisoners themselves, and every care and attention is given to the patients. The buildings used as prisoners' hospitals are illy adapted to the purposes to which they are applied. They are not sufficiently well ventilated and are badly arranged. As cleanliness and ventilation are the great essentials for a hospital no buildings would answer the purpose in the condition I found these. I attribute their condition to the indolence of the nurses and attendants, to the want of force in the medical officers in charge of the hospitals and to the general disregard of police regulations by the prisoners. Assistant Surgeon Merrifield is well aware of the wants of his hospitals, as that of the troops was in good condition. He has repeatedly given proper instructions, but has shown a want of energy and force in not enforcing them. The officers here have given many directions to the prisoners regarding their own comfort, but have permitted their instructions to be disregarded. The prisoners, indolent from confinement, will not perform the ordinary police duties of the camp demanded by all sanitary regulations without compulsion. There are two physicians employed by contract as assistants to Doctor Merrifield in the prisoners' hospitals. There are also three prisoners who represent themselves to be medical officers of the C. S. Army, and who are employed attending the sick prisoners, and render valuable service. Doctor Merrifield appears desirous of doing his duty, is active and industrious, but there is a looseness, want of discipline and system in the hospitals. There were three buildings used as prison hospitals which contained 207 patients. All of these were seriously sick and presented a case of suffering calculated to excite much sympathy. Besides those sick in hospitals there were 250 prisoners receiving medical treatment in the barracks. These prisoners were not seriously unwell and were able to visit the hospitals daily for their medicines. Besides the hospitals above referred to there was a small building separated from the camp and without the inclosure that is used as a smallpox hospital. It contained seven prisoners, all varioloid cases. The sanitary condition of the prisoners has improved but little since their arrival. The principal causes of their unhealthy condition are exposure in transportation to this camp; long confinement on transports without sufficient clothing to protect them from the weather; prostration and reduction before capture, together with a total neglect of all sanitary regulations and of personal cleanliness. The mortality of the camp is quite large; 103 persons died during the month of February. The prisoners' fund is rapidly accumulating and proper economy is exercised in its disbursement.

Quite a number of prisoners have taken the oath of allegiance. Before being permitted to do so each applicant is carefully questioned and examined and if there is reason to doubt the sincerity of his application this indulgence is not granted. I think that proper attention is not given to this subject and that the examination is not sufficiently thorough. The commanding officer is entirely too liberal in his indulgences in this respect. A number of the prisoners here are Texas conscripts and there is a great deal of professed loyalty among them.

Quite a number of them who were released by taking the oath of renunciation and allegiance have enlisted in the U. S. service. I would not permit any of those who enlisted in the U. S. troops at the camp to be placed as guards over their late companions. Sixty-one prisoners were released upon taking the oath of renunciation and allegiance during the month of February. The duties of provost-marshal are performed by Capt. R. W. Healy, Fifty-eighth Regiment Illinois Volunteers, but owing to a lack of force in the officers and a want of discipline they were not performed satisfactorily in every respect.

This camp might have been made a very satisfactory one in every respect but there was an apparent neglect in everything relating to discipline. There were no police regulations established. The commanding officer who had been a prisoner in the South seemed to care only for the security of the prisoners. They were closely confined within limits and no regard paid to their wants or comforts. He appeared to think this was all that was required of him. He has permitted the prisoners to take care of themselves; they have become indolent and have lived in filth and idleness until they have lost all energy and pride. I have given every necessary instruction at this camp for the complete compliance of all your instructions. I have instituted rigid police regulations and when I left everything indicated great improvement. With the aid of a few days of fine weather I have no doubt that the police and sanitary condition of the camp will be wonderfully improved.

I am, colonel, very respectfully, your obedient servant,

H. W. FREEDLEY,
Captain, Third Infantry.

WAR DEPARTMENT, *Washington, March 22, 1863.*
Hon. JOSEPH HOLT, *Judge-Advocate-General U. S. Army.*

COLONEL: A number of prisoners arrived here yesterday from Richmond who had been captured while on an expedition under the direction of Major-General Mitchel last spring. Several of the party sent out by General Mitchel are reported to have been put to death by the rebels and one of their number to have received 100 lashes on his bare back. I desire that you take measures to have the examination* of these witnesses taken and their testimony reduced to writing before a notary public for the purposes of this Department. They will be directed to report to you to-morrow.

Yours, truly,

EDWIN M. STANTON,
Secretary of War.

EXECUTIVE DEPARTMENT, *Wheeling, March 22, 1863.*
Colonel HOFFMAN, *Washington, D. C.*

DEAR SIR: I see in the papers that a number of the political prisoners at Richmond have been sent North for exchange. Will you please furnish me with the names of those residing in Virginia at as early a day as practicable?

I am, yours, &c.,

F. H. PEIRPOINT.

---

*For the Judge-Advocate-General's report in this matter and other documents relating to it, see Series I, Vol. X, Part I, p. 630 *et seq.*

HEADQUARTERS DEPARTMENT OF THE OHIO,
Cincinnati, Ohio, March 22, 1863.

Colonel HOFFMAN,
Commissary-General of Prisoners, Washington, D. C.:

I am directed by the department commander to acknowledge the receipt of your communication of the 16th instant and to call your attention to the inclosed special order.

Very respectfully, your obedient servant,

W. P. ANDERSON,
Assistant Adjutant-General.

[Inclosure.]

SPECIAL ORDERS, }   HDQRS. DEPARTMENT OF THE OHIO,
No. 103.   }   *Cincinnati, Ohio, March 21, 1863.*

I. As soon as the quartermaster's department can provide the necessary transportation via the Pittsburg and Baltimore route and so arrange for the movements as to time that different parties will not interfere with each other on the Pittsburg and Baltimore road all enlisted prisoners of the rebel army at Camp Chase, Ohio; Camp Morton, Indiana; Camps Douglas and Butler, Illinois, and Louisville, Ky., will be sent to City Point for delivery. Col. Thomas Swords, assistant quartermaster-general, U. S. Army, quartermaster-general Department of the Ohio, is charged with the duty of arranging the matter of transportation necessary and on being notified by him as to the proper time of starting the commanding officers at Louisville and the camps named will send the parties forward under proper guards.

By order of Major-General Wright:

W. P. ANDERSON,
Assistant Adjutant-General.

HEADQUARTERS PAROLED PRISONERS,
Near Annapolis, Md., March 22, 1863.

Col. W. HOFFMAN, *Commissary-General of Prisoners.*

SIR: I have the honor to inclose you a complete account of my savings and expenditures up to date since the 1st of September. It will be seen that the savings to the 1st of March, 1863, is $17,143.65 and the amount drawn $9,000. Out for that are vouchers for $8,232.74, leaving a balance on hand of $767.26, a part of which has gone per Adams Express to pay bills and return the proper vouchers, which will speak for themselves at the end of the month when I make up my final statement for this month. I have things so arranged in my office that my monthly accounts will be promptly sent you at the end of each month. You will perceive that these headquarters have cost on an average for the last six months $207 to pay clerks, &c., for the labor done in this office, and then I have worked my men at least fifteen hours per day. The commissary department of my camp has cost on an average of $140 per month. The quartermaster's department has cost on an average of $151 per month, and all the work otherwise done by the quartermaster of the post, who pays $25 per month, I have had done for $7.75 and $12 per month, $7.75 to the teamsters and laborers and $12 or $12.40 to clerks and chief men.

The whole work of my department has not cost the Government one cent beyond the wear and tear of horses and wagons. All the buildings for the departments and stables for over 140 horses are our property and cost the Government nothing, which I hope will give general satisfaction. The amount of bills due are $2,486.20 and the amount on hand $767.26. I have inclosed drafts for approval for $2,000 so as to be able to make as close a settlement at the end of this month as possible. Captain Lazelle informs me that you did not receive my return of savings for the month of February which I sent you on the 10th instant and inclose* now. It is the smallest monthly savings which I have yet had, which shows that such a commissary as Captain Ames was would never suit for this camp. For instance I find where there was a quart of molasses due he would issue one gallon and such like issues. I am much pleased with the visit of Captain Lazelle and believe the plans proposed by him to be of great importance. He is an officer of large experience and thoroughly acquainted with details which makes him fully adapted to make an investigation and suggestions such as are needed for such a camp as this. It encourages me much and I hope his suggestions will be adopted at once.

I am, colonel, with great respect, your obedient servant,

GEO. SANGSTER,
Lieutenant-Colonel, Commanding Paroled Prisoners.

QUARTERMASTER-GENERAL'S OFFICE,
Washington, March 22, 1863.

Col. WILLIAM HOFFMAN,
Commissary-General of Prisoners, Washington, D. C.

COLONEL: In reply to your note of this morning relative to the issue of clothing to certain citizen prisoners and asking how this issue can be made so as to have the clothing properly accounted for I am directed by the Quartermaster-General to inform you that there is a quantity of irregular clothing on hand from which such issues may be made and that you will be supplied with such garments as you may make requisition for for that purpose. The clothing being turned over to your control the issuing officer should be instructed to take the receipts of the parties receiving it as required by the regulations in the case of issues of like nature to soldiers, and in addition the receipts should be accompanied by certified copies of the Secretary's order authorizing the issue and the certificate of the officer that the issue is strictly in accordance therewith.

By order of the Quartermaster-General:

Very respectfully, your obedient servant,

ALEX. J. PERRY,
Assistant Quartermaster.

WAR DEPARTMENT, *Washington, March 22, 1863.*

J. C. WETMORE, Esq.,
344 Pennsylvania Avenue, Washington, D. C.

SIR: The Secretary of War requests that you will have the Ohio prisoners belonging to the detachment sent out by General Mitchel who have just returned from Richmond report at 11 o'clock to-morrow morning to the Judge-Advocate-General, Colonel Holt, in order to have their examinations taken touching the circumstances of their capture and their treatment and in respect to the execution of certain of their number.

Very respectfully, your obedient servant,

F. H. HALL.

---

* Not found.

WASHINGTON, D. C., *March 23, 1863.*

Brig. Gen. M. C. MEIGS, *Quartermaster-General.*

GENERAL: There are about 100 prisoners in the Old Capitol Prison sentenced to hard labor on the public works and the number is daily increasing.

The Secretary of War has proposed to send them to the Tortugas if proper transportation should offer. If your Department is sending any vessel to that place suitable for the purpose please inform me. The prison is already too much crowded.

Very respectfully, your obedient servant,

H. W. HALLECK,
General-in-Chief.

OFFICE COMMISSARY-GENERAL OF PRISONERS,
Washington, D. C., March 23, 1863.

Brig. Gen. M. C. MEIGS,
Quartermaster-General U. S. Army, Washington, D. C.

GENERAL: The Secretary of War directs that clothing of an irregular and inferior character be issued to destitute citizens recently released from the prisons in Richmond, and I have respectfully to request that you will cause to be furnished to Capt. E. M. Camp, aide de-camp, at the Soldiers' Rest, the following-named articles to be receipted for and issued by him, VIZ: 80 hats, 68 coats, 62 pants, 63 shoes, 79 shirts, 83 drawers, 62 stockings.

Very respectfully, your obedient servant,

W. HOFFMAN,
Colonel Third Infantry, Commissary-General of Prisoners.

OFFICE COMMISSARY-GENERAL OF PRISONERS,
Washington, D. C., March 23, 1863.

Col. D. H. RUCKER,
Aide-de-Camp, Chief Depot Quartermaster, Washington, D. C.

COLONEL: The Secretary of War directs that transportation to their homes be furnished to the destitute citizens recently released from the prisons in Richmond and now in this city and I have therefore to request that you will cause transportation to be provided for the persons named in the accompanying list to the places set opposite their respective names or to the nearest point which can be reached by railroad or water communication.

Very respectfully, your obedient servant,

W. HOFFMAN,
Colonel Third Infantry, Commissary-General of Prisoners.

Extract from testimony of Maj. Gen. John F. Reynolds before the Committee on the Conduct of the War.

WASHINGTON, *March 23, 1863.*

Maj. Gen. JOHN F. REYNOLDS sworn and examined.

By Mr. GOOCH:

Question. What is your rank and position in the Army?

Answer. I am a major-general of volunteers, at present commanding the First Corps of the Army of the Potomac.

Question. At what point were you when the rebellion first broke out and when did you join the Army in the field?

Answer. I was commanding the cadets at West Point when the war broke out and joined the Army in the field in September, 1861, from recruiting service. I had been appointed lieutenant-colonel of the Fourteenth Infantry and was recruiting one battalion of that regiment from the 4th of July until September. I joined the Army of the Potomac under General McClellan while it was opposite Washington.

Question. With what rank and position?

Answer. As a brigadier-general of volunteers, and was assigned to the command of a brigade in the Pennsylvania Reserves.

Question. When the Army moved from Washington to the Peninsula to what corps were you attached?

Answer. The division to which I belonged (General McCall's) was attached to General McDowell's corps—the First Corps.

* * * * * * *

Question. Were you present at the battle of Gaines' Mill?

Answer. I was; and my brigade was engaged for the greater part of the afternoon and until our line was broken on the left and the enemy succeeded in cutting off a portion of the troops engaged on the right; and unfortunately cut off myself, so that I was unable to make my way back to the bridges that night. I was made prisoner the next morning (Saturday morning) by their pickets. The position of Gaines' Mill I knew scarcely anything about, either the ground or the position of the troops. As my brigade had been in action the day before I was first ordered by General Porter to place it in reserve; but shortly after the action commenced I was called upon and my brigade was placed in action.

* * * * * * *

Question. Will you give an account of what befell you after you were taken prisoner and describe the treatment that you received?

Answer. When taken prisoner by the picket I was conducted to the rear into the presence of the general commanding that part of the line, General D. H. Hill, and I found several general officers of the enemy there with him. Among them were General Jackson, General Ripley and General C. S. Winder. I was received by them very properly and nothing occurred there to myself at all derogatory to my position as a general officer in our Army. In a very short time I was sent under escort on horseback to the rear on the Old Cold Harbor road as far as General Lee's headquarters. There we were halted. I was sent with some other prisoners, the most of them wounded, among them Major Clitz. We were sent in an ambulance to General Lee's headquarters until he was communicated with. After that we were conducted to Richmond over the battle-field of Mechanicsville. On arriving in Richmond we were taken to the provost-marshal, General Winder, who sent me to the Spotswood House, a hotel there, where I remained until after the battles were all over, confining myself entirely to my room. I gave General Winder assurance I think in some shape or other that I would remain in my quarters. I do not recollect now whether it was in writing or not. After the battle of Malvern Hill, having been joined by General McCall, we were taken one evening out of the hotel by the assistant provost-marshal and conducted to the prison for the officers which had been prepared—a tobacco warehouse—and placed in confinement there, where all the officers they had captured were confined, the field officers on one floor—a large floor. A space was partitioned off for General McCall and myself to occupy. The floor above us was occupied by the captains and the floor above that by the subalterns. In this prison we remained until some four or five officers escaped. After that circumstance we were paraded in public—marched down the streets to the Libby Prison. We understood that this was done because it was supposed that the remaining officers had connived at the escape of the others. At the Libby Prison we were all placed on two floors without any distinction as to rank being made. While in the first prison the officers were allowed by the authorities one ration each consisting of bread and meat only. There was a caterer to the prison who attended to the commissions of the officers and bought provisions for them, such things as they chose to buy themselves for their messes; and General McCall and myself were allowed to have our meals brought from a boarding house. After we were placed in the Libby Prison this was continued I believe with some restrictions. We remained in the Libby Prison until our exchange was effected when we were ordered to prepare to march to Aiken's Landing. There was some objection made by some of the officers—some who were sick and unable to march and some who thought they ought not to be made to march; and finally some five or six conveyances were provided—mule wagons—which were used for all the field officers and those who were sick and a light board wagon was given to General McCall and myself, and in that way we were conveyed to Aiken's Landing. The weather was extremely hot, and on the road down the officers and the guard who were marching were halted some three miles out of town in the shade and detained there until late in the afternoon, having given out in marching. We started between 12 and 1 o'clock in the middle of the day and we arrived at Aiken's Landing that night and we arrived at Harrison's Bar the next morning, the 12th or 13th of August I think.

Question. What was the character of the rations allowed to you by the authorities in Richmond?

Answer. The rations consisted only of bread and meat and was said to be the same as was allowed to their own soldiers. I do not know the amount of it; I never saw it; we would not touch it at all. If it was sent to the prison it went into the general mess of the officers and they used it there. Having our meals brought to us I did not see the rations at all. The bread I know was very good.

Question. What was the character of the quarters in which you were placed? Was it suitable all circumstances considered for officers of your rank?

Answer. The character of the quarters was very filthy and unsuitable to the character of a general officer in every way whatever. We all washed, ate, slept, &c., in the same room. The room consisted of the entire floor of a large tobacco warehouse, unobstructed except by the rows of posts supporting the upper part of the building. The reason they gave for it was that it was necessary to keep the officers under guard in that way—at least we understood that was the reason—because the people were so excited that it would not do to allow the officers any greater privilege.

Question. Can you describe the treatment of our private soldiers?

Answer. I only know that the men were encamped on an island in the James River above the town. I have personally no means of knowing what the treatment of the men was. I must say, however, that I consider the treatment of the officers unjustifiable for various reasons. There was no necessity for removing us from the first prison; especially the general officers. With the ordinary treatment of prisoners according to the rules of war we ought not to have been made responsible for any of the acts of those officers who escaped from the prison under any circumstances. We were kept under guard all the time and if the guard failed to do their duty there was no one to blame but themselves. If any pledge had been exacted from us to remain in a certain place without guards at all we would have felt bound as a matter of course to have kept that pledge. But the action of the prison authorities there implied a connivance on the part of the general officers which was entirely gratuitous, for which there was of course no foundation whatever so far as the general officers and a majority of the other officers were concerned. If those who escaped had any accomplices in the matter it must have been confined to one or two confidants.

Question. What was the rank of the officers who escaped?

Answer. There was one lieutenant-colonel—Lieutenant-Colonel Hatch—a captain I think, and the rest I think were subalterns. Two of them were recaptured. The others got away and joined the Army at Harrison's Landing.

Question. What was the treatment of the men who were retaken?

Answer. It was very harsh and barbarous. They were taken every night under guard out of the prison and confined in some close dungeon or something of that kind and brought back in the morning. They were not put back at any time with the other officers who were prisoners but were put in with the men or teamsters, that is Colonel Hatch and the other officer with him—I do not recollect his name or grade. The discipline of the prison and the control of the prisoners were vested in a very young officer whose character I myself know from transactions at West Point while he was a cadet under me. This officer and some persons from Maryland had the control in the prisons. The character of this officer had been such at West Point that when I met him in Richmond I refused to hold any intercourse with him. Those persons had the entire control so far as I could understand and were only responsible to the provost-marshal-general for the safe keeping of the prisoners.

* * * * * * *

WASHINGTON, D. C., *March 23, 1863.*

Colonel HOFFMAN, *Commissary-General of Prisoners.*

COLONEL: During my confinement in the South as a prisoner I spent for the benefit of the other Union prisoners there who were sick and suffering $350, for which expenditure I ask to be reimbursed as all my property has been destroyed and everything taken from me.

Very respectfully, your obedient servant,

S. A. PANCOAST.

We believe the above to be correct and just.

JNO. M. RICH.
PETER CHEEVERS.

I was a fellow-prisoner of Mr. S. A. Pancoast for three and a half months at Salisbury, N. C., and saw him furnish needful articles to our fellow-prisoners, for which I take pleasure in stating.

Very respectfully,

CHAS. WILLIAMS.
JAS. M. SEEDS.

[Indorsement.]

OFFICE COMMISSARY-GENERAL OF PRISONERS,
April 4, 1863.

Respectfully referred to the Secretary of War with the recommendation that the amount be refunded out of the money belonging to the prisoners' fund in my hands.

W. HOFFMAN,
Colonel Third Infantry, Commissary-General of Prisoners.

WASHINGTON, D. C., *March 4 [24], 1863.*

Colonel HOFFMAN.

RESPECTED SIR: Making out a list of items of the expenses I have incurred for the sick and suffering prisoners who have been with me in my confinement and for which I ask the Government to repay I find very difficult, as it was from day to day and without the idea at any time of remaining two weeks in prison (although I remained nearly seventeen months). Ragged and suffering to-day, sick, needing attention to-morrow; all of them feeling that to go to the hospital was a long step to the grave if not a certainty, as their medicines were very light, and Salisbury Prison a very hell of chill and fever. Quinine went up to a dollar for eight grains and of which they furnished none in the yard, and the cases of chills and fever, sometimes three or four a day, and their great unwillingness to go to the hospital to die as they said made me furnish so much of that article. The scurvy and dropsy cases were almost general there being no vegetables furnished and our doctor saying they could not be cured without and must die I ordered all sick to have them every day and paid for them myself; and as there was not half bread enough to eat I ordered a dollar's worth of corn bread every other day, not having any idea of the sum amounting to so much, as I expected to leave every week. You will see the utter impossibility of my making out a correct account; but this I can say in truth I gave where and whenever I thought it was needed most, and if I had had a thousand dollars I would have given it for their relief seeing the tremendous suffering. I therefore guess at what was given and the dates. I was in Richmond from the middle of November to the 15th of May; at Salisbury nearly ten months.

EXPENSES IN RICHMOND.

Medicines for the sick	$20
Clothing, &c	30
Victuals, &c	20

EXPENSES IN SALISBURY.

For medicines	70
Clothing	30
Vegetables and meat	80
Blankets, bed-ticks, &c	30
Bread and pies	50
Liquor for the old and sick	25
	355

Respectfully, &c.,

SAMUEL A. PANCOAST.

Affirmed that the above account is correct and just and acknowledged before me this 7th day of April, 1863, at Washington, D. C.

GEO. C. THOMAS,
Notary Public.

[Indorsement.]

WAR DEPARTMENT, *April 7, 1863.*

Approved.

To be paid from the prisoners' fund in the hands of the commissary-general of prisoners.

By order of the Secretary of War:

ED. R. S. CANBY,
Brigadier-General and Assistant Adjutant-General.

WAR DEPARTMENT, *Washington, March 24, 1863.*

Col. WILLIAM H. LUDLOW, *Fort Monroe, Va.:*

The Secretary of War directs me to say that the subject of the exchange of officers cannot be decided before Friday, if so soon as that. It will be communicated when received.

E. A. HITCHCOCK,
Major-General of Volunteers, &c.

GOLDSBOROUGH, N. C., *March 24, 1863.*

Maj. Gen. J. G. FOSTER, *Federal Army.*

SIR: Two communications have been referred to me as the successor of General French. The prisoners from Swindell's company and the Seventh North Carolina are true prisoners of war and if not paroled I will retaliate five-fold. In regard to your first communication touching the burning of Plymouth you seem to have forgotten two things. You forget, sir, that you are a Yankee and that Plymouth is a Southern town. It is no business of yours if we choose to burn one of our own towns. A meddling Yankee troubles himself about everybody's matters except his own and repents of everybody's sins except his own. We are a different people. Should the Yankees burn a Union village in Connecticut or a cod-fish town in Massachusetts we would not meddle with them but rather bid them God-speed in their work of purifying the atmosphere. Your second act of forgetfulness consists in your not remembering that you are the most atrocious house-burner as yet unhung in the wide universe. Let me remind you of the fact that you have made two raids when you were weary of debauching in your negro harem and when you knew that your forces outnumbered the Confederates five to one. Your whole line of march has been marked by burning churches, school-houses, private residences, barns, stables, gin-houses, negro cabins, fences in the row, &c. Your men have plundered the country of all that it contained and wantonly destroyed what they could not carry off. Before you started on your freebooting expedition toward Tarborough you addressed your soldiers in the town of Washington and told them that you were going to take them to a rich country full of plunder. With such a hint to your thieves it is not wonderful that your raid was characterized by rapine, pillage, arson and murder. Learning last December that there was but a single weak brigade on this line you tore yourself from the arms of sable beauty and moved out with 15,000 men on a grand marauding foray. You partially burned Kinston and entirely destroyed the village of White Hall. The elegant mansion of the planter and the hut of the poor farmer and fisherman were alike consumed by your brigands. How matchless is the impudence which in view of this wholesale arson can complain of the burning of Plymouth in the heat of action! But there is another species of effrontery which New England itself cannot excel. When you return to your harem from one of these Union-restoring excursions you write to your Government the deliberate lie that you have discovered a large and increasing Union sentiment in this State. No one knows better than yourself that there is not a respectable man in North Carolina in any condition of life who is not utterly and irrevocably opposed to union with your hated and hateful people. A few wealthy men have meanly and falsely professed Union sentiments to save their property and a few ignorant fishermen have joined your ranks but to betray you when the opportunity offers. No one knows better than yourself that our people are true as steel and that our poorer classes have excelled the wealthy in their devotion to our cause. You knowingly and willfully lie when you speak of a Union sentiment in this brave, noble and patriotic State. Wherever the trained and disciplined soldiers of North Carolina have met the Federal forces you have been scattered as leaves before the hurricane.

In conclusion let me inform you that I will receive no more white flags from you except the one which covers your surrender of the scene of your lust, your debauchery and your crimes. No one dislikes New England more cordially than I do, but there are thousands of honorable men even there who abhor your career fully as much as I do.

Sincerely and truly, your enemy,

D. H. HILL,
Major-General, C. S. Army.

OFFICE COMMISSARY-GENERAL OF PRISONERS,
Washington, March 24, 1863.

Hon. E. M. STANTON, *Secretary of War, Washington, D. C.*

SIR: In submitting the accompanying order* for the approval of the Secretary of War I think it my duty to state that I am informed by Mr. Wood, superintendent of the Old Capitol Prison, that prisoners of war are released there on taking the oath of allegiance every day or two by Captain Parker, provost-marshal, and if this is done here in the city it is scarcely worth while to go to the trouble and expense of sending deserters from the rebel army farther north before they can be

---

*Not found.

released on the same terms. The fact of their being deserters is a guaranty that they will not return to the rebel army.

Very respectfully, your obedient servant,

W. HOFFMAN,
Colonel Third Infantry, Commissary-General of Prisoners.

OFFICE COMMISSARY-GENERAL OF PRISONERS,
Washington, D. C., March 24, 1863.

Col. WILLIAM HOFFMAN,
Commissary-General of Prisoners, Washington, D. C.

COLONEL: I have the honor to submit the following report of the condition of the prisoners of war confined at Camp Morton, Ind.:

Camp Morton is located near Indianapolis and contains accommodations for a large number of prisoners. There are at present only 652 prisoners confined here. They are well provided with quarters and fuel and have ample space for exercise within the sentinels' lines. The prisoners confined here principally belong to Kentucky, Tennessee and Alabama regiments. They have all been either sick or wounded; nearly all were captured in the hospitals of Murfreesborough. All are well provided for; every care has been taken of the wounded and all appear as cheerful and happy as could be expected of men in their circumstances and conditions.

The prisoners are quartered in five large frame buildings in the center of the camp. The dimensions of the buildings are as follows, viz, one 40 by 24 feet, one 110 by 20, two 100 by 20, one 120 by 20 and three small buildings in which are quartered 4 commissioned officers, 3 female nurses and 8 non-commissioned officers. These non-commissioned officers and nurses are attached to the prisoners' hospitals.

This camp is commanded by Col. James Biddle, Seventy-first Indiana Volunteers and captain Fifteenth U. S. Infantry. His regiment, the Seventy-first, is stationed here and is employed in guarding the prisoners. The regiment is partly on parole and cannot be detailed for guard duty. There are 250 of the enlisted men of this regiment who are not paroled. Besides the Seventy-first there are two companies of the Sixty-third Indiana Regiment that assist in the duty of guarding the prisoners. The police of the camp was good; everything was in fine condition. The space allotted to the prisoners for exercise was kept neat and clean. The barracks were in good order, floors cleanly scoured and swept; bedding well aired and clean; everything about the barracks comfortable. The guards were attentive and well instructed in their duties; the sentinels vigilant on their posts. The command was well disciplined and the duties of the enlisted men were performed in a thorough and soldier-like manner.

The prisoners were divided into companies and the roll called daily; all changes and alterations reported to the commanding officer ; police and fatigue parties detailed and all other of the common details and duties of the camp performed. The prisoners here were held in better subjection, were more cleanly in their personal appearance, would perform the police duties of the camp with more willingness and alacrity and were apparently more cheerful and happy than at the other posts. They indulged in more active games of amusement and exhibited more life and activity.

The duties of the adjutant's office were properly performed. The rolls and records were kept as directed in your circular ; the money accounts faithfully recorded and receipts given. The quartermaster's department is under the charge of Capt. James A. Ekin, assistant quartermaster, U. S. Army, at Indianapolis, having for his assistant Capt. John H. Moore, assistant quartermaster, U. S.volunteers, stationed at the camp. The duties of this department at the camp are not at all complicated and require but little time and attention. Captain Moore is an officer of but little experience, but endeavors faithfully and correctly to perform all his duties.

The commissary department is also under the charge of Captain Moore. The reduced ration of last year is issued. It is somewhat smaller than the one you have adopted but it is quite sufficient. The commissary supplies are furnished by Capt. Thomas Foster, Jr., assistant commissary of subsistence, U. S. volunteers, at Indianapolis. The ration was found to be good and wholesome in all its parts.

The medical department is under the charge of Asst. Surg. A. N. Weir, Seventy-first Indiana Volunteers, having for his assistants Drs. D. Funkhauser and P. H. Jamison, physicians employed by contract, from the city of Indianapolis. I found the hospitals clean, well regulated but somewhat crowded. The dimensions of the buildings used as hospitals are as follows, viz, one 40 by 24 feet, the other 100 by 24. Besides these there were two small outbuildings. There were 172 prisoners under hospital treatment. The general health of this camp is quite good. Those in hospitals were all old cases, principally wounds. The mortality of this camp is not large. Twenty-three prisoners have died since their arrival. This is indeed quite small when the fact of all being sick or wounded on their arrival is taken into consideration. The cases now in hospital appear to be improving. There has been no smallpox at this camp. The prisoners' fund is rapidly accumulating. Proper economy has been exercised in its expenditure.

I must call your attention to the fact that the bake-house at this camp which not only bakes all the bread for the troops and prisoners in the camp but for those in adjoining camps is under the charge of the quartermaster-general of the State. As a saving of 25 per cent. can be made by baking the benefit of it should properly belong to the troops and prisoners to whom the rations are due. When we take into consideration the large number of troops and prisoners at this camp last year, the number of paroled troops there last winter and the present number of troops and prisoners this saving must have amounted largely above the expenditures. I find that during last year the full ration of flour was issued to the bake house for the benefit of the prisoners. The saving in baking was placed to the benefit of the bake-house. I was unable to ascertain by whose authority this bake-house is conducted by the quartermaster-general of the State.

There have been but few repairs made at this post and those have been at but little extra expense to the Government. No clothing has been issued to the prisoners. No escapes have been made.

Very respectfully, your obedient servant,
H. W. FREEDLEY,
Captain, Third Infantry.

SAINT LOUIS, *March 25, 1863.*

President LINCOLN:

James N. Burns, indicted for conspiracy at commencement of the rebellion, guilty no doubt, recommended for pardon by loyal men. Think it would be judicious.

H. R. GAMBLE,
Governor.

OFFICE COMMISSARY-GENERAL OF PRISONERS,
Washington, D. C., March 25, 1863.

Brig. Gen. J. H. MARTINDALE,
Commanding Military District of Washington, Washington, D. C.

GENERAL: From statements made by the following-named rebel officers now confined in the Old Capitol—viz, Capt. P. L. Darling, Lieuts. James J. Burch and J. T. McCarthy, Fifteenth Georgia Infantry; W. F. Barrett, White's cavalry, and John A. Billingsley, Ninth Virginia Cavalry—and from the dates of their commitments it appears that they have been exchanged, and if there is nothing on the records of your office to show to the contrary I request you will consider them exchanged and forward them to City Point on the State of Maine. All Confederate prisoners captured in Maryland or Virginia up to November 1, 1862, and all captured at Fredericksburg during the month of December have been exchanged. It appears from the statement of Clagett D. Fitzhugh, First Virginia Cavalry, that he was captured in Maryland on the 14th of September, 1862; that he was transferred from Fort Delaware to this city on the 29th November and that he was paroled from that time to the 5th of January when he was confined in the Old Capitol Prison. If he was captured at the time he says he too has been exchanged and should be sent to City Point unless there is something on the records in your office which would deprive him of the privilege of exchange. He is on the rolls as captain but he denies that he has ever held a commission. It is not a matter of any consequence whether he is a captain or private so far as the exchange is concerned. Please have separate rolls of these prisoners prepared.

Very respectfully, your obedient servant,

W. HOFFMAN,
Colonel Third Infantry, Commissary-General of Prisoners.

OFFICE COMMISSARY-GENERAL OF PRISONERS,
Washington, D. C., March 25, 1863.

Col. HENRY DENT, *Provost-Marshal-General, Louisville, Ky.*

COLONEL: I have the honor to request you to send to this office on the 1st of April next complete rolls of all prisoners in your charge, civil and military. Let the rolls be as complete as possible, giving under the head of remarks all necessary information not coming under the several headings, as time of arrival, where from, charges, &c. Separate rolls will be made for citizen prisoners belonging to the rebel army proper and guerrillas and other irregular organizations. These rolls are required for a new set of books and I hope they will be carefully prepared and forwarded to this office at the time named.

Very respectfully, your obedient servant,

W. HOFFMAN,
Colonel Third Infantry, Commissary-General of Prisoners.

(Same to Lieut. Col. F. A. Dick, provost-marshal-general, Saint Louis, Mo.; Maj. W. S Pierson, commanding military prison, Johnson's Island, Sandusky, Ohio; Col. John S. Williams, commanding Camp Morton, Indianapolis, Ind., and commanding officer military prison, Alton, Ill.)

FORT MONROE, *March 25, 1863.*

Major-General HITCHCOCK,
    Commissioner for Exchange of Prisoners :

It is very necessary to get our officers out of prison. They are suffering. If not authorized to deliver all Confederate officers and have the difference arranged by captured hereafter cannot authority be given to deliver an equal number or equivalent to ours and get the latter out of prison?

                                                WM. H. LUDLOW,
                                                Lieutenant-Colonel, &c.

FORT MONROE, *March 25, 1863.*

Col. W. HOFFMAN, *Commissary-General of Prisoners :*

Please send me if possible by to-morrow's mail a list of Confederate officers, prisoners, made up from returns already in your office.

                                                WM. H. LUDLOW,
                                                Lieutenant-Colonel, &c.

HEADQUARTERS MILITARY DISTRICT OF WASHINGTON,
            Washington, D. C., March 25, 1863.

Col. W. HOFFMAN,
    Commissary-General of Prisoners, Washington, D. C.

COLONEL: In to-day's communication to General Martindale Clagett D. Fitzhugh, who was captured in Maryland September 14, 1862, is mentioned as a claimant of the benefits of late exchanges. Fitzhugh has been for years clerk and manager of the iron-works of Messrs. Hughes at Mont Alto, Franklin County, Pa.; was such at the time he was captured. He was taken by the body of cavalry which cut its way from Harper's Ferry. Had a Confederate uniform beneath a civil dress and was piloting Longstreet's ammunition train. He is one of those pestilent scoundrels who induced the enemy to attempt the Maryland raid and who gave them information beforehand and aid and comfort when it could be safely attempted. This man during Lee's occupation is said to have discharged his office duties in the day and to have gone by night to their outposts. It would seem that he is not entitled to the treatment our policy indicates for those who have the pretext of State allegiance. His neighbors would have hung him at the time of his arrest could they have laid hands upon him.

I am, colonel, very respectfully, your obedient servant,

                                                THEODORE McGOWAN,
                                                Assistant Adjutant-General.

P. S.—The county of Franklin is my home, and these facts were learned in October last when there on leave.

[Indorsement.]

WAR DEPARTMENT, *June 25, 1863.*

Respectfully returned to the commissary-general of prisoners.

The Secretary of War will not give any orders in these cases at present.

                                                ED. R. S. CANBY,
                                                Brigadier-General.

OFFICE COMMISSARY-GENERAL OF PRISONERS,
Washington, March 26, 1863.

Col. J. C. KELTON,
Asst. Adjt. Gen., Headquarters of the Army, Washington, D. C.

COLONEL: I desire very respectfully to offer the following suggestions in relation to Camp Parole for the consideration of the General-in-Chief. After further and particular inquiries into the condition of the camp I am satisfied that from the accumulation of filth of every kind which surrounds it on all sides it will be absolutely necessary to occupy a new location during the coming summer, and as during the continuance of the war there must probably be from 2,000 to 10,000 men at the camp all the time I would urge as a matter of economy in men and money that immediate measures be taken to establish a permanent camp in the vicinity of the present one by erecting barracks of the character of those recently put up on Pennsylvania avenue above Twenty-second street. With paroled troops and such officers as can be spared to command them it is impossible to have huts erected that men can live in, and such as they are what one set builds another destroys. The use of tents is attended with great expense for besides the rapid destruction of them from want of care those which are vacated by the departure of troops are immediately seized upon by the men who remain and used to double the tents they occupy or to cut up for other purposes, and at the present rate the cost of tents for 100 men would be little less than barracks, while the tents would last only for a few months and the barracks would serve for the war. Besides the advantage of economy in barracks the men in them would be always comfortable, which would remove a great cause of the complaints and discontent which are now so often expressed. With a well arranged compact camp better discipline and better police can be maintained and the men will be more under the control of the guard. I have the honor to submit herewith a plan* of the new camp which shows the ground and the arrangement of the buildings for 6,000 men. The buildings are one story and will quarter 100 men, with one kitchen to three buildings. The plan is not complete in all its details but it is sufficiently so to give an idea how it may be arranged. By being near the railroad much expense in transportation will be saved. There is a good spring and well near the house and good water may be had by digging wells, as at the present camp. A camp of this kind for 6,000 men would cost at a rough estimate $20,000, which I feel very confident would be the best economy in the end. Two-story barracks are cheaper than one-story as the same roofing serves for both cases and the lower story makes kitchen and mess room; otherwise there must be a separate kitchen. The owner of the ground who is reported to be a good Union man asks $1,500 a year rent.

Very respectfully, your obedient servant,

W. HOFFMAN,
Colonel Third Infantry, Commissary-General of Prisoners.

OFFICE COMMISSARY-GENERAL OF PRISONERS,
Washington, D. C., March 26, 1863.

Colonel LUDLOW, *Agent for Exchange.*

COLONEL: I have placed in the hands of Captain Mulford duplicate rolls of the citizen prisoners just arrived from Sandusky and also duplicate rolls of prisoners of war sent from the Old Capitol Prison. You will

---

* Not found.

notice on the rolls from Sandusky a number returned as belonging to Kentucky regiments. Nothing was sent with them when arrested to show that they belonged to any military organization and the entry is made on their own statement. On the rolls from the Old Capitol are five officers who have heretofore been exchanged. Herewith you will find inclosed two rolls of deliveries of rebel prisoners at Baton Rouge. I inclose also a list of rebel prisoners paroled at Des Arc, Ark. I will hand to Captain Mulford rolls of rebel officers that we now hold at the various camps and military prisons. There may be some inaccuracies in the lists as some of them are probably already exchanged, but the records as we have them show the lists* as presented.

Very respectfully, your obedient servant,

W. HOFFMAN,
Colonel Third Infantry, Commissary-General of Prisoners.

OFFICE COMMISSARY-GENERAL OF PRISONERS,
Washington, D. C., March 26, 1863.

Maj. T. HENDRICKSON, *Commanding Alton Prison, Alton, Ill.*

MAJOR: Your letter of the 19th is received and I have the satisfaction of informing you that orders have been issued placing you in full control of the prison, for which a suitable guard will be detailed to be under your command. You will probably find ample instructions on file in the commanding officer's office to guide you in all matters connected with the prison. I have given particular instructions in relation to the authority of Colonel Dick over prisoners sent there by him and I think there will be no difficulty on that point. If my letters have been lost or destroyed, which is not improbable, please inform me and I will send you copies.

Very respectfully, your obedient servant,

W. HOFFMAN,
Colonel Third Infantry, Commissary-General of Prisoners.

FORT MONROE, *March 26, 1863.*

Major-General HITCHCOCK,
Commissioner, &c., Washington, D. C.:

I have additional information to-day of the sufferings of our officers growing out of scarcity of provisions at the South.

WM. H. LUDLOW,
Lieutenant-Colonel and Agent for Exchange of Prisoners.

MASSACHUSETTS MILITARY STATE AGENCY,
Washington, D. C., March 26, 1863.

L. THOMAS, *Adjutant-General U. S. Army.*

SIR: The paroled prisoners at Annapolis, Md., are ordered by the commandant of the post to work upon the barracks now being erected by the Government at that place. A refusal subjects them to confinement in the guard-house and subsistence upon bread and water. The ground of their objection is that they on being paroled took an oath not to render the United States Government any service directly or indirectly

---

* Omitted.

until duly exchanged. To perform the work thus required they conscientiously believe to be a violation of the oath they have taken. Will you if proper make some authoritative declaration which will determine the question of their duty in this particular?

Most respectfully, your obedient servant,

GARDINER TUFTS,
Massachusetts Military Agent.

[First indorsement.]

OFFICE COMMISSARY-GENERAL OF PRISONERS,
March 30, 1863.

Respectfully referred to the General-in-Chief with the request that the duties which paroled troops may be required to perform may be defined in general orders.

W. HOFFMAN,
Colonel Third Infantry, Commissary-General of Prisoners.

[Second indorsement.]

MARCH 31, 1863.

It is the opinion of the Secretary of War that it is no violation of the cartel to employ paroled prisoners of war to construct barracks and sheds for themselves any more than to erect tents to cover them. Such structures erected for the temporary purposes of a parole camp are not military works nor is labor on them military duty in the proper sense of that word. The names of those men who refuse to do this work for their own comfort will be taken down and reported to the Secretary of War, who will then decide upon the disposition to be made of them.

H. W. HALLECK,
General-in-Chief.

———

HEADQUARTERS DEPARTMENT OF THE GULF,
New Orleans, March 27, 1863.

ADJUTANT-GENERAL U. S. ARMY, *Washington, D. C.*

SIR: I have the honor to transmit herewith duplicate lists* of 21 U. S. prisoners of war captured on the U. S. steam ram Queen of the West; also duplicate lists* of 335 U. S. prisoners of war captured at Galveston, Tex., January 1, 1863; also duplicate lists* of 372 U. S. prisoners of war belonging to the First, Seventh and Eighth Regiments U. S. Infantry captured in Texas. All the above-named prisoners are at New Orleans.

Very respectfully, your obedient servant,

N. P. BANKS,
Major-General, Commanding.

———

WASHINGTON, *March 27, 1863.*

Col. WILLIAM H. LUDLOW:

The Secretary of War authorizes exchanges of officers man for man without reference to the cartel.

E. A. HITCHCOCK,
Major-General of Volunteers.

———

* Omitted.

FORT MONROE, *March 27, 1863.*

Col. WILLIAM HOFFMAN,
        Commissary-General of Prisoners, Washington, D. C.:

General Hitchcock informs me that the Secretary of War authorizes exchanges of officers man for man without reference to the cartel. Please send me immediately all Confederate officers you have at Washington, Baltimore and Fort Delaware, and order all at the West to be sent to you that I may use them for exchange. Our officers are suffering greatly.

WM. H. LUDLOW,
        Lieutenant-Colonel and Agent for Exchange of Prisoners.

————

OFFICE COMMISSARY-GENERAL OF PRISONERS,
        Washington, March 27, 1863.

Lieut. Col. GEORGE SANGSTER,
        Commanding Camp Parole, Annapolis, Md.

COLONEL: In examining your accounts I find a very large number of employés at your headquarters and in the departments. At your headquarters you can be allowed extra pay for the sergeant-major, if he is a clerk, and for 6 additional clerks, for 1 postmaster and for 1 mail carrier at 25 cents a day. Express agents and orderlies will not be allowed extra pay. The commissary will be allowed 1 commissary-sergeant who, if he is not paid by the department, will be allowed 40 cents a day; 2 clerks, 1 butcher at 40 cents per day and 3 laborers at 25 cents per day. There is no account of men employed in the quartermaster's department and I presume none have been employed since November.

There was no fund until November and yet I find large accounts paid out for September and October for which you had no authority. Under no circumstances will extra pay be allowed out of the fund to men who receive extra pay from either of the departments. On your January roll one clerk signs the names of three others. This is not proper nor can it be permitted. On the rolls presented for services in the quartermaster's department there are a number of men paid for loading wood. This cannot be permitted and if you have continued to employ men in this way you will pay them nothing. It is very commendable that the affairs of the camp have been managed with so much economy to the Government but it is expected at the same time that the fund which accumulates very rapidly should be judiciously expended and that employés in the several departments should be limited to the same numbers and the same rates of compensation as if paid in the usual way. The fund is mainly for the benefit of the men belonging to the camp and is not to be too liberally bestowed on individuals who have little to do. Your accounts should have been clos d and sent in at the end of each month according to my instructions and not allowed to accumulate for six months. By this means you have given me no opportunity to approve or disapprove your course and now I have no alternative but to approve what I may not think right or leave you involved in large debts. Hereafter your accounts must be presented punctually at the end of the month and if there is occasion to deviate from my instructions you must refer the matter to me. I am unable to tell from your accounts what part is paid and what part is unpaid. Make up a statement to show this, giving the amount due to each person, and then I will act on your estimates for $2,000 which

I presume is intended to pay the outstanding debts. It will perhaps save labor if you refer to the vouchers in my possession.

It is probable that a new camp will be established on other ground and until this is determined you will stop all work and purchase no more lumber and of course your engineer corps will receive no pay while they are unemployed. I notice that you pay them for every day in the month, Sundays included. This cannot be allowed, as you did not of course employ them on Sundays in violation of the orders of the President dated November 15, 1862.

I am informed that a number of the officers belonging to your camp take their meals in Annapolis and sleep there. You will put a stop to this practice immediately. No officer will be permitted to board or sleep in town nor will you give permission to do either on the surgeon's certificate. If officers are too unwell to remain in camp they must obtain a sick leave by the mode pointed out by the regulations. Make a report of what steps you took to carry out my instructions in relation to Sergeant Ewing.

Very respectfully, your obedient servant,

W. HOFFMAN,
Colonel Third Infantry, Commissary-General of Prisoners.

EXECUTIVE DEPARTMENT, *Wheeling, Va., March 28, 1863.*
Colonel HOFFMAN, *Commissary-General of Prisoners.*

SIR: I want two majors, four captains and ten lieutenants, rebel officers, prisoners of war, belonging to the Virginia rebel army. I desire them to be sent here immediately to be placed at my disposal. I desire to put them in a chain-gang and put them to breaking stone on the national road in this county. I desire to keep them there at hard labor until some Virginia officers are released from hard labor in the penitentiary at Richmond.

Please consult the Secretary of War or get his permission and send them immediately. I have some soldiers here that I can put over them as a guard in the daytime and can shut them up at night.

There is now a wicked devil named Keaton at Camp Chase who shot a Union man in cold blood and threw his little child in the fire in Putnam County, Va. I want him among them.

I am, yours, &c.,

F. H. PEIRPOINT,
Governor of Virginia.

[First indorsement.]

WASHINGTON, *April 1, 1863.*

Respectfully referred to the Secretary of War.

W. HOFFMAN,
Commissary-General of Prisoners.

[Second indorsement.]

WAR DEPARTMENT, *April 7, 1863.*

Respectfully returned to the commissary-general of prisoners.

It is expected that the prisoners now in the hands of the rebel authorities will soon be exchanged and action upon this application will be deferred for the present.

By order of the Secretary of War:

ED. R. S. CANBY,
Brigadier-General.

BEFORE VICKSBURG, *March 28, 1863.*

COMMANDING OFFICER CONFEDERATE FORCES,
                    Vicksburg, Miss.:

Herewith inclosed find a number of copies of General Orders,* No. 49, present series, from Headquarters of the Army, Washington, D. C. It is due that this order should have as great a circulation as possible among Southern commanders. I respectfully request that you will give the copies sent that circulation.

U. S. GRANT,
Major-General.

_____

HEADQUARTERS, *Cincinnati, Ohio, March 28, 1863.*

Hon. E. M. STANTON, *Secretary of War:*

The Seventy-first Indiana, about 700 strong, are at Camp Morton awaiting exchange. They are well organized and equipped. Can they not be included in the next exchanges so that they may be ordered into the field at once?

A. E. BURNSIDE,
Major-General, Commanding Department of the Ohio.

_____

HEADQUARTERS, *Cincinnati, Ohio, March 28, 1863.*

Maj. Gen. H. W. HALLECK, *General-in-Chief:*

The medical director reports very strongly against the condition of the camp at Camp Douglas and recommends the removal to Des Plaines. Have I the authority to change the location?

A. E. BURNSIDE,
Major-General, Commanding.

_____

OFFICE COMMISSARY-GENERAL OF PRISONERS,
                Washington, D. C., March 28, 1863.

Hon. E. M. STANTON, *Secretary of War, Washington, D. C.*

SIR: I desire very respectfully to call the attention of the Secretary of War to the course pursued by Mr. W. P. Wood, superintendent of the Old Capitol Prison, in connection with the recent transfer of prisoners to City Point. On the evening of the 12th instant Major-General Hitchcock addressed a note to Mr. Wood requiring of him a list of citizen prisoners to be furnished the following morning. This note was delivered by my orderly to the assistant superintendent of the prison who told him that an answer would be sent down in the morning if required and since that time the assistant superintendent has told the orderly that the letter was handed by him to Mr. Wood soon after it was received. On the 13th having received no roll from him I requested by note he would inform me of the probable number in his charge to be exchanged, to which I received no reply. I then called on General Hitchcock and requested him to endeavor to get this information for me. The general accordingly addressed a note to Mr. Wood requiring that if the rolls called for the previous evening were not ready he would report at once the probable number in his charge for exchange. On the morning of the 14th Mr. Wood called at my office with a list of about forty names and stated that he had not received General Hitchcock's first note, but he assured me he would have the roll com-

_____

*Omitted here; see p. 306.

pleted at once by the addition of some few more names and let me have it for examination in time to order the prisoners on board the transport at 3 o'clock. The name of D. T. Chandler was on his list who I told him was not to go, and I at the same time pointed out the name on a list which I gave him prepared by the provost-marshal, from which it was erased by drawing red lines through it across the sheet. Having heard nothing further from Mr. Wood at 4.30 I left my office after giving orders that as there was not time to prepare the rolls the prisoners would not embark on the steamer till the next morning. Between 5 and 6 o'clock Mr. Wood called on me in Georgetown and gave me the roll which he had completed and informed me that he had ordered the prisoners on board the steamer. This was wholly unexpected by me and contrary to my instructions, but as it was near dark I had no alternative but to have copies of the rolls prepared at once so that the steamer might be got away from the landing without delay. The following morning I learned that notwithstanding my orders D. T. Chandler had been sent in the steamer and I was obliged to telegraph to Fort Monroe to have him returned.

The accompanying report made to me by Captain Mulford, Third New York, who received the prisoners on board the steamer, gives Mr. Wood's explanation to him of the cause of the delay in furnishing the roll called for by General Hitchcock. It appears from this that as the first note was delivered by my orderly he supposed it came from me and was therefore not entitled to his notice. On the 25th instant I addressed a note to Mr. Wood requesting him to give me the names of any citizens in his charge who could be exchanged, informing him at the same time that if there was time to get them ready before the departure of the steamer I would give an order for them to be sent with the prisoners of war to City Point. As I heard nothing from him in reply I concluded there were no citizen prisoners in the Old Capitol Prison for exchange. About the time of the sailing of the steamer I ordered Captain Hartz, assistant adjutant-general, to go on board and see that my instructions in regard to the prisoners of war who were to go on her had been complied with. On his return he reported that the names of some twenty citizens were on the rolls furnished by Mr. Wood, who told him they were sent on board by order of General Martindale. The following morning I requested Mr. Wood to give me the names of these citizen prisoners and a copy of the order of General Martindale under which he acted. During the morning he brought me the list and the note which I had written him two days before as his authority for sending these prisoners away.

In both of these transactions besides not complying with the instructions which he received from me Mr. Wood has made statements which are contradicted by persons who would seem to have no possible object in deviating from the truth and the circumstances attending his conduct all go to corroborate the reports of those who contradict him. I report this matter only that the character of the man intrusted with so important a charge as that of the Old Capitol Prison may be fully understood. I inclose herewith copies of two notes from General Hitchcock to Mr. Wood and a copy of my note of the 25th to him.*

Very respectfully, your obedient servant,

W. HOFFMAN,
Colonel Third Infantry, Commissary-General of Prisoners.

---

* See also Hoffman to Wood, March 13, p. 354; Wood to Hoffman, March 19, p. 368, and Hartz to Hoffman, March 30, p. 413.

[Inclosure No. 1.]

WASHINGTON, *March 20, 1863.*

Col. W. HOFFMAN, *Commissary-General of Prisoners.*

SIR: On the evening of March 14, 1863, after I had received on board steamer State of Maine the detachment of citizen prisoners sent from Washington on that date to City Point, Va., I was speaking to Mr. Wood, keeper of the Old Capitol Prison, of the delay which had occurred in the delivery of said prisoners on board the steamer and questioning him as to the cause of the delay. He remarked that he knew all about it and that it need not have occurred if the proper orders had been given. I told him I knew you had given the order in time. He said he had received orders two days (I think) before from Colonel Hoffman to prepare the rolls and that the same order had been sent again, but he did not recognize the authority and paid no attention to them. He said he received his appointment direct from the War Department and recognized no other authority, &c. I inquired why he did not explain his objections and have the proper order given if your order was not recognized. He answered that was not his business. I then said I should see that I was not again detained from the same cause, to which he responded: "It is all right now," as the Secretary of War had issued an order instructing him to aid General Hitchcock in all matters pertaining to prisoners and that General Hitchcock had issued a like order in your favor which would make your order good in future. I have thought proper to call your attention to the facts herein stated that you may be able to understand and correct any delays which may possibly occur in future from like causes.

I have the honor to remain, your obedient servant,

JNO. E. MULFORD,
Captain, Commanding Detachment of Prisoners.

[Inclosure No. 2.]

WASHINGTON, D. C., *March 12, 1863.*

WILLIAM P. WOOD, *Superintendent Old Capitol Prison.*

SIR: You will please furnish me with a list of all prisoners not soldiers under your charge specifying the time and place of arrest in each case, the authority for the arrest and the charges. As the purpose of this is to make exchanges you are requested to make in the margin or column of remarks all such cases as in your opinion (from a knowledge of the parties or otherwise) are not proper subjects for exchange, with such reasons as you think proper to state. This list is required for use to-morrow morning.

Respectfully, your obedient servant,

E. A. HITCHCOCK,
Major-General of Vols., Commissioner for Exchange of Prisoners.

[Inclosure No. 3.]

WASHINGTON, D. C., *March 13, 1863.*

W. P. WOOD, *Superintendent Old Capitol Prison.*

SIR: You will please report at once the probable number (if you have not prepared the list requested yesterday) of those who may be the subject of exchange as citizen prisoners under your charge. This is required in order to know what arrangements to make for them and the list desired yesterday must be furnished as soon as practicable.

Very respectfully, your obedient servant,

E. A. HITCHCOCK,
Major-General of Vols., Commissioner for Exchange of Prisoners.

[Inclosure No. 4.]

OFFICE COMMISSARY-GENERAL OF PRISONERS,
Washington, D. C., March 25, 1863.

W. P. WOOD, *Superintendent Old Capitol Prison.*

SIR: Please inform me if there are any citizen prisoners in your charge who may be exchanged. If there are any furnish me with a list of their names and the charges against them and if there is yet time I will send them to City Point in the steamer which leaves to-morrow morning.

Very respectfully, your obedient servant,

W. HOFFMAN,
Colonel Third Infantry, Commissary-General of Prisoners.

OFFICE COMMISSARY-GENERAL OF PRISONERS,
Washington, D. C., March 28, 1863.

Maj. Gen. A. E. BURNSIDE,
Commanding Department of the Ohio, Cincinnati, Ohio:

By direction of the Secretary of War I have the honor to request you will give the necessary orders for the transfer to Fort Delaware of all rebel officers held as prisoners of war in your department. Please direct that lists of all prisoners so transferred be furnished to this office.

Very respectfully, your obedient servant,

W. HOFFMAN,
Colonel Third Infantry, Commissary-General of Prisoners.

(Same *mutatis mutandis* to General Curtis, Saint Louis, Mo.)

OFFICE COMMISSARY-GENERAL OF PRISONERS,
Washington, March 28, 1863.

Maj. Gen. R. C. SCHENCK,
Commanding Eighth Army Corps, Baltimore, Md.

GENERAL: By direction of the Secretary of War I have the honor to request you will give the necessary orders to transfer immediately to Fort Monroe, Va., for exchange all rebel officers held as prisoners of war at Forts McHenry and Delaware to report to Lieut. Col. W. H. Ludlow, agent for exchange of prisoners. Capt. R. W. Baylor, a prisoner at Fort Delaware, is charged with violating a flag of truce and murder and will be retained in confinement. If there are any enlisted prisoners at either of the forts they should be sent with the officers.

Very respectfully, your obedient servant,

W. HOFFMAN,
Colonel Third Infantry, Commissary-General of Prisoners.

OFFICE COMMISSARY-GENERAL OF PRISONERS,
Washington, D. C., March 28, 1863.

Brig. Gen. J. H. MARTINDALE,
Comdg. Military District of Washington, Washington, D. C.

GENERAL: By direction of the Secretary of War I have the honor to request you will give the necessary orders to forward immediately to Fort Monroe, Va., all rebel officers held as prisoners of war at the Old Capitol Prison to report for exchange to Col. W. H. Ludlow, agent for exchange of prisoners. If there are enlisted men among the prisoners please forward them with the officers. Duplicate lists should be sent with the prisoners and I have to request a copy may be furnished for this office.

Very respectfully, your obedient servant,
W. HOFFMAN,
Colonel Third Infantry, Commissary-General of Prisoners.

OFFICE COMMISSARY-GENERAL OF PRISONERS,
Washington, March 28, [*1863.*]

Col. JUSTIN DIMICK,
Commanding Fort Warren, Boston, Mass.

COLONEL: I have the honor to inform you that by direction of the Secretary of War rebel officers captured hereafter will be sent to Fort Warren. Please inform me how many can be provided for in the fort.

Very respectfully, your obedient servant,
W. HOFFMAN,
Colonel Third Infantry, Commissary-General of Prisoners.

WASHINGTON, *March 28, 1863.*

Lieutenant-Colonel LUDLOW:

Rebel officers here and at Forts McHenry and Delaware are ordered to Fort Monroe; from Western camps to Fort Delaware.

W. HOFFMAN,
Commissary-General of Prisoners.

HEADQUARTERS ARMY OF THE POTOMAC,
Camp near Falmouth, Va., March 28, 1863.

Brig. Gen. W. W. AVERELL, *Commanding Cavalry Division:*

Your report of the battle of Kelly's Ford mentions the fact that a certain number of prisoners were paroled on the field of battle. This action was entirely irregular and in disregard of the orders of the War Department, No. 49, February 28, 1863. Paragraph III states that "no paroling on the battle-field, no paroling of entire bodies of troops after a battle and no dismissal of large numbers of prisoners with the general declaration that they are paroled is permitted or of any value."

The major-general commanding desires to know if Colonel Duffié who by your report seems to have paroled prisoners on the field had been furnished with a copy of the order referred to above and he also desires to know if this order has been duly promulgated and published to your command.

Very respectfully, &c.,
S. F. BARSTOW,
Assistant Adjutant-General.

HEADQUARTERS PAROLED PRISONERS,
Near Annapolis, Md., March 28, 1863.

Col. W. HOFFMAN, *Commissary-General of Prisoners.*

SIR: I have the honor to acknowledge the receipt of yours of the 27th instant and will endeavor to make as full a reply as I can to all the points to which you call my special attention.

The sergeant-major spoken of has not been on my rolls since November, for by an order from the War Department he was mustered out of the service, he properly being a three-months' man but was for twelve months South and four months here before being discharged, since which time he has not been employed in these headquarters. While he was here he acted as a clerk and was very efficient. The number of clerks for headquarters as shown on the rolls do not estimate the true force, but it will be seen that they are always changing. For example the February roll will show twenty-six men including the post-office and express office and College Green Barracks, which is apart from these headquarters but on the rolls. Eight on this roll have gone away and only one of the eight worked for the whole month as shown on the rolls. Just as soon as arrivals or an exchange of men occurs in large bodies I have to employ more clerks so as to make out the rolls for you and the officer in charge of the detachment. The rolls for clothing and pay accounts and everything pertaining to them, in fact the real business of all the battalions is done in this office, from the fact that I cannot depend upon the officers or men in any of the battalion headquarters, hence the necessity for so many men for these headquarters. After I have an officer for every 600 men with a non-commissioned officer the labor of this office will be much reduced; besides I can hold the regular detailed officer responsible and can take his return as a true paper, which I could not do with the paroled officers or men; and the men will not do anything without being paid. Had I not paid them I could not get any work done, as of course I cannot compel them to do any military service and the work in the department is of a strictly military character. It will cost at least $700 per month for the 2,000 men. I only have now to work the battalions in accordance with the new plan which I hope will be carried out, and not till then can I with my force give the satisfaction required nor scarcely make my proper returns. I have on an average of thirty letters per day to answer independent of the business with the department and camp.

The number of clerks required at these headquarters for the work of this office alone is as follows: One for the business with the departments, your office, General Schenck's and Colonel Waite's; one book-keeper for the camp savings and accounts; one for the order book and business in general with the adjutant; one for the morning, seven-days' and monthly reports for your office and tri-monthly and monthly report to General Schenck and Colonel Waite; two for descriptive lists and discharges, which is very large in itself; one for clothing and pay accounts and requisitions, which for all departments are checked in this office; one for accounts of deserters, transportation, &c., which is a matter of great importance to the Government (thousands of dollars are refunded to the Government by this method which I have adopted, which was spoken of in Captain Lazelle's report); two for the business of College Green Barracks, where the men are first received; one for traveling to and from the departments and battalions, making copies of rolls, requisitions, issues, &c., which has always been necessary, having no confidence in officers or men in the battalions, and by doing so I can check any irregularity or attempt at fraud, making in all eleven clerks for the work of this office at all times. And if they were permanent you could depend upon all your orders being faithfully performed as I have always tried to do, but have only failed in some instances for want of proper support, which I have spoken of in person and by letter to you. As to the pay of clerks when you were here I asked you about the payment of clerks and extra-duty men; also as to the bills contracted by the hospital. I told you that I had then paid out $227, to which you replied as I understood you to say as well did Major Given that I should pay clerks 40 cents per day and laborers 25, and that I could pay what was due when you arranged for the camp savings. This I did in good faith, but if I have paid for the working of this department anything wrong I am willing rather than you should approve a wrong to pay any of the bills of labor I have incurred; or anything that I have done wrong in striving to serve my Government, with an average of 10,000 in my command since the 1st of September, 1862, with two officers to support me in the discharge of such arduous and responsible duties as such a disorganized and demoralized command as mine has been, with but little sympathy save from yourself.

The postmaster and mail carrier is a very important post, and thousands of letters and money pass through their hands. To get men of an honest character to take the responsibility is very hard. Hence the reason I paid one 40 cents per day and the other 25 is [that] they go three times to the city per day with heavy bags on their backs, a distance of two and one-half miles, in all weathers. When the camp was large our mail for the camp would go as high as 2,000 letters in one day. The express agent must be a man of great honesty, for he carries to and from the city thousands of dollars. All the money from the men which is sent home goes from this office, and last week we paid off and the men sent over $20,000 away to their families through this office, and I have never heard of anything going wrong. A good honest man to take such responsibilities ought to be paid at least 40 cents per day. If I allowed the men to go to town to express their money, &c., the country would be overrun with men. The commissary department may get along with the number specified in your letter at camp at present while the number is so low, but the moment an arrival of any amount comes it will be necessary to have men at the barracks at College Green and in the navy-yard to get out the goods, as the Government has no men for any of this work. I have to furnish everything in the form of laborers, teamsters, &c.; there is not a man in any of my departments that is paid by the Government anything extra save what they get here. For example, I have nine teamsters which I pay $7.75 per month, and one wagon-master $12, in all $81.25, which if paid by the quartermaster of the post, as all teamsters in his service, it would cost the Government $250 per month. In this alone I have saved to the Government $178.25 per month. These wagons do the business for the quartermaster's and commissary departments less the bringing of wood to camp, which is done by the quartermaster of the post.

The reason there are no rolls from the quartermaster's department is because I would not pay so many laborers as were employed by the quartermaster, and they have stood over since November; but if you refer to the schedule of bills unpaid you will find an account of my indebtedness to the quartermaster's department. A copy of the schedule I sent you I inclose* you now, showing the amount due, to whom and for what and what I have paid since I rendered you my statement. The business of the quartermaster is very large and will need quite a number of men, but if the quartermaster of the post has to furnish laborers for this department in Annapolis it will reduce the expenses very much, but it will cost the Government three times the amount paid by me. If you strike out the laborers on the rolls for December, Jan-

* Not found.

uary and February of the quartermaster's department it will reduce them considerably, but these men have worked faithfully through the storms at all hours, and now that they have come to their senses and willing to take 25 cents per day instead of 40 I will have to pay them myself for they deserve it, and hereafter no men will be employed except on your order, that is regularly detailed men for the work of any of the departments. The signing of the rolls by one clerk several times occurs from the fact that those men whom he signs for left the office for their regiments before the men on the pay-roll were paid and left an order with him to draw their money and send it to them, which I saw was done and the money sent to them. I have their orders and receipt. If they are needed I will send them. This occurs from the ever changing state of my office and camp, but if such is wrong it will not be done again; but as the men trusted to my honor in the matter to be faithful to them, as they have been to me, I thus acted. The working of my engineer corps on Sundays has been a work of necessity, for you will notice that all my arrivals from Richmond are on Sunday morning and evening, causing not only the engineer corps to work, but every department is busy on the day and night always on arrivals, and especially before I made my arrangements for the use of the barracks at College Green. I have never been able to leave my office but one Sunday since the 27th of last August and then I left the church before the service was over to care for 1,200 men who had just arrived. Their wants must be attended to on Sunday or any other day; but this might be altered. The flag-of-truce boat always leaves the fort on Friday for City Point and returns on Saturday, bringing them always here on Sunday, or very early on Monday morning. My seven-days' report required on Monday has to be made from my Saturday returns, hence to send it off it must be finished on Sunday as well as my reports for General Schenck. As far as my quartermaster's and commissary departments are concerned I have them arranged so that no work is done on Sunday except on the arrival of men. But these headquarters have no stoppage; there is always as much to be done on Sunday as any other day.

I have stopped all buildings since your last letter save finishing those on hand which required me to purchase some more lumber to finish with, but nothing more will be done in building. I had some 400 trees cut down in the woods dressed, and those I am having hauled in and piled up here which can be drawn to the new site with much ease, as I find upon examination of the woodland on the new site that there is not much good timber. When I get this done I will stop the work of the engineers as directed and will stop now if you think I had better not draw any more logs. The officers who are allowed to sleep in town are here from 9 a. m. to 5 p. m.; those who are sick and in the hospital at Annapolis dine in the city whom I have no control over; they are under the orders of Doctor McParlin. All the officers I have here for duty live in camp and those who were allowed to sleep in town, they being sick, I ordered to come to camp at once in obedience with your order. My orders have always been to officers that they must live in camp or hospital, but when I could get eight hours' work from a sick officer every day and know that if he slept in camp that I could get no work out of him at all, I preferred the former, always being short of officers.

I inclose you a statement* of bills due, as I did in my return to you on the 23d instant, marked "bills unpaid," and I have added to it the bills

---

* Omitted.

which I have paid since then. All the vouchers you have are paid, of which I have duplicates, as I take triplicate receipts for all moneys paid.

I am, colonel, very respectfully, your obedient servant,

GEO. SANGSTER,
Lieutenant-Colonel, Commanding Paroled Prisoners.

WASHINGTON, D. C., *March 28, 1863.*

Col. W. HOFFMAN.

SIR: The Quartermaster-General refers me to you in reference to instructions for forwarding prisoners of war from the West to Baltimore and Washington. We have just transported 200 from Wheeling to Baltimore, and as our road (the Baltimore and Ohio) presents the shortest and best route from the Southwest to either this city or Baltimore, we beg to suggest that you order the remainder by this line. We can forward them in lots of 200 by the passenger trains or in any number you may desire by troop trains. As our road passes through no great cities and there is no danger of escape, &c., we judge with our large capacity it will be to the interest of the Government to direct the transportation as suggested.

With great respect, your obedient servant,

J. W. GARRETT,
President.

HDQRS. MILITARY DISTRICT OF WASHINGTON, D. C.,
March 28, 1863.

Capt. H. B. TODD, *Provost-Marshal.*

CAPTAIN: By direction of the Secretary of War all rebel officers held as prisoners of war now confined in the Old Capitol Prison will be forwarded immediately to Fortress Monroe, Va., to report for exchange to Lieut. Col. W. H. Ludlow, agent for exchange of prisoners.

If there are any enlisted men, rebels, among the prisoners they will be forwarded with the officers.

Duplicate list will be sent with the prisoners and a copy furnished Col. W. Hoffman, commissary-general of prisoners.

By command of Brigadier-General Martindale:

JOHN P. SHERBURNE,
Assistant Adjutant-General.

WASHINGTON, *March 29, 1863.*

Colonel LUDLOW:

General Burnside reports that the Seventy-first Indiana, about 700 strong, are at Camp Morton awaiting exchange. Please say whether they have or have not been exchanged and if not procure their exchange as speedily as possible.

EDWIN M. STANTON,
Secretary of War.

FORT MONROE, *March 29, 1863.*

Hon. E. M. STANTON, *Secretary of War:*

If the Seventy-first Indiana was captured before the 10th of December last they have long ago been declared exchanged in general orders.

If captured since that date I will upon information of that fact arrange the exchange and send to you the necessary notice thereof as I make declarations of exchanges. I hand over to Colonel Hoffman all papers connected therewith. I am under the impression that this regiment was declared exchanged in General Orders, No. 191, November 19, 1862.

WM. H. LUDLOW,
Lieutenant-Colonel and Agent for Exchange of Prisoners.

WASHINGTON, *March 29, 1863.*

Colonel LUDLOW:

The Seventy-first Indiana was captured on the 28th of December last at Muldraugh's Hill, Ky. Please get them exchanged as soon as possible.

EDWIN M. STANTON,
Secretary of War.

WAR DEPARTMENT, *Washington, March 29, 1863.*

Major-General BURNSIDE, *Cincinnati:*

Camp Douglas cannot be changed without a full report and the order of the Secretary of War.

H. W. HALLECK,
General-in-Chief.

WAR DEPARTMENT, ADJUTANT-GENERAL'S OFFICE,
Washington, March 29, 1863.

Col. W. HOFFMAN, *Commissary-General of Prisoners.*

COLONEL: The Secretary of War desires to know when and where the Seventy-first Regiment Indiana Volunteers was captured.

Respectfully, your most obedient servant,

THOMAS M. VINCENT,
Assistant Adjutant General.

OFFICE COMMISSARY-GENERAL OF PRISONERS,
Washington, D. C., March 29, 1863.

Maj. THOMAS M. VINCENT, *Assistant Adjutant-General.*

MAJOR: No reports in relation to the capture of the Seventy-first Indiana Volunteers the second time have reached this office, except a telegram from General Wright, in which he states that the regiment was captured at Muldraugh's Hill, Ky. He does not give the date but states that rolls were forwarded to the Adjutant-General by the adjutant general of Indiana on the 19th of January, 1863.

Very respectfully, your obedient servant,

W. HOFFMAN,
Colonel Third Infantry, Commissary-General of Prisoners.

HEADQUARTERS DEPARTMENT OF VIRGINIA,
Fort Monroe, March 29, 1863.

Col. W. HOFFMAN, *Commissary-General of Prisoners.*

COLONEL: I have the honor to acknowledge the receipt, with other official papers, of lists of Confederate officers now held as prisoners of war. They amount to 649, 120 of whom including many surgeons have been exchanged. Good faith requires as speedy a delivery as possible of these exchanged officers, and the sufferings of our own officers in confinement at the South likewise call for a speedy delivery of equivalent numbers of Confederates. When will they probably reach Fort Delaware? If you could give me the time I will send a steamer from here directly there for them. Will you please instruct the commanding officer there to turn them over to me on my order? I shall go to City Point to-morrow and will ascertain how many I shall need for exchange.

I am, very respectfully, your obedient servant,
WM. H. LUDLOW,
Lieutenant-Colonel and Agent for Exchange of Prisoners.

P. S.—If there are any Confederate officers in surplus and not needed for exchange now they might remain at Fort Delaware subject to call.
W. H. L.

HEADQUARTERS DEPARTMENT OF THE GULF,
New Orleans, March 30, 1863.
Maj. Gen. J. B. MAGRUDER, *Commanding, &c., at Houston.*

SIR: I have the honor to acknowledge the receipt of your communication of the 6th ultimo offering to exchange one of the commissioned officers of the U. S. Army or Navy held by you as prisoners of war for Mr. Paine, taken by the steamer Cambria off Galveston. If it meets with your concurrence I will return Mr. Paine in exchange for Colonel Burrell, Forty-second Regiment Massachusetts Volunteers, taken prisoner at Galveston, the exchange to be effected agreeably to your suggestion on board the fleet off Galveston. The reports concerning Mr. Paine's ill-treatment to which you refer are without foundation.

I am, sir, very respectfully, your obedient servant,
N. P. BANKS,
Major-General, Commanding.

HDQRS. DEPT. OF MISSISSIPPI AND EAST LOUISIANA,
Jackson, March 30, 1863.
Maj. Gen. N. P. BANKS, *Commanding U. S. Forces, &c.*

GENERAL: I find that you still retain six prisoners of war who were captured some time last spring and who should have been returned by the terms of the cartel on the last exchange of prisoners. Their names and respective ranks are as follows: Sergt. Patrick Kane and Corpl. Edward C. Smith, First Louisiana, Company B; Sergt. George L. Williams, First Louisiana, Company E; Private William Stanley, First Louisiana, Company B; Private Daniel Doyle, First Louisiana, Company D; Private Abraham McLane, Twenty-third Louisiana Volunteers (Allen Guards).

Presuming that this was an unintentional omission it is believed that it is only necessary to remind you of their detention to secure their return. I have further to inquire whether an investigation has yet been made into the case of the murderers of Majors Prados and Bauduc, of the C. S. Army, on board the steamer Virtue; and if so is it your intention to turn them over to the Confederate authorities?

I am, general, very respectfully, your obedient servant,
J. C. PEMBERTON,
Lieutenant-General, Commanding.

SAINT LOUIS, *March 30, 1863.*

General BARTHOLOW, *Glasgow:*

All right. I am misinformed as to the locality of Sibley's Landing. I had telegraphed Loan, who has no doubt telegraphed commanders everywhere. Death to bushwhackers is the order. Have a commission always ready to try, determine and execute immediately if they are unfortunately taken alive.

S. R. CURTIS,
Major-General.

HEADQUARTERS U. S. FORCES,
Nashville, Tenn., March 30, 1863.

Col. STANLEY MATTHEWS, *Department of the Cumberland.*

COLONEL: I have the honor to transmit herewith a list of those whom I deem proper subjects for the operation of General Orders, No. 43,* Department of the Cumberland. This is composed almost altogether of the names of wealthy or very vindictive rebels who are more properly classed in the words of the order referred to as those "whose sympathies and connections are such as to surmount all the obligations that arise from their permission to remain within our lines, forbidding them to communicate with the enemy or act as spies against us." I also transmit testimony in some of the cases. I would for the information of the general commanding state that I have in the cases of very poor people coming under the classification of those "whose natural protectors and supporters are in arms against us" been in the practice of giving orders upon wealthy secessionists here to provide for their wants. Much suffering will inevitably ensue to people of this latter class if they are sent South to struggle with the destitution that prevails there and unless they manifest an active desire to aid the enemy I would most respectfully recommend that the policy of making wealthy rebels support the wives and children of those whom they have driven into the Southern Army be continued. The property left by wealthy expatriated rebels here might be made to yield an income for this purpose.

I am, colonel, your very obedient servant,

ROBT. B. MITCHELL,
Brigadier-General, Commanding.

HDQRS. DEPT. OF SOUTH CAROLINA, GEORGIA AND FLORIDA,
Charleston, S. C., March 30, 1863.

Commodore T. TURNER,
Commanding U. S. Naval Forces off Charleston Harbor.

SIR: I avail myself of the occasion to inform you that it is not within the knowledge of these headquarters if the U. S. naval officers who are in confinement at Columbia are in need of money or any assistance from the United States Government.

It is known, however, that Lieutenant-Commander Conover has been tendered any assistance wanted through a bank officer in this city and the papers herewith will show what instructions have been issued touching the treatment of these gentlemen.

---

*For General Orders, No. 43, see p. 339.

Of course any money, clothes or letters for them will be duly forwarded and delivered.

Respectfully, your obedient servant,

THOMAS JORDAN,
Brigadier-General and Chief of Staff.

OFFICE COMMISSARY-GENERAL OF PRISONERS,
Washington, D. C., March 30, 1863.

Col. G. LOOMIS, *Commanding Fort Columbus, N. Y.*

COLONEL: General Burnside writes that some time about June last he forwarded rolls of prisoners paroled at Salisbury, N. C., to the commanding officer at Fort Columbus, N. Y. If such rolls are on the files of your office will you please forward them to us at your earliest convenience?

Very respectfully, your obedient servant,

W. HOFFMAN,
Colonel Third Infantry, Commissary-General of Prisoners.

OFFICE COMMISSARY-GENERAL OF PRISONERS,
Washington, D. C., March 30, 1863.

Col. J. L. DONALDSON,
Quartermaster, U. S. Army, Baltimore, Md.

COLONEL: Lest you may not have been advised of the movement I think it well to inform you that some 5,000 or 6,000 rebel prisoners have been ordered from the West to be delivered at City Point via Baltimore. Near 300 will leave Saint Louis to-morrow.

Very respectfully, your obedient servant,

W. HOFFMAN,
Colonel Third Infantry, Commissary-General of Prisoners.

OFFICE COMMISSARY-GENERAL OF PRISONERS,
Washington, D. C., March 30, 1863.

Lieut. Col. D. D. PERKINS,
Commanding Fort Delaware, Delaware, Del.

COLONEL: Some 800 to 1,000 rebel officers have been ordered from the West to Fort Delaware and may be expected to arrive in a week or ten days.

Very respectfully, your obedient servant,

W. HOFFMAN,
Colonel Third Infantry, Commissary-General of Prisoners.

OFFICE COMMISSARY-GENERAL OF PRISONERS,
Washington, D. C., March 30, 1863.

Lieut. Col. W. H. LUDLOW,
Agent for Exchange of Prisoners, Fort Monroe, Va.

COLONEL: Your letter of the 25th* instant with its inclosures is received. There are on file in this office three lists of Federal prisoners

---

* Not found.

paroled at Salisbury, N. C., on the 27th, 28th and 29th May, 1862, amounting in all to 387 men. These rolls were forwarded to me from New Berne by General Wessells, and there is nothing to show that the men named have ever been exchanged. I inclose* them herewith. I spoke to General Burnside about the prisoners paroled at Salisbury but he could give me no information in relation to them. I have two other rolls of prisoners delivered in General Burnside's lines May 28 and June 2 amounting to 740 men. The Burnside deliveries declared exchanged in General Orders, No. 118. I will inquire of Colonel Loomis, commanding Fort Columbus, if he has the rolls we are looking for.

Very respectfully, your obedient servant,

W. HOFFMAN,
Colonel Third Infantry, Commissary-General of Prisoners.

OFFICE COMMISSARY-GENERAL OF PRISONERS,
Washington, D. C., March 30, 1863.

Col. W. HOFFMAN, *Commissary-General of Prisoners.*

COLONEL: I have the honor to inform you that on making inquiries of Mr. Wood as to the prisoners put on board of the steamer State of Maine on the evening of the 26th of March I was informed by him that there were about thirty-five prisoners amongst them, and when I told him it was contrary to your orders, or words implying the same, he told me they were sent by direction of the military commander of the district, or words to the same effect.

Very respectfully, your obedient servant,

W. T. HARTZ,
Captain and Assistant Adjutant-General.

SURGEON-GENERAL'S OFFICE,
Washington, March 30, 1863.

Col. W. HOFFMAN,
Commissary-General of Prisoners, Washington, D. C.

COLONEL: I have the honor to inclose herewith a partial list† of names of prisoners of war who have died in our hospitals during this rebellion. It has required considerable time to obtain the reports from all sections where our troops are serving and from the more distant sections the reports are daily arriving. It is thought, however, desirable to send this incomplete list to relieve as promptly as possible the anxiety of the friends of those persons whose names are herein mentioned. Another list embracing about 1,000 additional names will speedily be prepared. The Secretary of War upon the application of the Surgeon-General has given the authority to furnish this list, which you are respectfully requested to forward to Richmond with, should you deem it advisable, a copy of this letter.

By order of the Surgeon-General U. S. Army:

Very respectfully, your obedient servant,

JOS. R. SMITH,
Surgeon, U. S. Army.

---

* Omitted.   †Not found.

GENERAL ORDERS, ⎰   HEADQUARTERS PAROLED PRISONERS,
     No. 8.   ⎱   *Near Annapolis, Md., March 30, 1863.*

I. Pursuant to instructions from the commander-in-chief through Col. William Hoffman, commissary-general of prisoners, officers who have reported at these headquarters or may hereafter report will not be permitted to take their meals or sleep in the city of Annapolis but will at all times be in camp, and will be held to a strict accountability for the comfort of the men and the proper policing of the company streets and grounds of the battalion to which they are assigned for duty.

II. The provost-marshal at Annapolis, Md., will report to these headquarters any officer living in the city of Annapolis who has reported or should report to these headquarters.

III. Officers will not leave the camp without authority and when the leave is extended over six hours they must have it in writing from these headquarters.

By order of Lieut. Col. George Sangster:

JAMES E. DOUGHTY,
Lieutenant and Adjutant Paroled Prisoners.

FORT MONROE, VA., *March 31, 1863.*

Hon. E. M. STANTON:

I have just returned from City Point and have the honor to report to you that the Seventy-first Regiment Indiana Volunteers, captured on the 28th of December last at Muldraugh's Hill, Ky., are declared exchanged.

I am, very respectfully,

WM. H. LUDLOW,
Lieutenant-Colonel and Agent for Exchange of Prisoners.

GENERAL DEPOT RECRUITING SERVICE MISSOURI VOLS.,
Benton Barracks, Mo., March 31, 1863.

Col. W. HOFFMAN,
Commissary-General of Prisoners, Washington, D. C.

COLONEL: I have the honor to report that during the period commencing March 20 and ending March 31 the number of absentees who have reported to these headquarters is as follows: 1 commissioned officer, 525 enlisted men.

I am, colonel, very truly, your obedient,

B. L. E. BONNEVILLE,
Colonel, U. S. Army, and Supt. Recruiting Service Missouri Vols.

OFFICE COMMISSARY-GENERAL OF PRISONERS,
Washington, D. C., March 31, 1863.

Lieut. Col. W. H. LUDLOW,
Agent for Exchange of Prisoners, Fort Monroe, Va.:

Your letter of the 29th is just received. You must not forget that many rebel officers who have been heretofore exchanged have been retained in our hands unavoidably owing to the difficulty of delivering them in the West. I am not able to say when the officers ordered

to Fort Delaware will reach there—probably in about a week. I will
direct the commanding officer to forward them to Fort Monroe whenever you call for them. I will forward to you to-morrow rolls of paroled
Federal troops at the several camps that you may know how many are
to be exchanged. Please return these rolls to me and any others you
may have that you have no further use for.
    Very respectfully, your obedient servant,
                                W. HOFFMAN,
        Colonel Third Infantry, Commissary-General of Prisoners.

                          FORT MONROE, *March 31, 1863.*
Col. W. HOFFMAN, *Commissary-General of Prisoners.*
    COLONEL: The inclosed lists* are returned for certification that the
parties paroled were sent through our lines or are not now within them.
The officers taking the parole should state what disposition was made
of the paroled men. I hope you may be able to obtain the desired
certificates as we shall need every parole taken by us. Are you not
receiving any paroles of the many captures made by our troops? The
Confederates are making heavy deliveries of prisoners, and it would be
very desirable to get our paroled men declared exchanged as soon as
possible. When will the Arkansas Post and Murfreesborough prisoners arrive?
    I am, very respectfully, your obedient servant,
                                WM. H. LUDLOW,
        Lieutenant-Colonel and Agent for the Exchange of Prisoners.

    P. S.—Have there been any deliveries of Confederate prisoners made
at Vicksburg since the 1st of January?
                                W. H. L.

        HEADQUARTERS DEPARTMENT OF THE GULF,
                          New Orleans, March 31, 1863.
Brig. Gen. JAMES BOWEN,
        Provost-Marshal-General, New Orleans.
    SIR: The commanding general directs that you make immediate
arrangements to send all the prisoners of war taken from the enemy
and now in our hands, commissioned officers excepted, to the enemy's
lines at Port Hudson by a flag of truce. Before being delivered the
prisoners will be required to give the usual parole. You will send an
officer and guard in charge of them and will see that the movement is
made quietly and without producing disturbance or excitement.
    Duplicate lists of the prisoners should be made out, both to be signed
by the officers who receive the prisoners and forwarded to these
headquarters.
    The Quartermaster's Department will furnish the necessary trans-
portation. Please report when you are ready to send the prisoners up
in order that final instructions for the movement may be given and the
communications and letters prepared to accompany the flag.
    Very respectfully, your most obedient servant,
                                R. B. IRWIN,
                          Assistant Adjutant-General.

---

* Not found.

CITY POINT, *March 31, 1863.*

Lieutenant Colonel LUDLOW.

SIR: I inclose to you a slip* which I this morning cut from the Baltimore American of the 28th instant. It is only one of the many confirmations which I have lately seen of the truth of what I told you at our recent interview, to wit, that since your declaration that it was not the intention of your Government to make any more political arrests or arrests of non-combatants you have made more of such than during any previous equal space of time. I shall report that belief of mine to my Government for its action. I put it to any conscientious man whether it is fair that you should expect the release of all political prisoners held by us when you are daily making arrests and imprisoning the parties.

In this view of the case it makes no difference that the parties arrested hailed from a country claimed by both of us. You demand the release of men arrested by us in that country and insist upon your privilege of arresting and imprisoning. Is that fair? Is that right? If your understanding is that you are to be at liberty to imprison citizens of Virginia who are loyal to the South and that we are not to imprison or keep in confinement men who are disloyal to the South arrested in the same State I assure you it is one which will not be accepted by me in any shape or form. You have not asked that much in negotiation and yet your people are practicing it. These men and all others in their situation must be released and such practices abandoned. Otherwise it is worse than idle for us to talk about political prisoners.

Your obedient servant,

RO. OULD,
Agent of Exchange.

———

CITY POINT, *March 31, 1863.*

Lieutenant-Colonel LUDLOW, *Agent of Exchange.*

SIR: In the delivery of officers which you intend to make to us you must take into consideration the large number (more than 200) whom we have captured, paroled and released since the President's proclamation. I am entitled to equivalent for them. You can bring in any paroles of a like kind yourself. Upon your application I recognized this principle in the case of the Fredericksburg officers. Even after I had ceased delivering officers I surrendered to you of those in our possession a number equal to those whom you paroled at Fredericksburg. I ask the recognition of the same principle now.

Respectfully, your obedient servant,

RO. OULD,
Agent of Exchange.

———

FLEMINGSBURG, KY., *March 31, 1863.*

Hon. JO. HOLT,
Judge-Advocate-General U. S. Army, Washington, D. C.

DEAR SIR: Having noticed by the letters of the Washington correspondent of the Cincinnati Gazette that you were taking proof of the returned six prisoners of that expedition† consisting of twenty-two men sent out by General Mitchel to capture a train in Georgia, and that Parrott received 100 lashes to make him tell [who was] the main

———

*Not found.
†For "Railroad Raid" in Georgia, see Series I, Vol. X, Part I, pp. 630–639.

engineer that run the train—the main engineer and captain of that detachment was James J. Andrews, a resident of this place. He made a bequest of $1,200 to this county for the benefit of the poor. And in my official capacity as county attorney I proceeded to make the proof and elicited an important letter from Captain Andrews himself, written but two days before his execution, which is authentic and of record, and I inclose you a copy thereof, supposing of course it must aid in making out the case. Andrews was a good man, energetic, faithful and loyal from principle.

I also find a letter from James Pike, of the Fourth Ohio Cavalry, which turned up in some way at Murfreesborough, Tenn., as per printed letter herewith, all which is respectfully communicated to you, hoping it may aid you in the premises.

I remain, yours, truly,

W. H. CORD,
County Attorney.

[Inclosure No. 1.]

FLEMING COUNTY COURT, *January [10?], 1863.*

In the matter of the estate of James J. Andrews, deceased, a resident of this county.

On motion of the county attorney, David S. McGavic being sworn states that he knew James J. Andrews for more than one year prior to the 17th of February, 1862, when after several conversations with him, being intimate with him, he delivered to me the check before me in substance as follows, to wit:

FLEMINGSBURG, *February 17, 1862.*

Cashier of the Branch Bank of Louisville, at Flemingsburg, pay to David S. McGavic or bearer in coin twelve hundred dollars.

J. J. ANDREWS.

He was then in the secret military service of the Government of the United States and he remarked to witness that he was engaged in rather a critical business and might never get back and if he should not get back—

I want you to draw this money out of bank, loan it out and the proceeds to go to the poor of Fleming County perpetually.

He left here for Louisville, Ky., and I heard from him no more except from newspaper accounts of his arrest and execution at Atlanta, Ga. Shortly after that I received the letter mailed at Louisville July 3, 1862, which I knew to be in his handwriting and addressed to me in substance as follows:

CHATTANOOGA, TENN., *June 5, 1862.*
D. S. McGAVIC, Esq., *Flemingsburg, Ky.*

DEAR SIR: You will doubtless be surprised to hear from me from this place and more surprised to hear that I am to be executed on the 7th instant for attempting to capture and run a train of cars from the Western and Atlantic Railroad to Huntsville, Ala., for the use of General Mitchel. I had a party of twenty-one detailed men from the Second, Twenty-first and Thirty-third Ohio Regiments with me. We succeeded in getting possession of the train and traveled with it some eighty or eighty-five miles when on account of one extra train being on the road we were compelled to abandon the train, the party scattering and trying to make our way back on foot. The whole party, however, were captured. I was taken on the 14th of April. I am satisfied that I could very easily have gotten away had they not put a pack of dogs on my trail. It was impossible to elude them. I was tried by court-martial and received my sentence on the last day of May instant. One week before the time set apart for my execution, on Monday morning, the 2d, I made an attempt to escape. I succeeded in getting out of prison and ran by the guard, they shooting at me but not hitting me. The whole country was immediately swarmed with soldiers. I succeeded in eluding them until Tuesday about 2 o'clock when I was recaptured and will be executed on Saturday. The sentence seems a hard one for the crime proven against me, but I suppose the court that tried me thought otherwise. I have now calmly submitted to my fate and have been earnestly engaged in preparing to meet my God in peace; and I have found that peace of mind and tranquillity of soul that even astonishes myself. I never supposed it possible that a man could feel so entire a change under similar circumstances. How I would like to have one hour's chat with you, but this I shall never have in this life but hope and pray we may meet in heaven where the troubles and trials of this life never enter.

What the fate of the balance of the party will be I am unable to say, but I hope they will not share the fate of their leader. If they ever return some two or three of them will call on you and the rest of the friends and I hope you will receive them kindly. They are noble fellows and will give you a full history of the affair. Please acquaint my friends of my fate. I shall try to write to some two or three more before my execution. Tell J. B. Jackson should there be any little claims that I neglected to settle to pay them and keep the horse. I don't think there are any but may be. In regard to other matters do exactly as instructed before I left. I have received no letters from Flemingsburg since I left. I wrote several but never received any answers. Please read this letter to Mrs. Eckels and tell her that I have thought of her kindness many times and that I hope we may meet in heaven where we shall enjoy the presence of the Lord forever. Give my kindest regards to Mr. Eckels also. According to the course of nature it will not be long until we shall meet in that happy country. Blessed thought. Remember me also to the young ladies of Flemingsburg, especially to Miss Kate Wallingford and Miss Nannie Baxter.

Hoping that we may meet in that better country, I bid you a long and last farewell.

J. J. ANDREWS.

CHATTANOOGA, TENN., *June 5, 1862.*

D. S. McGAVIC, Esq., J. B. JACKSON, Mrs. SARAH ECKELS,
Flemingsburg, Fleming County, Ky.:

You will find one trunk and one black valise. The valise has my name in red letters on the end and the other had my name on a paper pasted on the end. These are at the City Hotel, Nashville, in care of the old porter, on third floor. These with contents I present to you. Mr. Hawkins, you will find at the Louisville Hotel a large lady's trunk, no mark on it and is entirely empty. Please take it to Mr. Lindsey's, near Mill Creek Church on the Maysville and Flemingsburg pike, and request him to present it to Miss Elizabeth J. Layton for me, and much oblige

J. J. ANDREWS.

I certify that the foregoing is a true copy as it purports from the record thereof as it remains on file in my office.

Given under my hand this 1st day of April, 1863, as clerk of the Fleming County court.

[SEAL.]   W. T. DUDLEY,
                                                   Clerk.

[Inclosure No. 2.]

MURFREESBOROUGH, TENN., *March 25, 1863.*

I have been all the forenoon at headquarters copying the following letters. I have not time before the express leaves to write even a few sentences by way of introduction; but of Pike I would say he was captured at Bridgeport, Tenn., April 24, 1862. I had not time to write out his account of his defense and capture. What I give, however, is copied *verbatim* from his own written statements.

The second letter, of January 3, I give as an illustration of the general feeling of Tennesseeans relative to the rebel defeat at Stone's River. Bragg and others may disguise their feelings as much as they please before the public but the sentiments of this letter are the true ones among the great majority of the Tennessee officers.

G.

ELEVEN MONTHS AMONG THE REBELS.

MURFREESBOROUGH, TENN., *March 22, 1863.*

*   *   *   *   *   *   *

I was taken to Chattanooga and confined in a jail. This was a two-story building. The upper story where I was confined was twelve feet square. In this room were confined nineteen Tennesseeans, a negro and myself. In the dungeon, which was only ten feet square, were confined twenty-one men out of the Second, the Twenty-first and the Thirty-third Ohio Infantry, charged with being spies. They were under the command of Captain Andrews, who was then under sentence of death by a court-martial held at Chattanooga. They were waiting for the Secretary of War at Richmond to ratify the proceedings of the court-martial previous to executing the captain, and they said they were satisfied the rest would certainly be hung. I was afterwards informed by the rebels that Andrews and six of the men were hung at Atlanta, Ga. Another time I was told by the rebel citizens that they hung Andrews and seventeen men. I went down into the dungeon to where these men were and found them handcuffed with close irons and chained in pairs by the neck, with a heavy chain locked around each man's neck with a padlock that would weigh two pounds. These padlocks were larger than a man's hand.

We were fed twice a day on tolerably good bread and spoiled beef, with coffee made of cane seed. There was no sink in the jail, so that our offal stood in a bucket in the room where we were confined day and night. This bucket was only emptied twice a day and of course the stench was intolerable. We were denied the privilege of washing our clothes or having it done. The jail was literally swarming with vermin, nor was it ever cleaned out.

From Chattanooga I was taken to Knoxville to another jail and confined in an iron cage. Here I was told by a man named Fox, the jailer, that I was brought to Knoxville to be tried by a court-martial as a spy and if I was tried I would no doubt be hung. This court-martial as did the one at Chattanooga adjourned without bringing me to trial. From there I was sent to Mobile, where another court-martial was in session; but after keeping me there about eight days I was sent to Tuscaloosa, Ala. From this place I was taken in company with all the prisoners at that post to Montgomery, Ala. The first day out I was taken sick with pneumonia and typhoid fever. The rebel surgeons refused me any medicines and even a bed and I was left for twelve days lying on the deck of the boat with nothing to eat but corn bread and beef which the rebels said had been packed five years. At Tuscaloosa they shot a man for looking out of a window and wounded another in the face for the same offense. At Montgomery they refused to let me go to a hospital although in a helpless condition. Here they shot a lieutenant* for us under the following circumstances: He had been allowed to go out for milk accompanied by a guard. They were waiting for a woman to hand the milk out through a window when the guard gave the order to "come on." "Wait a moment till I get my milk," said the lieutenant. The guard made no reply but shot him in the breast with a shot-gun, killing him instantly. From Montgomery I was taken to Macon, Ga., in company with 1,200 others. Here we were allowed seven pounds of corn meal and two and a half pounds of bacon of bad quality for seven days. We were allowed two surgeons and but very little medicine. Our men fared badly, being punished severely for the most trifling offenses. One man named Cory was kept tied up three days by the wrists to a tree just so that his toes touched the ground. This was because he helped kill a yearling calf that got into the camp. A Floridian and two Kentuckians, political prisoners, were confined in the jail at Macon on quarter rations for twenty-two days. The only offense they had committed was to escape from the prison lot. Our men were pegged down on the ground for any misdemeanor. This was done by stretching out the limbs and driving a forked stick down over them. The operation was completed by driving one down over the neck. It would be impossible to tell all of the hardships to which we were subjected. I have endeavored to portray a few of them. They may be summed up thus: We were confined in bad quarters; our dead were left unburied for days together; some were left unburied entirely, at least to our knowledge; we were denied medical attendance; our chaplains were forbidden preaching to us or praying for us (by order of Major Rylander); our men and officers were shot without cause; an insane man was shot at Macon, Ga., for no offense; we were compelled to bury men in river banks where their bodies were liable to be washed out; we were beaten with clubs (this was done on board of the steamer en route for Montgomery, Ala.); we were fed on foul and unwholesome diet, frequently left without any rations two or three days at a time, and our exchange was delayed as long as possible; we were kept confined in camp surrounded by swamps, as the rebels said, that we all might die. I find it impossible to enumerate all the hardships put upon us, but have enumerated such as were the most intolerable.

JAMES PIKE,
Company A, Fourth Ohio Volunteer Cavalry.

SPECIAL ORDERS, }
No. 90. }

HDQRS. DEPT. OF THE TENNESSEE,
Young's Point, La., March 31, 1863.

* * * * * * *

VIII. The commanding officer of the Sixteenth Army Corps will cause to be built on one of the islands of the Mississippi somewhere between

---

* See Vol. IV, this Series, p. 230, for report of the killing of Lieut. W. S. Bliss.

Columbus, Ky., and Memphis, Tenn., a suitable log or frame prison for the accommodation of 1,000 prisoners. The island so occupied will be garrisoned by such a force as the corps commander may deem necessary for the safe-keeping of all prisoners intrusted to them and for holding the post. One contract physician will be habitually kept to take charge of the sick in prison and more should the number requiring medical attendance make it necessary. The expense of building such structure will be defrayed by the quartermaster's department from funds received through the provost-marshal's department.

* * * * * * *

By order of Maj. Gen. U. S. Grant:

JOHN A. RAWLINS,
Assistant Adjutant-General.

WAR DEPARTMENT, *Washington, April 1, 1863.*

Major-General DIX, *Fort Monroe:*

General Burnside is sending a lot of secesh women to Fortress Monroe from Cincinnati. You will on their arrival put them beyond our lines.

EDWIN M. STANTON.

OFFICE COMMISSARY-GENERAL OF PRISONERS,
Washington, April 1, 1863.

Col. D. D. PERKINS,
Commanding Fort Delaware, Del.

COLONEL: You will receive orders from the headquarters Middle Department to forward rebel officers, prisoners of war in your charge, to Lieutenant-Colonel Ludlow, agent for exchange of prisoners at Fort Monroe, for exchange. If it should not be so stated in the order you will not include with them Capt. R. W. Baylor who is charged with serious crimes, nor any other officer who may be held on any other charge than that of being in the rebel army.

Very respectfully, your obedient servant,

W. HOFFMAN,
Colonel Third Infantry, Commissary-General of Prisoners.

OFFICE COMMISSARY-GENERAL OF PRISONERS,
Washington, April 1, 1863.

Lieut. Col. GEORGE SANGSTER,
Commanding Camp Parole, Annapolis, Md.

COLONEL: It has been reported that paroled prisoners at Camp Parole have complained that they are required to assist in the erection of barracks, which they think is a violation of their parole. The question has been submitted to the Secretary of War who has decided that it is no violation of the cartel to employ paroled prisoners of war to construct barracks and sheds for themselves any more than to pitch their own tents. Such works are not military works nor is the labor on them military duty in the proper sense of that word. You will report the names of all who refuse to do this work for their own comfort to be laid before the Secretary of War for his action.

Very respectfully, your obedient servant,

W. HOFFMAN,
Colonel Third Infantry, Commissary-General of Prisoners.

OFFICE COMMISSARY-GENERAL OF PRISONERS,
Washington, D. C., April 1, 1863.

Capt. E. L. WEBBER,
Commanding Camp Chase Prison, Columbus, Ohio.

CAPTAIN: Orders have been sent to you through the commanding general of the Department of the Ohio to forward all rebel officers to Fort Delaware, on the Delaware River below Philadelphia, and to-day in reply to your telegram of yesterday I telegraphed an order to you to the same effect. This order applies of course to the sick and wounded who are able to travel, but those who are too unwell to be moved will remain at Camp Chase till further orders. It is expected that all the prisoners at Camp Chase will be removed to Johnson's Island in a few days and I am only waiting for the list of prisoners of all kinds at the camp called for in my letter of the 16th ultimo to give you the necessary orders.

Very respectfully, your obedient servant,
W. HOFFMAN,
Colonel Third Infantry, Commissary-General of Prisoners.

OFFICE COMMISSARY-GENERAL OF PRISONERS,
Washington, April 1, 1863.

GARDINER TUFTS, Esq.,
Massachusetts Military Agent, Washington, D. C.

SIR: In reply to your letter of the 26th ultimo addressed to the Adjutant-General in relation to the duties which may be performed by paroled troops I have to inform you that it is the decision of the Secretary of War that it is no more violation of the cartel to employ paroled prisoners of war to construct barracks and sheds for themselves than to pitch their own tents. Such works are not military works nor is such labor military duty in the proper sense of the word.

Very respectfully, your obedient servant,
W. HOFFMAN,
Colonel Third Infantry, Commissary-General of Prisoners.

HEADQUARTERS CAMP OF INSTRUCTION,
Benton Barracks, Mo., April 1, 1863.

Col. W. HOFFMAN,
Commissary-General of Prisoners, Washington, D. C.

COLONEL: Herewith I have the honor to transmit returns of the paroled men at this post for the month of March, 1863, as required by your instructions containing 108 commissioned officers present; 19 commissioned officers absent; 2,132 enlisted men present; 969 enlisted men absent; aggregate present and absent 3,228.

Very respectfully, your obedient servant,
B. L. E. BONNEVILLE,
Colonel, U. S. Army, Commanding.

OFFICE COMMISSARY-GENERAL OF PRISONERS,
Washington, April 1, [1863.]

Maj. W. S. PIERSON, *Sandusky, Ohio.*

MAJOR: Orders have been issued through the headquarters of the Department of the Ohio for all rebel officers, prisoners of war, to be sent to Fort Delaware and all enlisted men to City Point for exchange via Baltimore and Fort Monroe. You will accordingly without delay forward all enlisted prisoners of war, including guerrillas, to Fort Monroe to report to Lieutenant-Colonel Ludlow, agent for exchange of prisoners. Send duplicate rolls with them and a roll to this office. Separate rolls should be made of those belonging to regular regiments and the guerrillas.

You will forward also all rebel officers in your charge except those charged as spies to Fort Delaware, on the Delaware River, about fifty miles below Philadelphia. Send rolls with them and a copy to this office.

Send the enlisted men under an officer and a suitable guard, not over one man to eight or ten prisoners. The officers may be permitted to travel on their parole in charge of an officer. They will not be permitted to have communication with any person by the way nor to make purchases of any kind except something to eat.

The paroles should be very specific. If they object to this arrangement send them under a guard.

Notify the quartermaster at Baltimore when the enlisted men will be there so that he may have water transportation provided.

Very respectfully, your obedient servant,
W. HOFFMAN,
Colonel Third Infantry, Commissary-General of Prisoners.

FORT MONROE, *April 1, 1863.*

Col. W. HOFFMAN, *Commissary-General of Prisoners:*

When will the Confederate officers be delivered at Fort Delaware? Our officers are suffering greatly in garrison.
WM. H. LUDLOW,
Lieutenant-Colonel, &c.

WASHINGTON, *April 1, 1863.*

Lieutenant-Colonel LUDLOW:

Rebel officers were ordered to Fort Delaware on the 28th ultimo. Will probably arrive in about a week. Wrote to you yesterday.
W. HOFFMAN,
Commissary-General of Prisoners.

HEADQUARTERS DEPARTMENT OF VIRGINIA,
Fort Monroe, Va., April 1, 1863.

Col. W. HOFFMAN, *Commissary-General of Prisoners.*

COLONEL: I returned yesterday from City Point. The following-named commissioned officers captured at Murfreesborough were delivered and declared exchanged for an equal number of equal rank of Confederates delivered at City Point: First Lieut. David Snodgrass, Seventy-fourth Ohio; Second Lieut. H. J. Gass, Eighty-sixth Indiana; First Lieut. G. H. Hollister, Second Ohio; First Lieut. J. P. Fleming, One hundred and first Ohio; Second Lieut. J. H. Anchors, Seventy-eighth Pennsylvania; Capt. W. C. Wheeler, Eighty-first Indiana; Capt.

J. P. Dufficy, Thirty-fifth Indiana; Capt. John Becker, First Kentucky; Capt. H. A. Bornemann, Twenty-second Illinois; Capt. A. McMoore, Seventy-fifth Illinois; Capt. A. Perry, Ninetieth Ohio; Surg. P. Treadwell, of the steamer Columbia, unconditionally released. All of the above officers were sent to Annapolis.

I am, very respectfully, your obedient servant,

WM. H. LUDLOW,
Lieutenant-Colonel and Agent for Exchange of Prisoners.

P. S.—Eight hundred and five men mostly captured on the march at Thompson's Station have been received and sent to Annapolis this morning. The Confederate exchanged officers and other prisoners from Camp Chase have just reached here and have been sent to City Point.

W. H. L.

FORT HAMILTON, *N. Y. Harbor, April 1, 1863.*

Brig. Gen. L. THOMAS,
Adjutant-General U. S. Army, Washington, D. C.

SIR: Inclosed you will receive a letter* written by a prisoner at Fort Lafayette which I think best to send through your office. There was no necessity of Mr. Laurent to send an abusive letter about the Government through its officers to the British consul, as not long ago Mr. Archibald was down here and Mr. Laurent could have said what he desired under the usual restrictions. He could have stated his case just as he pleased to the consul, who appears to be a fair as well as he is a gentlemanly man. I may state that the British consul has permission to see certain prisoners in presence of an officer. This order is of long standing, which makes the communications of such prisoners as Laurent and Vernon inexcusable. According to the rules of the post any person can write to his friends on business or family matters or he can state at any time his case or his grievance in proper language to the heads of the Government at Washington.

Very respectfully, your obedient servant,

MARTIN BURKE,
Lieutenant-Colonel Third Artillery.

MILITARY PRISON, *Alton, Ill., April 1, 1863.*

Col. W. HOFFMAN,
Commissary-General of Prisoners, Washington, D. C.

COLONEL: I have the honor to report that in compliance with instructions from the headquarters of the Department of the Missouri of March 25, 1863, 869 Confederate prisoners of war left here this morning by railroad for City Point, Va. They were escorted by a detachment of the Seventy-seventh Regiment of Ohio Volunteers, 136 officers and men, under the command of Capt. L. E. Sisson, and had rations for five days.

I have the honor to be, sir, with much respect, your obedient servant,

T. HENDRICKSON,
Major Third Infantry, Commanding Prison.

---

* Omitted.

OFFICE COMMISSARY-GENERAL OF PRISONERS,
Washington, D. C., April 1, 1863.

Surg. D. W. BLISS.

SIR: I am directed by the commissary-general of prisoners to inform you that transportation to their homes will be ordered for all the exchanged citizen prisoners now in your hospital as soon as they are able to travel, and by sending a note with them or by messenger to the quartermaster, Captain Curtis, corner Eighteenth and G streets, he will furnish the same, as instructions will be sent from this office authorizing the same.

Very respectfully, your obedient servant,
W. T. HARTZ,
Captain and Assistant Adjutant-General.

OFFICE FOR THE EXCHANGE OF PRISONERS OF WAR,
Vicksburg, April 1, 1863.

Maj. Gen. N. P. BANKS,
Commanding Department of the Gulf, New Orleans, La.

GENERAL: I call your attention to the inclosed paragraph from the Appeal showing that many of our citizens are now held in confinement at Fort Pickens in violation of an agreement between the Federal and Confederate commissioners for exchange of prisoners. Said agreement is as follows:

3. The Federal commissioner has formally agreed to treat as subjects of exchange all officers and men belonging to irregular military organizations, even though such military organizations and their officers do not derive their authority from the Confederate States. All therefore who are captured in "hostile array" are to be regularly exchanged.

4. The Federal commissioner has also agreed to release unconditionally all noncombatants captured in any one of the Confederate States. He has also stated in writing that it is not the purpose of his Government to make any more arrests of that description.

Under these two last agreements therefore all persons now confined by them whether military or civil are to be immediately released. I am credibly informed that many others are held in confinement in other forts and places of confinement, some of whom I have hitherto called to your attention. Many of the State organizations of troops are detained in New Orleans against their will who have been registered for exchange under the cartel. I call your attention to these facts believing you will promptly remedy the injustice. I especially call your attention again to the case of P. E. Walden, deputy collector of the port of New Orleans, said to be confined in Fort Jackson.

Col. Ig. Szymanski, C. S. Army, has kindly consented to be the bearer of this letter as I am now seriously indisposed. He will also deliver to any officer you may appoint to receive them about 120 Federal prisoners and 1 surgeon; for the latter no receipt required.

I am, general, very respectfully,
N. G. WATTS,
Major and Agent.

[Indorsement.]

APRIL 5, 1863.

Maj. G. Norman Lieber, judge-advocate, will receive and receipt for these prisoners.

By command:

RICHD. B. IRWIN,
Assistant Adjutant-General.

[Inclosure.—From Memphis Daily Appeal.]

FROM PENSACOLA—PRISONERS DETAINED.

We are indebted to the editors of the Mobile Tribune for a proof slip giving some particulars of the situation of affairs at Pensacola and Fort Pickens, obtained from Mr. Benjamin Leggett, who made his escape from Fort Pickens on last Thursday after a confinement there since the capture of New Orleans. The only forces now at the fort are one Vermont regiment numbering about 500 men and one company of regulars. There are only 700 men guarding the mainland, Fort Barrancas and the navy-yard. They are in command of a Captain Allen. All the other forces have been sent as previously reported to re-enforce General Banks. The only vessel blockading the port is the Potomac. Now lying near the navy-yard are the Preble and the Susquehanna guarding the city, which as we stated some days ago has been evacuated and partially burned.

Mr. Leggett also states that the Hon. John T. Monroe, mayor of New Orleans; J. B. Leefe, member of the late finance committee of that city; Gerard Stith, ex-mayor; Doctor Mackin, of the True Delta; R. L. Bruce, of the firm of Gregory & Bruce; Dr. William Booth, of the quarantine station; Mr. Laurason, Albert G. Middleton, of Pensacola, and about forty others, nearly all prominent and influential citizens of New Orleans, are there as prisoners kept in close confinement and subjected to hard labor and the most brutal treatment. He says that these unfortunate men express considerable dissatisfaction with their own Government which they think has abandoned them to their cruel fate—absolutely forgotten their existence. Perhaps this is not just, and there may be some insuperable obstacle to an interposition. Certainly no men are more deserving of the care of the powers at Richmond. They are generally men of excellent character and certainly have borne as much if not more suffering than any of the other prisoners of war. We trust that the matter may be looked into and some effort be made to restore them to their country.

SPECIAL ORDERS, }   HDQRS. DEPARTMENT OF THE OHIO,
      No. 115.   }   Cincinnati, Ohio, April 1, 1863.
  *   *   *   *   *   *   *

III. All rebel officers held as prisoners of war in this department will at once be sent under proper guard to Fort Delaware. A list of all prisoners so transferred will be forwarded to Colonel Hoffman, Third Infantry, commissary-general of prisoners, Washington, D. C. The Quartermaster's Department will provide the necessary transportation.

By order of Major-General Burnside:

W. P. ANDERSON,
Assistant Adjutant-General.

QUARTERMASTER-GENERAL'S OFFICE,
Washington, April 2, 1863.

Hon. E. M. STANTON, Secretary of War.

SIR: I have the honor to report that I have made inquiry in regard to the capacity of the Pea Patch Island, on which Fort Delaware is situated, for accommodation of prisoners and find that the total area of the island is 178 acres, of which there are 6¾ covered by the fort.   The inhabitable part of the island exclusive of the fort is about 45 acres. There are barracks for 5,000 persons already erected inside of the fort. On the upper end of the island it is estimated there is room to build barracks for about 10,000 more or to encamp 6,000.

M. C. MEIGS,
Quartermaster-General.

OFFICE COMMISSARY-GENERAL OF PRISONERS,
Washington, D. C., April 2, 1863.

Lieut. Col. W. H. LUDLOW,
    Agent for Exchange of Prisoners, Fort Monroe, Va.

COLONEL: I send you by mail to day five packages of rolls of paroled troops now at various camps who are to be exchanged as by the inclosed schedule*.   After using them in making exchanges please return them to this office.

The rolls show a large number at Camp Parole, but a large part of them are now at Camp Chase or Benton Barracks.

I inclose herewith three reports* of the capture of Federal troops to be included among the exchanges.

After you have arranged the exchanges with Mr. Ould please furnish me with the announcement he will make so that I may have no doubt of the position of those of their prisoners who may remain in our hands in hospitals.   We have had a number of officers and men of the rebel army captured in Virginia and Maryland remaining in our hospitals about whom I have been in doubt whether they were exchanged or not, though I think you told me that all captured in those two States up to November 1 have been exchanged.

I have this moment received your letter of yesterday.

Very respectfully, your obedient servant,

W. HOFFMAN,
Colonel Third Infantry, Commissary-General of Prisoners.

HEADQUARTERS DEPARTMENT OF VIRGINIA,
Fort Monroe, Va., April 2, 1863.

Col. W. HOFFMAN, *Commissary-General of Prisoners.*

COLONEL: I have the honor to acknowledge your letter of the 31st March.   The ninety-two Confederate officers declared exchanged were sent yesterday to City Point.   I will depend upon you for the information of arrival of Confederate officers (not exchanged) at Fort Delaware in order that I may send a steamer for them.   There can be no further declarations of exchange until deliveries of Confederate prisoners are made.   When will the Arkansas Post and Murfreesborough prisoners probably arrive?   Have you not many paroles which also can be used?   Mr. Ould alleges that many of our captured officers at the post have been paroled since Davis' proclamation.   Have you any information on this subject?

Yours, very respectfully,

WM. H. LUDLOW,
Lieutenant-Colonel and Agent for Exchange of Prisoners.

---

* Not found.

HEADQUARTERS PAROLED PRISONERS,
Near Annapolis, Md., April 2, 1863.

Col. W. HOFFMAN, *Commissary-General of Prisoners.*

SIR: I have the honor to report that last evening I received 11 officers and 815 men from Richmond and this morning I have received 400 men, and on Saturday 600 men will arrive. I will send you complete rolls as soon as the delivery is complete. I also inclose requisition* for clothing so as to be prepared for arrivals after receiving the 1,800 men this week. I have plenty of clothing for the arrivals of this week. Please approve and forward as soon as possible the inclosed requisition.

I am, colonel, very respectfully, your obedient servant,

GEO. SANGSTER,
Lieutenant-Colonel, Commanding Paroled Prisoners.

NAVY DEPARTMENT, *Washington, April 3, 1863.*

Hon. E. M. STANTON, *Secretary of War.*

SIR: The Department has directed the commandant of the navy-yard at Philadelphia to transfer to Fort Lafayette nine rebel prisoners sent to that post from the U. S. steamer New Ironsides.

The circumstances under which they were captured are such as to suggest the idea that it may be a trick on the part of the rebel authorities to obtain information concerning the squadron. I have therefore to request that they may not be exchanged for the present if it can be obviated, at least not until our immediate pending operations on the southern coast are completed.

Their names are M. P. Burke, sergeant, and William Kelly, Stephen Davis, Alex. Clarke, James Finerty, John Hook, Henry Battdine, James Jackson and Jacob Fields, privates.

I have the honor to be, sir, your obedient servant,

GIDEON WELLES,
Secretary of the Navy.

[First indorsement.]

WAR DEPARTMENT, *April 4, 1863.*

Respectfully referred to Major-General Hitchcock, commissioner for exchange of prisoners, who will give the necessary instruction to carry out the wishes of the Secretary of the Navy.

By order of the Secretary of War:

ED. R. S. CANBY,
Brigadier-General.

[Second indorsement.]

WASHINGTON, *April 4, 1863.*

Referred to Col. William Hoffman, commissary-general of prisoners, who will please see that the men named are not sent for exchange until further order.

E. A. HITCHCOCK,
Major-General of Vols., Commissioner for Exchange of Prisoners.

---

* Not found.

WAR DEPARTMENT, *Washington, April 3, 1863.*
The SECRETARY OF THE NAVY, *Washington, D. C.*

SIR: Your communication of this date in relation to rebel prisoners transferred by your direction from the navy-yard at Philadelphia to Fort Lafayette has been received and directions will at once be given not to exchange these prisoners until advised by you that it will no longer be necessary to retain them.

Very respectfully, sir, your obedient servant,

EDWIN M. STANTON,
Secretary of War.

HDQRS. DEPARTMENT OF WESTERN VIRGINIA,
Dublin, April 3, 1863.
Brig. Gen. E. P. SCAMMON, U. S. Army.

GENERAL: Your letter of the 2d was received on the 14th ultimo. The petition of citizens of Kanawha praying the release of certain men named and which you said you would send did not accompany your letter and has not been received. The men named are not within the limits of my department but I have applied to the proper officer to ascertain where they are and what charges are alleged against them, and I shall act in the matter just as I would have done had the petition been received.

Whether or not the proper authorities will release those men I can't say. The instructions which as I am informed General Halleck has recently given General Rosecrans concerning citizens of Tennessee and the fact that your Government has now in its prisons hundreds perhaps thousands of our citizens with no other charge against them than that of loyalty to their Government is not calculated to induce a favorable consideration of the petition in behalf of the men you name.

Your letter conveyed to me the first information I have of the shooting of Mr. Richmond, at Rich'd [Richmond] Ferry, by Confederate soldiers last autumn. I have inquired into the case and ascertain that if that crime was committed—and I have no doubt that it was—it was in direct violation of the orders of the major-general then commanding this department. He was greatly incensed and caused the officer by whose order Mr. Richmond was said to have been shot to be arrested and brought to trial by court-martial.

Before the case was concluded the exigencies of the service in an active campaign required that the members of the court should rejoin their respective commands and before they could assemble again to conclude the case the members were scattered; one has been killed in battle and others are now in distant departments.

You are in error in supposing that "no offense was charged against him (Richmond) save that of unswerving loyalty to the United States." The president of the court from whom I derive this information informs me that testimony was adduced which proved that Richmond not only guided the invaders but instigated them to the commission of many outrages on inoffensive citizens and committed himself all manner of outrages and crimes, including theft, arson, murder and rape.

The last-named crime was committed on the person of a daughter of a most estimable citizen of Western Virginia and the wife of an officer in the C. S. Army. If these statements are true, and they were generally believed to be true, you will I think admit that Mr. Richmond had little reason to expect mercy at the hands of soldiers from the neighborhood in which his crimes were committed; and yet the proper steps were taken to bring the offenders to punishment.

Doubtless many acts have been committed by the troops and adherents of both parties to this war which are condemned by the rules of civilized warfare. But we have had provocation; our country has been invaded and much of the fairest and best portions of it laid waste, as it was thought none but vandals and savages could waste, and every conceivable outrage committed by the invaders, and I must think that honorable and impartial Christian men will be apt to look with some measure of allowance on a few departures from the rules of civilized warfare by men who were exasperated by a war which has been conducted by your Government in a way to excite the just execration and detestation of enlightened men in all civilized countries, including many of the wisest and best in your own country. I fully appreciate the tone of your letters and have no doubt of your desire and purpose to do all in your power to keep your troops "within the limits of civilized warfare." In that effort you shall have my hearty co-operation so far as concerns the government of my own troops.

One other remark of yours I cannot permit to pass unnoticed. Disclaiming any "wish to enter upon ethical disputations" you say we have both sworn to defend the Government of the United States against all her enemies and to "bear true allegiance to the United States of America." You omit to say that the terms of our commissions pledged us to obey the "lawful orders" of the President; probably because you felt conscious that in conducting this war your Government has utterly disregarded and set at naught the Constitution and laws under which we served.

But you add that you do not say this "by way of reproach." I accept it in the spirit in which it is said, and I desire to say in the same spirit that by the acceptance of the resignation of my commission as an officer of the U. S. Army I was released from all obligations to serve a Government which places arms in the hands of our domestic servants, incites and encourages them to commit murder and all manner of outrages on defenseless women and children, and commands its officers (civil, military and naval) to aid and abet our servants in all the horrors of a servile insurrection.

Very respectfully, &c.,

SAM. JONES,
Major-General.

OFFICE COMMISSARY-GENERAL OF PRISONERS,
Washington, D. C., April 3, 1863.

Maj. Gen. S. A. HURLBUT,
Commanding Sixteenth Army Corps, Memphis, Tenn.

GENERAL: I have the honor to acknowledge the receipt of your letter of the 23d of March to the Adjutant-General inclosing roll of twenty-two prisoners captured within the lines of your command. Neither the letter nor the roll states what disposition was made of the prisoners, and I assume that they are all held as prisoners of war at Memphis. I have also to acknowledge the receipt of your letter of the 25th ultimo inclosing a list of two rebel prisoners of war captured and paroled. I beg leave to refer you to the first clause of General Orders, No. 49, current series, from which you will perceive that paroles are only to be recognized when duplicate receipts are signed as evidence of the delivery of the prisoners paroled to the forces to which they belong. I presume that one receipted roll is to be given to the officer who delivers the prisoners and one is to be retained by the officer who receives them and signs the roll. If the two men on the roll were not delivered and a receipt taken for them the parole cannot be recognized. Your letter of the 16th March with a descriptive roll of prisoners captured by your command has also been received. The roll does not show when or where they were captured nor what disposition was made of them and I can consequently make no use of the roll for exchange.

Very respectfully, your obedient servant,

W. HOFFMAN,
Colonel Third Infantry, Commissary-General of Prisoners.

OFFICE COMMISSARY-GENERAL OF PRISONERS,
Washington, D. C., April 3, 1863.

Col. C. A. WAITE, *Commanding, Annapolis, Md.*

COLONEL: I have the honor to acknowledge the receipt of your letter of the 1st instant in relation to furnishing transportation to destitute citizens who have been held in confinement by the rebels and in reply I would inform you that I am authorized by the Secretary of War to furnish transportation and provisions to their homes to the destitute citizen prisoners recently arrived from Richmond, and I will be much obliged to you if you will cause those referred to in your letter to be so provided. There may be others similarly situated arriving in a few days and I have to request you will cause them also to be provided with transportation and rations to the nearest point to their homes that can be reached by water or by railroad.

Very respectfully, your obedient servant,

W. HOFFMAN,
Colonel Third Infantry, Commissary-General of Prisoners.

WASHINGTON, *April 3, 1863.*

Lieutenant-Colonel LUDLOW:

Thirty-four officers have been forwarded from Sandusky to report to you for exchange. Do you want more citizen prisoners sent to City Point for exchange?

W. HOFFMAN,
Commissary-General of Prisoners.

HEADQUARTERS DEPARTMENT OF VIRGINIA,
Fort Monroe, Va., April 3, 1863.

Col. W. HOFFMAN, *Commissary-General of Prisoners.*

COLONEL: It would be a great convenience if the annexed parole taken from the cartel be printed at the head of all rolls of prisoners. Will you please order that the paroles of all prisoners of war be taken before leaving their places of detention for delivery for exchange? It is exceedingly difficult to take the paroles on board of vessels while in transition.

I am, very respectfully, your obedient servant,

WM. H. LUDLOW,
Lieutenant-Colonel and Agent for Exchange of Prisoners.

[Inclosure.]

We, the undersigned prisoners of war, do give our parole of honor that we will not take up arms again nor serve as military police or constabulary force in any fort, garrison or field-work held by the Confederates, nor as guards of prisons, depots or stores, nor to discharge any duty usually performed by soldiers, until exchanged under the provisions of the cartel entered into July 22, 1862.

HEADQUARTERS DEPARTMENT OF VIRGINIA,
Fort Monroe, Va., April 3, 1863.

Hon. ROBERT OULD, *Agent for Exchange of Prisoners.*

SIR: I send you to-day —— prisoners of war. Among them are nine officers, two of whom, Lieut. A. A. Scott, Sixth Alabama Volunteers, captured at South Mountain September 14, 1862, and Capt. C. K. Sherman, captured at Georgetown October 18, 1862, are exchanged.

For the others—Maj. C. Breckinridge, Second Virginia Cavalry; Maj. Rufus W. Wharton, North Carolina Sharpshooters; Capt. John Alexander, Second Virginia Cavalry; Lieut. H. B. Bicksler, Eighth Virginia Infantry; Lieutenant O. H. Cox, Twenty-first Mississippi Volunteers; Adjt. T. B. Hutchison, Eighth Virginia Infantry; Lieut. Charles C. Robinson, Ninth Virginia Cavalry—I ask equivalents from the Murfreesborough officers. Captain Mulford is instructed to bring them. Please send me Maj. D. J. Hall, Eighty-ninth Illinois, who is one of them. Please send me by Captain Mulford lists of our officers held by you that I may be enabled to arrange for the delivery of the equivalents in your officers. I desire to know when all our officers, naval and military, will be at Richmond ready for delivery. The revocation of the offensive order of Mr. Jefferson Davis relating to U. S. officers and the observance of the cartel will settle all questions relating to officers. Until this be done all exchange of officers must be special. I will deliver to you in exchange for U. S. officers equivalents in number or rank of Confederate officers. If we have not the equivalent number in rank enough of lower grade will be exchanged to secure the release of all you hold. The number of officers captured and paroled by us at Fredericksburg was in excess of U. S. officers captured at the same place and delivered by you at City Point. Sergeant Mullen, a prisoner of war, has not yet been delivered. Will you send him by this boat? The Murfreesborough and Arkansas Post prisoners are now on their way here and are expected to arrive at the rate of 500 daily. Some have already been sent to you.

I am, very respectfully, your obedient servant,
WM. H. LUDLOW,
Lieutenant-Colonel and Agent for Exchange of Prisoners.

HEADQUARTERS FIFTEENTH ARMY CORPS,
Camp before Vicksburg, April 4, 1863.

Major-General GRANT.

DEAR SIR: I inclose you a letter sent me by Major Watts, agent for the exchange of prisoners in Vicksburg, asking that we return a prisoner captured on Deer Creek. This prisoner is a large boy, dressed in a kind of uniform, found with a rifle which he attempted to conceal, and was confused in his statements, at one time admitting himself to be a soldier and again denying it. With your consent I will send the boy home, as from the scare of his mother I think he will give us no further trouble.

The package of money I showed you a few days ago was all Confed erate money—that is no money at all. Also with your consent I would send it as the sender is one of the most enthusiastic Kentuckians I know.

With great respect, yours,

W. T. SHERMAN,
Major-General.

[Inclosure.]

OFFICE FOR EXCHANGE OF PRISONERS,
Vicksburg, Miss., April 4, 1863.

Major-General SHERMAN, U. S. Army.

GENERAL: A youth named D. Clark was taken prisoner on Deer Creek about the 22d ultimo, and I am informed is now in charge of Colonel Smith, Eighth Missouri Regiment. I am also informed you are willing to exchange him for Sergeant Stevens, orderly to Colonel Smith, commanding brigade.

Sergeant Stevens was sent by me to New Orleans on the 1st day of this month to be delivered over to the Federal authorities as a prisoner of war. I have been compelled to adopt this way of delivering Federal prisoners on account of General Grant's refusal to receive them.

I hope, general, you will return the boy to me that I may return him to his distracted parents.

I am, general, very respectfully, your obedient servant,

N. G. WATTS,
Major and Agent, &c.

[Indorsement.]

APRIL 4, 1863.

Respectfully referred to General Grant with letter of this date.

Would recommend that this agent be notified we will exchange pris oners under the cartel strictly, officers being included. It must be inconvenient to our prisoners to go to New Orleans, where they can only reach us by a sea voyage.

W. T. SHERMAN,
Major-General, Commanding.

HEADQUARTERS FIFTEENTH ARMY CORPS,
Young's Point, La., April 4, 1863.

Maj. N. G. WATTS,
Agent for Exchange of Prisoners of War, Vicksburg, Miss.

DEAR SIR: Your note relating to young Clark is received and I send him to you in exchange for Sergeant Stevens already sent by you to New Orleans. Please send the usual receipt.

I would have promptly yielded to the mother's request but this young gentleman committed himself sadly and led me to conclude he was at the time of his arrest engaged in war on his own hook.

You are in error as to General Grant. He is perfectly willing to exchange prisoners of war according to the Dix-Hill cartel which is issued as a positive command to our whole Army. The reason why

General Grant refused to receive a certain lot of prisoners was that he understood yours or General Pemberton's proposition to be to send over the enlisted men but to retain the officers. He thought this unfair to our officers who were at one time threatened with punishment as criminals under State laws.

If you have any prisoners of war for exchange I undertake they will be received if not coupled with any condition other than that contained in the cartel.

Every officer who has conferred with you touching prisoners of war has borne testimony to your fair dealing, and we are always ready to acknowledge the fact and to reciprocate.

I am, with respect, your obedient servant,

W. T. SHERMAN,
Major-General, U. S. Forces.

OFFICE COMMISSARY-GENERAL OF PRISONERS,
Washington, D. C., April 4, 1863.

Lieut. Col. W. H. LUDLOW,
Agent for Exchange of Prisoners, Fort Monroe, Va.

COLONEL: Yours of the 2d instant is just received. I will notify you of the arrival of rebel officers from the West at Fort Delaware. The rolls of Federal prisoners of war which I forwarded to you on the 1st contain all the information I have of our paroled troops. If there are others paroled they have not been reported to me and it is unfortunate for us if it is so, for we lose the opportunity for exchanging them and are deprived of their services. Do not forget to provide for the case of Private H. C. Lilly, Company B, Fourteenth Kentucky Cavalry, for whom you declared a special exchange.

Very respectfully, your obedient servant,

W. HOFFMAN,
Colonel Third Infantry, Commissary-General of Prisoners.

HEADQUARTERS DEPARTMENT OF VIRGINIA,
Fort Monroe, Va., April 4, 1863.

Col. W. HOFFMAN, *Commissary-General of Prisoners.*

COLONEL: There arrived here last evening from City Point 286 prisoners of war and forty-three released citizens mostly from Virginia, Kentucky and Tennessee. Among the prisoners of war were the officers whose names are inclosed* and who have been exchanged and can with the others whose names I sent to you yesterday be put in the field. All were sent to Annapolis.

I am, very respectfully, your obedient servant,

WM. H. LUDLOW,
Lieutenant-Colonel and Agent for Exchange of Prisoners.

HEADQUARTERS DEPARTMENT OF VIRGINIA,
Fort Monroe, Va., April 4, 1863.

Col. W. HOFFMAN, *Commissary-General of Prisoners.*

COLONEL: Inclosed I have the honor to send to you a copy of communication from Hon. G. V. Fox, Assistant Secretary of the Navy.

---

* Omitted; included names of fourteen officers.

Will you please have all the persons referred to and who may be confined at Fort Lafayette sent to Fort Delaware to be ready for delivery to me at the same time with the Confederate officers now on their way here? If there are any others referred to in the letter of Mr. Fox who are confined in other places please have them sent to me in time for same delivery with those above mentioned. The Secretary of War has authorized me to exchange Zarvona. Will you also please have him sent from Fort Lafayette to Fort Delaware at the same time with the rest?

I am, very respectfully, your obedient servant,

WM. H. LUDLOW,
Lieutenant-Colonel and Agent for Exchange of Prisoners.

I inclose also a copy of letter to Mr. Fox to which his is a reply.

[Inclosure No. 1.]

HEADQUARTERS DEPARTMENT OF VIRGINIA,
Fort Monroe, Va., March 29, 1863.

Hon. G. V. FOX, *Assistant Secretary of the Navy.*

SIR: I have the honor to inform you that by the direction of the Secretary of War exchanges of officers will now be resumed. There are many naval officers now in confinement in the South. The Confederate authorities refuse to release them unless the captures on the sea which were declared exchanged by General Orders, No. 11, current series, and for which they have given equivalents are released. This rule they also declare their intention to apply to future captures. They ask that the rule of reciprocity be carried out in captures on the sea as on the land. You know how carefully I have endeavored to carry out the wishes of your Department and from a sense of courtesy have uniformly given to it in the arrangement of my declarations of exchange preference over our own branch of the service. I respectfully await instructions from you.

I am, very respectfully, your obedient servant,

WM. H. LUDLOW,
Lieutenant-Colonel and Agent for Exchange of Prisoners.

[Inclosure No. 2.]

NAVY DEPARTMENT, *Washington, April 1, 1863.*

Lieut. Col. WILLIAM H. LUDLOW, *Fort Monroe, Va.*

SIR: Your letter of the 29th of March has been received. I am directed by the Secretary of the Navy to inform you that the release of certain persons held by the Navy will be immediately proceeded with by turning them over to the proper officers for exchange.

Very respectfully,

G. V. FOX,
Assistant Secretary of the Navy.

SAINT LOUIS, *April 4, 1863.*

Col. W. HOFFMAN, *Commissary-General of Prisoners:*

Four thousand and sixty prisoners left here for Baltimore on the 2d instant.

F. A. DICK,
Provost-Marshal-General.

OFFICE COMMISSARY-GENERAL OF PRISONERS,
Washington, D. C., April 4, 1863.

Maj. W. S. PIERSON,
Commanding Depot of Prisoners of War, Sandusky, Ohio.

MAJOR: In reply to your communication of March 30, 1863, in relation to building a chapel I am directed by the commissary-general of prisoners to inform you that he is perfectly willing that you should erect a chapel and also that one-half of the expense can be paid from the camp fund.

Very respectfully, your obedient servant,

W. T. HARTZ,
Captain and Assistant Adjutant-General.

GENERAL SCHENCK'S HEADQUARTERS,
Baltimore, April 5, 1863.

Col. W. HOFFMAN, *Commissary-General of Prisoners:*

Please instruct officers to notify when I may expect prisoners to arrive in Baltimore. Twelve hundred have just arrived that I had no notice of and I am obliged to put them in public warehouses till I can procure a steamer.

J. L. DONALDSON,
Lieutenant-Colonel and Quartermaster.

OFFICE COMMISSARY-GENERAL OF PRISONERS,
Washington, April 5, 1863.

Lieut. Col. J. L. DONALDSON,
Quartermaster, U. S. Army, Baltimore, Md.

COLONEL: Your telegram of this date is just received and I have replied by telegram giving you all the information I have in relation to the movement of prisoners. When I sent instructions to the West for this movement I requested that you might have timely notice so that there might be no delay for transportation, and Colonel Swords was directed by General Wright, in the Department of the Ohio, to make the necessary arrangements. There must be some 8,000 to 10,000 prisoners to be forwarded in all and most or all of them are now on their way to Baltimore. About 5,000 are to come from Saint Louis and Alton (I gave you notice of 1,100 of these), 3,000 from Chicago and perhaps 2,000 from Camps Butler, Chase and Morton and the depot at Sandusky. These numbers will enable you to make an estimate of how much transportation you will require.

Very respectfully, your obedient servant,

W. HOFFMAN,
Colonel Third Infantry, Commissary-General of Prisoners.

HEADQUARTERS PAROLED PRISONERS,
Near Annapolis, Md., April 5, 1863.

Col. W. HOFFMAN, *Commissary-General of Prisoners.*

SIR: I have the honor to inclose you complete rolls* of officers and men which arrived here on the 1st and 2d of April, 1863, from Richmond on board of transport State of Maine, Capt. John E. Mulford,

---

* Omitted.

Third New York Volunteers, commanding, and transport steamer Met-amora. The number received on the 1st of April as shown on rolls was 12 officers and 804 men, and on the 2d of April as shown on rolls 404 men. They were all cleansed, clothed and fed in six hours after each arrival. Each man received a cup, plate, spoon, knife and fork and all were made very comfortable.

I am, colonel, very respectfully, your obedient servant,

GEO. SANGSTER,
Lieutenant-Colonel, Commanding Paroled Prisoners.

I expect to receive 600 men this p. m.

MURFREESBOROUGH, *April 5, 1863.*

Colonel HOFFMAN, *Commissary-General of Prisoners*:

Will you designate some point on the Ohio at which Confederate prisoners for this department shall be collected and make arrangements for forwarding them thence to Vicksburg promptly?

WM. M. WILES,
Captain and Provost-Marshal-General.

GLASGOW, *April 5, 1863.*

Doctor DAVIS:

I embrace the present opportunity of informing you of my where-abouts. I made my escape from prison on the 31st of March and have succeeded in getting this far from the city without any trouble and just as soon as I get money enough intend returning to Forrest, in Tennessee. I have seen a pretty hard time. The damned scoundrels had a twenty-four-pound ball and chain on my leg for three weeks. I succeeded in sawing the rivets of the chain with an old case-knife some of the boys gave me, threw a handful of pepper in one of the guard's eyes, knocked the other one down, making my way to the river; got into a skiff and bid Saint Louis good by. I would have escaped sooner but tried to make them believe that I was a good Union man, thinking I would be released. Got my Confederate money and watch. Finding I could not get my money I was determined to escape or die in the attempt. I effected the escape of six others with myself. I don't know what became of the others except one who is still with me, and he is a good soldier; belongs to Morgan's cavalry. I will write to my wife from Jacksonville and mail the letter to you. I am in good health and hope to live to kill 100 Yankees before I die. There is no use in talking; when they beat me they beat a trump. If the prisoners at Saint Louis had the nerve they could all make their escape but they are all too damned cowardly. It was all I could do to keep them from reporting on me. No more at present, but remain your friend,

WM. H. WHITE,
Assistant Adjutant-General, Forrest's Cavalry, C. S. Army.

[Indorsement.]

FORT DELAWARE, DEL., *April 13, 1863.*

Respectfully forwarded for the information of Colonel Hoffman.

This copy was furnished by Lieutenant Smith, of the Fifty-eighth Illinois, under whose charge White was brought to this post.

ROBT. C. BUCHANAN,
Lieutenant-Colonel Fourth Infantry, Commanding.

WAR DEPARTMENT, *Washington, April 6, 1863.*
Maj. Gen. E. A. HITCHCOCK,
    Commissioner for Exchange of Prisoners.

GENERAL: It has been reported to this Department by Mr. Charles McClure, now at the Kirkwood House in this city, that his son, Captain McClure, of the Sixteenth Ohio Volunteers, and ten other commissioned officers, who were captured in the first attack upon Vicksburg and paroled, are now confined in the jail at Jackson, Miss., as common felons. You will please examine as to the truth of this statement and report thereupon to the Department at your earliest convenience.

Very respectfully, your obedient servant,
                    EDWIN M. STANTON,
                            Secretary of War.

[Indorsement.]

The undersigned has already taken the necessary steps to reach the persons referred to and respectfully submits a report from Colonel Ludlow received this morning (6th of April) on the subject.
                    E. A. HITCHCOCK,
    Major-General of Vols., Commissioner for Exchange of Prisoners.

[Inclosure.]

HEADQUARTERS DEPARTMENT OF VIRGINIA,
                Fort Monroe, Va., April 4, 1863.
Maj. Gen. E. A. HITCHCOCK,
    Commissioner for Exchange of Prisoners.

GENERAL: I have the honor to acknowledge the receipt of your letter* of the 2d instant relating to officers captured near Vicksburg. I had previously received a communication from Col. Thomas C. Fletcher. Thirteenth Missouri Volunteers, dated Libby Prison, Richmond, March 30, informing me that he and twenty other officers captured near Vicksburg on the 29th December last were in the Libby Prison. He sends me their names and among them are those of eleven officers of the Sixteenth Regiment Ohio Volunteers. I presume that they are the same as referred to by you and have been transferred from Jackson, Miss. The arrangements made will release all our officers as soon as I can deliver an equivalent number of Confederates who as I am informed are now on their way here.

Sergeant Mullen in whom you took a personal interest is released and went to Annapolis to-day. He can give you information relating to the so-called Captain Stewart, sentenced by the Confederates to be hung. I know nothing of Stewart except from Mullen's account. No one else seems to know anything about him. Mullen says that Stewart did break his parole. I have not seen Mullen myself. The above information is brought to me by an officer whom I sent to see and talk with him.

I am, very respectfully, your obedient servant,
                    WM. H. LUDLOW,
    Lieutenant-Colonel and Agent for Exchange of Prisoners.

WAR DEPARTMENT, *Washington, April 6, 1863.*
Hon. WILLIAM H. SEWARD, *Secretary of State.*

SIR: The Secretary of War directs me to transmit the inclosed copies of reports received from the Adjutant-General, to whom was referred

---

* Not found.

your communication of the 10th of December last made to this Department at the instance of M. Mercier, the minister from France, in regard to the case of Mr. Le More, said to be a French subject, whom the Government had caused to be confined in Fort Pickens at hard labor with a ball and chain upon a charge by General Butler of having been engaged in supplying the insurgents with stores, and with contumacy in refusing to submit to an examination and to produce papers. From these reports it will appear that Mr. Le More is not now in confinement.

I have the honor to be, sir, your obedient servant,

P. H. WATSON,
Assistant Secretary of War.

[Inclosure No. 1.]

HEADQUARTERS, *Fort Pickens, Fla., February 4, 1863.*

Lieut. J. NOWLAND,
Acting Assistant Adjutant-General, Pensacola, Fla.

SIR: I have the honor to state that the communication inclosing letters from War Department in relation to the confinement of Messrs. Le More is received.* In reply I would say that Mr. Le More was confined at this fort on the 15th day of November, 1862, by the order of Major-General Butler; that on the 26th day of November he was ordered to appear at headquarters Department of the Gulf, New Orleans, in compliance with which order he left this post and proceeded to New Orleans since which time he has not been confined here. The communications received are herewith inclosed.

I am, sir, very respectfully, your obedient servant,

H. A. ALLEN,
Captain, Second Artillery, Commanding.

[Indorsements.]

HEADQUARTERS DEPARTMENT OF THE GULF,
New Orleans, February 21, 1863.

Respectfully forwarded with additional report from the commanding officer of Fort Pickens.

I understand that all the records in relation to the confinement and release of prisoners prior to December 17, 1862, are retained by my predecessor in command, Major-General Butler. There is nothing on the records of the adjutant-general's office of this department in relation to Mr. Le More.

N. P. BANKS,
Major-General, Commanding.

ADJUTANT-GENERAL'S OFFICE, *March 6, 1863.*

Respectfully referred to Maj. Gen. B. F. Butler, U. S. Volunteers, for report. To be returned.

By order of the Secretary of War:

E. D. TOWNSEND,
Assistant Adjutant-General.

I have the honor to report that Jules Le More and Alfred Le More were arrested as army contractors of the Confederate Government. One of them was ordered to answer questions and was ordered into confinement with punishment for contumacy, but I afterwards found the evidence and did not inflict the punishment. When I left New

---

* See Wolcott to Butler, December 12, 1862, p. 73.

Orleans he was in the parish prison awaiting trial. If he is not there now I suppose he has bribed the jailor and escaped—a favorite mode of jail delivery in former times at New Orleans.

BENJ. F. BUTLER,
Major-General, Commanding.

ADJUTANT-GENERAL'S OFFICE, *March 27, 1863.*

Respectfully submitted. General Butler's report is indorsed, and it appears from this and the report of General Banks that Mr. Le More is not now in confinement.

E. D. TOWNSEND,
Assistant Adjutant-General.

[Inclosure No. 2.]

BOARD OF PRISON INSPECTORS,
New Orleans, February 17, 1863.

Lieut. Col. RICHARD B. IRWIN, *Assistant Adjutant-General.*

COLONEL: Upon the communications referred to this board from the Departments of State and War at Washington in the case of Mr. Le More, the board would respectfully report that after inquiry and careful examination of all the reports and returns of prisoners confined in the military prisons within this department the board does not find the name of Le More in any of them, nor is he known to be in confinement in any of the prisons.

Respectfully submitted.　　　　　　JAMES SMITH,
Lieutenant-Colonel and President of Board.

[Inclosure No. 3.]

LOWELL, MASS., *March 23, 1863.*

Brig. Gen. L. THOMAS, *Adjutant-General.*

GENERAL: Having read Major-General Banks' report on the imprisonment of Messrs. A. and J. Le More, in which he says "there is nothing on the records in the adjutant-general's office of this department in relation to Mr. Le More," I beg leave to state that I had charge of the adjutant-general's office under Maj. George C. Strong, assistant adjutant-general, and that all the correspondence together with all other documents referring to the case are copied in the proper places in the record book of that office, which book has been turned over to Lieut. Col. Richard B. Irwin, the present assistant adjutant-general in the Department of the Gulf.

I have the honor to be, most respectfully, your obedient servant,

EMILE H. BRIL.

I certify that Emile H. Bril was clerk in the adjutant-general's office, having charge of the books and papers the same as stated by him above.

BENJ. F. BUTLER,
Major-General, U. S. Volunteers.

———

HEADQUARTERS DEPARTMENT OF THE GULF,
New Orleans, April 6, 1863.

Maj. N. G. WATTS, *Agent for Exchange of Prisoners, &c.*

MAJOR: It gives me pleasure to acknowledge the receipt of your letter of the 1st of April which I have this moment received by the hand of Captain Sargent. I regret the personal illness which has prevented your supervision of the transfer of prisoners under your charge, but it will give me pleasure to co-operate with Colonel Szymanski in the discharge of the duties assigned to him.

I am not aware that any communication has been made to me in reference to the political prisoners held in this department or to the case of P. E. Walden, deputy collector of the port of New Orleans, to whom your letter refers by name.

I beg you to accept my assurance that I will properly comply with all of the provisions of the cartel in reference to the discharge of this or any other class of prisoners held in this department.

As soon as opportunity offers I will investigate the facts and communicate the result of my inquiry to you in reference to all cases of this class. I have directed Lieutenant Colonel Abert, U. S. Army, to wait upon Colonel Szymanski and receive and receipt for the prisoners now in his charge.

With much respect, major, I am yours, &c.,

N. P. BANKS,
Major-General, Commanding.

HEADQUARTERS DEPARTMENT OF THE GULF,
New Orleans, April 6, 1863.

Lieut. Gen. J. C. PEMBERTON, *Commanding, &c., Vicksburg.*

GENERAL: I respectfully suggest that it will be on many accounts more convenient that communications by flag of truce in relation to the exchange of prisoners should be received at our lines near Baton Rouge, and that any future deliveries of paroled or exchanged prisoners should take place at some suitable point in the same neighborhood.

I have the honor to be, very respectfully, your obedient servant,

N. P. BANKS,
Major-General, Commanding.

HEADQUARTERS CAMP DOUGLAS, *Chicago, April 6, 1863.*

Col. W. HOFFMAN, *Commissary-General of Prisoners.*

SIR: The last detachment of prisoners left here Friday, April 3, 1863, except the sick in hospital and those detailed to attend them. The number forwarded was 2,534. The sick in hospital and attendants number about 350, but as some will not probably recover there will be a less number to forward. I made an examination of the hospitals this morning and suppose 150 or perhaps 200 will be in a condition to forward the last of this week or the first of next and will be sent unless you order to the contrary. Duplicate rolls were sent with each detachment. The rolls of those sent and those remaining will be forwarded to you to-morrow. Difficulties and troubles have prevented their earlier transmission.

Respectfully, your most obedient servant,   J. AMMEN,
Brigadier-General of Volunteers, Commanding.

ANNAPOLIS, MD., *April 6, 1863.*

Col. W. HOFFMAN, *Commissary-General of Prisoners:*

By Thursday we can vacate some buildings so as to afford tolerable shelter for 3,000 rebel prisoners. We cannot give shelter for a larger number at one time.

C. A. WAITE,
Colonel First Infantry, Commanding Annapolis City.

OFFICE COMMISSARY-GENERAL OF PRISONERS,
Washington, April 6, 1863.

Maj. Gen. A. E. BURNSIDE,
Commanding Department of the Ohio, Cincinnati, Ohio.

GENERAL: The General-in-Chief directs that Camp Morton, near Indianapolis, be used as a depot for rebel prisoners of war, and he also directs that you will please detail a suitable and permanent guard for the camp under a competent commander. I would respectfully suggest that at least six companies will be required for a guard to take charge of the average number of prisoners that may be expected to be received at the camp. It is only by having an energetic and reliable commander that I can hope to have the affairs of the camp properly managed.

Very respectfully, your obedient servant,
W. HOFFMAN,
Colonel Third Infantry, Commissary-General of Prisoners.

OFFICE COMMISSARY-GENERAL OF PRISONERS,
Washington, D. C., April 6, 1863.

Maj. Gen. S. P. HEINTZELMAN,
Commanding Defenses of Washington, Washington, D. C.

GENERAL: No rolls have been furnished to this office of the officers and men captured with General Stoughton, and as such rolls are required to effect their exchange I have the honor to request you will cause them to be furnished in duplicate as early as practicable.

Very respectfully, your obedient servant,
W. HOFFMAN,
Colonel Third Infantry, Commissary-General of Prisoners.

OFFICE COMMISSARY-GENERAL OF PRISONERS,
Washington, April 6, 1863.

Col. J. C. KELTON,
Assistant Adjutant-General, Washington, D. C.:

I beg leave again to call your attention to the urgent necessity for a permanent guard at Camp Parole. I am informed by a letter of the 3d instant from the commanding officer that the guard remains as it was at the date of my letter of the 7th ultimo, and while it so continues it is impossible that he can have any control over the paroled prisoners of war. There are now some 4,000 men at the camp and more are expected and it is unreasonable to expect that a guard of ninety men can preserve order in so large a camp.

Very respectfully, your obedient servant,
W. HOFFMAN,
Colonel Third Infantry, Commissary-General of Prisoners.

OFFICE COMMISSARY-GENERAL OF PRISONERS,
Washington, D. C., April 6, 1863.

Lieut. Col. W. H. LUDLOW,
Agent for Exchange of Prisoners, Fort Monroe, Va.

COLONEL: Your letter of the 3d instant is received and I will take immediate steps to have your wishes in relation to paroles carried out.

I have not yet been furnished with rolls of the officers and men captured with General Stoughton and that they may not be overlooked in the exchange I want to remind you of them. I have asked for rolls and will send them to you. Another of our generals was captured at Murfreesborough whose name you have but I am not sure it is on any of the rolls. Please find inclosed* a list of rebel prisoners who have died in our hospitals, furnished by the Surgeon-General. Lists are being prepared of those who have died at our Western camps which will be forwarded to you very soon. They will amount to 4,000 or 5,000. Your two letters of the 4th instant are this moment received and will be attended to. Thirty-nine officers will be with the prisoners from Sandusky.

Very respectfully, your obedient servant,
W. HOFFMAN,
Colonel Third Infantry, Commissary-General of Prisoners.

BALTIMORE, *April 6, 1863.*

Colonel HOFFMAN, *Commissary-General of Prisoners:*

Telegram received. There are no accommodations for prisoners here and those I cannot transport to City Point at once I will send to Annapolis to await transportation there. I have telegraphed Colonel Thomas to send me all the steamers he can.

J. L. DONALDSON.

SAINT LOUIS, *April 6, 1863.*

Col. W. HOFFMAN, *Commissary-General of Prisoners:*

Under your orders of March 28 to send rebel officers to Fort Delaware shall I forward bushwhacking officers of Porter or Poindexter?

F. A. DICK,
Lieutenant-Colonel and Provost-Marshal-General.

HEADQUARTERS DEPARTMENT OF THE GULF,
New Orleans, April 6, 1863.

Col. IG. SZYMANSKI, C. S. Army.

SIR: I am directed by the commanding general to inform you in reply to your communication of to-day that he has received no instructions in regard to the exchange of political prisoners, nor has he any official information of the agreement quoted as paragraph 3 in the letter of Maj. N. G. Watts, C. S. Army, of April 1, 1863. The commanding general will make this the subject of a communication to the War Department and will carry out such agreement as may have been entered into by the Governments for the exchange of political prisoners. All Confederate prisoners in this department registered for exchange were sent up the river to Port Hudson on the 4th instant.

Very respectfully, your obedient servant,
RICHARD B. IRWIN,
Assistant Adjutant-General.

---

* Not found.

HEADQUARTERS DEPARTMENT OF THE GULF,
New Orleans, April 6, 1863.

Brig. Gen. T. W. SHERMAN,
Commanding Defenses of New Orleans.

GENERAL: The commanding general directs me to communicate as follows:

You will please instruct the commanding officers at all our outposts that no flag of truce is to be received by them or any person accompanying the flag permitted to land or to enter our lines until the arrival of the flag, its purport and any communications accompanying it shall have been duly made known through the proper channels to you and until your orders in the case are received

If necessary you will communicate with these headquarters before giving such orders.

In all cases where prisoners of war taken from us by the enemy are sent here paroled or exchanged you will please see that their wants are supplied.

The commanding general has addressed a letter to Lieutenant-General Pemberton, commanding the enemy's forces at Vicksburg, requesting that all communications in relation to the exchange of prisoners may be sent to our lines near Baton Rouge and that all future deliveries of prisoners paroled or exchanged may take place at some suitable point in that neighborhood.

Very respectfully, your obedient servant,

RICHARD B. IRWIN,
Assistant Adjutant-General.

RICHMOND, *April 6, 1863.*

Lieut. Col. WILLIAM H. LUDLOW, *Agent of Exchange.*

SIR: I herewith inclose to you the receipt of Major Hall for the fifty dollar Federal note sent to him by you.

I will be much obliged to you if you will cause to be sent to City Point Thomas J. Dunn, Company E, Eighteenth Mississippi Regiment, captured and wounded at Antietam. He is now at Locust Springs, about two miles from Frederick, Md. I am very anxious about this matter and will take it as a great favor if you will give it your attention.

I have declared exchanged Private Walter Overton, Third Confederate Cavalry, captured and paroled at Murfreesborough.

Of course the citizen prisoners are released upon delivery from their paroles and every obligation contained in them, including any oath of allegiance. This is our distinct agreement. Why do you limit this release to such political prisoners as are delivered at City Point? Our clear and indisputable understanding was that all civilians who should be released or had been released upon giving a parole or any obligation should be considered as absolved from that parole or obligation. It made no difference where the parties were delivered or whether they had ever been in actual confinement even. It was a necessary incident to our agreement for the release of political prisoners. I have already acted upon this and given notice that all civilians whenever and wherever released were discharged from any parole or any obligation or any oath into which they may have entered before their release or at the time they were released. The parole and oath of Wardener only operated until he was delivered to you at City Point.

Respectfully, your obedient servant,   RO. OULD,
Agent of Exchange.

HEADQUARTERS IN THE WOODS, *April 6, 1863.*

COMMANDER OF THE POST, *Corinth.*

SIR: I write this dispatch to set forth the facts relative to S. White who is a prisoner in your hands. I do not approve of his conduct in a few particulars. He has an order from Lieutenant-General Pemberton to capture all goods coming from the enemy. I had him arrested for trial, and found this order in his possession, for the same thing that you accused him of being—a highway robber.

I will state the case to General Pemberton and you and him for it. He has been sworn in the Confederate service. Therefore I think you ought to treat him as a prisoner of war.

Captain Smith wants me to state to you that you have one of his men chained with a ball, so he has understood. He prays your clemency toward him, for he does not want to be forced to treat a prisoner amiss. The man's name is W. J. Morphis.

Yours,

T. W. HAM,
Major.

WAR DEPARTMENT, *April 7, 1863.*

Col. W. HOFFMAN, *Commissary-General of Prisoners.*

COLONEL: I have just received the inclosed dispatch from Mr. Stanton and desire you to make an instant investigation into the matter, using the telegraph, and report to-morrow morning.

Very respectfully,

P. H. WATSON,
Assistant Secretary of War.

[Inclosure.]

RELAY HOUSE, MD., *April 7, 1863.*

P. H. WATSON, *Assistant Secretary of War:*

I am informed that twenty-five prisoners having the smallpox are now at Locust Point in a railroad station there, having been brought there from places where they were confined, and are to be sent to Fort Monroe. I think it is outrageous that the commissary-general of prisoners should allow infected persons to travel through the States and be introduced to our posts. You will please see the commissary-general of prisoners and consult with Generals Halleck, Meigs and Hitchcock as to what shall be done with them, and inform the commissary-general of prisoners that I shall expect him to investigate the facts and see who is responsible for such acts if my information be correct.

E. M. STANTON,
Secretary of War.

HEADQUARTERS SIXTEENTH ARMY CORPS,
Memphis, April 7, 1863.

Brigadier-General CHALMERS, C. S. Army.

SIR: I have the honor to forward to you by orders from the War Department official copy of General Orders, No. 49,* Adjutant-General's Office, Washington, in the belief that hereafter no misapprehension may occur upon the subject of paroles to enlisted men of the U. S. service.

I have the honor to be, your obedient servant,

S. A. HURLBUT,
Major-General, U. S. Volunteers, Commanding.

---

* See p. 306.

JUDGE-ADVOCATE-GENERAL'S OFFICE, *April 7, 1863.*

Honorable SECRETARY OF WAR:

The policy which it has been deemed advisable to adopt of treating as prisoners of war traitors taken in arms against the Government may present a serious obstacle to the infliction of merited punishment on the offenders mentioned in the letter* of Commander Murray. In view of the existing cartel their precise legal status and consequently the disposition which should be made of them cannot be determined without reference to the pass and protection which they are represented to have held from Governor Stanly, U. S. Military Governor of North Carolina. It is recommended that the proper officer be directed to send to the department for its consideration one of the passes and protections found on the prisoners held for trial which will enable this office to report on its bearing upon the crimes which they are alleged to have committed.

J. HOLT,
Judge-Advocate-General.

OFFICE COMMISSARY-GENERAL OF PRISONERS,
Washington, April 7, 1863.

Maj. Gen. G. GRANGER, *Commanding Army of Kentucky.*

GENERAL: I have the honor herewith to return roll* of prisoners of war sent to Vicksburg for exchange, forwarded by you to the Adjutant-General January 17, 1863, and by him referred to this office. The rolls were sent to Colonel Ludlow, agent for exchange, and returned by him, as he could not make use of them for purposes of exchange unless furnished with the receipts showing that they had been properly delivered. Please inform me what disposition was made of them and if they are still in our hands at what point they are confined.

Respectfully, your obedient servant, W. HOFFMAN,
Colonel Third Infantry, Commissary-General of Prisoners.

(Same to several other commanding officers.)

OFFICE COMMISSARY-GENERAL OF PRISONERS,
Washington, April 7, 1863.

Lieut. Col. J. L. DONALDSON,
Quartermaster, U. S. Army, Baltimore, Md.

COLONEL: I have just dispatched to you a telegram asking for information in relation to smallpox cases among the prisoners from the West, and in addition I will be obliged to you if you will inform me from what camp the cases came; if the disease is prevailing as has been reported here. Please give all the information you have in relation to them, how you have disposed of them and what instructions are necessary to meet the case. If there is a hospital in Baltimore in which they can be received let them be placed there at once if it has not already been done.

Very respectfully, your obedient servant,
W. HOFFMAN,
Colonel Third Infantry, Commissary-General of Prisoners.

P. S.—Of course no person showing any symptoms of this disease must be permitted to go to Fort Monroe.

W. H.

* Not found.

FORT MONROE, *April 7, 1863.*

Hon. E. M. STANTON:

Shall such Confederate prisoners as arrive here *en route* to City Point who desire to take the oath of allegiance and enter our military service be permitted to do so?

WM. H. LUDLOW,
Lieutenant-Colonel and Agent for Exchange of Prisoners.

WAR DEPARTMENT, *April 7, 1863.*

Col. W. H. LUDLOW, *Fort Monroe:*

The rule is not to permit Confederate prisoners to join our Army. But in any case in which you are satisfied a prisoner is sincerely desirous of renouncing all connection with the rebels you may on his taking the oath of allegiance send him to Fort Delaware, to be released there after further investigation as to his sincerity and sent North to reside.

P. H. WATSON,
Assistant Secretary of War.

HEADQUARTERS DEPARTMENT OF VIRGINIA,
Fort Monroe, Va., April 7, 1863.

Col. W. HOFFMAN, *Commissary-General of Prisoners.*

COLONEL: Will you order an investigation into the case of Captain Baylor, detained at Fort Delaware under charges of murder and violation of flag of truce, that in case of acquittal he may be sent with other Confederate officers for exchange? The prisoners of war are daily arriving here and forwarded to City Point. When the detachments shall have all been delivered I will arrange exchanges. A package of rolls directed to you was taken by mistake from my desk on the 5th instant and mailed without full payment of postage. If not received will you inquire for them at the Washington post-office?

I am, very respectfully, your obedient servant,

WM. H. LUDLOW,
Lieutenant-Colonel and Agent for Exchange of Prisoners.

FORT HAMILTON, *New York Harbor, April 7, 1863.*

Brig. Gen. L. THOMAS,
Adjutant-General U. S. Army, Washington, D. C.

SIR: I have thought it would not be improper to send you a copy of a letter I have sent to Lieutenant Wood at Fort Lafayette in regard to a better regulation of the correspondence of the prisoners at that post.

Very respectfully, your obedient servant,

MARTIN BURKE,
Lieutenant-Colonel Third Artillery.

P. S.—A copy of the above has been sent to Colonel Hoffman, commissary-general of prisoners.

[Inclosure.]

FORT HAMILTON, *New York Harbor, April 7, 1863.*

Lieut. CHARLES O. WOOD,
Commanding at Fort Lafayette, New York Harbor.

SIR: A prisoner from Tampico wrote to me a day or two ago that he wished a lawyer to attend to his case. Also a Mr. Williamson, of Baltimore, a prisoner at Fort Lafayette, boldly asks to have a *habeas corpus* issued in his case. I wish that all letters sent from Fort Lafayette to me at Fort Hamilton to be mailed conform to all the original instructions that I communicated to you about twenty months ago. Please reject any letters that do not conform to those rules. Any complaint or objection made on this matter and addressed to the authorities in Washington will be duly forwarded. Please state this fact to the prisoners if necessary.

Very respectfully, your obedient servant,
MARTIN BURKE,
Lieutenant-Colonel Third Artillery.

SAINT LOUIS, *April 7, 1863.*

Lieut. J. GUYLEE, *Fourth Iowa Cavalry, Aide-de-Camp.*

LIEUTENANT: On the 31st ultimo Mrs. General Jeff. Thompson, her friend Mrs. Colhoun (wife of a rebel officer), a nurse and two children arrived in Saint Louis from Helena, claiming to be here on honest business and to have been properly passed through our lines at Helena. They are now in close custody in their rooms at the Everett House under charge of the U. S. police, having been arrested as being improper persons within our lines and under suspicious circumstances. You will take charge of the entire party and conduct them to Helena under close guard, to be passed through the lines in the direction they came from unless the commanding officer of the district may decide that the circumstances of their getting through there will justify their detention and trial. George Smizer, of Helena, is reported as having been instrumental in procuring the passes for these women and to have changed money for them. You will inquire particularly into this and report all facts proper for his information and action to the commanding officer at Helena. You receive herewith the pass by which they left their lines, the pass by which they came into ours and the one by which they left Helena and went toward Memphis. The circumstances attending the reaching Saint Louis by these rebel women are so suspicious that General Curtis desires particular information in regard to it. A W. Paul Bently was arrested at the same time and is now in Gratiot [Street] Prison. You will take him also through the lines as a suspicious person. He admits having run the blockade from the South. On your return you will make full report to this office.

By command of Major-General Curtis:

F. A. DICK,
Lieutenant-Colonel and Provost-Marshal-General.

HEADQUARTERS COMMANDANT OF PRISONS,
Camp Chase, Ohio, April 7, 1863.

Col. W. HOFFMAN,
Commissary-General of Prisoners, Washington.

COLONEL: I have the honor to this day forward to you by mail in separate packages, viz:

1. The monthly returns for March of the prisoners' savings fund and prison hospital fund together with abstract and vouchers for expenditures.

2. Complete rolls of all the prisoners of war and citizens at this post April 1, 1863.

The citizen list includes three female prisoners here from Nashville. There are: Commissioned officers, 468; enlisted men, 20; citizens, 41; total. 529.

The rolls for all the rebel commissioned officers at this post able to travel, 453 in number, are already made up and transportation to Fort Delaware will be ready for them Thursday, 9th instant. Of the list of twenty-four invalid rebel officers for Fort Delaware forwarded to you yesterday, three of them on parole in Columbus were unable to travel and were left, viz: Major Phillips, Capt. W. S. Malcombe and Capt. William P. Jones. Fifty-six prisoners of war, enlisted men, arrived here from Louisville, Ky., on the 5th instant. They were picked up at their homes and other places in Kentucky absent from the rebel ranks, and all claim to be deserters and the rolls with them bear the remark to that effect. Your further instructions are respectfully asked as to this class of prisoners.

EDWIN L. WEBBER,
Captain, Commanding Prisons.

HEADQUARTERS FIFTEENTH ARMY CORPS,
Camp before Vicksburg, Miss., April 8, 1863.

Col. J. A. RAWLINS,
Assistant Adjutant-General to General Grant.

SIR: This morning I went down the river in a flag-of-truce boat and had a full interview with Major Watts, agent for exchange of prisoners of war. I explained to him that the cartel or agreement made between the two contending parties was set forth in full in General Orders, No. 142, of 1862, a copy of which I carried with me, and was made obligatory upon all U. S. officers and would be fully carried out by yourself; that you declined to receive enlisted men without their officers because the agreement was that all prisoners taken in war should within ten days be paroled and sent to Aiken's Landing, Va., or Vicksburg, Miss., for exchange. He admitted his instructions from Richmond were not to exchange officers and he seemed under the impression our military authorities had made a similar order. He says he has delivered the enlisted men sent him for exchange to Baton Rouge when no objection was made to receive them. I told him I had seen a notice in a Saint Louis paper that Colonel Fletcher and other officers made prisoners at Chickasaw Bayou had been delivered at Baton Rouge, but he insisted he had not delivered for exchange any officers, and if Colonel Fletcher or other commissioned officers had thus escaped it was by misrepresenting their rank. This I considered impossible.

He wanted to surrender the sailors of the Indianola without officers but of course I declined to receive them. Your action is right. The agreement known as the Dix-Hill cartel is an entirety and must stand or fall as a whole. I do think General Banks ought to be advised as it is unfair that our officers should be held back, and also that our men be made to get home by the roundabout way of New Orleans, New York and Saint Louis. Major Watts was of same opinion, but his orders are imperative, although he expects daily to receive other orders restoring the cartel to its full effect.

I cannot find in my file of orders from the War Department anything modifying General Orders, No. 142, and infer that the moment the Confederate authorities make exchanges on that basis we will also.

The Mr. Montgomery inquired for by Major Watts died in the hospital at Young's Point March 8—a month ago. I delivered to him the evidence of the fact.

Our interview was full and frank and as far as was proper friendly. I send with this two newspapers of April 5 and 7, from Mobile and Jackson.

With respect, yours,

W. T. SHERMAN,
Major-General, Commanding.

————

LOUISVILLE, *April 8, 1863.*

Col. WILLIAM HOFFMAN:

Following dispatch just received:

MURFREESBOROUGH, *April 7, 1863.*

Commissary-general of prisoners has ordered us to send all rebel prisoners of war to Camp Morton. Please send any from this department sent to you forward to that place.

By order of General Rosecrans:

C. GODDARD,
Assistant Adjutant-General.

Shall we comply with this or with your last order to send them to Baltimore, received through headquarters Department of the Ohio?

H. G. WRIGHT,
Brigadier-General.

————

OFFICE COMMISSARY-GENERAL OF PRISONERS,
Washington, D. C., April 8, 1863.

Hon. P. H. WATSON,
Assistant Secretary of War, Washington, D. C.

SIR: Pursuant to your instructions of last evening requiring a report of the circumstances under which cases of smallpox were brought to Baltimore among the prisoners of war just arrived in that city from the West I have the honor to report that ten cases among the prisoners and one of the guards have been reported. It will be seen from the accompanying letter from the medical director at Baltimore that these cases were provided for without delay at the Marine Hospital. He informs me verbally that arrangements are made to take from the cars to the hospital without delay any further cases that may arrive.

It appears too from Surgeon Simpson's letter that on leaving the camp (it is not stated which one) the examination of the sick was intrusted to the rebel surgeon who was attending on the prisoners and he suffered nine slight cases to be brought with the well men. These are probably the cases which developed themselves on the way, for unless the infection was very strong it could not be so fully developed in the time required to make the journey.

I am informed by Colonel Donaldson, quartermaster, Baltimore, that these smallpox cases came from Camp Douglas, Chicago. Previous to the 1st of March they had a number of cases at that camp but measures were taken to isolate them from other prisoners, and on the 11th of March a favorable report of the sanitary condition of the camp was made and I did not think it necessary to call General Wright's particular attention to this matter, more especially as there was a general commanding the camp whose duty it would be to see that all necessary precautions were taken to prevent the spread of so dangerous a disease.

The disease had prevalence to some extent at Alton, and notwithstanding prisoners are passing from Saint Louis to the prison and returning perhaps daily. I took the precaution of calling the attention of Major General Curtis to the matter that he might decide on the propriety of sending prisoners from there to City Point.

I have the honor to inclose herewith a copy of my letter to General Curtis communicating the order of the General-in-Chief and an extract of my letter to General Wright, commanding Department of the Ohio, in which though I was not called upon by my duty to do I made suggestions which were intended to guard against there being any delay from want of transportation.

I have requested by telegraph of the commanders of Camp Douglas and Alton Prison to report what inspection was made of the prisoners before their departure with a view to prevent their carrying the smallpox with them.

Very respectfully, your obedient servant,
W. HOFFMAN,
Colonel Third Infantry, Commissary-General of Prisoners.

[Inclosure No. 1.]

MEDICAL DIRECTOR'S OFFICE,
Baltimore, Md., April 8, 1863.

Lieut. Col. J. L. DONALDSON, *Chief Quartermaster.*

COLONEL: I have the honor to inform you that from the Confederate prisoners who have recently passed through this city ten cases of smallpox have been admitted to the Marine Hospital (smallpox) by my order as well as one member of their guard. It is believed all the squads which have passed through have not been properly reported, but where they have been the effort has been made to stop them. I have been unofficially informed an attending Confederate surgeon took with him some cases that he considered "slight."

There is a hospital for such cases and if reported to this office can be cared for. If their anticipated arrival is reported with a view to their inspection it would be of benefit.

Very respectfully, your obedient servant,
J. SIMPSON,
Surgeon, U. S. Army, Medical Director.

[Inclosure No. 2.]

OFFICE COMMISSARY-GENERAL OF PRISONERS,
Washington, D. C., March 16, 1863.

Maj. Gen. S. R. CURTIS,
Comdg. Department of the Missouri, Saint Louis, Mo.

GENERAL: The General-in-Chief directs that all enlisted prisoners of war of the rebel army be forwarded to City Point for delivery and I have the honor to request you will give the necessary orders for the movement of the prisoners in the two prisons at Saint Louis and the Alton Prison. At the latter prison the prevalence of smallpox for some time past may make it objectionable to send prisoners from there more or less infected with the disease so far through the interior of the country, and it is left for you to decide how far the order in relation to these prisoners can be carried out. This order covers all guerrillas, rangers, &c.

The Pittsburg and Baltimore route will I presume be most, direct and convenient and I would respectfully suggest that the quartermaster at these two places be notified of the movement in time so that there may be no delay for transportation.

I will write to the provost-marshal-general at Saint Louis and the commanding officer at Alton Prison in relation to rolls, &c.

I am, general, very respectfully, your obedient servant,

W. HOFFMAN,
Colonel Third Infantry, Commissary-General of Prisoners.

[Inclosure No. 3.]

OFFICE COMMISSARY-GENERAL OF PRISONERS,
Washington, D. C., March 16, 1863.

Maj. Gen. H. G. WRIGHT,
Commanding Department of the Ohio, Cincinnati, Ohio:

*   *   *   *   *   *   *

The Pittsburg and Baltimore route I presume will be the most convenient and I would respectfully suggest that the quartermasters at these two places have timely notice to provide the necessary transportation, &c., and the movement should be so arranged as to time that the parties from different camps would not interfere with each other on the Pittsburg and Baltimore road.

*   *   *   *   *   *   *

Very respectfully, your obedient servant,

W. HOFFMAN,
Colonel Third Infantry, Commissary-General of Prisoners.

HEADQUARTERS DEPARTMENT OF THE CUMBERLAND,
Murfreesborough, Tenn., April 8, 1863.

General J. A. GARFIELD, *Chief of Staff.*

GENERAL: In obedience to Special Field Orders, No. 78, by which I was detailed on the 22d ultimo to superintend the execution of Department General Orders, No. 43, I have the honor to submit the following partial report:

For the purpose of a personal conference with Brig. Gen. Robert B. Mitchell, commanding U. S. forces at Nashville, the point at which the operation of the order would be most general, I visited him at his headquarters and consulted with him as to the best mode of its execution. I have since received from him a list of names of persons who on account of their sympathies with the rebellion he deems it unsafe to permit to remain within our lines, which with the papers* on the subject I transmit with this report. I have dropped a few names from this list as the reasons alleged against some and my personal knowledge in reference to others leads me to believe that action in reference to them is not necessary at present. The remainder I have divided into three classes, appending separate lists according to that classification to this report. Those named in list No. 1 I recommend to be sent through our lines by way of Vicksburg or some other point remote from the position of this army to the territory occupied by the rebels. Those named in list No. 2 I recommend to be sent to the rear of our lines in the loyal States, north of the Ohio River, for the reason that if permitted to go South they might

----

* Not found.

serve to swell the ranks of our enemies. In both cases they should be given to understand that if afterwards found within our lines they will be treated as spies and punished accordingly. List No. 3 contains the names of the most dangerous class against whom there are charges capable of proof of overt acts in violation of military law, who ought not to be sent South for the reason above assigned and who ought not to be suffered to go at large anywhere. I recommend that they be sent North to be confined in a military prison during the war or until released by competent authority and under the same penalties if found hereafter within our lines.

In reference to those persons designated in the general order as those "whose mutual protectors and supporters are in arms against us," General Mitchell informs me that he has been in the practice of giving orders upon wealthy secessionists to provide for their wants. He adds:

Much suffering will inevitably ensue to people of this class if they are sent South to struggle with the destitution that prevails there, and unless they manifest an active desire to aid the enemy I would most respectfully recommend that the policy of making wealthy rebels support the wives and children of those whom they have driven into the Southern Army be continued. The property left by wealthy expatriated rebels might be made to yield an income for this purpose.

In this recommendation I entirely concur.

Respectfully,   STANLEY MATTHEWS,
                                   Colonel Fifty-first Ohio Volunteers.

                                   WASHINGTON, *April 8, 1863.*
Maj. Gen. JOHN A. DIX, *Commanding:*
Some of the prisoners from the West are infected with the smallpox and the Secretary of War directs that all possible precaution be taken to prevent its spreading.

                                   W. HOFFMAN,
                                   Commissary-General of Prisoners.

OFFICE COMMISSARY-GENERAL OF PRISONERS,
                    Washington, D. C., April 8, 1863.
Hon. F. H. PEIRPOINT,
        Governor of Western Virginia, Wheeling, Va.
SIR: I have the honor to inform you that your letter of the 28th ultimo requesting that certain officers from Virginia belonging to the rebel army may be placed at your disposal has been laid before the Secretary of War and in reply he directs me to say that it is expected that the prisoners now in the hands of the rebel authorities will soon be exchanged and action on your application is therefore deferred for the present.

Very respectfully, your obedient servant,
                                   W. HOFFMAN,
        Colonel Third Infantry, Commissary-General of Prisoners.

OFFICE COMMISSARY-GENERAL OF PRISONERS,
                    Washington, D. C., April 8, 1863.
Brig. Gen. M. C. MEIGS,
        Quartermaster-General U. S. Army, Washington, D. C.
GENERAL: I have respectfully to request that the assistant quartermasters at Columbus, Indianapolis, Springfield and Chicago may be

directed to take charge of all property purchased with the prisoners' fund at the camps near those cities respectively, viz, Camp Chase, Camp Morton, Camp Butler and Camp Douglas, when those camps are vacated by the prisoners held at them from time to time. To insure a proper care of the property it is desirable if possible that the quartermaster send an agent to the camp occasionally to see that the property is not unnecessarily destroyed and when the camp is vacated that the property is collected and accounted for.

Very respectfully, your obedient servant,

W. HOFFMAN,
Colonel Third Infantry, Commissary-General of Prisoners.

GENERAL SCHENCK'S HEADQUARTERS,
Baltimore, April 8, 1863.

Col. W. HOFFMAN, *Commissary-General of Prisoners:*

Surgeon Simpson, medical director, is now on his way to see you about smallpox cases among the Confederate prisoners. They are from Camp Douglas.

J. L. DONALDSON,
Quartermaster.

OFFICE QUARTERMASTER, *Baltimore, Md., April 8, 1863.*

Col. W. HOFFMAN,
Commissary-General of Prisoners, Washington, D. C.

COLONEL: I am just in receipt of your letter and in addition to what I stated to you by telegram will say that most of the cases of smallpox among the prisoners came from Chicago. This is my opinion, as no report has been made to me by officers in charge. I have sent them all to the Marine Hospital, as accommodations are there to receive them. Some ten cases have been thus disposed of, one of which has been fatal. Doctor Simpson, medical director of this department, left here this morning to confer with you and has I presume by this time had a consultation with you. He can give you all the information that I have on the subject.

Very respectfully, your obedient servant,

J. L. DONALDSON,
Quartermaster.

OFFICE COMMISSARY-GENERAL OF PRISONERS,
Washington, April 8, 1863.

Lieut. Col. W. H. LUDLOW,
Agent for Exchange of Prisoners, Fort Monroe, Va.:

I send you by this mail an additional list of rebel prisoners of war who have died in our hospitals furnished by the Surgeon-General. I send also list of those who have died at the several stations where they have been held at Forts Warren and Delaware, Camps Chase, Butler, Morton and Douglas, Alton and Saint Louis Prisons and Johnson's Island. I inclose herewith a list* of Federal troops captured with General Stoughton and now held I believe at Richmond. The prisoners

---

*Omitted.

at Fort Lafayette captured by the Navy have not yet been placed at my disposal. As soon as they are I will give instructions to have them and Zarvona sent to Fort Delaware.

Very respectfully, your obedient servant,

W. HOFFMAN,
Colonel Third Infantry, Commissary-General of Prisoners.

HEADQUARTERS DEPARTMENT OF VIRGINIA,
Fort Monroe, Va., April 8, 1863.

Col. W. HOFFMAN, *Commissary-General of Prisoners.*

COLONEL: Your letters of the 2d and 6th instant with inclosures are just received. The lists of deceased Confederate soldiers are I suppose intended for the Confederate authorities. Please inform me by return mail whether I can depend upon the receiving of the prisoners held under the order of the Navy Department and also Zarvona at the same time with the officers. I cannot arrange exchanges of naval officers and men without the former and a very advantageous exchange can now be effected for the latter. I am very desirous to get these old matters out of the way and now seems to be the best time to do it. I sent to Annapolis last evening about 150 released prisoners. Among them and who are declared exchanged are the following-named officers.*

I am, very respectfully, your obedient servant,

WM. H. LUDLOW,
Lieutenant-Colonel and Agent for Exchange of Prisoners.

HEADQUARTERS, *Annapolis, Md., April 8, 1863.*

ASSISTANT ADJUTANT-GENERAL,
Hdqrs. Middle Department, Eighth Army Corps, Baltimore.

SIR: I have the honor to return to your office Captain Lazelle's report in relation to the condition of things at Camp Parole and Colonel Hoffman's letter which accompanied it.

I am, sir, with much respect, your obedient servant,

C. A. WAITE,
Colonel First Infantry, Commanding Post.

[Indorsement.]

HEADQUARTERS EIGHTH ARMY CORPS,
Baltimore, Md., April 9, 1863.

Respectfully returned to Col. C. A. Waite, calling his attention to the instructions contained in the indorsement of the major-general commanding of the 11th March, 1863, which he happens to have overlooked. Colonel Waite will report his views in relation to the matters contained in the report of the inspecting officer and state what changes and remedies he has already been able to make.

By order of Major-General Schenck:

W. H. CHESEBROUGH,
Assistant Adjutant-General.

---

* Nominal list of 13 officers omitted.

EXECUTIVE DEPARTMENT, *Boston, April 8, 1863.*

Lieut. Col. A. G. BROWNE, Jr.,
Military Secretary, &c., Washington, D. C.

COLONEL: I am directed by His Excellency the Governor to forward to you the inclosed copy of a letter from C. B. Burrell, quartermaster of the Forty-second Regiment Massachusetts Volunteers, concerning the sale into slavery in the State of Texas of two colored boys attached to the regiment, some companies of which were taken prisoners at Galveston.

The Governor desires that you shall present the facts in the case to the Secretary of War, the particulars of which are fresh in your mind. You will recollect that the grandfather of one of these boys was one of the colored soldiers of the Revolution, and that his widow, now residing in Concord, is one of the few surviving revolutionary pensioners in this State.

His Excellency desires that Mr. Stanton be made acquainted with these facts and that any relief possible may be obtained for these boys, Charles Fairfax Revaleon and Charles Gerrish Amos.

I have the honor to be, very respectfully, your obedient servant,
H. WARE,
Assistant Military Secretary.

[Indorsement.]

WASHINGTON, *April 13, 1863.*

The two colored boys mentioned within, Charles Fairfax Revaleon and Charles Gerrish Amos, were citizens of Massachusetts and were engaged in the military service of the United States as servants to the colonel and staff of the Forty-second Regiment Massachusetts Volunteer Infantry. As such they were taken prisoners by the rebels at the recapture of the city of Galveston, Tex., in February last, two companies of the Forty-second being at the same time forced to capitulate after a brave resistance. Lieut. C. B. Burrell, the writer of the annexed letter, is the quartermaster of the regiment and is a brother of the colonel, who still remains a prisoner in the hands of the rebels.

A. G. BROWNE, JR.,
Lieutenant-Colonel and Military Secretary.

[Inclosure.]

NEW ORLEANS, *March 2, 1863.*

EDWIN W. QUINCEY, *Dedham, Mass.*

DEAR SIR : The chance that I feared and warned poor Charley against has been his fate. He was sold into slavery at Houston, Tex., the second or third day of his captivity. My brother said all that man could do to save him without avail, as well as the other officers who liked the boy very much. His cousin shared a like fate. His aunt will remember that I tried to discourage the boy in every way that I could from going with us but without avail. Charley is smart and if he can only keep his tongue within bounds he will make his escape before any length of time elapses.

Our officers are all in close confinement and of course can do nothing for him. Tell his aunt to keep up her courage and hope as we all do for the best. The chances of war we all have to run and the end always follows the beginning. I will keep your address and if I learn anything of the boys I will write you.

One item may give his relations some little comfort in their trouble. Our men that were taken received very good treatment and the disposition seems to be to use Federals well that fall in their hands.

Yours, respectfully,

C. B. BURRELL.

[Indorsement.]

WASHINGTON, *April 14, 1863.*

Respectfully returned to the honorable Secretary of War with the remark that it seems impossible to do anything in this case except as a result of success in the war.

E. A. HITCHCOCK,
Major-General of Volunteers.

HEADQUARTERS DEPARTMENT OF VIRGINIA,
Fort Monroe, April 8, 1863.

Hon. ROBERT OULD, *Agent for Exchange of Prisoners.*

SIR: The best mode of arranging all questions relating to exchange of officers is to revoke formally or informally the offensive proclamation relating to our officers. I simply ask that you say by authority that such proclamation is revoked. The spirit of that proclamation was the infliction of personal indignities upon our officers, and as long as it remains unrepealed it can be at any moment put in force by your authorities. What assurance have we that it will not be?

I earnestly desire a return to the cartel in all matters pertaining to officers, and until such be the case and a uniformity of rule be thereby established our exchange of officers must be special. Some of our officers paroled at Vicksburg were subsequently placed in close confinement and are now so held. If hereafter we parole any of your officers such paroles will be offset against any which you may possess. At present the exchanges will be confined to such equivalents as are held in confinement on either side. I hope you will soon be able to remove all difficulties about officers by the revocation I have mentioned. By reference to the map you will see that Fort Delaware is *en route* to Fort Monroe. It is used as a depot for collecting of prisoners sent from other places for shipment here and is from its peculiar position well adapted for convenience for exchange.

If any mistake be found in the account of men paroled by Lieutenant-Colonel Richards at Oxford, Miss., on December 22, 1862, it can be rectified when we meet.

I am, very respectfully, your obedient servant,

WM. H. LUDLOW,
Lieutenant-Colonel and Agent for Exchange of Prisoners.

JUDGE-ADVOCATE-GENERAL'S OFFICE, *April 9, 1863.*

The SECRETARY OF WAR:

On the 27th of November, 1862, Brigadier-General Boyle issued a general order from which the following is an extract:

All slaves within camp will be placed beyond the guard lines and not be permitted to return.

The first question which arises on the letter* of Major Sherwood referred to this office for consideration is as to the legality of this order.

---

* Not found.

The right to determine who shall be permitted to remain within the camps of our armies belongs necessarily to the commanding generals. If they regard the presence of slaves within their camps as injurious or dangerous to the military service they may expel them without any violation of existing laws, but this power must be exercised in good faith and solely on the ground named. If such expulsion is based upon a decision made by the commander on any claim to the service or labor of such slaves or if the object of expelling such slaves from the camp is to place them within the reach of those claiming to be their owners then such order of expulsion would be a violation of the letter and spirit of the tenth section of the act of 17th of July, ch. 195. The conduct of Colonel Bond as stated by Major Sherwood was a palpable infraction of this law and Brigadier General Boyle should be required to report the facts in regard to it and also to communicate to the Secretary of War the ground upon which and the purpose for which his order of 27th November was issued. It has been alleged that the numerous class of negroes mentioned in the ninth section of the act referred to and who when found within any place occupied by the forces of the United States are declared to be free are under this order treated as slaves and driven from our military camps into the meshes of men who thrust them into prison as fugitives, with the intention of having them afterwards sold into servitude under the local laws. Any military officer detected in prostituting his police power over his camp to give aid, however remote, to such practices as these should be at once dishonorably dismissed the service.

J. HOLT,
Judge-Advocate-General.

OFFICE COMMISSARY-GENERAL OF PRISONERS,
Washington, April 9, 1863.

Hon. E. M. STANTON, *Secretary of War, Washington, D. C.*

SIR: Pursuant to instructions from the War Department I have the honor to report that in my judgment it would seem to be advisable to prepare barracks at Fort Delaware to accommodate in all 10,000 prisoners of war. It is possible that we may never have occasion to prepare for so many, but the chances are in favor of our having quite that number to take care of occasionally though it may be only for a short time, and it will probably be the best economy and certainly the most convenient course to be prepared permanently for any number that may be thrown in our hands at any one time. We may depend on the use of tents for any number over 10,000, though they make the most expensive kind of shelter for prisoners of war who feel no interest in preventing their destruction. Besides prisoners are more readily controlled while in barracks, for tents must necessarily occupy a large tract of ground which greatly increases the difficulty of guarding them.

Very respectfully, your obedient servant,

W. HOFFMAN,
Colonel Third Infantry, Commissary-General of Prisoners.

WASHINGTON, *April 9, 1863.*

Major-General GRANT, *Before Vicksburg:*

Please inform me if the crew of the Queen of the West belongs to Ellet's brigade.

W. HOFFMAN,
Commissary-General of Prisoners.

[Indorsement.]

HEADQUARTERS DEPARTMENT OF THE TENNESSEE,
Milliken's Bend, La., April 22, 1863.

Respectfully returned to Colonel Hoffman, commissary-general of prisoners, and attention invited to report* of Lieutenant-Commander Breese, Mississippi Squadron, accompanying for the information desired.

U. S. GRANT,
Major-General.

OFFICE COMMISSARY-GENERAL OF PRISONERS,
Washington, D. C., April 9, 1863.

Lieut. Col. W. H. LUDLOW,
Agent for Exchange of Prisoners, Fort Monroe, Va.

COLONEL: Your letter of the 7th is received. I have had inquiries made at the post-office for the package of rolls but it has not yet been found. I have called for the charges against Captain Baylor and his case will be laid before Colonel Holt, Judge-Advocate-General. On examining the rolls of deceased rebels I find that the Surgeon-General gives the names of some but not all who died at the Western stations. Wherever the same name is on both rolls I have had it marked.

When your exchanges are completed please furnish me with the names of all army employés and citizens who have been exchanged. If I understand it rightly none of the late deliveries, soldiers or citizens, have been exchanged except under General Orders, No. 10, or in some special cases. Please say if I am correct in this impression.

Can you effect anything in Doctor Rucker's case? If he will probably be released please inform me by telegraph that I may communicate it to his wife. The rolls mentioned in my letter of yesterday will be forwarded by to-day's mail.

Very respectfully, your obedient servant,

W. HOFFMAN,
Colonel Third Infantry, Commissary-General of Prisoners.

BALTIMORE, *April 10, 1853.*

Hon. E. M. STANTON:

Archbishop Kenrick again intercedes for Rev. T. A. Becker, Catholic priest at Martinsburg, and will probably appeal to you. I have examined Mr. Becker in person. Find him a thorough secessionist who prayed in his church for Jeff. Davis and the Confederacy but will not pray for the President and authorities of the United States. See former papers in his case. I think he should be sent through the lines.

ROBERT C. SCHENCK,
Major-General, Commanding.

WASHINGTON, *April 10, 1863.*

Lieut. Col. W. H. LUDLOW, U. S. Army.

SIR: I inclose a communication of the 31st [30th?] ultimo with sundry indorsements in relation to Major Withers, to which your attention is called, particularly in view of the indorsement by General Halleck,

---

*Not found; but see Breese to Rawlins, p. 499.

which you will please carry out and report the results as soon as they become known to you. Make the demand for Major Withers on general grounds that he is an officer and go into no details as to the particulars recited in the letter.

Very respectfully, your obedient servant,

E. A. HITCHCOCK,
Major-General of Vols., Commissioner for Exchange of Prisoners.

[Inclosure.]

HEADQUARTERS TENTH VIRGINIA,
Camp near Winchester, March 30, 1863.

Capt. JOHN O. CRAVENS,
Assistant Adjutant-General, Winchester.

CAPTAIN: I have heard though not authentically that Major Withers, of my regiment, who has been confined in Libby Prison at Richmond, has been turned over to the civil authorities to be tried for an alleged murder.

The facts in regard to the matter are these: Before he joined the Army he led a party of sixteen citizens and home guards into the town of Glenville, Gilmer County, Va., against a party of guerrillas under one Captain Parrill, who were then engaged plundering the town, and killed the captain with his own hands, one of the party led by him also killing the captain's son.

They drove this band of plunderers from the town and captured from eight to twelve horses, most of which turned out to be horses that had been stolen by these guerrillas from loyal men.

I desire through you to call the attention of the Government to this case, as I am convinced from the fact that he has been detained in prison that some evil is meditated against him. He was captured near Strasburg about the 20th December, 1862, and has been confined in Libby Prison ever since.

Very respectfully, your obedient servant,

T. M. HARRIS,
Colonel Tenth [West] Virginia Volunteer Infantry.

[First indorsement.]

HDQRS. SECOND DIVISION, EIGHTH ARMY CORPS,
Winchester, March 31, 1863.

Respectfully forwarded for the action of the War Department. Major Withers is an excellent young officer and should be released from the power of the enemy if possible.

R. H. MILROY,
Major-General, U. S. Volunteers, Commanding.

[Second indorsement.]

HEADQUARTERS EIGHTH ARMY CORPS,
Baltimore, Md., April 4, 1863.

Respectfully forwarded for the consideration of the General-in-Chief. If Major Withers be not treated as a prisoner of war I trust that some measure of retaliation may be ordered.

ROBERT C. SCHENCK,
Major-General, Commanding.

[Third indorsement.]

APRIL 5, 1863.

Major-General Hitchcock will demand the release of this officer and if not released or his confinement satisfactorily explained a Confederate officer of equal rank will be treated in like manner.

H. W. HALLECK,
General-in-Chief.

OFFICE COMMISSARY-GENERAL OF PRISONERS,
Washington, D. C., April 10, 1863.

Major-General HITCHCOCK, *Agent for Exchange of Prisoners.*

GENERAL: I have this morning received a list of Federal officers just arrived at Camp Parole from Richmond and among them is Maj. H. H. Withers, Tenth [West] Virginia Volunteers. This is the name of the officer for whose release you are forwarding a demand. Will it be advisable to send the letter to Colonel Ludlow?

Very respectfully, your obedient servant,

W. HOFFMAN,
Colonel Third Infantry, Commissary-General of Prisoners.

OFFICE COMMISSARY-GENERAL OF PRISONERS,
Washington, D. C., April 10, 1863.

Lieut. Col. W. H. LUDLOW,
Agent for Exchange of Prisoners, Fort Monroe, Va.

COLONEL: Your letters of the 8th instant are received. The list of prisoners at Fort Lafayette held by the Navy Department I have just received and I will give orders that they (thirty-two in number) and Zarvona shall be immediately forwarded to Fort Delaware. I have requested that the Surgeon-General would order Captain Dunn, Eighteenth Mississippi, to be sent to report to you at Fort Monroe. A few days since I received a letter from Colonel Webster, military superintendent of railroads in Memphis, reporting the capture by guerrillas of Capt. Carlos Dutton, assistant quartermaster, who is now supposed to be at Richmond. My impression is that this letter was referred to you but it is not so recorded on the books. Please bear the case in mind and arrange his exchange. The rolls of deceased rebel soldiers are to be forwarded to the rebel authorities at Richmond and it is expected they will furnish lists of our people in return. I inclose herewith a letter from Surg. J. R. Smith, which accompanied the rolls furnished by the Surgeon-General.

Very respectfully, your obedient servant,

W. HOFFMAN,
Colonel Third Infantry, Commissary-General of Prisoners.

[Inclosure.]

SURGEON-GENERAL'S OFFICE,
Washington, April 7, 1863.

Col. WILLIAM HOFFMAN, &c.

DEAR COLONEL: I send you an additional list* of Confederate prisoners who have died. We still have over 1,000 additional names to furnish.

Yours, truly,

JOS. R. SMITH,
Surgeon, U. S. Army.

---

* Omitted.

OFFICE COMMISSARY-GENERAL OF PRISONERS,
Washington, April 10, 1863.

Lieut. Col. W. H. LUDLOW,
Agent for Exchange of Prisoners, Fort Monroe, Va.

COLONEL: I omitted to say in my letter of this date inclosing a copy of one from Surg. J. R. Smith that I did not think it necessary to send a copy of that letter to Richmond with the rolls.

The package of rolls which you spoke of as having been mailed without postage stamps on it has not reached the post-office in this city.

Very respectfully, your obedient servant,

W. HOFFMAN,
Colonel Third Infantry, Commissary-General of Prisoners.

OFFICE COMMISSARY-GENERAL OF PRISONERS,
Washington, April 10, 1863.

Lieut. Col. GEORGE SANGSTER,
Commanding Camp Parole, Annapolis, Md.

COLONEL: The fourteen officers captured at Hartsville, Tenn., whose exchange is announced in General Orders, No. 10, and who arrived at Camp Parole on the 6th instant from Richmond, will be ordered to join their regiments without delay except such of them as may be required to conduct troops to Western camps. Hereafter whenever there are paroled prisoners of war at Camp Parole whose regiments are serving in the West and who should therefore be ordered to Camp Chase or Benton Barracks you will report the fact, giving the number for each camp and wait for instructions. I have understood unofficially that Lieutenant Eddy, aide-de-camp, has returned to duty with General Whipple. If this report be true please inform me by what authority he left Camp Parole and how you ascertained he was exchanged. A letter was addressed to him from this office soon after his arrival at the camp, sent to your care. Please say if it was received. Some of the rolls recently received from you are without signature of any kind. Your name is required to authenticate them.

Very respectfully, your obedient servant,

W. HOFFMAN,
Colonel Third Infantry, Commissary-General of Prisoners.

P. S.—Hereafter you will furnish only tri-monthly reports of troops at the camp on the 10th, 20th and last day. These will take the place of the weekly reports which you now make.

W. H.

HEADQUARTERS DEPARTMENT OF VIRGINIA,
Fort Monroe, April 10, 1863.

Col. W. HOFFMAN, *Commissary-General of Prisoners.*

COLONEL: Your dispatch relating to smallpox among the prisoners of war is just received. The utmost care has been taken here. I think that neglect has occurred at some point before arrival here. Some of the cases were of an aggravated character and the officers in charge ought to have been notified and reported them in Baltimore. Thirty smallpox cases were delivered from one steamer at City Point. Will you please inform me whether the prisoners alluded to in the letter of

Mr. Fox, and a copy of which I sent to you, are to be delivered? I ask because a very small detachment of other prisoners arrived here yesterday from Fort Lafayette.

I am, very respectfully, your obedient servant,
                                        WM. H. LUDLOW,
           Lieutenant-Colonel and Agent for Exchange of Prisoners.

                              MILITARY PRISON, *Alton, Ill., April 10, 1863.*
Capt. J. F. DWIGHT,
       Assistant Provost-Marshal-General, Saint Louis, Mo.

SIR: In reply to your inquiry of yesterday as to in what manner hard labor is imposed at Alton I have to state that hard labor is not imposed in any manner upon the prisoners in this prison and for this reason: there is no kind of labor other than the ordinary police of the place which is by no means hard labor at which they can be employed. It seems to me therefore to be a useless trouble and expense besides defeating the ends of justice to send to this place convicts thus sentenced with the expectation that a sentence to hard labor can be properly carried into effect. We have no means to do so, consequently these rogues invariably escape their deserts.

I am, sir, with much respect, your most obedient servant,
                                        T. HENDRICKSON,
                  Major Third Infantry, Commanding Prison.

                              HEADQUARTERS, *Louisville, April 10, 1863.*
Col. W. HOFFMAN, *Commissary-General of Prisoners:*
There are in military prison here 240 prisoners of war.
                                        STEPHEN E. JONES,
                                        Captain and Aide-de-Camp.

              HEADQUARTERS COMMANDANT OF PRISONS,
                         Camp Chase, Ohio, April 10, 1863.
Col. W. HOFFMAN,
       Commissary-General of Prisoners, Washington, D. C.

COLONEL: I have respectfully to state that since the receipt of your instructions of the 4th ultimo concerning the uniform and clothing of prisoners a considerable amount of clothing has been received here for prisoners in boxes and other packages, sent to them by their friends and acquaintances. As much of it was superfluous above the necessities of the prisoners while here in confinement what they did not need has been withheld and turned over to the keeping of the prison provost-marshal. On searching the baggage and persons of officers destined for Fort Delaware it was found that in many cases they had managed to purchase by some means more clothing than under your instructions was proper for them to carry off toward the point of exchange. In such cases a portion of the clothing was taken away and placed in charge of the provost-marshal of prisons. I respectfully ask your instructions as to the disposition to be made of such clothing, blankets, &c.; also of surgical instruments, arms and other articles deemed contraband. In regard to the contributed clothing in a number of cases instead of distributing large packages to but two or three individuals as originally intended it has been distributed partly to destitute prisoners.

I am, colonel, very respectfully, your obedient servant,

JOHN C. MOON,
Captain, Commanding Prisons.

GENERAL ORDERS, ╲   HDQRS. DEPARTMENT OF THE OHIO,
    No. 36.   ╱   *Cincinnati, Ohio, April 10, 1863.*

The commanding general has observed with surprise that in this department prisoners from the rebel service are frequently allowed unguarded the freedom of the vicinity in which they are confined. This practice must cease. Prisoners of this character must be constantly under guard and any officer permitting a violation of this order will at once be arrested and sent to these headquarters for such action as the commanding general may direct.

By command of Major-General Burnside:

LEWIS RICHMOND,
Assistant Adjutant-General.

WAR DEPARTMENT, *Washington, April 11, 1863.*

Maj. Gen. R. C. SCHENCK, *Commanding at Baltimore:*

Remove Mrs. Faulkner and her family beyond our lines if by their disloyal practices their presence within our lines in your judgment endangers the success of military operations or the safety of your troops.

P. H. WATSON,
Acting Secretary of War.

HEADQUARTERS OF THE ARMY,
Washington, April 11, 1863.

Major-General BURNSIDE, *Cincinnati:*

Reports have been received here that Senator Powell, candidate for Governor of Kentucky, has acted in a disloyal manner and advocated the secession of that State from the Union. You will cause his conduct to be closely observed and reported to these headquarters.

H. W. HALLECK,
General-in-Chief.

SUFFOLK, [VA.,] *April 11, 1863.*

Major-General KEYES:

I have arrested all the leading secessionists in this place and forbade the passing out of any individuals through the lines. Wives and families of our officers are ordered to leave and I advise that no more passes be given to citizens to visit Suffolk at the present time. All the reserve ammunition and tools for this command were thrown off the track last night a few miles this side of Norfolk. They are indispensable and should be sent forward without delay.

JOHN J. PECK,
Major-General.

BALTIMORE, *April 11, 1863.*

Hon. E. M. STANTON, *Secretary of War:*

I have permitted Mrs. Emma Moore, a secesh kinswoman of mine from Philadelphia, to go South via Fort Monroe on her parole not to attempt to come within the Union lines during the rebellion, her baggage and person also being strictly searched. Will you give an order to Lieutenant-Colonel Ludlow to let her pass by the flag-of-truce boat? Part of Mrs. Moore's trunks containing contraband goods were seized and held in Philadelphia.

ROBERT C. SCHENCK,
Major-General, Commanding.

OFFICE COMMISSARY-GENERAL OF PRISONERS,
Washington, April 11, [1863.]

Brig. Gen. J. H. MARTINDALE,
Comdg. Military District of Washington, Washington, D. C.

GENERAL: By direction of the General-in-Chief all the enlisted prisoners of war in the Old Capitol Prison will be forwarded with as little delay as practicable to City Point there to be paroled or exchanged.

Please direct duplicate rolls to be sent with them and one to this office. On their reaching Fort Monroe direct the officer in charge to report to Colonel Ludlow, agent for exchange of prisoners, for further orders.

It is desirable that these prisoners should be delivered without delay, and I would therefore suggest that they be sent via Baltimore unless a steamer can be obtained here more readily.

Very respectfully, your obedient servant,

W. HOFFMAN,
Colonel Third Infantry, Commissary-General of Prisoners.

OFFICE COMMISSARY-GENERAL OF PRISONERS,
Washington, D. C., April 11, 1863.

Col. B. L. E. BONNEVILLE,
Commanding Benton Barracks, Saint Louis, Mo.

COLONEL. The following prisoners of war belonging to the crew of the Queen of the West, recently captured on the Red River, have been ordered to report to you and to remain at Benton Barracks until further orders, viz: W. E. Taylor, first assistant engineer; Henry S. Duncan, third master; C. S. Edison, second master; James W. Foster, carpenter. Please request General Grant to direct that muster-rolls and all necessary information to show the position these men hold in the military service may be furnished you, a copy of which you will please send to this office.

Very respectfully, your obedient servant,

W. HOFFMAN,
Colonel Third Infantry, Commissary-General of Prisoners.

APRIL 12, 1863.

P. S.—Sixteen other men of the crew of the Queen of the West have been also ordered to report to you. A list of their names is herewith inclosed.

W. H.

OFFICE COMMISSARY-GENERAL OF PRISONERS,
Washington, D. C., April 11, 1863.

Col. HENRY DENT, *Provost-Marshal-General, Louisville, Ky.*

COLONEL: Your letter of 4th instant with rolls of political prisoners and deserters is received. The following extract* from a letter addressed to Capt. S. E. Jones, aide-de-camp, will instruct you how to dispose of deserters from the rebel army. Your letter of the 22d ultimo is received and I have to reply that deserters from the rebel army cannot be considered prisoners of war, but to insure their loyalty they should be required to take the oath of allegiance, with the penalty of death for its violation. If professed deserters come within our lines they may be spies and every commander should judge of each case after careful inquiries according to the circumstances.

Very respectfully, your obedient servant,

W. HOFFMAN,
Colonel Third Infantry, Commissary-General of Prisoners.

OFFICE COMMISSARY-GENERAL OF PRISONERS,
Washington, April 11, 1863.

Lieut. Col. MARTIN BURKE,
Commanding Fort Hamilton, New York Harbor:

By direction of the Secretary of War you will forward without delay the prisoners of war named on the accompanying list† now held at Fort Lafayette under the authority of the Navy Department to Fort Delaware for exchange. Please send duplicate rolls with them and one to this office. You will also forward to Fort Delaware at the same time Thomas alias R. T. Zarvona. The Quartermaster's Department will furnish the necessary transportation and you will call on General Brown, commanding New York Harbor, for a suitable guard. As an additional security and to avoid the necessity of a large guard please take the parole of these prisoners to be binding until exchanged.

Very respectfully, your obedient servant,

W. HOFFMAN,
Colonel Third Infantry, Commissary-General of Prisoners.

WASHINGTON, *April 11, 1863.*

Lieutenant-Colonel LUDLOW:

About eighty rebel officers are at Fort Delaware. Four hundred and fifty should arrive there in a day or two from Camp Chase. I will notify you when their arrival is reported. Prisoners from Fort Lafayette are ordered there to-day. Will send you lists of citizen prisoners.

W. HOFFMAN,
Commissary-General of Prisoners.

OFFICE COMMISSARY-GENERAL OF PRISONERS,
Washington, D. C., April 11, 1863.

Lieut. Col. GEORGE SANGSTER,
Commanding Camp Parole, Annapolis, Md.

COLONEL: The thirteen officers who arrived at Camp Parole from Richmond on the 8th instant under Maj. D. J. Hall, Eighty-ninth Illinois,

---

* Not found, but see Hoffman to Jones, p. 19.   † Omitted.*

having been declared exchanged, you will order them to join their regiments without delay. Those who belong to regiments which have paroled men at Camp Chase or Benton Barracks will be ordered to those stations to await the exchange of their men.

Very respectfully, your obedient servant,

W. HOFFMAN,
Colonel Third Infantry, Commissary-General of Prisoners.

OFFICE COMMISSARY-GENERAL OF PRISONERS,
Washington, D. C., April 11, 1863.

W. P. WOOD,
Superintendent Old Capitol Prison, Washington, D. C.

SIR: Please furnish me without delay the names of all citizen prisoners in confinement at the Old Capitol Prison on charges of disloyalty in any shape. In each case give the place of residence, the date and place of arrest, the charges and the authority for the arrest. If there are any who for special reasons known to you should not be exchanged please state these reasons under the head of remarks. To facilitate the preparation of the rolls I send herewith suitable blanks.

Very respectfully, your obedient servant,

W. HOFFMAN,
Colonel Third Infantry, Commissary-General of Prisoners.

OFFICE COMMISSARY-GENERAL OF PRISONERS,
Washington, D. C., April 11, 1863.

Capt. G. S. BLODGETT,
Assistant Quartermaster, U. S. Army, Annapolis, Md.

CAPTAIN: I expected to see you this evening but as I will probably not be able to do so I will give you an idea of the style of building I propose to put up at the new camp so that you may be making some arrangements for their construction. The soldiers' barracks will be one story, on the following ground plan:

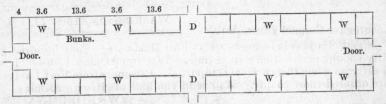

The buildings, balloon frame, eighty feet long, eighteen feet broad, nine feet elevation inside from the floor; weather-boarded; windows, two sashes, six lights each, ten by twelve glass; covered with the patent paper roofing; bunks for 120 men in each building; one kitchen for three buildings; barracks for officers of the same style. The barracks will be constructed by contract. The accompanying drawing* gives the proposed plan of the camp, but it will have to be modified in many particulars.

Very respectfully, your obedient servant,

W. HOFFMAN,
Colonel Third Infantry, Commissary-General of Prisoners.

---

* Omitted.

OFFICE COMMISSARY-GENERAL OF PRISONERS,
Washington, D. C., April 11, 1863.
HENRY S. DUNCAN,
Third Master, U. S. Ram Queen of the West, Newark, N. J.

SIR: Your letter of the 25th ultimo addressed to the Secretary of the Navy has been referred to the War Department with the indorsement that your name does not appear on the books of the Navy Department. Though there is no muster-roll of the crew of the Queen of the West on file in the Adjutant-General's Office it is not doubted that you belong to the military service, and being a paroled prisoner of war by direction of the General-in-Chief you will without delay report to the commanding officer at Benton Barracks, near Saint Louis, where you will remain till you are exchanged. In the meantime information will be obtained showing your position in the Army and on which you can be paid whatever may be due you. You will call on the quartermaster at New York, Maj. S. Van Vliet, for transportation to Benton Barracks.

Very respectfully, your obedient servant,
W. HOFFMAN,
Colonel Third Infantry, Commissary-General of Prisoners.

(Same *mutatis mutandis* to C. S. Edison, second master, New York City; James W. Foster, carpenter, New York City; William E. Taylor, first assistant engineer, and Asst. Surg. D. L. Booth, U. S. ram Queen of the West.)

QUARTERMASTER-GENERAL'S OFFICE,
Washington City, April 11, 1863.
Col. GEORGE H. CROSMAN,
Assistant Quartermaster-General, Philadelphia.

COLONEL: The Secretary of War directs the Quartermaster-General to cause to be constructed on Pea Patch Island additional barracks for 5,000 prisoners. You will take immediate measures to carry out this order of the War Department.

Very respectfully, your obedient servant,
E. S. SIBLEY,
Brevet Colonel, U. S. Army, Deputy Quartermaster-General.

(Copy to Col. William Hoffman, commissary-general of prisoners, Washington, D. C.)

OFFICE QUARTERMASTER, U. S. ARMY,
Baltimore, Md., April 11, 1863.
Col. W. HOFFMAN,
Commissary-General Prisoners, Washington, D. C.

COLONEL: I desire to call your attention to the fact that Confederate prisoners have been arriving here in large bodies without any previous intimation to me of their coming. The consequence is that I have been exceedingly embarrassed to find accommodations for them till transportation could be provided. I am this moment informed that nine Confederate prisoners were left at the Western police station last night sick with typhoid fever, &c. I have sent to the medical director and requested that a surgeon be sent at once to examine them and to designate a hospital in which they can be received. But where did these prisoners come from and who placed them in the station? This is a grave and serious matter and should be authoritatively regulated. Those who dispatch prisoners to the city as well as those who have them in charge should be instructed to give me timely notice of their being sent and when they may be expected to arrive. In such cases I can have the medical department notified to have a surgeon ready to inspect them on arrival and transportation ready to take them to their destination.

I cut a slip from the Sun of to-day in reference to the arrival of prisoners here. The first batch came in due season and have been sent forward. I am yet to learn of the second batch as I have received no information on the subject. Perhaps the nine sick were of this party.

Very respectfully, your obedient servant,

J. L. DONALDSON,
Quartermaster, U. S. Army.

[Inclosure.—Extract from the Baltimore Sun.]

ARRIVAL AND DEPARTURE OF CONFEDERATE PRISONERS.

Yesterday morning a special train of cars arrived at the Camden Street Depot from the West via the Baltimore and Ohio Railroad with 518 Confederate prisoners of war. Three females accompanied the party. They proceeded under guard to Locust Point, where they were placed on board the steamer Metamora, and at 1.30 o'clock yesterday afternoon the steamer started for Fortress Monroe from whence the prisoners will be sent up the James River to Richmond for exchange. At a late hour last night about 600 Confederate prisoners arrived at Bolton Depot from the West via the Northern Central Railway. It was also stated that another train would arrive this morning by the same route bringing about 500 more. They will all be sent to Fortress Monroe this afternoon. * * *

HEADQUARTERS, *Fort Monroe, Va., April 11, 1863.*

Col. W. HOFFMAN, *Commissary-General of Prisoners.*

COLONEL: All the citizen prisoners delivered to us have been declared exchanged, their equivalents having been delivered to the Confederates. All the officers delivered to us whose names I have from time to time sent you have been declared exchanged, their equivalents also having been delivered. I hope that the case of Captain Baylor may be speedily investigated that in case of acquittal he may be subject to exchange with other officers. It is vitally important to know whether the prisoners at Fort Lafayette captured by the Navy will be placed at your disposal in time for delivery with the officers expected to arrive at Fort Delaware. No officer of the Navy will be released by the Confederates until these men who have been declared exchanged and for whom equivalents have been given are delivered within the Confederate lines. Will you please communicate with the Secretary of the Navy on this subject and inform me of his decision by return mail? * * * Doctor Rucker's case is yet undergoing investigation. Doctor Green is held at Fort Norfolk as a hostage for him.

I am, very respectfully, your obedient servant,

WM. H. LUDLOW,
Lieutenant-Colonel and Agent for Exchange of Prisoners.

RICHMOND, *April 11, 1863.*

Lieut. Col. WILLIAM H. LUDLOW, *Agent of Exchange.*

SIR: Your letters of the 8th instant have been received. I am very much surprised at your refusal to deliver officers for those of your own who have been captured, paroled and released by us since the date of the proclamation and message of President Davis. That refusal is not only a flagrant breach of the cartel but can be supported by no rule of reciprocity or equity. It is utterly useless to argue any such matter. I assure you that not one officer of any grade will be delivered to you until you change your purpose in that respect.

You have charged us with breaking the cartel. With what sort of justice can that allegation be supported when you delivered only a few days ago over ninety officers most of whom had been forced to languish and suffer in prison for months before we were compelled by that and other reasons to issue the retaliatory order of which you complain? Those ninety odd are not one-half of those whom you unjustly hold in prison. On the other hand I defy you to name the case of one who is confined by us whom our Government has declared exchanged.

Is it your idea that we are to be bound by every strictness of the cartel while you are at liberty to violate it for months and that too not only in a few instances but in hundreds? You know that our refusal to parole officers was a matter exclusively of retaliation. It was based only upon your refusal to observe the requirements of the cartel. All that you had to do to remove the obnoxious measure of retaliation was to observe the provisions of the cartel and redress the wrongs which had been perpetrated.

Your last resolution if persisted in settles the matter. You need not send any officers to City Point with the expectation of getting an equivalent in officers so long as you refuse to deliver any for those whom we have released on parole in Tennessee and Kentucky.

If captivity, privation and misery are to be the fate of officers on both sides hereafter let God judge between us. I have struggled in this matter as if it had been a matter of life and death to me. I am heartsick at the termination but I have no self-reproaches.

Respectfully, your obedient servant,

RO. OULD,
Agent of Exchange.

CAMBRIDGEPORT, MASS., *April 11, 1863.*

Hon. ABRAHAM LINCOLN.

HONORED SIR: I cannot bring my mind into a state to apologize for addressing you on a subject calculated to arouse the deepest feelings of the human soul. I have before me in my office a weeping mother, a Christian woman, whose oldest son has been sold as a slave in Houston, Tex., having been captured in the city of Galveston with the Forty-second Regiment. He is a noble boy, born in Boston. His mother is a member of the First Baptist Church in this city of which I also am a member. He was a Sabbath scholar in the school connected with our church. This boy was earning about $8 per month in one of the houses connected with Harvard College. He gave it all to his mother, who is so white that she is not suspected as having any negro blood in her veins. She is well educated and in every respect a perfect lady. Her agony is intense, heartrending, and yet subdued by that Christian fortitude that sustains her in her thoughts and emotions of despair as she broods over her loss and the sufferings of her son, born in freedom, but which the might of thirty millions of men cannot because they will not protect. Information has been received from the quartermaster of the Forty-second that though earnest remonstrances were made against it and assurances given that he was born free in Boston that he was sold for the pitiful sum of $47. He was a servant of Doctor Cummings, surgeon of the Forty-second Regiment. His cousin, Charles G. Amos, sixteen years old, was sold at the same time. He was servant of Colonel Burrell, of the Forty-second Regiment. Who are these young men now slaves in Texas? I will tell you. Their great-grandfather was Prince Amos, who fought at Bunker Hill. His wife, the great-grandmother, now lives in Andover (I think) at the great age of ninety-seven years. She receives a pension from the United States Government now which enables her to live the few remaining hours of her prolonged existence. She hears with anguish that her great-grandchildren are in that slavery that none of the family ever knew before. During the long period of life they have intermarried with the Indians and whites. There is some (though remotely) negro blood, just enough to give a shade to the skin. The woman I plead for is poor. She has not yet received a dollar from the son who I presume has never seen a cent of pay since his departure from home.

For thirty-four years I have seen this result. I have always struggled to place it before the community in the business (a merchant) I have transacted. I have warned my countrymen. I voted for you as President. I have confidence in you but more in God. I know you are moved by the infernal influence of the border States slave-masters. I have stood with and among them in Washington. I heard their plans. But you have been no more moved to protract this war than God deems necessary to allow us to clean out with perfection the awful system that glories in making merchandise of God's poor men and women. If you have confidence in Him he will help you and make you a glorious instrument in doing the mighty work; if you shrink He has other agents who will accomplish it.

Can anything be done for this poor, suffering, praying, Christian woman? If there is power in the aggregation of immense power that has been concentrated in your hands do I presume in saying you ought to do something? Would to God I had the power. I would use it.

Yours, truly,   JOHN L. BARBOUR.

I am known to Charles Sumner and Henry Wilson, our Senators; to John B. Alley, Daniel W. Gooch, Samuel Hooper and other of our Representatives; to George W. McLellan, Assistant Postmaster-General; Dr. John Pierpont, in the Treasury Department; Judge Fernald and Charles H. Morse, esq., of the Quartermaster's Department, either of whom will testify to the reliableness of my statements.

[Indorsement.]

WASHINGTON, *April 29, 1863.*

With respect to the inclosed letter the undersigned respectfully refers to his indorsement April 14, 1863,* upon a letter from His Excellency Governor Andrew of the 8th instant on the same subject, and painful as the facts are feels obliged to repeat that it seems impossible to do anything for the relief of the boys except as the result of success in the prosecution of the war.

It is manifest that a formal demand for the boys except at the head of a conquering army would be met with insult.

E. A. HITCHCOCK,
Major-General of Vols., Commissioner for Exchange of Prisoners.

* See p. 456.

HEADQUARTERS FIFTEENTH ARMY CORPS,
Camp near Vicksburg, April 12, 1863.

Major-General GRANT, *Commanding, &c.*

DEAR SIR: A flag of truce brought on the family of Mrs. Mary M. Tompkins, of California, who wishes to go to San Francisco via New York City. She understands her obligations and duties, and I have promised she may with your approval pass to New York and San Francisco provided she respects the laws of propriety whilst passing through our territory. She has two daughters with her, Lilly and Rose, thirteen and eleven. Please give the necessary passes.

I send papers sent me by Major Watts, and have a message that in the gun-boat attack the Montauk was sunk. Major Watts sent me word that the attack on Charleston had been renewed. He says he has many prisoners he would like to deliver up, but his orders remain the same as before as to officers. Captain Brown has given his parole and gone up to Memphis from Jackson.

If Mr. Dana wants an excuse to see some secession officers and if you have any distinct proposition to make for the exchange of prisoners send them down and I will go on with the flag. Mr. Dana can go along. He asked me to notify him the first chance. General Thomas may advise you if it be proper to receive prisoners of war under the old cartel. I see in Northern papers so many notices of the renewal of exchanges that I believe there must be some truth in it, though Major Watts told me distinctly he had orders not to exchange officers and sent me word to-day that he had nothing new on this subject.

I am, &c.,

W. T. SHERMAN,
Major-General, Commanding.

HEADQUARTERS U. S. FORCES,
Franklin, Tenn., April 12, 1863.

Major-General VAN DORN,
Commanding Confederate Forces, Spring Hill, Tenn.

GENERAL: I am directed by the commanding general of the Army of the United States to forward to you under flag of truce the herewith inclosed General Orders, No. 49,* War Department, Washington, February 28, 1863, in reference to the rules and regulations in regard to paroles as established by the common law and usage of war, and which have been published for the guidance and instruction of said Army. These orders have just been received by me and I send them to you at this my earliest convenience.

I regret that I am compelled to inform you that some of your officers violated a well-recognized principle of war and an agreement lately entered into by representatives of the Government of the United States and the Government of the Confederate States in taking two of my medical officers prisoners at Brentwood, Tenn., on the 25th day of March last; and also as I am credibly informed that at the same time these officers so uncomfortably crowded some of my sick and wounded there taken prisoners into wagons and compelled them to undergo such hardships and exposure on the march that a large number of them died from the effects thereof.

---

* Omitted here; see p. 306.

Furthermore the horses, horse equipments and arms of four of my medical officers were then taken from them. I respectfully request that you have the same returned to me as soon as convenient.

I am, general, very respectfully, your obedient servant,

G. GRANGER,
Major-General, Commanding.

HEADQUARTERS U. S. FORCES,
Franklin, Tenn., April 12, 1863.

Maj. Gen. EARL VAN DORN,
Commanding Confederate Forces, Spring Hill, Tenn.

GENERAL: The commanding general of the Army of the Cumberland has just informed me that he has received information that our wounded men at Columbia are in a condition of great suffering, and he has authorized me to make arrangements if agreeable to you to have the men transferred here as soon as possible. I will give my receipt for them and will immediately return to you an equal number of your men now in our possession in exchange.

I am, general, very respectfully, your obedient servant,

G. GRANGER,
Major-General, Commanding.

OFFICE COMMISSARY-GENERAL OF PRISONERS,
Washington, D. C., April 12, 1863.

Col. G. LOOMIS,
Commanding Fort Columbus, New York Harbor.

COLONEL: By direction of the General-in-Chief you will please forward to Benton Barracks the sixteen men recently captured by the rebels on the Queen of the West and who have been turned over to you by Commodore H. Paulding, U. S. Navy, as paroled prisoners of war. The party will be placed under the charge of the senior officer or non-commissioned officer present, who will on his arrival at Benton Barracks report to the commanding officer. Asst. Surg. D. L. Booth, of the Queen of the West, has been ordered to report to you to accompany the party. The quartermaster will furnish the necessary transportation.

Very respectfully, your obedient servant,

W. HOFFMAN,
Colonel Third Infantry, Commissary-General of Prisoners.

WASHINGTON, *April 12, 1863.*

Lieutenant-Colonel LUDLOW,
Agent for Exchange of Prisoners:

There will not be more than 6,000 or 7,000 prisoners to be delivered. A mistake was made in the report from Saint Louis.

W. HOFFMAN,
Commissary-General of Prisoners.

OFFICE COMMISSARY-GENERAL OF PRISONERS,
Washington, April 12, 1863.

MILITARY PROVOST-MARSHAL, *Baltimore, Md.*

SIR: On the 22d of December last Capt. Robert W. Baylor, Twelfth Virginia Cavalry, was sent by an order from your office to Fort McHenry with a statement that he was charged with murder in having killed one of the men when bearing a flag of truce. If there are any written charges against him in your office or any evidence by which the charge can be established I have to request you will forward it to this office, to the end that the case may be investigated.

Very respectfully, your obedient servant,

W. HOFFMAN,
Colonel Third Infantry, Commissary-General of Prisoners.

MURFREESBOROUGH, TENN., *April 12, 1863.*
Lieut. Col. J. R. PAUL,
Commissary of Subsistence, Fourteenth Army Corps:

I beg leave to tender to you the circumstances and facts concerning a detachment of men sent from Shelbyville, Tenn., one year ago this April, 1863, with a view to collect if possible their loss in money and rations when absent. On the 7th day of April, 1862, a request was made by Brig. Gen. O. M. Mitchel, then commanding Third Division, Department of the Ohio, at Shelbyville, Tenn., that the several commanders of brigades through their intermediate commanders, colonels, should request of the captains of their respective companies to furnish a detachment of men (which should be a voluntary act on the part of the men) for the purpose of engaging in a hazardous expedition, such as scouting in the enemy's country and endeavor to effect a purpose of material aid to the Government in the form of cutting off communications between Atlanta, Ga., and Knoxville, Tenn., Richmond, Va., and Corinth, Miss.

After due consideration of the matter twenty-two volunteered their services from the different regiments and companies and left Shelbyville, Tenn., the 7th day of April, 1862, all under command of a Mr. [J. J.] Andrews, of Kentucky, noted for his daring and skill, having been engaged in such exploits before. Mr. Andrews was empowered with the authority sufficient to arm and equip them as the necessity of the expedition should demand, and by order of their commander, Mr. Andrews, they furnished themselves each with a Colt revolver and other necessary equipments, &c. In due time they met at or near Atlanta, Ga., as formerly agreed upon, and took possession of a locomotive, tender and two box cars, uncoupling at the time the regular train hands were at breakfast, and started toward Chattanooga, Tenn., with the view of burning certain bridges and thereby accomplish the design contemplated in the start. But by making some too hasty movements or not fully taking into consideration the necessary precautions, and in consequence of a speedy pursuit their attempts were foiled, and it resulted in the capture of the whole party after making fruitless efforts to escape. They were all lodged in jail in Chattanooga, Tenn., and from there taken to Knoxville, Tenn., and there eight of them were tried by a Confederate court-martial, sentenced and taken to Atlanta, Ga., and hung amidst the howling and jeers of a lawless mob of rebels.

The balance were lodged in jail in Atlanta to await trial and there remained confined over six months. They appealed to the provost-marshal of the place at various times to know what was going to be done with them, and after learning they were to be subjected to the same kind of treatment as their comrades a plot was contemplated and resolutions formed to break jail and escape if possible the treacherous designs of the rebel authorities and bloodthirsty mob who were present and threatened them daily, which was carried into effect the evening of the 16th day of October, 1862. Keys were made of the bones taken from meat they were fed upon and consequently they were enabled to unlock their handcuffs and shackles. When the jailer returned, after bringing them their supper, to take the dishes out of their cell they forced the keys from him and unlocked the door of each cell and fled, dividing off in pairs and each pair taking a different direction. They were run by bloodhounds, shot at and subjected to various kinds of treatment and the severest of hardships, such as living five and six days without food, traveling barefooted, sleeping in hollow logs, wet caves, &c., and by traveling only in the night with the North Star as their guide, the following-named persons below finally succeeded in arriving safely to their regiments and companies at various times, with the loss of the sums set opposite their names: Private William Knight, Company E, Twenty-first Ohio Volunteer Infantry, $60; Sergt. Wilson W. Brown, Company F, Twenty-first Ohio Volunteer Infantry, $29; Sergt. John R. Porter, Company G, Twenty-first Ohio Volunteer Infantry, $30; Corpl. Mark Wood, Company C, Twenty-first Ohio Volunteer Infantry, $125; Private J. Alfred Wilson, Company C, Twenty-first Ohio Volunteer Infantry, $15. Others who were not among the lucky to escape at first have since arrived safely via Washington, D. C., and been compensated for all their loss in full by the Secretary of War and assigned as a mark of honor a brevet lieutenancy and furloughed home for thirty days, a notice which we are happy to make of them, and which is no doubt justly their due.

Therefore we, the officers of the Twenty-first Ohio Volunteer Infantry, do each and severally ask and request most respectfully in consideration of the loss of the above-named enlisted men and trials they have undergone that they be compensated for said loss of private moneys and equipments and for rations not drawn; all which I have the honor to submit for your consideration.

I am, very respectfully, &c.,   J. M. NEIBLING,
Colonel, Commanding Twenty-first Ohio Volunteer Infantry.

[First indorsement.]

COMMISSARY DEPARTMENT, FOURTEENTH ARMY CORPS,
April. 20, 1863.

Lieutenant-Colonel FLYNT,
Assistant Adjutant-General, Fourteenth Army Corps:

This letter and the accompanying accounts* are respectfully referred to you. I am satisfied of the correctness of the accounts. The men were sent from the division of General O. M. Mitchel while I was connected with it. Most of their comrades suffered death on the scaffold. These escaped by most daring measures, and I think it just that they should be paid for the loss of private property and also commutation of rations during the time of their absence from their commands.

J. R. PAUL,
Lieut. Col. and Commissary of Subsistence, Fourteenth Army Corps.

[Second indorsement.]

HEADQUARTERS FOURTEENTH ARMY CORPS,
Murfreesborough, April 20, 1863.

Respectfully referred to Colonel Neibling to know if the men herein mentioned are as worthy of the compliment as those already complimented by the Secretary of War.

By command of Major-General Thomas:
J. P. WILLARD,
Captain and Aide-de-Camp.

* Not found.

[Third indorsement.]

HEADQUARTERS TWENTY-FIRST OHIO VOLUNTEERS,
Murfreesborough, Tenn., April 27, 1863.

The within-named soldiers are as worthy if not more so than those complimented by the Secretary of War. They made their escape and endured unaccountable hardships and privations for weeks while in the enemy's country before reaching the Federal lines. They also participated in the battle of Stone's River and behaved with great gallantry.

Very respectfully, your obedient servant,

J. M. NEIBLING,
Colonel, Commanding. Twenty-first Ohio Volunteer Infantry.

[Fourth indorsement.]

HEADQUARTERS FOURTEENTH ARMY CORPS,
Murfreesborough, April 29, 1863.

Respectfully forwarded.

The within-named soldiers of the Twenty-first Ohio Volunteer Infantry appear from the accompanying statement of Colonel Neibling to be as worthy of remuneration and honorable mention for their losses and daring conduct while on the expedition referred to as their comrades who have already been so deservedly rewarded by the Secretary of War.

GEO. H. THOMAS,
Major-General, U. S. Volunteers, Commanding.

[Fifth indorsement.]

HEADQUARTERS DEPARTMENT OF THE CUMBERLAND,
Murfreesborough, May 1, 1863.

Respectfully forwarded to the Adjutant-General of the Army.

The Secretary of War having made a special case of men engaged with these in their enterprise the accompanying papers are respectfully transmitted for his action.

W. S. ROSECRANS,
Major-General, Commanding.

[Sixth indorsement.]

ADJUTANT-GENERAL'S OFFICE, *May 12, 1863.*

Respectfully submitted to the Secretary of War.

The action of the Department alleged in the latter part of this letter is not of record in this office.

E. D. TOWNSEND,
Assistant Adjutant-General.

[Seventh indorsement.]

WAR DEPARTMENT, *May 21, 1863.*

The men referred to in this application will be placed upon the same footing as the other members of their party.

By order of the Secretary of War:

ED. R. S. CANBY,
Brigadier-General.

[Eighth indorsement.]

WAR DEPARTMENT, *May 24, 1863.*

Respectfully referred with reference to the claims for commutation of subsistence to the commissary-general of prisoners.

By order of the Secretary of War:

ED. R. S. CANBY,
Brigadier-General.

SPECIAL ORDERS, } HEADQUARTERS SIXTEENTH ARMY CORPS,
No. 68.   }   *Memphis, Tenn., April 12, 1863.*

*   *   *   *   *   *   *

V. In pursuance of orders this day received from the major-general commanding department it is ordered that Lieut. Col. M. Smith, provost-marshal, forthwith cause the entire press of the city of Memphis to be suppressed. He will take possession of the offices and material thereunto belonging, leaving the same in safe custody, not to be used without orders from these headquarters.

The editors of the Bulletin newspaper, Messrs. Hough and Nabors, will be immediately arrested and sent under guard to the headquarters of the commanding general by the first boat.

By order of Maj. Gen. S. A. Hurlbut:

HENRY BINMORE,
Assistant Adjutant-General.

MILLIKEN'S BEND, LA., *April 13, 1863.*

Maj. N. G. WATTS, *Agent for Exchange of Prisoners:*

On consultation with the Adjutant-General of the Army as to the propriety of receiving prisoners of war for exchange without the officers accompanying them he advises me to receive them.

The Dix-Hill cartel requires that officers and soldiers taken prisoners by either party should be sent to one of the two places agreed upon for exchange within ten days after their capture.

The order of Mr. Davis to hold officers I looked upon as a violation of this cartel or at least a revocation of it and that I had no right to make exchanges on any other basis without direct instructions to do so from the Government.

General Thomas informs me that notwithstanding this order to retain officers they are exchanging them in the East and that he has no doubt but that all will be exchanged. I will therefore receive all prisoners you may please to send and will return to you the same class of prisoners as they fall into my hands.

U. S. GRANT,
Major-General.

HEADQUARTERS CONFEDERATE FORCES,
Spring Hill, Tenn., April 13, 1863.

Maj. Gen. GORDON GRANGER,
Commanding U. S. Forces, Franklin, Tenn.

GENERAL: In reply to your communications received yesterday by flag of truce in the hands of Brig. Gen. Absalom Baird, U. S. Army, I have the honor to state that I have forwarded them to the general commanding the Army of Tennessee at Tullahoma and will send you his reply as soon as received. I have not the authority to act upon your propositions or to reply to the subject-matter of your letter.

Very respectfully, general, I am, your obedient servant,

EARL VAN DORN,
Major-General, Commanding Confederate Forces.

CAMP DOUGLAS, ILL., *April 13, 1863.*

Col. W. HOFFMAN, *Commissary-General of Prisoners.*

SIR: Having been assigned to the command of the District of Illinois, headquarters at Springfield, Ill., by General Orders, No. 35, Department of the Ohio, Col. Daniel Cameron, Sixty-fifth Regiment Illinois

Volunteer Infantry, is placed in command of Camp Douglas. I have the honor herewith to transmit his receipt* for books, vouchers, &c., relating to prisoners forwarded and for prisoners sick in hospital and money placed to their credit. April 9 I forwarded a report by mail to you of the inspection that had been made of prisoners before forwarding them to guard against smallpox occurring during the trip.

Very respectfully,

J. AMMEN,
Brigadier-General of Volunteers, Comdg. District of Illinois.

FORT DELAWARE, *April 13, 1863.*

Col. W. HOFFMAN, *Commissary-General of Prisoners.*

SIR: Believing that it is not only the policy but the wish of your Government that the conduct of the present unfortunate war in which we are engaged should be conducted as far as possible upon principles · of humanity and that every means should be adopted to insure a kind and humane treatment to those soldiers of your army who may in the varying fortunes of war fall into our hands, and believing that you are not cognizant of or do not approve of such conduct as is being perpetrated by certain officials of your Government, I desire to call your attention to and to enter my solemn protest against the conduct of the U. S. officials in charge of the Confederate prisoners lately confined at Camp Chase, Ohio.

Upon leaving there I was subjected to the grossest and most inhuman treatment, my person insulted, the clothing torn from my back, my baggage robbed of all it contained, my overcoat and gloves taken and some of the officers of my staff even had their shirts stripped from their persons. Certain little articles of no pecuniary value or use to your Government but of peculiar value to me (articles which I had purchased in and brought from the South and which had been reserved to me by General McClernand at the time of my capture) were taken from me apparently from no other motive than the meanest malice. My spurs were taken from my feet, my sash from my waist, my combs, brushes and all such necessary articles of comfort were ruthlessly taken.

And I am not alone in the above complaint but it was the common lot of my staff and all the officers (between 300 and 400) confined therein with me. They did not even have the money for which they held the post commandant's receipt returned to them and some of them were stripped to the skin and exposed to the vulgar gaze of the gaping crowd.

Believing as I said before that such conduct is not warranted by any order of yours and knowing the evil and unfortunate tendency it will have to embitter and prolong the struggle I in the name of humanity and in behalf of your own unfortunate soldiers who may be in our hands respectfully ask your serious attention to the above fact.

I have the honor to be, very respectfully, your obedient servant,

T. J. CHURCHILL,
Brigadier-General, C. S. Army.

[Indorsement.]

HEADQUARTERS, *Fort Delaware, Del., April 13, 1863.*

Respectfully forwarded.

I have been compelled to issue 422 blankets, all that were on hand at the post, to the prisoners who arrived last night and want some 30

---

* Omitted.

more to supply them all. These officers generally complain of their treatment at the time of their leaving Camp Chase.

ROBT. C. BUCHANAN,
Lieutenant-Colonel Fourth Infantry, Commanding.

HEADQUARTERS DEPARTMENT OF VIRGINIA,
Fort Monroe, April 13, 1863.

Major-General HITCHCOCK,
  Commissioner for Exchange of Prisoners, Washington, D. C.:

The Confederates have released a number of our officers on parole since the proclamation and message of Jeff. Davis. Shall I not exchange Confederate officers we hold for such after I have exhausted equivalents for our officers now in confinement? We have enough Confederate officers to cover both classes of cases. Please reply as soon as possible. A flag-of-truce boat is waiting.

WM. H. LUDLOW,
Lieutenant-Colonel and Agent for Exchange of Prisoners.

WASHINGTON, *April 13, 1863.*

Col. W. H. LUDLOW:

Make the exchanges indicated in your telegram of this morning. Ask Mr. Ould for information concerning a report of thirteen U. S. officers said to be confined at Atlanta, Ga., including Lieutenant-Colonel Hapeman and Major Widmer. They were taken at Hartsville, Tenn., December 7. Report specially the result.

E. A. HITCHCOCK,
Major-General of Volunteers.

FORT MONROE, VA., *April 13, 1863.*

Major-General HITCHCOCK:

All the Hartsville officers except Lieutenant-Colonel Hapeman and Major Widmer have been delivered. Mr. Ould promises to find and deliver these also.

WM. H. LUDLOW,
Lieutenant-Colonel, &c.

HEADQUARTERS DEPARTMENT OF VIRGINIA,
Fort Monroe, April 13, 1863.

Hon. ROBERT OULD, *Agent for Exchange of Prisoners.*

SIR: I have just received your letter of the 11th instant and am too much hurried to reply as I wish in detail to the several points therein contained. You are all wrong in your premises, arguments and conclusions. I agree with you that it is useless to argue the question and I unite with you in the expression of your earnest desire to alleviate the miseries of captivity of officers who have been so needlessly and so cruelly subjected to it by the proclamation and message of Mr. Jefferson Davis. I will acknowledge all proper paroles of our officers by delivering to you equivalents of your officers after the special exchanges of those now in confinement are carried out. This is I believe what you ask for. Will you frankly inform me if it be the intention of your authorities to put in force the offensive portion of the proclamation and message so often alluded to when the fortunes of war may place the greater number of our officers in your hands? Your officers are now in Fort Delaware ready for delivery and your reply will determine whether they are to come for exchange or to be returned to the West.

Please be clear, frank and explicit in your reply. Captain Mulford is instructed to bring it to me.

I am, very respectfully, your obedient servant,

WM. H. LUDLOW,
Lieutenant-Colonel and Agent for Exchange of Prisoners.

OLD CAPITOL PRISON, *Washington, April 13, 1863.*
Col. W. HOFFMAN, *Commissary-General of Prisoners.*

SIR: Accompanying this note I send you rolls* of citizen prisoners in confinement at this prison. The charges are in a great measure taken from the commitments. My experience is (satisfactory to myself) that not much reliance can be placed thereon. I am but the custodian of the prisoners and am unable to furnish you with the authority for the arrest. My duties are to receive the prisoner when committed by proper authority and hold him until released by proper authority. There may be many who for special reasons should not be exchanged. I have on previous occasions made such selections. There are no charges on file other than the commitment at this prison. All other information is obtained by individual examination. My clerical assistance will not warrant me in saying such selections (exchanges) can be made in less than three days to prepare the rolls and at least five hours to make the necessary preparations previous to a release for exchange when the number of state prisoners is equal to the present, 201. Hoping this will be satisfactory,

I remain, your obedient servant,   WILLIAM P. WOOD,
Superintendent Old Capitol Prison.

. WASHINGTON, D. C., *April 13, 1863.*
Brig. Gen. L. THOMAS, *Adjutant-General U. S. Army.*

GENERAL: It would appear from the recently published report of the Congressional Committee on the Conduct of the War that the immediate cause of my arrest and imprisonment on the 8th of February, 1862, was a document submitted to the honorable the Secretary of War by Maj. Gen. George B. McClellan, then General-in-Chief of the Army, by him described as "the written result of the examination of a Leesburg refugee." I have made application to Major-General McClellan for a copy of that document and for the name of the refugee, but have been informed in writing that he did not recollect the name of the refugee, and that the last time he saw the document was just previous to my arrest in the War Office. I respectfully request as a matter of justice to myself that I may be furnished from the War Department with a copy of the statement of this refugee, which seems to have produced such important impressions on the mind of Major-General McClellan.

Very respectfully, I am, general, your most obedient servant,

CHAS. P. STONE,
Brigadier-General.

---

* Omitted.

[First indorsement.]

ADJUTANT-GENERAL'S OFFICE, *April 13, 1863.*
Respectfully submitted to the Secretary of War.
                                    E. D. TOWNSEND,
                                        Assistant Adjutant-General.

[Second indorsement.]

Refused.
                                    E. M. STANTON,
                                        Secretary of War.

[Third indorsement.]

                                WAR DEPARTMENT, *April 17, 1863.*
Respectfully returned to the Adjutant-General.
By order of the Secretary of War:
                                    ED. R. S. CANBY,
                                        Brigadier-General.

———

GENERAL ORDERS, }   HDQRS. DEPARTMENT OF THE OHIO,
    No. 38.   }   *Cincinnati, Ohio, April 13, 1863.*

The commanding general publishes for the information of all concerned that hereafter all persons found within our lines who commit acts for the benefit of the enemies of our country will be tried as spies or traitors and if convicted will suffer death. This order includes the following class of persons:

Carriers of secret mails.

Writers of letters sent by secret mails.

Secret recruiting officers within the lines.

Persons who have entered into an agreement to pass our lines for the purpose of joining the enemy.

Persons found concealed within our lines belonging to the service of the enemy, and in fact all persons found improperly within our lines who could give private information to the enemy.

All persons within our lines who harbor, protect, conceal, feed, clothe or in any way aid the enemies of our country.

The habit of declaring sympathies for the enemy will not be allowed in this department. Persons committing such offenses will be at once arrested with a view to being tried as above stated or sent beyond our lines into the lines of their friends.

It must be distinctly understood that treason expressed or implied will not be tolerated in this department.

All officers and soldiers are strictly charged with the execution of this order.

By command of Major-General Burnside:
                                    LEWIS RICHMOND,
                                        Assistant Adjutant-General.

———

                HEADQUARTERS TENTH ILLINOIS CAVALRY,
                    Camp Totten, Mo., April 14, 1863.

Major-General HERRON, *Commanding Army of the Frontier.*

SIR: In answer to your communication of the 12th instant in reference to certain prisoners of war captured and paroled by me at Van

Buren, Ark., January 25, 1863, I have the honor to refer you to the accompanying certificate.*

I am, general, very respectfully, your obedient servant,

JAMES STUART,
Lieutenant-Colonel Tenth Illinois Cavalry.

HEADQUARTERS, *Fort Delaware, Del., April 14, 1863.*
Col. WILLIAM HOFFMAN,
Commissary-General of Prisoners, Washington, D. C.

SIR: The inclosed letters* contain an intimation from the Quartermaster's Department that additional barracks for prisoners are about being erected on this island. Should such be the intention of the Government I should be pleased to be informed of the number of prisoners it is proposed to quarter here and also the character of the buildings to be erected. As I have some little experience in such matters as building quarters of all kinds and as the health of my command is in a great degree connected with that of the prisoners I request that I may have the matter of plan as well as location intrusted to me. The present barracks are not fitted in their most essential details for the purpose for which they were built and will have to be altered. One set is very badly located and I propose to change it to another point. By so doing and altering the other so as to adapt it to the purposes for which it was constructed the additional buildings which it appears to be the purpose to erect may probably be diminished in size. We want a smallpox hospital and bake ovens, with cisterns or tanks in which to catch the water from the roofs, and other things which are essential to health or comfort. By having charge of this matter I can better take care of the interests of the Government with reference to the economy of construction.

I am, sir, respectfully, your obedient servant,

ROBT. C. BUCHANAN,
Lieutenant-Colonel Fourth Infantry, Commanding.

HEADQUARTERS. *Camp Douglas. Chicago Avril 14, 1863.*
Col. WILLIAM HOFFMAN,
Commissary-General of Prisoners, Washington, D. C.

COLONEL: Brigadier-General Ammen left here yesterday in obedience to orders from headquarters Department of the Ohio. The command of Camp Douglas devolves upon me as the senior officer. We had on the 10th, the day on which General Ammen received orders, 323 prisoners of war in hospital sick and as nurses. We have since that date received 48 additional prisoners sent to this camp by Major-General Hurlbut, commanding at Memphis. I inclose descriptive list.† Heretofore commissioned officers sent to this camp have been forwarded to Columbus, Ohio, for safer confinement, and I respectfully ask instructions in the case of Captain Smith and Lieutenant Johns, of the Confederate service, now here.

I have the honor to be, your obedient servant,

DANIEL CAMERON,
Colonel Sixty-fifth Illinois, Commanding Camp Douglas.

---

* Not found; but see Series I, Vol. XXII, Part I, pp. 220–222. † Omitted.

OFFICE COMMISSARY-GENERAL OF PRISONERS,
Washington, April 14, [*1863.*]
Lieut. Col. W. H. LUDLOW,
Agent for Exchange of Prisoners, Fort Monroe, Va.

COLONEL: By direction of the commissary-general of prisoners I have the honor to inclose to you by mail the following rolls, viz: Roll of prisoners of state at the Old Capitol Prison, Washington, D. C.; list of U. S. prisoners belonging to the Eighth U. S. Infantry and band and to the First and Seventh U. S. Infantry captured in Texas, paroled or accounted for and forwarded for exchange December 26, 1862; rolls 344 paroled Federal prisoners received at New Orleans March 13, 1863, from Maj. N. G. Watts, C. S. Army, by Col. W. Hoffman; muster-rolls of Federal prisoners forwarded to Vicksburg for exchange January 22, 1863; list of prisoners captured on board the Queen of the West on Red River, La.

Very respectfully, your obedient servant,

W. T. HARTZ,
Captain and Assistant Adjutant-General.

STATE OF OHIO, *Hamilton County, ss:*

Personally appeared before me, a notary public in and for said county, James M. Seeds, who is personally known to me, who being first duly sworn deposes and says that the several matters and things set forth in his certain letters addressed to Colonel Hoffman, commissary-general of prisoners, hereto attached, respectively marked A and B, and dated respectively March 24, 1863, and April 13, 1863, are true in substance and in fact, the same being a true statement of the nature and amount of expenditures by him for the purposes therein named.

JAS. M. SEEDS.

Sworn to before me and subscribed in my presence this 14th day of April, 1863.

WILLIAM M. RAMSEY,
Notary Public, Hamilton County, Ohio.

[Inclosure A.]

WASHINGTON, D. C., *March 24, 1863.*
Colonel HOFFMAN, *Commissary-General of Prisoners.*

COLONEL: Whilst I was a prisoner in the South I spent for the use of the sick and suffering Union men confined there $125, which I ask to have returned to me, as I have lost all my property, including $1,300 in money and my clothes.

Very respectfully, your obedient servant,

JAS. M. SEEDS.

[Inclosure B.]

CINCINNATI, OHIO, *April 13, 1863.*
Col. W. HOFFMAN, *Washington, D. C.*

SIR: The expenditures made by me individually whilst confined in the county jail at Richmond, Va., from the 13th November, 1861, to the 15th May, 1862, for medicines, provisions and clothing for Union soldiers and Union men confined with me, arrested as spies and being entirely destitute, was $40. I expended $85 for the same purposes at

Salisbury, N. C., from 17th May, 1862, to 5th March, 1863, which includes some expenditures for the benefit of destitute Union prisoners at Libby Prison, Richmond, Va., from the 6th March to 18th March, 1863.

There were with me in the county jail at Richmond, Va., three Federal soldiers and ten Union men, including Oscar C. Staunton and H. H. Smith, of New York, and [A. H.] Lee, of Washington City, held as Federal spies. There were with me in prison at Salisbury, N. C., held on charges of being spies, bridge burners, giving aid and information to the U. S. Army, sympathizing with the United States Government, &c., 245 civilians. After all possible attention and nursing by S. A. Pancoast, —— Patterson, —— Dibble and myself to alleviate and assist them 40 died for want of proper medical attention and from exposure and starvation.

If this statement of facts is not sufficient please inform me at early date and send an outline of what will be necessary to do. If the account is paid please send the amount to John Stanton, corner of Fifth and Race streets, Cincinnati, Ohio, by express.

I have the honor to be, very respectfully, your humble servant,
                                                        JAS. M. SEEDS.

[First indorsement.]

OFFICE COMMISSARY-GENERAL OF PRISONERS,
                                                April 20, 1863.

Respectfully referred to the Secretary of War with the recommendation that the amount expended ($125) be refunded out of prisoners' fund in my possession.

                                                W. HOFFMAN,
        Colonel Third Infantry, Commissary-General of Prisoners.

[Second indorsement.]

                                WAR DEPARTMENT, *April 23, 1863.*
Approved.
By order of the Secretary of War:
                                                ED. R. S. CANBY,
                                                Brigadier-General.

————

                        HEADQUARTERS ARMY OF KENTUCKY,
                                Franklin, Tenn., April 15 1863.
Col. W. HOFFMAN,
        Commissary-General of Prisoners, Washington, D. C.

COLONEL: Your letter of the 7th instant returning the roll of prisoners of war sent from Lexington, Ky., to Vicksburg, Miss., which was sent to me by the Adjutant-General of the Army January 17, 1863, has just been received. I cannot furnish you the receipts for the delivery of the prisoners as requested as they were never sent to me nor do I know that any were ever given. All prisoners sent to Vicksburg from my former command, the District of Central Kentucky, were first sent from Lexington, Ky., by me and delivered over to Brigadier General Boyle at Louisville, Ky.; after that I had no further control over them. These receipts may be in the possession of Brigadier-General Boyle or his provost-marshal, Colonel Dent, at Louisville, Ky.

I am, colonel, very respectfully
                                                G. GRANGER,
                                        Major-General, Commanding.

WAR DEPARTMENT, *Washington, April 15, 1863.*

His Excellency JOHN A. ANDREW,
    Governor of Massachusetts, Boston, Mass.

SIR: By direction of the Secretary of War I have the honor to inform you that your communication of the 8th instant in relation to the sale into slavery of two negro boys in Texas has been received and considered and that at present it appears impossible to do anything in this case except as a result of success in the war. The effort to reclaim them will be made.

Very respectfully, your obedient servant,

ED. R. S. CANBY,
Brigadier-General and Assistant Adjutant-General.

FORT DELAWARE, DEL., *April 15, 1863.*

Col. G. H. CROSMAN,
    Assistant Quartermaster-General, Philadelphia, Pa.

COLONEL: In consequence of a violent storm this evening since my arrival I have not been able to examine the barracks which were erected here for the prisoners last year, but from the report made to me about them by Colonel Buchanan and from my recollection of them as I saw them soon after their erection I am satisfied it will be absolutely necessary to make some considerable change in their plan and in the manner in which they are constructed to make them suitable for the purpose intended, and that the buildings about to be erected may be free from the faults of the present ones I have respectfully to request that you will defer closing the contracts for them until I am able after a personal inspection to suggest such changes as seem to be demanded. In fixing upon the plan there are many things to be considered and acted on which, though at first attended with some additional expense, will in the end lead to a saving of money, and as we are not in immediate want of the barracks I hope you will defer closing the contracts until the most appropriate plan can be decided on. It is probable that new proposals will have to be asked for. I will return to Washington to-morrow night and will write you again from there.

Very respectfully, your obedient servant,

W. HOFFMAN,
Colonel Third Infantry, Commissary-General of Prisoners.

MILITARY PRISON, *Alton, Ill., April 15, 1863.*

Col. WILLIAM HOFFMAN,
    Commissary-General of Prisoners, Washington, D. C.

COLONEL: Your letter of March 26, 1863, informing me of orders having been issued placing me in full control of the prison was duly received but the orders referred to themselves have failed as yet to come to hand. I therefore occupy about the same uncertain position here that I have from the first so far as the full control of the prison is concerned.

I have the honor to be, sir, with much respect, your most obedient servant,

T. HENDRICKSON,
Major Third Infantry, Commanding Prison.

GENERAL ORDERS, } HDQRS. DIST. OF IND., DEPT. OF THE OHIO,
    No. 9.   }   *Indianapolis, April 15, 1863.*

In assuming the command of the District of Indiana the general commanding deems it advisable and proper to issue the following order to the end that all may be advised of the principles which will govern his action:

I. He has no proclamation to issue nor policy to adopt. That has already been done and in his judgment well done by the commanding general of this department. He has no partisan feelings or interests he intends to advance, but desires to confer freely and fully with the prominent men of all political parties and invokes their hearty co operation in all measures calculated to restore harmony and good feeling in the State. He neither claims any right to interfere with civil matters in the State nor has any desire to do so.

II. The commanding general is charged with the duty of carrying into effect the provisions of General Orders, No. 38, recently issued by Major-General Burnside. He proposes doing so. Unmistakable evidence has reached him that the provisions of this order have been and are being violated in various parts of the State. This is unfortunately done in many instances by well-meaning men who are led astray by newspapers and public speakers. These latter will therefore be held to the most rigid accountability. There is no use in trying to dry the stream while its fountains are allowed to flow. All the newspapers and public speakers that counsel or encourage resistance to the conscription act or any other law of Congress passed as a war measure or that endeavor to bring the war policy of the Government into disrepute will be considered as having violated the order above alluded to and treated accordingly. The country will have to be saved or lost during the time that this Administration remains in power and therefore he who is factiously and actively opposed to the war policy of the Administration is as much opposed to his Government.

III. The commanding general indulges the hope that all citizens of the State will see the propriety and necessity of the observance of this order, and as they regard the true interest and welfare of the State and nation give him no occasion to take action on account of its violation.

By command of Brigadier-General Hascall:

                   ED. R. KERSTETTER,
            Captain and Assistant Adjutant-General.

                  FORT DELAWARE, *April 16, 1863.*
Lieut. Col. W. H. LUDLOW,
     Agent for Exchange of Prisoners:

Five hundred rebel officers are here. Prisoners from Lafayette not arrived.

                    W. HOFFMAN,
            Commissary-General of Prisoners.

         MILITARY PRISON, *Alton, Ill., April 16, 1863.*
Colonel HOFFMAN, *Commissary-General of Prisoners.*

COLONEL: I had the honor to receive yesterday your letter of the 11th instant in relation to certain errors and discrepancies in the return and rolls which accompanied it for the month of March last. I have endeavored to correct these errors as far as possible from the prison books which I find have not been kept in all respects as accurately as is desirable they should be. I have therefore made a roll* of officers transferred and a new return* which are inclosed herewith and which I request may be substituted for those previously sent you. The error in the field and staff pointed out by you arose from the adjutants and other staff officers being counted as company officers. That has been corrected, and you will perceive that there are now 14 field and staff officers and 64 company officers and 204 non-commissioned officers, privates, citizens, &c. To make this last number the two men, Joseph Bryant and Andrew J. Dye, should be stricken from the roll of transferred men. Bryant it appears was discharged on oath and bond and is accounted for on the roll of discharged men. Dye is still here in prison.

The frequent transfer and retransfer of prisoners to and fro between Saint Louis and this place makes it a difficult matter to keep the run of some of them and it is not surprising that mistakes should sometimes occur though we endeavor to avoid them. In regard to the exchanged roll it is possible that in our endeavors to correct this roll after the prisoners had been marched to the cars some few names may have been crossed off the rolls that should not and thus the number of names be made so much less in the count. This I can only ascertain by requesting you which I now do to cause to be forwarded to me a list of all the names that are crossed off this roll and for which I shall be much obliged.

It was believed that 869 prisoners left here for exchange, but this probably was a mistake. The officer who conducted the prisoners to City Point has returned hither and reports having delivered to the Confederate authorities at that place 855, for which number he got a receipt. He also reports that 3 prisoners died while en route to City Point; 2 were left in hospital in Baltimore; 2 and probably 3, the names of whom he could not learn at the time, effected their escape before he reached Baltimore, and 3 others who are under sentence and whose names got upon the rolls by mistake were brought back to this place, making in all 866 men who left the prison. It has been ascertained that some four or five men managed to leave here with the exchange whose names were not upon the roll at all by assuming as is supposed the names of a like number of men who managed to remain behind and who have since been found here. Such a fraud seems to be almost impossible to avoid when so large a body of men was being sent off at the same time. Captain Sisson states that when delivering the prisoners at City Point he found several men, four or five, among them whose names did not appear upon the roll, but they were included in the 855 turned over by him.

I hope the foregoing explanation, though somewhat prolix, will be satisfactory, and that the accompanying rolls* and return* will be found correct as I think they are

I am, &c.,

T. HENDRICKSON,
Commanding Prison.

HEADQUARTERS SECOND DIVISION, NINTH ARMY CORPS,
Winchester, Ky., April 16, 1863.

PROVOST-MARSHAL, *Mount Sterling, Ky.*

SIR: You will arrest all parties that have at any time been connected with the Confederate Army, whether discharged or otherwise dismissed,

---

* Omitted.

and have them forwarded to Lexington. They will be reported at these headquarters on their way through.

By order of Brigadier-General Sturgis:

HENRY R. MIGHELS,
Captain and Assistant Adjutant-General.

OFFICE COMMISSARY-GENERAL OF PRISONERS,
Washington, April 17, 1863.

Col. R. C. BUCHANAN, *Commanding Fort Delaware, Del.*

COLONEL: Please say to General Churchill that his letter of the 13th instant complaining of the treatment which he and his officers received on leaving Camp Chase at the hands of the guard is before me and in reply I can only repeat what I said to him personally that all such conduct on the part of any U. S. officer or soldier is wholly unauthorized. I need not say that the desire of the Government is that prisoners of war shall be treated with all the kindness which a proper humane feeling prompts and which is consistent with their position, for it is a well-known fact that clothing and blankets have been issued to the many destitute who have fallen into our hands. The sick and wounded have been as well and as promptly attended to as our own soldiers and all have been furnished with an abundant supply of rations, even including what may well be called luxuries.

But if I am rightly informed it has by no means been so with our troops when they have been captured as he may learn by inquiry on reaching Richmond. So far from receiving clothing it has frequently happened that they have been stripped of all their outer garments and then crowded into prisons inconceivably filthy, so much so that it would be shocking to humanity to confine in such a place even the most abandoned criminals. Here too were confined men of all ranks, from generals to privates, and all alike experienced the most insulting indignities and most unwarrantable harshness. So far as I have learned this has been the almost invariable treatment of our citizens and soldiers who have been held as prisoners of war at Richmond and there is scarcely room to doubt that it has been done by authority.

In this brief view of the case you will say then to General Churchill that though the indignities and outrages of which he and his officers complain are not only wholly unauthorized but are in violation of the instructions which have been given to govern in such cases yet the course pursued as it appears by his Government in similar cases takes from him all shadow of grounds for complaint. He has been made to suffer by an unauthorized retaliation for innumerable outrages which have been committed on our people if not by authority of his Government at least in its immediate presence and which have given rise to the bitter feelings he so much deprecates.

In conclusion say to the general that I trust the humane example which has been set by the Government of the United States in its care for the welfare of prisoners of war may be followed by the Government at Richmond, a course which cannot fail to greatly mitigate the hardships which must unavoidably be experienced by all who are so unfortunate as to be captured.

Very respectfully, your obedient servant,

W. HOFFMAN,
Colonel Third Infantry, Commissary-General of Prisoners.

ASSISTANT QUARTERMASTER-GENERAL'S OFFICE,
Philadelphia, Pa., April 17, 1863.

Col. WILLIAM HOFFMAN,
Commissary-General of Prisoners, Washington, D. C.

COLONEL: Your letter of the 15th instant has been received. Any alteration or improvement which you may suggest in the plans for the barracks about to be erected at Fort Delaware involving additional expense should come through the Quartermaster-General's Office, with his approval and orders thereon.

Very respectfully, your obedient servant,
G. H. CROSMAN,
Assistant Quartermaster-General.

OLD CAPITOL PRISON, Washington, April 17, 1863.

Hon. E. M. STANTON, Secretary of War.

SIR: I respectfully submit the following as a report on the communication and papers submitted to the War Department by W. Hoffman, colonel Third Infantry and commissary-general of prisoners:

As regards the note of General Hitchcock addressed to me on the 12th ultimo (March) I respectfully submit the documents marked A and B. On my discovery of Mr. Adamson's negligence in this matter I expressed myself in the strongest terms to him of the mortification and disappointment it had caused me in not having received the communication of General Hitchcock. The officer on duty at the prison will fully corroborate this fact. Some time previous to the issue of the note of General Hitchcock before alluded to Colonel Hoffman had endeavored to obtain information from me in relation to the prisoners under my charge, but as I had no authority to furnish him with such information he did not receive it. Subsequently he made application to the military governor and provost-marshal upon which he was furnished with a list of prisoners. On or about the 11th or 12th ultimo (March) while in the provost-marshal's office on business Captain Todd exhibited to me a list of prisoners which he said Colonel Hoffman was about to exchange. I remarked that that roll would only mislead Colonel Hoffman as but about one-half thereon were subjects of exchange, and that there were many of that class who were not on the list who had been committed since the list was gotten up. I informed Captain Todd of the propriety of notifying Colonel Hoffman of these facts as a prevention of the blunders of others being subsequently charged to me. Captain Todd requested me to call on Colonel Hoffman myself and give him this information which I declined to do, remarking that I did not recognize Colonel Hoffman as having jurisdiction or authority over the Old Capitol Prison or myself, nor had I ever seen any order giving him jurisdiction in the exchange of rebel prisoners, but that I would comply with Colonel Hoffman's requests if ordered to do so by the military governor. I further informed Captain Todd that I had an order from the Secretary of War authorizing me to obey all orders of General Hitchcock, and if that general should give orders to the effect that I should comply with such requests by Colonel Hoffman that I should promptly execute them. Upon this explanation Captain Todd immediately sent one of his clerks to Colonel Hoffman, and I am satisfied that the clerk's visit to Colonel Hoffman's office caused the issue of the letter of General Hitchcock of the 12th ultimo.

I have before stated I did not receive that letter on the 12th ultimo, nor did I know of its issue until I received the one in which that officer called for the probable number of civilians subject for exchange; also referring to the letter in which he had requested the rolls. I replied that I should immediately proceed to prepare the rolls. Captain Todd had furnished me with a new form of rolls which he said was forwarded to him by Colonel Hoffman with instructions that the place of arrest should be accurately inserted, together with several other matters not in my possession. I called on Colonel Hoffman on the 14th ultimo and informed him of the character of the lists furnished him by the provost-marshal and that entirely new rolls would have to be made out; that I would have them completed as soon as possible and would endeavor to have the prisoners ready for the boat at 3 p. m. I also stated that had I received earlier official notice of this exchange the number could have been increased about forty persons, many of whom were on parole. Colonel Hoffman then requested me to have them called in and have them ready to go on the next boat. From Colonel Hoffman's office I went direct to the military governor's office and requested clerical assistance to prepare the rolls in time to meet the request of Colonel Hoffman. I could not obtain this assistance from either the military governor or provost-marshal. I informed these officers of the trouble and difficulty in obtaining the information required on the new rolls; that each prisoner would have to be individually examined to obtain it. They then instructed me to do the best I could with the matter; conform as near as I could to Colonel Hoffman's request and get the prisoners on board the boat as early as possible. The rolls were not completed until nearly 3 p. m., and were used for the delivery of the prisoners to the officer and guard detailed for the purpose and the prisoners were started for the boat. An orderly was sent to General Hitchcock with the rolls to prevent the possibility of an error and I then proceeded to the residence of General Hitchcock to ascertain if all was right. I informed the general of my action which he appeared satisfied with, and assured me that Colonel Hoffman would have the matter properly attended to; that he had sent the rolls to Colonel Hoffman and that it was unnecessary for me to give the matter further attention.

Previous experience prompted me to follow up the rolls and accordingly I called at Colonel Hoffman's office and made inquiry about them. I was there informed that Colonel Hoffman, the officers and clerks had all left, leaving no one to give the matter attention. I obtained the rolls, went myself to Colonel Hoffman's residence in Georgetown and presented them for his inspection, informing him that the prisoners were waiting on the wharf for his orders, when he requested me to return the rolls to his office.

The name of D. T. Chandler I am satisfied must have been on the list furnished by the provost-marshal, but a comparison of that list with the one furnished by me will show that the former was neither guide, evidence or reference for the material of the latter. All exchanges heretofore made from this prison were based on the charges and evidence in the office of the provost-marshal. Mr. Chandler was committed as attempting to run the blockade and on that charge was entitled to the same judgment as his fellow-prisoners, and I do not recollect that Colonel Hoffman called my attention to his case. He may have done so, but when he called it the next day (Sunday) to the roll with the red line run through the name of Chandler, I expressed my regret at the oversight and have no excuse to offer now save that I was over-worked in making the hasty preparations required of me, not having had time to partake of any nourishment on that day (the 14th) from early in the morning until all the prisoners were on board of the boat.

The report of Capt. John E. Mulford, Third New York Volunteers, is referred to, and it is evident that if it is correct he has a fine memory for reporting details; but as I do not desire to flatter that officer I feel assured in saying that that report was made out for special purposes, because the second report exposes the promptings of the first wherein he says: "A number of the prisoners demanded of me their money," &c. He does not state the number, which I believe consisted of two Jews who had been brought on from Baltimore for exchange the day previous and who on board of the boat informed me that Provost-Marshal McPhail, of Baltimore, had taken their money from them. I informed them that no money belonging to prisoners had ever been in my possession; that the officials making the arrests were the responsible parties, and if they would make their statements in writing and give the same to Captain Mulford that on that officer's return I would endeavor to ascertain the whereabouts of their funds, and if not confiscated I had no doubt that Captain Mulford would be able to bring it to them on his return trip. Why Captain Mulford should insinuate that I had any knowledge of the prisoners' money is rather incomprehensible to me when I know from Judge Turner that Captain Mulford called on him in relation to the money of the prisoners previous to the writing of Colonel Hoffman's communication, who informed him that Provost-Marshal McPhail had placed the money in his (Judge Turner's) hands. The adage that hypocrites are often discovered by overacting their parts is in my opinion applicable in this case to Capt. John E. Mulford, of the Third New York Volunteers.

I received a note from Colonel Hoffman on the 25th ultimo as he states, but having to prepare rolls, provisions, transportation, &c., for the departure of nearly 500 prisoners and my clerical force being inadequate to the task I had little time to devote to preliminaries and acted as I believed in a manner to merit intelligent approbation. The selection of the prisoners for exchange had always been intrusted to me in accordance with the evidence I could obtain of their cases and my general knowledge of their respective characters. I had also been instructed by the military governor and by General Hitchcock not to stand upon technicalities, but to do the best I could to facilitate the requests of Colonel Hoffman in regard to exchanges; and on these verbal instructions I sent about twenty citizen prisoners on board of the boat, not one of whom has been named as an improper person for exchange. I have never released any prisoners from my custody except on orders from the Secretary of War or military governor. Hence my answer to Capt. W. T. Hartz.

Colonel Hoffman did make a request of me on the following morning, as he states. I furnished him with the list and exhibited his note, but did not do so as my authority for sending the prisoners, and reminded him of the request he had made on the 14th ultimo in relation to the forty prisoners (before alluded to), when he remarked that that was but a verbal request. I informed him of my instructions from the military governor and General Hitchcock and had acted accordingly.

Colonel Hoffman may not be aware that Washington is the home of my boyhood as well as the birthplace of my children. Yourself and the Assistant Secretary have known me for years and I flatter myself that you have never heard my veracity or honesty questioned by any citizen of Washington. Your Department has evidence of my services and knows the fidelity with which I have performed all the duties intrusted to me as superintendent of the Old Capitol Prison.

I have the honor to be, your obedient servant,

WILLIAM P. WOOD,
Superintendent Old Capitol Prison.

[Inclosure A.]

OLD CAPITOL PRISON, *Washington, March 27, 1863.*

Mr. S. E. ADAMSON.

SIR: When I inquired of you about receiving a letter from General Hitchcock in relation to making out rolls of prisoners you informed me you had received no such communication. On the receipt of said information from you I wrote to General Hitchcock and Colonel Hoffman accordingly. After I had thus written you found the communication above referred to the next day, the seal unbroken, and then informed me that you had not received said letter nor could account for its being in the office. Please state in writing your recollection of the subject-matter of this communication.

Very respectfully,

WILLIAM P. WOOD,
Superintendent Old Capitol Prison.

[Inclosure B.]

OLD CAPITOL PRISON, *Washington, March 27, 1863.*

W. P. WOOD, *Superintendent Old Capitol Prison.*

SIR: In answer to your letter of this date asking for an explanation why you did not get the letter from General Hitchcock relative to inquiries about rolls of prisoners: The letter was received by me from an orderly on the night of 12th instant, but was not opened; consequently I did not give a receipt for it. The next day having been interrogated by you about the letter I made a search for it, failing to find it; upon which and without due consideration or reflection I hastily told you no such letter was received. It having been mislaid and not finding it led me into the error and ignorance of its non-receipt. Upon again calling my attention to the letter referred to I made another search when I found it unopened and so gave it to you.

Very respectfully, your obedient servant,

S. E. ADAMSON.

OFFICE COMMISSARY-GENERAL OF PRISONERS,
Washington, D. C., April 18, 1863.

Maj. Gen. R. C. SCHENCK,
Commanding Eighth Army Corps, Baltimore, Md.

GENERAL: On December 22, 1862, the provost-marshal at Baltimore, Major Constable, committed to Fort McHenry as a prisoner of war Capt. Robert [W.] Baylor, Twelfth Virginia Cavalry, charged with murder, having killed one of our men when bearing a flag of truce. May I beg of you the favor to direct that any testimony in the possession of the provost-marshal or other officer which will establish the above charge may be forwarded to this office as early as practicable in order that Captain Baylor may be brought to trial?

Very respectfully, your obedient servant,

W. HOFFMAN,
Colonel Third Infantry, Commissary-General of Prisoners.

OFFICE COMMISSARY-GENERAL OF PRISONERS,
Washington, D. C., April 18, 1863.

Brig. Gen. M. C. MEIGS,
Quartermaster-General U. S. Army, Washington, D. C.:

I beg leave respectfully again to call your attention to Camp Douglas in its military aspect. In July, 1862, I had the honor to submit a plan for a system of sewerage for the camp by introducing a supply of water by pipes connecting with the city water works to flow through the sewers and by that means carry off all offensive deposits from kitchens, sinks and other sources. The ground was surveyed by an engineer of Chicago and a detailed plan prepared showing that a large sewer might be constructed to pass around three sides of the camp, terminating at the lake with sufficient descent to give a flow to the water that would carry with it all offal thrown into it. The plan can be readily carried out, and for all seasons except the coldest period in winter would I have no doubt answer well; but while the sewers would be closed by ice the police of the camp would have to depend on the ordinary means. The cost is estimated at about $5,000, but in this calculation it was expected that the labor of prisoners of war then at the camp might be used in constructing the part of the sewer within the camp. Though I was satisfied of the utility and practicability of the plan I did not at that time urge it strongly because of the expense and the prospect of an immediate exchange of the prisoners, but the camp is again occupied by prisoners and as it is probable that it will at all times be used as a depot for assembling new troops, for our own troops on parole and for rebel prisoners of war I would now respectfully recommend that the system of sewerage to which I refer, the plan of which Captain Potter, assistant quartermaster, can obtain, be immediately constructed. It is the more necessary now than a year ago, since in that time the space which could be conveniently set aside for sinks has probably been entirely appropriated. I make this recommendation on what I saw of the camp last summer and on a careful examination which I made of the place to which I refer, but I advise that nothing be done till the plan is carefully considered and the expense accurately estimated. There is a balance of the prisoners' fund amounting to $2,000 on hand at Camp Douglas which might be applied for this purpose.

Very respectfully, your obedient servant,

W. HOFFMAN,
Colonel Third Infantry, Commissary-General of Prisoners.

OFFICE COMMISSARY-GENERAL OF PRISONERS,
Washington, D. C., April 18, 1863.

Col. G. H. CROSMAN,
Assistant Quartermaster-General, U. S. Army, Philadelphia, Pa.

COLONEL: I have laid the matter of changes in the character of the barracks to be erected at Fort Delaware, mainly in the roofing, before the Quartermaster-General but he has not yet given a decision. It is proposed to substitute shingles for felt roofing, probably to secure more durability and better security against leakage, but principally with a view to collect in wooden tanks all the rainwater that falls on them. Large quantities of water will be required for the prisoners if the barracks are ever fully occupied, and the Quartermaster-General is considering the propriety of employing a steam water-boat which perhaps will be considered as obviating the necessity of change in the roofing. I will write you again as soon as a decision is made.

Very respectfully, your obedient servant,

W. HOFFMAN,
Colonel Third Infantry, Commissary-General of Prisoners.

[APRIL 18, 1863?]

Colonel HOFFMAN,
Commissary-General of Prisoners, Washington, D. C.

COLONEL: In obedience to an order of Major-General Grant, a copy of which I herewith forward you, I have the honor to report that a small force of the Nineteenth Michigan Infantry Volunteers stationed as a guard at the bridge on the railroad between Nashville and Franklin, Tenn., was captured by General Forrest, of the rebel army, on the morning of the 25th of March. This force consisted of Company D, of the above regiment of Michigan infantry, numbering about seventy men, and about 160 men who were fragments of the other nine companies of the regiment which were left to us after the battle of the 5th of March at Thompson's Station, in which 475 of the regiment were killed, wounded or made prisoners. Nearly 100 of the 160 named above were the sick and feeble men of the respective companies. Our total force at the bridge was about 230 men. At about 8 a. m. on the 25th Forrest surrounded this small force with three brigades, Forrest's, Armstrong's and Starnes', in all about 5,000 strong, accompanied by a section of artillery. Having got this into position he demanded our surrender. The officer in command, Capt. E. B. Bassett, judging it inadvisable to attempt to fight so large a force surrendered at once. Everything fell into the hands of the enemy, a large portion of which inclusive of tents, clothing, many overcoats, blankets and knapsacks belonging to those who had been made prisoners at the battle of Thompson's Station were burned on the spot. We were immediately marched a westerly course. When about four miles from Brentwood, as near as we could judge, our cavalry fell upon the rear guard of our captors producing a general stampede of the rear guard. The prisoners were put to the double-quick and by the personal exertions of Forrest and Armstrong the rout of their forces was stopped. We were, however, marched rapidly forward all day and most of the night, changing our course the next day, but keeping for the most part in the woods and unfrequented roads. We were hurried forward to Columbia, Tenn., which we reached on the evening of the third day. Here we were kept on the 28th, and officers and men except surgeons and chaplains were paroled. On the 29th we were sent to Shelbyville and thence to Tullahoma, which we reached on the 1st day of April. Here by order of General Bragg I was unconditionally released, furnished transportation and ordered out of the Confederacy via Vicksburg. I left Tullahoma on the 2d day of April and arrived at Vicksburg via Chattanooga, Montgomery, Selma and Meridian on the 5th, and on the 7th was sent by flag of truce to the U. S. fleet above Vicksburg. Chaplain C. D. Pillsbury, whose name appears in the order of General Grant, was taken on the same day and released at the [same] time as myself. He will doubtless report for himself. By this capture the regiment to which I belong are all prisoners of war, about 450 having been taken at Thompson's Station, and the balance except a few in hospitals on the 25th as herein stated. The men are already being received and sent to Camp Chase. Shall I join them there? I await orders. Until I receive them my address will be Coldwater, Mich.

With great respect, I have the honor to be, your obedient servant,
                                  I. COGSHALL,
               Chaplain Nineteenth Michigan Infantry Volunteers.

[Inclosure.]

SPECIAL ORDERS, }   HDQRS. DEPT. OF THE TENNESSEE,
     No. 97.   }   *Milliken's Bend, La., April 7, 1863.*
    Chaplains C. D. Pillsbury, of the Twenty-second Wisconsin Infantry Volunteers, and I. Cogshall, of Nineteenth Michigan Infantry Volunteers, captured at Brentwood, Tenn., on the 25th of March, having been unconditionally released by the Confederate authorities at Vicksburg (whilst their regiments are still held as prisoners), having reported at these headquarters, are directed to proceed to their respective homes and report by letter without delay to Major-General Rosecrans, commanding Department of the Cumberland, and to Colonel Hoffman, commissary-general of prisoners, Washington, D. C., such information as they may possess, and for orders. The Quartermaster's Department will furnish the necessary transportation.
    By order of Maj. Gen. U. S. Grant:
                                  JNO. A. RAWLINS,
                                  Assistant Adjutant-General.

———

                OFFICE COMMISSARY-GENERAL OF PRISONERS,
                       Washington, D. C., April 19, 1863.
Col. R. C. BUCHANAN, *Commanding Fort Delaware.*
    COLONEL: I am directed by the commissary-general of prisoners to request [you] to hold David Lynn until further orders. He is one of the rebel officers recently sent from Camp Chase. Telegram just received from Major Darr, provost-marshal-general, Wheeling, Va., says General Rosecrans confirms his report of the violation of parole of David Lynn.
    Very respectfully, your obedient servant,
                                  W. T. HARTZ,
                          Captain and Assistant Adjutant-General.

———

                OFFICE COMMISSARY-GENERAL OF PRISONERS,
                       Washington, D. C., April 19, 1863.
Maj. T. HENDRICKSON,
        Commanding Military Prison, Alton, Ill.
    MAJOR: In reply to appeal of Captain Melton which was referred by you to this office I am directed by the commissary-general of prisoners to inform you that the records in this office show that Captain Melton left Camp Chase for Johnson's Island the 26th of April, 1862, and that he was not delivered at the island. His statement that he escaped is therefore true, and his recapture only restored him to his position of prisoner of war. He will therefore be sent forward with the next party of prisoners of war ordered for exchange.
    Very respectfully, your obedient servant,
                                  W. T. HARTZ,
                          Captain and Assistant Adjutant-General.

OFFICE COMMISSARY-GENERAL OF PRISONERS,
Washington, D. C., April 19, 1863.
Capt. E. L. WEBBER,
Commanding Military Prison, Camp Chase, Ohio.

CAPTAIN: In reply to communication of Capt. John C. Moon, of April 10, 1863, in relation to clothing and other articles taken from prisoners of war I am directed by the commissary-general of prisoners to request you to have a list made of the various articles and to whom belonging, specifying the character of the articles, whether contraband or otherwise, and forward the list to this office. You are directed to place them in charge of the quartermaster for storage, taking his receipts for them.

Very respectfully, your obedient servant,

W. T. HARTZ,
Captain and Assistant Adjutant-General.

FRANKLIN, TENN., *April 20, 1863.*
General ROSECRANS:

All quiet in front. Received an answer to my dispatch from Van Dorn to-day about our wounded at Columbia. The matter was referred to Bragg, who ignores me, but is ready to enter into arrangements with you in reference to exchange.

G. GRANGER,
Major-General.

OFFICE COMMISSARY-GENERAL OF PRISONERS,
Washington, D. C., April 20, 1863.
Hon. E. M. STANTON, *Secretary of War, Washington, D. C.*

SIR: I have the honor to inclose herewith reports made by the commanders of Camp Douglas and the military prison at Alton of the inspection made of prisoners of war before being transferred to City Point with a view to prevent the communication of smallpox by them on the line of travel.

The report of Major Hendrickson, commanding Alton Prison, accompanied by the report of the medical officer in charge, shows that a careful inspection was made of the prisoners sent forward and that all proper precautions were taken to prevent the spread of the contagion, and it has not been reported to me that there were any cases among the prisoners sent from that prison.

The report of General Ammen, commanding Camp Douglas, gives no satisfactory details of the steps taken to guard against the possibility of the disease being communicated by prisoners from his camp.

So far from taking time for a thorough inspection and cleansing of those designated to leave some of them were ordered to move the day after the receipt of General Wright's order and it is not possible that in that brief time all proper and necessary preparations could have been made.

General Ammen states that the prisoners were examined by the principal surgeon (whose name is not given) and his assistants, but no report is made by the surgeon of the manner in which this inspection was made, nor what else was done if anything to insure that the contagion should not be carried with them. The general does not state who the assisting surgeons were, but some of them were possibly surgeons in the rebel army who were among the prisoners and who would be much inclined to take with them all whom they were not forced to reject. This fact goes to corroborate the report that nine slight cases were permitted to pass by the rebel surgeon who examined them.

Whatever injury may have resulted from the forwarding of prisoners of war from Camp Douglas to City Point by the spread of this dangerous disease General Ammen and his principal surgeon must be responsible for.

From the general's own report it does not appear that he gave any very explicit orders in the matter to guard against contagion or took any personal interest in it.

The surgeon makes no report, and the immediate result—the development of several aggravated cases before reaching Baltimore—shows there was great carelessness in the examination or willful neglect.

Two cases of varioloid from the Saint Louis Prison have been reported to me, but these were scarcely to be guarded against, for the prevalence of the disease in Saint Louis and the frequent interchange of prisoners between Saint Louis and Alton would give rise to cases when not at all looked for.

I do not think it at all necessary to offer any excuse for the manner and the time of issuing the order for the delivery of the prisoners of war at City Point, but that the case may be fully understood I will respectfully offer the following explanations:

This movement had been in contemplation for several weeks and had been determined upon early in February, but in consequence of the great expense attending the transfer and in the hope that the way to Vicksburg would soon be opened the order was postponed from time to time. At length, in order to relieve the Government from the cost of holding them, including the employment of a large force as guards, and to open the way by exchange for sending to the field a large force of our own troops now on parole, it was determined by the General-in-Chief on my representation to order all the prisoners in our hands to City Point, and by his direction I communicated the order to the generals commanding the Departments of the Ohio and the Missouri.

My report of the 8th instant will show how careful I was to guard against the omission of any essential point in the instructions. In addition I wrote to the several commanders directing what rolls should be prepared and if not otherwise ordered by the general commanding the department what guards should be detailed, what rations should be furnished, what instructions should be given to the guards to prevent all intercourse with any one at stopping places, &c.

To have delayed the order because of the possibility of there being a case of smallpox developed on the route would have compelled us to retain in our hands for an indefinite period several thousand prisoners of war, while for the same reason three regiments of infantry and a battery of artillery should now be detained from the field at Camp Douglas.

Cases of smallpox have been taken out of the street cars in this city and they have been picked up in the streets. There are cases among our soldiers at Camp Parole, there are cases at Fort Delaware, and the disease probably exists at other camps, and if the transfer of troops or prisoners of war can only be made from camps or places free of this disease a moment's reflection will show how much expense and how much embarassment to the service must grow out of such a rule.

If this rule had governed 3,000 to 4,000 prisoners could not have been sent to Camp Douglas for safe-keeping, and there was no other place to which they might have been sent.

My part in this transaction has been but a subordinate one, having generals on both sides of me to give and receive the orders, and I feel conscious that I performed my whole duty faithfully, carefully and with judgment, as is fully established by the foregoing report.

In closing my report I must beg leave to express my deep regret that my untiring efforts to perform the various duties of my office with ability and promptness should meet only with such harsh censure as is contained in your telegram to the Hon. Mr. Watson, Assistant Secretary of War.

Very respectfully, your obedient servant,

W. HOFFMAN,
Colonel Third Infantry, Commissary-General of Prisoners.

[Inclosure No. 1.]

MILITARY PRISON, *Alton, Ill., April 9, 1863.*

Col. WILLIAM HOFFMAN,
Commissary-General of Prisoners, Washington, D. C.

COLONEL: Your dispatch of the 8th in relation to Confederate prisoners of war sent from this prison for exchange to City Point, Va., on the 1st instant was received last evening and in compliance therewith I have the honor to report that so soon as I received the instructions from the headquarters Department of the Missouri to prepare these prisoners for the exchange (which was five or six days before they left the prison) I directed Doctor Wall, assistant surgeon of the Seventy-seventh Ohio Volunteers, the senior medical officer in charge of the prison hospital, to make a critical examination and inspection of the sick under his care with a view to their being sent away for exchange and to designate such of them only as were then free from any infectious disease, especially the smallpox, and able to perform the journey to City Point, Va., without inconvenience or difficulty. This inspection I have reason to believe was faithfully made and no prisoner was sent from here so far as I know who was not entirely free from smallpox. I was present when the prisoners were called out for exchange and saw each man take his place in the ranks previous to being marched to the cars, and with the exception of two or three of them who were somewhat lame from wounds or other injuries I saw none so far as I was capable of judging who were not in a condition to perform the journey.

The smallpox has prevailed here in the prison to a greater or less extent for some months past and it is not impossible but that some of the prisoners who left here on the 1st instant, though to all appearances entirely free from disease at the time, may have had the seeds of this disease in their system. But no one of them who was known to be thus affected was permitted to leave or did leave here at that time. I have not heard that the smallpox was carried away with the prisoners sent from here but I infer from the tenor of your dispatch that a report to that effect has been put in circulation.

I inclose herewith the report of Doctor Wall in relation to the inspection made by him as alluded to in the body of this my report.

I have the honor to be, sir, with much respect, your most obedient servant,

T. HENDRICKSON,
Major Third Infantry, Commanding Military Prison.

[Sub-inclosure.]

MILITARY PRISON HOSPITAL, *Alton, Ill., April 9, 1863.*
Maj. T. HENDRICKSON, *Prison Commandant.*

MAJOR: In answer to your query respecting the precautions that were taken to prevent the smallpox being carried from this prison by those who were sent on exchange I would say that every means were adopted that were possible under the circumstances when I learned of the intended movement. I issued orders to the effect that the prisoners should all perform daily ablutions of the whole body, and that all of their underclothing and as much of their outer as could be should be thoroughly washed, and that no prisoners, particularly those from the hospital, should be permitted to go out of the prison on the exchange unless his garments were as clean as was possible for him to get them. I feel confident that the disease would not be carried from here on the person or clothing of any of the prisoners, but it is possible that some of them might have received the infection into their system prior to their leaving and the disease develop itself on the way.

This could not be obviated, though it was my opinion that all those who were sent were protected by vaccination or by their previously having had smallpox. We had on hand at that time six cases of this disease and varioloid, but they were completely isolated from the rest of the sick and the well prisoners.

I made a personal inspection of all those connected with the hospital and all others complaining of indisposition the day previous to their start.

Respectfully, yours,

AND. WALL,
Surgeon in charge of Prison Hospital.

[Inclosure No. 2.]

CAMP DOUGLAS, *Chicago, Ill., April 9, 1863.*
Col. W. HOFFMAN, *Commissary-General of Prisoners.*

SIR: Yours of April 8 stating that "the Secretary of War directs that you report immediately what inspection was made of the prisoners at Camp Douglas before their departure for Baltimore," &c., received.

Soon after the arrival of the prisoners at Camp Douglas cases of smallpox were discovered. The prisoners were vaccinated as speedily as possible. They were examined daily and those taking the disease were removed to the hospital and allowed no intercourse with the others. The number of new cases daily diminished, and when any recovered their clothing was burned; they were cleansed and supplied with new clothing.

When orders were received to send the prisoners to City Point, Va., those occupying certain barracks were designated to move the next day. These prisoners were then examined by the principal surgeon aided by one or more of his assistants and all such as showed any symptoms of the disease were detained.

The surgeon assures me they were strictly examined and that none were sent who showed any sign of the disease at the time of leaving.

Very respectfully, your most obedient servant,

J. AMMEN,
Brigadier-General of Volunteers, Commanding.

OFFICE COMMISSARY-GENERAL OF PRISONERS,
Washington, D. C., April 20, 1863.

Brig. Gen. JOHN S. MASON, *Commanding, Columbus, Ohio.*

GENERAL: I have the honor to acknowledge receipt of your letter of the 17th instant suggesting that authority be given to you to grant short furloughs to paroled soldiers and in reply I have to inform you that your letter has been submitted to the General-in-Chief for his action. In accordance with it I have referred a recommendation heretofore made that a permanent guard be established at Camp Chase, the commander of which should be the permanent commander of the camp and the prison. In reply to your second letter of the same date I have to state that the control of the prison was placed entirely in the hands of the guard specially designated for it, the commander thereof having sole authority over the prison and prisoners. This arrangement was made with the understanding that General Cooper was to command the camp and avoid the continual changes which would otherwise take place by the frequent changes of the troops at the camp. The irregularities which are reported by Captain Drake are all in violation of my instructions for the government of the prison. The officer of the day of the camp should have nothing to do with the inside of the prison, and the improprieties committed by the violation of this rule show how necessary it is that there should be no interference with the prisoners by a person not under the authority of the commander of the prison. My letter to General Cooper and my instructions to the commander of the guard will explain how this command is to be understood. It is probable all the prisoners will be removed from Camp Chase to Johnson's Island very soon and this will obviate all the difficulties growing out of a divided command, but in the meantime I will be much indebted to you if you will have me informed of any irregularities occurring at the prison that may be brought to your notice.

Very respectfully, your obedient servant,

W. HOFFMAN,
Colonel Third Infantry, Commissary-General of Prisoners.

U. S. MISSISSIPPI SQUADRON, *April 20, 1863.*

JOHN A. RAWLINS, *Assistant Adjutant-General.*

SIR: Your communication of yesterday has been received. The crew of the Queen of the West do belong to Ellet's brigade, although not soldiers, being hired men for a specified time as master, pilots, mates, deck-hands, &c. The crew proper work the vessel, in addition to which they have soldiers who fight her.

Respectfully, your obedient servant,

K. R. BREESE,
Lieutenant-Commander, U. S. Navy.

HEADQUARTERS DEPARTMENT OF VIRGINIA,
Fort Monroe, April 20, 1863.

Hon. ROBERT OULD, *Agent for Exchange of Prisoners*

SIR: On the 11th instant I sent to City Point in charge of Lieutenant-Colonel Matson ten Confederate officers who had not been exchanged. I inclose herewith a copy of my letter of that date* giving

---

* Not found.

the names and rank of the officers. Lieutenant-Colonel Matson disobeyed his instructions in not bringing back with him equivalents for these officers. Please deliver these equivalents now to the officer bearing this.

In my letter of the 13th instant, a copy of which is inclosed* for your more convenient reference, I stated my willingness to exchange officers on the terms therein mentioned. I wish to know whether those terms are assented to by you and I desire a response to the other questions therein propounded. The peculiar position of this question of exchange of officers renders these questions proper, and I regret extremely having received through my agent so unsatisfactory and I may say exceptionable notice (not reply), of which I inclose a copy.† Until you think proper to inform me what your understanding is in reference to our officers I certainly cannot move one step farther toward sending to City Point any of the large number of Confederate officers now at Fort Delaware awaiting your action.

I again ask the release of Lieut. Col. Douglas Hapeman and Maj. J. H. Widmer, One hundred and fourth Regiment Illinois Volunteers, Hartsville officers declared exchanged and yet held by you. Please send them, and also one captain and one lieutenant due to me as you will see on reference to my letter of the 13th instant and which inclosed duplicate lists of officers sent to you.

I am, very respectfully, your obedient servant,

WM. H. LUDLOW,
Lieutenant-Colonel and Agent for Exchange of Prisoners.

MILITARY PRISON, *Alton, Ill., April 20, 1863.*

Col. W. HOFFMAN,
Commissary-General of Prisoners, Washington, D. C.

COLONEL: I find upon inspection that some of the buildings within the prison walls used as quarters and for hospital purposes require considerable repairs to make them comfortable for those purposes. The roof of the building used as the principal hospital leaks badly and should be repaired as early as practicable—now, while the number of its inmates is comparatively small. I wish to know how these repairs are to be made, whether by the Quartermaster's Department, the owners of the prison or must they be made from the prison fund?

I have the honor to be, sir, with much respect, your obedient servant,

T. HENDRICKSON,
Major Third Infantry, Commandant of Prison.

HEADQUARTERS U. S. FORCES,
Columbus, Ohio, April 21, 1863.

Brig. Gen. J. D. COX,
Commanding District of Ohio, Cincinnati, Ohio.

GENERAL: I would beg leave to suggest that all paroled prisoners now at Camp Chase who belong to Illinois, Missouri, Michigan, Pennsylvania, Indiana, Minnesota, Wisconsin and New York regiments or batteries be ordered to the camp of their respective States and that the

---

* Omitted here; Ludlow to Ould, p. 478.   † Not found.

paroled prisoners of the Regular Army now at Camp Chase be transferred to Camp Thomas.

I have the honor to be, very respectfully, your obedient servant,

JNO. S. MASON,
Brigadier-General of Volunteers, Commanding.

[Indorsement.]

HEADQUARTERS DISTRICT OF OHIO,
Cincinnati, April 28, 1863.

Respectfully referred to Colonel Hoffman, commissary-general of prisoners, Washington, for information whether prisoners already at the general camps can properly be transferred to other camps merely for the purpose of having them within the States where they were enlisted. General Orders, Nos. 72 and 191, of 1862, refer to the original mode of reporting and to the forwarding of paroled men from temporary stations, &c., but do not apparently decide the case made by General Mason's letter.

J. D. COX,
Brigadier-General, Commanding.

OFFICE COMMISSARY-GENERAL OF PRISONERS,
Washington, April 21, [1863.]

Maj. Gen. U. S. GRANT, *Commanding, Memphis, Tenn.*

GENERAL: I beg leave again to call your attention to the incomplete rolls of prisoners of war which are forwarded from the Department of the Tennessee to this office. Some of them give neither the time nor place of capture nor what disposition has been made of the prisoners and are wholly useless either for the records of this office or for the purpose of exchange.

I have the honor to inclose herewith one roll as a specimen. There is nothing upon it to show where it was made nor by whom, nor whether the prisoners are Federal or rebel except by the designation of the regiments.

Other rolls are more complete but still defective in parts. They should show at what place prisoners are held if still retained in our hands, or at what point delivered if sent beyond our lines.

Very respectfully, your obedient servant,

W. HOFFMAN,
Colonel Third Infantry, Commissary-General of Prisoners.

OFFICE COMMISSARY-GENERAL OF PRISONERS,
Washington, D. C., April 21, 1862.

Col. G. H. CROSMAN,
Assistant Quartermaster-General, Philadelphia, Pa.

COLONEL: The Quartermaster-General has decided to substitute shingles for the felt roofing on the prison barracks about to be erected at Fort Delaware. The object in part is to secure the water which falls on them, and to this end the Quartermaster-General directs that suitable wooden water-tanks be constructed for each building. The general also directs that the schooner employed in transporting water to the fort be so arranged as to carry it in bulk. Possibly a larger vessel may be necessary in anticipation of the arrival of large numbers of prisoners. I believe a force pump and hose have been ordered for use at the fort, which will serve to transfer the water from the water boat to such place as it may be required. The present buildings have their floor on the ground, which being always very damp makes them uncomfortable and unhealthy. The height of the buildings is such that the floor may be raised fifteen or eighteen inches from the ground and leave still sufficient from the floor to the eaves to admit of three tiers of bunks, about nine feet. The Quartermaster-General approves of this modification. Experience shows also that ventilation by an opening in the roof through its whole length just below the ridge is objectionable also, as in stormy weather rain and snow blow in, making the barracks wet and uncomfortable. Square ventilators some fifteen or twenty feet apart set into the comb of the roof with shutters on the four sides are suggested as more convenient.

Very respectfully, your obedient servant,

W. HOFFMAN,
Colonel Third Infantry, Commissary-General of Prisoners.

FORT MONROE, *April 21, 1863.*

Col. W. HOFFMAN, *Commissary-General of Prisoners:*

It is very important for me to know why and how those Confederate officers were released at Vicksburg and for what equivalents. Will you inquire and let me know as soon as possible?

WM. H. LUDLOW,
Lieutenant-Colonel, &c.

FORT MONROE, *April 21, 1863.*

Col. W. HOFFMAN, *Commissary-General of Prisoners:*

What shall I do with the lists of regulars captured in Texas which you sent me? They were long ago declared exchanged and are accounted for.

WM. H. LUDLOW,
Lieutenant-Colonel, &c.

FORT MONROE, *April 21, 1863.*

Col. W. HOFFMAN, *Commissary-General of Prisoners:*

Have equivalents been received for Colonel Looney, Captain Sanford and Lieutenant Bright, C. S. Army, delivered at Vicksburg to Major Watts on the 2d instant? If not, why were they sent there?

WM. H. LUDLOW,
Lieutenant-Colonel. &c.

CARTHAGE, JASPER COUNTY, MO., *April 21, 1863.*

Maj. JAMES H. STEGER, *Assistant Adjutant-General.*

SIR: A few days since two of my best soldiers were captured by a gang of guerrillas and taken ten or twelve miles from here to the camp of one Colonel Harrison (formerly lieutenant-colonel of MacDonald's regiment, now its colonel), from whom I received a note in some mysterious way stating that he had my men and would hold them until

Washington Petty and Eli Adams, of this county, were released from the guard-house in Springfield. From my previous knowledge of Colonel Harrison I believed I could effect the release of my soldiers immediately and learn some other things that would be of importance to me at this place and to the Government. I sent out a flag of truce to him under Captain Henslee; found him in a few hours; accomplished what I desired. My men arrived safely at home, but Colonel Harrison was fired upon under his flag before having gone more than three miles; his horse was shot under him, wounded severely; it and the rigging were captured, his private papers, and my letter to him in regard to the prisoners, the manner of exchange, &c. This was done by the Newtonia militia under Major Eno I suppose, and I learn that he has since declared that he would not return the trappings of the horse and my letters. As it was under a flag of truce proposed by me, an officer of the Government, for the good and welfare of that Government; as my command was kindly and safely guarded, picketed and protected by them during the existence of the flag, and as Colonel Harrison had not reached the point from which he started in order to meet my flag I maintain that they should not have been fired [upon] and that the property captured by them should be returned to me that I might return it, or be sent directly to Colonel Harrison; and I hope, major, that Colonel Cloud will issue an order upon Eno to that effect. I consider my honor involved, and if it commands any respect at your quarters I desire you if compatible with Colonel Cloud's views to issue such an order immediately. Colonel Harrison had my men treated remarkably well; horses returned with saddles and saddle equipments, and not one cent or one stitch of clothing taken from them; captured four in all, released two unconditionally.

I hope you will have Petty and Adams released as exchanged prisoners for Joseph McKinnon, Company L, and Elihu Maxwell, Company K, Seventh Cavalry Missouri State Militia. If such is not done I will be compelled to return my soldiers to Colonel Harrison. They are vigorous and active soldiers. I received such information from Colonel Harrison as would be of service to General Curtis and I communicated it directly to him. Colonel Harrison seems to be in command of all the squads, bands and gangs abroad in the country (outranking Tom R. Livingston, who is still absent but daily expected with 150 men), and who says he is gathering them together to make an expedition into Colorado Territory to capture the arms, mules, wagons and mail belonging to the Government. I will not be deceived by these specious stories.

Major, am I to remain here much longer? I make this inquiry because this place is in General Blunt's department. The Secessionists say that Tom R. Livingston (Chin Pagod) will sweep over this district like a tornado and will make the Fed's tremble from head to foot. Bah! My impression is they are preparing to make a heavy raid into Kansas and if General Blunt is not upon the alert they will burn and desolate that State furiously. It was reported to me on yesterday by Major Morgan, of the Enrolled Missouri Militia, stationed at Avilla, between here and Greenfield, that 150 men of Col. B. F. Parker's regiment had passed there going north; were under command of Captain Marchbanks. I ordered them to send word immediately to Colonel Phillips at Greenfield. Major, I am in hopes that you will not delay that order on Eno.

Yours, very truly,

T. T. CRITTENDEN,
Lieutenant-Colonel Seventh Cavalry, Missouri State Militia.

HEADQUARTERS COMMANDANT OF PRISONS,
Camp Chase, Ohio, April 21, 1863.

Col. W. HOFFMAN, *Commissary-General of Prisoners.*

COLONEL: I have the honor to state that several rebel commissioned officers have made application to me to be released upon the oath of allegiance to the United States Government, as please see the application of Capt. Frank May, herewith inclosed. Your instructions of February 17, 1863, contain the following paragraph:

It will be determined in a few days whether rebel officers can be permitted to take the oath of allegiance.

Since the date of that paper I find no orders on file relative to the release of this class of prisoners. Again and of same date:

You are not at liberty to grant paroles to rebel officers under any circumstances without the authority of the Secretary of War except in case of illness, which is provided for by the Circular of Regulations.

On reference to those regulations I do not discover that I as commandant of the post have any authority to parole prisoners on account of illness or to even transfer them from the prisons as a matter of safety in cases of contagious disease. Paragraph 9 of the Regulations appears only to refer to the visits of the friends and relatives of prisoners in cases of illness.

In this connection I would respectfully state that two smallpox cases became developed in the prisons recently and as a matter of safety to the other prisoners I caused their transfer from the prison to the pest-house. I would thank you to furnish me with specific instructions for my guidance in exercising authority in all matters concerning the prisons and prisoners in my charge.

Herein please notice a copy of General Orders, No. 36,* Department of the Ohio, issued by Major-General Burnside, which relates to prisoners from the rebel service on parole. Under this order I have directed the return to confinement at this post of several who were on parole in the city of Columbus by direction of His Excellency Governor Tod. I would thank you to designate the authority under which His Excellency has heretofore directed the parole of rebel prisoners placed in charge of the commanding officer of this post. There are now confined here perhaps over 100 prisoners of war who were sent here from Kentucky as deserters. No positive proof of their being deserters came with them more than that they were picked up at different points in Kentucky as having been in the rebel army, and the rolls with them state that some are deserters and others claim to be so. Since the last exchanges I prefer addressing myself to you to ascertain whether I am to go on and release such prisoners under your orders of February 18, 1863, as it would seem as though the authorities at Louisville could more properly have released them, possessing doubtless better information than I can have on the merits of their respective cases.

Very respectfully, your obedient servant,

ALEX. E. DRAKE,
Captain, U. S. Army, Commanding Post.

[Inclosure No. 1.]

PRISON HOSPITAL, *Camp Chase, Ohio, April 20, 1863.*

Captain DRAKE, *Commanding Post.*

SIR: I am sick in this hospital and as there is very little hope of my final recovery in this place I was recommended by the post surgeon for

*See p. 463.

a parole in order to get home and restored to health. I am perfectly willing and very anxious to take the oath of allegiance to the United States, and would have never joined the rebel army if not compelled by circumstances I was then unable to resist. All I wish now is to return home and live the few years which Providence may grant me in peace and loyalty to the United States Government.

Hoping for a compliance with my request as soon as convenient,

I am, respectfully, your obedient servant,

FRANK MAY,
Captain.

HEADQUARTERS U. S. FORCES,
Columbus, Ohio, April 21, 1863.

Report of the number of paroled prisoners belonging to Illinois, Missouri, Michigan, Pennsylvania, Indiana, Minnesota, Wisconsin, New York regiments and batteries and the Regular Army:

State.	Commissioned officers.	Enlisted men.	Total.
Illinois	1	41	42
Missouri		4	4
Michigan	5	354	359
Pennsylvania*		85	85
Indiana		333	†333
Minnesota		1	1
Wisconsin	2	21	23
New York*		5	5
U. S. Army		13	13
Total	8	857	865

*Annapolis. †Have been sent to Indianapolis, Ind., on the 20th instant.

WM. VON DOEHN,
Assistant Adjutant-General.

EXECUTIVE DEPARTMENT. Columbus, April 22, 1863.

Col. W. HOFFMAN,
Commissary-General of Prisoners, Washington, D. C.

DEAR SIR: As requested in your dispatch of this date I give you below a list of the bridge burners captured in Georgia:

E. H. Mason, Twenty-first Regiment Ohio Volunteer Infantry, now at Columbus, Ohio; Robert Buffum, Twenty-first Regiment Ohio Volunteer Infantry, now in Massachusetts; William Bensinger, Twenty-first Regiment Ohio Volunteer Infantry, now in Hancock County, Ohio; Jacob Parrott, Thirty-third Regiment Ohio Volunteer Infantry, now in Hardin County, Ohio; William H. Reddick, Thirty-third Regiment Ohio Volunteer Infantry, now in Adams County, Ohio; William Pittenger, Second Regiment Ohio Volunteer Infantry, now in Steubenville, Ohio. Please request the Secretary of War to extend their furloughs until exchanged, directing them to report to me from time to time.

Respectfully, yours,

DAVID TOD,
Governor.

MURFREESBOROUGH, *April 22, 1863.*

Col. W. HOFFMAN, *Commissary-General of Prisoners:*

Have my prisoners taken at Stone's River been exchanged? Please give official notice soon.

W. S. ROSECRANS,
Major-General.

SAINT LOUIS, *April 22, 1863.*

Maj. Gen. H. W. HALLECK, *General-in-Chief:*

I wish Major Major, Alton Prison, exchanged for Major McConnel, taken and paroled by-rebels yesterday. McConnel has important intelligence to disclose after exchanged. Immediate answer is desired. Rebels 10,000 strong in South Missouri. They hope to co-operate with forces raising in Illinois. Much excitement at Pilot Knob, but the enemy seems to move toward Cape Girardeau or Dallas to cut off Bloomfield forces. Their move seems daring and confident.

S. R. CURTIS.

OFFICE COMMISSARY-GENERAL OF PRISONERS,
Washington, D. C., April 22, 1863.

Col. HENRY DENT, *Provost-Marshal-General, Louisville, Ky.*

COLONEL: On comparing the rolls of prisoners of war forwarded from Lexington, Ky., by order of General Gillmore, with the roll of those forwarded to City Point for delivery it is found that those named on the accompanying rolls which are on the Lexington rolls are not accounted for. Will you please inform me whether these prisoners are still held at Louisville or have they been released?

I inclose herewith a copy of regulations* published in June last for the government of stations where prisoners of war are held and I have to request you will be guided by them as far as practicable.

Blank monthly returns were sent to you in November last but no return has ever been furnished to this office. Please forward me one for this month at its close, with such rolls and explanations as may be necessary to account for the alterations. I inclose herewith a scale† of rations to govern issues to prisoners and the savings go to make the prison fund. By this mail I forward to you blank returns.

Very respectfully, your obedient servant,

W. HOFFMAN,
Colonel Third Infantry, Commissary-General of Prisoners.

OFFICE COMMISSARY-GENERAL OF PRISONERS,
Washington, D. C., April 22, 1863

Capt. A. E. DRAKE, *Comdg. Camp Chase, Columbus, Ohio:*

The control of the Camp Chase Prison has heretofore been exclusively in the hands of Captain Webber and I have to request that it may remain so. The irregularities which you mention and which I am obliged to you for reporting have grown out of the unauthorized influence of the commander of the camp, who should not have opened the prison

---

* Omitted here; see Vol. IV, this Series, p. 152.   † Not found.

gate for the admission of officers who had little or no responsibility for their conduct when inside.

Very respectfully, your obedient servant,

W. HOFFMAN,
Colonel Third Infantry, Commissary-General of Prisoners.

RICHMOND, *April 22, 1863.*

Lieut. Col. WILLIAM H. LUDLOW, *Agent of Exchange, &c.*

SIR: Your communication of the 21st has been received. I did not answer your communication of the 13th instant because I really had nothing more to say in relation to the subject-matter than what was contained in the letter to which that was a reply. In my unofficial note to Captain Mulford I certainly did not intend to be discourteous or to write anything "exceptionable." You will do me the justice to acknowledge that in all the difficult and irritating subjects which have engaged our attention in correspondence I have never stepped beyond the bounds of decorous propriety. I take pleasure in saying the same in reference to yourself.

In my former communications and in personal interviews I demanded that equivalents should be given for the officers whom we had paroled and released since the 10th of December last in Tennessee and Kentucky. I distinctly put those officers upon the same footing as that of those whom we now hold in confinement. I only asked that in exchange officers paroled and released should be put in the same category as those who were retained.

You had complained that we did not parole your officers. Although in your communication of the 13th you agreed to give equivalents for such officers as we had retained you refused to give any at present for those whom we had paroled and released. In other words in cases where we had pursued a course which you had declared objectionable an equivalent would be given; but where we had conformed to your own demands in the release of officers none should be given.

I must confess I was very much surprised at your letter of the 8th instant. I expressed that surprise in perhaps very strong language in my communication of the 11th instant. I intended in that letter to say to you very distinctly that unless the released officers in the West were put upon the same footing as those whom we held in confinement no more deliveries of officers would be made to you. I came to the determination with great regret. Your letter of the 13th did not mend matters much. I thought our demand was so fair, so equitable, that no one could refuse it. When therefore you sought in your communication of the 13th to put the released Western officers upon a different footing from those held by us I considered that you refused to acknowledge our fair claim.

In your letter of the 13th instant you say: "I will acknowledge all proper paroles of our officers by delivering to you equivalents of your officers after the special exchanges of those now in confinement are carried out." That was not what I asked. I demanded simply that the Western released officers should be put upon the same footing with those held by us. I did not wish to have any controversy about "proper paroles," nor did I think it right that such cases should be postponed until all those in our custody were released. I thought and still think that the exchange should be simultaneous. You have an excess of officers—more perhaps than those now held by us added to such as we have paroled.

One boat can accommodate all. Why then postpone the delivery of equivalents except to allow distracting questions to intervene which might defeat the delivery? If you have any paroles I will acknowledge them; if any are hereafter presented by you up to the present date I will acknowledge *them* if you will give me the same privilege. What can be more fair, equal and reciprocal than all this? If you think I will press upon you paroles which are not "proper" let us meet together when the officers are brought up or before. I will offer none to you but such as are most clearly within our former rules of practice. If you will send to City Point all the officers you have you will receive no detriment.

If there are more than we have (counting paroles) I pledge you an equivalent, either in men already delivered to you or if you prefer it in officers hereafter captured and as soon as captured. No proclamation or message shall affect the surplus.

Respectfully, your obedient servant,

ROBERT OULD,
Agent of Exchange.

BURKE'S STATION, *April 22, 1863.*

Colonel HOFFMAN, *Commissary-General of Prisoners.*

DEAR SIR: Will you be so kind as to inform me per return mail whether the railroad men captured at this place last December and released from Richmond in February are yet exchanged?

Respectfully, yours,

A. E. CROCKER.

HEADQUARTERS OF THE ARMY,
Washington, April 23, 1863.

Major-General GRANT, *Near Vicksburg.*

GENERAL: Prisoners sentenced to hard labor, &c., in your department should not be sent to Alton Prison where there is no labor to be performed but should be made to work on fortifications, &c., in your department. Moreover Alton is not capable of accommodating the prisoners sent there.

Very respectfully, your obedient servant,

H. W. HALLECK.

HEADQUARTERS OF THE ARMY,
Washington, D. C., April 23, 1863.

Major-General CURTIS, *Saint Louis:*

All exchanges must be made under the cartel. Only two modes are provided—one by delivery at the points named and the other at the points agreed upon in the field. Exchange requires actual delivery across the lines. * * *

H. W. HALLECK,
General-in-Chief.

HEADQUARTERS OF THE ARMY,
Washington, D. C., April 23, 1863.

Colonel LUDLOW, *Fort Monroe.*

COLONEL: It has been officially reported that on the arrival at Tulla-homa of the prisoners of war of the Twenty-second Wisconsin Volunteers, captured at Thompson's and Brentwood Stations, up in Tennessee, they were by order of General Bragg stripped of their overcoats and blankets.

You will at your next interview with the officer appointed by the enemy for the exchange of prisoners present him with a copy of this letter and ask an answer whether this allegation be true and whether the Confederate authorities approve or disapprove the act alleged.

Very respectfully, your obedient servant,

H. W. HALLECK,
General-in-Chief.

[First indorsement.]

HEADQUARTERS DEPARTMENT No. 2,
[*May 21, 1863.*]

The complaint is true; my action was retaliatory. Prisoners captured from this army have not only been stripped of overcoats and blankets but money, watches and even small articles of priceless value to them, though of no earthly use to the robbers who took them.

I informed Major-General Rosecrans when I first gave the order early in December last and expressed my regret that the conduct of the officers of his Government imposed this unpleasant duty upon me. The staff officer of the general who received the prisoners with this notice acknowledged the precedent and told his men in the presence of my representative that he regretted the act but would not complain, the example having been set by them. Instead of checking such outrages the general has permitted them to a greater extent, and has recently by general orders required the uniform pantaloons to be taken from my men when captured. He has even pronounced the death penalty against prisoners who may be taken wearing the uniform prescribed by our Government and ordered that no quarter shall be shown them on the field. There is not one of us from the private up but will come within the terms of this general order.

BRAXTON BRAGG,
General, Commanding.

[Second indorsement.]

RICHMOND, VA., *May 29, 1863.*

Respectfully transmitted through Col. R. Ould, agent for the exchange of prisoners, to Maj. Gen. H. W. Halleck, commanding U. S. Army.

By command of Secretary of War:

S. COOPER,
Adjutant and Inspector General.

[Third indorsement.]

HEADQUARTERS OF THE ARMY, *June 2, 1863.*

The within letter of General Halleck to Colonel Ludlow and General Bragg's reply forwarded by General Cooper are referred to General Rosecrans for report. As the Government of the United States has uniformly treated prisoners of war with the utmost kindness, supplying them with clothing and blankets when needed and in all cases adopting the most lenient rules of civilized warfare, it is presumed that if there have been any such abuses as here complained of by General Bragg they have been committed by unknown persons on whom due punishment could not be imposed.

H. W. HALLECK,
General-in-Chief.

WASHINGTON, *April 23, 1863.*

General CURTIS:

The Secretary of War authorizes the exchange of Major Major for Major McConnel as recommended in your telegram to General Halleck of yesterday. You will please make the exchange and report your action to Colonel Hoffman.

E. A. HITCHCOCK,
Major-General.

JUDGE-ADVOCATE-GENERAL'S OFFICE, *April 23, 1863.*

Hon. E. M. STANTON, *Secretary of War.*

SIR: It appears from the letter of Major-General Negley, under date of the 7th instant, that while his forces were engaged in an expedition into East Tennessee in the summer of the past year two negro slaves escaped from their masters and joined his command where they were employed as servants; that one of them belonged to a Methodist clergyman, an active guerrilla, and the persecutor of citizens in Sweeden's Cove, and who was with Adams' cavalry at the time they were driven out from that place. The other belonged to a noted rebel residing near Fayetteville. It further appears that the latter negro had previously rendered valuable services to General Mitchel's command as he afterwards did to Major-General Negley by furnishing them secret information, of which fact he held a certificate from General Mitchel.

It is further shown that during the last fall when General Buell's army entered Kentucky these negroes, whose names are Sandy and George, accompanied it, having under the direction of the wagon-master of General Negley's division charge of some of the animals he was taking to Louisville, Ky. While *en route* they were seized as fugitive slaves by the civil authorities at Hardinsburg, Breckinridge County, in that State, where they have remained in jail until the present time, and as stated by the jailer of the county are advertised to be sold as slaves under the local laws of Kentucky on the third Monday in May.

These negroes were under the sixtieth Article of War virtually in the military service of the United States as retainers to the camp, though at the moment of their arrest they may have been separated from the main body of the army. Being on such service they were not liable to be seized by the civil authorities. But they have a more decided character assigned to them by the ninth section of the act of 17th July, 1862, ch. 195. Having been the property of men known to be in open rebellion against the Government of the United States, and taking refuge within the lines of our army, which was their status at the time of their arrest, they are declared by the section of the act referred to to be "captives of war and forever free of their servitude." This act is a part of the supreme law of the land to which the local legislation of the States must give way. The civil authorities have no more right to seize and detain in prison negroes falling within the purview of the section quoted than they have to seize and imprison other captives of war taken by the armies of the United States.

It is understood that the disgraceful practice of kidnapping negroes declared to be "captives of war and free" under the act of Congress with a view of their sale into slavery under local laws extensively prevails and it should be suppressed with a vigorous and decided hand. The supreme law and the right it gives to the military custody and control of the victims of these shameless oppressions should be enforced with the whole power of the Government if necessary. It should be added that the important services voluntarily and so loyally rendered by one of these negroes to the Union cause appeal strongly to the Government to interpose for his protection.

The claim of $250 for expenses set up against each of these negroes should not be recognized nor regarded. Those who have incurred these expenses, if indeed they have been incurred to the amount named, have done so in their own wrong and in violation of law and they have no right to look either to the Government or to their victims, the negroes, for redress.

Very respectfully, your obedient servant,

J. HOLT,
Judge-Advocate-General.

HEADQUARTERS U. S. FORCES,
Columbus, Ohio, April 23, 1863.

Col. W. HOFFMAN, *Commissary-General of Prisoners:*

The Governor of Ohio has in some instances granted paroles to rebel prisoners where in consequence of sickness it has been necessary to remove them from the prison. Yesterday he desired me to request that authority be vested in me to grant paroles in cases of this kind. He also suggested the propriety of paroling the female prisoners now here to the limits of this city. There are at present five female prisoners confined here, there being no suitable accommodations at Camp Chase. They were removed to the second story of a house in the city, placed in the immediate charge of a loyal female, strictly guarded and subjected to all of the regulations established by you for government of prisons. The house occupied was already in charge of the quartermaster and not rented for the purpose.

Your letter of the 20th has been received and your instructions with reference carried into effect, Captain Webber, of the Governor's Guards, being commandant of prisons.

Your obedient servant,

JNO. S. MASON,
Brigadier-General, Commanding.

OFFICE COMMISSARY-GENERAL OF PRISONERS,
Washington, D. C., April 23, 1863.

Hon. E. M. STANTON, *Secretary of War, Washington, D. C.*

SIR: Pursuant to your instructions of the 17th instant I have the honor to make the following report upon the necessity of constructing a new prison in the West for the detention of prisoners of war and disloyal persons, as suggested in the accompanying letter* of His Excellency Governor Tod, of Ohio: There is at this time in the West no suitable prison for the purpose referred to except that on Johnson's Island, in Sandusky Bay, which is in every way well located and complete except that in such a winter as the past, which was very unusual for its mildness, communication with it may be almost entirely cut off. In ordinary seasons the crossing is interrupted for a few days in the fall and spring, but not enough to be any great inconvenience. The other prison camps were not originally intended for the purpose, and though

---

* Not found.

modifications have been made from time to time to make them suitable they are of a very temporary character and generally affording little security for the prisoners. There are other great objections to them, viz: They are more or less connected with large camps, where from there being frequent changes in the troops there is little discipline and the management of the prisoners is unavoidably irregular and unsatisfactory.

At Camp Chase there are three inclosures in the midst of a large camp; the ground is very flat with little drainage and in wet weather it is very muddy; the stench from the sinks particularly during warm weather pollutes the air of the whole camp and soldiers and prisoners alike suffer in consequence of it.

Camp Morton, near Indianapolis, was originally a fair ground, and so far as the location is concerned is a very favorable place for a prison, but it occupies a large area requiring a large guard, and is inclosed by a very temporary fence which is used on two sides as the back of a shed which forms part of the barracks, giving prisoners ready egress if they are disposed to take advantage of it. The location has the advantage of a stream of water running through it and there are many shade trees standing, but the camp is required for the assembling of Indiana troops, and it is also a desirable place to assemble paroled troops when occasions require it and the appropriation of it to prisoners of war as has been the case is attended with much inconvenience.

Camp Butler, near Springfield, has accommodations for only 2,000 prisoners—too limited a number to be of much consequence; besides the camp is more or less occupied by our troops all the time.

Camp Douglas, at Chicago, can accommodate 8,000 prisoners with a suitable guard; but while so occupied it can be used for no other purpose. The possibilities are that it may be required for paroled troops, for whom it will form a good depot for all coming from the States of Minnesota, Wisconsin, Illinois and Michigan, or for the assembling of new levies from the same States.

It would seem then that it is very desirable that a new prison should be established for the exclusive use of prisoners of war at some point selected with a view to the advantage of easy access, the cheapness of supplies and facility for its construction. A place near Lake Michigan would have the advantage of the best market for lumber and supplies, but then it would lead to the necessity of a longer route and some additional cost of transportation. At points near to the river more easy of access there would be the objection of the presence of numerous sympathizers with the rebellion, which would lead to many inconveniences and a greater scarcity and increased cost of materials and supplies. Among the towns most convenient to the field of operations of our armies in the West and on the principal lines of travel are Vincennes, Terre Haute, Lafayette, Logansport, Fort Wayne, Michigan City and Chicago. The last has the advantage of all others in its large market for supplies of all kinds. Of the others, where the shorter route would give them an advantage worthy of consideration, the choice would seem to be between Terre Haute and Lafayette. Whether a good location can be found, possessing a good site and abundant supply of water, can only be decided by personal examination. If we go north of Lafayette it would be preferable to go at once to Chicago, where the abundant supplies and building materials would probably more than balance the additional cost of transportation.

Fort Warren will only accommodate 175 officers, and it will therefore not serve as a place of confinement for all officers that may be captured, and if a new prison be established in the West may be as heretofore appropriated exclusively for officers and citizens, and when not so required it will make an excellent depot for paroled troops.

For the foregoing considerations I respectfully recommend that a new prison be constructed of sufficient dimensions to accommodate 8,000 to 10,000 prisoners, to be inclosed by a substantial fence, with barracks outside for a guard of five companies of 100 men each, to be raised for this especial service. The cost of such a prison would probably be in the vicinity of $50,000.

Very respectfully, your obedient servant,
W. HOFFMAN,
Colonel Third Infantry, Commissary-General of Prisoners.

OFFICE COMMISSARY-GENERAL OF PRISONERS,
Washington, D. C., April 23, 1863.
Brig. Gen. G. M. DODGE, *Commanding, Corinth, Miss.*

GENERAL: I have the honor to acknowledge the receipt of your letter of the 13th instant and beg to say in reply that the roll returned is satisfactory in all the details given, and it was only necessary that I should be assured that the prisoners named were detained in Memphis subject to delivery for exchange when an opportunity offers. No reports have been made to me of prisoners of war being held at Memphis and as the heading of your roll stated that they were forwarded for exchange I was not sure that they had not been delivered at some point for exchange.

Very respectfully, your obedient servant,
W. HOFFMAN,
Colonel Third Infantry, Commissary-General of Prisoners.

HEADQUARTERS DEPARTMENT OF VIRGINIA,
Fort Monroe, April 23, 1863.
Major-General HITCHCOCK,
Commissioner for Exchange of Prisoners.

GENERAL: I have received a receipt (a copy of which is inclosed) from Colonel Hoffman, who informs me it is not reported that equivalents have been received for them. Can it not be ascertained by what authority and under what circumstances this delivery was made and for what equivalents if any?

I am, very respectfully, your obedient servant,
WM. H. LUDLOW,
Lieutenant-Colonel and Agent for Exchange of Prisoners.

[Inclosure.]

Received April 2, 1863, of Maj. Gen. S. A. Hurlbut, U. S. Army, the following paroled prisoners of war, viz: Col. R. F. Looney, C. S. Army, Capt. R. A. Sanford, Thirty-eighth Regiment Tennessee Volunteers, First Lieut. D. Bright, Eighteenth Regiment Mississippi Volunteers.

N. G. WATTS,
Major, C. S. Army,
Agent for Exchange of Prisoners of War at Vicksburg, Miss.

33 R R—SERIES II, VOL V

HEADQUARTERS DEPARTMENT OF VIRGINIA,
Fort Monroe, April 23, 1863.

Col. W. HOFFMAN, Commissary-General of Prisoners.

COLONEL: The postmaster here reports that the package of papers supposed to have been mailed here to you without prepayment of postage was forwarded to Washington to you and must either be in the city or dead-letter post office there. The package was made up of lists of paroled prisoners sent to you for additional proof of delivery within the enemy's lines.

I am, very respectfully, your obedient servant,

WM. H. LUDLOW,
Lieutenant-Colonel and Agent for Exchange of Prisoners.

OFFICE SPECIAL COMMISSIONER,
Camp Chase, Columbus, Ohio, April 23, 1863.

Maj. L. C. TURNER, Judge-Advocate:

As to Miss Fannie Battle, aged nineteen years, of Davidson County, Tenn., arrested on the 7th day of April, A. D. 1863, by order of Colonel Truesdail, chief of police at Nashville, and brought to Camp Chase on the 15th day of April, 1863, charged with being a spy, with smuggling goods and with getting a forged pass, I have the honor to report that the prisoner denies the allegation of having been a spy but admits that she is a rebel and she had a forged pass. She further denies that she was smuggling goods at the time she was arrested. There can be no doubt from the manner of the prisoner in replying to inquiries that she has been engaged in smuggling. The prisoner is affable and attractive and well qualified by manners and mind to be influential for evil to the loyal cause. She is a daughter of the rebel General Battle. I recommend that she be exchanged and sent beyond our lines as soon as it may be convenient to our Government.

Respectfully,

SAML. GALLOWAY,
Special Commissioner.

OFFICE SPECIAL COMMISSIONER,
Camp Chase, Columbus, Ohio, April 23, 1863.

Maj. L. C. TURNER, Judge-Advocate:

As to Miss Harriet Booker, aged twenty-four years, of Davidson County, Tenn., arrested on the 7th day of April, A. D. 1863, by order of Colonel Truesdail, chief of police at Nashville, and brought to Camp Chase on the 15th day of April, 1863, charged with being a rebel, a spy, with forging a pass and altering the same and with smuggling goods through the lines and conveying letters and information to the enemy, I have the honor to report that the prisoner denies the charge of smuggling, of being a spy or conveying letters to the enemy, but admits herself to be a rebel and to have altered a forged pass, knowing the same to have been forged for the purpose of being fraudulently used. The prisoner is less intelligent than Miss Battle and more ingenuous. She has been obviously under the control of Miss Battle. There can be no doubt as to her active and cordial co-operation in the acts of Miss Battle. If she could be removed from the influence of

[that] designing woman she would be harmless. I recommend that she be exchanged and sent beyond our lines, and if convenient and practicable that she be separated from the companionship of Miss Battle.

Respectfully,

SAML. GALLOWAY,
Special Commissioner.

WAR DEPARTMENT, *Washington, April 24, 1863.*
Major-General CURTIS, *Saint Louis:*

The exchange of Major Major for Major McConnel according to your request has been sent to General Hitchcock, commissioner of exchange.

EDWIN M. STANTON.

WAR DEPARTMENT, *Washington, D. C., April 24, 1863.*
Lieut. Col. F. A. DICK,
Provost-Marshal-General, Saint Louis, Mo.

SIR: The Secretary of War directs me to acknowledge the receipt, by reference from Col. W. Hoffman, commissary-general of prisoners, of your letter of the 5th ultimo, in the following words:*

Upon this letter several indorsements have been made of which the following are copies, viz:

WAR DEPARTMENT, *April 8, 1863.*

Referred to the Judge-Advocate-General to report what should be done in these cases.

By order of the Secretary of War:

P. H. WATSON,
Assistant Secretary of War.

JUDGE-ADVOCATE-GENERAL'S OFFICE, *April 24, 1863.*

The views of Provost-Marshal Lieutenant-Colonel Dick as expressed in the within letter are fully approved. The policy which he indicates for the treatment of incorrigible rebels is unquestionably the true one and a policy less lenient than this cannot be safely pursued anywhere but especially in the State of Missouri. I recommend that he be instructed to carry into execution promptly and inflexibly the opinion he has expressed as to the proper disposition to be made both of the men and women who are in rebellion against the Government in the State of Missouri or who are actively though secretly giving aid and comfort to those who are so.

J. HOLT,
Judge-Advocate-General.

WAR DEPARTMENT, *April 23, 1863.*

Opinion of Judge-Advocate-General approved.

EDWIN M. STANTON,
Secretary of War.

You will be governed in your action by these indorsements.

Very respectfully, your obedient servant,

P. H. WATSON,
Assistant Secretary of War.

FORT MONROE, *April 24, 1863.*
Hon. E. M. STANTON:

General Burnside has sent three ladies from Cincinnati to go to City Point by your permission. When Mr. Ould was advised that no one was to come North without previous permission from you he notified us

---

* Omitted here; see p. 319.

ЦЦЦЦЦЦ

that no one would be received at City Point to go South without previous permission from the authorities at Richmond and several persons sent up by your authority have been returned by the boat which took them there. I advised you at the time.

JOHN A. DIX,
Major-General.

MEMPHIS, *April 24, 1863.*

Brigadier-General ASBOTH:

If there is likely to be any trouble about the Anna prisoners remove them to Columbus. Do not surrender them to any one except U. S. marshal from Illinois, General Ammen or General Burnside.

S. A. HURLBUT,
Major-General.

COLUMBUS, KY., *April 24, 1863.*

Major-General HURLBUT, *Memphis, Tenn.:*

Pursuant to orders from General Burnside the twenty-three prisoners arrested at Anna and Jonesborough, Ill., were forwarded from here to Cincinnati this morning on steamer Lady Jackson under guard, Captain Cunningham, Twenty-seventh Wisconsin Infantry, in command, with orders to shoot any person interfering with his duties.

ASBOTH,
Brigadier-General.

HEADQUARTERS ARMY OF THE FRONTIER,
In the Field, April 24, 1863.

Maj. Gen. S. PRICE, C. S. Army.

GENERAL: In accordance with paragraph II, General Orders, No. 49, from War Department of the United States, I inclose you herewith as commander of the opposing forces a true copy of the rules and regulations* for paroling of prisoners of war.

These rules will govern the officers of my command and paroles given my men or officers not in accordance with the order will not be recognized by me.

I am informed that the above rules governing paroles have been adopted by the commanders of all the Confederate armies in the field.

I send this per flag of truce and would request that you communicate with me in regard to the matter.

I have the honor to be, general, very respectfully, your obedient servant,

F. J. HERRON,
Major-General, Commanding.

OFFICE COMMISSARY-GENERAL OF PRISONERS,
Washington, D. C., April 24, 1863.

Maj. Gen. A. E. BURNSIDE,
Commanding Department of the Ohio, Cincinnati, Ohio.

GENERAL: In reply to the accompanying letter† from Col. John W. Foster, commanding, Henderson, Ky., referred to me through your office,

---

*See General Orders, No. 49, p. 306.   † Not found.

I have the honor to inform you that no such order as the one referred to authorizing the release of prisoners by the Governor of Kentucky has been issued by the War Department. As far as possible to guard against impositions in petitions presented for the release of prisoners, even when presented and urged by Members of Congress, the Secretary of War decided that such petitions should not be entertained unless approved by the Governor of the State in which the petitioners and the prisoners reside and then a release can be granted only on his order. The great difficulty in selecting the good cases from the bad is that nothing reliable in the shape of charges is sent with the prisoners only suspected and those caught in the commission of serious offenses are alike classed on the rolls as guerrillas, aiding guerrillas, bushwhackers, &c. When a petition is presented in behalf of any such person it is impossible to tell to what class he belongs, the wrongly accused or the seriously guilty.

There are but two Fields, J. and W., on the rolls of Johnson's Island and both were sent to Vicksburg for exchange in November last, and the prisoners referred to by Colonel Foster could not have been released from that prison. There is a special commissioner at Camp Chase to investigate and decide in all cases at that prison and I do not know on what ground the discharges are granted. I expect to issue an order in a few days for the transfer of all prisoners from Camp Chase to Johnson's Island, and in order that such men as Colonel Foster alludes to may not be discharged to the detriment of the public interest through want of information I have respectfully to request that you will direct that where prisoners are sent to the island a full report of each case of the character of the man and the charges against him shall be sent with him. So long as prisoners are continued at Camp Chase like reports should accompany all sent there.

Very respectfully, your obedient servant,

W. HOFFMAN,
Colonel Third Infantry, Commissary-General of Prisoners.

OFFICE COMMISSARY-GENERAL OF PRISONERS,
Washington, D. C., April 24, 1863.

Maj. Gen. A. E. BURNSIDE,
Commanding Department of the Ohio, Cincinnati, Ohio.

GENERAL: Brigadier-General Mason, who has recently assumed command at Columbus, Ohio, reports the great want of discipline among the paroled troops at Camp Chase, a state of things which has been brought to my notice more than once in other ways, and I would respectfully invite your attention to the subject with the request that you will direct such steps taken as will establish the good order and proper discipline so much needed at the camp. The indispensable requisite in the camp is an active and efficient commander with a reliable guard of at least five full companies. Without a force to compel obedience in paroled prisoners of war nothing can be done with them and they desert from the camp almost as fast as they can be brought back. Commander should be either a lieutenant-colonel or colonel so as to insure his having sufficient command, but he should have an efficient adjutant, commissary and quartermaster. When the prisoners are removed to Johnson's Island, as I have in a letter of this date informed you is in contemplation, the prison guard now at the camp may make part of the permanent guard and the larger prison will again

be used as barracks for troops. One of the small prisons may be used
for the prisoners of the camp and the other will accommodate the few
prisoners of war or political prisoners who may be sent there *en route*
to Johnson's Island.

I beg leave respectfully to offer the foregoing suggestion of measures
which I think are calculated in some degree [to remedy the] evils which
are in many ways so detrimental to the interests of the service. It is
objectionable I know to detain efficient officers from the front, but it is
highly important that our paroled troops should be kept under better
discipline and better control than they have been heretofore.

Very respectfully, your obedient servant,

W. HOFFMAN,
Colonel Third Infantry, Commissary-General of Prisoners.

WASHINGTON, *April 24, 1863.*

Lieut. Col. W. H. LUDLOW:

I will direct the commanding officer at Fort Delaware to deliver
prisoners to you. He has not reported arrival of prisoners from
Lafayette. Will request him to report to you.

W. HOFFMAN,
Commissary-General of Prisoners.

NEW BERNE, N. C., *April 24, 1863.*

Maj. Gen. J. G. FOSTER,
Commanding Eighteenth Army Corps, New Berne, N. C.

GENERAL: I beg leave to report to you the following circumstances
connected with the capture of some of my men and their treatment as
prisoners of war. On the 12th of March, 1863, six of my men were
detailed to guard some negroes who were chopping wood near Elizabeth City for the use of the garrison. They were attacked by the
Partisan Rangers and 3 of their number were taken prisoners. Also 3
negroes were taken and 2 killed. On the 6th of April Lieut. L. A.
Bigger was sent down the river to Little Flatty Creek for a schooner-
load of wood. He had with him six men and some negroes. They went
ashore at night and were surrounded and taken by the Partisan Rangers. We got information of the affair on the morning of the 7th and
sent out an expedition in pursuit but did not succeed in retaking them.
I got a note from Lieutenant Bigger the next day stating the facts
above stated. On the 23d of April I received a letter from Lieutenant
Bigger dated April 13, at Fortress Monroe, saying that he had been
paroled but that the men would be confined in Castle Thunder, where
the three who were captured March 12 had been confined in an awful
dungeon, from the effects of which two of the men had died. A
description of the prison by Lieutenant Bigger was a gloomy cell 15 by
20 feet occupied by twenty-eight men.

Thus my men are treated as felons of the deepest dye instead of as
prisoners of war because they are North Carolina Union volunteers.
While I was in command at Elizabeth City I had some of the guerrilla
prisoners and treated them as prisoners of war, and they were released
by General Palmer's orders on taking the oath of neutrality and giving
$250 bonds not to take up arms against us again.

The following is a list of the prisoners taken from Company D, First North Carolina Union Volunteers, on the 12th of March, 1863: H. C. Palmer; A. W. Keaton, died March 31, 1863; Frank M. Tow, died April 6, 1863.

The following is a list of the men taken on the 6th of April, 1863: Lieut. L. A. Bigger, Corpl. Benjamin Pendleton, Privates Henry Luters, James Luton, John A. Mead, Henry Boyd and Lemuel James.

I have been informed that there were two men from a company at Washington, N. C., during the battle at that place last summer and that they were confined in same way as those of my company and one of them had died since being confined in prison, and that there had never been any demand made for their release.

Praying that there may be something done by the authorities in power to have these men treated as other U. S. volunteers, prisoners of war, I subscribe myself,

Very respectfully, your humble servant,

E. C. SANDERS,
Captain Company D, First North Carolina Union Volunteers.

[First indorsement.]

HEADQUARTERS EIGHTEENTH ARMY CORPS,
New Berne, April 26, 1863.

Respectfully referred to Colonel Ludlow with the request that he will take some action in the case, these men having been regularly mustered into the U. S. service.

J. G. FOSTER,
Major-General, Commanding.

[Second indorsement.]

FORT MONROE, *May 3, 1863.*

Respectfully referred to Hon. R. Ould, agent for exchange of prisoners, for information about and delivery of the persons within named.

WM. H. LUDLOW,
Lieutenant-Colonel and Agent for Exchange of Prisoners.

[Third indorsement.]

Respectfully referred to General Winder.

R. OULD,
Agent for Exchange.

[Fourth indorsement.]

HEADQUARTERS DEPARTMENT OF HENRICO,
Richmond, May 12, 1863.

Referred to Capt. T. P. Turner, commander C. S. military prison, for information concerning these men.

By order of Brigadier-General Winder:

W. N. STARKE,
Captain and Assistant Adjutant-General.

[Fifth indorsement.]

C. S. MILITARY PRISON, *Richmond, May 12, 1863.*

The within-mentioned men, excepting Palmer, were paroled and sent home by flag of truce on the 5th of May, 1863. Were captured in Pasquotank, N. C., April 6, 1863.

TH. P. TURNER,
Captain, Commanding.

[Sixth indorsement.]

HEADQUARTERS DEPARTMENT OF HENRICO,
Richmond, May 13, 1863.

H. C. Palmer is at present in Castle Thunder. Will be transferred to the C. S. military prison to be sent off by first flag of truce.

By order of Brig. Gen. J. H. Winder:

W. N. STARKE,
Assistant Adjutant-General.

[Seventh indorsement.]

FORT MONROE, *May 18, 1863.*

This copy of this communication with the indorsements thereon is respectfully forwarded to Major-General Foster. All the men seem to be accounted for. Those delivered before the 6th of May have been declared exchanged and are now at Camp Parole, Annapolis, ready for active service.

WM. H. LUDLOW,
Lieutenant-Colonel and Agent for Exchange of Prisoners.

[Eighth indorsement.]

HEADQUARTERS EIGHTEENTH ARMY CORPS,
May 30, 1863.

Respectfully referred to Lieutenant-Colonel McChesney, First North Carolina Union Volunteers, for his information. This paper to be returned.

By order of Maj. Gen. J. G. Foster:

S. HOFFMAN,
Assistant Adjutant-General.

LOUISVILLE, KY., *April 25, 1863.*

President LINCOLN:

Pray let my son, Maj. Clarence Prentice, now at Camp Chase, be paroled and be permitted to return to the Confederate Army to effect his own exchange. This course has been adopted in other cases and would be most agreeable to his parents.

GEO. D. PRENTICE.

HEADQUARTERS DEPARTMENT OF VIRGINIA,
Fort Monroe, Va., April 25, 1863.

Acting Rear-Admiral S. P. LEE,
Commanding North Atlantic Blockading Squadron.

ADMIRAL: The officers of the insurgent army confined at Fort Norfolk will be sent to Richmond on parole in two or three days. There have been some unsettled questions in regard to the exchange of officers but they have been adjusted by Colonel Ludlow and Mr. Ould and the delivery on both sides will proceed as usual. Please inform me whether Lieutenant Rogers, of General French's staff, shall be sent up with the others. If you desire to retain him I will send him to you. His detention by me would be improper as it is inconsistent with the articles of agreement for the exchange of prisoners. These articles were negotiated and signed by me and it would be embarrassing to me to have Mr. Rogers in my custody after the other officers are sent away.

I am, very respectfully, your obedient servant,

JOHN A. DIX,
Major-General.

HEADQUARTERS, *Cairo, April 25, 1863.*

Hon. E. M. STANTON, *Secretary of War.*

SIR: Your letter of the 21st instant is received. The instructions in it in reference to colored persons "captives of war" have and shall be faithfully carried out. It is not true that I have failed to afford them all the protection in my power "upon the ground that I have no sympathy with abolitionist" or any other ground. Personally I feel a deep sympathy with the colored refugees of the South who have escaped from slavery. I have published under my signature articles 15, 22, 23, and 33 of the code, received by me from General Hitchcock and Doctor Lieber, in the Chicago Tribune which is read by all General Grant's forces, believing that article 33 was of vast importance. On taking command of this post General Tuttle took with him the adjutant-general and left very scanty records of the post. He left me no record of his being "authorized to make arrangements with humane and benevolent persons in the State of Illinois to give them (the negroes) employment for their support." But I have understood that to be the design of the Government and have acted on it. I have given every respectable applicant of a free State permission to take any of these people under my charge to his home on condition that he support them in sickness as well as in health and [with] fair compensation. I have refused to let them be taken to Kentucky or the ports of Missouri opposite to this place.

I refused to let Mr. Trabue, of Kentucky, take any of these persons to Caseyville, Ky., because it was a slave State and they were liable to abduction, though he had General Rosecrans' recommendation. He went to Columbus and obtained permission from General Asboth to take about fifty of them. When they arrived here I telegraphed General Asboth that part of them were unwilling to go; they have since been returned here. Why I know not. I afforded them immediate protection. In answer to "whether any application for protection has been made to you and what has been your action on the subject," I answer that a resigned officer of the Army on his way to his home in Illinois told me when he got home he was informed he would be indicted for having sent two or three colored persons to his farm and requested protection. I answered the State of Illinois was not under my military jurisdiction except Cairo and Mound City. I could do nothing in anticipation of any wrong done to him. But I advised him the Government would protect him if he obeyed its laws. I recollect no other case. General Ammen, commanding the District of Illinois, applied to me to send a force to Anna to make arrests. I promptly complied. My force is there. Twenty-one prisoners have been arrested and sent to Columbus, Ky. General Burnside has ordered them to Cincinnati. General Asboth sent them yesterday. I have written three times to General Burnside that the thirty witnesses being citizens of Union County it would be advisable that they be tried at Anna, as the offenders, most of them, ought to be turned over to the civil authorities according to the late conscription act and that it would be difficult to get the witnesses to Cincinnati. One of the prisoners, Dr. Jeptha Randolph, is accused of heading a mob who drove off the party of forty or more contrabands whom I had permitted to be taken by Benjamin Fenton to a farm in Union County to plant 400 acres of cotton. Fenton sent back the negroes to this place with no explanation except his agent's statement to me. The people had banded together not to let them remain. If he had kept them and applied to me for protection I would have rendered it.

I am sorry to trouble you with so long a letter, but it seemed necessary that I should enter into details.

I have the honor to be, your obedient servant,

N. B. BUFORD,
Brigadier-General, Commanding.

FORT DELAWARE, *April 25, 1863.*

Col. W. HOFFMAN, *Commissary-General of Prisoners:*

Some of the prisoners to be exchanged wish to take the oath and not to be sent South.   Please reply.

A. SCHOEPF,
Brigadier-General, Commanding.

WASHINGTON, *April 25, 1863.*

Lieutenant-Colonel LUDLOW,
     Agent for Exchange of Prisoners:

Prisoners from Fort Lafayette have arrived at Fort Delaware.   No report has been received relative to Major Armesy and Lieutenant Davis. Please return them.

W. HOFFMAN.

FORT MONROE, *April 25, 1863.*

Col. W. HOFFMAN, *Commissary-General of Prisoners:*

Have those prisoners, including Zarvona, been sent from Fort Lafayette to Fort Delaware?   If not will you please give the necessary orders and I will delay sending up the steamer to Fort Delaware until their arrival there.   Please reply.

W. H. LUDLOW,
Agent for Exchange of Prisoners.

WASHINGTON, *April 25, 1863.*

Lieut. Col. W. H. LUDLOW:

Prisoners, including Zarvona, left Fort Lafayette April 16.   Arrival at Fort Delaware not reported.   I inquired yesterday and directed a report made to you.

W. HOFFMAN,
Commissary-General of Prisoners.

OFFICE COMMISSARY-GENERAL OF PRISONERS,
Washington, April 25, 1863.

Lieut. Col. W. H. LUDLOW,
     Agent for Exchange of Prisoners, Fort Monroe, Va.

COLONEL: I inclose herewith the rolls* of rebel prisoners captured and paroled at Van Buren, Ark., and the certificate of Lieutenant-Colonel Stuart, Tenth Illinois Cavalry, showing that they were delivered into the hands of the rebel authorities at Little Rock.

In answer to my inquiries you have informed me that all citizens delivered since the last declaration of exchanges have been exchanged,

---

* Omitted.

which I understand to include sutlers and army employés. If I am wrong you can correct me.

I inclose also a letter* in relation to the capture of Lieutenant Rushby and some others which you may not hear of in any other way.

Very respectfully, your obedient servant,

W. HOFFMAN,
Colonel Third Infantry, Commissary-General of Prisoners.

OFFICE COMMISSARY-GENERAL OF PRISONERS,
Washington, D. C., April 25, 1863.

Maj. THOMAS M. VINCENT, *Assistant Adjutant-General.*

MAJOR: I am not sure that I remember rightly what you said in relation to the discharge of men at Camp Parole. The final payment will in all cases be made on the mustering-out roll, and when men have their descriptive rolls they must be completed at the camp and forwarded to regimental commander for his guidance in preparing the rolls; or shall the descriptive rolls be given to the man to be by him presented to the colonel and notice given to the colonel by the commanding officer of what has been done?

Yours, truly,

W. HOFFMAN,
Commissary-General of Prisoners.

[Indorsement.]

ADJUTANT-GENERAL'S OFFICE, *April 25, 1863.*

MEMORANDA.—All men will be mustered out at time regiment is mustered out. Those absent will be mustered out as absent. (See paragraph 80, Mustering Regulations.) The men at Camp Parole should have transportation furnished to their place of enrollment, and they should take with them their descriptive lists to be presented to the regimental commander at place where regiment is mustered out. A certificate to keep them from being picked up as deserters should be furnished. A general order is to be issued covering all cases of the kind.

Respectfully,

THOS. M. VINCENT,
Assistant Adjutant-General.

OFFICE COMMISSARY-GENERAL OF PRISONERS,
Washington, D. C., April 25, 1863.

Maj. T. HENDRICKSON,
Commanding Military Prison, Alton, Ill.

MAJOR: Your letter of the 20th instant is received, and in answer I have to state that the prison at Alton is State property and being in use of the United States should be kept in repair at the public expense; but if the prison fund is sufficient to pay for the required repairs you will have them made and paid for out of the fund. Prepare an estimate of the probable cost and if the fund is not sufficient to meet it and leave a balance on hand I will ask for an order from the Quartermaster-General for the necessary repairs to be made by the Department.

Very respectfully, your obedient servant,

W. HOFFMAN,
Colonel Third Infantry, Commissary-General of Prisoners.

*Not found.

HEADQUARTERS, *Camp Chase, April 25, 1863.*

Col. WILLIAM HOFFMAN.
   Commissary-General of Prisoners, Washington City, D. C.

COLONEL: Inclosed I have the honor to submit a plan of a set of regimental quarters that at a period when by a large excess beyond the means to supply accommodation for prisoners it was rendered an imperative necessity on the part of the (then) commanding officer to set apart as a prison. The blue [black] line exhibits the entire space inclosed, while the red [dotted] indicates that portion exclusively used for prison purposes, the remaining portion being occupied by the Governor's Guards. A substantial fence (shown by the red lines) surrounded the prison proper, while that round the quarters of the Governor's Guards is in a state of dilapidation. My opinion is concurred in by not only the surgeon but the officers of the Governor's Guards and the post

Plan
of
Camp Chase, Ohio.

National Turnpike Road.

Parade Ground.

Line of Prison inclosure:———
Portion now appropriated:----

Prison.

b

a

Recently occupied by Confederate officers and more recently (a & b west end) by female prisoners. Now vacant.

Occupied by Battalion 88th O.V.I. (Governor's Guards.)

Headquarters.

generally that the presence of the last-named fence is injurious to the health of the command, shutting it out as it does from proper ventilation by a free circulation of air.

The location of this prison is most inappropriate, situated as it is immediately in front of (not more than a half dozen rods from) the commanding officer's headquarters, and besides being nearly in the center of the camp. The entire drainage (which by the bye is sadly deficient) from it passes to the east through an open ditch in the midst of the most eligibly located portion of the camp. In view of these facts I would respectfully recommend that the quartermaster be authorized to remove the fence and restore the quarters to their original use. Or if in the opinion of the commissary-general of prisoners a necessity exists for the present excess of prison room that at least that portion of it surrounding the quarters of the Governor's Guards be carefully removed by the quartermaster and used for the enlarging of Prisons Nos. 1 and 2, repairs thereon, &c. The subject of drainage for the camp is one that has occupied not a little of my consideration and is a problem of no little difficulty of solution. The only feasible mode in view of the monotonous flatness of the camp that presents itself is by a system of cesspools that may be kept deodorized by the use of lime or its chlorides. , I have already in progress the taking up of the unsightly and almost useless plank footways and am constructing neat and commodious graveled ones. Those completed have proven in the miserably wet weather that we have had a complete success.

I have the honor at the same time to acknowledge the receipt of your favor of the 22d instant. The entire control of the prisons was two days since in accordance with your directions placed in the hands of Captain Webber. I should have mentioned in my former letter that at the time I deemed it necessary to assume control of the prisons Captain Webber was absent commanding the escort of the prisoners sent to Fort Delaware and the day before his return here I received an order from General Burnside to send him to Cincinnati, Ohio, on court-martial business, from whence he has recently returned. The evils to which I called your attention will not I hope occur again, or at least shall not I assure you so far as any co-operation of mine to aid Captain Webber in the prosecution of his duties can prevent. During the time that I had charge I divided the prisoners into three companies, officered by their own officers, placing the whole under charge of one of their field officers whom I required to furnish daily the provost-marshal of prisons with a strong detail for police purposes. By this system I had the prisons thoroughly whitewashed inside and out and properly policed. And at this time they are in better condition than I have before known them.

I am, colonel, very respectfully, your obedient servant,
ALEX. E. DRAKE,
Captain, U. S. Army, Commanding Post.

HEADQUARTERS, *Camp Douglas, April 25, 1863.*
Col. WILLIAM HOFFMAN, *Third U. S. Infantry.*

SIR: I find no order recorded for an examination of the Confederate prisoners previous to their departure for City Point. George H. Park, surgeon of the Sixty-fifth Illinois Volunteers, was acting as post surgeon at that time and is now in Lexington, Ky., with his regiment. I cannot learn from the surgeon now left in charge any information that would facilitate your inquiry.

Very respectfully, your obedient servant,
JOHN C. PHILLIPS,
Captain, Commanding Post.

HEADQUARTERS DISTRICT OF EASTERN KENTUCKY,
Louisa, Ky., April 26, 1863.
Col. W. HOFFMAN, *Commissary-General of Prisoners.*

COLONEL: I have the honor to state that before the promulgation of General Orders, No. 49, War Department, two separate squads of the Fourteenth Kentucky Volunteer Infantry were taken by the enemy. The first party was returned into our lines without any agreement as provided for by the cartel of exchange, each man having a scrip of paper stating in effect "Paroled;" signed "Wm. Smith." No duplicates were taken nor was there any commissioned officer with the party.

The second party was paroled by General Humphrey Marshall, C. S. Army, exchanging duplicates with each individual, there being no officer of the U. S. Army in the party, and they were likewise returned to our lines without any agreement. This on 25th ultimo. The first party was taken some time before.

The question arises whether under the circumstances they should be returned to duty or be disposed of as awaiting exchange.

I remain, sir, very respectfully, your obedient servant,
JULIUS WHITE,
Brigadier-General, Commanding.

HEADQUARTERS, *Cincinnati, Ohio, April 27, 1863.*

Hon. E. M. STANTON:

There are about 1,100 paroled prisoners at Indianapolis that have not been paid since last October. Major McClure reports that he has sufficient funds to pay them to 28th of February if muster for pay-rolls can be furnished to that date. Can I have authority to have them mustered for pay on the 30th?

A. E. BURNSIDE,
Major-General.

HEADQUARTERS U. S. FORCES,
Columbus, Ohio, April 27, 1863

Col. W. HOFFMAN,
Commissary-General of Prisoners, Washington, D. C.

COLONEL: I respectfully request to be informed whether paroled officers and soldiers who were captured subsequent to December 10, 1862, and were not delivered to the U. S. authorities either at Aiken's Landing or Vicksburg, Miss., or at a place designated by the commanding generals of the opposing armies for the exchange of prisoners, are to be ordered to rejoin their respective regiments without further orders from your office?

I have the honor to be, very respectfully, your obedient servant,
JNO. S. MASON,
Brigadier-General of Volunteers, Commanding.

OFFICE COMMISSARY-GENERAL OF PRISONERS,
Washington, D. C., April 27, 1863.

Col. J. HOLT, *Judge-Advocate-General, Washington, D. C.:*

I have the honor to refer to you for your consideration the petition of Capt. Robert W. Baylor, an officer of the rebel army now a prisoner of war at Fort Delaware, for an investigation of the charges against him or for his exchange. The accompanying papers* are all that I have been able to obtain to support the charge against him. Previous to my indorsement of the 18th instant I addressed a letter to the military provost-marshal at Baltimore requesting him to furnish me any charges or evidence against Captain Baylor which might be in his office but to

---

* Not found.

this letter I received no reply. On the 18th instant I addressed a letter to Major-General Schenck, commanding Eighth Army Corps, requesting that he would direct that any testimony in the possession of the provost-marshal at Baltimore or any other officer bearing upon the case of Captain Baylor should be forwarded to this office; but to this letter also I have received no reply and I am therefore compelled to submit the case in this imperfect condition.

I submit also for your action papers* referred to me by Major Darr, at Wheeling, in the case of David Lynn, a prisoner at Fort Delaware, and charges* against Maria Murphy, of Braxton County, W. Va.; also a letter* from General Patrick, provost-marshal-general, Army of the Potomac, reporting the case of Private Frank St. Clair Smith, of General R. E. Lee's body guard, a prisoner of war at the Old Capitol Prison.

Very respectfully, your obedient servant,

W. HOFFMAN,
Colonel Third Infantry, Commissary-General of Prisoners.

OFFICE COMMISSARY-GENERAL OF PRISONERS,
Washington, April 27, [*1863.*]

Lieut. Col. W. H. LUDLOW,
Agent for Exchange of Prisoners, Fort Monroe, Va.

COLONEL: I send you by to-day's mail a number of applications for special exchange.

Very imperfect rolls are sent to me of small parties who never reach the camps of paroled prisoners and who consequently are not found on any full rolls, and the only way in which I can secure their exchange is to send these lists and applications to you.

I have not kept duplicates of any of the rolls of our paroled troops forwarded to you because I have expected that after an exchange was arranged you would return them to me, and I presume you will be able to do this.

General Hitchcock this morning presented to me your letter of the 23d instant in relation to the three rebel officers delivered at Vicksburg and receipted for by Major Watts. My telegram of the 22d instant you probably received after writing your letter in which I informed you that the officers had been released on parole and that no equivalents had been received for them [illegible] doubtless gives you all the information you require.

The packages forwarded by you without postage stamps have never reached the post-office in this city so I learn by inquiring there and I must request of you the favor to ask your postmaster to make some effort to trace them up. He could I presume give such information as to the time of their being forwarded as will lead to their recovery.

Very respectfully, your obedient servant,

W. HOFFMAN,
Colonel Third Infantry, Commissary-General of Prisoners.

LOUISVILLE, KY., *April 28, 1863.*

President LINCOLN.

DEAR SIR: It is long since I wrote to you. In some things I have differed with you. I think you know I have differed with you with

---

* Not found.

great pain. I have tried to serve our country. I know that I have served it. I will not undertake to say how much.

Mr. Lincoln, I have a great favor to ask of you. Hear me! My only child, Clarence J. Prentice, God help him, is a major in the Confederate service. A few weeks ago he came into Kentucky and being cut off from his command he came by night to his home to see me and his mother and his baby. He was seen coming and in a few hours arrested. He is now at Camp Chase and his mother in Columbus. He desires I know to serve no longer in the war. He would be a great loss to the Confederates, for he has been one of their most effective officers.

I do not suppose, Mr. Lincoln, that you can parole my boy upon his taking the non-combatant's oath to remain in the United States though I should be most happy if you could; but I fervently appeal to you to let him go upon his taking that simple oath anywhere outside of the United States and of the rebel Confederacy. I know his plans. His mother will go with him and he will never bear arms against us again. I will be surety for this with fortune and life. I have written to General Burnside to let my son remain at Camp Chase till I hear from you. Please let it be soon for I am most unhappy.

Ever your friend,

GEO. D. PRENTICE.

[First indorsement.]

JUDGE-ADVOCATE-GENERAL'S OFFICE,
Washington, May 16, 1863.

The SECRETARY OF WAR:

Clarence J. Prentice, born and residing in Kentucky, at the breaking out of the rebellion left his home and entered the military service of the rebels, where by his zeal and efficiency as an officer he attained the rank of major, which position he now holds. He joined in the recent military invasion of his native State and having by some means not explained become separated from his command he availed himself of the opportunity to make a clandestine visit to his father's house in Louisville, where he was captured. The authorities have not thought proper to proceed against him as a spy but have treated him as a prisoner of war. As such he is now confined at Camp Chase. His father, speaking of him in a letter to the President, says: "He desires I know to serve no longer in the war," and in consideration of this seeming weariness of the crime in which he has been engaged he asks that on his taking the simple oath of a non-combatant he may be allowed to go anywhere outside of the United States and of the rebel Confederacy.

Clarence J. Prentice himself has made no communication to the Government expressive of his feelings in regard to the war or of his future plans and purposes. When prisoners of war are willing to take the oath of allegiance it is the practice to permit them to do so. When they are not thus willing they have been invariably exchanged under the cartel. The intermediate course now proposed has not been pursued because the Government would thereby lose the advantage of the exchange and because no satisfactory or reliable guaranty would exist that the prisoner thus tenderly dealt with would not at the first opportunity re enter the rebel military service. Doubtless investigation would show that the treason of many officers and soldiers in the rebel armies is palliated by the pressure of an excited public sentiment and by the military despotism to which they have been subjected. Such, however, was not the case of Clarence J. Prentice. He left his home in a State then and still loyal and voluntarily and wantonly banded with traitors for the overthrow of the Government of his country. It is for the Secretary to determine whether the established policy which has prevailed in the treatment of prisoners of war shall be modified in his favor.

J. HOLT,
Judge-Advocate-General.

[Second indorsement.]

WAR DEPARTMENT, *May 22, 1863.*

COLONEL: I submitted this paper to the Secretary of War yesterday and he said that he was under the impression that the President had given an order permitting Prentice to go abroad. Has it been done?
Very respectfully,

ED. R. S. CANBY,
Brigadier-General.

[Third indorsement.]

GENERAL: There is no record in this office of any special orders in the case of Major Prentice. On the 13th instant he was sent from Camp Chase to City Point for exchange.
Very respectfully,

W. HOFFMAN,
Commissary-General of Prisoners.

NEW YORK, *April 28, 1863.*

Hon. E. M. STANTON:
Seventeen men and three women, Union prisoners, paroled and sent to New Orleans, thence to New York by General Sherman. Shall I give them transportation to their homes?

S. DRAPER.

HEADQUARTERS, *Annapolis, Md., April 28, 1863.*

ASSISTANT ADJUTANT-GENERAL,
Hdqrs. Middle Department, Eighth Army Corps, Baltimore.
SIR: I again return to your office Captain Lazelle's report on matters connected with Camp Parole and Colonel Hoffman's letter which accompanied it. I also return my letter of the 8th instant.
To comply as far as possible with the indorsement on the last-mentioned communication I inclose a copy of my report* of the 18th March last, which I then deemed to be, as far as it was in my power to make it, a full compliance with the remarks of the commanding general on Colonel Hoffman's letter, and to which I have nothing of importance now to add.
Camp Parole is an independent command under Lieutenant-Colonel Sangster, who is not subject to my orders in anything connected with its police, discipline or interior management. I have never inspected it or in any way interfered with Colonel Sangster's duties. As I am not authorized to exercise any control over that camp I have never

* See p. 360.

visited it, and the report I made is based entirely on such statements as I have received and not on a personal knowledge of the condition of things thére.

From a brief conversation I had with the commanding general in Baltimore when on my way to this place I received the impression that he considered Camp Parole a separate command and not subject to my orders.

I will here repeat that the suggestions of Captain Lazelle if carried out will in my opinion produce beneficial results.

It is not in my power to carry into effect any of his recommendations without in effect assuming command of the camp.

By direction of the commanding general indorsed on Colonel Hoffman's letter of the 7th March last five companies of the Third Regiment Potomac Home Brigade under Colonel Gilpin, consisting of 313 enlisted men, have been sent to Camp Parole for a guard. The three remaining companies of that regiment are detached, one guarding the general hospital and public property at this post, one guarding the railroad between this city and Annapolis Junction and one guarding the hospital at the Junction.

A larger force is wanted at each of these places.

I am, sir, with much respect, your obedient servant,

C. A. WAITE,
Colonel First Infantry, Commanding Post.

[Indorsement.]

HEADQUARTERS, *Baltimore, Md., May 1, 1863.*

Respectfully referred to Lieutenant-Colonel Sangster for his information and with reference to the instructions to Colonel Waite heretofore indorsed.

The papers were referred to Colonel Waite because of the explanation of his command as embracing Camp Parole contained in the letter of the Adjutant-General, a copy of which is herein now inclosed. It was not the intention of the general commanding in his interview and conversation with Colonel Waite to presume to relieve him of any part of the duty assigned to him by higher authority, but as Colonel Waite appears to have yielded the entire command and management of Camp Parole to Lieutenant-Colonel Sangster, correspondence so far as that camp and parole prisoners are concerned will be held hereafter directly with Lieutenant-Colonel Sangster.*

By order of Major-General Schenck:

W. H. CHESEBROUGH,
Assistant Adjutant-General.

HEADQUARTERS, *Fort Gibson, April 28, 1863.*

Brigadier-General COOPER, C. S. Army.

GENERAL: I received your note† by the bearers of the flag of truce. I appoint my judge-advocate, Lieutenant Moody, and Major Maynard, my medical director, to visit you [to] determine places of exchange and to make any other necessary arrangements in conformity to the cartel. I merely ask that those with whom they co-operate shall be officers of similar rank.

I have been in the habit in the absence of other known points of sending prisoners to Saint Louis to be exchanged as per general orders,

---

* For Sangster's reply, see p. 605.   † Not found.

but shall be willing for a suitable arrangement which would not subject the parties to such inconvenience.

We have a few prisoners here whose names will be given by the judge-advocate.

In reference to the prisoners paroled by you at Washita I would merely remark that only two of them ever reached our lines, and they had to swim Arkansas River in order to get away. I have no desire to be captious, but would of course require a prisoner to be put within our lines.

In reference to the Cherokees executed at Tahlequah you will pardon me for reminding you that you simply state the facts without any definite information as to what you propose doing in the future and permit me to doubt, which I shall be happy to do, that you approve of that tragedy. On this point I have instructed the gentlemen who visit you to be plain. I cannot for a moment admit any such proceeding, and if persisted in will have to try by court-martial and similarly punish officers and soldiers who deserted the service of the U. S. Army to join the so-called Confederate service.

By the strict law of nations, as it was a rebellion, all engaged in this war against this Government might have been executed as insurgents. Adopting a more humane policy the Government of the United States treated the insurgents as belligerents and have so far—although that point has never been formally determined on—liberated even officers and soldiers of the Regular Army who deserted it for your service. It does indeed appear strange to me that those who have so much to expect from tolerance should raise such a point, especially as the doctrine which professedly at least underlies secessionism is an assertion of the right to throw off ties of allegiance when they become irksome. In view of the whole matter I can only regard a disposition to kill prisoners in this war as growing out of a disposition to wage war in its most barbarous shape.

I deprecate such a system. I invite you by considerations of humanity to a more enlightened policy, but do not hesitate to assure you that I am prepared for the responsibilities of a different course.

Although I might have referred your proposition to a brigade commander I received it and answer it frankly myself, hoping that a candid discussion of the points involved will lead to a better understanding.

I have the honor to remain, yours, respectfully,

W. A. PHILLIPS,
Colonel, Commanding.

HDQRS. EIGHTH REGT. CAV. MISSOURI STATE MILITIA,
Lebanon, Mo., April 28, 1863.

Maj. JAMES H. STEGER,
Assistant Adjutant-General, District of Southwest Missouri.

MAJOR: I telegraphed to the colonel commanding Southwest District of Missouri on the 23d that seven men were taken prisoners on their return from Springfield as escort to paymaster. They were taken in Dallas County, carried about fifty miles into Cedar County, stripped, murdered and thrown into a heap like so many hogs. Three of the soldiers thus murdered belonged to Company D and four to Company E of this regiment. The rebels were dressed in Federal uniform, and the men rode up to them as friends, when they were captured and most cruelly murdered. The three men of Company D were as good soldiers as ever shouldered a musket, always obedient, but on this occasion had straggled behind the command. Major, I respectfully inquire of the colonel commanding district whether any rebel wearing the Federal uniform should be treated as a prisoner of war? If I capture any rebel thus attired I will have him shot unless otherwise ordered.

I have the honor to be, most respectfully, your obedient servant,

J. J. GRAVELY,
Colonel Eighth Regiment Cavalry Missouri State Militia.

WASHINGTON, *April 28, 1863.*

General S. R. CURTIS:

It is impossible to deliver prisoners of war at Vicksburg.

W. HOFFMAN,
Commissary-General of Prisoners.

OFFICE COMMISSARY-GENERAL OF PRISONERS,
Washington, April 28, [*1863.*]

Brig. Gen. J. H. MARTINDALE,
Comdg. Military District of Washington, Washington, D. C.

GENERAL: By direction of the Secretary of War I have the honor to request that you will send A. Carroll Hicks, a prisoner in the Old Capitol Prison, to Lieutenant-Colonel Ludlow, agent for the exchange of prisoners at Fort Monroe, to be forwarded for exchange on the first flag-of-truce boat.

The honorable Secretary of the Navy desires that upon the summons of the district commander at Philadelphia John Little and J. M. Wilson, prisoners at the Old Capitol Prison, charged with violating the blockade, may be delivered to such person as may present the same, and I have the honor to request you will deliver said persons as desired.

Very respectfully, your obedient servant,

W. HOFFMAN,
Colonel Third Infantry, Commissary-General of Prisoners.

OFFICE COMMISSARY-GENERAL OF PRISONERS,
Washington, D. C., April 28, 1863.

Brig. Gen. JOHN S. MASON, *Commanding, Columbus, Ohio.*

GENERAL: I have the honor to acknowledge the receipt of your letter of the 23d instant, and in reply have to say that by General Orders, No. 67, of 1862, a copy* of which is inclosed, paroles may be granted to prisoners of war by the commissary-general of prisoners on the recommendation of the medical officer attending the prison, but only in cases of extreme illness. I require the recommendations to be forwarded through the commanding officer and to be approved by him. This is the only authority given by the Secretary of War for granting paroles. Complaints have been made by people of Columbus of the presence of paroled prisoners in their city and I do not feel at liberty to ask that the authority be extended. In case of a contagious disease of course the person should be removed without delay to a suitable place, but in ordinary cases the delay of referring the applications to this office could not be attended with any inconvenience.

---

* See Vol. IV, this Series, p. 30.

I have to request you will order Captain Webber to send to this city to be delivered to the provost-marshal Mrs. Mary Samuels and her two daughters Anna and Roberta and her son John Samuels. If the two females referred to in your letter are committed for acts of disloyalty please have them forwarded at the same time, sending with them the charges upon which they were arrested. A roll giving time and place of arrest, &c., should be sent to the provost-marshal and a copy to this office. Heretofore I have generally sent orders for the transfer of prisoners direct to Captain Webber, but under existing circumstances it will probably be most to the interest of the service for them to pass through your hands.

I inclose for your information regulations* issued by authority of the War Department for the management of the affairs of military prisons. My impression is that Captain Webber has been very attentive to his duties and has conducted the affairs of the prison in a satisfactory manner.

The Secretary of War has in some few cases ordered the discharge of rebel officers on their taking the oath of allegiance but only when it has been shown that there were circumstances which gave them a claim to this indulgence. There is no general authority for such discharges. I have given particular instructions to Captain Webber in relation to the discharge of deserters from the rebel army. The proof must be quite clear that they are really deserters and then the case must be referred to this office.

Very respectfully, your obedient servant,
W. HOFFMAN,
Colonel Third Infantry, Commissary-General of Prisoners.

WASHINGTON, *April 28, 1863.*

Lieutenant-Colonel LUDLOW:

Do you wish more prisoners of war forwarded? Some have been captured in the West recently.

W. HOFFMAN,
Commissary-General of Prisoners.

WASHINGTON, *April 28, 1863.*

Lieut. Col. W. H. LUDLOW,
Agent for Exchange of Prisoners:

Paroled prisoners of war received at Annapolis since January 1 belonging to regiments serving in the West have been sent to Camp Chase and Benton Barracks. All others remain at Camp Parole.

W. HOFFMAN,
Commissary-General of Prisoners.

OFFICE COMMISSARY-GENERAL OF PRISONERS,
Washington, D. C., April 28, 1863.

Lieut. Col. GEORGE SANGSTER,
Commanding Camp Parole, Annapolis, Md.

COLONEL: Forward without delay to Camp Chase, Ohio, and Benton Barracks, Mo., all exchanged or paroled troops belonging to regiments

---

* See Vol. IV, this Series, p. 152.

serving in the West, including those in the general hospital at Annapolis who are recommended for the transfer by the surgeon in charge, in
accordance with General Orders, No. 72, of June last. Furnish cooked
rations for the route and send the usual rolls and accounts with the
officer in charge. Exchanged officers and men will on reaching Camp
Chase or Benton Barracks be ordered to join their respective regiments
without delay. In preparing the command for the movement be governed by the instructions heretofore given to you in such cases. Report
to me by return mail at what time the command will probably leave.
    By order of the General-in-Chief:
        Very respectfully, your obedient servant,
                                    W. HOFFMAN,
        Colonel Third Infantry, Commissary-General of Prisoners.

                HEADQUARTERS SIXTEENTH ARMY CORPS,
                            Memphis, April 28, 1863.
Major-General HURLBUT,
        Commanding Sixteenth Army Corps.
    GENERAL: In compliance with Special Orders, No. 77, Headquar-
ters Sixteenth Army Corps, Memphis, April 22, 1863, I have the honor
to report the following in regard to the islands in the Mississippi River
and a point below Columbus, Ky., and in contemplation as proper loca-
tions for a military prison to accommodate 1,000 prisoners. Islands 1,
2, 3 and 4 lie between Cairo, Ill., and Columbus, Ky. They all overflow, and with the exception of one (Island 2) have become attached to
the mainland. At Columbus there is a good location about one mile
from military headquarters and south.
    It is a location that can always be approached by steam-boats at low
and high water to land stores or prisoners. There is a large amount of
timber on the point and in the immediate vicinity. Island No. 5, better known as Wolfe Island and in view of Columbus, is about seven
miles long and is from three and one-fourth to two and one-half miles
in width. It is well timbered and has high land in the center, which
is cultivated to quite an extent, there being some six farms under cul-
tivation. This ridge running through the island was overflowed in
1862 and 1858, but in ordinary high water does not overflow. The
landing at this island is bad and would require much labor and heavy
expense to make a landing that could be used at all seasons. The low
places in the island between the shore and ridge would require filling
up or bridging. Islands 7 and 8 are small and overflow. No. 9 is not
to be seen or distinguished from the mainland. No. 10 is high and is
the only island that does not overflow at extreme high water. It is
now garrisoned by a small force of the U. S. Army. The timber on the
island could be used for fire-wood but only a small portion of it could
be used for building purposes. On the Tennessee shore and in the
immediate vicinity of the island there is good timber for building purposes if it was considered practicable to build a log prison. The upper
end of this island is fast washing away, but from information gained
from river men the channel may turn at low water and the island
remain without further wash. This, however, cannot be relied upon.
    A portion of Island No. 10 could be placed under cultivation and be
made advantageous to the Government and expense of the prison
made light. I would respectfully recommend Island No. 10 as the most

suitable of any of the islands in the Mississippi River between Cairo and New Madrid. Islands Nos. 11, 12, 13, 14, 15, 16 and 17 all overflow and could not be used for the purpose desired.

I have the honor to be, very respectfully, your obedient servant,

W. H. THURSTON,
Lieutenant-Colonel and Assistant Inspector-General.

———

MILITARY PRISON, *Alton, Ill., April 28, 1863.*
Dr. J. B. BROWN, *Surgeon, U. S. Army, Saint Louis, Mo.*

SIR: I received this morning your communication of yesterday's date in which you call my attention to certain extracts embodied in your letter "from the report of the medical inspector who recently inspected the prison and barracks under your (my) supervision" and beg to state in reply that the inspector has made a mistake in holding me responsible as he appears to have done in his report for the shortcomings of the volunteer troops stationed at this place. I have no control whatever over these troops except when they are on guard within the prison, and am therefore not responsible for them and their acts in any shape or manner. Their barracks and regimental hospital are in the town and outside the prison walls and are under the control exclusively of their own officers. Therefore the several items in the extract from inspector's report about the company officers not inspecting the messes, the condition of building B of the barracks and of the regimental hospital do not apply to me as these things are not under my supervision.

As to the condition of the roof of the prison hospital building and other buildings of the prison I some time since reported to Colonel Hoffman, commissary-general of prisoners at Washington, the necessity of their speedy repair and am looking for instructions daily in relation to this subject. I would wish it to be understood, doctor, that there are two separate commands here: one of the prison, the other of the troops or post. I am responsible for the prison but not for the troops.

I have the honor to be, sir, with much respect, your most obedient servant,

T. HENDRICKSON,
Major Third Infantry, Commanding the Prison.

———

GENERAL ORDERS, { WAR DEPT., ADJT. GENERAL'S OFFICE,
No. 108.   }   *Washington, April 28, 1863.*

I. Whenever volunteer troops are mustered out of service the entire regiment or other organization will be considered as mustered out at one time and place except prisoners of war, who will be considered as in service until their arrival in a loyal State, with an allowance of time necessary for them to return to their respective places of enrollment. With officers and men of this class commanding officers of regiments and companies will exercise great care in stating in the remarks on the muster-rolls the dates and places of capture, thus: Prisoner of war. Captured at ———, December —, 18—.

*   *   *   *   *   *   *

By order of the Secretary of War:

E. D. TOWNSEND,
Assistant Adjutant-General.

WASHINGTON, D. C., *April 29, 1863.*

Major-General BURNSIDE, *Cincinnati, Ohio.*

GENERAL: The Secretary of War has shown me a letter of General Negley in regard to two negroes formerly belonging to belligerent citizens who are now advertised under local laws of Kentucky to be sold for expenses of arrest, keeping, &c. The same game was attempted last year in Missouri under the local laws of that State to sell back into slavery those who by the law of Congress were made free by the acts of their former masters. I directed the sheriff to release them all and forbade the sales. He at first objected but on a full and frank discussion of the matter he obeyed the order. I retained the men a short time in the employ of the Quartermaster's Department, mainly as a precaution for their own security, and then let them go where they pleased.

There can be no doubt, general, that the law of Congress on this subject overrides any State law. Negroes freed by the operations of the war and taken into our service are under the protection of the military, and I have always considered it my duty to thwart and defeat the operations of negro stealers to have them resold into slavery. I will send you a copy of my letter to the sheriff to-morrow. The reasons there given are fortified by the law of last July on the same subject, and this last law is of much more general application than the former one.

Very respectfully, your obedient servant,

H. W. HALLECK,
General-in-Chief.

JUDGE-ADVOCATE-GENERAL'S OFFICE, *April 29, 1863.*

Major-General HALLECK:

The writer of the within letter,* E. M. Strange, was found within our picket-lines under circumstances which led to his arrest on suspicion of his being a spy. He admits that his arrest was proper. He surrendered up certain papers with a view of proving that although capable of inventing and selling to the rebel authorities machines for destroying the iron-clad ships of his own Government he is not capable of being a spy, a conclusion which is regarded as decidedly a *non sequitur* from the premises. He alleges that these papers show him to be the inventor of these machines and that he sold the privilege of using them (of course in destroying the war vessels of the United States) to the Confederate authorities for which he has a large claim against them. He asks that the papers be returned to him in order doubtless that he may be enabled to collect the claim of which they are written evidence. He seems to expect not only that this assistance shall be given to him in reference to a claim originating in action on his part intended to aid in overthrowing the Government, but also in the event he is not permitted to return with his papers South that facilities shall be extended to him for patenting his inventions at Washington with a view to their being used against Great Britain should a war which he thinks has been fully provoked occur with that power. He does not appear willing that any use should be made of these inventions against the rebels, but declares that no possible consideration of gain or power could induce him to take up arms against his people in Virginia. Because, however, of his natural animosity against Great Britain he would gladly assist in a war against her.

---

* Not found.

This man is evidently a traitor of the deepest dye. He resided in California but left his home in that loyal State and went into the South for the express purpose of aiding the rebels by furnishing them the machines referred to. According to his own confession he is guilty under the second section of act of 17th of July, 1862, of having given efficient " aid and comfort" to the rebellion and should at once be tried for this crime by a military commission, the ordinary criminal courts not being open in the State where the crime was committed. The papers taken from him should be carefully preserved as they probably furnish full evidence of his guilt.

J. HOLT,
Judge-Advocate-General.

OFFICE COMMISSARY-GENERAL OF PRISONERS,
Washington, D. C., April 29, 1863. .

Maj. Gen. A. E. BURNSIDE,
Commanding Department of the Ohio, Cincinnati, Ohio.

GENERAL: It is desirable that all the prisoners of war in our hands should be forwarded for delivery and exchange with as little delay as practicable, and I have therefore by authority of the General-in-Chief the honor to request that you will order all in the Department of the Ohio who can be moved without danger of spreading the contagion of smallpox to be immediately forwarded to City Point. Those now at Camp Douglas are perhaps too much infected with the disease to be sent through the country, but a careful examination by the surgeon in charge will determine how far this is the case. Please direct that the quartermaster at Baltimore be advised of the number and the time when they will reach that city so that he may have the transportation prepared to carry them to City Point, and please have me informed by telegraph of the time of their leaving and the number. Duplicate rolls should accompany them and a copy be sent to this office.

Very respectfully, your obedient servant,

W. HOFFMAN,
Colonel Third Infantry, Commissary-General of Prisoners.

OFFICE COMMISSARY-GENERAL OF PRISONERS,
Washington, D. C., April 29, 1863.

Maj. Gen. S. R. CURTIS,
Commanding Department of the Missouri, Saint Louis, Mo.

GENERAL: I have the honor to inclose herewith a copy of a letter* addressed to me by Lieutenant-Colonel Dick, provost-marshal general at Saint Louis, dated March 5, 1863, suggesting a certain policy to be pursued toward disloyal persons in Missouri, and I am instructed by the Secretary of War to say that the views expressed by Colonel Dick as to the proper disposition to be made both of the men and women who are in rebellion against the Government in Missouri or who are actively though secretly giving aid and comfort to those who are so must be promptly and inflexibly carried into execution.

Under instructions heretofore given all guerrillas and irregular military organizations are held as prisoners of war, and those now in our possession will be ordered through this office forward for exchange at the earliest opportunity. They can be released on taking the oath of

---

* Omitted here; see p. 319.

allegiance only by the authority of the Secretary of War on recommendations approved by the Governor of the State.

Citizen prisoners can only be exchanged with the consent of the rebel authorities, and at present I am not advised that such an exchange can be effected.

Very respectfully, your obedient servant,

W. HOFFMAN,
Colonel Third Infantry, Commissary-General of Prisoners.

OFFICE COMMISSARY-GENERAL OF PRISONERS,
Washington, D. C., April 29, 1863.

Brig. Gen. A. SCHOEPF, *Commanding Fort Delaware.*

GENERAL: When I was recently at Fort Delaware some suggestions were made by the then commanding officer relative to remodeling and repairing the old barracks occupied by our troops which I approved of, but the Quartermaster-General wishes before he gives orders for any change to have a detailed report of what is proposed to be done, and I have therefore to request if you think the modification referred to necessary that you will have a ground plan prepared to show what changes are proposed and what the probable expense will be. The buildings require new roofing, new bunks, floors and windows before they will be fit for occupation. Instructions have already been given for arranging the floors in the barracks occupied by the prisoners of war, and I believe that by the contract under which they were constructed if the roofing required repairs before the expiration of a year the contractors are bound to make them.

I have the honor to inclose herewith certain orders* and regulations heretofore issued in relation to the control and management of prisoners of war and political prisoners. Until recently there have been but few prisoners held at Fort Delaware and no regular reports or returns have been sent to this office, and as it is hereafter to be a principal depot I have to request you will have the prescribed regulations put in force at once.

The prison fund accumulates very rapidly and is to be used for the purchase of such things as are necessary for the welfare of the prisoners and to meet expenses which would otherwise have to be paid by the Government. There are now some funds on hand which may be used in erecting a bakehouse or in making necessary repairs. A bakehouse is a source of large receipts to the fund and it may soon pay for itself. I inclose also a scale † of rations which is used at the prison camp.

Very respectfully, your obedient servant,

W. HOFFMAN,
Colonel Third Infantry, Commissary-General of Prisoners.

OFFICE COMMISSARY-GENERAL OF PRISONERS,
Washington, D. C., April 29, 1863.

Colonel CAMERON, *Commanding Camp Douglas, Ill.*

COLONEL: On the 22d April, 1863, I addressed to you the following telegram:

Please inform me who was the principal surgeon who examined the prisoners sent to City Point.

---

*Omitted here; see Vol. IV, this Series, p. 152.   †Not found.

To which no reply has been received. Please report as required by the return mail.

Very respectfully, your obedient servant,

W. HOFFMAN,
Colonel Third Infantry, Commissary-General of Prisoners.

WASHINGTON, *April 29, 1863.*

Lieutenant-Colonel LUDLOW:

Have you exchanged any rebel prisoners delivered at City Point?

W. HOFFMAN,
Commissary-General of Prisoners.

OFFICE COMMISSARY-GENERAL OF PRISONERS,
Washington, April 29, 1863.

Lieut. Col. F. A. DICK,
Provost-Marshal-General, Saint Louis, Mo.

COLONEL: Your letter of the 5th of March has been submitted to the Secretary of War and the suggestions made by you therein have been approved and I have to-day communicated to Major-General Curtis, commanding the Department of the Missouri, with a copy of your letter, the instructions of the Secretary of War that your recommendations in regard to disloyal men and women in Missouri be fully carried out. Instructions will be sent from this office as soon as the movement is practicable for the forwarding for exchange of all guerrillas and other irregular military organizations. They can be released on taking the oath of allegiance only by authority of the Secretary of War on recommendation approved by the Governor of the State. Citizen prisoners cannot be exchanged unless the rebel authorities consent to it and at this time no such exchanges are being made.

Very respectfully, your obedient servant,

W. HOFFMAN,
Colonel Third Infantry, Commissary-General of Prisoners.

MURFREESBOROUGH, *April 29, 1863.*

Colonel HOFFMAN:

Have reliable information that all Confederate prisoners delivered at City Point are sent to their commands at once. We have recaptured some who were taken March 5. Were they exchanged?

WM. M. WILES.

OFFICE COMMISSARY-GENERAL OF PRISONERS,
Washington, D. C., April 29, 1863.

THOMAS J. WILLIAMS,
Twelfth Illinois Cavalry, Army of the Potomac.

SIR: In answer to your communication addressed to the Adjutant-General and which has been referred to this office I am directed to inform you that all prisoners of war taken in Missouri up to January 1, 1863, have been exchanged. See General Orders, No. 10, from War Department, Adjutant-General's Office, for 1863.

Very respectfully, your obedient servant,

W. T. HARTZ,
Captain and Assistant Adjutant-General.

MURFREESBOROUGH, *April 30, 1863.*

Colonel HOFFMAN:

Have the prisoners taken at the battle of Stone's River been exchanged?

W. S. ROSECRANS,
Major-General.

WAR DEPARTMENT, *Washington, D. C., April 30, 1863.*

Maj. Gen. JOHN A. DIX, *Comdg., &c., Fortress Monroe.*

GENERAL: I have the honor by direction of the Secretary of War to inclose you the within copy of letter just received from Hon. A. W. Clark, M. C., Watertown, N. Y., in relation to Mrs. Long, daughter of the late General Sumner. And I am also directed by the Secretary to say that you will not permit Mrs. Long to pass through our lines South; that if she comes to Fortress Monroe or within your department to detain her till further orders and thoroughly examine her baggage and that she must not be allowed to pass without the express permit of the Secretary of War.

I have the honor to be, general, very respectfully, your obedient servant,

L. C. TURNER,
Judge-Advocate.

[Inclosure.]

WATERTOWN, JEFFERSON COUNTY, N. Y.

Hon. L. C. TURNER, *Judge Advocate.*

DEAR SIR: A daughter of the late Major-General Sumner, the wife of an officer in the rebel army, Mrs. Long, is now here on a visit. She came through our lines on a Government pass as I am informed and is to return to Richmond soon. She is open-mouthed and shameless (even to the disgust of her own family) in proclaiming secession doctrines. But the matter of importance is this: She has, so she says, purchased over $2,000 worth of goods in New York to take back with her, and probably will bear dispatches to the South from Northern traitors.

Yours, truly,

A. W. CLARK, M. C.

HEADQUARTERS DEPARTMENT OF VIRGINIA,
Fort Monroe, April 30, 1863.

Colonel HOFFMAN, *Commissary-General of Prisoners.*

COLONEL: Your telegram of yesterday is received. About 1,000 Confederates delivered at City Point previously to the 1st of March last have been declared exchanged and their equivalents given in deliveries of our men at Vicksburg up to January 9, 1863. The non-delivery at Vicksburg of prisoners captured in the West has caused a loss to the United States directly and indirectly of at least 2,000 men. I knew that such would be the effect, and you may recollect my so stating to you when I last saw you. I am now awaiting the arrival of the prisoners from Fort Delaware to proceed to City Point and meet Mr. Ould. In addition to the exchanges of officers I have to arrange those of the numerous deliveries of enlisted men. I have no doubt that in the coming settlement Mr. Ould will present heavy accounts of paroles taken at the West and will show an excess of prisoners. The deliveries of U. S. prisoners at City Point have been in excess of those of Confederates at same place. If you have any more Confederate prisoners of war I think it will be best to deliver them as soon as possible. All the papers and rolls relating to exchanges will be forwarded to you after the exchanges have been made.

I am, very respectfully, your obedient servant,
WM. H. LUDLOW,
Lieutenant-Colonel and Agent for Exchange of Prisoners.

HEADQUARTERS DEPARTMENT OF VIRGINIA,
Fort Monroe, April 30, 1863.
Col. WM. HOFFMAN, *Commissary-General of Prisoners.*

COLONEL: I have the honor to inclose to you copy of letter just received with memoranda* inclosed. I think that Doctor Dixon had better be released. Of Tunstall's case I am not advised. Please show the letter to General Hitchcock and give me information in detail on each of the points presented. Please have noted on the copy of memoranda and opposite each name the position of the case named. I think many of them have been released. If the case of Captain Baylor, confined at Fort Delaware, has not been examined I would recommend that it be as soon as practicable. The effect of keeping the release of a Confederate officer suspended on charges is always to retain one of our own officers in confinement, for while official notice of retaliation is not given I am satisfied that such retaliation is really practiced.

I am, very respectfully, your obedient servant,
WM. H. LUDLOW,
Lieutenant-Colonel and Agent for Exchange of Prisoners.

[Inclosure.]

WAR DEPARTMENT, *Richmond, Va., April 22, 1863.*
Lieut. Col. WILLIAM H. LUDLOW, *Agent of Exchange.*

SIR: 1. I will be very much obliged to you if you will secure the return of Thomas Tait Tunstall who I believe is now confined in Washington as a rebel spy. He is the gentleman with reference to whom I read you the letter of the Hon. C. C. Clay. Mr. Tunstall is no spy in any sense of the term. I am well assured there was a lady in the case. You will do a good service to humanity if you procure his discharge.

2. I also bring to your attention again the case of Dr. Jos. E. Dixon, confined at Johnson's Island. I have already given you a statement of the facts in his case. I have in my possession cumulative evidence to the fullest extent of the truth of that statement. The injustice done to him is producing great excitement amongst our people. Why force retaliation in such matters? Doctor Dixon has been in confinement long enough to have been tried a dozen times and yet he is held without trial upon a charge the easiest that can be trumped up against any one. Is this right?

3. Privates Betts, Rider and Oliver, of Captain Gaither's company, First Virginia Cavalry, captured on the 25th February, are now in the Old Capitol Prison. I understand they have been tried as traitors by a court martial in General Hooker's camp because they are Marylanders. The rumor is they have been sentenced to death. Is this system to be

* Not found.

inaugurated? They were captured in fair fight. If such a rule is adopted what a new world of misery is opened. I hope you will look into this matter and see how it is.

4. A large number of the citizens of New Orleans, including Mayor Monroe, J. B. Leefe, Gerard Stith, Doctor Mackin, R. L. Bruce, Dr. William Booth, Mr. Laurason and about forty others are now confined at Fort Pickens. Is this to be continued? You know how long they have been in confinement. I beg that you will pay to this and other cases of confinement of citizens some attention. It is a grievous case. Can you expect the release of your own citizens in view of such a state of facts? Let me know whether they will be released. There are many other Louisianians at Fort Jackson also who have been confined for many months. What is to be done with them?

5. A large number of citizens of Virginia (on its eastern border) have recently been arrested. Most of them are confined in Washington. Are they to be held in confinement? Let me know the purpose of your Government in this respect. You know how earnestly I have protested against this arrest of non-combatants. You also know to what it must ultimately lead.

Respectfully, your obedient servant,

RO. OULD,
Agent of Exchange.

HEADQUARTERS DEPARTMENT OF THE NORTHWEST,
Milwaukee, Wis., April 30, 1863.

COMMISSARY-GENERAL OF PRISONERS, *Washington, D. C.*

SIR: Can you inform me whether the men of the Second, Third, Seventh, Eighth, Tenth, Eleventh, Fifteenth, Sixteenth, Seventeenth and Eighteenth and Eighth Wisconsin Battery, Wisconsin Volunteers, paroled prisoners, have been exchanged? The men I particularly wish information of are the companies formed of above men now at Bayfield and Superior, Wis., who came up to Prairie du Chien, Wis., last autumn and were there organized for service at the above posts.

Very respectfully, your obedient servant,

R. O. SELFRIDGE,
Major and Assistant Adjutant-General.

HEADQUARTERS DISTRICT OF WESTERN KENTUCKY,
Louisville, April 30, 1863.

Col. W. HOFFMAN, *Commissary-General of Prisoners:*

By command of Brigadier-General Boyle Colonel Dent has been relieved of his connection with the military prison in this city and of the charge of prisoners in this military district and I have been directed to assume a general supervision of both subjects. Accordingly I have to request that all orders relating to prisoners in this military district and all correspondence in regard to them be addressed to me at General Boyle's headquarters. The only orders from department commissary-general of prisoners which have been turned over to me are contained in a circular from the office of the commissary-general of prisoners, Detroit, Mich., July 7, 1862. If other and more recent orders have been issued I request that they may be furnished me without delay that I may have them uniformly enforced throughout this military district. The provisions of the first section of the circular referred to above, providing for the organization of the prisoners into companies, &c., can scarcely be carried out in the military prison in this city from the fact that the prisoners are usually retained in it only long enough to have their rolls made out, when they are forwarded for exchange or to more permanent depots for prisoners. I would therefore ask permission to modify that provision of section 1 to suit the exigencies of the case. I would also request that section 8 allowing contributions (other than money) to be distributed as the donors request may be so changed as only to allow contributions to be made to a common fund to be drawn on by the commandant of the prison at his discretion to supply the necessities. It has been found by experience here that to allow secessionists (of whom there are many) to select particular subjects for their contributions tends to stimulate and keep alive their party zeal. I would request to know if the provisions of section 9 apply equally to political prisoners and prisoners of war. I would also request to know if the provisions of section 11 apply to prisoners claiming to be deserters or discharged soldiers from the rebel army and desirous of taking the oath of allegiance. If so shall they be sent to Camp Chase with a statement of all the facts known in their cases, to make from there their application to the War Department or commissary-general of prisoners? Are prisoners sent into the enemy's lines permitted to take letters under any circumstances? The monthly report of prisoners for April will be promptly forwarded.

I have the honor to be, very respectfully, your obedient servant,
STEPHEN E. JONES,
Captain and Aide-de-Camp.

WAR DEPARTMENT, *Washington, May 1, 1863.*
SIMEON DRAPER, *Provost-Marshal, New York:*

You will consult Mr. Pierrepont and follow his advice. Turn over any other prisoners you may have to General Wool, to be disposed of as he may deem proper, and make no arrests without authority of this Department.

EDWIN M. STANTON,
Secretary of War.

OFFICE COMMISSARY-GENERAL OF PRISONERS,
Washington, D. C., May 1, 1863.
Maj. Gen. R. C. SCHENCK,
Commanding Eighth Army Corps, Baltimore, Md.

GENERAL: Permit me again to ask your attention to the case of Captain Baylor, a prisoner of war at Fort Delaware. He is charged with the commission of a very obnoxious crime and it is very desirable if possible to obtain evidence that will convict him. In the letter* of Maj. A. G. A. Constable, provost-marshal at Baltimore, of December 22, 1862, addressed to General Morris when Captain Baylor was sent to Fort McHenry, charges have been made, he having killed one of our men while bearing a flag of truce, and it is supposed that the major may be able to point to some source where the necessary evidence may be procured. The Judge-Advocate-General cannot decide as to what disposition shall be made of him until it is ascertained whether the charges against

---
* Not found.

him are true or false, and as the negotiations for the exchange of our officers are embarrassed by the detention of Captain Baylor I have respectfully to request you will direct such reports to be made by his captors, giving the names of the witnesses, as will establish whether he is guilty or not. I beg your early attention to this matter.

Very respectfully, your obedient servant,

W. HOFFMAN,
Colonel Third Infantry, Commissary-General of Prisoners.

OFFICE COMMISSARY-GENERAL OF PRISONERS,
Washington, D. C., May 1, 1863.

Brig. Gen. J.ʰH. MARTINDALE,
Commanding Military District of Washington.

GENERAL: A steamer will reach this city from Fort Monroe the latter part of this week for the purpose of taking on board for delivery at City Point the prisoners of war, officers and men, who may be at the Old Capitol Prison and I have the honor to request you will give the necessary orders for the movement. Please direct duplicate parole rolls to be prepared to go with them and one copy without the parole for this office. As soon as I am informed I will notify you of the day when the steamer will be here.

Very respectfully, your obedient servant,

W. HOFFMAN,
Colonel Third Infantry, Commissary-General of Prisoners.

OFFICE COMMISSARY-GENERAL OF PRISONERS,
Washington, D. C., May 1, 1863.

Capt. H. B. TODD, *Provost-Marshal, Washington.*

CAPTAIN: Two women charged with disloyal practices have been ordered from Camp Chase to be delivered to you and they may be expected here in a day or two. It is probable there will be other women of the same class ordered on soon.

Very respectfully, your obedient servant,

W. HOFFMAN,
Colonel Third Infantry, Commissary-General of Prisoners.

DEPOT PRISONERS OF WAR,
Near Sandusky, Ohio, May 1, 1863.

Col. W. HOFFMAN, *Commissary-General of Prisoners.*

COLONEL: General Burnside has postponed the execution of Thomas M. Campbell, spy, till the 8th, one week. I received your dispatch in which you direct no visitors on the island the day of execution. The doctor desires Doctor Donahoe and perhaps another physician. The chaplain said he would like another clergyman, especially if the prisoner desired. I also consented that the sheriff of one county (Sandusky) [be present] as I am under obligations to him for irons, &c., besides being very accommodating in taking prisoners sometimes in the winter. I also design to give passes to reporters of the press to a limited number.

I do not expect any others unless it should be that there may be some high military or civil officer of the United States. I shall have to picket the whole island. I see by the Cincinnati papers that two others will be sent here for execution—to be shot.

I hope the above will please your views and not be inconsistent with your dispatch, as I had arranged thus far before receiving it and I think proper that reporters be present. These executions make very great excitement in the northern part of Ohio and I hope unless Captain Scovill and Captain Linnell are very useful at Wheeling they will be back.

Very respectfully, your obedient servant,
WM. S. PIERSON,
Major Hoffman's Battalion, Commanding.

————

WHEELING, VA., *May 1, 1863.*
Maj. L. C. TURNER, *Judge-Advocate:*

George W. Thompson is held prisoner on account of suspicious movements of his for the past few days. He is also held as a hostage. His son is among the rebels now committing raids in West Virginia. I hold him by order of Governor Peirpoint and as an enemy of the Government whose surveillance for some days is requisite and demanded by the present state of affairs. I trust no influence can be brought to bear upon the Government to release him from custody until the rebels are driven out of this part of the State.

JOS. DARR, JR.,
Major and Provost-Marshal-General.

————

OFFICE COMMISSARY-GENERAL OF PRISONERS,
Washington, May 1, 1863.
Maj. JOSEPH DARR, Jr.,
Provost-Marshal-General, Wheeling, Va.

MAJOR: By direction of the commissary-general of prisoners I have the honor to inform you that no order has been published since General Orders, No. 10, announcing exchanges, but it is expected one will be issued in a few days.

Very respectfully, your obedient servant,
W. T. HARTZ,
Captain and Assistant Adjutant-General.

————

OFFICE COMMISSARY-GENERAL OF PRISONERS,
Washington, D. C., May 1, 1863.
Capt. H. B. TODD, *Provost-Marshal, Washington, D. C.*

CAPTAIN: By direction of the commissary-general of prisoners I have the honor to inquire how many prisoners of war are in the Old Capitol Prison who are subject to exchange.

Very respectfully, your obedient servant,
W. T. HARTZ,
Captain and Assistant Adjutant-General.

QUARTERMASTER'S DEPARTMENT,
Indianapolis, Ind., May 1, 1863.

Col. WILLIAM HOFFMAN,
Commissary-General of Prisoners, Washington, D. C.

COLONEL: I herewith inclose an account* for medical services in favor of Doctor Funkhauser. The service has been rendered exclusively for and to prisoners of war. Please indicate how the account can be paid. The contract spoken of in the account was I understand made with Colonel Carrington, commanding at this post, a copy of which was sent to Surgeon-General U. S. Army.

I am, colonel, very respectfully, your obedient servant,
JAMES A. EKIN,
Assistant Quartermaster, U. S. Army.

JUDGE-ADVOCATE-GENERAL'S OFFICE, *May 2, 1863.*

SECRETARY OF WAR:

The Executive Department of the Government has no power to absolve Walter H. Powell from the oath of allegiance which he has taken. He alleges that he was forced to take it by the imprisonment to which he was subjected in consequence of his having refused it. It does not otherwise appear for what cause he was imprisoned. If the imprisonment was illegal and the oath taken under its pressure such duress would deprive it of all obligatory force. If it is thus invalid it should be so treated in the forum of conscience and would be so declared in any proceeding in which the question of its legality might be involved. The Government has no authority to declare the oath in the abstract inoperative and void or to relieve the party from any obligations it may have imposed.

J. HOLT,
Judge-Advocate-General.

OFFICE COMMISSARY-GENERAL OF PRISONERS,
Washington, D. C., May 2, 1863.

Brig. Gen. J. D. COX,
Commanding District of Ohio, Cincinnati, Ohio:

In reply to your indorsement on the letter of Brigadier-General Mason, commanding at Columbus, Ohio, dated the 21st instant, I have the honor to inform you that General Orders, No. 72, of June 28, 1862, is the order which governs the disposition of paroled troops, and the camps therein designated are the only ones at which they are to be assembled. I am authorized where there is occasion for it to designate other camps in the West for their reception, but camps cannot be allowed to individual States. The difficulty of furnishing efficient commanders and suitable guard for such camps is a great obstacle to their being multiplied if there were no others, and another camp will not be selected until there is an absolute necessity for it. I have applied to Major-General Burnside, commanding the Department of the Ohio, for a permanent and reliable guard for Camp Chase, and with it I have no doubt better order and better discipline will prevail.

Very respectfully, your obedient servant,
W. HOFFMAN,
Colonel Third Infantry, Commissary-General of Prisoners.

---

* Not found.

OFFICE COMMISSARY-GENERAL OF PRISONERS,
Washington, D. C., May 2, 1863.

Col. J. HOLT, *Judge-Advocate-General, Washington, D. C.*

COLONEL: I have the honor to ask your attention to the case of Dr. Joseph E. Dixon, of the rebel army, a prisoner at Johnson's Island charged with being a spy, which I presented for your consideration in a letter dated February 26, 1863. This case has been brought to the notice of Lieutenant Colonel Ludlow, agent for exchange of prisoners, by the rebel authorities who complain that great injustice is done by the long detention without trial of Doctor Dixon whose innocence it is asserted can be fully established.

Very respectfully, your obedient servant,

W. HOFFMAN,
Colonel Third Infantry, Commissary-General of Prisoners.

[First indorsement.]

JUDGE-ADVOCATE-GENERAL'S OFFICE,
June 5, 1863.

The letter referred to by Colonel Hoffman is not believed to have been received. Nothing is known in this office in regard to the case of Dixon.

J. HOLT,
Judge-Advocate-General.

[Second indorsement.]

The letter referred to within was without doubt delivered to Colonel Holt. The two cases of Dr. J. E. Dixon and W. P. Dixon have been confounded.

W. H.

OFFICE COMMISSARY-GENERAL OF PRISONERS,
Washington, D. C., May 2, 1863.

Lieut. Col. W. H. LUDLOW,
Agent for Exchange of Prisoners, Fort Monroe, Va.

COLONEL: Your letter of the 30th ultimo with a copy of a letter from Mr. Ould and a memorandum is received and your several requests will receive immediate attention. H. J. Samuels, adjutant-general of Virginia, reports the following named gentlemen of Wayne County, Va., have been taken prisoners to Richmond, viz, Hiram Bloss, U. S. commissioner; Ezekiel S. Bloss, clerk of court; Morgan Garrett, enrolling officer, all good and loyal men which makes them obnoxious to the rebels. Major-General Hitchcock, commissioner of exchange, directs that you demand of the Confederate authorities the immediate and unconditional release of these gentlemen.

Very respectfully, your obedient servant,

W. HOFFMAN,
Colonel Third Infantry, Commissary-General of Prisoners.

OFFICE COMMISSARY-GENERAL OF PRISONERS,
Washington, D. C., May 2, 1863.

Maj. JOSEPH DARR, Jr.,
Provost-Marshal-General, Wheeling, Va.

MAJOR: Please deliver to the provost-marshal in this city Mary J. Green and Maria Murphy, of Braxton County, and Jennie De Hart, female prisoners now in your custody charged with disloyal offenses. If there are any charges of disloyalty against Marian McKenzie or Mary Jane Prater you will send them also. Wearing soldier's clothes in camp is not an offense for which they can be sent South and if that is all that is against them they must be disposed of in some other way. Elizabeth Hays and Mary Summers are very hard cases and will have to remain on your hands until you see a good opening to dispose of them which I hope will soon present itself.

Very respectfully, your obedient servant,

W. HOFFMAN,
Colonel Third Infantry, Commissary-General of Prisoners.

WHEELING, VA., *May 2, 1863.*

Hon. E. M. STANTON:

There are no charges against G. W. Thompson. He is held as hostage. He has been exchanged and has not violated his implied parole to Judge Turner.

J. THOMPSON.

HEADQUARTERS MIDDLE DEPARTMENT,
Baltimore, May 2, 1863.

Brigadier-General LOCKWOOD,
Commanding First Separate Brigade, Point Lookout, Md.

GENERAL: You will direct with as little delay as possible the arrest of Thomas K. Robson, the editor and proprietor of a disloyal newspaper published at Easton, Talbot County, Md., copies of which are herewith inclosed,* and send him under guard to the provost-marshal of the Eighth Army Corps to be passed through the lines to remain during the war among rebels in arms whose cause and course he so manifestly prefers and encourages. You will also prohibit and prevent the further publication of this disloyal and mischievous newspaper. Return this and the inclosures with report of your action in the case.

I am, very respectfully, your obedient servant,

[WM. H. CHESEBROUGH,]
Assistant Adjutant-General.

HEADQUARTERS, *Camp Douglas, May 2, 1863.*

Col. W. HOFFMAN, *Commissary-General of Prisoners.*

SIR: Yours of April 29 is duly acknowledged. In relation to the telegram of the 24th of April to Colonel Cameron, "Please inform me who was the principal surgeon who examined the prisoners sent to City Point," I can but comply with your instructions by forwarding the only information at my command. Doctor Park, of the Sixty-fifth Illinois Infantry, was post surgeon. I cannot learn that the prisoners were examined. Doctor Brown, an assistant surgeon connected with the medical staff and still at this post, thinks they were not. I find no record

---

* Not found.

of any order from General Ammen (who was then commanding post) for an examination of prisoners. I but assumed command of Camp Douglas after the departure of Colonel Cameron with his regiment on the morning of the 19th of April, 1863.

Very respectfully, your obedient servant,

JOHN C. PHILLIPS,
Captain, Commanding Post.

Per W. C. G. L. STEVENSON,
Lieutenant, Post Adjutant.

[MAY 3, 1863.—For records relating to "Streight's Raid" and the capture of his command by the Confederates near Cedar Bluff, Ala., see Series I, Vol. XXIII, Part I, p. 280 *et seq.* Also see Part II, same volume, for correspondence relating to Streight's operations, beginning at p. 224.]

HEADQUARTERS CONFEDERATE FORCES,
Jackson County, Mo., May 3, 1863.

Maj. Gen. S. R. CURTIS,
Commanding U. S. Forces, Saint Louis, Mo.

SIR: Having been ordered to this section of the State by the legitimate authorities of my Government to resist any and all invading forces that may have for their object the subjugation of our people I deem it proper to address you officially of the intention of my Government and the determination of the colonel commanding in the event that the unholy, savage and inhuman war carried on against the people of Cass, Jackson, La Fayette, Bates and Johnson Counties is still persisted in.

Sir, while your soldiers have been treated as ordinary prisoners of war and the Union people respected in person and effects our soldiers and citizens have been arrested and executed without trial, basing and resting those hellish and diabolical acts upon the testimony of one or two unscrupulous dogs—villains that are sworn to sell and barter away the lives and liberty of men. Your officers in command of regiments, battalions and companies stationed in our border counties have without warrant or justification arrested and shot private citizens, charging as a pretext to that cowardly act that they fed, harbored and gave encouragement to bushwhackers, thereby covering the atrocity of the crime.

The more brutal the act the stronger the praise awarded by your Government. Your officers with or without your [consent] have arrested and banished our ladies for vindicating the sacredness of their sex against the slanders and insults of the base and unmitigated scoundrels calling themselves U. S. soldiers. Yes: some have been thus dealt with for refusing to cook, and giving expression to the detestation and abhorrence so justly engendered and borne toward these hireling vandals. What, sir, can you expect from a people whose rights are trampled in the dust, whose property is taken ruthlessly without the least shadow of law and feloniously appropriated; whose families have been outraged and subjected to indignities unbecoming the savages; whose friends and kindred have been shot for opposing the unwarrantable and unconstitutional invasion of our rights and country? All this has been done and now you threaten us with extinction; to extirpate our race and name; to blot out the landmarks of constitutional liberty and reduce to a wilderness the land we once inhabited.

If this is civilized and honorable warfare; if this is the spirit which animates the American people—that people of whom you have so often boasted—then I say, proud and ancient name how basely have you been lied upon.

Now, sir, being vested with authority to operate in this section of the State and protect as far as possible the people claiming citizenship and protection from the Confederate States Government, I therefore make known that I exact the rights of belligerents as ratified upon the first and original agreement between your Government and the Confederate States Government to treat all men in arms if captured as prisoners of war, whether they be found in the woods or prairies.

By acts of savage cruelty you have driven our citizens to the woods, forcing them to take desperate steps to protect their lives from the hands of commissioned assassins. The men that are now in arms in this State with a few exceptions are C. S. soldiers fighting to redeem their homes from the desecrating tread of ruffian soldiers and themselves from thraldom.

The unwarrantable seizure of persons and the destruction of property by fire; the carrying off of citizens and imprisoning them in bastiles and felons' dens; the consuming of the people's grain and meat without compensation has precipitated upon the women and children starvation, and their cries are now piercing the throne of Heaven asking to be avenged. These, sir, are a part of the causes driving men to arms, forcing upon [them] the alternative of fighting or our reduction to a state of vassalage.

Can these things be tolerated any longer? Can and must the people fold their arms and say, "O Lord, Thy will be done?" Can men stand back and see their families insulted and their property carried off by armed mobs? No! every impulse that warms the human heart calls upon our people to arms! The blood of our martyred heroes urges our people forward. The bones of our aged citizens bleaching under the midday sun calls for revenge. The tears of the widows and orphans appeal to the sympathy of Southern hearts and ask them to bleed with their comrades that have fallen in defense of their homes and firesides. Outraged humanity bleeds at every pore; the earth is stained with the blood of the innocent, and yet you hunt us with the wild and frenzied madness of the bloodhound. Can you expect willing submission? Can you expect our arms to be surrendered up and we return to our former allegiance? No! fight is the watchword of our people, and fight we shall until the hordes that now invest our country are withdrawn and our rights acknowledged among the nations of the earth.

We are compelled by the instincts of our nature to resist the enforcement of obnoxious and unlawful measures; hence the sole reason for having our soldiers and citizens put to death. If total annihilation is the intention of your Government then we are ready. If our lives are required to pay the bond then we are ready for the struggle.

The perversion of the war for the Union to a war of extermination forces upon us retaliation. And if another Confederate soldier or citizen is executed without due process of law five Union soldiers or citizens shall with their lives pay the forfeit.

This, sir, shall be done independent of the consequences, to take effect from and after the 20th day of May, A. D. 1863.

B. F. PARKER,
Colonel, C. S. Army.

SAINT LOUIS, *May 19, 1863.*

Respectfully referred to Brigadier-General Loan, who will look out for this champion of Southern rights and give him such justice as he merits. I have been sending around to find him for a month past but his forces are so small or quick of flight no one can find them.

S. R. CURTIS,
Major-General.

FORT MONROE, *May 3, 1863.*

Col. WILLIAM HOFFMAN:

I will send a steamer to Washington for the rebel prisoners the latter part of this week. I will give [you] the lists of exchanged rebel prisoners on my return from City Point where I go to-morrow morning.

WM. H. LUDLOW,
Lieutenant-Colonel, &c.

SAINT LOUIS, *May 4, 1863.*

Hon. E. M. STANTON, *Secretary of War, Washington, D. C.*

SIR: The friends of that noble and unfortunate officer, Col. Thomas C. Fletcher, are greatly troubled at his long-continued confinement in Jackson, Miss. You are aware that he was taken prisoner while gallantly and in the face of almost certain death leading his regiment against the batteries at Vicksburg. His daring bravery failed of its reward and he fell into the hands of the enemy. With many others I have a warm attachment for Colonel Fletcher. He has been a true, outspoken and enthusiastic friend of the Government from the commencement of this civil war and if it is possible to procure his exchange at once his family and friends, the Union men of this city, and in fact all who know him and his worth as a Union man and a soldier, would be full of thanks and rejoicings. I write this communication hurriedly and may take another occasion to invite your attention more particularly to his case.

I am, sir, with the highest respect, your very obedient servant,

HENRY T. BLOW.

WAR DEPARTMENT, *May 9, 1863.*

Referred to the commissary-general of prisoners for report.
By order of the Secretary of War:

P. H. WATSON,
Assistant Secretary of War.

HEADQUARTERS DEPARTMENT OF THE GULF,
Opelousas, La., May 4, 1863.

Major-General HALLECK,
Commander-in-Chief of the Army of the United States.

GENERAL: *   *   *   *   *   *

On the march to this point I ordered the arrest of ex-Governor Mouton who occupied the gubernatorial chair in 1845 and subsequently. He is a man of large influence and intelligence and has wielded with an iron hand his power over the masses of the people in this part of the country. He was president of the convention that declared Louisiana to have separated from the Union. His influence is still important and at a time when the sentiment of the people was in transition from acquiescence in the Confederate Government to a recognition and renewal of their obligations to the Union it seemed important that such a man should at least be quiet. I have therefore ordered him to New Orleans in the custody of the provost-marshal-general with instructions to that officer to provide him comfortable quarters but not allow general intercourse with the people of the city, where he will remain until further orders from the Government of the United States. This is the only arrest made except for crime. The inclosed dispatch to the Secretary of State I beg may be transmitted to his Department.*

I have the honor to be, with great respect, your obedient servant,

N. P. BANKS,
Major-General, Commanding.

WAR DEPARTMENT, *Washington, May 4, 1863.*

Maj. Gen. S. P. HEINTZELMAN,
Commanding Department of Washington.

GENERAL: The Secretary of War directs that sufficient measures be taken by you for guarding and taking care of the prisoners of war now being sent up from the Army of the Potomac and that you furnish the commissary-general of prisoners any assistance that he may require in the execution of his duties.

Very respectfully, sir, your obedient servant,

ED. R. S. CANBY,
Brigadier-General.

(Copy to Colonel Hoffman, commissary-general of prisoners.)

OFFICE COMMISSARY-GENERAL OF PRISONERS,
Washington, D. C., May 4, 1863.

Brig. Gen. JULIUS WHITE,
Commanding District of Eastern Kentucky, Louisville, Ky.

GENERAL: I have the honor to inform you in reply to your letter of the 26th that paroles given by officers or men previous to the publication of General Orders, No. 49, are to be recognized, though not in conformity with the cartel, and the prisoners so paroled are not liable for duty until exchanged. Paroles given after the publication of the above order are not valid except when in accordance with its provisions, and any person giving a parole in violation of said order is liable to punishment as therein provided for.

Very respectfully, your obedient servant,

W. HOFFMAN,
Colonel Third Infantry, Commissary-General of Prisoners.

OFFICE COMMISSARY-GENERAL OF PRISONERS,
Washington, D. C., May 4, 1863.

Brig. Gen. JOHN S. MASON, *Commanding, Columbus, Ohio.*

GENERAL: Your letter of the 27th ultimo is received and in reply I have the honor to inform you that all paroles given previous to the

---

* For portion of letter omitted, and for Chase to Stanton, May 28, 1863, see Series III.

publishing of General Orders, No. 49, of the 28th February, from the War Department, will be recognized as binding until the officer or soldier giving it is regularly exchanged. Paroles given after the publication of the order referred to will only be recognized when given in accordance with its provisions, and any officer or soldier giving a parole in violation of said order should be punished as therein provided for. In order that prisoners who have been properly paroled may be exchanged at the earliest opportunity it is necessary that rolls of all such should be promptly forwarded to this office, and I have to request you will send me full rolls, giving rank, regiment and company and time and place of capture of all paroled prisoners who may be ordered to Camp Chase.

A very large fund may be raised from the surplus rations for the benefit of paroled prisoners, and I am authorized to create such a fund by turning the surplus rations over to the commissary, who pays for them just as for the savings of a company except that he acts as treasurer for the fund which he turns over to the commanding officer of the camp on my order, who disburses it for such articles as the prisoners require. As there are scarcely any full companies among the prisoners of war this arrangement puts into useful shape a large amount of rations which otherwise must be thrown away and contributes much to the welfare of the troops, while it saves expense in many ways to the Government, and I will be much obliged to you if you will have the system put in force at Camp Chase for all men who are not in organized companies. The savings at Camp Parole, near Annapolis, have amounted to many thousands of dollars. The accompanying scale of rations is about what is issued, with perhaps a slight increase in the sugar and coffee. It is left for you to decide what the reduction should be. The fund accumulates very rapidly and it is necessary to have it carefully accounted for to prevent misapplication of it.

Very respectfully, your obedient servant,

W. HOFFMAN,
Colonel Third Infantry, Commissary-General of Prisoners.

OFFICE COMMISSARY-GENERAL OF PRISONERS,
Washington, D. C., May 4, 1863.

Capt. S. E. JONES,
Aide-de-Camp, Commanding Military Prison, Louisville, Ky.

CAPTAIN: Your letter of the 30th reporting that you have been placed in charge of the military prison at Louisville is received, and hereafter all instructions for the command of the prison will be addressed to you.

The regulations for the management of military prisons are mainly contained in the circular of January 7, but there are some few points which this does not cover. You are authorized to modify the first paragraph so as to make it applicable to the condition of your prison, the object being to keep a daily record of all present, but the monthly return showing the number present on the last day with all the changes during the month must be furnished. Paragraph 8 may be modified as you suggest. Paragraph 9 is intended to apply equally to all prisoners. It has been found to be necessary to prohibit visitors to the prisons in States north of the Ohio, and my impression is that it must be more necessary in the border States where there are so many who sympathize with and encourage the rebels.

My letter of the 3d December, 1862, addressed to you directed what should be done with deserters from the rebel army. When it is clearly established that they are deserters they may be released on taking the oath of allegiance with the understanding that death is the penalty for its violation. No prisoner of war can be recognized as a discharged soldier unless the circumstances of his capture clearly establish that he is so. If he is on the rolls as a soldier or if he was captured South he must be held as a soldier. In all cases of doubt send them to Camp Chase where their cases can be investigated. Prisoners sent into the enemy's lines should in no case be permitted to carry letters.

I inclose a scale* of rations according to which issues to prisoners should be made. The surplus rapidly creates a fund with which may be purchased many essential articles for the comfort of the prisoners and thereby save much expense to the Government. I hope you will give your particular attention to this matter and see that whatever is proper (and only such things) be provided. Heretofore no attention has been paid to this fund at Louisville.

Very respectfully, your obedient servant,

W. HOFFMAN,
Colonel Third Infantry, Commissary-General of Prisoners.

OFFICE COMMISSARY-GENERAL OF PRISONERS,
Washington, D. C., May 4, 1863.

Capt. JOHN C. PHILLIPS,
Commanding Camp Douglas, Chicago, Ill.

CAPTAIN: Your letters of the 24th and 25th ultimo have been received. You will receive orders from the headquarters Department of the Ohio to forward to City Point, Va., all the prisoners of war at Camp Douglas whose condition in health will permit them to be moved, and this will so reduce the number that your guard will be sufficient to take charge of those who remain.

Please report if Colonel Cameron turned over to you any Confederate money belonging to prisoners, how much and what disposition has been made of it.

Very respectfully, your obedient servant,

W. HOFFMAN,
Colonel Third Infantry, Commissary-General of Prisoners.

MILITARY PRISON, *Alton, Ill., May 4, 1863.*

Col. W. HOFFMAN,
Commissary-General of Prisoners, Washington, D. C.

COLONEL: I have the honor to transmit herewith a return† of prisoners in this prison for the month of April, 1863, together with rolls† in explanation of alterations during the month. You will perceive that this return differs from the one for the previous month in that soldiers and citizens are reported separately upon this return. Of the 123 aggregate last month 58 were citizens and are so reported in the return for April now transmitted.

I have the honor to be, sir, with much respect, your most obedient servant,

T. HENDRICKSON,
Major Third Infantry, Commanding Prison.

---

* Not found.　　　　　　　† Omitted.

SANDUSKY, *May 4, 1863.*

Col. W. HOFFMAN, *Commissary-General of Prisoners:*

Shall I allow any interviews with prisoners sentenced to death? If so with whom? On whose orders besides yours shall I grant interviews with prisoners?

WM. S. PIERSON.

SANDUSKY, *May 4, 1863.*

Col. WILLIAM HOFFMAN:

General Burnside orders me to hang Thomas M. Campbell, convicted as a spy. Do I require the order of the President under General Orders, No. 71, 1862?

WM. S. PIERSON,
Major, Commanding.

HEADQUARTERS DEPARTMENT OF THE OHIO,
Cincinnati, May 4, 1863.

CHARLES G. HUTTON, *Aide-de-camp, &c.*

CAPTAIN: You will proceed at once to Dayton, Ohio, by special train and cause the arrest of the Hon. Clement L. Vallandigham, after which you will return at once to these headquarters. You will confer with the provost-marshal, who will await your arrival at Dayton, and see that the arrest is made as quietly as possible. Captain Murry will accompany you and will render you any assistance you may request of him. The superintendent of the Cincinnati, Hamilton and Dayton Railroad will make all the necessary arrangements for trains upon showing him this order.

You should endeavor to arrive here before daylight to-morrow morning. Much discretion is allowed to your good judgment in this matter.

By command of Major-General Burnside:

D. R. LARNED,
Captain and Assistant Adjutant-General.

OFFICE COMMISSARY-GENERAL OF PRISONERS,
Washington, May 4, 1863.

Capt. E. L. WEBBER,
Commanding Military Prison, Camp Chase, Ohio.

CAPTAIN: Your communication* of April 28, 1863, has been received. I am directed by the commissary-general of prisoners to say that J. T. Rowdin will be held until further orders. In reply to your question as to how prisoners reported as discharged from the Confederate Army shall be considered it will depend entirely on what circumstances they have been captured or the charges upon which they were committed. If captured in the company of military men or if they were committed on military rolls they will be considered as belonging to the rebel service. If captured at home and their names do not appear on any military rolls they will be considered as citizens. You are authorized to pay a portion of the expense for carrying the mail from the prison fund.

Very respectfully, your obedient servant,

W. T. HARTZ,
Captain and Assistant Adjutant-General.

---

* Not found.

GENERAL ORDERS, } WAR DEPT., ADJT. GENERAL'S OFFICE,
No. 114. } *Washington, May 4, 1863.*

I. Before a military commission which convened in the city of Cincinnati, Ohio, April 22, 1863, pursuant to Special Orders, No. 135, dated Headquarters Department of the Ohio, Cincinnati, Ohio, April 21, 1863, and of which Brig. Gen. R. B. Potter, U. S. Volunteers, is president, were arraigned and tried—

1. William F. Corbin, now or late of the so-called Confederate Army.

CHARGE I: Recruiting men within the lines of the U. S. forces for the so-called Confederate Army.
Specification.—In this that the said William F. Corbin on or about April 9, 1863, was arrested within our lines near Rouse's Mills, Pendleton County, Ky., acting under a recruiting commission from one H. Marshall, a brigadier-general in the so-called C. S. Army, empowering him to raise recruits for the said army, the said Corbin being at the time in charge of a number of recruits whom he was seeking to conduct to the said army.
CHARGE II: Being the carrier of mails, communications and information from within our lines to persons in arms against the Government.
Specification.—In this that on or about the 9th day of April, 1863, at or near Rouse's Mills, Pendleton County, Ky., the said William F. Corbin, now or late of the so-called Confederate Army, was arrested engaged in carrying mails and information from within the lines of the U. S. forces to persons in arms against the Government.
To which charges and specifications the accused, William F. Corbin, now or late of the so-called Confederate Army, pleaded not guilty.
FINDING: The commission having maturely considered the evidence adduced finds the accused, William F. Corbin, now or late of the so-called Confederate Army, as follows:
CHARGE I: Of the specification guilty.
Of the charge guilty.
CHARGE II: Of the specification guilty.
Of the charge guilty.
SENTENCE: And the commission does therefore sentence him, William F. Corbin, now or late of the so-called Confederate Army, to be shot unto death at such time and place as the commanding general shall direct; two-thirds of the members of the commission concurring in the sentence.

2. T. G. McGraw, now or late of the so-called Confederate Army.

CHARGE: Recruiting men within the lines of the U. S. forces for the so-called Confederate Army.
Specification.—In this that the said T. G. McGraw, now or late of the so-called Confederate Army in some capacity unknown, was on or about the 9th day of April, 1863, arrested within our lines near Rouse's Mills, Pendleton County, Ky., engaged in recruiting men for the so-called Confederate Army, and was at the time when arrested engaged in conducting recruits to the said army.
To which charge and specification the accused, T. G. McGraw, now or late of the so-called Confederate Army, pleaded not guilty.
FINDING: The commission having maturely considered the evidence adduced finds the accused, T. G. McGraw, now or late of the so-called Confederate Army, as follows:
Of the specification guilty.
Of the charge guilty.
SENTENCE: And the commission does therefore sentence him, T. G. McGraw, now or late of the so-called Confederate Army, to be shot unto death at such time and place as the commanding general shall direct; two-thirds of the members of the commission concurring in the sentence.

II. The proceedings, findings and sentences in the foregoing cases are approved and confirmed. The prisoners, William F. Corbin and T. G. McGraw, now or late of the so-called Confederate Army, will be sent in irons by the proper officer and delivered into the custody of the commanding officer on Johnson's Island, depot of prisoners of war, near Sandusky, Ohio.

The commanding officer of that post will see that the sentences are duly executed at that post between the hours of 12 o'clock noon and

3 o'clock p. m. of Friday, May 15, 1863. Subject to the approval of the President of the United States.

A. E. BURNSIDE,
Major-General.

III. The President approves the sentences in the cases of William F. Corbin and T. G. McGraw and directs that they be executed at the time and place appointed in the foregoing order of Major-General Burnside.

By order of the Secretary of War:

E. D. TOWNSEND,
Assistant Adjutant-General.

GENERAL ORDERS, }   HDQRS. DEPARTMENT OF THE OHIO,
No. 58.   }   *Cincinnati, Ohio, May 4, 1863.*

I. Anonymous communications addressed to these headquarters will receive no attention.

II. Letters preferring charges against parties for disloyalty or other offenses will not be noticed unless a specific statement is made of the offense committed, with the names and place of residence of witnesses to prove the same.

By command of Major-General Burnside:

LEWIS RICHMOND,
Assistant Adjutant-General.

CINCINNATI, OHIO, *May 5, 1863.*

Hon. E. M. STANTON:

Has Mr. Vallandigham been arrested by your orders? Will you please answer by telegraph?

Yours, truly,

J. J. FARAN.
GEORGE E. PUGH.
WASHINGTON McLEAN.
GEO. H. PENDLETON.

ANNAPOLIS, *May 5, 1863.*

Col. W. HOFFMAN:

We have buildings in the rear of the college which will hold 3,000 rebel prisoners and accommodate a guard of 250 men. A guard of that number will be necessary. We have not a single soldier to guard them.

C. A. WAITE,
Colonel of Infantry.

OFFICE COMMISSARY-GENERAL OF PRISONERS,
Washington, D. C., May 5, 1863.

Col. ROBERT NUGENT,
Acting Assistant Provost-Marshal-General, New York.

COLONEL: Your letter of the 4th instant giving the account of paroled prisoners of war from New Orleans [is received] and in reply I have to request that you will send these and all other paroled men who may report to you to Camp Parole, near Annapolis, where they will be properly provided for. Please send with them all information you may have of their military status, to what regiments they belong, where and when they were captured and when paroled.

Very respectfully, your obedient servant,

W. HOFFMAN,
Colonel Third Infantry, Commissary-General of Prisoners.

OFFICE COMMISSARY-GENERAL OF PRISONERS,
Washington, D. C., May 5, 1863.

Col. G. W. GALLUP,
Commanding District of Eastern Kentucky, Louisville, Ky.

COLONEL: Your letter of the 23d ultimo speaking of the release of certain prisoners on their taking the oath of allegiance and a prisoner's letter of the same date have been referred to this office. The order referred to in your letter requires a report in all cases where prisoners are released on taking the oath of allegiance, but it does not confer authority on any one to release on any terms prisoners who have been committed for disloyal acts. The War Department has placed control of all prisoners of war and all arrested for offenses connected with the rebellion in my hands, and prisoners who have been duly committed can only be released by authority of the Secretary of War. All prisoners should be reported to this office with the charges against them, and the place of detention and of arrest and authority therefor. Please report to me the prisoners in your charge and who is in immediate charge in order that a list may be made out giving particulars as to the charges, &c., and be furnished me immediately. I inclose herewith General Orders,* Nos. 32 and 72, of the War Department, which with current series, No. 9,† from the Department of the Ohio, covers matters connected with prisoners.

Very respectfully, your obedient servant,

W. HOFFMAN,
Colonel Third Infantry, Commissary-General of Prisoners.

OFFICE COMMISSARY-GENERAL OF PRISONERS,
Washington, D. C., May 5, 1863.

Maj. W. S. PIERSON,
Commanding Depot Prisoners of War, Sandusky, Ohio.

MAJOR: I have received your letter of the 1st instant and your two telegrams of the 4th instant. Below is a copy of a telegram dispatched to you this morning which answers your telegram:

WASHINGTON, D. C., *May 5, 1863.*

Maj. W. S. PIERSON,
Commanding Depot Prisoners of War, Sandusky, Ohio:

General Burnside is the proper officer to inquire of in relation to the execution. Permit according to usage only immediate relatives and ministers to have interviews with prisoners sentenced to death, always in the presence of an officer. Interviews can be granted only by the War Department and General Burnside.

W. HOFFMAN,
Colonel Third Infantry, Commissary-General of Prisoners.

It is not probable that either the War Department or General Burnside will give permits for interviews beyond this I have granted, but

---

*Omitted here; see Vol. III, p. 417, and Vol. IV, this Series, p. 94.   † See p. 259.

should they do so their order of course will be obeyed. As I have said in the telegram interviews must always be in presence of an officer and the time must be regulated by your discretion. The chaplain may have the assistance of any clergyman requested by the condemned, and you may allow the surgeon to have the aid of Doctor Donahoe and any other physician you may think advisable. If you can limit the permission to those as far as reported I have no objection to their admission to the island, but [with] the understanding that they are to have no interviews or conversations with any of the prisoners.

The two companies under Captain Scovill will be ordered back to the depot as soon as their services can be dispensed with at Wheeling. If you have not a supply of arms for pickets procure as many as you may require.

Very respectfully, your obedient servant,

W. HOFFMAN,
Colonel Third Infantry, Commissary-General of Prisoners

FORT MONROE, *May 5, 1863.*

Hon. E. M. STANTON, *Secretary of War:*

I have just returned from City Point and have brought with me all our officers who have been held by the Confederates and whom I send to Annapolis to-night. I have made the following declarations of exchanges:

1. All officers and enlisted men and all persons whatever may have been their classification or character who have been delivered at City Point, Va., up to the 6th of May, 1863.

2. All officers who have been captured and released on parole up to April 1, 1863, wherever they may have been captured.

3. All enlisted men who have been captured in North Carolina and Virginia and released on parole up to the 1st of March, 1863.

I will be in Washington on the 7th instant.

WM. H. LUDLOW,
Lieutenant-Colonel and Agent for Exchange of Prisoners.

(Same to General Hitchcock.)

WASHINGTON, D. C., *May 5, 1863.*

Major-General SCHENCK, *Commanding at Baltimore:*

No person who went South January 8 by flag of truce had any promise or intimation that he or she could return again, but it was expressly understood and stated that no such assurance or understanding could be entertained.

L. C. TURNER,
Judge-Advocate.

CIRCULAR.] HDQRS. THIRD DIV., SIXTEENTH ARMY CORPS,
Jackson, Tenn., May 5, 1863.

The general commanding intends to protect to the fullest extent of his power all citizens of this district in the enjoyment of life, liberty and the pursuit of happiness.

Knowing that this is the primary object of the Government he serves, and determined to devote all of his energies to the defeat of the enemies of the Government, he still can as a soldier feel a respect for the manliness of those openly in arms against it, and they will be treated and respected as true soldiers.

But robbers who under the name of guerrillas have taken advantage of the unsettled state of the country to steal horses, burn dwellings and insult women are in no respect soldiers and will not be treated as such.

He requires of all citizens that they remain at their homes and peaceably pursue their usual avocations; that they aid and assist the officers of the United States Government by giving information of the movements of the bands of robbers now infesting the country, and that they stand firm in their allegiance to the United States Government.

Persons who have been conscripted as guerrillas and are acting as such who will return to their homes and remain there as peaceable citizens will be treated as such and will be protected in person and property. Guerrillas who are captured will be summarily dealt with.

These requirements are made for the welfare of the people and will be enforced. The loyal shall be protected and sympathizers with the rebellion though they may have taken the oath of allegiance to the Government of the United States will be made to suffer unless they conform in word and act to the spirit of that oath.

By order of Brig. Gen. Nathan Kimball:

E. D. MASON,
Assistant Adjutant-General.

HEADQUARTERS MILITARY DISTRICT OF WASHINGTON,
Washington, D. C., May 6, 1863.

Colonel HOFFMAN, *Commissary-General of Prisoners.*

COLONEL: The number of prisoners is now swollen to more than 2,000 and I find it very difficult to dispose of them. When will you be able to relieve me of them?

Very respectfully, &c.,

J. H. MARTINDALE,
Brigadier-General and Military Governor.

OFFICE COMMISSARY-GENERAL OF PRISONERS,
Washington, D. C., May 6, 1863.

Brig. Gen. J. H. MARTINDALE,
Military Governor, Washington, D. C.

GENERAL: In reply to your note of this morning I have the honor to inform you 4,000 prisoners may be sent to Fort Delaware, and I have to request you will so dispose of any that you cannot immediately provide for in this city. Please retain the officers in the Old Capitol Prison until a more appropriate place can be found for them.

Very respectfully, your obedient servant,

W. HOFFMAN,
Colonel Third Infantry, Commissary-General of Prisoners.

P. S.—Please notify General Schoepf, commanding Fort Delaware, of the number that will be sent there.

W. H.

JUDGE-ADVOCATE-GENERAL'S OFFICE, *May 6, 1863.*

The SECRETARY OF WAR:

I am aware of no ground on which money can be confiscated because it is suspected or even known that it is the purpose of its owner or holder to invest it in goods designed for a contraband trade. The law punishes acts and not mere intentions, and for the obvious reason that such intentions may never be carried into execution or any attempt made to do so. A *locus penitentiæ* is allowed to all contemplating evil or illegal acts and up to their inception or consummation the probability of a change of purpose is recognized. The discovery of funds held under such circumstances of suspicion could stimulate the officers to increased vigilance in observing the subsequent conduct of the parties, but no other use can be made of the discovery. Could it be clearly shown that the money was the proceeds of goods sold in the course of a contraband trade the rule might be different. Notes or bonds of the so-called Confederate States cannot be recognized as possessed of any moneyed value. They should be treated as any other publications calculated to incite to a support or sympathy with the rebellion which may fall into the hands of the officers of the United States Government.

J. HOLT,
Judge-Advocate-General.

OFFICE COMMISSARY-GENERAL OF PRISONERS,
Washington, D. C., May 6, 1863.

Brig. Gen. J. H. MARTINDALE,
Military Governor, Washington.

GENERAL: Arrangements are being made by the quartermaster to provide transportation to Philadelphia and Fort Delaware for 3,000 prisoners of war to-morrow morning. It is possible that not more than 1,000 can be sent through at a time, but if the rolls can be prepared and the necessary transportation be obtained it is very desirable that all should leave to-morrow.

Very respectfully, your obedient servant,

W. HOFFMAN,
Colonel Third Infantry, Commissary-General of Prisoners.

OFFICE COMMISSARY-GENERAL OF PRISONERS,
Washington, D. C., May 6, 1863.

Brig. Gen. JOHN S. MASON, *Commanding, Columbus, Ohio.*

GENERAL: In reply to your letter of the 27th ultimo I have the honor to inform you that all soldiers and officers captured and paroled previously to the publication of General Orders, No. 49, of the 28th of February last are held bound by their parole though not delivered at City Point or Vicksburg and they cannot be ordered to do duty until exchanged. An order announcing the exchange of recent deliveries at City Point will be published in a few days.

Very respectfully, your obedient servant,

W. HOFFMAN,
Colonel Third Infantry, Commissary-General of Prisoners.

OFFICE COMMISSARY-GENERAL OF PRISONERS,
Washington, D. C., May 6, 1863.
Surgeon SIMPSON,
Medical Director Eighth Army Corps, Baltimore, Md.

SIR: By the accounts for expenditures for the hospital at Camp Parole made from the camp fund it appears that in the month of April stores of various kinds were purchased to the amount of $995, including among the articles twelve barrels of ale and one barrel of whisky. No account of a hospital fund has been made to me and I am therefore unable to say if there is such a fund or how much of it has been expended for the benefit of the sick. There are now 122 sick in hospital and it appears to me that the expenditures have been of the most extravagant character. But as this can only be determined by the examination of a medical officer I have the honor to request that you will immediately cause a minute inspection of the affairs of the hospital to be made and a report of the results forwarded to this office.

Very respectfully, your obedient servant,
W. HOFFMAN,
Colonel Third Infantry, Commissary-General of Prisoners.

OFFICE COMMISSARY-GENERAL OF PRISONERS,
Washington, D. C., May 6, 1863.
Lieut. Col. GEORGE SANGSTER,
Commanding Camp Parole, near Annapolis, Md.

COLONEL: I inclose herewith your draft on Captain Sullivan for $5,000 approved. Hereafter I desire that a full settlement be made at the end of each month, leaving no debts unpaid, and to effect this you will make timely estimates for funds, specifying as I have already directed for what purpose it is to be used. Your purchases for the hospital are very heavy. Have you a hospital fund; what is the amount of it, and what amount was expended in April for the benefit of the sick? The number of employés in the hospital seems to be unnecessarily large, and you will make no payment for extra services until you have reported the number employed and the number of sick, on which report you will wait my decision. Report also the number of team drivers. Pay the outstanding debts of April except the hospital rolls at once and send an account with vouchers, rolls of extra-duty men, &c. Your tri-monthly and monthly returns have too much ornamental labor on them which unnecessarily occupies the time of your clerks.

Very respectfully, your obedient servant,
W. HOFFMAN,
Colonel Third Infantry, Commissary-General of Prisoners.

OFFICE COMMISSARY-GENERAL OF PRISONERS,
Washington, D. C., May 6, 1863.
Maj. R. O. SELFRIDGE,
Asst. Adjt. Gen., Department of the Northwest, Milwaukee, Wis.

SIR: Your letter of the 30th ultimo making inquiries in relation to the exchange of certain volunteers from Wisconsin is received and in reply I have to inform you that I am unable to say whether the men referred to have been exchanged or not as no rolls of them have been furnished to this office, and until I received your letter I was not aware that there were any paroled troops in Wisconsin. By General Orders, No. 72, from the War Department of June last, paroled prisoners of war belonging to Wisconsin regiments were ordered to Benton Barracks, near Saint Louis, and that is where they should be to insure an exchange.

Very respectfully, your obedient servant,
W. HOFFMAN,
Colonel Third Infantry, Commissary-General of Prisoners.

OFFICE COMMISSARY-GENERAL OF PRISONERS,
Washington, D. C., May 6, 1863.

Capt. W. CURTIS, *Assistant Quartermaster, Washington, D. C.*

CAPTAIN: You will please furnish transportation for 3,000 prisoners of war with a guard of 500 to 800 men to Philadelphia as early to-morrow morning as practicable. They are to embark at Philadelphia on a steamer for Fort Delaware, and it is thought absolutely necessary that they should be delivered by the cars at the depot where they can be taken immediately on board the steamer. For the same reason it is very desirable that the prisoners should reach Philadelphia before dark to facilitate the transfer to the steamer. If a sufficient train cannot be furnished for the whole number at one trip two trains may be used. It may be that only 1,500 will be prepared to leave in the morning, of which you will be notified.

Very respectfully, your obedient servant,
W. HOFFMAN,
Colonel Third Infantry, Commissary-General of Prisoners.

HEADQUARTERS CAMP OF INSTRUCTION,
Benton Barracks, Mo., May 6, 1863.

Col. W. HOFFMAN,
Commissary-General of Prisoners, Washington, D. C.:

Your letter referring to the men captured on the Queen of the West is received. They arrived here on the 20th of April last in a very destitute condition and deeming it necessary both for their appearance and comfort that they should be provided with clothing I ordered clothing issued to them and directed that vouchers be made, one copy* of which I herewith transmit that you may have the amount to place against their pay account. Please inform me if I did right in ordering the issue.

I am, colonel, very respectfully, your obedient servant,
B. L. E. BONNEVILLE,
Colonel, U. S. Army, Commanding.

OFFICE ACTG. ASST. PROVOST-MARSHAL-GENERAL,
New York, May 6, 1863.

Col. W. HOFFMAN,
Commissary-General of Prisoners, Washington, D. C.

COLONEL: Your communication of yesterday is received. My letter had more particular reference to Confederate prisoners who have taken the oath of allegiance and wish to return to their homes within the Union lines, and also to laborers who have been employed on the railroads now in use by our forces who have been taken prisoners, paroled,

---

*Not found.

sent to New Orleans and from there sent to this city as the only way in which they can reach the West. I shall be pleased to receive your instructions how I am to be governed in such cases.

Very respectfully, your obedient servant,

ROBERT NUGENT,
Col. 69th N. Y. Vols., Act. Asst. Provost-Marshal-General.

HEADQUARTERS DEPARTMENT OF VIRGINIA,
Fort Monroe, May 6, 1863.

Col. W. HOFFMAN, *Commissary-General of Prisoners.*

COLONEL: I have just returned from City Point and have concluded the exchanges as announced in the inclosed declaration.* I intend to leave for Washington to-day or to-morrow and will call upon you on Friday morning, taking with me all the rolls and papers connected with the exchanges. I can then go more carefully and minutely into any necessary explanations. I have directed Captain Mulford, Third Regiment New York Volunteers, in charge of the steamer State of Maine, to report to you for prisoners of war after he shall have left at Annapolis all the officers and men whom he received at City Point yesterday. He will probably be able to report to you on Friday morning and can take on board 800 prisoners of war. All the officers held by the Confederates (with two or three exceptions) who have been released are declared exchanged and can be sent to their commands and regiments.

I am, very respectfully,

WM. H. LUDLOW,
Lieutenant-Colonel and Agent for Exchange of Prisoners.

WASHINGTON, D. C., *May 6, 1863.*

Brigadier-General MARTINDALE, *Military Governor.*

GENERAL: The General-in-Chief wishes you to notify General Schenck before sending Confederate prisoners of war into or through his department of the number you propose to send, their destination and time of their departure from Washington in order that he may make suitable arrangements to receive and forward them.

Very respectfully, your obedient servant,

J. C. KELTON,
Assistant Adjutant-General.

HEADQUARTERS DEPARTMENT OF THE MISSOURI,
Saint Louis, May 6, 1863.

Lieut. Col. A. V. COLBURN, *Assistant Adjutant-General.*

SIR: In obedience to instructions received from department headquarters I visited Gratiot Street Prison and have the honor to report as follows:

There are at this time 353 prisoners in confinement. The whole establishment is under the supervision of citizens. The principal, a Mr. Masterson, is designated captain and is paid $100 per month. He has as assistants a chief clerk who receives $70 per month, a commissary-sergeant, a pass clerk and two turnkeys at a salary each of $40 per month. The captain has no control over the guard about the prison.

* See Ludlow to Stanton, p. 559.

I found the police arrangements well conducted as well as the whole internal management. The culinary department is complete and cleanly. The hospital department could not be better arranged and conducted, the sick receiving every attention our own soldiers receive. The surgeons employed are one principal surgeon and two assistants, the latter two being contract physicians. I would respectfully suggest for the more complete comfort and convenience of the prisoners that a small outlay be made in setting wash kettles (the kettles being on hand) for a general wash-room.

I found the sentinels about the prison posted as follows: Two sentinels in the west flank of building in court-yard, one sentinel on west side of building, one at the strong room upstairs and one on the ambulatory upstairs, one at the south flank, three at the east flank and two at the north flank. I would suggest for the more perfect security of the prisoners that the sentinels be increased at least one at the north and one at the east, also that at least two sentinels be placed in the interior of the building who shall have no regular beat but whose duty shall be to constantly patrol the different parts of the building. I would further suggest that iron bars be placed over two windows of the west flank where Gilmer made his escape; also that the limb of a tree on the east side which comes near an upstairs window be sawed off as it affords an easy way of escape to any one desirous of making the attempt. My opinion is that with the outlay of $100 and due diligence of the sentinels the escape of prisoners may be effectually prevented. The escape of prisoners heretofore in part is owing to the insecurity of the building, but principally to the want of vigilance of the guard and officers commanding the same.

I would further recommend that the expenses of the prison be curtailed by detailing good, intelligent enlisted men to fill the places of all except the principal and that his place be filled by a competent commissioned officer who shall be permanently in command and to whom the officer of the guard shall report. This arrangement will save to the Government $370 per month.

Respectfully submitted.

T. I. McKENNY,
Major and Assistant Inspector-General.

SPECIAL ORDERS, } HDQRS. ADVANCE BRIG., U. S. FORCES,
Bayou Bœuf, Four and a half miles beyond
No. 41.   }   *Cheneyville, La., May 6, 1863.*

R. H. Glaze, formerly a sergeant of the Eighth Regiment Louisiana Volunteers, serving in Virginia and lately a private in Captain Murdock's independent company serving on the Bayou Bœuf, and now by his own admission being entirely disconnected with any regular military organization in the service of the so-called Confederate States of America, having been captured by our guard, he being mounted with his overcoat strapped upon his saddle, arms in his possession, to wit, a Kentucky rifle, evidently for the purpose of shooting down our soldiers, it is ordered by the brigadier-general commanding the advance that the said R. H. Glaze be shot to death at sunrise to-morrow morning, May 7, 1863, as a warning to all men not soldiers to remain peaceably at their homes if they desire the protection of the Government of the United States, and the fate of this man shall be the fate of every man found with arms in his hands not belonging to the so-called Army of the Confederate States of America.

Colonel Van Zandt, commanding the Ninety-first Regiment New York Volunteers, will detail one commissioned officer, one sergeant and five privates to carry this order into effect.*

By command of—

WILLIAM DWIGHT,
Brigadier-General, Commanding Advance Brigade U. S. Forces.

DAYTON, OHIO, *May 6, 1863.*

Major-General BURNSIDE.

GENERAL : Your order concerning the Daily [Dayton] Empire has been quietly enforced. I have arrested the editor, Logan, and confined him in the prison here with several other noted men. Shall I forward Logan in 4 o'clock train to Cincinnati ?

CHAS. G. HUTTON,
Captain and Aide-de-Camp.

DAYTON, OHIO, *May 6, 1863.*

Maj. Gen. JOHN G. PARKE, *Cincinnati, Ohio:*

Town quiet. I have closed all drinking shops and suggest that martial law be proclaimed. The mayor of Dayton and some dozen friends are absent in Cincinnati. The mayor and police of Dayton are all butternuts and are in favor of the riot; also the city marshal. Logan, of the Dayton Empire, is a very dangerous character ; has taken a prominent part in the disturbances here. His office is supposed to be a den for butternuts and I am having it searched. I have affidavits for proving him a prominent man in taking part in the riot of yesterday.

I find only 150 men here, troops fit for duty. I have seized and put in safety 200 muskets and a small swivel found in the Empire office.

There are several men in the town against whom I have written proof and who ought to be arrested.

I have forbidden all congregating in streets. Most of the rioters appear to come from the country. With decided measures I think order can be restored.

CHAS. G. HUTTON,
Captain and Aide-de-Camp.

POST-OFFICE DEPARTMENT, FINANCE OFFICE,
Washington, May 7, 1863.

P. H. WATSON, Esq., *Assistant Secretary of War.*

SIR: By letter from Major-General Dix of date 2d April last this Department was informed that no letters would be sent by flag of truce from Fort Monroe unless accompanied by a permit from the War Department. I now notice in the National Intelligencer what purports to be regulations in regard to letters to be sent beyond the Federal lines in which the "permission" above noted is not made a requisite. I have the honor to request that this Department may be advised of the rules established by the War Department relative to this class of letters.

Very respectfully, yours,

A. N. ZEVELY,
Third Assistant Postmaster-General.

---

* Order executed May 7, 1863.

CINCINNATI, *May 7, 1863.*

Maj. Gen. H. W. HALLECK, *General-in-Chief:*

On Tuesday morning last I caused the arrest of the Hon. C. L. Vallandigham. He is now in this city undergoing trial before a military commission for uttering sedition. Some trouble was caused in Dayton on account of his arrest but all is now quiet. I hope to maintain perfect order in other portions of this department. There is necessarily much excitement among his friends. We are all hoping to hear of the glorious and final success of General Hooker.

A. E. BURNSIDE,
Major-General.

OFFICE COMMISSARY-GENERAL OF PRISONERS,
Washington, D. C., May 7, 1863.

Brig. Gen. J. H. MARTINDALE,
Comdg. Military District of Washington, Washington, D. C.

GENERAL: By direction of the General-in-Chief I have to request that the prisoners of war paroled to go North, prisoners who have taken the oath of allegiance and deserters from the rebel army recently received at the Old Capitol Prison from the Army of the Potomac, whose names are mentioned in the accompanying rolls,* may be sent to Philadelphia to report to the commanding officer and there to be released. Those who have not already done so to take the oath of allegiance.

Very respectfully, your obedient servant,

W. HOFFMAN,
Colonel Third Infantry, Commissary-General of Prisoners.

ANNAPOLIS, *May 7, 1863.*

Col. WILLIAM HOFFMAN:

There are 200 army officers and Generals Willich and [E. H.] Stoughton arrived here this morning. All exchanged. Also thirty-two naval officers exchanged. Naval officers I will send to navy-yard at Washington this p. m. Shall I order army officers away, as I have no quarters for them here? The men who arrived are all cared for. Particulars will send by mail. Answer.

GEO. SANGSTER,
Commanding Paroled Prisoners.

HEADQUARTERS MILITARY COMMANDER,
Wheeling, May 7, 1863.

Hon. F. H. PEIRPOINT, *Governor of Virginia.*

SIR: The females enumerated below, now residents of this city and acknowledging themselves secessionists, were indicted in September, 1861, for treason and perjury: Dora Dunbar, Julia Dunbar, Elizabeth Phillips, Eliza C. Hughes, Amanda Goshorn, Belle Goshorn, Hannah Smith, Joanna Smith. For some unexplained reason these females have never been tried, but their cases have been postponed at every session of the U. S. district court since their indictment although I have been informed that the charge could be easily substantiated. I consider them fit subjects to be sent beyond our lines and so recommend, as the court will take no action.

---

* Omitted.

I will forward with your indorsements to the major-general commanding this department a copy of the indictment in one [case] which is similar to the rest.

Very respectfully, your obedient servant,

JOSEPH DARR, JR.,
Major and Provost-Marshal-General.

MURFREESBOROUGH, *May 8, 1863.*

Colonel HOFFMAN:

Please inform me if all the prisoners captured at Stone's River have been exchanged. It is reported that about 200 of the Thirty-ninth Indiana are at Indianapolis. Is it so? We want them here.

W. S. ROSECRANS.

HDQRS. SECOND ARMY CORPS, ARMY OF THE POTOMAC,
May 8, 1863.

Hon. E. M. STANTON:

General Hays is a prisoner.

D. N. COUCH,
Major-General.

OFFICE PROVOST-MARSHAL-GENERAL, *May 8, 1863.*

Brig. Gen. S. WILLIAMS, *Assistant Adjutant-General, &c.*

GENERAL: I beg leave through you to call the attention of the commanding general to the state prisoners now in my custody on board the prison ship. There are about sixty now there, not more than five or six having any charges made against them and probably not more than one or two against whom any charge can be substantiated. It is now time for making the crop, which alone will secure them from starvation. I have presented the cases of some of these men more than once and they have been examined several times by Captain Chester, judge-advocate, and by my own officers with reference to trial, but a case cannot be made out against more than two or three of them.

I respectfully request that authority may be given me to dispose of these cases according to my own judgment, believing that great injury is done to our cause as well as to the parties themselves by holding them longer in confinement. A list* is herewith inclosed of April 30, 1863.

Very respectfully, your obedient servant,

M. R. PATRICK,
Provost-Marshal-General.

OFFICE COMMISSARY-GENERAL OF PRISONERS,
Washington, D. C., May 8, 1863.

Maj. Gen. S. R. CURTIS,
Commanding Department of the Missouri, Saint Louis, Mo.

GENERAL: The following is a copy of a declaration of exchanges made by Lieutenant-Colonel Ludlow, agent for exchange of prisoners:

FORT MONROE, *May 6, 1863.*

The following officers and men have been declared duly exchanged as prisoners of war since the announcement in General Orders, No. 10, of January 10, 1863:

1. All officers and enlisted men and all persons whatever may have been their classification or character who have been delivered at City Point, Va., up to the 6th of May, 1863.

---

* Not found.

2. All officers who have been captured and released on parole up to April 1, 1863, wherever they may have been captured.

3. All enlisted men who have been captured in North Carolina and Virginia and released on parole up to the 1st of March, 1863.

WM. H. LUDLOW,
Lieutenant-Colonel and Agent for Exchange of Prisoners.

Yesterday I telegraphed to you the substance of the above with the request, by authority of the General-in-Chief, that all exchanged prisoners in your department might be ordered to join their respective commands. At the same time I directed all exchanged officers at Annapolis belonging to Western regiments serving west of the Mississippi to report to you to take charge of exchanged men now in your department and conduct them to their regiments, or to be ordered themselves to join directly as you might judge proper.

Very respectfully, your obedient servant,
W. HOFFMAN,
Colonel Third Infantry, Commissary-General of Prisoners.

(Same to Major-General Burnside, Cincinnati, Ohio, and Major-General Rosecrans, Murfreesborough, Tenn.)

OFFICE COMMISSARY-GENERAL OF PRISONERS,
Washington, D. C., May 8, 1863.
Brig. Gen. J. H. MARTINDALE,
Comdg. Military District of Washington, Washington, D. C.

GENERAL: The steamer State of Maine is expected here to-day to take on board prisoners of war for delivery at City Point and I have the honor to request that you will direct that 800 or 900 be prepared to embark on Sunday morning, the 10th instant. No officers will be forwarded at this time. I have also to request that all citizens confined at the Old Capitol for disloyal conduct who are proper subjects for exchange may be forwarded at the same time with the prisoners of war, the whole number not to exceed 850. I presume there will be more than fifty citizens. Please have Alfred Simmonds included among those to be delivered. The prisoner recommended for exchange by Richard Wallach (John Goldsmith I believe) will not be delivered at this time. If the female prisoners ordered from Camp Chase and Wheeling to this city have arrived please send them to City Point for delivery.

Very respectfully, your obedient servant,
W. HOFFMAN,
Colonel Third Infantry, Commissary-General of Prisoners.

MILITARY PRISON, *Alton, Ill., May 8, 1863.*
Col. WILLIAM HOFFMAN,
Commissary-General of Prisoners, Washington, D. C.

COLONEL: In compliance with your instructions received some days since I have the honor to forward herewith an estimate* of the probable cost of repairs required upon the buildings of the prison. The roof of the hospital building as it is at present being of some kind of composition material and being also very flat, having scarcely any pitch, it is thought cannot be repaired so as to prevent its leaking more

---

* Omitted. Total proposed expenditure, $2,000, approved by Colonel Hoffman.

or less in wet weather. It has therefore been thought best in order to have a good tight roof upon this building to make an entirely new roof over the old one like that proposed in the estimate. A building for a guard-house is much needed for the accommodation of the prison guard. This guard consists, including officers and non-commissioned officers, of fifty-six men, and to accommodate these but one small building about sixteen feet square is all we have for the purpose. The other items in the estimate are for necessary repairs only.

I have the honor to be, sir, with much respect, your most obedient servant,

T. HENDRICKSON,
Major Third Infantry, Commandant of Prison.

TUSCUMBIA, ALA., *May 8, 1863.*

General DODGE, *Corinth, Miss.*

DEAR SIR: I am authorized by Colonel Roddey, commanding, to parole the sick and wounded with their nurses left at this place, and as you have as prisoners some of our men at Corinth I hope some arrangement can be made for an exchange at this point. Lieut. Jas. Clark and Nathan Boddey are of that number. Will you be kind enough to let me hear from you on this subject at your earliest convenience?

Yours, &c.,

JOS. H. SLOSS,
Captain, C. S. Army.

GENERAL ORDERS,   HDQRS. DEPARTMENT OF THE OHIO,
No. 61.   *Cincinnati, Ohio, May 8, 1863.*

I. All residents of the State of Kentucky banished from their homes by any authority whatsoever not higher than that of the department commander by reporting to these headquarters on Saturday, May 9, at 12 m. or as soon thereafter as practicable can obtain a hearing of their cases and all against whom definite charges supported by sufficient proof to warrant a trial do not appear will be allowed to return to their homes upon taking the oath of allegiance to the Government of the United States.

II. The general order prohibiting the sale of fire-arms and ammunition in this department is hereby rescinded, but all persons guilty of selling arms or ammunition to disloyal persons or with a knowledge that they are to go into the hands of disloyal persons will be arrested and tried for giving aid and comfort to the enemy.

By command of Major-General Burnside:

LEWIS RICHMOND,
Assistant Adjutant-General.

HEADQUARTERS ARMY OF THE POTOMAC, *May 9, 1863.*

Maj. Gen. H. W. HALLECK, *General-in-Chief:*

General Hays is supposed to be on his way to Richmond wounded and a prisoner. Mrs. Hays' most direct way would be by way of City Point.

JOSEPH HOOKER,
Major-General.

WASHINGTON, *May 9, 1863.*

Major-General DIX:

In the late battle at Chancellorsville Brig. Gen. William Hays was severely wounded, fell into the hands of the enemy and is now at Richmond. His wife desires to join him in Richmond, or at City Point if his parole and release can be had. You will please communicate with the Richmond authorities and if possible procure his immediate release on parole and ascertain whether Mrs. Hays can be permitted to join him. She will leave here for Fort Monroe to-morrow.

EDWIN M. STANTON,
Secretary of War.

WASHINGTON, *May 9, 1863.*

Colonel LUDLOW:

Does the late exchange of paroled prisoners include the enlisted men of the Mercedita, Hatteras and other vessels who have not been delivered up at City Point nor captured on the coast of North Carolina and Virginia?

G. V. FOX,
Assistant Secretary of the Navy.

WINCHESTER, VA., *May 9, 1863.*

Col. JAMES B. FRY, *Provost-Marshal-General:*

I have very strong circumstantial evidence that Major Dixon, a paymaster in the U. S. Army, is a traitor and that his wife and daughter are paid spies in high favor with the highest rebel authorities at Richmond. His daughter is the wife of a major in the rebel army by the name of Saunders. She holds a commission in the rebel Treasury Department at Richmond for signing notes, and received a short time ago $500 in gold from Fitzhugh Lee to buy medicines in Washington, and gets passes through her father. She is probably now in Washington. Look sharp after this tribe.

R. H. MILROY,
Major-General.

HEADQUARTERS, *Jackson, Tenn., May 9, 1863.*

Brigadier-General DODGE.

SIR: I am directed by the general commanding to transmit to you the following communication:

HEADQUARTERS SIXTEENTH ARMY CORPS,
Memphis, Tenn., May 8, 1863..

Major-General OGLESBY:

The commanding general has considered the indorsement by you made the 6th instant on communication of Col. P. E. Burke and directs me to say that guerrillas and men acting without recognized authority if taken at all will not be dealt with as prisoners of war, but will be dealt with as robbers and murderers as the case may be.

H. BINMORE,
Assistant Adjutant-General.

You will comply with the above directions in dealing with the class of persons mentioned in the above communication.

By order of Maj. Gen. R. J. Oglesby:

S. WAIT,
Assistant Adjutant-General.

ANNAPOLIS, MD., *May 9, 1863.*

Col. W. HOFFMAN, *Commissary-General of Prisoners:*

I have received your telegram of to-day. I fear that when we have hot weather 3,000 prisoners will be too many for the buildings intended for their use. I think it better to not send more than 2,000 at first, unless there are no barracks for them elsewhere.

C. A. WAITE,
Colonel, Commanding.

OFFICE COMMISSARY-GENERAL OF PRISONERS,
Washington, D. C., May 9, 1863.

Brig. Gen. W. A. HAMMOND,
Surgeon-General U. S. Army, Washington.

GENERAL: I would respectfully inquire if there is a general hospital at Saint Louis to which paroled prisoners could be sent from Annapolis occasionally. There is an application by the parents of some sick at Annapolis for permission to take them home, and would like to know to what hospital they could report if they do not recover by the expiration of their leave.

Very respectfully, your obedient servant,

W. HOFFMAN,
Colonel Third Infantry, Commissary-General of Prisoners.

BALTIMORE, *May 9, 1863.*

Col. W. HOFFMAN, *Commissary-General of Prisoners:*

I am here with 133 exchanged officers. We are all entirely destitute and suffering for decent clothing. We ask that we may stop over here and be paid. We have no means even to procure subsistence on the route. Can I visit Washington this afternoon?

H. C. GILBERT,
Colonel Nineteenth Michigan Regiment.

OFFICE COMMISSARY-GENERAL OF PRISONERS,
Washington, D. C., May 9, 1863.

Col. T. P. ANDREWS,
Paymaster-General U. S. Army, Washington, D. C.

COLONEL: Colonel Gilbert, Nineteenth Michigan Volunteers, with 50 to 100 officers belonging to Western regiments who have just been exchanged and who are now in Baltimore en route to join their regiments are authorized by the General-in-Chief to delay until they can be paid, and I have respectfully to request that you will give the necessary instructions to the paymaster in that city to make the payment.

Very respectfully, your obedient servant,

W. HOFFMAN,
Colonel Third Infantry, Commissary-General of Prisoners.

OFFICE COMMISSARY-GENERAL OF PRISONERS,
Washington, D. C., May 9, 1863.

Lieut. Col. W. H. LUDLOW,
Agent for Exchange of Prisoners, Fort Monroe, Va.

COLONEL: I will send you on the State of Maine to-morrow about 800 enlisted men, prisoners of war, and some fifty citizen prisoners.

It has been impossible to arrange the rolls in any order whatever, they having been sent up from the Army of the Potomac in a very confused condition without alphabetical or regimental arrangement. Among the citizens are eight or ten females, two or three of whom are pretty hard cases, and they will be a happy riddance to us on any terms. There are nearly 200 more citizen prisoners at the Old Capitol and I will be glad to send them down to you as soon as you can conveniently dispose of them. As they have few or no more of this class to exchange can't you count them as irregular?

Very respectfully, your obedient servant,

W. HOFFMAN,
Colonel Third Infantry, Commissary-General of Prisoners

OFFICE COMMISSARY-GENERAL OF PRISONERS,
Washington, D. C., May 9, 1863.

Maj. T. HENDRICKSON,
Third U. S. Infantry, Comdg. Military Prison, Alton, Ill.

MAJOR: By direction of the commissary-general of prisoners I beg leave to call your attention to certain differences existing between your return and the rolls for the month of April. Your return shows non-commissioned officers and privates joined, 590; citizens, 80; non-commissioned officers and privates transferred, 320; citizens, none; soldiers released, none. The rolls show non-commissioned officers and privates joined, 570; citizens, 99; non-commissioned officers and privates transferred, 316; citizens, 4; soldiers released, 7.

Very respectfully, your obedient servant,

W. T. HARTZ,
Captain and Assistant Adjutant-General.

Habeas corpus proceedings in case of Clement L. Vallandigham.

The United States of America, on the relation of Clement L. Vallandigham *v.* Ambrose E. Burnside, major-general in the Army of the United States, commanding, &c.

On Saturday, May 9, 1863, in the circuit court of the United States for the Southern District of Ohio, Judge Leavitt presiding, the Hon. George E. Pugh made an application on behalf of Hon. Clement L. Vallandigham for the allowance of a writ of *habeas corpus* to be directed to Maj. Gen. Ambrose E. Burnside, commanding the Department of the Ohio, which application was as follows:

UNITED STATES OF AMERICA,
Southern District of Ohio, to wit:

To the honorable the Judges of the Circuit Court of the United States within and for the district aforesaid:

Your petitioner, Clement L. Vallandigham, says that he is a native-born citizen of the State of Ohio, residing in Montgomery County, and not enlisted or commissioned in the land or the naval forces of the United States, nor called into actual service as one of the militia of any State. Nevertheless on the 5th day of May instant, between 2 and 3 o'clock in the morning of said day, his dwelling-house (in which he and his family then were) in the city of Dayton and county of Montgomery aforesaid was surrounded by about 100 soldiers, armed and in uniform as such and acting under the direction of Ambrose E. Burnside, a major general in the Army of the United States, which soldiers then and there violently broke the outer door and two inner doors of your petitioner's said house and entered the same, and then and there seized your petitioner by overpowering numbers and thence carried him to the city of Cincinnati, in Hamilton County, in the State and southern district of Ohio, where they imprisoned him against his will in a building on Second or Columbia street, then used as a military prison. And your petitioner says that he has ever since been and now is detained in said city of Cincinnati under a military guard of which said Ambrose E. Burnside is commander.

Your petitioner alleges that he was thus violently seized in his own house in the nighttime without any warrant issued upon probable cause supported by oath or affirmation and in contempt of his rights as an American citizen. He says also that since his imprisonment as aforesaid a paper has been delivered to him (of which a true copy is herewith annexed)* purporting to contain a charge and a specification against him, signed by J. M. Cutts, captain and judge-advocate, on which charge and specification he has been arraigned against his will before a number of officers of the Army of the United States assembled in a room of the Saint Charles Exchange, on East Third street, in the city of Cincinnati, styling themselves a military commission and assuming to exercise judicial authority at the instigation of said Ambrose E. Burnside as major-general aforesaid. But your petitioner denies that he is subject to any such mode of arraignment or of trial and claims that all proceedings of that description are in his case forbidden by the Constitution and laws of the United States.

Therefore and to the end that he may be relieved from manifest oppression under color of military authority and that he may be charged in due course of law in this court or some other with whatsoever crime is intended to be imputed by the charge and specification above mentioned your petitioner moves your honors to grant him a writ of *habeas corpus* directed to said Ambrose E. Burnside and all persons assuming to act in obedience to his orders commanding him and them forthwith to bring the body of your petitioner before this court, together with the cause (if any) of his caption and detention. And your petitioner submits hereby to whatsoever the Constitution of the United States in this behalf may require.

C. L. VALLANDIGHAM.
By G. E. PUGH,
His Attorney.

SOUTHERN DISTRICT OF OHIO, *to wit:*

George E. Pugh being duly sworn says that he makes this application for a writ of *habeas corpus* at the request of Clement L. Vallandigham, the petitioner above named, and that he believes the matters alleged in the foregoing petition to be true.

G. E. PUGH.

Sworn to before me and subscribed in my presence this 9th day of May, A. D. 1863.

JOSEPH H. GEIGER,
Clerk Circuit Court United States, Southern District of Ohio.

CINCINNATI, OHIO, *May 11, 1863.*

The application on my behalf, on May 9, 1863, to the circuit court of the United States for a writ of *habeas corpus* to release me from illegal military custody was made by Hon. George E. Pugh at my express instance and request.

C. L. VALLANDIGHAM.

The court inquired if there was any one present representing the United States in this behalf, whereupon Flamen Ball, esq., district attorney of the United States, said that as he was the attorney of the United States in their legitimate legal business in this district he felt called upon to answer the inquiry of the court by saying he had no express authority to appear either for Major-General Burnside or the War Department; that he considered it would be indelicate in him to volunteer to act and he felt sure if he should do so all his acts might justly be held to be void. He declined appearing, but as *amicus curiæ* suggested that in accordance with the practice of the court notice should be given to General Burnside that there might be a hearing on the application.

Mr. Pugh objected and insisted on the prompt issue of the writ and that the hearing could be had when the body of the prisoner should be brought into court.

---

* Omitted here; see p. 634.

The court took the matter under advisement and in the afternoon decided to hear the argument on the application and directed the clerk to notify Major-General Burnside that the hearing would be had on Monday, May 11.

On the opening of the court, May 11, Hon. Aaron F. Perry and District Attorney Ball appeared for General Burnside and Hon. George E. Pugh appeared for Mr. Vallandigham.

The district attorney presented to the court the following:

HEADQUARTERS DEPARTMENT OF THE OHIO,
Cincinnati, Ohio, May 11, 1863.

To the honorable the Circuit Court of the United States within and for the Southern District of Ohio :

The undersigned, commanding the Department of the Ohio, having received notice from the clerk of said court that an application for the allowance of a writ of *habeas corpus* will be made this morning before your honors on behalf of Clement L. Vallandigham, now a prisoner in my custody, asks leave to submit to the court the following statement:

If I were to indulge in wholesale criticisms of the policy of the Government it would demoralize the army under my command and every friend of his country would call me a traitor. If the officers or soldiers were to indulge in such criticisms it would weaken the army to the extent of their influence, and if this criticism were universal in the army it would cause it to be broken to pieces, the Government to be divided, our homes to be invaded and anarchy to reign. My duty to my Government forbids me to indulge in such criticisms; officers and soldiers are not allowed so to indulge, and this course will be sustained by all honest men.

Now I will go further. We are in a state of civil war. One of the States of this department is at this moment invaded and three others have been threatened. I command the department and it is my duty to my country and to this army to keep it in the best possible condition; to see that it is fed, clad, armed and as far as possible to see that it is encouraged. If it is my duty and the duty of the troops to avoid saying anything that would weaken the army by preventing a single recruit from joining the ranks, by bringing the laws of Congress into disrepute or by causing dissatisfaction in the ranks it is equally the duty of every citizen in the department to avoid the same evil. If it is my duty to prevent the propagation of this evil in the army or in a portion of my department it is equally my duty in all portions of it, and it is my duty to use all the force in my power to stop it.

If I were to find a man from the enemy's country distributing in my camps speeches of their public men that tended to demoralize the troops or to destroy their confidence in the constituted authorities of the Government I would have him tried and hung if found guilty, and all the rules of modern warfare would sustain me. Why should such speeches from our own public men be allowed?

The press and public men in a great emergency like the present should avoid the use of party epithets and bitter invectives and discourage the organization of secret political societies which are always undignified and disgraceful to a free people, but now they are absolutely wrong and injurious; they create dissensions and discord which just now amount to treason. The simple names "patriot" and "traitor" are comprehensive enough.

As I before said we are in a state of civil war and an emergency is upon us which requires the operations of some power that moves more quickly than the civil.

There never was a war carried on successfully without the exercise of that power.

It is said that the speeches which are condemned have been made in the presence of large bodies of citizens who if they thought them wrong would have then and there condemned them. That is no argument. These citizens do not realize the effect upon the Army of our country who are its defenders. They have never been in the field, never faced the enemies of their country, never undergone the privations of our soldiers in the field and besides they have been in the habit of hearing their public men speak and as a general thing of approving of what they say; therefore the greater responsibility rests upon the public men and upon the public press, and it behooves them to be careful as to what they say. They must not use license and plead that they are exercising liberty. In this department it cannot be done. I shall use all the power I have to break down such license and I am sure I will be sustained in this course by all honest men. At all events I will have the consciousness before God of having done my duty to my country, and when I am swerved from the performance of that duty by any pressure, public or private, or by any prejudice I will no longer be a man or a patriot.

I again assert that every power I possess on earth or that is given me from above will be used in defense of my Government on all occasions, at all times and in all places within this department.   There is no party, no community, no State government, no State legislative body, no corporation or body of men that have the power to inaugurate a war policy that has the validity of law and power but the constituted authorities of the Government of the United States and I am determined to support their policy.   If the people do not approve that policy they can change the constitutional authorities of that Government at the proper time and by the proper method. Let them freely discuss the policy in a proper tone, but my duty requires me to stop license and intemperate discussion, which tends to weaken the authority of the Government and Army.   Whilst the latter is in the presence of the enemy it is cowardly so to weaken it.   This license could not be used in our camps; the man would be torn in pieces who would attempt it.   There is no fear of the people losing their liberties. We all know that to be the cry of demagogues and none but the ignorant will listen to it.   All intelligent men know that our people are too far advanced in the scale of religion, civilization, education and freedom to allow any power on earth to interfere with their liberties; but this same advancement in these great characteristics of our people teaches them to make all necessary sacrifices for their country when an emergency requires.   They will support the constituted authorities of the Government whether they agree with them or not.   Indeed the Army itself is a part of the people, and is so thoroughly educated in the love of civil liberty which is the best guaranty for the permanence of our republican institutions that it would itself be the first to oppose any attempt to continue the exercise of military authority after the establishment of peace by the overthrow of the rebellion.   No man on earth can lead our citizen soldiery to the establishment of a military despotism and no man living would have the folly to attempt it.   To do so would be to seal his own doom.   On this point there can be no ground for apprehension on the part of the people.

It is said that we can have peace if we lay down our arms.   All sensible men know this to be untrue.   Were it so ought we to be so cowardly as to lay them down until the authority of the Government is acknowledged?

I beg to call upon the fathers, mothers, brothers, sisters, sons, daughters, relatives, friends and neighbors of the soldiers in the field to aid me in stopping this license and intemperate discussion which is discouraging our armies, weakening the hands of the Government and thereby strengthening the enemy.   If we use our honest efforts God will bless us with a glorious peace and a united country.   Men of every shade of opinion have the same vital interest in the suppression of this rebellion, for should we fail in the task the dread horrors of a ruined and distracted nation will fall alike on all whether patriots or traitors.

These are substantially my reasons for issuing General Orders, No. 38, my reasons for the determination to enforce it and also my reasons for the arrest of Hon. C. L. Vallandigham for a supposed violation of that order for which he has been tried. The result of that trial is now in my hands.

In enforcing this order I can be unanimously sustained by the people or I can be opposed by factious, bad men.   In the former event quietness will prevail; in the latter event the responsibility and retribution will attach to the men who resist the authority and the neighborhoods that allow it.

All of which is respectfully submitted.

A. E. BURNSIDE,
Major-General, Commanding Department of the Ohio.

EX PARTE C. L. VALLANDIGHAM—HABEAS CORPUS.

LEAVITT, J., delivered the following opinion:

This case is before the court on the petition of Clement L. Vallandigham, a citizen of Ohio, alleging that he was unlawfully arrested at his home in Dayton, in this State, on the night of the 5th of May instant, by a detachment of soldiers of the Army of the United States acting under the orders of Ambrose E. Burnside, a major-general in the Army of the United States, and brought against his will to the city of Cincinnati where he has been subjected to a trial before a military commission and is still detained in custody and restrained of his liberty.   The petitioner also avers that he is not in the land or naval service of the United States and has not been called into active service in the militia of any State, and that his arrest, detention and trial as set forth in his petition are illegal and in violation of the Constitution of the United States.   The prayer is that a writ of *habeas corpus* may issue requiring General Burnside to produce the body of the petitioner before this court with the cause of his caption and detention. Accompanying the petition is a statement of the charges and specifications on which he alleges he was tried before the Military Commission. For the purposes of this decision it is not necessary to notice these charges specially, but it may be stated in brief that they impute to the prisoner the utterance of sundry disloyal opinions and statements in a public speech at the town of Mount Vernon, in the State of Ohio, on the 1st of May instant, with the knowledge "that they did aid and comfort and encourage those in arms against the Government and could but induce in his hearers a distrust in their own Government and sympathy for those in arms against it and a disposition to resist the laws of the land." The petitioner does not state what the judgment of the Military Commission is, nor is the court informed whether he has been condemned or acquitted on the charges exhibited against him.

It is proper to remark here that on the presentation of the petition the court stated to the counsel for Mr. Vallandigham that according to the usages of the court as well as of other courts of high authority the writ was not grantable of course and would only be allowed on a sufficient showing that it ought to issue. The court is entirely satisfied of the correctness of the course thus indicated. The subject was fully examined by the learned Justice Swayne when present, the presiding judge of this court, on a petition for *habeas corpus* presented at the last October term; a case to which further reference will be made. I shall now only note the authorities on this point which seem to be entirely conclusive.

In the case *Ex parte* Watkins (3 Peters, 193), which was an application to the Supreme Court for a writ of *habeas corpus*, Chief Justice Marshall entertained no doubt as to the power of the court to issue the writ and stated that the only question was whether it was a case in which the power ought to be exercised. He says in reference to that case "the cause of imprisonment is shown as fully by the petitioner as could appear on the return of the writ; consequently the writ ought not to be awarded if the court is satisfied the prisoner would be remanded to prison." The same principle is clearly and ably stated by Chief-Justice Shaw in the case *Ex parte* Sims, before the Supreme Court of Massachusetts. (7 Cushing's Rep., 285.) See also Hurd on *habeas corpus*, 223 *et seq.*

I have no doubt of the power of this court to issue the writ applied for. It is clearly conferred by the fourteenth section of the judiciary act of 1789; but the ruling of this court in the case just referred to and the authorities just cited justify the refusal of the writ if satisfied the petitioner would not be discharged upon a hearing after its return. The court therefore directed General Burnside to be notified of the pendency of the petition to the end that he might appear by counsel or otherwise to oppose the granting of the writ.

That distinguished general has accordingly presented a respectful communication to the court stating generally and argumentatively the reasons of the arrest of Mr. Vallandigham, and has also authorized able counsel to represent him in resistance of the application for the writ. And the case has been argued at great length and with great ability on the motion for its allowance.

It is proper to remark further that when the petition was presented the court made a distinct reference to the decision of this court in the case of Bethuel Rupert at October term, 1862, before noticed, as an authoritative precedent for its action on this application. On full reflection I do not see how it is possible for me sitting alone in the circuit court to ignore the decision made upon full consideration by Justice Swayne, with the concurrence of myself, and which as referable to all cases involving the same principle must be regarded as the law of this court until reversed by a higher court. The case of Rupert was substantially the same as that of the present petition. He set out in his petition what he alleged to be an unlawful arrest by the order of a military officer on a charge imputing to him acts of disloyalty to the Government and sympathy with the rebellion against it, and an unlawful detention and imprisonment as the result of such order. The application, however, in the case of Rupert differed from the one now before the court in this that affidavits were exhibited tending to disprove the charge of disloyal conduct imputed to him; and also in this that there was no pretense or showing by Rupert that there had been any investigation or trial by any court of the charges against him.

The petition in this case is addressed to the judges of the circuit court and not to a single judge of that court. It occurs from the absence of Mr. Justice Swayne that the district judge is now holding the circuit court as he is authorized to do by law. But thus sitting would it not be in violation of all settled rules of judicial practice as well as of courtesy for the district judge to reverse a decision of the circuit court made when both judges were on the bench? It is well known that the district judge though authorized to sit with the circuit judge in the circuit court does not occupy the same official position and that the latter judge when present is *ex officio* the presiding judge. It is obvious that confusion and uncertainty which would greatly impair the respect due to the adjudications of the circuit courts of the United States would result from the assumption of such an exercise of power by the district judge. It would not only be disrespectful to the superior judge but would evince in the district judge an utter want of appreciation of his true official connection with the circuit court.

Now in passing upon the application of Rupert Mr. Justice Swayne in an opinion of some length though not written distinctly held that this court would not grant the writ of *habeas corpus* when it appeared that the detention or imprisonment was under military authority. It is true that Rupert was a man in humble position unknown beyond the narrow circle in which he moved, while the present petitioner has a wide-spread fame as a prominent politician and statesman. But no one will insist that there should be any difference in the principles applicable to the two cases. If any distinction were allowable it would be against him of admitted intelligence and distinguished talents.

I might with entire confidence place the grounds of action I propose in the present case upon the decision of the learned judge in that just referred to. Even if I entertained doubts of the soundness of his views I see no principle upon which I could be justified in treating the decision as void of authority. But the counsel of Mr. Vallandigham was not restricted in the argument of this motion to this point but was allowed the widest latitude in the discussion of the principles involved. It seemed due to him that the court should hear what could be urged against the legality of the arrest and in favor of the interposition of the court in behalf of the petitioner. And I have been greatly interested in the forcible argument which has been submitted though unable to concur with the speaker in all his conclusions.

If it were my desire to do so I have not now the physical strength to notice or discuss at length the grounds on which the learned counsel has attempted to prove the illegality of General Burnside's order for the arrest of Mr. Vallandigham and the duty of the court to grant the writ applied for. The basis of the whole argument rests on the assumption that Mr. Vallandigham not being in the military or naval service of the Government, and not therefore subject to the Rules and Articles of War, was not liable to arrest under or by military power. And the various provisions of the Constitution intended to guard the citizen against unlawful arrests and imprisonments have been cited and urged upon the attention of the court as having a direct bearing on the point. It is hardly necessary to quote these excellent guaranties of the rights and liberties of an American citizen as they are familiar to every reader of the Constitution. And it may be conceded that if by a just construction of the constitutional powers of the Government in the solemn emergency now existing they are applicable to and must control the question of the legality of the arrest of the petitioner it cannot be sustained for the obvious reason that no warrant was issued "upon probable cause supported by oath or affirmation," as is required in ordinary arrests for alleged crimes. But are there not other considerations of a controlling character applicable to the question? Is not the court imperatively bound to regard the present state of the country and in the light which it throws upon the subject to decide upon the expediency of interfering with the exercise of the military power as invoked in the pending application? The court cannot shut its eyes to the grave fact that war exists, involving the most imminent public danger and threatening the subversion and destruction of the Constitution itself. In my judgment when the life of the Republic is imperiled he mistakes his duty and obligation as a patriot who is not willing to concede to the Constitution such a capacity of adaptation to circumstances as may be necessary to meet a great emergency and save the nation from hopeless ruin. Self-preservation is a paramount law which a nation as well as an individual may find it necessary to invoke. Nothing is hazarded in saying that the great and far-seeing men who framed the Constitution of the United States supposed they were laying the foundation of our National Government on an immovable basis. They did not contemplate the existence of the state of things with which the nation is now unhappily confronted, the heavy pressure of which is felt by every true patriot. They did not recognize the right of secession by one State, or any number of States, for the obvious reason that it would have been in direct conflict with the purpose in view in the adoption of the Constitution, and an incorporation of an element in the frame of the Government which would inevitably result in its destruction. In their glowing visions of futurity there was no foreshadowing of a period when the people of a large geographical section would be guilty of the madness and the crime of arraying themselves in rebellion against a government under whose mild and benignant sway there was so much of hope and promise for the coming ages. We need not be surprised, therefore, that in the organic law which they gave us they made no specific provision for such a lamentable occurrence. They did, however, distinctly contemplate the possibility of foreign war and vested in Congress the power to declare its existence and "to raise and support armies" and "provide and maintain a navy." They also made provision for the suppression of insurrection and rebellion. They were aware that the grant of these powers implied all other powers necessary to give them full effect. They also declared that the President of the United States "shall be Commander-in-Chief of the Army and Navy and of the militia of the several States when called into actual service," and they placed upon him the

solemn obligation " to take care that the laws be faithfully executed."
In reference to a local rebellion, in which the laws of the Union were
obstructed, the act of the 28th of February, 1795, was passed providing in substance that whenever in any State the civil authorities of
the Union were unable to enforce the laws the President shall be empowered to call out such military force as might be necessary for the
emergency. Fortunately for the country this law was in force when
several States of the Union repudiated their allegiance to the National
Government and placed themselves in armed rebellion against it. It
was sufficiently comprehensive in its terms to meet such an occurrence,
although it was not a case within the contemplation of Congress when
the law was enacted. It was under this statute that the President
issued his proclamation of the 15th of April, 1861. From that time the
country has been in a state of war the history and progress of which
are familiar to all. More than two years have elapsed during which
the treasure of the nation has been lavishly contributed and blood has
freely flowed and this formidable rebellion is not yet subdued. The
energies of the loyal people of the Union are to be put to further trials
and in all probability the enemy is yet to be encountered on many a
bloody field.

It is not to be disguised then that our country is in imminent peril
and that the crisis demands of every American citizen a hearty support
of all proper means for the restoration of the Union and the return of
an honorable peace. Those placed by the people at the head of the
Government it may well be presumed are earnestly and sincerely
devoted to its preservation and perpetuity. The President may not be
the man of our choice and the measures of his administration may not
be such as all can fully approve, but these are minor considerations
and can absolve no man from the paramount obligation of lending his
aid for the salvation of his country. All should feel that no evil they
can be called on to endure as the result of war is comparable with the
subversion of our chosen Government and the horrors which must follow from such a catastrophe.

I have referred thus briefly to the present crisis of the country as
having a bearing on the question before the court. It is clearly not a
time when any one connected with the judicial department of the Government should allow himself except from the most stringent obligations of duty to embarrass or thwart the Executive in his efforts to
deliver the country from the dangers which press so heavily upon it.
Now the question which I am called upon to decide is whether General
Burnside as an agent of the Executive Department of the Government
has transgressed his authority in ordering the arrest of Mr. Vallandigham. If the theory of his counsel is sustainable that there can be no
legal arrest except by warrant based on an affidavit of probable cause
the conclusion would be clear that the arrest was illegal, but I do not
think I am bound to regard the inquiry as occupying this narrow base.
General Burnside by the order of the President has been designated
and appointed to take the military supervision of the Department of
the Ohio, composed of the States of Kentucky, Ohio, Indiana, Illinois
and Michigan. The precise extent of his authority in this responsible
position is not known to the court. It may, however, be properly
assumed as a fair presumption that the President has clothed him with
all the powers necessary to the efficient discharge of his duties in the
station to which he has been called. He is the representative and
agent of the President within the limits of his department. In time
of war the President is not above the Constitution but derives his

power expressly from the provision of that instrument declaring that he shall be Commander-in-Chief of the Army and Navy. The Constitution does not specify the powers he may rightfully exercise in this character nor are they defined by legislation. No one denies, however, that the President in this character is invested with very high powers, which it is well known have been called into exercise on various occasions during the present rebellion. A memorable instance is seen in the emancipation proclamation issued by the President as Commander-in Chief and which he justifies as a military necessity. It is perhaps not easy to define what acts are properly within this designation, but they must undoubtedly be limited to such as are necessary to the protection and preservation of the Government and the Constitution which the President has sworn to support and defend. And in deciding what he may rightfully do under this power where there is no express legislative declaration the President is guided solely by his own judgment and discretion and is only amenable for an abuse of his authority by impeachment prosecuted according to the requirements of the Constitution. The occasion which justifies the exercise of this power exists only from the necessity of the case, and when the necessity exists there is a clear justification of the act.

If this view of the power of the President is correct it undoubtedly implies the right to arrest persons who by their mischievous acts of disloyalty impede or endanger the military operations of the Government. And if the necessity exists I see no reason why the power does not attach to the officer or general in command of a military department. The only reason why the appointment is made is that the President cannot discharge the duties in person. He therefore constitutes an agent to represent him clothed with the necessary power for the efficient supervision of the military interests of the Government throughout the department. And it is not necessary that martial law should be proclaimed or exist to enable the general in command to perform the duties assigned to him. Martial law is well defined by an able jurist to be " the will of a military commander operating without any restraint save his judgment upon the lives, upon the persons, upon the entire social and individual condition of all over whom this law extends." It cannot be claimed that this law was in operation in General Burnside's department when Mr. Vallandigham was arrested, nor is it necessary that it should have been in force to justify the arrest. The power vested by virtue of the authority conferred by the appointment of the President. Under that appointment General Burnside assumed command of this department. That he was a man eminently fitted for the position there is no room for a doubt. He had achieved during his brief military career a national reputation as a wise, discreet, patriotic and brave general. He not only enjoyed the confidence and respect of the President and Secretary of War but of the whole country. He has nobly laid his party preferences and predilections upon the altar of his country and consecrated his life to her service. It was known that the widely extended department with the military supervision of which he was charged was one of great importance and demanded great vigilance and ability in the administration of its military concerns. Kentucky was a border State in which there was a large element of disaffection toward the National Government and sympathy with those in rebellion against it. Formidable invasions have been attempted and are now threatened. Four of the States have a river border and are in perpetual danger of invasion. The enforcement of the late conscription law was foreseen as a positive necessity. In Ohio, Indiana and Illinois a class of mischievous politicians had succeeded in poisoning the minds of a portion of the community with the rankest feelings of disloyalty. Artful men, disguising their latent treason under hollow pretensions of devotion to the Union, were striving to disseminate their pestilent heresies among the masses of the people. The evil was one of alarming magnitude and threatened seriously to impede the military operations of the Government and greatly to protract the suppression of the rebellion. General Burnside was not slow to perceive the dangerous consequences of these disloyal efforts and resolved if possible to suppress them. In the exercise of his discretion he issued the order (No. 38) which has been brought to the notice of the court. I shall not comment on that order or say anything more in vindication of its expediency. I refer to it only because General Burnside in his manly and patriotic communication to the court has stated fully his motives and reasons for issuing it, and also that it was for its supposed violation that he ordered the arrest of Mr. Vallandigham. He has done this under his responsibility as the commanding general of this department and in accordance with what he supposed to be the power vested in him by the appointment of the President. It was virtually the act of the Executive Department under the power vested in the President by the Constitution, and I am unable to perceive on what principle a judicial tribunal can be invoked to annul or reverse it. In the judgment of the commanding general the emergency required it, and whether he acted wisely or discreetly is not properly a subject for judicial review.

It is worthy of remark here that this arrest was not made by General Burnside under any claim or pretension that he had authority to dispose of or punish the party arrested according to his own will without trial and proof of the facts alleged as the ground for the arrest but with a view to an investigation by a military court or commission. Such an investigation has taken place, the result of which has not been made known to this court. Whether the military commission for the trial of the charges against Mr. Vallandigham was legally constituted and had jurisdiction of the case is not a question before this court. There is clearly no authority in this court on the pending motion to revise or reverse the proceedings of the military commission if they were before the court. The sole question is whether the arrest was legal, and as before remarked its legality depends on the necessity which existed for making it, and of that necessity for the reason stated this court cannot judicially determine. General Burnside is unquestionably amenable to the Executive Department for his conduct. If he has acted arbitrarily and upon insufficient reasons it is within the power and would be the duty of the President not only to annul his acts but to visit him with decisive marks of his disapprobation. To the President as Commander-in-Chief of the Army he must answer for his official conduct. But under our Constitution which studiously seeks to keep the executive, legislative and judicial departments of the Government from all interference and conflict with each other it would be an unwarrantable exercise of the judicial power to decide that a co-ordinate branch of the Government acting under its high responsibilities had violated the Constitution in its letter or its spirit by authorizing the arrest in question. Especially in these troublous times when the national life is in peril and when union and harmony among the different branches of the Government are so imperatively demanded such interference would find no excuse or vindication. Each department of the Government must to some extent act on a presumption that a co-ordinate branch knows its powers and duties and will not transcend them. If the doctrine is to obtain that every one charged with and guilty of acts of mischievous disloyalty not within the scope of the criminal laws of the land in custody under the military authority is to be set free by courts or judges on *habeas corpus* and that there is no power by which he may be temporarily placed where he cannot perpetrate mischief it requires no argument to prove that the most alarming conflicts must follow and the action of the Government be most seriously impaired. I dare not in my judicial position assume the fearful responsibility implied in the sanction of such a doctrine.

And here without subjecting myself to the charge of trenching upon the domain of political discussion I may be indulged in the remark that there is too much of the pestilential leaven of disloyalty in the community. There is a class of men in the loyal States who seem to have no just appreciation of the deep criminality of those who are in arms avowedly for the overthrow of the Government and the establishment of a Southern Confederacy. They have not I fear risen to any right estimate of their duties and obligations as American citizens to a Government which has strewn its blessings with a profuse hand and is felt only in the benefits it bestows. I may venture the assertion that the page of history will be searched in vain for an example of a rebellion so wholly destitute of excuse or vindication and so dark with crime as that which our bleeding country is now called upon to confront and for the suppression of which all her energies are demanded. Its cause is to be found in the unhallowed ambition of political aspirants and agitators who boldly avow as their aim not the establishment of a government for the better security of human rights but one in which all political power is to be concentrated in an odious and despotic oligarchy. It is indeed consolatory to know that in most sections of the North those who sympathize with the rebellion are not so numerous or formidable as the apprehensions of some would seem to indicate. It may be assumed I trust that in most of the Northern States reliable and unswerving patriotism is the rule and disloyalty and treason the exception. But there should be no division of sentiment upon this momentous question. Men should know and lay the truth to heart that there is a course of conduct not involving overt treason or any offense technically defined by statute, and not therefore subject to punishment as such, which nevertheless implies moral guilt and a gross offense against their country. Those who live under the protection and enjoy the blessings of our benignant Government must learn that they cannot stab its vitals with impunity. If they cherish hatred and hostility to it and desire its subversion let them withdraw from its jurisdiction and seek the fellowship and protection of those with whom they are in sympathy. If they remain with us while they are not of us they must be subject to such a course of dealing as the great law of self-preservation prescribes and will enforce. And let them not complain if the stringent doctrine of military necessity should find them to be the legitimate subjects of its action. I have no fears that the recognition of this doctrine will lead to an arbitrary invasion of the personal security or personal liberty of the citizen. It is rare indeed that a charge of disloyalty will be made upon insufficient grounds. But if there should be an occasional mistake such an occurrence is not to be put in competition with the preservation of the life of the nation. And I confess I am but little moved by the eloquent appeals of those who while they indignantly denounce violations of personal liberty look with no horror upon a despotism as unmitigated as the world has ever witnessed.

But I cannot pursue this subject further. I have been compelled by circumstances to present my views in the briefest way. I am aware

there are points made by the learned counsel representing Mr. Vallan
digham to which I have not adverted. I have had neither time nor
strength for a more elaborate consideration of the questions involved
in this application. For the reasons which I have attempted to set
forth I am led clearly to the conclusion that I cannot judicially pronounce the order of General Burnside for the arrest of Mr. Vallandigham as a nullity, and must therefore hold that no sufficient ground has
been exhibited for granting the writ applied for. In reaching this
result I have not found it necessary to refer to the authorities which
have been cited and which are not controverted for the obvious reason
that they do not apply to the theory of this case as understood and
affirmed by the court. And I may properly add here that I am fortified in my conclusion by the fact just brought to my notice that the
Legislature of Ohio at its late session has passed two statutes in which
the validity and legality of arrests in this State under military authority are distinctly sanctioned. This is a clear indication of the opinion
of that body that the rights and liberties of the people are not put in
jeopardy by the exercise of the power in question and is moreover a
concession that the present state of the country requires and justifies
its exercise. It is an intimation that the people of our patriotic State
will sanction such a construction of the Constitution as without a
clear violation of its letter will adapt it to the existing emergency.

There is one other consideration to which I may perhaps properly
refer not as a reason for refusing the writ applied for but for the purpose of saying that if granted there is no probability that it would be
available in relieving Mr. Vallandigham from his present position. It
is at least morally certain it would not be obeyed. And I confess I am
somewhat reluctant to authorize a process knowing it would not be
respected and that the court is powerless to enforce obedience. Yet if
satisfied there were sufficient grounds for the allowance of the writ
the consideration to which I have adverted would not be conclusive
against it.

For these reasons I am constrained to refuse the writ.

GENERAL ORDERS, } WAR DEPT., ADJT. GENERAL'S OFFICE,
   No. 117.   }   *Washington, May 9, 1863.*

I. The following officers and men have been declared duly exchanged
as prisoners of war since the announcement in General Orders, No. 10,
of January 10, 1863:

1. All officers and enlisted men and all persons whatever may have
been their classificati n who have been delivered at City Point, Va.,
up to May 6, 1863.

2. All officers who have been captured and released on parole up to
April 1, 1863, wherever they may have been captured.

3. All enlisted men who have been captured in North Carolina and
Virginia and released on parole up to March 1, 1863.

II. The paroled troops herein declared to be exchanged will be without delay equipped for the field and forwarded to the armies to which
they belong from posts or camps wherever they may be collected.

All officers and enlisted men absent in virtue of being on parole will
now that they are exchanged immediately return to duty with their
proper commands.

By order of the Secretary of War:

                                      E. D. TOWNSEND,
                                      Assistant Adjutant-General.

HEADQUARTERS DIVISION OF CAIRO,
Cairo, May 10, 1863.

Major-General BURNSIDE.

DEAR SIR: This letter will introduce you to the Hon. John Dougherty, of Jonesborough, Ill., who goes to Cincinnati as counsel for some of the twenty-three prisoners arrested in that place and sent to you. Mr. Dougherty is a man of influence and has used it in behalf of the Union. He asked my counsel as to the propriety of his defending the parties arrested. Some of them he knows to be bad citizens and disloyal men. I said to him all men have the right to obtain counsel and he could legitimately defend them. I had the honor to suggest to you that these men should be tried at Anna but have had no reply to my letter. Some of them ought to be turned over to the civil authorities. The provost-marshal who arrested them has been relieved from duty at this post and is now near Vicksburg. I commend Mr. Dougherty to your kind consideration.

I have the honor to be, your obedient servant,

N. B. BUFORD,
Brigadier-General, Commanding.

WAR DEPARTMENT, *Washington, D. C., May 10, 1863.*
Col. W. HOFFMAN, *Commissary-General of Prisoners.*

COLONEL: It has been represented to the Secretary of War that a number of officers who have recently been exchanged and ordered to the West are still at Baltimore and Annapolis, and in consequence of not having been paid for several months have no means of paying their expenses on the road or purchasing clothing and other supplies of which they are greatly in need. The Secretary of War desires that you will make the necessary arrangements and give the necessary orders to enable these officers to be paid; at least so far as to relieve their present necessities.

Very respectfully, your obedient servant,

ED. R. S. CANBY,
Brigadier-General.

OFFICE COMMISSARY-GENERAL OF PRISONERS,
Washington, D. C., May 10, 1863.
Hon. E. M. STANTON, *Secretary of War, Washington, D. C.*

SIR: Pursuant to your verbal instructions I have the honor herewith to inclose* a report of the number of officers and enlisted men at Camp Parole, Camp Chase and Benton Barracks, paroled prisoners of war recently exchanged, who may now be ordered to the field. The officers exchanged without troops were mostly captured with the commands at Holly Springs and they and the troops to which they belong are now at Benton Barracks. I am informed by Colonel Ludlow that one delivery of rebel prisoners of war at City Point was not large enough to cover the enlisted men captured at Holly Springs, but that he has an arrangement partially completed by which he expects to be able to declare them exchanged in a few days.

On the 7th instant I announced to Major-Generals Burnside and Curtis the recent declaration of exchange and by order of the General-in-Chief directed them to order all exchanged troops in their respective

---

* Omitted.

departments to join their proper commands. At the same time I notified Brigadier-General Patrick, provost-marshal-general of the Army
of the Potomac, of the presence at Camp Parole of about 1,500
exchanged troops belonging to the Army of the Potomac and to day
an officer has reported to me by his order to take charge of them and
conduct them to the army. The within report of the number of men
at Camp Chase and Benton Barracks is based on the number sent to
those stations from Camp Parole and includes the officers recently
ordered West. It is probable there are many absentees.

Very respectfully, your obedient servant,

W. HOFFMAN,
Colonel Third Infantry, Commissary-General of Prisoners.

OFFICE COMMISSARY-GENERAL OF PRISONERS,
Washington, D. C., May 10, 1863.

Brig. Gen. A. SCHOEPF,
Commanding Fort Delaware, Del.

GENERAL: I have to acknowledge the receipt of your letters of the
5th and 6th instant with estimate for new barracks, and your letter of
the 7th reporting changes in the old barracks. Orders have already
been given by the Quartermaster-General to Colonel Crosman, assistant
quartermaster-general at Philadelphia, in relation to the erection of
the barracks. If the changes you are making in the old barracks are
only in raising the floors and repairing the bunks and windows it is
not necessary to refer the matter to the Quartermaster-General; but if
you propose to open the square by cutting through the barracks on
two sides of the square and to run a cross-line of barracks as was proposed it will be necessary to submit the plan for the approval of the
Quartermaster-General. I will ask authority for the construction of a
hospital on your estimate. Your letter of the 8th instant is received
and your recommendation will be attended to.

Very respectfully, your obedient servant,

W. HOFFMAN,
Colonel Third Infantry, Commissary-General of Prisoners.

OFFICE COMMISSARY-GENERAL OF PRISONERS,
Washington, D. C., May 10, 1863.

Col. T. P. ANDREWS,
Paymaster-General U. S. Army, Washington, D. C.

COLONEL: By direction of the Secretary of War please give the
necessary orders to enable officers who have recently been exchanged
and who are now in Annapolis and Baltimore to receive the pay that
is due them or so much of it as may be necessary to meet their present
wants. Most of these officers are in Baltimore, being the officers mentioned in my note of last evening, and it is desirable if possible that
they should be paid in that city. I inclose herewith a list* of the officers
referred to, many of whom have already gone West and will not apply
for pay.

Very respectfully, your obedient servant,

W. HOFFMAN,
Colonel Third Infantry, Commissary-General of Prisoners.

---

* Omitted.

OFFICE COMMISSARY-GENERAL OF PRISONERS,
Washington, D. C., May 10, 1863.

Col. ROBERT NUGENT,
Acting Assistant Provost-Marshal-General, New York City.

COLONEL: Your letter of the 6th instant is received. The Government furnishes transportation to employés who have been captured and released on parole only to some point convenient within our lines where they can find employment. They are entitled to pay up to the time of their delivery to our authorities. The laborers referred to in your letter if Government employés are entitled to pay up to the time of their arrival in New Orleans. Transportation and subsistence was furnished to them from there to New York and now they must find some new employment. No provision of any kind is made for rebel prisoners of war who are released on taking the oath of allegiance. They must be content to provide for themselves by their own labor as better Union citizens do.

Very respectfully, your obedient servant,
W. HOFFMAN,
Colonel Third Infantry, Commissary-General of Prisoners.

FORT MONROE, *May 10, 1863.*

Hon. G. V. FOX, *Assistant Secretary of the Navy:*

The last declaration of exchanges does not include the enlisted men of the Mercedita, Hatteras and other vessels who have not been delivered at City Point. Send me the names of all the vessels whose crews have been paroled and their probable number and I will send you a declaration of them immediately.

WM. H. LUDLOW,
Lieutenant-Colonel and Agent for Exchange of Prisoners.

HDQRS. DEPT. OF VIRGINIA, *Fort Monroe, May 10, 1863.*

Hon. G. V. FOX,
Assistant Secretary of the Navy, Washington, D. C.:

I have received no lists of names and number of captured navy officers and men; only the general mention of the vessel and date of capture. Your letter did not indicate clearly who had been paroled or who were yet in confinement. Please furnish me these data and the exchanges can be at once declared.

The arrangement declaring all naval captures exchanged to a certain date would require you to release all captured by you to that date. Will you do this? If not it will be better to have exchanged all your officers and men as soon as you give me their names and number by giving military captures as equivalents.

Please inform me where those who have not been paroled and released are now confined. Do you not think you have had every benefit of exchange as far as information furnished me could give it?

WM. H. LUDLOW,
Lieutenant-Colonel and Agent for Exchange of Prisoners.

NEW YORK, *May 10, 1863.*

Hon. E. M. STANTON, *Secretary of War.*

SIR: By direction of the executive committee of the United States Sanitary Commission I have the honor to ask your attention to the deplorable condition of the hospitals containing rebel prisoners at Camp Douglas, near Chicago, Ill., and in Gratiot Street [Prison], Saint Louis, Mo., which in the deliberate judgment of the committee is disgraceful to us as a Christian people and should be promptly remedied by those possessing authority.

More than a year ago the very bad condition of Camp Douglas and its hospital was recognized by the president of the Sanitary Commission on personal visit and inspection and reported to Colonel Hoffman, U. S. Army, agent of the War Department in charge of rebel prisoners. It was promised by this officer that the evil should be remedied.

By recent reports under date of April 5 ultimo from two eminent members of the medical profession, Drs. Thomas Hun and Mason F. Cogswell, of Albany, N. Y., employed by the Sanitary Commission as special inspectors of hospitals, it is evident that the improvements promised by Colonel Hoffman have not been made and that the state of the hospitals in question is many degrees worse than when his attention was called to the condition of its inmates.

The high character held in this community by Doctors Hun and Cogswell and their eminent fitness to form a sound and judicious opinion as to the requirements of humanity in the treatment of the sick under any circumstances make it proper for me to subjoin the words employed in their report, premising that the report was special in its character in consequence of the urgent necessity which was recognized for the prompt remedy of the evils it set forth:

ALBANY, *April 5, 1863.*

* * * We desire most earnestly to call the attention of the Sanitary Commission and the Government to the condition of these hospitals. In our experience we have never witnessed so painful a spectacle as that presented by their wretched inmates; without change of clothing, covered with vermin, they lie in cots without mattresses or with mattresses furnished by private charity, without sheets or bedding of any kind except blankets often in rags, in wards reeking with filth and foul air. The stench is most offensive. We carefully avoid all exaggeration of statement but we give some facts which speak for themselves. From January 27, 1863, when the prisoners (in number about 3,800) arrived at Camp Douglas, to February 18, the day of our visit, 385 patients have been admitted to the hospitals, of whom 130 had died. This mortality of 33 per cent. does not express the whole truth, for of the 148 patients then remaining in hospital a large number must have since died. Besides this about 130 prisoners had died in barracks, not having been able to gain admission even to the miserable accommodations of the hospital, and at the time of our visit 150 persons were sick in barracks waiting for room in hospital.

Thus it will be seen that 260 out of the 3,800 prisoners had died in twenty-one days, a rate of mortality which if continued would secure their total extermination in about 320 days. Under the circumstances the rate of mortality would increase rather than diminish. We read this morning in the papers that 100 died there last week.

* * * At Saint Louis we found the condition of the barracks far worse than that of the hospitals. The bunks in which the prisoners sleep are made to hold two persons in each tier and are three tiers high, and these are placed so close together that there is scarcely space to pass between them. As in the hospitals, no bedding is furnished, but blankets or bits of carpet to take the place of blankets. The floor is incrusted with dirt so as to be more like an earthen than a plank floor.

In these rooms the prisoners spend day and night, for the small yard of the prison is scarcely sufficient to contain a foul and stinking privy. The day we visited this prison was warm so that all the windows were open, and the air was more tolerable on that account, but it is difficult to conceive how human beings can continue to live in such an atmosphere as must be generated when the windows are closed at night or in stormy weather.

Here were persons lying sick with pneumonia, dysentery and other grave diseases waiting for admission to the hospital.

* * * As we were sent to inspect hospitals it may be said that we are going beyond our duty in speaking of the condition of prisons, but since in the prisoners' quarters there were numerous sick persons unable to gain admission to the hospitals and dying in great numbers before reaching the hospital it cannot be said we

exceeded the spirit of our instructions. Besides this the barracks in their crowded and filthy condition serve as a hot-bed for generating diseases for the hospital and for this cause also we feel bound to report their condition.

However this may be, the fact has come to our knowledge and we report it to the Commission that in these prisons and hospitals a condition exists which is discreditable to a Christian people. It surely is not the intention of our Government to place these prisoners in a position which will secure their extermination by pestilence in less than a year. We believe that this state of things cannot be known to those who have the power to cause it to cease. From the circumstances under which we were admitted we feel that we have not the right to speak publicly of what we have seen, but for this reason do we the more earnestly urge on the Commission the necessity of taking immediate steps to put a stop to such atrocities.

* * * We can suggest no remedy short of a complete change in these establishments; all the sick ought to be removed from Gratiot Street [Prison], Saint Louis.

* * * The ground at Camp Douglas is most unsuitable for a hospital or even for barracks, being wet and without drainage. We think it ought to be abandoned. We were told that within a short distance are high grounds, well drained and adapted for such purposes.

* * * * * * *

We are, with great respect, your obedient servants,

THOMAS HUN, M. D.
MASON F. COGSWELL, M. D.

I am directed to state that a digest of the report from which these extracts are made was laid before the Surgeon-General at once in accordance with the regulations of the central office of the Commission at Washington, and I am informed that this officer has taken the measures he deems proper in the case, but I am also aware that he does not possess the power to remedy the evil, that power resting alone in your hands or in those of His Excellency the President. The executive committee recognizing its responsibilities to the nation and the Government has therefore decided to move in the matter, and has directed me to ask you respectfully and most earnestly to issue such orders as will secure humane and proper treatment for the sick prisoners whom the fortunes of war under your energetic administration places in your power.

I have the honor to be, with much respect, your obedient servant,

WM. H. VAN BUREN, M. D.

COLUMBUS, OHIO, *May 11, 1863.*

Hon. E. M. STANTON:

A number of Ohio officers are here en route from Richmond to their regiments in destitute condition. Please order them mustered for pay here.

DAVID TOD,
Governor.

EXECUTIVE DEPARTMENT, *Indianapolis, May 11, 1863.*
Hon. E. M. STANTON, *Secretary of War.*

SIR: In July, 1862, Col. A. D. Streight, Fifty-first Regiment Indiana Volunteers, with his regiment left Decatur, Ala., and marched over the mountains some twenty-five miles below that place to the relief of a number of Union citizens who had been obliged to abandon their homes and seek refuge in the mountains, and while there Colonel Streight succeeded in enlisting about 400 of these Alabamians in his regiment. They were regularly mustered into the service and have been doing duty ever since.

Some days since Colonel Streight with the permission of General Rosecrans left with a mounted brigade for the purpose of cutting off General Bragg's communications which they partially succeeded in doing, but were finally defeated and captured near Rome, and the account from the rebel newspapers states that "the men were paroled except the four companies of renegade Alabamians who were sent to Richmond."

Now I take it that this is a direct and palpable violation of the cartel. These men are regularly mustered into the Fifty-first Regiment Indiana Volunteers, and I respectfully ask that 800 prisoners may be selected from those now in our possession and held as hostages for the safety of these loyal Alabamians. Col. J. B. Fry is acquainted with these facts.

I have the honor to be, very respectfully, your obedient servant,

O. P. MORTON,
Governor of Indiana.

[First indorsement.]

Referred to Major-General Hitchcock, commissioner of exchange.

E. M. STANTON.

[Second indorsement.]

WASHINGTON, *May 21, 1863.*

Respectfully returned to the honorable Secretary of War with the remark that the undersigned would unhesitatingly recommend the adoption of the suggestion to hold 800 rebel prisoners as hostages for the loyal Alabamians held at Richmond but for the fact that the rebel authorities now hold Union prisoners considerably in excess over rebels held as prisoners by the Government.

An attempt to retaliate in the manner proposed would be immediately followed by an insulting outrage perpetrated by the rebel Government upon other unfortunate Union prisoners in their hands.

I would recommend that a circular be addressed to Union commanders of separate departments or corps embodying a statement of the facts connected with this transaction thus far developed, that our troops may be advised of it and go into battle with that knowledge.

Respectfully submitted.

E. A. HITCHCOCK,
Major-General of Vols., Commissioner for Exchange of Prisoners.

FORT MONROE, *May 11, 1863.*

Hon. EDWIN M. STANTON, *Secretary of War:*

Mr. Ould has come down with a flag of truce to the vicinity of Newport News where he was stopped by Admiral Lee. He came down to ask Colonel Ludlow to send up to Richmond to receive 10,000 prisoners. Five thousand have arrived there and the other 5,000 will be there by the time the transports reach City Point. Admiral Lee has sent me some Richmond papers which I will send by the afternoon mail. They acknowledge 7,000 wounded, 900 killed and 1,200 missing. General Van Dorn is dead.

JOHN A. DIX,
Major-General.

HEADQUARTERS DEPARTMENT OF VIRGINIA,
Fort Monroe, Va., May 11, 1863.
JAMES HOLBROOK, Esq.,
Special Agent Post-Office Department, New York.

SIR: The rules adopted in regard to the transmission of letters across the lines are not to be considered as authorizing correspondence. It is not to be inferred that all letters complying with them will be forwarded. It is entirely discretionary with the commanding officer here, and there may be times or circumstances which will render all correspondence inexpedient except with prisoners of war. The published memorandum only intended to give notice that no letters of any description will be forwarded unless certain rules were complied with. In regard to your special inquiry I answer that letters should be sent unsealed otherwise we shall break them open.

I am, respectfully, yours,

JOHN A. DIX,
Major-General.

HEADQUARTERS DISTRICT OF EASTERN ARKANSAS,
Helena, Ark., May 11, 1863.
Maj. H. Z. CURTIS, *Assistant Adjutant-General.*

SIR: I have the honor to hand you herewith a communication addressed to the major-general commanding the Department of the Missouri which was this day received from Lieutenant-General Holmes, C. S. Army, commanding District of Arkansas.

Very respectfully, sir, your obedient servant,

B. M. PRENTISS,
Major-General.

[Inclosure.]

HEADQUARTERS DISTRICT OF ARKANSAS,
Little Rock, May 7, 1863.
Maj. Gen. S. R. CURTIS, U. S. Army, or
OFFICER COMDG. DEPT. OF THE MISSOURI, *Saint Louis.*

GENERAL: I have in good faith carried out the cartel agreed upon by our respective Governments and have paroled until exchanged and sent within your lines such prisoners as have been captured by the forces under my command.

I have indisputable evidence that many prisoners have been made by troops under your command in Northwestern Arkansas and South Missouri who have never been heard from and have been carried off without any known effort on your part to account for them, while they have not been paroled for exchange.

I shall parole no more prisoners until I find a disposition on your part to comply with the terms of the cartel. It is furthermore reported to me in a manner which precludes all doubt that General Blunt has issued orders for the execution of all prisoners whom he is pleased to style "guerrillas" or "bushwhackers" taken in arms. The persons to whom he thus alludes constitute a part of the Confederate forces, organized specially by me under authority of the acts of the Confederate Congress for the defense of the frontier and in accordance with the laws of all civilized nations.

The orders of General Blunt are contrary to all law and unless immediately rescinded I will retaliate by executing man for man of the prisoners I may have at any time in my hands.

On the 7th of December last in accordance with instructions from the President of the Confederate States of America I had the honor of addressing you a communication on the subject of the murder of ten citizens of Missouri by the orders of General McNeil, U. S. Army. As no reply has been received up to this date I am forced to the conclusion that you decline to give the information sought. I again call your attention to that letter and the request contained in it, furthermore inclosing to you a copy of the letter* of the President of the Confederate States addressed to me on this subject. If within a reasonable time I do not receive a satisfactory answer to this my communication I shall be forced to the conclusion that the conduct of General McNeil meets with the approval of your Government and no alternative will be left me but to carry into effect my instructions to the letter.

I have the honor to be, general, very respectfully, your most obedient servant,

TH. H. HOLMES,
Lieutenant-General, Commanding.

OFFICE COMMISSARY-GENERAL OF PRISONERS,
Washington, D. C., May 11, 1863.

Maj. Gen. N. P. BANKS,
Commanding Department of the Gulf, New Orleans, La.

GENERAL: By direction of the General-in-Chief I have the honor to recommend the following: It has been determined that all irregular military organizations when captured are to be recognized as prisoners of war subject to be exchanged, and I have the honor to request that this rule may be acted on in your department. An effort will be made to fix upon Baton Rouge for the delivery of prisoners of war and there is little doubt that it will be so arranged, of which you will be promptly notified. In the meantime if deliveries cannot be made at Vicksburg and you are embarrassed to take care of your prisoners please forward them to Fort Monroe for delivery at City Point. Duplicate rolls should accompany them on which each man should give his parole not to bear arms, &c. One of these rolls after the delivery with the receipt of the Confederate officer to whom they are delivered upon it must be forwarded to this office.. Blank rolls for this purpose will be forwarded by this mail. A full roll of all prisoners of war should be forwarded to this office with as little delay as practicable. The rolls should show where the prisoners are held. Blanks for such rolls will also be forwarded. I have to request also that you will cause me to be furnished with full rolls of all Federal troops who may be delivered on parole in your department. Names should be arranged in alphabetical order by company and regiment. Blanks for this purpose are sent by mail.

Very respectfully, your obedient servant,

W. HOFFMAN,
Colonel Third Infantry, Commissary-General of Prisoners.

OFFICE COMMISSARY-GENERAL OF PRISONERS,
Washington, D. C., May 11, 1863.

Maj. Gen. U. S. GRANT,
Commanding Department of the Tennessee.

GENERAL: I am instructed by the General-in-Chief to say that when a person is arrested charged with being a spy or the commission of any

---

* See Vol. IV, this Series, p. 946.

other specific offense requiring a trial an immediate investigation must be had before a military tribunal at the place where the offense was committed and where the witnesses are within reach. Many persons have been arrested as spies and sent to interior prisons and after months of detention it has been found that the charges had neither specifications nor evidence to sustain them. In cases where arrests are made on a general charge of disloyal conduct it is necessary that full details in each case with the character of the person should be given in order to a proper disposal of it. Please give the necessary instructions to insure compliance with the foregoing in your department.

Very respectfully, your obedient servant,

W. HOFFMAN,
Colonel Third Infantry, Commissary-General of Prisoners.

(Same to Maj. Gens. S. R. Curtis, A. E. Burnside, W. S. Rosecrans, R. C. Schenck and N. P. Banks.)

OFFICE COMMISSARY-GENERAL OF PRISONERS,
Washington, D. C., May 11, 1863.

Brig. Gen. JOHN S. MASON, *Commanding, Columbus, Ohio.*

GENERAL: By direction of the Secretary of War you are authorized to release on their taking the oath of allegiance all prisoners at Camp Chase who are deserters from the rebel army. Many prisoners of war will doubtless endeavor to claim to be deserters with a view of escaping from confinement by this means, and it is left for you to decide by careful inquiry in each case who are really deserters and entitled to this indulgence. Let it be clearly understood that death is the penalty for the violation of the oath. Please have full rolls of all so discharged forwarded to this office. It is intended that hereafter Camp Chase prison shall be used only as a temporary place of confinement for prisoners, and I am instructed by the Secretary of War to direct that you forward from time to time all prisoners received at the camp to the depot on Johnson's Island, Sandusky. Rebel officers, however, will be held by themselves in one of the small prisons for special instructions.

It is not probable that Prison No. 3 will again be required, but an emergency may render it necessary and I therefore request that the fence may be taken down only in places and the part removed so disposed of that it may be readily used if required.

Orders have probably been given from the headquarters Department of the Ohio for the transfer of all prisoners of war now at Camp Chase to City Point. Please furnish me with detailed report of all exchanged troops ordered from Camp Chase to their regiments, giving names of officers and regiments and company of men, and send like reports of all not exchanged. The movement will be ordered by General Burnside.

Very respectfully, your obedient servant,

W. HOFFMAN,
Colonel Third Infantry, Commissary-General of Prisoners.

OFFICE COMMISSARY-GENERAL OF PRISONERS,
Washington, D. C., May 11, 1863.

Maj. W. S. PIERSON,
Commanding Depot Prisoners of War, Sandusky, Ohio.

MAJOR: The following-named prisoners, held at Johnson's Island as spies, will be placed on the rolls as prisoners of war and will be forwarded with the next detachment for delivery: Col. J. C. Morehead, Dr. Joseph E. Dixon, Capt. or Lieut. James H. Baker, Private John W. Garrett, Company D, First Kentucky [Infantry] Volunteers. The two officers referred to in your letter of the 30th will accompany the first party ordered to City Point. Prisoners of war are not permitted to decline to be sent forward for exchange, and if there was no better reason for detaining Doctor Read at the depot than that it was not sufficient. General Burnside has been directed to order all prisoners of war in his department to City Point, and if you have not received the order notify me by telegraph.

Very respectfully, your obedient servant,

W. HOFFMAN,
Colonel Third Infantry, Commissary-General of Prisoners.

OFFICE COMMISSARY-GENERAL OF PRISONERS,
Washington, D. C., May 11, 1863.

Capt. H. M. LAZELLE,
Eighth U. S. Infantry, Washington, D. C.

CAPTAIN: You will proceed this afternoon to Camp Parole, near Annapolis, Md., with a view to ascertain and report on the progress making in the construction of the new camp. You will also examine into the affairs of the camp as far as may seem to be necessary.

Very respectfully, your obedient servant,

W. HOFFMAN,
Colonel Third Infantry, Commissary-General of Prisoners.

SANDUSKY CITY, OHIO, *May 11, 1863.*

Col. WILLIAM HOFFMAN, *Washington City.*

HONORABLE SIR: Permit me to trouble you for a pass to visit the rebel prisoners at Johnson's Island. I am Catholic pastor in Sandusky City and successor to Rev. L. Molon, to whom you generously gave a permit. I inclose a note from the major commanding, which will be for you a kind of testimony that all will be right. Excusing myself for troubling you,

I remain, honorable sir, respectfully,

R. A. SIDLEY.

[Inclosure.]

HDQRS. HOFFMAN'S BATT., DEPOT PRISONERS OF WAR,
Near Sandusky, Ohio, May 6, 1863.

Rev. R. A. SIDLEY.

DEAR SIR: I shall be pleased to see you at my quarters, but under my orders it will be necessary for you to have the order of Col. William Hoffman, commissary-general of prisoners, Washington, D. C., before you can be admitted to see the prisoners. He gave such an order to Father Molon, and I presume will to you; but I have not the authority.

Very respectfully,

WM. S. PIERSON,
Major, Commanding.

HEADQUARTERS DISTRICT OF EASTERN KENTUCKY,
Louisa, Ky., May 12, 1863.
Brig. Gen. L. THOMAS,
 Adjutant-General U. S. Army, Washington, D. C.

SIR: In accordance with General Orders, No. 44, of the War Department, series of 1861, I have the honor to state that Lewis Wells, residing in Lawrence County, Ky.; James Johnson, residing in Lawrence County, Ky., and Elijah Johnson, residing in Lawrence County, Ky., prisoners of war, have been released upon giving bond and taking the oath of allegiance.

I am, sir, very respectfully, your obedient servant,
JULIUS WHITE,
Brigadier-General, Commanding.

PROVOST-MARSHAL-GENERAL'S OFFICE,
Washington, D. C., May 12, 1863.
Col. E. A. PARROTT,
 Actg. Asst. Provost-Marshal-General for Ohio, Columbus, Ohio.

COLONEL: I have the honor to acknowledge the receipt of your communication of the 6th instant and to state in reply that the enrollment act does not authorize the arrest by provost-marshals of persons charged with disloyalty; neither does it give them power to take cognizance of disloyal practices except such as may come under the specifications of the twenty-fifth section of the enrollment act. If persons charged with disloyalty can be proved to be spies they will be arrested, confined and dealt with as prescribed by section 7. Your action in forwarding communications touching disloyal practices in the State of Ohio to the major-general commanding the department and in the other matters reported in your communication is approved.

I am, colonel, very respectfully, your obedient servant,
J. B. FRY,
Provost-Marshal-General.

OFFICE COMMISSARY-GENERAL OF PRISONERS,
Washington, D. C., May 12, 1863.
Brig. Gen. M. C. MEIGS,
 Quartermaster-General U. S. Army, Washington, D. C.

GENERAL: I have the honor to inclose herewith copies of my letters* of the 1st and 10th of July last in relation to the condition of Camp Douglas at that time, with the request that they may be considered with my letter of the 20th ultimo on the same subject.

Very respectfully, your obedient servant,
W. HOFFMAN,
Colonel Third Infantry, Commissary-General of Prisoners.

WAR DEPARTMENT, *Washington, D. C., May 12, 1863.*
Hon. JOSEPH HOLT, *Judge-Advocate-General.*

SIR: I have the honor to report the facts and circumstances of the arrest of Mr. George A. Lawrence (British subject), which you will find

---

*Omitted here; see Vol. IV, this Series, pp. 110, 166.

in the report made to the Secretary of State (a copy of which is herewith inclosed). I have also the honor to report that since reporting to the Secretary of State I have ascertained the following: Abijah Dolly, the man who arrested him, makes oath that Lawrence when captured stated that he had accidentally fallen in company with his companion (guide) whose name was Lambert. It also appears by Dolly's affidavit that the guide Shipley (not Lambert) at first escaped and took the saddle pockets and contents, and that the contents of the saddle pockets were not obtained. I further state in addition that Lawrence when a prisoner at Baltimore, as reported to me by Major-General Schenck, bribed the guard having him in charge, and instead of proceeding to Washington by the 3.30 p. m. train he spent the night in Baltimore with secessionists.

I also further state that by investigation I have obtained the following reliable information in addition: That Mr. Lawrence when he went to Baltimore with his letter of introduction to Mr. W. W. Glenn was introduced by Mr. Glenn to a secession family (Cameron) on Eager street, fifth door from Charles, where Mr. Lawrence made his headquarters while in Baltimore; that Mr. Glenn procured for Mr. Lawrence a commission in the rebel army in General George [H.] Steuart's cavalry regiment and was to be attached to the staff, and was taking his horses (two) over the mountains and through our lines for use as a staff officer; that E. M. Shipley was recommended by Glenn as a suitable person to take charge of Lawrence's horses and guide him through our lines; that Shipley took the horses by rail to Cumberland and then beyond in the mountains, and made a reconnaissance of the route by which he should conduct Lawrence. Shipley then returned and joined Lawrence and guided him by night through our lines till captured.

This last information fatally implicates Lawrence and materially affects the truthfulness of his profession as to his intentions, &c. It also implicates Mr. Glenn in rendering treasonable aid and assistance to the rebellion.

All which is respectfully submitted.

L. C. TURNER,
Judge-Advocate.

[Inclosure.]

WAR DEPARTMENT, JUDGE-ADVOCATE'S OFFICE,
Washington, D. C., April 10, 1863.

Hon. WILLIAM H. SEWARD, *Secretary of State.*

SIR: I have the honor to report upon the case of George A. Lawrence, British subject, in reply to your note and accompaniment of the 11th instant that said Lawrence was arrested the night of the 4th instant at Greenland, Va., while attempting to pass the Federal lines south to the rebel army; that he was taken to Wheeling, Va., thence to Baltimore and thence to my office in custody of military authority. At my office on the evening of the 9th instant said Lawrence made the following statements or disclosures, viz: That he is a citizen of England and came to the United States the 4th of January last; remained in New York City about ten days; thence to Philadelphia and remained two days; thence to Washington City and stopped at the Metropolitan Hotel; saw Lord Lyons and dined with him and also with the British embassy; remained in Washington three days and then returned to Baltimore, taking with him letters of introduction from Mr. Clay (attaché of the British Legation) to the British consul and Mr. Glenn; that he remained in Baltimore till about one week since, stopping at Guy's Hotel, at Mr. Meredith's, Glenn's and others, making occasional trips into the region round about; that he left Baltimore the 6th instant by railroad for Cumberland alone, having sent his horse ahead to that place by the cars; that he left Cumberland Tuesday, the 7th instant, on horseback alone to proceed over the mountains into the valley on the way to Petersburg; that he rode till Saturday in the night, when he was arrested at Greenland, twenty-one miles from New Creek. At this point in his narrative I asked him if he wished to be understood that he, a stranger, traveled from Tuesday till Saturday in the nighttime and over the Alleghany Mountains alone. He replied that he did have a guide by name of E. M. Shipley; that the guide came to him in Baltimore and was there engaged by him and by an arrangement was to meet him at Oakland, some twenty miles beyond Cumberland, and did meet him as agreed. Here I asked Mr. Lawrence to explain the circumstances, agencies and recommendations whereby the guide was employed. Mr. Lawrence then declined and refused to make any statement or disclosure as to the employment of Shipley as guide or by whose advice or recommendation he acted. Mr. Lawrence then proceeded as follows:

I am the author of Guy Livingston and other works of fiction. I took no letters from Baltimore to carry and none were found on me. It was about 12 o'clock at night when I was arrested and I was traveling with my guide through the fields. We traveled nights to avoid the pickets. We passed the pickets a mile and a half and while riding through the fields we were hailed from the road: "Stop, or I'll shoot." We kept on and two pistol-shots were fired, one shot hitting my guide's horse in the neck. We still kept on, pulling down fences, and while the guide was pulling down a fence we were again hailed in front, asking our names and business. I answered: "Come here and I'll tell you." We were hailed the second time and I replied as before, when there was a rifle-shot, killing my horse dead under me. My guide made his escape with his saddle-bags, but he was captured the next day. I was taken to the station at Greenland. The name of the man who shot my horse is Dolly, a well-known farmer there, and was doing independent duty on his own hook from Greenland. From Greenland I was taken to New Creek, thence to Wheeling, Baltimore and Washington. I intended to rove about among the Confederate troops and then find my way back through Winchester.

Mr. Lawrence was armed with a knife from six to ten inches in length and a weapon which he calls a hunting whip. The large end is loaded and has attached a hammer-shaped instrument and the smaller end has a loop strap fastened, through which the hand is inserted, the strap encircling the wrist. The knife and hunting whip are formidable weapons for hunting man or beast. There was also found on Mr. Lawrence's person a letter addressed to him by W. W. Glenn falsely representing that he was in search of land, advising him where to go, who were reliable and who not and assuring him "my friends will be glad to serve you." This letter was intended as directions to the place where Lawrence would find the guide and the route to take, the persons to trust and avoid. It was ingeniously devised (probably), but seen in the light of subsequent disclosures it reflects a disloyal and traitorous light, as straws are said to indicate the direction of the current. I would also state that Mr. Lawrence when in Wheeling gave a hackman 25 cents in postal currency on which was distinctly written: "Jeff. Davis rides a white horse, Abe rides a mule; Davis is a gentleman, Abe is a fool." I also respectfully state that the guide of Mr. Lawrence (E. M. Shipley) has also been before me but he refused peremptorily to make any statement or make any disclosures whatever. He had letters upon him of late date addressed to persons in rebellion and papers proving him to be a rebel soldier. Mr. Glenn, of Baltimore, is known to be (from intercepted letters) the confidential agent or correspondent of the rebels who congregate in Canada. He has once been arrested and imprisoned for disloyalty. He was the friend and adviser of Captain Wynne (of the British army) and it was at Glenn's house it is now said where he took refuge after escaping from the Old Capitol Prison. The fact that one of the British legation gave Mr. Lawrence a letter of introduction to a man so notoriously disloyal as Mr. Glenn; that Glenn gave Lawrence a letter of direction to reach the rebels through the Federal lines disguised by representing Lawrence as in search of land, and that neither Lawrence nor Shipley (the guide) will disclose a single word as to Glenn's connection with the expedition and the selection and employment of the rebel guide—these facts and suppressions seem to implicate Lawrence as being something else than a foolish adventurer impelled by curiosity into gross imprudence, and Messrs. Glenn and Clay without explanation cannot be relieved from unfavorable suspicions and imputations. Further investigations are being made and the result will be communicated, and in the meantime Mr. Lawrence will be held in custody.

I have the honor to be, very respectfully, your obedient servant,
L. C. TURNER,
Judge-Advocate.

———

FORT MONROE, VA., *May 12, 1863.*

Hon. E. M. STANTON, *Secretary of War:*

Mr. Ould informs me that he has about 10,000 of our Fredericksburg prisoners at Richmond. I have sent up transportation for them with a hospital steamer and corps of surgeons and nurses for the sick and wounded. As all the officers and men sent to Camp Parole from City Point to the present date have been declared exchanged I would respectfully recommend that they be sent away to their regiments and make room for the large number soon to be received there.
WM. H. LUDLOW,
Lieutenant-Colonel, &c.

[First indorsement.]

OFFICE COMMISSARY-GENERAL OF PRISONERS,
May 12, 1863.

Respectfully referred to the Surgeon-General with the request that he will give the necessary instructions for the care of the wounded and sick.
W. HOFFMAN,
Colonel Third Infantry, Commissary-General of Prisoners.

Please return telegram.
W. H.

[Second indorsement.]

SURGEON-GENERAL'S OFFICE, *May 12, 1863.*

Respectfully returned.
The medical director at Fort Monroe has been instructed to care for the sick and wounded.
By order of the Surgeon-General U. S. Army:
JOS. R. SMITH,
Surgeon, U. S. Army.

———

FORT MONROE, *May 12, 1863.*

Hon. E. M. STANTON:

I am informed on good authority that General Stonewall Jackson is not expected to live. He was shot by accident by his own men.

General Hays is reported not to be wounded and Mr. Ould promises to me his immediate delivery and also the delivery of the other captured officers.

WM. H. LUDLOW,
Lieutenant-Colonel, &c.

HEADQUARTERS DEPARTMENT OF VIRGINIA,
Fort Monroe, Va., May 12, 1863.

Hon. G. V. FOX, *Assistant Secretary of the Navy.*

SIR: I have the honor to inform you that the officers and men of the following-named vessels have been declared exchanged: Of the steamers Hatteras, Mercedita, Queen of the West, Harriet Lane, Isaac Smith, Columbia and of the schooner Vassar.

I am, very respectfully, your obedient servant,

WM. H. LUDLOW,
Lieutenant-Colonel and Agent for Exchange of Prisoners.

FORT MONROE, *May 12, 1863.*

Col. W. HOFFMAN, *Commissary-General of Prisoners:*

Our officers will be delivered. Send to me all the citizen prisoners and Confederate officers you have with other prisoners of war.

WM. H. LUDLOW,
Lieutenant-Colonel, &c.

OFFICE PROVOST-MARSHAL-GENERAL,
Saint Louis, Mo., May 12, 1863.

Maj. T. I. McKENNY, *Aide-de-Camp:*

In pursuance to the order and instructions of the Secretary of War of the 24th of April, 1863, a copy of which is herewith inclosed*, and under instructions from Maj. Gen. S. R. Curtis, commanding the department, I commit to your charge the persons whose names are upon the rolls herewith handed you as those of the class of disloyal citizens who are in rebellion against the Government, and for that cause are to be conducted under guard South and passed through the lines of the U. S. Army and within the military lines of the enemy in rebellion, with instructions not to return within our military lines without the permission of the Secretary of War. You will proceed hence by steam-boat or cars to Memphis, and thence either to Vicksburg or such other point as may be most proper for the delivery of these persons within the lines of the enemy. You will cause the baggage of these persons to be carefully examined; but as there are some families who voluntarily accompany their husbands permission has been given them to take an ample supply of clothing and those necessaries required for their use which they otherwise might be without. Every regard and humane indulgence should on the way and in the delivery of the women and children within the lines be given to them consistent with their being safely conducted. It has been left to the option of the husbands to take their wives and children, excepting in the case of Charles Clark. As to the proper point of passing the lines you should consult with the officer commanding the U. S. forces, exhibiting to him the annexed order* of the Secretary of War that the same may be duly

---

* Omitted here; see p. 515.

obeyed in a manner not to interfere with the existing military plans of such commanding officer. In view of this it must be left to your discretion as to the plan of passing these persons through and within the lines of the enemy. You will return the rolls of the prisoners in duplicate to this office, with indorsement thereon of the time, place and manner of executing this order.

Very respectfully, your obedient servant,

F. A. DICK,
Lieut. Col. and Provost-Marshal-General Dept. of the Missouri.

SPECIAL ORDER, }   OFFICE PROVOST-MARSHAL-GENERAL,
No. 74. }   *Saint Louis, Mo., May 12, 1863.*

The persons herewith delivered to you to be conducted through the lines are ordered not to return during the war within the lines of the U. S. Army upon pain of imprisonment for the war, and in addition thereto such other punishment as may be imposed upon them by military authority. You will communicate this order to said persons.

By command of Major-General Curtis:

F. A. DICK,
Lieutenant-Colonel and Provost-Marshal-General.

OFFICE COMMISSARY-GENERAL OF PRISONERS,
Washington, May 12, [1863.]

Mr. PHILIP SHREINER, *Columbia, Pa.*

I am directed by the commissary-general of prisoners to inform you that your letter to Lieutenant-Colonel Ludlow, agent for exchange, was referred to Mr. Ould, the rebel agent for exchange, and has been returned with the following indorsement:

We cannot permit the friends of a deceased prisoner to come within our lines to superintend the removal of his body. Where the death of a prisoner is well established and his place of interment can be identified with reasonable certainty we have no objection to the removal of his remains provided the application is accompanied with funds sufficient to defray the expenses of disinterring the body and transportation to City Point.

Very respectfully, your obedient servant,

W. T. HARTZ,
Captain and Assistant Adjutant-General.

NEW YORK, *May 12, 1863.*

ADJUTANT-GENERAL U. S. ARMY:

A detachment of 302 paroled prisoners and 70 men of the Eighth Regiment Infantry have arrived here from New Orleans on board the ship Undaunted, where they remain awaiting orders. The officer in charge had orders to report to you by letter, which he informs me has been done.

By order of Stewart Van Vliet, quartermaster:

D. STINSON,
Assistant Quartermaster.

WAR DEPARTMENT, *Washington, May 13, 1863.*

Hon. A. W. LOOMIS, *Pittsburg :*

Arrangements have already been made for the exchange of all prisoners taken in the battles near Fredericksburg and they are expected here in a few days. Your son shall have a furlough on his arrival.

EDWIN M. STANTON.

HEADQUARTERS DEPARTMENT OF VIRGINIA,
Fort Monroe, Va., May 13, 1863.

His Excellency A. LINCOLN,
President of the United States.

SIR: A month ago you pardoned William P. Phillips, of Elizabeth City County, sentenced by a military commission to imprisonment at hard labor for six months for shooting a negro boy who was stealing his corn. I was absent when the pardon was granted and since my return the presence of the enemy in this department has prevented me from writing to you on the subject. Though I never supposed the homicide to have been committed with malice I always thought and still think the shooting was unnecessary and unjustifiable and the punishment very light. Mr. Phillips is a quiet, respectable citizen and has many friends, some of whom are nearly connected with me as commander of this department. I was strongly pressed first not to bring him to trial at all and second to remit the punishment. Against all this pressure I was immovable because my opinion has always been that every man publicly charged with a crime should be tried, and when he has had a fair trial and the punishment not too great for the offense the sentence should be carried into execution.

We know that the efficacy of punishment as a restraint upon the bad passions of men depends mainly on its certainty. I am aware that one of the grounds on which the pardon of Mr. Phillips was urged was that his wife was so much disturbed by the prospect of his imprisonment as to be in danger of insanity. This was the opinion of a respectable army surgeon but I did not think such a hazard should defeat the ends of justice. It is not my purpose to find fault with the exercise of mercy in Mr. Phillips' case. The facts are stated for the purpose of presenting two other cases nearly coincident in point of time which were tried by the same commission in which a negro shot a white man and the other in which a negro shot a horse.

The first is that of Jack Banks. He was returning with several other negroes from a hog hunt as they called it—catching hogs running at large in the woods and carrying them off to kill them. The party were confessedly committing an unlawful act by taking property not their own. They were met by the owner of one of the hogs and on his claiming it they immediately let it go without objection. The owner's son was present with a double-barreled gun, and having asked one of the negroes to give his name without receiving satisfactory answer he shot him. Banks who was armed says (and there is no contradictory evidence) the second barrel was turned toward him, and he fired and shot the white man who had killed his companion.

Great stress was laid on the fact that Mr. Phillips immediately surrendered himself and made a full confession. It was certainly strongly in his favor. Jack Banks did the same thing and asked a trial. From the testimony I was strongly impressed with the belief that Banks had shot his assailant to save his own life; that it was a case of justifiable homicide and that he should have been acquitted. The court, however, sentenced him to imprisonment for eighteen months at hard labor. Mr. Phillips, a white man, for shooting a negro boy who was unarmed and running away from him was sentenced to six months imprisonment, and Jack Banks, a negro, for shooting a white man who was about to shoot him, was sentenced to imprisonment for eighteen months. I did not think these sentences bore a fair proportion in severity to the offenses which they were intended to punish. But courts are entitled to great consideration from those who review their judgment. They hear the testimony, they give weight to the appearance and manner of the witnesses and other circumstances which may not be as justly appreciated by those who only read the reports of the evidence. For this reason, notwithstanding a strong impression that Banks should have been discharged, I nevertheless after much hesitation approved the proceedings in both cases and ordered the sentences to be executed. Mr. Phillips was never confined for a day. He was held to bail before trial in a large sum but had no difficulty in finding sureties. Jack Banks being poor and without friends could not have found bail if he had tried and had to go to prison. He was confined a short time before trial and has been imprisoned four months at hard labor under sentence.

The other case was that of Reuben Willis, one of the colored companions of Banks. He was also armed, and he fired killing a horse. There was no evidence that he intended to kill any one, and I did not doubt that it was one of those chance shots which are made in an affray under the influence of fear and excitement without any definite purpose. Willis was sentenced by the same commission to hard labor for six months. Mr. Phillips for killing a boy and Willis for killing a horse received the same sentences. The latter was confined some weeks before trial and has been imprisoned four months at hard labor under sentence.

From high considerations connected with government and society in the United States I have never been in favor of putting negroes on the same footing with white men in regard to political rights and privileges, but I have always considered it a duty to treat them with kindness and humanity, and to do all in our power to elevate and improve their moral and intellectual condition. In the administration of justice in this department I have recognized no distinction of color. So far as depended on me crime has been punished firmly and impartially whether committed by negroes or white men. Indeed I have been disposed to hold the latter to a more rigid accountability in consideration of their superior moral and intellectual culture. I should have remitted the sentences pronounced on Banks and Willis as soon as Mr. Phillips was pardoned by you but for the principle which decided me not to interfere with the course of justice in the case of the latter. For the same reason I do not recommend their pardon to you, but I deem it my duty to present their cases and to suggest whether on every principle of equal justice these negroes should not receive the same mercy which was shown to a white man who was guilty of a higher crime.

The proceedings in all the cases are in the custody of the Judge-Advocate-General should you desire to consult them.

I have the honor to be, very respectfully, your obedient servant,
JOHN A. DIX,
Major-General.

JUDGE-ADVOCATE-GENERAL'S OFFICE,
Washington, D. C., May 13, 1863.

Respectfully returned to the Secretary of War. The sum of $1,000 taken from Don Ramon Mir while attempting to pass our lines without a pass was in the form of Confederate notes or bills of the Confederacy. As such they were seized by the provost court of New Orleans. Not only are these notes regarded by our Government as possessed of no pecuniary value, but they are also viewed as evidence of the existing rebellion and *indicia* of treason and as tending to excite a sympathy and an interest in the cause of the rebels on the part of those who may use or receive them. They are illegal and disloyal publications and as such are ordered to be destroyed wherever found. An application therefore to restore these notes to their former possessor either in their original form or in Federal currency cannot be entertained. If Don Ramon Mir has other and equitable claims against the United States for property destroyed by our forces he is entitled to have them adjusted upon presenting the proper vouchers, but his present claim is quite a separate and independent matter.

J. HOLT,
Judge-Advocate-General.

OFFICE COMMISSARY-GENERAL OF PRISONERS,
Washington, May 13, 1863.

Maj. Gen. A. E. BURNSIDE,
Commanding Department of the Ohio, Cincinnati, Ohio.

GENERAL: I desire respectfully to call your attention to the following matter: A few days since I received from Colonel Simonson, commanding Camp Carrington, muster and descriptive rolls of paroled prisoners at that camp, furnished as he states pursuant to General Orders, No. 46, current series. The order referred to applies to men absent without authority, paroled prisoners included, and requires that they should be sent to general camps designated in General Orders, No. 72, of June, 1862, and it requires that the military commandant shall make tri-monthly reports of men so forwarded. Colonel Simonson neither forwarded the men nor made the reports required, and from his rolls I am unable to say whether the names of these men have ever been presented for exchange or not or whether they are covered by the recent declaration of exchanges by having been delivered at City Point. General Orders, No. 72, names the camps at which paroled prisoners are to be assembled, and the commanders of these camps are required to furnish me with rolls of all men who join or leave, and with a monthly and semi-monthly return showing all alterations. Previous to November last it was permitted that paroled prisoners belonging to Indiana regiments should be assembled at Camp Morton, but since that time the Secretary of War has repeatedly refused to permit special camps to be appropriated to paroled troops of particular States. If the men on Colonel Simonson's rolls were delivered at City Point as I presume they were they were ordered from Annapolis to Camp Chase, from which place they deserted, being encouraged to do so in hopes they could go to Camp Carrington and remain there without fear of punishment, and in this it would seem they have been disappointed. You will readily understand the confusion and detriment to the service which must result from such a state of things, and I respectfully request you will give such instructions as will secure a compliance with the orders from the War

Department relative to paroled prisoners, and when they are deviated from with your approval may I ask the favor of being informed of the change?

Very respectfully, your obedient servant,

W. HOFFMAN,
Colonel Third Infantry, Commissary-General of Prisoners.

OFFICE COMMISSARY-GENERAL OF PRISONERS,
Washington, D. C., May 13, 1863.

Brig. Gen. J. H. MARTINDALE,
Comdg. Military District of Washington, Washington, D. C.

GENERAL: By authority of the General-in-Chief I have the honor to request you will order all prisoners of war in this city including officers, with the exceptions heretofore made of those having special charges against them, and all citizen prisoners who are subjects for exchange, to be delivered at City Point as early as practicable. Duplicate parole rolls should be sent with the prisoners, and a roll without the parole is required for this office. It is expected that paroled Federal prisoners of war will be delivered in this city in a few days and the returning steamer can take the rebel prisoners to be delivered at City Point. I will give you early notice on this point.

Very respectfully, your obedient servant,

W. HOFFMAN,
Colonel Third Infantry, Commissary-General of Prisoners.

OFFICE COMMISSARY-GENERAL OF PRISONERS,
Washington, May 13, 1863.

Col. B. L. E. BONNEVILLE,
Commanding Benton Barracks, Saint Louis, Mo.

COLONEL: I am authorized by the Secretary of War to create a fund for the benefit of paroled prisoners of war by the sale of the surplus rations to the Subsistence Department. These rations are to be turned over to the commissary who pays for them just as for the savings of a company, except that he holds the money in his hands and acts as treasurer of the fund, which he disburses on the order of the commanding officer of the camp. Proper books must be procured for keeping the accounts of the fund, and monthly accounts are required for this office, with vouchers showing the amount of savings and the amount expended. Of course the money after being accounted for in paying for the savings is dropped from his accounts to the Subsistence Department. The fund is used for promoting the welfare of the men by purchasing all necessary table and kitchen furniture, all proper articles for the sick, paying extra pay to clerks at headquarters, paying clerks and extra-duty men in quartermaster's and commissary departments, and cooks and attendants in hospital, whose duties are mainly with paroled prisoners, and in purchasing all utensils for preserving the police of the barracks. When detachments leave to join their regiments each man should be furnished with a cup, plate, knife, fork and spoon. As there are rarely any full companies among the prisoners of war this arrangement puts into a useful shape a large amount of rations which otherwise must be thrown away, and contributes much to the welfare of the troops, while it saves expense in many ways to the Government, and I have to request you will have the system put in force at Benton Barracks for all men who are not in organized companies. The accompanying scale* of rations is about what is issued, with perhaps a slight increase in the sugar and coffee. It is left for you to decide what the reduction should be. The fund accumulates very rapidly and it is necessary to have it carefully accounted for to prevent misapplication of it.

Very respectfully, your obedient servant,

W. HOFFMAN,
Colonel Third Infantry, Commissary-General of Prisoners.

WASHINGTON, *May 13, 1863.*

Lieut. Col. W. H. LUDLOW:

Telegram of yesterday is received. All prisoners of war and citizen prisoners will be sent to you.

W. HOFFMAN,
Commissary-General of Prisoners.

OFFICE COMMISSARY-GENERAL OF PRISONERS,
Washington, D. C., May 13, 1863.

Capt. W. C. THORPE,
Mustering and Disbursing Officer, Wheeling, Va.

CAPTAIN: Your letter of the 9th instant has been received, and in order to decide how far your duties under General Orders, No. 46, and Major Darr's under General Orders, No. 58, conflict I have referred your letter to Colonel Fry, Provost-Marshal-General, and the following is his indorsement thereon:

MAY 13, 1863.

The duties of Major Darr under my bureau give him no control over paroled prisoners nor has he received any instructions from me on which to base the notice he has published in the papers as shown within. I know of no instructions given to him by General Schenck, and I have regarded Major Darr as being exclusively under my orders so far as the enrollment act is concerned since his assignment as provost-marshal-general of Western Virginia.

JAMES B. FRY.

From this it appears that the duties devolved upon you by the first-named orders are not transferred to Major Darr by the second and you will therefore perform the duties required of you as the mustering and disbursing officer. Please show Colonel Fry's indorsement to Major Darr that he may understand the views of the Provost-Marshal-[General].

Very respectfully, your obedient servant,

W. HOFFMAN,
Colonel Third Infantry, Commissary-General of Prisoners.

HEADQUARTERS PAROLED PRISONERS,
Near Annapolis, Md., May 13, 1863.

Col. W. H. CHESEBROUGH,
Assistant Adjutant-General, Eighth Army Corps.

SIR: I have the honor to inform you that in accordance with instructions received from headquarters Eighth Army Corps I have examined

---

* Not found.

the report made by Captain Lazelle, Eighth U. S. Infantry, on Camp Parole and would most respectfully make the following report:

ARRIVALS OF PRISONERS.

Paroled prisoners arrive here without notice being given in any way to the commanding officer. My arrangements are perfect for the reception of 2,000 men at any moment, and can clean, clothe and feed 2,000 men in ten hours; but sometimes I receive more than 2,000 at one arrival. Would recommend that a telegram be sent from Fortress Monroe before the prisoners are sent that I may provide for any number, as I can with ten hours' notice.

THE GUARD.

The daily detail of sixty men for guard has been changed, and the Third Regiment Potomac Home Brigade have their headquarters now in Camp Parole and under my command, thus giving me a permanent guard and 100 men on duty every day instead of 60, thus affording a greater protection to the property of the Government and the maintaining of a stricter discipline in camp. The Purnell Cavalry has been very much reduced by Col. C. A. Waite's having sixty men as a provost-guard at Annapolis, Md., leaving me but twenty men to guard a district of ten miles. Would respectfully recommend that Col. C. A. Waite have a company sent to him that I may have my men back, to enable me to perform my duty in protecting the property in this district and enforcing order in my command.

PERMANENT OFFICERS FOR CAMP.

There have been four extra officers permanently detailed for duty with paroled prisoners which greatly relieves these headquarters and enables me to keep a correct record. Inclosed please find blank sheet of new record book which I have gotten up, giving the history of the man from his arrival until he leaves camp.

THE QUARTERMASTER'S DEPARTMENT.

Arrangements have been made to have at all times on hand 2,000 complete outfits of clothing; also 2,000 tin cups, plates, knives, forks and spoons; and each man on arriving receives a new suit of clothes and a set of table furniture which they take with them when they leave camp. All requisitions for clothing are made on the commissary-general of prisoners at Washington and are very punctually attended to, and all deficiencies heretofore are now amply supplied.

NEW QUARTERS.

The recommendations of the inspecting officer as to the erecting of new quarters for paroled prisoners have been adopted by the commander-in-chief and I have received orders to build new barracks. There are to be sixty buildings, each 100 by 20 feet and 9 feet high, of boards, and bunks for 120 men, giving accommodations for 7,000 men. I am to build twenty kitchens, each 50 by 25 feet, to cook for 400 men each. Also two large store-houses 200 by 25 feet for quartermaster's department and one for the commissary department same size. Also six buildings for the hospital with a large kitchen for their accommodation. There will also be built comfortable accommodations for the guard. The contract for lumber has been made and the labor is to be furnished by extra-duty men in this camp and will be paid from the camp fund. The property on which the barracks are to be built has been hired by the Government at $1,500 rent per year. The house on the farm will be used as headquarters for officers and the large brick barn will be used as an ordnance store-house. The woods adjoining the farm will be used to the best possible advantage in building the new barracks. Sinks will be built on the edge of the wood.

CAMP FUND.

The camp fund is made from the savings of rations, and from this fund the hospital receives all that is needed for the comfort of the sick, and everything needed for the camp is purchased with this fund. All the departments are worked and sustained by the fund and all the extra-duty men are paid from this fund, and I have a balance now on hand of $9,852.68, which is to be used for the benefit of the new camp.

The new camp will be completed in about six weeks from this date, and all transportation after the new camp is built will be by the rail-road, the camp being on the side of it, thus saving the roads in the city of Annapolis, so much complained of.

All of which is most respectfully submitted.

I am, colonel, with great respect, your obedient servant,

GEO. SANGSTER,
Lieutenant-Colonel, Commanding Paroled Prisoners.

WAR DEPARTMENT, *Richmond, Va., May 13, 1863.*
Lieut. Col. WILLIAM H. LUDLOW, *Agent of Exchange.*

SIR: I send to you officers equivalent to 431 privates. Only officers equal to 349 privates were due to you. You will recollect that the Columbia officers (Captain [Acting Lieutenant] Conover and others) reduced the number from 431 to 349. When will you deliver the officers recently captured by you?

I again call your attention to the large number of officers captured long since and still held by you. You can assure your Government that retaliation will be resorted to in every case where a party is unjustly detained. You will certainly give us credit for great forbearance even in the cases of officers lately released by you, but who had been held in captivity without any pretense of trial for many months. Nothing is left now as to those whom our protests have failed to release but to resort to retaliation. The Confederate Government is anxious to avoid a resort to that harsh measure. In its name I make a final appeal for that justice to our imprisoned officers and men which your own agreements have declared to be their due.

Respectfully, your obedient servant,

RO. OULD,
Agent of Exchange.

WAR DEPARTMENT, *Richmond, Va., May 13, 1863.*
Lieut. Col. WILLIAM H. LUDLOW,
Agent for Exchange of Prisoners, Fortress Monroe, Va.

COLONEL: My attention has again been called to the case of Michael S. Kennard, adjutant Fifteenth Texas [Cavalry] Regiment, captured at Arkansas Post, tried and convicted at Saint Louis, Mo., for violating an alleged oath of allegiance said to have been given long ago, and sentenced to hard labor during the war with ball and chain.

This officer is regularly in our service and by our former agreements is wholly and entirely released from any former oath of allegiance to the United States Government. If Adjutant Kennard is not promptly delivered no alternative will be left but to select one or more Federal officers of equal rank and subject them to like treatment.

I am, colonel, very respectfully, your obedient servant,

RO. OULD,
Agent of Exchange.

WAR DEPARTMENT, OFFICE EXCHANGE OF PRISONERS,
Richmond, Va., May 13, 1863.
Lieut. Col. WILLIAM H. LUDLOW,
Agent of Exchange, Fortress Monroe.

COLONEL: I have the honor to inform you that I have this day declared specially exchanged: Second Lieut. B. A. Marshall, Company H, Fifty-ninth Virginia; Lieut. R. F. Lefler, Company H, Fifty-seventh North Carolina; Sergt. G. J. Pollard, Company H, Fifty-ninth Virginia, captured May 30, 1863, at Ashland, Va., by Col. J. Kilpatrick, commanding First Brigade, Third Division, Cavalry Corps, and released on parole, which I will offset to this extent against the number due me on deliveries at City Point up to the time of our last interview.

I am, colonel, very respectfully, your obedient servant,

RO. OULD,
Agent of Exchange.

WAR DEPARTMENT, OFFICE EXCHANGE OF PRISONERS,
Richmond, Va., May 13, 1863.
Lieut. Col. WILLIAM H. LUDLOW,
Agent of Exchange, Fortress Monroe.

COLONEL: I have the honor to inform you that I have this day declared specially exchanged: Capt. Taliaferro Hunter, assistant quartermaster; D. T. White, teamster; Paul Lipscomb, teamster; J. B. Wright, teamster, captured May 3, 1863, at Hanover Junction, Va., by Lieut. Col. H. Davis, commanding Twelfth Illinois Cavalry, and released on parole, which I will offset to this extent against the number due me on deliveries at City Point up to the time of our last interview.

I am, colonel, very respectfully, your obedient servant,

RO. OULD,
Agent of Exchange.

CINCINNATI, OHIO, *May 14, 1863.*
Hon. E. M. STANTON, *Secretary of War, Washington:*

Vallandigham is still here under guard. Will not be sent till to-morrow. He is sentenced to confinement in Fort Warren, Boston Harbor, during the war.

A. E. BURNSIDE,
Major-General.

HEADQUARTERS, *Cincinnati, May 14, 1863.*
Colonel HOFFMAN, *Commissary-General of Prisoners:*

Shall rebel officers, prisoners of war, be released on taking the oath of allegiance? I would recommend that it be allowed.

A. E. BURNSIDE,
Major-General.

OFFICE COMMISSARY-GENERAL OF PRISONERS,
Washington, D. C., May 14, 1863.

General S. P. HEINTZELMAN,
    Commanding Department of Washington, Washington, D. C.

GENERAL: Will it be necessary to arm the exchanged prisoners belonging to your command now at Annapolis and about to join their regiments?

Very respectfully, your obedient servant,
                                W. HOFFMAN,
        Colonel Third Infantry, Commissary-General of Prisoners.

[Indorsement.]

HDQRS. DEPARTMENT OF WASHINGTON, *May 14, 1863.*

Respectfully returned to Colonel Hoffman, commissary-general of prisoners. It will not be necessary to arm the exchanged prisoners belonging to this command before they join their regiments.

By command of Major-General Heintzelman:
                                CARROLL H. POTTER,
                                Assistant Adjutant-General.

WASHINGTON, *May 14, 1863.*

Lieutenant-Colonel LUDLOW,
    Commissioner for Exchange of Prisoners:

Can you arrange to have Baton Rouge as a place for the delivery of prisoners? Do not cease to urge Doctor Rucker's release.

                                W. HOFFMAN,
                                Commissary-General of Prisoners.

HEADQUARTERS DEPARTMENT OF VIRGINIA,
                    Fort Monroe, May 14, 1863.

Col. JOSEPH HOLT, *Judge-Advocate-General.*

SIR: Will you please furnish me with such information as you may deem proper in relation to the trial and conviction of two men in Kentucky as spies and sentenced to death? Also in the cases of other men in General Hooker's command in the same situation. I am called on by the Confederate agent for information in these cases. He responded to my call satisfactorily in the case of Captain Webster, hung at Richmond, and I desire to be enabled to do the same.

                                WM. H. LUDLOW,
                Lieutenant-Colonel and Agent for Exchange of Prisoners.

[Indorsement.]

JUDGE-ADVOCATE-GENERAL'S OFFICE, *May 16, 1863.*

Respectfully referred to the Secretary of War.

The demand made by the rebel authorities for information in reference to the proceedings of our courts-martial which resulted in the conviction of certain spies and traitorous emissaries in Kentucky is deemed impertinent and the information sought will not be communicated unless specially directed by the Secretary. This Government is in no degree responsible to rebels in arms for the action of its military courts, and it seems to me that it would utterly degrade itself by recognizing any such responsibility. Any such recognition would involve an ignoring of the great truth that this is a war on crime and criminals which cannot be lost sight of without incurring the risk of becoming in the judgment of the world criminals ourselves.

J. HOLT,
Judge-Advocate-General.

HEADQUARTERS DEPARTMENT OF VIRGINIA,
Fort Monroe, May 14, 1863.

Col. W. HOFFMAN, <i>Commissary-General of Prisoners.</i>

COLONEL: My attention has been frequently called by Mr. Ould, the Confederate agent for exchange of prisoners, to the fact that many Confederate officers and men who have been declared exchanged and who are in the department of Major-General Banks are retained by him. Will you please have issued the necessary orders for their delivery within the Confederate lines? I am also informed that many members of so-called irregular organizations within the same department have been refused exchange. These come under the same rules that have regulated our past exchanges. Will you please to have the necessary orders issued in their cases and inform General Banks that they are proper subjects of exchange?

I am, very respectfully, your obedient servant,

WM. H. LUDLOW,
Lieutenant-Colonel and Agent for Exchange of Prisoners.

HEADQUARTERS DEPARTMENT OF VIRGINIA,
Fort Monroe, May 14, 1863.

Col. W. HOFFMAN, <i>Commissary-General of Prisoners.</i>

COLONEL: Will you please furnish me with a copy of your lists of all Confederate prisoners, military and civil, at the various camps and places of detention? I think you informed me that they were made monthly to you and you can send me those of the last month.

I am, very respectfully, your obedient servant,

WM. H. LUDLOW,
Lieutenant-Colonel and Agent for Exchange of Prisoners.

FORT MONROE, May 14, 1863.

Col. W. HOFFMAN, <i>Commissary-General of Prisoners.</i>

COLONEL: I have made a demand upon the Confederate agent for Hiram Bloss, Ezekiel S. Bloss and Morgan Garrett, citizens of Wayne County, Va. I inclose to you a copy of memorandum handed to me by Governor Peirpoint and which I desire may be shown to the Secretary of War. I hope I am correct in the opinion that Governor Peirpoint has no authority whatever over military captures and that some restriction may be promptly placed on this system of retaliation which seems to be going on without the knowledge or consent of the Secretary of War.

The only Virginia officers now in confinement at Richmond are Captain Gramm and Lieutenant Wade, of the Eighth Regiment [West]

Virginia Volunteers, detained as hostages for Captain Dusky and Lieutenant Varner, now at hard labor in the penitentiary at Albany on conviction of breaking into a post-office. The Confederate authorities claim these two latter as prisoners of war; state they were regularly mustered into the Virginia State service; assume the act as done by competent order of superiors and upon this footing clearly place Dusky and Varner as prisoners of war entitled to exchange. The readiest mode of releasing Captain Gramm and Lieutenant Wade is to accept this explanation of the Confederate authorities and exchange the men. Please obtain the direction of the Secretary of War on these two cases. I may add that a demand has been made for the sheriff of Barbour County but of course with no such alternatives as presented by Governor Peirpoint.

I am, very respectfully, your obedient servant,

WM. H. LUDLOW,
Lieutenant-Colonel and Agent for Exchange of Prisoners.

[First indorsement.]

OFFICE COMMISSARY-GENERAL OF PRISONERS,
May 18, 1863.

Respectfully referred to the Secretary of War and I would respectfully suggest that the interference ot any other authority than that of the War Department in the control and treatment of prisoners cannot but lead to much embarrassment.

W. HOFFMAN,
Colonel Third Infantry, Commissary-General of Prisoners.

[Second indorsement.]

WAR DEPARTMENT, *May 21, 1863.*

Respectfully referred to the Judge-Advocate-General for report.
By order of the Secretary of War:

ED. R. S. CANBY,
Brigadier-General.

[Third indorsement.]

JUDGE-ADVOCATE-GENERAL'S OFFICE, *June 5, 1863.*

Respectfully returned to the Secretary of War.

The recommendation of Colonel Ludlow, agent for exchange of prisoners, in reference to accepting the terms of the Confederate agent in case of exchange of Dusky and Varner for Captain Gramm and Lieutenant Wade is concurred in. The proceedings of Governor Peirpoint in seizing and confining suspected rebels in his vicinity, placing them in a chain gang and holding them at hard labor until certain civilians and officers of West Virginia are released and exchanged by the enemy is certainly an interference with the disposition and treatment of prisoners of war which must needs be very embarrassing to those officers to whom the control of prisoners and their exchange has been expressly delegated by the War Department. Unless some special authority has been given to Governor Peirpoint by the War or State Office to act in this matter he should be advised that he cannot without embarrassing the Government transcend the ordinary police power which he is authorized as Governor to exercise over rebels within his jurisdiction, and that by taking it upon himself to hold rebel prisoners for exchange for Union men he necessarily interferes with the formal arrangements made by the proper officers for the same purpose. The fearlessness and energy shown by Governor Peirpoint in making these arrests cannot be too highly commended, but they should be made by virtue of his general police powers if not expressly enlarged as aforesaid.

J. HOLT,
Judge-Advocate-General.

[Inclosure.]

MEMORANDUM.

APRIL 27, 1863.

The sheriff of Barbour County, Va. (name I think Trahern), was seized at his home last winter by Imboden's men and taken to Richmond. Propositions have been made to exchange a man named Jones, from Pendleton, a rebel and clerk of the county court of that county.

Benjamin Bassell, of Upshur County, who went into the rebellion, has been arrested also. Jones and Bassell are both in Camp Chase. I desire to exchange one or both of them for the sheriff of Barbour. Bassell is a member of rebel legislature, well known at Richmond. I have six rebels imprisoned now at Wheeling for the sheriff of Barbour.

I desire also to call attention to some of the officers of the loyal Virginia regiments who are in the penitentiary at Richmond on some pretense. I have made arrangements to place double the number of rebel Virginia officers of superior and equal rank in a chain gang in Ohio County and set them to breaking stone on the National road until those Virginia officers are released or exchanged. Two of the Union officers to whom I refer belong to the Eighth [West] Virginia Regiment. Please get an ultimatum in both these cases and inform me.

I have now at Camp Chase Lieutenant Samuels and Lieutenant Holderby, of Jenkins' brigade, taken at Point Pleasant, that will join the chain gang.

I do not want to go to this extremity, but if forced to the alternative I shall do it; and if the sheriff of Barbour is not released I shall send beyond the lines and arrest the most influential I can get and continue until he is released.

Please inform me of the reply.

F. H. PEIRPOINT.

WAR DEPARTMENT, *Washington, D. C., May 14, 1863.*

W. P. WOOD, *Superintendent Old Capitol Prison:*

You will discharge from custody T. T. Tunstall upon his signing the parole* here inclosed.

By order of the Secretary of War:

L. C. TURNER,
Judge-Advocate.

HEADQUARTERS MILITARY COMMANDER,
Wheeling, May 14, 1863.

Col. W. HOFFMAN, *Commissary-General of Prisoners.*

SIR: I have the honor to inclose copy of General Orders, No. 15,† Headquarters Middle Department, Eighth Army Corps, relating to the capture and paroling of U. S. troops by the rebels without forwarding them to the points indicated for exchanges. Under this order

---

*Not found.　　　　　　　　　　　† Omitted here; see p. 339.

Captain Godwin, Company A, Sixth West Virginia Volunteer Infantry, and forty-six men of his company, captured lately at Oakland, Md., on the Baltimore and Ohio Railroad and released on parole, have been directed to return at once to duty. The same course is to be pursued with others captured and released at different points in West Virginia, in compliance with above order.

Very respectfully,

JOS. DARR, JR.,
Major and Provost-Marshal-General.

OFFICE COMMISSARY-GENERAL OF PRISONERS,
Washington, D. C., May 14, 1863.

Col. W. HOFFMAN, *Commissary-General of Prisoners.*

COLONEL: Under instructions received from this office on the 11th instant I have the honor to submit the following report upon the progress making in the construction of the new camp for paroled prisoners near Annapolis, Md., and of the affairs of the present camp used for paroled prisoners so far as it seemed necessary to examine into and report upon them, and so far as they are not embraced in previous reports by me of the same camp:

Due notice has been given in the public prints by the assistant quartermaster at Annapolis, Captain Blodgett, in soliciting proposals for lumber, roofing and building material designed to be used in the construction of the buildings at the new camp, and these advertisements have been very freely responded to by parties willing to furnish what is required. The bids for lumber were opened on Saturday last and the lowest (and accepted) bid for white pine lumber was $23.90 per 1,000 feet, and for scantling, per 1,000 feet, $20. As yet no contract has been awarded, though the terms of the advertisement permitted the amount to be sufficiently varied and made the terms of delivery subject to the quartermaster's control. I submit an estimate, marked A,* by Captain Blodgett of the probable cost of one building of 100 by 20 feet, on the basis that the work is all done by regular employés and at the prices near the present market value of material, though I think that the estimate is rather more liberal in its terms than would be absolutely required even in using all new material and hired labor. There are now preparing at the old camp a large quantity of foundation logs or string pieces to be used in the new buildings. Several hundred have been squared and completed and are now on the ground to be occupied. This is I believe the extent of the progress made in the construction of the new camp. Your verbal instructions to me I placed upon paper for the use of Colonel Sangster and Captain Blodgett. I inclose a copy.

Independently of the positive instructions given from this office to the commanding officer at Camp Parole no material changes have been made in the affairs there more than would be slowly developed on the system heretofore pursued or previously to the date of my last report. These instructions concern the guard, the assistant officers sent there, the records, the furnishing of supplies to the men, the employment of clerks, construction of sinks, and generally speaking have been well carried out and what relates to them is assuming a more satisfactory condition. A daily guard of seventy-two men is mounted from the soldiers now stationed at the camp but formerly occupying the College

* Omitted.

Green Barracks. This guard, however, is not sufficient to form a con-nected chain of sentinels about the camp or even more than two-thirds of it, and as this is the case the sentinels' posts are confined to the vicinities of the public property and the upper portion of the camp, with the exception of two or three sentinels placed near the largest collection of permanent quarters at the lower end. This want of a continuous chain of sentinels renders the guard duty incomplete and not as efficient as it would otherwise be. It would be very desir-able if the nature of the ground and position of the permanent bar-racks admitted to keep the camp in a more compact form, but without abandoning entirely the barracks at the lower end this cannot be done since the chief and more important portion of the camp is at the upper end. The intermediate ground is to a great extent not fit to be used for camping purposes. Six officers are regularly detailed and constantly in charge of the six battalions into which the men at the camp are divided, and by their assistance the records of the men are much better kept than formerly and better discipline prevails. They are also now properly supplied with cooking materials and table furniture sufficient for each man's use. Temporary sinks have also been constructed and surrounded by brush screens and the soldiers com-monly use them, though from the absence of sufficient sentinels nuisances are often committed and the men range in and out at pleas-ure at those points where there is no guard. I have carefully inquired into and examined the labors of each of the seven clerks now employed by Colonel Sangster and am satisfied that the numerous reports which he is required to furnish, the rolls, abstracts, orders and accounts render the services of the present number necessary with the excep-tion of one, a record clerk so called and reported. This clerk is employed both as clerk and orderly and his duty is generally to obtain data of their position from the men themselves to fill out required rolls or records, or in reply to numerous inquiries from people not connected with the camp. It would seem that as this is an orderly's or an offi-cer's duty the information could be furnished to the commanding officer by them; and since each of the other six clerks performs all the duties embraced under one of each of the six classes of papers required, such as descriptive rolls, reports, copying of orders, letters, &c., general rolls of men, adjutant's duties, and one general clerk for miscellaneous duties required by the commanding officer, that the duties of this one might be dispensed with.

The police of the camp is quite bad and the duty very imperfectly performed when performed at all. The camp should in my opinion be divided into sections and one put under the charge of each battalion officer who should be held responsible for its cleanliness. As it is now the camp is very dirty and will certainly be unhealthful in warm weather if left in the present condition. The quarters and guard-house are in the same condition as when last reported upon by me, though the former are not occupied to their fullest capacity just now by one-half the facilities for accommodation. The medical department of Camp Parole has recently been placed under the supervising charge of Surg. Thomas A. McParlin. It is very desirable to prepare as rapidly as possible the new camp, that by an early removal more system, order, discipline and cleanliness may be introduced and preserved free from the surroundings and inconveniences so much calculated at present to interfere with these elements.

I am, colonel, very respectfully, your obedient servant,

H. M. LAZELLE,
Captain, Eighth Infantry, U. S. Army.

[Inclosure.]

ANNAPOLIS, MD., *May 13, 1863.*

Col. GEORGE SANGSTER,
    Commanding Paroled Camp, near Annapolis.

COLONEL: I beg to lay before you for future reference the following suggestions from Colonel Hoffman, commissary-general of prisoners, which he desires should be carried into effect with regard to the construction and arrangement of buildings at the new camp for paroled prisoners so far as these suggestions can be so carried out economically under the arrangements already made for putting up the buildings required. He desires, first, that in the progress of building that storehouses, hospitals, privies, kitchens and all other necessary buildings should progress in construction (with reference to number) so as to accommodate a proportional number of men to the barracks constructed; in other words the accommodation required in all of the buildings put up shall be proportioned to each other so that the camp as it progresses shall be complete. The building the commanding general desires to be commenced at the lower end of the camp or that end nearest the dwelling house which is to be occupied, so that if at any time the work is to be suspended the camp may be left in a compact form. The commissary-general desires that if practicable and consistent with economy the buildings to be used as quarters (of 120 men each) shall be increased in width to twenty-two feet and that the outside covering shall be of boards placed vertically and matched. The paroled mechanics now employed to be retained for the present. Their places will be filled by men selected for the purpose when so ordered by Colonel Hoffman, when the present mechanics will be sent to their regiments. The colonel desires that all the building material composing the permanent buildings of the present camp shall be used as far as is possible in the buildings now to be constructed at the new camp.

Very respectfully, your obedient servant,

H. M. LAZELLE,
    Captain, U. S. Army, Asst. to Com. Gen. of Prisoners.

HEADQUARTERS DEPARTMENT OF VIRGINIA,
    Fort Monroe, Va., May 15, 1863.

Hon. E. M. STANTON,
    Secretary of War, Washington, D. C.

SIR: I have the honor to acknowledge the receipt of your telegraphic dispatch in regard to correspondence to and from the rebel States through Fort Monroe and to report:

1. That when I assumed command of the department and relieved Major-General Wool on the 2d of June, 1862, I found letters passing freely in both directions. They were examined by his aides, and on assigning the duty to my own staff I found the time of two of them was fully occupied with this duty. Only such letters as were considered unexceptionable were transmitted. The rest were sent from time to time to the Dead-Letter Office.

2. On inquiry I was informed that letters were transmitted in this manner with the permission of the Government and at the discretion of the commanding general of the department. The system found in operation was merely continued, but as will be seen with great modifications.

3. Letters of three and four pages, even two sheets, were frequently received for transmission. They were often without signatures or

signed with initial letters. To put an end to these annoyances and to secure a certain degree of responsibility in correspondents some brief rules were adopted. They are inclosed and marked A.* The result has been to reduce correspondence so much that not more than two or three hours a day are required by one of my aides to examine letters, including those addressed to prisoners of war.

4. These rules imply no obligation to forward letters. Even when fully complied with the transmission is discretionary. In explanation I have the honor to inclose a copy of a letter† to J. Holbrook, esq., special agent Post-Office Department, New York, marked B.

5. This subject has been twice a matter of reference and explanation, once incidentally, between the War Department and myself, as will be seen by the inclosed indorsements* marked C and D. In a personal interview with you soon after they were made I also explained the matter. I had then stopped all letters, but I found there were cases of great hardship in which intelligence of the death or wants of relatives and the distresses of families were sought to be communicated, and under the strict rules I adopted letters are now forwarded as before.

6. As a sample of the correspondence which is permitted I send three letters taken without selection from a number waiting to be forwarded. If there is no objection they will go to their destination when returned.

7. You are under a misapprehension in supposing that letters have only been forwarded with the sanction of the War Department in "one or two isolated instances." I have directed Captain Lord who has charge of the correspondence to keep a memoranda of the letters forwarded to the President and Departments of the Government, and he reports the number received since November as follows: From the President, 5; from the War Department, 25; from the Post-Office Department, 5; from the State Department, 3. In addition to these a large number have been received from Major Turner, from officers of the Government and members of Congress. They are all, however, subjected to the usual scrutiny. No letter passes in either direction without being read.

I am, sir, very respectfully, your obedient servant,

JOHN A. DIX,
Major-General.

FORT MONROE, *May 15, 1863.*

Hon. E. M. STANTON:

I send you files of the Richmond papers for several days previous to the 14th by mail. The prisoners arriving here think the whole number received at Richmond from Fredericksburg do not exceed 4,500. Those captured by the rebel General Forrest have arrived in Richmond.

JOHN A. DIX,
Major-General.

FORT MONROE, *May 15, 1863.*

Hon. E. M. STANTON:

I send by to-day's mail from Richmond papers of the 14th. News from Tullahoma, Chattanooga and Charleston up to the 12th. Nothing important. The prisoners from Richmond are arriving. It is

---

* Not found.   † Omitted here; see p. 591.

thought they will not exceed 7,000. This does not probably include all the wounded captured near Fredericksburg.

JOHN A. DIX,
Major-General.

HEADQUARTERS CAMP OF INSTRUCTION,
Benton Barracks, Mo., May 15, 1863.
Col. A. V. COLBURN,
Assistant Adjutant-General, Department of the Missouri.

COLONEL: Col. William Hoffman's official telegram of the 8th instant announcing the exchange of certain officers and enlisted men, with your indorsement on same of this date requesting a report of the names of any officers or soldiers coming under the declaration of said exchange, is just received. I would say in answer that all the paroled commissioned officers at this post, numbering an aggregate of about 115, and about 1,050 enlisted men will come under the declaration of this exchange. If you require it I will have accurate lists giving name, rank, company and regiment forwarded to you as soon as practicable.

I am, very respectfully, your obedient servant,
B. L. E. BONNEVILLE,
Colonel, U. S. Army, Commanding.

HEADQUARTERS CAMP OF INSTRUCTION,
Benton Barracks, Mo., May 15, 1863.
Col. W. HOFFMAN,
Commissary-General of Prisoners, Washington, D. C.

SIR: I have the honor herewith to transmit returns of paroled prisoners at this post for the month of April, 1863, embracing 114 commissioned officers present; 4 commissioned officers absent with leave; 3 commissioned officers absent without leave; 3,067 enlisted men present; 36 enlisted men absent with leave; 578 enlisted men absent without leave; 18 Government employés present; 3,820, aggregate present and absent.

Very respectfully, your obedient servant,
B. L. E. BONNEVILLE,
Colonel, U. S. Army, Commanding.

OFFICE COMMISSARY-GENERAL OF PRISONERS,
Washington, D. C., May 15, 1863.
Maj. Gen. S. P. HEINTZELMAN,
Commanding Defenses of Washington, Washington, D. C.

GENERAL: Much embarrassment is experienced at the Old Capitol Prison in disposing of prisoners arrested for disloyal conduct in consequence of the failure by the parties arresting them to send with them anything in the shape of charges, and I have therefore the honor to request that you will direct all under your command who make arrests of this nature to forward with [them] the place of arrest, place of residence and specific charges. Without such information it is impossible to say who should be tried and who should be exchanged.

Very respectfully, your obedient servant,
W. HOFFMAN,
Colonel Third Infantry, Commissary-General of Prisoners.

WASHINGTON, *May 15, 1863.*

Lieut. Col. W. H. LUDLOW,
    Commissioner for Exchange of Prisoners:

Does the last declaration of exchanges cover officers or men belonging to the Navy? Those captured on the Hatteras for example.

W. HOFFMAN,
Commissary-General of Prisoners.

WASHINGTON, *May 15, 1863.*

Lieut. Col. W. H. LUDLOW,
    Commissioner for Exchange of Prisoners:

Can provide for 2,000 paroled prisoners here and 5,000 at Annapolis. If more are delivered they must be sent to Fort Delaware. Get a list of wounded who remain at Richmond. Please answer.

W. HOFFMAN,
Commissary-General of Prisoners.

WASHINGTON, *May 15, 1863.*

Lieut. Col. W. H. LUDLOW,
    Commissioner for Exchange of Prisoners:

There are 1,100 rebel prisoners at Fort Delaware. Will be delivered when you send for them. About 500 prisoners of war and 200 citizens in the Old Capitol for delivery.

W. HOFFMAN,
Commissary-General of Prisoners.

FORT MONROE, *May 15, 1863.*

Hon. E. M. STANTON:

I have every reason to believe that the whole number of our officers and men captured at Fredericksburg and sent to Richmond will not exceed 4,500. There are very few wounded among them. Over 100 of our officers (General Hays among them and not wounded) arrived here this morning. Colonel Streight's command, captured in Georgia, have been received at City Point. I shall know to-morrow the exact number.

WM. H. LUDLOW,
Lieutenant-Colonel and Agent for Exchange of Prisoners.

OFFICE COMMISSARY-GENERAL OF PRISONERS,
Washington, D. C., May 15, 1863.

Lieut. Col. F. A. DICK,
    Provost-Marshal-General, Saint Louis, Mo.

COLONEL: By direction of the commissary-general of prisoners I have the honor to inform you that when prisoners are sent for delivery duplicate rolls with parole headings, signed by the prisoners before they are sent forward, should accompany them.

Very respectfully, your obedient servant,

W. T. HARTZ,
Captain and Assistant Adjutant-General.

(Same to Maj. Joseph Darr, jr., provost-marshal-general, Wheeling, Va.; Col. James Biddle, commanding Camp Morton, Indianapolis;

Assistant Adjutant-General, Thirteenth Army Corps, Army of the West; Assistant Adjutant-General, Nineteenth Army Corps, Department of the Gulf; Assistant Adjutant-General, Fourteenth Army Corps, Department of the Cumberland; Capt. E. L. Webber, commanding Camp Chase Prison, Columbus, Ohio; Col. W. F. Lynch, commanding Camp Butler, Springfield, Ill.; Capt. S. E. Jones, commanding Military Prison, Louisville, Ky.; Brig. Gen. J. Ammen, commanding Camp Douglas, Chicago, Ill.; Maj. W. S. Pierson, commanding Depot of Prisoners of War, Sandusky, Ohio.)

OFFICE COMMISSARY-GENERAL OF PRISONERS,
Washington, D. C., May 15, 1863.

Capt. H. M. LAZELLE,
Eighth U. S. Infantry, Washington, D. C.

CAPTAIN: You will proceed to Annapolis this afternoon and confer with Captain Blodgett, assistant quartermaster, in relation to the establishment of the new camp for paroled prisoners and to give such instructions as may be necessary to carry out my views. You will also communicate my instructions to Lieutenant-Colonel Sangster relative to providing for the reception of paroled prisoners expected to arrive at the old camp in a few days. You will be required to visit the new camp once in ten days to superintend its progress.

Very respectfully, your obedient servant,
W. HOFFMAN,
Colonel Third Infantry, Commissary-General of Prisoners.

MILITARY PRISON, *Alton, Ill., May 15, 1863.*

Col. W. HOFFMAN,
Commissary-General of Prisoners, Washington, D. C.

COLONEL: I have the honor to forward herewith an application* of the female prisoner, Mrs. Clara Judd, now in confinement in this prison, for a parole to go to her friends in the State of Minnesota. She desires this indulgence on account of her health which for some time past has not been very good. The parole is recommended by her attending physician, Assistant Surgeon Wall, of the Seventy-seventh Ohio Volunteers, the prison physician. I inclose also a copy of the charges against Mrs. Judd. From what I have seen of Mrs. Judd since she has been under my control I am inclined to think if she were permitted to go to Minnesota she would probably remain there and give no further trouble during the war.

I have the honor to be, sir, with much respect, your most obedient servant,

T. HENDRICKSON,
Major Third Infantry, Commanding the Prison.

[Inclosure No. 1.]

ALTON MILITARY PRISON HOSPITAL,
Alton, Ill., May 12, 1863.

Maj. T. HENDRICKSON,
Third Infantry, U. S. Army, and Prison Commandant.

MAJOR: I beg leave to respectfully represent to you that the condition of Mrs. Judd's health (a prisoner of war confined in the above-named prison) is such that in my opinion she had better be paroled

---

* Not found.

outside the prison walls. The utter impossibility of having any of her own sex to attend her in sickness makes it impossible for her medical attendants to render her that assistance they could under other circumstances.

Respectfully, yours,

AND. WALL,
Surgeon in Charge Military Prison Hospital.

[Inclosure No. 2.]

OFFICE CHIEF OF POLICE, FOURTEENTH ARMY CORPS,
Nashville, January 13, 1863.

Capt. WILLIAM M. WILES,
Provost-Marshal-General, Fourteenth Army Corps.

SIR: The following is the substance of the testimony elicited in the case of Mrs. Clara Judd, arrested by the army police on charge of attempting to carry through the lines articles contraband of war such as quinine, morphine, nitrate of silver, besides other goods, and one knitting-machine carried as a pattern, which articles were found and have been purchased by her and brought within these army lines upon a pass obtained under false pretenses.

Mrs. Judd is the widow of an Episcopal clergyman who resides in Winchester, Tenn. He died some two years since leaving a large family of some seven children. Mrs. Judd passed through our lines with permission to take her three youngest children to Minnesota, from whence the family originally came. She took them, leaving them with a sister, she herself returning and passing through our lines to the rebel army. One of her oldest boys had found employment in the rebel establishment at Atlanta, Ga. During her absence her premises were seized on by the Confederates, and her children remaining were taken by this young man to Atlanta. In the autumn of 1862 she returned to Winchester, went thence to Atlanta, claims to have received some $500 Southern funds of her son, which she exchanged for money current in the North. She also received funds from persons who desired her to purchase articles from the North for them. Having thus provided herself she came through our lines and was, under her representations that she wished to go to her children in Minnesota, granted a pass North. She states that from conversation of officers of the Confederate service whom she met on the cars going from Atlanta to Murfreesborough she learned it was the intention of John Morgan to strike at our railroad communications near Gallatin at a certain time. She found a traveling companion in the person of a Mr. Forsythe northward. She went as far as Louisville and Jeffersonville or New Albany, procuring the goods specified; returned on a pass to Gallatin. She states that her intention was to stop at Gallatin and set up the knitting-machine and manufacture stockings, &c., for a living, her object in doing so being that she would be near her children in Atlanta; that her living would be cheaper than in Nashville; that she supposed it would be lawful for her to hold her goods in expectation that the enemy would occupy the country and that she would then fall into their lines. It appears that she was tolerably well informed because about the time she expected it Morgan did make an attempt on Gallatin and shortly after broke the road above there.

It is respectfully submitted that she is a dangerous person to remain in these lines; that she is probably a spy as well as a smuggler; that cases of this kind being of frequent occurrence by females examples should be made, and that as there is at present no proper tribunal for her especial trial or proper place of imprisonment at Nashville she be committed to the military prison at Alton, in the State of Illinois, for trial. It is well to state further that Mrs. Judd represents her son at Atlanta to be a very ingenious mechanic and that it was her intention to furnish him with the knitting-machine for the purpose of manufacturing others from it taken as a pattern.

Very respectfully,

JOHN FITCH,
Provost-Judge.

[Indorsement.]

DEPARTMENT OF THE CUMBERLAND,
Murfreesborough, January 13, 1863.

Mrs. Clara Judd will be confined in Alton (Ill.) Military Prison during the present war or until tried, unless sooner released by the commanding general of the department.

By command of Major-General Rosecrans:

WM. M. WILES,
Captain and Provost-Marshal-General.

[Inclosure No. 3.]

U. S. MILITARY PRISON, *Alton, Ill., May 11, 1863.*

Statement of Mrs. Clara Judd, who has been a prisoner in Alton Military Prison over three months as a spy.

She denies being guilty. Her health is failing very fast (having been in feeble health for several years) from confinement. She wishes to be paroled and go to her parents and little children who are living in Minnesota. She makes a statement here how she came in the South and how she came to be arrested:

"I am the widow of the Rev. B. S. Judd and a native of the State of New York. My parents live in Minnesota, where I also resided with my husband seven years prior to going South. We moved to Winchester in November, 1859, on account of my health and on account of there being a chance of educating our children and board them at home and keep them under home influences. We had eight children. Six of them were going to school in 1861, when my husband went to Nashville on business, and while there he went to view some statuary at the capitol; accidentally stepped off the parterre and was injured so that he died in just four weeks, leaving me with seven children (one having died in the fall) without money, with a great deal of unfinished business and not a relative or Northern person that I ever saw two years before. My friends in the North wrote to have me come home, but I had taken out letters of administration and had no means and the blockade soon closed all communication. I struggled on with my children's help who went to work at anything they could get to do until Christmas, 1862. I was censured very much because I did not put my oldest children, being boys, into the army. I could not think it my duty to let them go on either side, my health being so poor and I liable to die at any time with heart disease. I thought they ought to preserve their lives to take care of those younger. At Christmas I put two of them into a Government factory to keep them from being conscripted. The factory was removed to Atlanta, Ga., in May. I was blockaded from there and in the meantime I had sent the next oldest into the same business. I could not hear from them or from the North and I had no means to support my four remaining children but what I could do myself. Winchester was taken possession of five different times by the Federals. I always treated them as brothers; had a house full every time they were there. (I never had a Confederate soldier in my house.) The 1st of August Thomas took possession of the town. Among his troops I had many acquaintances who told me they were going to destroy all of the crops except enough to last six weeks. They advised me to get my little children to my parents in the North. I could not stay to dispose of anything. I had three cows and seven acres of crops and my household goods and husband's library. I got a protection from provost-marshal for my things and a little boy twelve years old; borrowed money and took my three youngest children out on the second train through from Decherd to Nashville. I was to be gone four weeks. I arrived in Minnesota on the 11th of August. Three days after I got there I had to take my children and flee from the Indians, which detained me three or four weeks instead of two. I then started with money enough as I supposed to take me to Nashville. I intended to go back and dispose of my effects if possible and get my boys out and go to Nevada Territory for two years. I had made arrangements for my sister to take care of my little children for three years, but when I arrived at Louisville they were expecting an attack from Bragg.

"I went to New Albany and was taken sick; was there six weeks. I after incredible trouble succeeded in hiring some money to pay my expenses and take me to Nashville where I was acquainted with the clergy and would get help there. I started but could not get my trunks through farther than Mitchellville. I was very deficient in clothing myself. I thought I would go to [Louisville] and get me some funds and come back to New Albany and pay the borrowed money and get a few clothes for myself and a hand knitting-machine which I had been talking of getting for several years. I accordingly did so. Told the officers at Nashville my whole business and tried to get a pass to go and come back, but could not get one to come back. When I got to Winchester I found everything destroyed except my husband's library and the son I left gone to the same business the others were at and that I could not get my sons out. When I left I supposed Buell would keep the country. I came back and was detained at Murfreesborough three days in trying to get a pass. When I got one I could not get any conveyance but walked eleven miles after 10 o'clock, the last three miles in my stocking feet, having blistered my feet the first three miles. I got a carriage at La Vergne to take me to where the flag officers were, as there was a flag that day. Just before I got there there came a carriage from Murfreesborough bringing a gentleman who was said to be a prisoner of the South. The Federal officers would not let me through until they had been to headquarters. I wrote a statement to Rosecrans. While waiting there the person from Murfreesborough commenced questioning me. He told me he was from Connecticut. My husband and parents were from there. We soon seemed like old acquaintances. He wished to know where I stopped in Nashville. I told. Said he stopped there, and then said he would see Rosecrans about my pass; said he thought he had more power there than Colonel Hepburn. The second day after this the flag officer came out; told me that I could go, but would have to go under guard. I told them I would; I was perfectly willing. I had nothing but some open letters—those I sent to Rosecrans. I walked almost seven miles, my guard mounted. After giving a statement to headquarters of everything I saw while in the South I went to the same hotel where Mr. Forsythe (that is the name of the prisoner from Murfreesborough) put up. He was not there and the house was full. I went to a private house where I was slightly acquainted. The next morning I went to the provost-marshal's office and got a pass to go to Louisville. I found there was a battle near and that I would either stop in New Albany or go to a god-son's in Illinois and wait until times were settled after the battle, but when the clerk gave me my pass he said I could not go. The next day I wanted to go to Mitchellville on account of getting some clothes. I accordingly sent a note to Mr. Forsythe asking him to call, wishing to have him provide me with a private conveyance to Mitchellville, he having informed me while out with the flag that he had been a merchant in Nashville for some time before he went to Murfreesborough. When he called he said he was going to Louisville the next day but one; wanted to see my pass. I finally told him my hurry to get through was mainly because I had heard about what time Morgan would interrupt that road and that I feared I would be left South which would trouble me very much on account of paying the money I had borrowed by a certain time, as the people had placed confidence in me. He said he was very glad I had told him as he had $30,000 worth of goods on the road or about to start, but wanted to know why I did not come back. I told him that at that time I feared to try and that I thought I would stop in Indiana. He urged me to come back; told me before he was a widower; said he would like to become better acquainted with me; said Rosecrans had given him a pass to take some of his goods to Murfreesborough to sell. I said I had thought first of stopping at Gallatin. He then urged me to let him take my pass and have it changed to come back to Gallatin, where I could get to Murfreesborough after awhile. He went to headquarters and came back with the pass changed but laughed about the wording of it. He said he would go with me in the morning and would be happy to render me any assistance I might need, and would introduce me to a merchant where I could get my things at wholesale.

"After we started in the morning I asked him how he came to have so much influence with Rosecrans. Said they were old neighbors, but after a little told me he was a Southern man as strong as any dared to be. I found I was in a close place. I could turn neither way, for the conductor would not wait for me to take my trunk aboard at Mitchellville, so that I could leave him in Louisville. He finally after we got there told me not to get anything contraband, but I told him there was nothing contraband while in the United States, and if I stopped at Gallatin I was inside the lines. He told me the price of drugs and finally urged me to buy. I told him I had no means; he offered me some money but I refused it. He then urged me to take the money I had brought to pay the debt I had contracted in New Albany. I was in debt in Winchester and thought if I had money it was a great temptation to buy, and to stop in Gallatin, and if Morgan took that part of the country it would help me out of debt, but I did not yield at first. I went to New Albany and found the lawyer gone from home. Forsythe went with me when he found how things were. He told the gentleman in the office that I had had to sacrifice a great deal of my money so that I had not got the clothing I needed and that he would vouch that I would send the money back in two or three weeks through his name to Cahill and Hues, Louisville, and gave his name and theirs in writing. Then as soon as we were in the street told me to buy drugs, and he would send me whatever I wanted in the drug line, and as soon as I could get to Atlanta he would visit me and set me up in a commission store. I supposed it was all understood between him and Rosecrans.

I need not worry about it when I bought my drugs. I traded where I had bought 50 cents worth of goods while I was boarding in town. He did not stop in the store when I traded; I wondered at it. We did not get back to Louisville till 12 at night on Saturday; the ferry-boat detained us. I had agreed to receive my knitting-machine at 7 o'clock that night; I could not get it on Sunday. On Sunday evening he told me he had got a pass to go from Boyle, but he telegraphed to Nashville to see if it was all right; seemed very much elated. I ought to have mentioned before that my drugs were brought from New Albany in a carpet bag. He carried it for me and some little bundles besides. While I lighted the gas he set my things into my room and bid me good night. Suddenly in the morning I wanted to open my satchel; it was not in my room. I called the landlord. He said the guard found it standing on the out door step. I told him he did not for there was a light in the hall; Forsythe preceded me upstairs and that he set it down by my door while I was unlocking it, and that after he bid me good night I looked to see if there was anything left but there was nothing there. The landlord said [he] had it put in the office. The facts were when he bid me good night he took the satchel to the office; had it examined (the key was in it); then telegraphed to Nashville. When I saw my pass I was astonished. It was to go to Louisville and back to Gallatin without molestation forthwith. My trunk was not opened. I told him on Sunday night I had to stay until Tuesday night on account of my knitting-machine. He said I must go with him and he would leave a line to have it expressed on the next train but I took a carriage and got it before the cars started. The officers from Nashville met us at Bowling Green and arrested me at Mitchellville, fifty miles this side of Gallatin; took me to Nashville where they confiscated everything.

"I was arrested on Monday before Christmas and have never known what evidence there was against me nor on what footing I was here until to-day. He has sworn falsely and misrepresented other things then said jocosely. The officer told me at Nashville that the fact of Gallatin being attacked the very night I would have got there made it look like a preconcerted plan, but it was a feint of some of his men while he attacked Elizabethtown, but I knew nothing whatever more than what I had learned by Morgan's adjutant two weeks before, and I had been delayed and so had he by the Hartsville fight, and it was purely accidental my starting that day. I never spoke with Morgan nor any other officer of the Confederacy higher than a lieutenant-colonel and then only about my pass. Perhaps I ought to except General Polk. He is an old acquaintance, but politics were never mentioned. I never had anything to do with political affairs, neither do I wish to have.

"I am perfectly willing to make oath that this is as near the truth as I can get it from memory.

"MRS. CLARA JUDD."

Statement of Lieutenant Leigh.

I was taken prisoner on Saturday, May 3, between 12 and 1 a. m. I was sent to the rear, the rebels thinking me a surgeon. The enemy were massed on the plank road about 30,000, five lines of battle on the left of the plank road and the artillery in position in the field where Major-General Howard's headquarters were. They said to me in a very confident way, "We got Dan. Sickles' corps cut off and we'll capture the whole of them." They asked if General Sickles was there. I told them they could always find him with his troops. They said: "We'll hang him, God damn him, when we catch him." Their troops were arriving all night. At daylight they marched us out the Orange road about four miles when a courier came up and we were ordered to about face and march back again, it having been reported that Stoneman was on the road. At 5.30 their men came running out of the woods into the open field to the number of 400 or 500 and their batteries which they had in position in the center of the field poured into the woods three rounds of grape and canister; at the least twenty pieces of artillery were there. About 9 o'clock I started on a march again [on] the road to the left of the Orange road, on which we walked about two miles and were about faced and marched back again. The men wanted to know if Stoneman was on that road too. After resting about half an hour we took up a march again and struck in through the woods and arrived at midnight at the Spotsylvania Court-House. We asked for some rations and they said there was not even a cracker in the place.

May the 4th, at 7 a. m., we marched off and reached Guiney's Station on Fredericksburg and Potomac Railroad at 2 p. m. They then had all their camp and garrison equipage in their wagons and were going toward Gordonsville. When asked where the wagons were going in such a hurry they replied they were going for subsistence and seemed very nervous, anxious and in a hurry. All their wounded who could walk had got as far as Guiney's Station and I am sure the wounded I saw and all the other officers agreed that they could not number less than 10,000. There were two regiments of Stuart's cavalry drawn up in line of battle about a mile south and east from the station. We received no rations until Tuesday, then they gave us a barrel of flour which we had to mix up with a little water and bake in the coal. We were in an open field without shelter or blankets from Monday until Thursday, when we were placed in the cars and forwarded to Richmond, being the first train that passed over since Monday when the railroad was destroyed. Their own wounded were without shelter or food and some died of starvation and exposure. We arrived in Richmond on Thursday evening about 7 o'clock and our guard consisted of citizens from the cars down to Libby Prison. While confined there the officers were allowed two-thirds rations bread and bacon. We were allowed to purchase sugar and rye coffee; sugar, $1.50, when Government price was 3½ cents. We asked why Government did not furnish to us at that price. Captain Turner remarked we were fortunate enough to get it anywhere at any price.

We were released from Libby on Wednesday, the 13th, at 4 p. m.; had to march from Richmond to Petersburg, a distance of twenty-two miles, the rain pouring down all night, and alongside of the railroad and a train passing us with three empty cars attached. The men were not allowed to halt but forced to march at the point of the bayonet.

We arrived at Petersburg in the morning about 7 o'clock, and going through the streets of Petersburg Lieutenant Dietrich, who was in command, would not allow the officers to purchase anything but damned them for Yankee sons of bitches and swore that if they did not cover files and march by fours he'd have the bayonet put into them. General Hays, Lieutenant Ford, Lieutenant Leigh, having always been mounted officers, were unused to walking; on arriving at Petersburg could go no farther and asked the privilege of having a conveyance to take them to City Point. The sergeant ordered a guard if we did not move on to put the bayonet into the Yankee sons of bitches. General Hays told them he could not walk; they might put him in jail if they liked, but as to walk to City Point it was impossible. The sergeant again ordered to put the bayonet into him when some citizens told him that these officers could not walk; that he should take us to the provost-marshal to see what he said. He did so and the provost-marshal put us into a dirty, filthy jail, about ten by twelve, where we were confined about an hour and a half. During that confinement the lieutenant of the guard brought a female in to show her some live Yankees and told her to look at us but not to speak to us as we might bite her.

Major Vaughan, a cavalry officer in the Confederate service, went to the provost-marshal, having become disgusted with our treatment, and persuaded the provost to allow the general and the aides to hire a conveyance as he might allow us that privilege, and we had to pay Robert Clark for a chaise to transport three of us from Petersburg to City Point $40 in greenbacks, amounting to $60 of their scrip. In asking the reason of the high prices they said that Stoneman having taken all the horses around the country from Government Government to get square on Stoneman seized the horses of all their loyal subjects.

On Sunday, May 10, Governor Letcher and several other officials visited us at the Libby. The Governor said if Lincoln did as he wanted him to do Virginia would not have seceded and there would have been no war; and if Lincoln would not have been elected the South would be blessed with peace. General Hays asked him if Douglas had been elected how it would have been. He replied it made no difference; they had been disunionists for fifty years.

When we arrived in Libby they took from the officers their belts, canteens, sashes and all writing paper about them; said it was contraband, and on coming away would not allow us even to bring a blanket with us. The same time they boast that certain of their officers are furnished with money when taken prisoners, and their friends in the North buy them trunks and fill them with contraband goods and the officers returning take these trunks with them as private baggage, our Government furnishing them transportation.

Second Lieutenant Ahlert, Forty-fifth New York, Eleventh Corps, and sergeants and privates of Sixty-sixth Ohio now at Camp Parole, Annapolis, state the time they were attacked they had no pickets or skirmishers in front and were playing cards and eating; taken so by surprise that most of them left their arms stacked. The rebels also say that had they known that the officers and soldiers were such cowardly poltroons they would have sent a note to General Hooker requesting him that he would place some troops there that would at least fire one round without running, as they did not want to fight sheep.

THOS. J. LEIGH,
Lieutenant and Aide-de-Camp.

WAR DEPARTMENT, *Washington City, May 15, 1863.*
His Excellency O. P. MORTON, *Indianapolis, Ind.*

SIR: The Secretary of War directs me to acknowledge the receipt of your communication of the 11th instant, in which you call attention to the announcement from the rebel newspapers that about 400 Alabamians, enlisted by Colonel Streight and regularly mustered into the Fifty-first Regiment Indiana Volunteers, captured near Rome, were refused their parole and sent to Richmond, and request that 800 prisoners may be selected from those now in our possession and held as hostages for the safety of these loyal Alabamians. In reply the Secretary instructs me to inform you that the same has been referred to General Hitchcock, commissioner for exchange of prisoners.

Very respectfully, your most obedient servant,

JOHN POTTS,
Chief Clerk, War Department.

LOUISVILLE, KY., *May 16, 1863.*

President LINCOLN:

Col. Samuel B. Churchill, of Saint Louis, formerly of this city, has been banished South with his wife and seven children, five of them very small. Colonel Churchill is a man of intelligence and high character, of moderate fortune. It will utterly ruin him to have to go South. I respectfully request that his sentence be commuted. He will take the oath and give bond if allowed. I ask this because I know him and rely on his honor, and he is a cousin of my children.

JAMES GUTHRIE.

WAR DEPARTMENT, *Washington, May 16, 1863.*

Hon. JAMES GUTHRIE, *Louisville, Ky.:*

Your dispatch of to-day is received. I personally know nothing of Colonel Churchill; but months ago and more than once he has been represented to me as exerting a mischievous influence at Saint Louis for which reason I am unwilling to force his continuance there against the judgment of our friends on the ground. But if it will oblige you he may come to and remain at Louisville upon taking the oath of allegiance and your pledge for his good behavior.

A. LINCOLN.

BALTIMORE, *May 16, 1863.*

Colonel HOFFMAN:

The prisoner, Captain Baylor, killed a man named Roher under a flag of truce at Harper's Ferry. Colonel Schley from Point of Rocks telegraphs that he will send statement in full and that witnesses can be obtained without trouble. Communicate this to judge-advocate.

ROBT. C. SCHENCK,
Major-General, Commanding.

FORT MONROE, *May 16, 1863.*

Colonel HOFFMAN, *Commissary-General of Prisoners:*

Two notorious prostitutes sent with citizen prisoners from the Old Capitol Prison to City Point have been denied permission to land and have been returned to Annapolis. Please give the necessary orders to Colonel Waite to send them to Old Capitol Prison and direct that no more such characters be sent here for exchange.

WM. H. LUDLOW,
Lieutenant-Colonel, &c.

HEADQUARTERS DEPARTMENT OF VIRGINIA,
Fort Monroe, May 16, 1863.

Col. W. HOFFMAN, *Commissary-General of Prisoners.*

COLONEL: I inclose to you a letter just received from Mr. Ould. The character of these women was of course not known to you, and they were probably sent by some mistake on a flag-of-truce boat instead of to a penitentiary.

I am, very respectfully, your obedient servant,

WM. H. LUDLOW,
Lieutenant-Colonel and Agent for the Exchange of Prisoners.

P. S.—The description of these women as given by Mr. Ould is fully sustained by the officer in charge of them.

W. H. L.

[Inclosure.]

CITY POINT, VA., *May 14, 1863.*

Lieutenant-Colonel LUDLOW, *Agent of Exchange.*

SIR: I send back to you two strumpets who were landed at this place yesterday in company with honorable and virtuous women. If after arriving here they had behaved themselves I should have stood the transaction, though with hard thoughts. A state of war even does not allow any outrage to be perpetrated upon the sanctity of a pure woman's character and last of all where a flag of truce is the vehicle. We are husbands and fathers and brothers and no form of war should stifle or subdue the holy feelings that spring from those relations. If I did not believe you were imposed upon I would be justified in taking this matter as a personal affront. These women since their arrival at City Point have descended to a depth of infamy that I hardly thought could be reached by the sex. They have delighted themselves with the foulest billingsgate that ever disgraced a fish-woman, courting prostitution at every turn and making themselves loud-mouthed in their denunciation of everything cherished and beloved by our people. Their conduct for one night has been so outrageous as to attract the attention of the press and engage the gossip of the streets. Though I cannot charge myself with blame in the affair I feel a deep sense of mortification that so infamous a proceeding should have had the countenance of the purity of a flag of truce. I have written strongly about this matter not only because every sensibility of my nature has been aroused but because of the further reason that I have a jealous regard for a flag whose honor and purity it is our special mission to uphold.

Very respectfully, your obedient servant,

RO. OULD,
Agent of Exchange.

FORT MONROE, *May 16, 1863.*

Col. W. HOFFMAN, *Commissary-General of Prisoners:*

Captain Mulford, with the steamer State of Maine carrying 800 men, will report to you on Monday. Please inform me whether there will be more than that number to come. If so I will order another transport. Complaint is made by Mr. Ould that twelve of Mosby's men were not sent with the others. Please send them now and all officers and men held as prisoners of war.

WM. H. LUDLOW,
Lieutenant-Colonel and Agent for Exchange of Prisoners.

NORFOLK, *May 16, 1863.*

Lieutenant-Colonel PELOUZE, *Assistant Adjutant-General:*

Send the prisoners to City Point with instructions to the officer in charge to have duplicate rolls of his prisoners; to deliver them with one of the rolls to the Confederate authorities at City Point, and take their receipt on the other roll which is to be brought back and left with me. The officer need not wait to bring any of our men. Cooked rations if necessary can be obtained from the commissary.

WM. H. LUDLOW,
Lieutenant-Colonel.

ANNAPOLIS, MD., *May 16, 1863.*

Col. W. HOFFMAN, *Commissary-General of Prisoners:*

Eighty officers and 3,000 men from Richmond this morning and 313 from New Orleans. Please have Major Dodge ordered to come down and pay the officers.

GEO. SANGSTER,
Lieutenant-Colonel, Commanding Paroled Prisoners.

OLD CAPITOL PRISON, *Washington, May 16, 1863.*

Col. W. HOFFMAN, *Commissary-General of Prisoners.*

SIR: I respectfully inform you that the number of persons will be less than 350 who are subjects of exchange, viz, 136 officers, 76 enlisted men and less than 150 state prisoners. These will leave sufficient room for at least 300 more prisoners. I am not informed whether Captain Todd has any other prisoners in Washington. I shall endeavor to have the rolls completed by 6 p. m. this evening and will wait instructions when they are to embark.

I have the honor to be, your obedient servant,

WILLIAM P. WOOD,
Superintendent Old Capitol Prison.

OLD CAPITOL PRISON, *Washington, D. C., May 16, 1863.*

Col. W. HOFFMAN, *Commissary-General of Prisoners.*

SIR: I beg you will excuse me for again drawing your attention to my case. I now again take the liberty as I learn we are upon the eve of an exchange. I have now been a prisoner for eight months and why I am longer held I cannot see. When I was captured on the 14th September, 1862, I was sent to Fort Delaware, there then being a charge of spy against me. This charge was entirely without foundation. I was there confined for three weeks in irons. I demanded a hearing upon this charge three different times but received no answer to any of my communications. After the expiration of three weeks I was released from close confinement and placed among the officers at Fort Delaware, not, however, because I was an officer but only through the kindness of my friend Major Burton, then in command. Major Burton informed me at this time that this charge had been removed entirely. After remaining at Fort Delaware for about three months I was ordered to report to Washington, which I did upon my parole. After reporting here my parole was extended by Major Sherburne without my even requesting it. I remained upon parole upward of two months and in that time reported several times to yourself.

I must again draw your attention to the fact that I am not an officer, but am a private belonging to the First Virginia Cavalry, and was taken in arms at the time the Confederates were retreating from Maryland. If the charge of being a spy or any other charge yet remains against me I most respectfully beg you will use your influence to gain me a trial as anything is preferable to imprisonment here and being kept in a constant state of suspense. Does it strike you very forcibly that if your Government had any serious charges against me it would permit me to be comfortably quartered here now among the officers, not to mention my having been allowed to enjoy a parole for about three months? Now, may I beg you to give this matter your personal attention? I know I have no right to ask this favor of you, but knowing you have the power to exchange me if you please, and believing you to be a just and upright gentleman, I trust you will take the matter in hand and permit me to leave with the next exchange.

I remain, sir, very respectfully, your obedient servant,

CLAGETT D. FITZHUGH.

GENERAL ORDERS, } HEADQUARTERS MIDDLE DEPARTMENT,
No. 32. } *Baltimore, Md., May 16, 1863.*

I. The following communication received from the commissary-general of prisoners is published for information:

OFFICE COMMISSARY-GENERAL OF PRISONERS,
Washington, D. C., May 11, 1863.

Maj. Gen. R. C. SCHENCK,
Commanding Eighth Army Corps, Baltimore, Md.

GENERAL: I am instructed by the General-in-Chief to say that when a person is arrested charged with being a spy or the commission of any specific offense requiring a trial an immediate investigation must be had before a military tribunal at the place where the offense was committed and where the witnesses are within reach.

Many persons have been arrested as spies and sent to interior prisons and after months of detention it has been found that the charges had neither specifications nor evidence to sustain them.

In cases where arrests are made on a general charge of disloyal conduct it is necessary that full details in each case with the character of the person should be given in order to a proper disposal of it.

Please give the necessary instructions to insure compliance with the foregoing in your department.

Very respectfully, your obedient servant,

W. HOFFMAN,
Colonel Third Infantry, Commissary-General of Prisoners.

II. Instructions similar in substance to those contained in the above letter have been given from time to time from these headquarters, and hereafter all commanding officers of divisions, brigades or detached commands and all provost-marshals will be held strictly responsible for a careful observance of them. When a prisoner is sent from any point to another to be detained in custody the charges, with all specifications, affidavits or other papers showing clearly the nature and character of the case must be forwarded with him, and when two or more prisoners are sent together there must be a separate statement and papers for each case.

By command of Major-General Schenck:

WM. H. CHESEBROUGH,
Lieutenant-Colonel and Assistant Adjutant-General.

LOUISVILLE, *May 17, 1863.*

His Excellency A. LINCOLN:

Samuel B. Churchill, of Saint Louis, was arrested in this city by order of General Curtis and taken to Saint Louis. We understand that he with his family, a wife and seven children, are ordered to leave for the South on Wednesday. We know Churchill well, being an old schoolmate and intimate friend to both of us. His father was a prominent citizen here and a warm Union man. He died a few months ago leaving a large estate and the prisoner one of his executors, with important and indispensable duties to discharge in which many of our and your friends are deeply interested, none of which can be discharged without his discretion. In view of all the circumstances we ask a revocation of the order, and we will hold ourselves bound for the faithful performance of any obligation which may be imposed on him. In justice to ourselves and to you we must say that we approve of the order sending active rebel sympathizers South, but we do not believe that Mr. Churchill is one who should be embraced in the order. From our intimate acquaintance with him we fear that some private enemy is abusing the power of the Government to wreak personal vengeance which we desire avoided on your account and on account of the cause. The duties alluded to in connection with his father's estate are here. If his presence is hurtful in Saint Louis can he be allowed to remain here? If this is granted we will hold ourselves in honor bound to inform on him and arrest him should he do anything wrong. If this cannot be done can a respite be granted till one of us can see you or the Secretary of War?

JOSHUA F. SPEED.
JAMES SPEED.

[Indorsement.]

LOUISVILLE, *May 17, 1863.*

The PRESIDENT:

I am assured Colonel Churchill will take the oath of allegiance and pledge myself he will be of good behavior, and feel greatly obliged by your decision.*

J. GUTHRIE.

HEADQUARTERS DEPARTMENT OF VIRGINIA,
Fort Monroe, May 17, 1863.

Col. W. HOFFMAN, *Commissary-General of Prisoners.*

COLONEL: I inclose to you a copy of letter just received from Mr. Ould. Please give especial orders that the men named in the letter are sent on the State of Maine.

The statement made by Mr. Ould removes these men from the charge of being bushwhackers and guerrillas. There are many Confederate officers and men who have been declared exchanged held in our prisons. The best interests of our own officers and men who have been or who may be captured demand their delivery. If there are clear, apparently well founded charges a prompt trial should be given. If not they should be promptly released and delivered. In taking this view I am influenced by considerations for our own people.

I am persistent in my demands upon Mr. Ould for them all, and insist upon knowing why any one is retained in confinement when

---

others are delivered. Please have the Old Capitol Prison cleaned out as far as is possible of both prisoners of war and civilians. I can hardly express to you the continual annoyance given by the reiterated demands and appeals made for the release and delivery of Confederate officers and men, many of whom have been declared exchanged and others who are held back in prisons when their comrades are delivered.

I am, very respectfully, your obedient servant,

WM. H. LUDLOW,
Lieutenant-Colonel and Agent for Exchange of Prisoners.

[Inclosure.]

WAR DEPARTMENT, *Richmond, Va., May 14, 1863.*

Lieut. Col. WILLIAM H. LUDLOW, *Agent of Exchange.*

SIR: I have now before me two men who were delivered by you yesterday who belong to Mosby's command. One of them I know well and can vouch for his truthfulness. They say that Thomas N. Green, J. H. Barnes, Thomas W. Howard, James Wilson, Samuel Underwood, John W. Martin, C. E. Smith, Samuel Anderson, A. J. Brown, C. W. Selden, Richard Moran and William Hibbs, who were captured about the 1st of May, 1863, are retained in the Old Capitol Prison. My informants tell me that the foregoing persons who belong to Mosby's command are retained and not allowed to come off, although they earnestly requested it. They are retained under the allegation that they are bushwhackers and guerrillas. Mosby's command is in the Confederate service in every sense of the term. He is regularly commissioned and his force is as strictly Confederate as any in our army. Why is this done? This day I have cleaned every prison in my control as far as I know. If there is any detention anywhere let me know and I will rectify it. I am compelled to complain of this thing in almost every communication. You will not deem me passionate when I assure you that it will not be endured any longer. If these men are not delivered a stern retaliation will be made immediately.

Respectfully, your obedient servant,

RO. OULD,
Agent of Exchange.

———

FORT MONROE, *May 17, 1863.*

Col. W. HOFFMAN, *Commissary-General of Prisoners:*

Eighty-four of our officers captured at Chancellorsville have been delivered to me and sent to Annapolis. Please send me all the Confederate officers you have and I will obtain the release of an equivalent number of our officers now in Richmond. How many Confederate officers have you?

WM. H. LUDLOW,
Lieutenant-Colonel and Agent for Exchange of Prisoners.

———

HEADQUARTERS MILITARY DISTRICT OF WASHINGTON,
Washington, D. C., May 17, 1863.

Col. W. HOFFMAN, *Commissary-General of Prisoners.*

COLONEL: By direction of the general commanding the district I have the honor to inform you that those of Mosby's men who are in confinement in this city are held to be subjects of exchange and can be forwarded for that purpose whenever it may be deemed desirable.

I am, colonel, very respectfully, your obedient servant,

THEODORE McGOWAN,
Assistant Adjutant-General.

HEADQUARTERS DEPARTMENT OF THE OHIO,
Cincinnati, Ohio, May 18, 1863.

Maj. Gen. H. W. HALLECK,
General-in-Chief, Washington, D. C.

GENERAL: I have the honor to forward by Lieut. W. G. Fitch to the Judge-Advocate-General the proceedings in the case of Hon. Clement L. Vallandigham who was arrested on the 4th instant for a violation of General Orders, No. 38, issued from these headquarters. The fact of his arrest and the proceedings of the court have been published in the newspapers from time to time and have no doubt reached you, but I have made no official report of my action in the matter to you feeling that it was better to be guided by the written and verbal instructions already received than annoy and harass you and delay the final result of the matter by asking for orders from time to time.

I have been fully sustained in my action by the Supreme Court* and trust the record will meet with the approval of the President and yourself.

The moral effect of the carrying out of the principles of that order is very apparent throughout the department and I am constrained to believe the policy adopted is the true one.

Hoping my course will meet with your approbation, I have the honor to remain,

Very respectfully, your obedient servant,

A. E. BURNSIDE,
Major-General, Commanding Department of the Ohio.

[Inclosure.]

Trial of Clement L. Vallandigham.

Proceedings of a military commission convened at Cincinnati, Ohio, by virtue of the following order:

SPECIAL ORDERS, } HEADQUARTERS DEPARTMENT OF THE OHIO,
No. 135. } *Cincinnati, Ohio, April 21, 1863.*

*   *   *   *   *   *   *

IV. A military commission is hereby appointed to meet at Cincinnati, Ohio, at 10 o'clock a. m. on Wednesday, the 22d instant, or as soon thereafter as practicable, for the trial of such prisoners as may be brought before it.

Detail for the commission: Brig. Gen. R. B. Potter, U. S. Volunteers; Lieut. Col. E. R. Goodrich, commissary of subsistence, U. S. Volunteers; Maj. J. L. Van Buren, aide-de-camp; Maj. J. M. Brown, Tenth Kentucky Cavalry; Maj. R. M. Corwine, aide-de-camp; Maj. A. H. Fitch, One hundred and fifteenth Ohio Volunteers; Capt. E. Gay, Sixteenth U. S. Infantry; Capt. P. M. Lydig, aide-de-camp; Capt. W. H. French, commissary of subsistence, U. S. Volunteers. Capt. J. M. Cutts, Eleventh U. S. Infantry, is appointed judge-advocate.

By command of Major-General Burnside:

W. P. ANDERSON,
Assistant Adjutant-General.

---

* See *habeas corpus* proceedings at p. 573 *et seq.*

[The commission met and adjourned from time to time, disposing of such business as was brought before it, till May 6, which was of its sittings the]

TWELFTH DAY.

CINCINNATI, OHIO, *Wednesday, May 6, 1863.*

The commission met pursuant to adjournment.

SPECIAL ORDERS, ?   HEADQUARTERS DEPARTMENT OF THE OHIO,
No. 161.   ζ   *Cincinnati, Ohio, May 5, 1863.*

*   *   *   *   *   *

III. Capt. W. H. French, commissary of subsistence, is hereby relieved from duty as a member of the military commission convened by paragraph IV, of Special Orders, No. 135, current series, from these headquarters, and of which Brig. Gen. Robert B. Potter is president.

IV. Col. John F. De Courcy, Sixteenth Regiment Ohio Volunteer Infantry, is hereby assigned to duty as a member of the military commission convened by paragraph IV, of Special Orders, No. 135, current series, from these headquarters, and of which Brig. Gen. Robert B. Potter is president.

By command of Major-General Burnside:

W. P. ANDERSON,
Assistant Adjutant-General.

Present, General Potter, Lieutenant-Colonel Goodrich, Major Brown, Captain Lydig, Colonel De Courcy, Major Van Buren, Major Fitch and judge-advocate.

The judge-advocate stated that the absence of Major Corwine and Captain Gay is sufficiently explained by the fact that they had recently been ordered on other duty by the general commanding the department.

The proceedings of the preceding day were read by the judge-advocate and approved.

The commission then proceeded to the trial of Clement L. Vallandigham, a citizen of the State of Ohio, who being called into court and having heard the foregoing orders read was asked if he had any objection to any of the members named therein, to which he replied in the negative.

The commission was then duly sworn by the judge-advocate, and the judge-advocate was sworn by the president in the presence of the accused, and Clement L. Vallandigham was arraigned on the following charge and specification of charge:

CHARGE: Publicly expressing in violation of General Orders, No. 38, from headquarters Department of the Ohio, sympathy for those in arms against the Government of the United States and declaring disloyal sentiments and opinions with the object and purpose of weakening the power of the Government in its efforts to suppress an unlawful rebellion.

Specification.—In this that the said Clement L. Vallandigham, a citizen of the State of Ohio, on or about the 1st day of May, 1863, at Mount Vernon, Knox County, Ohio, did publicly address a large meeting of citizens and did utter sentiments in words or in effect as follows, declaring the present war "a wicked, cruel and unnecessary war;" "a war not being waged for the preservation of the Union;" "a war for the purpose of crushing out liberty and erecting a despotism;" "a war for the freedom of the blacks and the enslavement of the whites;" stating "that if the Administration had so wished the war could have been honorably terminated months ago;" that "peace might have been honorably obtained by listening to the proposed intermediation of France;" that "propositions by which the Northern States could be won back and the South guaranteed their rights under the Constitution had been rejected the day before the late battle of Fredericksburg by Lincoln and his minions," meaning thereby the President of the United States and those under him in authority; charging "that the Government of the United States was about to appoint military marshals in every district to restrain the people of their liberties, to deprive them of their rights and privileges;" characterizing General Orders, No. 38, from headquarters Department of the Ohio, as "a base usurpation of arbitrary authority," inviting his hearers to resist the same by saying "the sooner the people inform the minions of usurped power that they will not submit to such restrictions upon their liberties the better;" declaring "that he was at all times and upon all occasions resolved to do what he could to defeat the attempts now being made to build up a monarchy upon the ruins of our free Government;" asserting "that he firmly believed, as he said six months ago, that the men in power are attempting to establish a despotism in this country more cruel and more oppressive than ever existed before."

All of which opinions and sentiments he well knew did aid, comfort and encourage those in arms against the Government and could but induce in his hearers a distrust of their own Government, sympathy for those in arms against it and a disposition to resist the laws of the land.

The accused asked delay to procure counsel, stating that he was engaged in preparing his plea and required advice.

The commission was duly cleared for deliberation, and on its reopening the judge-advocate announced as its decision that the commission would require the accused to plead guilty or not guilty to the charge and specification, and would then adjourn for half an hour to permit the accused to procure counsel when the commission would proceed to hear the evidence for the prosecution.

The accused denying the jurisdiction of the commission and refusing to plead as directed by the commission, the commission directed that the plea of not guilty to the specification and charge be entered for him by the judge-advocate.

The commission then adjourned for half an hour.

The commission reassembled pursuant to its adjournment.

All persons required to give evidence were directed to withdraw and remain in waiting till called for.

Capt. H. R. HILL, of the One hundred and fifteenth Regiment Ohio Volunteer Infantry, a witness for the prosecution, being duly sworn testifies as follows:

By the JUDGE-ADVOCATE:

Question. What is your rank and regiment?

Answer. Captain, One hundred and fifteenth Regiment Ohio Volunteers.

Question. Were you present at a meeting of citizens held at Mount Vernon on or about May 1, 1863?

Answer. I was.

Question. Did you hear the accused address that meeting?

Answer. I did.

Question. How near were you to him while speaking?

Answer. I was leaning on the end of the platform on which he was speaking. I was about six feet from him.

Question. Was this your position during the whole of the time he was speaking?

Answer. Yes.

Question. State what remarks he uttered in relation to the war now being waged, and any remarks he may have made in that connection.

Answer. [The witness stated that in order to state his remarks in the order in which they were made he would refresh his memory from manuscript notes made on the occasion. These the witness produced and held in his hands.]

The speaker commenced by referring to the canopy under which he was speaking—the stand being covered by an American flag—"the flag which," he said, "had been rendered sacred by Democratic Presidents—the flag under the Constitution."

After finishing his exordium he spoke of the designs of those in power being to erect a despotism; that "it was not their intention to effect a restoration of the Union; that previous to the bloody battle of Fredericksburg an attempt was made to stay this wicked, cruel and unnecessary war;" that the war could have been ended in February last; that a day or two before the battle of Fredericksburg a proposition had been made for the readmission of Southern Senators into the U. S. Congress and that the refusal was still in existence over the President's own signature, which would be made public as soon as the ban of secrecy enjoined by the President was removed; that the Union could have been saved if the plan proposed by the speaker had been adopted; that the Union could have been saved upon the basis of reconstruction, but that it would have ended in the exile or death of those who advocated a continuation of the war; that "Forney, who was a well-known correspondent of the Philadelphia Press, had said that some of our public men (and he, Forney, had no right to speak for any others than those connected with the Administration) rather than bring back some of the seceded States would submit to a permanent separation of the Union." He stated that "France, a nation that had always shown herself to be a friend of our Government, had proposed to act as a mediator," but that "her proposition, which if accepted might have brought about an honorable peace, was insolently rejected"—it may have been "instantly rejected;" that "the people had been deceived as to the objects of the war from the beginning;" that "it was a war for the liberation of the blacks and the enslavement of the whites We had been told it would be terminated in three months, then in nine months, and again in a year, but that there was still no prospect of its being ended; that Richmond was still in the hands of the enemy; that Charleston was theirs and Vicksburg was theirs; that the Mississippi was not opened and would not be so as long as there was cotton on its banks to be stolen or so long as there were any contractors or officers to enrich." I do not remember which word, contractors or officers, he used. He stated that a Southern paper had denounced himself and Cox and the "Peace Democrats" as having "done more to prevent the establishing of the Southern Confederacy than a thousand Sewards;" that "they proposed to operate through the masses of the people in both sections who were in favor of the Union." He said that "it was the purpose or desire of the Administration to suppress or prevent such meetings as the one he was addressing;" that "military marshals were about to be appointed in every district who would act for the purpose of restricting the liberties of the people," but that "he was a free-man;" that he "did not ask David Tod or Abraham Lincoln or Ambrose E. Burnside for his right to speak as he had done and was doing;" that his authority for so doing was higher than General Orders, No. 38—it was General Orders, No. 1—the Constitution;" that General Orders, No. 38, was a base usurpation of arbitrary power; that he had the most supreme contempt for such power. He despised it, spit upon it; he trampled it under his feet." That only a few days before a man had been dragged down from his home in Butler County by an outrageous usurpation of power and tried for an offense not known to our laws by a self-constituted court-martial—tried without a jury, which is guaranteed to every one; that he had been fined and imprisoned; that two men had been brought over from Kentucky and tried contrary to express laws for the trial of treason and were now under the sentence of death; that an order had just been issued in Indiana denying to persons the right to canvass or discuss military policy and that if it was submitted to would be followed up by a similar order in Ohio; that he was resolved never to submit to an order of a military dictator prohibiting the free discussion of either civil or military authority. "The sooner that the people informed the minions of this usurped power that they would not submit to such restrictions upon their liberties the better." "Should we cringe and cower before such authority?" That "we claimed the right to criticise the acts of our military servants in power;" that there never was a tyrant in any age who oppressed the people further than he thought they would submit to or endure; that in days of Democratic authority Tom Corwin had in face of Congress hoped that our brave volunteers in Mexico "might be welcomed with bloody hands to hospitable graves," but that he had not been interfered with. It was never before thought necessary to appoint a captain of cavalry as provost-marshal as was now the case in Indianapolis, or military dictators as were now exercising authority in Cincinnati and Columbus. He closed by warning the people not to be deceived; that "an attempt would shortly be made to enforce the conscription act;" that "they should remember that this war was not a war for the preservation of the Union;" that "it was a wicked abolition war and that if those in authority were allowed to accomplish their purposes the people would be deprived of their liberties and a monarchy established; but that as for him he was resolved that he would never be a priest to minister upon the altar upon which his country was being sacrificed."

Question. Will you state what other flags or emblems decorated the platform than the American flag?

Answer. There were frames covered with canvas all of which were decorated with "butternuts." One banner which was borne at the head of a delegation bore the inscription, "The Copperheads are coming."

Question. Did you see any badges worn by the citizens? How many and what were those badges?

Answer Yes; I saw hundreds of them wearing butternuts and many of them copperheads cut out of cents.

Question. Did you hear many and how many cheering for Jeff. Davis or expressing sympathy for him?

Answer. I heard no cheers for Jeff. Davis, but I heard a shout in the crowd that "Jeff. Davis was a gentleman and that was what the President was not."

Cross-examined by the ACCUSED:

Question. Did not the speaker refer to the Crittenden propositions and condemn the rejection of them?

Answer. In endeavoring to show that the restoration of the Union was not the object of the war he stated a number of means, this among others, by which the war could have been ended; he considered from the fact that none were adopted that this was proof that the restoration of the Union was not the object of the war.

Question. Did I not quote Judge Douglas' declaration that the responsibility for the rejection of those propositions was with the Republican party?

(Objected to by the judge-advocate.)

The commission was duly cleared for deliberation and on its reopening the judge-advocate announced as its decision that the question would not be admitted.

Question. When speaking in connection with Forney's Press did I not say that if other Democrats in Washington and myself had not refused all ideas and suggestions from some prominent men of the party in power to make peace on terms of disunion that I believed the war would have been ended in February?

Answer. When speaking of the proposition, viz, "that it was not a war for the restoration of the Union," he stated that if the Democrats in Washington had united in a plan for the permanent separation of the Union the thing would have been accomplished in February.

Question. Did I not expressly refer to myself in that connection and say that I had refused and always would refuse to agree to a separation of the States; in other words to peace on terms of disunion?

Answer. He stated something to that effect. He stated that he wished to have a voice in the manner in which the Union was to be reconstructed, and that he wished also our Southern brethren to have a voice.

Question. Referring to the Richmond Enquirer article did I not say that it, Jeff. Davis' organ, had called upon Dictator Lincoln to lock up Mr. Cox, Senator Richardson and myself in one of his military prisons because of our doing so much against Southern recognition and independence?

Answer. Yes; substantially he did say so.

Question. Referring to General Orders, No. 38, did I not say that in so far as it undertook to subject citizens not in the land or naval forces or militia of the United States in actual service to trial by court-martial or military commission I believed it to be unconstitutional and a usurpation of arbitrary power?

Answer. He did, except the words "in so far."

Question. Referring to two citizens of Kentucky tried by military court in Cincinnati did I not say that what they were charged with was actual treason punishable by death, and that if guilty the penalty by statute was hanging, and they ought to be hung after being tried by a judicial court and a jury; instead of which they had been tried by a military court as I understood and sentenced to fine and imprisonment, one of them a fine of $300?

Answer. That was in substance what he said.

Question. Did I not also say in that connection that the rebel officer who was tried as a spy by the military court at Cincinnati was legally and properly tried and convicted according to the Rules and Articles of War; that that was a clear case where the court had jurisdiction?

Answer. It is my recollection that he denounced the court as an unlawful tribunal and that he did use the above language, and then gave the instances referred to in my direct testimony. He probably did refer to Campbell's case.

(The judge-advocate stated that the accused did distinguish in his speech the different cases for the purpose of showing jurisdiction, condemning those cases in which he held the court to have no jurisdiction and approving the case of the spy.)

Question. Did I not distinctly in the conclusion of the speech enjoin upon the people to stand by the Union at all events, and that if war failed not to give the Union up; to try by peaceable means, by compromise, to restore it as our fathers made it, and that though others might consent or be forced to consent I would not myself be one of those who would take any part in agreeing to a dissolution of the Union?

Answer. Yes. He said he and the peace men were the only ones who wished the restoration of the Union.

Question. Did not one of the "banners" you refer to as decorated with "butternuts" bear the inscription, "The Constitution as it is and the Union as it was?"

Answer. One of them bore that inscription.

Question. Do you mean to be understood to say that I heard the reference to Jeff. Davis or gave any assent to it whatever?

Answer. I cannot say that he did. It was said loud enough for him to hear if his attention had been directed that way. He gave no assent neither did he give any dissent.

Question. What was the size of the crowd assembled there that day?

Answer. It was very large.

The commission adjourned to meet again at 9.30 o'clock a. m. on Thursday, the 7th instant.

ROBERT B. POTTER,
Brigadier-General of Volunteers, President.
J. M. CUTTS,
Captain, Eleventh Infantry, Judge-Advocate.

THIRTEENTH DAY.

CINCINNATI, OHIO, *Thursday, May 7, 1863.*

The commission met pursuant to adjournment.

Present, Brigadier-General Potter, Lieutenant-Colonel Goodrich, Major Brown, Captain Lydig, Colonel De Courcy, Major Van Buren, Major Fitch, and judge-advocate.

The proceedings of the preceding day were read by the judge-advocate and approved.

All persons required to give evidence were directed to withdraw and remain in waiting until called for.

The cross-examination of Captain HILL was continued.

By the ACCUSED:

Question. In speaking of the character of the war did I not expressly say, as Mr. Lincoln in his proclamation July 1, 1862, said: "This unnecessary and injurious civil war?"

Answer. I do not recollect that he did. The language he made use of I understood to be his own.

Question. Again in speaking of the character of the war did I not expressly give as proof the President's proclamation of September 22, 1862, and January 1, 1863, as declaring emancipation of the slaves in Southern seceded States, and as a proof that the war was now being waged for that purpose?

(The accused stated that he offered this question as an explanation of the purpose and object of his declarations as to the present character of the war and as his authority for his statement. If he stated what the President stated he (the accused) could not be held disloyal for so doing.)

The judge advocate stated that the question was one which clearly put in question, not the utterance of certain words, opinions and sentiments, but their propriety, truth and justice when uttered, and required the commission to pass judgment not upon sentiments uttered by the accused but upon certain proclamations of the President of the United States. He further objected to the question as one designed in his belief not to meet the merits of this case, but to prepare a record in this case of a political character and for political uses.

The commission was duly cleared for deliberation, and on its reopening the judge advocate announced as its decision that the question would not be admitted.

Question. Did you continue at the same place during the delivery of the whole speech?

Answer. I did.

Question. Were your notes taken at the time or reduced to writing after the speech was over?

Answer. They were taken at the time. All I used before the court were just as they fell from his [your] lips.

Question. Were you not in citizen's clothes, and how came you to be at Mount Vernon that day? Did you go to Mount Vernon for the purpose of taking notes and reporting the speech?

The accused insisted on the question on the ground that it would show the temper and spirit of the witness and his prejudices, and as showing that the notes were taken with reference to arrest and prosecution before this commission, he being in the service as captain and his regiment in Cincinnati.

(The question was objected to by the judge-advocate and the commission was duly cleared for deliberation, and on its reopening the judge-advocate stated that he had withdrawn his objection and the question would be admitted.)

The question was then put to the witness.

Answer. I was in citizen's clothes and I went up for the purpose of listening to any speech that might be delivered at that meeting. I had no order to take notes or report.

Question. Did you take notes of any other speech?

Answer. I commenced taking notes of the speech of Mr. Cox, but I considered it harmless after listening to him a short time and stopped. I took no notes of any other speeches.

Question. Were you not expressly sent to listen to my speech on that occasion?

Answer. I was not, any more than to the other speeches.

Question. By whom were you sent?

Answer. By Capt. Andrew C. Kemper, assistant adjutant-general of the military commandant of the city of Cincinnati, Ohio.

Question. Did you make report to him on your return?

Answer. I did not. I reported first to Colonel Eastman himself, and from there went to headquarters Department of the Ohio.

Capt. JOHN A. MEANS, One hundred and fifteenth Ohio Volunteers, a witness for the prosecution, being duly sworn, testifies as follows:

By the JUDGE-ADVOCATE:

Question. What is your rank and regiment?

Answer. Captain, One hundred and fifteenth Ohio Volunteers.

Question. Were you present at a meeting of citizens held at Mount Vernon, Ohio, on or about May 1, 1863?

Answer. I was.

Question. Did you hear the accused address that meeting?

Answer. I did.

Question. How near were you; and state your position with reference to the speaker and state whether you heard the whole or a part of his speech?

Answer. I was in two or three positions. Most of the time about ten feet in front of the stand—directly in front. I heard the whole of his speech.

Question. State what, if any, remarks you heard the accused make with reference to the war or upon subjects in that connection. Give as near as you can his language.

Answer. He stated at one time that the war was not waged for the preservation of the Union; that it was an abolition war; that it might have been stopped or peace restored some time ago and the Union restored if the plan which had been submitted had been accepted.

(Objected to by the accused on the ground that he had applied for a subpœna summoning Fernando Wood, esq., of New York, and directing him to bring with him a letter signed by the President referring to this plan, which had been refused by the judge-advocate.)

The judge-advocate stated that he would withdraw so much of the specification as related to remarks alleged to have been made by the accused with reference to the termination of the war.

The witness was directed to omit any testimony he might possess on that point.

The witness continued:

The accused stated that if the plan he had proposed himself had been adopted peace would have been restored, the Union saved by a reconstruction, the North won back and the South guaranteed in their rights. That our Army had not been successful; that Richmond was not taken, Charleston nor Vicksburg; that the Mississippi was not opened, and would not be so long as there was cotton to sell or contractors to enrich. He spoke in regard to the rebuke of the Administration at the last fall election; that no more volunteers could be had; that the Administration had to resort to the French conscription law; that he would not counsel resistance to military or civil law; that was not needed; that a people were unworthy to be freemen who would submit to such encroachments on their liberties. He was then speaking of the conscription act. He said he believed the Administration was attempting to erect a despotism; that in less than one month Mr. Lincoln had plunged the country into this cruel, bloody and unnecessary war. He stated that General Orders, No. 38, was a usurpation of power; that he despised it, spit upon it and trampled it under his feet, and that he for one would not regard it. He styled the officers of the Administration and the officers of the Army as minions of the Administration, or as Lincoln's minions. I do not recall anything else. I will add that he said he did not ask Tod or Lincoln or Burnside whether he might speak as he was doing and had done; that he was a free man; that he spoke as he pleased and where he pleased. He said that proclamations and military orders were intended to intimidate the people and to prevent them from meeting as they were then that day doing; that he claimed the right to discuss and criticise the actions of civil and military men in power. He advised at the close of his speech to come up together at the ballot-box and hurl the tyrant from his throne. In one part of his speech he styled the President as "King Lincoln."

Cross-examined by the ACCUSED:

Question. Did you make any notes at all of my speech or are you testifying solely from memory?

Answer. I took no notes at the delivery of the speech, but after Pendleton commenced speaking went to the hotel and made minutes. I made those minutes an hour and a half or thereabouts after I heard the speech.

Question. About what was the length of the speech?

Answer. I think about an hour and a half.

Question. You speak of my saying the North might be won back. Was it not that the South might be won back, her rights being guaranteed under the Constitution?

Answer. No; I noticed this particularly. It struck me very forcibly.

Question. You say that I said that I would not counsel resistance to military or civil laws. Did I not expressly counsel the people to obey the Constitution and all laws and to pay proper respect to men in authority, but to maintain their political rights through the ballot-box and to redress personal wrongs through the judicial tribunals of the country and in that way put down the Administration and all usurpations of power?

Answer. He said at the last of his speech to come up united at the ballot-box and hurl the tyrant from his throne. I did not understand him to counsel the people to submit to the authorities at all times. I do not remember the language as stated, but part of it I remember.

Question. Did I not say that my authority to speak to the people in public assemblages on all public questions was not derived from General Orders, No. 38, but from General Orders, No. 1, the Constitution of the United States—George Washington commanding?

Answer. I understood him to say that his authority to speak to the people was higher than General Orders, No. 38, by that military despot Burnside. It was Orders, No. 1, signed Washington.

Question. Were not the words "Tod, Lincoln and Burnside" used, and that I did not ask their consent to speak?

Answer. He did use these words at one time.

Question. Were not the remarks you say I made about spitting and trampling under foot expressly applied in reference to arbitrary power generally, and did I not in that connection refer to General Orders, No. 9, in Indiana, signed by General Hascall, denying the right to criticise the war policy of the Administration?

Answer. The remarks in reference to spitting upon, &c., were made in direct reference to General Orders, No. 38. He some time afterwards in speaking of the tyranny of the Administration said that a general order had been issued in Indiana denying the rights of the people to criticise the military power of the Administration, and if submitted to would be followed by a similar one in Ohio.

Question. Do you undertake to give any connected or methodical statement of my speech of an hour and a half on that occasion?

Answer. I do not pretend to give his speech just as he spoke it. I only remember part.

Question. Were you not present in citizen's clothes? How came you to be at Mount Vernon that day—by whose order, and were you sent for the purpose of listening to and reporting the speech?

Answer. I was present in citizen's clothes by order of Colonel Eastman. I was sent there to listen to the speech and report his language as near as I could, and I did make report to Colonel Eastman.

Question. Did you make report of any other speech on that occasion?

Answer. I related the substance of Mr. Cox's and Mr. Kenny's speeches.

Question. Were you directed to go to Mount Vernon and make a report of the speech with reference to the prosecution under General Orders, No. 38?

Answer. I was not.

Question. Was any object stated to you, and if so what, for your going there in citizen's clothes, listening to and reporting the speech?

Answer. Not any.

The judge-advocate stated that he did not propose to re-examine the witness, and having no other witnesses would here close the testimony for the prosecution.

The accused asked to consult with his counsel, who did not appear and had not appeared in the court-room during the trial, before entering upon his defense.

The commission adjourned for fifteen minutes to enable the accused to consult with his counsel.

The commission reassembled pursuant to adjournment.

Hon. S. S. Cox, a witness for the defense, being duly sworn testifies as follows:

By the PRISONER:

Question. Were you present at a public political meeting of citizens of Ohio at Mount Vernon on Friday, May 1, 1863, and if so in what capacity?

Answer. I was present as one of the speakers.

Question. Did you hear the speech of Mr. Vallandigham that day?

Answer. I did. I heard the whole of it.

Question. State where your position was during its delivery; what your opportunity for hearing was; whether you heard it all and whether and why your attention was particularly directed to it.

Answer. Before the speaking began I was on the stand a few feet from Mr. Vallandigham, most of the time standing near him, so that I could not fail to hear all that he said. I do not think my attention was distracted but for perhaps a few moments during the entire speech. I had not heard Mr. Vallandigham speak since the adjournment of Congress, and as I came in from the West I did not know that he was to be there. I took an especial interest in listening to his speech throughout. Having to follow him I naturally noted the topics which he discussed.

Question. Did you hear allusions to General Burnside by name, and if so what were they?

Answer. The only allusion he made to the general was I think near the beginning of his speech in which he said he was not there by the favor of Abraham Lincoln, Governor Tod or Ambrose E. Burnside.

Question. Was any epithet applied to him during the speech?

Answer. No, sir. If there had been I should have noticed it because General Burnside is an old friend of mine and I should have remembered any odious epithet applied to him.

Question. Did you hear the references to General Orders, No. 38, and if so what were they? State fully.

Answer. The only reference made to that order in that speech was something to this effect: that he did not recognize (I do not know that I can quote the language) Orders, No. 38, as superior to Orders, No. 1, the Constitution, from George Washington, commanding.

Question. Were any insolent epithets, such as spitting upon, trampling under foot or the like used at any time in the speech in reference to this Order 38; and if any criticism was made upon it what was that criticism?

Answer. I cannot recall any denunciatory epithets applied to that order. I did not hear any that I can remember. The only criticism I heard was that in reference to the Constitution. Mr. Vallandigham discussed these matters very briefly, taking up the larger portion of his speech with another proposition. The other proposition was in connection with closing of the war by separation. He charged that men in power were willing to make peace by separation. He exhausted some time in reading proofs from publications of Montgomery Blair and Forney. He also stated there were private proofs yet to be disclosed which time would disclose. He said they pursued this thing until they found that Democrats were unwilling to make peace except upon a basis of the restoration of the whole Union. He denounced bitterly any attempts to restore peace by a separation of the States.

Question. Do you remember to what if at all in connection with future usurpation of power he applied his strongest language?

Answer. I cannot say as to his "strongest language," for he always speaks pretty strongly. He denounced in strong language any usurpations of power to stop public discussions and the suffrage. He appealed to the people to protect their rights, as a remedy for every grievance of a private nature. He counseled no resistance except such as might be had at the ballot-box.

Question. Was anything said by him at all looking to forcible resistance of either laws or military orders?

Answer. Not as I understand it. He stated the sole remedy to be in the ballot-box and in the courts. I remember this distinctly for I had been pursuing the same line of remark at Chicago and Fort Wayne and other places where I had been speaking, and with the purpose of repressing any tendency toward violence among our Democratic people.

Question. Was anything said by me on that occasion in denunciation of the conscription bill or looking in any way to resistance to it?

Answer. My best recollection is that Mr. Vallandigham did not say a word about the conscription.

Question. Did he refer to the French conscription bill, and if not was such reference made and by whom?

Answer. He did not. I did.

Question. Do you remember his quotation from President Lincoln's proclamation of July 1, 1862, of the words "unnecessary and injurious war?"

Answer. I do not. He may have done so.

Question. Did you hear similar language used by him?

Answer. I did not.

Question. Do you remember his comments on the change of the policy of the war some year or so after its commencement and what references were made by him in that connection?

Answer. He did refer to the change in the policy of the war and I think devoted some time to show that the war had been deviated from a war for the restoration of the Union into a war for the abolition of slavery.

Question. What did he claim to have been its original purpose as avowed and how show it?

Answer. He referred in that connection to the Crittenden resolutions, declaring the war to be one for the restoration of the Union and not to break up the "institution" of a State.

Question. Did he counsel any other mode in that speech of resisting usurpations of arbitrary power except by free discussion and the ballot-box?

Answer. He did not.

Question. Were any denunciations of the officers of the Army indulged in by him or any offensive epithets applied to them?

Answer. He occasionally used the words "the President and his minions," but I did not understand him to use them in connection with the Army. It was not in that connection. It was in connection with arbitrary arrests.

Question. Do I understand you to say that the denunciations to which you refer were chiefly in reference to arbitrary arrests?

Answer. My recollection is that that is the connection in which they were used. He applied some pretty strong epithets to spies and informers whom he did not seem to like very much.

Question. Do you remember the connection in which some words to this effect were used at the close of the speech, with regard to the possibility of a dissolution of the Union and of his own determination in regard to such a contingency?

Answer. I could not give the exact words. I remember the metaphor that "he would not be a priest to minister at the altar of disunion." He was speaking about the Union and his attachment to it. I cannot give the words of the metaphor.

Question. What counsel did I give at the close of my speech upon that subject?

Answer. He invoked the people under no circumstances to surrender the Union.

Question. Do you remember any rebuke in connection with the Butler County case of men who hurrahed for Jeff. Davis?

Answer. Yes; I do. He denounced the applause of Davis.

Question. Was anything said in that speech in reference to the war except in condemnation of what he claimed to be the policy upon which it was now being waged and as a policy which he insisted could not restore the Union but must end finally in disunion?

Answer. I can only give my understanding I do not know about inferences people might draw. I understood his condemnation of the war to be launched at its perversion from its original purpose.

The court here adjourned to meet at 4 30 p. m. of the same day.

4.30 O'CLOCK P. M.

The court met pursuant to adjournment.

The witnesses Locky Harper, J. T. Irvine and Frank H. Hurd, summoned for the defense, not having appeared the judge-advocate stated that if it would avoid an adjournment he would admit that they if present would under oath testify substantially the same as Hon. S. S. Cox.

Thereupon the accused stated that he would close his defense and offer no further testimony.

The judge-advocate stated that he did not propose to offer any further testimony.

The accused then read to the commission the statement (of which Mr. Vallandigham has a copy) hereunto appended:

PROTEST OF MR. VALLANDIGHAM.

CINCINNATI, OHIO, *May 7, 1863.*

Arrested without due "process of law," without warrant from any judicial officer and now in a military prison I have been served with a "charge and specifications," as in a court-martial or military commission.

I am not in either "the land or naval forces of the United States nor in the militia in the actual service of the United States," and therefore am not triable for any cause by any such court, but am subject by the express terms of the Constitution to arrest only by due process of law, judicial warrant, regularly issued upon affidavit and by some officer or court of competent jurisdiction for the trial of citizens, and am now entitled to be tried on an indictment or presentment of a grand jury of such court, to speedy and public trial by an impartial jury of the State of Ohio; to be confronted with witnesses against me, to have compulsory process for witnesses in my behalf, the assistance of counsel for my defense and evidence and argument according to the common laws and the ways of judicial courts.

And all these I here demand as my right as a citizen of the United States and under the Constitution of the United States.

But the alleged "offense" is not known to the Constitution of the United States nor to any law thereof. It is words spoken to the people of Ohio in an open and public political meeting lawfully and peaceably assembled under the Constitution and upon full notice. It is words of criticism of the public policy of the public servants of the people, by which policy it was alleged that the welfare of the country was not promoted. It was an appeal to the people to change that policy, not by force but by free elections and the ballot-box. It is not pretended that I counseled disobedience to the Constitution or resistance to laws and lawful authority. I never have. Beyond this protest I have nothing further to submit.

C. L. VALLANDIGHAM.

The judge-advocate stated that he had no reply to make to the statement of the accused. In so far as it called in question the jurisdiction of the commission that question had been decided by the authority convening and ordering the trial, and he was not called upon to discuss it nor had the commission been willing at any time to entertain it. In so far as any implications or inferences designed or contemplated in the statement of his right of counsel and to have witnesses summoned for his defense were involved the judge-advocate had summoned such witnesses as the accused had requested, and he had had the benefit of three lawyers of his own choice as counsel, who had, however, remained continuously in an adjoining room during the continuance of the trial—the accused himself for some reason unknown not having introduced them before the commission, though the commission had expressly authorized him to do so and had adjourned to permit his obtaining their presence.

The facts alleged in the specification were to be decided upon the evidence before the commission and he believed it unnecessary to comment thereon.

The question of the criminality of the facts alleged if proved was also a question purely for the commission and which the judge-advocate deemed it unnecessary to enforce by argument. He therefore without further comment submitted the case to the consideration of the commission.

The commission was duly cleared for deliberation.

FINDING AND SENTENCE.

After maturely considering the evidence before them and the state-ment of the accused the commission find the accused, Clement L. Vallandigham, a citizen of the State of Ohio, as follows:

Of the specification (except the words "that propositions by which the Northern States could be won back and the South guaranteed their rights under the Consti-tution had been rejected the day before the battle of Fredericksburg by Lincoln and his minions," meaning thereby the President of the United States and those under him in authority, and the words "asserting that he firmly believed as he asserted six months ago that the men in power are attempting to establish a despotism in this country more cruel and more oppressive than ever existed before"), guilty.

And as to these words not guilty.

Of the charge guilty.

And the commission do therefore sentence him, the said Clement L. Vallandigham, a citizen of the State of Ohio, to be placed in close confinement in some fortress of the United States to be designated by the commanding officer of this department, there to be kept during the continuance of the war.

ROBERT B. POTTER,
Brigadier-General of Volunteers, President.
J. M. CUTTS,
Captain, Eleventh Infantry, Judge-Advocate.

The commission then adjourned to meet again at 10 o'clock a. m. on Monday, the 11th instant.

ROBERT B. POTTER,
Brigadier-General of Volunteers, President.
J. M. CUTTS,
Captain, Eleventh Infantry, Judge-Advocate.

GENERAL ORDERS, }   HDQRS. DEPARTMENT OF THE OHIO,
No. 68.   }   *Cincinnati, Ohio, May 16, 1863.*

I. At a military commission which convened at Cincinnati, Ohio, on the 6th day of May, 1863, pursuant to Special Orders, No. 135, of April 21, 1863, current series, from these headquarters, and of which Brig. Gen. Robert B. Potter, U. S. Volunteers, is president, was arraigned and tried Clement L. Vallandigham, a citizen of the State of Ohio, on the following charge and specification of charge, to wit:*

*   *   *   *   *   *   *

II. The proceedings, finding and sentence in the foregoing case are approved and confirmed, and it is directed that the place of confine-ment of the prisoner, Clement L. Vallandigham, in accordance with said sentence, be Fort Warren, Boston Harbor.

By command of Major-General Burnside:

LEWIS RICHMOND,
Assistant Adjutant-General.

HEADQUARTERS DEPARTMENT OF THE SOUTH,
Hilton Head, S. C., May 18, 1863.

Rear-Admiral S. F. DU PONT,
Commanding South Atlantic Blockading Squadron.

ADMIRAL: I have received intelligence that one of my captains who was recently taken prisoner of war by the rebels has been executed by them. I am anxious to obtain possession of as many as possible of

---

* Charge and specification omitted here; see p. 634.

the enemy who may be prisoners in our hands to be held answerable for the treatment which my officers and men may receive at the hands of their captors.

With this view I earnestly beg that if it can be done consistently the nine prisoners taken by the fleet at Edisto may be turned over to me.

I have the honor to be, admiral, very respectfully, your obedient servant,

D. HUNTER,
Major-General, Commanding.

HEADQUARTERS DEPARTMENT OF THE MISSOURI,
Saint Louis, May 18, 1863.
Lieut. Gen. T. H. HOLMES, C. S. Army,
Commanding District of Arkansas.

GENERAL: There has been no intentional departure on my part from the cartel to which you refer, but the changes of position of troops and departments have prevented me from preserving the current accounts which would otherwise have continued. Eastern Arkansas has fallen into the temporary command of the Department of the Tennessee. In relation to orders issued by General Blunt I send you a copy of my Orders, No. 30, current series, which you will perceive supersedes any order such as you name, as General Blunt is within this department. As there is no very exact meaning to the word "bushwhackers" I do not consider it necessary to determine the rights appertaining to them. Regular soldiers in bushes are very different from mere stragglers or murderers in the bush as you will readily understand. I have, therefore, in my order tried to define irregular troops according to established rules. In relation to the matter of General McNeil I send you a copy of my reply sent long ago and which must have been neglected by other commanders who were placed in command about the time.

Trusting that these explanations will be sufficient to satisfy you of my determination to restrain licentious warfare and pursue only such rules as seem most certain to terminate our unfortunate strife by honorable means,

I have the honor to remain, your obedient servant,

S. R. CURTIS,
Major-General, Commanding.

QUARTERMASTER-GENERAL'S OFFICE,
Washington, May 18, 1863.
Col. WILLIAM HOFFMAN,
Commissary-General of Prisoners, Washington City.

COLONEL: John Walker, late captain of the U. S. tug-boat Fox, with Martin B. Woolfley, engineer of the said boat, report that they represent the crew of the U. S. tug Fox, consisting of twenty-one men, including themselves, captured at Pass à l'Outre, April 12, midnight, and carried into Mobile, thence forwarded to Richmond and paroled for exchange and sent to Annapolis, thence to Washington City. They apply for transportation for themselves and crew to New Orleans. They have been directed to report to you, and upon a requisition approved by you Colonel Rucker, depot quartermaster, will send them by transport to New York to be forwarded thence by transportation to New Orleans.

    Very respectfully, your obedient servant,

M. C. MEIGS,
Quartermaster-General.

LEXINGTON, KY., *May 18, 1863.*

Major-General BURNSIDE:

    The following from General Carter with regard to Rogers and Deaton, two officers imprisoned for life in irons, calls for immediate action. Please confine two or more officers in like manner and let me have their names. I will communicate further with you in regard to the hostages for the two citizens:

    Through an assistant surgeon recently released from a rebel prison I learn that Lieut. Canada H. Rogers, of First Tennessee Infantry, and Captain Deaton, of I think the Sixth East Tennessee Infantry, are both in prison at Knoxville, Tenn., and are condemned to imprisonment for life and are heavily ironed. Both officers were captured in East Tennessee.

    Sam. Snapp, of Sullivan County, Tenn., and Preston Berry, from near Williamsburg, Ky., are also in Knoxville prison. I have ordered the arrest of a rebel citizen in Laurel County, Ky., to be held as a hostage for Berry. I hope you will order at least two rebel officers for each of ours to be imprisoned in irons till the release of Rogers and Deaton, and that some rebel citizen may be held for Snapp, who is a loyal man and had committed no other offense than that of being loyal.

CARTER.

O. B. WILLCOX,
Brigadier-General.

CAPE GIRARDEAU, *May 18, 1863.*

General DAVIDSON:

    I send by telegraph the following letter received from Colonel Shelby. An agreement between Generals Blunt and Marmaduke can of course have no effect in this district, nor do I believe you will regard wounded prisoners as neutrals. I have informed Captain Adams of my referring the whole matter to you. Please telegraph me upon the receipt of this. Under the advice of Surgeon Martin and your former permission I take first boat for Saint Louis, as I find myself unfit to discharge duties encumbent on me.

JOHN McNEIL,
Brigadier-General, Commanding.

[Inclosure.]

HDQRS. C. S. FORCES, NORTHEAST ARKANSAS,
May 11, 1863.

Brig. Gen. JOHN McNEIL,
    Comdg. U. S. Forces Southeast Missouri, Cape Girardeau, Mo.

    GENERAL: You have in your hands the following officers of this command: Maj. Y. H. Blackwell, Shelby's regiment Missouri cavalry; Capt. H. M. Woodsmall, Jeans' regiment Missouri cavalry; Lieut. J. N. Edwards, Shelby's regiment Missouri cavalry; Lieut. William H. Ferrill, Shelby's regiment Missouri cavalry, all wounded at the engagement at Cape Girardeau. According to the agreement between Brigadier-General Blunt and Major-General Hindman made after the battle of Prairie Grove all wounded are to be considered as neutrals and cannot be made prisoners. In the late expedition of part of this command into Missouri this agreement was strictly adhered to by all officers of the command.

I much desire to have these officers within our lines and under treatment with their friends, and I therefore by direction of the brigadier-general commanding send Captain Adams, Jeans' Missouri cavalry, with an escort of ten men under flag of truce for the above-mentioned officers, and have to request that you will give him assistance in the duty assigned him.

In case the agreement between Generals Blunt and Hindman is not recognized in this instance I am directed by the brigadier-general commanding to notify you that in no future instance will he recognize it as binding.

I also by direction of Brigadier-General Marmaduke and at the request of the prisoners return to you three prisoners of your command, Capt. H. A. Spencer, Company E, Third Iowa Cavalry; Capt. S. A. C. Bartlett, Company C, Third Cavalry Missouri State Militia, and Capt. T. J. Mitchell, Company K, Third Missouri Volunteer Cavalry. These officers are permitted to return under parole, and under parole of honor that unless the wounded officers C. S. Army above named are not allowed to return they will return to this command to be kept as prisoners of war.

I am, general, very respectfully,

J. O. SHELBY,
Colonel, Commanding Division.

HDQRS. SUB-DISTRICT, *Cape Girardeau, May 18, 1863.*

Col. J. O. SHELBY:

I have the honor to acknowledge the receipt of your communication of May 11, 1863, under flag of truce borne by Captain Adams, Jeans' Missouri cavalry, in which you propose the exchange of three captains therein named for Maj. Y. H. Blackwell, Capt. H. M. Woodsmall, Lieuts. J. N. Edwards and William H. Ferrill.

In reply I would say I am wrongly addressed as commanding forces in Southeast Missouri, Brigadier-General Davidson, commanding Saint Louis District of Missouri, being the commandant of all forces in Southeast Missouri. Your communication will be telegraphed to him and I will act as directed by him. Meanwhile without any reference to agreement between Generals Blunt and Marmaduke of which I have no knowledge if you are disposed to discharge those gentlemen on their parole of honor as stated by you I will see that its terms are complied with and consider your so doing as a favor which I will endeavor to reciprocate. Only one of the prisoners demanded is fit to be moved

I have the honor to be, colonel, your most obedient,

JOHN McNEIL,
Brigadier-General, Comdg. U. S. Forces, Cape Girardeau, Mo.

HEADQUARTERS DISTRICT OF NORTHWEST MISSOURI,
Saint Joseph, Mo., May 18, 1863.

Maj. J. M. BASSETT, *District Provost-Marshal.*

SIR: You will direct your assistants to arrest the most prominent and influential rebels and sympathizers with the rebellion in their respective districts. The assistant provost-marshals will in every case take testimony upon the following points, viz:

1. Disloyal conduct previous to July 25, 1862, the date of the President's proclamation.

2. Disloyal conduct since that period.

3. General reputation of the accused as to his sentiments and character, and as to whether he is or is not a dangerous man in his neighborhood. Women who are violent and dangerous secessionists must be arrested as well as men.

4. You will not arrest persons who were at one time disloyal but have been permitted to remain among us on taking the oath of allegiance and giving bond, provided they have since observed their obligations in the best faith.

The slightest departure from good faith in this matter, acts or words that would not be noticed if spoken or committed by Union men, will be sufficient to cause the arrest of such persons. Active loyalty is required at the hands of all citizens. Those whose best claim to the protection of the United States Government is that they "have done nothing" are rebels. It is the duty of every man to do something to uphold his Government. In clear cases of disloyalty and in those only the prisoners and the proofs will be sent forward to you. Their cases will be disposed of here.

I am, sir, very respectfully, your obedient servant,
CHESTER HARDING, Jr.,
Colonel, Commanding District.

FORT MONROE, *May 18, 1863.*

Col. WILLIAM HOFFMAN:

Transports leave to-night for prisoners at Fort Delaware. Will Captain Baylor be delivered with the other Confederate officers? His release is again demanded by Confederate agent.
WM. H. LUDLOW,
Lieutenant-Colonel, &c.

FORT MONROE, *May 18, 1863.*

Col. WILLIAM HOFFMAN:

Will Thomas Tait Tunstall, confined in the Old Capitol Prison, be sent? A pressing demand is made by Mr. Ould for Capt. Clagett D. Fitzhugh and Capt. George M. Shearer, who are said to be in Old Capitol Prison or Fort McHenry. The former was captured in July, 1862. Will they be delivered?

WM. H. LUDLOW,
Lieutenant-Colonel, &c.

FORT MONROE, *May 18, 1863.*

Col. W. HOFFMAN, *Commissary-General of Prisoners:*

Will you please direct that all prisoners be paroled before leaving their places of detention and especially before embarking on any transport. Unless done in this latter case there is great danger that they may overpower the guard and run away with the vessel. I have had intimations of such intentions. Two transports left last night to bring away prisoners from Fort Delaware.

WM. H. LUDLOW,
Lieutenant-Colonel, &c.

OFFICE COMMISSARY-GENERAL OF PRISONERS,
Washington, D. C., May 18, 1863.

Lieut. Col. W. H. LUDLOW,
Agent for Exchange of Prisoners, Fort Monroe, Va.

COLONEL: Your letters of the 14th, 16th and 17th instant and also several telegrams relating to the delivery of individual prisoners of war are in our hands. After many applications I have succeeded in getting a report in the case of Captain Baylor, and as it is represented that there is testimony to prove that he fired upon a flag of truce and caused the death of one of our men an order has been issued for his immediate trial.

Colonel Morehead, Doctor Dixon, Capt. or Lieut. James H. Baker and Private John W. Garrett, Company D, First Kentucky Infantry, at Johnson's Island, and Capt. David Lynn, at Fort Delaware, are ordered to be delivered for exchange immediately. The Secretary of War has not yet decided to order the delivery of Colonel Poindexter. Major Saunders is at Fort Lafayette at the disposal of the Navy Department.

I am unable to find the name of Arnold Harris, jr., on any of our books. Thomas Tait Tunstall was released some time since on his pledge to remain abroad during the war. Clagett D. Fitzhugh and George M. Shearer are in the Old Capitol Prison. The former denies that he is an officer in the rebel army. Says he is only a private. The latter says he was a lieutenant but is not now in the army. Both cases are held for the action of the War Department.

I did not know of the presence of the twelve men of Mosby's cavalry at the Old Capitol Prison till I received your telegram. Unless they are held for trial for some offense outside of their duty as soldiers they will be sent down on the State of Maine. I some days since obtained authority from the General-in-Chief to direct that in all cases where prisoners were arrested charged as spies or with any other act cognizable by a military tribunal they should be brought to immediate trial. This will prevent the great wrong of holding prisoners for months on charges which have little or no foundation. I have again and again ordered that all prisoners of war in our possession, including all irregular organizations, not spies, should be sent forward for delivery or exchange, and when it has not been done it has been from some obstacle not known or reported to me. Such things, however, are not done with a view to evade our obligations, but are thought to be necessary from some peculiar circumstances in the individual cases.

The two women sent down by the steamer on her last trip to whom Mr. Ould refers were not arrested nor sent forward on account of their personal character but for serious acts of disloyalty, being confirmed rebels, and it was not to be expected that in their position in life their morals could be very correct; nor was that examined into. They were sent South simply because they were determined to give the rebellion all the aid in their power. For their grossly outrageous conduct on the boat they should have been properly disposed of and punished on board the steamer, and certainly their obscene language should not have been permitted to reach the ears of ladies.

I will write to General Banks on the subject of exchanged prisoners and prisoners of irregular organizations as you request. I have not written to General Rosecrans about the canceling of oaths of allegiance taken by persons in Kentucky and Tennessee on either side of the line by way of an exchange as you suggested was desired by Mr. Ould because I do not think the Government could admit so formally that an American citizen could in that way set aside or throw off his allegiance. It would be a very favorable arrangement for the other party but might embarrass us very much.

I have laid your letters with the memorandum containing Governor Peirpoint's views before the Secretary of War. I have had blank parole rolls distributed, with instructions to use them when prisoners are sent forward for delivery.

Very respectfully, your obedient servant,
W. HOFFMAN,
Colonel Third Infantry, Commissary-General of Prisoners.

WASHINGTON, *May 18, 1863.*
Lieut. Col. W. H. LUDLOW:

Capt. David Lynn will be sent for exchange. The Secretary of War will not yet order the delivery of Colonel Poindexter. Two hundred and thirty prisoners left Camp Douglas for City Point 15th instant.
W. HOFFMAN,
Commissary-General of Prisoners.

MILITARY PRISON, *Alton, Ill., May 18, 1863.*
Col. W. HOFFMAN,
Commissary-General of Prisoners, Washington, D. C.

COLONEL: I have the honor to report that 708 Confederate prisoners of war, twenty-three of whom are commissioned officers, arrived here this morning from Mississippi and Tennessee.

I am, sir, with much respect, your obedient servant,
T. HENDRICKSON,
Major Third Infantry, Commanding the Prison.

MILITARY PRISON, *Alton, Ill., May 18, 1863.*
Col. W. HOFFMAN,
Commissary-General of Prisoners, Washington, D. C.

COLONEL: About a month ago, viz, on the 16th of April, I reported to you that this prison was being made the receptacle for all the deserters and other convicts from the various volunteer forces serving in the West. Since that time about thirty of this class of convicts have been received here, making the number of these Federals now confined in this prison about ninety. All of these men have been sentenced either formally or informally to hard labor with ball and chain, forfeiture of pay, &c., for longer or shorter periods, from six months to twenty years. Many of them are reckless and some of them are desperate men ready at all times for any enterprise however hazardous. They have made several attempts recently to escape from the prison by digging under the foundation of the prison walls, but in which attempts they were fortunately foiled by a discovery before their purpose was consummated. Having never been kept in proper subjection these men are highly insubordinate and mutinous, openly and publicly denouncing in unmeasured terms their officers who sent them here, and setting at defiance both by word and deed all who attempt to exercise control over them.

These ninety men by their bad conduct give us more trouble than all the Confederate prisoners confined here, and if they are kept here their insubordinate conduct cannot but have a pernicious effect upon the latter from whom it is almost impossible to keep them entirely separate. I have a dozen or so of the most prominent among the mutinous crew confined in the cells of the prison, but even here they continue their violent conduct by breaking up the balls and chains I have had put upon them and by battering down the walls of the cells and committing other outrages. As it is impracticable to carry out the sentences of these men here, there being no kind of hard labor at which they can be employed, and as it is equally as impracticable to keep them from mingling more or less with the Confederate prisoners, of whom we have now about 1,100, I would suggest that they (the Federals) be removed to some place (to one of the fortifications upon the Atlantic coast, for instance) where their sentence can be properly carried into effect.

I would suggest also that an order be issued by the proper authorities prohibiting the sending here in future any more convicts like those above mentioned.

I have the honor to be, sir, with much respect, your most obedient servant,

T. HENDRICKSON,
Major Third Infantry, Commanding the Prison.

GENERAL ORDERS, }   HDQRS. DEPARTMENT OF THE OHIO,
    No. 70.   }   *Cincinnati, Ohio, May 18, 1863.*

I. The intention of that portion of General Orders, No. 66, from these headquarters, relating to the "removal of wives and families of persons in arms against the United States," being merely to remove from this department those persons who from their intimate relations with the enemies of the Government would be presumed to exercise an active sympathy with the rebellion, and would therefore be dangerous as residents, and as arbitrary arrests or notices to remove under that order might occasion suffering and injustice, it is hereby ordered that in all such cases the proper officer having cognizance of the facts will forward to these headquarters a written statement of the circumstances before he takes any further action.

II. As the experience of this department has shown that cases exist where the persons to whom General Orders, No. 66, refers are notwithstanding their close relationship to the enemies of the country still loyal to the Government and are willing to testify it by taking the oath of allegiance, such persons when there is evidence of the honesty of the intention of the parties in taking the oath will not be molested.

III. The attention of all officers having charge of paroled prisoners is again directed to the orders of the War Department relative to paroled prisoners, the requirements of which must be strictly complied with. Negligence in this respect causes great confusion and injury to the service, and hereafter any officer guilty of such neglect will be held strictly accountable therefor.

General Orders, No. 46, current series, War Department, applies to men absent without authority, paroled prisoners included, and requires that they should be sent to the general camps designated in General Orders, No. 72, War Department, of June, 1862, and it requires that the military commandant shall make tri-monthly reports of men so forwarded. General Orders, No. 72, names three camps at which paroled prisoners are to be assembled, and the commanders of those camps are required to furnish the commissary-general of prisoners with rolls of all men who join or leave and with a monthly and semi-monthly return showing all alterations.

IV. All tenders of resignations or applications for leaves of absence or furloughs will be forwarded through the proper military channels to these headquarters for final action.

V. Officers in their official communications will be governed by the regulations requiring that such communications shall refer to "one subject only."

VI. With the exception of telegraphic communications from district commanders all official papers intended for the commanding general must be addressed to the assistant adjutant-general of the department and forwarded through the proper military channel.

By command of Major-General Burnside:

LEWIS RICHMOND,
Assistant Adjutant-General.

ALBANY, N. Y., *May 19, 1863.*

To His Excellency the PRESIDENT OF THE UNITED STATES:

The undersigned, officers of a public meeting held at the city of Albany on the 16th day of May instant, herewith transmit to Your Excellency a copy of the resolutions adopted at the said meeting and respectfully request your earnest consideration of them. They deem it proper on their personal responsibility to state that the meeting was one of the most respectable as to numbers and character and one of the most earnest in the support of the Union ever held in this city.

Yours, with great regard,

ERASTUS CORNING, *President.*
ELI PERRY, *Vice-President.*
PETER GANSEVOORT, *Vice-President.*
PETER MONTEITH, *Vice-President.*
SAMUEL W. GIBBS, *Vice-President.*
JOHN NIBLACK, *Vice-President.*
H. W. McCLELLAN, *Vice-President.*
LEMUEL W. RODGERS, *Vice-President.*
WILLIAM SEYMOUR, *Vice-President.*
JEREMIAH OSBORN, *Vice-President.*
WM. S. PADOCK, *Vice-President.*
J. B. SANDERS, *Vice-President.*
EDWARD MULCAHY, *Vice-President.*
D. V. N. RADCLIFFE, *Vice-President.*
WILLIAM A. RICE, *Secretary.*
EDWARD NEWCOMB, *Secretary.*
R. W. PECKHAM, JR., *Secretary.*
M. A. NOLAN, *Secretary.*
JOHN R. NESSEL, *Secretary.*
C. W. WEEKS, *Secretary.*

[Inclosure.]

Resolved, That the Democrats of New York point to their uniform course of action during the two years of civil war through which we have passed, to the alacrity which they have evinced in filling the ranks of the army, to their contributions and sacrifices, as the evidence of their patriotism and devotion to the cause of our imperiled country. Never in the history of civil wars has a Government been sustained with such ample resources of means and men as the people have voluntarily placed in the hands of this Administration.

Resolved, That as Democrats we are determined to maintain this patriotic attitude, and despite of adverse and disheartening circumstances to devote all our energies to sustain the cause of the Union; to secure peace through victory and to bring back the restoration of all the States under the safeguard of the Constitution.

Resolved, That while we will not consent to be misapprehended upon these points we are determined not to be misunderstood in regard to others not less essential. We demand that the Administration shall be true to the Constitution; shall recognize and maintain the rights of the States and the liberties of the citizen; shall everywhere outside of the lines of necessary military occupation and the scenes of insurrection exert all its powers to maintain the supremacy of the civil over the military law.

Resolved, That in view of these principles we denounce the recent assumption of a military commander to seize and try a citizen of Ohio, Clement L. Vallandigham, for no other reason than words addressed to a public meeting in criticism of the course of the Administration and in condemnation of the military orders of that general.

Resolved, That this assumption of power by a military tribunal if successfully asserted not only abrogates the right of the people to assemble and discuss the affairs of government, the liberty of speech and of the press, the right of trial by jury, the law of evidence and the privilege of *habeas corpus,* but it strikes a fatal blow at the supremacy of the law and the authority of the State and Federal Constitutions.

Resolved, That the Constitution of the United States—the supreme law of the land—has defined the crime of treason against the United States to consist "only in levying war against them or adhering to their enemies, giving them aid and comfort," and has provided that "no person shall be convicted of treason unless on the testimony of witnesses to the same overt act or on confession in open court." And it further provides that "no person shall be held to answer for a capital or otherwise infamous crime unless on a presentment or indictment of a grand jury except in cases arising in the land and naval forces or in the militia when in actual service in time of war or public danger;" and further that "in all criminal prosecutions the accused shall enjoy the right of a speedy and public trial by an impartial jury of the State and district wherein the crime was committed."

Resolved, That these safeguards of the rights of the citizen against the pretensions of the arbitrary power were intended more especially for his protection in times of civil commotion. They were secured substantially to the English people after years of protracted civil war and were adopted into our Constitution at the close of the Revolution. They have stood the test of seventy-six years of trial under our republican system under circumstances that show that while they constitute the foundation of all free government they are the elements of the enduring stability of the Republic.

Resolved, That in adopting the language of Daniel Webster we declare "it is the ancient and undoubted prerogative of this people to canvass public measures and the merits of public men." It is a "home-bred right," a fireside privilege. It had been enjoyed in every house, cottage and cabin in the nation. It is as undoubted as the right of breathing the air or walking on the earth. Belonging to private life as a right, it belongs to public life as a duty, and it is the last duty which those whose representatives we are shall find us to abandon. Aiming at all times to be courteous and temperate in its use except when the right itself is questioned we shall place ourselves on the extreme boundary of our right and bid defiance to any arm that would move us from our ground. "This high constitutional privilege we shall defend and exercise in all places—in time of peace, in time of war, and at all times. Living, we shall assert it; and should we leave no other inheritance to our children by the blessing of God we will leave the inheritance of free principles and the example of a manly, independent and constitutional defense of them."

Resolved, That in the election of Governor Seymour the people of this State by an emphatic majority declare their condemnation of the system of arbitrary arrests and their determination to stand by the Constitution. That the revival of this lawless system can have but one result: to divide and distract the North and destroy its confidence in the purposes of the Administration. That we deprecate it as an element of confusion at home, of weakness to our armies in the field and as calculated to lower the estimate of American character and magnify the apparent peril of our cause abroad. And that regarding the blow struck at a citizen of Ohio as aimed at the rights of every citizen of the North we denounce it as against the spirit of our laws and Constitution and most earnestly call upon the President of the United States to reverse the action of the military tribunal which has passed a "cruel and unusual punishment" upon the party arrested, prohibited in terms by the Constitution, and to restore him the liberty of which he has been deprived.

Resolved, That the president, vice-president and secretary of this meeting be requested to transmit a copy of these resolutions to His Excellency the President of the United States with the assurance of this meeting of their hearty and earnest desire to support the Government in every constitutional and lawful measure to suppress the existing rebellion.

WAR DEPARTMENT, *Washington, May 19, 1863.*
JOSHUA F. SPEED and JAMES SPEED, *Louisville:*

Before the receipt of your telegram of Sunday the President on the application of Hon. James Guthrie had directed that Colonel Churchill might remain at Louisville on condition of taking the oath of allegiance and Mr. Guthrie pledging himself that Colonel Churchill should be of good behavior and do no act of hostility against the United States and give no aid and comfort or information to the enemy. The Adjutant-General has been directed to telegraph the order to General Curtis and to the military officer commanding at Louisville and to Mr. Guthrie.

EDWIN M. STANTON,
Secretary of War.

WASHINGTON, *May 19, 1863.*
Major-General BURNSIDE, *Cincinnati:*

The President desires to know what you have done with Vallandigham, and if sent away by what route and where to.

EDWIN M. STANTON,

CINCINNATI, OHIO, *May 19, 1863.*

Hon. E. M. STANTON:

Vallandigham is still here under guard. Will not be sent till to-morrow. He is sentenced to confinement in Fort Warren, Boston Harbor, during the war.

A. E. BURNSIDE,
Major-General.

WAR DEPARTMENT, *Washington, May 19, 1863.*

Major-General BURNSIDE, *Cincinnati.*

SIR: The President directs that without delay you send C. L. Vallandigham under secure guard to the headquarters of General Rosecrans to be put by him beyond our military lines and that in case of his return within our lines he be arrested and kept in close custody for the term specified in his sentence.

By order of the President:

EDWIN M. STANTON,
Secretary of War.

WAR DEPARTMENT, *Washington, May 19, 1863.*

Major-General ROSECRANS,
Comdg. Dept. of the Cumberland, Murfreesborough, Tenn.:

The President has directed General Burnside to send C. L. Vallandigham to your headquarters to be put by you beyond our military lines and that if he returns to be arrested and kept in close custody during the war. The President also directs that when C. L. Vallandigham reaches your headquarters you keep him in close custody and send him beyond our military lines and that if he returns within your command you arrest and keep him in close custody during the war or until further orders.

By order of the President:

EDWIN M. STANTON,
Secretary of War.

NAVY DEPARTMENT, *Washington, May 19, 1863.*

Col. WILLIAM HOFFMAN,
Commissary-General of Prisoners, Washington, D. C.

SIR : I transmit herewith a list* of prisoners which has been communicated to Lieutenant-Colonel Ludlow as available for exchange. I also transmit a list* of others now confined in Fort Lafayette by order of this Department whom the Department does not wish exchanged at present if it can be avoided.

Very respectfully, &c.,   GIDEON WELLES,
Secretary of the Navy.

WASHINGTON, [*May 19, 1863.*]

General ROSECRANS:

The President has directed Burnside to send C. L. Vallandigham to your headquarters to be put by you beyond our military lines and that

---

* Not found.

if he returns he be arrested and put in close custody during the war. The President also directs that when C. L. Vallandigham reaches your headquarters you keep him in close custody and send him beyond our military lines and that if he returns within your command you arrest and keep him in close custody during the war or until further orders.

By order of the President:

E. R. S. CANBY,
Brigadier-General and Assistant Adjutant-General.

10 P. M.

Acknowledge receipt of this and report time when received is request of General Canby.

MURFREESBOROUGH, *May 19, 1863.*

Brigadier-General CANBY:

Your telegram respecting C. L. Vallandigham received. The President's orders will be obeyed. Burnside must send him with secrecy or he will be shot by some lawless person.

W. S. ROSECRANS,
Major-General.

MURFREESBOROUGH, *May 19, 1863.*

Major-General BURNSIDE:

The President orders me to receive C. L. Vallandigham from you at my headquarters and put him through our lines. Send him with great secrecy and caution or he will run the risk of a stray shot from some lawless person.

W. S. ROSECRANS,
Major-General.

HEADQUARTERS OF THE ARMY, *Washington, May 19, 1863.*
Colonel HOFFMAN, *Commissary-General of Prisoners.*

COLONEL: You will carry out the suggestions of Colonel Ludlow in the inclosed telegram to the Secretary of War.

Very respectfully, your obedient servant,

H. W. HALLECK,
General-in-Chief.

[Inclosure.]

FORT MONROE, VA., *May 19, 1863.*

Hon. EDWIN M. STANTON, *Secretary of War:*

Will you please direct that all prisoners be paroled before leaving their places of detention and especially before embarking on any transport. Unless done in this latter case there is great danger that they may overpower the guard and run away with the vessel. I have had intimations of such intentions. Two transports left last night to bring away prisoners from Fort Delaware.

WM. H. LUDLOW,
Lieutenant-Colonel, &c.

[Indorsement.]

Referred to the General-in-Chief to issue the necessary orders.

EDWIN M. STANTON.

FLAG-SHIP WABASH,
Port Royal Harbor, S. C., May 19, 1863.

Maj. Gen. D. HUNTER,
Comdg. Dept. of the South, Hdqrs. Hilton Head, S. C.

GENERAL: I have the honor to acknowledge the receipt of your communication of the 18th instant referring to the prisoners taken by the naval forces on Edisto Island and now on the Vermont.

I had reserved these men for a particular purpose, viz, to effect an exchange for the officers of the U. S. S. Isaac Smith captured in Stono or I should have delivered them over to you before.

By the papers and private sources I have learned that all these officers have been exchanged and therefore the object for retaining them has apparently ceased; but as I have written to the Department for special instructions in reference to these very prisoners I would prefer to wait a few days to give time for an answer to my communication.

I have the honor to be, general, very respectfully, your obedient servant,

S. F. DU PONT,
Rear-Admiral, Commanding South Atlantic Blockading Squadron.

QUARTERMASTER-GENERAL'S OFFICE,
Washington, May 19, 1863.

Col. S. B. HOLABIRD, *Chief Quartermaster, New Orleans, La.*

COLONEL: John Walker, late captain of the U. S. tug-boat Fox, Martin B. Woolfley, engineer of the said boat, and the crew, consisting of twenty-one men including the two named, will receive transportation from this place to New Orleans on the requisition of the commissary-general of prisoners. It is represented that they were captured at Pass à l'Outre 12th April, midnight, and carried into Mobile, thence forwarded to Richmond and paroled for exchange and sent to Annapolis, thence to Washington City. A court of inquiry should be held upon this affair as soon as the crew arrive in New Orleans.

M. C. MEIGS,
Quartermaster-General.

WAR DEPARTMENT, *Washington, May 19, 1863.*

Maj. Gen. E. A. HITCHCOCK,
Military Governor, &c., Washington, D. C.

SIR: The Secretary of War directs that unless specially authorized no Confederate prisoners of war will be released upon the condition of taking the oath of allegiance to the Government of the United States.

Very respectfully, sir, your obedient servant,

ED. R. S. CANBY,
Brigadier-General and Assistant Adjutant-General.

[Indorsement.]

WAR DEPARTMENT, *May 19, 1863.*

[Colonel HOFFMAN.]

COLONEL: The Secretary of War intends that this order shall have a general application.

Very respectfully,

ED. R. S. CANBY,
Brigadier-General.

SAINT LOUIS, MO., *May 19, 1863.*

General MCNEIL, *Commanding Cape Girardeau:*

The exchange by cartel must take place by delivery at Vicksburg of equal numbers and rank.

J. W. DAVIDSON,
Brigadier-General.

HEADQUARTERS SAINT LOUIS DISTRICT, *May 19, 1863.*

General MCNEIL, *Cape Girardeau:*

Say to General Marmaduke that the agreement between himself [Hindman] and General Blunt is not acknowledged by me as any rule of action. Retain your prisoners therefore until properly exchanged.

J. W. DAVIDSON,
Brigadier-General.

CAPE GIRARDEAU, *May 19, 1863.*

General DAVIDSON:

Your instructions in regard to prisoners have been complied with. He now proposes the following:

I, R. H. Adams, fully empowered to negotiate for the exchange of Maj. Y. H. Blackwell, Capt. H. M. Woodsmall and Lieuts. J. N. Edwards and William H. Ferrill and such privates as I think proper do hereby propose to exchange Major McConnel for Major Blackwell and Captain Spencer for Captain Woodsmall; and then I propose to exchange Captain Bartlett for Lieutenant Edwards and two enlisted men, and Captain Mitchell for Lieutenant Ferrill and two enlisted men.

R. H. ADAMS,
Captain, Jeans' Cavalry Regiment.

Adjutant Cramer who received the flag of truce saw his authority and order of discretion from General Marmaduke. If the exchange he proposes is not according to cartel he will make one that is.

Please answer immediately.

JOHN MCNEIL,
Brigadier-General, Commanding.

HEADQUARTERS SUB-DISTRICT,
Cape Girardeau, Mo., May 19, 1863.

Col. J. O. SHELBY,
Comdg. First Division of Forces in Arms against United States.

COLONEL: I am instructed by General Davidson to say that he does not acknowledge the agreement between Generals Blunt and Hindman as any rule of action. He instructs me to retain my prisoners until properly exchanged. Inclosed you will find statements of your officers now in hospital in regard to duties of humanity as discharged toward them.

You will accept my grateful acknowledgments for your kindness to and care of our officers who have fallen into your hands.

Under the terms of Captains Spencer's, Mitchell's and Bartlett's parole they will be returned to your custody.

In order to avoid all misapprehension on the part of yourself or of your brother officers in regard to prisoners in my hands I beg to assure you that all proper attention both to the sick and well will be accorded to all such men as the Government of the United States are certain to regard as entitled to belligerent rights. To guerrillas, horse-thieves and every description of outlaws I shall mete out proper justice.

I am, colonel, very respectfully,

JOHN McNEIL,
Brigadier-General, Commanding U. S. Forces.

[Inclosure.]

POST HOSPITAL, *Cape Girardeau, May 19, 1863.*
Col. J. O. SHELBY, *Commanding Missouri Cavalry Division.*

COLONEL: We, the wounded officers of your brigade, take pleasure in testifying that our treatment by the Federal authorities here has been kind, gentlemanly, generous and disinterested. All our wants have been supplied, our wishes gratified, and General McNeil and officers have shown by constant and repeated kindnesses that they have no enmity beyond the hot blood and the excitement of the battle-field and that Confederate prisoners deserve and do receive every attention which courtesy requires.

Three of us at present are unable to be moved as it is impossible for us to walk.

Y. H. BLACKWELL,
Major.
H. M. WOODSMALL,
Captain.
W. H. FERRILL,
Lieutenant.
J. N. EDWARDS,
Adjutant.

HEADQUARTERS, *Annapolis, Md., May 19, 1863.*
Col. W. HOFFMAN, *Commissary-General of Prisoners.*

SIR: Inclosed you will receive a list* of the names of the persons said to have composed the crew of the U. S. tug-boat Fox, who arrived here on the 17th instant with the paroled troops. These men had been prisoners in Richmond and were released on parole. As I did not doubt their having been in the U. S. service and as they were destitute of means I furnished them with transportation to Washington. I have just answered your telegram.

I am, sir, with much respect, your obedient servant,

C. A. WAITE,
Colonel First Infantry, Commanding Post.

HEADQUARTERS DISTRICT OF NORTHWEST MISSOURI,
Saint Joseph, Mo., May 19, 1863.
Maj. J. M. BASSETT.

SIR: You will direct your assistants to arrest the most prominent and influential rebels and sympathizers with the rebellion in their respective districts. The assistant provost-marshal will in every case take testimony upon the following points, viz: 1st. Disloyal conduct previous to July 25, 1862 (the date of the President's proclamation).

---

*Nominal list of twenty-one men, including the captain, omitted.

2d. Disloyal conduct since that period.   3d. General reputation of the accused as to his sentiments and character and as to whether he is or is not a dangerous man in his neighborhood.   In clear cases of disloyalty and in these only the prisoners and the proofs will be sent forward to you.   Their cases will be disposed of here.

CHESTER HARDING, JR.,
Colonel, Commanding District.

NOTE.—Women who are violent and dangerous secessionists must be arrested as well as men.

OFFICE COMMISSARY-GENERAL OF PRISONERS,
Washington, D. C., May 19, 1863.

J. C. KELTON,
> *Assistant Adjutant-General, Headquarters of the Army.*

COLONEL: Please to say to the General in-Chief that rolls and instructions to meet the wishes of Colonel Ludlow relative to the paroling of prisoners of war before delivery were distributed to the commanders of prison camps several days since.

Very respectfully, your obedient servant,
W. HOFFMAN,
Colonel Third Infantry, Commissary-General of Prisoners.

WASHINGTON, May 19, 1863.

Lieut. Col. W. H. LUDLOW,
> *Commissioner for Exchange of Prisoners:*

Instructions requiring prisoners to sign paroles before being sent forward were given several days since. I repeat them to Fort Delaware to-day.

W. HOFFMAN,
Commissary-General of Prisoners.

WASHINGTON, May 19, 1863.

Lieut. Col. W. H. LUDLOW:

Does the declaration of exchanges in general orders of May 9 apply to rebel prisoners?

W. HOFFMAN,
Commissary-General of Prisoners.

FORT MONROE, May 19, 1863.

Col. W. HOFFMAN, *Commissary-General of Prisoners:*

The declaration of exchanges in general orders of May 9 does apply to rebel prisoners.

WM. H. LUDLOW,
Lieutenant-Colonel and Agent for Exchange of Prisoners.

OFFICE COMMISSARY-GENERAL OF PRISONERS,
Washington, D. C., May 19, 1863.

Maj. W. S. PIERSON,
Commanding Depot Prisoners of War, Sandusky, Ohio.

MAJOR : You are authorized to permit the Rev. R. A. Sidley to visit the prisoners in your charge if they desire it, provided he is willing first to take the oath of allegiance. Of course the visits should be made under proper restrictions.

Very respectfully, your obedient servant,
W. HOFFMAN,
Colonel Third Infantry, Commissary-General of Prisoners.

OFFICE COMMISSARY-GENERAL OF PRISONERS,
Washington, D. C., May 19, 1863.

Capt. H. B. TODD, *Provost-Marshal, Washington, D. C.*

CAPTAIN : I am directed by the commissary-general of prisoners to inform you that Mosby's men, confined at the Old Capitol Prison, will be sent for exchange.

Very respectfully, your obedient servant,
W. T. HARTZ,
Captain and Assistant Adjutant-General.

OFFICE COMMISSARY-GENERAL OF PRISONERS,
Washington, D. C., May 19, 1863.

Mr. W. P. WOOD,
Superintendent of Old Capitol Prison, Washington, D. C.

SIR : I am directed by the commissary-general of prisoners to inform you that Mosby's men, now confined at the Old Capitol, will be sent for exchange. You are requested therefore to have their names put on the rolls to be sent.

Very respectfully, your obedient servant,
W. T. HARTZ,
Captain and Assistant Adjutant-General.

SEYMOUR, IND., *May 19, 1863.*

Major-General BURNSIDE, *Cincinnati :*

Everything arranged agreeably to your wishes; plan number one preferred and immediate action advised. I am delayed here by a train off the track; shall be in Cincinnati by 2 o'clock.
CHAS. G. LORING.

SPECIAL ORDERS, }
No. 223.   }

WAR DEPARTMENT,
Washington, May 19, 1863.

The President directs that the military order requiring the removal of Colonel Churchill from Saint Louis beyond the U. S. lines be so modified that Colonel Churchill may be allowed to reside at Louisville upon condition that he take the oath of allegiance to the Government of the United States and that the Hon. James Guthrie pledge himself to the officer commanding at Louisville that Colonel Churchill shall be of good behavior and do no act of hostility to the United States and communicate no information nor give any aid or comfort to the enemy. Please acknowledge receipt.

By order of the Secretary of War:

E. D. TOWNSEND,
Assistant Adjutant-General.

WAR DEPARTMENT, *Washington, May 20, 1863.*
CHARLES A. MAY, Esq., *Cashier Park Bank, New York.*

SIR: Your telegram received. W. T. Smithson being arrested* and in prison on charges of grave magnitude, subjecting his property to confiscation if they prove true, it is the desire of this Department and you are authorized and directed to retain any funds or property in your bank standing in his name until further order by this Department. It is my desire to save the property for his creditors and the Government and prevent its application or transfer to purposes inimical to the Government. Please notify me if any checks or drafts in his name should be presented.

EDWIN M. STANTON,
Secretary of War.

CONFIDENTIAL.]   HEADQUARTERS OF THE ARMY,
Washington, May 20, 1863.
Major-General BURNSIDE, *Cincinnati.*

GENERAL: I have just come from an interview with the President and Secretary of War during which the Vallandigham case was alluded to. No objections were made to your action in this matter but there was evidently some embarrassment in regard to the disposition of the prisoner. Outside friends have expressed fears that this case might do more harm than good. Not having read the trial I do not know how far the testimony justifies the finding and sentence. I, however, have always been of the opinion that in the loyal States like Ohio it is best to interfere with the ordinary civil tribunals as little as possible. Treasonable acts in those States unless of immediate and pressing danger should be left for trial by the courts as provided in the act of Congress. Districts of country where military operations are carried on and those which are actually in arms against the Government must necessarily be in a great measure subject to military control, and in the absence of proper civil courts offenses must be tried by military commissions. I am not objecting to what has been done in the Vallandigham case for I have no official information in regard to it further than that he was arrested and held for trial. I write simply to put you on your guard against inciting opposition to the Government by unnecessary arrests and military trials.

Again the Secretary of War is of opinion that appointment of military commanders in Illinois, Indiana and Ohio should be avoided

---

* Smithson appears to have been twice in arrest. For first arrest see Vol. II, this Series, p. 1354–1357.

as much as possible. Most of the duties of military commanders in these States can now be performed by provost-marshals under the law. Moreover it seems difficult to find military commanders of sufficient judgment and discretion to avoid conflicts with the civil authority in these States, and in many of these conflicts the officers have been entirely in the wrong, assuming powers which do not belong to them. All this does much harm by inciting party passions and political animosities.

The Secretary of War also alluded to another matter upon which I wrote you some time ago, viz, the importance of your taking the field, concentrating your forces and inflicting some blow upon the enemy especially while large re-enforcements are detached to operate against General Grant. If you and General Rosecrans can do nothing to injure the enemy while he is engaged with Grant he will certainly return in force and injure you.

I regret that your calls for re-enforcements cannot be met. There are no troops that can possibly be sent to you till more are raised. Moreover if we had 10,000 available troops to-morrow it would be necessary to send them to General Grant and General Banks where they are much the most needed.

Very respectfully, your obedient servant,

H. W. HALLECK,
General-in-Chief.

WASHINGTON, D. C., *May 20, 1863.**

Major-General HITCHCOCK, *Washington, D. C.*

GENERAL: I have just received your indorsement on the letter of Governor Morton in regard to newspaper statements that the enemy had refused to parole certain prisoners of war in accordance with the stipulations of the cartel. I fully concur with you in regard to the proposed retaliation, but I think a direct and positive demand should be made upon Mr. Ould for the execution of the cartel in regard to these prisoners before any further action should be decided upon.

Very respectfully, your obedient servant,

H. W. HALLECK,
General-in-Chief.

HEADQUARTERS, *Cincinnati, Ohio, May 20, 1863.*

Hon. EDWIN M. STANTON, *Secretary of War:*

The President's order in reference to Mr. Vallandigham is received and he is now on board of a gun-boat at anchor in the river preparatory to starting. I beg to make the following suggestions for the consideration of the President:

The commission which tried Mr. Vallandigham was organized to meet a supposed emergency in this department, and the necessity for that course as well as the action of the commission has been sanctioned by the U. S. court, thus giving to the existence of the commission a validity which is very necessary to it in the discharge of its important duties. The commission is composed of some of our best officers. In making up a verdict in the case the sentence to send the prisoner South was as I know fully discussed and decided against. In case he should now be sent South it would open the Government and myself to

---

* Void; see letter of proper date, p. 693.

the charge of having changed the sentence of the commission, which in a legally organized court is not possible. A sentence can be lessened or entirely remitted. And it would also take from the commission much of the validity with which it was invested by the U. S. court.

I will not state what I consider to be the disadvantages of sending him South after having taken a full view of the case, but beg most respectfully to suggest that I can be more useful in this department if the established and recognized course be pursued in reference to these courts than if we depart from that course. But notwithstanding my views on the subject, to which I have given my strictest and most honest attention, I will most cheerfully obey the order of the President in the matter, but hope I may be pardoned for keeping the gun-boat at anchor until I receive a response to this. In case it should be decided to have the original sentence carried out I would respectfully state that the plan is to send him to Pittsburg by gun-boat, thence to Baltimore without change of cars, thence by propeller to Boston direct or by way of New York. No one knows of this plan but myself. I should have sent this communication by mail but for the necessity of haste.

Respectfully, &c.,

A. E. BURNSIDE,
Major-General, Commanding.

WAR DEPARTMENT, *Washington, May 20, 1863.*

Major-General BURNSIDE:

Your dispatch of 3 this afternoon to Secretary Stanton has been received and shown to the President. He thinks the best disposition to be made of Vallandigham is to put him beyond the lines as directed in the order transmitted to you last evening, and directs that you execute that order by sending him forward under secure guard without delay to General Rosecrans.

By order of A. Lincoln, President:

ED. R. S. CANBY,
Brigadier-General.

Acknowledge receipt.

HEADQUARTERS DEPARTMENT OF THE SOUTH,
Port Royal, S. C., May 20, 1863.

Rear-Admiral S. F. DU PONT, U. S. Navy.

ADMIRAL: I have the honor to acknowledge the receipt of your note of the 19th instant in relation to the nine prisoners of war captured by the Navy on Edisto. I think it so important to the safety of my officers that I should have possession of these prisoners that I have deemed it my duty to write His Excellency the President on the subject requesting an order to have these prisoners delivered to me. My letter cannot go North till the next mail. Until I can hear from the President on the subject I beg, Admiral, that you will suspend the execution of any order you may receive on this subject from the Navy Department till I can have a reply from the President.

I have the honor to be, very respectfully, your most obedient servant,

D. HUNTER,
Major-General, Commanding.

HEADQUARTERS SUB-DISTRICT,
Cape Girardeau, Mo., May 20, 1863.

Col. J. O. SHELBY,
Comdg. First Div. of Forces in Arms against the United States.

COLONEL: The proposition made by Captain Adams, the representative of General Marmaduke, for an exchange of prisoners—as follows, Major McConnel for Major Blackwell, Captain Spencer for Captain Woodsmall, Captain Mitchell for Lieutenant Edwards and two enlisted men, Captain Bartlett for Lieutenant Ferrill and two enlisted men—was telegraphed to General Davidson who makes the following reply:

General McNEIL:

The exchange must take place by delivery at Vicksburg of equal number and rank.

J. W. DAVIDSON,
Brigadier-General, Commanding.

I therefore in obedience to their parole and orders from headquarters return to your custody the three captains you sent to this point for exchange.

I have the honor to be, colonel, your very obedient servant,
JOHN McNEIL,
Brigadier-General, Commanding

HEADQUARTERS CAMP OF INSTRUCTION,
Benton Barracks, Mo., May 20, 1863.

Maj. H. Z. CURTIS, *Assistant Adjutant-General.*

MAJOR: On examination I find that 115 officers and 1,200 enlisted men at this post are declared exchanged by General Orders, No. 117, Adjutant-General's Office, current series. The officers with one or two exceptions belong to the Department of the Tennessee while the men belong to the Department of the Cumberland. The men are organized into companies and comprise the Fourth Battalion Paroled Men, three companies of the Second Battalion and half a company of the First Battalion, commanded by officers detailed for that purpose as their proper officers have not yet reported here. As these officers have in charge the muster and descriptive rolls of the men and are familiar with all the records to prevent the confusion of accounts incidental to a change of commanders I recommend that they be retained here till the proper officers arrive; or if that is not practicable that they be instructed to take the men to their proper commands in the field, turning over all the military history in their possession. Besides these exchanged men we have about 3,000 paroled men present and absent who will require 45 or 50 officers for their command. As there are no paroled officers who can be used for this service I suggest the propriety of retaining here those exchanged officers who have no commands in the field and of sending the others to join their regiments at once. I would also suggest that it might be well to relieve from duty at this post those colonels and lieutenant-colonels whose commands are mainly here to enable them to act for the benefit of their regiments in the field and in their respective States.

Awaiting your instructions I am, major, very respectfully, your obedient servant,
B. L. E. BONNEVILLE,
Colonel, U. S. Army, Commanding.

[Indorsement.]

All men who have been exchanged will be sent to their commands without delay. When no officers of their commands are present with them others will be detailed (those at present in charge in preference) to conduct them, returning to this place as soon as the duty shall be performed. Exchanged officers not required in the field may be retained to take charge of paroled men.

J. M. S[CHOFIELD].

BENTON BARRACKS, MO., *May 20, 1863.*

Colonel HOFFMAN, *Commissary-General of Prisoners:*

In reply to yours of the 13th instant calling my attention to your former instructions I feel it due to myself to remark that my only desire is to do your wish and to do it exactly as you wish. When I do not succeed it is a cause of regret. My last report of the fragments of more than 100 regiments when finished upon examination was found incorrect and had to be made over again, which will explain the delay in forwarding it. Your communication respecting creating a fund from the saving of rations of paroled men reached me last evening. The 4,300 paroled men at this barracks are divided into companies of about 100 each, and these companies are divided into five battalions of paroled men, which organization is preserved over all parcels of scattered companies, and to the commanders of these battalions, together with principal surgeon and the commissary of subsistence as a board of officers, I have placed your letter for their consideration and to carry out your suggestions in the best possible manner.

Very respectfully, your obedient servant,

B. L. E. BONNEVILLE,
Colonel, U. S. Army, Commanding Post.

SPECIAL ORDERS,)   HEADQUARTERS CAMP OF INSTRUCTION,
No. 64.   )   *Benton Barracks, Mo., May 20, 1863.*

*   *   *   *   *   *   *

II. A board of officers is hereby convened to take into consideration a communication from the commissary-general of prisoners suggesting certain modifications of the rations of paroled men with a view of creating a fund from the savings thus made to be expended for the benefit of the men as indicated in said communication (a copy of which is furnished the board). The board will consist of Colonel Kinney, commanding First Battalion Paroled Men; Colonel Fox, commanding Second Battalion Paroled Men; Lieut. Col. Harry S. Smith, commanding Third Battalion Paroled Men; Maj. S. M. Meeker, commanding Fourth Battalion Paroled Men; Col. C. M. Ferrell, commanding Fifth Battalion Paroled Men; Lieut. P. Lucas, One hundred and fourteenth Illinois Volunteers (expected to put in execution any plan adopted), who will meet at the office of the post adjutant at 3 p. m. to-day or as soon thereafter as practicable and make report as to the best method of carrying into effect the views of the commissary-general of prisoners. The junior member will record the proceedings.

III. In addition to paragraph II, Special Orders, No. 64, from these headquarters, Captain Campbell, commissary of subsistence, is hereby announced as one of the board to take into consideration the saving of surplus rations. Also Dr. Ira Russell, surgeon in charge of hospitals.

Benton Barracks, will form one of the board unless his duties are such that he cannot, when he will appoint one of his surgeons to act in his place.

By order of Colonel Bonneville, U. S. Army, commanding:

A. J. NEWBY,
Lieutenant and Assistant Adjutant-General.

POST ADJUTANT'S OFFICE,
Benton Barracks, Mo., May 22, 1863.

In compliance with the above order the board met at 9 a. m. The order convening the board together with the communication from the commissary-general of prisoners, including the scale of reduced rations, having been read and duly considered the following recommendations were unanimously passed by the board: That they deem it inexpedient to interfere in any way with the rations of enlisted paroled men; and further the provisions of the U. S. Army Regulations and of existing orders from the War Department are entirely sufficient for the proper disposal of all the savings of companies and battalions.

Very respectfully submitted.

CHAS. H. FOX,
101st Illinois Infantry, Chairman Board.
P. LUCAS,
114th Illinois Infantry, Recorder.

OFFICE COMMISSARY-GENERAL OF PRISONERS,
Washington, D. C., May 20, 1863.

Maj. Gen. N. P. BANKS,
Commanding Department of the Gulf, New Orleans, La.

GENERAL: It is represented by the Confederate agent for exchange of prisoners that a number of officers and men of the rebel army who have been declared exchanged are still held as prisoners of war in the Department of the Gulf, and by direction of the General-in-Chief I have the honor to inform you that General Orders, No. 10, of January 10, and No. 117, of May 9, apply to rebel officers and soldiers as well as to our own forces, and I therefore request that if there are any prisoners of war still held whose exchange is covered by either of the above orders they may be delivered beyond our lines as early as practicable. These exchanges include irregular organizations—guerrillas, bushwhackers, &c.

Very respectfully, your obedient servant,

W. HOFFMAN,
Colonel Third Infantry, Commissary-General of Prisoners.

OFFICE COMMISSARY-GENERAL OF PRISONERS,
Washington, D. C., May 20, 1863.

Maj. Gen. U. S. GRANT,
Commanding Department of the Tennessee:

The Secretary of War directs that unless specially authorized no Confederate prisoners of war will be released on condition of taking the oath of allegiance.

W. HOFFMAN,
Colonel Third Infantry, Commissary-General of Prisoners.

(Same to Generals Dix, Banks and Rosecrans.)

OFFICE COMMISSARY-GENERAL OF PRISONERS,
Washington, D. C., May 20, 1863.

Maj. Gen. JOHN A. DIX, *Fort Monroe, Va.*

GENERAL: The following are extracts* from a letter to-day addressed to Lieutenant-Colonel Ludlow, commissioner for exchange of prisoners, in relation to paroling of prisoners of war, to be laid before the Confederate commissioner, as the rule which will govern the U. S. armies in the field.

There may be cases of a subsequent date when from peculiar circumstances it would be advisable to recognize irregular paroles, but in all such cases a special report with full rolls of the parties should be forwarded to this office as early as practicable.

W. HOFFMAN,
Colonel Third Infantry, Commissary-General of Prisoners.

(Copies of above letter sent to Maj. Gen. U. S. Grant, commanding Department of the Tennessee; Maj. Gen. J. M. Schofield, commanding Department of the Missouri, Saint Louis, Mo.; Maj. Gen. W. S. Rosecrans, commanding, Murfreesborough, Tenn.; Maj. Gen. N. P. Banks, commanding Department of the Gulf, New Orleans, La.; Maj. Gen. Joseph Hooker, commanding Army of the Potomac; Maj. Gen. A. E. Burnside, commanding Department of the Ohio, Cincinnati, Ohio; Maj. Gen. S. P. Heintzelman, commanding Defenses of Washington, Washington, D. C., and Maj. Gen. R. C. Schenck, commanding Eighth Army Corps, Baltimore, Md.

OFFICE COMMISSARY-GENERAL OF PRISONERS,
Washington, D. C., May 20, 1863.

Maj. Gen. S. P. HEINTZELMAN,
Commanding Defenses of Washington, D. C.

GENERAL: I have the honor to inclose herewith communications† from Col. W. G. Veazey, Sixteenth Vermont Volunteers, commanding at Union Mills; Lieut. Col. H. H. Wells, provost-marshal-general, Alexandria; Capt. W. D. Munson, provost-marshal, Union Mills, and Capt. E. M. Camp, commanding Soldiers' Rest, all covering paroles given by individual officers or soldiers in violation of General Orders, No. 49, current series, and are therefore void, and I am directed by the General-in-Chief to order these men to report to you to be proceeded against as you may direct. By the cartel all prisoners of war are to be delivered and paroled at certain named places and when this provision of the cartel is violated the paroles so given are invalid; but this does not relieve those who give such paroles from the penalties for violating General Orders, No. 49.

Very respectfully, your obedient servant,

W. HOFFMAN,
Colonel Third Infantry, Commissary-General of Prisoners.

OFFICE COMMISSARY-GENERAL OF PRISONERS,
Washington, May 20, [1863.]

Lieut. Col. W. H. LUDLOW,
Agent for Exchange of Prisoners, Fort Monroe, Va.

COLONEL: I inclose herewith General Orders, Nos. 49‡ and 100, current series, announcing regulations and instructions for the government

---

* Extracts omitted here; see Hoffman to Ludlow, following.
† Not found.
‡ Omitted here; see p. 306.

of the U. S. forces in the field in the matter of paroles.   These together with the stipulations of the cartel will govern our Army.   By the cartel all prisoners of war are to be delivered at certain named places, there to be exchanged or paroled, and all paroles exacted or accepted by the enemy from our troops in violation of this stipulation except in the case provided for by the cartel are null and void and troops so paroled will be ordered to duty as if no parole had been given.

Officers or soldiers who give paroles in violation of General Orders, No. 49, commit an offense for which they are liable to punishment by a court-martial, but the enemy have nevertheless no right to claim that the parole is binding.   You will perceive from the inclosed order* of General Schenck how the cartel is interpreted.

Orders will be immediately issued to our commanders to permit no paroles to be taken from the enemy except as provided for by the cartel and all paroles now in force not so taken will be declared of no effect.

Very respectfully, your obedient servant,

W. HOFFMAN,
Colonel Third Infantry, Commissary-General of Prisoners.

P. S.—Paroles given before the publication to the Army of General Orders, No. 49, though deliveries were not made as required by the cartel, will under the rule prevailing at that time be held as valid. The last paragraph of the above letter must be so understood.

W. H.

[Inclosure.]

GENERAL ORDERS, } WAR DEPT., ADJT. GENERAL'S OFFICE,
      No. 100.   }   *Washington, April 24, 1863.*

The following instructions for the government of armies of the United States in the field, prepared by Francis Lieber, LL. D., and revised by a board of officers of which Maj. Gen. E. A. Hitchcock is president, having been approved by the President of the United States, he commands that they be published for the information of all concerned.

By order of the Secretary of War:

E. D. TOWNSEND,
Assistant Adjutaut-General.

Instructions for the government of armies of the United States in the field.

SECTION I.

Martial law—Military jurisdiction—Military necessity—Retaliation.

1. A place, district or country occupied by an enemy stands in consequence of the occupation under the martial law of the invading or occupying army whether any proclamation declaring martial law or any public warning to the inhabitants has been issued or not.   Martial law is the immediate and direct effect and consequence of occupation or conquest.   The presence of a hostile army proclaims its martial law.

*   *   *   *   *   *   *

12. Whenever feasible martial law is carried out in cases of individual offenders by military courts; but sentences of death shall be executed only with the approval of the Chief Executive provided the urgency of the case does not require a speedier execution and then only with the approval of the chief commander.

---

* Not found.

13. Military jurisdiction is of two kinds: first, that which is conferred and defined by statute; second, that which is derived from the common law of war. Military offenses under the statute law must be tried in the manner therein directed; but military offenses which do not come within the statute must be tried and punished under the common law of war. The character of the courts which exercise these jurisdictions depends upon the local laws of each particular country. In the armies of the United States the first is exercised by courts-martial, while cases which do not come within the "Rules and Articles of War," or the jurisdiction conferred by a statute on courts-martial are tried by military commissions.

14. Military necessity as understood by modern civilized nations consists in the necessity of those measures which are indispensable for securing the ends of the war and which are lawful according to the modern law and usages of war.

15. Military necessity admits of all direct destruction of life or limb of armed enemies and of other persons whose destruction is incidentally unavoidable in the armed contests of the war; it allows of the capturing of every armed enemy and every enemy of importance to the hostile Government or of peculiar danger to the captor; it allows of all destruction of property and obstruction of the ways and channels of traffic, travel or communication and of all withholding of sustenance or means of life from the enemy; of the appropriation of whatever an enemy's country affords necessary for the subsistence and safety of the army and of such deception as does not involve the breaking of good faith either positively pledged regarding agreements entered into during the war or supposed by the modern laws of war to exist. Men who take up arms against one another in public war do not cease on this account to be moral beings responsible to one another and to God.

16. Military necessity does not admit of cruelty; that is infliction of suffering for the sake of suffering or for revenge, nor of maiming or wounding except in fight, nor of torture to extort confessions. It does not admit of the use of poison in any way, nor of the wanton devastation of a district. It admits of deception but disclaims acts of perfidy; and in general military necessity does not include any act of hostility which makes the return to peace unnecessarily difficult.

17. War is not carried on by arms alone. It is lawful to starve the hostile belligerent, armed or unarmed, so that it leads to the speedier subjection of the enemy.

18. When the commander of a besieged place expels the non-combatants in order to lessen the number of those who consume his stock of provisions it is lawful though an extreme measure to drive them back so as to hasten on the surrender.

*　　*　　*　　*　　*　　*　　*

26. Commanding generals may cause the magistrates and civil officers of the hostile country to take the oath of temporary allegiance or an oath of fidelity to their own victorious Government or rulers and they may expel every one who declines to do so. But whether they do so or not the people and their civil officers owe strict obedience to them as long as they hold sway over the district or country at the peril of their lives.

27. The law of war can no more wholly dispense with retaliation than can the law of nations of which it is a branch; yet civilized nations acknowledge retaliation as the sternest feature of war. A reckless enemy often leaves to his opponent no other means of securing himself against the repetition of barbarous outrage.

28. Retaliation will therefore never be resorted to as a measure of mere revenge but only as a means of protective retribution and moreover cautiously and unavoidably; that is to say retaliation shall only be resorted to after careful inquiry into the real occurrence and the character of the misdeeds that may demand retribution. Unjust or inconsiderate retaliation removes the belligerents farther and farther from the mitigating rules of a regular war and by rapid steps leads them nearer to the internecine wars of savages.

*   *   *   *   *   *   *

SECTION II.

Public and private property of the enemy—Protection of persons and especially women, of religion, the arts and sciences—Punishment of crimes against the inhabitants of hostile countries.

*   *   *   *   *   *   *

32. A victorious army by the martial power inherent in the same may suspend, change or abolish as far as the martial power extends the relations which arise from the services due according to the existing laws of the invaded country from one citizen, subject or native of the same to another. The commander of the army must leave it to the ultimate treaty of peace to settle the permanency of this change.

*   *   *   *   *   *   *

42. Slavery, complicating and confounding the ideas of property (that is of a thing) and of personality (that is of humanity), exists according to municipal or local law only. The law of nature and nations has never acknowledged it. The digest of the Roman law enacts the early *dictum* of the pagan jurist that " so far as the law of nature is concerned all men are equal." Fugitives escaping from a country in which they were slaves, villains or serfs into another country have for centuries past been held free and acknowledged free by judicial decisions of European countries, even though the municipal law of the country in which the slave had taken refuge acknowledged slavery within its own dominions.

43. Therefore in a war between the United States and a belligerent which admits of slavery if a person held in bondage by that belligerent be captured by or come as a fugitive under the protection of the military forces of the United States such person is immediately entitled to the rights and privileges of a freeman. To return such person into slavery would amount to enslaving a free person, and neither the United States nor any officer under their authority can enslave any human being. Moreover a person so made free by the law of war is under the shield of the law of nations, and the former owner or State can have by the law of *post-liminy* no belligerent lien or claim of service.

*   *   *   *   *   *   *

SECTION III.

Deserters—Prisoners of war—Hostages—Booty on the battle-field.

48. Deserters from the American Army having entered the service of the enemy suffer death if they fall again into the hands of the United States whether by capture or being delivered up to the American Army; and if a deserter from the enemy having taken service in the Army of the United States is captured by the enemy and punished

by them with death or otherwise it is not a breach against the law and usages of war requiring redress or retaliation.

49. A prisoner of war is a public enemy armed or attached to the hostile army for active aid who has fallen into the hands of the captor either fighting or wounded on the field or in the hospital by individual surrender or by capitulation. All soldiers of whatever species of arms; all men who belong to the rising *en masse* of the hostile country; all those who are attached to the army for its efficiency and promote directly the object of the war except such as are hereinafter provided for; all disabled men or officers on the field or elsewhere if captured; all enemies who have thrown away their arms and ask for quarter are prisoners of war and as such exposed to the inconveniences as well as entitled to the privileges of a prisoner of war.

50. Moreover citizens who accompany an army for whatever purpose, such as sutlers, editors or reporters of journals or contractors, if captured may be made prisoners of war and detained as such. The monarch and members of the hostile reigning family, male or female, the chief and chief officers of the hostile Government, its diplomatic agents and all persons who are of particular and singular use and benefit to the hostile army or its Government are if captured on belligerent ground and if unprovided with a safe-conduct granted by the captor's Government prisoners of war.

51. If the people of that portion of an invaded country which is not yet occupied by the enemy or of the whole country at the approach of a hostile army rise under a duly authorized levy *en masse* to resist the invader they are now treated as public enemies and if captured are prisoners of war.

52. No belligerent has the right to declare that he will treat every captured man in arms of a levy *en masse* as a brigand or bandit. If, however, the people of a country or any portion of the same already occupied by an army rise against it they are violators of the laws of war and are not entitled to their protection.

53. The enemy's chaplains, officers of the medical staff, apothecaries, hospital nurses and servants if they fall into the hands of the American Army are not prisoners of war unless the commander has reasons to retain them. In this latter case or if at their own desire they are allowed to remain with their captured companions they are treated as prisoners of war and may be exchanged if the commander sees fit.

54. A hostage is a person accepted as a pledge for the fulfillment of an agreement concluded between belligerents during the war or in consequence of a war. Hostages are rare in the present age.

55. If a hostage is accepted he is treated like a prisoner of war according to rank and condition as circumstances may admit.

56. A prisoner of war is subject to no punishment for being a public enemy nor is any revenge wreaked upon him by the intentional infliction of any suffering or disgrace, by cruel imprisonment, want of food, by mutilation, death or any other barbarity.

57. So soon as a man is armed by a sovereign Government and takes the soldier's oath of fidelity he is a belligerent; his killing, wounding or other warlike acts are no individual crimes or offenses. No belligerent has a right to declare that enemies of a certain class, color or condition when properly organized as soldiers will not be treated by him as public enemies.

58. The law of nations knows of no distinction of color, and if an enemy of the United States should enslave and sell any captured persons of their army it would be a case for the severest retaliation if not redressed upon complaint. The United States cannot retaliate by

enslavement therefore death must be the retaliation for this crime against the law of nations.

59. A prisoner of war remains answerable for his crimes committed against the captor's army or people committed before he was captured and for which he has not been punished by his own authorities. All prisoners of war are liable to the infliction of retaliatory measures.

60. It is against the usage of modern war to resolve in hatred and revenge to give no quarter. No body of troops has the right to declare that it will not give and therefore will not expect quarter, but a commander is permitted to direct his troops to give no quarter in great straits when his own salvation makes it impossible to cumber himself with prisoners.

61. Troops that give no quarter have no right to kill enemies already disabled on the ground or prisoners captured by other troops.

62. All troops of the enemy known or discovered to give no quarter in general or to any portion of the Army receive none.

63. Troops who fight in the uniform of their enemies without any plain, striking and uniform mark of distinction of their own can expect no quarter.

64. If American troops capture a train containing uniforms of the enemy and the commander considers it advisable to distribute them for use among his men some striking mark or sign must be adopted to distinguish the American soldier from the enemy.

65. The use of the enemy's national standard, flag or other emblem of nationality for the purpose of deceiving the enemy in battle is an act of perfidy by which they lose all claim to the protection of the laws of war.

66. Quarter having been given to an enemy by American troops under a misapprehension of his true character he may nevertheless be ordered to suffer death if within three days after the battle it be discovered that he belongs to a corps which gives no quarter.

67. The law of nations allows every sovereign Government to make war upon another sovereign State and therefore admits of no rules or laws different from those of regular warfare regarding the treatment of prisoners of war although they may belong to the army of a Government which the captor may consider as a wanton and unjust assailant.

68. Modern wars are not internecine wars in which the killing of the enemy is the object. The destruction of the enemy in modern war and indeed modern war itself are means to obtain that object of the belligerent which lies beyond the war. Unnecessary or revengeful destruction of life is not lawful.

69. Outposts, sentinels or pickets are not to be fired upon except to drive them in or when a positive order, special or general, has been issued to that effect.

70. The use of poison in any manner, be it to poison wells or food or arms, is wholly excluded from modern warfare. He that uses it puts himself out of the pale of the law and usages of war.

71. Whoever intentionally inflicts additional wounds on an enemy already wholly disabled or kills such an enemy or who orders or encourages soldiers to do so shall suffer death if duly convicted, whether he belongs to the Army of the United States or is an enemy captured after having committed his misdeed.

72. Money and other valuables on the person of a prisoner, such as watches or jewelry as well as extra clothing, are regarded by the American Army as the private property of the prisoner and the appropriation of such valuables or money is considered dishonorable and is prohibited. Nevertheless if large sums are found upon the persons of

prisoners or in their possession they shall be taken from them and the surplus after providing for their own support appropriated for the use of the army under the direction of the commander, unless otherwise ordered by the Government. Nor can prisoners claim as private property large sums found and captured in their train although they had been placed in the private luggage of the prisoners.

73. All officers when captured must surrender their side-arms to the captor. They may be restored to the prisoner in marked cases by the commander to signalize admiration of his distinguished bravery or approbation of his humane treatment of prisoners before his capture. The captured officer to whom they may be restored cannot wear them during captivity.

74. A prisoner of war being a public enemy is the prisoner of the Government and not of the captor. No ransom can be paid by a prisoner of war to his individual captor or to any officer in command. The Government alone releases captives according to rules prescribed by itself.

75. Prisoners of war are subject to confinement or imprisonment such as may be deemed necessary on account of safety, but they are to be subjected to no other intentional suffering or indignity. The confinement and mode of treating a prisoner may be varied during his captivity, according to the demands of safety.

76. Prisoners of war shall be fed upon plain and wholesome food whenever practicable and treated with humanity. They may be required to work for the benefit of the captor's Government according to their rank and condition.

77. A prisoner of war who escapes may be shot or otherwise killed in his flight; but neither death nor any other punishment shall be inflicted upon him simply for his attempt to escape which the law of war does not consider a crime. Stricter means of security shall be used after an unsuccessful attempt at escape. If, however, a conspiracy is discovered the purpose of which is a united or general escape the conspirators may be rigorously punished even with death; and capital punishment may also be inflicted upon prisoners of war discovered to have plotted rebellion against the authorities of the captors whether in union with fellow-prisoners or other persons.

78. If prisoners of war having given no pledge nor made any promise on their honor forcibly or otherwise escape and are captured again in battle after having rejoined their own army they shall not be punished for their escape, but shall be treated as simple prisoners of war although they will be subjected to stricter confinement.

79. Every captured wounded enemy shall be medically treated according to the ability of the medical staff.

80. Honorable men when captured will abstain from giving to the enemy information concerning their own army, and the modern law of war permits no longer the use of any violence against prisoners in order to extort the desired information or to punish them for having given false information.

SECTION IV.

Partisans—Armed enemies not belonging to the hostile army—Scouts—Armed prowlers—War-rebels.

81. Partisans are soldiers armed and wearing the uniform of their army but belonging to a corps which acts detached from the main body for the purpose of making inroads into the territory occupied by the enemy. If captured they are entitled to all the privileges of the prisoner of war.

82. Men or squads of men who commit hostilities, whether by fighting or inroads for destruction or plunder or by raids of any kind without commission without being part and portion of the organized hostile army and without sharing continuously in the war, but who do so with intermitting returns to their homes and avocations or with the occasional assumption of the semblance of peaceful pursuits, divesting themselves of the character or appearance of soldiers—such men or squads of men are not public enemies and therefore if captured are not entitled to the privileges of prisoners of war, but shall be treated summarily as highway robbers or pirates.

83. Scouts or single soldiers, if disguised in the dress of the country or in the uniform of the army hostile to their own employed in obtaining information, if found within or lurking about the lines of the captor are treated as spies and suffer death.

84. Armed prowlers by whatever names they may be called, or persons of the enemy's territory who steal within the lines of the hostile army for the purpose of robbing, killing or of destroying bridges, roads or canals, or of robbing or destroying the mail, or of cutting the telegraph wires, are not entitled to the privileges of the prisoner of war.

85. War-rebels are persons within an occupied territory who rise in arms against the occupying or conquering army or against the authorities established by the same. If captured they may suffer death whether they rise singly in small or large bands and whether called upon to do so by their own but expelled Government or not. They are not prisoners of war; nor are they if discovered and secured before their conspiracy has matured to an actual rising or to armed violence.

SECTION V.

Safe-conduct—Spies—War-traitors—Captured messengers—Abuse of the flag of truce.

*   *   *   *   *   *   *

88. A spy is a person who secretly in disguise or under false pretense seeks information with the intention of communicating it to the enemy. The spy is punishable with death by hanging by the neck whether or not he succeed in obtaining the information or in conveying it to the enemy.

89. If a citizen of the United States obtains information in a legitimate manner and betrays it to the enemy, be he a military or civil officer or a private citizen, he shall suffer death.

90. A traitor under the law of war or a war-traitor is a person in a place or district under martial law who unauthorized by the military commander gives information of any kind to the enemy or holds intercourse with him.

91. The war-traitor is always severely punished. If his offense consists in betraying to the enemy anything concerning the condition, safety, operations or plans of the troops holding or occupying the place or district his punishment is death.

92. If the citizen or subject of a country or place invaded or conquered gives information to his own Government from which he is separated by the hostile army or to the army of his Government he is a war-traitor and death is the penalty of his offense.

93. All armies in the field stand in need of guides and impress them if they cannot obtain them otherwise.

94. No person having been forced by the enemy to serve as guide is punishable for having done so.

95. If a citizen of a hostile and invaded district voluntarily serves as a guide to the enemy or offers to do so he is deemed a war traitor and shall suffer death.

96. A citizen serving voluntarily as a guide against his own country commits treason and will be dealt with according to the law of his country.

97. Guides when it is clearly proved that they have misled intentionally may be put to death.

98. All unauthorized or secret communication with the enemy is considered treasonable by the law of war. Foreign residents in an invaded or occupied territory or foreign visitors in the same can claim no immunity from this law. They may communicate with foreign parts or with the inhabitants of the hostile country so far as the military authority permits but no further. Instant expulsion from the occupied territory would be the very least punishment for the infraction of this rule.

99. A messenger carrying written dispatches or verbal messages from one portion of the army or from a besieged place to another portion of the same army or its Government, if armed and in the uniform of his army and if captured while doing so in the territory occupied by the enemy, is treated by the captor as a prisoner of war. If not in uniform nor a soldier the circumstances connected with his capture must determine the disposition that shall be made of him.

100. A messenger or agent who attempts to steal through the territory occupied by the enemy to further in any manner the interests of the enemy if captured is not entitled to the privileges of the prisoner of war and may be dealt with according to the circumstances of the case.

101. While deception in war is admitted as a just and necessary means of hostility and is consistent with honorable warfare the common law of war allows even capital punishment for clandestine or treacherous attempts to injure an enemy because they are so dangerous and it is so difficult to guard against them.

102. The law of war like the criminal law regarding other offenses makes no difference on account of the difference of sexes concerning the spy, the war-traitor or the war-rebel.

103. Spies, war-traitors and war-rebels are not exchanged according to the common law of war. The exchange of such persons would require a special cartel authorized by the Government or at a great distance from it by the chief commander of the army in the field.

104. A successful spy or war-traitor safely returned to his own army and afterwards captured as an enemy is not subject to punishment for his acts as a spy or war-traitor, but he may be held in closer custody as a person individually dangerous.

SECTION VI.

Exchange of prisoners—Flags of truce—Flags of protection.

105. Exchanges of prisoners take place number for number, rank for rank, wounded for wounded, with added condition for added condition, such for instance as not to serve for a certain period.

106. In exchanging prisoners of war such numbers of persons of inferior rank may be substituted as an equivalent for one of superior rank as may be agreed upon by cartel, which requires the sanction of the Government or of the commander of the army in the field.

107. A prisoner of war is in honor bound truly to state to the captor his rank, and he is not to assume a lower rank than belongs to him in order to cause a more advantageous exchange nor a higher rank for the purpose of obtaining better treatment. Offenses to the contrary have been justly punished by the commanders of released prisoners and may be good cause for refusing to release such prisoners.

108. The surplus number of prisoners of war remaining after an exchange has taken place is sometimes released either for the payment of a stipulated sum of money or in urgent cases of provision, clothing or other necessaries. Such arrangement, however, requires the sanction of the highest authority.

109. The exchange of prisoners of war is an act of convenience to both belligerents. If no general cartel has been concluded it cannot be demanded by either of them. No belligerent is obliged to exchange prisoners of war. A cartel is voidable so soon as either party has violated it.

110. No exchange of prisoners shall be made except after complete capture and after an accurate account of them and a list of the captured officers has been taken.

111. The bearer of a flag of truce cannot insist upon being admitted. He must always be admitted with great caution. Unnecessary frequency is carefully to be avoided.

112. If the bearer of a flag of truce offer himself during an engagement he can be admitted as a very rare exception only. It is no breach of good faith to retain such a flag of truce if admitted during the engagement. Firing is not required to cease on the appearance of a flag of truce in battle.

113. If the bearer of a flag of truce presenting himself during an engagement is killed or wounded it furnishes no ground of complaint whatever.

114. If it be discovered and fairly proved that a flag of truce has been abused for surreptitiously obtaining military knowledge the bearer of the flag thus abusing his sacred character is deemed a spy. So sacred is the character of a flag of truce and so necessary is its sacredness that while its abuse is an especially heinous offense great caution is requisite on the other hand in convicting the bearer of a flag of truce as a spy.

* * * * * * *

SECTION VII.

The parole.

119. Prisoners of war may be released from captivity by exchange and under certain circumstances also by parole.

120. The term parole designates the pledge of individual good faith and honor to do or to omit doing certain acts after he who gives his parole shall have been dismissed wholly or partially from the power of the captor.

121. The pledge of the parole is always an individual but not a private act.

122. The parole applies chiefly to prisoners of war whom the captor allows to return to their country or to live in greater freedom within the captor's country or territory on conditions stated in the parole.

123. Release of prisoners of war by exchange is the general rule; release by parole is the exception.

124. Breaking the parole is punished with death when the person breaking the parole is captured again. Accurate lists, therefore, of the paroled persons must be kept by the belligerents.

125. When paroles are given and received there must be an exchange of two written documents in which the name and rank of the paroled individuals are accurately and truthfully stated.

126. Commissioned officers only are allowed to give their parole and they can give it only with the permission of their superior as long as a superior in rank is within reach.

127. No non-commissioned officer or private can give his parole except through an officer. Individual paroles not given through an officer are not only void but subject the individual giving them to the punishment of death as deserters. The only admissible exception is where individuals properly separated from their commands have suffered long confinement without the possibility of being paroled through an officer.

128. No paroling on the battle-field; no paroling of entire bodies of troops after a battle, and no dismissal of large numbers of prisoners with a general declaration that they are paroled is permitted or of any value.

129. In capitulations for the surrender of strong places or fortified camps the commanding officer in cases of urgent necessity may agree that the troops under his command shall not fight again during the war unless exchanged.

130. The usual pledge given in the parole is not to serve during the existing war unless exchanged. This pledge refers only to the active service in the field against the paroling belligerent or his allies actively engaged in the same war. These cases of breaking the parole are patent acts and can be visited with the punishment of death; but the pledge does not refer to internal service such as recruiting or drilling the recruits, fortifying places not besieged, quelling civil commotions, fighting against belligerents unconnected with the paroling belligerents or to civil or diplomatic service for which the paroled officer may be employed.

131. If the Government does not approve of the parole the paroled officer must return into captivity, and should the enemy refuse to receive him he is free of his parole.

132. A belligerent Government may declare by a general order whether it will allow paroling and on what conditions it will allow it. Such order is communicated to the enemy.

133. No prisoner of war can be forced by the hostile Government to parole himself, and no Government is obliged to parole prisoners of war or to parole all captured officers if it paroles any. As the pledging of the parole is an individual act so is paroling on the other hand an act of choice on the part of the belligerent.

134. The commander of an occupying army may require of the civil officers of the enemy and of its citizens any pledge he may consider necessary for the safety or security of his army and upon their failure to give it he may arrest, confine or detain them.

*   *   *   *   *   *   *

SECTION IX.

Assassination.

148. The law of war does not allow proclaiming either an individual belonging to the hostile army or a citizen or a subject of the hostile

Government an outlaw who may be slain without trial by any captor any more than the modern law of peace allows such international outlawry; on the contrary it abhors such outrage. The sternest retaliation should follow the murder committed in consequence of such proclamation made by whatever authority. Civilized nations look with horror upon offers of rewards for the assassination of enemies as relapses into barbarism.

SECTION X.

Insurrection—Civil war—Rebellion.

149. Insurrection is the rising of people in arms against their Government or a portion of it, or against one or more of its laws, or against an officer or officers of the Government. It may be confined to mere armed resistance or it may have greater ends in view.

150. Civil war is war between two or more portions of a country or State, each contending for the mastery of the whole and each claiming to be the legitimate government. The term is also applied to war of rebellion when the rebellious provinces or portions of the State are contiguous to those containing the seat of Government.

151. The term rebellion is applied to an insurrection of large extent and is usually a war between the legitimate Government of a country and portions or provinces of the same who seek to throw off their allegiance to it and set up a government of their own.

152. When humanity induces the adoption of the rules of regular war toward rebels, whether the adoption is partial or entire, it does in no way whatever imply a partial or complete acknowledgment of their government if they have set up one of them as an independent or sovereign power. Neutrals have no right to make the adoption of the rules of war by the assailed government toward rebels the ground of their own acknowledgment of the revolted people as an independent power.

153. Treating captured rebels as prisoners of war, exchanging them, concluding of cartels, capitulations or other warlike agreements with them, addressing officers of a rebel army by the rank they may have in the same, accepting flags of truce, or on the other hand proclaiming martial law in their territory, or levying war taxes on forced loans, or doing any other act sanctioned or demanded by the law and usages of public war between sovereign belligerents neither proves nor establishes an acknowledgment of the rebellious people or of the government which they may have erected as a public or sovereign power. Nor does the adoption of the rules of war toward rebels imply an engagement with them extending beyond the limits of these rules. It is victory in the field that ends the strife and settles the future relations between the contending parties.

154. Treating in the field the rebellious enemy according to the law and usages of war has never prevented the legitimate Government from trying the leaders of the rebellion or chief rebels for high treason and from treating them accordingly unless they are included in a general amnesty.

155. All enemies in regular war are divided into two general classes; that is to say combatants and non-combatants or unarmed citizens of the hostile Government. The military commander of the legitimate Government in a war of rebellion distinguishes between the loyal citizen in the revolted portion of the country and the disloyal citizen. The disloyal citizens may further be classified into those citizens known to sympathize with the rebellion without positively aiding it and those

who without taking up arms give positive aid and comfort to the rebellious enemy without being bodily forced thereto.

156. Common justice and plain expediency require that the military commander protect the manifestly loyal citizens in revolted territories against the hardships of the war as much as the common misfortune of all war admits. The commander will throw the burden of the war as much as lies within his power on the disloyal citizens of the revolted portion or province, subjecting them to a stricter police than the non-combatant enemies have to suffer in regular war; and if he deems it appropriate or if his Government demands of him that every citizen shall by an oath of allegiance or by some other manifest act declare his fidelity to the legitimate Government he may expel, transfer, imprison or fine the revolted citizens who refuse to pledge themselves anew as citizens obedient to the law and loyal to the Government. Whether it is expedient to do so and whether reliance can be placed upon such oaths the commander or his Government have the right to decide.

157. Armed or unarmed resistance by citizens of the United States against the lawful movements of their troops is levying war against the United States and is therefore treason.

NEW YORK, *May 20, 1863.*

Brig. Gen. L. THOMAS.

GENERAL: Pursuant to orders from General N. P. Banks I have the honor to report my arrival at New York with 188 exchanged prisoners of the Eighth U. S. Infantry.

CHAS. S. FASSETT,
Lieutenant, Commanding Detachment U. S. Infantry.

CAPE GIRARDEAU, *May 20, 1863.*

We, R. H. Adams, captain, Jeans' Second [Twelfth] Missouri Cavalry, C. S. Army, the representative of General Marmaduke, and F. L. Cramer, first lieutenant and acting assistant adjutant-general, the representative of General McNeil, of the Army of the United States, make the following agreement:

I, F. L. Cramer, of the second part, in consideration of liberty being given to Captain Spencer, Captain Bartlett and Captain Mitchell, do agree to parole and send into the lines of the Army of the Confederate States of America three officers of equal rank, according to the cartel, with the distinct understanding that I do not recognize any agreement between Generals Blunt and Hindman and do not establish any agreement for an exchange upon the field or bind myself for anything further than the present agreement. Captain Adams, of the first part, agrees as the legal representative of General Marmaduke to permit the three captains herein mentioned to come within the lines of the Federal Army and there to remain until regularly exchanged.

R. H. ADAMS,
Captain, Second [Twelfth] Regiment Missouri Cavalry, C. S. Army.

F. L. CRAMER,
First Lieutenant and Acting Assistant Adjutant-General.

Witnesses:

FRANCIS W. CRANE,
Paymaster, U. S. Army.

S. C. NOLAND,
Orderly Sergt. Company E,
Second [Twelfth] Regiment Missouri Cavalry.

HEADQUARTERS SUB-DISTRICT,
Cape Girardeau, Mo., May 20, 1863.

W. H. Ferrill, a lieutenant in Company F, Gordon's regiment, C. S. Army, captured by the U. S. forces under command of Brig. Gen. John McNeil, is hereby released from custody upon condition that he will not take up arms against the United States, nor will he disclose nor give any information or knowledge he may have concerning the United States or forces of the same, nor in any manner perform any military service in the Army of the Confederate States until regularly exchanged as a prisoner of war by the proper authorities.

By order of John McNeil, brigadier-general, commanding:

F. L. CRAMER,
First Lieutenant and Acting Assistant Adjutant-General.

OFFICE COMMISSARY-GENERAL OF PRISONERS,
Washington, D. C., May 20, 1863.

Maj. JOSEPH DARR, Jr.,
Provost-Marshal-General, Wheeling, Va.

MAJOR: Your letter of the 14th instant is received. Major-General Schenck has been advised how the several orders in relation to paroles including the cartel are to be understood, and such instructions as he may give will be carried out. Custom has heretofore sanctioned paroling without delivering but it is to be discontinued.

Very respectfully, your obedient servant,

W. HOFFMAN,
Colonel Third Infantry, Commissary-General of Prisoners.

FORT MONROE, May 20, 1863.

Col. WILLIAM HOFFMAN:

Another detachment of prisoners has arrived here from the West without having been paroled before being sent on. I inform you of it that some one may be held responsible for disobedience of orders.

WM. H. LUDLOW,
Lieutenant-Colonel, &c.

HEADQUARTERS DEPARTMENT OF VIRGINIA,
Fort Monroe, May 20, 1863.

Hon. ROBERT OULD, Agent for Exchange of Prisoners.

SIR: I have received information from some of our prisoners captured at Chancellorsville and lately released which satisfies me that many of them were treated with great inhumanity, and some of them, officers, though worn out with marching and with sore and blistered feet, were brutally threatened with the bayonet if they fell out of the line of march. This information is without doubt correct. I have it from the officers themselves. I shall be glad to receive from you any information or explanation concerning it.

I am, very respectfully, your obedient servant,

WM. H. LUDLOW,
Lieutenant-Colonel and Agent for Exchange of Prisoners.

[First indorsement.]

Respectfully referred to Captain Turner for a report.

RO. OULD,
Agent of Exchange.

[Second indorsement.]

C. S. MILITARY PRISON, *Richmond, May 27, 1863.*
Lieut. JOHN LATOUCHE, *Acting Adjutant Military Prison.*

SIR: I refer to you a communication addressed by the Federal agent of exchange of prisoners to Hon. Robert Ould complaining that the Northern prisoners were while on the march to City Point treated with great inhumanity, were brutally threatened with the bayonet, &c. This is the first intimation I have had of any such brutalities (as alleged) being practiced and must believe that they are on a par with the slanderous falsehoods usually circulated by Northern prisoners. You were in charge of the batch of prisoners alluded to. You will therefore please report upon the communication referred to above.

Respectfully,   TH. P. TURNER,
                                        Captain, Commanding.

[Third indorsement.]

RICHMOND, *May 27, 1863.*
Capt. T. P. TURNER, *Commanding C. S. Military Prison.*

SIR: In answer to your communication referring me to a statement of the Federal commissioner dated May 20, 1863, that " some of the Federal officers were treated brutally and threatened with the bayonet" on the march to City Point I beg to state that previous to making arrangements for the march to City Point I informed the officers that the distance was thirty-two miles; that they could take their choice either to march down with the men or wait a few days for transportation by rail. The march was by no means rapid, taking thirty-one hours to go thirty-two miles. Our infantry guard did not complain although carrying arms and accouterments. As to any officer being threatened with the bayonet I believe this statement to be utterly false and unfounded in fact, and moreover I do not believe there is a single officer who will certify to such a fact or any intentional unkind treatment from any officer of this post.

I have the honor to be, your obedient servant,
                                        JOHN LATOUCHE,
                                Lieutenant and Acting Adjutant of Post.

[Fourth indorsement.]

Respectfully returned to Lieutenant-Colonel Ludlow.
                                        RO. OULD,
                                        Agent of Exchange.

[Fifth indorsement.]

FORT MONROE, *June 1, 1863.*

Respectfully forwarded to Col. William Hoffman, commissary-general of prisoners.

Major-General Hitchcock desired inquiries to be made about the within-mentioned matter. I am satisfied that the report of Lieutenant Latouche is false and that the inhumanity complained of was practiced.
                                        WM. H. LUDLOW,
                                Lieutenant-Colonel and Agent for Exchange.

———

MILITARY PRISON, *Alton, Ill., May 20, 1863.*
Col. W. HOFFMAN,
        Commissary-General of Prisoners, Washington, D. C.

COLONEL: I have the honor to report that another female prisoner, a Miss Mollie Hyde, of Nashville, Tenn., has been sent to this prison "for spying and other misdeeds," to be confined during the war or until released by competent authority. She was sent here by the order of General Rosecrans.

I have the honor to be, sir, with much respect, your most obedient servant,

T. HENDRICKSON,
Major Third Infantry, Commandant of Prison.

HEADQUARTERS MILITARY COMMANDER,
Wheeling, Va., May 20, 1863.

Col. W. HOFFMAN, *Commissary-General of Prisoners.*

SIR: I have been favored with a copy of a late letter from you to Capt. W. C. Thorpe, mustering and disbursing officer at this post, which includes an indorsement from Col. J. B. Fry, Provost-Marshal-General. In Captain Thorpe's letter to you he states that I claim to have control of all paroled prisoners, stragglers, &c., arriving here under paragraph III of General Orders, No. 58, War Department. The truth is that I have always done considerable of extra work at this post because no one else attended to it and I certainly shall not interfere with Captain Thorpe in discharging any of his duties. When General Orders, No. 46, February 20, 1863, War Department, reached Maj. B. H. Hill, Second Artillery, U. S. Army (Captain Thorpe's predecessor), that officer called upon me and requested me to attend to it stating he would write you on the subject. Please refer to my letter of March 7 relating to the same. Captain Thorpe was of course perfectly justified in writing to you to learn if he should carry out instructions of this order. My desire now is simply to explain how I came to make reports required by it. I would prefer that this explanation should go to Colonel Fry in connection with the other papers.

Very respectfully, your obedient servant,

JOS. DARR, JR.,
Major and Military Commander.

WAR DEPARTMENT, *Washington, May 21, 1863.*

Major-General BURNSIDE, *Cincinnati, Ohio:*

In the case of Thomas M. Campbell, convicted as a spy, let execution of the sentence be respited until further order from me, he remaining in custody meanwhile.

A. LINCOLN.

Major-General BURNSIDE:

Please acknowledge receipt of above telegram and time of delivery.

THOS. T. ECKERT.

NEAR VICKSBURG, MISS., *May 21, 1863.*

COMMANDING OFFICER CONFEDERATE FORCES,
Jackson, Raymond, Edwards Station and Intermediate Places:

Captain Durbin, assistant quartermaster, U. S. Army, goes with supplies for the wounded men of the two armies who from the nature of their wounds would not bear removal after the late engagements near the places named. As soon as practicable I will be pleased to get all the wounded men within our lines, where they can receive care and attention without being a tax upon the communities where they now are. If the places named have been garrisoned so as to make it improper for me to send flag of truce with provision trains I would be pleased to know it and will conform with any plan for the relief of such wounded as were necessarily left near the battle-field as may be agreed upon. My only desire is to know that there is no unnecessary suffering among the unfortunate wounded. This I will feel satisfied of the moment I know they are in the hands of a military commander or that I am free to look after them.

U. S. GRANT,
Major-General.

OFFICE COMMISSARY-GENERAL OF PRISONERS,
Washington, D. C., May 21, 1863.

Hon. E. M. STANTON, *Secretary of War, Washington, D. C.*

SIR: I have the honor to submit the following report in reply to the communication of Doctor Van Buren, of the U. S. Sanitary Commission, on the condition of the hospitals for rebel prisoners at Camp Douglas and Saint Louis:

In July last, "not more than a year ago," the hospital at Camp Douglas was in a very fair condition. Ample provisions had been made of bedding, including sheets and pillow cases and all other necessary articles, but the general sanitary condition of the camp was very bad in consequence of its unfavorable location, being on flat, low ground with very little drainage, and in part owing to the want of proper attention to the police by the garrison. I made a full report of the state of the camp at that time to the Quartermaster-General and recommended a system of sewerage which it was thought would remedy much of the evil complained of. With my report I sent a letter from Doctor Bellows written in July upon the necessity for improvements. At the same time I gave precise instructions as to what should be done by the troops and the prisoners to produce a more healthful state of things, but soon after it was decided to exchange the prisoners of war and as the guard was composed of three-months' men little or no attention was paid to my orders. When the prisoners left the camp in September my control over it ceased.

In the latter part of January between 3,000 and 4,000 prisoners of war arrived at the camp with some 800 under medical treatment. The smallpox prevailed at the camp and it soon spread among the prisoners. A medical board was appointed by the Board of Health of Chicago to inspect and recommend what course should be taken, and General Ammen, then in command, adopted measures to carry out their recommendations.

About the same time Captain Freedley, U. S. Army, who had been ordered by me to inspect Camp Douglas, reported in relation to the hospital as follows:

The medical department is under the charge of Dr. George H. Park, surgeon Sixty-fifth Illinois Infantry. I found the hospitals generally neat and clean and well supplied with cots and bedding. The sick prisoners were well cared for. The medical supplies were sufficient. Doctor Park is kind in his treatment of the sick prisoners and endeavors to perform his duties satisfactorily. He is zealous, energetic and attentive and will endeavor faithfully to carry out your instructions.

There are now but little over —— prisoners at Chicago and there ought to be no want of anything for the few who are in hospital.

On the 20th of April I made a report to the Quartermaster-General urging that immediate steps should be taken to improve the sanitary condition of Camp Douglas by the introduction of the system of sewerage recommended a year ago, and on the 12th instant I again called attention to this subject.

When there are such frequent changes of commanders and medical officers as there have been at Camp Douglas it is almost impossible to have instructions properly carried out. There is no responsibility and before neglects can be traced to any one he is relieved from duty. To remedy these evils in part I have recommended that suitable medical officers be stationed permanently at the Western camps where our own paroled prisoners or prisoners of war may be assembled, and that permanent commanders with reliable guards may be assigned to them.

By a report made to the Surgeon-General some two or three weeks since by the medical inspector at Saint Louis it appears that proper steps have been taken to introduce in the prison hospital at Saint Louis all necessary reforms, and at the date of the report it was represented to be in a very satisfactory condition.

To insure a proper administration of the hospital department at camps under my control I have applied to the Surgeon-General for the detail of a surgeon as medical inspector whose special duty it will be to attend to this service.

Very respectfully, your obedient servant,

W. HOFFMAN,
Colonel Third Infantry, Commissary-General of Prisoners.

OFFICE COMMISSARY-GENERAL OF PRISONERS,
Washington, D. C., May 21, 1863.

Brig. Gen. J. T. BOYLE,
Commanding Western District of Kentucky, Louisville, Ky.

GENERAL: On the 30th ultimo 255 prisoners of war arrived at Baltimore from Louisville *en route* to City Point without rolls or papers of any kind and it was not till the 4th instant that the rolls were received. In the meantime they were forwarded to City Point. Such omissions cause much embarrassment and I have to request that you will direct that hereafter when prisoners are sent for delivery duplicate parole rolls signed together with necessary orders may be sent with them, and a roll without paroles to this office.

Very respectfully, your obedient servant,

W. HOFFMAN,
Colonel Third Infantry, Commissary-General of Prisoners.

WASHINGTON, *May 21, 1863.*

Lieut. Col. W. H. LUDLOW:

Please give me early notice of expected arrivals of prisoners from Richmond and the number.

W. HOFFMAN,
Commissary-General of Prisoners.

FORT MONROE, *May 21, 1863.*

Col. WILLIAM HOFFMAN:

I send to City Point to-day prisoners from Washington. No arrivals yet from Fort Delaware. I shall go to City Point to-morrow. All our officers will be delivered, Captain Brownson among the number. He has not been sent. When can you send me replies to the memoranda given to me by Mr. Ould?

WM. H. LUDLOW,
Lieutenant-Colonel, &c.

HEADQUARTERS PAROLED PRISONERS,
Near Annapolis, Md., May 21, 1863.

Col. W. HOFFMAN,
Commissary-General of Prisoners, Washington, D. C.

SIR: I have the honor to make application if consistent with the good of the service for the permission to retain the band of the One hundred and fourteenth Pennsylvania Volunteers now at this camp. They were paroled, having been taken at Fredricksburg December 13, 1862. Their instruments were taken from them, and since arriving at this camp new instruments have been purchased by the men composing the band which are private property. These men are privates of the aforesaid regiment. My reasons for wishing to retain them are that they have an immense influence through the medium of the national and other airs played upon the disorganized and undisciplined command I am intrusted with, so much so that its effects are very visible to any one acquainted with the camp before and since their arrival. The band is used morning and night, at funerals and all arrivals and departures of men of this camp and has a great tendency to keep the men together and from straggling, saving much trouble and annoyance in the absence of a sufficient guard. I would respectfully refer you to Captain Lazelle who expressed himself much in favor of this proposi tion. I hope it may be compatible with the interests of the service.

Please find inclosed a list* of the musicians.

I am, colonel, with great respect, your obedient servant,

GEO. SANGSTER,
Lieutenant-Colonel, Commanding Paroled Prisoners.

ADJUTANT'S OFFICE, *Fort Delaware, Del., May 22, 1863.*

Col. W. HOFFMAN, *Commissary-General of Prisoners.*

SIR: I have the honor to inform you that all the prisoners of war were sent off yesterday, the 21st instant, for exchange. Triplicate parole rolls are forwarded this day to you.

By order of General Schenck, commanding Middle Department, Captain Baylor will be sent to-day to Harper's Ferry for trial.

A. SCHOEPF,
Brigadier-General, Commanding Post.

OFFICE COMMISSARY-GENERAL OF PRISONERS,
Washington, D. C., May 22, 1863.

Col. J. C. KELTON,
Asst. Adjt. Gen., Hdqrs. of the Army, Washington, D. C.

COLONEL: The interests of the service require that an officer of higher rank, more experience and one more specially fitted for the position should be detailed to relieve Lieut. Col. George Sangster in

---

* Omitted.

the command of Camp Parole, and I have the honor to request that Col. J. B. McIntosh, Third Pennsylvania Cavalry, be detailed for this duty. Colonel McIntosh is now serving with the Army of the Potomac but I am informed his regiment is so much reduced that his presence may readily be dispensed with. It is very important that an officer of the character and ability which I am assured he possesses should be placed in command of Camp Parole, and I trust he may be assigned to this position without detriment to the service elsewhere.

Very respectfully, your obedient servant,

W. HOFFMAN,
Colonel Third Infantry, Commissary-General of Prisoners.

[First indorsement.]

HEADQUARTERS OF THE ARMY, *May 22, 1863.*

Respectfully referred to Major-General Hooker, commanding, to report if Colonel McIntosh can be spared from his command.

By order of Major-General Halleck:

J. C. KELTON,
Assistant Adjutant-General.

[Second indorsement.]

HEADQUARTERS ARMY OF THE POTOMAC,
May 27, 1863.

Respectfully returned.

In my judgment the commander of a cavalry regiment in the field should not be detailed for the duty within indicated. Colonel McIntosh has reluctantly been granted a leave of absence by me to attend to what he considered very important personal interests. It was my expectation that he would rejoin this army at the expiration of his leave and I trust he will not be detailed for any duty. It is presumed that his regiment, though now reduced in numbers, will at no distant day be filled up.

JOSEPH HOOKER,
Major-General, Commanding.

[Third indorsement.]

MAY 28, 1863.

Detail will not be made.

H. W. H.

FORT MONROE, *May 22, 1863.*

Major-General HITCHCOCK:

I had before the receipt of your telegram called the attention of the Confederate agent to the reported inhuman treatment of our men. I expect a reply* to-morrow when I go to City Point.

WM. H. LUDLOW,
Lieutenant-Colonel, &c.

FORT MONROE, *May 22, 1863.*

Col. W. HOFFMAN, *Commissary-General of Prisoners:*

I would advise that the orders referred to in the last paragraph of your letter of the 20th, and also the Orders, No. 15, of General Schenck,

---

* See indorsement on Ludlow to Ould, May 20, p. 683.

be prospective from this date and not retroactive. Many paroles have been taken by us from the enemy in the field in the South and Southwest; many in Stoneman's late expedition and have been accounted for. I shall meet Mr. Ould to-morrow and serve upon him copies of Orders 49 and 100, with notice that article 7 of cartel must be literally complied with.

WM. H. LUDLOW,
Lieutenant-Colonel and Agent for Exchange of Prisoners.

Copy to Hon. E. M. Stanton.)

———

HEADQUARTERS DEPARTMENT OF VIRGINIA,
Fort Monroe, Va., May 22, 1863.

Hon. ROBERT OULD, <i>Agent for Exchange of Prisoners.</i>

SIR: I have the honor to inclose to you copies of General Orders,* No. 49 and No. 100, of War Department, announcing regulations and instructions for the government of the U. S. forces in the field in the matter of paroles. These together with the stipulations of the cartel will govern our army. I would invite your special attention to article 7 of the cartel which provides that all prisoners of war shall be sent to places of delivery therein specified. The execution of this article will obviate much discussion and difficulty growing out of the mode, time and place of giving paroles. No paroles or exchanges will be considered binding except those under the stipulations of said article and permitting commanders of two opposing armies to exchange or release on parole at other points mutually agreed on by said commanders.

I am, very respectfully, your obedient servant,

WM. H. LUDLOW,
Lieutenant-Colonel and Agent for Exchange of Prisoners.

———

WAR DEPARTMENT, Richmond, Va., May 22, 1863.

Lieut. Col. WILLIAM H. LUDLOW, <i>Agent of Exchange.</i>

SIR: You are very well aware that for the last six months I have been presenting to you lists of Confederate officers and soldiers and Confederate citizens who have been detained by your authorities in their prisons. Some of these on my remonstrance have been released and sent to us. By far the greater number remain in captivity. I am satisfied that you have made strenuous exertions to have these persons released and to carry out in good faith the agreements which we have made. Even those exertions have proved of little avail. Nothing now remains but for me to give you formal notice that our Government will resort to retaliation in every case which has heretofore been brought to your attention where the wrong complained of has not been redressed. The Confederate authorities will exercise their discretion in selecting such prisoners as they think best, whether officers or privates, in this purpose of retaliation. You will be notified in each case. I am now preparing a list of officers and men such as are reserved for retaliation. As soon as the parties for whom they are held are delivered to us the hostage will be released. I have thus frankly informed you of our purposes before they are put into actual execution for the double purpose of preventing any imputation of bad faith and of giving you an opportunity of saving a resort to so stern

* Omitted here; see pp. 306 and 671 for these orders.

a remedy. You have at this moment in your prisons Confederate officers whom you have held over twelve months without charges or trial. They have been fairly exchanged by our agreements and ought to have been delivered long ago.

Respectfully, your obedient servant,   RO. OULD,
Agent of Exchange.

WAR DEPARTMENT, *Richmond, Va., May 22, 1863.*
Lieut. Col. WILLIAM H. LUDLOW, *Agent of Exchange.*

SIR: I perceive by the Northern papers that Captains McGraw and Corbin were shot to death with musketry on Friday, the 15th instant, at or near Sandusky, Ohio.

These are the cases which I brought to your attention when last I saw you. These men were duly authorized to recruit within the limits of Kentucky. They were tried by a court-martial upon the charge of recruiting within your lines. They were sentenced to be shot and that sentence was approved by General Burnside and President Lincoln.

The Confederate Government has ordered that two captains now in our custody shall be selected for execution in retaliation for this gross barbarity. The order will be speedily executed.

Your papers refer to other cases of parties condemned to death upon the same charge. They are some five or six in number.

In view of the awful vortex into which things are plunging I give you notice that in the event of the execution of these persons retaliation to an equal extent at least will be visited upon your own officers, and if that is found ineffectual the number will be increased.

The Great Ruler of nations must judge who is responsible for the initiation of this chapter of horrors.

Respectfully, your obedient servant,   RO. OULD,
Agent of Exchange.

WAR DEPARTMENT, *Richmond, Va., May 22, 1863.*
Lieut. Col. WILLIAM H. LUDLOW, *Agent of Exchange.*

SIR: In several of your late communications you have appealed to me for the release of political prisoners held by us. I am ready to deliver every one of them when you do the same charity. Until then not one of them shall be released except at our own pleasure. You asked in a late communication for the release of the sheriff of Barbour County. Are you aware that you now hold some half dozen or more of harmless and inoffensive old men as hostages whom you do not even pretend to release, and yet ask the sheriff's deliverance? You have now thousands of helpless non-combatants in your prisons not arrested as dangerous persons to your army, but incarcerated because it is supposed they are loyal to their own country. Their number is increasing every day. I will listen to no proposition for the release of non-combatants that is not based upon the delivery of all whom you have in custody coupled with some distinct written understanding as to future conduct in respect to such captures. If this is not agreeable let God save the right. I hope there will be no further mistake between us in regard to this matter. I trust I have made myself sufficiently distinct.

Respectfully, your obedient servant,   RO. OULD,
Agent of Exchange.

WAR DEPARTMENT, *Richmond, Va., May 22, 1863.*

Lieutenant-Colonel LUDLOW, *Agent of Exchange.*

SIR: The President of the Confederate States has this day received the following dispatch:

Your interference in behalf of Sergt. John R. Lyle is earnestly invoked. He is sentenced by court-martial at Bowling Green, Ky., to be hung as a spy on Friday, the 27th of May, on Johnson's Island, near Sandusky, Ohio.

He was not a spy, and if execution can be suspended until General John A. Logan* can be heard from he will prove that Mr. Lyle belongs to his command and was by him sent into Kentucky to notify some of his men who had been captured and paroled to report for exchange to avoid being treated as deserters, and whilst in the execution of that service he was captured in the dress he had worn all the time in service.

A. O. P. NICHOLSON.

I am entirely satisfied upon further inquiry that Mr. Nicholson's representation is correct. I implore you as an act of humanity to lose no time in notifying your authorities of the foregoing facts and securing at least a suspension of the sentence. Of course we cannot deny your military authority to execute spies. That right, however, must never be used as a cloak to other designs. If it ever is our right is clear when we are satisfied of the entire innocence of the party and when the true facts are brought to the attention of the adversary to resort to retaliation.

I say this in no spirit of threatening. I appeal as a man in behalf of one whom I know to be unjustly accused and convicted.

Respectfully, your obedient servant,

RO. OULD,
Agent of Exchange.

[First indorsement.]

HEADQUARTERS OF THE ARMY, *June 3, 1863.*

Respectfully referred to Major-General Burnside who will communicate with Maj. Gen. John A. Logan and report his opinion whether there are any good reasons for pardoning John R. Lyle or of commuting his sentence.

H. W. HALLECK,
General-in-Chief.

[Second indorsement.]

HEADQUARTERS DEPARTMENT OF THE OHIO,
Cincinnati, Ohio, June 6, 1863.

Respectfully referred to Captain Cutts, judge-advocate, Department of the Ohio, who will retain proceedings in this case until General Logan can be heard from. Captain Cutts will forward this to General Logan with a statement of the facts as appear from the records and ask for General Logan's immediate answer.

By order of Major-General Burnside:

W. P. ANDERSON,
Assistant Adjutant-General.

GENERAL ORDERS, } HDQRS. 1ST. DIV., 16TH ARMY CORPS,
No. 86. } *La Grange, Tenn., May 22, 1863.*

Hereafter when citizen prisoners are apprehended charges and specifications will be made by commanding officers making the arrests; these charges and specifications with names of witnesses annexed to be

---

* This is evidently an error on the part of the writer; he meant General John H. Morgan, of the Confederate service.

lodged with provost-marshals when the prisoners are delivered into their custody.

Military commissions will be convened at the headquarters of each brigade of this division for the trial of citizens upon the charges and specifications so prepared.

The provost-marshal will present the charges and specifications to those commissions and secure the attendance of the witnesses named.

Every effort will be made to secure an early hearing of each case.

By order of Brig. Gen. William S. Smith, commanding First Division, Sixteenth Army Corps:

> W. H. HARLAND,
> *Acting Assistant Adjutant-General.*

> WASHINGTON, D. C., *May 23, 1863.*

Major-General HITCHCOCK, *Washington.*

GENERAL: I have just received your indorsement on the letter of Governor Morton in regard to newspaper statements that the enemy had refused to parole certain prisoners of war in accordance with the stipulations of the cartel. I fully concur with you in regard to the proposed retaliation but I think a direct and positive demand should be made upon Mr. Ould for the execution of the cartel in regard to these prisoners before any further action should be decided upon.

Very respectfully, your obedient servant,

> H. W. HALLECK,
> *General-in-Chief.*

> OFFICE COMMISSARY-GENERAL OF PRISONERS,
> *Washington, D. C., May 23, 1863.*

Maj. Gen. J. M. SCHOFIELD,
Commanding Department of the Missouri, Saint Louis, Mo.

GENERAL: By direction of the General-in-Chief I have the honor to request that you will order all prisoners of war now held at Saint Louis or Alton to be forwarded for delivery at City Point, Va. This order embraces all military organizations, guerrillas and others, and if there are any of this class held on charges of an indefinite character or on which they cannot be immediately tried I request that they may be included among those sent forward. I inclose a list* of some such cases found on the files of this office.

The Confederate authorities complain that we retain in our prisons prisoners of war who have been exchanged, and it is desirable that they should have no shadow of ground to accuse us of bad faith. Please direct that the quartermaster at Baltimore be notified of the time when they will reach that city in order that he may have a steamer ready to take them directly on board. In consequence of the prevalence heretofore of the smallpox at the prisons it will be necessary to take every proper precaution to prevent the spread of the disease along the route. It is possible that before this order can be put in force it will be possible to deliver prisoners at Vicksburg or some other point on the river, and in that case I have to request you will inform me by telegraph.

Very respectfully, your obedient servant,

> W. HOFFMAN,
> *Colonel Third Infantry, Commissary-General of Prisoners.*

---

* Not found.

OFFICE COMMISSARY-GENERAL OF PRISONERS,
Washington, D. C., May 23, 1863.

Col. B. L. E. BONNEVILLE,
Commanding Benton Barracks, Saint Louis, Mo.

COLONEL: Your letter of the 6th instant was received some days since, and in reply I have to say that the issue of clothing to the crew of the Queen of the West was very proper. These men belong to Ellet's brigade, though not soldiers, and it is proper that an account of the issues made to them should be sent with them when they join their command.

Very respectfully, your obedient servant,
W. HOFFMAN,
Colonel Third Infantry, Commissary-General of Prisoners.

———

OFFICE COMMISSARY-GENERAL OF PRISONERS,
Washington, D. C., May 23, 1863.

Lieut. Col. F. A. DICK,
Provost-Marshal-General, Saint Louis, Mo.

COLONEL: Orders have been sent to-day to the general commanding the Department of the Missouri directing that all prisoners of war at Saint Louis and Alton be forwarded via Baltimore to City Point. In executing the order you will receive from General Schofield you will be governed by his instructions and those heretofore given from this office on similar occasions. All military organizations, regular or irregular, are classed as prisoners of war, and none will be detained except by the order or approval of the general commanding the department. Send duplicate parole rolls signed by each prisoner with them and a roll without parole to this office. Give the commander of the guard particular instructions to permit no person to hold communication with the prisoners by the way nor will he allow officers or others to go to eating or drinking houses. If you have money belonging to them in your possession turn it over to the commander of the guard with the names of those to whom it belongs, to be handed to them on arriving at City Point. The commander of the guard should notify the quartermaster at Baltimore of the time of his arrival there, giving the number of prisoners, so that he may have rations prepared for them.

Very respectfully, your obedient servant,
W. HOFFMAN,
Colonel Third Infantry, Commissary-General of Prisoners.

(Same *mutatis mutandis* to Major Hendrickson, Alton Military Prison.)

———

OFFICE COMMISSARY-GENERAL OF PRISONERS,
Washington, D. C., May 23, 1863.

Capt. H. B. TODD, *Provost-Marshal, Washington, D. C.*

CAPTAIN: I am directed by the commissary-general of prisoners to request you to furnish this office with a list of persons now in the Old Capitol Prison claiming to be deserters from the rebel army.

Very respectfully, your obedient servant,
W. T. HARTZ,
Captain and Assistant Adjutant-General.

MURFREESBOROUGH, *May 24, 1863.*

Colonel HOFFMAN:

Up to what date are prisoners exchanged? Is Streight and his command exchanged yet?

W. S. ROSECRANS,
Major-General.

U. S. FLAG-SHIP MINNESOTA,
Off Newport News, May 24, 1863.

Hon. GIDEON WELLES, *Secretary of the Navy.*

SIR: At 8.30 this morning the steamer James Brooks came down from City Point with 620 paroled prisoners including 80 officers and the crew of the Indianola.

*   *   *   *   *   *

S. P. LEE,
Acting Rear-Admiral.

FORT MONROE, *May 24, 1863.*

Col. W. HOFFMAN, *Commissary-General of Prisoners:*

Ninety-six officers and about 500 men go to Annapolis to-morrow. All officers who have been sent to Annapolis have been exchanged. I expect to send forty more officers on Monday or Tuesday. I send this from City Point, where I shall remain until Monday.

WM. H. LUDLOW,
Lieutenant-Colonel and Agent, &c.

SPECIAL ORDERS, }   HDQRS. DEPT. OF THE TENNESSEE,
    No. 130.   }   *Young's Point, La., May 24, 1863.*

*   *   *   *   *   *

III. Lieutenant-Colonel Graham, Twenty-second Iowa Volunteers (paroled), is appointed to take charge of paroled prisoners at this place and will report to Lieut. Col. L. Kent, provost-marshal, for orders.

By order of Maj. Gen. U. S. Grant:

T. S. BOWERS,
Acting Assistant Adjutant General.

SPECIAL ORDERS, }   HDQRS. DEPT. OF THE TENNESSEE,
    No. 139.   }   *In Field, near Vicksburg, Miss., May 24, 1863.*

I. Col. Clark B. Lagow, aide-de-camp, U. S. Army, will immediately proceed to Memphis, Tenn., with the prisoners of war captured in recent battles and now at or in the vicinity of Young's Point, La. He will deliver one certified list or roll of said prisoners to Maj. Gen. S. A. Hurlbut, at Memphis, Tenn., who will send said prisoners to Island No. 10 and furnish strong guards for them until he can communicate with the General-in-Chief of the Army as to the disposition to be made of them. One roll or list of said prisoners will be retained by Major

Bowers, judge-advocate. The troops now guarding the prisoners will accompany them as guards to Memphis from where they will immediately return to this place. The prisoners not to be debarked at Memphis but sent immediately on to Island No. 10. Lieut. Col. J. D. Bingham, assistant quartermaster, will furnish the necessary transportation. Colonel Lagow will request Admiral D. D. Porter to furnish a gun-boat to escort the transports conveying prisoners.

*   *   *   *   *   *   *

By order of Maj. Gen. U. S. Grant:

JOHN A. RAWLINS,
Assistant Adjutant-General.

WAR DEPARTMENT, *Washington, D. C., May 25, 1863.*
Maj. Gen. R. C. SCHENCK,
　　Commanding Middle Department, Baltimore.

GENERAL: Information has reached this Department this morning that a man named J. H. Warring, who owns a large plantation near the mouth of the Patuxent, has been accustomed to make of his premises a place of rendezvous for harboring rebel officers. He is now confined in the Old Capitol Prison, three rebel officers being taken in his house with a large amount of rebel mails, uniforms, &c. I am also informed that one of your men was killed in the effort to make the arrest. The object of this communication is to instruct you immediately to take military possession of that plantation, to remove the family beyond the U. S. lines and to seize and convert to the use of the Government all the property which may be found on the plantation and to hold the premises for military uses. This order should be executed with diligence and efficiency.

Very respectfully, your obedient servant,

EDWIN M. STANTON,
Secretary of War.

WAR DEPARTMENT, *Washington, D. C., May 25, 1863.*
Major-General BURNSIDE, *Cincinnati:*

The Secretary of War directs that the execution of the sentence of John R. Lyle be suspended till further orders. No more Confederate officers will be paroled or exchanged till further orders. They will be kept in close confinement and strongly guarded.

H. W. HALLECK,
General-in-Chief.

WAR DEPARTMENT, *Washington, D. C., May 25, 1863.*
General SCHOFIELD:

No Confederate officers will be paroled or exchanged till further orders. They will be kept in close confinement and be strongly guarded. Those already paroled will be confined.

H. W. HALLECK,
General-in-Chief.

(Same to Major-Generals Rosecrans, Hurlbut (for General Grant), Dix, Foster, Hooker, Schenck, Banks, Hunter and Col. W. Hoffman, commissary-general of prisoners; Major-General Herron, Army of the

Frontier; Brigadier-General Davies, District of Rolla; Col. Lewis Merrill, District of Northeast Missouri; Col. Chester Harding, jr., Saint Joseph, District of Northwest Missouri; Brigadier-General Loan, Jefferson City, Mo., District of Central Missouri; Col. W. F. Cloud, Springfield, District of Southwest Missouri; Major-General Blunt, Leavenworth City, District of Kansas; Col. J. M. Chivington, District of Colorado, Denver City; Brigadier-General Craig, District of Nebraska, Omaha.)

FORT MONROE, VA., *May 25, 1863.*

Hon. E. M. STANTON, *Secretary of War:*

Mr. Kirby who has been in prison six months in Richmond is here. If it is your wish to see him please apprise me.

JOHN A. DIX,
Major-General.

FORT MONROE, *May 25, 1863.*

Major-General HALLECK, *General-in-Chief:*

I request that no officers may be sent from Fort McHenry or elsewhere here for confinement. Fort Wool is given up to the engineers. We have nothing but a small guard-house at Fort Monroe and we have no other place except Fort Norfolk, which has always a large number of political prisoners and soldiers under sentence or awaiting trial.

JOHN A. DIX,
Major-General.

HEADQUARTERS DEPARTMENT OF THE SOUTH,
Port Royal, S. C., May 25, 1863.

Admiral S. F. DU PONT,
Comdg. South Atlantic Blockading Squadron, Flag-ship Wabash.

ADMIRAL: I have been already so much mortified with regard to the nine prisoners of war, the sons of leading secessionists—Seabrook, &c.—recently captured by the Navy, that I have concluded not to address His Excellency the President on the subject.

I must say, however, in view of all the facts and in justice to the officers of my command who have all been condemned to death by the rebel Congress that the delivering up of these aristocrats, the sons of leaders in this rebellion, to be exchanged as ordinary prisoners of war instead of being kept to be hanged for every one of my officers injured would be one of the grossest outrages ever committed on the American people, and I think you will find that the people will so decide.

I hope, Admiral, on a full review of the case you will think with me and will decide at once to turn these prisoners over to me. The recent release of some of our prisoners is only intended by the rebels to induce us to release these pets of the aristocracy; they would then commence their old game and laugh at us for our folly. I am thus earnest feeling conscious if I were not so that all the bloodshed this folly would inaugurate would be justly chargeable to me.

I have the honor to be, very respectfully, your most obedient servant,

D. HUNTER,
Major-General, Commanding.

HEADQUARTERS DEPARTMENT OF THE SOUTH,
Hilton Head, S. C., May 25, 1863.

Admiral S. F. DU PONT,
    Comdg. South Atlantic Blockading Squadron, Port Royal Harbor.

ADMIRAL: I hasten to acknowledge that I find from an unofficial interview with Capt. C. R. P. Rodgers, your chief of staff, that a portion of my letter to you of this day's date was based on a misapprehension of the third paragraph of your letter to me under date May 19, 1863, a misapprehension which if you will review that letter you will easily understand. I also find that certain expressions in my letter have been construed as indicating a feeling unfriendly to yourself or at least of personal dissatisfaction with your conduct while their true purport was exclusively directed against what I deemed and must continue to deem an impolitic act on the part of one branch of the Government.

I feel that it can hardly be necessary for me to disavow any intention of slight in the letter which I now beg to withdraw or to reassure you of my sincere respect and friendship. Considering the delicate nature of the relations subsisting between the two branches of the service it is rather to be wondered at that so few misunderstandings should have occurred than that this one misunderstanding should have arisen. And now having I trust fully put away anything of personal unpleasantness in this controversy I must reiterate my opinion that in view of the action of the rebel Congress as reported placing all the men and officers of my command outside the laws and usages of civilized warfare and condemning us to death if captured that no grosser outrage or folly could be committed by the Government than to tolerate in any part of the theater of war any exchange of prisoners until this act of the rebel Congress shall have been repealed or disavowed by the military despotism controlling the Confederacy; and more especially should such exchanges cease in the case of prisoners captured in the Department of the South against which this legislation is more pointedly aimed. That the prisoners captured by the forces under your command and now in your hands are of less intrinsic value than an equal number of prisoners of similar grades belonging to the forces of the Union may be at once admitted, but in view of the essentially aristocratic character of the rebellion and the fact that the prisoners referred to are cadets of the best families in South Carolina I thought and still think that they are eminently prisoners who should be held as hostages for the safety of any officers or men of this command who may fall into the enemy's hands. It is now nearly a year since I and the members of my staff were declared outlaws to be executed wherever found by a general order from the rebel War Department and no protest was made by our Government against this order even when returning me to duty on what appeared to be and may yet prove a hazardous expedition. In my own case I had no protest to offer, but against continuing exchanges while the officers and men of my command are threatened with disgraceful deaths if captured I must and do protest with all the energy of my nature. The employment of negroes as soldiers is now a settled part of the policy of our Government and it is unjust to the negroes and to the white troops who will have eventually to serve with them that exchanges should be continued which tacitly admit the right of the rebel Government to violate the laws and usages of war at pleasure.

I have the honor to be, admiral, very respectfully, your most obedient servant,
                                          D. HUNTER,
                                        Major-General, Commanding.

CINCINNATI, *May 25, 1863.*

Col. W. HOFFMAN, *Commissary-General of Prisoners:*

Governor Morton, of Indiana, asks that the Fifty-first and Seventy-third Regiments Indiana Volunteer Infantry, paroled prisoners at Camp Chase, be sent to Indianapolis to be filled up. Will the War Department authorize their being sent there?

J. D. COX,
Brigadier-General.

JUDGE-ADVOCATE-GENERAL'S OFFICE,
Washington, May 25, 1863.

Hon. E. M. STANTON, *Secretary of War:*

In the case of W. T. Smithson, a political prisoner lately arrested and placed in confinement by authority of the Secretary of War and whose case is referred to me to advise as to its disposition, I have the honor to report as follows:

Smithson was in the early part of the war arrested and confined at Fort Lafayette as being one of the most prominent and dangerous of rebel sympathizers in Washington. He was released after an imprisonment of four months upon taking the oath of allegiance and (as it is said) voluntarily pledging himself in no way to aid or abet the enemies of the country. It now appears from researches of the provost-marshal of the War Department that Smithson has for a considerable period been largely engaged in the purchase and sale of Southern securities and Southern bank currency; that he has negotiated sight drafts on Richmond as well as 8 per cent. Confederate bonds, and that he has filled orders for Confederate notes in amounts from $500 to $50,000, purchasing them in some cases from parties known to him to have come direct from Richmond.

It is further shown that Smithson has to a large extent assisted in the correspondence with rebels and rebel sympathizers at the South, and correspondence of a dangerous character in reference to running the blockade has been discovered in his possession while apparently passing through his hands. It is also proved that Smithson has been acting as business agent in Washington for friends at the South and especially for Mrs. Rose O'N. Greenhow, an avowed rebel. A power of attorney from this lady to Smithson is produced by which she empowers him to sell, collect, &c., as her agent all stocks, securities, dividends, &c., which she may hold in the United States, and there was found in his bank since his arrest one certificate of 120 shares of railroad stock belonging to Mrs. Greenhow. A letter from this lady accompanies the power of attorney in which she urges Smithson to sell the stock for her as soon as possible and remit to her the proceeds by a party whom she names. She also advises him to join her in cotton and tobacco speculations in Richmond which she represents as promising large profits.

Smithson may without doubt be prosecuted under the act "to prevent correspondence with rebels" of February 25, 1863 (Chapter LX), as having promoted and assisted in such correspondence. He may also be proceeded against as for perjury on account of the violation of his oath of allegiance. Moreover the facts of his promoting a treasonable correspondence with a well-known and influential rebel and his acting as her business agent in the sale of her property which should be forfeited to the Government, and of his largely negotiating and aiding to give currency and value to the securities of the Confederate Government—these facts taken together would seem to bring his case within the general act of July 17, 1862 (Chapter CXCV), entitled "An act to suppress insurrection, to punish treason and rebellion, to seize and confiscate the property of rebels," &c. Section 2 of this act includes the case of any one who assists or gives aid and comfort to the rebellion (without actually engaging in it) and fixes a very severe punishment for the offense. It is believed that Smithson's case comes within this section, his whole course from the beginning having been that of a person desiring directly or indirectly to give aid and comfort to the rebellion and to rebels. Certainly in no way could he more directly give them aid and comfort than by acting as their banker and broker in Washington, assisting them to realize the illegal securities and currency of their Government and aiding to give it value and use by his negotiations.

Under section 5 of this act all Smithson's property and estate in Washington, &c., may be at once seized and the proceeds applied to the support of the Army of the United States as his case would come within the sixth enumerated clause of this section. In seizing his property, however, all Confederate notes and securities found belonging to him should be destroyed by the provost-marshal. They are not held to possess any pecuniary value; are simply disloyal utterances or publications and *indicia* of treason and therefore to be suppressed. The certificates mentioned or any other property of Mrs. Greenhow found in Smithson's possession may be seized and applied by virtue of the same enactment. Or if the certificate was sent here by her with her letter and power of attorney, as appears to be the case, it may be confiscated under section 5, Chapter CXX, of act of March 3, 1863, which provides for the confiscation of any property coming from a disloyal State to a loyal one, or within the lines of the United States through or by a person other than an agent duly appointed by the provisions of the act. It may be noted that the act of August 6, 1861 (Chapter LX), entitled "An act to confiscate property used for insurrectionary purposes," would probably apply to any property of actual pecuniary value purchased or acquired by Smithson for himself or any one for whom he was agent in the course of his negotiations as financial agent of the Southern Confederacy or its members with intent to use the same in aiding, abetting or promoting in any way the insurrection.

But his case as to the subject of the confiscation of property is more readily brought under the general act of July 17, 1862, than any other. It is proper to remark further that a case of this grave and aggravated character requiring as it does a summary and decisive treatment eminently calls for the exercise of the power given to the President by a recent act of Congress of suspending the writ of *habeas corpus*. That this course be pursued by the President is therefore earnestly recommended in the present instance for the reason that if such action is not taken the result must be that the prisoner will be admitted to bail by the civil courts and will without doubt be enabled to resume and follow with impunity his disloyal and traitorous occupations. Inasmuch as the process of the civil courts would necessarily be slow and uncertain in the cases of the offenses created by the acts of Congress above alluded to it must certainly have been contemplated or designed in framing the acts that the jurisdiction of these courts and their authority over prisoners should be aided by precisely the measure now recommended, the suspension of the writ of *habeas corpus* by the President. That this was the design and that this design should be carried out in the case of so conspicuous a traitor as Smithson cannot it is believed be questioned.

Respectfully submitted: J. HOLT,
Judge-Advocate-General.

WASHINGTON, *May 25, 1863.*

Lieut. Col. W. H. LUDLOW:

If it is not convenient to hold rebel officers at Fort Monroe send them back to Fort Delaware

W. HOFFMAN,
Commissary-General of Prisoners.

BALTIMORE, *May 25, 1863.*

Major-General MILROY, *Winchester:*

The following order was received from the War Department to-day:

No Confederate officer will be paroled or exchanged until further orders. They will be kept in close confinement and be strongly guarded. Those already paroled will be confined.

H. W. HALLECK.
General-in-Chief.

DONN PIATT,
Lieutenant-Colonel and Chief of Staff.

(Same to Brigadier-General Averell, Weston, W. Va.; Brigadier-General Kelley, Parkersburg, W. Va.; Brigadier-General Scammon, Charleston, W. Va.`

FORT MONROE, *May 25, 1863.*

Col. W. HOFFMAN, *Commissary-General of Prisoners:*

I have just returned from City Point and will see you in Washington in a day or two. No paroles will hereafter be acknowledged except such as are strictly in accordance with article 7 of the cartel. I would advise that orders be issued to release on parole no more Confederate officers and men. All captured enlisted rebels can be delivered at Baton Rouge or City Point. All captured rebel officers should be sent to Old Capitol Prison or Fort Delaware to be convenient for disposition. All our captured officers will be sent to Richmond. All future captures will be reduced to possession, except special cases under the direction of the commanding general.

WM. H. LUDLOW,
Lieutenant-Colonel and Agent for Exchange of Prisoners.

FORT MONROE, *May 25, 1863.*

Col. WILLIAM HOFFMAN:

The Confederates threaten to execute two of our officers in retaliation for the two rebels executed at Johnson's Island. I will bring with me to Washington all the correspondence in the case. I would advise the retention of every Confederate officer at present, even those who have been declared exchanged. Please notify General Banks as he might otherwise release those he has. The Confederates will keep all of Colonel Streight's officers. I have had just enough Confederate officers to exchange for all our officers except Colonel Streight. Particulars when I see you. Send Doctor Dixon, as for him I can get Doctor Sanger, one of our surgeons, who will be insane unless speedily released.

WM. H. LUDLOW,
Lieutenant-Colonel, &c.

HEADQUARTERS DEPARTMENT OF VIRGINIA,
Fort Monroe, May 25, 1863.

Col. W. HOFFMAN, *Commissary-General of Prisoners.*

COLONEL: I inclose herewith copy* of letter from Mr. Ould. I telegraphed you this morning in relation to paroles. A fair construction of article 7 of the cartel requires all captures to be reduced to possession and delivered at the two places agreed on. The Confederates will accept Baton Rouge at the West (though they have not yet officially so informed me). City Point is of course already agreed on at the East. All questions relating to officers must be adjusted at City Point, and I hope that instructions will be issued to send all rebel captured officers to some place at the East to await disposition. I am anticipating much trouble in relation to officers, and am of opinion we should hold on to all we have, even if declared exchanged, to abide action on the part of the enemy. With this view I shall retain Colonel Morehead and others at Fort Monroe.

I am, very respectfully, your obedient servant,
WM. H. LUDLOW,
Lieutenant-Colonel and Agent for Exchange of Prisoners.

P. S.—All our officers will be sent to Richmond.

W. H. L.

HEADQUARTERS DEPARTMENT OF VIRGINIA,
Fort Monroe, May 25, 1863.

Hon. ROBERT OULD, *Agent for Exchange of Prisoners.*

SIR: You threaten retaliation in your letter of the 22d instant in case certain parties whom you have demanded are not delivered to you. I beg leave to inform you that no deliveries of any kind will be made to you under such threats. If such threats are withdrawn deliveries can be made of parties properly entitled to release but not otherwise. Three-fourths or nine-tenths of the cases of which you have furnished memoranda have been released and delivered to you. If before the necessary investigations in the remaining cases have been made you put in practice retaliation either upon our officers or men I give you formal notice that the United States Government will exercise their discretion in selecting such persons as they think best, whether officers or privates, for the purpose of counter retaliation.

I am, very respectfully, your obedient servant,
WM. H. LUDLOW,
Lieutenant-Colonel and Agent for Exchange of Prisoners.

HEADQUARTERS DEPARTMENT OF VIRGINIA,
Fort Monroe, May 25, 1863.

Hon. ROBERT OULD, *Agent for Exchange of Prisoners.*

SIR: Captains McGraw and Corbin were executed upon conviction of being spies. They were also guilty of recruiting within our lines.

---

* Not found, but see *ante.*

Without waiting to know the facts or evidence in these cases (for you have admitted that you are acting on mere general newspaper statements which give neither facts nor evidence) orders have been given as you inform me that two of our officers now in your custody are to be selected for execution in retaliation for what you term "gross barbarity," and that the order will be speedily executed.

I give you formal notice that for each officer so executed one of your officers in our hands will be immediately put to death and if this number be not sufficient it will be increased.

The United States Government have been most lenient in their treatment of prisoners who have fallen into their hands. This leniency has been abused. And by your own admission your officers and men have come within our lines for the purpose ostensibly of recruiting but really as spies. They have been taken in citizens' dress under all the circumstances clearly surrounding the character of a spy. And in accepting such service they have taken upon themselves all its responsibility and the consequence of capture. And yet you propose to select brave and honorable officers who have been captured in fair and open fight on the battle field and barbarously put them to death in retaliation for the just punishment of spies.

I call to your mind among numerous other instances the barbarous execution of the brave men who under the orders of General Mitchel captured a locomotive and train and penetrated with it into the interior of Georgia for the sole purpose as was and is well known of destroying the railroad communications. They were executed as spies and yet the United States Government has not retaliated for this act.

Were I in your place I should hardly dare to invoke the judgment of the Great Ruler of nations upon the responsibility for the initiation of this what you most properly term chapter of horrors.

I am, very respectfully, your obedient servant,

WM. H. LUDLOW,
Lieutenant-Colonel and Agent for Exchange of Prisoners.

HEADQUARTERS DEPARTMENT OF VIRGINIA,
Fort Monroe, May 25, 1863.

Hon. ROBERT OULD, *Agent for Exchange of Prisoners.*

SIR: In reply to your communication of the 23d in relation to citizen prisoners I have to state that I have demanded them, and not as you inform me appealed to you for them; you probably, however, mean the same thing. I have demanded them because I have delivered you their equivalent with the understanding you were to release them. I bring to your mind the cases of Lewis and Scully. You distinctly and without reservation told me that these men should be delivered on the day following the delivery to you of a large number of citizen prisoners; their names were especially mentioned and I have not yet received them. I shall deliver to you no more political or citizen prisoners except at "our own pleasure," and no such agreement or understanding such as you propose will be for a moment entertained.

I am, very respectfully, your obedient servant,

WM. H. LUDLOW,
Lieutenant-Colonel and Agent for Exchange of Prisoners.

HEADQUARTERS DEPARTMENT OF VIRGINIA,
Fort Monroe, May 25, 1863.

Hon. E. M. STANTON, *Secretary of War.*

SIR: I have the honor to inclose to you copies* of recent correspondence between Mr. Ould and myself. I hope that my replies will meet your approval.

I am satisfied from close observation that the ground I have taken is one upon which the rebels can be most successfully met.

I am, most respectfully, your obedient servant,

WM. H. LUDLOW,
Lieut. Col. and Assistant Inspector-General Seventh Army Corps.

[First indorsement.]

MAY 27, 1863.

Referred to Major-General Hitchcock.

E. M. STANTON,
Secretary of War

[Second indorsement.]

ANNAPOLIS, *June 1, 1863.*

The undersigned returns the accompanying papers transmitted by Lieutenant-Colonel Ludlow and respectfully recommends that a letter be addressed to Colonel Ludlow approving the course taken by him in his letters to Mr. Ould as having been rendered necessary by the tenor of Mr. Ould's communications. But it is deemed proper to suggest before any further steps are taken in following out the barbarian practice threatened by the rebel Government that the subject should be laid before the President of the United States who may think it proper to advise with the members of his Cabinet in relation to it.

The practice proposed by the rebel Government is not simply an offense against the laws of war but an outrage upon civilization and humanity and cannot fail to call forth the condemnation of the historian and the execration of mankind. The United States Government is clearly in the right in the execution of the "spies" even according to the rebel statement of the facts, and it may be possible to reach the authors of the proposed criminal retaliation by a vigorous prosecution of the war.

E. A. HITCHCOCK,
Maj. Gen. of Vols., Commissioner for Exchange of Prisoners.

FORT MONROE, *May 25, 1863.*

Col. W. HOFFMAN, *Commisary-General of Prisoners:*

Colonel Morehead, Doctor Dixon and other rebel officers have arrived here. I will hold on to them.

WM. H. LUDLOW,
Lieutenant-Colonel and Agent for Exchange of Prisoners.

FORT MONROE, *May 25, 1863.*

Hon. E. M. STANTON:

I mailed to you this p. m. copy of correspondence with Mr. Ould relative to threatened execution of our officers and other matters.

WM. H. LUDLOW,
Lieutenant-Colonel and Agent for Exchange of Prisoners.

---

*Omitted here; see correspondence in its proper chronological order.

HEADQUARTERS PAROLED PRISONERS,
Near Annapolis, Md., May 25, 1863.

Col. W. HOFFMAN,
Commissary-General of Prisoners, Washington, D. C.

SIR: I have the honor to acknowledge the receipt of your letter of the 23d instant directing me to explain why I sent but 771 men to Washington instead of 1,000, on which I would respectfully report that I sent all the men that had clothing sufficient to cover their nakedness; and not having clothing to give the others I thought it would be prudent to keep them here until I could get clothing for them instead of sending them naked to a new camp. I would also respectfully report the reason I did not send officers to Washington to remain with the men was that I had no orders to send officers. The order was to send men, and a telegram previous to that gave me orders to hold all eastern officers until further orders; that is, officers in the Army of the Potomac. I acted on that order and did not send any officers to remain there. I have ordered twenty-four officers to proceed to report to Colonel McKelvy which will be a great relief to me, I having but poor quarters for them.

I am, colonel, very respectfully, your obedient servant,

GEO. SANGSTER,
Lieutenant-Colonel, Commanding Paroled Prisoners.

WHEELING, VA., *May 25, 1863.*

Lieut. Col. W. H. CHESEBROUGH,
Assistant Adjutant-General.

SIR: I beg leave to call your attention to a paper dated May 7, 1863, approved by Governor Peirpoint, submitted to the major-general commanding recommending that eight females of this city indicted for treason and perjury in September, 1861, but not tried should be sent beyond the lines. If the communication I refer to has been mislaid or miscarried I will forward copy.

Very respectfully, your obedient servant,

JOS. DARR, JR.,
Major and Military Commander.

OFFICE PROVOST-MARSHAL-GENERAL,
Murfreesborough, May 25, 1863.

Brigadier-General GARFIELD,
Chief of Staff, Department of the Cumberland.

GENERAL: As directed by the major-general commanding I proceeded at 11 p. m. yesterday with a guard of six men to the railroad depot and received the person of C. L. Vallandigham, a prisoner from the Department of the Ohio, conducted him to my office and after furnishing him with refreshments I in company with Col. J. C. McKibbin, aide-de-camp, and with two companies of the Fourth U. S. Cavalry as escort conveyed him to the house of Mr. Butler, five miles south from Murfreesborough on the Shelbyville pike, where the prisoner was kept under close guard until daylight when we proceeded as far as to our cavalry vedettes. Here the escort was halted and the prisoner left in charge of Lieutenant-Colonel Ducat, inspector-general of the department.

45 R R —SERIES II, VOL V

Colonel McKibbin and myself proceeded under flag of truce to the Confederate cavalry vedettes, when Colonel McK. sent a note to the officer commanding outpost informing him of the object of our visit. We remained there nearly two hours when the officer in command (Colonel Webb, Alabama cavalry) appeared and stated that Mr. Vallandigham would not be received under a flag of truce or in any official manner, but that if he were set beyond our lines and approached those of the Confederate Army to request admittance he would be received and treated as any other citizen.

Feeling that it was necessary to dispose of him within the rebel lines I insisted upon the permission and it was granted to take him within a short distance of their lines where I delivered him to an orderly sent from the rebel lines to receive him. In the presence of Captain Goodwin and myself Mr. Vallandigham delivered himself up as a prisoner, stating that he was a citizen of the State of Ohio and the United States of America.

I am, general, very respectfully, your obedient servant,

WM. M. WILES,
Major and Provost-Marshal-General.

HEADQUARTERS ARMY OF THE POTOMAC,
Office of the Provost-Marshal-General, May 25, 1863.

Col. W. HOFFMAN, *Commissary-General of Prisoners.*

COLONEL: Major-General Reynolds, commanding First Army Corps, and whose command captured Lieutenant-Colonel Critcher, states that the prisoner should be retained in custody as long as possible. Colonel Critcher has undoubtedly been detailed to remain on the north side of the Rappahannock to organize bushwhacking parties and to furnish information of our movements to the enemy. One dispatch from him to General Lee was intercepted which led to his capture. There is not sufficient evidence to hold him as a spy but it is requested that every impediment possible be thrown in the way to prevent his exchange for some time to come.

Very respectfully, your obedient servant,

L. F. LYTTLE,
Captain and Provost-Marshal.

GENERAL ORDERS, ⎱   HDQRS. DEPT. OF THE CUMBERLAND,
No. 118.   ⎰   *Murfreesborough, Tenn., May 25, 1863.*

By direction of the General-in-Chief all officers of the Confederate Army who are now held as prisoners of war and any who may be hereafter captured will until further orders be placed in close confinement and strongly guarded; none will be paroled or exchanged.

By command of Major-General Rosecrans:

C. GODDARD,
Assistant Adjutant-General.

WASHINGTON, D. C., *May 26, 1863.*

Major-General HURLBUT, *Memphis:*

Tell General Grant to send captured officers to Sandusky and soldiers up the river for Camp Douglas or Fort Delaware. I will tell you which place to-morrow. Officers and men should be immediately separated.

H. W. HALLECK,
General-in-Chief

CINCINNATI, *May 26, 1863.*

PRESIDENT OF THE UNITED STATES:

The extension of time to Campbell and Lyle in justice requires the same extension to the others condemned to be hung on Johnson's Island next Friday, and I have therefore ordered that the executions be postponed one week till I can hear more definitely from you.

A. E. BURNSIDE,
Major-General.

HEADQUARTERS DEPARTMENT OF THE CUMBERLAND,
Murfreesborough, May 26, 1863.

Brig. Gen. L. THOMAS,
Adjutant-General U. S. Army, Washington, D. C.

GENERAL: I have the honor to inclose herewith a copy of a letter just received from Colonel Hoffman, commissary-general of prisoners, and to ask your attention in connection therewith to the marked passage in General Orders, No. 31, from these headquarters, series of 1862.

Colonel Hoffman's letter seems to convey the idea that it is not the wish of the Secretary that any persons who are or have been in the Confederate service should be treated otherwise than as prisoners of war. I desire specific instructions on this point as I am well assured that large numbers of men now in the Confederate Army, especially the Kentuckians, would desert if they were sure they would not be returned for exchange. As it is many deserters are admitted within our lines who express great unwillingness to be returned and who desire to become peaceable and law abiding citizens. Great care and judgment has to be exercised in liberating these men, but there is little room to doubt that in most cases their statements are true and the desires they express honest.

Very respectfully, your obedient servant,

W. S. ROSECRANS,
Major-General of Volunteers, Commanding Department.

[Inclosure No. 1.]

OFFICE COMMISSARY-GENERAL OF PRISONERS,
Washington, D. C., May 20, 1863.

Maj. Gen. W. S. ROSECRANS, *Murfreesborough, Tenn.*

GENERAL: The Secretary of War directs that unless specially authorized no Confederate prisoners of war will be released on condition of taking the oath of allegiance.

Very respectfully, your obedient servant,

W. HOFFMAN,
Colonel Third Infantry, Commissary-General of Prisoners.

NOTE IN PENCIL.—This letter was laid before General-in-Chief June 30. He had no instructions to give.

[Inclosure No. 2.]

GENERAL ORDERS, } HDQRS. FOURTEENTH ARMY CORPS,
　　　　　　　　　　　DEPARTMENT OF THE CUMBERLAND,
No. 31. 　　　　　　　*Nashville, Tenn., December 4, 1862.*

* 　　　* 　　　* 　　　* 　　　* 　　　* 　　　*

For this reason the general commanding is disposed to hold out every encouragement to these misguided men to lay down their arms, abandon the desperate cause in which they are embarked, return to their homes and families and resume once more the tranquil occupations of peace.

All that will be exacted of those who will honestly do so will be to take the non-combatant's parole and give proper security that they will keep it. So long as they faithfully observe this parole, obey the laws and deport themselves as peaceable citizens they shall not be molested by any officer or soldier belonging to this army.

    *   *   *   *   *   *   *

By command of Major-General Rosecrans:

JULIUS P. GARESCHÉ,
Assistant Adjutant-General and Chief of Staff.

FLAG-SHIP WABASH,
Port Royal Harbor, S. C., May 26, 1863.

Maj. Gen. D. HUNTER, *Comdg. Department of the South.*

GENERAL : I have read with great pleasure your letter of yesterday. It would have greatly pained me if any misapprehension should have interrupted the cordial relations which have ever marked our official intercourse, holding as we do such important commands on this coast, each of which has its special difficulties, and I am also certain that you would equally have regretted any such circumstance. I inclose a copy of the only letter I have written to the Navy Department on the subject of the prisoners in question. The reply to which dated the 13th instant, received 21st, informs me of the paroling of the officers of the Isaac Smith and directs me to send the prisoners to Lieut. Col. William H. Ludlow, at Fortress Monroe. I will continue to hold them on board the Vermont until I can inform the Department of your request to hold them as hostages. And I would respectfully recommend, general, that you follow your first intention of writing to the President or Secretary of War, for as the naval prisoners on this coast including the officers of the Isaac Smith and Flambeau have now been exchanged the Navy Department might have the intention of exchanging these men for naval prisoners in the West or elsewhere.

In the meantime I think their presence on board the Vermont will have all the moral effect you can desire and prevent any attempt on the part of the rebels carrying out what you and I would so quickly resent. You will ever find me ready to co-operate in any duties which may pertain to us in common and especially desire to express my heartfelt sympathy in those delicate circumstances of your command which you have so powerfully and clearly set forth in your interesting communication of last evening.

Perhaps I was not sufficiently particular in explaining to you that I had no other object in reference to the matter of the prisoners than to keep myself technically right with the Navy Department.

I have the honor to be, general, with great respect, your obedient servant,

S. F. DU PONT,
Rear-Admiral, Comdg. South Atlantic Blockading Squadron.

[Inclosure.]

FLAG-SHIP WABASH,
Port Royal Harbor, S. C., May 5, 1863.

Hon. GIDEON WELLES,
Secretary of the Navy, Washington, D. C.

SIR: I desire to call the attention of the Department to the officers of the Isaac Smith, captured on board of that vessel in Stono River, and who are now prisoners in Columbia jail, S. C., however, a military prison; and also to one of the officers of the Flambeau, Acting Master Sheldon, taken on Bull's Island.

There are at present on board the U. S. steamer Vermont nine prisoners, a sergeant and eight privates, captured on Edisto Island in April last by an armed expedition from the U. S. bark Kingfisher under Acting Master Dutch. Five at least of these prisoners, though only privates, belong to wealthy and influential families, and if the Department cannot effect an exchange for the officers of the Isaac Smith and the Flambeau at the North I might be able should the Department give me authority to effect that exchange here.

As at present advised I do not suppose I have authority either to exchange or parole prisoners without the consent of the Department. On this point I would be pleased to have instructions.

The names of the officers of the Isaac Smith and Flambeau who are now at the military prison, Columbia, so far as I have information, are: Acting Lieut. F. S. Conover, commanding; Acting Master J. W. Dicks, Acting Master Robert Tarr, Acting Ensign W. Chase, Acting Ensign F. J. Brenton, Acting Ensign H. S. Borden, Acting Assistant Paymaster F. C. Hills and Acting Third Assistant Engineer E. Barry, of the U. S. S. Isaac Smith, and Acting Master W. B. Sheldon, of the U. S. S. Flambeau.

The names of the prisoners on the Vermont are: Sergt. Townsend Mikell and Privates R. E. Seabrook, J. J. Wescoat, A. C. Lee, W. S. Murray, W. B. Whaley, H. M. Bailey, Joseph Edings and W. G. Baynard, of the Third South Carolina Cavalry.

Very respectfully, your obedient servant,

S. F. DU PONT,
Rear-Admiral, Comdg. South Atlantic Blockading Squadron.

HEADQUARTERS, *Jackson, Miss., May 26, 1863.*
Maj. Gen. ULYSSES S. GRANT, *Commanding U. S. Forces.*

GENERAL: I have the honor to acknowledge the receipt of your communication under flag of 21st instant.

I am directed by the general commanding the Army of Mississippi to assure you that the sick and wounded Federal officers and soldiers who have fallen or who by the casualties of war may hereafter fall into our hands will receive all the attention we can bestow.

There can be no possible objection to the military authorities of the United States bringing or sending supplies and medicines for their sick and wounded in our possession to outposts where military operations have recently taken place.

I avail myself of this opportunity to state that the friends and relatives of Maj. J. W. Anderson, the chief of artillery of General Stevenson's division who was wounded in the recent engagement at Baker's Creek, would be grateful for any information respecting him, whether wounded and if a prisoner in your hands.

I am, very respectfully, your obedient servant,

W. W. LORING,
Major-General, Commanding.

LOUISVILLE, KY., *May 26, 1863.*
Col. JOSEPH HOLT, *Judge-Advocate-General:*

Colonel Mundy, post commander here, has Doctor Cheatham and wife in custody until Mr. Cheatham is able to travel. Please telegraph him an order to hold them here until further orders from the War Department or General Rosecrans.

ANDREW JOHNSON,
Military Governor.

WAR DEPARTMENT, *Washington, May 26, 1863.*

Maj. Gen. W. S. ROSECRANS,
Comdg. Dept. of the Cumberland, Murfreesborough, Tenn.:

The Secretary of War has received your telegram of the 23d instant and directs that you proceed with the execution of the sentence against Doctor and Mrs. Cheatham.

ED. R. S. CANBY,
Brigadier-General and Assistant Adjutant-General.

WAR DEPARTMENT, *Washington, May 26, 1863.*

Colonel MUNDY, *Commanding, Louisville, Ky.:*

General Rosecrans reports that Doctor Cheatham and wife entertained a spy from General Morgan; sent letters and goods through lines and advised spy to dress in Federal uniform; go about city and learn and inform Morgan where our stores were located and where our troops were posted. General Rosecrans has been directed to proceed with the execution of this sentence. Please inform Governor Johnson. Duplicate by mail.

ED. R. S. CANBY,
Brigadier-General and Assistant Adjutant-General.

FORT MONROE, *May 26, 1863.*

Hon. G. V. FOX:

The officers and men of the Indianola have been released and are declared exchanged. The officers have arrived here and go to Annapolis to-night. The men went on Sunday night.

WM. H. LUDLOW,
Lieutenant-Colonel, &c.

FORT MONROE, *May 26, 1863.*

Col. W. HOFFMAN, *Commissary-General of Prisoners:*

Eighteen Confederate officers have been brought back to me from City Point by the officer in charge according to my instructions, equivalents in our own officers not having been delivered for them. I have sent them to Fort Norfolk. Thirty-six more of our officers came down from City Point this morning, the officers of the Indianola among them. The Confederates have retained Captain McKee and Lieutenant Shepherd for execution; also all of Colonel Streight's officers, about ninety-six in number. All our officers who have been delivered are declared exchanged. I send lists by mail this afternoon.

WM. H. LUDLOW,
Lieutenant-Colonel, &c.

WAR DEPARTMENT, *May 26, 1863.*

G. D. SHELDON, *Fort Monroe, Va.:*

Address and forward copy of General Halleck's telegram of 25th in relation to paroling Confederate officers to General Hunter, Department of the South, Port Royal, by first conveyance.

T. T. ECKERT,
Major and Assistant Superintendent U. S. Military Telegraph.

GENERAL ORDERS, }   HDQRS. SIXTEENTH ARMY CORPS,
No. 65.   }   *Memphis, Tenn., May 26, 1863.*

*   *   *   *   *   *   *

VIII. An entire year of occupation of this city by the United States has given abundant opportunity for all persons to make their deliberate election of the sovereignty to which they owe their allegiance. The so-called Confederate Congress by acts passed at an early period of the rebellion ordered peremptorily from the limits of the revolted States those true citizens who adhered to the country of their fathers. The same sentence will be pronounced after one year's patient waiting upon all who while denying their allegiance to the United States yet have found protection beneath its flag. These persons will be sent where their affections are.

IX. Giving aid and comfort to the public enemy is punishable with death and the leniency with which such persons have been treated must cease. Any person who shall hereafter offer insult by word or act to the United States or who shall express sympathy with the enemy or satisfaction at any imagined or real success of the Confederate arms will be arrested at once and severely punished.

*   *   *   *   *   *   *

By order of Maj. Gen. S. A. Hurlbut :

HENRY BINMORE,
Assistant Adjutant-General.

EXECUTIVE MANSION, *Washington, May 27, 1863.*

Major-General SCHENCK, *Baltimore, Md.:*

Let the execution of William B. Compton be respited or suspended till further orders from me, holding him in safe custody meanwhile. On receiving this notify me.

A. LINCOLN.

HEADQUARTERS DEPARTMENT OF THE SOUTH,
Hilton Head, S. C., May 27, 1863.

His Excellency A. LINCOLN,
President of the United States:

SIR: I have most urgently to request that orders may be issued to the Secretary of the Navy to cause to be turned over to me by Admiral S. F. Du Pont nine prisoners of war captured by an expedition from the U. S. bark Kingfisher on Edisto Island, S. C., and now held on board the U. S. S. Vermont, to be held by me as hostages against the execution of the retaliation resolutions passed by the late rebel Congress. Five of these nine prisoners are known to be the sons of some of the wealthiest and most influential rebels of the Sea Islands; and though we have no positive information as to the status of the remaining four it may be inferred from their association that they are the cadets of families from whom it would be of importance to hold hostages.

The retaliation resolutions announced by the Charleston Mercury and other semi official papers of the rebellion as having been passed by the late rebel Congress condemn to death if captured all white officers commanding or acting in concert with colored troops, thus condemning to death every officer of my command, and they further declare that colored soldiers shall not be held entitled to exchange or to the rights and usages of war. This declaration would seem to be only a formal announcement of what has for some time been the practice in the Western departments where many colored teamsters, laborers and servants employed by the army when captured by the enemy have been sold into slavery.

I submit that the flag should protect and cover all its defenders irrespective of their color and am well convinced that in this statement I only express your policy. I submit that until the retaliation resolutions of the rebel Congress shall have been formally disavowed by the Government at Richmond all exchanges of prisoners should cease, more especially in those departments where this class of soldiers is employed.

All prisoners captured and more particularly those of the aristocratic caste should be held as hostages to be hung man for man with any who may be executed by the rebels under the resolutions in question.

Five of the prisoners now on board the Vermont are of the best class to be held as hostages, their families being rich, powerful and malignant; and I could not but regard it as an act of great injustice to the officers and men of my command to have these "young darlings" of the South exchanged for an equal number of non-commissioned officers and privates captured elsewhere.

Begging most respectfully your favorable attention to the request of this letter, I have the honor to be, sir,

Very respectfully, your most obedient servant,
D. HUNTER,
Major-General, Commanding.

HEADQUARTERS DEPARTMENT OF THE SOUTH,
Hilton Head, Port Royal, S. C., May 27, 1863.

Hon. GIDEON WELLES,
Secretary of the Navy, Washington, D. C.

SIR: I have the honor to call your attention to certain prisoners now on board the U. S. S. Vermont, captured on Edisto Island in April last by an armed expedition from the U. S. bark Kingfisher and have most respectfully to ask under the peculiar circumstances of the case that these prisoners, nine in number, may be turned over to my custody.

From copies of the Charleston Mercury, regarded as a semi-official paper, and from extracts from the Richmond papers reproduced in the Northern press, it appears that the late rebel Congress passed an act condemning to death all white officers commanding or acting in concert with colored troops, thus in fact condemning to death all the white officers of this department, and further declaring that colored soldiers if captured should not be held subject to exchange as other prisoners of war.

Until this alleged act of the rebel Congress shall have been disproved or disavowed by the rebel Government I most respectfully but earnestly urge that all prisoners captured in this department whether by the Army or Navy shall be retained as hostages for the safety of the officers and troops under my command if captured by the enemy; the alleged act of the rebel Congress not declaring outlaws the officers of the Navy inasmuch as colored men in the Navy so far as I have any knowledge are not armed but are merely used as boat's crews and other laboring duties.   On this point it is possible that I may be misinformed, but if so the retaliation resolutions will then apply to the Navy as well as to the Army and will furnish an additional reason why these prisoners should not be exchanged, paroled or discharged from custody in this department.

Five at least of these prisoners as Admiral Du Pont has doubtless informed you are the sons of some of the wealthiest and most influential rebels on the Sea Islands—Seabrook, Edings, Baynard, &c.

With reference to the status of the others we have no positive information but from their association with the sons of those who owned the Sea Islands it may be fairly inferred that they are of families from which it may prove of importance to hold hostages.

At my earnest request Admiral Du Pont has agreed to hold them until your further instructions shall have been received.

I have the honor to be, sir, with the highest respect, your very obedient servant,

D. HUNTER,
Major-General, Commanding.

OFFICE COMMISSARY-GENERAL OF PRISONERS,
Washington, D. C., May 27, 1863.

Hon. EDWIN M. STANTON,
    Secretary of War, Washington, D. C.

SIR: I have the honor to inclose herewith a check for $36, the amount of the claim presented through the Department of State by M. M. Kimmey, U. S. consul at Monterey, Mexico, for money paid by him for the relief of destitute soldiers of the U. S. Army who having been taken prisoners of war in Texas made their escape from San Antonio and returned to the United States through Monterey. This money is advanced out of prisoners' fund in my possession. The account with the vouchers is retained in this office with a view to having the amount refunded out of allowances for commutation of rations about to be paid the parties concerned. I have the honor to return herewith the other papers submitted by the honorable Secretary of State through whom it would probably be safer to forward the checks.

Very respectfully, your obedient servant,

W. HOFFMAN,
Colonel Third Infantry, Commissary-General of Prisoners.

OFFICE COMMISSARY-GENERAL OF PRISONERS,
Washington, D. C., May 27, 1863.

Brig. Gen. JOHN S. MASON, *Commanding, Columbus, Ohio.*

GENERAL: I have the honor to acknowledge the receipt of your letter of the 21st instant and in reply beg to inform you that instructions have been given to generals commanding departments in relation to the validity of paroles, and they will doubtless communicate these instructions for the government of all subordinate commanders.

Very respectfully, your obedient servant,

W. HOFFMAN,
Colonel Third Infantry, Commissary-General of Prisoners.

HEADQUARTERS,
In Field, before Vicksburg, May 27, 1863.

Brig. Gen. P. J. OSTERHAUS,
Comdg. U. S. Forces, Big Black R. R. Bridge, Miss.

GENERAL: Your communication of this date inclosing dispatch* by flag of truce from Major-General Loring, of the Confederate Army, is received. Your action in requiring the Confederate officer bearing the dispatch to remain outside of our lines is approved.

You will please acknowledge the receipt of it and say that the major-general commanding the Army of the Tennessee knows nothing of Maj. J. W. Anderson about whom inquiry is made; that steps will be immediately taken to ascertain if he is in our lines a prisoner and his condition.

If any information should be obtained relative to him it will be communicated to his friends; add anything else in answer you may deem proper. A copy of the dispatch of General Loring to be answered is herewith inclosed.

By order of Major-General Grant:

JNO. A. RAWLINS,
Lieutenant-Colonel and Assistant Adjutant-General.

HDQRS. FIRST DIVISION, SIXTEENTH ARMY CORPS,
La Grange, Tenn., May 27, 1863.

Capt. [SOL. G.] STREET, C. S. Army.

SIR: Information has reached me from perfectly reliable sources that two of your men, Kesterson and Robinson, have been guilty of murdering two Union soldiers in cold blood who were prisoners in your hands.

Their excuse that the prisoners were trying to escape was so notoriously false that your own men heaped upon them the execration that they so richly deserve. These criminals, a disgrace to humanity, are within your reach and under your control, while six of your men are prisoners in my hands and thus far treated as prisoners of war. I will to-day order four of them put in irons to be shot if Kesterson and Robinson are not delivered into our hands within a reasonable length of time to suffer the penalty due to their infamous crime. If there is any indisputable proof that the charges against Kesterson and Robinson are false please send it to me and the men ironed shall be restored to the conditions of prisoners of war.†

WILLIAM SOOY SMITH,
Brigadier-General, Commanding First Division.

WASHINGTON, *May 28, 1863.*

MY DEAR SIR: Surg. S. F. Myers, of the Seventy-third Indiana Volunteers, a townsman of mine captured by Forrest in Georgia at

---

*See Loring to Grant, May 26, p. 709.
†See Street to Ruggles, June 4, 1863, p. 967.

the time Streight's brigade was taken, was released on parole and is now at Annapolis. The military officers of that brigade are all held by the rebels who refuse to exchange them. Five other surgeons of that same brigade are with him. Their regiments were all paroled and are now at Camp Chase, Columbus. These Western surgeons desire authority to report to the Surgeon-General here as to their treatment and to confer with the authorities here as to their brother officers so unjustly detained. I hope as their regiments are not with them you will grant this authority. If you will not for all I trust you will for the Indianians. I have several townsmen in Libby Prison. See names of surgeons on next page.

Yours, truly,

SCHUYLER COLFAX.

Western surgeons at Camp Parole, Annapolis, Md.: Surg. S. F. Myers, Seventy-third Indiana Volunteers; Asst. Surg. Wilson Pottenger, Seventy-third Indiana Volunteers; [Assistant] Surgeon King, Fifty-first Indiana Volunteers; Surg. W. L. Peck, Third Ohio Volunteers; Asst. Surg. T. C. Clason, Third Ohio Volunteers; [Asst.] Surg. A. Davidson, Forty-seventh Ohio Volunteers.

RICHMOND, VA., *May 28, 1863.*

Lieut. Col. WILLIAM H. LUDLOW, *Agent of Exchange.*

SIR: Your communications of the 25th have been received. That in relation to the execution of Captains McGraw and Corbin contains statements which I am sure upon further reflection you will retract. You say:

By your own admissions your officers and men have come within our lines ostensibly for the purpose of recruiting but really as spies.

I have never made any such admission. I have not done it in the cases of Captains McGraw and Corbin or in any other. All the information heretofore received both from your own side and our own people agreed as to the fact that these officers were engaged in a recruiting service and were tried and condemned for that reason. It would indeed be amazing if I had admitted them to be spies when I was not possessed of a single fact which would warrant such a conclusion.

You say that Captains McGraw and Corbin were executed upon conviction of being spies. More than three weeks ago I asked you for the records in these cases. You then promised to furnish them. You promised the same thing at our last interview. It has not been done yet. The unanimous statements of your newspaper press before, during and after trial, the order of General Burnside, the form of death inflicted upon these unfortunate men, all united in proclaiming that they were tried for recruiting within a State represented in our legislative councils and in the ranks of our Army. If they were tried as spies why were they shot instead of being hung? Will you say your military courts are so ignorant of the unvarying judgment pronounced by such tribunals upon spies as to make so strange a mistake? Even if the evidence showed them to be spies no military court had the right to convict them as such upon a charge of recruiting within your lines. No man even before a military tribunal can be convicted of a higher crime than that with which he is charged. In addition to all this it is within the knowledge of this Government that these officers were not in Kentucky as spies. They had no motive to go there as spies. The

Confederate authorities therefore in view of this array of facts and in the absence of conclusive proof to the contrary on the 22d of this month gave you notice that two captains would be selected for speedy execution in retaliation for the gross barbarity of which we complained. I now reiterate the same. The Confederate Government is too well satisfied of the justice of its proceeding in this matter to be in any manner deterred from the execution of its purpose by your threat that our officers in your hands "will be immediately put to death."

If any such issue is made whatever responsibilities or duties it imposes will be promptly met.

Respectfully, your obedient servant,

RO. OULD,
Agent of Exchange.

EXECUTIVE DEPARTMENT, *Springfield, Ill., May 29, 1863.*
Hon. E. M. STANTON, *Secretary of War, Washington.*

DEAR SIR: A number of citizens of Alabama, now residents of this State, have addressed me by letter asking me to interest myself in securing for citizens of Alabama, relatives and friends of theirs captured with Colonel Streight's command, the rights and immunities of prisoners of war. These men have claims upon the Government in this regard of the highest character. They have run fearful risks in their devotion to the Union and the Government should never desert them in their peril. Their lives are in danger but should a hair of their heads suffer instant retaliation should be enforced. I cannot help thus most forcibly pressing the claims of these noble men upon the protection of the Government and trust that you will immediately take such action as respects them as shall not fail to secure their safety.

I am, dear sir, most respectfully, your obedient servant,

RICHD. YATES,
Governor.

[First indorsement.]

WAR DEPARTMENT, *June 5, 1863.*

Referred to Major-General Hitchcock, commissioner for exchange of prisoners.

By order of the Secretary of War:

JAS. A. HARDIE,
Assistant Adjutant-General.

[Second indorsement.]

ANNAPOLIS, MD., *June 8, 1863.*

Everything possible under the circumstances has been done in this case. The question involved is plainly that which brought on the war and can only be ended with the war, to wit, the right of a State over its own people in denial of their obligations as citizens of the United States. Measures of mere retaliation beyond the refusal to make any further exchanges cannot determine this question. It can only be settled on the battle field. No further exchanges ought to be made until the men captured with Colonel Streight shall be restored.

E. A. HITCHCOCK,
Major-General of Vols., Commissioner for Exchange of Prisoners.

HEADQUARTERS, *Cincinnati, Ohio, May 29, 1863.*

His Excellency A. LINCOLN,
  President of the United States:

A messenger from Governor Morton came to me this morning in reference to the arrest by the military authorities of a citizen of Indiana. I understood from him that my action in the administration of affairs in this department was not approved by a single member of your Cabinet. This taken in connection with your dispatch to me several days ago approving of my course convinces me that my action here has been a source of embarrassment to you. My views as to the proper policy to be pursued in this department are only changed in the belief that the present policy should be increased in rigor. You know my views upon the subject of command and you must not allow me to stand in the way of the carrying out of any general policy which you may choose to adopt, and I should be glad to be relieved if the interest of the public service requires it but at the same time I am willing to remain and assume the responsibility of carrying out the policy which has been inaugurated if it is approved.

A. E. BURNSIDE,
Major-General.

WASHINGTON, D. C., *May 29, 1863.*

Major-General BURNSIDE, *Cincinnati, Ohio:*

Your dispatch of to-day received. When I shall wish to supersede you I will let you know. All the Cabinet regretted the necessity of arresting for instance Vallandigham—some perhaps doubting that there was a real necessity for it, but being done all are for seeing you through with it.

A. LINCOLN.

MEMPHIS, TENN., *May 29, 1863.*

Maj. Gen. H. W. HALLECK, *General-in-Chief:*

Forty-five hundred prisoners from Vicksburg have arrived this morning. Where shall I send them? General Grant has called for all spare infantry from this corps and I can scarcely furnish more than transportation guard by river and obey his late order.

S. A. HURLBUT,
Major-General, Commanding.

HEADQUARTERS OF THE ARMY,
  Washington, D. C., May 29, 1863.

Colonel HOFFMAN, *Commissary-General of Prisoners.*

COLONEL: Copy of the following telegram is respectfully furnished for your information:

WASHINGTON, D. C., *May 29, 1863.*

Major-General HURLBUT, *Memphis:*

The officers will be sent to Sandusky, and half of the men to Indianapolis and the other half to Fort Delaware, Del.

H. W. HALLECK,
General-in-Chief.

[H. W. HALLECK,
General-in-Chief.]

CINCINNATI, *May 29, 1863.*

General W. S. ROSECRANS:

Will you please forward by flag of truce the following dispatch to General Bragg? Please answer.

General BRAXTON BRAGG, *Commanding Army of Tennessee:*

Your letter in reference to John R. Lyle, convicted as a spy at Bowling Green, Ky., is received. The execution is deferred until further orders.

I take this opportunity to say that information has reached me that Captain McKee and another Federal officer are in close confinement in Richmond and sentenced to death in retaliation for the execution of McGraw and Corbin at Sandusky City. These two men were found within my lines in citizens' clothes recruiting for the enemies of my country. Every man so found will be tried and if convicted will suffer death.

Officers and soldiers taken in open warfare against my Government will be treated as prisoners of war. There can certainly be no complaint in your army of my treatment of such captives as I was the first general officer of our service who initiated a general system of parole by the release of the entire garrison captured on Roanoke Island, and I have ever since endeavored to treat prisoners of war according to the usages of modern warfare, but secret recruiting officers and spies as well as men from the country occupied by my forces who have become homesick and visit their families within our lines must expect to suffer death if caught and convicted by a court ordered by me, particularly if they are found in citizens' clothes. If they wish to spare their lives let them wear uniform, carry their arms and travel in a soldierly manner.

Every general in your army is at liberty to apply the same rule to my forces. I desire to make the following statement to the authorities at Richmond through you and ask you to forward it as the only means I have of communicating with them:

All officers of your army taken in open arms which I now hold and all that I may hereafter take will be placed at once in solitary confinement and there held till McKee and the other Federal officer now in Richmond are released in accordance with the cartel agreed upon, and for every officer of my department taken in open arms who suffers death by direction of your authorities in the way of retaliation or otherwise ten of your officers, and in the absence of officers to fill up the number I will take the relatives and sympathizers of the officers from this department now in your army.

This is not made as a threat but is established as a rule to be inflexibly observed in this department.

Hoping your authorities may be influenced to adopt the policy of carrying on this war according to the modern code of civilized warfare,

I remain, respectfully, yours,

A. E. BURNSIDE,
Major-General.

A. E. BURNSIDE,
Major-General.

HEADQUARTERS SIXTEENTH ARMY CORPS,
Memphis, Tenn., May 29, 1863.

Lieut. Col. JOHN A. RAWLINS, *Assistant Adjutant-General.*

COLONEL: I have the honor to report that Col. C. B. Lagow, aide-de-camp, reported to me early this morning with 4,408 prisoners. Pursuant to your orders the guard was relieved about 12 m. to-day and Colonel Lagow was verbally directed by me to send his guard down at once.

Colonel Lagow does not appear to have paid any attention to this duty or to have taken any care of the officers and men under his charge, nor even to have known how many men constituted the guard. He informed me that they were about 1,000 and were to go below on the Emerald. Although I considered 1,000 a very heavy load for the Emerald still I thought it might be done. Three boats left here to-day, the Champion, the Courier and another with State authorities, sanitary stores, &c., any of which could have taken 250 men and would have been thus guarded.

Colonel Lagow leaves for Vicksburg himself and Colonel Mansfield, Fifty-fourth Indiana, reports to me for orders, having received none. He reports 1,400 men. I have ordered all that can go on the Emerald to go on that boat; the remainder await transportation at Fort Pickering. Colonel Mansfield also reports that the prisoners have suffered for want of provisions.

I send them by order of General Halleck, officers to Sandusky, men, half to Indianapolis and half to Fort Delaware.

Very respectfully, your obedient servant,

S. A. HURLBUT,
Major-General.

OFFICE COMMISSARY-GENERAL OF PRISONERS,
Washington, D. C., May 29, 1863.
Maj. Gen. A. E. BURNSIDE,
Commanding Department of the Ohio, Cincinnati, Ohio.

GENERAL: I have the honor to inclose herewith a copy of a letter* which I addressed to the commander of the District of Eastern Kentucky in reply to two letters received from him reporting the release of prisoners. By a similar report of the release of prisoners of war from General White of May 12† made through your headquarters, which I have the honor to inclose herewith, it appears that the general puts a very different construction from mine upon the orders of the War Department referred to, and I have therefore respectfully to request that you will take such action in the matter as you may deem proper. As it now stands I have no means of knowing anything about the prisoners held in the Eastern District of Kentucky except as I receive occasionally a report from the officer in command of prisoners that he has released.

Very respectfully, your obedient servant,

W. HOFFMAN,
Colonel Third Infantry, Commissary-General of Prisoners.

OFFICE COMMISSARY-GENERAL OF PRISONERS,
Washington, D. C., May 29, 1863.
Maj. Gen. A. E. BURNSIDE,
Commanding Department of the Ohio, Cincinnati, Ohio.

GENERAL: I had yesterday the honor to communicate to you the authority of the General-in-Chief to transfer the Fifty-first and Seventy-third Indiana Regiments on parole at Camp Chase to Indianapolis until exchanged, and I have most respectfully to request you will direct the officer in command at that camp to which they are assigned to furnish me rolls of them with a return at the end of this month if the transfer is made in the meantime, and to furnish me hereafter such report as I may call for.

Very respectfully, your obedient servant,

W. HOFFMAN,
Colonel Third Infantry, Commissary-General of Prisoners.

---

* Omitted here; see Hoffman to Gallup, May 5, p. 558.
† See White to Thomas, p. 595.

RICHMOND, VA., *May 29, 1863.*

Lieut. Col. WILLIAM H. LUDLOW, *Agent of Exchange.*

SIR: The names of several Confederate officers including that of Colonel Morehead who were long since declared exchanged under our agreements appear upon one of your recent rolls. These officers were not delivered to us. I understand they are detained at or near Old Point. Are these officers to be delivered to us or not? One of them is a Confederate surgeon, Doctor Read. Do you intend to retain surgeons?

There is not a single Federal officer in our custody who has been declared exchanged unless it may be Rucker and for him you hold Doctor Green. On what pretense are these officers held? I will be obliged to you if you will inform me what course you intend to pursue in reference to such cases.

Respectfully, your obedient servant,

RO. OULD,
Agent of Exchange.

BALTIMORE, MD., *May 29, 1863.*

Brigadier-General KELLEY, *Harper's Ferry, Va.:*

Captain Baylor, rebel army, will be placed in close confinement according to orders.

By order:

W. H. CHESEBROUGH,
Assistant Adjutant-General.

MURFREESBOROUGH, *May 30, 1863.*

Major-General HALLECK:

There are 600 men of Willich's brigade, 200 from Thirty-ninth Indiana alone, loafing around Indianapolis and Cincinnati. Please issue general orders releasing all paroled soldiers belonging to this army.

W. S. ROSECRANS,
Major-General.

OFFICE CHIEF COMMISSARY OF SUBSISTENCE,
Saint Louis, Mo., May 30, 1863.

Lieut. Col. A. V. COLBURN,
Asst. Adjt. Gen., Hdqrs. Dept. of the Missouri, Saint Louis, Mo.

COLONEL: I have the honor to invite the attention of the general commanding to what I deem the unauthorized and improper expenditure of the "prison fund" at the military prisons in this city. I find upon the examination of the accounts that shovels, spades, blankets, handcuffs, leg irons, padlocks, hammers, planes, window guards, iron doors, &c., are charged to this fund and the accounts have been paid. This fund arises from savings of rations and is intended to be expended for the health and comfort of the prisoners and not for articles which should be furnished by the Quartermaster's Department.

Very respectfully, your obedient servant,

T. J. HAINES,
Colonel and Commissary of Subsistence.

Give orders to correct this error.

J. M. S.

HEADQUARTERS DEPARTMENT OF VIRGINIA,
Fort Monroe, May 30, 1863.
Brig. Gen. L. THOMAS, *Adjutant-General U. S. Army.*

GENERAL: I have the honor to report that the following officers and men have been declared duly exchanged as prisoners of war since the announcement in General Orders, No. 117, of May 9, 1863:

1. All officers, naval and military, delivered at City Point up to May 30, 1863.

2. All the officers and men of the steamers Hatteras, Mercedita, Queen of the West, Harriet Lane, Isaac Smith, Columbia, Indianola and schooner Vassar.

3. All the officers and enlisted men captured and paroled at Holly Springs, Miss., in December, 1862.

4. All the officers and enlisted men of the Seventy-first Regiment Indiana Volunteers captured at Muldraugh's Hill, Ky., in December, 1862.

5. All the officers and enlisted men of the Ninety-first Regiment Illinois Volunteers captured at Elizabethtown, Ky., in December, 1862.

6. All the officers and enlisted men captured at Mount Sterling, Ky., March, 1863.

7. All the officers and enlisted men of the Fifty-first Regiment Indiana Volunteers, of the Seventy-third Regiment Indiana Volunteers, of the Third Regiment Ohio Volunteers, of the Eightieth Regiment Illinois Volunteers and of the First Tennessee Cavalry, forming part of Streight's brigade and captured near Cedar Bluff, Ga., about the 1st of May, 1863.

8. All persons specially exchanged and who have been specially notified of such exchange either individually or through their commanding officer.

I am, very respectfully, your obedient servant,
WM. H. LUDLOW,
Lieutenant-Colonel and Agent for Exchange of Prisoners.

(Copy to the Secretary of the Navy.)

WAR DEPARTMENT, *Washington, D. C., May 31, 1863.*
Major-General ROSECRANS, *Murfreesborough:*

All exchanged prisoners have been ordered to their regiments. Paroled prisoners cannot be released and ordered to their regiments till exchanged.

H. W. HALLECK,
General-in-Chief.

CINCINNATI, OHIO, *May 31, 1863.*
General H. W. HALLECK, *General-in-Chief:*

Your dispatch received. I had already given the order several days ago but the commissary-general of prisoners held the men until they could be paid, and it has been understood at these camps that the prisoners were under the immediate control of the commissary-general of prisoners.

A. E. BURNSIDE,
Major-General.

CINCINNATI, *May 31, 1863.*

General AMMEN, *Springfield, Ill.*
General HASCALL, *Indianapolis, Ind.*
General BOYLE, *Louisville, Ky.:*

All Confederate officers now held as prisoners of war in this department will be placed in close confinement and no exchange will be made or allowed till further orders.

A. E. BURNSIDE,
Major-General.

MURFREESBOROUGH, TENN., *May 31, 1863.*

Maj. Gen. H. W. HALLECK, *General-in-Chief:*

There are 200 men belonging to the Thirty-ninth Indiana and 400 more of Willich's brigade detained at Indianapolis. There are also large numbers in the aggregate now at other parole camps in the North belonging to my command who have been exchanged and yet I cannot get them back. Will you please issue orders to have them returned?

W. S. ROSECRANS,
Major-General.

MURFREESBOROUGH, TENN., *May 31, 1863.*

Maj. Gen. H. W. HALLECK, *General-in-Chief:*

I understand from the commissioner for exchange that Coburn's brigade and all the prisoners captured at Stone's River are exchanged. Sheridan alone reports 600 men not returned though exchanged. The habit appears to be to let them go home after exchange.

W. S. ROSECRANS,
Major-General.

MEMPHIS, TENN., *May 31, 1863.*

Brigadier-General BUFORD:

Forty-four hundred prisoners and guard of 400 under Lieutenant-Colonel Spaulding left here yesterday for Cairo. Provide transportation by railroad to Indianapolis for the whole, not to change cars if possible, and telegraph to officer in charge at Indianapolis at what time they will leave. Half of the men will remain at Indianapolis and half proceed to Fort Delaware, officers to Sandusky. The division will be made and rolls perfected at Indianapolis. Colonel Spaulding's guard will take them to their several destinations. You will see that they are properly provisioned and permit no intercourse between the prisoners and citizens. Give Colonel Spaulding copy of this dispatch.

S. A. HURLBUT,
Major-General.

CITY POINT, *May 31, 1863.*

Lieut. Col. WILLIAM H. LUDLOW, *Agent of Exchange.*

SIR: I call your attention again to a matter of which I often heretofore complained. By to-day's arrival you have sent several citizens as prisoners of war and several discharged soldiers as also prisoners of war.

One of the men, T. H. Moreland, is put down as belonging to the First Kentucky Cavalry who never was in our service in any sort of capacity in his life; who never was in the field and not even a guerrilla or bushwhacker. Captain Mulford heard his statement. He says he was compelled to sign a parole at Louisville as a member of the First Kentucky Cavalry under a threat if he did not so do he would be put in prison with ball and chain during the war. He protested against it in the hearing of more than fifty men here who were here this very day. There are four or five other cases of exactly the same sort in your roll delivered to me this day.

The memoranda are made on your roll. Is this to be allowed?

Respectfully, your obedient servant,

RO. OULD,
Agent of Exchange.

———

EXECUTIVE MANSION, *Washington, June 1, 1863.*

Colonel LUDLOW, *Fort Monroe:*

Richardson and Browne, correspondents of the Tribune captured at Vicksburg, are detained at Richmond. Please ascertain why they are detained and get them off if you can.

A. LINCOLN.

———

FORT MONROE, VA., *June 1, 1863.*

His Excellency A. LINCOLN,
President of the United States:

Your telegram is received. Everything will be done that can be done to obtain the release of the parties named.

WM. H. LUDLOW,
Lieutenant-Colonel and Agent for Exchange of Prisoners.

———

WAR DEPARTMENT, *Washington, June 1, 1863.*

Maj. Gen. A. E. BURNSIDE,
Commanding Department of the Ohio.

GENERAL: The President replied briefly to your telegram of the 29th of May, and upon consultation in regard to the subject it refers to he desires me to say that his attention has been directed to various orders and letters made by Brigadier-General Hascall, commanding in the State of Indiana, some of which are herewith inclosed, and to submit to your consideration whether it would not be better to withdraw General Hascall from that command.* Whatever dissatisfaction there may exist in the State of Indiana or in other States north of

———

*See Series I, Vol. XXIII, Part II, p. 369, for Morton to Stanton and Davis to Stanton recommending the removal of Hascall.

the Ohio within your department is liable to be increased by the presence of an indiscreet military officer, who will unnecessarily interfere with the political condition of the State and produce irritation by assuming military powers not essential to the preservation of the public peace. Great care is to be exercised in those States not to excite the apprehensions of the State Executives who are loyal and diligent in maintaining the authority of the Government.

Governor Morton has been distinguished for the zeal, ability and patriotism which he has on every occasion manifested during this war, and the necessity for a good understanding with him and with the Executives of Ohio and Illinois the President feels sure will not be underrated by you. So far as it can be done with safety to the Government it is well to leave the administration within those States to their respective Governors and to consult them in regard to any coercive measures in respect to persons not in the military service or not engaged in actual hostility. Their familiarity with the temper of the people will enable you to judge to what extent such measures may or may not be advisable. It is not designed by the President to restrict you in the powers exercised by the commanders of other military departments but only to make such suggestions as are thought to be expedient for the public service. The natural aversion of our people to the exercise of military powers without necessity will be greatly stimulated by any feeling in the State Executives that the General Government is disposed to interfere in matters of administration which properly belong to them or which they are able to manage. The proper limit of military power in such cases is at their request to aid and not supersede the State authority.

No one can understand better than yourself what harm may be done by an indiscreet or foolish military officer, who is constantly issuing military proclamations and engaging in newspaper controversies upon questions that agitate the public mind. For this reason it is thought by the President that General Hascall is not adapted to the service in which he is engaged in the State of Indiana, and that if there be a necessity for a military officer in that State his place can be supplied by one of more prudence and discretion than he manifests.

The subject is commended by the President to your considerate judgment as one requiring immediate attention. It is not expected that with the arduous and responsible duties of your office you will be able under any circumstances to satisfy every one. The utmost that can be expected is to avoid unnecessary irritation.

Yours, truly,

EDWIN M. STANTON,
Secretary of War.

P. S.—Since writing the above letter the President has been informed that you have suppressed the publication or circulation of the Chicago Times in your department. He directs me to say that in his judgment it would be better for you to take an early occasion to revoke that order. The irritation produced by such acts is in his opinion likely to do more harm than the publication would do. The Government approves of your motives and desires to give you cordial and efficient support. But while military movements are left to your judgment, upon administrative questions such as the arrest of civilians and the suppression of newspapers not requiring immediate action the President desires to be previously consulted.

EDWIN M. STANTON,
Secretary of War.

[Inclosure No. 1.—Extract from New York Times.]

INTERESTING CORRESPONDENCE BETWEEN AN EDITOR AND A BRIGADIER-GENERAL ON ORDERS, NO. 9, ETC.

Some days since the editors of the Express received a letter from Brig. Gen. Milo S. Hascall, dated Indianapolis. Never having heard of this military gentleman until his now famous Orders, No. 9, came out we thought that when he sent us the following letter somebody was making a fool of him and his profession and therefore we wrote to inquire if the letter was genuine or a forgery. In a scurrilous reply he admits the letter to be genuine. We therefore publish the letter and our reply,* which we have mailed for him to-day:

HEADQUARTERS DISTRICT OF INDIANA, *Indianapolis, May 5, 1863.*
To the EDITORS OF THE NEW YORK EXPRESS.

GENTLEMEN: Some one has been kind enough to inclose me a slip from your paper containing a copy of my Orders, No. 9, and your remarks thereon. They are exceedingly witty and smart, and in your judgment probably dispose of the whole case. It may surprise you some to know that the order was issued after mature deliberation and consultation and is being and will be carried out to the letter. It is fortunate for you that your paper is not published in my district.
Very truly, yours,   MILO S. HASCALL.

[Inclosure No. 2.]

HEADQUARTERS DISTRICT OF INDIANA,
Indianapolis, May 8, 1863.
EDITOR OF COLUMBIA CITY NEWS.

SIR: A copy of your paper of May 5 has been handed me and my attention called to your comments on General Orders, No. 9, from these headquarters. You can now take your choice—publishing an article taking back your threats of resistance to that order and your comments designed to destroy its usefulness and hereafter publish a loyal paper or you can discontinue the publication of your paper until further orders. Any violation of this order will receive prompt attention.
MILO S. HASCALL,
Brigadier-General of Volunteers, Commanding District.

[Inclosure No. 3.]

HEADQUARTERS DISTRICT OF INDIANA,
Indianapolis, May 8, 1863.
EDITOR OF SOUTH BEND FORUM, *South Bend, Ind.:*

A half dozen copies of your paper of the 3d instant have been sent to me marked, in which you boast of your intention to violate General Orders, No. 9, from these headquarters. You can now publish an order retracting all this and publish a loyal paper hereafter or you can discontinue its publication till further orders. A violation of this notice will receive immediate attention.
MILO S. HASCALL,
Brigadier-General of Volunteers, Commanding District.

[Inclosure No. 4.]

HEADQUARTERS DISTRICT OF INDIANA,
Indianapolis, May 11, 1863.
E. VAN LONG, Esq., *Editor Warsaw Union:*
I have received a copy of your paper of the 8th instant in which you boldly proclaim your intention to violate Orders, No. 9. My object in

* Reply not found.

addressing you is to give you a fair warning and to give you an opportunity to retract the objectionable matter in your paper of the 8th. A failure to attend promptly to this admonition will not be overlooked.

I am, sir, yours, very truly,

MILO S. HASCALL,
Brigadier-General of Volunteers, Commanding District.

WAR DEPARTMENT, *Washington, D. C., June 1, 1863.*

Major-General BURNSIDE, *Cincinnati:*

You will see that all exchanged prisoners in your department are immediately sent to their regiments. The Governors of States can exercise no control over such exchanged prisoners. Your particular attention is called to General Orders, No. 117, May 9.

H. W. HALLECK,
General-in-Chief.

(Same to General Schofield, Saint Louis.)

WAR DEPARTMENT, *Washington, D. C., June 1, 1863.*

Major-General ROSECRANS, *Murfreesborough:*

General Orders, No. 117, May 9, covers the case of all exchanged prisoners. Generals Burnside and Schofield have been directed to see that this order is immediately carried into effect.

H. W. HALLECK,
General-in-Chief.

HEADQUARTERS, *Saint Louis, June 1, 1863.*

H. W. HALLECK, *General-in-Chief:*

I have sent all exchanged men to their regiments and all officers except a few whose men are not exchanged.

J. M. SCHOFIELD,
Major-General.

SAN FRANCISCO, CAL., *June 1, 1863.*

Hon. E. M. STANTON:

Secretary's telegraph* of 30th of May received. Alfred Rubery from the evidence is one of the principals in the Chapman affair. Correspondence with sympathizers in victories was conducted by him. He is in confinement at Alcatraz Island. The case is in hands of the U. S. district attorney. No facts have been elicited showing him to be an object of Executive clemency. The feeling here is strong against all such actions.

G. WRIGHT,
Brigadier-General, Commanding.

CINCINNATI, OHIO, *June 1, 1863.*

General AMMEN, *Springfield, Ill.:*

I have issued an order suppressing the Chicago Times. You will please see that no more publications of it are made, and if necessary you will take military possession of the office.

A. E. BURNSIDE,
Major-General.

---

* Not found.

HEADQUARTERS FIRST DIVISION,
Harper's Ferry, Va., June 1, 1863.

Lieut. Col. W. H. CHESEBROUGH,
Assistant Adjutant-General, Baltimore, Md.

COLONEL : I have the honor to report that on or about the 26th day of April, 1863, near Burlington, Hampshire County, Va., a detachment of Seventh Virginia Cavalry, under Captain Kuykendall, C. S. Army, captured Lieut. W. T. Singleton, regimental quartermaster First [West] Virginia, Lieut. D. F. Gordon, regimental quartermaster Fifty-fourth Pennsylvania Volunteers, Lieut. H. A. Myers, Ringgold Cavalry, and Private John A. Meeks of same command.

At and shortly after the capture it was proposed to release these prisoners upon parole, and this led to a discussion of the general order of the major-general commanding declaring inoperative paroles taken in violation of the cartel of exchange. The Federal officers gave their decided opinion that such parole would not be regarded by "their military superiors as of binding effect." They were kept for over two days among the mountains in the neighborhood by a detachment of the rebel cavalry, forced to travel at night from one point to another resting a few hours in daytime, and without adequate clothing or other protection against the weather, until wearied out they consented to give the usual parole with the addition that if not recognized by the Federal authorities they would report themselves within the enemy's lines for exchange.

They desire to be fully advised regarding the course proper to be pursued ; whether they shall return to duty with their commands or report in pursuance of their parole or whether they can be exchanged without such action on their part. They regard the parole given under these circumstances as binding and express some delicacy in going to duty until exchanged.

I am, very respectfully, your obedient servant,
B. F. KELLEY,
Brigadier-General.

[First indorsement.]

BALTIMORE, *June 3, 1863.*

Respectfully referred to Colonel Hoffman, commissary-general of prisoners, with request for his instructions.

This I suppose to be one of those irregular paroles which ought, however, to be recognized as binding because of the peculiar circumstances of the case. I forward this special report therefore in accordance with the last clause of the letter of instructions received by me from the commissary-general of prisoners dated May 20, 1863.

ROBERT C. SCHENCK,
Major-General, Commanding.

[Second indorsement.]

OFFICE COMMISSARY-GENERAL OF PRISONERS,
June 6, 1863.

This is one of those cases where it is left for the major-general commanding to decide whether the parole shall be recognized or not. If it is held as binding the parties should be sent to Camp Parole to await their exchange. On the 22d ultimo Mr. Ould, the Confederate agent for exchange, was notified that from that date no paroles would be binding except such as were given under the stipulations of the seventh article of the cartel.

Respectfully returned:

W. HOFFMAN,
Colonel Third Infantry, Commissary-General of Prisoners.

HDQRS. DISTRICT OF CAIRO, *Cairo, Ill., June 1, 1863.*

Major General BURNSIDE, *Commanding:*

Four boats have this day arrived from Memphis with 4,400 prisoners of war of whom 180 are officers. General Hurlbut's order to me is to send them all by rail to Indianapolis, at which place half of the enlisted men are to be confined, the other half sent to Fort Delaware and all the officers to Sandusky. The Illinois Central Railroad will transport all the prisoners to Indianapolis without change of cars. They are under charge of Lieutenant-Colonel Spaulding, Twenty-seventh Ohio Volunteers, with 400 men for guard. I shall provide attendance for the prisoners who are too sick to bear removal. The whole will be sent forward in four trains, two to-day and two to-morrow. I telegraph you to-day, also the commanding officer at Indianapolis, but write more fully.

I have the honor to be, your obedient servant,

N. B. BUFORD,
Brigadier-General.

OFFICE COMMISSARY-GENERAL OF PRISONERS,
Washington, D. C., June 1, 1863.

Brig. Gen. L. THOMAS, *Adjutant-General, Washington, D. C.*

GENERAL: I have the honor to inform you that the following officers and enlisted men, prisoners of war, have been declared exchanged, viz:

1. All officers delivered at City Point on the 14th, 23d and 25th May, 1863. 2. Enlisted men captured near Holly Springs, Miss., December 20, 1862 3. Ninety-first Regiment Illinois Volunteers, captured at Bacon Creek and Nolin, Ky., December 26, 1862; Elizabethtown, Ky., December 27, 1862, and Muldraugh's Hill, Ky., December 28, 1862. 4. Seventy-first Regiment Indiana Volunteers, captured at Muldraugh's Hill, Ky., December 28, 1862. 5. Enlisted men captured at Mount Sterling, Ky., 22d and 23d March, 1863. 6. Fifty-first and Seventy-third Regiments Indiana Volunteers, Third Regiment Ohio Volunteers, Eightieth Regiment Illinois Volunteers, and two companies First Tennessee cavalry, of Streight's brigade, captured near Cedar Bluff, Ga.

Generally the officers exchanged belong to troops still on parole, who are now at Camp Parole or the Convalescent Camp, and it will be necessary to detain a portion of them at these camps to take charge of their men. As soon as I am informed of the number of paroled men of each regiment present I will be able to designate those who may be ordered to duty in the field.

Very respectfully, your obedient servant,

W. HOFFMAN,
Colonel Third Infantry, Commissary-General of Prisoners.

FORT MONROE, *June 1, 1863.*

Colonel HOFFMAN:

Please answer my questions about prisoners at Washington. The flag-of-truce boat has just returned from City Point and can go to

Washington if the number of prisoners there demand it. Has the execution of William B. Compton, sentenced to be hung as a spy, been suspended?

WM. H. LUDLOW,
Lieutenant-Colonel.

WASHINGTON, *June 1, 1863.*

Lieut. Col. W. H. LUDLOW,
Commissioner for Exchange of Prisoners:

About 200 prisoners of war at Old Capitol and some citizens and 140 prisoners left Louisville May 25. The papers say the execution of W. B. Compton has been suspended. I can learn nothing officially.

W. HOFFMAN,
Commissary-General of Prisoners.

CITY POINT, *June 1, 1863.*

Lieut. Col. WILLIAM H. LUDLOW, *Agent of Exchange.*

SIR: I was about proceeding to Fortress Monroe or as near to it as I would be allowed to go when Captain Mulford came up the river. I am afraid your proceeding in relation to declarations of the exchange of your men will lead to complication and difficulty. The Holly Springs capture according to my recollection pays off the number due to you at our last interview. You have not sent more than 600 since including to-day's arrival. For that number you declare exchanged five regiments (Ninety-first Illinois, Fifty-first Indiana, Seventy-third Indiana, Third Ohio and Eightieth Illinois), also the captures at Mount Sterling and the men of the Indianola.

How many the Mount Sterling capture are I do not know but I am very sure the aggregate of the above greatly exceeds the balance due to you.

I protest against the declarations of exchange where the number is not known and agreed upon by us. You can readily perceive without my statement what grave objections might be made to such a proceeding. Why not make exchanges by rolls of which we can have a copy and in relation to which we have mutually agreed as in the Holly Springs capture? How am I to know how many men of the Eightieth Illinois Regiment were taken prisoners or when or where they were captured? I throw out these observations as suggestions for your reflection. I think you will agree with me that when we or you are in excess of prisoners neither party should declare any exchange except where the lists have been adjusted between us and the number declared to be exchanged known and agreed on between us. I do not so much object to your over-running the number due to you as the certainty of great complication and prospect of misunderstanding by pursuing the course you have done in this case.

You have not given me any reply even yet to my inquiries in relation to your declaration of exchange as to parties captured at Muldraugh's Hill or the Sixty-sixth Indiana. I hope I shall not be compelled to wait much longer.

Respectfully, your obedient servant,

RO. OULD,
Agent of Exchange.

WHEELING, VA., *June 1, 1863.*

Lieut. Col. W. H. CHESEBROUGH,
        Assistant Adjutant-General.

SIR: On the 21st ultimo I had the honor to submit the case of Rev. Daniel O'Connor, late Catholic priest at Weston, Va., sent here as a prisoner by order of Brigadier-General Roberts. Mr. O'Connor has solicited to-day an early decision regarding himself. As he does not hesitate to follow in the footsteps of his bishop and declares his sympathy with the rebels while claiming that he is not an American citizen, I respectfully suggest that he be ordered to leave this State, and if possible that he be directed to leave the United States. He has relatives in Canada.

Very respectfully,

JOS. DARR, JR.,
        Major and Military Commander.

SAINT LOUIS, *June 1,* [1863.]

His Excellency H. R. GAMBLE, *Governor of Missouri.*

GOVERNOR: I have the honor to acknowledge the receipt of your letter of this date concerning the case of Mrs. Polk in her being sent through our lines. I fully appreciate the service which it would be to Mrs. Polk to be sent toward Little Rock, and spoke to Major-General Schofield on the subject in reference to Mrs. Polk and others who desire to go to the Rock instead of being sent east of the river, but it was deemed inexpedient to take that course for the reason among others that it would be unsafe in a military point of view to permit these persons to remain on our immediate border, and because Vicksburg falling in a short time we should find Arkansas itself within our lines. I think Your Excellency will when looking upon this question in this light agree with this decision, for at this time above all others it is desirable that the military commanders in Arkansas should not be possessed of such information as Mrs. Polk and others of her intelligence and means of observation would be able to communicate.

I have the honor to be, very respectfully, your obedient servant,

JAMES F. DWIGHT,
        Captain and Provost-Marshal-General.

OLD CAPITOL PRISON, *Washington, June 1, 1863.*

Capt. W. T. HARTZ, *Assistant Adjutant-General.*

SIR: The number of prisoners of war now at Old Capitol Prison is 185.

Respectfully, your obedient servant,

WM. P. WOOD,
        Superintendent Old Capitol Prison.

OFFICE PROVOST-MARSHAL-GENERAL,
        New Orleans, June 2, 1863.

Maj. Gen. JOHN A. DIX, *Comdg. Dept. of Virginia.*

GENERAL: There will be sent by the steamer Cahawba, in charge of Colonel Wilson, Sixth New York Volunteers, forty-six Confederate officers, prisoners of war, to be landed at Fort Monroe. The rebel leaders at Richmond have excepted from exchange such U. S. officers serving in this department as may be captured by their forces and they propose to turn them over to the authorities of the rebel States for execution.

I respectfully suggest that the rebel officers now sent may be held until the final determination of the rebels in respect to officers of the United States captured in this department shall have been ascertained.

I have the honor to be, general, your obedient servant,

JAMES BOWEN,
Brigadier-General, Provost-Marshal-General.

Four Confederate officers have just arrived and I have orders to send them, which will make a total of fifty.

C. W. KILLBORN,
Provost-Marshal New Orleans.

HEADQUARTERS, *New Orleans, June 2, 1863.*

Lieutenant-Colonel VAN BUREN,
Assistant Adjutant-General, Fort Monroe.

COLONEL: Since directing Colonel Cassidy to take these prisoners to New York I have received orders to send them to Fort Monroe. There are forty-six of them, all officers of the Confederate service captured in this department, and duplicate rolls are inclosed herewith. I suppose they will not be and should not be exchanged until the decree issued by the Confederate authorities is revoked which directs all Federal officers captured in this department to be retained.

I have the honor to be, your obedient servant,

W. H. EMORY,
Brigadier-General, Commanding.

[Inclosure.]

Roll of commissioned officers captured in the Department of the Gulf, at New Orleans, sent to Fort Monroe.

Capt. J. J. Atkinson, gun-boat Hart; Lieut. Samuel Alston, Crescent Regiment; Lieut. W. H. Andrews, First Alabama Regiment; Lieut. T. N. Brown, Lee Battery; Lieut. B. F. Broyles, Seventh Texas Cavalry; Lieut. A. Brugnions, Crescent Regiment; Lieut. E. A. Carmouche, Fourth Louisiana Volunteers; Capt. D. T. Crath [?], General Beauregard's staff; Lieut. C. L. Camford, Eleventh Louisiana Cavalry; Lieut. J. Dubecq, gun-boat Diana; Lieut. D. N. Estes, Ninth Tennessee Cavalry [Battalion]; Capt. G. L. Fusilier, General Taylor's staff; Capt. E. W. Fuller, Queen of the West; Lieut. H. L. Fisk, Beauregard Regiment; Capt. J. Gieseck, Fourth Texas Cavalry; Lieut. Charles Gilbeau, Thirtieth Louisiana Volunteers; Capt. E. Holmes, Crescent Regiment; Capt. G. W. Holloway, Eleventh Louisiana Battalion; Lieut. J. Hinson, Miles Legion; Lieut. D. M. C. Hughes, Miles Legion; Lieut. R. S. Jackson, Eighth Louisiana Volunteers; Lieut. W. G. Jeter, Fourth Louisiana Volunteers; Lieut. J. D. Kirkland, Ninth Louisiana Battalion; Lieut. Samuel W. Kelsey, Tenth Arkansas Regiment; Capt. J. H. Long,

Fourth Texas Cavalry; Lieut. William H. Lilley, Tenth Arkansas Regiment; Lieut. T. D. Melville, Eighteenth Louisiana Volunteers; Capt. F. J. McLean, Ninth Tennessee Cavalry [Battalion]; Purser E. McGowen, gun-boat Diana; Lieut. J. M. Mobley, First Choctaw Battalion; Lieut. A. P. Morse, Ordnance Corps; Lieut. J. M. Musselman, Fourteenth Louisiana Volunteers; Capt. Ludwick W. Mathews, Fifteenth Arkansas Regiment; Lieut. William S. Nelson, Crescent Regiment; Lieut. David A. Nation, Fifteenth Arkansas Regiment; Lieut. Z. M. Porter, Arizona Battalion; Capt. W. H. Pruett, First Alabama Regiment; Lieut. Charles Roussel, Tenth Louisiana Volunteers; Lieut. W. H. Rogers, Crescent Regiment; Capt. O. J. Semmes, light artillery; Capt. E. A. Scott, Ninth Louisiana Battalion; Lieut. A. Schlick, Fourth Texas Cavalry; Lieut. John M. Smith, Arizona Brigade; Lieut. G. W. Stafford, Eighth Louisiana Volunteers; Lieut. John Webre, Twenty-eighth Louisiana Volunteers; Lieut. William Welsh, Arizona Battalion; Lieut. H. W. Wilkinson, Steede's battalion; Col. Allen R. Witt, Tenth Arkansas Regiment; Capt. J. B. Wolf, Fourteenth Arkansas; Capt. J. W. Youngblood, General Gardner's staff.

[First indorsement.]

OFFICE PROVOST-MARSHAL,
New Orleans, June 2, 1863.

I do hereby certify that I have this day by order of Brigadier-General Bowen, provost-marshal-general Department of the Gulf, delivered to Lieutenant-Colonel Cassidy, Sixth New York Regiment Volunteers, the above-named fifty commissioned officers of the C. S. Army to be conveyed by him to Fort Monroe and there delivered to Maj. Gen. John A. Dix, commanding Department of Virginia.

C. W. KILLBORN,
Captain and Provost-Marshal, New Orleans.

Received this day of Capt. C. W. Killborn, provost-marshal Parish of Orleans, the above-named fifty commissioned officers of the C. S. Army.

J. W. BURGESS,
Major Sixth New York Volunteers, Commanding.

[Second indorsement.]

HEADQUARTERS DEPARTMENT OF VIRGINIA,
Fort Monroe, June 8, 1863.

These prisoners of war, fifty in all, are to be sent to Fort Delaware together with the others (officers) now confined in Fort Norfolk and not exchanged pursuant to instructions from the War Department.

By command of Major-General Dix:

D. T. VAN BUREN,
Assistant Adjutant-General.

HEADQUARTERS VALLEY DISTRICT, June 2, 1863.
Major-General MILROY,
Commanding U. S. Forces, Winchester, Va.

GENERAL: I am instructed by General Lee to send you the inclosed communication.

I have the honor to be, very respectfully, &c.,

A. G. JENKINS,
Brigadier-General, Commanding.

[Inclosure.]

GENERAL ORDERS, ⎞ HDQRS. ARMY OF NORTHERN VIRGINIA,
No. 67.   ⎠   *May 26, 1863.*

A general order lately issued by General Schenck, commanding U. S. forces in the Department of Maryland (General Orders, No. 21, Middle Department, March 29, 1863), directs that any officer or soldier of the Confederate States who shall be found within his lines or otherwise wearing any article of clothing or accouterments belonging to the uniform of the U. S. Army shall be dealt with as a spy. And further that proof of the possession and wearing of such uniform by any commissioned officer or soldier shall be taken as sufficient evidence in itself of his character as a spy.

It is hereby declared that articles of clothing and accouterments are legitimate objects of capture under the rules of war and may be used by the captors at their pleasure for the equipment of their troops and that steps will be taken to repress any attempt to treat as spies or punish in any manner officers or soldiers of the Confederacy who may be captured and condemned by the enemy solely on account of their possessing or wearing clothing or accouterments which formerly belonged to the officers, soldiers or Government of the United States.

By command of General R. E. Lee:

R. H. CHILTON,
Assistant Adjutant and Inspector-General.

[Indorsement.]

HEADQUARTERS, *Winchester, Va., June 6, 1863.*

The within order was received this day by flag of truce and is respectfully forwarded for the information of the major-general commanding Eighth Army Corps.

R. H. MILROY,
Major-General, U. S. Volunteers, Commanding.

OFFICE COMMISSARY-GENERAL OF PRISONERS,
Washington, D. C., June 2, 1863.

Hon. G. V. FOX,
Assistant Secretary of the Navy, Washington, D. C.

SIR: I am required by Lieutenant-Colonel Ludlow, commissioner [agent] for exchange of prisoners, to inform you that by an error of the copyist the word "officers" was inserted in the seventh section of the declaration of exchanges dated May 30, a copy of which he furnished to you. None but enlisted men are exchanged by that section.

Very respectfully, your obedient servant,

W. HOFFMAN,
Colonel Third Infantry, Commissary-General of Prisoners.

OFFICE COMMISSARY-GENERAL OF PRISONERS,
Washington, D. C., June 2, 1863.

Lieut. Col. S. McKELVY,
Commanding Convalescent Camp, Va.

COLONEL: Please notify paroled officers at your camp that all officers delivered at City Point up to May 30, 1863, have been declared exchanged, and as soon as I have your report of the paroled men at the camp all officers whose services are not required with them will be ordered to join their regiments immediately. It appears on comparing your rolls of officials arrived from Camp Parole with the roll of officers ordered to report to you by Colonel Sangster that the following-named had failed to obey the order, viz: F. D. Sloat, captain Company A, Twenty-seventh Connecticut Volunteers; O. Eschrich, captain Company K, Twenty-seventh Connecticut Volunteers; H. L. Morey, captain Company G, Seventy-fifth Ohio Volunteers; Samuel Surbrug, captain Company K, One hundred and seventh Ohio Volunteers; Frank M. Chapman, first lieutenant Company A, Twenty-seventh Connecticut Volunteers; Hiram Van Buren, first lieutenant Company H, Forty-third New York Volunteers. Capt. R. C. Hopkins had a leave of absence for ten days commencing on the 27th instant. Please call on Capt. M. Esembaux, Fifty-eighth New York Volunteers, who was in charge to explain why these officers failed to join as ordered.

Leaves of absence to officers or furloughs to enlisted men (paroled) are only granted by the Secretary of War on my recommendation and therefore applications should not be sent unless in very extreme cases. It is not necessary to send blank furloughs for when a furlough is granted the necessary papers are issued from the War Department.

Very respectfully, your obedient servant,

W. HOFFMAN,
Colonel Third Infantry, Commissary-General of Prisoners.

HEADQUARTERS THIRTEENTH ARMY CORPS,
Camp near Vicksburg, Miss., June 2, 1863.

Brig. Gen. P. J. OSTERHAUS,
Big Black River Railroad Bridge.

GENERAL: I have the honor to acknowledge the receipt of your favor of this date and am sorry that the ambulance train could not go out to the hospitals. An assistant surgeon left in the hospital will hand you this and can give you further information in relation to the hospitals and wounded.

This surgeon says that it has been informally agreed not to molest ambulances. We have allowed theirs to come in for their wounded at Edwards Station and they have promised not to molest ours.

The general commanding desires you to try this under a small train or send a train under a flag of truce. Talk with the bearer and act as wisdom and exigencies may approve and require. But if possible get the wounded able to travel away and send them North.

Your most obedient servant,

WALTER B. SCATES,
Lieutenant-Colonel and Assistant Adjutant-General.

NEW YORK, *June 2, 1863.*

Col. W. HOFFMAN:

The steamer United States put in here in distress. She has fifty-five paroled prisoners belonging to Western States. The vessel is bound to Boston. Commanding officers here will give no orders in regard to the prisoners. What shall be done with them? Answer.

STEWART VAN VLIET.

WAR DEPARTMENT, *Washington, June 3, 1863.*
Major-General SCHOFIELD, *Commanding at Saint Louis:*

In the month of January last the President directed the release of William P. Dixon, held in military custody. Whether this order failed to reach its destination or has been overlooked information has been received that Mr. Dixon is still in custody. If this be so you will please discharge him from custody. Please report.

EDWIN M. STANTON,
Secretary of War.

HEADQUARTERS, *New Berne, June 3, 1863.*
H. W. HALLECK, *General-in-Chief, Washington, D. C.*

GENERAL: I have the honor to acknowledge the receipt of your telegram* of the 25th of May concerning Confederate prisoners and beg leave to inform you that no prisoners of war have been paroled here for some time ; those taken in this department have been sent to Colonel Ludlow, Fortress Monroe, for exchange. The last lot, numbering about 300, taken at Gum Swamp and on previous expeditions, were sent to Colonel Ludlow ten days since.

I have the honor to be, general, very respectfully, your obedient servant,

J. G. FOSTER,
Major-General, Commanding.

OFFICE COMMISSARY-GENERAL OF PRISONERS,
Washington, D. C., June 3, 1863.
Maj. Gen. A. E. BURNSIDE,
Commanding Department of the Ohio, Cincinnati, Ohio.

GENERAL: I have the honor to inform you that the following declaration of exchanges of prisoners of war was made on the 30th ultimo, viz:†

Some of the officers now at Camp Parole near Annapolis and the Convalescent Camp near this city belonging to regiments or companies of which the men are not yet exchanged will remain on duty with their men. The remainder will be ordered to join their respective regiments.

The regiments of Streight's brigade—Third Ohio, Fifty-first and Seventy-third Indiana, Eightieth Illinois, and two companies First [Middle] Tennessee Cavalry—now at Camp Chase and Camp Morton, have been exchanged with a view to serve as guards at those camps till their officers who are now held as prisoners at Richmond join them. The Eightieth Illinois was improperly sent to Camp Chase. Benton Barracks is its proper station and they should be sent there unless you have occasion for their services.

Very respectfully, your obedient servant,

W. HOFFMAN,
Colonel Third Infantry, Commissary-General of Prisoners.

(Same to Maj. Gen. J. M. Schofield, Saint Louis, Mo., with the exception of the last paragraph.)

---

* See p. 696.
† Schedule omitted here; see Ludlow to Thomas, May 30, p. 721.

OFFICE COMMISSARY-GENERAL OF PRISONERS,
Washington, D. C., June 3, 1863.

Maj. Gen. W. S. ROSECRANS,
Commanding, Murfreesborough, Tenn.

GENERAL: I have the honor to inform you that the following declaration of exchanges of prisoners of war was made on the 30th ultimo, viz:* The regiments of Streight's brigade—Third Ohio, Fifty-first and Seventy-third Indiana, Eightieth Illinois and two companies First [Middle] Tennessee Cavalry—now at Camp Chase and Camp Morton have been exchanged with a view to serve as guards at those camps till their officers who are now held as prisoners at Richmond join them. There are other paroled troops belonging to your army at Benton Barracks whose exchange will be made as soon as they can be classified. They were captured in small parties and at different times.

Very respectfully, your obedient servant,
W. HOFFMAN,
Colonel Third Infantry, Commissary-General of Prisoners.

OFFICE COMMISSARY-GENERAL OF PRISONERS,
Washington, D. C., June 3, 1863.

Maj. Gen. W. S. ROSECRANS,
Commanding, Murfreesborough, Tenn.

GENERAL: Your letter of the 26th ultimo addressed to the Adjutant-General in relation to the release of deserters from the rebel army has been referred to this office and in reply I have the honor to say that the order of the Secretary of War directing that prisoners of war shall not be released on taking the oath of allegiance does not apply to deserters.

Very respectfully, your obedient servant,
W. HOFFMAN,
Colonel Third Infantry, Commissary-General of Prisoners.

OFFICE COMMISSARY-GENERAL OF PRISONERS,
Washington, D. C., June 3, 1863.

Col. WILLIAM H. LUDLOW, Agent for Exchange.

COLONEL: Please find inclosed a copy † of the declaration of exchange as I have corrected it in the fifth and seventh sections. I inclose also a list of captures † at a number of places and at various times amounting in all to 1,181 men who are now at Benton Barracks. Can't you declare them exchanged en masse? And I will announce it in a special order, giving the names of the men exchanged.

I return herewith three papers received from you making inquiries in relation to prisoners. In two of the cases replies are given. You probably did not notice the offensive indorsement in pencil on the third one. I respectfully request that you return the papers that the indorsement may be removed and the matter will be properly attended to. Other similar papers referred to this office will be acted on as soon as possible.

Many inquiries are made for missing wounded soldiers captured at the battle of Chancellorsville. Some are possibly in hospital at Richmond and many probably have died. I will be greatly obliged to you

---

* Schedule omitted here; see Ludlow to Thomas, May 30, p. 721.
† Not found.

if you can obtain the names of all such cases as early as practicable. The guide or scout, J. Harvey Sherman, who was said to have been captured near Winchester and hung by some of Mosby's Rangers it appears is confined in Castle Thunder. Please make some inquiries about him and if you can make some arrangement for his exchange. I mentioned to you that there were eight men of Ohio regiments who were captured near Chattanooga imprisoned at Atlanta and from there made their escape. They are of the party which were sent on a railroad expedition by General Mitchel, some of whom were executed as spies. It is desirable that these eight men should be exchanged to prevent in case of recapture their being liable to trial as spies, and I request you will make some arrangement to accomplish this. Please send me Mr. Ould's declaration of exchange.

Very respectfully, your obedient servant,

W. HOFFMAN,
Colonel Third Infantry, Commissary-General of Prisoners.

HEADQUARTERS DEPARTMENT OF VIRGINIA,
Fort Monroe, Va., June 3, 1863.

Hon. ROBERT OULD, *Agent for Exchange of Prisoners.*

SIR: Will you please furnish me with a copy of the act of the Confederate Congress* which you promised me and which directs some certain disposition of our captured officers commanding negro troops and also of the troops themselves? Will you also please inform me if it be the intention of your authorities to execute this act?

I am, very respectfully, your obedient servant,

WM. H. LUDLOW,
Lieutenant-Colonel and Agent for Exchange of Prisoners.

HEADQUARTERS DEPARTMENT OF VIRGINIA,
Fort Monroe, June 3, 1863.

Hon. ROBERT OULD, *Agent for Exchange of Prisoners.*

SIR: You informed me at our last interview that you were instructed not to deliver any of the officers of Colonel Streight's command captured at or near Cedar Bluff, Ala., about the 1st of May last.

I now make a formal demand for them under the cartel and tender to you their equivalents in your own officers now in our hands. If this demand and tender be refused please state the reasons therefor frankly that the issues presented may be fully understood and promptly met.

I am, very respectfully, your obedient servant,

WM. H. LUDLOW,
Lieutenant-Colonel and Agent for Exchange of Prisoners.

MILITARY PRISON, *Alton, Ill., June 3, 1863.*

Col. W. HOFFMAN,
Commissary-General of Prisoners, Washington, D. C.

COLONEL: I have the honor to transmit herewith a return† of prisoners of war in confinement in this prison for the month of May, 1863, with rolls† in explanation of alterations and changes during the month. The officers and privates reported as having escaped are supposed to

---

* See p. 940. † Omitted.

have left the prison under assumed names with the detachment which was sent hence to City Point on the 28th of April. Their absence was first discovered a few days after that detachment left this place and I telegraphed to the officer in charge of it to Fortress Monroe to search for these men before they (the prisoners) were delivered to the Confederate authorities. The dispatch I believe did not reach its destination in time to effect the object desired. The name of the officer is Samuel G. Barr and he belonged to the Missouri State Guard. He joined us on the 25th of April and left 28th. The prisoners to be exchanged have been in readiness for two or three days and I only wait instructions from department headquarters to send them forward.

I have the honor to be, sir, with much respect, your most obedient servant,

T. HENDRICKSON,
Major Third Infantry, Commanding the Prison.

MILITARY PRISON, *Alton, Ill., June 3, 1863.*

ASSISTANT ADJUTANT-GENERAL,
Headquarters Department of the Missouri, Saint Louis, Mo.

SIR: The frequent application by friends of the Confederate prisoners in this prison to visit them which if granted would very much interfere with the proper duties of the prison has induced me to send you the following extract from my instructions from the commissary-general of prisoners at Washington in regard to this matter:

It is the direction of the Secretary of War that no visitors be allowed in the Alton Prison.

I have the honor to be, sir, with much respect, your obedient servant,
T. HENDRICKSON,
Major, U. S. Army, Commanding Prison.

MILITARY PRISON, *Alton, Ill., June 3, 1863.*

ASSISTANT ADJUTANT-GENERAL,
Headquarters Department of the Missouri, Saint Louis, Mo.

SIR: I have the honor to report that the Confederate prisoners of war in this prison are now ready to be sent to City Point, Va., for exchange and only await orders from department headquarters to be forwarded.

I have the honor to be, sir, with much respect, your most obedient servant,

T. HENDRICKSON,
Major, U. S. Army, Commanding the Prison.

OFFICE COMMISSARY-GENERAL OF PRISONERS,
Washington, D. C., June 3, 1863.

Maj. Gen. U. S. GRANT,
Commanding Department of the Tennessee, Memphis, Tenn.

GENERAL: I have the honor to inform you that the following declaration of exchanges of prisoners of war was made on the 30th ultimo, viz:*

All officers and men whose exchange is announced in the above

---

*Schedule omitted here; see Ludlow to Thomas, May 30, p. 721.

declaration will be ordered to join their proper commands as soon as practicable.

Very respectfully, your obedient servant,

W. T. HARTZ,
Captain and Assistant Adjutant-General.

OFFICE COMMISSARY-GENERAL OF PRISONERS,
Washington, D. C., June 3, 1863.

W. P. WOOD,
Superintendent Old Capitol Prison, Washington, D. C.

SIR: I am directed by the commissary-general of prisoners to request you to furnish him with the number of citizen prisoners now at the Old Capitol Prison subject to discharge.

Very respectfully, your obedient servant,

W. T. HARTZ,
Captain and Assistant Adjutant-General.

GENERAL ORDERS, }   HDQRS. DEPARTMENT OF THE OHIO,
No. 90.   }   *Cincinnati, Ohio, June 3, 1863.*

The general commanding directs that General N. C. McLean, provost-marshal general, at once institute an investigation into the cases of all citizen prisoners now confined in this department, and in all such cases as do not clearly show premeditated disloyalty on the part of the accused or when a desire is manifested to atone for past faults by future good conduct the prisoners will be released on taking the oath of allegiance and giving bonds for the strict observance thereof. The general commanding is convinced that a large majority of the men arrested have been misled by dishonest and designing politicians and he prefers to strike at the sources of the evil and allow those who have been led astray to return to their loyalty and allegiance if they have seen the folly and sin of opposing the Government.

The United States in striving to put down a rebellion unparalleled in history requires that every man at home or in the field shall each in his sphere be enlisted in the cause. The necessity demands a sacrifice from all. In responding to this call the devotion of the citizen soldier stands foremost and his sacrifice is greatest. He gives up all that is dear to the citizen—his home, his freedom of speech and action, the prospect of gain and often gives his life. He exacts no conditions, but surrenders himself wholly to his country as represented by the constituted authorities placed over him. But while he thus yields up his civic rights so entirely to his country he is none the less a citizen; he waives them temporarily to give greater efficiency to his efforts and looks forward to the time when, the authority of the Government restored, he shall again exercise the rights he has patriotically laid down. While the duties of a citizen are of a more peaceful and less exacting character he is none the less a soldier, and it becomes him to appreciate the grandeur and entireness of the devotion of his brethren in the field and to remember that he too has sacrifices to make; but the country's demand upon him is comparatively but small. The country demands from him no physical sacrifice, no personal hardships; it merely asks that he shall imitate the loyal example of the soldiers in the field so far as to abate somewhat of that freedom of speech which they give up so entirely. The citizen would be unjust to the soldier as well as unfaithful to his country if while enjoying the comforts of home he were unwilling to give up a portion of a privilege which the soldier resigns altogether. That freedom of discussion and criticism which is proper in the politician and journalist in time of peace becomes rank treason when it tends to weaken the confidence of the soldier in his officers and his Government. When this insidious treason striking at the very root of that military power which is for the time being the country's protection makes its appearance it is the bounden duty of the commanding general to expel it from his lines with a heavier hand than he would drive from his camp the villain who would scatter a material poison that would enervate and decimate his soldiers. The general commanding desires to again call the attention of the officers, provost-marshals and others in authority to the necessity of great care in the making of arrests which should in all instances be founded upon full affidavits sustaining distinct charges, except when the exigencies of the case demand instant action. Carelessness in this respect is only less censurable than negligence in the detection and punishment of crime.

With the exercise of scrupulous care and sound discretion on the part of officers, and a candid consideration on the part of all citizens of the relations of the people and the Army to each other as above set forth, the general commanding is full of hope that mutual co operation in putting down the rebellion will become more hearty and effective, the necessity for arrests will be diminished and the tendency to factious opposition to the Government and hurtful criticisms of its measures be removed.

By command of Major-General Burnside:

LEWIS RICHMOND,
Assistant Adjutant-General.

NEAR VICKSBURG, MISS., *June 4, 1863.*

COMMANDING OFFICER CONFEDERATE FORCES,
Near Edwards Station, Miss.:

I send Assistant Surgeon Darrow, of the Federal Army, in charge of ambulances and supplies for the wounded soldiers left near that place. I would be pleased to send and get all of my wounded at Baker's Creek, Raymond and Jackson so that they may be sent to Northern hospitals for care. Will you please communicate this desire to the general commanding department with the request that he will inform me how these wounded men may be recovered?

U. S. GRANT,
Major-General.

OFFICE COMMISSARY-GENERAL OF PRISONERS,
Washington, D. C., June 4, 1863.

Col. B. L. E. BONNEVILLE,
Commanding Benton Barracks, Saint Louis, Mo.

COLONEL: I have the honor to acknowledge the receipt of your letter of the 20th ultimo covering the proceedings of a board of officers which was ordered by you to take into consideration certain instructions from this office in relation to a camp fund. My letter of instruction of the 13th ultimo was by authority of the Secretary of War, and it was not contemplated that the propriety of putting it in force would be referred to a board of officers nor can the opinion of any such board be admitted as a sufficient reason for failing to comply with the Secretary's order. I presume the proceedings are intended to be considered only as suggestions. The Regulations of the Army provide for but one mode of disposing of surplus rations and that is by the sale of those saved by companies to the Commissary Department. So far as you have regularly organized companies this regulation applies, but for the large body of fragments of companies at Benton Barracks there is no authority for disposing of one pound of saved rations except as authorized by my letter of the 13th ultimo. The ration is much larger than can be consumed by the men, and if there is no responsible company commander to take charge of and dispose of the surplus it must either be sold by unauthorized persons in violation of regulations or converted into a camp fund according to my instructions, or it must remain in the Subsistence Department. The object is to convert a large saving of rations into a fund which may be used for the benefit of the troops and to remove the temptation it offers to irresponsible persons to convert it into a source of personal profit. If the sick are well provided for in every way you can make no use of a fund to promote the general welfare of the camp or of individuals. Please report your own views on the subject and inform me what disposition is made of the surplus rations which unavoidably accumulate in every command. At a camp of paroled troops near this city it is found that rations for two days are ample to last three days and the excess of one day's rations remains in the Subsistence Department.

Very respectfully, your obedient servant,

W. HOFFMAN,
Colonel Third Infantry, Commissary-General of Prisoners.

GENERAL ORDERS, }   HDQRS. DEPARTMENT OF THE OHIO,
No. 91.   }   *Cincinnati, Ohio, June 4, 1863.*

I. By direction of the President of the United States the order suppressing the publication of the Chicago Times is hereby revoked.

II. The circulation of the New York World in this department having been suppressed for the same reasons that caused the suppression of the publication of the Chicago Times that portion of the general order relating to said newspaper is hereby revoked and it will be allowed to resume its circulation.

By command of Major-General Burnside:

W. P. ANDERSON,
Assistant Adjutant-General.

INDIANAPOLIS, *June 4, 1863.*

General M. C. MEIGS:

Additional hospital accommodations are required for rebel prisoners at Camp Morton. It can be done economically by a temporary extension of the present hospital building to the extent absolutely necessary for the emergency. Prisoners all in camp.

JAMES A. EKIN,
Quartermaster.

WASHINGTON, D. C., *June 4, 1863.*

Col. W. HOFFMAN, *Commissary-General of Prisoners.*

COLONEL: I have the honor to inform you that the transport United States on which I embarked at New Orleans in charge of certain Choctaw Indians, prisoners of war, bound to Boston, having been driven by stress of weather into the harbor of New York the prisoners were landed at Fort Columbus. By direction of the commander-in-chief I report to you for further orders in relation to the disposal of the prisoners. The within is a copy of the orders under which I sailed from New Orleans.

Respectfully, your obedient servant,

J. B. NOTT,
Captain and Commissary of Subsistence.

[Inclosure.]

OFFICE PROVOST-MARSHAL-GENERAL,
New Orleans, May 19, 1863.

Captain NOTT:

You will take charge of the Choctaw Indians, prisoners of war, now at Algiers and proceed by steamer United States to Boston. When you shall have placed the prisoners in safe custody there you will report to the Provost-Marshal-General in Washington and receive his orders in respect to the further disposition of the prisoners. Captain Killborn, provost-marshal, is charged with preparing the proper papers of the names of the prisoners and the battalion in the rebel service to which they are attached.

JAMES BOWEN,
Brigadier-General and Provost-Marshal-General.

WASHINGTON, *June 5, 1863.*

Hon. E. M. STANTON, *Secretary of War.*

SIR: We are informed by Captain Brown, of the Indianola, that the Confederates hold as prisoners some seven or eight men of the Kansas Seventh Regiment; that they do not recognize them as prisoners of war but as jayhawkers; that every possible cruelty is practiced against them; that they are kept heavily ironed and are threatened with hanging.

We call your attention to the subject and earnestly pray you take such retaliatory steps as the outrage demands. The only cause which can be urged for the outrage is that Kansas soldiers have their heart in this war and pursued a course to crush it out. Captain Brown is in the city and can give you all the particulars.

Yours,

J. H. LANE,
U. S. Senator.
A. C. WILDER,
Member of Congress.
T. A. OSBORN,
Lieutenant-Governor of Kansas.

[First indorsement.]

FORT MONROE, *June 17, 1863.*

Respectfully referred to Hon. Robert Ould, agent for exchange of prisoners.

WM. H. LUDLOW,
Lieutenant-Colonel and Agent for Exchange of Prisoners.

[Second indorsement.]

Respectfully returned to Lieutenant-Colonel Ludlow. Where are these men? What are their names? I think the facts will show that Captain Brown is mistaken. If you will furnish me with a starting point (the place of alleged confinement) I will find out the facts and have justice done. You will find out I have no doubt that Captain Brown's information is based on rumor only. I do not believe a U. S. soldier is in irons in our Confederacy.

RO. OULD,
Agent of Exchange.

SAINT LOUIS, *June 5, 1863.*

Hon. E. M. STANTON, *Secretary of War:*

The records of the provost-marshal's office show that William P. Dixon was by order of the President on the 29th of January released on oath and bond and to remain in Iowa north of Burlington during the rebellion. Is it your pleasure that these restrictions be removed?

Respectfully,

J. M. SCHOFIELD,
Major-General.

OFFICE COMMISSARY-GENERAL OF PRISONERS,
Washington, D. C., June 5, 1863.

Col. E. D. TOWNSEND,
Assistant Adjutant-General, Washington, D. C.

COLONEL: I would respectfully suggest the following as the concluding paragraph of the order announcing recent exchanges:

The paroled officers and men herein declared exchanged will without delay be forwarded to the commands to which they belong from the camps at which they have been assembled except such officers belonging to companies not yet exchanged as the commissary-general of prisoners may think necessary to retain to take charge of their own men. Exchanged officers and men absent on leave will at the expiration of their leaves join their respective commands.

Very respectfully, your obedient servant,

W. HOFFMAN,
Colonel Third Infantry, Commissary-General of Prisoners.

OFFICE COMMISSARY-GENERAL OF PRISONERS,
Washington, D. C., June 5, 1863.

Capt. H. B. TODD, *Provost-Marshal, Washington, D. C.*

CAPTAIN: It is very desirable that the two female prisoners, Mrs. and Miss Thomas, at the Old Capitol, Mr. Thomas Popper, a political prisoner on parole in this city, and Rev. Bennett Smedes, a political prisoner on parole in Baltimore, should be forwarded for exchange, and I have therefore to request that you will send these prisoners under a suitable officer via Baltimore to Fort Monroe there to report to Lieutenant-Colonel Ludlow, agent for exchange of prisoners. Mr. Smedes' address is 134 Biddle street, Baltimore. Please give him notice by telegram. Send rolls with them.

Very respectfully, your obedient servant,

W. HOFFMAN,
Colonel Third Infantry, Commissary-General of Prisoners.

FORT MONROE, *June 5, 1863.*

Col. W. HOFFMAN, *Commissary-General of Prisoners:*

I cannot make any more declarations of exchange until we shall deliver more rebel prisoners. Send me the names of the eight men of Ohio regiments captured near Chattanooga and I will immediately arrange their exchange. How many prisoners have you at Washington? Shall I send for them? Please answer.

WM. H. LUDLOW,
Lieutenant-Colonel, &c.

WASHINGTON, *June 5, 1863.*

Lieutenant-Colonel LUDLOW:

Have 200 prisoners of war [and] about 50 citizens for exchange. If the steamer can be spared please send for them. Please reply.

W. HOFFMAN,
Commissary-General of Prisoners.

WAR DEPARTMENT, *Richmond, Va., June 5, 1863.*

Lieut. Col. WILLIAM H. LUDLOW, *Agent of Exchange.*

SIR: Will you be good enough to inform me when it is to be considered that General Orders, No. 100,* went into effect. Is the date of the order April 24, 1863, or the date of its communication to me, 23d May, 1863, the true time? Do you recognize the rules of General Orders, No. 100, to be as binding against you as for you?

Permit me also to call your attention to the flagrant outrages that have recently been perpetrated in Gloucester, Mathews, King and Queen and the adjacent counties. Are they a fair interpretation of your celebrated general order? I am aware it gives a license for a man to be either a fiend or a gentleman. He can find abundant authority for either role in the order. What is the interpretation in General Dix's department? The country has always esteemed him as an honorable gentleman. I inclose a slip† which is inside the truth recounting some of the doings of Colonel Kilpatrick. Does General Dix approve of this style of conducting war even with belligerent rebels? It is in his own department. Perhaps the higher powers may have something to do with this question some of these days. "Silent spectators of the destruction of their agricultural implements."

Respectfully, your obedient servant,

RO. OULD,
Agent of Exchange.

WAR DEPARTMENT, *Richmond, Va., June 5, 1863.*

Lieut. Col. WILLIAM H. LUDLOW, *Agent of Exchange.*

SIR: I again ask you will you deliver the officers and men whom our agreements have declared exchanged? Will you not give me an answer to this inquiry? Allow me to quote you: "I now make a formal demand for them under the cartel. If this demand be refused please frankly state the reason therefor that issues presented may be fully understood and promptly met."

---

* See p. 671. † Not found.

You say I am mistaken in stating that no Federal officers are in our prisons who have been declared exchanged. You promise to furnish memoranda.

You actually refer to one case, that of one Spencer Kellogg. I have no recollection of ever having heard of him before. I have already caused inquiry to be made and if he is here he shall be delivered to you. So shall each and every other oficer or man who has been declared exchanged if you will say you will do the same. I do not care whether there are charges against them or not If you wish to limit this to officers I will agree to it. I would prefer it should include the men. Prepare your lists. I have prepared mine. Bring even the men whose deliverance I have asked and who are already exchanged and you shall have at City Point every prisoner whom you can name as being confined in our territory. If any one is wanting I will pay you tenfold. Will you agree to this? I have told you often and repeat it now that there is no reciprocal and fair proposition as to prisoners and exchanges to which I will not agree.

I again say that it is my deliberate conviction that there is not one solitary exchanged Federal officer now in confinement in the South unless Doctor Rucker is made an exception. I honestly believe that you have now in your prisons or on parole confined at the North more than 200 exchanged Confederate officers. You must allow me to say that I was amused at the list which you returned me some time ago; I refer to that which purported to be an answer to the specific cases I had brought to your attention. More than one-half of the cases had "no record" appended to them. Such an entry was made in reference to Doctor Green; the same as to Clagett D. Fitzhugh, to Parson Cameron, to Kerchival, and to a hundred others who have been seen by scores of people within a month or two. Every man on that list except such as you have already delivered is now in some one of your prisons. He may not be in the one named; if not it is because he has been removed in accordance with the tactics of your Government or its jailers. I ask again will you deliver our exchanged officers and men?

Respectfully, your obedient servant,

RO. OULD,
Agent of Exchange.

WAR DEPARTMENT, *Richmond, Va., June 5, 1863.*
Lieut. Col. WILLIAM H. LUDLOW, *Agent of Exchange.*

SIR: You ask me for a frank statement of the reason for the detention of the officers of Streight's command. I will give it to you as I will in every case when you ask it. I think you will find it franker than your answer to my inquiry as to whether you intended to deliver the officers who have heretofore been declared exchanged.

Allegations have been officially received from the highest authority in Alabama charging these officers with grave offenses as well against the laws of that State as the usages of civilized warfare. They are detained until the proper inquiry can be made and the fact ascertained when a determination will be made by the Confederate Government whether they come within the obligations of the cartel as prisoners of war or are to be dealt with as criminals against the laws of war and the State. These men have never been declared exchanged. I believe I have given you a better and certainly a more detailed reason for their detention than you did with reference to Colonel Morehead and other exchanged officers of whom I inquired and about whom all I could learn was that they were confined in Fort Norfolk under recent orders from the Secretary of War.

Respectfully, your obedient servant, RO. OULD,
Agent of Exchange.

WAR DEPARTMENT, *Richmond, Va., June 5, 1863.*
Lieut. Col. WILLIAM H. LUDLOW, *Agent of Exchange.*

SIR: You seem to have misunderstood me in relation to the cases of Captains Corbin and McGraw. I did not ask for detailed information to be "prepared." I asked for the records. You refer to the case of Captain Webster. In his case I offered to produce the record for your inspection but you expressed no desire to see it. If you have any such desire now I will immediately produce it upon notice. I will not give you a copy but show you the original and furnish you a copy at the same time. I understood you were satisfied with our proceedings in his case. If you want the record say so and it will be furnished.

If any person in our Confederacy with its means of intercommunication is so unfortunate as to be subjected to the penalty of death by judgment of a court-martial and you call for the record I will not wait one month for "detailed information" to be "prepared." More especially will it be so when the proceedings and findings are approved by our President and the record thus necessarily be brought under his notice.

I again respectfully ask you will you produce the records in the case of Captains Corbin and McGraw?

Respectfully, your obedient servant, RO. OULD,
Agent of Exchange.

RICHMOND, *June 5, 1863.*
Lieut. Col. WILLIAM H. LUDLOW, *Agent of Exchange.*

SIR: In one of your communications of the 2d you refer to the correspondents of the press and say it has been the practice "to treat them as non-combatants and not to retain them." I have been struggling for nearly twelve months to establish just such a rule as to non-combatants without success. The only difficulty I met was in your consent.

When was the rule established that non-combatants were not to be retained? What was the date of its adoption by Burnside or Rosecrans or Milroy? What peculiar immunity should the correspondents of the Tribune have over an old gray-headed grandfather who never shouldered a musket or followed in the wake of an army? Wherein are they privileged over delicate and noble-souled women who are either languishing in your prisons or "released" to the rigors and dangers of the wilderness?

It seems to me that if any exception be made as to any non-combatants it should be against such men as the Tribune correspondents who have had more share even than your soldiery in bringing rapine, pillage and desolation to our homes. I have no compassion for any such, even if their miseries were ten-fold greater. You ask me why I will not release them. 'Tis because they are the worst and most obnoxious of all non-combatants. Yet bad as they are, deeply as they have wronged and outraged us, they will be released if you will only discharge from imprisonment men and women "the latchets of whose shoes they are unworthy to unloose."

Mr. Colburn was released because Mr. Barr, a correspondent of the Grenada Appeal, was held by your authorities for one of the three correspondents and it came within the rule of our "sovereign will and pleasure" to release him.

Moreover if I had been disposed to ignore Mr. Colburn it would have given me a great deal of trouble to make a selection between the Tribune's correspondents.

Respectfully, your obedient servant,

RO. OULD,
Agent of Exchange.

WAR DEPARTMENT, *Richmond, Va., June 5, 1863.*
Lieut. Col. WILLIAM H. LUDLOW, *Agent of Exchange.*

SIR: I have been very much gratified by your two letters informing me that the orders for the execution of W. B. Compton and John R. Lyle have been suspended. If your own personal influence has been exercised in this matter, as I believe it has, allow me to express my deep personal gratification that you have so used it.

Nothing is nearer to my heart than to prevent on either side a resort to retaliation. Even if made necessary by the course of events it is much to be deplored. These are not only my own personal views but those of my Government. I believe that all of its acts will show it.

Respectfully, your obedient servant,

RO. OULD,
Agent of Exchange.

MILITARY PRISON, *Alton, Ill., June 5, 1863.*
Col. W. HOFFMAN,
Commissary-General of Prisoners, Washington, D. C.

COLONEL: I have the honor to inclose herewith a copy of an order issued by General Schofield, commanding Department of the Missouri, on the 1st instant, in relation to the prison fund in this department.

This order was handed to me this morning by Captain Rutherford, commissary of subsistence at this station, and as it conflicts in some respects with instructions previously received from you upon which I have heretofore acted I have thought it proper to send you this order and to ask how far I am to be governed by it in the future management of the prison fund. The quartermaster of the post—there is no such officer for the prison—is not subject to my orders; I can therefore only request him to do what I might under other circumstances direct.

I have the honor to be, sir, with much respect, your obedient servant,

T. HENDRICKSON,
Major Third Infantry, Commanding the Prison.

[Inclosure.]

SPECIAL ORDERS, } HDQRS. DEPARTMENT OF THE MISSOURI,
No. 147.   }   *Saint Louis, June 1, 1863.*

X. * * * Hereafter the prison fund arising from the savings of rations of the military prisons in this department will in no case be expended except for the "health and comfort" of the prisoners, and will in no case be used for the purchase of articles that can be furnished by the Quartermaster's Department.

By command of Major-General Schofield:

A. V. COLBURN,
Assistant Adjutant-General.

SAINT LOUIS, *June 5, 1863.*

Col. N. P. CHIPMAN, *Aide-de-Camp.*

COLONEL: There is confided to your charge under special orders herewith delivered a detachment of prisoners of war (officers) to be transferred hence to City Point, Va., for exchange. The prisoners are all paroled here and have signed duplicate rolls. Transportation is furnished to Baltimore for prisoners by railroad. From Baltimore you will proceed by steam-boat to Fortress Monroe (making requisition on the quartermaster at Baltimore for transportation) where Lieutenant-Colonel Ludlow, U. S. Army, has his headquarters, and report to him the arrival of prisoners and for further orders. Colonel Ludlow may see fit to send you on to City Point. You will act under his orders in the matter of these prisoners, and on being relieved by him and on returning hitherward will report to Col. William Hoffman, commissary-general of prisoners, at Washington, the delivery of the prisoners and whatever else of interest may have occurred on the route. There have been incidents during the passage of other detachments which Colonel Hoffman has been made acquainted with, and I desire him to know how these prisoners are treated along the road and how they conduct themselves.

You will take particular care that no person is allowed to hold communication with the prisoners by the way, and the prisoners will not be permitted to go to eating or drinking houses. Sufficient rations for the prisoners will be taken with them, and it will not be necessary for them to quit the cars except for special purposes. If there should be found on the way any persons who at the stopping places manifest strong sympathy with the prisoners I recommend that you take such persons under your custody, carrying them along as proper persons to be included with your prisoners, and report them specially to Colonel Ludlow and the circumstances to Colonel Hoffman. Many of these prisoners have money. This will be delivered to you here in separate envelopes, with the name of the prisoner and the amount written on the outside and a list of names and amount. You will give receipts to the quartermaster at this office on a duplicate list. You will deliver this money to the prisoners at City Point or elsewhere as directed by Lieutenant-Colonel Ludlow. You will notify the quartermaster at Baltimore by telegraph of the probable time of your arrival there so that he may have transportation by steam-boat ready and also rations, if you find those taken from here will not be sufficient. Duplicate signed parole rolls of the prisoners (eighteen in number) will be delivered to you here. These you will take with you and report to Lieutenant-Colonel Ludlow.

Very respectfully, your obedient servant,

JAMES F. DWIGHT,
Captain and Provost-Marshal-General.

WAR DEPARTMENT, *Washington, June 6, 1863.*

Brigadier-General KELLEY, *Harper's Ferry:*

A gang of spies from Richmond among whom is Captain Alexander, provost-marshal of that place, have been in Washington but may have left last night or may leave here to-day or to-night. One or more will be in disguise of the U. S. uniform, that being a common trick, and others as citizens. They expect to cross our lines at Point of Rocks, Berlin or Harper's Ferry. Every person not well known that arrives at either point by train or carriage for the next forty-eight hours should be arrested and examined. Alexander or some one of them has plans of the forts around Washington. They say that Colonel Schley of your command is in with them and will pass them; also that they have an understanding with Captains Means and Marsh who will help them. No effort should be spared to arrest this gang and get their papers. I have telegraphed Colonel Fish, provost-marshal at Baltimore, but rely greatly on your vigilance and activity for their arrest. Please acknowledge this. No communication should be made to Colonel Schley until a further investigation in respect to him can be had.

> EDWIN M. STANTON,
> *Secretary of War.*

WAR DEPARTMENT, *Washington, June 6, 1863.*
Col. A. B. JEWETT, *Commanding at Poolesville:*

Some rebel spies who have been in Washington within the last few days will attempt to day, to-night or to-morrow to cross our lines and escape. Watch Edwards Ferry closely; arrest and examine and search every stranger; detain them and make immediate report, unless they are well known. Much may depend on your vigilance in preventing their escape through our lines. Acknowledge the receipt of this.

> EDWIN M. STANTON,
> *Secretary of War.*

POOLESVILLE, MD., *June 6, 1863.*
Hon. E. M. STANTON, *Secretary of War:*

Your telegram is received. Every effort will be made to arrest the spies.

Respectfully,

> A. B. JEWETT,
> *Colonel, Commanding Brigade.*

WAR DEPARTMENT, *Washington, June 6, 1863.*
Colonel FISH, *Provost-Marshal, Baltimore:*

Captain Alexander, provost-marshal of Richmond, and three perhaps four other rebel spies, some in the military service, are or were yesterday in Washington and design leaving here for Richmond or Culpeper to-day or to-night. They will probably go by Point of Rocks, Berlin or Harper's Ferry, probably Berlin. Their plan last night was to take the train for Harper's Ferry at the Relay House, going from here either in a carriage or by train as might be most prudent. One or more of them will be disguised in the U. S. uniform as officers or privates. Alexander has a large amount of Confederate money and plans of the forts around Washington and other valuable papers. He will be disguised. Some officer at Berlin or Harper's Ferry is treacherous and acting with them. They say that Colonel Schley is the man, and also that Captains Means and Marsh will pass them.

These spies must be arrested at all hazards. They will perhaps escape from Washington but you may be able to take them. You are directed to give the matter your personal attention and spare no effort. Every person leaving the train at the Relay House, Harper's Ferry or any point between should be arrested, examined and held unless known to be loyal. You should have a force on the lookout at Baltimore and every point to Harper's Ferry and beyond where our lines may be crossed. Colonel Schley and Captains Means and Marsh should be watched and every method taken that your skill and experience can devise. You can render no service equal to the arrest of Alexander and this gang of spies. Acknowledge the receipt of this telegram and keep me advised during the next forty-eight hours where you can be communicated with.

EDWIN M. STANTON.

I have telegraphed General Kelley. You had better communicate with him.

WAR DEPARTMENT, *Washington, June 6, 1863.*
Colonel FISH, *Baltimore:*
Alexander is said to be about five feet eight inches high, erect and well made, with keen black eyes and black hair. He wore a heavy black beard a short time ago but may have shaved it off. Captain Summers, who was with Thomas in stealing the steam-boat last year, is one of the party. Another is Leon Ellinger; another is Fritz [Fitzpatrick], keeper of the Bull Run Hotel in Richmond. The description of these I have not got. Summers designed to travel in the uniform of an officer of the United States. It is not certain whether they will travel by rail or in a buggy or on horseback, or whether they will go to Baltimore. The fact of their being here yesterday is certain. All strangers on the line should be carefully examined. I will give you any further details as soon as they can be had.

EDWIN M. STANTON.

WAR DEPARTMENT, *Washington, June 6, 1863.*
Colonel FISH, *Baltimore:*
Have Poolesville and Edwards Ferry closely watched.
EDWIN M. STANTON,
Secretary of War.

RELAY HOUSE, *June 6, 1863.*
Hon. E. M. STANTON, *Secretary of War:*
The operator at this place was able to read by ear and as I had cause to suspect his loyalty I politely requested him to give me possession of the office. He is also the postmaster here and was somewhat indignant; but I told him I would take the responsibility to do as I have and he could report me if he chose. He said he could go into the next room and read everything and I instructed the officer in command here if he did so to arrest him.

W. S. FISH,
Lieutenant-Colonel and Provost-Marshal.

HEADQUARTERS OF THE ARMY,
Washington, D. C., June 6, 1863.

Colonel HOFFMAN, *Commissary-General of Prisoners.*

COLONEL : Copy of the following telegram is respectfully furnished for your information :

WASHINGTON, D. C., *June 5, 1863.*

Major-General SCHOFIELD, *Saint Louis:*

At the present time citizen prisoners cannot be conveniently sent through Fortress Monroe.

H. W. HALLECK,
General-in-Chief.

[H. W. HALLECK,
General-in-Chief.]

MURFREESBOROUGH, *June 6, 1863.*

Major-General HALLECK :

Your orders in regard to exchanged prisoners have not been complied with in the case of Coburn's brigade. It is now six weeks since they were exchanged and nothing has been heard from them.

W. S. ROSECRANS,
Major-General.

SPECIAL ORDERS, } WAR DEPT., ADJT. GENERAL'S OFFICE,
No. 253. } *Washington, June 6, 1863.*

*   *   *   *   *   *   *

XV. First Lieut. G. S. Carpenter, Eighteenth U. S. Infantry, will report in person without delay to Col. William Hoffman, Third U. S. Infantry, commissary-general of prisoners, for duty in his office in this city.

*   *   *   *   *   *   *

By order of the Secretary of War :

E. D. TOWNSEND,
Assistant Adjutant-General.

GENERAL ORDERS, } HDQRS. DEPARTMENT OF THE OHIO,
No. 95. } *Cincinnati, Ohio, June 6, 1863.*

I. The following officers and men have been declared by the commissary-general of prisoners duly exchanged as prisoners of war since the announcement in General Orders, No. 60, current series, from these headquarters.*

II. All prisoners exchanged by the above will at once proceed to join their regiments. The commanding officers at depots of prisoners will organize the enlisted men into detachments and send them under the proper officers to their regiments. The Quartermaster's Department will furnish the necessary transportation.

III. Prisoners belonging to regiments out of this department will hold themselves in readiness to join as soon as the proper arrangements shall be made.

By command of Major-General Burnside:

LEWIS RICHMOND,
Assistant Adjutant-General.

---

* Schedule omitted here; see Ludlow to Thomas, May 30, p. 721.

CINCINNATI, *June 6, 1863.*

General HASCALL, *Indianapolis:*

I am glad to have you in this department and will as soon as you are relieved by Willcox assign you to important duty. You can make my telegram of last night public if you wish.

A. E. BURNSIDE,
Major-General.

HEADQUARTERS IN THE FIELD,
Near Okolona, June 6, 1863.

Brig. Gen. WILLIAM S. SMITH,
Comdg. First Div., Federal Army Corps, La Grange, Tenn.

GENERAL: Your communication of the 27th ultimo to Capt. S. G. Street, of the Mississippi State troops, now of the Confederate service, relative to an alleged murder of two Union soldiers by men of Captain Street's command while prisoners of war having been referred to me I have to state that no criminal conduct such as is charged against the soldiers of Captain Street's command within my knowledge has ever been encouraged much less sanctioned in our service, and I have ordered Kesterson and Robinson to be arrested and immediate and rigid inquiry to be made as to the facts and circumstances under which the two prisoners in their charge were killed, and will see that punishment be inflicted for any violation of the rules of civilized warfare or of common humanity. But it cannot be expected that I should place them in the hands of an enemy who have already and without the means of ascertaining all the facts prejudged them.

I regret that assuming the prisoners to have been "murdered in cold blood" you should have proceeded as is stated in your communication to put in irons four of Captain Street's men prisoners in your hands "to be shot if Kesterson and Robinson are not delivered into our (your) hands within a reasonable length of time to suffer the penalty due to their infamous crimes," as it obliges me, as I have done, to issue a like order in the case of four of the men of your command captured by Captain Street and now prisoners in our hands to be thus held as hostages for the safety of the four men you have placed in irons and until they shall be treated as prisoners of war.

Very respectfully, your obedient servant,
DANIEL RUGGLES,
Brigadier-General, Commanding District.

OFFICE COMMISSARY-GENERAL OF PRISONERS,
Washington, D. C., June 6, 1863.

Col. G. LOOMIS,
Commanding Fort Columbus, New York Harbor:

By direction of the Secretary of War the fourteen Indian prisoners of war belonging to the rebel army reported in your letter of the 2d instant will remain at Fort Columbus until further orders. Please inform me what accommodations you have for them and if you require supplies of any kind for them. Brigadier-General Martindale has been instructed to send via Fort Columbus to the Department of the Gulf and the Department of North Carolina certain deserters from the army in those departments, and by direction of the General-in-Chief I have the honor to request you will forward these men by the earliest opportunity with troops going south so as to avoid the necessity of a special guard. There is also one deserter to be sent to Fort Warren and one to Fort Preble.

Very respectfully, your obedient servant,

W. HOFFMAN,
Colonel Third Infantry, Commissary-General of Prisoners.

FORT MONROE, *June 6, 1863.*

Col. W. HOFFMAN, *Commissary-General of Prisoners:*

On the 22d May I gave to Mr. Ould General Orders, Nos. 49 and 100, with notice that no paroles would be binding after that date except those under the stipulation of article 7 of the cartel which provides for the delivery of prisoners at certain points unless otherwise agreed upon by commanders of opposing armies. Please send me copies of all orders of courts-martial in cases of execution.

WM. H. LUDLOW,
Lieutenant-Colonel, &c.

OFFICE COMMISSARY-GENERAL OF PRISONERS,
Washington, D. C., June 6, 1863.

Capt. H. B. TODD, *Provost-Marshal, Washington, D. C.*

CAPTAIN: I am directed by the commissary-general of prisoners to inform you that the steamer will be here as soon as she returns from City Point, which will probably be on Monday, and all prisoners of war now at the Old Capitol and as many citizen prisoners as are eligible will be sent for exchange. The prisoners Arnold, Hite, Bettison and McCorkle will be sent with the rest. Samuel Clawson, wife, daughter and son, now at Camp Chase, have been telegraphed for. If they arrive in time they will also be sent for exchange.

Very respectfully, your obedient servant,

W. T. HARTZ,
Captain and Assistant Adjutant-General.

HEADQUARTERS SECOND DIVISION,
Convalescent Camp, June 6, 1863.

Hon. HENRY WILSON,
Member of Congress, Chairman Committee on Military Affairs.

HONORABLE SIR: I feel it my duty to draw your attention to a defect in the system of paroling prisoners of war. A number of such persons having lately come into camp I learned from officers and men the following facts:

1. That the rebels administer the oath to privates and non-commissioned officers direct and parole them in the absence of officers of our Army. This is in direct violation of General Orders, No. 100, section VII, paragraph 126, issued April 24, 1863.

2. That the oath so administered contains the words "not to aid and abet the United States by bearing arms or otherwise," which is loose and too wide an application of parole, disquieting, by its contradiction

to same order and section, paragraph 130, the consciences of the honest and affording a seemingly just excuse to the dishonest, who are opposed to military discipline after they come to Annapolis or here.

3. That the latest form of the oath concocted by the traitors contains a clause by which officers (I could not learn whether men also) are bound not to go into any camp or fortress or other place devoted to military purposes belonging to the United States until exchanged. This in direct conflict with orders establishing camps for paroled prisoners.

The officers and men from whom I learned these facts were taken prisoners between May 2 and 5 and sent to Annapolis May 14 from City Point. The order from our Government must have been communicated to the rebels before that time, having been issued April 24. The additional clause forbidding any military discipline seems to have been the answer to the liberal and just provisions of Orders, No. 100. The state of discipline and cleanliness at Annapolis or rather absence of either seems to be shocking if the statement of officers and gentlemen are to be believed. I know of an officer who went to New York from there and staid five days. All the officers describe it as the filthiest place they have seen. We can keep our camp clean. The soldiers (paroled) are not made to do anything there. When they came here we had very hard work to get them to obey orders. They were very unclean.

I have the honor to be, sir, very respectfully, your obedient servant,

G. A. SCHMITT,
Captain, Twentieth Mass. Vols., Comdg. Second Div. Convalescents.

FORT MONROE, VA., *June 7, 1863.*

Hon. E. M. STANTON:

I see no objection to allowing all women and children to go South who desire it on the condition that they do not return; or women and children to come North on the same condition. There are as you say many fearful I might add distressing cases. I think it would be well to fix a day a little more distant than you suggest, say Wednesday, the 1st of July, and give public notice as you did before. I have no doubt Mr. Ould will consent and fix a day for women and children desiring to come North.

JOHN A. DIX,
Major-General.

UNOFFICIAL.]   ANNAPOLIS, MD., *June 7, 1863.*

Hon. EDWIN M. STANTON.

DEAR SIR: I think night and day of the late correspondence between Mr. Ould and W. H. Ludlow touching the safety of Union men whose lives have been threatened by the rebel Government in alleged retaliation for the execution of two spies in Burnside's department.

I am of opinion that while it was proper to justify Colonel Ludlow in writing his letter of the 25th ultimo threatening re-retaliation should the rebels carry out their threats, the letter being calculated to check them in the execution of their barbarous threats, still I would on no account follow their savage example. If they choose in the South to act as barbarians we as a civilized people ought not to follow their example.

We have now more of their officers in our power than they have of ours and are therefore in the right position for holding up their conduct to the eyes of the world and drawing down upon them the abhorrence of mankind.

The immediate effect on the field of battle would be that our men would not suffer themselves to be taken prisoners while the rebels may the sooner yield; and as to other nations such a course on our part would naturally command their sympathies in our favor, and in case of interference it would be to put down a people disposed to act like savages.

I am the more earnest in this view the more I think of the subject, and though I mark this note "unofficial" I shall be glad to have my opinion communicated to the President or used in any manner you may think proper.

Very respectfully, your obedient servant,

E. A. HITCHCOCK,
Major-General, &c.

SURGEON-GENERAL'S OFFICE,
Washington, D. C., June 7, 1863.

Col. W. HOFFMAN,
Commissary-General of Prisoners, Washington, D. C.

COLONEL: With a view to the provision of sufficient hospital accommodation at Fort Delaware I request such information as you may be able to give as to the probable number of rebel prisoners destined to occupy this post and the probable time of their stay.

Very respectfully, your obedient servant,

JOS. R. SMITH,
Acting Surgeon-General.

HEADQUARTERS,
Fort Columbus, New York Harbor, June 7, 1863.

Col. WILLIAM HOFFMAN,
Commissary-General of Prisoners, Washington, D. C.

COLONEL: The prisoners of war are confined in one of the casemate rooms of the castle. They may need some clothing. If so I will send you a list of the articles needed. These Choctaws say they were forced into the rebel service. I have no knowledge of any troops going South, but will do my best to send the deserters as you request. I do not know where Fort Pueblo [Preble] is to which one of the deserters is to be sent.

Very respectfully, your obedient servant,

G. LOOMIS,
Colonel Fifth Infantry, Commanding.

HEADQUARTERS DEPARTMENT OF VIRGINIA,
Fort Monroe, June 7, 1863.

Col. W. HOFFMAN, *Commissary-General of Prisoners.*

COLONEL: What information have you in relation to the effect of the time when General Orders, No. 100, went into effect? It was served upon Mr. Ould on the 23d of May last (as I telegraphed to you) with the notice that all captures must be reduced to possession as provided for in article 7 of the cartel. Am I correct in the supposition that Orders, No. 100 is to be recognized as binding against us as for us?

I am, very respectfully, your obedient servant,

WM. H. LUDLOW,
Lieutenant-Colonel and Agent for Exchange of Prisoners.

HEADQUARTERS DEPARTMENT OF VIRGINIA,
Fort Monroe, June 7, 1863.

Col. W. HOFFMAN, *Commissary-General of Prisoners.*

COLONEL: I inclose* to you two receipts for money sent to City Point, one for $20 and one for $925; also some papers referred for information. Can you not send to me by return mail two copies each of the general order containing court-martial proceedings in cases of spies and other Confederate prisoners sentenced to death? I am again and again called upon for them by Mr. Ould. It is clearly our interest to furnish all proper information of such cases as I intend to call for it from the Confederates when necessary and if we do not give it we certainly cannot expect to receive it. I wrote to Judge Holt on this subject about four weeks ago. I telegraphed about ten days ago to General Burnside on the same and up to this time have not heard from either. It seems to me that the orders asked for should be obtained. I want them not only in the cases of McGraw and Corbin, but of all others of executions of Confederates.

I am, very respectfully, your obedient servant,

WM. H. LUDLOW,
Lieutenant-Colonel and Agent for Exchange of Prisoners.

FORT MONROE, *June 7, 1863.*

Col. W. HOFFMAN, *Commissary-General of Prisoners:*

Please send me copies of all orders containing proceedings of courts-martial in cases of execution of spies. I have received none as yet and need them most pressingly. Captain Mulford will report to you on Tuesday morning to bring away prisoners. No exchanges can be at present made of citizens but the Confederates will receive such as are sent to them.

WM. H. LUDLOW,
Lieutenant-Colonel, &c.

BALTIMORE, MD., *June 7, 1863.*

Hon. EDWIN M. STANTON, *Secretary of War:*

I have positive information that one of the party in question went to New York yesterday. The principal in the matter was in Washington this morning. I feel quite sure from the knowledge I have of his habits and affairs that he will visit this city, as his wife and mother reside here, and he also has a lady-love whom it is just to presume he will use every endeavor to procure an interview with particularly as she is of easy virtue. I shall probably hear more from this before midnight and will advise you.

W. S. FISH,
Lieutenant-Colonel and Provost-Marshal.

---

* Omitted.

MILITARY PRISON, *Alton, Ill., June 7, 1863.*

ASSISTANT ADJUTANT-GENERAL,
Headquarters Department of the Missouri, Saint Louis, Mo.

SIR: A week or two since I notified the provost-marshal-general of the department at Saint Louis that this prison was full and that we could not accommodate any more prisoners without great inconvenience until some of the number now here were removed or sent away. But notwithstanding this prisoners in squads are being sent here almost daily till the prison is full to repletion. Upward of fifty prisoners have been received here since Friday last, the 5th instant, and I have been informed that several hundred are now en route up the river for this place. Should these latter arrive here before the prisoners now ready for exchange can be sent off I shall be compelled in our crowded state to refuse them admittance into the prison.

I have the honor to be, sir, with much respect, your most obedient servant,

T. HENDRICKSON,
Major Third Infantry, Commanding the Prison.

SAINT LOUIS, *June 7,* [*1863.*]

J. M. HEATH, Esq.,
Provost-Marshal of the Border, Keokuk, Iowa.

SIR: In the case of Henry Clay Dean reported on your regular report just received as being in the guard-house, I wish you would take full evidence against the man, and if you think it justifies sending [him] South under the instructions forwarded to you from this office heretofore transfer him here with all the proof and I will send him through the lines. Without knowing specially of this Dean my impression is that he is very disloyal and a man of dangerous influence. He probably is not worth the trial accorded his compeer, Vallandigham, but I hope you will be able to find sufficient evidence to justify his transfer here to that same destination which the other one has attained.

Very respectfully, your obedient servant,

JAMES F. DWIGHT,
Captain and Provost-Marshal-General.

OLD CAPITOL PRISON, *Washington, June 7, 1863.*

Brigadier-General MARTINDALE,
Military Governor of the District.

SIR: I herein respectfully beg leave to call your attention to my case. I have now been a prisoner for nearly nine months, the first three months of which I spent at Fort Delaware; was then ordered to report to this place. Upon doing so I was paroled and remained upon parole for three months. During my parole I reported for exchange (although my parole did not order me to do so) three different times. Upon reporting on the 1st of March I was committed to this place where I have since remained. It appears I have been held as an officer in the Confederate Army. I never was an officer in the Confederate Army. I am a private in Company K, of the First Virginia Cavalry. Joined the army in September, 1862, when the Confederates were in Maryland. Was regularly mustered in and was captured in endeavoring to cross the river. You have no charges whatever against me. Four men who were captured with me who were from the same place I am and who joined the army at the same time I did were exchanged six weeks after they were captured. I really know of no reason why I should be longer held unless it is because I am a Marylander. But this Government is exchanging Marylanders who belong to the Southern Army at every exchange which takes place from here. This I know to my own certain knowledge. You have not nor is there any charge anywhere against me whatever, and I know not what this Government means by holding me so long in confinement. As to taking the oath I will not do it nor will I accept anything but an unconditional release or an exchange. I know that I am entitled to an exchange. Your having no charges against me and my not wishing to take the oath and desiring to be sent to Richmond certainly entitles me to one. May I beg you will take the matter in hand and see that I am no longer deprived of my just rights; or if you imagine you have any charges against me, why for God's sake let me know what they are and grant me a trial, as anything is preferable to this.

Very respectfully, your obedient servant,

CLAGETT D. FITZHUGH.

HEADQUARTERS MILITARY DISTRICT OF WASHINGTON,
Washington, D. C., June 8, 1863.

Col. W. HOFFMAN, *Commissary-General of Prisoners.*

COLONEL: Clagett D. Fitzhugh, prisoner of war, is still confined in the Old Capitol Prison. Is it the desire that he remain there or be sent for exchange? Perhaps you recollect he was the one who violated his parole in failing to report to you as ordered. He is also suspected of being a spy. He has been confined some months.

I am, colonel, very respectfully, your obedient servant,

JOHN P. SHERBURNE,
Assistant Adjutant-General.

GENERAL ORDERS, } WAR DEPT., ADJT. GENERAL'S OFFICE,
No. 167.   }   *Washington, June 8, 1863.*

I. The following officers and men have been declared duly exchanged as prisoners of war since the announcement in General Orders, No. 117, of May 9, 1863:*

II. The paroled officers and men herein declared exchanged will without delay be forwarded to the commands to which they belong from the camps at which they have been assembled, except such officers belonging to companies not yet exchanged as the commissary-general of prisoners may think necessary to retain to take charge of their own men.

Exchanged officers and men absent on leave will at the expiration of their leaves join their respective commands.

By order of the Secretary of War:

E. D. TOWNSEND,
Assistant Adjutant-General.

---

*Schedule omitted here; see Ludlow to Thomas, May 30, p. 721.

Order in relation to passes.

WAR DEPARTMENT, *Washington, June 8, 1863.*

Ladies desiring passes to go to or return from the rebel States can receive permits under the following regulations:

1. All applications for passes to go South must be made in writing and verified by oath, addressed to Maj. L. C. Turner, judge-advocate, Washington, D. C., as follows:

I, A—— B——, applicant for a pass to go to City Point, Va., and now residing at ——, do solemnly swear that if said pass be granted I will not take any property excepting my wearing apparel, and that all the articles to be taken with me are contained in the trunk or package delivered or to be delivered to the quartermaster on the transport steamer on which I am to go to City Point; that I have not been in any insurgent State nor beyond the military lines of the United States within thirty days last past; that I will not return within the military lines of the United States during the present war, and that I have not in my trunk nor on my person any papers or writings whatsoever, nor any contraband articles.

No person will be allowed to take more than one trunk or package of female wearing apparel weighing not over 100 pounds and subject to inspection, and if anything contraband be found in the trunk or on the person the property will be forfeited and the pass revoked.

2. A passenger boat will leave Annapolis, Md., on the 1st day of July next to deliver those permitted to go South at City Point, and the baggage of each applicant must be delivered to the quartermaster on said boat at least twenty-four hours previous to the day of departure for inspection.

3. Children will be allowed to accompany their mothers and relatives and take their usual wearing apparel, but the name and age of each child must be given in the application.

4. Ladies and children desiring to come North will be received on the boat at City Point and taken to Annapolis, and every adult person coming North will be required to take and subscribe the oath of allegiance to the Government of the United States before the boat leaves Fortress Monroe.

L. C. TURNER,
Judge-Advocate.

———

CINCINNATI, OHIO, *June 8, 1863.*

General HASCALL, *Indianapolis:*

You are granted thirty days' leave. After which you will report to these headquarters for duty.

A. E. BURNSIDE,
Major-General.

———

OFFICE COMMISSARY-GENERAL OF PRISONERS,
Washington, D. C., June 8, 1863.

Maj. Gen. S. P. HEINTZELMAN,
Commanding Defenses of Washington, Washington, D. C.

GENERAL: I have the honor to inform you that all the prisoners of war confined in the Old Capitol will be sent for exchange by the boat that is expected to arrive to-morrow and have therefore to request that the prisoners now at Alexandria may be sent to the Old Capitol Prison to be sent with them.

Very respectfully, your obedient servant,

W. HOFFMAN,
Colonel Third Infantry, Commissary-General of Prisoners.

OFFICE COMMISSARY-GENERAL OF PRISONERS,
Washington, D. C., June 8, 1863.

Surg. JOSEPH R. SMITH,
Acting Surgeon-General, Washington, D. C.

SIR: I have the honor to acknowledge the receipt of your letter of the 7th instant making inquiries as to the probable number of sick rebel prisoners to be provided for at Fort Delaware and in reply I have to say that barracks for 8,000 or 10,000 prisoners are being erected there and a hospital corresponding in size will be built, but whether so large a number of prisoners will ever be collected there and how long they remain depends on circumstances which cannot be foreseen. If provision is made for the usual proportion of sick in 5,000 men for forty-five days I think you will have ample time to obtain any additional supplies that may be required.

Very respectfully, your obedient servant,

W. HOFFMAN,
Colonel Third Infantry, Commissary-General of Prisoners.

OFFICE COMMISSARY-GENERAL OF PRISONERS,
Washington, D. C., June 8, 1863.

Lieut. Col. W. H. LUDLOW,
Agent for Exchange of Prisoners, Fort Monroe, Va.

COLONEL: I inclose herewith orders* announcing the proceedings of courts-martial by which spies have been sentenced to be executed. On Friday I mailed to you the orders directing the executions at Johnson's Island. I inclose also a newspaper slip† giving an account of the recent executions at Johnson's Island, which will go to show that the whole proceedings were tempered with as much kind feelings as was consistent with a prompt and humane administration of justice. I have just received the inclosed communication† addressed to Mrs. Rucker, from which it appears that her husband is to be released. I hope this may be so, and if it depends on us in any way that whatever is possible will be done at once to secure his return to his family.

On Saturday I was shown a copy of General Cooper's order announcing the last declaration of exchange which is more comprehensive than ours and I am quite sure is not according to your understanding with Mr. Ould. It says as well as I can recollect that all prisoners captured on the sea or waters flowing into the sea are exchanged, and all persons who have taken the oath of allegiance to the United States and given bond for loyal conduct or who have been released on parole under any circumstances are exchanged. I give only the substance of one or two sections. There are other features which I don't think you have agreed to. On the 3d instant I requested you would obtain Mr. Ould's declaration so that I might understand how far it covers prisoners in our hands.

I inclose herewith a further list† of deaths of prisoners of war in our hospitals, and I hope you will be able soon to obtain corresponding lists of deaths of our people in rebel hospitals. You will also find inclosed $40 Confederate money belonging to Maj. A. De Blanc, Eighth Louisiana Regiment, and $12 belonging to Lieut. H. D. Verble, Fifty-seventh North Carolina, who have been delivered at City Point. The money was placed in the hands of Captain Camp, in charge of the

---

*See General Orders, No. 114, p. 556.   † Not found.

Soldiers' Rest, where they remained a few days, and he has turned it over to me. Please forward it through Mr. Ould.

Very respectfully, your obedient servant,

W. HOFFMAN,
Colonel Third Infantry, Commissary-General of Prisoners.

OFFICE COMMISSARY-GENERAL OF PRISONERS,
Washington, D. C., June 8, 1863.

Lieut. Col. GEORGE SANGSTER,
Commanding Camp Parole, near Annapolis, Md.

COLONEL: Your letter of the 14th reporting on the shipment of exchanged prisoners to Fort Columbus is received. As these men were to be reshipped at Fort Columbus it was necessary and proper that you should address a letter to the commanding officer explaining why they were sent there and requesting that they might be forwarded. The simple statement in the order given to the corporal in charge that they belonged to the Department of the South was not sufficient. There was no excuse for sending fifty-seven men to so distant a point under the charge of a corporal. I am sure I have given you no orders prohibiting you from sending officers on such duty when you had them to spare as you had on this occasion. Send me a copy of the order to which you refer. The excuses offered by the corporal for the unsatisfactory manner in which the duty was done are not reliable. His best excuse is that he should not have been sent on the duty and that having been sent he was not properly instructed. Whatever papers are prepared to go with men detached should be signed before they leave your office. I don't understand your explanations on this point.

Very respectfully, your obedient servant,

W. HOFFMAN,
Colonel Third Infantry, Commissary-General of Prisoners.

HEADQUARTERS MOUNTED INFANTRY,
Near Edwards Depot, Miss., June 8, 1863.

Brigadier-General OSTERHAUS, U. S. Army:

Your ambulances under flag of truce will be permitted to move your sick and wounded from Champion Hill Hospital and the hospitals in its vicinity. I will be glad to have your ambulance train move the Confederate wounded from the hospitals near the Big Black bridge.

I hope for the honor of your Government you will not permit violations of your flag of truce.

I cannot grant the request of F. Tunica, engineer, U. S. Army, to make a sketch of the battle-field near Baker's Creek.

I am, sir, very respectfully, your obedient servant,

H. B. LYON,
Colonel Eighth Kentucky Regiment, Commanding.

OFFICE COMMISSARY-GENERAL OF PRISONERS,
Washington, D. C., June 8, 1863.

Rev. [J. R.] BURGETT.
(Care of Brown Brothers & Co., Baltimore, Md.)

SIR: I am directed by the commissary-general of prisoners to inform you that no arrangements have been made for the exchange of citizen prisoners as yet and will therefore be unable to send you orders for several days.

Very respectfully, your obedient servant,

W. T. HARTZ,
Captain and Assistant Adjutant-General.

OFFICE COMMISSARY-GENERAL OF PRISONERS,
Washington, D. C., June 8, 1863.

Mr. JOHN SHARP, Jr., *Philadelphia Post-Office.*

SIR: I am directed by the commissary-general of prisoners to inform you that your letter to His Excellency the President in relation to your son has been referred to Mr. Robert Ould, the rebel agent for exchange, and is returned with the following indorsement:

No prisoner captured at the first battle of Fredericksburg is in any of our prisons. If he was it is a libel to say that he is suffering from starvation.

Very respectfully, your obedient servant,

W. T. HARTZ,
Captain and Assistant Adjutant-General.

INDIANAPOLIS, *June 8, 1863.*

General M. C. MEIGS:

Attention is respectfully requested to telegram of 4th instant relative to enlargement to hospital accommodations for rebel prisoners at Camp Morton, Ind. Direction is urgent.

JAS. A. EKIN.

SPRINGFIELD, ILL., *June 8, 1863.*

Col. W. HOFFMAN,
Commissary-General of Prisoners, Washington, D. C.

COLONEL: In a printed circular of Col. T. J. Haines, chief commissary of subsistence, Department of the Missouri, there is one from you dated Detroit, July, 1862, giving scale of rations to prisoners of war in which five pounds of green coffee or four of ground to the 100 rations is required to be issued. In the scale furnished to me from your office dated May 4, 1863, nine pounds of raw coffee is the amount required, and in the list given by Captain Freedley to the commandant of the post at Camp Butler the quantity is seven pounds. Please inform me which is right. Since the receipt of the inclosed copy of act* of Congress I have refused to pay out of prisoners' savings extra pay to soldiers detailed to duty in attending on prisoners. The law makes no exceptions. Am I right? Please return act of Congress.

Respectfully, your obedient servant,

N. W. EDWARDS,
Captain and Commissary of Subsistence.

[JUNE 8, 1863.—For the capture, trial, condemnation and execution as spies of William Orton Williams and Walter G. Peter, officers of the Confederate Army, at Franklin, Tenn., see Series I, Vol. XXIII, Part II, p. 397 *et seq.*

---

*Not found.

MURFREESBOROUGH, *June 9, 1863.*

Brig. Gen. L. THOMAS:

Last evening a dispatch from Col. J. P. Baird, commanding post at Franklin, Tenn., was received as follows:

Two men came in camp about dark dressed in our uniforms, with horse equipments to correspond, saying that they were Colonel Auton, inspector-general, and Major Dunlap, assistant, having an order from Adjutant-General Townsend and your order to inspect outposts, but their conduct was so singular that we arrested them, and they insisted that it was very important to go to Nashville to-night.

Colonel Baird asked if there were any such persons in the army and if so their description. I replied at once that they were probably spies and directed him to order a court, and if they proved to be spies to execute them immediately, which was done, and they were tried, condemned to be hung and the sentence was carried into execution before 10 o'clock this morning. On being discovered they confessed that they were officers in the Confederate Army, one a colonel named Lawrence W. Orton, formerly W. Orton Williams. One claims [to be] first cousin to Robert E. Lee [and] to have been chief of artillery on General Bragg's staff, and formerly to have been on General Scott's staff, of Second Regular Cavalry. A full history of the case will be forwarded you by mail.

W. S. ROSECRANS,
Major-General.

WAR DEPARTMENT, *Washington, June 9, 1863.*

Major-General ROSECRANS, *Murfreesborough:*

Your dispatch to the Adjutant-General in respect to the execution of the spies that came into your camp has just been received. Your prompt action is approved.

EDWIN M. STANTON,
Secretary of War.

SURGEON-GENERAL'S OFFICE,
Washington, D. C., June 9, 1863.

Col. W. HOFFMAN, *Commissary-General of Prisoners.*

COLONEL: Your reply of the 8th instant to a letter from this office of the 7th relative to the probable number of rebel prisoners to be provided for at Fort Delaware has been received. The Surgeon-General directs me to inquire whether in connection with the barracks at Fort Delaware any steps have been taken toward the erection of hospitals.

By order of the Surgeon-General U. S. Army:

Very respectfully, your obedient servant,

JOS. R. SMITH,
Surgeon, U. S. Army.

[First indorsement.]

OFFICE COMMISSARY-GENERAL OF PRISONERS,
June 10, 1863.

My recommendation to the Quartermaster-General to have a hospital for prisoners at Fort Delaware was referred to the Surgeon-General on the 27th ultimo and has not yet been returned. On the Surgeon-General's approval the hospital will be erected.

Very respectfully returned:

W. HOFFMAN,
Colonel Third Infantry, Commissary-General of Prisoners.

[Second indorsement.]

SURGEON-GENERAL'S OFFICE, *June 10, 1863.*

Respectfully returned to Colonel Hoffman with the information that his recommendation to the Quartermaster-General (to have a hospital for prisoners erected at Fort Delaware) said to have been referred to this office on the 27th ultimo has not been received.

By order of the Surgeon-General:

> JOS. R. SMITH,
> *Surgeon, U. S. Army.*

HEADQUARTERS DISTRICT OF EASTERN KENTUCKY,
Louisa, Ky., June 9, 1863.

Lieut. Col. LEWIS RICHMOND,
Assistant Adjutant-General, Hdqrs. Department of the Ohio.

COLONEL: I have the honor to acknowledge the receipt of a copy of a letter,* date of May 29, 1863, from the commissary-general of prisoners to the major-general commanding the department, referred to me, and which with its inclosures is herein inclosed. The prisoners in question† were arrested as we arrest many persons—upon only probable suspicion. In this region where a great portion of the inhabitants are actively engaged in [giving] aid, comfort and information to the enemy it is impracticable to arrest only those against whom charges are preferred in regular form backed by proper evidence. That would be to allow the most dangerous persons in the community to go free. In our scouts we seize those who we have reasonable grounds by hearsay or otherwise to believe are aiding the enemy. We have no time to investigate but take them along. Upon arrival at the headquarters of the troops their cases are investigated by a military commission appointed for that purpose and dealt with as a general thing in accordance with its suggestions. If found to be harmless, neutral, or if no positive proof can be obtained of their complicity with the enemy and they are not themselves good loyal citizens they are usually discharged upon taking the oath of allegiance and giving bond for their good behavior in future.

It has never been supposed that such cases were to be referred to the commissary-general of prisoners. The instructions contained in a letter of February 26, 1863, from Major-General Wright, then commanding the department, a copy of which is herewith inclosed,‡ have been followed as far as possible. The above-named persons were not properly prisoners of war though so reported. But General Orders, No. 44,§ War Department, series of 1861 (as published in General Orders, No. 9, Department of the Ohio, current series, the original never having been obtained though repeatedly applied for), directs that the names, &c., of all prisoners be reported, &c., and it was in accordance with this that the within report was transmitted.

The commissary-general of prisoners appears to have supposed that all these men were taken into custody upon known grounds, whereas a more proper view of the matter is that they are so taken only to determine whether they shall be considered as prisoners at all. The reasons for reporting their names, however, appears to be the same, whether retained or not. Rolls of prisoners of war according to the blanks

---

*Omitted here; see Hoffman to Burnside, p. 719.
† See White to Thomas, May 12, p. 595.
‡ Omitted here; for Wright's instructions, see p. 299.
§ See Vol. III, this Series, p. 9.

furnished by Adjutant-General's Office are regularly forwarded as therein directed and the parties sent to Camp Chase, Ohio. Those persons retained as political prisoners are also sent to Camp Chase with the charges and testimony. Deserters from the enemy are also sent to Camp Chase with a statement of their position. No rolls of the last-named two classes have been forwarded and none it is believed are required from these headquarters. The returns now required from the provost-marshal and other officers having prisoners in charge will it is conceived give all necessary information regarding them.

I am, sir, very respectfully, your obedient servant,

JULIUS WHITE,
Brigadier-General, Commanding.

JUDGE-ADVOCATE-GENERAL'S OFFICE,
Washington, June 9, 1863.

Hon. E. M. STANTON, *Secretary of War.*

SIR: Pursuant to instructions received from you under date of March 23, 1863, I have the honor to transmit herewith lists* of political prisoners of which duplicates have been furnished to the judges of the circuit and district courts of the United States in compliance with the requirements of the act of Congress of March 3 last, entitled "An act relating to *habeas corpus* and regulating judicial proceedings in certain cases." Your instructions to me were to see that the provisions of that law are observed in regard to all persons held in military custody. For the preparation of the lists required by those provisions there were furnished me by you rolls of prisoners confined in the Government prisons at Saint Louis, Alton, Louisville, Sandusky, Wheeling, Camp Chase (Ohio), Fort Lafayette, Fort McHenry, Fort Delaware and in the Old Capitol Prison at Washington.

In consequence of the late date of your letter of instruction and of the receipt of the rolls, as well as on account of the pressure of business the lists have not been furnished within the twenty days specified in the act. This delay, however, cannot affect the privileges of the prisoners in question as will be seen by reference to the third section of the act alluded to at the end of this communication. Most of the rolls furnished are incomplete in view of the requirements of the act in that they do not state where the offenses were committed or by whose authority the arrests were made, and some of them do not specify in many cases what the offense was or charge. The residence of prisoners, however, is generally given, and this in nearly every case affords a venue for trial according to the terms of the act. It not being generally stated in the rolls by whose authority the arrests which are the subject of this communication were made it has been presumed (for the purposes of the present lists) that all were made by the authority either directly or indirectly of the President, acting through the Secretary of War.

In point of fact, however, it is believed that these arrests were generally made by military commanders and provost-marshals without any intervention on the part of the President or Secretary. A considerable number of the prisoners enumerated in some of the rolls, especially those from the prisons of Saint Louis and Alton, are not included in the lists prepared by me for the U. S. judges. The act does not appear to have been carefully framed and has been found to be extremely difficult of construction. In view of this fact and of the deficiencies in the

* Omitted.

rolls as well as in consideration of the exigencies of the service the act has been strictly construed by me, and those cases which are clearly triable by court martial or military commission and which are being every day thus tried and readily and summarily disposed of are not generally included in the lists. Such are cases of prisoners arrested as guerrillas or bushwhackers or as being connected with or aiding these. So too of those arrested for communicating intelligence to the enemy in the sense of the Fifty-Seventh Article of War and of those taken as spies.

It is not believed that it was intended in the act to invite attention to cases of persons charged with purely military offenses or of persons suffering under sentences of military tribunals. The cases of parties confined under sentence pronounced by military courts previous to the date of the act are, therefore, not contained in the present lists. But the large class of prisoners in whose case no charge or offense is set forth in the rolls or who are noted as awaiting charges, and the numerous class of those who are specified as confined during the war (without its being added that they are under sentence) are both included. The lists also embrace those cases in which the charge is stated in general terms as by the words rebel, disloyal, &c., and further comprise prisoners held as hostages merely or as refugees.

The construction of the act which has been adopted by me is supported by the consideration that under its provisions such construction cannot impair the rights of any prisoner not placed in the lists, for it is provided in the third section that in case a prisoner is omitted to be presented by the Secretary to the judge in the formal list he may obtain by a process therein prescribed the judge's order for his discharge upon the same terms as those which govern the case of the prisoners whose names, &c., have been furnished in the list by the Secretary.

Very respectfully, your obedient servant,

J. HOLT,
Judge-Advocate-General.

OFFICE COMMISSARY-GENERAL OF PRISONERS,
Washington, D. C., June 9, 1863.

Maj. Gen. N. P. BANKS,
Commanding Department of the Gulf, New Orleans, La.

GENERAL: I have the honor to inform you that Baton Rouge has been selected as a place for the delivery of prisoners of war as provided for in the cartel. Please require rolls of all deliveries made to be forwarded to this office.

Very respectfully, your obedient servant,

W. HOFFMAN,
Colonel Third Infantry, Commissary-General of Prisoners.

OFFICE COMMISSARY-GENERAL OF PRISONERS,
Washington, D. C., June 9, 1863.

Maj. Gen. J. M. SCHOFIELD,
Commanding Department of the Missouri, Saint Louis, Mo.

GENERAL: I have just received from the commanding officer of the Alton Prison a copy of your order of the 1st instant directing for what purposes the prison fund at that and other places in your department should be used. Supposing it possible that your attention may not have been called to General Orders, No. 67, of June last, I have the honor to inclose it herewith* together with a copy of the regulations I issued by the authority placed in my hands by said order for the creation and disbursement of a prison fund, and I would respectfully inquire whether the system now in force under these regulations at the several prisons is to be set aside by the order issued from your headquarters.

Very respectfully, your obedient servant,

W. HOFFMAN,
Colonel Third Infantry, Commissary-General of Prisoners.

OFFICE COMMISSARY-GENERAL OF PRISONERS,
Washington, D. C., June 9, 1863.

Brig. Gen. A. SCHOEPF,
Commanding Fort Delaware, Del.:

The enlisted prisoners of war ordered from the West to Fort Delaware will be ordered forward for delivery at City Point in a few days and I have to request you will have prepared to be sent North with them duplicate parole rolls signed and a roll for this office. These rolls should be made by regiments and companies. Please inform me when the rolls are completed.

Very respectfully, your obedient servant,

W. HOFFMAN,
Colonel Third Infantry, Commissary-General of Prisoners.

OFFICE COMMISSARY-GENERAL OF PRISONERS,
Washington, D. C., June 9, 1863.

Lieut. Col. W. H. LUDLOW,
Agent for Exchange of Prisoners, Fort Monroe, Va,

COLONEL: Your two letters of the 7th are received. I have forwarded to you at three different times orders which have been published, announcings of courts-martial in the cases of rebel spies and others sentenced to death, all of which I hope reached you safely. General Orders, No. 100, went into effect with us as soon as published. We hold the enemy bound by it from the time you presented it to Mr. Ould and it is as operative against us as for us. Its provisions so far as paroles are concerned are about the same as General Orders, No. 49, which I stated in my letter to you of the 20th ultimo was in force from the time it was published to the army, and all paroles taken or given in violation of it are not binding except in some particular cases when for special reasons generals commanding think proper to recognize paroles heretofore given by our troops. The enemy can take no exceptions to our recognizing irregular paroles which they have exacted. No such cases will occur hereafter. A few days since I returned to the Army of the Potomac a roll of prisoners of war captured and paroled by General Stoneman's command with the decision of the General-in-Chief that the paroles were not valid inasmuch as they had been taken in violation of General Orders, No. 49.

The State of Maine will leave to-morrow with some 300 prisoners of war and about forty citizen prisoners for delivery at City Point. Among them is Surg. W. A. McCorkle, Second Tennessee [Cavalry] Regiment, who under the cartel should be unconditionally released,

---

* Omitted here; see Vol. IV, this Series, pp. 30 and 152 for this order and the regulations.

but under present circumstances while they refuse to deliver the officers they hold you will decide on the propriety of holding or delivering him as may seem best to you.

I inclose to you a letter* addressed to me by Surgeon Hewitt, of General Grant's army, in which he requests a statement made by Right Rev. Bishop Green, of Jackson, Miss., in relation to the murder of Col John N. Cromwell in the streets of Jackson, Miss., which he placed in the hands of General Winder, may be returned to him. The importance which attaches to this document will be apparent to you and will I am sure secure your immediate attention.

I send you by this mail some rolls of rebel prisoners of war paroled in the West some months since with certificate showing that they were delivered within the rebel lines. I am not sure you will be able to use them.

Very respectfully, your obedient servant,

W. HOFFMAN,
Colonel Third Infantry, Commissary-General of Prisoners.

BALTIMORE, *June 9, 1863.*

Hon. E. M. STANTON:

I have learned by telegraph that the men I sent to New York have arrested one of the party, Simon Rosenfelt, but he refuses to tell the whereabouts of Alexander. They are on the track and I think will be successful. Please instruct civil authorities not to interfere in New York City.

W. S. FISH,
Lieutenant-Colonel and Provost-Marshal.

MILITARY PRISON, *Alton, Ill., June 9, 1863.*

Col. W. HOFFMAN,
Commissary-General of Prisoners, Washington, D. C.

COLONEL: I have the honor to report that the following detachments of prisoners have been received at this prison since the 1st instant, viz: From Nashville on the 5th, 18 men and 1 woman, Mrs. Trainor; from Memphis on the 6th, 37, including 4 commissioned officers; from Saint Louis on the 6th, 16 sentenced men, 3 commissioned officers included, and several Federals, and from Vicksburg and Memphis last night, 111, 8 of whom are commissioned officers.

Including the Federal prisoners, of whom there are 110 now confined here, we have about 1,600 persons confined in this prison—a number far too great for convenient and comfortable accommodation. The prison buildings cannot conveniently accommodate more than 1,000 persons and I would be glad if arrangements could be made so that the number of prisoners confined here at any one time should not exceed that number, especially in warm weather. The prisoners of war for exchange have been ready for a week or more but I have not yet received instructions from department headquarters to send them forward. I telegraphed the assistant adjutant-general at headquarters this morning in relation to this subject.

I have the honor to be, sir, with much respect, your most obedient servant,

T. HENDRICKSON,
Major Third Infantry, Commanding the Prison.

---

* Omitted.

SAINT LOUIS, *June 9, 1863.*

Major HENDRICKSON, *Commanding Military Prison, Alton:*

In compliance with instructions from the War Department you will forward at once to City Point, Va., all the prisoners of war now in the Alton Prison. A sufficient guard will be furnished by the commanding officer at Alton Prison.

By order of Major-General Schofield:

A. V. COLBURN,
Assistant Adjutant-General.

———

HEADQUARTERS DEPARTMENT OF THE CUMBERLAND,
Murfreesborough, June 10, 1863.

Major-General HALLECK, *General-in-Chief.*

GENERAL: The copy of General Bragg's letter* justifying the stripping of Coburn's brigade of their clothing as an act of retaliation for similar outrages perpetrated by our troops on his prisoners has been received, with your indorsement requesting from me a report on our practice toward their prisoners.

I regret to say after full consideration of all the possible or probable grounds for making such assertions by General Bragg that in my opinion a statement more radically at variance with truth and justice was never written. When I remonstrated with General Bragg for robbing the Hartsville prisoners of their blankets and overcoats in December last (see copies of our correspondence* marked from I to XXIV) he stated that they had done so following a very bad precedent set by our troops and admitted by our officer in command of the Hartsville troops. I replied that no such conduct was sanctioned nor did I believe that there had been any such practice; that so far as my information went we had on the contrary furnished their prisoners when destitute (as they usually are when taken) with clothing and blankets to prevent their suffering. But I subsequently called on the officer whom Bragg alleges to have admitted the existence of the bad practice and learned from him that General Bragg's statement was one of those tricky misrepresentations by a play on words which have marked that general's correspondence with me as will appear in his letters herewith inclosed. The officer said: "If such has been the practice I suppose we should not complain."

1. I now assure you that no order or permission expressed or implied has ever authorized the stripping of prisoners taken from the enemy of their blankets or clothing.

2. That I never heard of a single instance of such conduct nor has any general of whom I have inquired ever heard of an instance of such stripping of prisoners of their overcoats, blankets or other clothing by troops of this command, nor do we believe that there ever has been any such instances in any public manner or with any official sanction whatever, nor have I heard of any of those acts of private robbery which must sometimes occur.

3. I believe that when General Bragg made the statement he knew it was not true in the sense in which he knew his words would be taken.

4. Neither General Bragg nor any other Confederate officer has ever reported to me a single instance of any such practice nor asked for any redress.

———

* Not found.

5. General Bragg's assertion that orders have been issued stripping his men of their pantaloons and pronouncing the death penalty on those who wear the uniform "prescribed by our (meaning as I suppose the Confederate) Government" is confronted by the inclosed General Orders,* No. 16, which you will see is against those and those only who with less magnanimity than savages sneak up to our lines disguised in our own uniform. If the Confederate Government has adopted our uniform then General Bragg's statement may be correct and the responsibility—doing what the savages scorn to do, stealing the marks of other tribes—belongs to his Government. But if as I believe they have not been guilty of authorizing any such cowardly deceit then the responsibility of making a false assertion rests on General Bragg and is in keeping with his official course on other matters.

6. I have to say that General Bragg's cavalry have sneaked in behind their own flag of truce and captured our pickets in its presence. He has been furnished with official evidence thereof and made no reparation. That he has been officially furnished with list of personal property robbed from thirty-eight of our surgeons at the battle of Stone's River and given neither redress nor excuse; that he has been informed that Wheeler's cavalry robbed even our wounded soldiers on the hospital boat at Harpeth Shoals of their blankets, medicines, food and pocket money and given no redress; that they stripped our dead on the field at Stone's River and gave no excuse; that their guerrilla cavalry rob private persons of their clothing, money and other valuables whenever they attack our railroad trains without scruple or so far as I know any official disapprobation.

Official reports of these transactions having been sent from time to time for the information of the War Department the forwarding of duplicate copies thereof with this communication is deemed unnecessary. I am determined to deal most justly and humanely with our enemies, but I solemnly affirm that while there are many shining examples of individual chivalry and honor among them I have found the prevailing characteristics of their official conduct like that of General Bragg's letter to his own Government, wanting not only in magnanimity but in regard for truth and justice.

I have the honor to be, general, very respectfully, your most obedient servant,

W. S. ROSECRANS,
Major-General, Commanding.

HEADQUARTERS DEPARTMENT OF THE SOUTH,
Hilton Head, Port Royal, S. C., June 10, 1863.

Col. JAMES MONTGOMERY,
Commanding Raids, Georgia and Florida.

COLONEL: Every rebel man you may capture, citizen or soldier, you will send in irons to this place to be kept as hostages for the proper treatment of any of your men who may accidentally fall into the hands of the enemy.

Very respectfully, your most obedient servant,

D. HUNTER,
Major-General, Commanding.

* See p. 264.

HEADQUARTERS, *Fort Delaware, June 10, 1863.*
Col. W. HOFFMAN, *Commissary-General of Prisoners:*

One thousand nine hundred and ninety-four prisoners of war were received here last night from the West. Plenty of room to accommodate 4,000 more.

A. SCHOEPF,
Brigadier-General, Commanding.

HEADQUARTERS,
Fort Columbus, N. Y. Harbor, June 10, 1863.
Col. WILLIAM HOFFMAN,
Commissary-General of Prisoners, Washington, D. C.

COLONEL: I inclose herewith a list* of clothing required for use of the Choctaw Indians confined at this post as prisoners of war.

Very respectfully, your obedient servant,

G. LOOMIS,
Colonel Fifth Infantry, Commanding.

HEADQUARTERS DEPARTMENT OF VIRGINIA,
Fort Monroe, June 10, 1863.
Col. W. HOFFMAN, *Commissary-General of Prisoners.*

COLONEL: Section No. 8 in the Exchange Notice, No. 5,† published by Mr. Ould is not in accordance with agreement with me and he has been so informed. Exchanges of civilians and their releases from paroles and oaths are confined to those delivered at City Point and to a few special cases in which special notice has been given to the parties themselves.

Section No. 9 in same notice is also without agreement with or authority from me. We are only bound by what I agree to and not by what the Confederates publish. It is of course expected that parties declared exchanged are to be delivered to their friends. There are a few officers of ours who have been declared exchanged yet in the hands of the Confederates who are willing to deliver them. We have some of theirs in like situation. Please ask the consent of the General-in-Chief that such may be delivered and inform me by return mail of his directions.

A request has been made of Mr. Ould for lists of our deceased prisoners. The money inclosed to me ($52) belonging to Confederate prisoners will be forwarded to City Point.

I am, very respectfully, your obedient servant,

WM. H. LUDLOW,
Lieutenant-Colonel and Agent for Exchange of Prisoners.

MILITARY PRISON, *Alton, Ill., June 10, 1863.*
Col. W. HOFFMAN,
Commissary-General of Prisoners, Washington, D. C.

COLONEL: I have the honor to report that 1,192 prisoners of war including 67 commissioned officers were sent hence to City Point, Va.,

---

* Not found.   † See p. 949.

for exchange on the 12th instant the triplicate rolls* of whom are herewith transmitted.

I have the honor to be, sir, with much respect, your most obedient servant,

T. HENDRICKSON,
Major Third Infantry, Commanding Prison.

HEADQUARTERS DEPOT PRISONERS OF WAR,
Near Sandusky, Ohio, June 10, 1863.

Col. WILLIAM HOFFMAN,
  Commissary-General of Prisoners, Washington, D. C.

COLONEL: I am in receipt of your dispatch that I am not under orders of the provost-marshal; only General Burnside. I inclose you order† from General Cox on the 2d instant. I furnished under this order on the requisition of the provost-marshal of Erie County, Ninth Congressional District, Ohio, a force under Captain Benson to go to Crawford County, Ohio, and arrest deserters and those who harbor them. They were successful and arrested six who are now here, and two men who concealed or employed them, and they were taken to Cleveland and await trial before U. S. court. I forwarded you the roll of deserters last Saturday. Of course I am willing the battalion should render any proper service to the Government and as we had so few prisoners the men could be spared at that time. It is inconvenient to keep the deserters here, at least would be in large numbers very long, as I do not like to mix them with rebel prisoners and am keeping them separate I shall do in all respects on the subject as you direct.

Major Bascom, adjutant-general on General Cox's staff, is in the habit of sending me all the orders which issue from the District of Ohio. They are designed I suppose mostly for troops in the field. Among other things I am ordered to send morning reports four times a month; also am called on for rolls of prisoners, &c. As I am made responsible for the command by your orders I believe I understand the matter as well as can be done at Cincinnati, and I suppose that it is only incidental from this post being in this District of Ohio that has led to it. I have no complaint on the subject, but I believe the service has been as faithfully performed heretofore as it will be with this increase of clerical labor. I should not have mentioned the matter at all only there would seem to be rather a conflict between your dispatch and the inclosed order, and I thought proper to advise you that probably more from accident than design I seem to have many orders of late from the District of Ohio, and regarding you as my commanding officer I have no disposition to change, and least of all have any conflict. I will add that it would be convenient for the provost-marshal at Sandusky to call on me if he needs help and I shall be pleased to be permitted to help him.

Very respectfully, your obedient servant,

WM. S. PIERSON,
Major Hoffman's Battalion.

[First indorsement.]

OFFICE COMMISSARY-GENERAL OF PRISONERS,
June 15, 1863.

Respectfully referred to the Secretary of War.

Heretofore the depot has been under my exclusive control subject only to such orders as the general commanding the Department of the

---

* Omitted.   † Not found.

Ohio thought proper to issue, and there does not seem to be any necessity for the interference of a subordinate commander.

W. HOFFMAN,
Colonel Third Infantry, Commissary-General of Prisoners.

[Second indorsement.]

WAR DEPARTMENT, *June 16, 1863.*

The depot of prisoners of war at Johnson's Island, Ohio, and its guard are under the direct control of the commissary-general of prisoners, and the commander of the guard is immediately responsible for the security of the prisoners under his charge and is the judge of the propriety of making any detachments from his force.

By order of the Secretary of War:

ED. R. S. CANBY,
Brigadier-General.

HEADQUARTERS DISTRICT OF KENTUCKY,
Louisville, June 10, 1863.

Col. WM. HOFFMAN, *Commissary-General of Prisoners:*

Prisoners of war are frequently sent to the military prison in this city from the Department of the Cumberland with instructions to dispose of them otherwise than as directed by you in your general orders, as for instance to send the prisoners to Camp Morton and the officers to Camp Chase. Shall these be complied with or shall I only regard those received from you?

I have the honor to be, very respectfully, your obedient servant,

STEPHEN E. JONES,
Captain and Aide-de-Camp.

CONFEDERATE CORRESPONDENCE.

JACKSON, MISS., *December 1, 1862.*

Maj. Gen. M. L. SMITH, *Vicksburg:*

Measures will be taken to take care of the sick prisoners when forwarded here. Please state whether contagious disease exists among them and also at what time they will be forwarded.

DANIEL RUGGLES,
Brigadier-General.

ADJUTANT AND INSPECTOR GENERAL'S OFFICE,
Richmond, December 1, 1862.

Lieut. Col. F. L. HUBBELL, *Third Missouri Infantry.*
(Through Lieut. Gen. J. C. Pemberton.)

COLONEL: In reply to your communication of 9th ultimo I am directed by the Adjutant and Inspector General to say that the Confederate Government does not recognize the right of the United States Government to capture unarmed citizens not connected with any military organization. Any oaths or bonds entered into by such persons will not be respected by the Confederate Government.

Very respectfully, &c.,

J. S. WHITING,
Assistant Adjutant and Inspector General.

QUARTERMASTER-GENERAL'S OFFICE,
Richmond, December 1, 1862.

Maj. JOHN AMBLER, Quartermaster, Richmond, Va.

MAJOR: The Secretary of War has decided the officers and men taken prisoners of war by the enemy at Rich Mountain are entitled to pay to the date they were exchanged; that the disbandment of a portion of the Twentieth Virginia Regiment was without authority of law, and therefore the companies disbanded as well as those retained in service are to be allowed pay to date of exchange.

Respectfully, your obedient servant,

RICH'D S. COX,
Major and Quartermaster.
(For Quartermaster-General.)

[Indorsement.]

The Rich Mountain paroled prisoners were exchanged on the 12th of August, 1862.

WM. ROBINSON.
(For R. Ould, Agent for Exchange of Prisoners.)

———

VICKSBURG, December 1, 1862.

Lieutenant-General PEMBERTON, Oxford:

Nine hundred prisoners just arrived. Shall I return the Yankee prisoners on hand? I do not mean those held as hostages.

N. G. WATTS,
Major and Agent.

———

CASTLE THUNDER, December 1, 1862.

Hon. JAMES A. SEDDON, Richmond, Va.

SIR: I am a private in the First Battalion Connecticut Cavalry. On the 7th of October last I was with my battalion encamped near Centerville. Pickets at night patrolled within two miles and a half of Gainesville. Twice a day a patrol was sent to Thoroughfare Gap to reconnoiter. On the 7th of October in the afternoon I was sent there. I was returning and when near Haymarket I was surprised by a party of the Twelfth Virginia Cavalry and taken prisoner. When taken I was within the Federal lines and as near as I can judge forty miles— at least that was the distance I had to travel before I reached the Confederate lines. I have been held since the 12th of October in this prison. Am I not a prisoner of war? And if so why should I not be exchanged? Does my case not come under the cartel? I am here without friends or money. True I am a poor private and that must be the reason I am overlooked. I am confined with all classes of criminals. I respectfully solicit an inquiry into my case.

I am, respectfully, your obedient servant,

CHAS. H. MARSH,
First Battalion Connecticut Cavalry.

[First indorsement.]

General WINDER:

I would suggest the propriety of inquiring into this case. The writer is evidently of some intelligence and tells a plausible tale. He may be really a mere prisoner of war entitled to exchange.

J. A. SEDDON,
Secretary of War.

[Second indorsement.]

HDQRS. DEPARTMENT OF HENRICO, *December 20, 1862.*

Respectfully referred to the Secretary of War with the inclosed letter* of the prisoner. He was charged with being a spy and his statement in that letter tended to confirm the suspicion.

JNO. H. WINDER,
Brigadier-General.

DEPARTMENT OF STATE, *Richmond, December 2, 1862.*
Hon. JAMES A. SEDDON, *Secretary of War.*

SIR: I inclose a copy of a letter to this Department dated 27th ultimo from Mr. Robert Bunch, consul of Her Britannic Majesty at Charleston, S. C. It will be seen that Mr. Bunch states that one Gabriel Cueto, claiming to be a British subject, has informed him that he has been arrested and confined nine months at Salisbury, N. C., without trial or charges, and that another British subject named John Carfoot has also been confined for several months without being made acquainted with the accusation against him. I respectfully request that you will direct an immediate and careful investigation to be made of the truth of these allegations and especially whether the parties named are British subjects and that the result may be communicated to this Department.

With great respect, your obedient servant,

J. P. BENJAMIN,
Secretary of State.

[Inclosure.]

BRITISH CONSULATE FOR NORTH AND SOUTH CAROLINA,
Charleston, November 27, 1862.
Hon. J. P. BENJAMIN,
Secretary of State, Richmond, Va.

SIR: I have just received a letter from a person named Gabriel Cueto who describes himself as a British subject born at Edinburg who has never relinquished his allegiance to the Queen. He writes from Salisbury Political Prison, N. C., in which he states that he has been imprisoned for nine months without any charges having been brought against him and consequently without trial. He adds that he came to America as the correspondent of a Scotch newspaper. He gives me no clue to his alleged offense and professes entire ignorance respecting it. Mr. Cueto mentions that there is another British subject named John Carfoot who has been likewise confined in the same prison for several months and who is equally ignorant of the reasons for his detention. It is stated by my correspondent that both he and Mr. Carfoot have been debarred from writing to me and I am led to infer that their present application is made surreptitiously. Under these circumstances I have the honor to request that you will be so good as to inform me as speedily as may be practicable why these arrests have been made and also why these British subjects have been detained in confinement for so long a period without a trial. I feel assured that such abuses of authority if they have really occurred will meet with the prompt reprobation of your Government and that they will be at once redressed.

I beg leave to remain, with the highest consideration, sir, your most obedient, humble servant,

ROBERT BUNCH,
Her Majesty's Consul.

---

* Omitted here; see Marsh to Wood (inclosure), p. 777.

RICHMOND, VA., *December 2, 1862.*

Hon. JAMES A. SEDDON, *Secretary of War.*

SIR: I have the honor to acknowledge the receipt of the inclosed papers* indorsed with a request for my opinion and report.

The prisoners who are held by the Federal authorities are citizens of one of the Confederate States. So also are those who are held by us. The proposition made is to release one set on condition of the discharge of the other. In other words it is a proposal to exchange our own citizens who have been arrested for disloyalty to our Government for other citizens of the Confederate States who in defiance of the usages of civilized warfare have been arrested by the enemy.

I am well satisfied from the course of the Federal authorities that it is their anxious desire to consummate just such a system as is contained in this proposal. It is a deeply laid design to interfere with the administration of justice in the Confederate States and to give practical immunity to such of their friends and partisans in the Confederate States as may preach and practice disloyalty.

There is no sort of reciprocity in the proposed arrangement. We are asked to exchange our own people for our own people. One or more of these parties is subject to the conscript act. In a military point of view what real equivalent do we get for him? Moreover would not the acceptance of a proposal like this be a practical invitation to every man who was inclined to be disloyal to proclaim his hostility to our Government in order that by arrest and subsequent exchange he might relieve himself from conscription? If this request is granted other parties in similar circumstances will claim the benefit of the precedent and demand the exchange of such loyal citizens as the enemy may have wrongfully captured for our own disloyal people.

Our Government has already formally protested against the arrest of such of our people as are not connected with military organizations. We have officially declared to the enemy that persons so taken will not be recognized as lawful captures and therefore not subject to exchange. We have further declared that if persisted in such a course will be met by retaliation.

An acquiescence in the present proposal is substantially an invitation to a future arrest of our non-combatant citizens. Even if the exchange were made there is no guaranty that the same persons would not be arrested again within a week. My own course heretofore has been to refuse any such negotiation as the one proposed.

I shall not consummate any such arrangement unless I am specifically instructed to do so.

With great respect, your obedient servant,

RO. OULD,
Agent of Exchange.

CASTLE THUNDER, *December 2, 1862.*

Hon. JAMES A. SEDDON, *Richmond, Va.*

DEAR SIR: I am a prisoner of war belonging to the First Battalion of Connecticut Cavalry and have been confined here since the 12th of October, and I beg that you will please investigate the matter as there have been several exchanges since I have been here.

I remain, very respectfully, your obedient servant,

CHAS. H. MARSH,
First Battalion Connecticut Cavalry.

---

* Not found.

[First indorsement.]

I find from our books that the within-named prisoner was received here and delivered to Captain Alexander on 24th of October charged with being a spy.

TH. P. TURNER,
Captain, &c.

[Second indorsement.]

CASTLE THUNDER, December 8, 1862.

The record against Charles H. Marsh, who is here, is that he was taken at Bull Run August 9 as a Yankee spy. Papers with General Winder. Brought here October 24, 1862.

G. W. ALEXANDER,
Assistant Provost-Marshal.

[Third indorsement.]

HEADQUARTERS DEPARTMENT OF HENRICO,
December 10, 1862.

Respectfully returned to the Secretary of War inclosing letter from the prisoner, which was deemed of itself sufficient to establish a grave suspicion and to warrant his detention.

JNO. H. WINDER,
Brigadier-General.

[Inclosure.]

CASTLE THUNDER, Richmond, October 25, 1862.

Mr. WOOD, Commissioner of the United States.

SIR: I am a private of Company D, First Battalion Connecticut Cavalry. On Tuesday, the 6th day of October, 1862, I was detailed by Capt. L. N. Middlebrook, who was stationed with his company at Fairfax Court-House and Centerville, Va., to go to Thoroughfare Gap of Bull Run Mountain for the purpose of watching the enemy. One man was detailed each day for that purpose. After I had passed Haymarket I was captured by eleven members of the Twelfth Virginia Cavalry who got into my rear. I was mounted upon a gray horse with my military saddle and armed with my revolver. My company are without sabers. I was clothed in my uniform. As I was coming up to Haymarket I found on the road a gray jacket which I put on over my blouse as it was a very cool morning. I have been informed that I am charged with being a spy. I claim the protection of the United States.

Yours, truly,

C. H. MARSH,
Private, Company D, First Battalion Connecticut Cavalry.

VICKSBURG, December 3, 1862.

General PEMBERTON:

The flag-of-truce officer is instructed by General Grant to retain four of the returned prisoners in place of the four held in custody here, subject to the same treatment and fate. Do you wish any reply sent?

M. L. SMITH.

HEADQUARTERS MILITARY POST,
Atlanta, Ga., December 3, 1862.

Brigadier-General WINDER, Commanding, Richmond.

SIR: I have the honor to inclose list of prisoners herewith sent by an order from General Beauregard, commanding Department of South

Carolina and Georgia. They have been confined here some time and are many of them a desperate, bad set of men. You will please send by return guard a receipt for them, and also order the guard furnished with rations for their return to this post.

I am, general, very respectfully, your obedient servant,

G. W. LEE,
Commanding Post

[Inclosure.]

List of Federal prisoners in barracks.

Name.	Company and regiment.	Date of capture.	Charge.
		1862.	
P. Pierce	Company B, 1st Tennessee	Apr. 25	Bridge burning.
J. J. Barker	Company E, 2d Tennessee	May 3	Do.
T. McCoy	Company G, 2d Tennessee	Mar. 28	Do.
W. Bensinger	Company G, 21st Ohio	Apr. 13	Engine thief.
G. Smith	Company H, 2d U. S. Artillery	May 20	Prisoner of war.
H. Hebling	Company G, 10th Wisconsin	July 3	Do.
G. W. Walton	Company H, 2d U. S. Artillery	May 20	Do.
T. W. Coleman	Company G, 10th Wisconsin	July 3	Do.
B. Powers	Company G, 19th Kentucky	May 5	Do.
Jacob Parrott	Company K, 33d Ohio	Apr. 3	Engine thief.
William Pittenger	Company G, 2d Ohio	Apr. 14	Do.
Robert Buffum	Company H, 21st Ohio	Apr. 13	Do.
Elihu H. Mason	Company K, 21st Ohio	Apr. 14	Do.
William H. Reddick	Company B, 33d Ohio	Apr. 18	Do.
John Walls	Citizen, East Tennessee	Mar. 25	Disloyalty.
H. Mills	do	Mar. 12	Do.
R. White	do	Mar. 21	Do.
John Green	do	Mar. 24	Do.
G. W. Barlow	do	Mar. 11	Do.
J. Tompkins	do	May 11	Do.

All except the five prisoners of war were delivered to Captain Alexander December, 1862.

ATLANTA, Ga., *December 3, 1862.*

GRENADA, *December 4, 1862.*

Maj. J. R. WADDY:

Bragg's prisoners can go if there is an officer of his to take charge of them.

J. C. PEMBERTON,
Lieutenant-General, Commanding.

VICKSBURG, *December 4, 1862.*

Major WADDY, *Assistant Adjutant-General:*

The prisoners were guarded on board the train and sent to Jackson, General Ruggles being notified by telegraph of their departure. The prisoners sent over are exchanged and not paroled.

M. L. SMITH.

HEADQUARTERS FIRST MILITARY DISTRICT,
DEPT. OF MISSISSIPPI AND EAST LOUISIANA,
Jackson, Miss., December 4, 1862.

Maj. J. R. WADDY, *Assistant Adjutant-General.*

SIR: I have the honor to acknowledge the receipt to-day of Special Orders, No. 43, of November 29, assigning to me the duty in charge of exchanged and paroled prisoners. I am desirous of information as to the authority invested in me from the lieutenant-general commanding.

First. Is there any established hospital to which I have authority to send the sick and wounded; and if not have I authority to establish one for that purpose?

Second. Have I authority to order supplies from the quartermaster's, subsistence, ordnance and medical departments for the use and benefit of these prisoners?

Third. Have I authority to employ any of the exchanged prisoners as guards in the absence of other good and sufficient guards?

Fourth. In the absence of supplies of clothing for the exchanged prisoners am I authorized to apply to the War Department at Richmond for supplies?

Fifth. My quartermaster and commissary having been assigned to other duties am I entitled to their official services or not?

I shall hope to receive information at an early moment on this subject.

Very respectfully, your obedient servant,

DANIEL RUGGLES,
Brigadier-General, Commanding District.

VICKSBURG, *December 5, 1862.*

Major WADDY, *Assistant Adjutant-General:*

Four transports with prisoners instead of two have arrived. Having no place for them here will send forward as rapidly as possible.

M. L. SMITH.

INSPECTOR-GENERAL'S OFFICE,
Murfreesborough, December 6, 1862.

INSPECTOR-GENERAL, *Lieutenant General Polk's Corps.*

SIR: Accompanying you will find a list* of 179 paroled prisoners belonging to Lieutenant-General Polk's command. These men are at Chattanooga and in want of pay, &c., to obtain which their descriptive lists are necessary. You will please have them made out and sent to this office as soon as possible.

By order:

A. J. HAYS,
Lieutenant-Colonel and Assistant Inspector-General.

VICKSBURG, *December 6, 1862.*

Maj. J. R. WADDY, *Assistant Adjutant-General:*

Five hundred political prisoners. None landed and will not be landed until definite instructions are received regarding them.

D. BELTZHOOVER.

IUKA HOSPITAL, *Iuka, Miss., December 7, 1862.*

Lieutenant-General PEMBERTON,
Commanding C. S. Army of the West.

SIR: Occupying the position that I do I feel impelled from a sense of duty to report to you the conduct of Colonel Roddey and officers and men under his command. They have not only violated the condition

---

* Omitted.

upon which the Federal authorities established this hospital, but have insulted Surg. A. B. Stewart whom it was the pleasure of the Federal authorities to place here in charge in a manner which in my opinion demands that a just Government should no less than ask for an explanation and redress. About two weeks ago Capt. Richard W. Johnson entered Iuka in violation of the agreement upon which the Federal lines were extended thus far, and embracing this village and the line of railroad between here and Corinth, and when politely requested to withdraw from the town in reply cast an ungentlemanly reflection upon Surgeon Stewart. And yesterday during the absence of Surgeon Stewart on business for the hospital Major Johnson, accompanied by his brother, Captain Johnson, and about 300 armed men passed through this town, Captain Johnson and one man entering the room where Surgeon Stewart's wife lay sick and under pretense of searching for a contraband (a body servant of Surgeon Stewart's from Northern Kentucky) made a complete search of the room even to the bed upon which Mrs. Stewart was lying, from which she has suffered greatly. General, permit me to say that such conduct must be punished or this hospital located here by the special request of your surgeons will be closed, although many of the wounded of your command are pronounced by the surgeons in charge not in a condition to be safely moved. It has been our pleasure to treat with the most circumspect deference the wounded who have fallen into our hands and the Confederate surgeons in charge of them, and we look for an honorable and speedy redress of those outrages.

I am, general, very respectfully,

J. C. CAMERON,
Capt., U. S. Army, and Provost-Marshal-General, Dist. of Corinth.

GENERAL ORDERS, } ADJT. AND INSP. GENERAL'S OFFICE,
No. 100. } *Richmond, December 8, 1862.*

* * * * * * *

XIII. Commanding officers may order necessary issues of clothing to prisoners and convicts, taking deserters' or other damaged clothing when there is such in store.

* * * * * * *

By order:

S. COOPER,
Adjutant and Inspector General.

HDQRS. C. S. TROOPS ON SHENANDOAH MOUNTAIN, VA.,
December 9, 1862.

His Excellency the PRESIDENT.

SIR: Day before yesterday Mr. Job Parsons, a citizen of Tucker County in this State, personally well known to me as a man of the highest respectability, came to this camp to enlist under my command. He was pursued by eight of the enemy's cavalry for many miles, but his superior knowledge of the mountains enabled him to elude his pursuers and escape. He handed me the inclosed original papers* which had been served upon him by the military authorities at Saint George. A similar assessment was made upon Mr. Parsons' father for $300 and on another relative for $700, and payment coerced under the same diabolical threats. The pretext of robberies of Union men by bands of guerrillas is a falsehood. The fact is that Union men have conspired to run off each other's horses to Pennsylvania where they are secretly sold, the owners afterwards setting up a claim for reparation on the false ground that guerrillas have robbed them. I inclose this evidence of the atrocity of General Milroy for such action as Your Excellency may deem expedient in retaliation, either as a restraint upon this savage or a punishment should his horrible threat ever be carried into execution. This is only one of a thousand barbarities practiced here in these distant mountains of which I have almost daily heard for the last four months. Oh, for a day of retribution!

With the highest respect, your obedient servant,

JOHN D. IMBODEN,
Colonel, Commanding.

Medical director's remarks in reference to statements made by Brig. Gen. D. Ruggles in a communication to department commander of December 6, 1862. Referred to medical director by assistant adjutant-general December 8, 1862.

MEDICAL DIRECTOR'S OFFICE,
Jackson, Miss., December 9, 1862.

Maj. J. R. WADDY,
Assistant Adjutant-General, Jackson, Miss.:

The statement of General Ruggles that I was in any way the cause of much exposure to the sick of exchanged prisoners is unjust in the extreme as will at once be seen from the following facts:

On the morning after the arrival of the prisoners I was informed (not officially or by General Ruggles) that the piazza at the Bowman House was crowded with paroled prisoners seeking shelter from the rain. I at once sent for the surgeon whose duty it is to attend the prisoners arriving here and directed him to notify General Ruggles of the above fact. He told me he had been to see General Ruggles but was unable to obtain an audience with him. I directed him to go again and to say his business was urgent. I believe that he then succeeded. General Ruggles soon afterwards requested me to call at his office, which I did. I met Major Waddy, the assistant adjutant-general, there and the propriety of sending the sick to Brandon or to any other of the general hospitals was then discussed. I advised against it as I thought there was danger of spreading smallpox over the department. It was then understood between General Ruggles, Major Waddy and myself that the surgeon in charge of the prisoners was to treat all ordinary diseases among them in camp, and if any cases of smallpox occurred they were to be sent to the Deaf and Dumb Institute Hospital where some eighteen cases were already under treatment. I have approved for the surgeon a number of requisitions for hospital tents and other camp equipage, and supposed that all necessary arrangements had been or were being made for the comfort of the prisoners.

It was about 9 or 10 o'clock on the morning referred to that I sent to notify General Ruggles of the prisoners being at the Bowman House. I had heard nothing from him on the subject and did not know whether any of the prisoners were sick or not. I was actuated by sentiments of humanity in sending to notify him. It is I believe General Ruggles' duty to provide for paroled prisoners arriving here and not that of the medical department except as far as relates to those that are sick, and I will do what I can to provide hospital accommodations for such when due notice of their arrival is given me by him. To avoid the risk of spreading smallpox I recommended in my letter of November 29 to the department commander to keep the prisoners in camp for twenty days after their arrival. I have had no reasons to change my views on that subject and I believe that the wisdom of that measure is concurred in by a majority if not all of the medical officers at this post. My prohibitions to sending prisoners to Brandon or to any other general hospital amounted to advice only as it would have been presumptuous in me to have prohibited it while the assistant adjutant-general, the representative of the department commander, was present and could have ordered the sick sent there had General Ruggles convinced him of the policy of doing so notwithstanding my prohibition. I expected no credit from General Ruggles for anything I did but had still less reasons to expect censure from him for not attending to his duties. I was credibly informed yesterday that the night previous the proprietors of the Bowman House had lodged and fed free of charge 200 paroled prisoners who it appears from this up to that time had not been provided for. Will General Ruggles reproach me with that also? Or rather will he not give said proprietors credit for their hospitality and thank them for their kindness in thus relieving him from what might have appeared a neglect of duty on his part had the prisoners been compelled to sleep out of doors.

Very respectfully, your obedient servant,

N. S. CROWELL,
Surgeon, C. S. Army, Medical Director.

RICHMOND, *December 10, 1862.*

Hon. J. P. BENJAMIN, *Secretary of State.*

SIR: Orders were given some time ago for the release of Cueto whenever the British consul in this city should require him for removal beyond the limits of the Confederacy. An order has been issued to-day to General Winder to hold John Carfoot subject to your orders.

Very respectfully, your obedient servant,

J. A. CAMPBELL.
(For Secretary of War.)

HDQRS. DIST. OF TEXAS, NEW MEXICO AND ARIZONA,
Houston, Tex., December 10, 1862.

Colonel REILY, *Comdg. Sibley's Brigade, Millican, Tex.*

SIR: I am instructed by Major-General Magruder to communicate to you the existence of the following order from the Adjutant and Inspector General's Office at Richmond, November 12, 1862, for the information of all concerned:

EXCHANGE NOTICE, No. 3.]   [NOVEMBER 11, 1862.]

*   *   *   *   *   *   *   *

3. All Confederate officers and men who have been delivered at Vicksburg, Miss., previous to November 1, 1862, and including said date have been duly exchanged and are hereby so declared.

RO. OULD,
Agent for Exchange.

I am further instructed by the major-general commanding to say that all officers and men of your command who have been delivered at the above place will be ordered at once by you to join their respective regiments and companies without the least delay. None of your command except those delivered in conformity with the above order have been exchanged.

I am, sir, very respectfully, your obedient servant,

E. P. TURNER,
Assistant Adjutant-General.

SPECIAL ORDERS, ⎰ HEADQUARTERS DEPARTMENT No. 2,
No. 26.   ⎱   *Murfreesborough, December 10, 1862.*

* * * * * * *

II. All paroled prisoners who have been or who hereafter may be delivered at Vicksburg are declared by the agent at that point as exchanged. They will therefore report for duty with their respective regiments.

By command of General Bragg:

GEORGE G. GARNER,
Assistant Adjutant-General.

WAR DEPARTMENT, *Richmond, Va., December 11, 1862.*

Lieutenant-General PEMBERTON,
    Commanding, Jackson, Miss.

GENERAL: Your letter* of the 19th ultimo containing the correspondence between yourself and Generals Butler and Rosecrans, of the Army of the United States, has been received. The papers will be referred to Major Ould, commissioner of the Confederate States to arrange the exchange of prisoners with the United States.

Your own correspondence is approved by the President.

By order of the Secretary of War:

Very respectfully,

J. A. CAMPBELL,
Assistant Secretary of War.

HEADQUARTERS DEPARTMENT OF HENRICO,
December 11, 1862.

Captain TURNER.

SIR: You will parole all the prisoners of war now in your custody to be sent by flag of truce to-morrow.

By order of General Winder:

W. S. WINDER,
Assistant Adjutant-General.

SPECIAL ORDERS, ⎰ HEADQUARTERS DISTRICT OF TEXAS,
                NEW MEXICO AND ARIZONA,
No. 11.   ⎱   *Houston, Tex., December 11, 1862.*

* * * * * * *

V. Brig. Gen. H. P. Bee, commanding Sub-Military District of the Rio Grande, will at once cause the officers and men of the U. S. Army who were captured early last year in this State, including the Eighth

---

* See Vol. IV, this Series, p. 948.

U. S. Infantry, to be sent under a guard of cavalry to Vicksburg, Miss., there to be delivered to the commanding officer at that point to be placed by him at some convenient point in possession of the enemy. General Bee will direct the necessary transportation and subsistence arrangements to be made for the above purpose.

By command of Major-General Magruder:

A. G. DICKINSON,
Major and Assistant Adjutant-General.

BRITISH CONSULATE, *Charleston, December 12, 1862.*

Hon. J. P. BENJAMIN, *Secretary of State, Richmond.*

SIR: I have the honor to acknowledge the receipt of your letter of the 9th instant with which you have been so good as to convey to me certain information which has been furnished to you by the War Department on the subject of the imprisonment at Salisbury, N. C., of Gabriel Cueto. I observe also that the Secretary of War promises to acquaint you with the reasons for the detention at the same place of John Carfoot, who as well as Mr. Cueto is a subject of the Queen. I beg leave to return my thanks to you for your compliance with my request for information respecting these men. As regards the first of them I shall reserve any further action until I can consult with Her Majesty's consul at Richmond, by whom the investigation into his case has been commenced. With reference to the other I must await the report to you of the War Department.

I have the honor to remain, with the highest consideration, sir, your most obedient, humble servant,

ROBERT BUNCH,
Her Majesty's Consul.

STEVENSON, JACKSON COUNTY, ALA.,
December 12, 1862.

Honorable SECRETARY OF WAR, *Richmond, Va.*

DEAR SIR: I have belonged to the Confederate Army almost since the commencement of the war until a few months since, when I was taken prisoner by the Abolitionists. After being confined in the cells of a loathsome jail and other prisons and told I would not be exchanged I was induced to accept their terms by which I could be released which was taking the oath and giving a heavy bond, which I complied with. These being the facts of the case I wish to know if our Government forces me by conscription back into the service, not allowing me even the privilege of other soldiers who have been taken and released by parole or exchanged. If such is the case I submit as it is our law, but at the same time do not believe it is religiously or morally right. Besides which death is my penalty should I ever again fall into their hands for the violation of this oath or parole. I simply ask for the same as other prisoners—an exchange; but if it is not granted I am willing to do my country all the good I can. Without troubling you more upon this subject I close, hoping to hear from you soon.

Very respectfully, your obedient servant,

JOHN T. FITZPATRICK.

[Indorsement.]

Answer that if the writer of this letter was in the Confederate service and while so was taken a prisoner until his exchange is made he is not liable to conscription; but if he was not in the Confederate service but a citizen peaceably employed the Department does not acknowledge the authority of the United States to take him a prisoner or to exact from him an oath and will defend him against the consequences of re-entry into service.

HEADQUARTERS CAVALRY,
La Vergne, Tenn., December 13, 1862.

Col. GEORGE WILLIAM BRENT,
Assistant Adjutant-General and Chief of Staff.

COLONEL: I have the honor to forward you per courier three letters addressed to General Braxton Bragg which have this day been brought in with flag of truce. I inclose note* of Major Prentice which explains circumstances of the capture of three men from the Fifth Kentucky Cavalry. They were vedettes on the enemy's outpost and were captured by Criswell and a party of six others—a party of six scouts authorized to act by Colonel [General] Wheeler. At the time of the capture a Federal flag of truce under command of Captain Buford was in front at our picket-lines covering the dispatches herewith sent. The Federal flag officer entered his protest against the capture under the circumstances. I have the honor to inquire what disposition shall be made of the prisoners, their arms and equipments.

Respectfully, colonel, your obedient servant,
JNO. T. MORGAN,
Colonel, Commanding Outpost.

HEADQUARTERS ARMY OF MISSISSIPPI,
Grenada, December 14, 1862.

General S. COOPER,
Adjutant and Inspector General, Richmond, Va.

GENERAL: I had the honor to forward to the War Department sometime since a letter from Major-General Butler, commanding U. S. forces, New Orleans, in which he said he would hold Brigadier-General Clark and fourteen other prisoners subject to retaliation for the pretended murder of certain parties in Louisiana, also my reply stating that I would consequently retain all U. S. prisoners until I received instructions from my Government.

I would respectfully ask directions from the honorable Secretary of War for action in the premises.

Very respectfully, &c., your obedient servant,
J. C. PEMBERTON,
Lieutenant-General, Commanding.

HEADQUARTERS ARMY OF TENNESSEE,
Murfreesborough, December 14, 1862.

Brig. Gen. JOSEPH WHEELER,
Chief of Cavalry, La Vergne.

GENERAL: The general commanding directs me to inclose you the accompanying communications* from Colonel Allen and Major Prentice

---

*Not found.

in relation to certain Federal vedettes captured on yesterday whilst a flag of truce from the enemy was within our lines.

The general desires you will investigate fully and report all the facts in the case, especially the localities and relative position of the flag and the parties captured.

I am, general, very respectfully, your obedient servant,

GEO. WM. BRENT,
Assistant Adjutant-General.

HEADQUARTERS, *Ponchatoula, La., December 14, 1862.*

General PEMBERTON :

*   *   *   *   *   *   *

I have the further honor to inform you that I this day send to the provost-marshal at Jackson five Federal prisoners captured by one of my scouting parties. Some three months ago a picket of four men belonging to Rhodes' Partisan Rangers were captured by the enemy and taken to New Orleans. I have been informed that their exchange has been refused by the commanding Federal officer. I therefore respectfully request your permission to order a flag of truce with instructions to ascertain whether General Butler will exchange them or the reasons for his refusal.

I am, general, very respectfully, your obedient servant,

A. R. WITT,
Colonel, Commanding Post.

[Indorsement.]

Say to Colonel Witt that the case of the four men referred to will be brought to the notice of General Butler by first flag of truce.

J. C. P.,
Lieutenant-General.

HEADQUARTERS CAMP OF INSTRUCTION,
Macon, Ga., December 14, 1862.

Hon. JAMES A. SEDDON, *Secretary of War, Richmond.*

SIR : I have the honor to transmit the following copy of a letter received on yesterday from Lieut. J. M. Brittian, enrolling officer of the Sixth Congressional District in this State. I telegraphed the Attorney-General upon the subject immediately upon receipt of the information.

The circuit judge alluded to was the first judicial officer in this State who pronounced the conscript act to be unconstitutional.

Very respectfully, your obedient servant,

JNO. B. WEEMS,
Lieutenant-Colonel, Commanding, &c.

[Inclosure.]

DECATUR, GA., *December 10, 1862.*

Maj. CHARLES S. HARDEE,
Commanding Conscript Camp No. 2:

Judge Thomas W. Thomas of the northern circuit is releasing men again on writ of *habeas corpus.* He ordered J. M. N. Glenn, sub-enrolling officer of Oglethorpe County, to be confined in jail because he did not bring the person of R. S. Freeman before his honor to be tried on the writ. The sub-enrolling officer informed me of Freeman's refusal to go to camp at the appointed time whereupon I ordered the squad to proceed to the residence of Freeman and arrest him and put him under guard to be forwarded to camp the next morning with the squad. It seems that Glenn had been warned to bring Freeman before his honor for trial, but I had no evidence of it before I issued the order for the arrest of Freeman. I sent him to camp previous to the trial ordered by Judge Thomas because he had refused to go. Glenn proceeded to Judge Thomas' quarters at the time specified whereupon his honor ordered him to be put in jail until the person of Freeman was brought before him.

JABEZ M. BRITTIAN,
Enrolling Officer Sixth Congressional District of Georgia.

WAR DEPARTMENT, *Richmond, December 15, 1862.*
Brig. Gen. J. H. WINDER.

GENERAL: The Secretary of State desires to have a report of the time when Carfoot was arrested and the exact circumstances of his arrest and the facts elicited at his examination.

Very respectfully, your obedient servant,

J. A. CAMPBELL,
Assistant Secretary of War.

HEADQUARTERS DEPARTMENT No. 2,
Murfreesborough, Tenn., December 15, 1862.

Col. B. S. EWELL,
    Assistant Adjutant-General, Chattanooga.

SIR: I have the honor to inclose for the information of the general commanding the following papers:*

Field return of the Army of Tennessee; tabular form of the organization of same; copies of general orders in same; copy of correspondence with Major-General Rosecrans, commanding enemy's forces in my front; a map of the country in my front and flanks.

I invite your special attention to the correspondence with General Rosecrans. With that as a basis I have refused to exchange political prisoners; have discharged the only one in my command and have demanded a like discharge on his part.

I am, sir, very respectfully, your obedient servant,

BRAXTON BRAGG,
General, Commanding.

WAR DEPARTMENT, *Richmond, December 16, 1862.*
Brig. Gen. J. H. WINDER.

GENERAL: You will discharge from arrest and confinement J. G. Anderson, confined at Castle Thunder as a political prisoner.

By order of the Secretary of War:

J. A. CAMPBELL,
Assistant Secretary of War.

---

* Not found.

HEADQUARTERS, *Jackson, Miss., December 16, 1862.*
Maj. J. R. WADDY, *Assistant Adjutant-General.*

MAJOR: I have the honor to state for the information of the lieutenant-general commanding that it is apparently important to send a
flag of truce to Major-General Butler in relation to the release or
exchange of Brigadier-General Clark who was captured after having
been severely wounded at the battle of Baton Rouge, and some other
prisoners. If this meets with the approval of the lieutenant-general
I shall cause preparations to be made accordingly.

Very respectfully, your obedient servant,
DANIEL RUGGLES,
Brigadier-General, C. S. Army, Commanding District.

[Indorsement.]

Inform Brigadier-General Ruggles that the matter of communication
with the enemy is exclusively under the control of department headquarters.

J. C. P.,
Lieutenant-General.

HEADQUARTERS ARMY OF TENNESSEE,
Murfreesborough, Tenn., December 16, 1862.
Brig. Gen. JOSEPH WHEELER,
Chief of Cavalry, La Vergne, Tenn.

GENERAL: I am directed by the general commanding to instruct
you to return to their lines the three vedettes captured on the 13th
together with their entire equipments—arms. The passing of the flag
implied protection to all in its rear. He exonerates the officers and
men of your command involved in the matter from all intention to violate the flag and has so explained to General Rosecrans.

Respectfully, &c.,

J. STODDARD JOHNSTON,
Lieutenant-Colonel and Aide to General Bragg.

RICHMOND, VA., *December 17, 1862.*
Lieut. Gen. J. C. PEMBERTON.

SIR: Several communications of yours to the War Department have
been referred to me. One of them refers to the case of Captain Murphy. On the 21st September last Captain Murphy was exchanged for
Maj. Charles E. Livingston, Seventy-sixth New York Volunteers. General Butler has therefore no claim for any further equivalent for Captain
Murphy. The exchange was a special one and was made by me in
consequence of an urgent letter from Governor Moore, of Louisiana, in
whose service Captain Murphy had been acting. I informed Governor
Moore of the consummation of the exchange nearly three months ago.
If General Butler will refer to General Orders, No. 147, issued by the
United States Government, September 30, 1862, he will see the above
exchange therein published. The same communication refers to Partisan Rangers.

The following agreement has been made between the respective
commissioners of exchange, to wit:

The body of Confederate troops known by the designation of Partisan Rangers
and whose officers are commissioned by the Confederate Government and who are
regularly in the service of the Confederate States are to be exchanged when
captured.

The Federal Government has recently professed to carry out the above agreement to its full extent. I am inclined to believe it has done so in the East. Perhaps General Butler has not as yet been notified of the action of his Government. The agreement above quoted comes from the War Department at Washington and is signed by their agent of exchange.

It is yet an open question as to what action the Federal Government will take as to Partisan Rangers whose officers are not commissioned by the Confederate Government. We demand also their exchange as prisoners of war. To this the Federal Government has not formally acceded, though many such have been delivered for exchange by the Federals. I am in hopes they will soon embrace them as proper subjects of exchange.

Some time ago I informed Major Watts at Vicksburg that all Confederate officers and men who had been delivered at Vicksburg on or before November 1, 1862, and all officers and men who should after that date be delivered there until I informed him to the contrary were duly exchanged. Has he not so informed you? I presume you have not been so informed as the Secretary of War to-day refers a letter of Capt. James Clark, Company A, Seventh Missouri Cavalry, forwarded by you under date of November 29, 1862, inquiring as to his exchange. Captain Clark and all officers and men, Partisan Rangers of all classes included, who have been delivered at Vicksburg up to this present date have been exchanged. This arrangement will continue until you are notified to the contrary. I will be obliged to you if you will let me hear from you on the receipt of this letter.

Respectfully, your obedient servant,

RO. OULD,
Agent of Exchange.

HEADQUARTERS ARMY OF TENNESSEE,
Murfreesborough, December 18, 1862.

Brigadier-General WHEELER, *Chief of Cavalry.*

GENERAL: In reply to your communication* of this date on the subject of the three Federal vedettes captured on the 12th instant the general commanding directs me to say that you will destroy the paroles of these men and discharge them from the obligation.

I am, general, very respectfully, your obedient servant,

GEO. WM. BRENT,
Assistant Adjutant-General.

PROVOST-MARSHAL'S OFFICE,
Murfreesborough, Tenn., December 18, 1862.

General JOSEPH WHEELER, *La Vergne.*

GENERAL: I herewith send under guard the following-named Federal prisoners: Benjamin Leach, private, Company I, Fifth Kentucky Regiment; Thomas Leach, private, Company I, Fifth Kentucky Regiment; John Williams, private, Company I, Fifth Kentucky Regiment. The prisoners have been paroled and are sent in obedience to your order of the 17th instant.

I am, general, very respectfully, your obedient servant,

CHAS. W. PEDEN,
Captain and Provost-Marshal.

---

* Not found.

SPECIAL ORDERS, }   HEADQUARTERS DEPARTMENT No. 2,
     No. 66.   }   *Murfreesborough, Tenn., December 18, 1862.*

*   *   *   *   *   *   *

II. All paroled prisoners who have been or may hereafter be deliv ered at Vicksburg are declared by the agent at that place as exchanged. They will therefore promptly report for duty with their respective regiments.

*   *   *   *   *   *   *

By command of General Bragg:

[GEO. WM. BRENT,]
Assistant Adjutant-General.

WAR DEPARTMENT, *Richmond, December 19, 1862.*
THOMAS W. WHITE, Esq., *White's Battalion.*

SIR: You are respectfully informed in reply to your letter of the 24th ultimo that this Government does not recognize the paroles that were extorted from prisoners who were not engaged in hostilities between the Confederate States and the United States.

Very respectfully, your obedient servant,
JAMES A. SEDDON,
Secretary of War.

RICHMOND, VA., *December 20, 1862.*
Hon. JOHN LETCHER, *Governor of Virginia.*

SIR: I have the honor to report the results of my mission to Fincastle at your instance for the trial of Dr. William P. Rucker on various charges. The first indictment found against him was for the murder of one Michael Joyce in July, 1861. Before the death of the party he was examined by a justice for feloniously stabbing with intent to kill and was committed to answer to that charge before an examining court. At the regular term next thereafter he appeared and was examined after the death of Joyce for the charge of feloniously stabbing, &c., and was discharged.

The grand jury indicted him after an examination for the murder for that crime at the special term of the circuit court of Alleghany held in November. To that charge the prisoner pleaded *autrefois acquit* and relied upon his discharge by the examining court upon the charge of feloniously stabbing, &c. To the filing of that plea the Commonwealth objected and moved its rejection for insufficiency. Upon full argument the court overruled the Commonwealth's motion, and adjudging the discharge to be a bar to the prosecution for murder allowed the plea to be filed. The Commonwealth then tendered a replication to the plea averring the examination and judgment to have been procured by the prisoner's fraud in the absence of the attorney for the Commonwealth. To this replication the prisoner's counsel objected for insufficiency and the court adjourned it for argument at the next term.

The prisoner was then arraigned upon a charge of larceny of a horse of Joseph H. Persinger in January, 1862. To this he pleaded not guilty, and the Commonwealth not being ready to try it owing to the absence of a material witness it was continued to the next term.

Then came on the case of treason with those of arson of the Cow-Pasture bridge on the Central Railroad and a number of other cases therewith connected, all of which were committed in the month of May,

1862. To these charges the prisoner pleaded to the jurisdiction of the court on the ground that he was at the time of the commission of the several offenses charged a citizen and subject of the United States and in their military service, and that he was while so in their military service taken a prisoner of war by the Confederate States and that as such prisoner of war he is not liable to indictment and prosecution by a State court for any of the said offenses. To this plea the Commonwealth objected and after a very elaborate argument the court rejected the said plea as insufficient. A further plea in abatement was tendered and rejected and then the prisoner pleaded not guilty to all the indictments except in the case of treason. In the case of treason the prisoner, his pleas to jurisdiction and in abatement having been overruled, demurred to the indictment. His demurrer was in some respects to matters of form which were unimportant and of no consequence to the main question. But he demurred principally upon the ground that the war in which we are engaged is a war between the United States and the Confederate States, and that the act of the prisoner in levying war in combination with the Army of the United States and in adhering to the public enemy, giving them aid and comfort, was treason against the Confederate States and not against the State of Virginia. This ground of demurrer goes not to the form of the proceeding but is of the gist of the prosecution.

One count is not liable to the objection. Some of the overt acts of levying war and adhering to the enemy in other counts are not open to the objection but many of them are so liable. I desire to argue the point with due care and after ample preparation.

The cases will continue over until the spring term when I hope to be able to dispose of them.

I have the honor to be, with high respect, your obedient servant,
J. R. TUCKER.

PETERSBURG, VA., *December 22, 1862.*

Hon. JAMES A. SEDDON,
Secretary of War C. S. A., Richmond, Va.

SIR: I represent to you the case of Charles A. J. Collins. He was a citizen of Prince George County, Va., and a constituent of mine as State senator. He was arrested by military orders on or about the 10th of July, 1862. He was put in the jail of this city shortly after his arrest. He was kept in jail until about the 1st instant when he was sent a prisoner to Salisbury, N. C., where he is still confined. I do not know why he was arrested, but have reason to believe that he is not guilty of any act of disloyalty. But this I can knowingly represent, to wit, that he was a civilian at the time of his arrest and so remains of course, in no way attached to the army, and is denied not only a speedy trial but any trial at all, for the authorities are ordered not to subject civilians to trial by courts-martial (see General Cooper's letter to General French under date November 21,* 1862), and he is not delivered over to the civil authority to be tried. I do therefore most respectfully and with the solemn earnestness which it seems to me every lover of civil liberty should, nay must, participate in and affectionately appreciate apply to you or to the President, if he alone is competent, to order the military commanders in whose custody the said Collins is to deliver him over to the civil magistracy of Prince George County where he was arrested.

* See Vol. IV, this Series, p. 950.

I write you this letter at the instance of the wife of Collins, my sense of public duty as a citizen and my opinion as counsel concurring in the application. She has three small children, poor and a refugee from her humble home. She is now with her mother in this city, who is also a poor woman.

I have the honor to be, sir, your obedient servant,
ROBT. R. COLLIER,
Senator of Virginia.

[Indorsement.]

Answer that an examination of the political prisoners at Salisbury has been made to a great extent and it was supposed that all had been examined who had been arrested so long ago as July. Directions will be given for the examination of Collins.

J. A. S.

Statements of Messrs. Mulford, Florance, Giffin (December 23) and Borland (December 26.)

James H. Mulford, a citizen of New Orleans, having been required by the undersigned, Secretary of State, to make a statement of the facts connected with the gathering of the crops from the plantations in Lower Louisiana by the U. S. forces, declares the following facts to be within his knowledge: Andrew J. Butler, the brother of the commanding general, bought from Mr. Zunts, a planter below the city, his sugar crop as it stood in the field for the sum of $25,000 and informed this witness that he had gotten back his money in the first twelve days of grinding the cane; that he, Butler, took off the crop; that the plantation yielded a crop of about 1,200 hogsheads of sugar; that Butler said he had bought and was taking off the crops from several other plantations. Witness also saw the agent of the commercial house of Brown, Johnstone & Co.; the name of the agent is Tucker, and he was accompanied by 120 white laborers. The said Tucker was then on his way, as he informed witness, to take off the crops from the plantations of said Brown, Johnstone & Co., and Frank Webb, on joint account with the Yankees. This was done after the plantation of Mr. Webb had been stripped of everything, even to his wife's wardrobe and jewels, and the negroes driven off. It was well understood in New Orleans that no planter was allowed to take off his crop for himself. If he did his sugar was seized by order of General Butler as fast as it reached New Orleans.

JAMES H. MULFORD.

Signed in my presence.

J. P. BENJAMIN,
Secretary of State.

DECEMBER 23, 1862.

Henry Florance, a citizen of New Orleans, states that it is to his knowledge that all the slaves were taken away from the plantation of Mr. Zunts, a planter below New Orleans, who being thus left without means to gather his growing crop was applied to by Col. Andrew J. Butler, who offered to buy his crop as it stood for $25,000. The crop under ordinary circumstances is one of the largest in the State, worth perhaps five times that amount if taken off. The witness left New

Orleans before the season for grinding cane and has no knowledge how the crop was taken off, but it was sold as above to Colonel Butler. An arrangement was also made, as witness was informed by Clement Story, who is a sugar planter below New Orleans, to take off his crop on joint account with some of the U. S. officers in New Orleans. It was a well understood fact in New Orleans that no planter could obtain permission to gather his crop unless he would agree to share it with Colonel Butler or some of the Yankee officers.

HENRY FLORANCE.

Signed in my presence.

J. P. BENJAMIN,
Secretary of State.

DECEMBER 23, 1862.

——

Adam Giffin, a citizen of New Orleans, states that he knows Mr. Zunts, a sugar planter, who lives below New Orleans; that many of the negroes having been abducted from said plantation said Zunts informed witness that Andrew J. Butler, the brother of General Butler, had made him a proposition to buy his crop as it stood in the field; that Zunts being without any means of gathering his crop was forced to accept the offer, and that a bargain was made that Butler should restore the negroes to the plantation, or at least an equal number; that the crop should be taken off under the supervision of Zunts for account of Butler, and that the plantation should be restored to Zunts in the spring in full and complete order with all the slaves, and Zunts received in payment for his crop $25,000. Zunts told witness he had cane enough to make 700 hogsheads of sugar. A hogshead of sugar made by the process used on the plantation of Zunts is worth over $100, in addition to which is the molasses. It was well understood in New Orleans that no planter could take off his crop without some arrangement being made for the profit of the Yankee officials.

ADAM GIFFIN.

Signed in my presence.

J. P. BENJAMIN,
Secretary of State.

DECEMBER 26, 1862.

——

Dr. Euclid Borland says he is the owner of a plantation on the Mississippi River below New Orleans; that he was on a visit to the plantation of Mr. Zunts when he was introduced to a person by the name of Weed, and was informed by Zunts that he had made a bargain with Colonel Butler and Weed and another person connected with the quartermaster's or commissary department of General Butler's army. Witness cannot recollect the name of this last-mentioned person, although it was stated to him. The bargain was that the slaves which had left the plantation were to be brought back and that the crop of Zunts was to be made for account of Colonel Butler and his associates who had paid $25,000 for it; that the purchasers were to pay the overseer's wages and pay for some hogsheads that Zunts had bought, and were to pay for all expenses of taking off the crop, except such supplies as were then on the plantation. The purchasers agreed to bring back the negroes by aid of U. S. soldiers, and witness learned that a portion of the slaves were brought back to the place under a guard of soldiers. Zunts suggested to witness to make a similar bargain, as many of the slaves of witness had left his plantation, and witness then had a conversation with Weed who stated that he was trying to make bargains with numbers of the planters below the city; that he would not make with others the same bargain as he had made with Zunts; that he could not undertake to restore to each planter the identical slaves that he had lost but that he would furnish a number sufficient to take off the crop and share the proceeds with the owner; that if a sufficient number of planters would make this agreement he would station guards above and below the plantations so as to prevent any escape of the negroes. The witness told Weed that his mind was made up to hold on to his own property unless it was taken from him by force; that he would not share his property with the enemies of his country, but that if the Federal authority thought proper to place guards of soldiers to keep the negroes in order witness was willing to pay his share of the expense of so doing. During the conversation Weed said that the negroes would be forced to come down and work the plantations by guards of U. S. soldiers in all cases where the bargain was made with him. When Zunts' negroes were returned to his plantation under guard, as he understood, there were some negroes of Mr. Baylie, a neighboring planter, mixed with them. Baylie's negroes escaped from Zunts' plantation and went back to their owner. Witness was present in the office of Mr. Judson, a broker in New Orleans, when the written contract between Zunts and Colonel Butler was read in presence of witness. The contract had been drawn up by Isaac E. Morse, esq., as attorney for Zunts, and witness heard the contract read and remembers it well. Witness understood that the Saint Anne and the Concession Plantations, in the parish of Plaquemine, were to be worked in the manner above mentioned, in partnership with Weed and his associates, and that a portion of the negroes had been carried back to the Concession place. Weed was in treaty with Mr. E. Lawrence for the same purpose with respect to his plantation, but witness does not know whether Lawrence accepted the offer. Zunts told witness that he, Zunts, had been formerly in partnership with Colonel Butler as negro traders.

EUCLID BORLAND.

Signed in my presence. The erasures* were made on a second reading of the statement, witness requiring the modifications to be made as more accurate.

J. P. BENJAMIN,
Secretary of State.

DECEMBER 26, 1862.

EXECUTIVE DEPARTMENT, *Raleigh, December 24, 1862.*
His Excellency JEFFERSON DAVIS.

DEAR SIR: In accordance with the request of the General Assembly of this State I have the honor to send you herewith by the hands of A. C. Cowles, esq., a joint resolution of that body in relation to the seizure of one R. J. Graves, a citizen of North Carolina, and his transportation beyond the limits of the State. An answer to the demand therein contained at your earliest convenience will oblige,

Most respectfully, your obedient servant,

Z. B. VANCE.

---

* In the original on file.

[Inclosure.]

Whereas, the General Assembly of North Carolina is informed that one R. J. Graves, a citizen of the county of Orange, hath been seized at his residence in said county by a person professing to be a police officer from Richmond, in Virginia, and hath been transported to and is now detained as a prisoner in the said city of Richmond; and whereas the said Graves nor any other citizen of this State is liable thus to be seized and transported beyond the limits thereof without the order and approbation of the proper authority of this State, but on the contrary he and they are not liable to arrest except only on the warrant of a proper judicial officer; and if crime be imputed they are by the express provisions of the Confederate and the State constitutions amenable only to the civil tribunals and have a right to a hearing and trial before the courts of the Confederacy or of the State, according to the nature of the offense with which they stand charged, such trial to be had in open court according to due course of law; and whereas it is the duty of the government of North Carolina to protect from unlawful violence as far as possible every one of her citizens and to insure to each a fair trial in a lawful court having jurisdiction of his case: Therefore,

Resolved, That His Excellency the Governor be requested immediately to demand of the authorities at Richmond by whose order the said R. J. Graves was seized and transported and is now detained that he be immediately returned to this State to the end that he may be delivered over to the civil authorities here either of this State or of the Confederate States for examination and if sufficient cause appear for commitment and trial, so that if innocent of the matter laid to his charge he may be acquitted, or if guilty be convicted and punished by due course of law.

R. S. DONNELL,
Speaker of the House of Commons.

GILES MEBANE,
Speaker of the Senate.

GENERAL ORDERS, }   ADJT. AND INSP. GENERAL'S OFFICE,
    No. 111.   }   *Richmond, December 24, 1862.*

I. The following proclamation of the President is published for the information and guidance of all concerned therein:

BY THE PRESIDENT OF THE CONFEDERATE STATES.

A PROCLAMATION.

Whereas a communication was addressed on the 6th day of July last (1862) by General Robert E. Lee, acting under the instructions of the Secretary of War of the Confederate States of America, to General H. W. Halleck, General-in-Chief of the U. S. Army, informing the latter that a report had reached this Government that William B. Mumford, a citizen of the Confederate States, had been executed by the U. S. authorities at New Orleans for having pulled down the U. S. flag in that city before its occupation by the forces of the United States, and calling for a statement of the facts with a view to retaliation if such an outrage had really been committed under sanction of the authorities of the United States;

And whereas (no answer having been received to said letter) another letter was on the 2d August last (1862) addressed by General Lee under my instructions to General Halleck renewing the inquiry in relation to the said execution of said Mumford, with the information that in the event of not receiving a reply within fifteen days it would be assumed that the fact alleged was true and was sanctioned by the Government of the United States;

And whereas an answer, dated on the 7th August last (1862) was addressed to General Lee by General H. W. Halleck, the said General-in-Chief of the Armies of the United States, alleging sufficient cause for failure to make early reply to said letter of 6th July, asserting that "no authentic information had been received in relation to the execution of Mumford, but measures will be immediately taken to ascertain the facts of the alleged execution," and promising that General Lee should be duly informed thereof;

And whereas on the 29th November last (1862) another letter was addressed under my instructions by Robert Ould, Confederate agent for the exchange of prisoners under the cartel between the two Governments, to Lieut. Col. W. H. Ludlow, agent of the United States under said cartel, informing him that the explanations promised in the said letter of General Halleck of 7th August last had not yet been received, and that if no answer was sent to the Government within fifteen days from the delivery of this last communication it would be considered that an answer is declined;

And whereas by letter dated on the 3d day of the present month of December the said Lieutenant-Colonel Ludlow apprised the said Robert Ould that the above-recited communication of 29th of November had been received and forwarded to the Secretary of War of the United States;

And whereas this last delay of fifteen days allowed for answer has elapsed and no answer has been received;

And whereas in addition to the tacit admission resulting from the above refusal to answer I have received evidence fully establishing the truth of the fact that the said William B. Mumford, a citizen of this Confederacy, was actually and publicly executed in cold blood by hanging after the occupation of the city of New Orleans by the forces under the command of General Benjamin F. Butler when said Mumford was an unresisting and non-combatant captive, and for no offense even alleged to have been committed by him subsequent to the date of the capture of the said city;

And whereas the silence of the Government of the United States and its maintaining of said Butler in high office under its authority for many months after his commission of an act that can be viewed in no other light than as a deliberate murder, as well as of numerous other outrages and atrocities hereafter to be mentioned, afford evidence only too conclusive that the said Government sanctions the conduct of said Butler and is determined that he shall remain unpunished for his crimes:

Now therefore I, Jefferson Davis, President of the Confederate States of America, and in their name do pronounce and declare the said Benjamin F. Butler to be a felon deserving of capital punishment. I do order that he be no longer considered or treated simply as a public enemy of the Confederate States of America but as an outlaw and common enemy of mankind, and that in the event of his capture the officer in command of the capturing force do cause him to be immediately executed by hanging; and I do further order that no commissioned officer of the United States taken captive shall be released on parole before exchange until the said Butler shall have met with due punishment for his crimes.

And whereas the hostilities waged against this Confederacy by the forces of the United States under the command of said Benjamin F. Butler have borne no resemblance to such warfare as is alone permissible by the rules of international law or the usages of civilization but have been characterized by repeated atrocities and outrages, among the large number of which the following may be cited as examples:

Peaceful and aged citizens, unresisting captives and non-combatants, have been confined at hard labor with balls and chains attached to their limbs, and are still so held in dungeons and fortresses. Others have been subjected to a like degrading punishment for selling medicines to the sick soldiers of the Confederacy.

The soldiers of the United States have been invited and encouraged by general orders to insult and outrage the wives, the mothers and the sisters of our citizens.

Helpless women have been torn from their homes and subjected to solitary confinement, some in fortresses and prisons and one especially on an island of barren sand under a tropical sun; have been fed with loathsome rations that had been condemned as unfit for soldiers, and have been exposed to the vilest insults.

Prisoners of war who surrendered to the naval forces of the United States on agreement that they should be released on parole have been seized and kept in close confinement.

Repeated pretexts have been sought or invented for plundering the inhabitants of the captured city by fines levied and exacted under threat of imprisoning recusants at hard labor with ball and chain.

The entire population of the city of New Orleans have been forced to elect between starvation, by the confiscation of all their property, and taking an oath against conscience to bear allegiance to the invaders of their country.

Egress from the city has been refused to those whose fortitude withstood the test, even to lone and aged women and to helpless children; and after being ejected from their homes and robbed of their property they have been left to starve in the streets or subsist on charity.

The slaves have been driven from the plantations in the neighborhood of New Orleans till their owners would consent to share the crops with the commanding general, his brother Andrew J. Butler, and other officers; and when such consent had been extorted the slaves have been restored to the plantations and there compelled to work under the bayonets of guards of U. S. soldiers.

Where this partnership was refused armed expeditions have been sent to the plantations to rob them of everything that was susceptible of removal, and even slaves too aged or infirm for work have in spite of their entreaties been forced from the homes provided by the owners and driven to wander helpless on the highway.

By a recent general order (No. 91) the entire property in that part of Louisiana lying west of the Mississippi River has been sequestrated for confiscation and officers have been assigned to duty with orders to "gather up and collect the personal property and turn over to the proper officers upon their receipts such of said property as may be required for the use of the U. S. Army; to collect together all the other personal property and bring the same to New Orleans and cause it to be sold at public auction to the highest bidders"—an order which if executed condemns to punishment by starvation at least a quarter of a million of human beings of all ages, sexes and conditions; and of which the execution although forbidden to military officers by the orders of President Lincoln is in accordance with the confiscation law of our enemies which he has directed to be enforced through the agency of civil officials. And finally the African slaves have not only been excited to insurrection by every license and encouragement but numbers of them have actually been armed for a servile war—a war in its nature far exceeding in horrors the most merciless atrocities of the savages.

And whereas the officers under the command of the said Butler have been in many instances active and zealous agents in the commission of these crimes, and no instance is known of the refusal of any one of them to participate in the outrages above narrated;

And whereas the President of the United States has by public and official declaration signified not only his approval of the effort to excite servile war within the Confederacy but his intention to give aid and encouragement thereto if these independent States shall continue to refuse submission to a foreign power after the 1st day of January next, and has thus made known that all appeals to the laws of nations, the dictates of reason and the instincts of humanity would be addressed in vain to our enemies, and that they can be deterred from the commission of these crimes only by the terms of just retribution:

Now therefore I, Jefferson Davis, President of the Confederate States of America and acting by their authority, appealing to the Divine Judge in attestation that their conduct is not guided by the passion of revenge but that they reluctantly yield to the solemn duty of repressing by necessary severity crimes of which their citizens are the victims, do issue this my proclamation, and by virtue of my authority as Commander-in-Chief of the Armies of the Confederate States do order—

1. That all commissioned officers in the command of said Benjamin F. Butler be declared not entitled to be considered as soldiers engaged in honorable warfare but as robbers and criminals deserving death, and that they and each of them be whenever captured reserved for execution.

2. That the private soldiers and non-commissioned officers in the army of said Butler be considered as only the instruments used for the commission of the crimes perpetrated by his orders and not as free agents; that they therefore be treated when captured as prisoners of war with kindness and humanity and be sent home on the usual parole that they will in no manner aid or serve the United States in any capacity during the continuance of this war unless duly exchanged.

3. That all negro slaves captured in arms be at once delivered over to the executive authorities of the respective States to which they belong to be dealt with according to the laws of said States.

4. That the like orders be executed in all cases with respect to all commissioned officers of the United States when found serving in company with armed slaves in insurrection against the authorities of the different States of this Confederacy.

In testimony whereof I have signed these presents and caused the seal of the Confederate States of America to be affixed thereto at the city of Richmond on this 23d day of December, in the year of our Lord one thousand eight hundred and sixty-two.

[L. S.]   JEFF'N DAVIS.

By the President:

 J. P. BENJAMIN, *Secretary of State.*

II. Officers of the Army are charged with the observance and enforcement of the foregoing orders of the President. Where the evidence is not full or the case is for any reason of a doubtful character it will be referred through this office for the decision of the War Department.

 By order:

S. COOPER,
Adjutant and Inspector General.

NEW MARKET, *December 26, 1862.*
General S. COOPER, *Adjutant and Inspector General:*

Please retain Major Withers, Tenth [West] Virginia (Federal) Regiment, until I can send you copies of orders recently issued by General Milroy.

W. E. JONES,
Brigadier-General, Commanding.

WAR DEPARTMENT, *Richmond, December 27, 1862.*
His Excellency Z. B. VANCE, *Governor of North Carolina.*

SIR: In the absence of the President now on a visit to the armies of the West and South your letter of the 24th instant communicating a preamble and resolution of the General Assembly of North Carolina relative to the seizure and transportation from the State of R. J. Graves, a citizen of Orange County, and making in conformity with the resolution a demand for the return of the said R. J. Graves to the State and his delivery to the authorities there for examination and if sufficient cause appear for commitment and trial, has been handed by A. C. Cowles, esq., to me as Secretary of War for my action thereon. It will doubtless be matter of regret to you and the General Assembly of your State as it certainly is to me that the matter cannot receive the more satisfactory consideration and determination of the President, and as the subject shall on his return be promptly submitted to his revision it is not improbable that he may deem it worthy of further special communication from himself.

Still the imposing source of the application and the gravity of the subject demanding from its nature prompt action in my estimation impose on me the responsibility of exercising my imperfect judgment in rendering a decision. Some brief statement of the connection of t' e department with the detention of Mr. Graves and of the circumstances of his case will naturally and appropriately precede and explain both the action heretofore taken and the conclusion arrived at in his case.

Only some few days since was I informed as head of this Department of the detention of Mr. Graves in one of the military prisons of the city to which he had been consigned by the order of Brigadier-General Winder, military commandant of the district and acting provost-marshal of the city. When apprised of the fact I inquired briefly as to the ground of charge and was assured by General Winder that he was charged and held as a spy and that he did not consider it safe that he should be dismissed. I then directed that he should be examined by the commissioner, Mr. Sydney S. Baxter, a lawyer of high repute, charged with the duty of inquiring into the cases of prisoners in the military prison and of either discharging them or handing them over to their proper tribunals for trial. A day or two afterwards on the application of the Reverend Mr. Brown, of North Carolina, learning that the examination had not been had I reiterated the order, and being informed that the cause of delay had been the absence of a soldier and officer in the army who were wanted as witnesses I immediately directed that they should be ordered from the field here. Thus the matter stood to-day on the delivery of your letter.

On the fuller investigation immediately made of the circumstances of the arrest and of the grounds on which it was based I learn from General Winder that on the 6th of November last there appeared in the Richmond Enquirer a long letter written by the Rev. R. J. Graves proffered as giving to our people just views of the purposes of our enemies. A number of the paper containing the letter will be submitted to you with this. Without pretending to judge the real intent or probable effect of this letter it is sufficient to say it seemed to many well calculated to cause distrust and discouragement among our people as to the result of the war and that the loyalty of the writer was greatly doubted.

Not very long after the publication of this article two letters addressed to the editor of the Enquirer elicited by the distrust which this letter had aroused as to the character and purposes of the writer were submitted by that editor to General Winder. Copies* of these two letters are transmitted herewith. One was from Capt. T. E. Upshaw, a gallant officer of the army, giving the intelligence derived from one of his soldiers, a returned prisoner vouched as entirely truthful, that this reverend gentleman (Mr. Graves) who had come down with the flag of truce to Harrison's Landing while there was heard by him giving information to the enemy of all he knew "about our matters at Richmond and especially about the gun-boat Richmond," in respect to which "so elaborate were the discussion and explanation that the drawings and plans of the Monitor were brought and shown to him." Other particulars tending to strengthen suspicion and identify the Reverend Mr. Graves are given on which as you will have the letter it is needless to dwell.

In this connection it may be added that subsequently it has been ascertained that after his return from the North the Reverend Mr. Graves voluntarily stated to a leading clergyman of this city (Mr. Norwood) that finding difficulty interposed to his going North he had obtained his permit to proceed by affecting to give information which he believed would be of no avail to the enemy and had among other topics made statements respecting the gun-boat Richmond. This attitude, confessed by himself, of a minister of the gospel for an end of private advantage affecting to act the spy is certainly not calculated to diminish the suspicion of his conduct while it identifies him with the person charged by the soldier and confirms the general accuracy of his statement.

The other letter laid before General Winder signed "An old citizen," but submitted by Mr. George B. Miles, appears to have been written by a zealous citizen of North Carolina fully acquainted with the origin and antecedents of the Reverend Mr. Graves and characterizes him as a Northern man, a Yankee undeserving of trust and more than doubtful loyalty having neither home nor people in North Carolina. On applying to General Winder for a passport at the time of his trip to Harrison's Landing Mr. Graves had represented himself as a New Yorker desirous of returning to the North. Other oral suggestions General Winder informs me were made from various sources against this man, but the letters constituted the main grounds for his actions. He sent an officer under his command to North Carolina, had him arrested and brought to this city.

You will observe his information was that the reverend gentleman had acted the spy and might naturally be expected to continue the same line of conduct. He did not know him to be a North Carolinian, but believed him an alien enemy (being described as a Yankee without home in the State), and as such being charged with giving information to the enemy he considered him as a spy, to be arrested anywhere in the Confederacy and brought for examination and trial to the military district within which his alleged offense had been committed. General Winder in the judgment of the Department acted with over-zeal in not

---

* Not found.

first fully satisfying himself that the party charged was not a citizen of North Carolina. As such while amenable to arrest on sufficient grounds as a spy or even as a traitor he could with no propriety or legality be removed from the State but should have been handed over to the appropriate authorities, military or civil, in that State to be dealt with according to the law. While doubt on the subject of the citizenship of this party may have been on the information possessed pardonable heretofore, now that the assurance of this citizenship is afforded by the deliberate act of the General Assembly of North Carolina, there can be neither pretense nor justification for not promptly admitting the error committed by his removal and rectifying it by his immediate return and delivery under Your Excellency's demand. He will accordingly be cheerfully and at once placed at the disposition of Mr. Cowles or at his option sent under the escort of an officer to be delivered in Raleigh to such authority as you may direct. Should any proceedings be instituted against him requiring the presence of witnesses I need not add that all facilities will be afforded by the Department here to secure their due attendance.

While regretting the mistake committed in this case I find compensative satisfaction in evincing the sincere respect entertained by the Department for the rights of citizenship and sovereignty of the States, and avail myself of the opportunity to assure Your Excellency and through you the General Assembly of North Carolina that the Department so far from countenancing infringement on either regards it as its highest privilege as well as plainest duty by the utmost effort of its powers to preserve them both inviolate against all enemies.

I have the honor to be, with high consideration and esteem, most respectfully, your obedient servant,

JAMES A. SEDDON,
Secretary of War.

WAR DEPARTMENT, *Richmond, December 27, 1862.*
Brig. Gen. J. H. WINDER, *Richmond, Va.*

SIR: I have concluded to surrender the Rev. R. J. Graves to the authorities of the State of North Carolina. You will therefore hold the prisoner in readiness to be delivered to the agent of the Governor or to be sent to that State in charge of your officers as may be preferred by the agent.

Respectfully,

JAMES A. SEDDON,
Secretary of War.

INSPECTOR-GENERAL'S OFFICE,
Murfreesborough, December 27, 1862.
Col. B. S. EWELL, *Assistant Adjutant-General, Chattanooga.*

COLONEL: In the absence of General Bragg who has gone to the front and the matter not admitting of delay I send you some Federal prisoners for your disposal, General Rosecrans having declined to receive them through his lines. The officer in charge, Captain Cunningham, is instructed to report the enlisted men to you and to convey the officers to Atlanta to be held as hostages until further orders. Colonel Moore and his aide-de-camp, Lieutenant Dewald, having been paroled and receipted for by General Rosecrans I respectfully ask that they be sent to Richmond to be forwarded through our lines.

I am, colonel, very respectfully, your obedient servant,

W. K. BEARD,
Inspector-General.

BRITISH CONSULATE, *Charleston, December 28, 1862.*
Hon. J. P. BENJAMIN, *Secretary of State, Richmond.*

SIR: It is now nearly a month since you were so good as to promise to procure from the War Department some information respecting the reasons which may have led to the imprisonment at Salisbury, N. C., of John Carfoot, a subject of Her Majesty. As this person is still so far as I know held in confinement I beg leave to again direct your attention to the matter in order that he may be either brought at once to trial or speedily released.

I have the honor to be, sir, your very faithful and obedient servant,

ROBERT BUNCH.

WAR DEPARTMENT, *Richmond, December 30, 1862.*
Hon. R. R. COLLIER, *Petersburg, Va.*

SIR In the absence of the President your letter to him of the 23d instant has been referred to this Department for answer and you are respectfully informed that an additional person has been appointed to examine all prisoners and has instructions to discharge all those who are illegally detained.

Very respectfully, your obedient servant,

JAMES A. SEDDON,
Secretary of War.

WAR DEPARTMENT, *Richmond, December 30, 1862.*
BEVERLY R. WELLFORD, Jr., Esq.

SIR: You have been selected by this Department to proceed to Petersburg, Va., and Salisbury, N. C., for the purpose of making an examination of the entire body of prisoners who are detained in prison in either of those places under the military authority of the Confederate States and where the persons do not belong to the army of the Confederacy. You are authorized to call upon the provost-marshals and the officers having charge of the prisons in either of those places for the books and papers kept by them and for all the information they have respecting the cause of arrest and detention of any person held in confinement. You may examine any witnesses they have or can produce against them and may hear the statement of the prisoners themselves. You will make a record of all your proceedings under this commission and a report of your judgment in each particular case.

You are authorized to set at liberty all those against whom no well-grounded cause of suspicion exists of having violated any law or done any act hostile or injurious to the Confederate States. And as to those against whom suspicion is found properly to exist you will make a report of the facts and of your opinion and recommendation concerning them. You will notify the commanding officers of this commission and of the time you will commence your investigation and they will be ordered to grant you every facility and to carry into effect all your recommendations.

Very respectfully, your obedient servant,

JAMES A. SEDDON,
Secretary of War.

WAR DEPARTMENT, *Richmond, Va., December 31, 1862.*
Lieut. Gen. J. C. PEMBERTON, *General Commanding, &c.*

SIR: I have the honor to acknowledge your letter of the 14th instant which has just reached me through the Adjutant-General. Your determination to retain the U. S. prisoners under your control until General Clark and the fourteen other officers held by General Butler contrary to good faith and the obligation of the cartel for the exchange of prisoners between the United States and the Confederate Government are returned is fully approved. The pretense on which General Clark and the other officers are withheld is wholly unjustifiable and untenable. In the first place the evidence which is offered of the alleged ground of action, being the mutilated fragment of the supposed proceedings of a court-martial, is too imperfect and unsatisfactory to be the basis of such action, but giving full credence to it and viewing it as conclusive it would still only show the action of an officer of the State of Louisiana and of a court-martial held under his authority upon a man subject to the militia service of the State.

Now, the Government of the United States has explicitly refused to recognize the applicability of the cartel to officers or soldiers merely in State service and it is consequently precluded from avoiding the obligation of that cartel by reference to the action of such State officers, but the most conclusive reason against their pretense is that the exchange of General Clark and his companions in confinement seems to have been actually arranged and on our part carried out by the delivery of the Federal officers agreed on. A grosser breach of faith than the retention of those officers and the refusal to deliver these for whom they were returned could not well be exhibited. You will therefore continue the course you have adopted until adequate redress is obtained.

With high consideration and esteem, very respectfully, your obedient servant,

JAMES A. SEDDON,
Secretary of War.

HEADQUARTERS WESTERN SUB-DISTRICT OF TEXAS,
San Antonio, January 2, 1863.
Maj. A. G. DICKINSON,
Assistant Adjutant-General, Houston, Tex.

SIR: I have the honor to report that the U. S. prisoners of war under the escort of Capt. F. V. D. Stucken's company of cavalry, Taylor's battalion, have taken up the line of march for Vicksburg via Shreveport, and would request that the necessary orders may be sent on to meet them.

I am, very respectfully, your obedient servant,

H. P. BEE,
Brigadier-General, Provisional Army.

DEER CREEK, *January 2, 1863.*

GENERAL COMMANDING, *Grenada, Miss.*

GENERAL: I have the honor to hand inclosed list* of prisoners, C. S. Army, left at Greenville, Miss., this county, by the steamer Minnehaha on the 31st ultimo. These prisoners were sick and were put off without any provision being made for their well-being and comfort. Without bedding, rations or medicines, these disabled soldiers are roughly thrown into a deserted hotel in a small village on the river, whose inhabitants may be numbered by the half dozen, beyond the reach of everything like material comfort. The citizens in the neighborhood have already given away all their surplus bedding, have no medicines and can barely supply the poor soldiers with enough to eat; and besides the recent raids and destruction of property along the river-bank will deter the people from sending that aid which they otherwise would.

These soldiers are a portion of the prisoners brought down for exchange and ordered back by the Federal commander at Vicksburg. Eight hundred and fifty remained on the boat and were to be carried to Memphis or Helena. I understand the Minnehaha put off a case of smallpox below Greenville. The obvious effect if not intent of this policy will be to scatter a violent plague throughout the whole country. Escaped prisoners report that Grant's army from above and Banks' army from below are ordered to co-operate in the attack upon Vicksburg. Whether this be true or not I cannot say.

I cannot close without calling the attention of the general commanding to the iniquity of the course thus pursued by the Yankees in attempting to scatter through this whole country and that too without warning the most violent epidemic disease known.

I have the honor, general, to be, your obedient servant,

W. L. NUGENT,
Lieutenant, &c.

[Indorsements.]

Respectfully referred to Doctor Moses for his consideration. I should like to see him to converse with him on the subject. Return this. I wish to reply and send it to General Pemberton.

W. W. LORING,
Major-General.

I have ordered Doctor Moses to send a surgeon with medicines and comforts for the sick.

Respectfully forwarded.

W. W. LORING,
Major-General, Commanding.

OFFICE PROVOST-MARSHAL,
Knoxville, Tenn., January 3, 1863.

Maj. H. L. CLAY, *Assistant Adjutant-General.*

SIR: Below you will please find a list of free negroes confined in jail: Moses Sliger, Knoxville, confined by order of Brigadier-General Davis, commanding post, December 8, 1862; Jesse Malone, Campbell County, Tenn., committed December 5, 1862; Simon Malone, Campbell County, Tenn., committed December 5, 1862; Manuel Cox, Campbell County, Tenn., committed December 5, 1862.

---

* Omitted.

The first-named negro was arrested by order of Brigadier-General Davis, commanding post, on account of a riot at his house. The other three, from Campbell County, Tenn., ran away to Powell's Valley some time since and perhaps have been to Kentucky. They were captured by a scouting party from Big Creek Gap and sent to this place by Colonel Palmer, Fifty-eighth North Carolina Regiment.

I respectfully recommend that the first-named negro be turned over to Messrs. McGee & Co. What disposition shall be made of the others?

Respectfully,

JOHN E. TOOLE,
Colonel and Provost-Marshal.

[Indorsement.]

Turn them all over to McGee & Co.
By command of Lieut. Gen. E. Kirby Smith:

H. L. CLAY,
Assistant Adjutant-General.

HEADQUARTERS SECOND CORPS,
Grenada, January 4, 1863.

Hon. G. G. VEST, *Member of Congress.*

SIR: General Price directs me to acknowledge the reception of your communication* of the 30th ultimo in relation to the murder of Col. Frisby H. McCullough by the Federal authorities in Northern Missouri, and to state in reply that the general is under the impression that Colonel McCullough obtained recruiting authority from him at Springfield last winter. He does not know whether Colonel McCullough organized troops under this authority or not. Your communication has been referred to Adjutant-General Hough, to whom all the books, &c., pertaining to the Missouri State Guard were delivered with the request that he will furnish to you a copy of the recruiting authority given to Colonel McCullough.

The general further directs me to say that he will cordially co-operate with you in any endeavor that you may make to prevent the murder of citizens and soldiers of Missouri.

I am, sir, &c.,

JAMES M. LOUGHBOROUGH.

WAR DEPARTMENT, *Richmond, January 5, 1863.*

Hon. JOHN B. BALDWIN, *Staunton, Va.*

SIR: I have the honor to inclose to you a copy* of the report of S. S. Baxter, esq., who was charged with the investigation anew of the case of Samuel Simmons. It appears from this report and the accompanying certificates that Simmons was received at the C. S. Military Prison in this city on the evening of the 7th of September last, was transferred to the hospital on the 12th and died there on the 18th or 19th of the same month. The seeming loss of all trace of this unfortunate man while in the custody of the military authorities presented a case sufficiently startling to arouse the anxious attention of the Department. The illness of Mr. Simmons unhappily occurring so speedily after he was brought to Richmond issuing in his death in the brief space of six days doubtless prevented his case being the subject of examination

---

* Not found.

while fresh in the memory of those in whose custody he had been placed. Changes in the officers at the prisons, the large number of prisoners of war as well as others in confinement there and the clerical error in the name as explained by Mr. Baxter account for the difficulty which has existed in tracing him. While sparing no effort to guard the interests of the Confederacy in the life struggle in which we are engaged it is my earnest desire and purpose that the personal rights of the citizen shall be as jea'ously observed as in time of peace so far as is consistent with the safety of the State.

Respectfully, yours,

JAMES A. SEDDON,
Secretary of War.

JASPER, TENN., *January 6, 1863.*

His Excellency JEFFERSON DAVIS,
President of the Confederate States of America.

SIR: I take the liberty to inform you how I have been treated by the Federal forces for my opinions' sake. On the 1st of last May eighty-three men belonging to General O. M. Mitchel's division came from Bridgeport, Ala., and pillaged my store of every article of any worth, and on the 5th of June last General Negley sent ten soldiers (Federal) piloted by one of our tories and demanded $500 in cash and my person. The captain said he was directed by General Negley if I did not pay the $500 to take property to that amount. Not getting the cash they took $900 or $1,000 of property, some the relics of my deceased wife to her little son. They took me from a sick bed and made me march with troops trained without anything to eat except crackers and bacon; no tents to lie in or blankets to cover with, but was compelled to lie on the cold ground without any covering whatever. From our homes we were marched near Chattanooga, Tenn., and put in a filthy stable; from thence to Shelbyville, Tenn., and put in a slaughter-house, 140 feet deep without ventilation and a hospital above head with large cracks in the floor, and nothing to eat but crackers and hot water which they termed coffee. General Negley issued an order prohibiting the ladies or citizens of Shelbyville from furnishing us with any article of diet whatever saying we were furnished with the same rations that the Federal soldiers were, which was false. From thence we were taken to the State Penitentiary and incarcerated with thieves, murderers and assassins and such men as do God and man's laws at defiance set (for no crime save my love and devotion to my home and native South and her constitutional rights), where I remained near four months, while my little children were robbed of everything they had to eat and scared and insulted by a brutal soldiery, they having come twelve miles to do it. I never lived in their lines. General Negley sent his cavalry six miles from his road of travel to rob and arrest me. He killed one of our citizens by marching him while sick for no cause except his opinions' sake, and other citizens of our county have been sent to Camp Chase, and are there now, if alive. Their names are William H. Ballard and Claiborn Gott. Neither of us was ever connected with politics or the army. I understand that General Negley was taken prisoner at Murfreesborough. If so, please give orders concerning his case.

With sentiments of high regard, I am, President, yours, devotedly,

WASHINGTON TURNER.

P. S.—For my veracity I refer you to Generals John B. Floyd and John B. Gordon; Col. P. Turney, First Tennessee Regiment; Dr. J. G.

Barksdale, Shelbyville, Tenn.; Revs. E. W. Sehon, Atlanta, Ga., and William T. Smithson, formerly of Washington, D. C.

                                                                W. T.

———

WAR DEPARTMENT, *Richmond, Va., January 8, 1863.*
Hon. J. P. BENJAMIN, *Secretary of State.*

SIR: Instructions have been again addressed to Brigadier-General Winder to procure the testimony you have asked for in your letter of yesterday relative to John Carfoot, a prisoner lately confined at Salisbury, N. C. As soon as he makes his report of the cause of the arrest of Carfoot and the proof that was produced against him it will be communicated to you.

Very respectfully, your obedient servant,
                                        JAMES A. SEDDON,
                                              Secretary of War.

———

C. S. MILITARY PRISON, *Richmond, January 8, 1863.*
Hon. ROBERT OULD, *Agent of Exchange.*

SIR: Although you desired that no citizens be sent by flag of truce to-morrow yet General Winder wishes that exceptions be made in the cases of three men, viz: D. C. Bull, citizen of New York; William Bull, his son, and Wm. J. Peters, citizen of Delaware. Mr. John O. E. Sowers, citizen of Virginia, arrived yesterday on parole to obtain the release of Mr. Bull and his son. The Secretary of War is only willing that D. C. Bull be returned for Mr. Sowers.

William Bull is on parole for thirty days to obtain permission for the release of Charles Henry Smith, son of Col. Larkin Smith. The other, Wm. J. Peters, paroled for thirty days to effect exchange of any citizen of the Confederate States who may be confined in prison at the North.

I am, sir, your obedient servant,
                                        THOS. P. TURNER,
                                        Captain, Commanding Prison.

———

C. S. MILITARY PRISON, *Richmond, January 8, 1863.*
Captain MULFORD.

SIR: I send by Lieutenant Bossieux, C. S. Army, seven rolls of money belonging to the above-named* persons, late prisoners here. Owing to some haste and confusion at the time of the departure of the prisoners last Tuesday we unavoidably failed to remit to them all their dues. Please receipt to Lieutenant Bossieux for the same.

Respectfully,
                                        THOS. P. TURNER,
                                        Captain, Commanding Prison.

———

HEADQUARTERS ARMY OF NORTHERN VIRGINIA,
                                              January 10, 1863.
Hon. JAMES A. SEDDON, *Secretary of War.*

SIR: In view of the atrocious orders issued by the Federal General Milroy with regard to citizens of the Valley District I would respect-

———

* Omitted.

fully recommend that prisoners from his command captured by our forces be not exchanged but that they be held as hostages for the protection of our people against the outrages which he is reported to be committing.

I have the honor to be, very respectfully, your obedient servant,

R. E. LEE,
General.

VICKSBURG, *January 10, 1863.*

Colonel WADDY:

Under date of 6th instant I was informed by Assistant Adjutant-General B. S. Ewell, from Chattanooga, that 3,500 Federal prisoners are on their way here. Instructions regarding them are asked for.

M. L. SMITH,
Major-General.

JACKSON, MISS., *January 10, 1863.*

General J. C. PEMBERTON:

Thirty-five hundred Federal prisoners are on their way here from Bragg's army. What shall I do with them?

J. R. WADDY,
Assistant Adjutant-General.

SPECIAL ORDERS, }   HEADQUARTERS FIRST DISTRICT,
                 DEPT. OF MISS. AND EAST LA.,
No. 2.   }   *Jackson, Miss., January 11, 1863.*

*   *   *   *   *   *   *

II. The command of that portion of the district recently embraced within and now separated from the First Military District, as well as the city of Jackson, is hereby relinquished to Brigadier-General Adams, who has been appointed to the command.

III. The office of commissioner of exchanged and paroled prisoners is also turned over to Brigadier-General Adams.

By order of Brigadier-General Ruggles:

R. M. HOOE,
Assistant Adjutant-General.

Extract from President's Message, January 12, 1863.

To the SENATE AND HOUSE OF REPRESENTATIVES OF THE CONFEDERATE STATES:

*   *   *   *   *   *   *

The public journals of the North have been received containing a proclamation dated on the first day of the present month signed by the President of the United States in which he orders and declares all slaves within ten States of the Confederacy to be free, except such as are found in certain districts now occupied in part by the armed forces of the enemy.

We may well leave it to the instincts of that common humanity which a beneficent Creator has implanted in the breasts of our fellow-men of all countries to pass judgment on a measure by which several millions of human beings of an inferior race, peaceful and contented laborers in their sphere, are doomed to extermination, while at the same time they are encouraged to a general assassination of their masters by the insidious recommendation "to abstain from violence unless in necessary self-defense." Our own detestation of those who have attempted the most execrable measure recorded in the history of guilty man is tempered by profound contempt for the impotent rage which it discloses. So far as regards the action of this Government on such criminals as may attempt its execution I confine myself to informing you that I shall unless in your wisdom you deem some other course more expedient deliver to the several State authorities all commissioned officers of the United States that may hereafter be captured by our forces in any of the States embraced in the proclamation that they may be dealt with in accordance with the laws of those States providing for the punishment of criminals engaged in exciting servile insurrection. The enlisted soldiers I shall continue to treat as unwilling instruments in the commission of these crimes and shall direct their discharge and return to their homes on the proper and usual parole.

*   *   *   *   *   *

JEFF'N DAVIS.

HEADQUARTERS DEPARTMENT OF HENRICO,
Richmond, January 12, 1863.

Hon. GEORGE MOORE, *Her British Majesty's Consul.*

SIR: * * * John Carfoot has been released. The charges against him are at Salisbury, N. C., and have been telegraphed for. They will be communicated to you upon their arrival.

Very respectfully, your obedient servant,
JOHN H. WINDER,
Brigadier-General.

VICKSBURG, *January 13, 1863.*

Colonel WADDY:

If prisoners arrive locate them in most convenient place for encampment, and employ the whole of Taylor's brigade to guard them.
J. C. PEMBERTON,
Lieutenant-General.

HDQRS. C. S. FORCES ON SHENANDOAH MOUNTAIN,
January 13, 1863.

Hon. JAMES A. SEDDON, *Secretary of War.*

SIR: In reply to a letter from Robert Ould, esq., agent of exchange, to H. B. Davidson, of date January 2, 1863, which was referred to me, I have the honor to transmit herewith proof of the authenticity of certain orders of Brig. Gen. R. H. Milroy, U. S. Army, which were forwarded by me to the President some weeks ago. In addition to the deposition of Job Parsons and myself I furnish you as cumulative evidence a copy of The Crisis, of date December 24, 1862, a newspaper published at Columbus, Ohio, in which the orders of Milroy are published as part of the history of the times. I have not seen Adam Harper, who is the subject of this published order, but two of his sons, one of whom is my scout, have stated to me that their father was compelled to pay the assessment of $285 to save his life. The whole amount of money raised by these illegal assessments in the small county of Tucker as near as I can ascertain it is about $6,000. Were I to report every case of outrage of this character which has come to my knowledge it would astound all Christian people who read it. Permit me, sir, to express the opinion that we have an effectual remedy for these crimes by the adoption of an inexorable rule of retaliation. The oppressions of our people cannot be increased but I believe will be mitigated by the enforcement of the fullest measure of retaliation on these bloodthirsty savages.*

Respectfully, your obedient servant,

J. D. IMBODEN,
Colonel, Commanding.

[Inclosure No. 1.]

VIRGINIA, *Augusta County, to wit:*

This day Job Parsons (son of Abraham Parsons), a citizen of Tucker County, Va., personally appeared before the undersigned justice of the peace in and for the county aforesaid and being by me duly sworn deposes and says that on the 27th day of November, 1862, being at his father's house on Cheat River, in Tucker County, eight miles above Saint George, the county seat of said county, a Federal lieutenant with five men came there and handed to deponent a paper of which Exhibit A hereto attached is a literal and exact copy. That at the same time and place a similar paper was handed to Abraham Parsons, deponent's father, and on the same day similar notices were served on from thirty to forty citizens of Tucker County by the same authority. On the next day, November 28, 1862, deponent repaired to Saint George where he found a company of the One hundred and twenty-third Ohio Regiment stationed in the court-house under command of Capt. Horace Kellogg. As soon as deponent arrived Captain Kellogg in person handed him a paper of which Exhibit B, herewith filed, is an exact and literal copy. On reading this paper deponent remarked to Captain Kellogg that it was a very rigid and unreasonable order and he thought it very unjust to hold private citizens responsible for the acts of the military authorities, to which Captain Kellogg replied that he thought not, that the old man (General Milroy) was in earnest. Deponent further says that on the same day (November 28) he saw a similar order, exactly, served upon his father, Abraham Parsons, who was assessed with the sum of $340 and that fifteen or twenty other citizens received the same orders at the same time who were assessed with various sums. Deponent did not pay his assessment but made his escape from the county and came through the mountains to the camp of Col. John D. Imboden at Shenandoah Mountain and delivered to him the papers of which Exhibits A and B are true copies. And further saith not.

JOB PARSONS.

Subscribed and sworn to before me this 10th day of January, 1863.

WM. W. MONTGOMERY,
Justice of the Peace.

[First indorsement.]

VIRGINIA, *Augusta County Court, Clerk's Office:*

I, William A. Burnett, deputy clerk of said court, certify that on this the 12th of January, 1863, Col. John D. Imboden personally appeared before me in my office aforesaid, and being by me duly sworn deposes and says that he is personally acquainted with Job Parsons, whose deposi-

---

* For other correspondence, etc., relating to Milroy's orders, see Series III.

tion is above taken, and that he knows the general reputation and character of said Job Parsons and does not hesitate to say that said Parsons is a man of excellent moral character and worthy of full credit as a truthful man and witness. Deponent further states that he forwarded to Richmond the originals of Exhibits A and B, which were furnished to him early in December last by said Parsons, and that he has no doubt of the genuineness of said orders nor of the fact that a large number of the loyal citizens of Tucker County have had similar orders served upon them by Captain Kellogg and that large sums of money have by this means been extorted from them. And further saith not.

JOHN D. IMBODEN.

[Second indorsement.]

I further certify that William W. Montgomery, whose name is signed to the foregoing deposition of Job Parsons, was at the date of said deposition and now is a justice of the peace in and for the county aforesaid. In testimony whereof I have hereunto set my hand and affixed the seal of my court the day and year above written.

WM. A. BURNETT,
Deputy Clerk.

[Exhibit A.]

SAINT GEORGE, TUCKER COUNTY, VA.,
November 27, 1862.

Mr. JOB PARSONS:
(Son of Abraham Parsons.)

You are hereby ordered to report in person or by your representative at my headquarters in Saint George Court-House on the 28th of November, 1862, to attend to business of vital importance to yourself, and in case of your failure to comply with the above order you must suffer the penalty.

By order of Brig. Gen. R. H. Milroy:

HORACE KELLOGG,
Captain and Post Commandant.

[Exhibit B.]

SAINT GEORGE, TUCKER COUNTY, VA.,
November 28, 1862.

Mr. JOB PARSONS:
(Son of Abraham Parsons.)

SIR: In consequence of certain robberies which have been perpetrated upon Union citizens of Tucker County, Va., by bands of guerrillas you are hereby assessed to the amount of $14.25 to make good their losses, and upon your failure to comply with the above assessment by paying the money over to me by the 1st day of December, 1862, the following order will be executed, viz:

If they fail to pay at the end of the time you have named their houses will be burned and themselves shot and their property all seized, and be sure that you carry out this threat rigidly and show them that you are not trifling or to be trifled with. You will inform the inhabitants for ten or fifteen miles around your camp on all the roads approaching the town upon which the enemy may approach that they must dash in and give you notice, and that upon failure of any one to do so their houses will be burned and the men shot.

By order of Brig. Gen. R. H. Milroy:

HORACE KELLOGG,
Captain, Commanding Post.

[Inclosure No. 2.]

[Extract from The Crisis newspaper, December 24, 1862.]

ANOTHER MILROY ORDER.

The following letter comprising an order from General Milroy belongs to the history of the times:

SAINT GEORGE, TUCKER COUNTY, VA.,
November 28, 1862.

Mr. ADAM HARPER.

SIR: In consequence of certain robberies which have been committed on Union citizens of this county by bands of guerrillas you are hereby assessed to the amount of $285 to make good their losses. And upon your failure to comply with the above assessment by the 8th day of December the following order has been issued to me by Brig. Gen. R. H. Milroy:

"You are to burn their houses, seize all their property and shoot them. You will be sure that you strictly carry out this order.

"You will inform the inhabitants for ten or fifteen miles around your camp on all the roads approaching the town upon which the enemy may approach that they must dash in and give you notice, and that upon any one failing to do so you will burn their houses and shoot the men."

By order of Brig. Gen. R. H. Milroy:

H. KELLOGG,
Captain, Commanding Post.

* The above Adam Harper the subject of this order is an old Dutchman over eighty-two years of age, a cripple and infirm, and can neither read nor write.

The above is a little ahead of anything that has yet met our eye. Because Adam Harper could neither read nor write, eighty-two years old and a cripple General Milroy to the disgrace of the nation orders a tax of $285 levied on him, and the whole country for ten or fifteen miles round is to be laid waste! "You are to burn their houses, seize all their property and shoot them. You will be sure that you strictly carry out this order."

And what did those people do? Nothing! But a band of guerrillas is charged with robbing Union citizens. That is all. Can we be surprised to hear of fist fights in the councils of a Cabinet guilty of carrying on such a war? We are not surprised after the above that The Crisis was prohibited circulation through the mails in Western Virginia by military order if such conduct as this is the order of the day.

The bogus government at Wheeling of course comes into existence with a very excellent record of civil and modest pretensions.

VICKSBURG, *January 13, 1863.*

Lieutenant-General PEMBERTON:

I have been informed by Major Fairbanks that General Bragg's prisoners are all paroled.

N. G. WATTS,
Major and Agent.

GENERAL ORDERS, }   ADJT. AND INSP. GENERAL'S OFFICE,
No. 5.   }   *Richmond, January 13, 1863.*

I. The following order is published for the information of all concerned:

EXCHANGE NOTICE, No. 4.]   RICHMOND, *January 10, 1863.*

The following officers and men have been duly exchanged and are hereby so declared:

1. All officers and men captured in Kentucky, Tennessee, Alabama, Mississippi, Georgia, Florida and South Carolina up to December 10, 1862.

2. All officers and men captured in Missouri, Kansas, New Mexico, Arizona, Arkansas and Louisiana up to January 1, 1863.

3. The two foregoing sections apply not only to officers and men of the Confederate service but also to persons captured in arms or hostile array against the United States whatever may have been the character of the military organization to which they were attached and whatever may have been the terms of the paroles given by them. If any are in Federal prisons they are to be immediately released and delivered to the Confederate authorities.

4. All persons who have been captured on the sea or sea coast of the Confederate or United States up to December 10, 1862. If any such are in Federal prisons they are to be immediately released and delivered to the Confederate authorities.

5. All Confederate officers and men who have been delivered at City Point up to January 6, 1863.

6. All Confederate officers and men who have been delivered at Vicksburg up to December 23, 1862, and including said date.

7. All paroled Confederate officers and men receipted for at Vicksburg up to December 23, 1862, and including said date.

8. All Confederate officers and men captured and paroled at Fredericksburg, Va., in December, 1862.

9. All Confederate officers and men captured and paroled at Goldsborough, N. C., in December, 1862.

10. Other miscellaneous and minor exchanges of which the appropriate officers will be duly informed.

RO. OULD,
Agent of Exchange.

By order:

S. COOPER,
Adjutant and Inspector General.

WAR DEPARTMENT, Richmond, Va., January 14, 1863.

Lieut. Gen. J. C. PEMBERTON.

SIR: Yours of the 1st instant has been received. It is entirely irregular for the enemy to send either paroles or copies of them to Vicksburg. They ought not to be in any way regarded and I shall so instruct Major Watts. There is no guaranty that the paroles of the same parties will not be sent here to me again for double exchange. To prevent inextricable confusion and vast cheating it is absolutely necessary that there should be but one place of exchange, and but one official to make and declare the exchange. The War Department accordingly has made such an order. There is only one exception to this rule and that is where the commanders of two opposing armies exchange and deliver prisoners captured from each other.

I have already specifically instructed Major Watts that he cannot make any exchange at all.

You will perceive in a moment that if any person other than myself were permitted to make exchanges parties might and probably would be exchanged more than once. The exchange of prisoners is only consummated when after conference with the Federal commissioner and after the giving and receiving of equivalents a publication of exchange is made. The proper course in the case put by you would be for the Federal officer who made the captures to transmit to his Government the paroles given by our men. The United States Government would then deliver those paroles (or a list of them) to their commissioner of exchange who in his turn would present them to me as the evidence of capture. It would then be my duty to give an equivalent for them and to declare them exchanged.

If this plan is not strictly pursued untold difficulties will surround the matter and every avenue of fraud will be opened. How otherwise can we prevent the enemy from claiming that our men shall be exchanged over and over again? Under this plan as I record every man who is exchanged I can soon see if they are playing false.

You will perceive by my published notice and general order issued under it that all officers and men of our army captured in your department before December 10, 1862, are fully exchanged.

If at any time you wish any special exchange made sooner than would likely be the case in the ordinary routine notify me by letter or telegraph and I will see that it is done. I most heartily congratulate you on your brilliant and successful defense of Vicksburg. I perceive that all Yankeedom is howling, and I am happy to know that "your praise is in all our cities."

Yours, very truly,   RO. OULD,
                                                    Agent of Exchange.

HEADQUARTERS MORGAN'S DIVISION,
McMinnville, January 15, 1863.

Col. G. W. BRENT,
    Asst. Adjt. Gen. and Chief of Staff, Army of Tennessee.

SIR: I forward you for the consideration of the general commanding the inclosed communication* from Captain Thruston, additional aide-de-camp to Major-General Rosecrans, to Lieut. F. Brady, an officer of my command now in confinement within the Federal lines, and beg leave to make the following statements in regard to the matter:

1. On the morning of the 10th instant two ladies came to my head-quarters at Smithville and stated that they had received information that a brother of one of the ladies was lying mortally wounded at Murfreesborough. They desired to gain access to him as speedily as possible. In order to effect this it was decided to send them under a flag of truce to the Federal lines and an order was issued to Captain Quirk, commanding a company stationed at Liberty, to furnish them with a suitable escort. This escort is now held in confinement by Major-General Rosecrans.

2. The road pursued by the escort was the public turnpike road between Liberty and Murfreesborough.

3. I was not aware of the agreement entered into between General Bragg and Major-General Rosecrans, spoken of in Captain Thruston's communication, and we have never been informed either officially or privately of any such agreement.

I am, colonel, very respectfully, your obedient servant,
                                            JNO. H. MORGAN,
                                                Brigadier-General.

C. S. MILITARY PRISON, *Richmond, Va., January 16, 1863.*
Brig. Gen. JOHN H. WINDER, *Commanding, &c.*

GENERAL: Having occupied the Mayo Factory as a prison I necessarily require an additional number of men for guard duty. The least number I can do with in addition to what has heretofore been furnished me is 1 commissioned officer, 3 non-commissioned officers and 32 privates. These I would wish to report regularly at this (the Libby) prison at 9 o'clock a. m.

I am, sir, your obedient servant,
                                            TH. P. TURNER,
                                                Captain, Commanding.

---

*Omitted here; see p. 170.

SPECIAL ORDERS, }   HDQRS. DEPARTMENT OF HENRICO,
       No. 12.   }   Richmond, Va., January 16, 1863.

I. It appearing from the report of the board of officers appointed to inquire into the cause of the escape of certain prisoners from the military prison in the western district in this city that it was caused by the negligence of the officer of the guard at that post, the general commanding the department takes this occasion to remind the officers in charge of the military prisons in this city of the great responsibility of their position and to warn them that too much vigilance on their part cannot be observed.   They having complete control of the guards at their respective posts will be held responsible for their discipline, and for the further maintenance of the same the following order is issued:

At the respective military prisons in this city there will be detailed daily an officer of the guard who must be a commissioned officer.   He will serve his regular tour of twenty-four hours and will not be allowed to absent himself from his post during that time under any consideration whatever except in case of sickness, and then only when regularly relieved by another officer.

II. The officers in charge of the military prisons in this city will furnish a morning report to these headquarters.

By order of Brig. Gen. John H. Winder, commanding department:

J. W. PEGRAM,
Assistant Adjutant-General.

C. S. MILITARY PRISON HOSPITAL,
Richmond, January 18, 1863.

General JOHN H. WINDER.

DEAR SIR: Allow me to bring to your notice the fact that there is an assistant surgeon belonging to the U. S. Army here in prison, and I am informed that surgeons and assistant surgeons are not considered as prisoners of war by either party.   I hope he may be allowed to accompany the wounded that go by the first flag of truce; in case there should be no further exchange of prisoners that he be sent across the lines according to his request as soon as possible.   His name is George F. Mish, Fifteenth Pennsylvania Cavalry.   There are two wounded lieutenants here wounded in such a way that they will never be fit to enter service again, one having (as he says) been exchanged, taken prisoner on the 8th of June last; his thigh is amputated high up.   The other has his right arm amputated at the shoulder joint.

There are other officers here who from the nature of their wounds may be able to enter service again, for which reason I did not think of asking for their exchange.   I ask that these two lieutenants be exchanged for the reason that they have been treated in a ward in which the hospital gangrene has made its appearance.   There are many reasons for asking particularly for their exchange and I address you this letter at your own suggestion.   Judge Ould seems to have misunderstood me in speaking of them as officers though his clerk so understood me.   Had the flag of truce gone this morning the ward in which the gangrene is would have been empty of wounded except one captain.

From the number here, if they are not exchanged, I cannot empty this ward.   I therefore ask that there may be some place temporarily assigned in which these men may be placed until this ward is thoroughly cleaned and ventilated.   This need not be for a longer time than a week when I think they may be safely brought back, in case the place in which they are removed is wanted.

A. W. THOMSON,
Surgeon in Charge.

[Indorsement.]

Captain TURNER.

SIR: You will call the attention of Surgeon Thomson to the fact that all communications must be sent through the proper channel. You will call his attention to the Army Regulations on the subject of correspondence. Also the orders of the Adjutant-General upon the same subject.

By order of Brigadier-General Winder:

W. S. WINDER,
Assistant Adjutant-General.

HDQRS. PAROLED AND EXCHANGED PRISONERS,
Jackson, Miss., January 19, 1863.

Lieut. Col. J. R. WADDY,
Assistant Adjutant-General, Jackson, Miss.

COLONEL: In answer to your inquiry to what date the paroled prisoners have been undoubtedly exchanged I have the honor to state that there is no record in this office specifying any general exchange except proclamation marked A, issued by Brig. Gen. John Gregg, declaring the prisoners brought by Federal transports under flag of truce and delivered to Maj. N. G. Watts, agent paroled and exchanged prisoners, at Vicksburg. The Federal prisoners coming by railroads from enemy's lines reporting themselves in person at these headquarters are sent to camp and their names forwarded to Major Watts, agent for paroled and exchanged prisoners, for exchange, and when that is accomplished I am notified, and they are forwarded in squads under proper officers to their commands; but lately under instructions from the lieutenant-general commanding this department and in accordance with telegram from Robert Ould to Major Fairbanks, marked B, all the prisoners paroled previous to the 10th December have been forwarded to their respective commands, and the assistant adjutant-general of the corps to which each squad was ordered is notified by a letter with muster-roll attached of officers, non-commissioned officers and privates.

Inclosed you will also find copy of dispatch marked C, to Robert Ould, and when answer is received the matter will be I hope definitely settled.

I am, colonel, most respectfully, your obedient servant,

JOHN ADAMS,
Brigadier-General, Provisional Army, C. S., Commanding.

[Inclosure A.]

HEADQUARTERS EXCHANGED PRISONERS,
Jackson, Miss., November 23, 1862.

By authority from the War Department I hereby proclaim that an exchange has been completed of all prisoners (Confederate officers and men) delivered at Vicksburg up to this date. I also make proclamation that those delivered at Vicksburg from this time forth are exchanged upon delivery.

JOHN GREGG,
Brigadier-General, Provisional Army, C. S.

[Inclosure B.]

RICHMOND, *January 11, 1863.*

Maj. G. R. FAIRBANKS:

If the 900 men were captured before December 10 they have been already exchanged. If they were captured since I hereby declare them to be exchanged. Let me know, however, by telegraph where they were captured. Do not register them at Vicksburg. The Yankees will present the paroles.

RO. OULD,
Agent of Exchange.

[Inclosure C.]

HDQRS. PAROLED AND EXCHANGED PRISONERS,
Jackson, Miss., January 18, 1863.

ROBERT OULD,
Agent for Exchange of Prisoners, Richmond, Va.:

Maj. G. R. Fairbanks has communicated to me your telegram of the 11th instant declaring men captured before 10th December already exchanged. Does this refer to all men captured before 10th December or only to 900 referred to by Fairbanks?

JOHN ADAMS,
Brigadier-General.

———

WAR DEPARTMENT, *Richmond, January 20, 1863.*

Brig. Gen. JOHN H. WINDER,
Commanding Richmond, Va., &c.

GENERAL: You are instructed to dispose of the following-named prisoners as hereinafter specified: (1) John Roche, parole to work as a coal miner under direction of Captain Warner on such wages as he shall prescribe; (2) Patrick Kelly, administer oath to observe all State and Confederate laws and parole to work in city of Richmond; (3) Elbert Flynn, (4) John Murphy, (5) Edward Vickell, (6) John Ward, administer oath of allegiance and parole to work under direction of Captain Warner; (7) Roger Byron, administer oath of allegiance and allow him to enlist in some South Carolina regiment; (8) Amos Hemmings, (9) Frederick Cullen, (10) James McLaughton, (11) Francis T. Treanor, (12) Peter Blair, (13) Aaron Ankrum, (14) William H. Maguire, (15) Thomas Hankls, (16) Felix Willett, (17) John Green, (18) John Miller, administer oath of allegiance and parole to work under direction of Capt. G. W. Alexander, assistant provost-marshal, city of Richmond; (19) Chauncey Ward, administer oath of allegiance and as he prefers let him enlist in some regiment or parole him to go to work; (20) Charles Willis, send him to Captain Pegram, C. S. Navy, and if he gives him a good character administer the oath of allegiance and let him enlist in the Navy; (21) John Newton, employ him on wages at his trade about the prisons until the officers can form some idea of his character; (22) August Sheran, (23) James Smith, send North by first flag-of-truce boat; (24) McNeil—if Colonel Ould thinks this man is entitled as a sutler to be sent home on parole send him North, if not, retain as a hostage for our citizen prisoners; (25) J. F. May, (26) E. McWee, (27) E. Whitney, (28) P. McChesney, (29) William Conner, (30) D. C. Georgia, (31) Caleb May, (32) Thomas Ward, (33) James Cail, (34) John Elliott, retain as hostages for our citizens held as prisoners by the enemy; (35) Hiram Hale, (36) —— Hale (his son), administer oath of allegiance and give them transportation home; (37) Jacob

Thrasher, (38) George Thrasher, administer oath of allegiance, give transportation to Staunton and commutation of rations to their home; (39) Annie D. Brown, (40 and 41) her two mulatto nieces; (42 and 43) their two children and (44) ——— Brown (her son), (45 and 46) William Edwards and his daughter, release on parole to work in city of Richmond under direction of Capt. G. W. Alexander, assistant provost-marshal; (47) Lewis H. Call, send to enrolling officer as a conscript; if incapable of military service employ him as a teamster under some C. S. officer; (48) Joseph Kennan, parole to work in the interior of the country under direction of some C. S. officer; (49) Robert B. Wright, send to some hospital or send home; (50) J. H. Trout, retain as a prisoner until demanded by the authorities of Virginia; (51) C. B. Humwell, order Lieutenant-Colonel Critcher, Fifteenth Virginia Cavalry to send names of witnesses and retain this man for trial; (52) Charles H. Marsh, treat as prisoner of war; (53) George W. Steele, (54) John Buntain, (55) David Bowers, retain as prisoners; (56) James Gilmer, retain as prisoner until the length of confinement renders any information he might communicate valueless to the enemy, when he may be exchanged for some citizen prisoner; (57) Pat. Leonard, parole not to bear arms against Confederate States and return to Baltimore by first flag of truce; (58) George Miller, retain as prisoner suspected of being a spy until the length of confinement renders any information he might communicate valueless to the enemy, when if no evidence in the meantime shall be furnished he may be exchanged for a citizen; (59) Wilson Gleason, (60) Thomas Gallan, (61) John Whitehead, (62) Bernard Harkell, (63) Thomas W. B. Phillips, (64) Edward Lent, (65) George B. Heath, (66) John Berden, (67) Edward Farrell, (68) Theodore McCary, (69) Edward Welsh, (70) C. Fuher, (71) Charles Christopher Callum, (72) Hiram Scovell, (73) Solomon Howe, (74) Richard T. Sinton—these are deserters from the enemy and may be treated as prisoners of war and paroled under the cartel if they desire it. If any of them do not and will not take the oath of allegiance and give their parole to work, administer the oath, exact the parole and assign them to some C. S. officer who can make them useful, with due caution to observe their deportment; all such as do not work to return under the cartel and [such as] will not take the oath and give the parole you will for the present retain as prisoners. (75) William B. Taylor, (76) Jacob R. Taylor, send the first of these brothers to the hospital for medical treatment and employ the other as an attendant about the hospital on wages if his health will permit. As soon as the circumstances of their home will render it prudent administer the oath of allegiance and send them home. (77) James Clarke, parole him to go to work under direction of the provost-marshal of Richmond City.

Very respectfully, &c.,

J. A. CAMPBELL,
Assistant Secretary of War.

———

SALISBURY, *January 20, 1863.*

Brig. Gen. J. H. WINDER, *Richmond, Va.:*

Ship to come through with second lot of prisoners 150 large-size tents. It will be necessary owing to the peculiar position of prison inclosure and buildings to have at least two or three more companies for guard duty.

H. McCOY.

SALISBURY, *January 20, 1863.*

General J. H. WINDER, *Richmond, Va.:*

Dispatch received concerning prisoners. Will try and have everything in readiness. Can two independent companies be sent for guard duty?

Ship by express 2,000 tin cups and plates and any bedding you can spare for prisoners.

HENRY McCOY,
Captain, Commanding Prison.

HEADQUARTERS C. S. MILITARY PRISON,
Salisbury, January 20, 1863.

Brig. Gen. J. H. WINDER, *Richmond, Va.*

SIR: Your telegram concerning prisoners of war was received late last night. I will as near as possible try and have everything in readiness for their reception.

The buildings will not possibly hold more than from 1,200 to 1,500 consequently it will be necessary to put the balance in tents. I telegraphed you to-day to send me with the second lot of prisoners 150 large-size army tents, likewise 2,000 tin cups and plates with if possible bedding for the prisoners as we have none of the above-named articles here.

Owing to the peculiar location of the buildings in the prison grounds, they being very much scattered, it will be necessary for the safety of the prisoners to have my force increased at least two or three companies. I hope you will be able to send them with the prisoners.

Very respectfully, your obedient servant,

HENRY McCOY,
Captain and Assistant Quartermaster, Commanding.

CHARLESTON JAIL, *January 20, 1863.*

General G. T. BEAUREGARD.

SIR: One week ago last Friday I in connection with S. T. Riddell, C. Rowell and O. F. French were captured by a detachment of cavalry under command of Captain Dickison near Saint Augustine, Fla. We had been out by invitation to see them grind cane and were returning when we were captured. We were taken to Captain Dickison's camp, near the Saint John's River, and from thence to General Finegan at Lake City, where we were paroled and sent to this place in charge of Captain Mays, who has our paroles. On our arrival here we were lodged in jail where we now are. I would state further that there are two other prisoners with us who belong at Key West, Fla., and also two others who claim to be deserters. They have all been paroled.

Permit me now, general, to call your attention to the following facts: First, we have no clothing except what we have on, and, second, our means for providing ourselves with these articles are very limited; consequently we would most respectfully ask that we may be sent North as soon as possible.

Very respectfully, your obedient servant,

VIRGIL H. CATE,
First Lieutenant Company C, Seventh Regt. New Hampshire Vols.

HDQRS. DEPT. OF S. CAROLINA, GEORGIA AND FLORIDA,
Charleston, S. C., January 21, 1863.
Lieut. VIRGIL H. CATE,
Seventh Regt. N. H. Vols., U. S. Army, Charleston Jail.

SIR: Your communication of the 20th instant has been considered and I am instructed to inform you that some or all of you prisoners of war will be either sent to Richmond or Port Royal as soon as practicable. As for yourself, a commissioned officer, you are not subject to exchange and will probably be turned over to the local authorities of the State of Florida for trial under the statutes made and provided in that State for the punishment of persons engaged in exciting negro slaves to insurrection. It is needless for me to inform you that this course is a necessary consequence of the proclamation of the President of the United States by which the Army and Navy of the United States were instructed to aid negroes against their masters. Should you wish to secure clothing and money I will forward any open communication on the subject to the commanding general at Port Royal by flag of truce.

Respectfully, your obedient servant,
THOMAS JORDAN,
Brigadier-General and Chief of Staff.

C. S. MILITARY PRISON, *Richmond, January 21, 1863.*
Capt. W. S. WINDER, *Assistant Adjutant-General.*

SIR: In reference to the list of men sent me yesterday containing the names of twenty-nine prisoners taken in the Valley to be held as hostages I have to say that they were all paroled and sent home via City Point on Monday last except the first on the list, viz, Lieutenant Dawson, of Company K, First [West] Virginia Cavalry, who still remains in the prison.

I am, sir, your obedient servant, T. P. TURNER,
Captain, Commanding.

PONCHATOULA, *January 22, 1863.*
Lieut. Col. J. R. WADDY,
Assistant Adjutant-General, Jackson, Miss.:

I inclose herewith letter addressed to Confederate Army officers by Colonel Clark, U. S. Army, which was left at Madisonville yesterday and forwarded to this place this morning. None of the citizens mentioned have arrived at this place.

Very respectfully, your obedient servant,
THOMAS SHIELDS,
Lieutenant-Colonel and Acting Assistant Inspector-General.

[Inclosure.]

MADISONVILLE, *January 21, 1863.*
ANY OFFICER OF CONFEDERATE ARMY:

Under flag of truce and in absence of any officer to confer with I have taken the liberty to land some 250 citizens, mostly women and children. They have been left at their own request and without restraint. I commend them to your kindness.

Respectfully, your obedient servant,
JOHN S. CLARK,
Colonel and Aide-de-Camp to Maj. Gen. N. P. Banks.

WAR DEPARTMENT, *Richmond, January 23, 1863.*
Col. G. W. LEE, *Atlanta, Ga.:*

Hon. H. C. Burnett, of the Senate, desires reply to his letter concerning correspondence with H. C. Payne, a prisoner in your custody. The Department requests you to answer his letter.

J. A. SEDDON,
Secretary of War.

VICKSBURG, *January 23, 1863.*
Lieutenant-General PEMBERTON:

Major Watts applies for a boat to go up with flag of truce and exchange the prisoners now in jail here. What reply shall I make?

M. L. SMITH,
Major-General.

[Indorsement.]

VICKSBURG, *January 23, 1863.*

Reply that I am ordered by Secretary of War not to exchange any prisoners until General Clark and the thirteen chiefest others at New Orleans are given up.

J. C. PEMBERTON,
Lieutenant-General, &c.

HEADQUARTERS DEPARTMENT OF HENRICO,
January 23, 1863.
Captain TURNER.

CAPTAIN: Please furnish me the name of the Yankee officer who was sent here by Colonel Imboden from the northwest and with reference to whom an order was issued that he should be retained. This order will still be insisted upon and you will see that it is enforced.

Very respectfully,

JNO. H. WINDER,
Brigadier-General.

P. S.—He will probably be called for in a few days.

JACKSON, MISS., *January 23, 1863.*
Maj. Gen. M. L. SMITH, *Commanding, Vicksburg:*

Orders from Secretary of War not to exchange any prisoners until General Clark and the thirteen "chiefest" others at New Orleans are given up.

J. R. WADDY,
Assistant Adjutant-General.

C. S. MILITARY PRISON, *Richmond, January 23, 1863.*
Capt. W. S. WINDER, *Assistant Adjutant-General.*

SIR: I wish to report a matter which I should have mentioned before but for a press of other business. With the batch of prisoners sent off by flag of truce on the 11th instant a sutler named Marcus McNeil, from New York, went off under the name of Turner, a prisoner of war, the latter remaining in his (McN.'s) place. I did not discover it until the prisoners had left and then it was made known by a deserter who moreover stated that McNeil had paid Turner a sum of money for so doing. Upon searching Turner the sum of $196 was found upon his person and he acknowledged that it had been paid to him for the purchase stated above. Will you please inform me what disposition shall be made of the money?

I am, sir, your obedient servant,

THOMAS P. TURNER,
Captain, Commanding.

P. S.—The money is in bullion bank notes and is said to be spurious.

T. P. T.

C. S. MILITARY PRISON, *Richmond, January 24, 1863.*
Capt. W. S. WINDER, *Assistant Adjutant-General.*

SIR: In answer to the inquiry made yesterday as to the name of the Yankee officer sent here by Colonel Imboden from the northwest, &c., I have to say that his name is A. Dawson, lieutenant, Company K, First Regiment [West] Virginia [Cavalry] (Peirpoint Volunteers), captured at Moorefield, Va., January 3, 1863.

I am, sir, your obedient servant,

TH. P. TURNER,
Captain, Commanding.

HDQRS. RICHARDSON'S PARTISAN RANGERS, C. S. ARMY,
January 25, 1863.

Whereas Col. J. K. Mizner, commanding U. S. forces at Brownsville, Tenn., has issued a proclamation addressed to James Whitelaw, H. W. Colter, James Bond, Dr. E. A. Taylor, Wiley Mann, Robert Wilson, Dr. E. Davis, Charles F. Read, T. P. Livingston, R. Y. Longley, George T. Taylor, F. Maclin, Dr. J. S. Peete, C. P. Taliaferro and all indefinitely alleging that the persons and property of many Union citizens having been threatened by guerrillas and persons claiming allegiance to or sympathy with the so-called Confederate States, and notifying all persons in Haywood and Tipton Counties that in case of molestation of the person or property of all loyal citizens living within the military district of Jackson, Tenn., the above-mentioned persons to be held responsible in person and property for all acts of violence; that in case of the arrest of any loyal citizen double the number will be arrested and held as hostages and twice the amount of property taken or injured will be levied from citizens therein named: Now therefore in reply to this paper bullet fired across the Hatchie River by the brave Colonel Mizner at unoffending non-combatants be it known that for each man named and every other good and loyal citizen of the Confederate States living in Haywood and Tipton Counties, Tenn., who may be arrested under the aforesaid proclamation I will have shot twice the number of Yankee soldiers taken in battle or on duty, and for each dollar's worth of property taken under said proclamation I will take or destroy twice the amount from the United States, their soldiers and Union men. It may be as well to proclaim hereby also that for every house burned by the U. S. soldiers I will shoot five U. S. soldiers on duty or taken in battle. The impudence of the aforesaid brave's proclamation consists in the fact that while he, his officers and men are stealing from all Southern men horses and mules, negroes and chickens and arresting unoffending men, women and children he threatens to do these things if "loyal citizens" as he calls them are molested in person and property. From such men and infamous Government to which they render such disgraceful service Southern men have nothing to hope except what their arms can secure.

To all soldiers in the Army of the United States who have become tired of a war waged to free negroes and enslave white men I extend an invitation to lay down their arms and seek my command for protection; all such shall be treated as friends and brothers.

R. V. RICHARDSON,
Col., Comdg. First Tennessee Regt. of Partisan Rangers, C. S. Army.

WAR DEPARTMENT, *Richmond, January 27, 1863.*
Brig. Gen. JOHN H. WINDER, *Richmond, Va.*

GENERAL: You will dispose of the prisoners below named as follows: (1) Joseph Stiles, to be returned as a prisoner. If a case cannot be made out against him as a spy he will be valuable as a hostage for our citizens held as prisoners. (2) John Flagg, to be held as a hostage for citizens; (3) Jim Allen, to be paroled under cartel, if he is entitled to it, but if not to be held as hostage for citizens; (4) Stanley Lees, to be held as a hostage for citizens; (5) Solomon Fisher, to be discharged and furnished transportation to his home; (6) Henry Mallard, to be paroled as a British subject to work but not to go into any region of our country which may have been or which may hereafter be the theater of hostilities; (7) George William White, to be sent to provost-marshal at Staunton with instructions to parole him to remain in Augusta County and administer oath to demean himself as a good citizen; (8) S. Dickinson, to be discharged and furnished transportation to Christiansburg, Va.; (9) Aaron Bennett, to be sent to Staunton, and instruct provost-marshal to administer oath of allegiance and parole him to remain in such part of Augusta or adjacent counties where he may reside without injury to our cause; (10) Thomas Raleigh, to be discharged as a British subject on parole of good conduct; (11) George Miller, to be held as a hostage for our citizens.

Very respectfully, your obedient servant,
J. A. CAMPBELL,
Assistant Secretary of War.

JACKSON, *January 27, 1863.*
General PEMBERTON:

I have obtained from city authorities use of part of bridge remaining standing. By to-morrow afternoon I will be ready for 500 prisoners. It is perfectly safe and secure; can be guarded by few men. For more prisoners I will have to construct a high wall to pitch tents; no buildings to be obtained. Shall wall be made?

JOHN ADAMS,
Brigadier-General.

C. S. MILITARY PRISON, *Richmond, January 28, 1863.*
Capt. W. S. WINDER, *Assistant Adjutant-General.*

SIR: In reference to the accident which occurred yesterday morning when the prisoners were being sent off I wish to report the following: The prisoners were started from this prison at 4 o'clock a. m. and were marched by the nearest and usual route to the Petersburg depot. The train was waiting to receive them but had backed nearer to the foot bridge that spans the canal than is usually the case, in consequence of which the prisoners had to be halted before they were all over which left a portion on the bridge and on this side. Before those in front could be gotten on board the bridge gave way and about sixty or seventy were thrown into the canal. All were rescued except two whose names I inclose.* This is clearly proven from the fact that at City Point the roll was called and the prisoners counted in the presence of the Abolition officer in charge of the Yankee boats and only two were missing. The rolls sent down called for 794 and I have the Federal officer's receipt for 792.

Proper persons were engaged all day yesterday in dragging for the bodies supposed to be drowned. Two were discovered as mentioned above. The coroner took charge of them. None of the guard who accompanied the prisoners were drowned.

I am, sir, your obedient servant,

T. P. TURNER,
Captain, Commanding.

BRITISH CONSULATE, *Charleston, January 30, 1863.*
Hon. J. P. BENJAMIN, *Secretary of State, Richmond.*

SIR: I beg leave to call your attention for the third time to the imprisonment of John Carfoot, a British subject, in the political prison at Salisbury, N. C. It is now nearly two months since I first addressed myself to you respecting this matter. As yet no information has been furnished to me, although there is no reason why the particulars of the arrest should not have been conveyed to me in fifteen days after my first application. In again urging your attention to this case I feel it my duty to suggest to you the grave responsibility which will undoubtedly attach to those who have confined a subject of the Queen for upward of nine months without affording him an opportunity of proving his innocence, if indeed any charges have been preferred against him.

I have the honor to be, sir, your very obedient, humble servant,
ROBERT BUNCH,
Her Majesty's Consul.

CHARLESTON JAIL, *February 2, 1863.*
General G. T. BEAUREGARD, *Commanding Department.*

SIR: I respectfully represent to you that I, as the late commander of the gun-boat Isaac Smith, with my brother officers have been confined as prisoners in the common jail. We are here upon the same footing with criminals, subject to even stricter rules, as we are not allowed what is called "the liberty of the yard" and provided with the same quarters and food. Under these circumstances, so humiliating to officers of our rank and position, I most respectfully but earnestly ask if we cannot be paroled, as has heretofore been the custom, as soon as the necessities of your service will permit.

Very respectfully, your obedient servant,
F. S. CONOVER,
Acting Lieutenant-Commander, U. S. Navy.

---

* Not found.

HDQRS. DEPT. OF S. CAROLINA, GEORGIA AND FLORIDA,
Charleston, S. C., February 2, 1863.

Lieut. F. S. CONOVER, U. S. Navy, *Charleston.*
    (Through Colonel Gaillard.)

SIR: In reply to your note of this date I am instructed to inform you that you cannot be paroled and for these reasons: The Army and Navy of the United States under the late proclamation of your President are instructed to assist slaves in servile war against their lawful masters, which is not only a high crime under the local laws of the State in whose waters you were captured but is contemned by all people as a means or appliance of war wholly illegitimate between civilized nations. It is purposed that the officers of a service thus found employed shall be held amenable to the laws made and provided in South Carolina for the punishment of those who incite our slaves to rebellion against their masters.

You and your associates will, however, be permitted all possible liberty compatible with your secure confinement, to which end instructions have been given to the provost-marshal. The usual ration allowed to prisoners of war has been directed to be furnished you in strict accordance with the regulations of the United States; that is "one ration without regard to rank" for each officer or man, and such a ration as is issued to our men. You and your associates, however, will be allowed to make any additions to your table at your own expense without restrictions.

Respectfully, your obedient servant,

T. JORDAN,
Brigadier-General and Chief of Staff.

CHARLESTON, S. C., *February 3, 1863.*

General S. COOPER,
    Adjutant and Inspector General, Richmond, Va.:

Shall I send prisoners of war (sailors) captured in Stono to Salisbury, N. C., or Richmond, holding officers?

G. T. BEAUREGARD.

RICHMOND, *February 3, 1863.*

General BEAUREGARD, *Charleston, S. C.:*

Send the prisoners to Richmond, retaining the officers.

S. COOPER,
Adjutant and Inspector General.

CHARLESTON JAIL, *February 4, 1863.*

General G. T. BEAUREGARD, *Commanding Department.*

SIR: I have the honor to acknowledge the receipt of your communication of the 2d instant and although no reply to it may be thought necessary I cannot permit myself to pass over part of its contents in silence. I do not understand that the proclamation of President Lincoln instructs as you say officers of the Army and Navy to assist slaves in servile war against their masters and cannot conceive that it is so understood by the officers of my Government. On the contrary I am happy to believe that an idea so repugnant to the laws of humanity finds no place in their minds. This I say, sir, only in justice to myself and those who for years have been my associates. The chief object of this letter, however, is to ask if my brother officers and myself can be permitted to communicate with our families.

Very respectfully, your obedient servant,

F. S. CONOVER,
Acting Lieutenant, U. S. Navy.

SPECIAL ORDERS, } HDQRS. DEPT. OF S. C., GA. AND FLA.,
No. 32. } *Charleston, February 4, 1863.*

I. All prisoners of **war** in this city (except officers and negroes) of the land and naval service of the United States will be sent forthwith and turned over to Brigadier-General Winder at Richmond, Va.

* * * * * * *

III. All officers of the land and naval service of the United States at present prisoners in the custody of the provost-marshal near these headquarters will be sent for further confinement to Columbia, S. C., until further orders.

* * * * * * *

By command of General Beauregard:

JNO. M. OTEY,
Assistant Adjutant-General.

WAR DEPARTMENT, *Richmond, February 5, 1863.*

Brigadier-General WINDER,
Hon. R. OULD:

Your letter of the 20th ultimo relative to the intercourse between citizens of the United States and Confederate States by the boat coming to City Point under flag of truce has been received. The intercourse should be regulated on terms of equality and reciprocity. If the Federal Government adhere to the rule that none shall pass to the United States except with the permission of the Secretary of War the requisition should be made that none should be permitted to land here without a previous permission from the War Department. No permission of the Secretary of War of the United States should be respected the application for which was not made through the commissioner of exchange (Mr. Ould). The Department does not perceive any necessity of placing those who are permitted to land nor those who shall make application to depart from the Confederate States under a special surveillance. None of the latter class are allowed to leave at this time without affording satisfactory references to their good character. That precaution will be continued. The Department is quite willing to place the subject in the hands of the commissioners of exchange of prisoners, and that they may determine who shall be allowed to go and return on either side. It does not desire to impose restrictions or embarrassments in the way of such intercourse as it is willing to allow at all. The adoption of any rules by the United States Government may require the adoption of corresponding rules on the part of this Government, but the Department would prefer rules which would not subject persons on either side to inconvenience, expense or delay.

Very respectfully, your obedient servant,

J. A. SEDDON,
Secretary of War.

WAR DEPARTMENT, *Richmond, Va., February 6, 1863.*
Hon. J. P. BENJAMIN, *Secretary of State:*

Inclosed you will find a report from General Winder of all the information that can be extracted from him on the subject of John Carfoot. A letter has been written to Mr. Wellford, at Salisbury, to make further inquiry on the subject.

For Secretary of War.

Very respectfully, your obedient servant,

J. A. CAMPBELL,
Assistant Secretary of War.

[Inclosure.]

HEADQUARTERS DEPARTMENT OF HENRICO,
Richmond, February 5, 1863.
Hon. JAMES A. SEDDON, *Secretary of War.*

DEAR SIR: In reply to yours of 4th instant relative to John Carfoot I have the honor to report that the said John Carfoot was arrested near New Berne, N. C., by Captain Boothe in April, 1862, and sent to Salisbury, N. C., by General Ransom. The inclosed letter, a copy of one addressed to the Adjutant-General and the original of which is on file in the Adjutant-General's Office, will explain the nature of the charges against him. He was discharged on the 3d day of January, 1863, and I am informed he is now at work in Salisbury, N. C., having taken the oath of allegiance to the Confederate States. I also inclose an extract* from a letter to the British consul notifying him of Carfoot's release. I am under the impression the former inquiry came through the Adjutant-General's Department and hence the reference was addressed to that office.

I am, respectfully, your obedient servant,

JOHN H. WINDER,
Brigadier-General.

[Sub-inclosure.]

HEADQUARTERS DEPARTMENT OF HENRICO,
Richmond, January 14, 1863.
General S. COOPER,
Adjutant and Inspector General C. S. Army, Richmond, Va.

GENERAL: I have the honor to transmit the following information concerning John Carfoot: He was arrested near New Berne, N. C., in the month of April, 1862, by Captain Boothe and sent to Salisbury by General Ransom. He was supposed at the time to have come to the above-named place in company with General Burnside. There are no papers on file.

Very respectfully, your obedient servant,

JNO. H. WINDER,
Brigadier-General.

WAR DEPARTMENT, *Richmond, Va., February 7, 1863.*
General J. C. PEMBERTON, *Jackson, Miss.:*

Use your own discretion about the deserters. Parole and discharge if you think best.

JAMES A. SEDDON,
Secretary of War.

---

* See p. 808.

WAR DEPARTMENT, *Richmond, February 7, 1863.*

R. T. CLARKE, Esq., *Conrad's Store, Va.*

SIR: You are informed in reply to your letter of the 2d instant that General Orders, No. 64, paragraph V, announces that no oath of allegiance to the United States and no parole by a person not in military service pledging himself not to bear arms against the United States will be regarded as an exemption from service in the armies of the Confederate States; but persons liable to conscription taking such oath or giving such parole will be enrolled for service. If captured by the enemy they will be demanded as prisoners of war. The Department therefore is not authorized to exempt you on the grounds stated.

Respectfully,

JAMES A. SEDDON,
Secretary of War.

HDQRS. DEPT. SOUTH CAROLINA, GEORGIA AND FLORIDA,
Charleston, S. C., February 7, 1863.

Lieut. F. S. CONOVER, U. S. Navy.
(Through Col. John S. Preston, commanding, &c., Columbia.)

SIR: Your letter of the 4th instant has just been received and I am instructed to say that of course you and your brother officers will be permitted to communicate in writing with your families to whom any letters will be forwarded with all possible dispatch. In connection with the cause of your present situation I have only to say that were the language of President Lincoln's proclamation of doubtful import the meaning would be made clear by the fact that there are now at Hilton Head or that vicinity negro troops, fugitive slaves who have recently been employed in armed expedition against the people of Georgia and South Carolina.

Respectfully, your obedient servant,

T. J[ORDAN,]
Chief of Staff.

AUSTIN, TEX., *February 8, 1863.*

General J. B. MAGRUDER, *Galveston.*

SIR: General Pelham, a most worthy citizen of this vicinity, was in New Mexico at the beginning of the present war, and when General Sibley reached that country with his brigade and found it untenable General Pelham shouldered his gun to fight for Southern independence, and on his way down from Santa Fé with arms in his hands was taken prisoner and paroled, but inasmuch as he had not joined the service formally and had his name placed upon the muster-roll the enemy deny him the benefits of a prisoner of war and claim him to be a political prisoner and as such refuse to exchange him. He feels the injustice done him in this regard by the enemy and is exceedingly anxious to be exchanged, so that he may be in a condition to aid in the defense of our country against the Abolitionists, and particularly to be enabled to defend his family without violating his parole. General W. R. Scurry is referred to for full particulars in regard to General Pelham. Now if you can consistently with your duties aid in disenthralling a brave, true and valuable citizen by procuring his exchange the people of Texas will consider it not only as an act of justice but another evidence of your devotion to her cause. Not having a personal acquaintance with you that would justify this appeal induces me to address you over my official signature.

Hoping you will find it compatible with your public duties and sense of justice to use your best efforts in behalf of General Pelham,

I have the honor to be, your most obedient servant,

C. W. BURNLEY,
Speaker of the House of Representatives, Ninth Legislature.

HDQRS. DEPT. SOUTH CAROLINA, GEORGIA AND FLORIDA,
Charleston, S. C., February 8, 1863.

Col. JOHN S. PRESTON, *Commanding, &c., Columbia.*

COLONEL: Assistant Surgeon Marvin, U. S. Navy, should not have been sent to Columbia but to Richmond, whither you will send him in charge of some officers when convenient; that is, without detailing an officer for that special service. Of course it will not do to let him run at large, though it is desired that he shall have as much liberty as practicable. He will be delivered to General Winder at Richmond.

Respectfully, your obedient servant,

T. J[ORDAN,]
Chief of Staff.

EXECUTIVE DEPARTMENT, *Richmond, February 9, 1863.*

Honorable SECRETARY OF WAR.

SIR: I am directed by the President to forward for your attention and the proper action the following copy of a resolution of the House of Representatives of the 5th instant:

Resolved, That the President be requested to communicate to this House a list of all civilians now in custody under authority of the War Department, giving as to each his name, residence and occupation, with the date of his arrest, the offense charged against him and the place of his imprisonment.

Your obedient servant,

BURTON N. HARRISON,
Private Secretary.

C. S. MILITARY PRISON,
Salisbury, N. C., February 9, 1863.

B. R. WELLFORD, Esq., *C. S. Commissioner.*

SIR: Although I understand that your visit to this place is made only for the purpose of investigating the cases of parties confined here for political offenses and therefore myself and the eleven officers lately attached to U. S. steamer Columbia who are held as prisoners of war are not directly included among its objects I take leave to submit to you a brief statement of our case and to request that you will do me the favor of bringing to the notice of the proper authorities at Richmond the exceptional circumstances under which we became rather than were made prisoners.

The Columbia, at that time one of the blockading squadron in the vicinity of New Inlet, N. C., while running in in the evening of the 14th ultimo with the intent to anchor for the night in obedience to orders, some three miles from shore and when by the soundings she should have been at that distance and the order had been given to bring ship to anchor found herself (owing to an error of the leadsman in calling the depth of water) close in with breakers, and before her engines could be reversed she struck on the reef off Masonborough Inlet, where all efforts to get her off by lightening her of her guns and coal proving fruitless she became a total wreck. At midnight the foremast was cut away to prevent her canting broadside to the surf, in which case all on board would probably have perished. On the afternoon of the 15th the U. S. steamer Penobscot hove in sight and toward 4 p. m. two of her boats succeeded in approaching near enough to catch a small line thrown from the end of the bowsprit. By means of a strong rope attached to this thirty of our crew were dropped overboard and hauled some hundred and fifty yards through the surf to the boats, all but two reaching them alive. An end was put to this effort to rescue us by the coming on of the night, which brought a heavy gale from southwest that raised a violent surf, causing the vessel to strike with fearful force and exposing us momentarily through the long hours of the night to be swept from the quarter-deck where all hands were crowded for greater safety, drenched by the seas that broke over them and the rain which fell in torrents and toward morning half frozen by the bitter cold which followed a sudden shift of the gale northwest.

While in this helpless and perishing condition, with no vessel in sight and our only chance for life being apparently an escape to the shore, a fire was opened upon the wreck from two batteries a short distance back of the beach several of whose shells passed just over the vessel, on which I ordered the white flag to be hoisted at the peak in token of our surrender (not having a gun to reply with) and the ensign to be set union down in the rigging as a signal of distress. Soon after this the southernmost battery ceased its fire, but the other kept it up nearly two hours longer not seeing as I was afterwards told our white flag. Between 9 and 10 a. m. (16th) two U. S. steamers made their appearance in the offing, and the firing on the wreck from the northern battery being still kept up I dispatched to the commander of the nearest a boat that narrowly escaped being swamped by the surf with a note requesting him to send in his boats and endeavor to take us off. To our astonishment, however, instead of doing this after his communication with the other vessel both of them commenced replying to the batteries at long range. Upon seeing this I at once (although the wind was at the time blowing a violent gale offshore) lowered my last boat and ordered an officer to pull in for any practicable point with a flag of truce and inform the commander of the post of our defenseless condition and surrender when the battery ceased firing on us.

On the return of the boat I went on shore myself at the request of Colonel Lamb but surrendered to Colonel Wilson, of one of the Georgia regiments, who informed me that he was the senior officer on the station.

It was not till the following morning (17th) that the ship's company could be got on shore when we were taken to Wilmington and ordered thence to Richmond the same night by General Whiting.

On reaching Goldsborough, however, the twenty eight seamen only who accompanied us pursued the route to Richmond, myself and officers being sent on to this place by order as I have since been told of General Smith.

Never having seen the proclamation of President Davis issued on the 12th ultimo I am not competent to speak with confidence of its tenor or bearing on our case; but if I have been correctly informed that it is directed in express terms only against officers of the Army of the United States who shall be found in arms on the soil of any of the Confederate States endeavoring to foment a servile insurrection I

would respectfully inquire whether naval officers not being referred to
in it can under the strict construction to which all such documents are
subject be fairly held to come within its scope, and whether in view of
this alone the officers (myself and fellow prisoners) might not *non
obstante* the proclamation be granted a release on parole?

But without presuming to decide a question in regard to which my
information is limited permit me to urge as a far stronger argument
in favor of our being paroled the peculiar nature of the circumstances
which led to our becoming prisoners—defenseless, shipwrecked mari-
ners barely escaping with life to the shore which for eighteen hours it
was doubtful whether we should survive to reach. Our situation is one
which has ever been recognized by civilized nations as establishing a
claim upon the hospitality of even their enemies which I shall not
readily believe the Confederate Government will be the first to deny,
and I cannot suffer myself to doubt that on the facts of our case being
fairly in its possession it will have no hesitation in according to us the
parole we request.

I subjoin the names* and rank of the officers who are my companions
in captivity, and have the honor, sir, to remain,

Very respectfully, your obedient servant,
JAS. P. COUTHOUY,
Lieut., U. S. Navy, late Comdg. U. S. Steamer Columbia.

[First indorsement.]
FEBRUARY 26, 1863.

Respectfully referred to the President.
The fact that this party came into our possession by shipwreck and
that he asserts ignorance of the President's proclamation commends
his case to favorable consideration.
J. A. SEDDON,
Secretary of War.

[Second indorsement.]

SECRETARY OF WAR:
For the reasons set forth let the exception be made.
JEFF'N DAVIS.

[Third indorsement.]

Referred to Brigadier-General Winder to carry into effect the order
of the President hereon.
By order of Secretary of War:
J. A. CAMPBELL,
Assistant Secretary of War.

[Fourth indorsement.]
HEADQUARTERS DEPARTMENT OF HENRICO,
March 23, 1863.

Respectfully returned to the Secretary of War with the remark that
these men have been ordered to Richmond and the President's order
will be carried into effect upon their arrival in the city.
JNO. H. WINDER,
Brigadier-General.

HEADQUARTERS DEPARTMENT OF HENRICO,
Richmond, February 10, 1863.

Capt. T. P. TURNER, *Commanding C. S. Prison.*

SIR: Some boxes of clothing will be sent to you to-day for the prisoners of war now in your custody. You will please send to these head-

* Omitted.

quarters a list of clothing and what disposition has been made of them. You will be held responsible for it after you have received them.

By order of General Winder:

W. S. WINDER,
Assistant Adjutant-General.

ALLEYTON, [TEX.,] *February 10, 1863.*
Maj. Gen. J. BANKHEAD MAGRUDER.

DEAR SIR: The political prisoners that were arrested by detachments from the Arizona Brigade I have turned over to the civil authorities in the counties in which they resided according to your orders. I am sorry to inform you that the arrests were made with much cruelty and violence to women and children and to the prisoners arrested. Affidavits have been made to be forwarded you, and I will thoroughly investigate the matter, and if true I will have the men arrested and punished and the officers who commanded the detachments arrested and held subject to your order. I have assured the citizens you will punish severely any injury inflicted on their rights, persons or property. I learn some are disposed to doubt my authority to act as your adjutant-general as they say they have never seen it published that I was authorized to act for you. Would it not be well to publish in the newspapers that I must be respected and obeyed as one of your adjutant-generals? My only desire is to carry out your views in enforcing subordination, a proper regard for the civil law and the rights and privileges of our citizens. The officers of the Arizona Brigade do not enforce proper order, and until under the immediate command of a strict disciplinarian will not be efficient but will always make trouble. Colonel Hardeman is yet very sick, unable to leave his bed. Colonel Madison is in command. I hope you will pardon the liberty I have taken in addressing you personally as I believed it best to do so in this case. I will keep you regularly informed of all matters and transactions that take place in this country through the proper channel. All opposition to the General or State government has apparently subsided. I will prepare a history of the evidences that made it necessary to declare martial law for transmission to Richmond and send it to you for your approval.

With sentiments of esteem and respect, I am, very truly, your obedient servant,

HENRY L. WEBB.

OFFICE PROVOST-MARSHAL, *Greeneville, February 10, 1863.*
Col. JOHN E. TOOLE, *Provost-Marshal.*

SIR: Some arrangement should be made at once for taking possession of and preserving all property subject to confiscation in this department. Men are continually leaving for Kentucky who always leave their property in the hands of some friend who disposes of it, thus defrauding the Government or rather the citizens of such property. A few days since one of the enrolling officers reported to me some property left in his district by Doctor Taylor, the notorious Lincolnite, which he said some women with whom Taylor had been living were removing. I told him to take possession of it, which he did of all to be found. A fine case of surgical instruments had been removed, also some other property. Shall he retain this property as I have ordered? If retained to whom shall I send it or report it? Another enrolling officer reports a cow or two belonging to the notorious Fry which I told him to hold subject to orders from the authorities. Stockbridge left some property, mostly books, which his wife has been selling. Stockbridge having spent nearly all the property she had when he married her this may all be well enough. Shall I interfere? I would be glad to have some instructions on this point.

I am, sir, your humble servant,

JAS. H. ROBINSON,
Assistant Deputy Provost-Marshal.

HEADQUARTERS DEPARTMENT OF HENRICO,
Richmond, February 13, 1863.

Gen. J. E. JOHNSTON, *Commanding, &c.*

GENERAL: At the request of Mr. Robert Ould, agent of exchange, the Secretary of War directs that the following prisoners be brought to this city:

All the Federal commissioned officers who were captured previous to the 10th of December, 1862.

All the citizens of the United States not in the Confederate States at the commencement of the war who have been captured or arrested and are now confined in the military prisons of the department.

All officers and men belonging to the home guards of Virginia, Tennessee and Kentucky.

If any of the above mentioned are within the limits of your command will you please have them sent to this city as soon as practicable.

I am, very respectfully, your obedient servant,

JOHN H. WINDER,
Brigadier-General.

[Indorsement.]

Sent copies to General Bragg and Lieutenant-General Pemberton ordering them to execute.

J. E. J.

C. S. MILITARY PRISON, *Richmond, February 13, 1863.*

Surg. JOHN WILKINS,
In charge of C. S. Military Prison Hospital.

SIR: I send you to-day six boxes marked "Thos. T. May, Libby Prison Hospital, care Agent of Exchange, Fort Monroe." The boxes contain articles of various kinds for the use of the Federal sick and wounded in your hospital. I am directed by General Winder to turn these boxes over to you with the request that you examine them, make an inventory of the articles they contain and distribute them as your judgment may suggest. Please acknowledge the receipt of this and when the inventory is made out send me a copy to be forwarded to headquarters.

I am, sir, your obedient servant,

TH. P. TURNER,
Captain, Commanding.

C. S. MILITARY PRISON HOSPITAL,
Richmond, Va., February 13, 1863.

Capt. THOMAS P. TURNER, *Commandant of Post.*

SIR: I have the honor to acknowledge the receipt of your letter and six boxes marked "Thos. T. May, Libby Prison Hospital, care Agent of Exchange, Fort Monroe." In obedience to your instructions I have examined their contents and inclose you an inventory of same.

Very respectfully,

JOHN WILKINS,
Surgeon in Charge.

[Inclosure.]

Inventory of six boxes marked "Thos. T. May, Libby Prison Hospital, care Agent of Exchange, Fort Monroe," sent on by the Sanitary Committee of New York for the use of the sick and wounded in this hospital, received February 3, 1863:

Cotton shirts, 83; condensed milk, 20 cans; ink bottles, 3; cotton drawers, 55 pairs; corn starch, farina, &c.; tapers, 30; lead pencils, 4; woolen shirts, 41; sponges, 9 pieces; chocolate cakes, 5; woolen drawers, 40 pairs; tin plates, 1 dozen; assorted pickles, 5 gallons; socks, 35 pairs; tin cups, $1\frac{9}{12}$ dozen; pickled peaches, 5 gallons; slippers, 42 pairs; writing paper, 2 reams; 1 lot of rags and 2 cloth coats; envelopes, 10 packages; 1 lot of assorted dried fruit; vests, 2; penholders, 2 dozen; towels, 9 dozen; steel pens, 4 dozen; assorted soap, 2 bags; combs, 3; cans soup, 1 dozen; scissors, 6 pair.

JOHN WILKINS,
Surgeon in Charge.

HDQRS. C. S. FORCES, N. E. ARKANSAS AND S. E. MISSOURI,
Batesville, Ark., February 15, 1863.

Capt. A. D. BROWN, C. S. Army:

Capt. A. D. Brown, C. S. Army, is directed to proceed with his party under flag of truce and deliver official communications to Brigadier-Generals Brown and Davidson, U. S. Army, as addressed.

By command of Brigadier-General Marmaduke:

E. G. WILLIAMS,
Assistant Adjutant-General.

[Indorsement.]

HEADQUARTERS, &C., *February 16, 1863.*

This party is armed with pistols and sabers for their protection against jayhawkers and bushwhackers.

J. S. MARMADUKE,
Brigadier-General.

C. S. MILITARY PRISON, *Richmond, February 19, 1863.*

Capt. G. W. ALEXANDER,
Assistant Adjutant-General and Assistant Provost-Marshal.

SIR: In accordance with General Winder's instructions I send you four boxes marked as follows: No. 1, Castle Thunder, 75 coats or jackets; No. 2, Castle Thunder, 75 pairs of boots; No. 3, Castle Thunder, 75 flannel shirts and 100 pairs socks; No. 4, Castle Thunder, 75 trousers or pants.

The general wishes that you will have the articles carefully counted and distributed as requested in Colonel Ludlow's letter to Hon. Robert Ould, a copy* of which I send you, and in delivering the articles to the

---

* Not found.

prisoners make them receipt for each article and take duplicate copies of same.

You will please, captain, also receipt to me for the above-named boxes.

I am, sir, your obedient servant,

TH. P. TURNER,
Captain, Commanding.

SAN ANTONIO, *February 19, 1863.*

Major-General MAGRUDER,
Comdg. Department of Texas, New Mexico and Arizona.

GENERAL: On the 19th of January, ultimo, I wrote you a note inclosing a parole pass requesting to be exchanged for some civil prisoner held by the Confederate States Government. My note was returned indorsed:

JANUARY 28, 1863.

The within is not a subject of exchange. This is only a pass.
By command of Major-General Magruder:

E. P. TURNER,
Assistant Adjutant-General.

On the 2d February following I again wrote asking a reconsideration of the foregoing decision. My letter was returned indorsed:

FEBRUARY 12, 1863.

Were an exchange to be made that exchange would not release you from the oath you took unless the prisoner going North would consent to take a similar oath to the Confederate States Government, consequently the major-general commanding can only refer you to his original decision as final.
By order of Major-General Magruder:

STEPHEN D. YANCEY,
Lieutenant and Acting Assistant Adjutant-General.

Since entering upon the foregoing correspondence I have been shown by Major Russell, of General Bee's staff, an order from Richmond which directly and positively refuses to acknowledge such passes as that issued by General Butler in the light of paroles, said order especially stating that such parole passes will not exempt parties from military duty. In taking said pass I knew full well that it was contrary to all the usages of war, it being manifestly illegal and unprecedented to subject non-combatants to permanent military disability and without the privileges of exchange; but this not being the first departure from the rules of civilized warfare on the part of our enemy I had hoped that this like other departures from common usage might be rectified by reprisal and therefore availed myself of the pass to escape the Yankee lines, promising myself to use my best endeavors to effect an exchange. Having failed I now accept your original decision, general, as final, to wit, that I am not a subject of exchange and that my supposed parole is not a parole but only a pass. I therefore consider myself released from now henceforth. But I must beg to file an answer to the indorsement of the 12th February made upon my letter of the 2d February.

Neither my pass nor any letters hint in the most shadowy form that I have ever taken an oath in presence of any U. S. officer or in favor of the United States Government. Yet by some misconception it has been inferred in said indorsement that I have taken some kind of an oath while within the Yankee lines. This I now most clearly and emphatically deny. My pass was obtained strictly as a personal favor to myself through Mr. G. S. Denison, Federal collector of New Orleans, and before whom I had positively refused to take the oath of allegiance to the United States. He saw General Butler and not I. I was asked no questions and subjected to no tests. The pass was drawn by General Butler's adjutant. I signed my name to it. It was then handed me and so the matter ended. I did with a willing heart and free conscience take the oath of allegiance to the Confederate States of America in San Antonio months before going to Louisiana, and by that oath alone with the help of God I ever expect to abide.

I have the honor to be, general, your most obedient servant,

THEODORE HEERMANN.

HEADQUARTERS DEPARTMENT OF HENRICO,
Richmond, Va., February 20, 1863.

General JOSEPH E. JOHNSTON,
Commanding, &c., Tullahoma.

GENERAL: At the request of Mr. Robert Ould, agent of exchange, the Secretary of War directs that the following prisoners be brought to this city: All the Federal commissioned officers who were captured previous to the 12th of January, 1863.

Very respectfully, your obedient servant,

JNO. H. WINDER,
Brigadier-General.

CIRCULAR.]   HEADQUARTERS HINDMAN'S DIVISION,
Little Rock, February 22, 1863.

It has frequently happened that officers and men of this command captured and paroled by the enemy have remained a considerable time without exchange either with their companies or else at home rendering no service. Brigade commanders are directed to forward reports promptly setting forth the name, company, regiment and rank of every such paroled prisoner, when and where captured and whether in hospital or not when taken, so that they may be exchanged and returned to duty without delay. Regimental and company commanders must be required to make similar reports from time to time.

By command of Major-General Hindman:

R. C. NEWTON,
Assistant Adjutant-General.

HDQRS. DEPT. OF MISSISSIPPI AND EAST LOUISIANA,
Jackson, February 23, 1863.

General S. COOPER,
Adjutant and Inspector General, Richmond, Va.

GENERAL: I have the honor herewith to inclose for the information of the War Department a copy of a notice* which purports to have been issued by Admiral D. D. Porter, of the U. S. Navy, and a copy of a retaliatory notification† which I have caused to be communicated to the Federal authorities near Vicksburg.

I have the honor to be, general, very respectfully, your obedient servant,

J. C. PEMBERTON,
Lieutenant-General, Commanding.

---

* Omitted here; see Stevenson to Grant, February 24, and inclosure, p. 293.
† Omitted here; see Grant to Pemberton, Porter to Grant and Porter to Stevenson, March 2, pp. 308 and 309. For Seddon to Pemberton, March 20 and 28, see Series I, Vol. XXIV, Part III, pp. 679 and 696.

ASHEVILLE, N. C., *February 24, 1863.*

[Hon. Z. B. VANCE.]

GOVERNOR: In obedience to your direction to do so I have made inquiries and gathered facts such as I could in reference to the shooting of certain prisoners on Laurel Creek, in Madison County. I have to report to you that I learn that the militia troops had nothing to do with what was done on Laurel. Thirteen prisoners at least were killed by order of Lieut. Col. J. A. Keith. Most of them were taken at their homes and none of them made resistance when taken. Perhaps some of them ran. After they were taken prisoners the soldiers took them off to a secluded place, made them kneel down and shot them. They were buried in a trench dug for the purpose. Some two weeks since their bodies were removed to a graveyard. I learn that probably eight of the thirteen killed were not in the company that robbed Marshall and other places. I suppose they were shot on suspicion. I cannot learn the names of the soldiers who shot them. Some of them shrank from the barbarous and brutal transaction at first, but were compelled to act. This is a list of the names of those killed:

Elison King (desperate man), Jo. Woods (desperate man), Will Shelton (twenty years old, [son] of Sipus), Aronnata Shelton (fourteen years old, [son] of Sipus, not at Marshall), James Shelton (Old Jim, about fifty-six years old), James Shelton, jr. (seventeen years old), David Shelton (thirteen years old, was not in the raid), James Madcap (forty years old, was not in the raid), Rod Shelton (Stob Rod, was not in the raid), David Shelton (brother of Stob Rod, was not in the raid), Joseph Cleandren (fifteen or sixteen years old, was not in the raid), Halen Moore (twenty-five or thirty years old, was not in the raid), Wade Moore, twenty or twenty-five years old, was not in the raid.

It is said that those whose names I have so marked did not go to Marshall. The prisoners were captured on one Friday and killed the next Monday. Several women were severely whipped and ropes were tied around their necks. It is said Col. L. M. Allen was not in command and that Keith commanded. Four prisoners are now in jail, sent here as I learn by order of General Davis. These are Sipus Shelton, Isaac Shelton, William Norton and David Shelton, son of Sipus.

I think the facts stated are about true. One thing is certain, thirteen prisoners were killed—shot without trial or any hearing whatever and in the most cruel manner. I have no means of compelling witnesses to disclose facts to me and I do not know that I shall be able to make a fuller report to Your Excellency at any early day. I hope these facts will enable you to take such steps as will result in a more satisfactory development of the true state of the matter.

I am, &c., yours, truly,   A. S. MERRIMON.

GENERAL ORDERS, ⎫   HEADQUARTERS FIRST DISTRICT,
                     ⎬   DEPT. OF MISS. AND EAST LA.,
     No. 6.   ⎭   *Columbus, Miss., February 25, 1863.*

*   *   *   *   *   *   *

VII. The passing of paroled Federal prisoners through this district northward is positively prohibited without special orders from these headquarters or from higher authority for that purpose.

*   *   *   *   *   *   *

By order of Brigadier-General Ruggles:

                                   R. M. HOOE,
                                   Assistant Adjutant-General.

WAR DEPARTMENT, *Richmond, February 26, 1863.*

W. H. SYME, Esq., *Lewisburg, Va.*

SIR: Your letter of the 14th instant has been received, and in reply you are informed, first, that all prisoners who have been captured and paroled that were taken anywhere in Virginia prior to the 1st of November have been exchanged; second, the pay of a volunteer private continues during his captivity though paroled; third, the private should report to his regiment at once and if disabled placed on special duty; fourth, the provost-marshal has no right to appoint your son assistant provost-marshal. The application for duty should be made through the officers of your son's regiment and proof of disability presented, and in that form be communicated to the Secretary of War.

Respectfully,

JAMES A. SEDDON,
Secretary of War.

WAR DEPARTMENT, *Richmond, February 26, 1863.*

M. J. SAFFOLD, Esq., *Montgomery, Ala.*

SIR: You have been selected by this Department and are hereby commissioned to make a full examination into the cases of all prisoners (not connected with the Confederate Army) now held in confinement by the military authorities of the Confederate States at any military post or prison in the State of Alabama or the Department of Western Georgia.

You will communicate this appointment to the military commanders in the said State and department and inquire where such prisoners are confined, and with as little delay as practicable will repair to the respective posts or prisons and enter upon the discharge of the duties assigned.

You are authorized to require the production of all documentary testimony and military orders respecting such prisoners; may examine any witnesses who can be produced for or against them, and may hear any statements which the prisoners desire or are willing to make.

You are authorized to discharge, either absolutely or upon such oath or parole as you may think proper, all prisoners against whom no well-founded suspicion of having violated any law of the Confederate States may exist, or whose longer detention you may think not demanded by the public interests.

Orders will be issued to the commanding officers in the State of Alabama and the Department of Western Georgia to render you every facility in the discharge of your duties and to obey your instructions in regard to the prisoners you may examine.

A full report of your proceedings under this commission and your opinion with regard to each prisoner examined will be made by you as promptly as practicable.

You will notify the Department on receipt of this communication whether you will accept the position assigned you and when it will comport with your convenience to enter upon the discharge of the duties.

By way of compensation for your services you will be allowed the sum of $125 per month, and transportation will be furnished for all necessary travel by the commandants of the several posts.

Very respectfully, your obedient servant,

J. A. CAMPBELL,
Assistant Secretary of War.

WAR DEPARTMENT, *Richmond, February 27, 1863.*
To the PRESIDENT OF THE CONFEDERATE STATES:

In answer to a resolution of the House of Representatives I have the honor to inclose a list* of the civilian prisoners now in custody in this city and at Salisbury, N. C., under military authority.

No arrests have been made at any time by any specific order or direction of this Department. The persons arrested have been taken either by officers of the Army commanding in the field or by provost-marshals exercising authority of a similar nature, and the ground for arrest is or ought to be founded upon some necessity or be justified as a proper precaution against an apparent danger. The Department has had commissioners to examine these persons with directions to "discharge those against whom no well-grounded cause of suspicion exists of having violated a law or done an act hostile or injurious to the Confederate States."

The Department appointed in November last a commissioner to examine prisoners in the Southwestern Department, embracing a portion of Georgia, Alabama and a portion of Mississippi. This commissioner found some obstructions in the performance of his duties from the provost marshals and some difficulty in obtaining reports from them. He resigned in the latter part of January without making a report of the prisoners remaining in the department for which he was appointed. These commissioners have been found useful and I recommend that the Department may be authorized to appoint them for the objects before mentioned and that they be clothed with the authority of commissioners under the act of the Provisional Congress, No. 273, respecting commissioners appointed by the district courts.

In conclusion I have to say that under the examinations that have been made a large number of prisoners have been discharged and none are retained unless there be a cause of suspicion supported by testimony rendering it probable that the discharge of the prisoner would be prejudicial to the public interest.

Most respectfully,

JAMES A. SEDDON,
Secretary of War.

———

EXECUTIVE DEPARTMENT, *Raleigh, February 27, 1863.*
Brigadier-General DAVIS, *Knoxville, Tenn.*

GENERAL: In my last letter to you I referred to a report that a number of prisoners taken on Laurel had been shot in cold blood and expressed the hope it might not prove true. I fear, however, that it is even worse than was first reported. I beg leave to ask your attention to the copy inclosed† of a part of a letter from A. S. Merrimon, esq., attorney for the State in that district, and to respectfully request you to make inquiry into the truth of the statements therein with a view to proceedings against the guilty parties. Whilst expressing again my thanks for the prompt aid rendered by your command in quieting the troubles in that region I cannot reconcile it to my sense of duty to pass by in silence such cruel and barbarous conduct as is alleged to have characterized a portion of them, and more especially as the officers mentioned are citizens of this State.

Very respectfully, your obedient servant,

Z. B. VANCE.

———

*Not found.   †See also Merrimon to Vance, February 24, p. 836.

[Inclosure.]

ASHEVILLE, N. C., *February 16, 1863.*

Governor Z. B. VANCE, *Raleigh, N. C.*

GOVERNOR: Your letter of the 9th instant is just received. I beg to assure you that I shall at the next term of the court prosecute vigorously such of the prisoners to whom you direct my attention as may be turned over to the civil authorities. The late expedition to Laurel sent only four prisoners to jail and one of them was admitted to bail on yesterday by Judge Bailey. I understand there are no more to send. I have no knowledge of my own touching the shooting of several prisoners on Laurel. I have learned, however, from a most reliable source that thirteen of them were killed; that some of them were not taken in arms but at their homes; that of all the men shot thirteen if not more were prisoners at the time they were shot; that they were taken off to a secluded cove or gorge in the mountains and then made to kneel down and were thus shot. One man was badly and mortally shot in the bowels and while he was writhing in agony and praying to God for mercy a soldier mercilessly and brutally shot him in the head with his pistol. Several women were whipped.

This I learn from one who got his information from some of the guilty parties. I learn that all this was done by order of Lieut. Col. James A. Keith. I know not what you intend doing with the guilty parties, but I suggest they are all guilty of murder. I do not suppose they had any order to do so barbarous a deed, but if they had the order was void absolutely, no matter by whom issued. Such savage and barbarous cruelty is without a parallel in this State and I hope in every other. I am gratified that you intend to take the matter in hand. I will make such investigation as I can, but I have no means of compelling any one to disclose facts to me. It will not be difficult I learn to prove that the prisoners were killed. I assure you that I will prosecute all persons who have committed criminal offenses in this circuit at the next term of the court and in the meantime I will do all in my power to suppress crime and violence. These are fearfully on the increase in this section of the State. A report might be made that would astonish you. I have done all I could in reference to the complaints made to you from Jackson and Cherokee Counties.

*   *   *   *   *   *   *

I am, &c., yours, truly,

A. S. MERRIMON.

SPECIAL ORDERS, }   ADJT. AND INSP. GENERAL'S OFFICE,
No. 49.   }   *Richmond, February 27, 1863.*

*   *   *   *   *   *   *

VIII. Capt. W. H. Hatch, assistant adjutant-general, will proceed without delay to Tullahoma, Tenn., on business in connection with the exchange of prisoners. He will report to Col. Robert Ould in this city for instructions. Having discharged these duties he will report at the office of the Adjutant and Inspector General in this city.

*   *   *   *   *   *   *

By command of the Secretary of War:

JNO. WITHERS,
Assistant Adjutant-General.

ADJUTANT AND INSPECTOR GENERAL'S OFFICE,
Richmond, February 28, 1863.

General R. E. LEE, Commanding, &c., Fredericksburg, Va.

GENERAL: I have received your letter of the 24th instant and it seems only necessary to say that I concur in your views respecting the Sixty-fifth and Eighty-ninth Articles of War.

I am, general, very respectfully, your obedient servant,

S. COOPER,
Adjutant and Inspector General.

CHATTANOOGA, February 28, 1863.

General S. COOPER, Adjutant and Inspector General.

SIR: I respectfully submit the accompanying papers* to the War Department to show the fact that Major-General Rosecrans declines to correspond with General Bragg and upon what grounds.

To Major-General Rosecrans' letters to myself I replied† that the correspondence which he desired me to undertake was one of General Bragg's functions which I could not assume.

Most respectfully, &c.,

J. E. JOHNSTON,
General.

INSPECTOR-GENERAL'S OFFICE, ARMY OF TENNESSEE,
Tullahoma, Tenn., February 28, 1863.

ASSISTANT ADJUTANT-GENERAL, Army of Mississippi.

SIR: I have the honor in obedience to instructions from the commanding general to forward to your headquarters under guard George U. Thatcher, who purports to be a citizen of Missouri and who has twice been arrested within the lines of our army under suspicious circumstances, with the request that Thatcher be sent across the Mississippi River. The circumstances of Thatcher's arrest are as follows: When the Army of Mississippi entered Kentucky Thatcher was found within our lines. Not being able satisfactorily to account for himself General Bragg had him arrested and ordered to the rear, directing him to remain at Chattanooga, Tenn., until the return of the army. Instead of doing this Thatcher preceded the army in its advance through Kentucky, arriving at Louisville simultaneously with General Buell, U. S. Army. Shortly after this an article appeared in a Louisville paper giving the organization of the Army of Mississippi (at that time so-called). Authorship of this article was attributed to the prisoner. On the return of the army Thatcher is again found within the lines with military goods for sale ; also a negro which he claims as his property. Negro boy is identified by a citizen of Rutherford County and Thatcher is arrested as a spy but is released at the solicitations of Honorable Phelps, Member of Congress from Missouri, with the distinct understanding that he is to proceed immediately across the Mississippi River. Violating this Thatcher is re-arrested and is now sent to Lieutenant-General Pemberton with the request that he be immediately sent across the Mississippi River as too dangerous a man to be allowed to remain within our lines.

---

* See Rosecrans to Johnston, January 18 and 19, pp. 188, 191.
† See Johnston to Rosecrans, February 12, p. 266.

You will pardon, sir, the apparent discourtesy in not giving you your title and rank as I am unacquainted with both.

I am, sir, very respectfully, your obedient servant,

W. CLARE,
Major and Assistant Inspector-General.

EXECUTIVE DEPARTMENT, *Raleigh, February 28, 1863.*

Hon. JAMES A. SEDDON, *Secretary of War.*

SIR: Some six months since a disturbance occurred in Madison County, N. C., near the Tennessee border, by some disloyal persons capturing the little country town and seizing a lot of salt and other plunder. An armed force was promptly sent from Knoxville under command of General Davis to suppress the insurrection which was accomplished before the local militia could get there, though ordered out immediately. But in doing so a degree of cruelty and barbarity was displayed, shocking and outrageous in the extreme on the part of Lieut. Col. J. A. Keith, Sixty-fourth North Carolina Troops, who seems to have been in command and to have acted in this respect without orders from his superiors so far as I can learn. I beg leave to ask you to read the inclosed letter* (copy) from A. S. Merrimon, State's attorney for that judicial district, which you will perceive discloses a scene of horror disgraceful to civilization. I desire you to have proceedings instituted at once against this officer, who if the half be true is a disgrace to the service and to North Carolina. You may depend upon the respectability and fairness of Mr. Merrimon who made an investigation officially by my order. I have also written General Davis.

Very respectfully, your obedient servant,

Z. B. VANCE.

HEADQUARTERS DEPARTMENT OF HENRICO,
Richmond, February 28, 1863.

Hon. JAMES A. SEDDON, *Secretary of War.*

SIR: In reply to the letter from the House of Representatives dated February 24, 1863, containing copy of a resolution passed by that body calling for the "authority by which a number of Yankee prisoners have been admitted to take the oath of fidelity to the Confederate States and have been allowed to locate as free laborers in Rockbridge County, Va.," which letter was indorsed to these headquarters on the 26th instant for report, I have the honor to state that upon representation to the War Department that a large number of Yankee deserters had accumulated in the military prisons I was instructed by the Secretary of War to allow such of them as were willing to take the oath of allegiance to the Confederate States and permit them to seek work wherever it could be found.

These instructions referred exclusively to deserters and my action was in strict conformity thereto.

I would further beg leave respectfully to state that those men mentioned in the resolution above referred to as having located in Rockbridge County, Va., were employed by Joseph R. Anderson, esq., of the Tredegar Works, who forwarded them to that county to labor.

Very respectfully, your obedient servant,

JNO. H. WINDER,
Brigadier-General.

---

* Omitted here; see Merrimon's two letters, pp. 836, 839.

WAR DEPARTMENT, *Richmond, Va., March —, 1863.*

All matters relating to the exchange of prisoners and flag-of-truce boats will be under the direction and control of Robert Ould, agent for the exchange of prisoners, subject only to the orders of the Secretary of War.

JAS. A. SEDDON,
Secretary of War.

BROWNSVILLE, TEX., *March 1, 1863.*

Hon. J. P. BENJAMIN, *Richmond.*

SIR: On the 20th ultimo I learned that one Henry Safford, formerly of Galveston, Tex., and lately from New York, had arrived at Matamoras with $50,000 in counterfeit Confederate money. I immediately notified General Bee of it and spoke with the Mexican authorities to have said Safford arrested. On the 26th a Spaniard named Manuel Lluro visited Brownsville and endeavored to negotiate the sum of $2,000 in paper which upon examination was found to be counterfeited. The bearer was arrested and in his voluntary statement asserted that he had received said paper from Safford. On the same day I visited Matamoras and succeeded in obtaining from the proper authorities an order for the arrest and delivery of Safford. Both he and Lluro are now at Fort Brown to be tried.

The Mexican Government is to receive (at the mouth of the Rio Grande) 40,000 stand of arms from New York which have been contracted for by J. Bustamente, an agent of said Government. As the arms are to be paid for on delivery and the Mexican authorities cannot dispose of the full sum needed I at the request of General Bee have spoken with the custom-house inspector (Mr. Zambrano) who has agreed to let us have part of said arms. The consignee who resides at Matamoras is also willing to contract with us. As soon as our object is accomplished it will not be amiss to forward the proper information to the C. S. agent at Havana that the French Government may be apprised of the neutrality of the United States. I shall leave here to-morrow for Monterey.

I have the honor to be, your obedient servant,

J. A. QUINTERO.

COLUMBUS, *March 3, 1863.*

Lieut. Gen. J. C. PEMBERTON:

Twelve Federal prisoners sent to Okolona to go North. Shall they pass? I have endeavored to stop this indiscriminate passing of paroled prisoners acting as spies.

DAN'L RUGGLES,
Brigadier-General.

VICKSBURG, *March 4, 1863.*

Colonel WADDY:

Colored prisoners from Indianola sent over to-day by 12 o'clock train. Ninety-four in all.

M. L. SMITH,
Major-General.

C. S. MILITARY PRISON, *Richmond, March 4, 1863.*

[Capt. W. S. WINDER.]

CAPTAIN: The number of prisoners having greatly increased in the last few days, and having just received from Robert Ould, esq., rolls containing nearly 4,000 names of paroled prisoners of war that have been sent North which he has referred to me in order to compare them with the prison books that I may certify as to date of capture, which he says is necessary to have with his next interview with the Federal commissioner of exchange of prisoners, my time will consequently be so much occupied at the prison as to prevent me from attending closely to the temporary duty at provost-marshal's office to which I was assigned by Special Orders, No. 49. I therefore respectfully request that I may be relieved from that duty if in your judgment no inconvenience may result from it.

Your obedient servant,

TH. P. TURNER,
Captain, Commanding.

P. S.—The provost-marshal's assistant who has been sick for some time returned to duty to-day and I suppose my services can be dispensed with without serious inconvenience.

T. P. T.

WAR DEPARTMENT, *Richmond, March 5, 1863.*

His Excellency Z. B. VANCE,
Governor of North Carolina, Raleigh, N. C.

SIR: I received your letter of the 28th ultimo in reference to the conduct of Lieut. Col. J. A. Keith, Sixty-fourth North Carolina Regiment, and have directed General Donelson, commanding at Knoxville, to investigate the matter and report the facts to the Department.

Very respectfully, your obedient servant,

JAS. A. SEDDON,
Secretary of War.

VICKSBURG, *March 5, 1863.*

Lieutenant-General PEMBERTON:

General Grant will not receive non-commissioned officers and privates without the commissioned officers. Please do not send the prisoners to this place.

N. G. WATTS,
Major and Agent.

[Indorsement.]

MARCH 5, 1863.

Respectfully referred to Brigadier-General Adams who will not forward any of the prisoners to Vicksburg.

By order of Lieutenant-General Pemberton:

J. C. TAYLOR,
Aide-de-Camp.

GENERAL ORDERS, }   ADJT. AND INSP. GENERAL'S OFFICE,
    No. 25.   }   *Richmond, March 6, 1863.*

I. The following act of Congress and regulations to enforce the same are published for the information of all persons concerned:

CHAP. LXII.—*An act to protect the rights of owners of slaves taken by or employed in the Army.*

The Congress of the Confederate States of America do enact, That every person connected with the Army or Navy of the Confederate States arresting or coming into possession of any slave by capture from the enemy or otherwise than by lawful authority shall immediately report the same to the commanding officer of the post or brigade or station to which he may be attached. The said commanding officer shall with as little delay as practicable send the slaves so reported to the nearest depot described in the next section, with a register of the place and date of their arrest: *Provided, however,* That the said slaves or any of them may at once be delivered to their respective owners if claim is made and established on satisfactory evidence.

SEC. 2. The Secretary of War shall establish depots for recaptured slaves at convenient places, not more than five in number, in each State, and all slaves captured in such State shall be kept in such depots. Public notice shall be given of the places so selected.

SEC. 3. Lists of the slaves in each of such depots, showing the name and color of such slaves, the place and time of their arrest, and the names of their owners, as given by themselves or otherwise ascertained, shall be regularly advertised in each State in one or more newspapers of general circulation.

SEC. 4. While such slaves are in depot they may be employed under proper guard on public works; but no slave shall be removed from the depot to which he is first carried for at least one month after the first advertisement of his being there, nor then unless an exact register is made of the removal and due advertisement made in the newspapers as aforesaid.

SEC. 5. Free access shall be permitted to all persons desiring to inspect the said slaves for the purpose of identifying them and establishing ownership, and upon due proof they shall be immediately restored to the persons claiming them.

SEC. 6. It shall further be the duty of the Secretary of War to require the names of all slaves in the employment of an officer or soldier of the Confederate Army or Navy, with the names and residence of their owners, and of the person by whom hired out, and of the officer or soldier hiring, to be reported to his department and a full register thereof to be kept for public inspection.

SEC. 7. The President shall prescribe regulations for carrying this act into effect and provide for the subsistence of said slaves while in such depots.

[Approved October 13, 1862.]

II. Depots for recaptured slaves are hereby established at the following places, viz:

At the Camps of Instruction at Richmond, Petersburg and Dublin Station, in the State of Virginia; Camp of Instruction at Raleigh, in the State of North Carolina; Camp of Instruction at Columbia, in the State of South Carolina; Camps of Instruction at Macon and Decatur, in the State of Georgia; Camps of Instruction at Notasulga and Talladega, in the State of Alabama; Camp of Instruction at Tallahassee, in the State of Florida; Camps of Instruction at Brookhaven and Enterprise, in the State of Mississippi; Camps of Instruction at Monroe, Camp Moore and New Iberia, in the State of Louisiana; Camp of Instruction at Houston, in the State of Texas; Camps of Instruction at Knoxville and McMinnville, in the State of Tennessee; Camp of Instruction at Little Rock, in the State of Arkansas.

III. The commandants of the several camps of instruction will provide necessary quarters for all negroes sent to the depots; will detail sufficient guards for their safe-keeping; provide for their custody, employment and subsistence; require full and accurate registers to be kept, and advertisements as prescribed by the act of Congress to be regularly made, and afford all facilities to claimants to establish their ownership, and on due proof surrender the slaves to their owners.

IV. Commanding generals will require all persons connected with the Army to make immediate report of all slaves arrested or coming into their possession; and if claim is not promptly made and established by the owner will send such slaves with a register of the place and date of their arrest with as little delay as practicable to the nearest depot in the State wherein the capture is made. They will also require all officers and soldiers now employing slaves forthwith to report the same and those hereafter employing them within ten days thereafter, with the names and residence of their owners and of the person by whom they were hired out and of the officer or soldier hiring, and return such reports as soon as received to this office; and will in all other respects enforce from the officers and men under their command a strict and prompt observance of the requirements of the above-recited act of Congress.

By order:

S. COOPER,
Adjutant and Inspector General.

WAR DEPARTMENT, *Richmond, March 7, 1863.*

General J. C. PEMBERTON, *Jackson, Miss.:*

Use your discretion with regard to men taken as prisoners of war. Enlist if any are willing. Let any willing take the oath of allegiance. Put any willing to work. Parole and dismiss toward their own country such as you may deem safe.

JAMES A. SEDDON,
Secretary of War.

PROVOST-MARSHAL'S OFFICE,
Charleston, S. C., March 7, 1863.

Capt. J. M. OTEY, *Assistant Adjutant-General.*

SIR: Under the approval of Brigadier-General Ripley I expect to send to Richmond in a few days the wounded prisoners of war captured on board the Isaac Smith together with sundry prisoners belonging to Confederate regiments now in North Carolina and Virginia. I would respectfully ask if the prisoner of war Calvin Jones shall be sent at same time or be detained longer. He belongs to Company D, Ninth Maine Regiment, and was sent here by Brigadier-General Walker on the 19th February last, and was captured but a short time previous to that date. I omitted to state that he is not a commissioned officer.

Very respectfully, your obedient servant,

P. C. GAILLARD,
Lieutenant-Colonel and Provost-Marshal.

VICKSBURG, *March 8, 1863.*

Lieutenant-General PEMBERTON:

Can I send Federal prisoners to Jackson?

C. L. STEVENSON,
Major-General.

SHELBYVILLE, *March 9, 1863.*

Maj. THOMAS M. JACK, *Assistant Adjutant-General.*

MAJOR: In obedience to instructions from the lieutenant-general commanding (through Col. W. B. Richmond, aide-de-camp) of this date I have the honor to submit the following explanation: On the 7th instant the general informed me that he had received a communication from General Van Dorn stating that the prisoners captured by his (General Van Dorn's) command at Thompson's Station would pass through this place en route to Tullahoma; that they numbered about 2,200 men and would need rations. The general directed me to see that they had rations provided for them on their arrival; that General Van Dorn could not furnish them with cooking utensils, consequently I should have the rations properly prepared. The general suggested that I could use the utensils left in camp by a portion of Withers' division, then on outpost duty, and to make the detail left in charge of the camp cook them. He also directed me to send a courier on the Lewisburg road to meet them with a communication to the officer in charge asking for the number of men and the number of days' rations required and any other information that would facilitate their speedy transportation from this point to Tullahoma. Immediately after leaving the general I dispatched a courier as directed with a letter to the officer in charge of the prisoners making the inquiries named. I charged the courier to be as prompt as possible. I then sent for Captain Spence and directed him to go out to the camp of Withers' division and see the officer in command and notify him that he would have to superintend the preparation of the rations. Captain Spence returned and reported that he found Colonel Walker (the senior officer present) and that the colonel signified to him that he was ready to carry out the order as soon as he received the rations.

I also saw Major Mason, assistant quartermaster, and directed him to furnish transportation for the rations when required. I then went to the post commissary store-house to see Captain Cromwell, assistant commissary of subsistence. The captain being absent I directed his chief clerk (a Mr. Baugh) to furnish the rations when called on without delay. I then awaited the return of the courier. The courier not having returned on the morning of the 8th (when I expected him to return on the preceding night at the latest) I reported the fact to the general. The general directed me to send Captain Spence with another courier on the same road with instructions similar to those given the first courier. The first courier returned about 3 o'clock on the afternoon of the 8th with a note from Lieutenant-Colonel Gordon, commanding the escort in charge of the prisoners, giving the number 1,205, but said nothing about when their rations were out. The colonel also stated in his note that he would send his regimental commissary in to attend to the wants of his own command. Immediately on the receipt of Colonel Gordon's communications I directed Captain Spence to have two days' rations for 1,205 men sent out to Colonel Walker with instructions to have them prepared without delay. I also directed that the wagons used for hauling them out should remain and bring the rations back when prepared to the court-house. Captain Spence returned and reported that he had carried out my instructions. About 5 p. m. a violent rain came on which continued with more or less violence until a late hour at night and materially interfered with the cooking of the rations. In order to be certain that the prisoners would get their rations I saw Major Mason about 11 o'clock last night and asked him what directions he had given about the wagons. He replied that he had "directed them to remain at the camp until the rations were cooked and then bring them in if they had to remain all night." I sent Captain Spence out to the camp at an early hour this morning to inquire why the rations were not prepared and sent in. He reports that Colonel Walker had them ready at 2 a. m., but that the wagons had left before that time and that he had no other available transportation. These are all the facts in the case, and I earnestly hope that they will exonerate me from all culpable neglect in the premises.

Respectfully submitted.

T. F. SEVIER,
Assistant Inspector-General.

HDQRS. POLK'S CORPS, ARMY OF TENNESSEE,
March 9, 1863.

Maj. THOMAS M. JACK, *Assistant Adjutant-General.*

MAJOR: The general directs that you place Colonel Sevier, the inspector-general, under arrest, and instruct the commandant of the post to instantly prepare food for the Federal prisoners now here.

Very respectfully,

W. B. RICHMOND,
Aide-de-Camp.

SHELBYVILLE, *March 11, 1863.*

Lieutenant-General POLK, *Commanding.*

GENERAL: I would state that some time during the evening of Sunday, the 8th instant, Captain Spence called upon me for two wagons to haul rations for the prisoners. All my wagons being employed in moving stores for the depot and post commissaries I told him to go there and take any two of the wagons that he saw, which he did. About 7 o'clock in the evening I was called on to furnish wood for the prisoners at the court-house yard which I accordingly furnished. Later in the night Colonel Sevier asked me if the wagons had been furnished to haul the rations and I told him that they had, and I do not remember any further conversation on the subject with Colonel Sevier. I heard nothing about where the rations were to be hauled from or to until the next morning when Captain Spence called on me for two wagons to haul rations from Walker's regiment, Chalmers' brigade, which wagons I sent immediately.

Respectfully submitted.

R. M. MASON,
Major and Assistant Quartermaster.

C. S. MILITARY PRISON, *Richmond, March 12, 1863.*

Capt. W. S. WINDER, *Assistant Adjutant-General.*

CAPTAIN: I herewith inclose communication* from Major Boyle dated 11th instant containing a list of Yankee prisoners, twenty-nine in number. In connection with these prisoners allow me to make the following statement: They reached here yesterday about 7.30 o'clock p. m. The roll being called it was found that four of the prisoners on the list, viz, Brig. Gen. E. H. Stoughton, Captain Barker, Privates B. F. Pratt and R. B. Wardener did not answer, and Lieutenant Bossieux, the officer in charge of the prison during my absence, was informed that they were

---

* Not found.

at the Ballard Hotel for the night which fact was reported to me when I returned to the prison.

Deeming it my duty as the officer in command of the prison to see that the prisoners mentioned in an official communication as being sent here for confinement were delivered at the proper place, being quite sure that it was contrary to the wishes of the commanding general of this department that any such discriminations should be made in permitting a few of a batch of prisoners to obtain lodgings at a hotel while a majority of the same batch were committed to prison, and also as acting assistant provost-marshal considering that it was a part of my duty to see that prisoners are delivered at the proper time and place, I directed Lieutenant Bossieux to proceed to the Ballard Hotel and request of the officer or whoever might be in charge of the prisoners that they be delivered into his custody to be brought to prison. But for some reason unknown to me the officer, Lieutenant McClellan, refused to deliver them. I then went to the hotel myself after 12 o'clock p. m. and after a parley of nearly an hour Lieutenant McClellan reluctantly consented that the prisoners should be delivered into my custody.

I make this statement in order to vindicate myself from any charge of officiousness or assumption of authority. Please bear in mind that the unsealed official communication in reference to and containing a list of prisoners (the four mentioned included) was in my hands. Further, the train reached the city at 7.30 o'clock p. m. The provost-marshal's office is open all night. I was there myself till 8 o'clock p. m., and a portion of the prisoners were properly delivered before 8 o'clock p. m. at the C. S. Military Prison.

I am, sir, your obedient servant,

T. P. TURNER,
Captain, Commanding.

HEADQUARTERS RIVER BATTERIES, *March 13, 1863.*

Col. EDWARD HIGGINS,
Commanding River Batteries, Vicksburg.

COLONEL: I beg leave to submit to your consideration certain facts connected with the imprisonment by the Federal authorities in New Orleans of several non-commissioned officers and men formerly under your command at Fort Jackson, La. Their names and respective rank are as follows: Sergt. Patrick Kane, Corpl. Edward C. Smith and Private William Stanley, First Louisiana Artillery, Company B; Private Daniel Doyle, First Louisiana Artillery, Company D; Private Abraham McLane, Twenty-third Regiment Louisiana Volunteers (Allen Guards); Sergt. George L. Williams, First Louisiana Artillery Volunteers, Company E.

These men were arrested in New Orleans in May or June last under the charge of a conspiracy while they were prisoners of war on parole to recruit a company for the Confederate service. They were tried by a military commission,* found guilty and sentenced to be shot. On the appointed day they were taken out for execution, but just after the firing squad had received the last commands, "ready," "aim," an order was produced by the provost-marshal which commuted their sentence to imprisonment at hard labor on Ship Island during the pleasure of the President of the United States.

A short time before the day on which they were to be executed the men belonging to my old company (Company B) sent to request that I

---

* See Vol. III, this Series, p. 616, for the order relating to these men.

would come to see them. I obtained a permit from the provost-marshal and was admitted to their prison. There they told me that their trial had not been a fair one. They had no notice; no means of preparing a defense. One or two witnesses were examined by the military commission. They were asked if they had any rebutting evidence to produce, and in the face of their earnest protest were found guilty and condemned.

They were denounced by one of the traitors who had gone over to the enemy and it was chiefly on his testimony that they were condemned. They solemnly declared to me that the whole charge was a malicious fabrication; that they had never been concerned in any attempt to raise a company; that they had never in any way violated their parole. A few days ago Doctor Bradbury, who as you will remember volunteered his professional services and was with us at the fort during the bombardment, came out from New Orleans on the boat, the Cartel, which recently brought up the exchanged prisoners. He met with a gentleman who had just been released from Ship Island. While there this gentleman had frequently met our men and had brought with him a memorandum of their names to see if something could not be done for them. He states that men were never more faithful to a cause than they are to ours. They have frequently been offered their release on the sole condition of taking the oath of allegiance to the Federal Government; and this, although with the exception of Smith they are foreigners without ties of family or interest to bind them to the Confederacy, they have steadily refused.

As to the former good character of the men from my regiment (the First Louisiana) I can bear strong testimony. Stanley was employed in the magazine on ordnance duty. Sergeant Kane was gunner on the 8-inch columbiad in the upper river bastion of Fort Jackson. Corporal Smith was stationed with Captain Robertson in the Water Battery. Doyle was head carpenter in the quartermaster's department. No men could have done their duty better, either during the long period for which we garrisoned the forts or during the fatiguing length of the bombardment. They were brave, active, willing and in the mutiny faithful among traitors.

They well deserve that efforts should be made to procure their release. This imprisonment is plainly a violation of the articles of capitulation under which we surrendered, their trial and condemnation a flagrant instance of the many similar hollow mockeries which helped disgrace General Butler's rule in New Orleans. In regard to the men belonging to the Allen Guards it will be easy to obtain from Capt. S. Jones, who is at present in command of the Twenty-third Regiment Louisiana Volunteers, a statement of their character and of the points which bear upon their case.

I am, colonel, very respectfully, your obedient servant,

BEVERLY [C.] KENNEDY,
Lieutenant and Ordnance Officer, River Batteries.

[Indorsement.]

VICKSBURG, *March 18, 1863.*

Respectfully transmitted with the recommendation that the agent for exchange of prisoners be directed to demand their exchange or a new trial with counsel.

M. L. SMITH,
Major-General.

CAMP ON DEER CREEK,
Washington County, March 13, 1863.

Maj. J. J. REEVE, *Assistant Adjutant-General.*

MAJOR: I have the honor to make the following report: On the 15th [14th] of February, ultimo, I received by the hand of a citizen a letter from Capt. E. W. Sutherland, U. S. Navy, a copy of which is herewith* forwarded. The department was at once informed of the result of that interview and furnished with the notice† of Admiral Porter, then communicated by Captain Sutherland, who expressed his willingness to communicate at any time that it should be necessary by flag of truce.

On the 25th of same month I received instructions from Lieutenant-General Pemberton which I was ordered to communicate to Captain Sutherland or any other Federal officer. I at once sent by flag of truce a letter,‡ a copy of which is herewith forwarded. After keeping the party with the flag of truce at Greenville for several days in the fruitless effort to communicate the ravages of the Abolitionists on Lake Washington compelled me to withdraw the party except a sergeant and one man, whom I left at Greenville with the flag and letter. I accidentally learned from a citizen that on or about the 4th instant a gun-boat, the Curlew, landed a party who met the flag of truce, disarmed the bearers and took them on board, where they were rudely treated and their dispatch broken open and read. It was then returned to them with the remark that Captain Sutherland should be informed the letter was for him. About the time this news reached me and before I could communicate with the sergeant referred to I heard from a citizen that a gun-boat had landed and taken off two men.

I at once dispatched another party with flag of truce and letter,§ a copy of which please find inclosed, as well as a copy of the answer I received to it. I cannot learn by what boat they were taken and have not received an answer from Admiral Porter. Their horses and horse equipments I found at Greenville. Since the receipt of Captain Prichett's letter I have posted a picket at or near Greenville, but from the 23d instant to that time I had no troops nearer there than twenty miles except the party with the flag, and I need not add that the assertion of Captain Prichett in regard to flags of truce is utterly false and that none but those mentioned herein have been sent or been seen there.

Very respectfully, your obedient servant,

S. W. FERGUSON,
Lieutenant-Colonel, Commanding.

[Inclosure.]

U. S. GUN-BOAT PRAIRIE BIRD,
Greenville, March 9, 1863.

Lieutenant-Colonel FERGUSON,
Commanding C. S. Forces, Washington County:

Your letter in regard to two of your men having been carried off while under a flag of truce has been received. In reply must state that I am not acquainted with the matter. I will immediately forward your letter to Rear-Admiral D. D. Porter, commanding Mississippi Squadron, and he will give you the direct information. It has been reported that flags of truce are almost constantly presenting themselves at this place

---

*See Series I, Vol. XXIV, Part III, p. 55.
† See p. 294.
‡ See Series I, Vol. XXIV, Part III, p. 67.
§ Not found.

upon very trivial business which are not in accordance with the usages of civilized warfare. I hope to see no more here except on very important business.

Very respectfully, your obedient servant,

JAS. M. PRICHETT,
U. S. Navy, Senior Officer, Commanding Naval Forces.

EXECUTIVE DEPARTMENT, *Raleigh, March 14, 1863.*

GEORGE V. STRONG,
Attorney for the District of North Carolina.

DEAR SIR: His Excellency Governor Vance directs me to inform you that Henry Hanbury, Green Mason, W. Jackson, Josiah Lufton, William Hodges, Charney Kenyon, E. H. Gerkin, M. L. Strausbery or Strasbury [Stransbury] and W. A. Foreman are now confined as prisoners at Camp Holmes. It is due the public as well as these individuals that the offenses with which they are charged should be speedily investigated in order that they may be retained for trial if guilty or be discharged if innocent. Unless some action is taken in the matter at an early day His Excellency will deem it his duty to have them discharged.

Yours, very respectfully,

DAVID A. BARNES,
Aide-de-Camp to the Governor.

HDQRS. DEPT. SOUTH CAROLINA, GEORGIA AND FLORIDA,
Charleston, March 14, 1863.

Col. JOHN S. PRESTON, *Commanding, &c., Columbia, S. C.*

COLONEL: I am instructed by the War Department to direct that all Federal officers captured before the 12th day of January, A. D. 1863, shall be forwarded to Richmond to Brigadier-General Winder.

Respectfully, your obedient servant,

T. JORDAN,
Chief of Staff.

A similar letter to Lieutenant-Colonel Gaillard, provost-marshal.

T. J.

RICHMOND, *March 14, 1863.*

Lieut. Gen. J. C. PEMBERTON:

Colonel Garland has not been delivered yet. I expect to receive him next Monday but there is no certainty.

RO. OULD,
Agent, &c.

PORT HUDSON, *March 16, 1863.*

Lieutenant-General PEMBERTON:

I request to parole Midshipman Francis, from [of the] Mississippi, who exerted himself to save our men overboard from flag-of-truce boat at Baton Rouge.

FRANK GARDNER,
Major-General.

MOBILE, *March 16, 1863.*

Hon. JOHN A. CAMPBELL, *Assistant Secretary of War.*

DEAR SIR: In your communication to me of February last appointing me commissioner to investigate cases of prisoners now held in confinement by the military authorities it would seem that my authority to investigate only applied to arrests and imprisonments which have already been made. The object of this is to inquire whether the cases of prisoners which may arise daily during the time I may hold the commission are subject to my investigation. I have not been able to ascertain even who are the military commanders in the northern part of the State and Western Georgia to whom I am instructed to communicate my appointment. I suppose General Bragg commands north of General Buckner's district, but I should be glad to be referred to the order or orders dividing the State and western part of Georgia into geographical departments and districts and appointing the commanders. What is it contemplated that I am to do with prisoners whom I think have committed offenses against the Government and should not be discharged? Are they to be remanded to the custody of the military authorities and their cases reported to the Department for further action of the Department or am I to turn them over to the civil authorities for trial? Is it expected that I will make one general report of my proceedings under the commission after going through with the departments assigned me or am I to make reports from each post or prison?

I take this occasion, judge, to say that in conferring this appointment upon me you have doubtless rendered me a far greater service than you were aware of at the time. I am almost entirely without an income now except the compensation of this office and even now am compelled to rely upon assistance from others almost in the shape of gratuities for the support of my family, my income derived heretofore almost entirely from my profession having been cut off by the war. Though the compensation of the commissionership is a considerable help to me it is still inadequate to pay my heavy hotel bill and leave me any sufficient contribution to my family. I would therefore consider myself peculiarly fortunate if I could have the satisfaction so to execute this commission to commend me to the favorable consideration of the Department for an appointment the salary of which would be from $2,000 to $2,500, and for any assistance you may render me in promoting this end it could but add to the debt of gratitude I already owe you personally. Will you do me the favor to address an answer to my inquiries at Montgomery?

I have the honor to be, very respectfully,

M. J. SAFFOLD.

HOUSTON, TEX., *March 16, 1863.*

Maj. B. BLOOMFIELD, *Chief Quartermaster, &c.*

SIR: In accordance with your order of date 22d January last I took charge of and proceeded with the U. S. prisoners of war captured at Galveston 1st [of the] same month and proceeded by the New Orleans and Texas Railroad to Beaumont where railroad transportation was broken on account of extreme high water. Thence by your order of the same month I proceeded by the way of Sabine River on steamer Roe-Buck to Barr's Ferry. Arrived there the 5th and on the 9th left for Alexandria, having had to await for the transportation wagons and teams. On my trip up the Sabine two of the prisoners, one D. Chapin, of Company I, Forty-second Massachusetts Regiment, and H. C. Sellea, of Company D, same regiment, died and were buried, the former at Stark's Ferry, Tex., and the other at Barr's Ferry, La. On my arrival at Alexandria I found no preparations made to receive the prisoners and was detained there and on river below until the 22d February when I was ordered by Major-General Taylor to parole all my prisoners and proceed under a flag of truce to Port Hudson and report to General F. Gardner, commanding there, with the intention of proceeding by the way of Clinton to Tangipahoa and thence up the New Orleans and Jackson Railroad. On the 23d I arrrived at Port Hudson meeting Major Watts and Colonel Szymanski, exchange officers on the part of Confederate States Government, returning from Baton Rouge with C. S. prisoners that day exchanged. I was ordered immediately to proceed accompanied by Colonel Szymanski to Baton Rouge and there turn over the prisoners in my charge to the U. S. exchange officer. On the 24th we arrived at and turned over all save and except two sent back sick from Beaumont to this place, one left in the hospital [at] Beaumont and the two who had died as herein reported. I herewith hand you the receipt of Colonel Szymanski, the exchange officer on the part of the Confederate States Government, for the 330 prisoners under my charge.

Having thus reported the manner of the discharge of my duty under your orders I await your further orders and have the honor to be, sir, your very obedient servant,

W. J. HOWERTON,

Lieut., Prov. Army, C. S., Comdg. Escort and Guard U. S. Prisoners.

CITY POINT, *March 17, 1863.*

Brigadier-General WINDER.

SIR: A flag-of-truce boat has arrived with 350 political prisoners, General Barrow and several other prominent men amongst them. I wish you to send me at 4 o'clock Wednesday morning all the military prisoners (except officers) and all the political prisoners you have. If any of the political prisoners have on hand proof enough to convict them of being spies or of having committed other offenses which should subject them to punishment so state opposite their names. Also state whether you think under all the circumstances they should be released.

The arrangement I have made works largely in our favor. We get rid of a set of miserable wretches and receive some of the best material I ever saw.

Tell Captain Turner to put down on the list of political prisoners the names of Edward G. Eggling and Eugenia Hammermister. The President is anxious they should get off. They are here now. This of course is between ourselves. If you have any female political prisoners whom you can send off safely to keep her company I would like you to send her. Two hundred and odd more political prisoners are on their way. I would be more full in my communication if I had time.

Yours, truly,

RO. OULD,
Agent of Exchange.

[First indorsement.]

Send all called for in this letter unless they are charged with some criminal offense.

JNO. H. WINDER,
Brigadier-General.

[Second indorsement.]

Executed and returned.

T. P. TURNER,
Captain, &c.

SPECIAL ORDERS, }   ADJT. AND INSP. GENERAL'S OFFICE,
      No. 67.   }   *Richmond, March 19, 1863.*

*   *   *   *   *   *   *

XVIII. Paragraph XXVII, Special Orders, No. 62, current series, is hereby revoked, and Capt. W. H. Hatch, assistant adjutant-general, Provisional Army, C. S., will report to Col. Robert Ould for assignment to duty.

*   *   *   *   *   *   *

By command of the Secretary of War:

JNO. WITHERS,
Assistant Adjutant-General.

[MARCH 21, 1863.—For Quintero to Benjamin, with inclosures relative to the arrest of Col. E. J. Davis and others, see Series I, Vol. XXVI, Part II, pp. 67–71.]

WAR DEPARTMENT, *Richmond, March 21, 1863.*
EDWARD M. CLARK, Esq., *Richmond, Va.*

SIR: Your letter of the 12th instant was referred to the Commissary-General who replies that it has been decided that paroled soldiers could have their rations commuted from the date of parole up to the period of exchange at the cost price of the ration. No commutation is allowed during the time the soldier is in the hands of the enemy. The accounts for commutation must be certified to by a commissioned officer cognizant of all the facts and dates.

Respectfully,   JAMES A. SEDDON,
Secretary of War.

HEADQUARTERS ARMY OF NORTHERN VIRGINIA,
March 21, 1863.
Hon. JAMES A. SEDDON, *Secretary of War.*

SIR: I have received from General Hooker General Orders, No. 49, of General Halleck dated Washington, February 28, 1863, a copy of which I submit* herewith.

I would respectfully call your attention to this order which in my judgment conflicts with the cartel for the exchange of prisoners and solicit such instructions with regard to it as you may deem requisite.

I have the honor to be, with great respect, your obedient servant,

R. E. LEE,
General.

[Indorsement.]

WAR DEPARTMENT, *March 31, 1863.*

Mr. Ould will please examine this and report wherein he thinks it violates the cartel.

J. A. S.,
Secretary of War.

---

* Omitted here; see p. 306.

WAR DEPARTMENT, *Richmond, Va., March 21, 1863.*
Col. A. C. MYERS.

MY DEAR SIR: If the exigencies of our army require the use of trains for the transportation of corn pay no regard to the Yankee prisoners. I would rather they should starve than our own people suffer. I suppose I can safely put it in writing "Let them suffer." The words are memorable and it is fortunate that in this case they can be applied properly and without the intervention of a lying quartermaster.

Very truly, your faithful friend,

RO. OULD.

GENERAL ORDERS, ⎱ HDQRS. DEPT. OF MISS. AND EAST LA.,
No. 51.   ⎰   *Jackson, Miss., March 23, 1863.*

I. The following act of Congress and regulations to enforce the same are published for the information of all persons concerned:*

II. Depots for recaptured slaves are hereby established at the following places, viz: Brookhaven, Miss., Enterprise, Miss., Camp Moore, La.

III. All persons connected with the Army will make immediate report of all slaves arrested or coming into their possession, and if claim is not promptly made and established by the owner they will send such slaves, with a register of the place and date of their arrest, with as little delay as practicable, to the nearest depot in the State wherein the capture is made. All officers and soldiers now employing slaves will forthwith report the same, and those hereafter employing them within ten days thereafter, with the names and residence of their owners, and of the person by whom they were hired out, and of the officer or soldier hiring, and return such reports as soon as received to this office; and will in all other respects enforce from the officers and men under their command a strict and prompt observance of the requirements of the above-recited act of Congress.

By order of Lieutenant-General Pemberton:

R. W. MEMMINGER,
Assistant Adjutant-General.

HEADQUARTERS FOURTH MILITARY DISTRICT,
Jackson, Miss., March 24, 1863.
Maj. R. W. MEMMINGER, *Assistant Adjutant-General.*

MAJOR: I have the honor to submit the following report of U. S. prisoners of war received at this post from Port Hudson on the 21st instant. The following is a list† of officers:

In obedience to orders from the lieutenant-general commanding the above-named H. B. Francis, master's mate, was paroled and sent through the lines North. Amongst the seamen there is one negro, who is said to be a free negro. He is reported a seaman, but Captain Fontaine says he has been employed as cook. I respectfully ask for instructions in his case. He is at present confined with the others.

I am, major, respectfully, your obedient servant,

JOHN ADAMS,
Brigadier-General, Provisional Army, C. S., Commanding.

---

* Omitted here; see p. 844.   † Omitted.

HEADQUARTERS FOURTH MILITARY DISTRICT,
Jackson, Miss., March 24, 1863.

Maj. R. W. MEMMINGER, *Assistant Adjutant-General.*

MAJOR: I have the honor to submit the following report* of U. S. prisoners of war received at this post on the 12th instant captured on the U. S. gun-boat Indianola.

Forty-three seamen; 20 firemen, boys, &c. Total number of prisoners, 85.

I am, major, respectfully, your obedient servant,
JOHN ADAMS,
Brigadier-General, Provisional Army, C. S., Commanding.

HEADQUARTERS, *Jackson, March 24, 1863.*

Maj. R. W. MEMMINGER, *Assistant Adjutant-General.*

MAJOR: In obedience to orders from the Secretary of War the following named U. S. prisoners of war (officers) were sent to Richmond, Va., on the 14th instant in charge of Captain Tabb, Fourteenth Mississippi Regiment: T. C. Fletcher, colonel; P. Kershner, lieutenant-colonel; F. Jaensch, major; A. Gallfy, captain; John C. Ander Egg, captain; James S. McMurtry, captain; A. S. McClure, captain; F. Doherty, captain; C. Cunningham, captain; M. Mills, captain; W. P. Van Doorn, captain; J. J. Cole, first lieutenant; P. M. Smith, first lieutenant; S. H. Corn, first lieutenant; H. S. Wood, second lieutenant; R. H. Vorhes, second lieutenant; B. F. Heckert, second lieutenant; M. Menne, second lieutenant; G. W. Wilson, second lieutenant; W. H. Rogers, second lieutenant; William Buchanan, second lieutenant; J. M. Cady, second lieutenant. All of the above-named officers were captured previous to the 12th of January, 1863.

I am, major, respectfully, your obedient servant,
JOHN ADAMS,
Brigadier-General, Provisional Army, C. S., Commanding.

HEADQUARTERS, *Fort Brown, Tex., March 24, 1863.*

Maj. E. F. GRAY,
Acting Assistant Adjutant-General, Fort Brown, Tex.

SIR: Inclosed herewith please find the parole† in triplicate of the crew of the U. S. schooner C. C. Pinckney, recently captured at the mouth of the Rio Grande, which was this day granted them by me.

I have the honor to be, very respectfully, your obedient servant,
P. N. LUCKETT,
Colonel Third Texas Infantry, Commanding.

WAR DEPARTMENT, *Richmond, Va., March 25, 1863.*

His Excellency Z. B. VANCE,
Governor of North Carolina, Raleigh, N. C.

SIR: I have received your letter with regard to the arrest of citizens of North Carolina by a party of cavalry from Georgia. In reply I have the honor to say that the Department has no information at present concerning the alleged arrest and removal referred to by Your Excellency but will proceed to institute inquiry and require a report of

---

*Names of prisoners omitted.   † Omitted.

all the facts and redress of any injustice done. I will advise you of the result of my inquiries.

With high regard, your obedient servant,

JAMES A. SEDDON,
Secretary of War.

———

RALEIGH, N. C., *March 25,* [1863.]

Hon. JAMES A. SEDDON, *Richmond, Va.:*

General Pillow has sent a detachment of cavalry into Western North Carolina to enroll and arrest conscripts without the shadow of law and in defiance of the proper authorities. Please order it stopped through Colonel Coltart, Greeneville, Tenn., or there will be resistance and bloodshed.

———

Z. B. VANCE.

HEADQUARTERS EASTERN SUB-DISTRICT OF TEXAS,
Houston, March 25, 1863.

Capt. EDMUND P. TURNER, *Assistant Adjutant-General.*

CAPTAIN: I desire to know whether the major-general commanding has any suggestions to make or instructions to give in relation to the exchange of the Morning Light prisoners; what route they are to take, if they are to be sent forward for exchange and the course to be pursued in the premises in case he thinks proper to send them forward. The officer charged with the delivery of the prisoners taken at Galveston has returned having completed his mission. •

I have the honor to be, very respectfully, your obedient servant,

W. R. SCURRY,
Brigadier-General, Commanding.

[Indorsement.]

The privates, sailors, petty officers, non-commissioned officers, &c., to be sent to Vicksburg for exchange. The commissioned officers to be kept prisoners; all the commissioned officers to be sent to the prisons or the penitentiary at Huntsville if the Governor will consent. General Magruder has broached the subject to him and he has not yet answered. Brigadier-General Scurry will correspond with the Governor and if it can be done will send them to Huntsville under proper guard.

———

J. B. M.

WAR DEPARTMENT, *Richmond, March 28, 1863.*

J. M. BAKER, Esq., *Richmond, Va.*

SIR: You are informed in reply to yours of the 14th instant that you are entitled to pay during your detention by the enemy according to your position in the army at the time of your capture.

Respectfully,

JAMES A. SEDDON,
Secretary of War.

———

WAR DEPARTMENT, *Richmond, March 28, 1863.*

Hon. JAMES M. BAKER, *House of Representatives.*

SIR: Your letter of the 22d instant inclosing a communication from Dr. H. Bacon asking intervention of the Government in behalf of certain citizens of Saint Mary's, Ga., taken prisoners by the enemy, has been received and referred to Mr. Ould, commissioner for exchange of prisoners.

Very respectfully, your obedient servant,
                              JAMES A. SEDDON,
                                        Secretary of War.

                    HEADQUARTERS, *Charleston, S. C., March 28, 1863.*
General SAMUEL COOPER,
      Adjutant and Inspector General, Richmond.

GENERAL: I have the honor to transmit herewith a copy of General Orders,* No. 49, War Department of the United States, dated Washington, D. C., February 28, 1863, in relation to paroles.

I do not suppose that the observance of the order in question will affect this department in any way; that is it is not anticipated that it will be desirable at any time to release prisoners of war on the field of battle in this department; yet as this may not be the case at all times in other departments I have deemed it my duty to bring the matter to your attention in this way.

Respectfully, your obedient servant,
                              G. T. BEAUREGARD,
                                        General, Commanding.

HDQRS. DEPT. SOUTH CAROLINA, GEORGIA AND FLORIDA,
                    Charleston, S. C., March 30, 1863.
Col. JOHN S. PRESTON, *Commanding, Columbia, S. C.*

COLONEL: A communication from Commodore T. Turner, U. S. Navy, has been received at these headquarters in which he inquires particularly if the U. S. naval officers who are in confinement at Columbia are in need of money or any assistance from the United States Government. The general commanding desires that you will furnish the above information as soon as practicable.

Very respectfully, your obedient servant,
                              CLIFTON H. SMITH,
                                        Assistant Adjutant-General.

                              KNOXVILLE, *March 30, 1863.*
His Excellency Z. B. VANCE, *Governor of North Carolina.*

SIR: Your letter† of the 22d of February addressed to me at Warm Springs was not received by me until now owing to the fact that I was absent from the department. I am obliged to you for the complimentary manner in which you have been pleased to speak of the small service which I had the honor to perform while on duty in your State. I assure you that I agree entirely in the sentiments you express relative to the reported shooting of prisoners by the troops under the command of Colonel Keith. I know nothing of the facts, the transaction having taken place before I was placed in command of the troops operating in North Carolina. No report was made to me of the affair before I left. I have forwarded your letter to General D. S. Donelson, commanding department, who will no doubt give the matter proper attention.

I have the honor to be, with great respect, Your Excellency's obedient servant,
                              W. G. M. DAVIS,
                                        Brigadier-General.

---

* Omitted here; see p. 306.   † Not found.

MILITARY PRISON, *Alton, Ill., March 30, 1863.*

Hon. HENRY C. BURNETT, *Member Confederate Senate.*

MY DEAR SIR: In the utmost extremity I address you. I can say but a few words as danger threatens both the medium of my communication and self. Hear me I conjure you, and demand of my Government immediate intervention for my deliverance.

Let hard facts speak for themselves and stern justice vindicate my claims:

I, J. F. Melton, of Calloway County, Ky., commanded a company of cavalry at Fort Henry in Tilghman's division. At the surrender of Fort Henry I retreated to Fort Donelson and was thrown under Col. (now General) N. B. Forrest; was captured after the surrender of Donelson on the 16th of February, 1862; made my escape *en route* from Camp Chase to Sandusky on the 26th of April, 1862; returned South for the purpose of raising a new company and while so engaged was recaptured on the 13th of July, heavily ironed with log chain and ball, transported to this prison, thrown into a cell 6 by 3 feet with my iron fetters on, kicked, cuffed, taunted, jeered and maltreated in every conceivable form. I remained the inmate of this living tomb until my life was despaired of. I was then removed to the hospital where I have remained ever since, denied the privileges of a common culprit, denied a parole, denied an exchange, several of which have left here during my imprisonment. To my demands they have replied by adding insult to injury, in renewed insult and cruelty. I have had to run the gauntlet of every disease which human flesh is heir to—smallpox, measles, mumps, pneumonia; in a word all the ills of Pandora.

Oh! the horrors of this place, the cruelty of my persecutors, tongue cannot tell, neither hath it entered into the heart of man to conceive. I have seen thousands of my companions in arms consigned to a premature and untimely grave here by the cruelty and injustice of my enemies, murdered in cold blood in this lazar house of disease and death.

With me "the sands of life are nearly run." There is but little left now. I rejoice that it was freely offered upon the altar of my country as a last libation to liberty, sacrificed to that country which I so devotedly love, and which I have the proud consciousness of knowing I have faithfully served. Will not that country now interpose her strong arm and rescue me from this charnel house, this living death, and save the little of life left me to my country and family?

Will you abandon me in this dire extremity? Will you leave me to my unhappy fate in the iron hands of my most cruel and unnatural persecutors?

I do not, I cannot believe it. I will not think so meanly of my country. She does not know my wrongs. She cannot have heard of my most foul and unsoldierly treatment.

Oh! my countrymen, how long will you suffer these abuses; how long will you permit your patience to be abused, your forbearance outraged and your humanity scoffed at by these unlettered and unthinking monsters? Act at once and deliver me from worse than death.

How? Demand me under the cartel of exchange; unless surrendered throw into close confinement some influential Yankee officer and hold him as a hostage in pledge for me; make it known to the Federal Government and you will compass my immediate release. Refuse and I am lost. The grave will soon be my end, yet one reflection will illume my tomb and take away the sting of death, the consciousness that I fall a martyr to my country, blessing her with my last sigh in death.

Hear me I adjure you, for my cause, your cause, as sacred a cause as ever brought and bound a people together—the cause of our country and our God. Believing that you will instantly lay my case before the authorities at Richmond and demand that justice so long denied me, I am, your unfortunate but faithful friend,

                                                J. F. MELTON.

[Indorsement.]

                                                APRIL 22, 1863.
Mr. OULD:

Demand explanation and exchange else I shall feel constrained to set aside an officer of the Federal Army for retaliatory treatment.

                                                J. A. S.,
                                                    Secretary.

          HEADQUARTERS, *Columbia, S. C., March 31, 1863.*
Brig. Gen. THOMAS JORDAN, *Chief of Staff, Charleston, S. C.*

GENERAL: In answer to your communication of March 30 desiring to know if the U. S. naval officers who are in confinement at Columbia are in need of money or any assistance from the United States Government I have the honor to forward you the inclosed communication* from F. S. Conover, acting lieutenant-commander.

Your obedient servant,

                                                JNO. S. PRESTON,
        Colonel and Assistant Adjutant-General, Commanding Post.

                                        RICHMOND, *April 1, 1863.*
Hon. JAMES A. SEDDON, *Secretary of War.*

SIR: In the matter of Halleck's General Orders, No. 49, I have the honor to make the following report:

The cartel of exchange only incidentally treats of the parole of prisoners. The only provisions in it relating to paroles are as follows, to wit:

1. All prisoners of war to be discharged on parole in ten days after their capture, and the prisoners now held and those hereafter taken to be transported to the points mutually agreed upon at the expense of the capturing party.
2. Each party upon the discharge of prisoners of the other party is authorized to discharge an equal number of their own officers or men from parole, &c.
3. Nothing in this article contained shall prevent the commanders of the two opposing armies from exchanging prisoners or releasing them on parole at other points mutually agreed on by said commanders.

I see nothing in article 1 of general orders which in any manner conflicts with the cartel.

Articles 2 and 3 are restrictions upon giving paroles. There are no regulations in the cartel as to when paroles may be given or not given.

I do not think that these paragraphs can be said to be in violation of the cartel. They certainly establish a new practice. Is it, however, not within the power of a belligerent in the absence of an express agreement to the contrary to forbid its soldiers from entering into any paroles? These provisions, however, taken in connection with others of the general order are so sweeping that it would not be safe here-

---

*Not found; but see p. 823.

after to take any paroles. The only sure course left is to hold at least until an explanation is had.

Article 4 is a penalty for the violation of one branch of the preceding article.

In article 5 it is difficult to understand what General Halleck means by "wholesale paroling." The first [second] says " none but commissioned officers can give the paroles for themselves or their commands, &c." The sixth provides that " no non-commissioned officer or private can give his parole except through an officer." Article 1 [2] forbids any but a commissioned officer from giving paroles for himself or his men and article 6 seems to allow a non-commissioned officer or private to give his parole through an officer.

This discrepancy is complicated by the fifth article which declares that " for the officer the pledging of his parole is an individual act and no wholesale paroling by an officer for a number of inferiors in rank is permitted or valid." Are these provisions consistent ?

Article 6 makes the whole matter still more confused. What is meant by " giving a parole through an officer?" Is it that the officer is to approve it and sign that approval ? If so how can lists of paroled prisoners who are about to be sent off be made at the Libby Prison ? If it was not for the last clause of the sixth article it might be well supposed that all the provisions of the general order related to paroles given at the time of capture. That clause, however, speaks of "long confinement." It only allows a private to give his individual parole after he has "suffered long confinement without the possibility of being paroled through an officer." What is long confinement ? According to this clause if he has been at the Libby a short time and no officer is there in confinement he cannot be paroled; moreover is he not according to article 1 compelled to remain a long time in prison until one of his own officers happens to be captured?

Article 7 declares that no prisoner of war can be forced by the hostile Government to pledge his parole, &c. The cartel [article 4] says " all prisoners of war shall be discharged on parole in ten days after their capture." If the soldier under the injunction of his Government refuse his parole how can we discharge him on parole ?

Articles 8, 10, 11 and 12 require no other comment than that the cartel and not the common law of war establishes the terms of the parole and gives the consent of both Governments to those terms.

Article 9 is in clear violation of the cartel. Article 4 of the cartel says :

The surplus prisoners not exchanged shall not be permitted to take up arms again nor serve as military police or constabulary force in any fort, garrison or field-work held by either of the respective parties, nor as guards of prisons, depots or stores, nor to discharge any duty usually performed by soldiers, until exchanged.

Although I was only required by your indorsement to report wherein I thought the general order violated the cartel yet I deemed it my duty to make special mention of the foregoing matters in order that I might receive your instructions respecting the same. Had I not better bring the subject to the attention of the Federal agent of exchange, protesting against so much of the general order as is in violation of the cartel and asking explanations of that which is doubtful, ambiguous or contradictory ?

With great respect, your obedient servant,

RO. OULD,
Agent of Exchange.

RICHMOND, *April 2, 1863.*
General J. H. WINDER, *Richmond, Va.*

GENERAL: The Secretary of War has suspended until the 10th instant the sentence of death against Capt. A. C. Webster, of Peirpoint's army. Please direct the necessary measures in the matter.

Very respectfully,

S. COOPER,
Adjutant and Inspector General.

WAR DEPARTMENT, *Richmond, Va., April 3, 1863.*
Hon. J. P. BENJAMIN, *Secretary of State.*

SIR: Inclosed you will find sundry papers respecting John Carfoot, late prisoner at Salisbury, N. C., of whose detention complaint has been made as you advised this Department by the British consul. The reports of General Winder, commanding the military prison at Salisbury, N. C.; of General Ransom, by whose order Carfoot was sent to Salisbury, and of Mr. Wellford, who at the time of the reception of your letter was engaged in the examination of political prisoners at Salisbury and who was specially instructed to make inquiries into Carfoot's case, with their inclosures, are respectfully submitted.

For Secretary of War.

Very respectfully, your obedient servant,

J. A. CAMPBELL,
Assistant Secretary of War.

[Inclosure No. 1.]

SALISBURY, N. C., *January 3, 1863.*
Capt. H. McCOY, *Commanding C. S. Prison.*

SIR: You will discharge the following-named prisoners in accordance with an order from the Secretary of War, viz: Edward Barnes, John Carfoot, John Delaney, Charles Deckwer, James Graham, Henry Knipping, William McKinney, Samuel McLure, James E. Robertson, Daniel Scholly.

By order of General Winder:

W. S. WINDER,
Assistant Adjutant-General.

[Inclosure No. 2.]

WAR DEPARTMENT, *Richmond, Va., March 9, 1863.*
Hon. JAMES A. SEDDON, *Secretary of War.*

SIR: I inclose an unofficial letter from Capt. Samuel B. Waters, C. S. Army, stationed at the C. S. military prison at Salisbury, N. C., in reference to certain prisoners some time since discharged from that prison. Captain Waters' letter was written in reply to one from myself asking information in reference to these parties, demanded by certain letters forwarded to me during my recent visit to Salisbury, but which not arriving before I had left were returned to me by mail in this city. Information about the Moomans was called for by the Hon. W. R. Staples, of Virginia, and about John Carfoot by the British consul.

Very respectfully, yours,

B. R. WELLFORD, JR.

[Sub-inclosure to inclosure No. 2.]

HEADQUARTERS C. S. MILITARY PRISON,
Salisbury, February 26, 1863.

Mr. B. R. WELLFORD, Jr.

DEAR SIR: Your favor of February 23 duly received and in reply will state that a communication came to these headquarters some time since in regard to the prisoners Mooman. They were exchanged and sent North through [William P.] Wood, the Federal commissioner, on October 28, 1862. In regard to John Carfoot we have no papers whatever. The circumstances of his arrest were these: He was at New Berne at the time of the battle and did not leave when our forces evacuated the place. Some two or three days after he with another party went about three miles from the town to look after some cotton and were arrested by our pickets, who suspected them of endeavoring to get the cotton in the Yankee lines. He was taken before General Ransom and by him sent up here. Afterwards he was examined by Lieutenant Talley and released by the order of the Secretary of War January 3, 1863. He was captured April 7, 1862. During his confinement at this post he was allowed the parole of the grounds. Previous to his arrest and also to the battle of New Berne he was in the employment of the Confederate States as engineer on one of our steamers. Since his release he has been in the employment of the Western North Carolina Railroad Company.

I am, sir, very respectfully, your obedient servant,

SAMUEL B. WATERS,
Captain Company A.

The Moomans were sent to Richmond to be exchanged through [William P.] Wood. If they are not now there they were sent on North. You can find it out by inquiry of General Winder. He has the list of the prisoners who were exchanged I suppose.

S. B. W.

[Inclosure No. 3.]

WAR DEPARTMENT. *Richmond, Va., March 12, 1863.*

Brig. Gen. JOHN H. WINDER.

GENERAL: The Secretary of War is informed by the British consul that John Carfoot reported by you February 3 as having taken the oath of allegiance to the Confederate States denies the fact stated and the Secretary of State asks to be furnished with any evidence in your possession respecting him, with a copy of the oath and an account of the circumstances attending its administration and acceptance. You will give this matter your early attention and communicate the result of your investigation to this Department to be transmitted to the Secretary of State.

By order of the Secretary of War:

J. A. CAMPBELL,
Assistant Secretary of War.

[First indorsement.]

HEADQUARTERS DEPARTMENT OF HENRICO,
March 13, 1863.

Respectfully referred to Captain McCoy, commanding C. S. military prison at Salisbury, N. C., for immediate answer.

JNO. H. WINDER,
Brigadier-General.

[Second indorsement.]

HEADQUARTERS C. S. MILITARY PRISON,
Salisbury, N. C., March 16, 1863.

John Carfoot was discharged from the C. S. military prison at this post January 3, 1863. His discharge was unconditional, he not being required to take any oath whatever, it being by order of the Secretary of War forwarded through Brigadier-General Winder's headquarters.

H. McCOY,
Captain, Commanding.

[Third indorsement.]

HDQRS. DEPARTMENT OF HENRICO, *March 18, 1863.*

Respectfully returned to the honorable Secretary of War with the indorsement of Captain McCoy.

JNO. H. WINDER,
Brigadier-General.

[Inclosure No. 4.]

HEADQUARTERS BRIGADE,
Camp near Wilmington, N. C., March 13, 1863.

General S. COOPER,
Adjutant and Inspector General C. S. Army.

SIR: In reply to letter from the Secretary of War of 10th instant asking information relative to the arrest and sending to Salisbury, this State, of one John Carfoot I have the honor to state that the man was arrested by our pickets and brought to me. Upon an examination of his case it seemed he either had had or was trying to have communication with the enemy. It was customary in detaining parties for them to be sent by me to department headquarters with a statement of the case and the evidence thereon and the commanding general determined what it was proper to do with them. I was in charge of the outposts and did not take final action in such cases. This statement is from memory. I am certain though that at the time he was sent up the evidence was sufficient for his detention and imprisonment or he would not have been. It has not unfrequently happened that from long delay the evidence in such cases has been lost. I do not remember anything of the man having been employed by our authorities.

I am, sir, very respectfully, your obedient servant,

R. RANSOM, JR.,
Brigadier-General.

[Inclosure No. 5.]

WAR DEPARTMENT, *Richmond, Va., April 3, 1863.*

Hon. JAMES A. SEDDON, *Secretary of War.*

SIR: I inclose an unofficial letter this day received from Capt. S. B. Waters, C. S. Army, Salisbury, N. C., in regard to John Carfoot, late prisoner at that place, respecting whom complaint has been made by the British consul. Captain Waters incloses a written statement of Carfoot showing that he had been previous to his arrest in employment of the Confederate Government.

Very respectfully, yours,   B. R. WELLFORD, JR.

[Sub-inclosure to No. 5.]

SALISBURY, N. C., *March 30, 1863.*

Mr. B. R. WELLFORD, Jr.

DEAR SIR: Inclosed you will find a written statement in John Carfoot's own hand which will show you plainly that he was not only in the employment of the Confederate States as an engineer but was also employed by our ordnance officer, Major Boone. I had him to write the statement himself in the presence of a witness. It was his own confession that I alluded to in my last letter to you, and if my affidavit is necessary I can give it to that effect. I go to Charleston on some business on Wednesday but will only be gone for a few days. In the meantime should you wish any further information you can write, as it will be but a short time ere I return.

I am, sir, very respectfully, your obedient servant,

SAMUEL B. WATERS,
Captain.

[Sub to sub-inclosure to No. 5.]

SALISBURY, N. C., *March 28, 1863.*

I run as engineer on the steamer North State for Dibble and owned by Dibble & Brothers but employed by the Confederacy; and next I was employed by Major Boone on the repairs of some machinery; and next I run as engineer on the steamer Johnston owned by Pender, also employed by the Confederacy. I was still in Major Boone's employ while the steamer run on Neuse River, but when we moved down to Fort Macon Captain Devine was our paymaster.

JOHN CARFOOT.

Attest:
his
PETER x BOWLIN.
mark.

———

WAR DEPARTMENT, *Richmond, Va., April 3, 1863.*
Maj. Gen. S. G. FRENCH, *Petersburg, Va.*

GENERAL: Your attention is invited to the inclosed letter with the request that you will cause an early investigation to be made and have the grievances removed if you find that the complaints are well founded.

Your obedient servant,

JAMES A. SEDDON,
Secretary of War.

[Inclosure.]

PETERSBURG, VA., *April 1, 1863.*

We, the undersigned citizens of Fairfax County, have been confined in the Old Capitol Prison for some four weeks and were sent to Richmond for exchange. We have been at Camp Parole at this place for three days without having anything done in our case and scarcely anything to eat and nothing to sleep [on] or cover with.

Your earliest attention to this will be gratefully received.

Yours, with respect,   F. G. FOX,
[And 11 others.]

P. S.—We wish to be sent to Richmond so we can form or join some company on the front.

[Indorsement.]

MODEL FARM, *Near Petersburg, April 1, 1863.*

DEAR SIR: I was at the camp of the paroled prisoners just now and had an interview with them, and when some of them mentioned you I advised this letter to you, and I beg to add my request that you will interest yourself in their behalf. They have been sufferers.

I am, respectfully,

R. R. COLLIER.

Resolution of the C. S. House of Representatives adopted April 4, 1863.

Resolved, That a special committee of five be appointed to inquire into and report to this House as early as practicable—

1. What punishment if any in violation of law has been inflicted upon prisoners confined in Castle Thunder; the kind and character of the punishment inflicted by the officers of the prison.

2. How many have been killed, by whom and the circumstances under which they were killed.

3. That the committee have power to send for persons and papers.

WAR DEPARTMENT, *Richmond, April 6, 1863.*

W. O. TUGGLE, Esq., *La Grange, Ga.*

SIR: In answer to your letter of the 23d ultimo you are informed that if you were actually in custody as a prisoner after your parole and made your escape from such custody you are entitled to join your command at once; but if you were enjoying liberty under your parole and were merely on your way to a place from which you might more easily reach home and abandoned the officers who were conducting you under an impression that you might be detained there you would be bound by your parole notwithstanding your escape. It is probable that your exchange has been effected ere this as there were no such orders as is represented in your letter.

Respectfully,

JAS. A. SEDDON,
Secretary of War.

MONTEREY, *April 6, 1863.*

Hon. J. P. BENJAMIN, *Richmond.*

SIR: Herewith you will find duplicate copies of the correspondence* between General Bee and Governor Lopez, of Tamaulipas (marked A, B, C and D), in regard to the parties abducted at the mouth of the Rio Grande on the 15th ultimo and reporting their return to the right bank of the river. E. J. Davis and three others, all that have come into General Bee's possession and of whom he could obtain some information, are now in Matamoras. I hope that no serious consequences will ensue and that amicable relations will be continued. No news from the interior of Mexico.

I have the honor to be, your obedient servant,

J. A. QUINTERO.

TARBOROUGH, EDGECOMBE COUNTY, N. C.,
April 7, 1863.

Mr. SECRETARY.

SIR: I write you a few lines asking you how a paroled prisoner is to know when he is exchanged for certain. Does the Richmond Enquirer give all the notices or not? Or where the enrolling officer gets his authority from. My sons were taken prisoners and I want to be certain of the exchange before they go back. I have asked some men and there seems to be a difference of opinion about it. I

---

* See Series I, Vol. XV, pp. 1128–1132,

also ask if they can leave the infantry and go to the artillery or not when they are exchanged, for one of my sons is not able to march. You will please to answer me soon.   Direct your letter to Tarborough, N. C., Edgecombe County.

Yours, most obediently,

WILLIAM COKER.

[First indorsement.]

Notices are published in the newspapers and in general orders.

[Second indorsement.]

A publication is made in the Richmond papers of the exchanges which take place.   All North Carolina prisoners taken prior to orders have been exchanged.

———

HDQRS. DEPT. OF MISSISSIPPI AND EAST LOUISIANA,
Jackson, April 7, 1863.

Maj. Gen. C. L. STEVENSON, *Commanding, &c., Vicksburg.*

GENERAL: The lieutenant-general commanding directs me to send you the inclosed copies* of communications from the War Department and to say that he regrets that the tenor of your correspondence with Admiral Porter was not in accordance with his instructions; that hereafter your communications with the enemy will be guided by the considerations set forth in the indorsement of the President.

Very respectfully, your obedient servant,

J. C. PEMBERTON,
Lieutenant-General, Commanding.

———

WAR DEPARTMENT, *Richmond, April 8, 1863.*

Lieut. Gen. J. C. PEMBERTON,
Commanding, &c., Jackson, Miss.

GENERAL: Your letter of 26th ultimo asking instructions in regard to a negro captured on the U. S. steamer Mississippi has been received. In answer you are respectfully informed that the negro can be put to work in any of the workshops of the Government or on the fortifications or in any manner that may be regarded by you as advisable. The Department has determined that negroes captured will not be regarded as prisoners of war.

Very respectfully, your obedient servant,

JAS. A. SEDDON,
Secretary of War.

———

EXECUTIVE DEPARTMENT, *Richmond, April 8, 1863.*

Honorable SECRETARY OF WAR.

SIR: I am directed by the President to forward for your attention and the proper action the following copy of a resolution of the House of Representatives of the 4th instant:

Resolved, That the President be requested to cause this House to be informed whether or not any special efforts have been yet made to obtain the release from imprisonment of Surg. Joseph E. Dixon, of the Ninth Battalion of Tennessee Cavalry, commanded by Lieut. Col. George Gantt, Surgeon Dixon being now in close confinement in the military prison of Johnson's Island, near Sandusky, in the State

———

* See Series I, Vol. XXIV, Part III, p. 696.

of Ohio; and that the letter of Surgeon Dixon and that of Lieut. John W. Dunnington herewith presented be transmitted to the President for his consideration with a view to facilitating such action in the case as may secure the early release of Surgeon Dixon from his present state of captivity.

Inclosed please find the letters referred to.

Very respectfully, your obedient servant,

BURTON N. HARRISON,
Private Secretary.

[Inclosure.]

JOHNSON'S ISLAND MILITARY PRISON,
Near Sandusky City, Ohio, March 3, 1863.

Hon. H. S. FOOTE, *Member of Congress, Richmond, Va.*

DEAR SIR: Inclosed you will find a letter from Lieut. John W. Dunnington, C. S. Navy, which I hope will receive your kind consideration. Though a stranger to you I address you this letter hoping to interest you in my behalf that justice may be done myself and the Confederate Government, to which I claim allegiance and of which I expect protection. I am a Tennesseean, a citizen of the Confederate States and a surgeon in the army. I was appointed surgeon of the Ninth Battalion of Tennessee Cavalry, commanded by Lieut. Col. George Gantt, of Columbia, Tenn. The Ninth Battalion was mustered into the State service the last of November, 1861, and was transferred to the Confederate service between the 1st and middle of December, 1861. Lieutenant Colonel Gantt's battalion was at Fort Donelson and was included in the surrender which took place February 16, 1862, after which I was held a prisoner for four months, then unconditionally released as a surgeon. I went to my home near Columbia, Maury County, Tenn., where I remained a short time and then procuring the required passes, &c., I proceeded South to rejoin the army, &c. I had no trouble whatever until I arrived at the headquarters of General McCook (since killed) who commanded at Battle Creek. Upon examining my pass he consented for me to proceed, but after delaying some time caused me to be arrested and returned to Huntsville, Ala. From there I was sent to Camp Chase and from there to this island.

For seven long dreary months I have been an occupant of either guard-house or prison, an innocent sufferer. I have done nothing to justify the treatment I am receiving and I think certainly my Government is not aware of the outrage. I have appealed to the authorities at Washington time and again but all to no purpose. So far I have been denied either an exchange or release, the latter of which is due every surgeon as they are non-combatants and so far as I am aware is extended by our authorities to all Federal surgeons. My treatment would have been intolerable did I not have the pleasing satisfaction of knowing that General McCook who ordered my arrest has gone to reap the reward of his doings—a reward richly deserved by him and all others engaged like him in this unholy nigger war. Several gentlemen have left here on exchange who promised faithfully to represent the outrageous conduct of the Lincoln Government in disregarding previous agreements, &c. (in holding surgeons as prisoners, of which I am the unfortunate subject and sufferer), but they have failed to comply with their promise, which was a duty they owed their Government, or else the authorities at Richmond have disregarded the report and thereby neglected their duty in allowing a citizen and soldier of the Confederate States to be grossly imposed upon. I appeal to you as a Representative of Tennessee to use every means in your power for my release from prison. Urge upon the authorities an immediate demand for my immediate exchange as the treatment I am receiving is unjust. Having every confidence that you will give a son of Tennessee your aid, I remain, very respectfully, your obedient servant,

JO. E. DIXON,
Surgeon, Provisional Army, C. S.

[Sub-inclosure.]

JOHNSON'S ISLAND MILITARY PRISON,
Near Sandusky, Ohio, February 16, 1863.

Hon. H. S. FOOTE, *Member of Congress, Richmond, Va.*

SIR: You will excuse me for addressing you this letter when I state it is to claim your assistance and aid in getting released from this prison a much wronged Tennesseean, Dr. J. E. Dixon, of Maury County. Doctor Dixon was the surgeon of Col. George Gantt's battalion, C. S. Army, and taken a prisoner at Fort Donelson a year ago this month. After a short imprisonment he was released to go South, a pass being given him through the Federal lines. He went to Maury County to see his family and there the Federal officer in command indorsed his permit and passed him through his lines. He had no trouble until he reached General McCook's army at Huntsville. He showed his pass to General McCook who at first gave him permission to go South but soon after caused him to be arrested and placed in prison. He was shortly after sent to Camp Chase, Ohio, and from there to this place. He has been confined since July last, no charges being made against him. He was arrested with this pass in his possession. Although there have frequently been prisoners sent South for exchange he has never been permitted to go and sees no hope of getting away from this place. As he is a regular Confederate officer taken at the surrender of Fort Donelson he certainly is entitled to the protection and care of his Government, and I beg you as a matter of justice to a son of Tennessee and as a personal favor to me to insist that the Government demand his exchange at once. As I am but slightly acquainted with you and probably unremembered, I will state that I am a brother of F. C. Dunnington.

I am, sir, very respectfully, your obedient servant,

JNO. W. DUNNINGTON,
Colonel, Provisional Army, C. S., Prisoner of War.

PRISON BOAT, *Aquia, April 8, 1863.*

Hon. JAMES A. SEDDON, *Secretary of War.*

SIR: I learn that Capt. Stephen Chester, of the Engineer Corps, Fifteenth New York, was arrested about two months since on the banks of the Rappahannock and is now in the Libby Prison, Richmond City. Since his confinement he has had lost or stolen from him his coat and all the money he had with him, about $200, and is in a state of destitution and want. These facts are given me by his brother, of General Berry's staff, who as judge-advocate under a military commission has shown me as much kindness as is consistent with his duty. I feel it due to him as well as to the cause of humanity to acquaint you with these facts and to solicit an interest in behalf of Captain Chester. If advisable or proper I most respectfully ask that he be included in the next list of exchange for an officer of equal rank or such equivalents as may be agreed upon. Otherwise I hope it may accord with your views of propriety to allow his friends through any safe channel you may designate to send him such supplies of money or clothing as he may need.

Any communication respecting this matter addressed to Capt. William H. Chester, assistant inspector-general, care of General Berry, will receive immediate attention and be thankfully received.

Very respectfully, your obedient servant,

R. A. CLAYBROOK.

P. S.—My prison life here will close I hope now in a few days.

R. A. C.

[Indorsement.]

OFFICE EXCHANGE OF PRISONERS,
Richmond, April 25, 1863.

Respectfully returned.

Capt. Stephen Chester, U. S. Army, Engineer Corps, Fifteenth New York Regiment, was sent North via City Point and flag-of-truce boat April 23, 1863.

RO. OULD,
Agent of Exchange.

HDQRS. DEPARTMENT OF SOUTHERN VIRGINIA,
Petersburg, April 9, 1863.

Hon. J. A. SEDDON, *Secretary of War.*

DEAR SIR: On the receipt of your letter which I return that you may at a glance have the whole matter before you I directed Maj. W. H. Ker, adjutant-general's department, to proceed to the Model Farm Barracks and investigate the alleged grievance. On the back of the letter you will find his report.

I have a great deal of trouble with these prisoners. Those that are not in service cannot be supplied with clothing until they are conscripted and mustered into service.

These men have the same clothing to protect them now that they have had ever since they left the prisons in the United States, and cannot be worse off with fires in the barracks than they were *en route* to this place.

Money paid to pettifogging lawyers I apprehend has often had something to do with the numerous complaints that come before you.

You may remember that the militia were called out and after all the trouble of mustering them into service and when the expense had been incurred and when they were rendering good service in guarding the paroled prisoners you caused them to be discharged, thus requiring me to take old soldiers from the field to relieve them.

That you may see the patriotism and influence that may have induced men to appeal to you for their discharge I inclose you a copy of a letter from the captain of the militia. You will perceive that Mr. Collier was hired to get you to discharge them.

He is also their agent to get them their pay and I am told by the captain has the power of attorney to draw it for many of them.

I have the honor to be, yours, respectfully,

S. G. FRENCH,
Major-General.

[Inclosure No. 1.]

PETERSBURG, VA., *April 8, 1863.*

Maj. Gen. S. G. FRENCH, *Commanding, &c., Petersburg.*

GENERAL: I have investigated the matters referred to in the within letter and submit the following report:

J. N. Mills, A. B. Williams, G. W. Cook and Richard Richardson have been discharged; the other signers of the letter are retained at the Model Farm [Barracks] for enrollment as conscripts. They receive the same rations as other soldiers but are without bed-clothing.

I am, very respectfully, your obedient servant,

WM. H. KER,
Major and Assistant Adjutant-General.

[Inclosure No. 2.]

➡️PETERSBURG, *April 9, 1863.*

Maj. Gen. S. G. FRENCH.

SIR: In answer to the inquiry whether or not the men of my company agreed to pay Mr. R. R. Collier for procuring their discharge from the service I will say that many of them did inform me that they had done so. The sums they agreed to pay I do not know.

Very respectfully, your obedient servant,

JOHN BATTE,
Captain Company A, Militia.

GENERAL ORDERS, ⎫   HEADQUARTERS ARMY OF TENNESSEE,
No. 76.   ⎬   *Tullahoma, April 9, 1863.*

*   *   *   *   *   *   *

IV. The general commanding has been informed that a free and unrestricted intercourse with prisoners of war has been allowed to the officers and soldiers of this army and citizens. This practice is most pernicious to the well-being and discipline of the Army. Such intercourse will not hereafter be allowed except upon written permission.

*   *   *   *   *   *   *

By command of General Bragg:

GEO. WM. BRENT,
Assistant Adjutant-General.

CONSULATE OF FRANCE AT RICHMOND,
Richmond, April 10, 1863.

Hon. W. M. BROWNE, *Assistant Secretary of State, Richmond.*

SIR: I have received with the letter of the 5th of this month which you have done me the honor to write three copies of the supplementary report of the Secretary of War relative to the exchange of prisoners between the Government of the Confederate States and that of the United States. I thank you for sending the documents, which in conformity to the desire which you have verbally expressed to me will be transmitted by me to the Department of Foreign Affairs at Paris.

I beg you, sir, to accept the assurances of the high consideration of your very humble and very obedient servant,

ALFRED PAUL.

Treatment of Prisoners in Castle Thunder, Richmond, Va.

Evidence taken before the committee of the House of Representatives of the Confederate States appointed to inquire into the treatment of prisoners at Castle Thunder.

SATURDAY, *April 11, 1863.*

WILLIAM CAUSEY sworn:

I live in Elizabeth City County but have been in Richmond since January, 1861, employed as a detective in General Winder's detective police force.

I know something of the treatment of the prisoners. They are put in huddles, sometimes 500 and 700 in one building. Sometimes they are treated well by the commandant and the wardens, but I have seen them severely punished. I have seen them tied by the thumbs and raised up on their toes. I don't think theirs could have been very aggravated offenses; rather think it was for disagreements among themselves. I don't know how long they remained tied up, but from the best information they were kept sometimes eight hours. I don't know that any of the sick prisoners were thus treated. I saw a man handcuffed around a post, raised up at first and afterwards cut down when his blood had stagnated. I don't know what offense he had committed. On another occasion a canteen of gunpowder was exploded in the prison room by some of the prisoners. The powder was collected from cartridges and was not much in quantity. I heard the report of it ten minutes after its occurrence and rode up to General Winder's office with Captain Alexander. While in General Winder's office Captain Alexander reported the circumstances of the powder explosion. I don't know what the general said, but Captain Alexander went back to the prison and put the men down in the pen outside, where they remained two or three days. They had no covering and it was raining. The men in the pen were those in the room where the powder was exploded. Captain Alexander demanded the names of those who put the powder in the stove, and because the men refused to tell put them all in the pen. It was last fall, in the month of November I think. I heard of some of them dying shortly afterwards. They died after that I am positive, but I never knew their names. Prisoners guilty of bad offenses have irons on them generally, but I don't think any of the men put in the pen had irons on.

I think two men have been shot at the prison since Captain Alexander has been in charge, and one on Franklin street at the guard-house. The man killed at the guard-house was shot while attempting to escape. In my opinion all could have been arrested without being shot. The desperate men were generally put in Castle Godwin. The soldiers picked up on the street are put in this prison. Castle Godwin is not part of Castle Thunder. Thunder was Godwin's successor in cognomen after removal. The man shot a few nights ago at Castle Thunder certainly could have been captured without shooting. There is a standing order to shoot only if he cannot otherwise be arrested.

I have seen prisoners whipped, but I don't know by whose or what authority. I have seen men severely whipped on the buttocks with straps; don't know how many lashes were laid on, but I should think about fifty. I only saw one whipping. On this occasion the officers were requested by Captain Alexander to go up into the prison room and see the men whipped. The whipping strap was secured onto wooden handles. They were made of harness leather or sole leather from eighteen inches to two feet in length. The blows were laid on about as hard as a man could do it. I have seen prisoners wear the same clothes for months until they were ready to drop off in rags. I think there have been instances of attempts to bribe the guard.

J. F. SCHAFFER sworn:

I reside in Richmond and am a detective in General Winder's force. The prisoners are treated according to their behavior. Some of them I think have been cruelly treated. They were punished sometimes for fighting, sometimes for stealing. I have seen them whipped, one received fifteen lashes, another twenty-five and a third fifty lashes. The prisoner that received fifty lashes was pretty severely cut.

I know something about putting the prisoners out in the back yard. It was in November, and it was raining during a portion of the time. They were put there for exploding gunpowder in the building. The prisoners who were put out were put there because they would not tell who did it. Some of those men died afterwards. I could not say who gave the order to put the men in the yard, but I suppose Captain Alexander ordered them to be put there. They had generally woolen clothes on. Two men have been killed in Castle Thunder and one in Franklin street guard-house. The man last mentioned was attempting to escape when shot. Of the other men one of them was a deranged man and was put in a cell. He got out of the cell and in attempting to get away was halted by the sentinel, but not heeding was shot by him. He was a Yankee prisoner brought from the Libby Prison and shot the same night. I have seen two men whipped in Castle Thunder, but it was done by order of the court-martial.

I have seen prisoners "bucked" for one or two hours. Some of them had attempted to escape, others had been insulting to the officers of the prison. Some of the prisoners are well clad and others very poorly. Some have no bed clothing. I have been connected with the prison over one year. I know the prisoners need clothing, and common decency requires that they should be better clothed. The prison is kept very clean—as clean as it well can be. The printed rules require this. I have never heard the officers of the prison abuse the prisoners unless the prisoners were refractory. One prisoner's clothing is very frequently stolen by the others.

ROBERT B. CROW sworn:

I am a resident of Richmond and have been for forty years. I am one of the detective force under the provost-marshal or rather General Winder. Of the treatment of the prisoners at Castle Thunder I know very little except from hearsay, as my position does not require me [to go] beyond the office. I can recall an instance or two of their treatment. On one occasion I remember Captain Alexander had one of the prisoners whipped for garroting or robbing another prisoner. I did not see him whipped, but heard that he was whipped and I presume the captain gave the order to have him whipped. I do not know whether he was whipped on his bare back or not; I say I do not know it of my own knowledge, but I think he was. I know of the prisoners being turned out in the Castle yard but do not know what their offense was. It was in quite cold weather and rainy and they had nothing to cover them but the clothing they had on and no roof covering to shelter them. I do not know what their offense was; do not know what rations they had while out there nor whether they had bed clothing or not. The yard is an ordinary one, walled in; do not know how large it is. I know two or three prisoners to have been killed at the Castle. One was the case of a Yankee who was shot and the other case that of the deserter (Carroll) shot the other night in trying to escape. The one that was shot last was shot lying down, dragging himself along the balcony trying to get out. I was not present at the time. Some of the prisoners are well clad and others again are very indifferently clothed. The prison room is comfortable; there is a very large stove in it.

T. G. BLAND sworn:

I am from Louisiana and was former steward of the prison hospital. I went there on the 10th of November last and was relieved from duty on the 4th of the present month. In regard to the treatment of the prisoners confined there I myself was a prisoner four months in Fort Delaware, and from experience I consider the prisoners treated well there to what they are here. I consider them most barbarously and inhumanly treated. On one occasion ten or fifteen of the prisoners were brought out in a large hall, two of them accused of stealing from the prisoners. Two out of the number brought out were not whipped; they were sick I believe, and that was the reason. I do not think the whipping was done by order of the court-martial as Captain Alexander had the men brought out himself. The prisoners were stripped and whipped on the bare back, each receiving ten or twelve lashes laid on by the strongest man in Captain Bossieux's company. The words Captain Alexander used while the whipping was going on were, "Lay it on!" They were whipped for stealing money; and as they were all hard cases, every one of them, some of them did steal it no doubt, but none had a chance of vindicating themselves. They were tied up to a post and whipped. The general treatment of the prisoners is very good but some of the officers of the prison treat the prisoners as though they were dogs instead of soldiers fighting in the common cause of the Confederacy.

Captain Alexander here suggested that the witnesses be kept separate from the witness delivering his testimony as customary in proceedings of the kind before the committee. The chairman of the committee said he judged the witnesses present were all honorable men and would not suffer their own ideas to be influenced by the testimony of a witness. He, however, yielded the point and all the witnesses except the one under investigation were sent from the committee room.

Mr. BLAND resumed:

I have heard of men being killed at the prison. I helped to put one in a coffin myself and sent the corpse to the undertaker. He was shot while trying to escape. I have seen men handcuffed around a large pillar and one of these I saw so punished was taken from the hospital. His offense was trying to bribe the guard. Neither had irons on them. The sick man was under the surgeon's care then. He was handcuffed around the pillar between 5 and 6 o'clock in the afternoon, and when I got back to the prison at 11 o'clock the same night he was still there, and I do not know how long after that. The worst characters in the prison are handcuffed and wear ball and chain; the others who are not so desperate are left to go free. Those tied up could not have been in for very serious offenses. I know the prisoners were put out in the yard and kept there for two or three days. Some of them were thinly and badly clothed and others were well clad. The citizen prisoners are generally clothed well and the soldiers poorly, having no change. Some of those exposed in the yard were brought up into the hospital afterwards sick with the pneumonia, and I heard the surgeon, Doctor Coggin, say that the exposure in the yard made them ill and nothing else. Several of them died in the hospital of pneumonia. The season was in November, with cold, rainy weather. I know of one direct violation of the Army Regulations of the Confederate States and that was in regard to treatment received by myself. It was for disobeying an order of Captain Alexander. The order was to prescribe for a patient. I am not a graduated physician and it was against the orders of the surgeon in charge. I was ordered to a dungeon in which I could not stand up straight—a cell about six feet square. I had no chance to vindicate myself as I sent for Captain Alexander and he did not visit me. I was kept in the dungeon until the next morning. I have known prisoners to be kept there three or four days. I have seen on one or two occasions fifteen or twenty prisoners "bucked" and "gagged" at a time. The "gag" is effected by a stick inserted crosswise in the mouth, and the "buck" is to tie the arms at the elbows to a cross-piece beneath the thighs. They were generally ironed, wore ball and chain, and were charged with various offenses. I recollect now I only "gagged" one. I have seen the "barrel shirt" worn by a prisoner. The shirt is made by sawing a common flour barrel in twain and cutting armholes in the sides and an aperture in the barrel head for the insertion of the wearer's head. The one I saw have the barrel shirt on wore it as a punishment for fighting. He was tied up by the thumbs to the roof and stood on his feet, wearing it one day and part of the next day. Do not know how much longer he wore it.

JOHN CAPHART sworn:

I have been employed with Captain Alexander eleven months on the detective force; seven months of that time I have been at the prison. I have never seen a prisoner harshly treated except by orders. It was really dangerous at times for the officers to go among the prisoners, some of them were such desperate characters. A new prisoner sent in among them was usually knocked down, beat and robbed if he had anything about him. I was off and on duty at the prison, sleeping there. One night I would be off duty and go to my room at 8 o'clock and another night at 10 o'clock. I remember the occasion of the difficulty between Captain Alexander and Mr. Bland. The captain gave him an order to render service to a sick child. Bland refused to obey and Captain Alexander again reiterated his order and Bland again refused with an oath. I then put him in the cell by the order of Captain Alexander. Bland was intoxicated on that occasion. I have seen men whipped at the prison by order of the court-martial and General Winder and by order of Captain Alexander through General Winder (by the latter generally), for stealing from prisoners and the maltreatment of prisoners. I have seen prisoners tied up by the arms. They were two men whom nobody could manage. They were not tied up by the thumbs. The whipping was all done with a leather thong or strap about two feet long. In regard to the barrel shirt I saw one of Captain Bossieux's men walking in one by order of the court-martial.

—

MONDAY, *April 13, 1863.*

The examination of witnesses was resumed.

JOHN CAPHART, detective, was recalled to the stand.

By Captain ALEXANDER:

Question. Mr. Caphart, how many years of your life were you connected with prisons before you came with me?

Answer. Thirty-one years, sir.

Question. How does my treatment of prisoners compare with what you have seen in other prisons?

Answer. Very favorable. For offenses such as have been committed in the Castle by the prisoners they would be put in irons. As I said before, at one time it was dangerous to go into the prison room It was necessary to observe great caution in going in among them. I did not feel safe unless I went with one hand on my pistol.

Question. Do you think you ever saw a worse set in any jail?

Answer. No; I never did. They would be ironed down to ringbolts in the floor for conduct such as I have seen at the Castle.

Question. They chain men down in jails then do they?

Answer. Yes; I have seen it done and helped to do it.

Question. You have been eleven months with me as commandant of Castle Thunder post; what is my manner and demeanor toward the prisoners?

Answer. Usually kind on all occasions. Men reported to you for misconduct you have sometimes imprisoned them.

Question. Have you not seen persons who came to the Castle spit upon by the prisoners from the windows and the sentinels cursed and abused?

Answer. Yes; I have seen it done many times.

Question. When prisoners are brought in under arrest and I am present, do I not attempt to discriminate and instruct the officers to separate and classify them and assign them different quarters according to their appearance or offense?

Answer. Yes; I have seen it done and know it was done.

Question. Do you know anything of the plot gotten up among the prisoners to assassinate me and other officers, set the board yard [fence] on fire and liberate the prisoners?

Answer. Yes; I heard of it and it is a well-established fact, and A. C. Webster who was hanged was the ringleader of the plot.

Question. And [after] all this when Webster was afterwards condemned to death what was my conduct toward him?

Answer. You cut and fixed his food and set up with him after he received his injuries in attempting to escape.

Question (by Mr. WARD, counsel for Captain Alexander). Mr. Caphart, tell the committee how James Tyree was treated by the prisoners when first put into the Castle.

Answer. Yes; I remember when Tyree was brought to the prison; he was dressed in a suit of black and looked genteel and nice. He was sent upstairs and put in one of the rooms. In a few minutes I heard a tremendous noise of shouting, yelling and hallooing mingled with cries. I went up as fast as I could and found Tyree all beaten and gory with blood and stripped to his drawers. He was so bloody and bruised that I could hardly recognize him. I rescued him and took him out from among the prisoners and they followed and crowded around yelling, "Let me at him once more, the son of a bitch; kill the son of a bitch," &c. I carried him outside of the railing and the prisoners attempted to come over the railing after him. Tyree had nothing but his drawers on then. The clothing was never found.

Question (by the COMMITTEE). How many more cases of this kind do you know about?

Answer. I know of one case—an old man fifty years old who was beaten and died from the effects of it.

Captain ALEXANDER. That was a case of murder outright.

Question (by Mr. WARD). Did you ever see more lenient treatment by the captain of such incorrigible prisoners?

Answer. Never in my life, sir; never saw prisoners better treated. Such misbehavior elsewhere would have led to their close confinement.

Question (by the CHAIRMAN OF THE COMMITTEE). You say the prisoners are dangerous to each other and visitors?

Answer. Not now, sir; since the whipping.

Question. How many do the guards number?

Answer. Fourteen, or about that number.

Question. Did you ever know visitors to the prison to be attacked?

Answer. Yes, sir; always told visitors to look out when they went where the prisoners were. I have seen beef bones large enough to knock a man down thrown at visitors. Once the commandant and all of his officers had to retreat from a shower of beef bones.

Question. How long since were the prisoners so desperate?

Answer. Before the whipping of the ringleaders. The conduct of the prisoners has improved since.

Question. Were some of the men whipped brought from the room from whence the beef bones were hurled?

Answer. Yes, sir.

Question. What for?

Answer. For fighting, stealing and other offenses.

Question. How did you know they were the men?

Answer. They were pointed out by the other prisoners. The captain said he would have them all whipped unless they pointed out the guilty ones. They did so and the guilty ones stepped out.

Question. How many men were brought out to be whipped?

Answer. I think there were eight or ten.

Question. Were these men whipped for fighting?

Answer. Yes, sir; they were.

Question. How do you know they were the right men?

Answer. I do not know for certain whether the men whipped were the right ones or not, but the other prisoners said so. They were engaged among others and were pointed out by the other prisoners.

Question. How many prisoners were beaten in that fracas?

Answer. Several. One old man named Mitchell was beaten so dreadfully that he has been crazy ever since.

Question. Do you know the provocation for the fight, and was it inquired into?

Answer. I know of no provocation. The case was inquired into by Captain Alexander. There was a great change after the whipping. All was quiet and we could go in and out without molestation.

Question. How many rooms are there in the prison?

Answer. In the second story there is a large hall and beyond that a large-sized room where citizens and disloyal persons are confined, and on the third story is a very large room for the soldiers, and partitioned cells, or rather rooms, for prisoners tried by court-martial and prisoners awaiting trial by court-martial.

Captain ALEXANDER (to the committee). We get so accustomed to the men received at Castle Thunder that we know their character as soon as they come in and are thus guided in our disposition of them.

Mr. WARD (counsel for Captain Alexander, to the committee). Men are often received from the commanding officer of a company accompanied by an order running something like this:

Take this man and put him in a cell and feed him on bread and water till I send for him for he is one of the damnedest rascals in the world.

Captain ALEXANDER. Such irresponsible orders are never observed nor followed out, though.

Question (by the COMMITTEE). Was the whipping referred to by order of General Winder?

Answer. Yes, sir, it was. I carried the order myself from the general to the captain.

WILLIAM CAUSEY, detective, was recalled to the stand.

By the COMMITTEE:

Question. Do you know anything about prisoners who were whipped; and if so, whether they were Confederate volunteers?

Answer. Yes, sir; and I think they were volunteer soldiers, for there are no others there.

Question. Do you know what was their crime?

Answer. No, sir.

Question. Did not you hear something about a row among the prisoners?

Answer. No, sir; I only saw some men whipped.

Question. How long have you been a detective?

Answer. Since March last, twelve months ago. I left the Castle six or eight days ago and was transferred to the provost-marshal's office.

Question. Up to the time you left were the prisoners there all Confederate volunteers?

Answer. Yes, sir.

Question. Were there any Yankee prisoners there?

Answer. Yes; there were some in the lower room, sent from the Libby Prison when it was full.

Question. What is Caphart's character as an officer?

Answer. I should say he was rather rough.

Question. In his general deportment toward the prisoners is he humane or otherwise?

Answer. He was otherwise, I should think. He would curse them, shake his stick and talk of how he would serve them.

Question. From the tenor of his remarks would you suppose he would be gratified rather than humiliated at the chastisement of a soldier?

Answer. Rather gratified, I think.

Question (by Mr. WARD). Causey, don't you think Caphart a good officer and detective?

Answer. I do not, sir.

Question. Did you ever hear Caphart exult over a man whom he thought was punished properly or justly?

Answer. I don't know his thoughts. I can't answer that question.

Question. From his conversation did you think he thought the men were justly punished?

Answer. No, sir; I did not.

Question. Did you ever hear him express any regrets that they were whipped?

Answer. No, sir.

Question (by Captain ALEXANDER). Do you know whether the prisoners whipped were Yankees or Confederate volunteers?

Answer. I think they were Confederate volunteers.

Question (by Mr. WARD). Have you been in the habit of visiting the prisoners?

Answer. Rarely or never except on business.

Question. Did you see the men whipped?

Answer. I did.

Question (by Captain ALEXANDER). How many lashes were given them, and did you hear the sentence of the court-martial?

Answer. I think it was by order of the court-martial.

Question. Where was the whipping done?

Answer. Upstairs.

Question. On what part of the body was the lash laid on?

Answer. On the buttocks I think.

Question. Did you see any prisoners tied up?

Answer. Yes; lifted up on their toes.

Question. Did you ever knock a prisoner down?

Answer. No, sir.

Question. Did you ever strike a prisoner?

Answer. Yes; after the prisoner struck me.

Question (by the CHAIRMAN OF THE COMMITTEE). What is Captain Alexander's treatment of the prisoners generally?

Answer. He is sometimes kind and sometimes the reverse of kindness.

Question (by Mr. WARD). Do you know what provocation the captain had in thus speaking?

Answer. No; but I have heard him speak very snappish when prisoners were being put in. He expressed himself only in language.

Question. What was his language?

Answer. Well, something like, "Shove them in there." "Put them in there, God damn them."

Question (by Mr. WARD). Did not the prisoners refuse to be put back sometimes and resist—so much so as to require the exercise of force?

Answer. I never had a prisoner to refuse to go in, but I have had them to resist me on the street.

J. F. SCHAFFER, detective, was recalled to the stand.

By the CHAIRMAN OF THE COMMITTEE:

Question. What is the deportment of Caphart toward prisoners?

Answer. I have known him to be very abusive, generally, when prisoners were impudent to him. I have heard him curse prisoners under arrest when they held back or resisted him.

Question. Did you ever see men tied up by the thumbs?

Answer. I have seen prisoners tied up either by the thumbs or the wrists It is called "trysting up" and is a sailor's punishment.

Question (by Mr. WARD). Did you ever examine to see by which they were tied, the thumbs or the wrists?

Answer. No, sir.

Question (by the CHAIRMAN OF THE COMMITTEE). For what offenses were those you saw tied up?

Answer. For bribing the guard I believe. I don't know whether they were Yankees or Confederate volunteers.

Question. Do you remember on a certain occasion when eight or ten men were whipped?

Answer. I heard it rumored; didn't see it.

Question. Is Caphart's conduct toward prisoners abusive?

Answer. No; except on occasions; he was rather kind.

Question (by Mr. WARD). Mr. Schaffer, don't you think Caphart as good an officer as there is on the force?

Answer. I must say I have heard him abuse the prisoners very much. I have heard him use some very harsh language toward them.

Question (by Captain ALEXANDER). Who is the most passionate of the two, Causey or Caphart?

Answer. I couldn't say.

Question (by the CHAIRMAN OF THE COMMITTEE). Is Caphart kind and humane toward the prisoners or the reverse?

Answer. I cannot say.

Question (by Captain ALEXANDER). You know him to be a kind husband and father don't you?

Answer. I never saw him in the midst of his family so I cannot say.

ROBERT B. CROW, detective, was recalled to the stand.

By the CHAIRMAN:

Question. You know Caphart?

Answer. Yes, sir; I do.

Question. What is his general disposition; is he kind?

Answer. He is exactly the reverse of that.

Question. Did you ever hear him express any regrets for punishment inflicted upon soldiers?

Answer. No, sir; he rather exulted at it. I have heard him say, " Damn them, I'd take a knife and cut them in pieces."

Question. Does he treat them roughly or kindly?

Answer. Very roughly indeed.

Question. Without provocation?

Answer. He is generally rough; it is natural with him. I have seen him shove and push prisoners about as though they were negroes. I never heard him express any regrets but rather exulted at their treatment.

Question. How many prisoners are usually confined in the Castle?

Answer. Between 400 and 500; sometimes more and sometimes less. They are constantly being received and discharged.

Question. How often is it found necessary to punish the prisoners?

Answer. I don't know. I seldom go up among the prisoners. I have seen whippings inflicted three or four times.

Question. Is it necessary to flog them as often as once a week? As often as once a fortnight?

Answer. I cannot say.

Question (by the CHAIRMAN). What is Captain Alexander's conduct among the prisoners under his charge?

Answer. He is sometimes rough and sometimes pleasant.

Question. Have you seen him rough without provocation?

Answer. Well, the captain has a good deal to excite and provoke him, but I have seen him speak to and treat the prisoners harshly when I thought there was no occasion for it

Question (by Mr. WARD). Don't you know that the captain has an excited manner and when he swears like a sailor oftentimes he does not mean anything?

Answer. I don't know.

Question (by Captain ALEXANDER). Did you ever, Mr. Crow, regret a punishment you saw inflicted on a prisoner at the Castle and thought it was wrong?

Answer. I have, sir.

Question. Have not you, Crow, exulted over the seizure of liquor from poor women at the depots when you caught them smuggling it into the city?

Answer. Yes, sir; that was my business, sir.

Question (by the CHAIRMAN). Did you see the whipping of a man for knocking the eye out of another man?

Answer. Yes; I was ordered up along with other officers to witness it.

Question. Was it a powerful man who laid the blows on?

Answer. Yes, sir; about the strongest man they could get. They gave him I don't know how many lashes.

Question. Was the thong made of heavy leather?

Answer. Yes, sir; a heavy, thick strap.

Question. Was the man whipped tried by the court-martial or was he lashed by Captain Alexander's order alone?

Answer. I think it was by Captain Alexander's order.

Question (by Captain ALEXANDER). Mr. Crow, do you like Caphart?

Answer. I do not, sir.

Question. Haven't you had a quarrel with him?

Answer. I have, sir.

T. G. BLAND was recalled to the stand.

By the CHAIRMAN:

Question. Do you know Caphart?

Answer. Only since I have been at the prison.

Question. What is his general conduct toward the prisoners?

Answer. Very rough and uncouth.

Question. Did you ever hear him express regrets at their harsh treatment?

Answer. No; on the contrary I always found him willing and assisting to carry out the tyrannical orders of Captain Alexander.

Question. Did he exult over it or appear gratified?

Answer. I can't say as to that, colonel.

Question. How long have you known Caphart?

Answer. Four or five months I reckon.

Question. Were you present at the whipping of the two prisoners referred to by the other witnesses?

Answer. I was, sir.

Question. Who did the whipping?

Answer. Two men did the whipping; one laid it on light and the other very heavy. It was in the case of an old man named Mitchell who had been badly beaten or in a case of stealing money from prisoners.

Question. The prisoners you saw whipped, were they Confederate soldiers?

Answer. They were, and I don't think they were whipped by order of the court-martial.

Question. Do you know anything of the case of George Wright, a deranged prisoner?

Answer. Yes. I found him lying down behind a door in the prison room mired in his own filth with no clothing on but a short swallow-tailed coat. He was completely covered with scabs and vermin. Some of the prisoners said he had been lying there a week and more. I took him up into the hospital and treated him medically.

Question. What is Captain Alexander's treatment of prisoners under his charge?

Answer. He is in some instances very kind, in others very different.

Question. With or without provocation?

Answer. I can't say; but whether with provocation or not he might treat prisoners as an officer should treat them.

Question. Were you ever in the room where the prisoners are confined?

Answer. Yes; I was in there every day.

Question. Did the prisoners ever assault or throw beef bones at you?

Answer. No; not to my knowledge.

Question. Did you ever see them throw beef bones at anybody?

Answer. No; I never did.

Question. How many prisoners do you know to have been killed at the Castle?

Answer. I can't say, as I was only there five months. One or two killed in that time.

Question (by Captain ALEXANDER). Mr. Bland, is there not a place in the Castle called the "sick bay," where the warden puts the prisoners who need to be examined by the surgeon?

Answer. I know there is such a place.

Question. Is it not the duty of the surgeon to look after these sick cases and have them removed to the hospital?

Answer. Yes; it is his duty I believe.

Question. Have you not made threats of personal violence toward me?

Answer. I have not, sir.

Question. Don't you know the cause of Wright's dementedness or insanity?

Answer. Yes. Masturbation.

Question. When you were put in the cell by my order were you not possessed of a candle and a bottle of whisky?

Answer. Yes, sir; I was.

Question (by Mr. WARD). Was the cell not naturally lighted?

Answer. Yes; through the keyhole.

Question. Do you not harbor an animosity against Captain Alexander?

Answer. That makes no difference just now. I will tell you: Once the captain sent a negro boy with a bottle to the steward's hospital room for a bottle of whisky. My orders were to give nothing of the kind out and I so informed Captain Alexander. He then wrote me an order for the whisky and I wrote in reply that it could not be done. Captain Alexander then sent for me to come to his room. I went to his room and there was a little dinner party going on. He asked me to sit down, and after I rose asked me to furnish whisky for the party and I told him I could not. He said: "Suppose a man was suffering from a broken leg and I was to order you to furnish whisky for his relief and you refuse; I would put you in the cell." I was afterwards put in the cell for refusing to prescribe for a patient because I was not a graduated physician and knew nothing about the disease.

GEORGE W. THOMAS sworn.

By the CHAIRMAN OF THE COMMITTEE:

Question. Mr. Thomas, state what you know concerning the treat-ment of prisoners in Castle Thunder and any other circumstances bearing on this investigation.

Answer. I am from Henrico County and have been a detective to Captain Alex-ander since the 13th of March, last year. The general treatment of the prisoners I must say is good as far as my knowledge extends. Two classes of desperadoes are to be found in the Castle, one from far down south and the other from Baltimore; the "wharf rats" of New Orleans and the "plugs" from Baltimore. A third class is the inoffensive soldiers who are the great majority.

Question. Is in your opinion the conduct of the officials toward the prisoners humane and kind?

Answer. Generally kind except on occasions.

Question. On what occasion was that?

Answer. When the prisoners were put in the back yard as a punishment for out-rages committed among the prisoners—robbing and beating the more inoffensive of them—I looked into the yard and seeing the prisoners suffering I reported the condition of the prisoners to Captain Alexander and he had them brought immedi-ately. Some of the prisoners were warmly clad, but the more desperate of the pris-oners generally stole the blankets from the others.

Question. Where did Captain Alexander receive his orders for the punishment of the prisoners?

Answer. From General Winder I think.

Question. How often were the prisoners put out into that yard?

Answer. Only on that one occasion that I recollect.

Question. Had they any blankets?

Answer. Some of them had, but the strongest and more desperate got them.

Question. Was there any covering to the yard to shelter them from the storm?

Answer. No, sir.

Question. What is your duty in connection with the prison?

Answer. I am a detective.

Question. Are all of the prisoners without blankets?

Answer. No, sir; not all. Men go in there and their blankets are taken from them by the desperadoes to make ropes wherewith to escape.

Question. Are there any benches or seats in the prison rooms?

Answer. No, sir; nothing of the kind; they would break and burn them up if there was.

Question. Have you seen men whipped there?

Answer. I have on one or two occasions.

Question. Was the punishment inflicted by order of General Winder?

Answer. It was by his order which was carried [out] by Caphart. There were eight of them whipped on one occasion. Some two or three were struck a dozen or more blows; others were let off with less.

Question. What other kind of punishment did you ever see inflicted there? Did you ever see prisoners wearing barrel shirts?

Answer. Yes, sir; I have.

Question. Did you ever see men tied up by the thumbs?

Answer. No, sir; I never did.

Question. Have you known men to be killed there?

Answer. Yes; several were killed there.

Question. Do you know the circumstances?

Answer. General Winder's orders were after the discovery of the plot to escape to fire upon any prisoner thrusting his head from the windows in defiance of the guard or attempting to escape.

Question. Do you think the men shot and shot at could not have been recaptured without shooting?

Answer. I know of one instance myself in the case of Campbell, a deserter, who escaped and he led me a hard race. I fired at him twice and he would have escaped but for the guard coming up in his front.

Question. Do you know of any cases of whipping at the prison?

Answer. Yes; several cases. One case, that of an old man, Captain Alexander interested himself very much in because of his age and through his influence with General Winder got the sentence of the court-martial remitted.

Question (by Captain ALEXANDER). Thomas, do you think I am a cruel man?

Answer. No, sir; I do not.

TUESDAY, *April 14, 1863.*

GEORGE W. THOMAS was recalled.

By the CHAIRMAN OF THE COMMITTEE:

Question. Do you know anything of Caphart?

Answer. I am associated with him as a detective.

Question. Is he kind and humane?

Answer. I have seen him treat prisoners with unnecessary harshness and cruelty I thought.

Question. Do you think his rough deportment natural with him?

Answer. He has a rough way and is fond of talking.

Question. Does he seem to regret the punishment of any prisoner?

Answer. Caphart has filled the office of jailer to prisons for a great number of years and in the habit of dealing with bad fellows; he has perhaps grown callous and unfeeling.

Question. Have you ever heard him regret or exult over the punishment of any prisoner?

Answer. I couldn't say he was a kind man especially to bad prisoners. Never saw him exult over the punishment of any man, even the hardest villains, with which he had to do. He viewed it in the light of a moral corrective. Toward these he was rather rough. I have heard him curse them, but at such times he had provocation. The prisoners often brickbatted the sentinels; they never threw bones at me; they threw bones at Caphart because they hated him generally. He is not popular with the prisoners.

Question. If Caphart had been kind to them do you think they would throw beef bones at him?

Answer. I can't say as to that. I have seen them throw missiles at the sentinels.

Question. How are the prisoners clad generally?

Answer. I have seen some badly clothed, but not more indifferently than at other prisons. Some of the prisoners steal from each other. To relieve their destitution after the battle around Richmond Captain Alexander sent out men to gather up the clothing and blankets from the battle-fields to clothe the prisoners who were destitute.

Question. Was sufficient clothing obtained in that way to clothe all the destitute prisoners?

Answer. I can't say that every one was furnished, but a great many were.

Question. Have you seen a prisoner with more than one suit of clothing?

Answer. Yes; some of them have, not many.

Question. Do you know such a man as George Wright, once a prisoner in the Castle?

Answer. Yes, sir; he was in the hospital when I saw him. His condition was very bad.

Question. Do you know anything of a deranged Yankee prisoner who was brought from the Libby Prison to the Castle and shot in attempting to escape?

Answer. Yes; he was brought from the Libby Prison for safe-keeping having attempted to get out of that place. He was shot at the Castle in attempting to run the sentinel. The sentinels had been changed and the sentinel who shot him did not know I think that he was crazy. I don't know whether Captain Alexander was present there or not.

Captain ALEXANDER. No, Mr. Chairman, I was not at the Castle at that time.

Question. What officer received him?

Answer. I don't know, sir.

Question. Was it not the duty of the officer who received him to notify all that he was deranged?

Answer. I think it should have been done.

Question. Have you seen barrel shirts worn by the prisoners?

Answer. Yes; two of them by sentence of the court-martial.

Question. When soldiers are arrested on the street and taken to the Castle is it customary for an examination to be made into the charges against them?

Answer. They are never arrested except without papers and the returns are made every morning to the provost-marshal and General Winder.

Question. Then you put them all in among the "wharf rats" of New Orleans and the "plug uglies" of Baltimore?

Answer (by Mr. WARD). If the committee will allow me I will explain that point. When men are arrested on the street and elsewhere and sent to the prison their papers are examined. If regular they are discharged; if irregular they are put back until a case can be substantiated or disproved. If the prisoners are sent by the provost-marshal or General Winder the commandant of the prison has no authority to discharge and they are put back. If at the expiration of a reasonable time their case remains undisposed of a letter detailing the facts is forwarded asking an investigation. Some prisoners have remained in the prison a long time it is true, the difficulty of getting testimony and collecting witnesses operating against an early investigation. Again instances have occurred where they have been taken out on writs of *habeas corpus*.

Question. Are not a great many soldiers taken up and confined there who have merely overstaid their furlough?

Answer (by Mr. WARD). Yes; men are sent there frequently from the provost-marshal or General Winder's office with an order to this effect—"Confine these men and send them to their regiments," and such men are sent daily to the army or to Sergeant Crow, at the barracks, or under a guard and escort of the commandant of the prison post.

Question. You turn the prisoners all in together; the desperadoes with the inoffensive soldiers?

Answer. There are four or five large rooms for their accommodation and we discriminate as much as possible in our classification of them.

Question (by Captain ALEXANDER). Mr. Thomas, have I anything in the world to do with the clothing of prisoners?

Answer. I think not unless it was a voluntary act.

Question (by Mr. WARD). Have you been in the Army; are not the prisoners in Castle Thunder clothed and fed as well as the soldiers now in the Army?

Answer. I should say fully as well.

Question. Has not Captain Alexander exerted himself to clothe the more destitute of them?

Answer. Yes; I know of many instances of it.

Question (by the CHAIRMAN OF THE COMMITTEE). Do you know Mr. Bland?

Answer. I don't know much about him.

Question (by Captain ALEXANDER). Is Bland a drinking man?

Answer. I don't know anything about him.

Question (by Mr. WARD). If prisoners were put in Caphart's charge do you think he would beat them if they would go along quietly and peaceably?

Answer. I don't think he would.

Question (by Captain ALEXANDER). Don't you think there are as hard cases here as anywhere else?

Answer. Yes, indeed; it would be hard to match.

STEPHEN B. CHILDREY sworn:

By the CHAIRMAN:

Question. What is your position at prison?

Answer. I am the commissary of the prison.

Question. What is the general treatment of the prisoners confined there?

Answer. Good, very good; good as persons in the same situation could be treated.

Question. Did you ever see any whipping there without the authority of a court-martial?

Answer. I never saw any of the prisoners whipped.

Question. What is the general deportment of the officers toward the prisoners; is it kind?

Answer. As kind as could be expected. Of course harsh measures have to be used sometimes.

Question. What is the necessity or excuse for rough language?

Answer. Because they have some very rough characters to deal with. If they were treated differently they would run over them and take the prison.

Question. You have never seen any whipping, then?

Answer. No.

Question. Seen any other kind of punishment inflicted?

Answer. I have seen prisoners "bucked." They were of the more desperate characters.

Question. Do you know of any prisoners being killed there?

Answer. I know of one man dying from the effects of a beating at the hands of some of the prisoners and I know of another who was shot by the guard in attempting to escape.

Question. Do you think it was absolutely necessary to shoot this man to have recaptured him?

Answer. I suppose it was.

Question. Was the man outside of the building when fired upon and killed?

Answer. No, sir; he was on the balcony of the second story on Cary street about jumping down. The sentinel was on the pavement below him.

Question. Do you know anything about a crazy man who was shot in attempting to escape?

Answer. Yes; I heard of the circumstance.

Question. Do you know anything about the case of George Wright, a prisoner, and his condition when sent to the hospital?

Answer. Yes; his condition was very bad. I furnished him with clothing but he would tear the clothes off his person.

Question. In what condition was he when removed to the hospital?

Answer. He was traveling about the prison like the other prisoners but in a demented state of mind. I gave him his food. No filth is allowed to collect in the prison. It is I will venture to say one of the cleanest prisons in the State. Captain Alexander is as particular in this respect as any man I ever saw. His usual disposition when not provoked is kind and urbane.

Question (by Mr. WARD). You are the commissary of the prison are you not?

Answer. I am.

Question. And as such you came in contact with the prisoners a great deal?

Answer. Yes, sir.

Question. From your knowledge what is the character of the prisoners, or some of them?

Answer. I consider them desperate indeed.

Question. Did they ever make threats toward you?

Answer. Yes; the whipping had an excellent effect on them. They are getting worse now again since the law was passed by Congress abolishing whipping in the Army. Something will have to be done to stop their insubordination.

Question. You know about the clothing collected by Captain Alexander for the use of prisoners?

Answer. Yes; I distributed the clothing to the prisoners. I am at liberty to sell them anything in the way of food, luxuries or necessaries; anything they want if they have money to buy. I consider their rations better in quantity and quality than the soldiers in the field.

Question (by the CHAIRMAN OF THE COMMITTEE). Do you know anything about the whipping at the prison?

Answer. I never saw any whipping although it was done.

Question. Do you know anything about the shooting of prisoners?

Answer. Yes, sir.

Question. Who gave the order to shoot the prisoners?

Answer (by Captain ALEXANDER). I gave the order to the sentinels based on the orders of General Winder. I was not at the prison when the shooting occurred, but it is a general standing order to shoot at prisoners cursing or abusing the sentinels from the windows.

Question (by Captain ALEXANDER). Mr. Childrey, do you consider me a cruel man?

Answer. I do not; but I consider you a positive man—one who wants discipline and orders carried out.

Question. How many poor women am I now feeding from the milk obtained at the Castle?

Answer. Yes; I know you are supplying a good many.

Question. Did I not start a hospital and place my wife in it to attend to the sick and wounded?

Answer. Yes; I know that, captain.

Question. And did the Government ever pay me one cent for my money expended?

Answer. Not that I am aware of.

BALDWIN T. ALLEN sworn.

By the CHAIRMAN OF THE COMMITTEE:

Question. What is your position at Castle Thunder?

Answer. I am warden.

Question. What is the treatment of the prisoners?

Answer. That is rather a comprehensive question. In answering it I must take into consideration the character of some of the prisoners. The commandant has found it necessary to enforce very rigid rules. If they had been less rigid he would have been unable to keep one of them there.

Question. Does Captain Alexander and the other officers speak kindly or roughly to the prisoners?

Answer. I don't know of any officer being unkind to well-behaved prisoners.

Question. Have you seen whipping there without order of a court-martial?

Answer. I have seen whipping inflicted but whether with or without the order of a court-martial I cannot say.

Question. Do you know that General Winder gave the order or not?

Answer. I heard so; but I am not positive by whose authority it was done.

Question. Did you ever see any whipping?

Answer. Yes; I have seen fifty lashes laid on by order of the court-martial.

Question. Have you seen persons receive six, eight and ten lashes?

Answer. Yes; frequently.

Question. Were the men you saw whipped Confederate prisoners and soldiers of the Confederate service?

Answer. I think not. I think they were Yankee deserters.

Question. Were any of them Confederate soldiers?

Answer. I can't say; but I can get the names to-morrow.

Question. Do you know anything about the killing of some prisoners?

Answer. Yes; last fall a Yankee deserter who was deranged attempted to run the guard and was killed. Another was killed recently in attempting to escape. His name was Charles Carroll and he was a Confederate soldier.

Question. Have you seen men wear barrel jackets?

Answer. Yes, sir.

Question. Have you known prisoners to be put out in the prison yard without fire or shelter in cold weather?

Answer. Yes; several months ago. Their offense was robbing and stealing, breaking windows and gross violation of the rules.

Question. How long did they remain there?

Answer. All one day and night and part of another day.

Question. Any other instance?

Answer. The next time the prisoners were put into the back yard it was in October or November. They had no covering or shelter except their blankets and clothing.

Question. You say you found out they were suffering. Suppose you had not taken them in promptly what do [you] think would have been the consequences?

Answer. I suppose they would have been cold. They could have stood it though. Our soldiers stand it. They had fuel to make a fire.

Question. Of those placed in the yard last fall do you know of any who were taken sick afterwards?

Answer. Some of them may have been sick but whether from that cause or not I can't say.

Question. Did you ever see men tied up by the thumbs?

Answer. Yes; once or twice I saw men tied by the thumbs.

Question. What was their offense?

Answer. Stealing, &c.

Question. Were they Confederate prisoners?

Answer. Yes.

Question. Who was one?

Answer. Martin Darby, a young man twenty-five years of age. He was tied up several hours.

Question. Have you seen men bucked there?

Answer. Yes, and helped to buck a good many of them myself.

Question. What was their crime?

Answer. For various offenses. And I may say here that all the punishment inflicted is necessary to keep up the discipline of the prison.

Question. Did you ever see the hands of any of the men tied up black from the stagnation of the blood in them?

Answer. Yes, I have frequently I think.

Question. Did you ever see men handcuffed and their hands bloody from the effects of the tying up?

Answer. Yes; one was named William Campbell. He slipped up his handcuffs to his elbows I believe to cause stagnation of the blood.

Question (by Mr. WARD). You are the warden?

Answer. Yes, and in that capacity I am generally among the prisoners.

Question. What is the character of some of the men confined there?

Answer. I consider many of them the most desperate men in the Southern Confederacy. It would not do to treat them leniently.

Question. Are not all picked up and put together in these rooms appropriated to the prisoners?

Answer. But we try to separate the quiet from the quarrelsome prisoners.

Question. Have you seen prisoners there with one suit on constantly?

Answer. A change of clothing is beneficial to the health and comfort of the prisoners but few of them had it.

Question. Is it a rare or common case for the prisoners to be whipped?

Answer. Rather rare; but it has had a beneficial effect whenever it has been done.

Question (by Captain ALEXANDER). They say you let George Wright lay for two weeks in the prison room sick without attending to his wants?

Answer. I think there must be some mistake about that. I go around every morning and call the breakfast roll, and when I find a man down by sickness I take his name and report him to the surgeon.

Question (by Captain ALEXANDER). I handle a great many prisoners do I not, but whipping is comparatively rare?

Answer. Yes, it is; for so many.

Question (by Mr. WARD). Are not the prisoners in the Castle constantly changing?

Answer. Yes; those there to-day are sent off to-morrow.

Doctor LUNDAY sworn.

By the CHAIRMAN OF THE COMMITTEE:

Question. State to the committee what you know of the condition and treatment of prisoners at Castle Thunder.

Answer. I know nothing particular about the military conduct of the prison. I have been there to get prisoners out and have received notes from the prisoners. I have been through the prison and hospital and the condition of the hospital and prison apartments were much better than I expected to find. Below there is a good conduit for carrying off the filth but the building is not well ventilated, but that is the fault of the building. The hospital is clean beyond comparison, and the surgeon from what I saw pays all the necessary attention. While there I saw an inclosure, the back yard, containing a large number of prisoners. They were in a most woeful state as regards clothing and comfort and I remarked that it looked like pandemonium. The prisoners were growling and cursing and I heard the clanking of the chains. One of them accosted me as I passed along and asked me to get him out. I saw Captain Alexander and asked him to let the fellow out. Captain Alexander remarked: "To keep order here I have had to kill ten men."

(Captain Alexander here explained that he had used the expression "killed ten men" in a jocose manner in response to Doctor Lunday's remarks.)

—

WEDNESDAY, *April 15, 1863.*

The examination of witnesses for the Government was resumed.

J. T. KIRBY sworn:

I am at present an inmate of Castle Thunder where I have been held a prisoner as a spy for some months past. I am an Englishman, a resident of Niagara, Canada, where I have a wife and children. I came through the lines on business with the Government which will be explained as I proceed. God knows I wish to go back there.

By the CHAIRMAN OF THE COMMITTEE:

Question. State what you know about the treatment of the inmates of the prison.

Answer. At times I have known Captain Alexander to be extremely kind to prisoners; at times the very opposite, extremely harsh and domineering. I have been the recipient of his kindnesses and on the contrary I have received treatment from him which to describe [witness excited] I would prefer being interrogated as I proceed.

CHAIRMAN OF THE COMMITTEE. Go on and give your testimony in your own way.

Question. Is Captain Alexander kind?

Answer. I consider him the very opposite of kindness and it is so as a general rule. I myself have experienced some of his inhumanity.

Question. What is the character of his usual intercourse with prisoners?

Answer. At times he is kind and at other times extremely rough and uncouth, then kind again and then rough as the fit takes him. Simply for going into the hospital by order of the surgeon in charge, Doctor Coggin, Captain Alexander threatened to put me in the cell. I was ordered to the hospital by the surgeon to be treated for an affection of the throat. I was requested or rather invited by Doctor Coggin to visit the hospital daily for medical treatment; also to while away a few moments of my confinement in pleasant conversation. This privilege was refused me by Captain Alexander with the threat if I violated his instructions he would put me in the cell. I am in the hospital now. I was taken from cell No. 3 last Friday and given the range of the citizens' room. On Monday morning following while engaged in cleaning my teeth at the pump, the prisoner Campbell being present, Captain Alexander came up to his room. We were talking together of the captain and matters about the Castle, and as Captain Alexander came up I turned on my heel to enter my room saying to Campbell (suiting the action to the words), "I have no more respect for Captain Alexander than I have for my royal Bengal stern." I immediately went to my room and the officers came and took me out and confined me again in cell No. 3, a room about fifteen feet square and one window therein which was covered with boards. I had belonged to a mess in the prison room and the mess resolved to supply me with my meals. Mr. Allen, the warden, refused to let me have the food sent me and sent it back. I wrote a note to the mess and learned that it was refused. I was not allowed to purchase anything from the commissary. I asked for rations and they were refused me. I had nothing to eat from Friday morning to Saturday, some time during the day.

Question. On what charge are you confined?

Answer. I have been in prison since the 8th day of November last on suspicion of being a spy. I applied for and obtained a writ of *habeas corpus*, and on the 6th of March Mr. Aylett, the counsel for the Confederate States, closed the case announcing that no evidence had been adduced to hold me on the charge. On the 11th of March judgment was rendered in the case by Judge Lyons and I was informed that I was at liberty to return to the North by flag of truce which I refused to do, &c.

Question. What is Captain Alexander's treatment of the other prisoners under his charge?

Answer. Captain Alexander has his favorites. There are prisoners there whose sentences of court-martial condemning them to wear ball and chain have not been carried out. I know of two instances and others have been told me by the prisoners. Any person or prisoner could be Captain Alexander's favorite if he would become his pimp. I could have been one I reckon.

Question. Relate what instances you know of sentences not being carried out.

Answer. I know of one young man who was sentenced by court-martial to wear a ball and chain whose sentence was not carried out. He was sentenced to ball and chain and hard labor. He was a fine young man and I assisted him to write a letter to the President of the Confederate States asking a commutation of the sentence. The charge against him was assaulting his superior officer and desertion. He was in the citizens' room and never had the ball and chain on.

Question. Did you ever see any Confederate soldiers whipped there?

Answer. I have seen several whipping operations.

Question. Without the order of a court-martial?

Answer. I don't know. One James McAlister I was told was whipped twelve lashes for being quarrelsome in the prisoners' room. I have seen Yankee prisoners whipped for quarreling. I saw four whipped at one time. I was not where I could see at all times. I think two were whipped without the order of the court-martial. They were whipped on the bare back with a leather strap. Do not know that the lash drew blood; heard that it did in one instance.

Question. What other kinds of punishment have you seen inflicted?

Answer. I have seen prisoners bucked. One in the condemned cell was bucked for speaking to persons in the citizens' room.

Question. How long do they remain bucked?

Answer. I have seen them part of two days in that condition.

Question. Have you seen men wear barrel shirts?

Answer. Yes; I have seen two prisoners with them on about the prison.

Question. Is the punishment of the shirt severe?

Answer. No; not painful; not so severe as either thumbing or bucking. The humiliation is greater than the punishment.

Question. Have you seen any thumbing?

Answer. Yes; I have seen prisoners tied up by the thumbs as high as they could reach on their tiptoes. They were tied with a small-sized whip cord.

Question. How many hours have you known them to remain in that condition?

Answer. I have known them to remain in that condition from morning until night.

Question. Did you ever examine to see if any blood was drawn by the cord?

Answer. Once I did. The prisoner had pulled and loosened the cord and his thumbs were black and blue. He didn't complain of pain but rather took it as a good joke. I have seen men tied up around a post so tightly that they couldn't lie down or sit down. In one instance I was told that it was the orders of Captain Alexander that they should remain so all night but some of the officers had let them down so they could sit and lie down.

Question. What was the crime?

Answer. Attempting to bribe the guard I believe.

Question. Are the foregoing all the instances you know of?

Answer. They are all I can recall at present.

Question. How many prisoners were put into the yard on one occasion?

Answer. All in room No. 2—about one hundred.

Question. How long did they remain there?

Answer. For several days I think. It was in the latter part of November or December. Their offense was putting powder in the stove.

Question. Were any of them sick afterwards?

Answer. I cannot say but I understood some were ill from the effects of the exposure. They had neither covering, fire nor shelter except the high walls and it was raining part of the time.

Question. Did Captain Alexander give an order to have a fire built in the yard?

Answer. I never heard of any.

Question. How many days were they kept there?

Answer. Four or five I understood. .

Question. Were any men shot at the prison?

Answer. Yes; I have heard of men being shot and shot at for putting their heads out of the window. I myself was threatened with shooting. I know Captain Alexander gave an order to the guard to shoot me while I was looking out of an open window once. I drew down the window without moving my head and defied them. I remonstrated with Captain Alexander and told him my head was not outside of the window, and neither was it.

Question. Are there any female prisoners?

Answer. Yes; two I believe.

Question. Do you know anything of their treatment?

Answer. No; only what has been told me.

Question (by Mr. WARD). Mr. Kirby, where are you from?

Answer. From Niagara, Canada, sir, and have been confined eight months in the citizens' room.

Question. What were you sent from that room for?

Answer. A difficulty I had with the captain I suppose. We were ordered to scrub and prepare the room for the visit of the inspection committee and the guard would allow but two of us to go to the pump for water at one time. I remonstrated with Captain Alexander, when he called me "a damned son of a bitch" and I called him "a damned coward." I was put in the cell but that night ordered back to the citizens' room. I apologized for my conduct.

Question. Then you were put out of the citizens' room last Friday?

Answer. Yes; my difficulty with Captain Alexander caused it.

Question. You have a good room and a good bed?

Answer. Yes. The captain hasn't taken them away yet but I am not indebted to him for my bed.

Question (by Captain ALEXANDER). You say I didn't carry out the sentence of Leary who was condemned to wear ball and chain?

Answer. No; you did not.

Question. Did not you yourself petition the President for his reprieve? And did not you sit down in my office and write a letter to the President for Leary concerning his case? And did I not allow you to receive your meals from the hotels and faro banks and gave you many privileges not enjoyed by the other prisoners?

Answer. Yes, captain, you did all that.

Question. You say Mr. Allen's treatment of the prisoners is inhuman?

Answer. He is generally intoxicated and it is the merest exception in the world that I ever got a kind answer out of him.

Question (by the COMMITTEE). What is your opinion of Caphart?

Answer. I consider him in all respects a vile, low, inhuman person.

Question. Do you find prisoners like kind and humane officers?

Answer. I have heard prisoners say they could have escaped at times when it was Mr. Riggs' night on, but they would not do it for fear of compromising his character. All the officers are down on him. I have known the captain to treat him kindly and at other times snub him.

Question. Do you know Mr. Bland?

Answer. Yes; his deportment is generally kind.

Question. Do you know about the case of George Wright?

Answer. Yes; but I never saw him until I saw him in the hospital.

Question. Are you as a prisoner allowed to see persons from without the prison?

Answer. Once Hon. Mr. Boteler called to see me and I was refused an interview with him. I have sent for persons who have been refused to see me. I have been allowed to communicate with counsel several times under seal and this privilege was also stopped. I once gave a letter to Mr. Riggs to carry to the captain to read. He said it must go to General Winder and I gave it to Mr. Ward. On Sunday morning following, some four or five days after, Mr. Ward said he had given the letter to Captain Alexander.

Question. What became of the letter?

Answer. I don't know, sir.

Captain ALEXANDER. Mr. Chairman, shall I send to General Winder's and get it? The letter is on file there.

Mr. WARD. There is an order from General Winder that all communications from the prison shall go through his office. Accordingly all letters from the prisoners are put in a box and taken up to General Winder daily.

Question (by the COMMITTEE). What did you come here for, Mr. Kirby?

Answer. I had special business to the Confederate Government.

Question. Was that business made known on your arrival here?

Answer. It was.

Question. Are the authorities aware of your arrest?

Answer. They are.

JOHN SHEHAN sworn.

By the COMMITTEE:

Question. You are a prisoner at the Castle and a Confederate soldier?

Answer. Yes, sir.

Question. What is the treatment of the prisoners generally at the Castle?

Answer. In a majority of cases I think they are treated kindly. Men are whipped there. I have seen them whipped without the sentence of the court-martial. Captain Alexander I saw present at the whipping.

Question. How many lashes were laid on?

Answer. From six to eight lashes I should judge. They were laid on hard. The offense in one case was rioting and fighting in the prison room.

Question. Have you seen any bucking there?

Answer. Yes, and men whipped who were Confederate soldiers. The bucking was for the rioting in the prison. I have known men to remain bucked as long as four hours.

Question. Have you seen prisoners tied up by the thumbs?

Answer. Yes; I think so. He was a Confederate soldier belonging to Rodgers' cavalry. His offense was thieving I believe.

Question. What about the prisoners put out into the yards?

Answer. It was in November and they were kept there several days. A few had bed covering. Some were in bad health when put out there and looked miserable enough. Some were sick immediately after their exposure and I remember of one dying in the hospital.

Question. Have you seen any men shot there?

Answer. Yes; one was Carroll who attempted to escape.

Question. Could he not have been captured without shooting?

Answer. He was in the act of getting out of a window onto the portico beneath which was the guard. I think he could have been easily taken without killing.

Question. Was there any investigation into the shooting?

Answer. I didn't hear of any. I have known prisoners to be shot at for putting their heads out of the windows. The orders are to shoot them if they will not obey the sentinels. They have been told that often enough. I have put my head out of the window a thousand times and never was shot at.

Question. Have you got a cell or "sweat house" for the solitary confinement of prisoners?

Answer. Yes; it is a room about eight feet square. I was confined there once in irons. I could lay down. There are no windows. There is no protection from either the heat or cold.

Question. What were you put in the cell for?

Answer. For going out as corporal of the prison and getting drunk. I am in prison for being absent from my regiment without leave. My sentence will be out to-day or to-morrow. I have been in prison six months. I was there one month before any charge was preferred.

Question (by Captain ALEXANDER). You are a sailor are you not, Shehan?

Answer. Yes, sir.

Question. Is it not my habit to treat prisoners kindly?

Answer. No, sir; it is cruel and inhuman.

Question (by the CHAIRMAN OF THE COMMITTEE). What is Captain Alexander's deportment toward prisoners?

Answer. Sometimes he is kind as can be and at other times he is the very opposite.

Question. You know Caphart?

Answer. I knew him in Norfolk. He has little to do with the prison. Never saw him arrest a man.

Question (by Mr. WARD). Has my conduct been kind?

Answer. Yes; you are a gentleman as far as I know.

Question (by Captain ALEXANDER). Have I not a great deal to provoke and make me angry?

Answer. Yes; I know you have. You have treated me well. I do not find fault with the harshness of the rules but it is impossible to keep so many men in perfect order.

CHARLOTTE GILMAN sworn:

I have been in Castle Godwin and Thunder going on twelve months altogether—the last time about one month.

Question. What are you in prison for?

Answer. I am a witness against George W. Elam for counterfeiting.

Question. What is the general treatment of the prisoners?

Answer. I have always been well treated. All the ladies there spoke of Captain Alexander in the highest terms. All like him. I know nothing of the treatment of the other prisoners.

Question (by Captain ALEXANDER). Did I not go to General Winder and get an order for your washing?

Answer. Yes, you did; you have been very kind, and you let me go out very often.

WILLIAM CAMPBELL sworn:

I have seen no cruelty on the part of Captain Alexander toward the prisoners. I think I am the only one who ever suffered. I was among the number put into the yard. I was also bucked and put in the yard. The charge against me is desertion. I am from Louisiana.

Question. Have you been tried by court-martial?

Answer. No, sir.

Question. How long have you been in prison?

Answer. Only one month the last time. I have escaped three or four times.

———

THURSDAY, *April 16, 1863.*

The examination of witnesses was resumed.

V. T. CRAWFORD sworn:

I am located in Richmond and am a practicing lawyer. I was admitted to the bar some eight months ago. I know nothing of the treatment of the prisoners confined in Castle Thunder, but I do know something of the conduct of its officers [towards those] who are called upon to visit the prison in a professional way. After I had visited the prison once or twice without interruption obstacles began to be thrown in my way. First, an order forbidding conversation between myself and clients without a third person in the shape of an officer being present. At another time I was refused admittance beyond the guard, and all the conversation I could hold with my clients had to be carried on through a wire gauze screen. At another time Mr. Ward informed me I would have to get an official permit from General Winder to see prisoners. I went to General Winder for the pass and after some delay I was furnished with a general pass which had to be renewed on the occasion of every visit. General Winder asked me about the prisoners I wished to see, and said there were some men there whom they did not wish to have counsel. I asked him what men? And he replied, "We have our rights and you yours," and something more which I do not recollect. I have continued visiting the prison up to Tuesday last on a pass to be admitted at the discretion of the commandant. Day before yesterday I wrote out a pass to admit me to an interview with two prisoners, George Summers and Lieut. George Brown. I carried it to Captain Winder in a back room at the headquarters and he signed it. Both of the men sent letters requesting to see me six days after that. I never got the letter. Inquired and found he had given it to Mr. Allen who said he had handed it to Mr. Ward to forward to General Winder. Went to General Winder but found no letter there. Eight or ten days after that the letter reached me.

Question (by the CHAIRMAN OF THE COMMITTEE). Did Captain Alexander obstruct your intercourse with the prisoners?

Answer. He told me to do my speaking to them through the guard.

Question. Did he know your visits were professional ones?

Answer. Yes; he was well aware of that fact.

Question. Were not some of your clients citizens?

Answer. Yes; one. A man named Weeks; was a citizen of Loudoun or Fauquier. He was finally tried and discharged after an imprisonment of four or five months.

Question. Do you know anything else bearing on the subject before the committee?

Answer. I know another affair which first raised my suspicions. I was called professionally to see a soldier named Miller belonging to Captain Thornton's company, of Caroline County. I agreed to undertake his case for $50, and he said he would give that. Miller was discharged and when I saw him he said Mr. Ward had told him not to pay me the $50 fee, as he (Mr. Ward) had done more for him than I had. Previous to this Miller told Ward to keep a note for $65 and give it to me. I inquired for the note of Mr. Ward and it was not to be found.

Question. Did Miller pay Mr. Ward?

Answer. I cannot say that he did.

Mr. WARD (to the committee). I deny the statement Mr. Crawford has made. He called on me on one occasion and desired that I should solicit practice for him, or in other words take advantage of my position to drum up clients for him at the Castle. He said he understood such a procedure was customary at the Richmond bar and offered to give me half of the proceeds of such a joint operation. I told him I would not be a party to any such arrangement; that it was unprofessional, and that a party who stooped to it would most certainly lose standing and position at the bar. I did say that in case Mr. Crawford was inquired for I would notify him of it.

DENNIS O'CONNOR sworn:

I was an inmate of Castle Thunder. I am paroled to report there until I make a choice of the branch of the service I shall enter. I prefer the Navy.

By the COMMITTEE:

Question. How were you treated while there?

Answer. I was taken up on the street late at night by the guard and sent to Castle Thunder as a supposed deserter. I had been drinking. I was put in a dungeon, a small room called the "sweat house." I was kept there from Thursday to Saturday at 3 o'clock when I was taken upstairs to be flogged by order of Captain Alexander. I was ordered to take off my clothes and I stripped. I was tied up by my wrists to a post and one of the members of Captain Bossieux's company laid on the lashes and he would spring on his toes at every lick. Captain Alexander was present and told the man with the lash to lay it on to me. That was the only time I was ever whipped.

Question. Who arrested you?

Answer. Caphart arrested me. I don't know anything about his general disposition as he never came among the prisoners much. He looked as if he would treat them rough if he had anything against them. The prisoners all liked Riggs. He could go among them without molestation at all times. Mr. Allen, the warden, is a rough man. I was put into the yard along with the other prisoners. It was for exploding powder in the room. There was no danger of blowing up the building. It was done to frighten some North Carolina soldiers who were lying by the wall asleep.

Question. Did Captain Alexander find out the guilty parties?

Answer. No, sir; they were all put down into the yard because none would tell. The orders were to take no blankets or extra covering but some were lowered from the windows afterwards. Some of the prisoners were in bad health; several died from it and several were taken into the hospital.

Question. Had the prisoners any fire in the yard?

Answer. The commissary gave them some wood, a dozen sticks or so at night, but none in the daytime. I don't remember the month, but it was in November I think. It snowed the first night and the next night it rained. The ground was not very muddy until our feet cut it up.

Question. Did you see any other whipping there?

Answer. O, yes. I don't know whether by order of court-martial or not. I saw ten whipped for being concerned in stealing one coat. All except one were whipped, and he was a Federal prisoner. The others were Confederate soldiers and two Yankee deserters.

Question. They were whipped because the coat could not be found?

Answer. They did not know anything about it I reckon. The coat was found. The prisoner who lost the coat selected the prisoners whom he suspected to be whipped. Captain Alexander was present and ordered the lashes to be laid on hard.

Question. How many lashes did they strike each?

Answer. Well, some six, some eight and some twelve.

Question. Have you seen any men bucked there?

Answer. Yes; for such offenses as disobeying orders, cutting the walls, transgressing the rules, &c.

Question. Is bucking severe?

Answer. No; not very severe.

Question. Do you know of any men being killed there?

Answer. Yes; several men were shot.

Question. Do prisoners who are confined in the sweat room suffer much?

Answer. There is air but no light and the fare is bread and water. I did not suffer for water. The corporal of the guard brought me water and I had a bucket for slops. I could go out once a day myself.

Question. When arrested were you taken before the provost-marshal or to the Castle?

Answer. I was taken to the Castle.

Question (by Captain ALEXANDER). I had your brother Thomas there once, O'Connor; what was my treatment of him?

Answer. Well, captain, you treated me rather rough.

Question. Are not all the prisoners glad to see me when I come among them?

Answer. Yes; because they wanted you to transact some business for them. Sometimes I wanted to get little things in, such as clothing, &c., and I could not get them; and persons wishing to see me have been denied I suppose by your order.

MARION C. RIGGS sworn.

By the CHAIRMAN OF THE COMMITTEE:

Question. What is your position at the Castle, Mr. Riggs?

Answer. I was warden.

Question. What is the deportment of Captain Alexander toward the prisoners confined there?

Answer. I have seen many instances of cruelty by order of Captain Alexander. I regard the treatment of the prisoners by Captain Alexander and his officers as cruel and inhuman.

Question. Have you seen men whipped there?

Answer. Yes, on several occasions; some I knew were not by the order of a court-martial. They were charged with stealing from other prisoners upstairs. Others were whipped for beating, breaking out of cells and interfering with the guard, &c.

Question. What number of lashes did they receive?

Answer. I have known as many as twelve to be laid on.

Question. Did you see any bucking done there?

Answer. Yes, and prisoners put into the back yard and kept there two or three days and nights in succession. It was in cold weather. Some were well provided with clothing. There was no sheltering except the wall and no extra covering. They were fed on bread and water during that time.

Question. Do you know of any men dying there after being taken out?

Answer. I know of none, though several were sick.

Question. The sweat house—do you know of men being confined there?

Answer. Generally men caught in attempting to escape were put in there on bread and water.

Question. What is bucking? Describe it.

Answer. It is a severe and degrading punishment. It is done by passing a splint across the elbows and tying them beneath the thighs after the manner of a calf going to market.

Question. Were any men shot there?

Answer. I recollect one man who was shot while rushing past the sentinel out of a cell. He was shot in the inclosed yard. He could have been secured without shooting. He was making his way upstairs and was fired upon at the foot of the stairs. He died in three or four days. He seemed to be insane.

Question. What was Captain Alexander's deportment then? Did he seem to regret it?

Answer. I cannot say.

Question. What was the man's name; was he a Confederate soldier?

Answer. I never could find out his name. It was in October or November, 1862.

Question. Was there an investigation into the shooting?

Answer. I do not know.

Question. Did Captain Alexander give orders to shoot men attempting to escape?

Answer. I never heard of such an order.

Question. Did you hear any regrets expressed among the officers for the shooting of this man?

Answer. Yes, several, but not Caphart or Allen. I heard the surgeon of the post wasn't in, and sent for Doctor Rucker, a prisoner. I picked him up. He was crazy, and no mistake.

Question. Was it known that he was deranged?

Answer. I could tell he was. He was brought from the Libby Prison where he was fired upon for the same offense, and was killed at the Castle the day he entered.

Question. What is the general character of Caphart? Is he kind?

Answer. I would say not; rather brutal. I have known instances where he has been ordered to tie up and buck prisoners and he seemed to take a special pleasure in it. He would tie them up as tight as possible, and I myself have let them down. I never heard him curse prisoners, but have seen him shake his stick over them when brought in. I never heard him express any regrets for them.

Question. What of Allen? Is he kind and humane?

Answer. I never saw him use physical force. I have heard him curse the prisoners.

Question. Is there any difficulty in managing prisoners?

Answer. Sometimes there is insubordination. They never resisted me nor threw beef bones at me, and I was frequently among them.

Question. Do you think they would be insubordinate if kindly treated?

Answer. I don't believe they would.

Question. Are you connected with the prison now?

Answer. I was discharged on the first of the month; it was said by the board or investigating committee to reduce force and expenses.

Question. Do you know at whose instance you were discharged?

Answer. I do not.

Question. Are persons allowed to see prisoners?

Answer. Yes, if they have passes.

Question. Do you know of obstacles being thrown in the way of attorneys wishing to see clients?

Answer. I have known instances. They are permitted to go in and stand at a screen window and talk through it.

Question. Do you consider Allen cruel?

Answer. Sometimes he is kind and at other times crabbed. I like him very much.

Question. Do you regard Captain Alexander as cruel?

Answer. I have thought his punishments more severe than the cases demanded. He always had some friend whom he shielded.

Question. Do you know of any cases where the captain has taken the responsibility of remitting the sentences of court-martial?

Answer. No, sir; I do not. I was connected with the prison six months and saw punishments once or twice a week.

Question. Hear of any complaints about food?

Answer. Yes, there were some complaints. There was plenty of food though; a pound of meat and a loaf of bread each. The floors were swept once or twice a day and washed once a week, generally on a Saturday.

Question (by Captain ALEXANDER). What are the characters of the prisoners confined there?

Answer. Very desperate fellows many of them. I saw the cases of Mitchell and Tyree who were beaten by them, and the men who were struck by a slung-shot. The guilty were afterwards whipped by orders from headquarters, General Winder's. My position was on the same floor with the mass of prisoners.

Question (by Captain ALEXANDER). What is the cry when a new prisoner enters?

Answer. "Fresh fish!" They are then generally beat and robbed if they have anything worth while.

Question (by Mr. WARD). Has Captain Alexander been kind to you and the other officers?

Answer. Yes.

Question (by Captain ALEXANDER). Do you think I am unkind?

Answer. Yes; in some instances.

Question (by the COMMITTEE). When Captain Alexander sent the prisoners into the yard was it done by order of General Winder?

Answer. I don't know that it was.

Question. Was it in the newspapers?

Answer. Yes; I think it was.

Question. Do you think Captain Alexander by nature a cruel man?

Answer. Yes; I consider his treatment cruel.

Question. What do the prisoners think of Captain Alexander?

Answer. I have heard him spoken of with disrespect.

Capt. CYRUS BOSSIEUX sworn.

By the COMMITTEE:

Question. You are stationed at the prison are you?

Answer. Yes, sir.

Question. What punishments have been inflicted there in violation of law?

Answer. I don't know that I have seen any in violation of law. I know of whipping and bucking and men being put into the yard to find out the perpetrators of outrages on prisoners.

Question. Have you seen any tied up by the thumbs?

Answer. No; but I have seen them bucked. It is not severe, but is esteemed humiliating. I have seen men tied up to a post; I can't swear that I saw them tied by the thumbs; but the punishment can either be made light or severe. I know one who was tied up for attempting to bribe my guard. The guard told me of it and I reported the case to Captain Alexander. Captain Alexander ordered him to be handcuffed and tied to a post. He sent for me and I examined his ropes. I loosened them and he was afterwards set at liberty. There were two connected in the bribing and they were Confederate soldiers.

Question. Do you know Riggs?

Answer. Yes; I do.

Question. Do the prisoners like him?

Answer. Yes; they do as one of the wardens.

Question. Do you know Caphart?

Answer. I don't think him inhuman if prisoners don't resist him hard; I don't consider him kind by any means. On one occasion Caphart while having two prisoners—Dennis and O'Connor—in charge one of the prisoners knocked a guard down and Caphart ordered the guard to fire, which they did not do.

Question. Do you know of any men shot there?

Answer. One of my guard shot a man who was attempting to escape. The orders are not to shoot a man of whom there was a possibility of capturing.

Question. Were these orders from the captain?

Answer. Yes; but I don't know that the orders were peremptory to shoot every one.

Question. Is there any necessity of shooting deranged men?

Answer. I did not see the shooting; never heard of that; I didn't speak of that.

Question. Did you ever hear of orders to the guard by the military commandant of prisoners to kill them were they to put their heads out of the windows?

Answer. Persistent effort in that way would insure their firing upon because it was against the rules.

Question (by Captain ALEXANDER). The night that Riggs and Dillard had the fight Riggs says I was drunk; was he not drunk or under the influence of liquor?

Answer. I heard he was, sir.

Question. Do you think I am a cruel man?

Answer. No, sir; I do not think so.

Question. I have sometimes hard cases to deal with?

Answer. You have some of the hardest cases in the Confederacy. I have heard of no persons being privately punished; all openly, and exhibitions for the public.

Question. Has the captain no disposition to be cruel?

Answer. No, sir.

Question. Nor Caphart?

Answer. Good officer, sir.

Question. Ever see Allen drunk?

Answer. I have seen him in liquor.

Question. How many times have you seen Riggs drunk?

Answer. He was very drunk once from the way he acted.

Question. Did he get *mania a potu?*

Answer. I don't know.

HENRY EDENBOROUGH sworn.

By the COMMITTEE:

Question. What are you?

Answer. I was a captain in the East India Royal Navy. I came through from Washington in November last. The Yankees had taken my papers and I was taken and locked up in Castle Thunder by order of the Secretary of War. I experienced there excellent treatment by Captain Alexander. I had a good room and opportunity to see the treatment of other prisoners. Never heard of harsh treatment; never experienced any myself. Any person who conforms to the rules will never be harshly treated. I have visited and commanded military prisons in Europe, in Naples, Sardinia, in 1860 and 1861; have visited and seen the hulks in India and China, and have seen nothing so lenient as at Castle Thunder in America. In regard to the rations I consider them fine. I got my meals sent frequently from the hotels, and dined there often, and always got more than I wanted. Nothing was refused to come in to any of the prisoners. Many small favors the prisoners were the recipients of. Men being sent off to their regiments were allowed to go into town under guard to get clothing. I have seen prisoners leave the prison who would take an affectionate and cordial leave of the captain and express regrets to him at parting.

Question. Do you know of any soldiers put in as comfortable quarters as you occupied?

Answer. Yes; the citizens' room was very comfortable indeed, and I have seen men put there.

Question. Then it depends on general appearance and conduct how treated?

Answer. Yes; it depends upon behavior in a great measure.

Question. Did the Secretary of War order your release?

Answer. No; my arrest was by order of the Secretary of War, and my release was effected through the courts.

Question (by Captain ALEXANDER). Do you think me a cruel man?

Answer. No, not exactly; but you make men toe the mark.

Question. Did you ever see Riggs drunk?

Answer. Yes; he came in my room once very drunk.

Question (by Captain ALEXANDER). Have you been offered a position in the Confederate Army?

Answer. Yes; major of artillery.

Question (by the COMMITTEE). Then you consider the punishments at Castle Thunder humane in the highest degree?

Answer. Yes, I do; considering.

Question. Would you take it as a mild punishment to be stripped naked and whipped upon the bare back without the order of a court-martial?

Answer. Well, in the service I belonged to whipping was an ordinary punishment. It was not considered a great indignity in the English service to be whipped with a cat o' nine tails.

Question. Is that all you know?

Answer. That's all I know.

—

WEDNESDAY, *April 22, 1863.*

JOHN ADAMS sworn:

I am from this city and have been in Castle Thunder seven months for leaving my regiment without leave and going home.

By the COMMITTEE:

Question. What was your treatment there?

Answer. Well, I was treated pretty tolerably rough. The charge against me was never established. There was an attempt to bribe the sentinel and I was taken and handcuffed and ironed around a post and tied up by my thumbs with a rope, my toes just touching the floor. I was in that condition for one hour or more when Captain Bossieux came along and released me. Then I was put into the sweat house, the floor of which was covered with mud and water. I was kept there two days and nights. It was in March, 1862, I think, and very cold. There was no dry spot in it. I could only stand up in it half bent.

Question. How were you fed?

Answer. I wasn't fed at all. I got nothing except what I bought from the commissary. I happened to have some money. I was put into the back yard and kept there a day and a half. I was bucked once, with a relief of fifteen or twenty minutes at intervals.

Question. Were your wrists tied tight then?

Answer. Yes; I can show the scars of handcuffs on my wrists now.

Question. Were you ever before a court-martial?

Answer. Yes. I was sent to wear a ball and chain for six months and to be sent to my company. The reason I don't go to my company is the captain wants me to stay here.

Question. Are your thumbs swollen from the tying up?

Answer. Yes; it was very painful. I have seen others tied up like me.

Question. Have you seen parties whipped without the authority of a court-martial?

Answer. Yes; some five or six. Their offense was stealing from other prisoners.

Question. How many lashes did they receive?

Answer. Some five or six and some more. Captain Alexander was present and said once: "Damn him, give him hell; if he don't need it now he will." He seemed to take delight in punishing us and he had a very rough manner in the administration of his punishments.

Question. Has his general deportment been such that you consider him cruel and inhuman?

Answer. Yes, I do; and I think it gave him pleasure to punish the prisoners.

Question. Do you know anything about the shooting of men at the Castle?

Answer. Yes; I know of the man who was shot at for sitting in the window. The sentinel ordered him to get out of the window. I don't know whether he got out or not, but he fired and put a buckshot through his hat.

Question. Was that by order of Captain Alexander?

Answer. I have heard him tell the sentinel to shoot the first man who put his head out of the window.

Question. Do you know Caphart?

Answer. Yes, sir; and he is no gentleman. He is a harsh and cruel man. Mr. Allen is rough spoken and I have heard him speak so when a kind word would have done as well.

Question. Did you ever see Mr. Allen drunk?

Answer. I have seen him out of the way four or five times; never saw him so far gone that he couldn't attend to his business.

Question. Do you know Riggs?

Answer. Yes; he is a kind man and all the prisoners like him.

Question. Do you know prisoners who like Captain Alexander?

Answer. Yes; some speak in favor of him.

Question. Do you think if Riggs had commanded there you would hear of any fighting or throwing of bones?

Answer. I don't believe they would; we would get along well. I never heard of prisoners who had made their arrangements to escape and would not because it was Riggs' night on.

Question (by Mr. WARD). When you were tied up by the thumbs did you not ask me to let you down?

Answer. Yes; you let me go.

Question. Wasn't the rope around your wrists and thumbs and over the nail and not around your thumbs?

Answer. I don't recollect now.

Question. What about your attempt to bribe the guard?

Answer. The money was sent to me for that purpose. I had not been accused of stealing.

—

FRIDAY, *April 24, 1863.*

The testimony for the defense was commenced. Mr. Farrar, M. D., made a statement of facts that fell under his notice while visiting the Castle in the capacity of one of the medical committee appointed to inspect the sanitary condition of the prisons and hospitals. The impression made upon his mind was that every care was taken of the prisoners that it was possible to take. This feature and the well ordered condition of everything about the prison was remarked by all the committee.

Capt. JACKSON WARNER, assistant quartermaster and assistant commissary, sworn.

Question. How long have you known Captain Alexander?

Answer. Since June, 1861—never before.

Question. Did you ever see him intoxicated?

Answer. I never saw him drunk but I suppose he drinks sometimes. I always found him attentive to his duties. I see him twice a week or oftener. I never saw or heard of him being drunk.

Question. What do you think of his treatment of prisoners?

Answer. I know nothing of his associations with the prison. I never heard him curse in my life. Think he is a member of church.

Question. Did you ever see him treat a prisoner roughly?

Answer. Never in my life.

Question. What are your ideas of the management of the prison?

Answer. I always thought the prison was managed well, and I have had opportunities to see and know. I have no prison experience myself.

Question. How long have you known Captain Alexander?

Answer. Since June, 1861; and since that time intimately so.

Question. Do you know any instances where Captain Alexander showed kindnesses to prisoners?

Answer. Yes, I do. In the case of Mr. L'Hommedieu, my clerk. He was put into the Castle for drunkenness. He had a sick wife at home and I went to Captain Alexander and stating the case asked him to let him go home and I would be responsible for his return. He did so and the next morning he reported. He was again arrested when sent to his regiment and again released on his parole by Captain Alexander upon a statement of facts I represented to him.

Question. In what room was he confined?

Answer. In the room in which the clerk slept so he told me.

Question. Do you know anything in regard to the case [waste] of Government property?

Answer. I never saw any waste. If waste had existed I would have taken notice of it as it is my business.

WILLIAM F. WATSON, C. S. commissioner, sworn.

Captain ALEXANDER. Judge, some complaints have been made of my treatment of lawyers coming to the Castle on business. You have been there frequently; tell the committee how you were treated and how I deal with the profession.

Answer. I am a practicing lawyer and have frequently called at the Castle on business. I have always been treated by Captain Alexander with uniform kindness; not only by the captain himself but by all his officers. I had no difficulty at all in gaining access to the prisoner I wished to see. All I had to do was to go [to] the proper officer and they were either sent down to me or I up to them. So far as the character of the majority of the prisoners are concerned I must say, to express it in common parlance, they are a hard crowd. It must require great coolness and determination to manage them. I as commissioner have had some of them before me.

Question. Do you regard the captain as a cruel man?

Answer. No; I should say he was rather of a kindly disposition, rather impulsive. He can manage by an appeal about as well as any official I know.

Question. Do you think Captain Alexander a man not to be swayed from his purpose?

Answer. I consider him impulsive but positive; one to do a thing under the excitement of a moment.

Question. Do you think the prisoners could be managed better under a milder or kinder man?

Answer. Mild men are not always the best for such posts; a little blending of the severe is better.

JOHN DE BUTTS, M. D., sworn.

I am surgeon of Castle Thunder Hospital. So far as I have opportunities of observation I regard the management of the prison as good, very good. I have never had any prison experience before.

By Captain ALEXANDER:

Question. Have I not told you, doctor, that your orders in regard to the sick were supreme?

Answer. Yes; you have told me so.

Question. Do you think I am a cruel man?

Answer. I never saw any cruelty practiced by you.

Question. Doctor, what was Mr. Bland discharged from the post of steward of the hospital for?

Answer. Moral incompetency I call it.

Question (by the COMMITTEE). What is moral incompetency?

Answer. He was in the habit of appropriating the hospital liquor to his own private use. No one else had access to it for he had the key. I don't know how much was taken but a great deal more was used than went to the patients.

Question (by Captain ALEXANDER). Is Kirby, the prisoner, comfortably fixed now?

Answer. Yes; he has the best room in the prison; the best ventilated and situated.

Question (by the CHAIRMAN). Has Kirby the privilege of buying his meals?

Captain ALEXANDER (to committee). Gentlemen, I wish to prove by Doctor De Butts that I never refused an appeal of sickness. When a man is to be branded I direct the surgeon to indicate where the iron is to be placed and when men are sentenced to be whipped the lashes are remitted if in the opinion of the surgeon the party's health is unequal to the punishment.

Question (by the CHAIRMAN). Do you know of any prisoners being placed in the yard of the Castle?

Answer. Yes; a number were confined there. They were brought in at night. I knew nothing of the whipping; never saw it done. I know of one man who escaped and was shot, and another was shot at for blackguarding the sentinel. His face was lacerated by splinters and I dressed it for him.

Col. ROBERT MAYO, member of the Legislature from Henrico County, sworn.

Captain ALEXANDER. You have known me a long time, colonel; tell the committee what you know of me.

Answer. My first acquaintance with Captain Alexander was on an occasion of a visit to him in his official capacity in relation to some abuse near my residence, which he speedily caused to be corrected. I found him pleasant and kind. This was when he was at Castle Godwin. When he moved down to Castle Thunder I saw him oftener. A great many of my neighbors were in the guard and I was frequently called to see prisoners. I often remarked that I never saw so many prisoners together under the same circumstances kept so orderly. They were as sprightly as any people I ever saw. It was wonderful to me.

Mr. WARD. Colonel, tell about the shooting you saw there.

Answer. One day I was about going into the Castle; a sentinel was about shooting a prisoner at a window for a violation of the rules when Captain Alexander interfered, ordered him to desist—not to shoot; that he would order the prisoner to be put in irons instead. I saw two prisoners shot at the Libby Prison, but Captain Alexander had nothing to do with that.

Question (by the COMMITTEE). What other kinds of punishment did you see there?

Answer. I saw prisoners wearing a barrel shirt, but that inflicts no pain.

Question. Is it not degrading to the soldier?

Answer. The one I saw did not think so; he was jesting about it.

Question (by Mr. WARD). From your knowledge of Captain Alexander and his treatment of prisoners, do you think him a cruel man?

Answer. I do not consider him a cruel man, by no means. If the prisoners conduct themselves well there is no trouble whatever.

Question. Do you know Mr. Childrey?

Answer. Yes, and a more honest and correct man cannot be found in the city of Richmond. I also know Mr. Caphart and Mr. Thomas, another officer at the prison and one of my neighbors. I have seen them all in the discharge of their duties and found them very attentive. I have called on Captain Alexander to send a squad of men to my neighborhood when disturbed and peace has been restored.

Capt. THOMAS P. TURNER, commandant of the Libby Prison, sworn.

By Captain ALEXANDER:

Question. Captain, describe in your own terms your ideas of my treatment of prisoners.

Answer. Well, I regard the prison as exceedingly well regulated; the discipline maintained has been good while the character of the inmates is the worst in the land. I regard none of the means employed to control them too severe or unnecessary punishment.

Question. What kind of punishment do you inflict when any is necessary?

Answer. For slight offenses I make them "mark time" and for graver offenses I buck them.

Question. Your prisoners are Yankees and not Confederate soldiers?

Answer. Yes, sir; all of them.

Question (by Mr. WARD). You have sent your worst cases to the Castle have you not?

Answer. Yes, I have.

Question. Is the order to shoot an escaping prisoner a standing order?

Answer. No; I make my own orders and have them approved by General Winder. I would allow no man to be shot who could be caught without shooting.

Question. If a prisoner was to attempt to escape from your prison by running upstairs as one did at the Castle would you consider it the duty of that sentinel to shoot him?

Answer. Not unless that man was about to escape and there was no possibility of capturing him.

Question. Well, does a prisoner ever escape by running upstairs?

Answer. Not in my prison, sir.

Question. Would you investigate a case of the kind?

Answer. Yes, certainly, and report the facts to headquarters.

Question. Did you send a deranged man to Castle Thunder and who was killed there in attempting to escape?

Answer. No, sir; it was done by my predecessor.

Question. If a deranged man was brought to your prison would you not consider it your duty to warn all hands that he was deranged in order to guard against accidents or to confine him?

Answer. It would be very difficult to know what to do with him. The deranged man, Silas Richmond who was killed at the Castle was a Yankee. He passed the guard several times in my prison, but the guard understood he was crazy. As for keeping the prisoners in the yard at the Castle over night I don't know anything about that.

———

SATURDAY, *April 25, 1863.*

The testimony was resumed for the defense.

Capt. THOMAS P. TURNER recalled.

By Mr. WARD:

Question. Were you ever present at Castle Thunder when punishment was being inflicted?

Answer. Yes; I witnessed one whipping not by order of court-martial. I think General Winder authorized it. Three were whipped I think for maltreatment of other prisoners, stealing, &c. The lashes were laid on tolerably hard, one receiving twelve and the other six, and a third only three lashes. The lashes were laid on with a leather strap about eighteen inches long and weighing about one pound and a half. The lashes were laid on tolerably hard but left no mark; the skin was not broken. Captain Alexander had been instructed to administer twelve lashes, but he used his own discretion and lessened the number. After it was over he congratulated the prisoners on the manliness they exhibited and said he was sorry the necessity for the infliction of such punishment existed.

Question. Did you hear Captain Alexander say "Lay it on harder?"

Answer. No, sir. They were tied up by the wrists around a post except one who said he could not stand it and he was allowed to clasp his arms around the post.

The above was the only punishment I saw inflicted there. I know Captain Alexander well, am often with him and regard him as a kind man.

Question. Is Captain Alexander temperate?

Answer. I never saw him intoxicated in my life. I have seen him drink. He is a sociable man and will take a drink with his friends.

Question. What is the character of the inmates of the Castle; are they mutinous?

Answer. Their characters are various; some of the most desperate men in the Confederacy are there. I was for a time the officer of that post and all passed through my hands. Once I ordered the arrest of two of my guard and sent them to the Castle. They were no sooner put in the prisoners' room than they were set upon, beat, their clothing torn off and robbed of everything. The offenders in this offense were whipped. I don't think there is a cleaner prison anywhere. It is kept remarkably neat and orderly.

Question. Did you ever hear any complaints respecting Captain Alexander's conduct?

Answer. No, sir; not until this committee met. I know he is a strict disciplinarian and keeps things straight around him. His punishment is not more stringent than necessary I suppose. At my prison where all are Yankees I have no need for such modes of punishment. No robberies are committed among the prisoners for their money is all taken away from them when they enter and given back to them when they leave. This is to prevent bribery.

Mr. WARD. This plan was for some time in practice at the Castle, but the prisoners would hide it about their persons and in their boots.

Question. Have you.any instances of bribery?

Answer. No; nothing positive though there have been attempts.

Lieut. DENNIS CALLAHAN sworn:

I am the adjutant of the Castle and have been there three months.

By Mr. WARD:

Question. What is the general treatment of the prisoners?

Answer. In my opinion judging from the time I have been there the prisoners are treated as well as they could be under the circumstances.

Question. What is the character of the prisoners?

Answer. Some of them are of very bad repute. I have seen whipping and bucking as punishment for stealing.

Question. Are not the prisoners fed on soldiers' rations.

Answer. Yes; and as far as I know they get more to eat than our soldiers.

Question. Are not the soldiers among the prisoners as well dressed as the soldiers in the field?

Answer. As a general thing I should say they were. The captain has interested himself in obtaining clothing from the Government authorities.

JAMES JENNINGS sworn:

I have been six months in the Castle and am from Maryland. I left my company on sick leave and was walking around getting well when arrested. I broke out after two months' confinement and started for my company and was arrested and sent back, my company being disbanded.

By Mr. WARD:

Question. Have you been kindly treated?

Answer. Yes; as well as could be expected.

Question. Have you been punished?

Answer. No, sir; I was put in the cell four days; I thought that perfectly right. It was for writing a letter and sending it out of the prison without submitting it to the captain. The cell is not a comfortable place; it is dry but cold. I suffered from the cold and was fed on bread and water. I think I was kept there five days. I thought the letter would go quicker and surer by sending through private hands. I am seventeen years old. I don't know what I am detained for. .

JOHN DOYLE sworn:

I have been in the Castle now four weeks. I don't know Captain Alexander; would not know him if I was to see him. I am treated as well as the others, I reckon. I never was punished; in fact I don't deserve it. I was shot at once in the window, or at least I thought I was shot at; but I don't believe he intended to hit me, for I don't deserve it.

By Mr. WARD:

Question. Didn't a shot go through your hat?

Answer. Can't tell; there is a hole through it.

JAMES MCALISTER sworn:

I am a seaman and came from Wilmington, N. C. I came here when the war broke out. I have not been treated by Captain Alexander as a man should be treated. I have been tied up and flogged like a negro.

By Mr. WARD:

Question. How many lashes did you receive?

Answer. Twelve I think, and by Captain Alexander's order they were laid on as hard as I could well have stood it.

Question. Was the blood cut out of you?

Answer. No; but I was black and blue and was sore for a month afterwards. I was whipped with a strap three inches wide and the blows were laid on by Caphart. I have been bucked for four hours in front of the office entrance where everybody could see me. Bucking is not painful but it mortifies and makes one ashamed.

Question. Do you know of any other punishments?

Answer. Yes; I was shot at once for standing at a window and looking out. The ball passed my head and went up through the hospital which was full of patients.

Mr. Wynne, doorkeeper of the House of Representatives, detailed before the committee some circumstances of his treatment at the prison when he went down to summon some officers and the purport of his conversation with several witnesses, which not being to the point here is omitted.

———

MONDAY, *April 27, 1863.*

Hon. Judge OULD sworn.

By Captain ALEXANDER.

Question. You, as judge-advocate of the court-martial, can give the committee some idea of the character of the prisoners?

Answer. The most of the cases brought before me were cases of desertion, coupled with theft and cases of insubordination.

Question. Do you think I am a cruel man?

Answer. I do not know about that. I do not think you are.

Question. What do you think about me carrying out an order?

Answer. Being a military man you would see any reasonable order carried out. I have conversed at times with persons who have been in Castle Thunder and have questioned them as to their treatment there. Never heard them mention any cases of cruelty but generally the reverse. There has been half a dozen sentenced to be shot and two condemned to be hung. We have never resorted to the death penalty unless the case presented the two aggravated phases—first, desertion, and secondly, desertion in face of the enemy. I know nothing of the punishments by the commandant of the Castle; never visited it in my life that I know of. In all sentences of court-martial the lashes were laid on except in one instance.

Lieut. PETER CALLAHAN sworn.

By Captain ALEXANDER:

Question. What is my conduct toward the prisoners?

Answer. Your conduct toward the prisoners has been as kind as it well could be under the circumstances.

Question. What is my conduct toward visitors?

Answer. I always thought your conduct gentlemanly.

Question. One of the witnesses swore that he saw fifteen men bucked and gagged in the prison; did you ever see such punishment?

Answer. I never did, and never heard of a man being gagged there. I do not regard bucking as adding anything to the disgrace of a man who lays himself liable to be put in Castle Thunder.

Question. How do you know that these men were guilty of any crime? Innocent men are sometimes put there. Were those men that were bucked found guilty of any crime?

Answer. I do not know that they were. I have seen soldiers in the Army more severely punished than at Castle Thunder. Have heard of men standing on a barrel all day with the word "thief" written on their backs by order of their officers. Men are often bucked in the Army and tied up by the thumbs.

Question. What is the condition of Castle Thunder?

Answer. I believe it is very good.

Question. You inspect the prison every morning?

Answer. Almost every morning.

Question. Then it would be impossible for a man to lie in his filth behind the door without you knowing it?

Answer. It certainly would be difficult.

FREDERICK F. WILEY sworn.

By Captain ALEXANDER:

Question. How long have you been at the Castle?

Answer. Ever since it was established.

Question. How long have you known me?

Answer. Ever since you escaped from Fort McHenry.

Question. What is the condition of the prison?

Answer. As clean as such a place can be kept.

Question. What is the position of your room?

Answer. Where I can hear any conversation in the prisoners' room.

Question. What language have you heard Kirby use?

Answer. I have heard him curse General Winder and yourself and other officials.

Question. Did I ever do anything with him?

Answer. No; although it was reported to you.

Question. Is there a cell in the Castle that a man cannot stand up erect in?

Answer. No; there is not.

Question. What about the whipping?

Answer. I have seen eight men whipped without order of the court-martial and by order of General Winder.

Question. How many lashes did they receive?

Answer. I don't think they received six lashes apiece. Some of them were Yankee deserters and I have no doubt some of them were Confederate soldiers.

Question. Were all these men concerned in the beating of the old man who died?

Answer. The prisoners pointed them out and they were their accusers.

Question. What authority had General Winder or anybody else to whip a soldier on his bare back?

Answer. I don't know, sir.

Question. Do you know anything about prisoners being put out in the back yard?

Answer. Yes; they were put out there. They had fire and some of them had blankets. It was cold weather and the wood must have been furnished them or they could not have got it. There were about sixty men in the yard. Captain Alexander ordered me to pick out any that were sick and I picked out a number. The second night I picked out a number more who were sick.

Question. Were all these men guilty of attempting to blow up the building?

Answer. I don't know, sir.

Question. Is it reasonable to suppose these men would blow up the building and themselves with it?

Answer. There are men without one redeeming trait in their character; would be guilty of any crime from murder down.

TUESDAY, *April 28, 1863.*

The testimony for the defense was continued.

FREDERICK F. WILEY recalled.

By Captain ALEXANDER:

Question. Do you know the characters of McAlister, Shehan and Adams?

Answer. I was informed some months ago that they had made a rope to escape; went to McAlister's cell and asked him for it. He said he had none, and I made a search. McAlister resisted with a spade or shovel. The other had a razor and the other had a ball and chain. I defended myself and drew a pistol. I found the rope in McAlister's bag. These are the characters of men we have to deal with. I would not believe McAlister on oath. One-third of the blankets distributed there I believe are cut up to make ropes wherewith to escape. Men are brought there sometimes with plenty of clothing and blankets and if we were not careful they would all be stolen for the above purpose.

Question. What do you think of Caphart?

Answer. I think him one of the best officers I ever saw. If you give him an order he will carry it out. I have roomed with him and consider him a kind-hearted man. I never saw him strike a man unless he had cause.

Question. On the night the prisoners were put into the yard were not those who looked sick taken back?

Answer. Yes; by your order and I helped to select them.

Question. Do you remember people on the street being in danger from missiles thrown from the windows?

Answer. Yes; and the mayor sent down word that it must be stopped.

Question. Did you not report the conduct of prisoners to the commanding general?

Answer. Yes; and he sent an order to have the guilty whipped.

Question. Have I not always expressed solicitude for the sick?

Answer. Yes; you supplied many of them with clothing obtained from the battle-fields around Richmond.   Men are brought there very badly off for clothing.

Question. Do you know Mr. Riggs?

Answer. Yes, sir; I know him.

Question. Did you ever see him drunk?

Answer. Yes; very drunk and abusive to you in your office.   You said you would discharge him but for his wife and children.

Question. Do you recollect the time Riggs went into the citizens' room?

Answer. I have known Riggs to be in there with the prisoners, disloyal persons, Unionists, &c., up to midnight, associating with them, drinking whisky.   My room adjoins the citizens' room and I can hear everything said.

Question. Do you think Captain Alexander a cruel man?

Answer. No, sir.

Question (by Captain ALEXANDER). How did I treat my soldiers I took down to the army?

Answer. Better than most of them in the army.

Question. Was the Yankee who was shot running in the direction that he could escape?

Answer. The steps he was running up lead to a porch from whence he could have escaped.   (The witness related the circumstances of the escape of the prisoner from the Libby Prison and his reception at the Castle for safe-keeping.)   I did not know he was crazy and was not told so.   He called me to him before he died and asked my forgiveness for anything against him.   (Witness related the killing of Charles Carroll, alias Byzer, over the portico while attempting to escape.)   I believe Campbell was the cause of his death as he got Carroll to draw the fire of the guard so he could get out unharmed.

Question. How long have you been at the prison?

Answer. Since its establishment.

Question. How many men have you seen whipped there without court-martial?

Answer. Only eight.   They were whipped for beating an old man sixty years of age from which he liked to have died, and for stealing.   There is no order to take the money or valuables of prisoners.   If they want to give them up we take them and give them receipts.   This was until recently.

Question. What is the condition of the yard?

Answer. It is a hard dirt floor or clay.

By Captain ALEXANDER:

Question. It appears from the evidence that one man was tied up by the thumbs.

Answer. Yes; the only man I ever saw and by your order I lowered him down. His offense was stealing money and beating a negro.

Question. Did I not punish a man for punishing a servant without my order?

Answer. Yes; your orders are to that effect.

Lieutenant BOSSIEUX sworn.

By Captain ALEXANDER:

Question. Do you remember the putting of some men in the yard?

Answer. In one instance a number were in the yard for attempting to blow up the building with powder.   The first night others attempted to cut out.   I staid there with the guard and caught fifteen when they came out.   It was very pleasant weather. On another occasion when some men were in the yard there came up a storm and I notified Mr. Ward and they were taken in. On another occasion four Yankees were put out, and it snowed. They were taken in.

Question. Do you think me a cruel man?

Answer. No, sir; I do not.

Question. Are not the doors of the cells often left open?

Answer. Yes; I have opened them myself often.

Question (by Mr. WARD). What is your opinion of the character of the men there?

Answer. Yes; there are some of the worst men in the world and I don't believe there is an hour that they are not concocting some plan to escape. I don't think they could be managed with less strictness.

Question. Do you know of a cell a man cannot stand up in?

Answer. No, sir.

Question. You never knew of any secret punishment?

Answer. No, sir; the prisoners are generally brought out where all can see them.

Question. What month was it the men were put into the yard?

Answer. It was pleasant weather. I was out all that night without my overcoat. They staid there two days and the third day they were taken up.

Question. Do you know of any whipping?

Answer. I have heard of whipping; never saw it. The whipping was by order of court-martial and was laid on by the corporal of police of the Castle.

Question. Do you know any punishment not of an ordinary character?

Answer. I recollect one circumstance. It was two men tied up to a post. Don't know whether by the thumbs or the wrists. Was told it was for robbing some prisoners upstairs. Don't know how long they remained in that position.

Question (by Captain ALEXANDER). Do you remember me telling you once to abstain from shooting some whose intended escape we had discovered?

Answer. Yes.

Question (by the COMMITTEE). What are your instructions in regard to prisoners putting their heads out of the windows?

Answer. We warn them and if they persist the sentinels fire over them. I remember when on Franklin street some of the prisoners threw the sashes out of the windows and tried to hit some of my men. They also threw bricks from the front windows. They climbed to the chimney and took bricks and threw them down.

Question. How many men have been shot by your guard?

Answer. None by guard. I only know of two shot there at all, the crazy Yankee and the man Carroll. We could have shot a hundred men there if the sentinels had been so disposed.

Question (by Captain ALEXANDER). Then you think if the prisoners behave themselves they will be well treated?

Answer. Yes, I do; I know it.

GEORGE W. WAYMACK, a prisoner, sworn.

By Captain ALEXANDER:

Question. Do you think a man put in the Castle if he behave well would he not be treated well?

Answer. I do.

Question. Did you ever see any act of cruelty there?

Answer. I never did, sir.

Question. When you were sick did I not let you go home?

Answer. You did.

Question. When before the court-martial did I not act as your counsel?

Answer. Yes; you did.

Question (by the COMMITTEE). Where are you from?

Answer. I am from Manchester and am in the Castle on the charge of desertion.

—

WEDNESDAY, *April 29, 1863.*

Judge BAXTER sworn.

Question. Judge, state what you know of the condition and treatment of prisoners.

Answer. Captain Alexander has sent for me to examine into such cases as presented mitigating circumstances and recommended their discharge or detention as the case might be. I have opportunities of seeing Captain Alexander and the prisoners. My belief is that he is peculiarly qualified to control such a body. I think his course has been one of great humanity. At his suggestion I have discharged prisoners. There have been cases of wrong imprisonment and hardship. The management of the prison my belief is has been conducted with ability and by measures of stringency required by the character of the prisoners. What was the police regulations of the cells I don't know.

Question. Do you know Kirby?

Answer. I was once at the prison for the purpose of examining into cases and Kirby was in the room, and I requested him to leave and he complained. Captain Alexander had indulged him, so as to exclude him from the mass of prisoners.

Question (by Captain ALEXANDER). Judge, do you think I am a cruel man?

Answer. I would rather take you to be a kind man but firm and resolute and not disposed to allow any of your orders to be transgressed.

Here testimony closed.

Testimony of DENNIS O'CONNOR—Continued.

Prisoner is still required to report every morning at Castle Thunder upon parole. Mr. F. F. Wiley, an officer in Castle Thunder, cursed and abused witness this morning; charged him with being a thief. The abuse was caused by witness having been called upon to testify before the committee. Wiley has been in the habit of abusing witness. He told Wiley that he was in his power and compelled to submit to his abuse. Wiley cursed the Irish generally and is in the habit of abusing prisoners who do not report upon their comrades. Witness is acquainted with Lieutenant Bossieux; don't know what character he bears. At one time he heard Mr. Wiley curse a prisoner who was in irons. Witness intended to join Captain Rodgers' company, Robertson's battalion; denies having voted in the election for officers; never joined Nineteenth Mississippi Regiment; never was a substitute for any one.

Testimony of Capt. W. N. STARKE—Continued.

Witness states that he has been assigned to duty by General Winder for the purpose of investigating all cases of political, citizen and military prisoners and of obtaining all the necessary evidence in relation thereto. Has been in the office but a short time and the failure to bring to trial or discharge many prisoners is attributed to the difficulty in obtaining the necessary evidence both for the prosecution and defense. Witness has been in the prison several times and found it well regulated and cleanly.

W. N. STARKE,
Captain and Assistant Adjutant-General.

Mr. RIGGS' testimony—Continued.

Question. State what you know of Mr. Wiley's treatment of prisoners.

Answer. It is brutal in my opinion. He cursed Webster who was hung the other day while Webster was in double irons. His language is brutal to prisoners, in my opinion.

Question. Was any complaint ever made to Captain Alexander or any report ever made in regard to Wiley's treatment of prisoners?

Answer. I don't know.

Question. You being there as acting assistant warden do you not think it was your duty to report all such things?

Answer. You told me to make reports in writing. I did not consider it my duty.

Question. Did you not curse the guard on one occasion?

Answer. I have no recollection of so doing.

STATEMENTS TAKEN UNDER OATH AND MADE BEFORE ROBERT D. WARD, ATTORNEY.

Statement of Lewis J. Blankenship.

Question. How long have you been in Castle Thunder?

Answer. I came about the 29th of July, 1862, and have been wardmaster of the hospital most of the time.

Question. State whether you know that Kirby had a conversation with McAlister, Adams and Shehan in regard to giving testimony before the Congressional committee. If so state all you know about it.

Answer. On the day that Mr. Kirby was subpœnaed to go before this committee Mr. Shehan sent down into No. 4 room and got James McAlister out and asked me to pass him into No. 2 hospital with Mr. Kirby, and there all three of these men consulted over the evidence which they were to give before the committee. Mr. Shehan made a statement of his evidence which he was going to testify to before the committee; wrote it out and gave it to McAlister. Mr. Shehan also wrote out Mr. Kirby's evidence and gave it to McAlister, and McAlister gave his evidence to Shehan and Kirby. Each one of the three had a written statement of the testimony which they proposed to give before the committee. The morning that Mr. Adams was summoned to go before the committee Mr. Shehan took Mr. Adams into Mr. Kirby's room, and he and Mr. Kirby told Adams what they had testified to, and they wanted Mr. Adams to come as near as he could stating the same things before the committee, and also told him as near as they could their own testimony and requested him to repeat the same as near as he could.

Question. Do you think there was a combination on the part of these men to injure Captain Alexander if possible?

Answer. I do, sir. I know that from the conversation they have had with me.

Question. State what conversation you allude to.

Answer. I have heard Mr. Shehan say that Captain Alexander was nothing but a God damned loafer; that he intended to get him out of here if he possibly could; that nobody suited this place but Mr. Riggs, and that if Mr. Riggs were captain of this prison he could get out whenever he pleased; that Captain Alexander was not fit to have command of a parcel of hogs. Long before this committee was appointed I have heard McAlister say that Captain Alexander had done all he could to have him shot and that if he ever had it in his power he would have his revenge out of him. About two days before he was summoned he said every dog had his day and that his day had just come. Mr. Kirby, Mr. Shehan and McAlister all knew that the committee was going to enter into the examination of Castle Thunder, and the three wrote a letter to Mr. Riggs about the committee before it was appointed and after Mr. Riggs had been discharged from Castle Thunder. I don't know that Mr. Riggs ever got the letter but I am confident the letter went out of the building by private hands. That letter stated that a committee was going to be appointed to examine into things here at Castle Thunder and they wished him to lay the letter before Congress, and if he did not like to do it himself to give it to Mr. Bland, the hospital steward.

Question. State what was the character of these men.

Answer. In regard to McAlister I staid in No. 4 room with him for about four weeks, and during the time I was in the room I don't think a night passed that some robbery of clothes, hats, shoes or money was not committed by some one in the adjacent large room and handed to McAlister through a crack or hole which he had cut through the partition which separated the two rooms, and received by him and sold by him whenever he got opportunity to sell. Frequently these stolen things were handed to McAlister through the crack by Shehan, who was then on his parole and acting as corporal of the police about the building. I don't know anything dishonest about Mr. Kirby, but I know of Mr. Adams having stolen a pair of boots and selling them to McAlister; and also he stole four sheets out of the hospital which I found in his knapsack. He also stole a blanket from the hospital which I also found in his possession.

Question. What is the conduct of the men generally who have been in Castle Thunder?

Answer. The largest proportion of the men are real rascals, guilty of cutting the building for the purpose of escaping, fighting, abusing each other, committing robberies and bribery of sentinels.

Question. Have you seen any punishments inflicted in this prison?

Answer. None, sir, but what I thought were well deserved. I saw a man of Wheat's battalion whipped for desertion by sentence of court-martial. I heard Captain Alexander tell him he was sorry to have it to do, but he was obliged to do it. Samuel Lebrick, the name of the man who was whipped, shook hands with the corporal of the police and asked him for a drink of whisky, which was given him by order of Captain Alexander. He was whipped very lightly.

Statement of J. B. Evans.

Question. How long have you been in Castle Thunder?

Answer. I have been here about ten weeks.

Question. Do you know of any combination among the prisoners to injure the reputation of Captain Alexander in any manner? If so please state it.

Answer. I saw Shehan, Adams and McAlister before they went before the committee go to Mr. Kirby and they asked him what they should say before the committee. I have heard McAlister and Adams both say that they would swear to anything to injure the captain. Adams said that if he had one more chance to go before the committee he would swear that Captain Alexander was always drunk.

Question. What is the character of these men?

Answer. They are of a desperate character. Adams told me he had been in the penitentiary twice. I have heard Shehan say that he has received money from prisoners to get them out when he was corporal of the police, and I heard Adams say that he had taken $50 from Captain Callan. I heard McAlister send word to Kirby to have him summoned; that he would like to have a chance to swear against the captain. He would do all he could to injure him.

Question. Do you know whether Mr. Kirby ever sent out letters privately from the building?

Answer. Yes; I have seen him send them out and receive them through private sources.

STATE OF VIRGINIA, *City of Richmond, to wit:*

I, Robert D. Ward, do certify that the foregoing statements made by Lewis J. Blankenship and J. B. Evans were sworn to by them respectively before me. Given under my hand this 28th day of April, 1863.

R. D. WARD,
Notary Public.

WALKER'S ARTILLERY BATTALION,
Camp Maury, near Milford, April 26, 1863.

[Capt. G. W. ALEXANDER.]

DEAR CAPTAIN: The summons of Hon. C. C. Herbert directing me to appear before the special committee of Congress on the 23d instant did not reach me until yesterday, the 25th instant. I immediately applied for leave of absence to enable me to obey the summons but found that no officer of the army will be allowed to take the cars except upon the special order of General Lee.

My application for two days leave, inclosing the summons, has been forwarded through the regular channels to General Lee and it will be over a week before it can be heard from. I fear that the deliberations of the committee will be closed before I can obtain permission to leave camp.

If you think it important for me to appear before the committee without delay you might procure an order from the Secretary of War directing my immediate appearance.

If the committee anticipates remaining in session over a week please advise me of the fact and I will go down as soon as General Lee's permit is received.

I assure you it will afford me pleasure to bear testimony to the systematic and able manner in which you have managed the provost prison under your charge and to the humanity and kindness with which you have treated the prisoners in your custody.

You have the greatest talent for controlling and managing desperate characters, and I have often said that I do not believe there is another man in the Southern Confederacy who can fill your present position.

Hoping that the report of the committee will triumphantly vindicate you, as it will do, from the malicious charges which have been preferred against you,

I remain, your friend,

GREENLEE DAVIDSON.

—

HEADQUARTERS DEPARTMENT OF HENRICO,
Richmond, April 28, 1863.

Captain ALEXANDER.

SIR: In reply to your communication I state that in consequence of the violent proceedings of the prisoners in blowing up the building, garroting and using slung-shots upon the newly-arrived prisoners, robbing and endangering their lives, I gave you orders to punish these ruffians severely and if necessary to resort to corporeal punishment.

Respectfully,

JNO. H. WINDER,
Brigadier-General.

—

Captain Alexander's Defense.

CASTLE THUNDER, *Richmond, April 13, 1863.*

*To the Honorable Committee of the House of Representatives, C. S. A.,
for the investigation of Castle Thunder.*

GENTLEMEN: Bonaparte said that "the first requisite in an officer was health, the second temper; without the first the second is seldom found, and without the second a good officer, mingling the gentleman with the commander, cannot exist."

> The elephant is never won with anger,
> Nor should the man who would reclaim the lion
> Take him by the teeth.

There is nothing so degrading to an officer of rank as an intemperate reprimand, and before his inferiors. If he be respectful, as he would have others respect him, *and forgets not that he is a gentleman*, his conduct is said to have merited the rebuke from his not having defended it. If both parties lose their temper a court-martial follows and neither party gains by the result. To make a good officer a man must be a gentleman, and they are inseparable. The man who cannot command his tongue is the worst man to intrust with any command. The supercilious and the arrogant always meet from men endowed with common sense the contempt such frivolity deserves.

So much for my opinion of a man placed at the head of any public affair. Now, I will proceed to state in as concise a manner as possible my views which I respectfully submit to your honorable notice. This subject I feel I cannot handle, although fraught with some interest to you and much anxiety to me. When this cruel war was forced upon us on the secession of Virginia I was among the first to resign from the old Navy and take up arms. I chose the Army, and shouldering my musket enrolled myself as a private. My career and advancement since then is known. I followed my unfortunate leader far within the enemy's lines, *never questioning an order*, but obeyed all; never asking, where go we? We fell. I suffered; but, thank God, escaped from the tyranny of the "usurper of rights" and have tried to deal them some good blows. My injuries placed me in command of this post. Here I have tried to do my duty, and no matter what may be said or done you cannot keep this strong right arm idle; it shall work either as an officer or private until we achieve what we are all struggling for—the vindication of a sacred right—self-government. I trust I have clearly demonstrated to this honorable body the character of the men who have been committed to my care—the murderer, the robber, the deserter, the substitute deserter, the pickpocket, and worst of all the skulker—the man who by his skulking endangers his comrades, therefore worse than the murderer—the spy, the reconstructionist, the disloyal; all, all that are inimical to our glorious cause are thrust upon me. Why? Because this Castle is the only penitentiary the Confederacy has. I have proved that rules and regulations were regularly distributed; that they were repeatedly told that punishment would follow a persistency in wrong-doing; that the place only acquired a bad name by the conduct of the fiends that inhabited it, and that punishment was only resorted to when it became absolutely necessary and it had become unsafe for a man to enter the wards. I have proved that while our noble army was in the field subsisting on corn these fiends were being fed on full rations and then would refuse positively to rejoin their suffering comrades, and could only be forced there at the point of a bayonet.

That some men were whipped on the back is true. *Does it appear in the voluminous evidence* that there was a single man not by the order of a court-martial or one from a State represented by any representative in our legislative halls? It was represented by one of the witnesses that men were tied up by the thumbs and gagged. The witness, who by the way was proven to have been discharged from his place for "moral incapacity," is certainly mistaken, or saw it in one of his drunken dreams, for it does not appear in the evidence, *and I say it is not so.* In fact I think that if those horrid brutalities existed the witnesses or whoever made the statement were very culpable to report them only when they were turned disgracefully away from this place. A man who knows a wrong to exist and reports it not is more guilty than the wrong-doer. I might here state that evidence also shows that when the hordes of the invader threatened close [to] our walls I did not rest safe within but threw myself into the breach, and when the smoke of battle receded and we were again free from their accursed presence I turned my attention to the care of those brave men who shed their blood in our defense and who, maimed, were borne to my doors. Many remember the little hospital of the "Angel of Mercy" where thirty beds were always kept and the brave were cared for by a pale little Virginia woman—my wife. Do the records show the loss of a single limb or life from that hospital or do they show a single bill paid by the Confederate States Government for its support? I do not like, gentlemen, to recount these things, but I am a stranger to you and I would rather you would condemn me to be shot than to promulgate upon such evidence as you have had before you from your legislative halls that I am cruel. There are men in your honorable body who know me and know my career. All men conversant with military law know that if a man persists in passing a sentry without the countersign he risks his life. That two men have been shot here is also true; one an Irishman who substituted for a gentleman from Halifax, and the same night deserted while in sight of the enemy, afterwards captured, locked up here and persisting in an attempt to escape was killed. Another, a Yankee, who rushing past the sentry attempted to fly by the back entrance—killed; they say he was crazy. The sentry did not know it nor I; or I might for I believe one-half of them are crazy.

I have demonstrated here before this honorable committee that some characters that have been committed here to my charge have been without a redeeming point. I have appealed in every way to them until at last endurance was worn out and corporeal punishment did much good. Does it appear from the evidence that Southern volunteers were ever struck except by Officer Causey in self-defense? The committee have been made aware of the immense number of prisoners I have handled—*thousands*—and yet it appears that only about twenty have been punished. Does that look cruel?

Are not soldiers in camp when guilty of little peccadilloes bucked and made to ride a cannon or a wooden horse? These fiends are only bucked; is that comparison cruel? This being a receptacle for all that is bad would I not have been justifiable had I been present when that master-fiend Webster, who expiated his crimes on the gallows, contemplated murder and attempted to escape to have shot him or ordered my guard to do so?

Have I not proven by the very prisoners themselves whom I have taken *ad libitum* that the character of many of the prisoners is terrible and that I have been lenient? Have I not proven that I have done many acts of kindness and charity—yea, many, far outnumbering the alleged cruelties? Have I not proven that the only witnesses who seem to think I have been the least cruel knew of these things before and only reported them when they had been sent away from prison as being no further of any use? Have I not proven my vigilance and strict adherence to right and my energy in carrying out all orders of my superiors? Have I not proven my economy and personal supervision to prevent extravagance or waste of all Government stores committed to my charge? Have I not proven that by my own individual exertions I have clothed many prisoners who were being sent to the field? When as some of the witnesses say were men exposed to the weather? Have I not proven their infernal character, and were not their comrades at that time whom they had shamefully deserted fighting our battles and sleeping on the cold ground without tent or other cover than the canopy of heaven?

I would here say a few words about the witnesses examined. Mr. Bland, a hospital steward, whom it appears from the evidence was a man not fit to be about a public institution; his depravity was such that he was disgracefully ordered away. He says he was five months in a Yankee prison and saw better treatment. I rather think that that argues badly for Mr. Bland, for while I was a prisoner among that hateful people the only one I saw treated well was one who sycophant-like courted favor at their hands. I was kept in a cell seven by four for three weeks, that cell underground and no window; moreover prisoners of war are entitled to better treatment than murderers, deserters, spies, &c.

Witness No. 2. Kirby, the spy. I hardly think it fair to take prisoner's evidence; but I waive that and challenge the whole prison. His evidence shows that although he is incarcerated as that most hateful of all things, a spy, yet he is put in the best room in the Castle, has a fire, good bed and is allowed to purchase anything from the outside that he may require. Oh! gentlemen, does this look cruel? And then he is only removed from this room when the true instincts of the beast were developed and he proves to be a lowborn blackguard.

Witness No. 3. One Adams, who served out a term in the penitentiary, was pardoned during a second term and deserted in sight of the enemy.

Witness No. 4. A man who will not tell where he is from and is sentenced to three years' imprisonment.

Witness No. 5. Shehan, a deserter, a man who has broken his parole and since he has given his evidence has again deserted his comrades. One or two others close the list and the least said about them the better.

Gentlemen, I leave the matter in your hands, well satisfied the action you take will be just action. I stand before the people and press of this country and invite at any time the strictest investigation.

I am, respectfully, your obedient servant,

G. W. ALEXANDER,
Asst. Adjt. Gen. and Asst. Provost-Marshal, Comdg. Castle Thunder.

—

Majority report of the committee of Congress to investigate the management of Castle Thunder.

[RICHMOND, *May 1, 1863.*]

The special committee to which was referred certain resolutions requiring investigation into the management of Castle Thunder, a military prison in this city, have instructed me to report that after a diligent examination of a large number of witnesses your committee find that the prison as to cleanliness and comfort has been well managed. Its discipline has been rigid, but good and successful, and the general treatment of prisoners as humane as the circumstances would allow. The evidence discloses some cases of severe corporeal punishment; some prisoners have been whipped with the lash, the blows numbering from five to twelve. This we condemn as inhuman and inconsistent with our system of government. But it does not appear that this punishment has been inflicted except on persons of abandoned characters, and for such offenses as stealing, fighting and abusing more helpless fellow-prisoners.

It should be observed also that this mode of punishment is common in military prisons, and that all these cases happened before Congress had passed a law prohibiting this mode of punishment in the Army. Some persons have been put out of the prison into a walled yard and so confined for several days; and in one instance two or three prisoners were allowed to remain out a short time in bad weather. This we condemn, but it is proper to state that in one of these instances the prisoners so punished had attempted to blow up or injure the building by firing and exploding a canteen of powder, and all the prisoners in that particular room were so taken to this yard, the object seeming to be to force some of them to reveal the names of the ringleaders. It does not appear that any of these persons suffered materially. In another instance of this yard punishment the offense was beating a fellow-prisoner, an old man of sixty-five years, so severely that he afterwards died from the effects of the beating. Captain Alexander in excusing himself for these acts exhibits a statement signed by General Winder in which he is directed to use corporeal punishment if necessary to enforce discipline.

In one instance a sentinel discharged his gun at the window of the prison where a prisoner was putting his head out in violation of rules and otherwise annoying the sentinel. The ball struck the frame of the window and tore off some splinters, which scarred the face of another prisoner standing near. This we condemn as barbarous in the extreme, but the evidence discloses that the order was not to shoot in such cases so as to endanger the person of the prisoner but only to terrify him. Captain Alexander would say in the hearing and presence of the prisoners that if they broke the rules by putting their heads out of the window they should be shot, but he would instruct his sentinels not to shoot so as to hurt but around the window so as to frighten.

Without pretending to review all the particular cases of punishment the undersigned referring to the evidence in the case have come to the conclusion, considering the nature of military prisons and especially in view of the desperate and abandoned characters of the inmates of Castle Thunder who are described by the witnesses as being in the main murderers, thieves, deserters, substitutes, forgers and all manner of villains, that the management of it by Captain Alexander has not been marked by such acts of cruelty and inhumanity as to authorize his condemnation, but on the contrary we are satisfied that he has exhibited such traits of character as in our opinion eminently fit him for such a position. In the successful management of a military prison promptness and a determination to enforce rigid discipline are essential and in these qualities we conclude that Captain Alexander excels.

All of which is respectfully submitted.

W. R. SMITH.
AUGUSTUS R. WRIGHT.
D. C. DE JARNETTE.

———

First minority report on the management of Castle Thunder.

[RICHMOND, *May 1, 1863.*]

The undersigned, one of the special committee of five appointed under a resolution of this House to investigate and report upon certain charges of cruelty and improper conduct on the part of Captain Alexander, the keeper of the military prison known as Castle Thunder, begs leave respectfully to report:

That the acts most complained of have been the killing of two prisoners, the shooting at a third, the infliction of corporeal punishment by whipping on the bare back and the confining of prisoners in the prison yard exposed to the weather.

As to the two prisoners killed, one of them was a lunatic, a Yankee prisoner brought to Castle Thunder from the Libby Prison and shot during the night of the day on which he was brought there by a sentinel while the lunatic prisoner was in the act of trying to pass said sentinel. The other was one who was out upon the balcony at night attempting to escape; in this attempt he was shot by a sentinel. The third case of shooting was also by a sentinel at one of the prisoners who was violating orders by putting his head out of a window overlooking the street. This shot did not take effect, though it appears it may have done so as the contents of the gun were lodged in the facing of the window. This appears to have been done in conformity with instructions from Captain Alexander, that such as put their heads out of the window were to be fired upon. In the judgment of the undersigned this remedy was not justifiable, though alleged to have been intended only as intimidation. The offense was such as could have been sufficiently punished by measures less hazardous to life and limb; the identification of the offender which no doubt could easily have been effected would have put it in Captain Alexander's power to have applied ample corrections and yet in such manner as not to have endangered the life or limb of the prisoner.

As to the whipping: On two occasions Captain Alexander ordered one or two men each to be whipped on the bare back. On another occasion he ordered some eight men to be similarly punished. In all these cases the punishment was inflicted without the intervention of a court-martial. In this in the opinion of the undersigned Captain Alexander was again in fault. The punishment in the two first cases was for fighting and general insubordination, offenses which it would appear might have been adequately punished without subjecting the prisoners to such humiliating infliction.

The other case it is true was more aggravated, to wit, a combination on the part of the offenders for the maltreatment of an aged prisoner recently brought to the prison. It appears Captain Alexander had instructions from General John H. Winder to use this kind of punishment when necessary. Still the undersigned thinks General Winder's instructions were not a sufficient warrant for resort to a mode of punishment unsupported by law and so odious to our people. And even had General Winder's instructions been sufficient authority for the use of such punishment its application should have been tempered with such discretion as to have prevented the infliction of this extraordinary punishment except in cases where other punishments not so revolting would have been inadequate.

As to exposing prisoners in the yard this was resorted to on three occasions; one time against two persons for fighting; at another time against fifteen or twenty for fighting and general insubordination; at another against eighty or a hundred, the inmates of the same room, because some one or more had ignited a flask of gunpowder causing it to explode under such circumstances as induced the belief that there had been an attempt to blow up a portion of the prison building and thus enable prisoners to escape. Without stopping to discuss whether Captain Alexander was right or wrong in punishing all in that room indiscriminately it may be remarked generally and with equal force as to persons guilty or innocent that this mode of punishing (long exposure to weather in winter) is improper, because it cannot be measured and assigned with that definiteness which should characterize all punishment.   One thus punished for so simple an offense as a fisticuff might have entailed upon him permanent loss of health if not loss of life.   Hence the undersigned thinks this treatment was either no punishment at all in consequence of mildness of the weather or if the weather was severe enough to make the punishment felt it might continue in fact long after it was intended and entirely beyond Captain Alexander's control.

Upon the general conduct of Captain Alexander as resting on the mere opinion of witnesses there was some difference.   Some of the witnesses charged great severity and cruelty, but it should be also stated that when this class of witnesses were pressed for facts to sustain their opinion they referred principally to the facts above recited. On the other hand it is but just to Captain Alexander to say the testimony was both satisfactory and abundant that the prison in everything relating to its sanitary condition and the general comfort of its inmates was well kept; that Captain Alexander to the mass of the prisoners is as kind and indulgent as could be expected or desired, in many cases allowing prisoners to send out and get better supplies than are furnished in their rations.   The undersigned thinks the above contains a fair summary of the most material portions of the testimony, speaking from impressions as made during the progress of the investigation, not having since examined the manuscript, it having gone immediately into the hands of the printer.

The conclusion of the undersigned therefore is that in view of the great and delicate responsibility devolved upon the keeper of such a prison, embracing among its inmates the most lawless and desperate characters, while it may be much regretted that such modes of punishment were used he is yet not prepared to recommend Captain Alexander's dismissal.   The undersigned thinks the infliction of corporeal punishment as administered by Captain Alexander was illegal and improper; that the punishing by exposing prisoners to the weather was improper and unwarranted, and that the order to shoot at those at the window was also unjustifiable.   But inasmuch as it is not known that any serious consequences have resulted from any of these acts, and inasmuch as they appear to have been resorted to by Captain Alexander not from any wantonness or cruelty but from a desire to maintain proper discipline and perhaps from an erroneous conception of his rights and powers as keeper of such a prison, the undersigned recommends that no further action be taken by the House.

There is one other fact in connection with this prison which should be remarked upon but for which Captain Alexander from the testimony does not seem to be responsible.   It is that persons are sometimes arrested and incarcerated there for days and weeks and sometimes for months without being either brought to trial or even having charges preferred against them; sometimes confined simply under virtue of orders of superior officers "till called for."   It is true this evil does not seem to exist to any great extent but it is an infringement of personal liberty and the exercise of unauthorized power which should meet no encouragement and which should be abolished.

Respectfully submitted.

W. D. SIMPSON,
One of the Committee.

Second minority report on the management of Castle Thunder.

Hon. THOMAS S. BOCOCK,
        Speaker of the House of Representatives:

The undersigned, a member of the special committee appointed under certain resolutions of the House of Representatives directing the committee to investigate the treatment of prisoners confined in the prison known as Castle Thunder, in the city of Richmond, and make report to the House thereon, begs leave to submit the following minority report:

The first resolution of the series adopted instructs the committee to inquire and report "What punishment if any in violation of law has been inflicted upon prisoners confined in Castle Thunder, the kind and character of punishment inflicted by the officers of that prison?" It was proven by witnesses brought before the committee that punishment of the most degrading and cruel character had been inflicted at various times by order of the officer in charge of this prison upon the prisoners confined therein. Some ten or twelve prisoners, all, with the exception of two, Confederate soldiers, were by order of Brig. Gen. J. H. Winder punished by lashes on the bare back. The offenses charged to have been committed by them in violation of the prison rules were fighting and stealing. The charges were preferred by their associates in the prison and the persons selected for punishment were chosen with the permission of the officers by the general vote of all the prisoners. In other words the parties making the charge and acting as witnesses sat as jurymen upon the case instituted by themselves and assessed the punishment. This novel and original method of enforcing the discipline of a prison invented by the officer having control of Castle Thunder deserves in my opinion the severest censure at the hands of Congress.

It was also in evidence before the committee that in the month of November one hundred or more of the prisoners were sent out into the back yard of the prison and kept there exposed to snow, rain and sleet, many of them having insufficient covering and comparatively unprotected against the weather. This punishment was inflicted by order of Captain Alexander to force from the prisoners a confession of who amongst them had been guilty of placing some powder in a canteen.

It was also proven before the committee that upon various occasions prisoners were punished by bucking, handcuffing and tying to a post with their arms stretched as tightly as possible and kept in this position for hours.

Witnesses also testified that Captain Alexander had during extremely cold weather refused fire to the prisoners and they were compelled to rely upon their own ingenuity and their precarious resources inside of the prison to supply fuel.

All the punishment inflicted except that by whipping was by order of Captain Alexander. Upon one occasion a sentinel discharged his gun at a prisoner in one of the windows and the splinters from the frame of the window wounded another prisoner.

Upon the facts elicited by the examination before the committee the undersigned is of the deliberate opinion that the punishments inflicted in Castle Thunder have been not only degrading and cruel but barbarous and inhuman. It is no excuse for the officers who are guilty of this conduct that Castle Thunder is a military prison and its inmates frequently of desperate character. The object of establishing and maintaining such an institution is the protection of society by the confinement of persons dangerous to its peace. To effect this object it is not necessary that men should be subjected to lashes, exposed to the inclemency of a severe climate, kept huddled together without fire and put to the rack by having their muscles corded to extreme tension for hours together. Firmness and promptness are very different from torture and inhumanity. The fact that a man is confined in a military prison under charges of even the gravest character is no justification for the officer who responsible alone for his safe-keeping anticipates the functions of a court and punishes the prisoner in advance of a trial.

The second resolution adopted by the House is as follows: " How many prisoners have been killed, by whom and the circumstances under which they were killed ?"

It was proved beyond any doubt before the committee that upon one occasion a deranged prisoner whilst running up the steps into the main building of the prison was shot by the sentinel and killed. Another prisoner was shot on the balcony by one of the guard and killed after he had begged the sentinel not to shoot. Under the circumstances attending both these cases the undersigned can regard them in no other light than as deliberate and willful murders. The unprotected and defenseless condition of a prisoner, confined and disarmed, no matter what his moral character, should appeal strongly to the sympathy of any man with proper sensibility, and to deprive him of life whilst in the condition of a prisoner can only be justified by the most extreme danger of the prisoner's escape. In neither of these cases did such danger exist. One of the victims was insane, the other had abandoned any attempt to escape and was asking for mercy when killed. There was no evidence before the committee that the sentinels perpetrating these outrages had been punished by the officers in charge of the prison.

From the foregoing specific instances and from the general tenor of the evidence adduced before the committee the undersigned is of opinion that Brigadier-General Winder and Captain Alexander, who have had the superintendence of Castle Thunder, have shown a want of judgment and humanity in the management of that prison deserving not only the censure of Congress but prompt removal from the position they have abused. Not only were the charges of cruelty and injustice sustained against Alexander by the evidence before the committee but it was also shown that he had been partial in his treatment of the prisoners under his charge and that some of his subordinates had imitated his example. It is but just to state that Mr. Riggs, an officer of the prison, is entitled to praise instead of censure for the course pursued by him, a course the more commendable as it is so remarkable an exception to the cruelty practiced by his superiors.

Captain Alexander and his friends and attorney were present at the examination of witnesses and put such questions to the witnesses as they thought proper.

[This report, dated May 1, 1863, is unsigned but indorsed " Herbert."]

HEADQUARTERS, *Tuscumbia, Ala., April 12, 1863.*
Captain SPENCER, *Commanding Flag of Truce.*

CAPTAIN: I am directed by the general commanding district to inform you that all prisoners of war held by him were paroled on the 7th instant and sent to the Federal lines.

Very respectfully, your obedient servant,

P. D. RODDEY,
Colonel, Commanding Cavalry.

HDQRS. DEPT. OF MISSISSIPPI AND EAST LOUISIANA,
Jackson, April 12, 1863.

Maj. Gen. C. L. STEVENSON, *Vicksburg.*

GENERAL: The lieutenant-general commanding acknowledges receipt of your communication of 11th instant inclosing that of Mrs. Mary James and directs that you place a prisoner taken from the enemy whilst on that movement from the Mississippi River in irons, and inform Admiral Porter of the fact and of its being done in retaliation for the arrest of Mr. John James, upon whose release the man will be relieved from irons and close confinement.

Very respectfully, your obedient servant,

J. C. TAYLOR,
Aide-de-Camp.

———

WAR DEPARTMENT, *Richmond, Va., April 13, 1863.*

General R. E. LEE, *Commanding, &c.*

GENERAL: I have had under consideration the General Orders, No. 49, issued by General Halleck, inclosed to me with your letter of the 21st ultimo and have delayed answering your letter longer than I designed.

The cartel of exchange only incidentally treats of the parole of prisoners, no restrictions as to when paroles may or may not be given; no regulations of the practice to be followed in taking paroles are contained in the cartel. The first four paragraphs of the general orders do not appear to be in violation of the cartel. It is supposed that a belligerent in the absence of an express agreement to the contrary would have the right to forbid its soldiers entering into any paroles. They may operate to establish a new practice, and taken in connection with the provisions of the general orders are so sweeping in their operation that it might hardly be safe to take paroles at least until an explanation is had, and it may be necessary to hold all prisoners that are taken.

The fifth and sixth paragraphs taken in connection with the preceding are ambiguous if not contradictory. By the second paragraph "none but commissioned officers can give paroles for themselves or their men;" by the eighth paragraph "no non-commissioned officer or private can give his parole except through an officer;" by the fifth it is declared that "for the officer the pledging his parole is an individual act and no wholesale paroling by an officer of a number of his inferiors in rank is permitted or allowed."

Does the term "inferiors in rank" refer only to commissioned officers? What is meant by "wholesale paroling?" What by "giving a parole through an officer?" Again these paragraphs might well be understood as only referring to paroles taken at the time of capture except for the last clause in the sixth paragraph, admitting, as the only exceptions to the prohibition against non-commissioned officers and privates giving them their paroles otherwise than through an officer, instances where individuals being separated properly from their commands have suffered long confinement without the possibility of being paroled through an officer. What is meant by long confinement? How are the lists of prisoners in confinement as at Libby Prison for example to be made out? Explanations of these are clearly necessary.

Paragraph 7 declares that "no prisoner of war can be forced by the hostile Government to pledge his parole," &c. The cartel says "all prisoners of war shall be discharged on parole in ten days after their capture." If the soldier under the injunction of his Government refuse to pledge his parole how can we discharge him on his parole? Paragraphs 8, 10, 11 and 12 require no other comment than that the cartel and not the common law of war establishes the terms of the parole and gives in advance the approval and ratification of both Governments to these terms.

Paragraph 9 is in clear violation of the cartel. Article 4 of the cartel says:

> The surplus of prisoners not exchanged shall not be permitted to take up arms again, nor to serve as military police or constabulary force in any fort, garrison or field work held by either of the respective parties, nor as guards of prisons, depots or stores, nor to discharge any duty usually performed by soldiers, until exchanged.

I desire that you will communicate with General Hooker and through him protest in such manner as you may deem appropriate and expedient against so much of that general order as conflicts with the cartel of exchange and ask explanations of what is doubtful, ambiguous or contradictory.

With high esteem, yours,

JAMES A. SEDDON,
Secretary of War.

WAR DEPARTMENT, *Richmond, April 13, 1863.*
WILLIAM COKER, Esq., *Tarborough, N. C.*

SIR: In answer to your letter of the 7th instant you are informed that a publication is made in the Richmond papers of the exchanges which take place. All North Carolina prisoners who have been taken at Goldsborough, on the sea coast, or who have been delivered up at City Point prior to the 13th of January have been exchanged.

Respectfully,

JAS. A. SEDDON,
Secretary of War.

RICHMOND, *April 13, 1863.*
General PEMBERTON:

If you approve of the exchange between General Rust and General Buford you are authorized to make it and inform General Holmes it was done by direction of the Secretary of War. I will answer your dispatch respecting your absence as soon as I see the President.

S. COOPER,
Adjutant and Inspector General.

OFFICE EXCHANGE OF PRISONERS,
Richmond, Va., April 13, 1863.
J. THOMPSON, *Inspector-General, Jackson, Miss.:*

I herewith respectfully return you the paroles of ten prisoners released by Capt. Thomas Henderson, Jackson's regiment of cavalry, forwarded by you to Maj. N. G. Watts, agent at Vicksburg, Miss., and by him forwarded to this office. In their present condition their paroles are entirely valueless as we cannot demand equivalents for them.

Every parole or list of paroled prisoners presented for exchange must show upon its face in addition to the name and rank of the prisoner where the capture was made, when made and the disposition made of the prisoner; that is whether retained or sent to or permitted to go to the lines of the enemy. The usual method is to retain the original paroles on file in the office of the inspector-general of the department in which the capture was made and forward to this office a list of the prisoners showing upon its face the facts before mentioned and certified as a true copy of the original roll of paroles by the inspector-general, and countersigned "official" by the adjutant-general of the department. Please have the inclosed paroles perfected and return to this office at your earliest convenience.

I have the honor to be, very respectfully, your obedient servant,

W. H. HATCH,
Captain and Assistant Adjutant-General.

COLUMBIA, TENN., *April 13, 1863.*

Hon. JAMES A. SEDDON, *Secretary of War.*

DEAR SIR: Under ordinary circumstances I would not intrude upon your valuable time, but I am constrained from a sense of duty to ask your attention to a few words in relation to a worthy citizen, a neighbor of mine. To be brief, Dr. Joseph E. Dixon, a citizen of Maury County, Tenn., was taken prisoner at Donelson and was released, being surgeon. He returned to his home in this county then in the enemy's lines, reported himself to General Negley, in command of the Federal forces, and in some fifteen or twenty days General Negley gave him a pass to go to Richmond and Doctor Dixon went via Huntsville, Ala. There he reported himself to General Buell and received a pass to Decatur, but when next morning it was reported that fighting was going on in the neighborhood of Decatur and he called to have his route changed and General Buell being out, General Rousseau gave him a pass to go by way of Battle Creek to Chattanooga. With this pass he arrived upon Battle Creek and unfortunately for him a battle was expected there and General McCook, in command of the Federals, complained to General Buell of General Rousseau for granting said pass and General Buell had him arrested and sent to Johnson's Island, where he has been confined ever since, now seven or eight months. I have the facts upon reliable information. Doctor Dixon was surgeon of the Ninth Battalion of Tennessee Cavalry, commanded by Lieutenant-Colonel Gantt. He was released as a surgeon while his battalion was still in prison and was on his way to report to his Government and with the pass of the Federal general in his possession. There have been several general jail deliveries since his imprisonment but he seems to be forgotten. His wife and family and friends are in deep distress. I beg leave to suggest for your consideration that you make a special demand for his case and if possible that you have him released.

With my best wishes for your official and personal success, I am, your friend,

JAMES H. THOMAS.

[First indorsement.]

Is not this the case in reference to which Mr. Ould made a report to the Secretary of War?

[Second indorsement.]

APRIL 28, 1863.

Respectfully referred to Hon. R. Ould.
By order of the Secretary of War:

J. A. CAMPBELL,
Assistant Secretary of War.

[Third indorsement.]

OFFICE EXCHANGE OF PRISONERS,
Richmond, Va., April 30, 1863.

Respectfully returned.
The case of Surg. J. E. Dixon will receive special attention. I have already made a report to the Secretary of War in this case.

RO. OULD,
Agent of Exchange.

[Fourth indorsement.]

Answer that the special attention of Colonel Ould, agent, &c., has been directed to the case of Surgeon Dixon.

HEADQUARTERS SECOND DISTRICT,
DEPARTMENT OF MISSISSIPPI AND EAST LOUISIANA,
Vicksburg, April 15, 1863.

Maj. R. W. MEMMINGER, *Assistant Adjutant-General, Jackson.*

MAJOR: The following is an extract from a letter of Colonel Ferguson of the 12th instant:

In this connection I would call your attention to the five prisoners sent down who acknowledged that they had been led to the east bank of Deer Creek by their captain to steal horses and mules and burn everything. They were caught on stolen animals and had in their possession articles of private property stolen from residences, and were recognized as those who had set fire to the corn on the De Holb Plantation. Will not our Government make an example of them?
Can these men be held in retaliation for James?

I am, major respectfully, your obedient servant,

C. L. STEVENSON,
Major-General, Commanding.

HEADQUARTERS FOURTH MILITARY DISTRICT,
Jackson, Miss., April 16, 1863.

Maj. R. W. MEMMINGER, *Assistant Adjutant-General.*

MAJOR: I have the honor to submit the following report of U. S. prisoners of war and deserters from U. S. Army received at this post on yesterday from Panola: 1 prisoner of war, 4 deserters, U. S. Army. Total number of prisoners and deserters, 5.

I am, major, very respectfully, your obedient servant,

JOHN ADAMS,
Brigadier-General, Commanding.

[First indorsement.]

HEADQUARTERS, *Jackson, April 14, 1863.*

Respectfully referred to General Adams to know if he reports the U. S. prisoners received, to Major Watts in charge, &c.
By order of Lieutenant-General Pemberton:

R. W. MEMMINGER,
Assistant Adjutant-General.

[Second indorsement.]

HEADQUARTERS FOURTH MILITARY DISTRICT,
Jackson, April 17, 1863.

The U. S. prisoners on their arrival are paroled but confined in guard-house. The list of prisoners is sent to Major Watts for exchange upon notification from Major Watts. Lists of all those at present in Jackson have been forwarded, but Major Watts has not heretofore been informed daily or immediately upon the receipt of Federal prisoners. Report like the within is furnished department headquarters in accordance with instructions from lieutenant-general commanding.

Respectfully,

JOHN ADAMS,
Brigadier-General, Commanding.

HEADQUARTERS FOURTH MILITARY DISTRICT,
Jackson, April 16, 1863.

Major MEMMINGER, *Assistant Adjutant-General.*

MAJOR: In reply to communication from department headquarters just received asking of the whereabouts of the negro captured from the sloop of war Mississippi I have the honor to state that the negro captured from the said sloop is now confined in Pearl River Bridge Prison.

I am, major, yours, respectfully,

JOHN ADAMS,
Brigadier-General, Commanding.

RICHMOND, *April 17, 1863.*
General EARL VAN DORN, *Columbia, Tenn.:*

All prisoners delivered at City Point to this date are exchanged.

S. COOPER,
Adjutant and Inspector General.

RICHMOND, VA., *April 18, 1863.*
His Excellency JOHN LETCHER, *Richmond, Va.*

SIR: In response to your letter of the 7th ultimo covering a copy of the preamble and resolutions of the General Assembly of Virginia relative to the imprisonment of C. A. J. Collins I have the honor to forward a report* of the Secretary of War on the case.

Very respectfully and truly, yours,

JEFFERSON DAVIS.

WAR DEPARTMENT, *Richmond, April 18, 1863.*
Col. WILLIAM T. WITHERS,
First Mississippi Light Artillery, Tuskeegee, Ala.

SIR: I cannot at this time assure you positively when I can declare exchanged the men whose names you report in the two lists under date

---

* Not found.

of the 7th instant. I hope it will not be long. At present there are insurmountable difficulties. I hope I can declare the exchange in a month.

Respectfully, your obedient servant,

RO. OULD,
Agent of Exchange.

RICHMOND, VA., *April 20, 1863.*

To the HOUSE OF REPRESENTATIVES:

I herewith transmit for your information a communication from the Secretary of War in response to your resolution of January 24 in reference to the exchange or release " of persons who taken from civil life have been transported and confined beyond the limits of the Confederacy."

JEFFERSON DAVIS.

[Inclosure.]

WAR DEPARTMENT, *April 18, 1863.*

To the PRESIDENT OF THE CONFEDERATE STATES.

SIR: In compliance with a resolution of the House of Representatives of January 24 last I have the honor to submit the report of the Hon. R. Ould, agent of exchange of prisoners, as to the steps that have been taken to procure the liberation and exchange of prisoners who taken from civil life have been transported and confined beyond the limits of the Confederate States, and whether any and what persons so confined at the instance of the Government have been set at liberty.

Very respectfully, your obedient servant,

JAMES A. SEDDON,
Secretary of War.

[Sub-inclosure.]

RICHMOND, *April 14, 1863.*

Hon. JAMES A. SEDDON, *Secretary of War.*

SIR: In the matter of the accompanying resolution of the House of Representatives relating to citizen prisoners I have the honor to make the following report:

The subject of the arrest and detention of civilians has been a matter of controversy between the Federal agent of exchange and myself ever since the establishment of the cartel. I have again and again protested against such arrests as illegal and contrary to the usages of civilized warfare.

At an early stage of the cartel I urged the adoption of the following rule, to wit:

That peaceable non-combatant citizens of both the Confederate and United States who are not connected with any military organization should not be arrested by either the Confederate or U. S. Armies within the territory of the adverse party; that if such a proposition was considered as being too broad let the only exception be in the case of a temporary arrest of parties within army lines where the arresting party has good reason to believe that their presence is dangerous to the safety of the army from the opportunity afforded of giving intelligence to the enemy, that then the arrest should cease as soon as the reason for making it ceased in the withdrawal of the army or for any other cause, and finally that the foregoing proposal should apply to and include such arrests and imprisonments as were then in force.

The proposition was declined. I have urged it frequently since but without success.

The Federal authorities on the other hand have always been anxious to institute a system of exchange of political prisoners man for man. It was a deeply laid scheme to interfere with the administration of justice in the Confederate States and to give practical immunity to such of their friends and partisans in the South as felt disposed to preach or practice disloyalty.

Under the instructions of the War Department I have constantly refused to engage in any such system of exchanges. There was no reciprocity in the arrangement. It amounted to an exchange of Confederate citizens for Confederate citizens owing to the fact that the enemy was in possession of portions of our own country and had therefore more frequent opportunities of making arrests. If any such proposal had been accepted we should soon have released every civilian held by us leaving many hundreds of our own people to languish in Northern prisons for whom we had no equivalent to offer. I repeatedly offered to release all political prisoners held by us except such as were held upon very aggravated charges if the Federal authorities would do the same. Lately they agreed to this proposition, coupling it with a written statement that it was not their intention to make any more arrests of non-combatants. I had very great doubts as to their good faith both as to the delivery of all political prisoners and their disavowal of any intention to make any more arrests.

The sequel has proved that these doubts in both respects were well founded. A few weeks ago in pretended compliance with the agreement they delivered some six hundred persons whom they called political prisoners. About one-half of that number were persons who had been in our service in the West belonging to irregular military organizations and who long ago had been declared exchanged under the agreement made between the Federal agent and myself. Finding they could not get any equivalent for them as military prisoners they attempted to palm them off as political prisoners. The false pretense was too apparent to deceive anybody. Some political prisoners held in this city against whom the charges were not aggravated were sent off in return. The number delivered by me bore about the same proportion to the whole number held by us as the number delivered by the Federal agent did to all the political prisoners held by the Federal authorities. They were not exchanged one against the other; they were simply released upon both sides—discharged from any paroles heretofore given by them. The Federal agent demanded that I should deliver to him political prisoners equal in number to those released by him. I refused to do so as the agreement was for the release of all political prisoners, and it was necessary that the proper proportion should be maintained on our side to secure the release of the hundreds still in captivity at the North. If all our prisoners had been delivered I am very sure no more deliveries would have been made by the Federal agent.

Even less faith has been shown by the Federal authorities in the matter of political arrests. Since the date of their declaration they have made more of such arrests than during any other equal space of time, embracing an unusual proportion of old men and helpless women.

The resolution of the House of Representatives specifically inquires "what steps if any have been taken to procure the liberation of persons who taken from civil life have been transported and confined beyond the limits of the Confederacy." In answer I respectfully state that at every interview, without exception, between the Federal agent and myself I have, under the instruction of the War Department, brought the subject to his attention in as forcible and as earnest manner as possible. That I have demanded the release of all civilians held in confinement and have threatened retaliation. In addition, whenever I have been specifically informed of cases of incarceration I have made them the subjects of correspondence with the Federal agent. In many cases I have been successful in procuring the release of the parties named; in others I have not succeeded. Some have been released at the North and allowed to make their way to their own homes, and others have been brought on flag-of-truce boats to Varina and City Point. Some have been discharged unconditionally and others put on parole. With reference to the latter class all such have been relieved from any obligation contained in the parole whether it was to return at a certain time to secure the release of another person or any other obligation.

Some nine hundred so-called political prisoners have been received by me at Varina and City Point. About five or six hundred were really non-combatants.

I have no means of knowing how many have been allowed to make their way to their own homes. Such parties do not report to me. They amount, however, to several hundred.

I have only a record of the names of such as were delivered at Varina and City Point and Vicksburg. Only a very few have been delivered at the latter place. If it be the pleasure of the House of Representatives that the names of all such be presented I will cause them to be separated from the rolls.

I have delayed until the present time this report because until within a few days past the whole subject was undetermined. I thought it best under the circumstances to wait long enough to ascertain whether the Federal authorities intended to carry out their agreement. I am now fully satisfied they have no such purpose.

Respectfully, your obedient servant,

RO. OULD,
Agent of Exchange.

———

[APRIL 20, 1863.—For Quintero to Benjamin, with inclosures, relative to the arrest of Col. E. J. Davis and others, see Series I, Vol. XXVI, Part II, pp. 48–53.]

———

CIRCULAR.]   HEADQUARTERS DEPT. OF MISS. AND EAST LA.,
Jackson, Miss., April 20, 1863

Heretofore in taking the parole of prisoners captured great irregularity has prevailed, and to obviate difficulty in future all officers who may parole prisoners will be guided by the following instructions received from the office for the exchange of prisoners at Richmond, viz: Each parole or list of paroled prisoners must show upon its face in addition to the name and rank of the prisoner his regiment and company, where the capture was made, when made and the disposition made of the prisoner; that is whether retained in prison or sent to or permitted to go to the lines of the enemy. The paroles thus made out will be sent to the office of the inspector-general of the department.

By order of Lieutenant-General Pemberton:

R. W. MEMMINGER,
Assistant Adjutant-General.

RICHMOND, VA., *April 22, 1863.*

[Honorable SECRETARY OF WAR.]

SIR: I was delegated by the soldiers of the division under General T. J. Churchill, captured at Arkansas Post, to petition in the name of the entire command that they might be sent back to Trans-Mississippi Army. The command which has been much reduced are anxious to return to that department as numbers of the different regiments are west of the river. Colonel Portlock's regiment, Captain Nutt's Louisiana cavalry, Johnson's (Texas) Spy Company and several other commands have a large portion of their command left on that side of the river, and most earnestly request that they may be allowed to replace them.

I am, sir, very respectfully, your obedient servant,

JNO. W. DUNNINGTON,
Ex-Colonel, Provisional Army, C. S.

CAMP HOLMES, *Near Raleigh, N. C., April 22, 1863.*

His Excellency JEFFERSON DAVIS:

SIR: Some time since I wrote to you informing you that myself and a boy some fifteen years of age were taken prisoners on the 17th day of February and incarcerated the 2d day of March. In answer to this letter I am informed that my case has been referred to Colonel Ould, Confederate agent for the exchange of prisoners. I have nothing from Colonel Ould in regard to the matter. My condition here is deplorable, nothing to sleep on or under and destitute of clothing. I hope, sir, you will have my case investigated as soon as convenient. I hereby transmit a copy of my appointment as captain of the Long Shoal Light Ship:

ON BOARD STEAMER HETZEL, *October 10, 1862.*

Mr. M. L. STRANSBURY:

SIR: You are hereby appointed keeper of the Long Shoal Light Ship, subject to the approval of the Secretary of the Treasury of the United States.

H. K. DAVENPORT,
Commander, Commanding Sounds of North Carolina.

Respectfully, yours,

M. L. STRANSBURY,
Captain.

[First indorsement.]

EXECUTIVE OFFICE, *April 27, 1863.*

Respectfully referred by the President to the honorable Secretary of War.

G. W. C. LEE,
Colonel and Aide-de-Camp.

[Second indorsement.]

Respectfully referred to Brigadier-General Winder. Is there any reason why these men should not be discharged under the cartel?

By order of Secretary of War:

J. A. CAMPBELL,
Assistant Secretary of War.

[Third indorsement.]

MAY 1, 1863.

Respectfully returned to the Secretary of War. Mr. Ould informs me that this man cannot be exchanged by reason of being an officer.

JNO. H. WINDER,
Brigadier-General.

———

MAYFIELD, *Near Petersburg, Va., April 24, 1863.*

Hon. JAMES A. SEDDON, *Secretary of War.*

SIR: A large number of the Arkansas Post prisoners are quartered near my residence. From frequent conversations with these men I discover that many of them desire to be employed on the public defenses now being constructed around Petersburg. If there is no impediment to their being thus employed it has occurred to me that the money expended on other laborers would be worthily bestowed upon these men. The works have progressed to a point near their quarters and will each day approach nearer. I thought the matter of sufficient importance to warrant me in so far trespassing upon your valuable time as to place the facts before your better knowledge and judgment, and am,

Most respectfully, your obedient servant,

TH. WHITWORTH.

[First indorsement.]

APRIL 25, 1863.

Respectfully referred to Chief of Engineers.
By order of the Secretary of War:

J. A. CAMPBELL,
Assistant Secretary of War.

[Second indorsement.]

ENGINEER BUREAU, *May 15, 1863.*

Understanding that these troops have been armed and placed again in service within a few days past this letter is respectfully returned to the honorable Secretary of War.

J. F. GILMER,
Colonel of Engineers and Chief of Bureau.

———

APRIL 24, 1863.

Lieutenant CAMPBELL:

Send the exchanged men to Franklin to rejoin their companies.
By order:

G. M. SORREL,
Assistant Adjutant-General.

———

BRIGADE HDQRS., *Chaffin's Farm, Va., April 26, 1863.*

Maj. Gen. A. ELZEY, *Commanding, &c.*

GENERAL: I beg to submit the inclosed General Orders,* No. 49, War Department, Adjutant-General's Office, Washington, February 28, 1863, and copies of papers received last night by flag of truce from Williamsburg. This morning I sent a reply to be forwarded to Colonel West, commanding Federal forces, Fort Magruder, informing him that I claim the prisoners that were paroled by Colonel Tabb and my assistant

———

* Omitted here; see p. 306.

adjutant-general, Captain [J. H.] Pearce, and that if the parole is not admitted hereafter such cases will not be paroled.

I am, general, very respectfully, &c.,

HENRY A. WISE,
Brigadier-General.

[Inclosure No. 1.]

HEADQUARTERS CAVALRY, WISE'S BRIGADE,
Barhamsville, Va., April 24, 1863.

Lieut. Col. JOSEPH JONES [*Fifty-ninth Virginia*], Comdg., &c.:

I have the honor to inclose a communication received per flag of truce from the Federal commander at Fort Magruder. It is I am satisfied only a means of ascertaining the locality of our picket-post. Please forward to General Wise.

I am, colonel, very respectfully, your obedient servant,

J. R. ROBERTSON,
Major, Commanding.

[Inclosure No. 2.]

HDQRS. ADVANCE BRIGADE, FOURTH ARMY CORPS,
OFFICE OF THE ASSISTANT ADJUTANT-GENERAL,
Fort Magruder, Va., April 24, 1863.

To the CONFEDERATE COMMANDER IN FRONT.

SIR: I am directed by my commanding general to forward to you under flag of truce the inclosed General Orders,* No. 49, from the War Department at Washington, in reference to paroles.

I have the honor to remain,   ROBT. M. WEST,
Colonel, Commanding.

RICHMOND, *April 26, 1863.*

Col. ROBERT OULD.

COLONEL: From the exchanged Confederate prisoners and other trustworthy persons I have learned that a large number of rank and file of Louisiana State troops paroled at New Orleans after the occupation of that city by Federal forces are now detained there and are not allowed the privilege of exchange in direct violation of Exchange Notice, No. 4, issued from your office. My attention among others was especially called to the case of Capt. Gustave Le Gardeur, [jr.,] of Louisiana artillery, who after the battle of Shiloh went to New Orleans on recruiting service and there was arrested on arrival of General Butler and afterwards paroled by his order. Many citizens are also confined in different forts and other places as political prisoners whose names it is difficult to ascertain in full, and it is merely by chance we learn of their fate as for instance in the case of James P. Shortridge who has been arrested by order of General Butler and is still in custody. Mr. Walden, formerly sheriff of New Orleans, has been taken prisoner while defending his home at Ponchatoula, La., during the raid of Federal troops at that place in the latter part of last month and not returned with others who were delivered to us at Port Hudson on the 8th of this month. I have the honor to submit the above statements for your consideration, and remain,

Very respectfully, your obedient servant,

I. SZYMANSKI,
Assistant Adjutant and Inspector General,
In Charge of Paroled and Exchanged Prisoners at Jackson, Miss.

---

* Omitted here; see p. 306.

HEADQUARTERS, *April 26, 1863.*

Judge R. OULD,
   Commissioner for Exchange, Richmond, Va.:

Have the prisoners captured recently with Stribling's battery been exchanged?

G. M. SORREL,
Assistant Adjutant-General.

———

TULLAHOMA, *April 27, 1863.*

General PEMBERTON:

Have you any prisoners who could be exchanged for Maj. R. A. Howard who was captured near the mouth of Red River?

J. E. JOHNSTON.

———

RICHMOND, *April 27, 1863.*

Maj. G. M. SORREL, *Assistant Adjutant-General.*

SIR: Stribling's men and all others who were delivered at City Point to this date have been fully exchanged.

RO. OULD,
Agent of Exchange.

———

HOUSE OF REPRESENTATIVES, *April 27, 1863.*

President DAVIS, *Richmond, Va.*

SIR: I beg to inclose a letter from General De Saussure, of South Carolina, for your consideration.

I have the honor to be, very respectfully, your obedient servant,

W. D. SIMPSON.

[First indorsement.]

Respectfully referred to the Secretary of War by the President.

WM. M. BROWNE,
Colonel and Aide-de-Camp.

[Second indorsement.]

MAY 4, 1863.

Referred to Hon. Robert Ould.
By order of the Secretary of War:

J. A. CAMPBELL,
Assistant Secretary of War.

[Third indorsement.]

OFFICE OF EXCHANGE OF PRISONERS,
Richmond, Va., May 8, 1863.

Respectfully returned.

Capt. D. B. Vincent was delivered by the Federal authorities at City Point May 5, 1863, and regularly exchanged.

RO. OULD,
Agent for Exchange.

Per W. H. HATCH,
Captain and Aide-de-Camp.

[Inclosure.]

CHARLESTON, S. C., *April 24, 1863.*

Hon. W. D. SIMPSON, *Richmond, Va.*

DEAR SIR: Will you permit me to call to your view a case of very great hardship and oppression and respectfully to ask your aid? Mr. Miles has been laboring in the same cause and I am sure will zealously co operate with you. Capt. Daniel B. Vincent, a seaman of great experience and one of our most worthy and respected citizens, was captured together with the vessels under his command by the enemy's fleet off Bull's Bayou June, 1862, while attempting to run the blockade. From that time until now he has been kept a close prisoner in Fort Lafayette, and as his friends are informed for a great portion of the time in solitary confinement. The officers and crew captured with him have long since been released but this gentleman is still kept a prisoner. No other cause can be given for this but that he is thoroughly acquainted with the harbors and rivers of this and the adjoining States and would therefore be a very useful man to the Confederacy. Surely the seamen and citizens are entitled to ask from the Confederate Government some of the protection afforded the soldier, particularly when the former are made prisoners in the effort to discharge a duty to the public. I would respectfully ask that this case be brought to the notice of the President in behalf of a citizen of South Carolina.

I am, sir, with great respect, your obedient servant,

WILMOT G. DE SAUSSURE.

RICHMOND, *April 28, 1863.*

General J. E. JOHNSTON, *Tullahoma:*

If Maj. R. A. Howard has been released on parole and is within our lines he will be declared specially exchanged and one officer of equal rank sent to the enemy's lines. If he is held in custody by the enemy he cannot be exchanged until an interview is had with the Federal agent, which will be in a few days.

S. COOPER,
Adjutant and Inspector General.

C. S. SENATE, *April 28, 1863.*

Mr. PRESIDENT:

I inclose you statement of the Seventeenth Texas Regiment. It shows now under General Holmes in Arkansas 1 lieutenant-colonel, 1 major, 4 captains, 8 lieutenants, 1 assistant quartermaster, 1 assistant commissary of subsistence and 350 privates. Of those captured at the Post of Arkansas there are now here only 180 privates and there are no officers. All the regiments and companies captured at the Post of Arkansas are in much the same condition. The whole of these exchanged prisoners are anxious to be sent back to Arkansas. They are conscripts and men of families, and there being no law to break up these regiments or to assign them to other regiments or to make of them new organizations I trust you will not allow them or their legal rights and the law of the land to be so treated and so disregarded. We must look to you for the enforcement of the law and for fair play.

Most truly, yours,

R. W. JOHNSON.

[Inclosure.]

BARRACKS CAMP, MODEL FARM,
Petersburg, Va., April 22, 1863.

Below is as true a statement of the condition of the Seventeenth Texas Cavalry as I am able to form under present circumstances without data, &c.:

Trans-Mississippi: 1 lieutenant-colonel, 1 major, 4 captains, 8 lieutenants, 1 assistant quartermaster, 1 assistant commissary of subsistence, 350 privates under command of above officers. At present camp 180 privates. The balance of officers not being exchanged.

C. S. BLALOCK,
Sergeant-Major Seventeenth Texas Cavalry.

HDQRS. SIXTEENTH REGIMENT VIRGINIA CAVALRY,
Salem, Va., April 29, 1863.

[Brig. Gen. A. G. JENKINS.]

GENERAL: The three prisoners handed over to you, to wit, Ezekiel S. Bloss, Hiram Bloss and Morgan Garrett, are citizens of Wayne County and officials of the usurped government of Virginia. They were arrested last fall during our occupation of the Kanawha Valley and in obedience to the proclamation of General Loring were released upon parole, and since that time they have so far as I know kept that parole and were not found fleeing from us upon the occasion of their late capture although fully aware of our presence for eight days. They are all men of influence and before the present war were men of good character and are now arrested as hostages for Charles W. and William Ferguson. I have been informed and believe that these prisoners have long since become repentant and are convinced of their error and are now willing to renounce in writing their allegiance to the United States Government and the usurped government of Virginia and take the oath to support the Constitution of the Confederate States and State of Virginia. If they will do this I hope they may be at once returned to their homes, not doubting that they will religiously respect their obligations, and I cheerfully recommend their release upon the aforesaid terms.

I am, general, yours, respectfully,

M. J. FERGUSON,
Colonel, Commanding Sixteenth Regiment Virginia Cavalry.

[First indorsement.]

Approved.

A. G. JENKINS,
Brigadier-General.

[Second indorsement.]

HEADQUARTERS DEPARTMENT OF HENRICO,
May 9, 1863.

Respectfully submitted with the recommendation that these men be released on their taking the oath of allegiance to the Confederate States Government.

W. N. STARKE,
Captain and Assistant Adjutant-General.

[Third indorsement.]

Approved and respectfully referred to Secretary of War.

JNO. H. WINDER,
Brigadier-General, Commanding.

[Fourth indorsement.]

Brigadier-General Winder's recommendation concurred in.
By order of the Secretary of War:

J. A. CAMPBELL.

ABINGDON, VA., *April 29, 1863.*

Brig. Gen. H. MARSHALL,
First Brigade, Army of East Tennessee.

GENERAL: We, the undersigned regularly enlisted soldiers of your brigade, Lieut. Col. Thomas Johnson's battalion Kentucky Mounted Rifles, having been taken prisoners of war by the forces of the United States and having been returned to our command, desire to make a statement of the inhuman treatment to which we and other Confederate soldiers are subjected when by the fortune of war we are thrown into the hands of the forces of the United States Government and ask that, if it is possible, some action may be taken by our Government to secure for prisoners of war humane treatment and if possible the treatment universally recognized by civilized nations engaged in war. We were captured, our horses and equipments were taken as they had a right; but they did not stop at this, but they by order of the provost-marshal of Lexington, Ky. (a Captain Hurlbut), robbed us of our clothing, blankets and money, even our pocket combs and knives. Some of us were put into a filthy negro jail, unhealthy and loathsome upon account of the vermin. Some of us were placed in iron cells and closely confined. Our food at Lexington and Louisville was unwholesome in character and even if it had been of a good quality totally insufficient for the use of the men. Captain Gray, commanding Company L, Tenth [Kentucky] Regiment Federal Cavalry, having captured three of the undersigned placed us in the county jail of Fleming County and kept us there for two days and three nights without making the least arrangement for our food or necessities. When we were taken the weather was very cold and disagreeable. They now have in close confinement handcuffed Henry Greenway, a private in Capt. Pete Everett's company, First Battalion Kentucky Mounted Rifles, C. S. Army. They decline to exchange him as a prisoner of war and we understood from Greenway that he was to be shot and he desired that his case should be presented to you. On account of the inhuman neglect of those in charge of the U. S. prisoners at Louisville and at Lexington, Ky., and those having charge of the transportation of our men from the different points at which they are confined to the Confederate lines many a soldier fails to reach his command. They often are left to die on the road and to our own knowledge men died from neglect belonging to the party to which we belonged in coming from Louisville, Ky., to City Point. While at Louisville, Ky., were under the charge of negroes who gave us our food in such quantity as suited them and gave us the privilege of coming under shelter as they pleased.

JOS. HIBLER.
JOHN CRAIG.
JACOB JOHNSON.
THOMAS B. FISHBACK.
JOHN M. FISHBACK.
JAMES L. SHIELDS.

Joint resolutions adopted by the Confederate Congress on the subject of retaliation April 30–May 1, 1863.

Resolved by the Congress of the Confederate States of America in response to the message of the President transmitted to Congress at the commencement of the present session, That in the opinion of Congress the commissioned officers of the enemy ought not to be delivered to the authorities of the respective States as suggested in the said message, but all captives taken by the Confederate forces ought to be dealt with and disposed of by the Confederate Government.

2. That in the judgment of Congress the proclamations of the President of the United States dated respectively September 22, 1862, and January 1, 1863, and the other measures of the Government of the United States and of its authorities, commanders and forces designed or tending to emancipate slaves in the Confederate States or to abduct such slaves or to incite them to insurrection, or to employ negroes in war against the Confederate States or to overthrow the institution of African slavery and bring on a servile war in these States would if successful produce atrocious consequences, and they are inconsistent with the spirit of those usages which in modern warfare prevail among civilized nations; they may therefore be properly and lawfully repressed by retaliation.

3. That in every case wherein during the present war any violation of the laws or usages of war among civilized nations shall be or has been done and perpetrated by those acting under the authority of the Government of the United States on the persons or property of citizens of the Confederate States or of those under the protection or in the land or naval service of the Confederate States or of any State of the Confederacy the President of the Confederate States is hereby authorized to cause full and ample retaliation to be made for every such violation, in such manner and to such extent as he may think proper.

4. That every white person being a commissioned officer or acting as such who during the present war shall command negroes or mulattoes in arms against the Confederate States or who shall arm, train, organize or prepare negroes or mulattoes for military service against the Confederate States or who shall voluntarily aid negroes or mulattoes in any military enterprise, attack or conflict in such service shall be deemed as inciting servile insurrection, and shall if captured be put to death or be otherwise punished at the discretion of the court.

5. Every person being a commissioned officer or acting as such in the service of the enemy who shall during the present war excite or attempt to excite or cause to be excited a servile insurrection or who shall incite or cause to be incited a slave to rebel shall if captured be put to death or be otherwise punished at the discretion of the court.

6. Every person charged with an offense punishable under the preceding resolution shall during the present war be tried before the military court attached to the army or corps by the troops of which he shall have been captured or by such other military court as the President may direct and in such manner and under such regulations as the President shall prescribe; and after conviction the President may commute the punishment in such manner and on such terms as he may deem proper.

7. All negroes and mulattoes who shall be engaged in war or be taken in arms against the Confederate States or shall give aid or comfort to the enemies of the Confederate States shall when captured in

the Confederate States be delivered to the authorities of the State or States in which they shall be captured to be dealt with according to the present or future law of such State or States.

TH. S. BOCOCK,
Speaker of the House of Representatives.
ALEXANDER H. STEPHENS,
President of the Senate.

Approved May 1, 1863.

JEFFERSON DAVIS.

CHARLESTON, *May 1, 1863.*
Doctor CROWELL, *Medical Director Hospitals, Charleston, S. C.*

SIR: The prisoners who have died in the Queen Street Hospital have left in my hands $475.54. I have also $98.75 belonging to two paroled prisoners which amount was accidentally omitted to be returned in the hurry of moving. I have also four silver watches, a note of $200 and a few articles of little or no value. Be pleased to notify me at your earliest convenience what disposition is to be made of these effects, and oblige,

Your obedient servant,

JOHN L. DAWSON, M. D.,
Prisoners' Hospital.

WAR DEPARTMENT, *Richmond, May 2, 1863.*
M. J. SAFFOLD, Esq., *Montgomery, Ala.*

SIR: Your reports of the examinations of political prisoners at Mobile and Pollard, Ala., have been received and examined. Your action in the premises meets the entire approbation of the Department.

J. A. CAMPBELL,
Assistant Secretary of War.

WAR DEPARTMENT, *Richmond, Va., May 2, 1863.*
Hon. JAMES A. SEDDON, *Secretary of War.*

SIR: I respectfully recommend that of the Federal officers now held by us a sufficient number be set aside to retaliate for the unjust detention of the following-named persons all of whom have been in prison for more than six months, and all of whom are already declared exchanged by the Federal agent of exchange, to wit: Surg. Joseph E. Dixon, at Johnson's Island; Col. John A. Poindexter, at Saint Louis jail; Col. J. C. Morehead, Lieut. James H. Baker and [Private] J. W. Garrett, at Johnson's Island; Daniel B. Vincent, merchant captain, and John C. Lea, Isaac B. Smith, Thomas Murray, Samuel Burrows, pilots, at Fort Lafayette or Delaware; Colonel Zarvona (Thomas), Fort Delaware, and Surgeon Green, held as a hostage for the infamous Rucker.

Respectfully, your obedient servant,

RO. OULD,
Agent of Exchange.

CIRCULAR.]   HEADQUARTERS ARMY OF TENNESSEE,
                        Tullahoma, May 2, 1863.

The following telegram from General S. Cooper, Adjutant and Inspector General, Richmond, is published for the information of all concerned:

All men delivered by the Federal authorities at City Point are duly exchanged and fully released from their paroles.

                                          S. COOPER,
                                Adjutant and Inspector-General.

All soldiers so delivered belonging to this army are hereby ordered to join their proper commands without delay.

By command of General Bragg:

                                KINLOCH FALCONER,
                                Assistant Adjutant-General.

                            FIRST LOUISIANA HOSPITAL,
                            Brookhaven, Miss., May 2, 1863.

Lieut. Gen. J. C. PEMBERTON,
    Comdg. Dept. of Mississippi and East Louisiana, Jackson, Miss.

GENERAL: On 29th ultimo the Federal cavalry force under Colonel Grierson entered this place and made prisoners the sick soldiers, their nurses and the other attendants of this hospital. They were regularly paroled and a correct list* of them is herewith forwarded. Having been short of provisions since 26th of April and unable to obtain supplies from Jackson in consequence of injury to the railroad I was compelled to send off with leave of absence for twenty days such men as could without difficulty reach their homes. A list* of these men is also forwarded. I have to state that the conduct of the enemy toward the hospital and its officers was entirely proper. Nothing was injured or disturbed in the slightest particular. There are here remaining fifty-eight men, paroled prisoners, awaiting your orders.

I have the honor to be, very respectfully, your obedient servant,

                                R. B. MAURY,
                                Surgeon in Charge.

                                    JACKSON, *May 3, 1863.*

Lieutenant-General PEMBERTON:

General Buckner says Federal prisoners can be sent to Selma, Ala. Shall I send them?

                                JOHN ADAMS,
                                Brigadier-General.

                                    JACKSON, *May 3, 1863.*

Lieutenant-General PEMBERTON:

Have not heard from Montgomery. Telegraphed Selma. Commanding officer there says he can take the Federal prisoners if General Buckner is willing. Have telegraphed General Buckner. Received no answer yet. What shall I do?

                                JOHN ADAMS,
                                Brigadier-General.

---

* Not found.

JACKSON, *May 3, 1863.*

Lieutenant-General PEMBERTON:

The following dispatch has just been received from Robert Ould:

All officers and men who have been delivered at City Point, Va., by the Federal authorities up to this date are fully exchanged and fully released from their parole.

RO. OULD.

JOHN ADAMS,
Brigadier-General.

EXECUTIVE OFFICE, *Tullahoma, Tenn., May 4, 1863.*

Hon. JAMES A. SEDDON.

SIR: I send you herewith a note which I have just received from Col. Joel A. Battle upon the subject of the arrest and imprisonment at Camp Chase of his daughter Miss Fannie Battle and Miss Booker. They are refined and very excellent young ladies belonging to the best families in the county, and were arrested alone upon the ground of their strong and openly avowed sympathies with the Confederate cause. Miss Battle has had two brothers killed in battle and her father dangerously wounded at the head of his regiment (the Twentieth Tennessee) at the battle of Shiloh. General Bragg tells me that he can do nothing here in the premises and advises me to address you upon the subject. I trust that the peculiar character of this case will be held to justify the most speedy and decided action. If these ladies are not liberated is it not legitimate to retaliate by placing in close confinement a number of Federal officers?

Very respectfully,

ISHAM G. HARRIS.

[First indorsement.]

Mr. S..

Answer Governor Harris and inform him of what I have done.

J. A. SEDDON.

[Second indorsement.]

MAY 11, 1863.

Mr. OULD:

Another shameful outrage of the enemy in spite of their promise to cease such arrests. Do all you can to procure the release of these ladies.

J. A. SEDDON,
Secretary.

[Third indorsement.]

OFFICE EXCHANGE OF PRISONERS,
Richmond, May 19, 1863.

Respectfully returned to Hon. James A. Seddon, Secretary of War. Miss Battle and Miss Booker were delivered at City Point, Va., May 13, 1863, via flag-of-truce boat.

RO. OULD,
Agent of Exchange.

[Inclosure.]

WINCHESTER, TENN., *May 4, 1863.*

Hon. I. G. HARRIS.

DEAR SIR: A rumor reached me some days since that one of my daughters, Fannie, has been arrested by the Federal authorities and

would probably be sent to a Northern prison. Yesterday I learned for
the first time that the report was certainly true and that she was confined closely at Camp Chase in a room adjoining a hospital. Another
young lady, Miss Harriet Booker, a daughter of one of our friends in
my neighborhood, was arrested at the same time and is confined with
my daughter. I have no personal acquaintance with either General
Johnston or General Bragg and I would take it as a very great kindness in you if you will see them and know if anything can be done by
which my daughter and Miss Booker can be exchanged or the Federals
induced to give them up. I am not advised as to whether we have any
ladies prisoners in the South, but if their newspaper accounts are true
there are some in our lines who ought to be if they persist in their
policy of incarcerating our women and burning our houses. A copy of
the Nashville Union now before me of a late date gives an account of
the cordial reception of Federal prisoners by the ladies of Shelbyville.
For a less offense my daughter is to be closely confined in a loathsome
Northern prison. Will you do me the favor of attending to the foregoing request at your earliest convenience and write me at this place?
    Respectfully, your friend,

                                        JOEL A. BATTLE.

SPECIAL ORDERS, }   ADJT. AND INSP. GENERAL'S OFFICE,
    No. 108.   }   Richmond, May 5, 1863.
    *   *   *   *   *   *   *

    XXIII. The officers now in Petersburg who have lately been prison-
ers will proceed to rejoin their proper commands as soon as they shall
have been declared exchanged.
    By command of the Secretary of War:
                                        JNO. WITHERS,
                                Assistant Adjutant-General.

                                        RICHMOND, May 7, 1863.
General EARL VAN DORN, Columbia, Tenn.:
    All officers captured prior to 1st day of April last and who have been
released upon parole are duly and regularly exchanged and should
rejoin their proper commands at once.
                                        S. COOPER,
                                Adjutant and Inspector General.

                                        HEADQUARTERS, May 7, 1863.
Hon. J. A. SEDDON, Secretary of War.
    SIR: I have the honor to acknowledge the receipt of your letter of
to-day. If the returned prisoners are intended to re-enforce General
Pemberton they should start to join him to-morrow. There is no good
reason that I know of why they should not—that is if that is their
destination. I fear that they may be too late to be useful there or elsewhere if they start. Any delay will increase the probabilities of losing
their services in the present campaign. I hope therefore that they
will be sent at once or not at all.
    I remain, sir, with great respect, &c., your most obedient servant,
                                        J. LONGSTREET,
                                Lieutenant-General, Commanding.

WAR DEPARTMENT, *Richmond, Va., May 7, 1863.*
SECRETARY OF WAR.

SIR: While a prisoner of war at Memphis Lieutenant-Colonel Woods, of the C. S. Army, a prisoner confined in the Irving Block Prison, was shot dead while he was asleep by Lieutenant Lewis [Denis Daily], of the U. S. Army. Colonel Woods had paid Lieutenant Lewis money to aid him in making his escape. After Colonel Woods made his escape Lewis had him (Lieutenant-Colonel Woods) rearrested. After Colonel Woods was rearrested he said Lewis did not act the gentleman with him; he had given Lieutenant Lewis his money and then he (Lewis) betrayed him.

Lieutenant-Colonel Woods was in charge of Lieutenant Larkin and his company. When Lieutenant Lewis went to the prison and asked to see Lieutenant-Colonel Woods he was shown to him. Colonel Woods was asleep. He (Lieutenant Lewis) drew his pistol and shot Colonel Woods in the head, which produced instant death.

Lieutenant Lewis was tried by a court-martial but was not confined and he went to parts unknown. The decision of the court was not made known.

I have the honor to be, sir, very respectfully, your obedient servant,

JAS. HOEY,
Lieutenant, Company A, Seventeenth Arkansas, C. S. Army.

[First indorsement.]

OFFICE EXCHANGE OF PRISONERS,
Richmond, May 20, 1863.

Respectfully referred to Lieut. Col. William H. Ludlow, agent of exchange for further information in connection with this most extraordinary case.

RO. OULD,
Agent of Exchange.

[Second indorsement.]

FORT MONROE, *May 26, 1863.*

Respectfully referred to Col. William Hoffman, commissary-general of prisoners.

WM. H. LUDLOW,
Lieutenant-Colonel and Agent for Exchange of Prisoners.

[Third indorsement.]

OFFICE COMMISSARY-GENERAL OF PRISONERS,
Washington, June 11, 1863.

Respectfully referred to Major-General Hurlbut with the request that the facts in this case may be given.*

W. HOFFMAN,
Colonel Third U. S. Infantry, Commissary-General of Prisoners.

RICHMOND, *May 8, 1863.*
CHARLES D. MYERS,
Assistant Adjutant-General, Petersburg:

All officers delivered by the Federal authorities at City Point up to May 6 are duly and regularly exchanged.

S. COOPER,
Adjutant and Inspector General.

---

* See Vol. VI, this Series, for Hurlbut to Hoffman, June 23, 1863, making report upon this matter.

EXECUTIVE DEPARTMENT,
Montgomery, Ala., May 8, 1863.

Hon. JAMES A. SEDDON, Secretary of War, Richmond, Va.

SIR: I am advised that among the prisoners recently captured near Rome, Ga., by General Forrest are officers found serving within the limits of the State of Alabama with armed slaves inciting slaves to insurrection within this State. If this information proves to be correct the departure from the rules of civilized warfare will and should deprive them of the benefit of any convention giving them the privileges of prisoners of war and render them amenable to the laws of the State of Alabama as criminals. In order that the military authorities might not be trammeled by any action in advance which might prejudice the claim of the State of Alabama upon these prisoners I telegraphed to General Bragg my intention to demand them for trial under the laws of this State, and the propriety of granting it can easily be determined upon the reports which General Forrest will make of the results of his expedition. If his report should state the fact to be as I have been informed the case of these officers will be clearly within the announcement of the intention of the President in relation to the proclamation of President Lincoln that they shall be surrendered on demand to the State authorities for trial.

But another matter has been brought to my notice in reference to this capture to which I wish especially to call your attention, not with a view of embarrassing the action of the Government, but to arrive at just and correct conclusions as to the proper course to pursue not only in relation to the present but to future captures of our own citizens willingly serving in the ranks of the enemy. Among the prisoners captured by General Forrest I understand there are two companies of Alabamians who have enlisted as such in the army of the enemy, and having been engaged with known enemies of the State and the Confederate States in acts not justified by any rule of war or by necessity have been captured on the soil of Alabama not only levying war against the State but instigating slaves to rebellion and committing deeds of rapine and destruction upon the property of its citizens without the excuse which can pertain to military necessity or the course of war. If the uniform of our enemy is to continue to protect their officers and men in their depredations upon private property and wanton destruction of commodities which cannot be classed as munitions of war to say nothing of assaults upon peaceful citizens and inhuman treatment of the helpless and unprotected or their instigation of our slaves to leave their service is it also to protect our recreant and traitorous citizens who still claiming themselves as Alabamians afford to our enemies the means of striking at the heart of the State and when captured claim the flag of our enemy as their protection? Ample opportunity was given to these traitors to cast their lot with the enemy and remove this reproach and stigma from the State. With a forbearance before unknown one of the earliest acts of the Confederacy was to invite those who preferred the rule of our enemies to leave our borders in peace and establish themselves in the Government of their choice. But these traitors preferred to remain that their crime might strike deeper and their blow fall heavier, and having chosen their status as citizens of a State of the Confederacy they should not be allowed to escape the penalty of treason which they have invited. They stand as citizens levying war as well as giving aid and comfort to our enemies.

They have chosen this position deliberately well knowing the penalty, rejecting the clemency of the Government, leaving in many instances their dependent families upon our soil to be supported by the charity of our people and proclaiming their intention to lead or accompany the armies of our enemy for our overthrow and destruction. If there could be any doubt as to their position if captured in legitimate warfare in the ranks of our enemies that doubt must be resolved when they abandon such warfare to engage in pillage of private property and murderous destruction of life. No commission can justify deeds of rapine and violation of the rules of civilized warfare. Even if through motives of policy we suspend the proper and fitting punishment of our known enemies, citizens of hostile States or aliens serving in their ranks who under orders of their superiors commit such acts of wanton depredation, the same reasons cannot apply to these marauders who flaunt the flag of their treason in our faces and dare and defy us in their malice. I do not wish to discuss the question whether their treason to their own State is merged in their treason against the Confederacy nor to embarrass the Confederate Government with questions of jurisdiction. It will be enough for me and the State I represent if these traitors be taught that impunity is not to be bought with bravado, and it will be a matter of indifference whether they receive the reward of their treason at the hands of the Confederacy or by the laws of the State. It is then with a view of disembarrassing the Confederate Government that I respectfully request that these marauders be delivered up to the authorities of this State for trial by her civil tribunals for their acts of violence and rapine against our citizens and their treason against the State whose citizens they claim to be. It cannot be alleged for them as it might be for traitorous citizens of border States that there are conflicting claims of hostile governments to jurisdiction or that the State has failed through the calamity of war to afford protection and redress to her citizens. Their position has been voluntarily sought, their treason openly avowed and boastingly vindicated, their attack upon the State premeditated, their violence wanton and malicious. They have braved the penalty of treason in avowing themselves Alabamians and as such serving with marauding bands of the enemy within the borders of our State and are not entitled to the privileges of prisoners of war. If it is preferred by the Confederate authorities to retain and try them for their treasonable acts I am willing to waive the demand on the part of the State; but believing that justice will be fully and fairly meted out to them by the judicial tribunals of Alabama it would be more agreeable to me that both the officers mentioned and the men alluded to be turned over upon my demands to the State authorities. Proper arrangements will be made for their safekeeping until they can have a fair and impartial trial.

Very respectfully, your obedient servant,

JNO. GILL SHORTER,
Governor of Alabama.

N. B.—It may become expedient in order to satisfy the public mind now much exercised on these questions to publish our correspondence. I shall be pleased to receive any suggestion from you on this point.

J. G. S.

TULLAHOMA, *May 9, 1863.*

General S. COOPER:

In my dispatch of the 7th instant I intended to ask whether I should send the officers who commanded the party of the enemy by whom negroes were seized to Richmond or turn them over to the Governor of Alabama.

B. BRAGG.

HEADQUARTERS DIVISION, *May 9, 1863.*

Maj. A. S. PENDLETON, *Assistant Adjutant-General.*

MAJOR: I understand that a very great number of prisoners taken have on their knapsacks shelter-tents. These are beyond a doubt public property, having been issued to them by the United States Government. These things are very useful and I would respectfully suggest that steps be taken to secure them for our Government.

Very respectfully, your obedient servant,

H. HETH,
Brigadier-General.

[First indorsement.]

HEADQUARTERS SECOND ARMY CORPS, *May 10, 1863.*

Respectfully forwarded and recommended that the authorities in Richmond be written to to secure these articles.

A. P. HILL,
Major-General, Commanding.

[Second indorsement.]

MAY 11, 1863.

Respectfully referred to Brigadier-General Winder. It is thought that nearly all the shelter-tents were secured before the prisoners were sent down.

By order of General Lee:

W. H. TAYLOR,
Assistant Adjutant-General.

[Third indorsement.]

HEADQUARTERS DEPARTMENT OF HENRICO,
Richmond, May 13, 1863.

Respectfully referred to Captain Turner, who will carry the suggestion of General Heth into execution. Please return this paper.

By order of General Winder:

J. W. PEGRAM,
Assistant Adjutant-General.

[Fourth indorsement.]

C. S. MILITARY PRISON, *May —, 1863.*

Nearly all the shelter-tents had been taken from the prisoners before they reached this prison.

T. P. TURNER,
Captain, Commanding.

[Fifth indorsement.]

HEADQUARTERS DEPARTMENT OF HENRICO,
Richmond, May 16, 1863.

Respectfully forwarded to Brig. Gen. R. H. Chilton, assistant adjutant and inspector general, with the remarks of Captain Turner.

JNO. H. WINDER,
Brigadier-General.

GENERAL ORDERS, }   ADJT. AND INSP. GENERAL'S OFFICE,
    No. 58.   }   *Richmond, May 11, 1863.*

I. The following notice relative to exchanged prisoners is published for the information of all concerned:

EXCHANGE NOTICE, No. 5.]   RICHMOND, *May 9, 1863.*

The following Confederate officers and men have been duly exchanged and are hereby so declared:

1 All officers and men who have been delivered at City Point at any time previous to May 6, 1863.

2. All officers captured at any place before the 1st of April, 1863, who have been released on parole.

3. All men captured in North Carolina or Virginia before the 1st of March, 1863, who have been released on parole.

4. The officers and men captured and paroled by General S. P. Carter in his expedition to East Tennessee in December last.

5. The officers and men captured and paroled by Lieutenant-Colonel Stuart at Van Buren, Ark., January 25, 1863; by Colonel Dickey in December, 1862, in his march to the Mobile and Ohio Railroad and by Captain Cameron at Corinth, Miss., in December, 1862.

6. The officers and men paroled at Oxford, Miss., on the 23d of December, 1862; at Des Arc, Ark., on the 17th of January, 1863, and at Baton Rouge, La., on the 23d February, 1863.

7. All persons who have been captured on the sea or the waters leading to the same or upon the sea-coast of the Confederate or United States at any time previous to December 10, 1862.

8. All civilians who have been arrested at any time before the 6th of May, 1863, and released on parole are discharged from any and every obligation contained in said parole. If any such person has taken any oath of allegiance to the United States or given any bond or if his release was accompanied with any other conditions he is discharged from the same.

•9 If any person embraced in any of the foregoing sections or in any section of any previous exchange notice wherein they are declared exchanged are in any Federal prison, they are to be immediately released and delivered to the Confederate authorities.

                        RO. OULD,
                        Agent of Exchange.

II. All persons whether citizens or soldiers are expressly prohibited from using or in any manner interfering with fuel or wood cut and delivered for the use of railroads or railroad companies. It is of the first importance that this order should be observed and it will be strictly obeyed and enforced by the Army.

By order:

                        S. COOPER,
                        Adjutant and Inspector General.

———

                        RICHMOND, *May 11, 1863.*

Lieutenant-General PEMBERTON:

All newspaper correspondents, traders and citizens of the United States captured on board steamers plying [the] Mississippi will be sent directly to this place to be disposed of by the authorities here.

                        RO. OULD,
                        Agent for Exchange of Prisoners.

SPECIAL ORDERS, }   ADJT. AND INSP. GENERAL'S OFFICE,
No. 113.   }   *Richmond, May 11, 1863.*

*   *   *   *   *   *   *

XIV. The Missouri officers and enlisted men who were exchanged at City Point on the 4th instant will immediately be sent to report for duty to General E. K. Smith at Alexandria.

By command of the Secretary of War:

JNO. WITHERS,
Assistant Adjutant-General.

RICHMOND, *May 13, 1863.*

General B. BRAGG, *Tullahoma, Tenn.:*

Send at once to this city all captured officers and men.

S. COOPER,
Adjutant and Inspector General.

OFFICE EXCHANGE OF PRISONERS,
Richmond, Va., May 13, 1863.

[General B. BRAGG:]

All Federal officers and men captured by our forces and not released on parole will be sent direct to this place to be disposed of by the authorities here.

RO. OULD,
Agent of Exchange.

RICHMOND, VA., *May 14, 1863.*

Honorable SECRETARY OF WAR.

SIR: I take this opportunity of dropping these few lines. I was taken prisoner at the late fights on the Rappahannock and have taken the oath of allegiance to support the Confederate States of America. My reason was one which all true Southern men come to. I am a son of Frank P. Blair, of Missouri, and a nephew of Hon. Montgomery Blair, Lincoln's Postmaster-General. I was in the Yankee Army about seven months. I have served about three months as a private soldier and four months as a lieutenant. I hereby offer my services to the Southern Confederacy in any capacity that you may think proper.

I am, very respectfully, your obedient servant,

FRANK P. BLAIR, JR.*

[Indorsement.]

JUNE 20, 1863.

I have heard privately the suggestion that the motive of this young man is to save from sequestration some property of his own or his family in the South. *Timeo Danaos.*

R. G. H. K[EAN].

CHRISTIANSBURG, VA., *May 14, 1863.*

Hon. JAMES A. SEDDON.

DEAR SIR: At the commencement of the war there was a young man in this place who volunteered in Captain Trigg's company, called the

---

* Evidently an impostor.

Wise Fencibles, afterwards the Montgomery Fencibles. He remained in service until the battle of Kernstown when he was taken prisoner. He was confined in Fort Delaware for a considerable time. He was on General Jackson's staff at the time of his capture. His father lives in Pennsylvania or New Jersey, who visited him in his confinement and urged him to take the oath of allegiance to the Northern Government and be released. He refused most peremptorily and the old man finding that no argument would induce his son thus to take the oath returned home and after some time returned and represented to his son that his mother was deranged and obtained certificates from physicians to prove the fact, and represented that it was on his account that this derangement existed and urged him to take the oath and obtain his release in order that he might visit his mother and thereby be the means of restoring her mind. Making such an issue as this with his son and having previously arranged the matter with Lincoln not to have him exchanged he consented on his mother's account for whom he entertained the most tender regard to take the oath, but which was done at the time under a protest. When he arrived at his father's he found that his father had deceived him and that his mother was not deranged, and was dissatisfied with the course pursued by his father. From these considerations and the bad treatment he received from his father he determined to make his escape and return to Virginia, which he effected. He is now a captain of a company in Col. Henry A. Edmundson's battalion, and was very near being again captured at the fight on Blackwater under General Pryor. He is now on his march to Kentucky where he took a trip some weeks ago and returned. It has occurred to me that if he should again be taken prisoner he might be dealt with very severely, and I have therefore felt it a duty to bring his case to your attention and see if he could not be exchanged or something done to relieve him of his present situation. He is devoted to the South and is willing to sacrifice even his life in her cause. His name is George G. Junkin. I should be much pleased to hear from you on this subject. I have stated his case precisely as I understand it, having received the information from him.

Very respectfully, your humble servant,

R. D. MONTAGUE.

[Indorsement.]

WAR DEPARTMENT, *May 18, 1863.*

The gentleman referred to herein was a brother-in-law of General T. J. Jackson. On his return from the North he sent through General Jackson a resignation of his command with a very touching narration of the circumstances by which he had been induced to take the oath and his deep humiliation and contrition for having done so. The resignation was accepted.

R. G. H. K[EAN,]
Chief of Bureau of War.

GENERAL ORDERS, }   ADJT. AND INSP. GENERAL'S OFFICE,
No. 62.   }   *Richmond, May 16, 1863.*

I. In accordance with an act to amend an act entitled "An act to better provide for the sick and wounded of the army in hospitals," approved May 1, 1863, the following modifications in General Orders, No. 95, last series from this office, are published:

The commuted value of rations for sick and disabled soldiers in hospitals (field or general) will until further orders be $1.25.

II. Hospital laundresses will be paid $25 per month and allowed rations and quarters.

By order:

S. COOPER,
Adjutant and Inspector General.

EXECUTIVE DEPARTMENT, *Raleigh, May 18, 1863.*

Hon. JAMES A. SEDDON, *Secretary of War, Richmond, Va.*

SIR: I had the honor to request of you some time since an examination into the case of Lieut. Col. J. A. Keith, Sixty-fourth North Carolina Troops, charged with the murder of some unarmed prisoners and little boys during the recent troubles in the mountains of this State. I have heard by rumor only that he was brought before a court-martial and honorably acquitted by producing an order for his conduct from General Davis, commanding in East Tennessee. I have also been officially notified of his resignation. Will it be consistent with your sense of duty to furnish me a copy of the proceedings of the court-martial in his case? Murder is a crime against the common law in this State and he is now subject to that law.

Very respectfully, &c.,

Z. B. VANCE.

WAR DEPARTMENT, *Richmond, May 19, 1863.*

General BRAXTON BRAGG, *Tullahoma, Tenn.:*

Governor J. G. Shorter writes that he had requested to retain the officers and the two companies of Alabamians among prisoners captured by General N. B. Forrest as he designs requesting their delivery to him for trial. If not previously sent hold them subject to further orders.

JAMES A. SEDDON,
Secretary of War.

CHARLESTON, S. C., *May 19, 1863.*

Hon. PIERRE SOULÉ, *Havana, Cuba.*
(Care of Señor Don Juan de Bances.)

DEAR SIR: I send you herewith inclosed a letter* from the Hon. Charles M. Conrad inclosing me an order of the War Department at Richmond containing a notice from Mr. Robert Ould, C. S. agent for the exchange of prisoners, which I think embraces your case and releases you from any obligations or parole to the U. S. authorities. I hope then that you will take the earliest opportunity to return amongst us and accept the position of volunteer aide on my staff which you desired last year before the fall of New Orleans, or should I be able to serve you in any other way pray let me know and it shall be done with much pleasure.

I suppose you have heard by this time of our success here and near Fredericksburg, but unfortunately without visible or marked results on the present struggle. The people of the North appear to be as determined as ever to wage upon us a war of extermination. Our country is being gradually overrun, and although we recover the lost ground occasionally still the damages incurred cannot be repaired.

---

* Not found.

*Ceux qui nous gouvernent doivent sûrement se nourrir de "Hatchie,"
car malgré nos malheurs, ils croient toujours à une paix dans soixante
jours!*

But I have faith in the future; our people are resolved to die rather
than submit to Yankee rule! With that determination they cannot be
conquered.

Hoping to have the pleasure of seeing you soon, I remain, truly,
your friend,

G. T. BEAUREGARD.

SPECIAL ORDERS, }   HEADQUARTERS,
   No. —. }   *Near Canton, Miss., May 21, 1863.*

I. When the services of Federal medical officers are not required for
the care of Federal wounded in hospital at Jackson they will be at
once sent to Richmond. ·

II. All Federal sick and wounded in hospital at Jackson who can
bear transportation will be sent immediately to hospital at Montgomery, Ala.

The necessary number of medical officers will be sent with them.

By command of General Johnston:

B. S. EWELL,
Assistant Adjutant-General.

RALEIGH, *May 22, 1863.*

Hon. J. A. SEDDON, *Richmond, Va.:*

I send you thirteen prisoners captured by my State troops, having
no place to keep them. Please retain them until I notify you that they
may be exchanged. The enemy murdered two of my men and I wish
to retaliate as soon as I can communicate with General Foster.

Z. B. VANCE.

KNOXVILLE, *May 22, 1863.*

Hon. GEORGE BROWN,
Judge of the Third Judicial Circuit of Tennessee:

Respondent John E. Toole for answer and return to your honor's
writ of *habeas corpus* issued upon the petition of Stephen McKee,
Michael Malone and Jonathan Summit would respectfully state and
show unto your honor that the statement of petitioners that they are
restrained of their liberty upon a charge of the murder of John Cunningham, who was a citizen of Monroe County, &c., is wholly untrue
and without foundation. Petitioners were not arrested and have not
been held upon the charge of the murder of John Cunningham.

Respondent here begs leave to submit to your honor a full and correct statement of facts as to the manner in which petitioners came into
the custody of respondent:

On the 3d of this month Col. G. Troup Maxwell, an officer of the
C. S. Army, commandant of the post at Loudon, Tenn., sent said petitioners as prisoners under guard to respondent as provost-marshal for
the Department of East Tennessee charged with disloyalty and treason
against the Government of the Confederate States in harboring and
feeding a band of bushwhackers who were committing acts of violence
upon the citizens of Monroe County, Tenn., and in discharge of my
duty as a subordinate officer of the Confederate Army and in obedience

to general orders and instructions from the commanding general of the Department of East Tennessee said petitioners were committed to the military prison at Knoxville to await such further disposition as the Confederate authorities might make in the premises. Afterwards, to wit, on the 12th instant Michael Malone, one of said petitioners, was released from custody upon my application and permitted to return home, and a few days since after the service of the writ upon me petitioners Stephen McKee and Jonathan Summit were arrested and taken out of the custody of the military authorities by the C. S. marshal for the District of East Tennessee upon a warrant for treason issued by Confederate Commissioner Elliott. Consequently none of said petitioners are in my custody or under my control or the control of the military authorities, but are in the custody and under the control of the civil officers of the Confederate Government, and for this reason I have no power or authority to have the bodies of petitioners before your honor at Sweet Water Depot on the 23d instant as directed and required by your honor's writ.

Now, having made full answer and return of my doings in the premises I pray to be hence dismissed.

JOHN E. TOOLE,
Colonel and Provost-Marshal Department of East Tennessee.

HEADQUARTERS IN THE FIELD,
Okolona, Miss., May 22, 1863.

Maj. R. W. MEMMINGER, <i>Assistant Adjutant-General.</i>

SIR: I have the honor to report for the information of the lieutenant-general commanding the department that on the 20th instant some forty persons, citizens of Missouri, reached the vicinity of Pontotoc under Federal military escort, exiled from their homes by the mandates from the Federal Government. The circumstances were such that it seemed to be incumbent upon me to receive them, especially as a large proportion of them are ladies and children driven to the alternative of exile from their homes, coming within our military lines or imprisonment at the North. This act of hospitality to our citizens who have become victims of political oppression after having fallen under the enemy's power seems due alike from motives of humanity and public courtesy.

A complete copy of the Federal orders and other papers accompanying these exiles is herewith* communicated for the information of the honorable Secretary of War. It will be seen that the Federal system of espionage, their orders of arrest, their despotic mandates of exile in the cases of delicate ladies and innocent children, their seizure of property of the wealthy exiles, their instigation of servile war, combined with the general and unrestrained license to plunder, rob and destroy which marks the movements of their military forces indicate the speedy inauguration of a reign of terror unparalleled in the history of civilized races of men. It is also to be observed that this Federal system of exile is designed to strike terror among loyal citizens in all border communities and to paralyze their actions and sympathies as well as to throw upon us on any pretense their spies, their outlaws and degraded classes at all times and for most unjustifiable causes.

The Federal authorities have prohibited exiles from bringing with them over $200 to each single person and $1,000 to each family, and

----

* Not found.

that not in gold or Confederate money but in Federal paper which is valueless and not currency within the Confederate lines.

Under these circumstances I feel constrained to recommend that in future persons thus forced from their homes under this system of tyranny be not received within our military lines with such special exceptions as it may be deemed expedient to make, and that explicit instructions be furnished me as to the policy and intentions of the Government on this subject.

Very respectfully, your obedient servant,

DANIEL RUGGLES,
Brigadier-General, Commanding District.

WAR DEPARTMENT, *Richmond, Va., May 23, 1863.*

His Excellency JOHN GILL SHORTER,
Governor of Alabama, Montgomery, Ala.

SIR: I have the honor to acknowledge the receipt of your communication of the 8th instant advising that among the prisoners captured near Rome, Ga., were officers found serving within the limits of the State of Alabama with armed slaves, inciting slaves to insurrection within the State, and that also among the prisoners captured at the same time were two companies of Alabamians who had enlisted as such in the army of the enemy and having been engaged with known enemies of the State and Confederate States in acts not justified by any rule of war or necessity had been captured upon the soil of Alabama not only levying war against the State but inciting slaves to rebellion and committing rapine and destruction on the property of its citizens. You informed the Department that you had telegraphed General Bragg to retain both the officers and the two companies of Alabamians with the intention of demanding that they should be delivered to you for trial by the courts of your State for their offenses against its laws and sovereignty. At the same time you state a willingness to waive such demand on the part of the State if it be preferred by the Confederate Government to retain and try these offenders for their crimes.

This communication has been submitted to the President and has been the subject of advisement and grave consideration, and I have been instructed to inform you that while on the statement of facts presented the offenses of these parties against the laws and dignity of the State are recognized yet considerations of public policy in his judgment make it more advisable that the cases should be brought under the cognizance of the tribunals of the Confederacy and remain subject to the final determination of its Executive. This it is not doubted will prove equally satisfactory not only to yourself but to the people of the State whose confidence in the Confederacy and its authorities has been so nobly evinced under all the trying ordeals of the war. It is proper to say, however, that some delay may arise in disposing of these cases from the necessity of awaiting the receipt of the official report of General Forrest.

I regret to inform you that before the receipt of your letter through the speedy action of the officials intrusted with the duty of exchanging prisoners the larger number of these alleged criminals have for the present escaped a just retribution. Without knowledge of their offenses or of your telegram to General Bragg the Adjutant-General had ordered the prisoners taken to be forwarded for exchange to this city, and under that order they were accordingly sent. This I learned from General Bragg in reply to a telegram directing their retention. On inquiry here I find there was no Alabama regiment (so-called) among the prisoners, but of a so-called Tennessee regiment there were two companies which are believed to have been composed of Alabamians. The privates had before the receipt of your letter been sent off under the cartel. Some of the officers of these companies as well as of the other regiments captured by General Forrest remain, and they will suffice perhaps to exhibit the determination of the Government and serve as exemplars of the punishment which will be visited on such crimes. The measure of forbearance so long exhibited by the authorities and people of the South under the outrages and atrocious violations of all the usages of civilized warfare by the enemy has been at last exhausted, and it only remains to vindicate by unavoidable retaliation the wrongs of our army and people and if possible deter by fear our unscrupulous foes insensible to all higher influences from a repetition of their atrocities.

Yours, with esteem,

JAMES A. SEDDON,
Secretary of War.

WAR DEPARTMENT, *Richmond, Va., May 23, 1863.*
His Excellency Z. B. VANCE, *Governor of North Carolina.*

SIR: Your letter of the 18th instant has been received. The resignation of Lieutenant-Colonel Keith was accepted at the office of the Adjutant and Inspector General the 15th instant. No proceedings of a court-martial in his case have been received. His resignation was accepted on the recommendation of Colonel Palmer, commanding the brigade, and Major-General Maury, the examining board having reported against his competency. The Adjutant and Inspector General was not aware of the facts of the alleged murder as applying to this officer at the time of his action on the resignation, there being no reference to the facts in the papers before him. In a communication to the Department by Lieutenant-Colonel Keith he claims that Brigadier-General Heth gave him a verbal order to this effect: "I want no reports from you about your course at Laurel. I do not want to be troubled with any prisoners and the last one of them should be killed;" that he went on further to state that he had been troubled with several prisoners from Laurel, N. C., and he did not want any more brought to Knoxville. This statement is supported by the deposition of a Doctor Thompson, and Keith states in his letter that he can prove it by another witness. The communication of Keith and the deposition of Thompson were submitted to General Heth for remarks. He says that he gave written instructions to Keith which will be found on the books of the Department of East Tennessee. He admits that he told Keith that those found in arms ought not to be treated as enemies, and in the event of an engagement with them to take no prisoners as he considered that they had forfeited all such claims, but he denies in strong terms the making use of any remarks which would authorize maltreatment of prisoners who had been accepted as such or to women and children.

Very respectfully, your obedient servant,

JAMES A. SEDDON,
Secretary of War.

PROVOST-MARSHAL'S OFFICE, *Weldon, May 23, 1863.*

General D. H. HILL, *Commanding Troops in North Carolina.*

GENERAL: I send you under guard with evidence against him James Dutton, a man of disloyal sentiment and no doubt an enemy of the first grade to the Confederate States. The guard that accompanies this man heard him publicly use sentiments detrimental to our cause and you may elicit from them sufficient evidence to cause his arrest. I inclose a soldier's discharge and his oath of allegiance.* The former you will discover is very imperfect, it not having been filled up. I believe the discharge a forgery. He was very impudent to me in questioning him and unreservedly uttered sentiments that would justify my pronouncing him a dangerous character.

I am, general, very respectfully, your obedient servant,

W. BRENAN,
Lieutenant and Provost-Marshal.

[Inclosure.]

WELDON, N. C., *May 24, 1863.*

Evidence of Sergt. L. LEWIS, Company A, Nineteenth Georgia:

I met prisoner at Weldon, N. C., under car-shed. He asked me to what regiment I belonged and where we were going. I told him we were going to Goldsborough or near there. He then replied that if we would behave ourselves and quit fighting we would all get to go home soon. I asked him what he meant by behaving ourselves and he made no answer. I then asked him where he lived. He said, "I live near Weldon; was born in Alabama." I then asked him if he belonged to the army. He answered, "That is none of your business." I then asked him what he was doing there and if he had any showing. He said, "I have, but won't show them to you," and at the same time tried to get away. I caught him by his coat collar and ordered him to show his papers. He told me that he was an old soldier and had been a member of the Fifth Alabama Regiment. I then had him put under arrest and sent to the provost-marshal.

Evidence of J. P. MERRITT, Company H, Nineteenth Georgia:

I first met prisoner at Weldon Hotel. He had his hand full of tobacco and asked me if I wanted to buy. After learning the price I told him no. He then asked me how we were getting along with the war in Virginia. I told him that we had whipped them there. He then said, "If you fellows will just only behave yourselves you will get to go home in a few days." I then asked him his reasons for using such expression as that. He replied to me, "You damned rebel, is that any of your business?" I then asked him what regiment he belonged to. He said, "I belong to no regiment." I asked him where he was from. He said, "From close about here;" then turned off to another gentleman and said, "I wouldn't give ten Yankees for the whole Southern Army." I then asked him if he was an Abolitionist. He said, "I have a right to be what I please. Is that any of your business?" I told him it was. He then said, "Well, make it your business, you damned scamp." I then quit him and went and told Sergeant Lewis about him.

Evidence of R. E. GARNER, Company G, Twenty-third Georgia:

I first met prisoner in the eating saloon under car-shed. He was making sport of the proprietor about some tobacco he had bought.

* Oath of allegiance, &c., omitted.

They got to talking then and I was a listener. He told the proprietor he had been in service two years. The proprietor replied: "I have been in service about two years, too." He then said: "You shall not go into service any more, nor I don't intend to go, either." He then turned around and said: "If you all had done as I wanted you to do you would have had peace and been at home now." He said: "If we would go home and stay there about two months we would have peace anyhow." We then wanted to know upon what terms peace could be made in so short a time. He then replied, addressing me: "I can send you home now if I would." I told him I would like to go for I had been in service about two years and had never yet been home. He then said: "You wouldn't go when I wanted you to and now you will have to stay here some time before you go." We then asked him what authority he had to send us home. He said he had the authority, but refused to tell us what authority it was. He said then to the crowd that there were some few Yankees six of whom he wouldn't give for every Confederate soldier. We spoke then of having him arrested for using such language. He said we had no authority for arresting him; that he had a right to say what he pleased. We asked him what right he had and wanted to see his authority for talking so. He had a small stick, a splinter, in his hand and said: "This is all the authority I want," referring to the stick. We then thought he might have some office there and outranked us and that we would have no more to say to him right then but had better watch him awhile. We watched him till he fell in company with Sergeant Lewis and heard part of the conversation between him and the sergeant.

This is the evidence of the three witnesses as given to me by each one separately.

J. A. RICHARDSON,
Lieutenant, Company C, Nineteenth Georgia Regiment.

HEADQUARTERS DEPARTMENT NO. 2,
Shelbyville, Tenn., May 26, 1863.

Hon. C. L. VALLANDIGHAM, of Ohio, *Shelbyville.*

SIR: I inclose you the passport desired and congratulate you on your arrival in our land of liberty where you will find the freedom of speech and of conscience secured to all. Your sojourn amongst us as a private citizen, exiled by a foreign Government with which we are at war, will of course impose some restraints upon you which our people will fully appreciate. But I am satisfied you will ever receive the courtesy due your unfortunate position and the respect of all who learn the quiet and retired position you have determined to occupy.

I am, sir, very respectfully, your obedient servant,
BRAXTON BRAGG,
General, C. S. Army.

[Inclosure.]

SHELBYVILLE, TENN., *May 26, 1863.*

Mr. Vallandigham, the bearer, a citizen of the State of Ohio, is permitted to pass as any citizen of the Confederacy within the limits of this department.

BRAXTON BRAGG,
General.

SPECIAL ORDERS, }   ADJT. AND INSP. GENERAL'S OFFICE,
    No. 125.   }   *Richmond, Va., May 26, 1863.*
  *   *   *   *   *   *   *

XI. The depot for recaptured slaves at McMinnville, Tenn., as announced in General Orders, No. 25, current series, is hereby changed to Chattanooga, Tenn.

  *   *   *   *   *   *   *

By command of the Secretary of War:

JNO. WITHERS,
Assistant Adjutant-General.

HEADQUARTERS ARMY OF NORTHERN VIRGINIA,
May 27, 1863.

Hon. JAMES A. SEDDON, *Secretary of War.*

SIR: Since the receipt of your letter of April 13 with regard to the general orders (No. 49) issued by Major-General Halleck, commanding U. S. forces, on the subject of paroles and prisoners of war, I have had no fit opportunity of communicating to General Hooker your views concerning that order.

Upon a full examination of the subject I beg leave respectfully to submit for your consideration that in my opinion no good can be accomplished by a discussion with General Hooker of the various points suggested.

From the conduct of the United States Government for some time past in the long detention of our prisoners, &c., they do not seem to regard the late cartel as binding, nor is this order (No. 49) the rule of their conduct since they administer the oath to all prisoners who will take it, a clear violation of paragraph 8 of that order.

In their late expedition to Ashland they paroled our wounded men and others in violation of paragraph 6 of the same order.

This is an order issued for the guidance of all the armies of the United States, and I think some more satisfactory understanding might be arrived at by causing Commissioner Ould to present the subject to the Commissioner of the United States for the consideration of his Government. If he could effect only the more prompt return of our prisoners by the enemy it would be a considerable improvement on the state of things which has prevailed for some months past, and might prevent in a measure the suffering and loss incurred by long imprisonment.

Any letter which I might write to General Hooker would be referred by him to his Government, and would most probably lead to recrimination and end in a long and useless correspondence.

I am, with great respect, your obedient servant,

R. E. LEE,
General.

HEADQUARTERS DEPARTMENT No. 2,
Shelbyville, May 27, 1863.

ADJUTANT AND INSPECTOR GENERAL, *Richmond, Va.*

SIR: On the 25th instant the Hon. C. L. Vallandigham, of Ohio, United States, was brought by an armed guard of the enemy to the neutral ground between our pickets on the road from Murfreesborough to this place and was there abandoned by them. I have admitted him within my lines and recei-. ed him with the courtesy due any unfortunate exile seeking a refuge from tyranny. He desires to go to the State of Georgia and I have granted him permission for that purpose. Should the Government desire any other policy in similar cases I shall be pleased to receive instructions.

I am, sir, very respectfully, your obedient servant,

BRAXTON BRAGG,
General, Commanding.

HARRISONBURG, *May 28, 1863.*

Hon. JAMES A. SEDDON, *Secretary of War:*

Allow an old Fredericksburg schoolmate of yours to suggest as to the disposal of the prisoners, both officers and privates, belonging to the negro regiments who may fall into our hands that they be employed in the Chesterfield coal-pits. The subject is difficult of solution and I will not undertake to elaborate the idea but would respectfully throw it out as my opinion worthy of the serious consideration of our Government.

Your friend and well-wisher,

J. M. W.

A communication addressed to surgeon in charge hospital at this place will reach me.

Very respectfully,

J. M. W.

WAR DEPARTMENT, *Richmond, May 28, 1863.*

General BRAXTON BRAGG, *Tullahoma, Tenn.:*

In General N. B. Forrest's report of capture of enemy near Rome no mention is made of armed negroes being engaged as has been represented by Governor J. G. Shorter. Request from General Forrest special report on that point.

JAMES A. SEDDON,
Secretary of War.

SPECIAL ORDERS, }   ADJT. AND INSP. GENERAL'S OFFICE,
No. 127.   }   *Richmond, May 28, 1863.*

*   *   *   *   *   *   *

II. The Department of North Carolina will hereafter include the Department of Southern Virginia as far north as to embrace the city of Petersburg and its environs and including the Appomattox River. All the troops within this department thus extended will be under the command of Maj. Gen. D. H. Hill.

The arrangements for the parole and exchange of prisoners by the Appomattox River will as heretofore be under the control of the agent for exchange, Colonel Ould, and the disposal of the prisoners after parole and exchange will be directed by the orders of Brigadier-General Winder, commanding the Department of Henrico.

      *   *   *   *   *   *   *

By command of the Secretary of War:

JNO. WITHERS,
Assistant Adjutant-General.

WAR DEPARTMENT, *Richmond, May 29, 1863.*

General B. BRAGG:

It was clearly an abuse of the flag of truce to employ it to cover a guard over expelled citizens, non-combatants, found at their homes by an invading army. Your right to hold soldiers so employed as prisoners of war or even to deal with them as spies is not questioned, but lest the men implicated may have ignorantly offended let them have the benefit of the flag so far as to be sent back with a warning to their commanding general against the repetition of such an outrage on the usages of war to aid him in his greater outrage against humanity and the usages of civilized nations.

J. A. SEDDON,
Secretary of War.

MOUNT STERLING, KY., *May 30, 1863.*

The AUTHORITIES AT RICHMOND, VA.

GENTLEMEN: Having learned through the newspapers and other sources that Capt. Samuel McKee, of the Fourteenth Regiment of Kentucky Cavalry, now in Richmond, Va., a prisoner, has been condemned to be executed as a retaliatory measure for Captain Corbin, recently executed at Cincinnati, I desire in behalf of Captain McKee to offer the following suggestions and most respectfully and earnestly to ask that the sentence may be reversed. I have resided in the same county with Captain McKee and have known him somewhat intimately for quite a number of years. He was born and raised in the county of Montgomery, Ky., where he still resides and where he has always maintained an irreproachable moral character. For several years past he has been a member of the church, since which time he has been regarded in this community as an exemplary Christian. At the time of his capture Captain McKee was stationed at this place and for some time previous thereto had been acting as provost-marshal here, during which period and up to his capture I never heard a charge or complaint against him save in the case of Capt. F. Ferguson, of the Confederate service, captured in November last, and for that I do not think Captain McKee should be blamed. He was not at the time the commander of this post but was under a superior officer. While Captain McKee had the custody of Captain Ferguson his treatment was not only humane but kind, permitting him to visit and remain with his family all night; nor is there any reason to believe that this course toward Captain Ferguson would have been changed if Captain McKee had been left to pursue his own course, and the change was no doubt made in obedience to the positive order of his superior officer superinduced by some imprudence doubtless upon the part of Captain Ferguson himself. This in relation

to Captain Ferguson's case, however, may have been wholly unnecessary as it is not for any crime or offense that Captain McKee has
committed that he is condemned to suffer. Certainly no humane or
Christian tribunal ever had the sentence of death executed even upon
a guilty criminal without sorrowing over the necessity which required
it. How much deeper must that sorrow be when the dread sentence is
to be executed upon one who has been guilty of no offense but has to
die for another; and who would not in sorrow see the innocent suffer?
May I not then in view of the innocence of Captain McKee implore
you to spare his life? He has a wife and two innocent, helpless babes,
all dependent upon him for a support and who will be left in helpless
widowhood and orphanage. If you should deem it proper to hold him
a prisoner of war and modify the sentence to that extent it would be
infinitely better it seems to me for all concerned. But a reversal of
the judgment and that Captain McKee may be exchanged is most
sincerely asked, and in this I believe our whole community without
distinction of parties concurs.

Very respectfully,

B. J. PETERS.

[Indorsement.]

ABINGDON, *June 6, 1863.*

President DAVIS:

The writer of the within letter, the Hon. B. J. Peters, is a true
Southern man. I have known him long and well. The bearer of this,
Doctor Hannah, is likewise a true man to the South and has done
much for us and suffered much. While I cannot concur in the Hon.
B. J. Peters' opinion of McKee's character I will respectfully ask that
the President will cause the execution of the sentence on Captain
McKee to be suspended, for the present at least. I ask this for the
personal security of our people at home. Doctor Hannah will give the
President full information in regard to our situation, and he is every
way reliable.

J. W. MOORE.

MOUNT STERLING, KY., *May 30, 1863.*

We, the undersigned citizens of Montgomery County, Ky., learning
of the fact that Capt. Samuel McKee, of the Fourteenth Kentucky
Cavalry, now a prisoner at Richmond, Va., is soon to be executed by the
Confederate authorities, by way of retaliation, because Major-General
Burnside did on the [15th] day of [May], 1863, execute Captain Corbin,
of the Confederate Army, would most respectfully entreat the Confederate authorities at Richmond to spare the life of Capt. Samuel McKee
and to release him from the sad fate which we learn awaits him. Captain McKee though decided in his political course was ever kind and
lenient to those who may have differed with him in political sentiments.
Captain McKee is a gentleman of high social standing in our midst,
and his Southern Rights friends of this community, many of whose
names are appended below, offer up this petition humbly to the Confederate authorities at Richmond, Va., to spare the life of Captain
McKee, of the Fourteenth Kentucky Cavalry, and hold him merely as
a prisoner of war, of which you have a perfect right.

WM. FERGUSON,
The Father of Capt. Franklin Ferguson, of C. S. Army.
K. FARROW,
R. P. B. CALDWELL,
(And 8 others.)

[First indorsement.]

ABINGDON, VA., *June 6, 1863.*

The gentlemen whose names are signed to this paper are all known to me and are all good and true Southern men.

J. W. MOORE.

[Second indorsement.]

JUNE 10, 1863.

Referred to General Winder for consideration in connection with the arrest of the parties bearing the petition.

J. A. S.,
Secretary.

[Third indorsement.]

Respectfully returned to honorable Secretary of War. The bearers of this petition have been released and sent home.

JNO. H. WINDER,
Brigadier-General.

HEADQUARTERS DEPARTMENT No. 2,
Shelbyville, Tenn., May 31, 1863.

Hon. C. L. VALLANDIGHAM.

DEAR SIR: The general commanding instructs me to inclose you a copy of a dispatch just received from Hon. J. A. Seddon, Secretary of War, Richmond, and to request you to give a response in writing in order that he may answer the inquiry contained in the dispatch. The general desires also that you will return the passport given you as pending further instructions from Richmond. It is evident that its issue is in conflict with the views which have prompted the dispatch.

[GEO. WM. BRENT],
Assistant Adjutant-General.

[Inclosure.]

WAR DEPARTMENT, *Richmond, May 30, 1863.*

General B. BRAGG, *Tullahoma, Tenn.:*

If Hon. Mr. Vallandigham has come or been forced within our lines ascertain and report in what character and under what circumstances he thus stands. If he claims to be a loyal citizen of the United States he must be held in charge or on parole as an alien enemy. He may be allowed on parole to proceed to Wilmington and there report to General Whiting.

JAMES A. SEDDON,
Secretary of War.

SHELBYVILLE, TENN., *May 31, 1863.*

General BRAGG, C. S. Army, *Commanding, &c.*

SIR: In answer to your note of this morning allow me to say that it was my offer upon first entering your lines to surrender myself a prisoner, and the order or suggestion of the Secretary of War is entirely consonant to my original desire and purposes, though I sincerely trust that the parole may allow my departure at any time as this is most important to me in every way. Please report also that I came to your lines upon compulsion and against my consent as a citizen of Ohio and of the United States in exile, banished from my country for no other offense than love of constitutional liberty, my political opinions and resolute, undaunted opposition to the principles and policy of the party and administration in power in the United States. The order of the President was absolute forbidding me to return under penalty of imprisonment during the war and therefore left me no alternative, and it was executed by military force. It is better for me doubtless for several reasons to be deemed a prisoner on parole while I remain in the Confederate States, but my most earnest desire is for a passport if necessary and permission to leave as soon as possible either through some Confederate port or by way of Matamoras for Canada where I can see my family, communicate with my friends and transact my business as far as practicable unmolested.

I am still a citizen of Ohio and of the United States, recognizing my allegiance to both and retaining the same opinions and position which I have always held at home. As the President of the United States will certainly not exchange me I trust I may be allowed to depart on parole for the place which I have above designated.

Very respectfully, &c.,

C. L. VALLANDIGHAM.

[HOUSTON, TEX., *June 1, 1863.*]

Maj. Gen. J. BANKHEAD MAGRUDER, C. S. Army,
  Comdg. the Dept. of Texas, New Mexico and Arizona, &c.

GENERAL: My stay in this department being rendered no longer necessary professionally on account of the removal of the officers of my command to Huntsville and the recovery of my wounded in the hospital and by the exchange of all my command except the officers and wounded with the exception of four privates, and as Acting Assistant Surgeon Sherfy, late of the ship Morning Light, is here to take care of his men and accompany them when they shall go to be exchanged, I very respectfully ask to be allowed to return to New Orleans as soon as can be convenient. My health is very infirm and has been for three weeks or more, and I have been unable to leave my room most of the time for that period. I very respectfully ask for this reason that I may be allowed to go by water by way of our fleet either at Galveston or Sabine—of course under such restrictions and regulations as your honor may deem necessary.

There are also here ten wounded and infirm men, five of my own regiment all wounded, the whole ten unable to walk any distance and all of whom will be discharged from the service as soon as they reach our lines. It would be a matter of great satisfaction to me if you would allow them to go with me, either paroling them as our forces did your sick and wounded recently in Louisiana, or allowing them to be receipted for by myself or the commander of the blockading fleet. All those remaining here save those ten are able to march, thus saving transportation for any invalids or wounded when they are sent forward for exchange. For nearly five months I have remained here and at Galveston, during which time I have given my undivided attention to the care of the sick and wounded, Confederate as well as Federal, and now I am desirous for reasons above named to return to my regiment that I may be useful, as I have ever tried to be heretofore, in striving to relieve the sufferings of frail humanity wherever found and whoever they are. I trust I may be of service as heretofore to the Confederate sick and wounded in the hands of the Federal forces as well as to those of my own command more immediately depending upon my care, and also to any medical officers of the Confederate Army who like myself believe it to be their duty to remain with their sick and wounded for a time in the hands of the Federal forces. As there are but eight men of my command (except the officers) remaining here and five of them are wounded it would give me great pleasure if possible to take them with me as well as the few others of the Harriet Lane and Morning Light who are unable to march.

Inclosed is a list* of all my own men remaining, those wounded marked, and also of the few others unable to march who only wait to get back to our lines to be discharged from the service. The term of service of my (present) regiment will expire on the 1st of July, and I trust the officers will not be kept longer than is absolutely necessary and that the men of the late ship Morning Light will be forwarded for exchange as soon as possible. Permit me, general, to return to you my most cordial and heartfelt thanks for your uniform kindness to me and for many favors shown me since I have been in your department; and I have the honor to remain, general,

Your humble servant,

A. J. CUMMINGS, M. D., LL. B.,
Surg. 42d Regt. Mass. Vols., late Post Med. Director, &c.

SHELBYVILLE, *June 1, 1863.*

General S. COOPER,
Adjutant and Inspector General, Richmond:

Hon. C. L. Vallandigham is here on parole. He was brought under guard by the enemy and abandoned in front of my lines with orders from his Government not to return under penalty of imprisonment for the war. Fearing assassination by a licensed soldiery he made his way to my outposts and surrendered as an alien enemy owing allegiance to the State of Ohio and the United States but exiled by the present Government for maintaining his civil rights as a freeman. He awaits orders but desires to make his way by the most expeditious route to Canada. I suggest a conference with him personally or by a confidential agent.

BRAXTON BRAGG.

(Copy sent to the President.

S. COOPER.)

RICHMOND, *June 2, 1863.*

General B. BRAGG, *Shelbyville:*

Your dispatch to Adjutant-General received. Send Hon. C. L. Vallandigham as an alien enemy under guard of an officer to Wilmington where further orders await him.

JEFF'N DAVIS.

SHELBYVILLE, *June 2, 1863.*

JEFFERSON DAVIS, *President of Confederate States:*

Upon Mr. Vallandigham's earnest request he was permitted to go this morning to Lynchburg to confer with a distinguished friend of Virginia. He reports from there on parole to the War Department.

BRAXTON BRAGG.

---

* Omitted.

RICHMOND, *June 2, 1863.*

General R. E. LEE, *Fredericksburg, Va.:*

The prisoners captured and paroled by Stoneman have not yet been exchanged, but will be as soon as the list is completed, now nearly ready.

S. COOPER,
Adjutant and Inspector General.

HAMPDEN SIDNEY COLLEGE, VA., *June 2, 1863.*

Hon. JAMES A. SEDDON, *Secretary of War.*

SIR: There seems no longer to be the slightest doubt that the Hon. C. L. Vallandigham, of Ohio, is within our lines, and the rumors of the last two days seem to indicate that he is or soon will be in Richmond if permitted by the Government to go there. I am not forgetful of the many delicate questions touching the dignity and policy of our Government raised by this attempt of Mr. Lincoln to make a "Botany Bay" of the Confederacy, nor can I undertake to say how they can be or ought to be settled. I have the utmost confidence in the wisdom of the Government to settle them in such a way as best comports with our dignity and affords the Government of the United States no possible advantage either over us or over Mr. Vallandigham. It seems most probable to me that our Government will allow Mr. Vallandigham to remain in the Confederacy on parole if he desires it. If so his residence must be subject to your control. It ought to be known to you whether he is paroled or not. I therefore write to you to ask your permission or if this matter is not under your control the permission of the proper authorities to invite Mr. Vallandigham to reside with me here in Prince Edward County during his exile. I extend this invitation to him under permission of the Government because I know him well, having been in college with him, where we were intimate friends, and having corresponded with him since, especially during the session of the Federal Congress immediately preceding Mr. Lincoln's inauguration. I know him to be a gentleman and a man of honor for whom I may safely undertake any obligation which the Government may require of me as his host while he remains with us. As I do not know where to address Mr. Vallandigham I inclose my invitation* to him unsealed in this letter and ask you to read it; and if you give me leave to invite him will you do me and him the kindness to add his address which I take for granted is known to you, and having sealed it to have it forwarded to him? You will very naturally desire to know something about me. I therefore take the liberty of referring you to Capt. Richard Morton, of the Niter Bureau; Reverend Doctor Brown, editor of the Central Presbyterian, and Reverend Doctor Moore, pastor of the First Presbyterian Church of Richmond. I deem it unnecessary to multiply references.

I remain, respectfully, your obedient servant,

CHARLES MARTIN.

WAR DEPARTMENT, *Richmond, June 3, 1863.*

J. M. W.

(Care surgeon in charge of hospital, Harrisonburg, Va.)

SIR: Your letter of the 28th ultimo with suggestions in regard to the negroes and officers of negro regiments that may be captured by us has

---

* Not found.

been received. In reply you are informed that the law has made provisions for the disposition of such slaves by directing them to be turned over to the State authorities. As negroes without free papers when not claimed by the owners they will be liable to be sold as slaves.

Respectfully, JAMES A. SEDDON,
Secretary of War.

HEADQUARTERS PAROLED AND EXCHANGED PRISONERS,
Demopolis, Ala., June 3, 1863.

Col. B. S. EWELL,
Assistant Adjutant-General, Jackson, Miss.

COLONEL: I would most respectfully request that you give me some instructions in regard to future action in providing for paroled and exchanged prisoners. Many of the men are in a destitute condition, having no clothes or money, and the quartermaster here declares that the men are still under the jurisdiction of General Pemberton and not that of General Maury. The men are very comfortably situated here, requiring no tents, as they occupy the Fair Grounds, and they are much less liable to desert or straggle from camp than when in Jackson, Miss. My own opinion is that this would be a most desirable place for a permanent camp, and if your views are consonant with mine I trust you will authorize me to make public such orders as will insure the prompt dispatch of paroled prisoners from other posts, Mr. Robert Ould, agent for exchange, Richmond, Va., having notified me of the necessity of keeping these men in camp in order to effect exchange. As I cannot longer permit the men to suffer I have ordered Lieutenant Gillenwater to proceed to Jackson and procure the payment of men and officers now in camp and those attached to my department.

Awaiting your instructions and orders as to the foregoing, I am, colonel, very respectfully, your obedient servant,

HENRY C. DAVIS,
Major, Commanding Paroled and Exchanged Prisoners.

P. S.—I have daily applications for leave of absence from men who live within this and adjoining States who have not seen their families for nearly two years. Am I at liberty to grant them a short furlough for ten, fifteen or twenty days?

H. C. D.

OFFICE EXCHANGE OF PRISONERS,
Richmond, Va., June 4, 1863.

Capt. W. H. Hatch, assistant adjutant-general, Provisional Army, C. S., having reported to me for assignment to duty by order of the Secretary of War is hereby authorized and empowered to act for me in all matters connected with the exchange of prisoners as fully and completely as I am empowered to act and will be respected and obeyed accordingly.

RO. OULD,
Agent of Exchange.

OKOLONA, MISS., *June 4, 1863.*

[General D. RUGGLES.]

GENERAL: About 13th ultimo I was detached from the First [Second] Mississippi State Cavalry with my company to reconnoiter the country adjoining the Memphis and Charleston Railroad in Tippah County. I proceeded to Tippah Ford, on Tippah Creek, some eight miles west of

Ripley, and then halted. Whilst there Alex. Robinson came up and said he had two Federal prisoners, Twelfth Michigan Regiment, and wanted me to take charge of and turn them over to the proper authorities. I detailed Private John Kesterson to accompany Robinson with the prisoners and ordered them to be taken and delivered to Colonel Smith, commanding First [Second] Mississippi State Cavalry. They started to the point of destination about 10 o'clock in the morning (about 15th May) with the prisoners and returned to my camp about 4 o'clock in the evening, stating that the prisoners had attempted to escape and that they had shot them.

I received a communication from General Smith, commanding First Division, Sixteenth Army Corps, La Grange, Tenn., May 27, 1863, which was referred to Colonel Smith, commanding First [Second] Mississippi State Cavalry, and by him referred to you. I ask your earliest attention in the premises.*

I am, general, yours, very respectfully,
SOL. G. STREET,
Captain, Comdg. Co. A, First [Second] Mississippi State Cavalry.

WAR DEPARTMENT, *Richmond, Va., June 5, 1863.*
ROBERT OULD, Esq., *Commissioner, &c.*

SIR: C. L. Vallandigham, a citizen of the United States and late a Representative in the Federal Congress, having been thrust by the violence and oppression of his Government within our Confederate lines has been held as an alien enemy, avowing himself to be still a loyal citizen of the United States, under arrest or on parole by General Braxton Bragg, commanding the Army of Middle Tennessee, and has been permitted while so under arrest or on parole to proceed to Lynchburg, Va. It is not the desire or purpose of this Government to treat this victim of unjust and arbitrary power with other than lenity and consideration, but as an alien enemy he cannot be received to friendly hospitality or allowed a continued refuge in freedom in our midst. This is due alike to our safety and to him in his acknowledged position as an enemy. You have therefore been charged with the duty, not inappropriate to the commission you hold in relation to prisoners, &c., of meeting him in Lynchburg and there assuming direction and control of his future movements. He must be regarded by you as under arrest, permitted unless in your discretion you deem it necessary to revoke the privilege to be at large on his parole not to attempt to escape nor hereafter to reveal to the prejudice of the Confederate States anything he may see or learn while therein. You will see that he is not molested or assailed or unduly intruded upon, and extend to him the attentions and kind treatment consistent with his relations as an alien enemy. After a reasonable delay with him at Lynchburg to allow rest and recreation from the fatigues of his recent exposure and travel you will proceed with him to Wilmington, N. C., and there deliver him to the charge of Major-General Whiting, commanding in that district, by whom he will be allowed at an early convenient opportunity to take shipping for any neutral port he may prefer, whether in Europe, the Islands, or on this Continent. More full instruction on this point will be given to General Whiting, and your duty will be discharged when you shall have conducted Mr. Vallandigham to Wilmington and placed him at the disposition of that commander.
JAMES A. SEDDON,
Secretary of War.

---

* See Smith to Street, May 27, 1863, p. 714.

RICHMOND, VA., *June 8, 1863.*

General BRAGG, &c.

GENERAL: Your letter of the 3d instant was received this morning. My dispatch in relation to the Hon. Mr. Vallandigham indicated a course but little different from that which in the absence of instructions you had adopted. In furtherance of our purpose Mr. Ould, commissioner for the exchange of prisoners of war, has been sent to Lynchburg to meet Mr. Vallandigham and to conduct him to Wilmington, whence his departure for a neutral port will be facilitated by all the courtesy and kindness due to his condition.

Very respectfully and truly, yours,

JEFF'N DAVIS.

WAR DEPARTMENT, *Richmond, Va., June 8, 1863.*

His Excellency JOHN GILL SHORTER, *Governor of Alabama.*

SIR: The official reports of General Forrest relative to the operations in Alabama and Georgia resulting in the capture of a body of the cavalry of the enemy near Rome, Ga., have been received. It does not appear from these reports that any slaves were associated as soldiers with the enemy's troops and if there were any Alabamians enlisted among them they made their escape before the capture. The probability is that Your Excellency has been misinformed on the subject.

Very respectfully, your obedient servant,

JAMES A. SEDDON,
Secretary of War.

WAR DEPARTMENT, *Richmond, June 10, 1863.*

Brig. Gen. JOHN H. WINDER.

GENERAL: S. S. Baxter, esq., commissioner for the examination of political prisoners in the city of Richmond, in his report of the 9th instant has submitted the following recommendations. The parties are almost all deserters from the Federal Army and as such the subjects of natural and unavoidable distrust. The Department is reluctant therefore to embarrass you with positive instructions as to the disposition to be made of them. With the lights before it just now there appears no reason to overrule the recommendations of the commissioner, but as circumstances presenting themselves to yourself may indicate a wiser disposition, the suggestions of Mr. Baxter are submitted to your consideration with full discretion in the premises:

Daniel McCullough, Martin Schwartz, James Gedney, Harrison Jones, John Kenney, William Gardner, William Seymour, John Fisher, Charles A. Freeman desire to enlist in the Confederate Navy, and if the Navy officers are willing to receive them may be permitted to do so. Benningham (Alfred) send to Conscript Bureau. James Barry desires to enlist in Sixth Louisiana Regiment; let him do so. William Morgan, J. D. Anderson, William Maguire, Fred. Coghn, Herman Wells—these men for various reasons object to go into service. They may perhaps be made useful as laborers or mechanics and put to work under direction of provost-marshal.

By order of the Secretary of War:

J. A. CAMPBELL,
Assistant Secretary of War.

EXECUTIVE DEPARTMENT, *Richmond, June 10, 1863.*
Honorable SECRETARY OF WAR.

SIR: I am informed that Maj. John P. Thompson (late of First Kentucky Regiment), authorized by you to raise a battalion in Kentucky, has been arrested in Owensborough, Ky., and sentenced to be shot as a spy. He was a gallant soldier and has probably been taken attempting to recruit.

WM. PRESTON JOHNSTON,
Colonel and Aide-de-Camp.

JOHN'S ISLAND, S. C., *June 10, 1863.*
Brigadier-General HAGOOD.

GENERAL: I beg leave to bring to your attention that the prisoners from the Rebel Troop taken while on duty beyond our picket-lines on the Edisto are still in the hands of the enemy, while Yankee prisoners since taken by Captain Mickler have been sent forward to be exchanged. These unfortunate young men we have reason to apprehend are now confined in the jail at Beaufort. The usual programme being to send their prisoners North to be kept in some of their bastiles till exchanged. There must be some special reason for treatment so extraordinary, and perhaps the insolent communication to President Davis (recently published of General Hunter), in relation to his threatened disposition of officers and slave-holders taken prisoners by him furnishes the explanation. They are doubtless kept as hostages for the safety of officers commanding negro troops and negro troops themselves who may be captured in some of their raids. They are the sons of wealthy planters or themselves owners of slaves and of some of those very negroes now in Yankee service. Just such as a cruel ingenuity would select for such a purpose. I would respectfully request that you bring to the notice of the general commanding this department this information as to their place of confinement, confident that he will take immediate steps to know why they are so kept contrary to the terms of the cartel for exchange of enlisted men still pretended to be acted upon by the Federal authorities. These unfortunate young men who have been hastily and harshly judged upon conjectural inferences from circumstantial evidence procured by daily exposure to capture on the extreme outpost and gave valuable information of the movements of the enemy in North Edisto River before the attack on Charleston, affording the information that the iron-clads were taking aboard their ammunition, by which the department commander received advice of the impending attack two days before it was made. Their friends look to your influence and instrumentality and solicit your earnest effort in using all the means in your power to effect their early exchange. I think something should be done and that quickly to know why they have not been exchanged to which they are entitled and for which there has been ample time.

JOHN JENKINS,
Major, Commanding Advanced Forces.

[Indorsement.]

HEADQUARTERS SECOND MILITARY DISTRICT,
Adams' Run, June 13, 1863.
Respectfully forwarded.

The subject-matter is earnestly brought to the attention of the general commanding.

JOHNSON HAGOOD,
Brigadier-General, Commanding.

INDEX.

Brigades, Divisions, Corps, Armies, and improvised organizations are "Mentioned" under name of commanding officer; State and other organizations under their official designation.

(971)

INDEX. 977

Brugnions, A., 731.
Brune, John C., 202.
Brune, William, 202.
Bryant, George W., 236, 258.
Bryant, Joseph, 486.
Buchanan, Robert C.
Correspondence, W. Hoffman, 436, 477, 481, 487, 494.
Mentioned, 484.
Buchanan, William, 856.
Buckingham, Catharinus P.
Correspondence. See *War Department, U. S.*
Mentioned, 58.
Buckley, William, 120.
Buckner, Simon B.
Correspondence, I. Dyer, 242.
Mentioned, 242, 852, 942.
Buell, Don Carlos, 14, 15, 17, 18, 107, 510, 622, 840, 927.
Buell, Ezekiel P., 155.
Buffum, Robert, 505, 778.
Buford, L. M., 785.
Buford, Napoleon B.
Correspondence:
Burnside, A. E., 585, 728.
Hurlbut, S. A., 722.
War Department, U. S., 521.
Mentioned, 926.
Bulger, A., 120.
Bull, D. C., 806.
Bull, James M., 214.
Bull, William, 806.
Bullard, Henry B., 156.
Bulloch, James D., 211.
Bunch, Robert.
Correspondence, State Department, C. S., 775, 784, 801, 823.
Mentioned, 775, 862-864.
Buntain, John, 817.
Burbank, Sidney.
Correspondence, H. G. Wright, 43.
Burbank, Sullivan W., 375.
Burbridge, Stephen G., 44.
Burch, James J., 393.
Burford, E. Spruel, 182, 183, 220, 285.
Burgess, James W., 732.
Burgett, J. R.
Correspondence, W. Hoffman, 761.
Burke, M. P., 427.
Burke, Martin.
Correspondence:
Adjutant-General's Office, U. S. A., 123, 423, 446.
Hoffman, W., 241, 271, 465.
Morgan, J. S., 123.
War Department, U. S., 80, 244.
Wood, C. O., 446.
Burke, Patrick E., 571.
Burlington, W. Va. Skirmish, April 26, 1863.
Paroled prisoners, 727, 728.
Burnett, E. H., 93.
Burnett, Henry C.
Correspondence, J. F. Melton, 859.
Mentioned, 820.
Burnett, William A., 809, 810.
Burnley, C. W.
Correspondence, J. B. Magruder, 827.
Burns, James N., 392.

Burnside, Ambrose E.
Correspondence:
Adjutant-General's Office, U. S. A., 148.
Ammen, J., 722, 726.
Army Headquarters, 400, 409, 463, 536, 567, 633, 664, 692, 696, 721, 726.
Boyle, J. T., 722.
Bragg, B., 718.
Buford, N. B., 585, 728.
Cutts, J. M., 692.
Eckert, T. T., 685.
Hascall, M. S., 722, 752, 759.
Hoffman, W., 403, 441, 516, 517, 537, 569, 593, 603, 608, 670, 719, 735, 764.
Hutton, C. G., 555, 566.
Lee, R. E., 98.
Lincoln, Abraham, 685, 707, 717.
Longstreet, J., 115, 116.
Loring, C. G., 663.
Rosecrans, W. S., 658, 718.
War Department, U. S., 400, 526, 608, 656, 657, 665, 666, 723.
White, J., 764.
Willcox, O. B., 648.
Mentioned, 37, 85, 89, 103, 104, 116, 117, 148, 160, 171, 172, 175, 178, 408, 412, 413, 420, 421, 463, 480, 485, 496, 504, 515, 516, 521, 525, 528, 544, 546, 555-568, 573-578, 580-582, 584, 585, 593-595, 634, 636, 641, 643, 654, 657, 658, 691, 715, 726, 739, 740, 746, 754, 756, 764, 772, 826, 962.
Request to be relieved, 717.
Burr, Raymond, 5.
Burrell, Charles B.
Correspondence, E. W. Quincey, 455.
Mentioned, 455.
Burrell, Isaac S., 410, 470.
Burrows, Samuel, 941.
Burton, Henry S., 629.
Bush, Thomas J.
Correspondence, H. Hinkley, 15.
Mentioned, 14, 17.
Bushwhackers.
Treatment, etc. See *Guerrillas.*
Bussey, Cyrus.
Correspondence, S. R. Curtis, 46.
Bustamente, Juan, 842.
Butler, Andrew J., 792-794, 797.
Butler, Benjamin F.
Correspondence:
Adjutant-General's Office, U. S. A., 438.
State Department, U. S., 56.
War Department, U. S., 73, 438.
Denounced as a felon and outlaw, 795-797.
Mentioned, 20, 56, 57, 73, 102, 119, 127, 145, 156, 187, 192, 253, 438, 439, 783, 785, 786, 788, 789, 792, 793, 796, 797, 802, 834, 835, 849, 935.
Butler, Camp, Ill.
Care and preservation of public property, 452, 453.
Inspections, 254, 255, 379-382.
Management, needs, etc., 250, 251, 254, 255, 272, 308, 379-382, 512.
Savings of rations, 762.
Smallpox, 381.
Byron, Roger, 816.
Byzer, ———. See *Charles Carroll.*

*Also called 1st Battery.

Laundresses.
Compensation of hospital, 9**52.**
Laurason, George C., 425, 542.
Laurent, A. P., 423.
Lawley, F., 197.
Lawrence, E., 794.
Lawrence, George A., 595–598.
Layton, Elizabeth J., 418.
Lazelle, Henry M.
Correspondence:
Henley, J. C., 138.
Hoffman, W., 122, 132, 303, 328, 594, 613, 619.
McMurray, J., 137.
Sankey, A., 138.
Tiffany, D. B., 139, 141.
Webber, E. L., 137, 210.
See also *William Hoffman.*
Mentioned, 3–5, 114, 193, 317, 326, 327, 348, 351, 352, 360, 361, 384, 405, 454, 529, 530, 606, 688.
Lea, John C., 941.
Leach, Benjamin, 789.
Leach, Thomas, 789.
Leak, Thomas W.
Correspondence, J. T. Boyle, 16.
Mentioned, 14–16, 18.
Leary (Prisoner), 892.
Leaves of Absence.
Paroled prisoners, officers, 734.
Leavitt, Humphrey H.
Mentioned, 573, 576.
Opinion, case of C. L. Vallandigham, 576–584.
Lebrick, Samuel, 915.
Lee, A. C., 709.
Lee, A. H., 483.
Lee, Fitzhugh, 197, 203, 571.
Lee, G. W.
Correspondence:
War Department, C. S., 820.
Winder, J. H., 777.
Lee, G. W. Custis.
Correspondence. See *Jefferson Davis.*
Mentioned, 197, 203.
Lee, Robert E.
Correspondence:
Adjt. and Insp. Gen.'s Office, C. S. A., 840, 966.
Burnside, A. E., 98.
Hill, A. P., 948.
War Department, C. S., 806, 854, 925, 959.
Winder, J. H., 948.
Mentioned, 104, 115, 116, 386, 394, 706, 732 763, 795, 796, 916.
Lee, S. Phillips.
Correspondence:
Dix, J. A., 287, 520.
Navy Department, U. S., 695.
Mentioned, 590.
Lee, S. S., 197.
Lee, William H. F., 98.
Leefe, J. B., 425, 542.
Lees, Stanley, 822.
Lefler, R. F., 608.
Le Gardeur, Gustave, jr., 935.
Leggett, Benjamin, 425.
Leigh, Thomas J.
Complaint of ill-treatment, 624–626.
Mentioned, 625.
Le More, Alfred, 56, 73, 438, 439.

Le More, Jules, 73, 438, 439.
Lent, Edward, 817.
Leonard, Abiel, 21.
Leonard, Pat., 817.
Letcher, John.
Correspondence. See *Virginia, Governor of.*
Mentioned, 34, 74, 110, 147, 212, 222, 223, 266, 286, 626.
Levy, Joseph, 120.
Lewis, Bryce, 703.
Lewis, Charles, 945.
Lewis, John M., 156.
Lewis, L., 957, 958.
Lexington, Mo. Siege of, Sept. 13–20, 1861.
Paroled prisoners, 76, 77, 85, 87–89, 95, 108, 121, 208.
L'Hommedieu, Charles, 903.
Lieber, Francis.
Instructions for government of armies in the field, 671–682, 690, 744, 753–756, 767.
Mentioned, 521, 671.
Lieber, G. Norman, 424.
Lillard, J. D., 93.
Lilley, William H., 732.
Lilly, H. C., 355, 433.
Lincoln, Abraham.
Correspondence:
Barbour, J. N., 469.
Burnside, A. E., 685, 707, 717.
Carrington, H. B., 235.
Corning, E., 654.
Dick, F. A., 99.
Dix, J. A., 358, 601.
Gansevoort, P., 654.
Gibbs, S. W., 654.
Guthrie, J., 627, 631.
Hunter, D., 711.
Judge-Advocate-General's Office, U. S. A., 256.
Ludlow, W. H., 286, 723.
McClellan, H. W., 654.
Missouri, Governor of, 392.
Monteith, P., 654.
Mulcahy, E., 654.
Nessel, J. R., 654.
Newcomb, E., 654.
Niblack, J., 654.
Nolan, M. A., 654.
Osborn, J., 654.
Padock, W. S., 654.
Peckham, R. W., jr., 654.
Perry, E., 654.
Prentice, G. D., 520, 527.
Radcliffe, D. V. N., 654.
Rice, W. A., 654.
Rodgers, L. W., 654.
Sanders, J. B., 654.
Schenck, R. C., 711.
Seymour, W., 654.
Sibley, H. H., 84, 86, 125.
Speed, J., 631.
Speed, J. F., 631.
Virginia, Governor of, 147, 266.
War Department, U. S., 124.
Weeks, C. W., 654.
Mentioned, 3, 24, 27, 57, 73, 99, 100, 108, 148, 151, 164, 170, 174, 177, 179, 187, 192, 211, 216, 221, 222, 248, 260, 266, 312, 313, 315, 338, 363, 365, 399, 458, 528, 529, 555, 557, 579–582, 589, 597, 616, 626, 631.

---

* Also called 1st Mounted Rifles.

Hill, Daniel H.
Correspondence:
Brenan, W., 957.
Foster, J. G., 389.
Mentioned, 1, 27, 216, 231, 238, 256, 339, 386, 432, 448, 476, 960.
Hill, Harrington R.
Mentioned, 635, 639.
Trial of C. L. Vallandigham, 635–640.
Hill, John A., 156.
Hill, Robert, 156.
Hills, Frederick C., 709.
Hindman, Thomas C.
Agreement with Blunt, 648, 649, 660, 661.
Correspondence, J. G. Blunt, 94.
Mentioned, 21, 53, 273–276, 648, 649, 660, 682, 835.
Hinkley, H.
Correspondence:
Boyle, J. T., 16.
Bragg, B., 14.
Bush, T. J., 15.
Mentioned, 15, 16, 18, 44.
Hinson, Joseph, 731.
Hitchcock, Ethan A.
Correspondence:
Army Headquarters, 460, 665, 693.
Curtis, S. R., 510.
Hoffman, W., 198, 356, 427, 460.
Ludlow, W. H., 181, 199, 212, 221, 244, 265, 268, 286, 351, 389, 394, 396, 397, 437, 458, 478, 513, 559, 689.
War Department, U. S., 90, 192, 228, 299, 325, 427, 437, 456, 470, 590, 659, 704, 716, 754.
Wood, W. P., 229, 251, 402.
Mentioned, 95, 172, 181, 215, 225, 243, 269, 277, 278, 325, 350, 354, 368, 369, 398, 400–402, 424, 444, 488–491, 515, 521, 527, 541, 547, 627, 671, 684, 722, 930, 931, 959.
Views on retaliation, 754, 755.
Hite, George, 753.
Hixon, Noah H., 214.
Hobdy, Charles, 120.
Hodges, William, 851.
Heey, James.
Correspondence, War Department, C. S., 945.
Hoffman, Samuel, 326.
Hoffman, Southard.
Correspondence. See *John G. Foster.*
Hoffman, William.
Correspondence:
Adjutant-General's Office, U. S. A., 24, 37, 176, 178, 217, 218, 267, 302, 350, 409, 523, 728, 743.
Ammen, J., 176, 230, 235, 257, 262, 281, 321, 358, 367, 440, 476, 498, 619.
Army Headquarters, 153, 280, 326, 338, 373, 374, 395, 397, 441, 658, 662, 688, 696, 717, 751.
Arnold, I. N., 287.
Bailhache, W. H., 296.
Banks, N. P., 290, 592, 593, 619, 669, 670, 766.
Biddle, J., 618.
Bliss, D. W., 424.
Blodgett, G. S., 466.
Bonneville, B. L. E., 128, 130, 160, 176, 195, 231, 315, 341, 378, 414, 421, 464, 563, 604, 617, 668, 694, 740.
Booth, D. L., 467.

Hoffman, William—Continued.
Correspondence:
Boyle, J. T., 687.
Buchanan, R. C., 436, 477, 481, 487, 494.
Burgett, J. R., 761.
Burke, M., 241, 271, 465.
Burnside, A. E., 403, 441, 516, 517, 537, 569, 593, 603, 608, 670, 719, 735, 764.
Cameron, D., 110, 214, 481, 538.
Carrington, H. B., 349.
Cheevers, P., 388.
Chester, J. N., 318.
Churchill, T. J., 477.
Cogshall, I., 493.
Constable, R. A., 316.
Cooper, J., 113, 168, 175, 185, 204.
Cox, J. D., 501, 546, 699.
Crocker, A. E., 508.
Crosman, G. H., 484, 488, 492, 501.
Curtis, S. R., 58, 76, 87, 89, 95, 98, 108, 121, 153, 201, 203, 218, 294, 357, 403, 450, 532, 537, 568, 593.
Curtis, W., 563.
Darr, J., jr., 71, 81, 121, 130, 155, 165, 187, 271, 301, 340, 545, 547, 612, 618, 683, 685.
De Korponay, G., 6, 46, 295, 300.
Dent, H., 263, 393, 465, 506.
Dick, F. A., 21, 25, 48, 49, 54, 73, 74, 79, 166, 179, 195, 226, 245, 272, 274, 277, 282, 285, 310, 311, 317, 319, 338, 368, 393, 434, 442, 539, 618, 694.
Dimick, J., 404.
Dix, J. A., 341, 452, 669, 670.
Dodge, G. M., 231, 513.
Donaldson, J. L., 290, 412, 435, 442, 445, 453, 467.
Doster, W. E., 54, 121, 201, 218, 227, 270, 272.
Drake, A. E., 504, 506, 524.
Duffield, W. W., 46.
Duncan, H. S., 467.
Edison, C. S., 467.
Edwards, L. A., 84.
Edwards, N. W., 762.
Ekin, J. A., 546.
Elliott, W. L., 172.
Fish, W. S., 472.
Fitzhugh, C. D., 629.
Forney, J. W., 221.
Foster, J. W., 467.
Freedley, H. W., 34, 51, 92, 150, 205, 227, 233, 239, 258, 308, 343, 379, 391, 686.
Gallup, G. W., 558, 719.
Garrett, J. W., 408.
Gilbert, H. C., 572.
Granger, G., 445, 483.
Grant, U. S., 457, 458, 501, 592, 669, 670, 738.
Hartz, W. T., 401, 413.
Heintzelman, S. P., 370, 441, 609, 617, 670, 759.
Hendrickson, T., 367, 369, 393, 396, 423, 484, 485, 494, 497, 500, 523, 554, 569, 573, 619, 652, 684, 694, 737, 738, 747, 768, 771.
Henley, J. C., 306.
Hildebrand, J., 109, 179, 277, 341.
Hill, B. H., 340.
Hitchcock, E. A., 198, 356, 427, 460.
Hooker, J., 670.
Hurlbut, S. A., 429, 945.
Hursam, N. A., 164.
Illinois, Adjutant-General of, 292.

---

*Also called 1st Battery.

---

* Also called 1st Mounted Rifles.